Rand Morimoto, Ph.D., MCITP

Michael Noel, MVP, MCITP

Omar Droubi, MCSE

Ross Mistry, MVP, MCITP

Chris Amaris, MCSE, CISSP

Technical Edit by Guy Yardeni

# Windows Server® 2008 R2

## UNLEASHED

 800 East 96th Street, Indianapolis, Indiana 46240 USA

# Windows Server® 2008 R2 Unleashed

Copyright © 2010 by Pearson Education, Inc.

ISBN-13: 978-0-672-33092-6
ISBN-10: 0-672-33092-X

The Library of Congress Cataloging-in-Publication Data is on file.

Printed in the United States of America

Sixth Printing January 2013

## Trademarks

All terms mentioned in this book that are known to be trademarks or service marks have been appropriately capitalized. Sams Publishing cannot attest to the accuracy of this information. Use of a term in this book should not be regarded as affecting the validity of any trademark or service mark.

## Warning and Disclaimer

Every effort has been made to make this book as complete and as accurate as possible, but no warranty or fitness is implied. The information provided is on an "as is" basis. The authors and the publisher shall have neither liability nor responsibility to any person or entity with respect to any loss or damages arising from the information contained in this book or from the use of it.

## Bulk Sales

Sams Publishing offers excellent discounts on this book when ordered in quantity for bulk purchases or special sales. For more information, please contact

**U.S. Corporate and Government Sales**
**1-800-382-3419**
**corpsales@pearsontechgroup.com**

For sales outside of the U.S., please contact

**International Sales**
**international@pearson.com**

**Editor-in-Chief**
Karen Gettman

**Executive Editor**
Neil Rowe

**Development Editor**
Mark Renfrow

**Managing Editor**
Kristy Hart

**Project Editor**
Betsy Harris

**Copy Editor**
Karen Annett

**Indexer**
WordWise Publishing Services

**Proofreaders**
Water Crest Publishing

Williams Woods Publishing

**Technical Editor**
Guy Yardeni

**Publishing Coordinator**
Cindy Teeters

**Book Designer**
Gary Adair

**Compositor**
Jake McFarland

**Contributing Writers**
Alex Lewis, CISSP, MVP

Colin Spence, MCP, MCTS

Jeff Guillet, MVP, MCITP, CISSP

Jon Skoog, MCSE, CISSP

Stefan Garaygay, MCSE

Tyson Kopczynski, CISSP, GSEC, GCIH, MCTS

# Contents at a Glance

# Table of Contents

**Part VIII    Desktop Administration**

**Part IX    Fault-Tolerance Technologies**

# About the Authors

**Rand H. Morimoto, Ph.D., MVP, MCITP, CISSP**, has been in the computer industry for over 30 years and has authored, coauthored, or been a contributing writer for dozens of books on Windows, Security, Exchange, BizTalk, and Remote and Mobile Computing. Rand is the president of Convergent Computing, an IT-consulting firm in the San Francisco Bay area that has been one of the key early adopter program partners with Microsoft, implementing beta versions of Microsoft Windows Server 2008 R2, Windows 7, Exchange Server 2010, and SharePoint 2010 in production environments over 18 months before the initial product releases.

**Michael Noel, MCITP, CISSP, MVP,** is an internationally recognized technology expert, best-selling author, and well-known public speaker on a broad range of IT topics. He authored multiple major industry books that have been translated into more than a dozen languages worldwide. Significant titles include *SharePoint 2010 Unleashed*, *Microsoft Exchange Server 2010 Unleashed*, *SharePoint 2007 Unleashed*, *Exchange Server 2007 Unleashed*, *ISA Server 2006 Unleashed*, and many more. Currently a partner at Convergent Computing (www.cco.com) in the San Francisco Bay area, Michael's writing and extensive public-speaking experience across six continents leverage his real-world expertise in helping organizations realize business value from Information Technology infrastructure.

**Omar Droubi, MCSE**, has been in the computer industry since 1992 and during this time has coauthored several of Sams Publishing best-selling books, including *Microsoft Windows Server 2003 Unleashed* and *Windows Server 2008 Unleashed*, and Omar has been a contributing writer and technical reviewer on several other books on Windows Server 2003, Windows Server 2008, and Exchange Server 2000, 2003, and 2007. Omar has been involved in testing, designing, and prototyping Windows Server 2008 and Windows Server 2008 R2 infrastructures for the past four years, and has primarily focused on upgrading existing networks and utilizing many of the new roles and features included in the product. Also during this time, Omar has assisted several organizations with the development of technical road maps, planning and executing domain and server consolidation and virtualization projects, and deploying Exchange Server 2007 for organizations of all sizes.

**Ross Mistry, MVP, MCITP,** is a principal consultant and partner at Convergent Computing, an author, and a Microsoft MVP. With over a decade of experience, Ross focuses on designing and implementing Windows, Active Directory, Hyper-V, Exchange Server, and SQL Server solutions for Fortune 500 organizations located in the Silicon Valley. His specialties include upgrades, migrations, high availability, security, and virtualization. Ross has also taken on the roles of lead author, contributing writer, and technical editor for many best-selling books published by Sams. His recent works include *SQL Server 2008 Management and Administration*, *Exchange Server 2010 Unleashed*, and *Windows Server 2008 Unleashed*. Ross writes technical articles for many sites including TechTarget.com and frequently speaks at international conferences around the world. You can follow him on Twitter *@RossMistry*.

**Chris Amaris, MCSE, CISSP/ISSAP, CHS III**, is the chief technology officer and cofounder of Convergent Computing. He has more than 20 years experience consulting for Fortune 500 companies, leading companies in the technology selection, design, planning, and implementation of complex Information Technology projects. Chris has worked with Microsoft Windows since version 1.0 in 1985. He specializes in messaging, security, performance tuning, systems management, and migration. A Certified Information Systems Security Professional (CISSP) with an Information System Security Architecture Professional (ISSAP) concentration, Certified Homeland Security (CHS III), Windows 2003 MCSE, Novell CNE, Banyan CBE, and a Certified Project Manager, Chris is also an author, writer, and technical editor for a number of IT books, including *Network Security for Government and Corporate Executives, Microsoft Exchange Server 2010 Unleashed*, and *Microsoft Operations Manager 2005 Unleashed*. Chris presents on messaging, operations management, security, and Information Technology topics worldwide.

# Dedications

*Kelly and Chip asked that I dedicate this book to our cat Lady. Meow!*

**—Rand H. Morimoto, Ph.D., MVP, MCITP, CISSP**

*This book is dedicated to my brother Joey, his wife Mary, and my new nephew Avery. Your love for life is an inspiration and a joy to behold.*

**—Michael Noel, MCSE+I, CISSP, MCSA, MVP**

*This book is dedicated to my lovely wife Colby Lucretia Crews Droubi and my two boys Omar Khalil Droubi and Jamil Kingsley Droubi— Love you guys.*

**—Omar Droubi**

*I dedicate this book to my parents Aban and Keki Mistry. Thanks for constantly pushing me in the right direction. Your hard work and sacrifices throughout the years are much appreciated. And in loving memory of my uncle Minoo Mistry. Thanks for treating Sherry and me like gold when we last visited Vancouver. You will be missed.*

**—Ross Mistry, MVP, MCITP**

*I dedicate this book to my lovely wife, Sophia, whose love and support I cherish. And to my children, Michelle, Megan, Zoe, Zachary, and Ian, for whose sake all the hard work is worthwhile. I also want to dedicate the book to my late father, Jairo Amaris, who taught me to think on many different levels.*

**—Chris Amaris, MCSE, MVP, CISSP/ISSAP, CHS III**

*I dedicate this book to my parents, Tsvi and Rachel, for teaching me to always do my best, starting my love for computers, kicking off a life-long addiction with a Commodore 64, and always supporting and nurturing the nerd within.*

**—Guy Yardeni, MCSE, MCITP, CISSP**

# Acknowledgments

**Rand H. Morimoto, Ph.D., MVP, MCITP, CISSP** I want to thank Microsoft (including Kevin Lane) for allowing us the opportunity to work with the technologies months before general release so that we could put together content for this book! A big thanks goes out to the Sams Publishing team (Neil, Mark, and all the folks behind the scenes) in working with our tight time schedule as we write, edit, and produce a book of this size literally in weeks! A special thanks to Betsy Harris and Karen Annett for really thinking through our writing and editing our content to catch stuff that we would otherwise never catch!

I also want to thank the consultants at Convergent Computing and our early adopter clients who fiddle with these new technologies really early on and then take the leap of faith in putting the products into production to experience (and at times feel) the pain as we work through best practices. The early adopter experiences give us the knowledge and experience we need to share with all who use this book as their guide in their production environments based on the lessons learned.

To Kelly and Chip, okay, two 1300+ page books back-to-back in 7 months, I might actually not be asleep on my laptop keyboard on the kitchen table in the morning when you wake up! And thank you, Mom, for your constant love and support! For all those afternoons and evenings that you struggled to help me get my homework done because I couldn't string together words into a sentence to write a book report; I guess after all these years and several books later, I can finally say I figured it out.

**Michael Noel, MCITP, MVP** You'd think that after the amount of writing it takes to finish a book like this that writing the acknowledgments would be relatively easy, but the reality is that there are so many people who are involved with the process of getting a book on the shelves (or in your e-reader) that it is impossible to thank them all. Book publishing is a messy, exhaustive business, and I'm eternally grateful to the folks at Sams Publishing for their years of hard work turning the scatterbrained ideas of a handful of technical authors into something that is of real value to our readers. A big thanks especially to Neil Rowe, our editor, for putting up with us yet again.

I couldn't do any of this without the help of my fellow authors, notably lead author Rand Morimoto. The expertise and cumulative years of experience in this book is mind-boggling, especially when you add in the efforts of the additional contributing writers and of Guy Yardeni, the highly proficient technical editor.

And of course, thanks once again to my family—Marina, Julia, Val, and Liza—for putting up with what is now the fifteenth time that I have disappeared into my lab to furiously write another of these books. Your love and devotion is the fuel that keeps me going.

**Omar Droubi**   There are many people I would like to thank and acknowledge. Many of the customers, colleagues, and business associates I currently work with and have done business with in the past have inspired me and assisted me in my career as an Information Technology consultant and in my writing career. First, without question, I would like to thank Rand Morimoto, Sams Publishing, and the other coauthors and contributing writers of this book and my previous books. Without them, my book-writing achievements would not be possible. Next, I would like to personally thank Jim McBee, Ricardo Hernandez, Marcus Bradford, Hadi Droubi, Stefan Garaygay, Ray Wan, Raul Alcaraz, Domenic Pacini, and Roberto Alcantar. Thank you all for your support over the years.

**Ross Mistry, MVP, MCITP**   I would like to thank my wife Sherry for doing an exceptional job raising our children in my absence. I know it is not easy with my long hours, clients, conferences, and writing back-to-back books. For this I am very grateful and recognize all the hard work and dedication you devote to our children Kyanna and Kaden.

Many thanks to Rand Morimoto, my fellow coauthors, and the team at Sams Publishing. It has been great working together on another title.

A special thinks to my children. I am so proud of both of you. Live life to the fullest—chase happiness and good health, not money.

Finally, to my long-time mentor Rustom Saddiq, thank you for guiding me through. The time is now…

**Chris Amaris, MCSE, MVP, CISSP**   Thanks, Rand, for the opportunity to work with you again on another book. The books keep getting bigger, the chapters longer, and the technologies more complicated, all of which I'm sure helps keep my brain young. Your guidance and example is invaluable.

I'd also like to thank Microsoft for developing the sophisticated virtualization technologies like Hyper-V and Remote Desktop, which make developing and working with the complicated virtual lab environments for the book incredibly easier.

And, as always, a huge thanks to my children for their hard work and efforts to do well in school while I'm lost in those virtual labs.

# We Want to Hear from You!

As the reader of this book, *you* are our most important critic and commentator. We value your opinion and want to know what we're doing right, what we could do better, what areas you'd like to see us publish in, and any other words of wisdom you're willing to pass our way.

You can email or write me directly to let me know what you did or didn't like about this book—as well as what we can do to make our books stronger.

Please note that I cannot help you with technical problems related to the topic of this book, and that due to the high volume of mail I receive, I might not be able to reply to every message.

When you write, please be sure to include this book's title and author as well as your name and phone or email address. I will carefully review your comments and share them with the author and editors who worked on the book.

Email:   feedback@samspublishing.com

Mail:    Neil Rowe
         Executive Editor
         Sams Publishing
         800 East 96th Street
         Indianapolis, IN 46240 USA

# Reader Services

Visit our website and register this book at informit.com/register for convenient access to any updates, downloads, or errata that might be available for this book.

# Introduction

Windows Server 2008 R2 is the latest release of the Windows Server operating system. Over the years, it has evolved quite dramatically from the early days of Windows NT Server, Windows 2000, Windows 2003, or even Windows 2008. With the release of Windows Server 2008 R2, Microsoft again has introduced a number of new technologies intended to help IT professionals improve their ability to provide network services to the clients they serve.

We've had the opportunity to write a book on every version of Windows Server over the past two decades, and when we set out to write this book, we wanted to once again provide you, the reader, with a lot of really valuable information. Instead of just marketing fluff that talks about features and functions, we wanted to really dig down into the product and share with you best practices on planning, preparing, implementing, migrating, and supporting a Windows Server 2008 R2 environment.

Even though the original Windows Server 2008 released in early 2008 and Windows 2008 R2 released late in the summer of 2009, we've been fortunate enough to work with these operating system releases for more than 2 years in priority early adopter programs. The thing about being involved with a product so early on is that our first experiences with these products were without any documentation, Help files that provided guidance, or any shared experiences from others. We had to learn Windows Server 2008 R2 from experience, usually the hard way, but that has given us a distinct advantage of knowing the product forward and backward better than anyone could ever imagine. And we started to implement Windows Server 2008 R2 in production environments for a select group of our enterprise customers more than a year before the product release—where organizations were depending on the server operating system to run key areas of their business.

So the pages of this book are filled with years of experience with Windows Server 2008 and 2008 R2, live production environment best practices, and fully updated with RTM code specifics that will hopefully help you design, plan, prototype, implement, migrate, administer, and support your Windows Server 2008 R2 environment!

This book is organized into 11 parts, each part focusing on core Windows Server 2008 R2 areas, with several chapters making up each part. The parts of the book are as follows:

▶ **Part I: Windows Server 2008 R2 Overview**—This part provides an introduction to Windows Server 2008 R2 not only to give a general technology overview, but also to note what is truly new in Windows Server 2008 R2 that made it compelling enough for organizations to implement the technology in beta in production environments. We also cover basic planning, prototype testing, and migration techniques, as well as provide a full chapter on the installation of Windows Server 2008 R2 as well as the GUI-less Windows Server Core.

▶ **Part II: Windows Server 2008 R2 Active Directory**—This part covers Active Directory planning and design. If you have already designed and implemented your Active Directory, you will likely not read through this section of the book in detail. However, you might want to look through the Notes and Tips throughout the chapter, and the best practices at the end of each chapter because we highlight some of the tips and tricks new to Windows Server 2008 R2 that are different from Windows 2000, 2003, and 2008. You might find that limitations or restrictions you faced when designing and implementing Active Directory 2003 and 2008 have now been revised. Topics such as federated forests, lightweight directory services, and identity lifecycle management capabilities might be of interest.

▶ **Part III: Networking Services**—This part covers DNS, DHCP, domain controllers, IPv6, and IIS from the perspective of planning, integrating, migrating, and coexisting. Again, just like in Part II, you might find the Notes, Tips, and best practices to have valuable information on features that are new in Windows Server 2008 R2; you might find yourself perusing these chapters to understand what's new and different that you can leverage after a migration to Windows Server 2008 R2.

▶ **Part IV: Security**—Security is on everyone's mind these days, so it was a major enhancement to Windows Server 2008 R2. We actually dedicated three chapters of the book to security, breaking the information into server-level security such as Public Key Infrastructure (PKI) certificate services; transport-level security such as IPSec and NAT traversal; and security policies, Network Access Protection (NAP), and Network Policy Server (NPS) that have been updated in Windows Server 2008 R2.

▶ **Part V: Migrating to Windows Server 2008 R2**—This part is dedicated to the migrations from Windows 2003 and 2008 to Windows Server 2008 R2. We provide a chapter specifically on tips, tricks, best practices, and lessons learned on the planning and migration process to Windows Server 2008 R2. We also have a chapter on application-compatibility testing of applications currently running on earlier versions of Windows Server and how to test and migrate applications to a Windows Server 2008 R2 platform.

▶ **Part VI: Windows Server 2008 R2 Administration and Management**—After you get Windows Server 2008 R2 in place, you end up spending the rest of your time managing and administering the new operating system platform, so we've dedicated six chapters to administration and management. This section covers the administration and management of users, sites, organizational units, domains, and forests typical of a Windows Server 2008 R2 environment. Although you can continue to perform tasks the way you did in Windows 2000, 2003, and 2008, because of significant changes in replication, background transaction processing, secured communications, Group Policy management, and Windows PowerShell management tools, there are better ways to work with Windows Server 2008 R2. These chapters drill down into specialty areas helpful to administrators of varying levels of responsibility. This part of the book also has a chapter on managing Windows Server 2008 R2 using System Center Operations Manager 2007.

▶ **Part VII: Remote and Mobile Technologies**—Mobility is a key improvement in Windows Server 2008 R2, so this part focuses on enhancements made to Routing and Remote Access Service (RRAS), significant improvements in Remote Desktop Services (formerly Terminal Services), and the introduction of a new remote access technology called DirectAccess. Instead of just providing a remote node connection, Windows Server 2008 R2 provides true end-to-end secured anytime/anywhere access functionality. The chapters in this part highlight best practices on implementing and leveraging these technologies.

▶ **Part VIII: Desktop Administration**—Another major enhancement in Windows Server 2008 R2 is the variety of new tools provided to support better desktop administration, so this part is focused on desktop administration. The chapters in this part go in depth on client-specific group policies, the Group Policy Management Console, Active Directory Administrative Center, Windows PowerShell-based group policies, Windows Deployment Services (WDS), and desktop administration tools in Windows Server 2008 R2.

▶ **Part IX: Fault-Tolerance Technologies**—As networks have become the backbone for information and communications, Windows Server 2008 R2 needed to be reliable and more manageable, and sure enough, Microsoft included several new enhancements in fault-tolerant technologies. The four chapters in this part address file system management and file-level fault tolerance in Distributed File System (DFS), clustering, Network Load Balancing, and backup and restore procedures. When these new technologies are implemented in a networking environment, an organization can truly achieve enterprise-level reliability and recoverability.

▶ **Part X: Optimizing, Tuning, Debugging, and Problem Solving**—This part of the book covers performance optimization, capacity analysis, logging, and debugging to help optimize and solve problems in a Windows Server 2008 R2 networking environment.

▶ **Part XI: Integrated Windows Application Services**—The last part of this book covers core application services integrated in Windows Server 2008 R2, including updates to Windows SharePoint Services and the Windows Media Services component.

It is our hope that the real-world experience we have had in working with Windows Server 2008 R2 and our commitment to relaying to you information that will be valuable in your planning, implementation, and migration to a Windows Server 2008 R2 environment will help you get up to speed on the latest in the Windows Server operating system software!

# Windows Server 2008 R2 Technology Primer

Windows Server 2008 R2 became available in the summer of 2009. In many ways, it is just the next-generation server operating system update to Windows Server 2008, but in other ways, it is more than just a service pack type update with significant feature enhancements introduced in the version release. To the authors of this book, we see the similarities that Windows Server 2008 R2 has in terms of usability and common graphical user interfaces (GUIs) with previous versions of Windows Server that make it easy to jump in and start implementing the new technologies. However, after over two years of early adopter experience with Windows Server 2008 R2 and the Windows 7 client operating system, when properly implemented, the new features and technologies built in to Windows Server 2008 R2 really address shortcomings of previous versions of Windows Server and truly allow IT organizations to help organizations meet their business initiatives through the implementation of key technologies now included in Windows Server 2008 R2.

This chapter provides an overview of what's in Windows Server 2008 R2, explains how IT professionals have leveraged the technologies to improve IT services to their organization, and acts as a guide on where to find more information on these core technology solutions in the various chapters of this book.

## Windows Server 2008 R2 Defined

Windows Server 2008 R2 is effectively the seventh generation of the Windows Server operating system. Upon initial boot, shown in Figure 1.1, Windows Server 2008 R2 looks like Windows 7 relative to icons, toolbars, and menus. However, because Windows Server 2008 R2 is more of a business functional operating system than a consumer or user operating system, things like the cute Windows Aero 3D interface are not installed by default, and the multimedia features found in the Windows 7 Home or Ultimate versions of the operating system are also not installed and enabled by default.

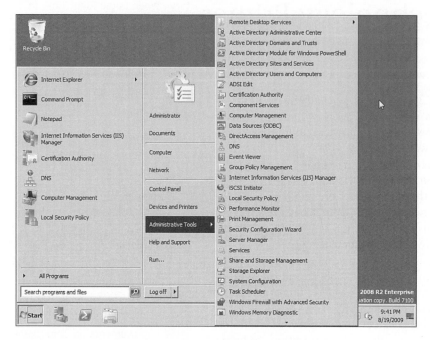

FIGURE 1.1    Windows Server 2008 R2 desktop screen.

Under the surface, though, and covered through the pages of this chapter are the new technologies and capabilities built in to Windows Server 2008 R2.

## Windows Server 2008 and Windows Server 2008 R2 Under the Hood

Although there are a lot of new features and functions added in to Windows Server 2008 and Windows Server 2008 R2 that are covered in chapters throughout this book, one of the first places I like to start is around the things in Windows Server 2008/2008 R2 that you don't see that make up some of the core capabilities of the new operating system. These are technologies that make the new operating system faster, more reliable, and do more things—but they aren't features that you have to install or configure.

### Self-Healing NTFS

One of the new embedded technologies in Windows Server 2008 and Windows Server 2008 R2 is self-healing NTFS. Effectively, the operating system has a worker thread that runs in the background, which makes corrections to the file system when NTFS detects a corrupt file or directory. In the past when there was a file system problem, you typically had to reboot the server for chkdsk to run and clean up file and directory corrupt errors.

This self-healing function is not something you will ever see running; however, it is an added capability under the hood in Windows Server 2008 R2 that keeps the operating system running reliably and with fewer system problems.

### Server Message Block 2.0

Introduced in Windows Vista and Windows Server 2008 is Server Message Block 2.0, more commonly called SMB2. SMB2 is a protocol that handles the transfer of files between systems. Effectively, SMB2 compresses file communications and, through a larger communications buffer, is able to reduce the number of round-trips needed when transmitting data between systems.

For the old-timers reading this chapter, it is analogous to the difference between the copy command and the xcopy command in DOS. The copy command reads, writes, reads, writes information. The xcopy command reads, reads, reads information and then writes, writes, writes the information. Because more information is read into a buffer and transferred in bulk, the information is transmitted significantly faster.

Most users on a high-speed local area network (LAN) won't notice the improvements when opening and saving files out of something like Microsoft Office against a Windows Server 2008/2008 R2 server; however, for users who might be copying up large image files or data sets between systems will find the information copying 10 to 30 times faster. The performance improvement is very noticeable in wide area network (WAN) situations on networks with high latency. Because a typical transfer of files requires short read and write segments of data, a file could take minutes to transfer across a WAN that can transfer in seconds between SMB2-connected systems because the round-trip chatter is drastically reduced.

For SMB2 to work effectively, the systems on both ends need to be Windows Server 2008/2008 R2 systems, Windows Vista or Windows 7 systems, or a combination of the two. A Windows XP client to a Windows Server 2008/2008 R2 server will communicate over SMB 1.0 for backward compatibility and will not gain from this new technology.

SMB2 and the benefits of this embedded technology are discussed in more detail in Chapter 32, "Optimizing Windows Server 2008 R2 for Branch Office Communications."

### Hyper-V

Hyper-V is a technology built in to the core of the operating system in Windows Server 2008 and expanded in Windows Server 2008 R2 that greatly enhances the performance and capabilities of server virtualization in a Windows environment. In the past, virtual server software sat on top of the network operating system and each guest session was dependent on many shared components of the operating system.

Hyper-V provides a very thin layer between the hardware abstract layer of the system and the operating system that provides guest sessions in a virtualized environment to communicate directly with the hardware layer of the system. Without having the host operating system in the way, guest sessions can perform significantly faster than in the past, and guest sessions can operate independent of the host operating system in terms of better reliability from eliminating host operating system bottlenecks.

Hyper-V and server virtualization is covered in more detail in Chapter 37, "Deploying and Using Windows Virtualization."

### Core Parking

A technology enhanced in the core Windows Server 2008 R2 operating system is a power-management technology called core parking. Normally, when a multicore server runs, all cores on all processors run at the highest speed possible, regardless of whether the server is being utilized. For organizations that need high capacity during the weekdays when employees are working, that means their systems are effectively idle during evenings and weekends, or more than two thirds of the time, yet consuming power and expending heat. With core parking, servers with the latest processors that recognize core parking protocols will shut down cores on a system when not in use. So, on a 16-core server, if only 2 cores are needed, the other 14 cores are powered off automatically. This dramatically improves power management and decreases the cost of operations of server systems.

## Windows Server 2008 R2 as an Application Server

As much as there have been significant improvements in Windows Server 2008 R2 under the hood that greatly enhance the performance, reliability, and scalability of Windows Server 2008 R2 in the enterprise, Windows servers have always been exceptional application servers hosting critical business applications for organizations. Windows Server 2008 R2 continues the tradition of the operating system being an application server with common server roles being included in the operating system. When installing Windows Server 2008 R2, the Server Manager Add Roles Wizard provides a list of server roles that can be added to a system, as shown in Figure 1.2.

The various server roles in Windows Server 2008 R2 typically fall into three categories, as follows:

- ▶ **File and print services**—As a file and print server, Windows Server 2008 R2 provides the basic services leveraged by users in the storage of data and the printing of information off the network. Several improvements have been made in Windows Server 2008 R2 for file security (covered in Chapter 13, "Server-Level Security") and file server fault tolerance (covered in Chapter 28, "File System Management and Fault Tolerance").

- ▶ **Domain services**—In enterprise environments running Windows networking, typically the organization is running Active Directory to provide centralized logon authentication. Active Directory continues to be a key component in Windows Server 2008 R2, with several extensions to the basic internal forest concept of an organization to expanded federated forests that allow Active Directories to interconnect with one another. There are several chapters in Part II, "Windows Server 2008 R2 Active Directory," that address Active Directory, federated forests, lightweight directories, and so on.

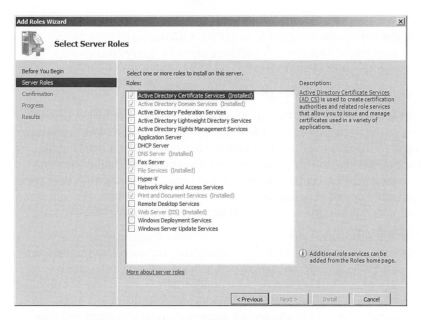

FIGURE 1.2    Server roles in Windows Server 2008 R2.

▶ **Application services**—Windows Server 2008 R2 provides the basis for the installation of business applications such as Microsoft Exchange, Microsoft Office
SharePoint Services, SQL Server, and so on. These applications are initially made to
be compatible with Windows Server 2008 R2, and later are updated to leverage and
take full advantage of the new technologies built in to the Windows Server 2008 R2
operating system. Some of the applications that come with Windows Server 2008 R2
include Remote Desktop Services for thin client computing access (covered in
Chapter 25, "Remote Desktop Services"), Windows Media Services for video and
audio hosting and broadcasting (covered in Chapter 36, "Windows Media Services"),
utility server services such as DNS and DHCP (covered in Chapter 11,
"DHCP/WINS/Domain Controllers," and Chapter 10, "Domain Name System and
IPv6"), SharePoint document sharing and collaboration technologies (covered in
Chapter 35, "Windows SharePoint Services"), and virtual server hosting (covered in
Chapter 37).

This book focuses on the Windows Server 2008 R2 operating system and the planning,
migration, security, administration, and support of the operating system. Windows Server
2008 R2 is also the base network operating system on top of which all future Windows
Server applications will be built.

## Windows Server 2008 R2 Active Directory

Although Windows Server 2008 R2 provides a number of new server roles for application
services, the release of Windows Server 2008 R2 also brings with it an update to Active
Directory. Unlike the shift from Windows NT to Active Directory a decade ago that
required a major restructuring of domain functions, Active Directory 2008 R2 is more

evolutionary than revolutionary. AD 2008 R2 adds a handful of new features that organizations might or might not choose to upgrade to AD 2008 R2 immediately; however, many organizations have found that the new enhancements in Active Directory 2008 R2 were the primary reason for their migration.

The new features in Active Directory 2008 R2 are as follows:

▶ **Active Directory Recycle Bin**—The AD Recycle Bin provides administrators an easy way to undelete objects in Active Directory. In the past, when an administrator inadvertently deleted an Active Directory object like a user, group, organizational unit container, or the like, the object was effectively gone and the administrator would have to create the object from scratch, which would create a whole new series of security principles for the new/unique object. The AD Recycle Bin now enables an administrator to simply run the recovery tool and undelete objects.

▶ **Managed Service Accounts**—Applications in a network frequently use service accounts associated with the security to start a database, conduct data searches and indexing, or launch background tasks. However, when an organization changes the password of a service account, all servers with applications using the service account need to be updated with the new password, which is an administration nightmare. With Active Directory 2008 R2 mode, service accounts can be identified and then managed so that a password change to a service account will initiate a process of updating the service account changes to application servers throughout the organization.

▶ **Authentication Mechanism Assurance**—Another Active Directory 2008 R2 feature is the enhancement of claims-based authentication in Active Directory. With authentication mechanism assurance, information in a token can be extracted whenever a user attempts to access a claims-aware application to determine authorization based on the user's logon method. This extension will be leveraged by future applications to improve claims-based authentication in the enterprise.

▶ **Offline Domain Join**—For desktop administrators who create system images, the challenge of creating images is that a system needs to be physically connected to the network before the system can be joined to the domain. With Offline Domain Join, a system can be prejoined with a file created with a unique system credential written to a file. When a Windows 7 client system or Windows Server 2008 R2 server system needs to be joined, rather than physically connecting the system to the network and joining the system to the domain, this exported file can be used offline to join the system to the Active Directory domain.

# When Is the Right Time to Migrate?

When Windows Server 2008 R2 first shipped in the summer of 2009, many organizations wondered about the right time to migrate to the new operating system. It used to be that you waited until the first service pack shipped before installing any Microsoft product; however, Windows Server 2008 R2 is effectively an update to Windows Server 2008 that is post–Service Pack 2. And early adopter beta participants found Windows Server 2008 R2

1

(and Windows 7) to be extremely stable and reliable and, thus, began implementation of the operating systems in production environments six+ months before the operating systems were released. So, the decision of when to implement Windows Server 2008 R2 comes down to the same decision on migration to any new technology—identify the value received by implementing Windows Server 2008 R2, test the solution in a limited environment, and roll out Windows Server 2008 R2 when you are comfortable that the product meets the needs of your organization.

This introductory chapter notes the many features and functions built in to Windows Server 2008 R2 that have helped other organizations make the decision that Windows Server 2008 R2 has significant value to plan a migration and new server implementation. Improvements in security, performance, and manageability provide benefits to organizations looking to minimize administration costs, while providing more functionality to users.

The cost and effort to migrate to Windows Server 2008 R2 vary based on the current state of an organization's networking environment, as well as the Windows Server 2008 R2 features and functions the organization wants to implement. Some organizations begin their migration process to Windows Server 2008 R2 by adding a Windows Server 2008 R2 member server into an existing Windows 2000/2003/2008 network. Others choose to migrate their Active Directory to Windows Server 2008 R2 as their introduction to the new operating system.

### Adding a Windows Server 2008 R2 System to a Windows 2003/2008 Environment

Many organizations want to add in a specific Windows Server 2008 R2 function such as Windows Server 2008 R2 Remote Desktop Services (previously called Terminal Services), Hyper-V R2 virtualization, DirectAccess, or BranchCache. Such functions can be installed on Windows Server 2008 R2 member servers in an existing Active Directory 2003 networking environment. This allows an organization to get Windows Server 2008 R2 application capabilities fairly quickly and easily without having to do a full migration to Active Directory 2008 R2. In many cases, a Windows Server 2008 R2 member server can simply be added to an existing network without ever affecting the existing network. This addition provides extremely low network impact but enables an organization to prototype and test the new technology, pilot it for a handful of users, and slowly roll out the technology to the client base as part of a regular system replacement or upgrade process.

Some organizations have replaced all their member servers with Windows Server 2008 R2 systems over a period of weeks or months as a preparatory step to eventually migrate to a Windows Server 2008 R2 Active Directory structure.

### Migrating from Windows 2003 and Windows 2008 Active Directory to Windows Server 2008 R2 Active Directory

For organizations that already have a Windows 2003 or Windows 2008 Active Directory environment, migrating to Windows Server 2008 R2 for Active Directory functionality can provide access to several additional capabilities that require a Windows network to be running on Windows Server 2008 R2. Some of the Windows Server 2008 R2 technologies that require implementation of the Windows Server 2008 R2 Active Directory include Active Directory Recycle Bin, Managed Service Accounts, PowerShell Administration, and Offline Domain Join capabilities as the most popular solutions.

Fortunately, organizations that already have Windows 2003 or 2008 Active Directory in place have completed the hard part of the Active Directory implementation process. Effectively, Windows Server 2008 R2 uses the same Active Directory organizational structure that was created with Windows 2003 or 2008, so forests, domain trees, domains, organizational units, sites, groups, and users all transfer directly into Windows Server 2008 R2 Active Directory. If the organizational structure in Windows 2003 or 2008 meets the needs of the organization, the migration to Windows Server 2008 R2 is predominantly just the insertion of a Windows Server 2008 R2 global catalog server into the existing Windows 2003 or 2008 Active Directory domain to perform a global catalog update to Windows Server 2008 R2 Active Directory.

Of course, planning, system backup, and prototype testing—covered in Chapter 16, "Migrating from Windows 2003/2008 to Windows Server 2008 R2"—help minimize migration risks and errors and lead to a more successful migration process. However, the migration process from Windows 2003 and Windows Server 2008 to Windows Server 2008 R2 is a relatively easy migration path for organizations to follow.

# Versions of Windows Server 2008 R2

Windows Server 2008 R2 comes in the same release versions as the more recent server version releases from Microsoft with the addition of a Server Core version that provides a lighter GUI-less version of Windows Server 2008 R2. The main versions of Windows Server 2008 R2 include Windows Server 2008 R2, Standard Edition; Windows Server 2008 R2, Enterprise Edition; Windows Server 2008 R2, Datacenter Edition; Windows Web Server 2008 R2; and Windows Server 2008 R2 Server Core.

## Windows Server 2008 R2, Standard Edition

The Windows Server 2008 R2, Standard Edition is the most common server version of the operating system. Unlike previous versions of Windows Server where basic functions and scalability for memory and processor support was limited to only the Enterprise or Datacenter Editions of the operating system, Windows Server 2008 R2, Standard Edition is now the default version deployed by organizations.

A basic Windows Server 2008 R2 x64-bit Standard Edition system supports up to four x64 professor sockets and 32GB of memory and supports all of the server roles available in Windows Server 2008 R2, with the exception of clustering, cross-file replication (DFS-R technology), and Active Directory Federation Services.

The Standard Edition is a good version of the operating system to support domain controllers, utility servers (such as DNS or DHCP), file servers, print servers, media servers, SharePoint servers, and so on. Most organizations, large and small, find the capabilities of the Standard Edition sufficient for most network services. See Chapter 34, "Capacity

Analysis and Performance Optimization," for recommendations on choosing and tuning a Windows Server 2008 R2 system that is right for its intended purpose.

> **NOTE**
>
> One of the first things an organization becomes aware of is that Windows Server 2008 R2 ONLY comes in 64-bit (x64 or IA64) versions. 32-bit hardware and a 32-bit installation is no longer supported. The last version of the Windows Server operating system that supported 32-bit is Windows Server 2008.

## Windows Server 2008 R2, Enterprise Edition

With the Windows Server 2008 R2, Standard Edition taking on the bulk of network services, the Windows Server 2008 R2, Enterprise Edition is really focused on server systems that require extremely large-scale processing and memory capabilities as well as clustering or Active Directory Federation Services. From the basis of scalability of processing and memory capacity, applications like Windows virtualization or enterprise-class Exchange 2010 or SQL 2008 servers would benefit from the capabilities of the Enterprise Edition of Windows Server 2008 R2.

Any time an organization needs to add clustering to its environment, the Enterprise Edition (or the Datacenter Edition) is needed. The Enterprise Edition is the appropriate version of operating system for high availability and high-processing demands of core application servers such as SQL Servers or large e-commerce back-end transaction systems.

For organizations leveraging the capabilities of Windows Server 2008 R2 for Thin Client Remote Desktop Services that require access to large sets of RAM (up to 2TB) and multiple processors (up to eight sockets), the Enterprise Edition can handle hundreds of users on a single server. Remote Desktop Services are covered in more detail in Chapter 25.

The Enterprise Edition, with support for server clustering, can provide organizations with the nonstop networking demands of true 24/7, 99.999% uptime capabilities required in high-availability environments. Windows Server 2008 R2, Enterprise Edition supports a wide variety of regularly available server systems, thus allowing an organization its choice of hardware vendor systems to host its Windows Server 2008 R2 application needs.

## Windows Server 2008 R2, Datacenter Edition

Windows Server 2008 R2, Datacenter Edition is a high-end datacenter class version of the operating system that supports very large-scale server operations. The Datacenter Edition supports organizations that need more than eight core processors. The Datacenter Edition is focused at organizations that need scale-up server technology to support a large centralized data warehouse on one or limited numbers of server clusters.

As noted in Chapter 34 on performance and capacity analysis, an organization can scale-out or scale-up its server applications. Scale-out refers to an application that performs better when it is distributed across multiple servers, whereas scale-up refers to an application that performs better when more processors are added to a single system. Typical scale-out applications include web server services, electronic messaging systems, and file and print servers. In those cases, organizations are better off distributing the application server functions to multiple Windows Server 2008 R2, Standard Edition or Enterprise Edition systems, or even Windows Web Server 2008 R2 systems. However, applications that scale-up, such as e-commerce or data warehousing applications, benefit from having all the data and processing on a single server cluster. For these applications, Windows Server 2008 R2, Datacenter Edition provides better centralized scaled performance as well as the added benefit of fault tolerance and failover capabilities.

> **NOTE**
>
> The Windows Server 2008 R2, Datacenter Edition used to be sold only with proprietary hardware systems; however, Windows Server 2008 R2, Datacenter Edition can now be run on "off-the-shelf" servers with extensive core, processor, and memory expansion capabilities. This update now allows organizations to purchase nonproprietary servers and get the scalability of the Datacenter Edition of the operating system for enterprise-class performance, reliability, and supportability.

## Windows Web Server 2008 R2 Edition

The Windows Web Server 2008 R2 Edition is a web front-end server version of the operating system focused on application server needs that are dedicated to web services requirements. Many organizations are setting up simple web servers as front ends to database servers, messaging servers, or data application server systems. Windows Web Server 2008 R2 Edition can be used as a simple web server to host application development environments or can be integrated as part of a more sophisticated web farm and web services environment that scales to multiple load-balanced systems. The Windows Server 2008 R2 operating system has significant improvements in scalability over previous versions of the Windows operating system, and an organization can license multiple web services systems at a lower cost per server to provide the scalability and redundancy desired in large web farm environments.

> **NOTE**
>
> For organizations looking to purchase a low-cost Windows Web Server Edition to set up a simple file and print server or utility server (DNS, DHCP, domain controller), the Web Server Edition does not provide traditional multiuser file or print access or utility services. You need to purchase the Windows Server 2008 R2, Standard Edition to get capabilities other than web services.

## Windows Server 2008 R2 Server Core

New to Windows Server 2008 and continued support with Windows Server 2008 R2 is a Server Core version of the operating system. Windows Server 2008 R2 Server Core, shown in Figure 1.3, is a GUI-less version of the Windows Server 2008 R2 operating system.

When a system boots up with Server Core installed on it, the system does not load up the normal Windows graphical user interface. Instead, the Server Core system boots to a logon prompt, and from the logon prompt, the system drops to a DOS command prompt. There is no Start button, no menu—no GUI at all.

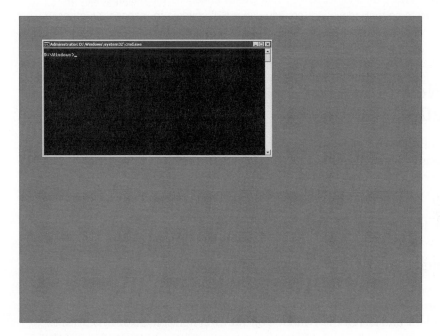

FIGURE 1.3    Windows Server 2008 R2 Server Core.

Server Core is not sold as a separate edition, but rather as an install option that comes with the Standard, Enterprise, Datacenter, and Web Server Editions of the operating system. So, when you purchase a license of Windows Server 2008 R2, the DVD has both the normal GUI Edition code plus a Windows Server 2008 R2 Server Core version.

The operating system capabilities are limited to the edition of Server Core being installed, so a Windows Server 2008 R2, Enterprise Edition Server Core server has the same memory and processor limits as the regular Enterprise Edition of Windows Server 2008 R2.

Server Core has been a great version of Windows for utility servers such as domain controllers, DHCP servers, DNS servers, IIS web servers, or Windows virtualization servers being that the limited overhead provides more resources to the applications running on the server, and by removing the GUI and associated applications, there's less of a security attack footprint on the Server Core system. Being that most administrators don't play Solitaire or use Media Player on a domain controller, those are applications that don't need to be patched, updated, or maintained on the GUI-less version of Windows. With fewer applications to be patched, the system requires less maintenance and management to keep operational.

**NOTE**

With the new remote administration capabilities of Windows Server 2008 R2, covered in Chapter 20, "Windows Server 2008 R2 Management and Maintenance Practices," administrators can now remotely manage a Server Core system from the Server Manager GUI interface on another server. This greatly enhances the management of Server Core hosts so that administrators can use a GUI console to manage the otherwise GUI-less version of Windows Server.

# What's New and What's the Same About Windows Server 2008 R2?

From a Microsoft marketing perspective, Windows Server 2008 R2 could be said to be faster, more secure, more reliable, and easier to manage. And it is true that the Windows Server 2008 R2 operating system has all these capabilities. However, this section notes specifically which changes are cosmetic changes compared with previous Windows operating systems and which changes truly improve the overall administrative and end-user experience due to improvements in the operating system.

## Visual Changes in Windows Server 2008 R2

The first thing you notice when Windows Server 2008 R2 boots up is the new Windows 7-like graphical user interface (GUI). This is obviously a simple cosmetic change to standardize the current look and feel of the Windows operating systems. Interestingly, with the release of Windows Server 2008 R2, Microsoft did away with the "Classic View" of the administrator Control Panel. For all the network administrators who always switched their server Control Panel to the Classic View, that is now gone, and you will need to figure out the "updated" Control Panel that was the standard starting with Windows XP.

## Continuation of the Forest and Domain Model

Windows Server 2008 R2 also uses the exact same Active Directory forest, domain, site, organizational unit, group, and user model as Windows 2000/2003/2008. So if you liked how Active Directory was set up before, it doesn't change with Windows Server 2008 R2 Active Directory. Even the Active Directory Sites and Services, Active Directory Users and Computers (shown in Figure 1.4), and Active Directory Domains and Trusts administrative tools work exactly the same.

There are several changes to the names of the Active Directory services as well as significant improvements within Active Directory that are covered in the section "Changes in Active Directory" a little later in this chapter.

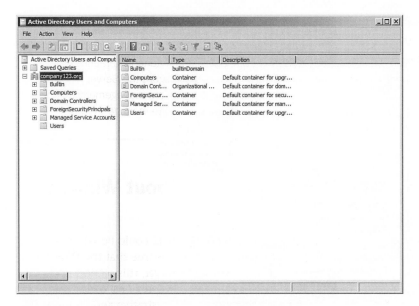

FIGURE 1.4    Active Directory Users and Computers tool.

## Changes That Simplify Tasks

Windows Server 2008 R2 has added several new capabilities that simplify tasks. These capabilities could appear to be simply cosmetic changes; however, they actually provide significant benefits for administrative management.

### New Server Manager Tool

A tool that was added in Windows Server 2008 is the Server Manager console, shown in Figure 1.5. Server Manager consolidates all of the administrative management consoles from Windows 2000/2003 into a single management tool. Now instead of having to open up the Active Directory Users and Computers console, Control Panel system properties, the DNS management console, and so on, and then toggle to the appropriate console you want, all of the information is now available in one screen.

Updated in Windows Server 2008 R2 is the ability for an administrator to use the Server Manager tool to access not only the server resources on the current server system, but also to remotely access server resources through the Server Manager tool on remote server systems. This remote capability of Server Manager minimizes the need of the administrator to remotely log on to systems to manage them; it allows the administrator to sit at a single Server Manager console and gain access to other servers in the organization.

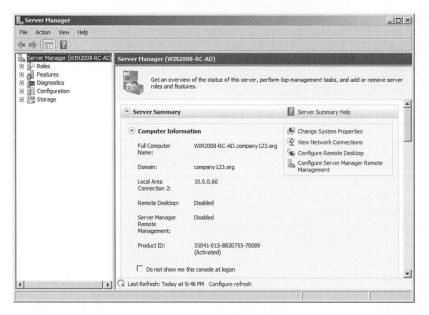

FIGURE 1.5    Server Manager.

Additionally, other tools like the Group Policy Management Console (GPMC) show up in Server Manager under the Features node and provide an administrator with the ability to edit group policies, change policies, and apply policies from the same console to which the administrator can make DNS changes, add users, and change IP configuration changes to site configuration settings.

### PowerShell for Administrative Tasks

Another updated server feature in Windows Server 2008 R2 is the extension of PowerShell for server administration and management. PowerShell has now been extended to be a full scripting language for administration tasks in Windows Server 2008 R2. PowerShell was first introduced in Exchange 2007 as the Exchange Management Shell (EMS) that underlies all functions of Exchange 2007 administration. PowerShell (version 2.0) is now installed by default in Windows Server 2008 R2, as opposed to being an add-in feature in Windows Server 2008. As a built-in component, all administrative tasks are now fully PowerShell enabled.

PowerShell in Windows Server 2008 R2 provides the ability for administrators to script processes, such as adding users, adding computers, or even more complicated tasks such as querying a database, extracting usernames, and then creating Active Directory users, and to provision Exchange mailboxes all from a PowerShell script. Additionally, PowerShell in Windows Server 2008 R2 allows an administrator to script installation processes so that if, for example, the administrator creates a Remote Desktop server or web server with specific settings, the administrator can use a PowerShell script and deploy additional servers all identically configured using the same script over and over.

And with PowerShell 2.0 built in to Windows Server 2008 R2, PowerShell scripts and commands can be run against remote servers. This enables an administrator to sit at one server and remotely execute scripts on other servers in the environment. Using secured server-to-server session communications, an administrator can configure a group of servers, manage a group of servers, and reboot a group of servers all from a series of PowerShell commands.

All future server products released from Microsoft will have the PowerShell foundation built in to the core Windows Server 2008 R2 operating system, thus making it easier for products running on Windows Server 2008 R2 to use the same administrative scripting language. PowerShell is covered in detail in Chapter 21, "Automating Tasks Using PowerShell Scripting."

### Active Directory Administrative Center

New to Windows Server 2008 R2 and built on PowerShell v2.0, the Active Directory Administrative Center is a customizable console that an organization can create for specific administrators in the organization. As an example, an organization might have an administrator who only needs to reset passwords, or another administrator who only needs or manage print queues. Rather than giving the administrator access to the full Active Directory Users and Computers or Print Management consoles, an Active Directory Administrative console can be created with just a task or two specific to the administrator's responsibilities.

The console is built on PowerShell, so underlying the GUI are simple PowerShell scripts. Anything that can be done in PowerShell on a Windows Server 2008 R2 server can be front-ended by the administration console. An example of the console is shown in Figure 1.6, and the tool is covered in detail in Chapter 18, "Windows Server 2008 R2 Administration."

## Increased Support for Standards

The release of Windows Server 2008 introduced several industry standards built in to the Windows operating system that have since been updated in Windows Server 2008 R2. These changes continue a trend of the Windows operating system supporting industry standards rather than proprietary Microsoft standards. One of the key standards built in to Windows Server 2008 and Windows Server 2008 R2 is IPv6.

Internet Protocol version 6 (or IPv6) is the future Internet standard for TCP/IP addressing. Most organizations support Internet Protocol version 4 (or IPv4). Due to the Internet numbering scheme running out of address space in its current implementation of addressing, Internet communications of the future need to support IPv6, which provides a more robust address space.

Additionally, IPv6 supports new standards in dynamic addressing and Internet Protocol Security (IPSec). Part of IPv6 is to have support for the current IPv4 standards so that dual addressing is possible. With Windows Server 2008 R2 supporting IPv6, an organization can choose to implement a dual IPv6 and IPv4 standard to prepare for Internet communications support in the future. IPv6 is covered in detail in Chapter 10.

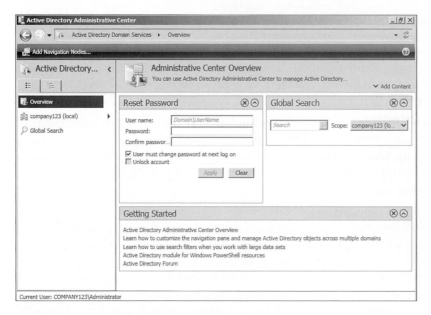

FIGURE 1.6    Active Directory Administrative Center.

# Changes in Active Directory

As noted earlier in this chapter, Active Directory in Windows Server 2008 R2 hasn't changed to the point where organizations with solid Active Directory structures have to make changes to their directory environment. Forests, domains, sites, organizational units, groups, and users all remain the same. There are several improvements made in Active Directory and the breadth of functionality provided by directory services in Windows Server 2008 R2.

The changes made in Active Directory are captured in the name changes of directory services as well as the introduction of a Read-Only Domain Controller service introduced in Windows Server 2008.

## Renaming Active Directory to Active Directory Domain Services

In Windows Server 2008, Active Directory was renamed to Active Directory Domain Services (AD DS), and Windows Server 2008 R2 continues with that new name. Active Directory Domain Services refers to what used to be just called Active Directory with the same tools, architectural design, and structure that Microsoft introduced with Windows 2000 and Windows 2003.

The designation of Domain Services identifies this directory as the service that provides authentication and policy management internal to an organization where an organization's internal domain controls network services.

For the first time, AD DS can be stopped and started as any other true service. This facilitates AD DS maintenance without having to restart the domain controller in Directory Services Restore Mode.

## Renaming Active Directory in Application Mode to Active Directory Lightweight Directory Service

Another name change in the directory services components with Windows Server 2008 from Microsoft is the renaming of Active Directory in Application (ADAM) to Active Directory Lightweight Directory Services (AD LDS). ADAM has been a downloadable add-in to Windows 2003 Active Directory that provides a directory typically used in organizations for nonemployees who need access to network services. Rather than putting nonemployees into the Active Directory, these individuals—such as contractors, temporary workers, or even external contacts, such as outside legal counsel, marketing firms, and so on—have been put in ADAM and given rights to access network resources such as SharePoint file libraries, extranet content, or web services.

AD LDS is identical to ADAM in its functionality, and provides an organization with options for enabling or sharing resources with individuals outside of the organizational structure. With the name change, organizations that didn't quite know what ADAM was before have begun to leverage the Lightweight Directory Services function of Active Directory for more than resource sharing but also for a lookup directory resource for clients, patients, membership directories, and so on. Active Directory Lightweight Directory Services is covered in detail in Chapter 8, "Creating Federated Forests and Lightweight Directories."

## Expansion of the Active Directory Federation Services

That leads to the third Active Directory service called Active Directory Federation Services, or AD FS. Active Directory Federation Services was introduced with Windows 2003 R2 edition and continues to provide the linking, or federation, between multiple Active Directory forests, or now with Windows Server 2008 R2 Active Directory Federation Services, the ability to federate between multiple Active Directory Domain Services systems.

Effectively, for organizations that want to share information between Active Directory Domain Services environments, two or more AD DS systems can be connected together to share information. This has been used by organizations that have multiple subsidiaries with their own Active Directory implemented to exchange directory information between the two organizations. And AD FS has been used by business trading partners (suppliers and distributors) to interlink directories together to be able to have groups of users in both organizations easily share information, freely communicate, and easily collaborate between the two organizations.

Active Directory Federation Services is covered in detail in Chapter 8.

### Introducing the Read-Only Domain Controller

Another change in Active Directory in Windows Server 2008 that was continued in Windows 2008 R2 was the addition of a Read-Only Domain Controller, or RODC. The RODC is just like a global catalog server in Active Directory used to authenticate users and as a resource to look up objects in the directory; however, instead of being a read/write copy of the directory, an RODC only maintains a read-only copy of Active Directory and forwards all write and authentication requests to a read/write domain controller.

RODCs can also be configured to cache specified logon credentials. Cached credentials speed up authentication requests for the specified users. The cached credentials are stored in cache on the RODC system, not every object in the entire global catalog. If the RODC is shut down or powered off, the cache on the RODC is flushed, and the objects in cache are no longer available until the RODC connects back to a global catalog server on the network.

The RODC is a huge advancement in the area of security being that a RODC cannot be compromised in the same manner that a global catalog server can be in the event of a physical theft of a domain server. Organizations that require the functionality of a global catalog server for user authentication that have the global catalog server in an area that is not completely secure, such as in a remote office, in a branch office location, or even in a retail store outlet, can instead put a RODC in the remote location.

# Windows Server 2008 R2 Benefits for Administration

Windows Server 2008 R2 provides several new benefits that help organizations better administer their networking environment. These new features provide better file and data management, better performance monitoring and reliability tracking tools to identify system problems and proactively address issues, a new image deployment tool, and a whole new set of Group Policy Objects that help administrators better manage users, computers, and other Active Directory objects.

### Improvements in the Group Policy Management

Windows Server 2008 R2 introduces over 1,000 new Group Policy Objects specific to Windows Server 2008 R2 and Windows 7, along with several new components that expand on the core capabilities of Group Policy management that have been part of Windows 2000/2003 Active Directory. The basic functions of Group Policy haven't changed, so the Group Policy Object Editor (gpedit) and the Group Policy Management Console (GPMC) are the same, but with more options and settings available.

As mentioned earlier, the Group Policy Management Console can either be run as a separate MMC tool, or it can be launched off the Features branch of the Server Manager console tree, as shown in Figure 1.7. Group policies in Windows Server 2008 R2 provide more granular management of local machines, specifically having policies that push down to a client that are different for administrator and non-administrator users.

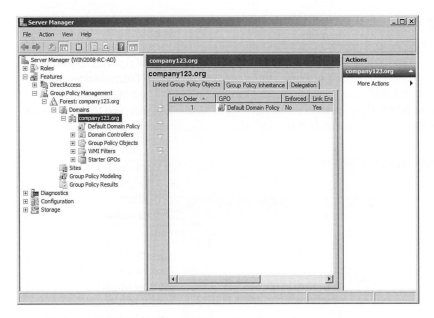

FIGURE 1.7    Group Policy Management Console.

Additionally, applications can now query or register with a network location awareness service within Group Policy management, which provides the identity where a user or computer object resides. As an example, a policy can be written that allows users to have access to applications and files if they are on a local network segment, but blocks users from accessing the same content when they are on a remote segment for security and privacy reasons. This addition to group policies adds a third dimension to policies so that now administrators can not only define who and what someone has access to, but also limit their access based on where they are.

Group policies are covered in detail in Chapter 27, "Group Policy Management for Network Clients," as well as in Chapter 19, "Windows Server 2008 R2 Group Policies and Policy Management."

**NOTE**

When running the Group Policy Management Console to manage a Windows Server 2008 R2 Active Directory environment, run the GPMC tool from a Windows Server 2008 R2 server or a Windows 7 client system to have access to all the editable objects available. If you run the GPMC tool from a Windows 2003 server or Windows XP client, you will not see all the features nor have full access to edit all objects available.

This is because Windows Server 2008 R2 now supports new template file formats (ADMX and ADML) that are only accessible from Windows Server 2008, Windows Server 2008 R2, Windows Vista, and Windows 7 systems.

## Introducing Performance and Reliability Monitoring Tools

Windows Server 2008 R2 introduces new and revised performance and reliability monitoring tools intended to help network administrators better understand the health and operations of Windows Server 2008 R2 systems. Just like with the Group Policy Management Console, the new Reliability and Performance Monitor shows up as a feature in the Server Manager console. By clicking on the Performance Diagnostic Console, the tool shows up in the right pane, as shown in Figure 1.8.

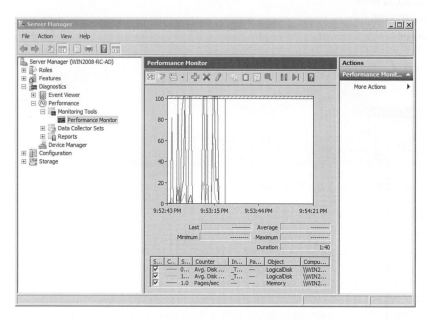

FIGURE 1.8    Windows Reliability and Performance Monitor.

The new tool keeps track of system activity and resource usage and displays key counters and system status on screen. The Reliability Monitor diagnoses potential causes of server instability by noting the last time a server was rebooted, what patches or updates were applied, and chronologically when services have failed on the system so that system faults can potentially be traced back to specific system updates or changes that occurred prior to the problem.

By combining what used to be three to four tools into a single console, administrators are able to look at system performance, operational tasks, and historical event information in their analysis of a server problem or system operations instability. You can find more details on performance and reliability monitoring in Chapter 34.

## Leveraging File Server Resource Manager

File Server Resource Manager (FSRM) was a feature pack add-in to Windows 2003 R2 and has been significantly improved with the release of Windows Server 2008 R2. FSRM is a quota management system of files on network shares across an enterprise. Rather than allowing employees to copy the entire content of their laptop to a network, or potentially back up their MP3 audio files onto a network, FSRM provides the ability to not only limit the amount of content stored on network shares, but also to set quotas (or limit storage altogether) on certain file types. So, a user could be limited to store 200GB of files on a network share, but of that limit, only 2GB can be allocated to MP3 files.

FSRM, shown in Figure 1.9, in Windows Server 2008 R2 has been improved to allow the nesting of quotas to ensure the most restrictive policy is applied. Quotas can also transcend subfolders, so as new folders are created, or as policies are applied at different levels in a folder hierarchy, the policies still apply, and the rules are combined to provide varying levels of quota allocation to user data. Additionally, quotas are now based on actual storage, so if a file is compressed when stored, the user will be able to store more files within their allocated quota.

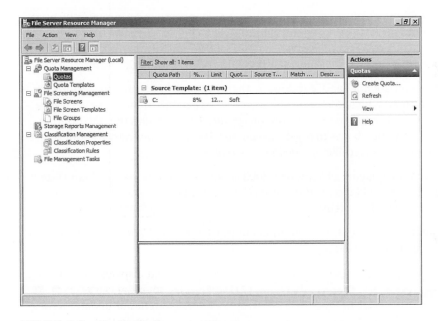

FIGURE 1.9   File Server Resource Manager.

File Server Resource Manager is covered in detail in Chapter 28.

## Leveraging the Best Practice Analyzer

Included in Windows Server 2008 R2 is a built-in Best Practice Analyzer. Found in the Server Manager console tool, the Best Practice Analyzer runs a series of tests against Active Directory roles, such as the Hyper-V role, the DNS role, and the Remote Desktop Services role, to assess whether the role has been installed and configured properly and to compare the installation with tested best practices.

Some of the results from the Best Practice Analyzer could tell an administrator they need to add more memory to a server, to move a role to a separate server to improve role optimization, or to shift a database to a different drive on the server to distribute disk performance demands on the system. More details on the Best Practice Analyzer are covered in Chapter 20.

### Introduction of Windows Deployment Services

Windows Server 2008 introduced a new tool called Windows Deployment Services (WDS), which was effectively an updated version of the Remote Installation Services (RIS) that has been available for the past several years. Unlike RIS, which was focused on primarily scripted installations and client images, WDS in Windows Server 2008 R2 can distribute images of Windows 7 clients or Windows Server 2008 R2 servers in a significantly more flexible and modifiable deployment process.

Like with RIS, Windows Deployment Services allows a client system to initiate a Preboot Execution Environment (PXE), effectively "booting" to the WDS server to see a list of images that can be deployed on the system. Alternately, an organization can create a Windows PE boot disc and have an image initiated from a CD or DVD.

With Windows Server 2008 R2 and Windows 7, the image can be created in Windows Imaging (WIM) format, which allows for the injection of patches, updates, or even new code to a WIM file without even booting the image file. This provides the organization with more than just static images that get pushed out like in RIS, but rather a tool that provides ongoing and manageable updates to image files.

WDS also supports the imaging of Windows 2003 servers and Windows XP client systems in the same manner that RIS did in terms of pushing out images or using an unattend script file to send images to systems.

Windows Deployment Services is covered in detail in Chapter 26, "Windows Server 2008 R2 Administration Tools for Desktops."

# Improvements in Security in Windows Server 2008 R2

Significantly more than just cosmetic updates are the security enhancements added to Windows Server 2008 R2. As organizations are struggling to ensure that their environments are secure, employees can depend on information privacy, and content is protected for regulatory compliance reasons; having the tools to secure the environment is critical.

### Enhancing the Windows Server 2008 R2 Security Subsystem

Part IV of this book, "Security," is focused on security in the different core areas. Chapter 13 addresses core security subsystems of Windows Server 2008 R2 as it relates to server systems. This includes the basics of server hardening, patching, and updating but also extends into new server security areas added to Windows Server 2008 R2, such as device control level security, wireless access security, and Active Directory Rights Management Services (RMS). Windows Server 2008 R2 has continued the "secure by default" theme at

Microsoft and no longer installs components like Internet Information Services (IIS) by default. The good part about it is that components that are not core to the operation of a server are not installed on the system; however, it means every time you install software, you need to add basic components and features. Getting to remember what has to be installed, configured, or made operational is important as servers are being built and added to a Windows Active Directory environment.

## Transport Security Using IPSec and Certificate Services

Chapter 14, "Transport-Level Security," addresses site-to-site and server-to-server security, addressed through the implementation of IPSec encryption. Not new to Windows, IPSec has finally gotten several new Group Policy management components added to aid in the implementation and management of IPSec in the enterprise. Also not new to Windows, but something that has been greatly enhanced, is Microsoft's offering around Public Key Infrastructure (PKI), specifically Certificate Services. It seems like everything security related is somehow connected to certificates, whether that is file encryption using Encrypting File System (EFS), email encryption using S/MIME, remote mobile device synchronization using certificate access, or transport security using IPSec. Everything needs a certificate, and the ability of an organization to easily create and manage certificates is the focus of Chapter 14.

## Security Policies, Policy Management, and Supporting Tools for Policy Enforcement

Completely new to Windows Server 2008, updated in Windows Server 2008 R2, and a major focus for organizations are security policies and policy management around security systems. It used to be we would just lock down systems, make sure they were secure by default, and use our best judgment and best effort to secure a network. However, with laws and regulations, or even human resource departments getting involved in information security, the root of all IT security practices fall on having set security policies defined so that IT can implement technologies to address the organization policies around information security. This is covered in detail in Chapter 15, "Security Policies, Network Policy Server, and Network Access Protection."

Chapter 15 goes beyond the policies and common best practices around policy management in an enterprise, and also digs into the underlying technologies that help organizations turn security policies into IT-managed technology services. Tools like the Network Policy Server in Windows Server 2008 R2 allow policies to be defined, and the Network Policy Server enforces those policies, specifically around remote logon access, access over wireless network connections, or the integration of Network Access Protection (NAP) in querying a device and making sure the device (desktop, laptop, or mobile device) has the latest patches, updates, and antivirus software dictated by management to ensure a device is secure.

# Improvements in Mobile Computing in Windows Server 2008 R2

As organizations find their workforce becoming more and more mobile, Microsoft has made significant improvements to mobility in Windows Server 2008 R2. New technologies provide a more seamless experience for users with laptops to move from office, to home, to Internet Wi-Fi hot spots and maintain connectivity to network resources. These improvements do require mobile users to run the latest Windows 7 client operating system on their laptop system to gain access to these new services; however, once implemented, users find the functionality to greatly support easier access to network resources no matter where the user resides.

## Windows Server 2008 R2 DirectAccess

One of the significant remote access enhancements in Windows Server 2008 R2 is the DirectAccess technology. DirectAccess provides a remote user the ability to access network resources such as file shares, SharePoint shares, and the like without having to launch a virtual private network (VPN) to gain access into the network.

DirectAccess is an amazing technology that combines sophisticated security technology and policy-based access technology to provide remote access to a network; however, organizations do find it challenging to get up to speed with all the technology components necessary to make DirectAccess work. So, although many organizations will seek to achieve DirectAccess capabilities, it might be months or a couple of years before all the technologies are in place for the organization to easily enable DirectAccess in their enterprise environment.

Some of the technologies required to make DirectAccess work include the following:

- ▶ **PKI certificates**—DirectAccess leverages PKI certificates as a method of identification of the remote device as well as the basis for encrypted communications from the remote device and the network. Thus, an organization needs to have a good certificate infrastructure in place for server and client certificate-based encrypted communications.

- ▶ **Windows 7 clients**—DirectAccess only works with clients that are running Windows 7. The client component for encryption, encapsulation, and policy control depend on Windows 7 to make all the components work together.

- ▶ **IPSec**—The policy control used in DirectAccess leverages IPSec to identify the destination resources that a remote user should have access to. IPSec can be endpoint to endpoint (that is, from the client system all the way to the application server) or IPSec can be simplified from the client system to a DirectAccess proxy server where the actual endpoint application servers do not need to be IPSec enabled. In any case, IPSec is a part of the security and policy structure that ensures the remote client system is only accessing server resources that by policy the remote client should have access to as part of the DirectAccess session connection.

## 1

▶ **IPv6**—Lastly, DirectAccess uses IPv6 as the IP session identifier. Although most organizations have not implemented IPv6 yet and most on-ramps to the Internet are still IPv6, tunneling of IPv6 is fully supported in Windows 7 and Windows Server 2008 R2 and can be used in the interim until IPv6 is fully adopted. For now, IPv6 is a requirement of DirectAccess and is used as part of the remote access solution.

More details on DirectAccess are provided in Chapter 24, "Server-to-Client Remote Access and DirectAccess."

## Windows 7 VPN Reconnect

VPN Reconnect is not a Windows Server 2008 R2–specific feature but rather a Windows 7 client feature; however, with the simultaneous release of the Windows 7 client and Windows Server 2008 R2, it is worth noting this feature because Microsoft will be touting the technology and network administrators will want to know what they need to do to implement the technology. VPN Reconnect is simply an update to the VPN client in Windows 7 that reestablishes a VPN session on a client system in the event that the client system's VPN session is disconnected.

VPN Reconnect effectively acknowledges that a client VPN session has been disconnected and reestablishes the session. Many longtime administrators might wonder why this is new because client systems in the past (Windows XP, Vista, and so forth) have always had the ability to retry a VPN session upon disconnect. However, the difference is that instead of simply retrying the VPN session and establishing a new VPN session, the VPN Reconnect feature of Windows 7 reestablishes a VPN session with the exact same session identification, effectively allowing a session to pick up exactly where it left off.

For example, a Windows 7 client user can be transferring a file on a wired VPN connected session and then switch midstream to a Wi-Fi VPN-connected session, and the file transfer will continue uninterrupted.

VPN Reconnect utilizes the IKE v2 protocol on the client and on the Windows Server 2008 R2 side with an established session identification so that upon reconnect, the session ID remains the same.

Chapter 24 provides more details on VPN Reconnect.

## Windows 7 Mobile Broadband

Another Windows 7–specific technology for mobile users is Windows 7 Mobile Broadband. Again, something that has nothing to do specifically with Windows Server 2008 R2, Windows 7 Mobile Broadband is an update to the carrier-based (for example, AT&T, Sprint, Verizon) mobile connection devices and services in Windows 7.

In the past, a user plugged in a Mobile Broadband card to their Windows XP or Vista system and then had to launch an application such as the AT&T Connection Manager. With Windows 7 and the latest Mobile Broadband drivers for the device and for Windows 7, the insertion of the Mobile Broadband card into a mobile system automatically connects the user to the Internet. Just like if the user turns on a Wi-Fi adapter in a system and automatically establishes a connection to a Wi-Fi access point, Mobile Broadband automatically connects the user to the Internet.

When the Windows 7 Mobile Broadband adapter is disconnected from the user's system, the Mobile Broadband session disconnects, and if the system has a Wi-Fi or wired Ethernet connection available, the user's system automatically connects to an alternate connection point. Combine Mobile Broadband with VPN Reconnect or with DirectAccess and a mobile user has seamless connection access back into their organization's network.

# Improvements in Windows Server 2008 R2 for Better Branch Office Support

Windows Server 2008 R2 has greatly enhanced the technology offerings that provide better IT services to organizations with remote offices or branch offices. Typically, a remote or branch office has limited IT support or at least the site needs to have the same functionality and reliability as the main corporate or business office, but without the budget, to have lots of redundant hardware and devices for full operational support. With the new Windows Server 2008 R2 branch office resources, a remote location can now have high security, high performance, access to data without significant latency, and operational capabilities, even if the remote site is dropped off the network due to a WAN or Internet connection problem.

The tools and technologies new or improved in Windows Server 2008 R2 include Read-Only Domain Controllers, BitLocker Drive Encryption, distributed file server data replication, and distributed administration.

Details on the new technologies built in to Windows Server 2008 R2 that better support remote and branch offices are covered in Chapter 32.

## Read-Only Domain Controllers for the Branch Office

As covered in the section "Introducing the Read-Only Domain Controller" earlier in this chapter, the RODC provides a copy of the Active Directory global catalog for logon authentication of select users and communications with the Active Directory tree without having the security exposure of a full global catalog server in the remote location. Many organizations concerned with distributed global catalog servers chose to not place a server in a remote location, but rather kept their global catalog and domain controllers centralized. What this meant for remote and branch offices is that all logon authentication had to go across the WAN or Internet connection, which could be very slow. And in the event of a WAN or Internet connection failure, the remote or branch office would be offline because users could not authenticate to the network and access network resources until the WAN or Internet connection was restored.

Read-Only Domain Controllers provide a way for organizations to distribute authentication and Active Directory access without increasing their security risk caused by the distribution of directory services.

## BranchCache File Access

New to Windows Server 2008 R2 is a role called BranchCache. BranchCache is a technology that provides users with better access to files across a wide area network (WAN). Normally, if one user accesses a file, the file is transferred across the WAN for the user, and then when another user accesses the same file, the same file is again transferred across the WAN for the other user. BranchCache acknowledges that a file has been transferred across the WAN by a previous user, and instead of retrieving the file across the WAN, the file is accessed locally by the subsequent user.

BranchCache requires Windows 7 on the client side and can be set up so that the file is effectively retrieved in a peer-to-peer manner from another Windows 7 client that had previously accessed a file. Or, a Windows Server 2008 R2 server with the BranchCache server role can be set up in the remote location where remotely accessed files are temporarily cached for other Windows 7 client users to seamlessly access the files locally instead of being downloaded across the WAN.

BranchCache does not require the user to do anything differently. Users simply accesses files as they normally do (either off a Windows file system or from a SharePoint document library), and the combination of Windows 7 and Windows Server 2008 R2 does all the caching automatically. BranchCache has proven to improve access time on average 30%–45% for remote users, thus increasing user experience and potentially user productivity by having faster access to information in remote locations.

## BitLocker for Server Security

BitLocker is a technology first introduced with Windows Vista that provides an organization with the ability to do a full partition encryption of all files, documents, and information stored on the encrypted partition. When BitLocker was first introduced in Windows Server 2008 as a server tool, it was hard to understand why a server would need to have its drive volume encrypted. It made sense that a laptop would be encrypted in the event the laptop is stolen—so that no one could get access to the data on the laptop hard drive. However, when considering that servers are placed in remote locations—many times not in a locked server rack in a locked computer room but rather sitting in a closet or even under a cash register in the situation of a retail store with a server acting as the point-of-sale system—servers with sensitive data are prevalent in enterprise environments.

So, BitLocker provides encryption of the volume of a Windows Server 2008 R2 server; for organizations that are concerned that the server might be physically compromised by the theft of the server or physical attack of the system, BitLocker is a great component to implement on the server system.

## Distributed File System Replication

Introduced in Windows 2000, improved in Windows 2003, and now a core component of the branch office offerings in Windows Server 2008 R2, Distributed File System Replication (DFSR) allows files to be replicated between servers, effectively providing duplicate information in multiple locations. Windows Server 2008 R2 has a much improved Distributed File System than what was available in Windows 2000/2003. In most organizations, files are distributed across multiple servers throughout the enterprise. Users access file shares that are geographically distributed but also can access file shares sitting on several servers in a site within the organization. In many organizations, when file shares were originally created years ago, server performance, server disk capacity, and the workgroup nature of file and print server distribution created environments in which those organizations had a file share for every department and every site. Thus, files have typically been distributed throughout an entire organization across multiple servers.

Windows Server 2008 R2 Distributed File System Replication enables an organization to combine file shares to fewer servers and create a file directory tree not based on a server-by-server or share-by-share basis, but rather an enterprisewide directory tree. This allows an organization to have a single directory spanning files from multiple servers throughout the enterprise.

Because the DFSR directory is a logical directory that spans the entire organization with links back to physical data, the actual physical data can be moved without having to make changes to the way the users see the logical DFS directory. This enables an organization to add or delete servers, or move and consolidate information, however it works best within the organization.

For branch office locations, DFSR allows for data stored on a file server in a remote location to be trickled back to the home office for nightly backup. Instead of having the remote location responsible for data backup, or the requirement of an organization to have tape drives in each of its branch offices, any data saved on the branch office can be trickle replicated back to a share at the main office for backup and recovery.

If the main office has data that it wants to push out to all remote offices, whether that is template files, company policy documents, standard company materials, or even shared data that a workgroup of users needs to access and collaborate on, DFSR provides the ability to push out data to other servers on the network. Users with access rights to the data no longer have to go across a WAN connection to access common data. The information is pushed out to a server that is more local to the user, and the user accesses the local copy of the information. If any changes are made to remote or centralized copies of data, those changes are automatically redistributed back to all volumes storing a copy of the data.

One of the enhancements made in Windows Server 2008 R2 specific to DFS-R is the ability for an administrator to set a DFS replica to be read-only. In the past, DFS replicas were all read/write replicas so that a user in a remote location could accidentally overwrite files that then replicate to all replicas in the environment. Administrators have compensated for this potential issue by setting file-level permissions across files and folders; however, for many remote branch offices, if the administrator could simply make the entire replica read-only, it would simplify the security task dramatically. Thus, read-only replicas can now be set so that an entire server or branch of a DFS tree can be set to replicate to a remote server on a read-only basis.

Distributed File System Replication is covered in detail in Chapter 28.

## Improvements in Distributed Administration

Finally, for remote or branch offices that do have IT personnel in the remote locations, administration and management tasks have been challenging to distribute proper security rights. Either remote IT personnel were given full domain administrator rights when they should only be limited to rights specific to their site, or administrators were not given any administrative rights because it was too difficult to apply a more limiting role.

Windows Server 2008 R2 Active Directory has now defined a set of rights specific to branch office and remote site administrators. Very similar to site administrators back in the old Exchange Server 5.5 days—where an administrator was able to add users, contacts, and administer local Exchange servers—now network administrators in Active Directory can be delegated rights based on a branch or remote site role. This provides those administrators with the ability to make changes specific to their branch location. This, along with all the other tools in Windows Server 2008 R2 specific to branch office and remote office locations, now provides better IT services to organizations with multiple offices in the enterprise.

# Improvements for Thin Client Remote Desktop Services

Windows Server 2008 R2 has seen significant improvements in the Terminal Services (now called Remote Desktop Services [RDS]) capabilities for thin client access for remote users and managed users in the enterprise. What used to require third-party add-ons to make the basic Windows 2000 or 2003 Terminal Services functional, Microsoft included those technologies into Windows Server 2008 and further enhanced them in Windows Server 2008 R2. These technologies include things such as the ability to access Remote Desktop Services using a standard Port 443 SSL port rather than the proprietary Port 3389, or the ability to publish just specific programs instead of the entire desktop, and improvements in allowing a client to have a larger remote access screen, multiple screens, or to more easily print to remote print devices.

These improvements in Windows Server 2008 R2 Remote Desktop Services have made RDS one of the easiest components to add to an existing Windows 2003 Active Directory to test out the new Windows Server 2008 R2 capabilities, especially because the installation of a Windows Server 2008 R2 Remote Desktop Services system is just the addition of a member server to the domain and can easily be removed at any time.

All of these new improvements in Windows Server 2008 R2 Remote Desktop Services are covered in Chapter 25.

## Improvements in RDP v6.x for Better Client Capabilities

The first area of significant improvement in Windows Server 2008 Terminal Services was addressed in the update to the Remote Desktop Protocol (RDP) v6.x client, shown in Figure 1.10.

FIGURE 1.10    Remote Desktop Protocol client for Remote Desktop Services.

The RDP client with Windows Server 2008 provided the following:

▶ **Video support up to 4,096 x 2,048**—Users can now use very large monitors across an RDP connection to view data off a Windows Server 2008 Terminal Services system. With Windows Server 2008 R2 Remote Desktop Services, the latest support has been extended to support DirectX 9, 10, and 11 redirection.

▶ **Multimonitor support**—Users can also have multiple (up to 10) monitors supported off a single RDP connection. For applications like computer-aided design (CAD), graphical arts, or publishing, users can view graphical information on one screen and text information on another screen at the same time.

▶ **Secured connections**—The new RDP client now provides for a highly encrypted remote connection to a Remote Desktop Services system through the use of Windows Server 2008 R2 security. Organizations that need to ensure their data is protected and employee privacy is ensured can implement a highly secured encrypted connection between a Windows Server 2008 R2 Remote Desktop Services system and the remote client.

## Remote Desktop Services Web Access

Also new to Windows Server 2008 and extended in Windows Server 2008 R2 Remote Desktop Services is a new role called Remote Desktop Services Web Access. Remote Desktop Services Web Access allows a remote client to access a Remote Desktop Services session without having to launch the RDP 6.x client, but instead connect to a web page that then allows the user to log on and access their session off the web page.

This simplifies the access method for users where they can just set a browser favorite to link them to a web URL that provides them with Terminal Services access.

> **NOTE**
>
> Remote Desktop Services Web Access still requires the client system to be a Windows XP, Windows Vista, Windows 7, Windows 2003, Windows Server 2008, or Windows Server 2008 R2 server system to connect to a Remote Desktop Services session. A browser user cannot be running from an Apple Macintosh or Linux system and access Remote Desktop Services Web Access. For non-Windows-based web clients, third-party vendors like Citrix Systems provide connector support for these types of devices.

## Remote Desktop Services Gateway

Remote Desktop Services Gateway is an update to Windows Server 2008 R2 Remote Desktop Services and provides the connectivity to a Remote Desktop Services session over a standard Port 443 SSL connection. In the past, users could only connect to Windows Remote Desktop Services using a proprietary Port 3389 connection. Unfortunately, most organizations block nonstandard port connections for security purposes, and, thus, if a user was connected to an Internet connection at a hotel, airport, coffee shop, or other location that blocked nonstandard ports, the user could not access Terminal Services.

Now with Remote Desktop Services Gateway, the remote user to the Remote Desktop Services Gateway connection goes over Port 443 just like surfing a secured web page. Because of the use of SSL in web page access (anytime someone accesses a web page with https://), effectively now a user can access Windows Server 2008 R2 Remote Desktop Services from any location.

## Remote Desktop Services RemoteApps

Another new server role added to Windows Server 2008 and updated in Windows Server 2008 R2 is called Remote Desktop Services RemoteApps. Remote Desktop Services RemoteApps allows administrators to "publish" certain applications for users to access. These applications could be things like Microsoft Outlook, Microsoft Word, the company's time sheet tracking software, or a customer relationship management (CRM) program. Instead of giving users full access to a full desktop session complete with a Start button and access to all applications on the session, an organization can just publish a handful of applications that it allows for access.

Leveraging group policies and Network Policy Server, along with Remote Desktop Services RemoteApps, the administrators of a network can publish different groups of applications for different users. So, some users might get just Outlook and Word, whereas other users would get Outlook, Word, and the CRM application. Add in to the policy component the ability to leverage network location awareness (new to Windows Server 2008 R2 covered in the earlier section "Improvements in the Group Policy Management"), the administrators of the network can allow different applications to be available to users depending on whether the user is logging on to the network on the LAN or from a remote location.

Beyond just limiting users to only the programs they should have access to by policy, Remote Desktop Services RemoteApps minimizes the overhead for each user connection because the user no longer has a full desktop running, but only a handful of applications deemed necessary for the remote user's access.

## Remote Desktop Services Connection Broker

Formerly called the Session Broker in Windows Terminal Services, the Remote Desktop Services Connection Broker is a system that manages Remote Desktop sessions to ensure that if users are disconnected from a Remote Desktop server, the users can reestablish a connection to their session without loss of the session state. Without a Connection Broker, users who attempt to reconnect to Remote Desktop Services after a session disconnect might end up logging on to a completely different Remote Desktop server and have to go back to where they last saved data to pick up where they left off.

Other than the name change from Session Broker to Connection Broker, new to Windows Server 2008 R2 Connection Broker is the ability to cluster this role. In the past, this role was a single server instance. In the event that this server session was down, the connection states would not be preserved and the Session Broker would not do its job. By clustering the Connection Broker role, an organization can now add redundancy to a critical role for an organization that has several Remote Desktop servers and wants to provide users with the ability to reconnect back to their session after a temporary disconnect.

## Virtual Desktop Infrastructure (VDI)

Lastly, a completely new role added to Windows Server 2008 R2 is the Virtual Desktop Infrastructure, or VDI role. Instead of Remote Desktop Services that provides a one-to-many experience, where effectively a single server instance is shared across multiple users, VDI provides a one-to-one virtual guest session relationship between the server and remote client. When a VDI client user logs on to a guest session, a dedicated guest session is made available to the user with a separate client boot-up shell, separate memory pool allocated, and complete isolation of the guest session from other guest sessions on the host server.

Windows Server 2008 R2 VDI provides two different VDI modes. One mode is a personalized desktop and the other is a pooled desktop. The personalized desktop is a dedicated guest session that users have access to each and every time they log on to the VDI server. It is basically a dedicated guest session where the image the guest uses is the same every time. A pooled desktop is a guest session where the user settings (favorites, background, and application configuration settings) are saved and reloaded on logon to a standard template. Actual guest session resources are not permanently allocated but rather allocated and dedicated at the time of logon.

VDI is covered in more detail in Chapter 25.

# Improvements in Clustering and Storage Area Network Support

Although clustering of servers has been around for a long time in Windows (dating back to Windows NT 4.0, when it was available, but really didn't work), clustering in Windows Server 2008 R2 now not only works, but also provides a series of significant improvements that actually make clustering work a whole lot better.

As IT administrators are tasked with the responsibility of keeping the network operational 24 hours a day, 7 days a week, it becomes even more important that clustering works. Fortunately, the cost of hardware that supports clustering has gotten significantly less expensive; in fact, any server that meets the required specifications to run Windows Server 2008 R2, Enterprise Edition can typically support Windows clustering. The basic standard for a server that is used for enterprise networking has the technologies built in to the system for high availability. Windows Server 2008 R2, Enterprise Edition or Datacenter Edition is required to run Windows Server 2008 R2 clustering services.

Clustering is covered in detail in Chapter 29, "System-Level Fault Tolerance (Clustering/Network Load Balancing)."

## No Single Point of Failure in Clustering

Clustering by definition should provide redundancy and high availability of server systems; however, in previous versions of Windows clustering, a "quorum drive" was required for the cluster systems to connect to as the point of validation for cluster operations. If at any point the quorum drive failed, the cluster would not be able to failover from one system to another. Windows Server 2008 and Windows Server 2008 R2 clustering removed this requirement of a static quorum drive. Two major technologies facilitate this elimination of a single or central point of failure, which include majority-based cluster membership verification and witness-based quorum validation.

The majority-based cluster membership enables the IT administrator to define what devices in the cluster get a vote to determine whether a cluster node is in a failed state and the cluster needs to failover to another node. Rather than assuming that the disk will always be available as in the previous quorum disk model, now nodes of the cluster and shared storage devices participate in the new enhanced quorum model in Windows Server 2008 R2. Effectively, Windows Server 2008 R2 server clusters have better information to determine whether it is appropriate to failover a cluster in the event of a system or device failure.

The witness-based quorum eliminates the single quorum disk from the cluster operation validation model. Instead, a completely separate node or file share can be set as the file share witness. In the case of a GeoCluster where cluster nodes are in completely different locations, the ability to place the file share in a third site and even enable that file share to serve as the witness for multiple clusters becomes a benefit for both organizations with distributed data centers and also provides more resiliency in the cluster operations components.

## Stretched Clusters

Windows Server 2008 R2 also introduced the concept of stretched clusters to provide better server and site server redundancy. Effectively, Microsoft has eliminated the need to have cluster servers remain on the same subnet, as has been the case in Windows clustering in the past. Although organizations have used virtual local area networks (VLANs) to stretch a subnet across multiple locations, this was not always easy to do and, in many cases, technologically not the right thing to do in IP networking design.

By allowing cluster nodes to reside on different subnets, plus with the addition of a configurable heartbeat timeout, clusters can now be set up in ways that match an organization's disaster failover and recovery strategy.

## Improved Support for Storage Area Networks

Windows Server 2008 R2 also has improved its support for storage area networks (SANs) by providing enhanced mechanisms for connecting to SANs as well as switching between SAN nodes. In the past, a connection to a SAN was a static connection, meaning that a server was connected to a SAN just as if the server was physically connected to a direct attached storage system. However, the concept of a SAN is that if a SAN fails, the server should reconnect to a SAN device that is now online. This could not be easily done with Windows 2003 or prior. SCSI bus resets were required to disconnect a server from one SAN device to another.

With Windows Server 2008 R2, a server can be associated with a SAN with a persistent reservation to access a specific shared disk; however, in the event that the SAN fails, the server session can be logically connected to another SAN target system without having to script device resets that have been complicated and disruptive in disaster recovery scenarios.

# Addition of Migration Tools

Beyond the standard migration tools that help administrators migrate from one version of Active Directory to another, or to perform an in-place upgrade from one version of Windows to another, Windows Server 2008 R2 has migration tools to help administrators move entire server roles from one system to another. These new tools provide migration paths from physical servers to virtual servers, or from virtual servers to physical servers. Other tools allow for the migration of DHCP configuration and lease information from one server to another. These tools and the prescriptive guidance help administrators migrate servers more easily than ever before.

## Operating System Migration Tools

Windows Server 2008 R2 provides tools that help administrators migrate from older versions of the Windows Server operating system to Windows Server 2008 R2. The supported migration paths are as follows:

▶ **Windows Server 2003, Windows Server 2003 R2, Windows Server 2008, and Windows Server 2008 R2**—These operating systems can be migrated to Windows Server 2008 R2 using the operating system migration tools and guidance documentation.

▶ **x86 and x64**—Servers can be migrated from x86 to x64 and from x64 to x64 with limitations. Because Windows Server 2008 R2 is an x64 operating system only, there is no in-place upgrade support from x86 to x64, so the upgrade path is a server-to-server transition, not in-place. However, x64 to x64 in-place is supported as long as any applications sitting on the server can be upgraded from one x64 platform to the Windows Server 2008 R2 x64 platform.

▶ **Full Server and ServerCore**—Operating system migration from Full Server to ServerCore and from ServerCore to Full Server are supported typically as a server-to-server migration because in-place migrations between Full Server and ServerCore have limitations. The GUI needs to be added or removed and, thus, applications are typically migrated rather than complete operating system migrations between the platforms.

▶ **Physical and virtual**—Virtualization of guest sessions is the de facto standard in data centers these days and the implementation of applications on virtual guest sessions is the norm. As such, organizations wanting to migrate from physical server configurations to virtual guest sessions can leverage the migration tools and guidance available in performing server and application migrations to virtual server roles.

## Server Role Migrations

Included in Windows Server 2008 R2 are tools and guidance that help administrators migrate server roles to Windows Server 2008 R2 server systems. The supported migration paths are as follows:

▶ **Active Directory Domain Services**—The migration from Active Directory 2003 and Active Directory 2008 to Active Directory 2008 R2 is fully supported and covered in Chapter 16 of this book.

▶ **DNS and DHCP migrations**—New migration tools are available that help administrators migrate their DNS and DHCP servers from running on previous versions of Windows to servers running Windows Server 2008 R2, and not only just the service configurations but also DNS and DHCP data. In the past, the migration of DHCP to a new server usually meant the loss of DHCP lease information. With the new migration tools in Windows Server 2008 R2, an administrator can now migrate the server configuration as well as the lease data, including lease expiration data, as part of the migration process. These migration tools are covered in Chapters 10 and 11 of this book.

▶ **File and print migrations**—Included in the migration tools for Windows Server 2008 R2 are features that migrate file data, included file permissions, and the migration of print server configurations and settings from older servers to new Windows Server 2008 R2 configurations. These migration tools help simplify the process of updating servers from old server systems to new systems with the least amount of impact on the organization and drastically simplify the process of migration for domain administrators.

# Improvements in Server Roles in Windows Server 2008 R2

The introduction of Windows Server 2008 R2 added new server roles to Windows as well as enhanced existing roles based on feedback Microsoft received from organizations on features and function wish lists. Server roles are no longer installed by default on a Windows Server 2008 R2 server and have to be selected for installation after the initial installation of the Windows operating system.

Some of the new or improved server roles in Windows Server 2008 R2 include Internet Information Services 7.5, SharePoint Services, Rights Management Service, and Windows virtualization.

## Introducing Internet Information Services 7.5

Internet Information Services 7.5 (IIS) is the seventh-generation web server service from Microsoft. Microsoft completely redesigned IIS 7.0 in Windows Server 2008 rather than just adding more functions and capabilities to the exact same IIS infrastructure as they have done for the past several years. The good part of the new IIS 7.x is that it now provides organizations with the ability to manage multiple web servers from a single console, rather than having to install components and configure each web server individually. This requires organizations to rethink and redesign their web management tasks from pushing the same content to dozens of servers individually to a process where information is pushed to a Shared Configuration store, where common information is posted and shared across all IIS 7.x servers. Organizations can continue to post information the old way by pushing information individually to each server; however, to gain the advantage of the new IIS 7.x services, redesigning how information gets posted should be changed to meet the new model.

The advantage of the new model of content posting is that information is stored, edited, and managed in a single location. At a designated time, the information in the single location is posted to each of the servers in the shared application hosting farm. This is a significant improvement for organizations managing and administering a lot of IIS web servers. This ensures that all servers in a farm are using the same content, have been updated simultaneously, and any changes are ensured to be propagated to the servers in the farm. Web administrators no longer have to worry that they forgot a server to update, or to stage an update at a time when each individual server could be updated in a fast enough sequence that the experience of all users was going to occur at around the same time.

IIS 7.5 is covered in detail in Chapter 12, "Internet Information Services."

## Windows SharePoint Services

A significant update provided as part of the Windows Server 2008 client access license (CAL) is the ability to load and run Windows SharePoint Services. Now in its third generation, Windows SharePoint Services (WSS) is a document-storage management application that provides organizations with the capability to better manage, organize, and share documents, as well as provide teams of users the ability to collaborate on information. Windows SharePoint Services sets the framework from which the Microsoft Office SharePoint Services 2007 (MOSS) is built. MOSS leverages the core functionality of WSS and extends the capability into enterprise environments. WSS is the basis of document sharing and communications for organizations in the evolution of file and information communications.

Windows SharePoint Services is covered in detail in Chapter 35.

## Windows Rights Management Services

Windows Rights Management Services (RMS) was available as a downloadable feature pack in Windows 2003 and is now included as an installable server role in Windows Server 2008 R2. Windows Rights Management Services sets the framework for secured information sharing of data by encrypting content and setting a policy on the content that protects the file and the information stored in the file.

Organizations have been shifting to RMS rather than the old secured file folder primarily because users who should be saving sensitive information into a file folder frequently forget to save files in the folder, and thus sensitive information becomes public information. By encrypting the content of the file itself, even if a file with sensitive information is stored in the wrong place, the file cannot be opened, and the information in the file cannot be accessed without proper security credentials to access the file.

Additionally, RMS allows the individual saving the file to set specific attributes regarding what the person would like to be secured about the file. As an example, a secured file in RMS can be set to not be edited, meaning that a person receiving the file can read the file, but he or she cannot select content in the file, copy the content, or edit the content. This prevents individuals from taking a secured file, cutting and pasting the content into a different file, and then saving the new file without encryption or security.

RMS also provides attributes to enable the person creating a file to prevent others from printing the file. The file itself can have an expiration date, so that after a given period of time, the contents of the file expire and the entire file is inaccessible.

Rights Management Services is covered in Chapter 13.

## Windows Server Virtualization

A new technology that wasn't quite available at the time Windows Server 2008 shipped in 2008, but has since been released and available on the original Windows Server 2008 R2 DVD, is Windows server virtualization known as Hyper-V. Hyper-V provides an organization with the ability to create guest operating system sessions, like those shown in Figure 1.11, on a Windows Server 2008 R2 server to get rid of physical servers, and instead make the servers available as virtual server sessions.

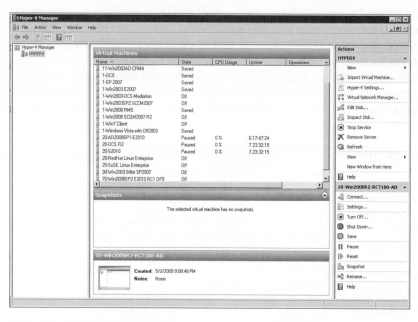

FIGURE 1.11    Windows virtualization guest sessions.

Instead of purchasing a new physical server every time a new server system needs to be placed on the network, a virtual server can be created that has all the same operations and functions as the physical server itself. Or, for organizations that are putting in place disaster recovery centers and server clustering for better server reliability and redundancy, virtualization allows the addition of these additional servers within the guest operating system space of a single server system.

Virtualization in Windows Server 2008 R2 supports 64-bit and 32-bit guest sessions; has a built-in tool that allows a snapshot of a virtual session so that the session can be protected or rolled back in the event of a guest image failure or corruption; and has virtual sessions that can span terabytes of disk storage and use 16GB, 32GB, or more of memory per guest session. Windows Server 2008 R2 Hyper-V supports "live migrations," which allows for a faster failover and recovery of a virtual guest session across host servers.

More details on Windows Server 2008 R2 virtualization are covered in Chapter 37.

# Identifying Which Windows Server 2008 R2 Service to Install or Migrate to First

With the release of Windows Server 2008 R2, organizations need to create a plan to install or migrate to Windows Server 2008 R2 in a logical manner. Covered so far in this chapter have been all the top features, functions, and technologies built in to Windows Server 2008 R2 that organizations have found as key technologies they implemented to improve technology-driven business processes.

Because Windows Server 2008 R2 provides many different functions, each organization has to choose how to best implement Windows Server 2008 R2 and the various networking features that meet its own needs. In small network environments with fewer than 20 to 30 users, an organization might choose to implement all the Windows Server 2008 R2 features on a single server. However, in larger environments, multiple servers might be implemented to improve system performance, as well as provide fault tolerance and redundancy; thus, a more staged implementation of core services needs to be taken.

## Windows Server 2008 R2 Core to an Active Directory Environment

For an organization that does not have Windows Active Directory already in place, that is one place to start because Active Directory Domain Services is key to application and user authentication. For organizations that already have a fully operational Active Directory running on Windows 2003 or Windows 2008, upgrading to Active Directory Domain Services on Windows Server 2008 R2 might be something that is addressed a little later in the upgrade cycle when AD DS 2008 R2 functionality is needed. To get a lot of the Windows Server 2008 R2 server functionality like 2008 R2 DFS, SharePoint Services, Hyper-V virtualization, and so on, an organization can still run on an older Active Directory environment (typically Active Directory 2003 native mode). However, the point is that Active Directory 2008 R2 is not a prerequisite to get Windows Server 2008 R2 server role functionality.

Because Active Directory is more than a simple list of users and passwords for authentication into a network, but rather a directory that Microsoft has embedded into the policy-based security, remote access security, and certificate-based security enhancements in Windows Server 2008 R2, AD DS 2008 implementation does occur earlier in the migration cycle for organizations wanting to implement many of the new Active Directory 2008 R2 technologies, such as Active Directory Recycle Bin, Offline Domain Join, Managed Service Accounts, and the ability to use PowerShell cmdlets within a Group Policy Object.

Windows Server 2008 R2 extends the capabilities of the Active Directory by creating better management tools, provides for more robust directory replication across a global enterprise, and allows for better scalability and redundancy to improve directory operations. Windows Server 2008 R2 effectively adds in more reliability, faster performance, and better management tools to a system that can be leveraged as a true enterprise directory provisioning, resource tracking, and resource management tool. Because of the importance of Active Directory to the Windows Server 2008 R2 operating system, plus the breadth of capabilities that Active Directory can facilitate, six chapters in Part II of this book are dedicated to Active Directory.

## Windows Server 2008 R2 Running Built-in Application Server Functions

As much as many administrators think of Active Directory as one of the key areas to upgrade when a new release of the operating system becomes available, in reality, Active Directory tends to not be the first thing updated. Instead, the real business drivers for migrating to Windows Server 2008 R2 typically come from the built-in application server programs that are available on Windows Server 2008 R2.

Windows Server 2008 R2 comes with several programs and utilities to provide robust networking capabilities. In addition to the basic file and print capabilities covered earlier in this chapter, Windows Server 2008 R2 can provide name resolution for the network and enable high availability through clustering and fault tolerance, connectivity for mobile users, web services functions, and dozens of other application server functions.

When convincing management that an upgrade to Windows Server 2008 R2 is important, the IT professional needs to sift through the technologies built in to Windows Server 2008 R2 and pick those services that help an organization use technology to achieve its business initiatives. When planning the implementation of Windows Server 2008 R2, a network architect needs to consider which of the server services are desired, how they will be combined on servers, and how they will be made redundant across multiple servers for business continuity failover.

For a small organization, the choice to combine several server functions to a single system or to just a few systems is one of economics. However, an organization might distribute server services to multiple servers to improve performance (covered in Chapter 34), distribute administration (covered in Chapter 18), create server redundancy (covered in Chapter 29), create a disaster recovery strategy (covered in Chapter 31, "Recovering from a Disaster"), enable security (covered in Chapter 13), or to serve users in other remote site locations of the organization (covered in Chapter 32).

Some of the built-in application server functions in Windows Server 2008 R2 include the following:

▶ **Domain controller**—Like in previous versions of the Windows operating system, the domain controller enables users to authenticate to the domain for access to network resources.

▶ **Global catalog server**—The global catalog server is a domain controller that also stores a subset of AD DS objects from other domains in the forest. When an internal or external user with appropriate security rights wants to look at a list of Active Directory users in the forest, the global catalog server provides the list.

▶ **DNS server**—The domain name system (DNS) maintains a list of network servers and systems and their associated IP addresses, so a DNS server provides information about the devices connected to the network.

▶ **DHCP server**—The Dynamic Host Configuration Protocol (DHCP) assigns IPv4 and/or IPv6 network addresses to devices on the network. Windows Server 2008 R2 provides the service function to facilitate DHCP addresses to network devices.

▶ **Cluster server**—When fault tolerance is important to an organization, clustering provides failover from one system to another. Windows Server 2008 R2 provides the ability to link systems together so that when one system fails, another system takes over.

▶ **Network Policy Server**—NPS is the Microsoft implementation of a Remote Authentication Dial-in User Service (RADIUS) server and proxy. NPS performs centralized connection authentication, authorization, and accounting for many types of network access, including wireless and virtual private network (VPN) connections. NPS routes authentication and accounting messages to other RADIUS servers. It also acts as a health evaluation server for Network Access Protection (NAP).

▶ **Remote Desktop server**—Instead of having a full desktop or laptop computer for each user on the network, organizations have the option of setting up simple, low-cost thin terminals for users to gain access to network resources. Windows Server 2008 R2 Remote Desktop Services allows a single server to host network system access for dozens of users.

▶ **Remote access server**—When a remote user has a desktop or laptop system and needs access to network services, Windows Server 2008 R2 provides remote access services that allow the remote systems to establish a secure remote connection.

▶ **Web server**—As more and more technologies become web-aware and are hosted on web servers, Windows Server 2008 R2 provides the technology to host these applications for browser-based access.

▶ **Media server**—With information extending beyond text-based word processing documents and spreadsheets into rich media such as video and audio, Windows Server 2008 R2 provides a source for hosting and publishing video and audio content.

▶ **Virtualization server**—Windows Server 2008 R2 provides the core capabilities to do server virtualization, providing the capability for an organization to consolidate physical servers into fewer host server systems, thus decreasing the total cost of IT operations.

▶ **Distributed File System (DFS) server**—For the past decade, data files have been stored on file servers all around an organization. Windows Server 2008 R2 provides Distributed File Systems that allow an organization to take control of distributed files into a common unified namespace.

These plus several other functions provide robust networking services that help organizations leverage the Windows Server 2008 R2 technologies into solutions that solve business needs.

## Windows Server 2008 R2 Running Add-in Applications Server Functions

Although some of the newer, built-in server application functions in Windows Server 2008 R2—such as Network Policy Server, server virtualization, Remote Desktop Services Web Access, Media Server, and so on—provide key areas for organizations to select as initial areas to implement Windows Server 2008 R2 technologies, other organizations might find add-in applications as being the key areas that drive an initial implementation of Windows Server 2008 R2. Some of the add-in applications come from Microsoft, such as the Microsoft Exchange Server 2010 messaging system or Microsoft SQL Server 2008 database system. Other add-ins to Windows Server 2008 R2 are provided by companies that provide human resource management applications; accounting software; document management tools; fax or voicemail add-ins; or other business, industry, or user productivity capabilities.

In earlier Windows Server operating systems, the core operating system provided simple logon and network connectivity functions; however, with Windows Server 2008 R2, the operating system includes many core capabilities built in to the Windows Server 2008 R2 operating environment. With integrated fault tolerance, data recovery, server security, remote access connectivity, web access technologies, and similar capabilities, organizations creating add-ins to Windows Server 2008 R2 can focus on business functions and capabilities, not on core infrastructure reliability, security, and mobile access functionality. This off-loading of the requirement of third-party add-in organizations to implement basic networking technologies into their applications enables these developers to focus on improving the business productivity and functionality of their applications. Additionally, consolidating information routing, security, remote management, and so on into the core operating system provides a common method of communication, authentication, and access to users without having to load up special drivers, add-ins, or tools to support each and every new application.

Much of the shift from application-focused infrastructure components to core operating system-focused functionality was built in to Windows 2000 and then later enhanced in Windows 2003 and Windows Server 2008. There were many challenges to earlier versions of the Windows operating system; however, after being on the market for many years now, Windows Server 2008 R2 add-ins have had several revisions to work through system functionality and component reliability between application and operating system. Fortunately, Windows Server 2008 R2 uses the same application/operating system technology used in Windows 2003 and Windows Server 2008, so applications written for Windows 2003 and Windows Server 2008 typically need just a simple service pack update to be able to run on Windows Server 2008 R2, if anything at all.

# Summary

This introductory chapter was intended to highlight the new features, functions, migration tools, and management utilities in Windows Server 2008 R2 that will help administrators take advantage of the capabilities of the new operating system. If Windows Server 2008 R2 is seen as just a simple upgrade to Windows 2000/2003/2008, an organization will not benefit from the operating system enhancements. However, when fully leveraged with the capabilities of the Windows Server 2008 R2 operating system, an organization can improve services to its employees through the use of new tools and technologies built in to the operating system.

Because Windows Server 2008 R2 is a relatively simple migration from existing Windows 2003 and Windows 2008 Active Directory environments, and Windows Server 2008 R2 application servers can be added to existing Active Directory 2000/2003/2008 domains, the migration process really is one where the IT administrators need to prioritize which Windows Server 2008 R2 services to install or migrate to first, and to then plan and test the new technologies to make sure they improve IT services to the organization.

# Best Practices

The following are best practices from this chapter:

▶ When implementing Windows Server 2008 R2 for the first time, or migrating to Windows Server 2008 R2 from a previous version of Windows, choose to implement the technologies in Windows Server 2008 R2 that will provide the organization with the most value in terms of employee productivity enhancements or regulatory compliance security improvements first.

▶ When considering adding a Windows Server 2008 R2 server to an existing Windows 2000/2003/2008 Active Directory environment, consider implementing things like Remote Desktop Services Web Access, SharePoint Services, or Windows virtualization, which have proven to be pretty easy to implement and provide a lot of value to organizations.

▶ To ultimately improve Windows security, tune and optimize Windows Server 2008 R2 for a secured networking environment.

▶ Use Remote Desktop Services in Windows Server 2008 R2 to provide users with access to local hard drives, as well as to redirect the audio from a centralized Terminal Server to a remote system.

▶ Use Windows Deployment Services (WDS) to create client system images that can be quickly and easily rolled back through Group Policy.

▶ Windows Server 2008 R2 virtualization can help organizations deploy clustering and add in disaster recovery data centers without having to add additional physical servers to the network.

▶ Remote and branch office locations greatly benefit from the use of Read-Only Domain Controllers, Distributed File System Replication, BitLocker security, and distributed administration tools built in to Windows Server 2008 R2.

▶ Using the new Windows Server 2008 R2 Server Manager can simplify the task of a network administrator trying to access information residing on different servers and in different server roles in the environment.

▶ It is best to run the Group Policy Management Console on a Windows Server 2008 R2 or Windows 7 system to have access to all the policy features available (compared with running GPMC on a Windows XP or Windows Server 2003 system).

# CHAPTER 2

# Planning, Prototyping, Migrating, and Deploying Windows Server 2008 R2 Best Practices

The technical process to implement or to migrate to a Windows Server 2008 R2 environment is similar to the migration processes that have been available for migrations to Windows 2000/2003 in the past; however, the requirements and expectations of organizations have made it important for IT professionals to do better planning, preparation, and testing before merely shoving in a CD and performing an upgrade. Organizations are extremely dependent on the reliability of their network systems and less tolerant to downtime such that the migration process needs to be planned and executed with great attention paid to minimizing user impact and system downtime.

This chapter examines how a structured multistep process for migrating to the Windows Server 2008 R2 environment can enhance the success of the project. Consisting of discovery, design, testing, and implementation phases, this methodology can be scaled to meet the needs of the wide variety of organizations and businesses that use Microsoft technologies. The results of this methodology are three very important documents created to map out the implementation process: the design document, the migration document, and the migration plan.

The examples used in this chapter assume that the environments being migrated are primarily Windows 2000/2003–based, but the concepts and process can certainly apply to other environments.

# Determining the Scope of Your Project

As outlined in the preceding chapter, the Windows Server 2008 R2 platform contains such a wealth of features that planning a migration to it can seem quite daunting at first. This chapter provides some guidance and best practices that can assist with the process and assist organizations in creating a well-thought-out and structured implementation plan.

Rather than forging ahead with no plan or goals and simply building new servers, loading application software, and inserting them into an existing network environment, a more organized process will control the risks involved and define in detail what the end state will look like.

The first steps involve getting a better sense of the scope of the project, in essence writing the executive summary of your design document. The scope should define from a high level what the project consists of and why the organization is devoting time, energy, and resources to its completion.

Creating this scope of work requires an understanding of the different goals of the organization, as well as the pieces of the puzzle that need to fit together to meet the company's stated goals for the project. For Windows Server 2008 R2, the primary pieces are servers that handle key network functionality, servers that handle and manage the data, servers that control or provide access to the information, and servers that handle specific applications.

# Identifying the Business Goals and Objectives to Implement Windows Server 2008 R2

It is important to establish a thorough understanding of the goals and objectives of a company that guide and direct the efforts of the different components of the organization, to help ensure the success of the Windows Server 2008 R2 project. It might seem counterintuitive to start at this very high level and keep away from the bits- and bytes-level details, but time spent in this area will clarify the purposes of the project and start to generate productive discussions.

As an example of the value of setting high-level business goals and objectives, an organization can identify the desire for zero downtime on file access; this downtime could be facilitated through the implementation of the Distributed File System (DFS) technology or the Windows Clustering feature. Starting with the broad goals and objectives will create an outline for a technical solution that will meet all the criteria the organization wants, at a lower cost, and with an easier-managed solution.

In every organization, a variety of different goals and objectives need to be identified and met for a project to be considered successful. These goals and objectives represent a snapshot of the end state that the company or organization is seeking to create. For a smaller company, this process might be completed in a few brainstorming sessions, whereas larger companies might require more extensive discussions and assistance from external resources or firms.

## High-Level Business Goals

To start the organizational process, it is helpful to break up business goals and objectives into different levels, or vantage points. Most organizations have high-level business goals, often referred to as the "vision of the company," which are typically shaped by the key decision makers in the organization (such as the CEO, CFO, CIO, and so on); these goals are commonly called the "50,000-foot view." Business unit or departmental goals, or the "10,000-foot view," are typically shaped by the key executives and managers in the organization (such as the VP of sales, HR director, site facilities manager, and so on). Most organizations also have well-defined "1,000-foot view" goals that are typically very tactical in nature, implemented by IT staff and technical specialists.

It is well worth the time to perform some research and ask the right questions to help ensure that the networking system implementation will be successful. To get specific information and clarification of the objectives of the different business units, make sure the goals of a technology implementation or upgrade are in line with these business goals.

Although most organizations have stated company visions and goals, and a quick visit to the company's website or intranet can provide this information, it is worth taking the time to gather more information on what the key stakeholders feel to be their primary objectives. Often, this task starts with asking the right questions of the right people and then opening discussion groups on the topic. Of course, it also matters who asks the questions because the answers will vary accordingly, and employees might be more forthcoming when speaking with external consultants as opposed to co-workers. Often, the publicly stated vision and goals are "the tip of the iceberg" and might even be in contrast to internal company goals, ambitions, or initiatives.

High-level business goals and visions can vary greatly among different organizations, but generally they bracket and guide the goals of the units that make up the company. For example, a corporation might be interested in offering the "best" product in its class, and this requires corresponding goals for the sales, engineering, marketing, finance, and manufacturing departments. Additional concepts to look for are whether the highest-level goals embrace change and new ideas and processes, or want to refine the existing practices and methods.

High-level business goals of a company can also change rapidly, whether in response to changing economic conditions or as affected by a new key stakeholder or leader in the company. So, it is also important to get a sense of the timeline involved for meeting these high-level goals.

> **NOTE**
>
> An example of some high-level business goals include a desire to have no downtime, access to the network from any of the organization's offices around the world, and secured communications when users access the network from home or a remote location.

## Business Unit or Departmental Goals

When the vision or "50,000-foot view" is defined, additional discussions should reveal the goals of the different departments and the executives who run them. Theoretically, they should "add up" to the highest-level goals, but the findings might be surprising. Whatever the case turns out to be, the results will start to reveal the complexity of the organization and the primary concerns of the different stakeholders.

The high-level goals of the organization also start to paint the picture of which departments carry the most weight in the organization, and will most likely get budgets approved, which will assist in the design process. Logically, the goals of the IT department will play a very important role in a network operating system (NOS) migration project, but the other key departments shouldn't be forgotten.

As an example of the business unit or departmental goals for an organization, an HR department may typically influence the decision for right-to-privacy access to core personnel records. Or a legal department may typically influence security access on information storage rights and storage retention.

If the department's goals are not aligned with the overall vision of the company, or don't take into account the needs of the key stakeholders, the result of the project might not be appreciated. "Technology for technology's sake" does not always fulfill the needs of the organization and in the long run is viewed as a wasteful expenditure of organizational funds.

In the process of clarifying these goals, the features of the network operating system and network applications that are most important to the different departments and executives should become apparent. It is safe to assume that access to company data in the form of documents or database information; to communications tools, such as email, faxing, and Internet access; and to vertical market software applications that the company relies upon will affect the company's ability to meet its various business goals.

The sales department will most likely have goals that require a specific customer relationship management (CRM) application as well as access to key company data and communications tools. Likewise, the finance department will have applications that track specific AR and AP information and that most likely tie into applications used by other departments. The IT department will have its key technologies that support the applications in use, store and maintain the company's data, and manage key servers and network devices.

It is also worth looking for the "holes" in the goals and objectives presented. Some of the less-glamorous objectives, such as a stable network, data-recovery abilities, or protection from the hostile outside world, are often neglected.

A by-product of these discussions will ideally be a sense of excitement over the possibilities presented by the new technologies that will be introduced, and will convey to the executives and key stakeholders that they are involved in helping to define and craft a solution that takes into account the varied needs of the company. Many executives look for this high-level strategy, thinking, and discussions to reveal the maturity of the planning and implementation process in action.

**NOTE**

An example of some departmental goals include a desire to have secured storage of human resource and personnel information, 30-minute response time to help desk questions during business hours, 24-hour support for sales executives when they are traveling, and easy lookup of files stored on servers throughout the organization.

## 2

# Identifying the Technical Goals and Objectives to Implement Windows Server 2008 R2

Although an operating system upgrade to Windows Server 2008 R2 might not initially seem integral to the highest-level company goals, its importance becomes clearer as the goals get close to the "1,000-foot view." When the business goals are sketched out, the technical goals should fall into place quite naturally.

At this point in the process, questions should focus on which components and capabilities of the network are most important, and how they contribute to or hinder the goals expressed by the different units.

As with business goals, the technical goals of the project should be clarified on different levels (50,000-foot, 10,000-foot, 1,000-foot, and so on). At the highest level, the technical goals might be quite vague, such as "no downtime" or "access to data from anywhere." But as the goals are clarified on a departmental and individual level, they should become specific and measurable. For example, rather than identifying a goal as "no downtime," ferreting out the details might result in a more specific goal of "99.99% uptime during business hours, and no more than four-hour downtime during nonbusiness hours scheduled at least two days in advance." Instead of stating a goal of "access to data from anywhere," a more specific goal of "high-speed remote logon from any corporate regional office around the world and dial-up or VPN access from the home offices of the organization's senior managers" can more reasonably be attained.

Part of the art of defining technical goals and objectives also resides in limiting them. Data can be accessed in many different ways, and the complexity of the network environment can boggle even the veteran IT manager's mind. So, for example, rather than setting a goal of "remote access to all employees," a more focused goal such as "access to email for all employees, remote access to email and the accounting software for the finance department, and remote access to email and the customer relationship management software for sales executives" is more actionable.

Departmental technical goals can include "10,000-foot" items—for example, implementing a new software application or set of functions that require other network changes, such as an operating system upgrade to Windows Server 2008 R2. The marketing department might require some of the advanced features of the latest version of Microsoft Exchange, as well as enhanced website capabilities that necessitate the implementation of Windows Server 2008 R2. Or, the sales department might require better remote access to the company's data through mobile devices and the Internet, and a solution was already chosen that requires Windows Server 2008 R2 as the core operating system platform.

Two key components should also be included in these discussions: budget and timeline. A huge amount of time in the design phase can be saved if these components are clarified (and agreed upon) early in the process. Some projects have to happen "yesterday," whereas others can happen over a period of quarters or even years. In most cases, the budget will vary with the time frame involved because longer timelines enable organizations to train resources internally and migrate in a more gradual fashion. Even if a firm budget or timeline isn't available, order of magnitude ranges can be established. If $500,000 is too much, how about $250,000? $100,000? $50,000? If a year is too long, but the budget won't be available for four months, the time frame becomes better clarified.

## Defining the Scope of the Work

By now, the list of goals and objectives might be getting quite long. But when the myriad of business and technical objectives as well as the overall priorities start to become clear, the scope of work starts to take shape. A key question to ask at this point, to home in on the scope of the project, is whether the migration is primarily an operating system upgrade or an application upgrade. Often the answer to this question seems clear at first but becomes more complex as the different goals of the business units are discussed, so the scope of work that is created might be quite different than it appeared at first.

Specifically, a decision needs to be made whether the entire network operating system (NOS) needs to be upgraded or only a subset of it, and what other infrastructure components need to be changed or replaced. This section focuses on the server components, but later chapters focus on other hardware and software areas that should be reviewed.

Upgrading to the latest version of a key network application (CRM solution, document management system, or remote access solution) might require a network operating system upgrade, but it might need to involve only a limited portion of the network (perhaps only one server). However, if this application needs to be accessed by every member of the organization, in several offices, and requires upgrades to data storage solutions, tape backup software, antivirus software, remote access, and connectivity among offices, a full NOS upgrade might make more sense. An upgrade to Windows Server 2008 R2 enterprisewide can allow centralization of resources, consolidation of servers, enhanced management tools, and other features that can make a larger project more attractive.

It is important to also examine how the business and technology goals fit into this plan. If one of the goals of the organization is 99.99% uptime during business hours, this might affect the migration process and limit changes to the network to weekends or after hours. Or, a goal that involves a dramatically short timeline might likewise affect the strategy and require a partial NOS upgrade.

Questions raised at this point might require further discussion and even research. The section, "The Discovery Phase: Understanding the Existing Environment," later in this chapter examines some areas that generally need review. But with a solid understanding of the different departmental and companywide goals for the project, you can sketch out a basic outline of the required configuration.

You need to get answers to these sample questions:

▶ How many servers need to be upgraded?

▶ Where do these servers reside?

▶ What core business applications need to be upgraded?

▶ What additional applications and devices need to be upgraded or modified to support the new servers and applications?

▶ How will this affect the desktop configurations?

Based on the goals and objectives for the project and the answers to these types of questions, the high-level scope of the work begins to take shape. Here are some general rules to consider:

▶ Keep it as simple as possible.

▶ Break up the project into logical segments.

▶ Don't forget that the staff and user community will need to learn new skills to be productive.

Often, it makes sense to upgrade the operating system first; then add directory services and file and print functionality; and, finally, ensure the system is properly protected with a compatible backup solution, virus protection, and disaster recovery plan. When this foundation is in place, the applications can be migrated in a more gradual process. In other cases, the new application must be installed in advance of the operating system upgrade, for testing purposes, or because of budget limitations or a tight timeline.

Implementing the latest version of Exchange is a good example; this implementation not only requires a core operating system like Windows 2003, Windows Server 2008, or Windows Server 2008 R2, but also requires that the Windows Active Directory is properly implemented. On the other hand, for an organization implementing Windows SharePoint Services (WSS), because WSS does not require Active Directory to make the application fully functional, the organization can choose to implement just Windows Server 2008 R2 as an application server and can delay the implementation of Windows Server 2008 R2 Directory Services or other Windows Server 2008 R2 components to a future date.

Note, however, that if the NOS in use is too old or no longer supported by the manufacturer, the upgrade choices might be limited. You might simply have to implement a completely new collection of servers with compatible network applications and phase out the old ones.

Often, an application-focused upgrade will introduce a limited number of new servers but also set the stage for the eventual migration. This can be an effective way to implement the new technology in a faster method than an enterprisewide operating system upgrade. A partial upgrade can also defer the costs of purchasing new server licenses, client access licenses, and other enterprisewide applications, including virus protection and tape backup. Ideally, the servers that are upgraded for the new application(s) should be designed to integrate into the NOS after a full-fledged upgrade. In other words, ideally these servers won't need to be rebuilt later.

As discussed in Chapter 9, "Integrating Active Directory in a UNIX Environment," Windows Server 2008 R2 is designed for compatibility and coexistence with other network operating systems in addition to Windows 2000/2003 servers. An important point to consider during the design process is whether it makes sense to upgrade the entire NOS even though doing so might not be absolutely essential. There might be convincing arguments for a complete upgrade because management of a uniform environment can be easier to administer organizationwide, and an upgrade to Windows Server 2008 R2 might solve a number of existing issues.

Again, the answers might not be obvious at this point in the design process. But by asking the questions and engaging in "what-if" discussions and speculations, the primary pieces of the puzzle can be identified. The next step is to determine how best to fit those pieces together.

## Determining the Time Frame for Implementation or Migration

An equally important component of the migration is the time frame, and this component will affect the path and process that need to be followed to create the results desired. Often, the goals for the project will dictate the timeline, and the technology upgrade can drastically affect other critical business project dependencies. Other upgrades might not have strict timelines, and it is more important that the process be a smooth one than a quick one.

Dependent on the scope of the project, a time frame of two to four months could be considered to be a short time frame, with four to six months offering a more comfortable window. Within these time constraints, several weeks are available for discovery and design, a similar amount of time is available for the testing process, and then the implementation can proceed.

A fundamental point to remember is that change will bring with it a learning curve to both the user communities and the administrative staff. And the greater the amount of change that employees need to adjust to, the more support and training will be required to ensure their productivity when the new platform is rolled out. This is especially true when the applications change along with the operating system.

A safe strategy to take when sketching out the timeline is to start by setting a completion date and then working backward from it, to get a sense for the time available to each component of the process. As this chapter discusses, the project has several key phases— discovery, design, prototype, and implementation—and sufficient time should be allowed for each one of them. Although there are no hard-and-fast rules of how the time should be split up among each of these phases, each phase tends to take longer than its predecessor, and the discovery and design phases typically take as long, combined, as the testing phase (that is, discovery + design = prototype time frame).

The implementation phase will vary tremendously based on the scope of the project. For simpler projects, where the implementation consists only of a new server housing a new application, the implementation might be as simple as "flipping a switch" over a weekend (assuming the solution has been thoroughly tested in the lab environment). At the other end of the spectrum, a full NOS upgrade, happening in several locations, with changes required on the desktop, can take a period of months or quarters.

Even when the deadline for the completion of the project is the infamous "by yesterday," time should be allocated for the design and planning process. If time and energy are not invested at this point, the prototype testing process might be missing the mark because it might not be clear exactly what is being tested, and the implementation might not be smooth or even successful. A good analogy here is that of the explorer who sets off on an adventure without planning what should go in her backpack or bringing a map along.

Slower, phased migrations typically occur when the existing environment is fairly mature and stable, and the vertical applications are still fairly current and meet the company's needs.

Slower time frames should allow a period of weeks or months for the staff to fully understand the goals of the project and requirements of the key stakeholders, review the existing environment, and document the design. Time will also be available to choose the right partner for the project, train the internal resources who will assist in (or lead) the process, and prototype the solution in a safe lab environment. Assuming the testing is successful, a phased implementation can further limit the risks of the project, and the pilot phase of the implementation will allow the staff to learn lessons that will smooth out the remaining phases.

Milestones should be set for the completion of the phases, even if they aren't essential to the project's success, to keep momentum going and to avoid the "never-ending project." Projects without periodic dates set as interim milestone points will almost certainly not meet an expected completion date. Projects that extend too far beyond the allotted time frame add costs and risks such as employee turnover, changing business conditions, and new revisions of hardware and software products.

Naturally, projects with shorter timelines bring their own challenges, and typically, some compromises need to be made to successfully complete a large project in a limited amount of time. However, it is important not to abandon the basic principles of discovery, design, and testing. If these steps are skipped and an upgrade is kicked off without planning or a clear understanding of the desired results, the result will often be flawed. In fact, the result might never even be reached because "showstoppers" can suddenly appear in the middle of the project.

It is usually possible to meet a quick timeline (a number of weeks at the very least) and have the results make the stakeholders happy. The real key is to understand the risks involved in the tight time frame and define the scope of the project so that the risks are controlled. This might include putting off some of the functionality that is not essential, or contracting outside assistance to speed up the process and leverage the experience of a firm that has performed similar upgrades many times.

Hardware and software procurement can also pose delays, so for shorter time frames, they should be procured as soon as possible after the ideal configuration has been defined. Note that often the "latest and greatest" hardware—that is, the fastest processors and largest-capacity drives—might take longer to arrive than those a step down. The new equipment should still be tested, or "burned in," and fine-tuned in a lab environment, but can often be moved right into production with the pilot implementation. For most medium and large organizations, it is recommended that a permanent lab be set up; this step is discussed in more depth in the section, "The Prototype Phase: Creating and Testing the Plan," later in this chapter.

## Defining the Participants of the Design and Deployment Teams

Division of labor is a key component of the implementation process. Organizations should evaluate the capabilities of their internal staff and consider hiring an outside firm for assistance in the appropriate areas. If the organization understands and defines the roles that internal staff can play, as well as defines the areas where professional assistance is needed, the project will flow more smoothly.

The experience levels of the existing resources should be assessed, as well as the bandwidth that they have available for learning new technologies or participating in a new project. If the staff is fully occupied on a daily basis supporting the user base, it is unlikely that they will be able to "make more time" to design and plan the new implementation, even with outside assistance. The track record of the existing staff often reveals how the next project will turn out, and if there are existing half-finished or unsuccessful projects, they can interfere with a new project.

Although classroom-style training and manufacturer-sponsored training do not guarantee expertise, they do indicate the IT staff's willingness to learn and illustrate that they are willing to dedicate time to learning new technologies. A new implementation can be a great opportunity to test the commitment levels of the existing staff and also to encourage them to update their skills.

Consider also how the changes to the environment will affect the complexity of the environment that will need to be supported. For example, an upgrade to Windows Server 2008 R2 might enable a company to consolidate and reduce the number of servers on the network and replace "flaky" applications with more stable ones. An upgrade might also introduce brand-new tools that can add support duties in unfamiliar areas to the existing staff.

After the organization takes an inventory of resources at this level and determines roughly what percentage of the project can be handled internally, an external partner should be considered. Even a smaller organization faced with a relatively simple project of, say, installing a Windows Server 2008 R2 server handling one new application can benefit from outside assistance. Some tight time frames necessitate delegating 90% of the tasks to outside resources, whereas other, more leisurely projects might require only 10% assistance levels.

A key distinction to make at this point is between the design resources and the deployment resources. The company or individuals in charge of the design work must have significant experience with the technologies to be implemented and be able to educate and lead the other members of the project team. For projects of moderate or greater complexity, these resources should be dedicated to the design process to ensure that the details are fully sketched out, and the solution designed is as well thought out as possible. Often, the design team has the challenging task of negotiating with the key stakeholders concerning the final design because not all the staff will get everything they want and wish for in the project. The deployment team can contain members of the design team, and these individuals should have training and hands-on experience with the technologies involved and will have more end-user interaction.

There are certain prerequisites to look for when choosing an independent consultant or solution provider organization as a partner. Without going into too much detail, the individual or firm should have proven experience with the exact technologies to be implemented, have a flexible approach to implementing the solution, and have specialized resources to handle the different components of the project. No one person can "do it all," especially if he gets sick or goes on vacation, so breadth and depth of experience should be considered. Obviously, the hourly fees charged are important, but the overall costs, if a firm is willing to commit to a cap or not to exceed a certain price, can be more important. In the current business environment, it makes sense to invest your time wisely in choosing a firm that is very good at what it does, or it might not be around in future months when your project reaches its critical phases.

Soft skills of the partner are also important because many projects are judged not only by whether the project is complete on time, on scope, and on budget, but also by the response of the stakeholders and user community. Communications skills, reliability, and willingness to educate and share knowledge along the way bring great value in the long run.

## The Discovery Phase: Understanding the Existing Environment

Assuming that the previous steps have been taken, the high-level picture of the Windows Server 2008 R2 upgrade should be very clear by now. It should be clear what the business and technology goals are from a "50,000-foot view" business standpoint all the way down to the "1,000-foot" staff level. The components of the upgrade, or the scope of the work, and priorities of these components should also be identified as well as the time constraints and who will be on the design and implementation teams.

The picture of the end state (or scope of work) and goals of the project should start becoming more clear. Before the final design is agreed upon and documented, however, it is essential to review and evaluate the existing environment to make sure the network foundation in place will support the new Windows Server 2008 R2 environment.

It is an important time to make sure the existing environment is configured the way you think it is and to identify existing areas of exposure or weakness in the network. The level of effort required will vary greatly here, depending on the complexity and sheer scope of the network. Organizations with fewer than 200 users and a single or small number of locations that use off-the-shelf software applications and standard hardware products (for example, Hewlett-Packard, IBM, Cisco) will typically have relatively simple configurations. In contrast, larger companies, with multiple locations and vertical-market custom software and hardware will be more complex. Companies that have grown through the acquisition of other organizations might also have mystery devices on the network that play unknown roles.

Another important variable to define is the somewhat intangible element of network stability and performance. What is considered acceptable performance for one company might be unacceptable for another, depending on the importance of the infrastructure and type of business. Some organizations lose thousands of dollars of revenue per minute of downtime, whereas others can go back to paper for a day or more without noticeable impact.

The discovery work needs to involve the design team as well as internal resources. External partners can often produce more thorough results because they have extensive experience with network reviews and analysis and predicting the problems that can emerge midway through a project and become showstoppers. The discovery process will typically start with onsite interviews with the IT resources responsible for the different areas of the network and proceed with hands-on review of the network configuration.

Developing standard questionnaires can be helpful in collecting data on the various network device configurations, as well as recording input on areas of concern of the network. Key end users can reveal needs that their managers or directors aren't aware of, especially in organizations with less-effective IT management or unstable infrastructures. Special attention should be paid to ferreting out the problem areas and technologies that never worked right or have proven to be unstable.

For the most part, the bigger the project, the more thorough the discovery should be. For projects involving a complete NOS upgrade, every affected device and application will need to be reviewed and evaluated to help determine its role in the new environment.

If network diagrams exist, they should be reviewed to make sure they are up to date and contain enough information (such as server names, roles, applications managed, switches, routers, firewalls, and so on) to fully define the location and function of each infrastructure device.

If additional documentation exists on the detailed configuration of key infrastructure devices, such as "as built" server documents with details on the server hardware and software configurations, or details on router configurations or firewalls, they should be dusted off and reviewed. Information such as whether patches and fixes have been applied to servers and software applications becomes important in the design process. In some cases, the desktop configurations need to be inventoried if client changes are required. Software inventory tools can save many hours of work in these cases.

Certain documented company policies and procedures that are in place need to be reviewed. Some, such as disaster recovery plans or service-level agreements (SLAs), can be vital to the IT department's ability to meet the needs of the user community.

The discovery process can also shed light on constraints to the implementation process that weren't considered previously, such as time restrictions that would affect the window of opportunity for change. These restrictions can include seasonal businesses as well as company budgeting cycles or even vacation schedules.

Ultimately, while the amount of time spent in the discovery process will vary greatly, the goals are the same: to really understand the technology infrastructure in place and the risks involved in the project, and to limit the surprises that might occur during the testing and implementation phases.

## Understanding the Geographical Depth and Breadth

At the same time that data is being gathered and verified pertaining to what is in place and what it does, connectivity among devices should also be reviewed, to review the logical as well as the physical components of the network. This information might be available from existing diagrams and documentation, or might need to be gathered in the field.

Important items to understand include answering the following questions: How are DNS and DHCP being handled? Are there VPNs or VLANs in place? How are the routers configured? What protocols are in use? What types of circuits connect the offices: DSL, T1, fiber? What is the guaranteed throughput or the SLAs that are in place?

Has connectivity failure been planned for through a partially or fully meshed environment? Connections to the outside world and other organizations need to be reviewed and fully understood at the same level, especially with an eye toward the security features in place. The best security design in the world can be defeated by a modem plugged in a plain old telephone line and a disgruntled ex-employee.

Along the same lines, remote access needs, such as access to email, network file and print resources, and the support needs for PDAs and other mobile devices, should be reviewed.

Geographically diverse companies bring added challenges to the table. As much as possible, the same level of information should be gathered on all the sites that will be involved in and affected by the migration. Is the IT environment centralized, where one location manages the whole environment, or decentralized, where each office is its own "fiefdom"?

The distribution of personnel should be reviewed and clarified. How many support personnel are in each location, what key hardware and software are they tasked with supporting, and how many end users are there? Often, different offices have specific functions that require a different combination of support personnel. Some smaller, remote offices might have no dedicated staff at all, and this can make it difficult to gather updated information. Accordingly, is there expansion or contraction likely in the near future or office consolidations that will change the user distribution?

Problems and challenges that the wide area network (WAN) design has presented in the past should be reviewed. How is directory information replicated between sites, and what domain design is in place? If the company already has Active Directory in place, is a single domain with a simple organizational unit (OU) structure in place, or are there multiple domains with a complex OU structure? Global catalog placement should also be clarified.

How is the Internet accessed? Does each office have its own Internet connection, firewall, router, and so on, or is it accessed through one location?

The answers to these questions will directly shape the design of the solution, as well as affect the testing and rollout processes.

## Managing Information Overload

Another area that can dramatically affect the design of the Windows Server 2008 R2 solution to be implemented is the place where the company's data lives and how it is managed.

At this point, you should know what the key network software applications are, so it is worth having some numbers on the amount of data being managed and where it lives on the network (1 server? 10 servers?). The total number of individual user files should be reviewed, and if available, statistics on the growth of this data should be reviewed.

Database information is often critical to an organization, whether it pertains to the services and products the company offers to the outside world, or enables the employees to perform their jobs. Databases also require regular maintenance to avoid corruption and optimize performance, so it is useful to know whether maintenance is happening on a regular basis.

Mail databases pose their own challenges. Older mail systems typically were quite limited in the size of their databases, and many organizations were forced to come up with interesting ways of handling large amounts of data. As email has grown in importance and become a primary tool for many companies, the Inbox and personal folders have become the primary storage place for many email users. If the organization uses Microsoft Exchange for its email system, users might have personal stores and/or offline stores that might need to be taken into account.

How the data is backed up and stored should also be reviewed. Some organizations have extremely complex enterprise storage systems and use clustering, storage area networks, and/or a distributed file system to ensure that data is always available to the user community. Sometimes, hierarchical storage processes are in place to move old data to optical media or even to tape.

An overall goal of this sleuthing is to determine where the data is, what file stores and databases are out there, how the data is maintained, and whether it is safe. It might also become clear that the data can be consolidated, or needs to be better protected through clustering or fault tolerance disk solutions. The costs to the company of data loss or temporary unavailability should also be discussed.

# The Design Phase: Documenting the Vision and the Plan

With the completion of the discovery process and documentation of the results, it should now be very clear what you have to work with in terms of the foundation the new solution will be implemented upon. Essentially, the research is all done, and many decisions will now need to be made and documented.

By now, a dozen documents could be written; however, the most important document that needs to be created is the design document. This document is a log of the salient points of the discussions that have taken place to date; it should make very clear why the project is being invested in, describe what the scope of the project is, and provide details of what the results will look like. A second document that needs to be created is the migration document, which provides the road map showing how this end state will be reached.

Often, companies strive for an all-in-one document, but as explained in the next section, there are specific advantages to breaking up this information into two key components. A simple analogy is that you want to agree on what the floor plan for a house will look like (the design) and what the function of each room will be before deciding on how to build it (the migration/implementation).

## Collaboration Sessions: Making the Design Decisions

The design team is most likely not ready to make all the decisions yet, even though quite a bit of homework has already been done. A more formal collaborative and educational process should follow to ensure that the end state of the project is defined in detail and that the design team members fully understand the new technologies to be introduced. The collaborative process involves interactive brainstorming and knowledge-sharing sessions, in which the stakeholders work with facilitators who have expertise with the technologies in question.

Ideally, a consultant with hands-on experience designing and implementing Windows Server 2008 R2 will provide leadership through this process. Well-thought-out agendas can lead the design team through a logical process that educates them about the key decisions to be made and helps with the decisions.

Whiteboards can be used to illustrate the new physical layout of the Windows Server 2008 R2 environment, as well as to explain how the data will be managed and protected on the network. Notes should be taken on the decisions that are made in these sessions. If the sessions are effectively planned and executed, a relatively small number of collaboration sessions will provide the key decisions required for the implementation.

With effective leadership, these sessions can also help establish positive team dynamics and excitement for the project itself. Employees might feel negative about a major upgrade for a wide variety of reasons, but through contributing to the design, learning about the technologies to be implemented, and better understanding their own roles in the process, attitudes can change.

Through these sessions, the details of the end state should become crystal clear. Specifics can be discussed, such as how many servers are needed in which locations, which specific functions they will perform (file and print or application servers, firewalls, and so on), and which key software applications will be managed. Other design decisions and logistical concerns will come up and should be discussed, such as whether to use existing server and network infrastructure hardware or to buy new equipment. Decisions also need to be made concerning secondary applications to support the upgraded environment, such as tape backup software, antivirus solutions, firewall protection, and network management software.

Ideally, some of the details of the actual migration process will start to become clear. For instance, the members of the testing and deployment teams, the training they will require, and the level of involvement from outside resources can be discussed.

## Organizing Information for a Structured Design Document

The complexity of the project will affect the size of the document and the effort required to create it. As mentioned previously, this document summarizes the goals and objectives that were gathered in the initial discovery phase and describes how the project's result will meet them. It should represent a detailed picture of the end state when the new technologies and devices have been implemented. The amount of detail can vary, but it should include key design decisions made in the discovery process and collaboration sessions.

The following is a sample table of contents and brief description of the design document:

▶ **Executive Summary**—Provides a brief discussion of the scope of the Windows Server 2008 R2 implementation (what are the pieces of the puzzle).

▶ **Goals and Objectives**—Includes the "50,000-foot view" business objectives, down to the "1,000-foot view" staff level tasks that will be met by the project.

▶ **Background**—Provides a high-level summary of the current state of the network, focusing on problem areas, as clarified in the discovery process, as well as summary decisions made in the collaboration sessions.

▶ **Approach**—Outlines the high-level phases and tasks required to implement the solution (the details of each task will be determined in the migration document).

▶ **End State**—Defines the details of the new technology configurations. For example, this section describes the number, placement, and functions of Windows Server 2008 R2.

▶ **Budget Estimate**—Provides an estimate of basic costs involved in the project. Whereas a detailed cost estimate requires the creation of the migration document, experienced estimators can provide order of magnitude numbers at this point. Also, it should be clear what software and hardware are needed, so budgetary numbers can be provided.

### The Executive Summary

The executive summary should set the stage and prepare the audience for what the document will contain, and it should be concise. It should outline, at the highest level, what the scope of the work is. Ideally, the executive summary also positions the document in the decision-making process and clarifies that approvals of the design are required to move forward.

### The Goals and Objectives

The goals and objectives section should cover the high-level goals of the project and include the pertinent departmental goals. It's easy to go too far in the goals and objectives sections and get down to the "1,000-foot view" level, but this can end up becoming very confusing, so this information might better be recorded in the migration document and the detailed project plan for the project.

### The Background

The background section should summarize the results of the discovery process and the collaboration sessions, and can list specific design decisions that were made during the collaboration sessions. Additionally, decisions made about what technologies or features not to include can be summarized here. This information should stay at a relatively high level as well, and more details can be provided in the end state section of the design document. This information is extremely useful to have as a reference to come back to later in the project when the infamous question "Who made that decision?" comes up.

### The Approach

The approach section should document the implementation strategy agreed upon to this point, and will also serve to record decisions made in the discovery and design process about the timeline (end to end, and for each phase) and the team members participating in the different phases. This section should avoid going into too much detail because in many cases the end design might not yet be approved and might change after review. Also, the migration document should provide the details of the process that will be followed.

### The End State

In the end state section, the specifics of the Windows Server 2008 R2 implementation should be spelled out in detail and the high-level decisions that were summarized in the background section should be fleshed out here. Essentially, the software to be installed on each server and the roles that Windows Server 2008 R2 will play (global catalog servers, domain controllers, DNS services) are spelled out here, along with the future roles of existing legacy servers. Information on the organizational unit (OU) structure, group structures, and replication sites should be included. Diagrams and tables can help explain the new concepts, and actually show what the solution will look like, where the key network devices will be located, and how the overall topology of the network will change. Often, besides a standard physical diagram of "what goes where," a logical diagram illustrating how devices communicate is needed.

**The Budget Estimate**

The budget section will not be exact but should provide order of magnitude prices for the different phases of the project. If an outside consulting firm is assisting with this document, it can draw from experience with similar projects with like-sized companies. Because no two projects are ever the same, there needs to be some flexibility in these estimates. Typically, ranges for each phase should be provided.

## Windows Server 2008 R2 Design Decisions

As the previous section mentioned, the key Windows Server 2008 R2 design decisions should be recorded in the design document. This is perhaps the most important section of the document because it will define how Windows Server 2008 R2 will be configured and how it will interact with the network infrastructure.

Decisions should have been made about the hardware and software needed for the migration. They should take into account whether the existing hardware will be used in the migration, upgraded, left in place, or retired. This decision, in turn, will determine how many server software licenses will be required, which will directly affect the costs of the project.

The level of redundancy and security the solution will provide should be detailed. Again, it is important to be specific when talking about data availability and discussing the situations that have been planned for in the design.

The server and other infrastructure hardware and software should be defined in this section. If upgrades are needed for existing hardware (more processors, RAM, hard drives, tape drives, and so on) or the existing software (upgrades from the existing NOS, server applications, and vertical market applications), they should be detailed here.

Other key technologies such as messaging applications or industry-specific applications will be included here, in as much detail as appropriate.

## Agreeing on the Design

The final step in the design document process actually takes place after the document has been created. When the document is considered complete, it should be presented to the project stakeholders and reviewed to make sure that it does, in fact, meet their requirements, that they understand the contents, and to see whether any additional concerns come up that weren't addressed in the document.

Although it is unlikely that every goal of every stakeholder will be met (because some might conflict), this process will clarify which goals are the most important and can be met by the technologies to be implemented.

Specific decisions made in the design document that should be reviewed include any disparities between the wish lists the stakeholders had and what the final results of the project will be. Also, the timeline and high-level budget should be discussed and confirmed. If the design document outlines a budget of $500K for hardware and software, but the stakeholders won't be able to allocate more than $250K, the changes should be made at this point, rather than after the migration document is created. A smaller budget might require drastic changes to the design document because capabilities in the solution might need to be removed, which will have ripple effects throughout the project.

If the time frame outlined in the design document needs to be modified to meet the requirements of the stakeholders, this should be identified prior to expending the effort of creating the detailed implementation plan as well.

Bear in mind as well that the design document can be used for different purposes. Some companies want the design document to serve as an educational document to inform not only what the end state will look like, but why it should be that way. Others simply need to document the decisions made and come up with budgetary information.

Having this level of detail will also make it easier to get competitive bids on the costs to implement. Many organizations make the mistake of seeking bids for solutions before they even know what the solution will consist of.

# The Migration Planning Phase: Documenting the Process for Migration

Before the migration document is created, the end state of the project has been documented in detail and agreed upon by the key stakeholders in the organization. There should not be any question as to exactly what the next evolution of the network will be composed of and what functionality it will offer. In addition, an estimated budget for the hardware and software required and an estimated timeline for the project have been identified. In some cases, depending on the size and complexity of the project, and whether outside consulting assistance has been contracted, a budget has also been established for the implementation services.

So, now that the end state has been clearly defined, the migration document can be created to document the details of the steps required to reach the end state with minimal risk of negative impact to the network environment.

The migration plan should not contain any major surprises.

A key component of the migration document is the project plan, or migration plan, that provides a list of the tasks required to implement the solution. It is the road map from which the migration document will be created. The migration document will also provide a narrative, where needed, of the specifics of the tasks that the project plan does not provide, and provide other details as outlined next.

## Time for the Project Plan

As mentioned previously, the primary stepping stones needed to reach the end point have been sketched out in the discovery process, and in collaboration sessions or design discussions that have taken place. The project plan in the migration document provides a tool to complement the design document, which graphically illustrates the process of building and testing the technologies required as well as provides an outline of who is doing what during the project.

By using a product such as Microsoft Project, you can organize the steps in a logical, linear process. The high-level tasks should be established first. Typically, they are the phases or high-level tasks involved in the project, such as lab testing, pilot implementation, production implementation, and support. Then, the main components of these tasks can be filled in.

Dates and durations should be included in the project plan, using the basic concept of starting with the end date when everything needs to be up and running, and then working backward. It's important to include key milestones, such as acquiring new software and hardware, sending administrative resources to training classes, and provisioning new data circuits. Slack time should also be included for unexpected events or stumbling blocks that might be encountered. Each phase of the project needs to be outlined and then expanded.

A good rule of thumb is not to try to list every task that needs to take place during the phase, but to have each line represent several hours or days of work. If too much detail is put into the project plan, it quickly becomes unmanageable. For the detailed information that does not necessarily need to be placed in the project plan (Gantt chart), the information can be detailed in the migration document. The migration document adds in technical and operational details that will help clarify more specific project information.

> **NOTE**
>
> The terms *project plan* and *Gantt chart* are commonly interchanged in IT organizations and might have different meanings to different individuals. In this book, the term project plan refers to the chronological steps needed to successfully plan, prepare, and implement Windows Server 2008 R2. The term Gantt chart is used to refer to the chronological steps, but also the inclusion of resource allocation, start and end dates, and cost distribution.

The plan should also assign resources to the tasks and start to define the teams that will work on the different components of the project. If an outside organization is going to assist in the process, it should be included at the appropriate points in the project. Microsoft Project offers an additional wealth of features to produce reports and graphical information from this plan; they will prove extremely helpful when the work starts. Also, accurate budgetary information can be extracted, which can take into account overtime and after-hours rates and easily give what-if scenario information.

## Speed Versus Risk

The project plan will also enable you to test what-if scenarios. When the high-level tasks are defined, and the resources required to complete each task are also defined, you can easily plug in external contractors to certain tasks and see how the costs change. After-hours work might take place during working hours in certain places.

If the timeline still isn't acceptable, tasks can be stacked so that multiple tasks occur at the same time, instead of one after the other. Microsoft Project also offers extensive tools for resource leveling to make sure that you haven't accidentally committed a resource to, for example, 20 hours of work in 1 day.

The critical path of the project should be defined as well. Certain key events will need to take place for the project to proceed beyond a certain point. Ordering the hardware and having it arrive will be one of these steps. Getting stakeholder approval on the lab environment and proving that key network applications can be supported might be another. Administrative and end-user training might need to happen to ensure that the resulting environment can be effectively supported.

You might need to build contingency time into the project plan as well. Hardware can get delayed and take an extra week or two to arrive. Testing can take longer, especially with complex configurations and when customization of the NOS is required or directory information needs to be modified.

## Creating the Migration Document

The migration document can now narrate the process detailed in the project plan. The project plan does not need to be 100% complete, but the order of the steps and the strategies for testing and implementing will be identified. Typically, the migration document is similar to the structure of the design document (a reason why many organizations combine the two documents), but the design document relates the design decisions made and details the end state of the upgrade, whereas the migration document details the process and steps to be taken.

The following is a sample table of contents for the migration document:

- Executive Summary
- Goals and Objectives of the Migration Process
- Background
- Risks and Assumptions
- Roles and Responsibilities
- Timeline and Milestones
- Training Plan

▶ Migration Process

   ▶ Hardware and Software Procurement Process

   ▶ Prototype Proof of Concept Process

   ▶ Server Configuration and Testing

   ▶ Desktop Configuration and Testing

   ▶ Documentation Required from Prototype

   ▶ Pilot Phase(s) Detailed

   ▶ Migration/Upgrade Detailed

   ▶ Support Phase Detailed

   ▶ Support Documentation Detailed

▶ Budget Estimate

   ▶ Labor Costs for Prototype Phase

   ▶ Labor Costs for Pilot Phase

   ▶ Labor Costs for Migration/Upgrade Phase

   ▶ Labor Costs for Support Phase

   ▶ Costs for Training

▶ Project Schedule

### The Executive Summary Section

The executive summary should set the stage and prepare the audience for what the document will contain, and it should be concise. It should outline, at the highest level, what the scope of the work is. Ideally, the executive summary also positions the document in the decision-making process and clarifies that approvals of the design are required to move forward.

### The Goals and Objectives Section

The goals and objectives section might seem redundant because the design documents documented the objectives in great detail, but it is important to consider which specific goals and objectives are important to the success of the migration project that might not have been included in the design document. For example, although the design document outlined what the final server configuration will look like, it might not have outlined the tools needed to migrate key user data or the order that the company offices will be migrated. So, the goals and objectives in the migration document will be very process specific.

### The Background Section

A summary of the migration-specific decisions should be provided to answer questions such as "Why are we doing it that way?" because there is always a variety of ways to implement new messaging technologies, such as using built-in tools as opposed to using third-party tools. Because a number of conversations will have taken place during the planning phase to compare the merits of one method versus another, it is worth summarizing them early in the document for anyone who wasn't involved in those conversations.

### The Risks and Assumptions Section

Risks pertaining to the phases of the migration should be detailed, and typically are more specific than in the design document. For example, a risk of the prototype phase might be that the hardware available won't perform adequately and needs to be upgraded. Faxing, virus protection, or backup software might not meet the requirements of the design document and, thus, need upgrading. Custom-designed messaging applications or Windows add-ons might turn out not to be Windows Server 2008 R2 compatible.

### The Roles and Responsibilities Section

In the roles and responsibilities section, the teams that will do the work should be identified in detail. If an outside company will be performing portions of the work, which tasks it will be responsible for and which ones internal resources will take ownership of should be documented.

### The Timeline and Milestones Section

Specific target dates can be listed, and should be available directly from the project schedule already created. This summary can be very helpful to executives and managers, whereas the Gantt chart contains too much information. Constraints that were identified in the discovery process need to be kept in mind here because there might be important dates (such as the end of the fiscal year), seasonal demands on the company that black out certain date ranges, and key company events or holidays. Again, be aware of other large projects going on in your environment that might impact your timeline. There's no point trying to deploy new servers on the same weekend that the data center will be powered off for facility upgrades.

### The Training Plan Section

It is useful during the planning of any upgrade to examine the skill sets of the people who will be performing the upgrade and managing the new environment to see if there are any gaps that need to be filled with training. Often, training will happen during the prototype testing process in a hands-on fashion for the project team with the alternate choice being classroom-style training, often provided by an outside company. Also ask yourself if the end users will require training to use new client-side tools. Also pay attention to how the new environment will integrate into existing systems such as backup or monitoring. Determine if those groups will need any training specific to interacting with Windows Server 2008 R2 components.

### The Migration Process Section

The project schedule Gantt chart line items should be included and expanded upon so that it is clear to the resources doing the work what is expected of them. The information does not need to be on the level of step-by-step instructions, but it should clarify the process and results expected from each task. For example, the Gantt chart might indicate that a Windows Server 2008 R2 server needs to be configured, and in the migration document, information would be added about which server roles need to be installed, how the hard drives are to be configured, and which additional applications (virus protection, tape backup, faxing, network management) need to be installed.

If the Gantt chart lists a task of, for example, "Configure and test Windows client access," the migration document gives a similar level of detail: Which image should be used to configure the base workstation configuration, which additional applications and version of Windows should be loaded, how is the workstation to be locked down, and what testing process should be followed (is it scripted or will an end user from the department do the testing)?

Documentation also should be described in more detail. The Gantt chart might simply list "Create as built documents," with as built defined as "document containing key server configuration information and screenshots so that a knowledgeable resource can rebuild the system from scratch."

Sign-off conditions for the prototype phase are important and should be included. Who needs to sign off on the results of the prototype phase to indicate that the goals were all met and that the design agreed upon is ready to be created in the production environment?

Similar levels of information are included for the pilot phase and the all-important migration itself. Typically during the pilot phase, all the upgraded functionality needs to be tested, including remote access, file encryption access, and access to shared folders. Be aware that pilot testing might require external coordination. For example, if you are testing remote access through a VPN connection, you might need to acquire an additional external IP address and arrange to have an address record created in DNS to allow your external testers to reach it without having to disturb your existing remote access systems.

The migration plan should also account for support tasks that need to occur after the Windows Server 2008 R2 infrastructure is fully in place. If you are using an outside consulting firm for assistance in the design and implementation, you should make sure that they will leave staff onsite for a period of time immediately after the upgrade to be available to support user issues or to troubleshoot any technical issues that crop up.

If documentation is specified as part of the support phase, such as Windows maintenance documents, disaster recovery plans, or procedural guides, expectations for these documents should be included to help the technical writers make sure the documents are satisfactory.

### The Budget Section

With regard to the budget information, although a great amount of thought and planning has gone into the design and migration documents, as well as the project plan, there are still variables. No matter how detailed these documents are, the later phases of the project might change based on the results of the earlier phases. For instance, the prototype testing might go flawlessly, but during the pilot implementation, performing data migration simply takes longer than anticipated; this extra time will require modifications to the amount of time required and the associated costs. Note that changes in the opposite direction can happen as well, if tasks can occur more quickly than anticipated. Often, the implementation costs can be reduced by keeping an eye on ways to improve the process during the prototype and pilot phases.

### The Project Schedule Section

Whereas the project plan provides the high-level details of the steps, or tasks, required in each phase, the approach sections of the migration document can go into more detail about the details of each step of the project plan, as needed. Certain very complex tasks are represented with one line on the project plan, such as "Configure Windows Server 2008 R2 #1" and might take several pages to describe in sufficient detail in the migration document.

Data availability testing and disaster recovery testing should be discussed. In the design document, you might have decided that clustering will be used, as well as a particular tape backup program, but the migration plan should outline exactly which scenarios should be tested in the prototype lab environment.

Documents to be provided during the migration should be defined so that it is clear what they will contain.

# The Prototype Phase: Creating and Testing the Plan

The main goal of the prototype phase is to create a lab environment in which the key elements of the design as defined in the design document can be configured and tested. Based on the results of the prototype, you can determine whether any changes are needed to the implementation and support phases as outlined in the migration document.

The prototype phase is also a training phase, in which the members of the deployment team get a chance to get their hands dirty with the new hardware and software technologies to be implemented. If an external consulting firm is assisting with the prototype testing, knowledge transfer should occur and be expected during this process. Even if the deployment team has attended classroom training, the prototype process is an environment that will more closely reflect the end state of the network that needs to be supported, and will involve technologies and processes not typically covered in classroom-style training. The deployment team can also benefit from the real-world experience of the consultants if they are assisting in this phase.

This environment should be isolated from the production network so that problems created by or encountered in the process don't affect the user community.

The design details of testing applications, confirming hardware performance, testing fault tolerance failover, and the like should be verified in a safe lab environment. If changes are needed to the design document, they should be made now.

## How Do You Build the Lab?

Although the details of the project will determine the specifics of exactly what will be in the prototype lab, certain common elements will be required. The migration document should clearly outline the components of the lab and what applications and processes

should be tested. A typical environment will consist of the primary Windows Server 2008
R2 server required for the implementation, as well as network switches, sample workstations, and printers from the production environment. Connectivity to the outside world
should be available for testing purposes.

A key decision to make is whether the lab will be implemented into the environment or
stay as a lab. Some companies will proceed from the prototype phase to the pilot phase with
the same equipment, whereas others prefer to keep a lab set up for future use. The advantages of having a lab environment for a Windows Server 2008 R2 environment are many,
and include testing NOS and application updates, upgrades and patches, as well as having
hardware available for replacement of failed components in the production environment.

Real data and applications should be installed and tested. Data can be copied from live
production servers, or data from tape can be restored to the test server. Applications
should be installed on the servers according to a manufacturer's installation instructions;
however, compatibility validation with Windows Server 2008 R2 should be conducted as
outlined in Chapter 17, "Compatibility Testing."

After the software applications have been installed, representative users from the different
company departments could be brought into the lab to put the applications through their
paces. These users will be best able to do what they normally do in the lab environment
to ensure that their requirements will be met by the new configuration. Areas that don't
meet their expectations should be recorded and identified as either "showstoppers" that
need to be addressed immediately or issues that won't harm the implementation plan.

## Results of the Lab Testing Environment

In addition to the valuable learning that takes place, a number of other things come out
of the lab testing process. If time permits, and there is room in the budget, a variety of
documents can be produced to facilitate the pilot and implementation process. Another
key result of the lab is hard evidence of the accuracy and completeness of the design and
migration documents.

Some of the documents that can be created will assist the deployment team during the
migration process. One key document is the "as built" document, which provides a snapshot of the key configuration details of the primary servers that have been configured and
tested. Whereas the design document outlines many of the key configuration details, the
"as built" document contains actual screenshots of the server configurations as well as the
output from the Windows Server 2008 R2 Computer Management administrative tool that
provides important details, such as physical and logical disk configuration, system
memory and processor information, services installed and in use on the system, and so on.

Another important document is the disaster recovery document (or DR document). This
document should outline exactly which types of failures were tested and the process for
rectifying these situations. Keep in mind that a complete disaster recovery plan should
include offsite data and application access, so the DR document that comes out of the
prototype phase will, in most cases, be more of a hardware failure document that discusses
how to replace failed components, such as hard drives or power supplies, and how to
restore the server configuration from tape backup or restore data sets.

If you need to implement multiple servers in the pilot and implementation phases, you can document checklists for the step-by-step processes in the prototype phase. Bear in mind that creating step-by-step documents takes a great deal of time (and paper!), and a change in process requires drastic changes to these documents. Typically, creating a step-by-step "recipe" for server builds is not worth the time unless lower-level resources need to build a large number in a short period of time.

When the testing is complete, the migration plan should be revisited to make sure that the timeline and milestones are still accurate. Ideally, there should be no major surprises during the prototype phase, but adjustments might be needed to the migration plan to ensure the success of the project.

Depending on the time frame for the pilot and implementation phases, the hardware and software that will be needed for the full implementation might be ordered at this point. As the cost of server hardware has decreased over the past several years, many companies "overspec" the hardware they think they need, and they might determine during the prototype phase that lesser amounts of RAM or fewer processors will still exceed the needs of the technologies to be implemented, so the hardware requirements might change.

# The Pilot Phase: Validating the Plan to a Limited Number of Users

Now that the prototype phase has been completed, the deployment team will be raring to go and have hands-on experience with all the new technologies to be implemented. The process documented in the migration document and migration plan will have been tested in the lab environment as completely as practical, and documentation detailing the steps to be followed during the pilot implementation will be at hand.

Although the pilot process will vary in complexity based on the extent of the changes to be made to the network infrastructure, the process should be well documented at this point.

It is important to identify the first group of users who will be moved to the new Windows Server 2008 R2 environment. Users with a higher tolerance for pain are a better choice than the key stakeholders, for the most part.

> **NOTE**
>
> In many organizations, the CEO, CIO, VP of sales, or other key executives might want to be part of the initial pilot rollout; however, we suggest not making these individuals part of the initial rollout. These individuals typically have the most complex user configuration with the lowest tolerance for interruption of network services. Users in the production environment with simpler needs can be used for the initial pilot. If necessary, create a prepilot phase so that the senior executives can be part of the official pilot phase, but don't make the challenges of pilot testing more difficult by starting with users who have the most complex needs.

A rollback strategy should be clarified, just in case.

Test the disaster recovery and redundancy capabilities thoroughly at this point with live data but a small user group to make sure everything works as advertised.

Migration processes can be fine-tuned during this process, and time estimates can be nailed down.

## The First Server in the Pilot

The pilot phase is begun when the first Windows Server 2008 R2 server accessed by users is implemented in the production environment. Dependent on the scope of the migration project, this first server might be a simple application server running Terminal Services or Windows SharePoint Services, or the first server might be an Active Directory domain controller.

Just as in the prototype phase, the testing to be conducted in the pilot phase is to verify successful access to the server or application services the system provides. One of the best ways to validate functionality is to take the test sequences used in the prototype phase and repeat the test steps in the pilot production environment.

The major difference between the prototype and pilot phases is interconnectivity and enterprisewide compatibility. In many lab-based prototype phases, the testing is isolated to clean system configurations or homogeneous system configurations; however, in a pilot production environment, the new technology is integrated with old technology. It is the validation that the new setup works with existing users, servers, and systems, and software that is the added focus of the production pilot phase.

## Rolling Out the Pilot Phase

The pilot phase is usually rolled out in subphases, with each subphase growing in number of users affected, uses of system technology by the pilot users, and the distribution of users throughout the organization.

### Quantity of Pilot Users

The whole purpose of the pilot phase is to slowly roll out users throughout the organization to validate that prototype and test assumptions were accurate and that they can be successful in the production environment. An initial group of 5 to 10 pilot users (typically members of the IT department overseeing and managing the migration) are first to be migrated. These users test basic functionality.

After successful basic testing, the pilot users group can grow to 1%, then to 3%, on to 5%, and finally to 10% of the user base in the organization. This phased rollout will help the migration team test compatibility, connectivity, and communications with existing systems, while working with a manageable group of users that won't overwhelm the help desk services in place during the pilot and migration process.

The pilot phase is also a time when help desk and migration support personnel build the knowledge base of problems that occur during the migration process so that if or when problems occur again (possibly in the full rollout phase of the product), lessons have been learned and workarounds already created to resolve stumbling blocks.

### Application Complexity of Pilot Users

In addition to expanding the scope of the pilot phase by sheer quantity, selecting users who have different application usage requirements can provide a level of complexity across software platforms. Application compatibility and operation are critical to the end-user experience during the migration process. Often, users won't mind if something runs a little slower during the migration process or that a new process takes a while to learn; however, users will get upset if the applications they require and depend on each day to get their job done lock up while they use the application, data is lost due to system insta-bility, or the application just won't work. So testing applications is critical in the early pilot phase of the project.

### Role Complexity of Pilot Users

Pilot users should also be drawn from various roles throughout an organization. In many migrations, all pilot users are tested from a single department using just a single set of applications, and it isn't until the full migration process that a feature or function that is critical to everyone in the organization (except the pilot group users' department) doesn't work. An example might be a specific financial trading application, a proprietary health-care tracking application, or a critical sales force automation remote access tool that causes the entire project to come to a halt far into the full rollout phase.

### Geographical Diversity of Pilot Users

The pilot group should eventually include members geographically distributed throughout the organization. It is important to start the pilot phase with a set of users who are local to the IT or help desk operation so that initial pilot support can be done in person or directly with the initial pilot group. Before the pilot is considered complete, however, users from remote sites should be tested to ensure their user experience to the new networking environment hasn't been negatively affected.

## Fixing Problems in the Pilot Phase

No matter how much planning and testing are conducted in the earlier phases of the project, problems always crop up in the pilot phase of the project. It is important to have the prototype lab still intact so that any outstanding problems can be re-created in the lab, tested, and resolved to be tested in the pilot production phase again.

## Documenting the Results of the Pilot

After the pilot, it is important to document the results. Even with the extensive discovery and design work, as well as the prototype lab testing and pilot phases that have taken place, problems might reoccur in the postpilot phases, and any documented information on how problems were resolved or configurations made to resolve problems in the pilot phase will help simplify the resolution in future phases. If you take some extra time to give attention to the pilot users, you can fine-tune the solution to make sure the full implementation is a success.

# The Migration/Implementation Phase: Conducting the Migration or Installation

By this point in the project, more than 10% of the organization's users should have been rolled out and tested in the pilot phase, applications thoroughly tested, help desk and support personnel trained, and common problem resolution clearly documented so that the organization can proceed with the migration and installation throughout the rest of the organization.

## Verifying End-User Satisfaction

A critical task that can be conducted at this point in the project is to conduct a checkpoint for end-user satisfaction, making sure that users are getting their systems, applications, or functionality upgraded; questions are answered; problems are resolved; and, most important, users are being made aware of the benefits and improvements of the new environment.

Not only does this phase of the project focus on the sheer rollout of the technology, but it is also the key public relations and communications phase of the project. Make sure the user community gets the training and support it needs throughout the process.

Plan on issues arising that will need support for several days after each department or user group is upgraded.

Don't forget the special users with unique requirements and remote users because they will require additional support.

## Supporting the New Windows Server 2008 R2 Environment

Before the last users are rolled into the new networking environment, besides planning the project completion party, you need to allocate time to ensure the ongoing support and maintenance of the new environment is being conducted. This step not only includes doing regular backups of the new servers (covered in detail in Chapter 30, "Backing Up the Windows Server 2008 R2 Environment"), but also includes planning for regular maintenance (Chapter 20, "Windows Server 2008 R2 Management and Maintenance Practices"), monitoring (Chapter 23, "Integrating System Center Operations Manager 2007 R2 with Windows Server 2008 R2"), and tuning and optimization (Chapter 34, "Capacity Analysis and Performance Optimization") of the new Windows Server 2008 R2 environment.

Now is the time to begin planning for some of the wish-list items that didn't make sense to include in the initial migration—for example, a new antiviral solution, knowledge-management solutions, enhanced security, and so on.

If you have a lab still in place, use it for testing patches and software updates.

# Summary

One analogy used in this chapter is that of building a house. Although this analogy doesn't stand up to intense scrutiny, the similarities are helpful. When an organization is planning a Windows Server 2008 R2 implementation, it is important to first understand the goals for the implementation, and not only the "50,000-foot" high-level goals, but also the "10,000-foot" departmental and "1,000-foot" IT staff goals. Then, it is important to more fully understand the environment that will serve as the foundation for the upgrade. Whether this work is performed by external resources or by internal resources, a great deal will be learned about what is really in place, and where there might be areas of risk or exposure. Collaboration sessions with experienced and effective leadership can then educate the stakeholders and deployment resources about the technologies to be implemented as well as guide the group through the key decisions that need to be made. Now all this information needs to be documented in the design document so that the details are clear, and some initial estimates for the resources required, timeline, and budget can be set. This document serves as a blueprint of sorts, and defines in detail what the "house" will look like when it is built. When all the stakeholders agree that this is exactly what they want to see, and the timeline and budget are in line, the migration document can be produced.

The migration document includes a detailed project plan that provides the tasks that need to take place to produce the results detailed in the design document. The project plan should not go into step-by-step detail describing how to build each server, but should stick to summary tasks from four hours to a day or more in duration. The migration document then provides a narrative of the project plan and supplies additional information pertaining to goals, resources, risks, and deliverables, as well as budgetary information accurate in the 10% to 20% range.

Based on these documents, the organization can now proceed with building the solution in a lab environment and testing the proposed design with actual company data and resources involved. The results of the testing might require modifications to the migration document, and will prepare the deployment team for live implementation. Ideally, a pilot phase with a limited, noncritical group of users will occur to fine-tune the live implementation process and put in place key technologies and Windows Server 2008 R2. Now the remainder of the implementation process should proceed with a minimum of surprises, and the result will meet the expectations set in the design phase and verified during the prototype and pilot phases.

Even the support phase has been considered, and during this phase, the "icing on the cake" can be applied as appropriate.

Although this process might seem complex, it can be molded to fit all different sizes of projects and will yield better results.

# Best Practices

The following are best practices from this chapter:

▶ Use a migration methodology consisting of discovery, design, testing, and implementation phases to meet the needs of your organization.

▶ Fully understand the business and technical goals and objectives of the upgrade and the breadth and scope of benefits the implementation will provide before implementing a new application or upgrade.

▶ Create a scope of work detailing the Windows Server 2008 R2 network functionality, data management, information access, and application hosting.

▶ Define high-level organizational goals.

▶ Define departmental goals.

▶ Determine which components and capabilities of the network are most important and how they contribute to or hinder the goals expressed by the different units.

▶ Clearly define the technical goals of the project on different levels ("50,000-foot," "10,000-foot," "1,000-foot," and so on).

## The Discovery Phase

▶ Review and evaluate the existing environment to make sure the network foundation in place will support the new Windows Server 2008 R2 environment.

▶ Make sure the existing environment is configured the way you think it is, and identify existing areas of exposure or weakness in the network.

▶ Define the current network stability and performance measurements and operation.

▶ Use external partners to produce more thorough results due to their extensive experience with network reviews and analysis and predict the problems that can emerge midway through a project and become "showstoppers."

▶ Start the discovery process with onsite interviews.

▶ Review and evaluate every affected device and application to help determine its role in the new environment.

▶ Maintain and protect database information that is critical to an organization on a regular basis.

▶ Determine where data resides, what file stores and databases are out there, how the data is maintained, and whether it is safe.

## The Design Phase

- ▶ Create a design document including the salient points of the discussion, the reasons the project is being invested in, the scope of the project, and the details of what the results will look like.

- ▶ Create a migration document providing the road map showing how the end state will be reached.

- ▶ Use a consultant with hands-on experience designing and implementing Windows Server 2008 R2 to provide leadership through this process.

- ▶ Determine what hardware and software will be needed for the migration.

- ▶ Determine how many server software licenses will be required to more accurately calculate project costs.

- ▶ Detail the level of redundancy and security that is required and that the solution will ultimately provide.

- ▶ Present the design and migration documents to the project stakeholders for review.

## The Migration Planning Phase

- ▶ Create a migration document containing the details of the steps required to reach the end state with minimal risk or negative impact to the network environment.

- ▶ Create a project plan that provides a list of the tasks, resources, and durations required to implement the solution.

## The Prototype Phase

- ▶ Create a lab environment in which the key elements of the design as defined in the design document can be configured and tested.

- ▶ Isolate the lab environment from the production network so that any problems created or encountered in the process don't affect the user community.

- ▶ Thoroughly test all applications.

## The Pilot Phase

- ▶ Identify the first group of users who will be moved to the new Windows Server 2008 R2 environment. Users with a higher tolerance for pain are a better choice than the key stakeholders, for the most part.

- ▶ Clarify a rollback strategy, just in case unexpected problems occur.

- ▶ Test the disaster recovery and redundancy capabilities thoroughly.

- ▶ Fine-tune the migration processes and nail down time estimates.

## The Migration/Implementation Phase

▶ Verify that applications have been thoroughly tested, help desk and support personnel have been trained, and common problem resolution is clearly documented.

▶ Conduct a checkpoint for end-user satisfaction.

▶ Allocate time to ensure that ongoing support and maintenance of the new environment are being conducted before the last users are rolled into the new networking environment.

▶ Plan a project completion party.

# CHAPTER 3

# Installing Windows Server 2008 R2 and Server Core

This chapter describes the step-by-step process for installing a clean version of the Windows Server 2008 R2 operating system, upgrading an existing system to Windows Server 2008 R2, and, finally, installing a Windows Server 2008 R2 Server Core installation.

Even though the installation process is very intuitive and has been simplified, an administrator must make several key decisions to ensure that the completed installation will meet the needs of the organization. For example, is it beneficial to upgrade an existing system to Windows Server 2008 R2, or is it preferred to conduct a clean install from scratch? What are the ramifications of these alternatives? Will I lose my existing settings, programs, and configurations? This chapter covers these prerequisite planning tasks to address administrators' questions and concerns.

In addition, this chapter also focuses on how to install and manage Server Core on Windows Server 2008 R2.

## Preplanning and Preparing a Server Installation

Before you begin the actual installation of Windows Server 2008 R2, you must make several decisions concerning prerequisite tasks. How well you plan these steps will determine how successful your installation is—as many of these decisions cannot be changed after the installation is complete.

## Verifying Minimum Hardware Requirements

Whether you are installing Windows Server 2008 R2 in a lab or production environment, you need to ensure that the hardware chosen meets the minimum system requirements. In most situations, the minimum hardware requirements presented will not suffice; therefore, Table 3.1 provides not only the minimum requirements, but also the recommended and maximum system requirements for the hardware components.

TABLE 3.1    Windows Server 2008 R2 System Requirements

| Component | Minimum Requirement | Recommended | Maximum |
| --- | --- | --- | --- |
| Processor | 1.4GHZ 64-bit | 2GHZ or faster | Not applicable |
| Memory | 512MB RAM | 2GB RAM or greater | 32GB RAM Standard Edition<br>2TB RAM Enterprise and Datacenter Editions |
| Disk Space | 32GB | 40GB Full installation<br>or<br>10GB Server Core installation | Not applicable |

**Take note:** When designing and selecting the system specifications for a new server solution, even the optimal system requirements recommendations from Microsoft might not suffice. It is a best practice to assess the server specifications of the planned server role while taking the load during the time of deployment and future growth into consideration. For example, a Windows Server 2008 R2 system running the Exchange Server 2010 Mailbox Server role will require much more than 2GB of RAM to run adequately. In addition, SQL Server 2008 R2 running on a Windows Server 2008 R2 server that is providing business intelligence solutions for 10,000 users might require 32GB of RAM. Therefore, size the system accordingly and test the load before going live into production.

---

**CAUTION**

Windows Server 2008 R2 ONLY supports 64-bit processor architectures. A server running 32-bit processors is NOT supported.

---

## Choosing the Appropriate Windows Edition

There are four main editions in the Windows Server 2008 R2 family of operating systems. The editions include Windows Server 2008 R2, Standard Edition; Windows Server 2008 R2, Enterprise Edition; Windows Server 2008 R2, Datacenter Edition; and Windows Server 2008, Web Edition. An organization or administrator must understand their workload needs and requirements when selecting the operating system to utilize. For example, the Enterprise Edition might be selected if there is a need to sustain a 16-node failover cluster or autoenrollment with Microsoft Certificate Services. Or the Standard Edition could be utilized if there is a need to implement virtualization with Hyper-V.

Each edition supports a Server Core version. For a full list of Windows Server 2008 R2 features and functionality, see Chapter 1, "Windows Server 2008 R2 Technology Primer." This chapter covers the editions in their entirety.

## Choosing a New Installation or an Upgrade

If you have an existing Windows environment, you might need to perform a new installation or upgrade an existing server. There are benefits to each of these options. The next two sections outline the benefits for each.

### Should You Perform a New Installation?

The primary benefit of a new installation is that, by installing the operating system from scratch, you are starting with a known good server. You can avoid migrating problems that might have existed on your previous server—whether due to corrupt software, incorrect configuration settings, or improperly installed applications. Keep in mind, however, that you will also lose all configuration settings from your previous installation. In addition, required applications on the legacy server will need to be reinstalled after the installation of the new operating system is complete. Make sure you document your server configuration information, have all the appropriate software you plan on reinstalling, and back up any data that you want to keep.

When performing a new installation, you can install on a new hard drive (or partition) or in a different directory on the same disk as a previous installation. Typically, most new installations are installed on a new or freshly formatted hard drive. Doing so removes any old software and gives you the cleanest installation.

### Should You Upgrade an Existing Server?

Upgrading, on the other hand, replaces your current Windows files but keeps existing users, settings, groups, rights, and permissions intact. In this scenario, you don't have to reinstall applications or restore data. Before choosing this option, keep in mind that you should test your applications for compatibility before migration. Just because they worked on previous versions of Windows does not mean they will work on Windows Server 2008 R2.

As always, before performing any type of server maintenance such as a Windows Server 2008 R2 installation, you should perform a complete backup of any applications and data that you want to preserve. Do not forget to include the System State when backing up the legacy Windows operating system. It is required when performing a restore if you want to maintain the existing Windows settings.

To upgrade to Windows Server 2008 R2, you must be running a server-level operating system. You cannot upgrade Workstation or Home Editions of operating systems such as Windows XP, Windows Vista, or Microsoft's latest desktop operating system, Windows 7 to Windows Server 2008 R2. To upgrade your existing server, you must be running Windows Server 2008 or Windows Server 2003. An upgrade from Windows NT 4.0 and Windows 2000 Server are not supported. Table 3.2 lists the available upgrade paths to Windows Server 2008 R2.

TABLE 3.2    Windows Server 2008 R2 Upgrade Paths

| Previous Operating System | Upgrade to Windows Server 2008 R2 |
| --- | --- |
| Microsoft Windows Server 2008, Standard, Enterprise, or Datacenter Edition | Yes, fully supported |
| Microsoft Windows Server 2008, Standard, Enterprise, or Datacenter Server Core Edition | Yes, fully supported to Server Core |
| Microsoft Windows Server 2003 R2, Standard, Enterprise, or Datacenter Edition | Yes, fully supported |
| Microsoft Windows Server 2003 operating systems with Service Pack 1 (SP1), Standard, Enterprise, or Datacenter Edition | Yes, fully supported |
| Microsoft Windows Server 2003 operating systems with Service Pack 2 (SP2), Standard, Enterprise, or Datacenter Edition | Yes, fully supported |
| Windows NT 4.0 | Not supported |
| Windows 2000 Server | Not supported |
| Windows XP | Not supported |
| Windows Vista | Not supported |
| Any 32-Bit Windows Edition | Not supported |

> **NOTE**
>
> A direct upgrade from any version of Windows Server 2003 to Windows Server 2008 R2 Server Core is not supported. If a Windows Server 2008 R2 Server Core is warranted, a fresh Windows Server 2008 R2 Server Core install or an upgrade from Windows Server 2008 Server Core is necessary.

> **NOTE**
>
> If there is a need to preserve settings and upgrade a legacy operating system such as Windows NT 4.0 or Windows 2000 Server, the system should first be upgraded to Windows Server 2003 and then again to Windows Server 2008 R2. Typically, this is not the recommended approach as the hardware is typically outdated; however, the multiple upgrade approach is doable.

## Determining the Type of Server to Install

You have the choice of making your server an Active Directory Domain Services (AD DS), a member server, a standalone server, or a Server Core installation. After you determine the tasks the server will perform, you can determine the role or roles that you will assign to it.

Domain controllers and member servers play a role in a new or existing domain. Standalone servers are not joined to a particular domain. Finally, Server Core installations were introduced with the release of the Windows Server 2008 family of operating systems and only consist of a minimal installation footprint. On a Server Core installation, the traditional graphical user interface (GUI) tools are not available and some of the roles that are supported include Active Directory Domain Services, Active Directory Lightweight Directory Services (AD LDS), DHCP Server, DNS Server, File Services, Print Server, Streaming Media Services, and Web Server (IIS) roles. Type `oclist` at a Server Core command prompt to determine the available server roles. However, with the release of Windows Server 2008 R2, Microsoft has introduced a new command called SCONFIG that allows for an easier configuration of a Server Core installation.

As in earlier versions of Windows, you are able to promote or demote server functions as you desire. Standalone servers can be joined to the domain to become member servers. Using the dcpromo utility, you can promote member servers to domain controllers. And, by uninstalling the Active Directory Domain Services role from a domain controller, you can return it to member server status. In addition, with Windows Server 2008 R2, server roles such as Web Server (IIS), DHCP, and DNS can be added or removed via the Server Manager tool.

## Gathering the Information Necessary to Proceed

During the installation of Windows Server 2008 R2, you will have to tell the setup wizard how you want your server configured. The wizard will take the information you provide and will configure the server settings to meet your specifications.

Taking the time to gather the information described in the following sections before starting your installation will likely make your installation go faster, smoother, and easier.

> **NOTE**
>
> Although items such as the server name and IP address are required for a server to function, they are manually entered after the installation is complete, unless an unattended installation with an answer file is used.

### Selecting the Computer Name

Each computer on a network must have a name that is unique within that network. Many companies have a standard naming convention for their servers and workstations. If not, you can use the following information as a guideline for creating your own.

Although the computer name can contain up to 63 characters, workstations and servers that are pre–Windows 2000 recognize only the first 15 characters.

It is widely considered a best practice to use only Internet-standard characters in your computer name. This includes the letters A–Z (upper- and lowercase), the numbers 0–9, and the hyphen (-).

Although it's true that implementing the Microsoft domain name system (DNS) service in your environment could allow you to use some non-Internet standard characters (such as Unicode characters and the underscore), you should keep in mind that this is likely to cause problems with any non-Microsoft DNS servers on your network. You should think carefully and test thoroughly before straying from the standard Internet characters noted in the preceding paragraph.

### Name of the Workgroup or Domain

After the server installation is complete, you need to determine the name of the work-group or domain that the server will be joining. You can either enter the name of an existing Windows domain or workgroup to join, or create a new workgroup by entering in a new name.

Users new to Microsoft networking might ask, "What is the difference between a work-group and a domain?" Simply put, a domain is a collection of computers and supporting hardware that shares the same security database. Grouping the equipment in this manner allows you to set up centralized security and administration. Conversely, a workgroup has no centralized security or administration. Each server or workstation is configured inde-pendently and locally for all security and administration settings.

### Network Protocol and IP Address of the Server

When installing Windows Server 2008 R2, you must install and configure a network protocol that will allow it to communicate with other machines on the network.

Currently, the most commonly used protocol is called TCP/IP version 4, which stands for Transmission Control Protocol/Internet Protocol. This protocol allows computers throughout the Internet to communicate. After you install TCP/IP, you need to configure an IP address for the server. You can choose one of the following three methods to assign an IP address:

▶ **Automatic Private IP Addressing (APIPA)**—APIPA can be used if you have a small network that does not have a Dynamic Host Configuration Protocol (DHCP) server, which is used for dynamic IP addresses. A unique IP address is assigned to the network adapter using the LINKLOCAL IP address space. The address always starts with 169.254 and is in the format 169.254.x.x. Note that if APIPA is in use, and a DHCP server is brought up on the network, the computer will detect this and will use the address that is assigned by the DHCP server instead.

▶ **Dynamic IP address**—A dynamic IP address is assigned by a DHCP server. This allows a server to assign IP addresses and configuration information to clients. Some examples of the information that is distributed include IP address, subnet mask, default gateway, DNS server address, and the Windows Internet Naming Service (WINS) server address. As the dynamic portion of the name suggests, this address is assigned to the computer for a configurable length of time, known as a lease. Before the lease expires, the workstation must again request an IP address from the DHCP server. It might or might not get the same address that it had previously. Although servers and workstations can both be configured to use this method of addressing, it is generally used for workstations rather than servers.

▶ **Static IP address**—Using a static IP address is the most common decision for a serv-er configuration. By static, we mean the server or workstation will not leverage DHCP; the IP address and settings are configured manually. The address will not change unless you change the configuration of the server. This point is important because clients and resources that need to access the server must know the address to be able to connect to it. If the IP address changed regularly, connecting to it would be difficult.

> **NOTE**
>
> Windows Server 2008 R2 includes the latest TCP/IP protocol suite known as the Next Generation TCP/IP stack. The legacy protocol stack was designed in the early 1990s and has been modified to accommodate future growth of computers networked together. The new TCP/IP stack is known as Internet Protocol version 6 (IPv6).

### Backing Up Files

Whether you are performing a new installation on a previously used server or upgrading an existing server, you should perform a complete backup of the data and operating system before you begin your new installation. This way, you have a fallback plan if the installation fails or the server does not perform the way you anticipated.

When performing a new installation on a previously used server, you overwrite any data that was stored there. In this scenario, you will have to use your backup tape to restore any data that you want to preserve.

On the other hand, if you are going to upgrade an existing server, a known good backup will allow you to recover to your previous state if the upgrade does not go as planned.

> **NOTE**
>
> Many people back up their servers but never confirm that the data can be read from the backup media. When the time comes to recover their data, they find that the tape is unusable or unreadable, or that they do not know the proper procedures for restoring their server. You should perform backup/recovery procedures on a regular basis in a lab environment to make sure that your equipment is working properly, that you are comfortable with performing the process, and that the recovery actually works.

# Installing a Clean Version of Windows Server 2008 R2 Operating System

The setup GUI for Windows Server 2008 R2 is a significant departure from the blue background and white text of previous versions. After the installation software loads into memory, the configuration setup pages have a consistent look and feel. Each step outlined in the following sections also has integrated links to relevant Help topics. Many of the choices and options that were part of the preinstallation setup process in Windows 2000/2003 are now relegated to postinstall configuration after the base OS installation has completed. Thus, the steps required during initial installation are minimized, allowing for a faster installation and more streamlined initial process, consolidating operations pertaining to settings specific to the final role of the server to the postinstallation phase.

The following sections outline the elements that must be entered during a clean installation of Windows Server 2008 R2.

## 1. Customizing the Language, Time, Currency, and Keyboard Preferences

The first element when installing Windows Server 2008 R2 is entering the Language to Install of the server. Typically, the language selected is English; however, the language selections vary based on a region. Examples of languages include English, Arabic, French, Dutch, Spanish, and much more. The next element to be specified is the Time and Currency Format. This setting dictates how the server will handle currencies, dates, and times, including daylight savings. The final element is the Keyboard or Input Method. Specify the country code, such as US, Canada, or China, and click Next to begin the installation. These languages and other preferences can be seen in Figure 3.1.

FIGURE 3.1    Specifying the language and other preferences.

## 2. The Install Now Page

The next page in the installation process prompts you with an action to Install Now. Click Install Now to commence the Windows Server 2008 R2 installation. Alternatively, before running the installation, you can click on the two operational links such as What to Know Before Installing Windows and Repair Your Computer. The What to Know Before Installing Windows link provides a list of prerequisite tasks, error messages, and general information about the installation. The Repair Your Computer link should be utilized if there is a need to fix a Windows Server 2008 R2 operating system that is already installed.

## 3. Selecting the Type of Operating System to Install

The next page is Select the Operating System You Want to Install. One of the first items that needs to be addressed on every new installation of Windows Server 2008 R2 is which type of operating system will be installed. The options include a Complete installation or a Server Core installation. A Complete installation is a traditional installation of Windows and includes all of the user interfaces and supports all the server roles. As mentioned earlier, a Server Core installation is a scaled-down installation of Windows Server 2008 R2 with the intent to reduce surface attack and management. A subset of the server roles is present and the server is managed through the command prompt; therefore, the GUI does not exist. Click Next to continue, as depicted in Figure 3.2.

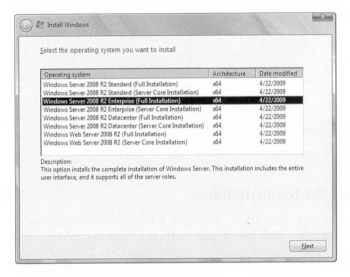

FIGURE 3.2    Specifying which operating system to install.

## 4. Accepting the Terms of the Windows Server 2008 R2 License

The Please Read the License Terms page is invoked next. Review the license terms and check the I Accept the License Terms check box if you comply with these terms. Click Next to continue.

## 5. Selecting the Type of Windows Server 2008 R2 Installation

On the Which Type of Installation Do You Want page, you have the ability to either select to upgrade an existing Windows server or install a clean copy of Windows. Because this is a clean installation and a legacy operating system does not exist, the Upgrade selection will present a message to this effect and prevent the installation from proceeding. Therefore, in this scenario, select Custom (Advanced) to perform a client installation of Windows Server 2008 R2. Click Next to continue, as shown in Figure 3.3.

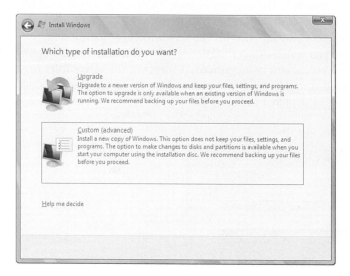

FIGURE 3.3    Specifying whether to upgrade or install a clean copy of Windows.

## 6. Selecting the Location for the Installation

On the next page, the Install Windows Wizard asks where you want to install Windows. You need to specify where you want to install the OS and then click Next to continue, as illustrated in Figure 3.4. This section replaces the portion of both Windows 2000/2003 server installs where decisions about disk partitioning and formatting are made during the initial steps of the installation. At this point, you can supply additional disk drivers, or add, delete, extend, or format partitions in preparation for the install. It's another small change to the process for preparing a system for loading the OS, but that change simplifies and organizes the process in a logical way.

> **NOTE**
>
> With older versions of the Windows operating system, you had two options when partitioning the hard drive: NTFS or FAT/FAT32. When creating and formatting partitions with Windows Server 2008 or Windows Server 2008 R2, FAT and FAT32 are no longer supported as NTFS is the only file system that can be sustained.

## 7. Finalizing the Installation and Customizing the Configuration

After the Windows Server 2008 R2 Install Windows Wizard collects the information and installs the Windows operating system, the system will restart. The administrator must set a password before logging in to complete the installation process. When logged in, the

Initial Configuration Tasks Wizard is automatically invoked. This wizard presents the following tasks, as shown in Figure 3.5, to initially configure the server. The high-level initial configuration tasks include the following:

1. Provide Computer Information

   ▶ Activate Windows

   ▶ Set Time Zone

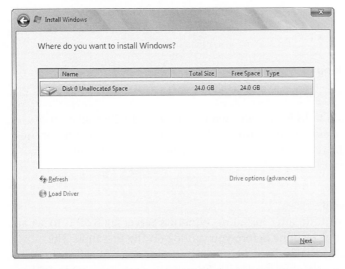

FIGURE 3.4    Specifying the location for the installation.

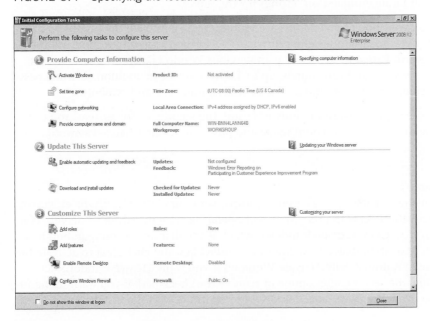

FIGURE 3.5    The Initial Configuration Tasks Wizard.

▶ Configure Networking

▶ Provide Computer Name and Domain

2. Update This Server

▶ Enable Automatic Updating and Feedback

▶ Download and Install Updates

3. Customize This Server

▶ Add Roles

▶ Add Features

▶ Enable Remote Desktop

▶ Configure Windows Firewall

Traditionally, these configuration tasks were addressed during the initial installation of Windows; however, now these elements are configured after the initial installation of the operating system is complete. By removing these elements from the installation, the installation process is much faster.

### Setting the Administrator Password

The first configuration task to perform after installing Windows Server 2008 R2 is to set an administrator password. This must be done before you can log on the first time. The installation process automatically creates the default administrator account called, surprisingly enough, Administrator. This account has local administrative privileges and enables you to manage all local configuration settings for the server.

As a best practice, you should rename this account after you complete the installation and assign a strong password. You must enter it twice: first in the Password text box and then again in the Confirm Password text box. As in previous Windows operating systems, the password is case sensitive and can contain up to 127 characters. In addition, a strong password should include both upper- and lowercase letters, numbers, and symbols.

You should choose your password carefully to ensure the security of the system. You can change both the Administrator account name and password in the Change Password dialog box.

### Activate Windows

Once the administrator password has been set, initial configuration tasks can be executed, starting with Activation. As with other Microsoft operating systems, Windows Server 2008 R2 must be activated. Click Activate Windows, which is the first initial configuration task. In the Windows Activation dialog box, enter the product key and click Next to activate the product. Choose to Automatically Activate Windows if you want to have Windows activate the next time the server comes online or remove the checkmark if you want to manually choose to activate Windows later. Click Next to continue with the installation process.

### Setting the Time Zone

Next on the initial task list is setting the date and time of the server. Click the Set Time Zone link in the Initial Configuration Tasks Wizard to invoke the Date and Time dialog box. On the Date and Time tab, set the time zone where the server will operate by clicking the Change Date and Time button. In addition, click the Change Time Zone button to configure the time zone for the server. The next tab, Additional Clocks, as displayed in Figure 3.6, should be utilized if there is a need to display the time in another time zone. Up to two clocks can be configured on this tab. The final tab, Internet Time, is where you configure a time server for the server to synchronize its clock with. Time.windows.com is the default time server; however, other time servers can be selected by clicking the Change Settings button.

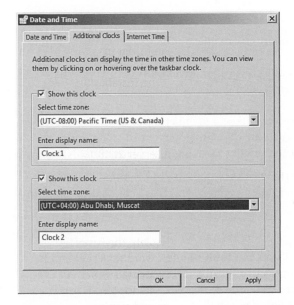

FIGURE 3.6    Configuring additional clocks.

### Configuring Networking

The third setting in the Provide Computer Information section of the Initial Configuration Tasks Wizard is Configure Networking. You need to decide on network settings for the server so it can connect to other computers, networks, and the Internet. By default, Windows Server 2008 R2, as with previous versions of Windows, installs Client for Microsoft Networks, File and Printer Sharing for Microsoft Networks, and TCP/IPv4. In addition, Windows Server 2008 R2 installs QoS Packet Scheduler, Internet Protocol version 6 (TCP/IPv6), Link-Layer Topology Discovery Mapper I/O Driver, and Link-Layer Topology Discovery Responder.

Don't be alarmed. The default client, service, and protocols that are installed by default will meet most companies' needs and require little manual configuration. You will, however, likely want to change the TCP/IPv4 settings and assign a static address for the server.

**NOTE**

Windows Server 2008 R2 utilizes IPv6 as the default protocol. If you do not have plans to utilize IPv6, you might want to disable this protocol to facilitate future server role installation. Many server roles, such as Domain Controller, DNS Server, and DHCP Server, require static IP addresses. You will either need to disable IPv6 or assign the server a static IPv6 address to install these roles. You can disable IPv6 by clearing the check box for Internet Protocol Version 6 (TCP/IPv6) and clicking OK.

For more details on configuring TCP/IP and the new protocol stack, review the chapters in Part III of this book, "Networking Services."

### Providing the Computer Name and Domain

Use the Provide Computer Name and Domain link to change the name of your computer and to add your computer to a domain or workgroup. If you are joining an existing domain, you will need the logon name and password for an account with appropriate domain permissions. Alternatively, you can have the administrator of the domain add your computer name into the domain so that your server can connect. If you do not know the name of the domain that the server will be a member of, or if you do not have the administrative rights to join the server to the domain, you can still change the computer name and you can always join the server to a domain at a later time.

Now that we configured the elements in the Provide Computer Information section of the Initial Configuration Tasks Wizard, the next step is to focus on the second configuration section called Update This Server.

### Enabling Automatic Updating and Feedback

The Enable Automatic Updating and Feedback link in the Update This Server section is used to configure how your system maintains its health and security by automatically downloading and configuring software updates and the degree to which you want to participate in Microsoft's information gathering efforts.

Although it's easy to dismiss these features, the tools do provide you an easy way to patch your systems and contribute your experience with Microsoft products with very little or no effort. Anonymous information gathered from users shapes Microsoft products and technologies, so if you don't have corporate policies around sharing technical information outside of your organization, give some thought to participating. If selected, the following options can be configured automatically, or you can manually configure the settings:

▶ **Automatic Updates**—Automatic Updates are not configured by default. You can leave this setting as is or configure the server to check for updates automatically on a schedule that fits your maintenance procedures. When patching large enterprise environments, it is a best practice to control software updates via a patching solution, such as System Center Configuration Manager 2007 R2 or WSUS 3.0 SP1.

▶ **Windows Error Reporting**—Windows Error Reporting, by default, prompts you to send detailed information to Microsoft when errors occur on your server. You can turn this function off or configure it to automatically send the error information to Microsoft. Reports contain information that is most useful for diagnosing and solving the problem that has occurred.

▶ **Customer Experience Improvement Program**—The Customer Experience Improvement Program (CEIP) gathers anonymous information and periodically sends it to Microsoft. CEIP reports generally include information about the features and general tasks performed by a user as well as any problems encountered when using the Microsoft product.

### Downloading and Installing Updates

Even though you might have selected the option in the previous steps to automatically configure server updates, it is still possible to download and install updates manually by selecting the Download and Install Updates link in the Update This Server section of the Initial Configuration Tasks Wizard. When selected, the server will connect to the Microsoft Windows Update site. Before configuring roles or features or making your server available to users on the network, it is a best practice to install the latest updates and patches from Microsoft. If your environment uses an automated tool such as WSUS, tested and approved patches might already be installed by your update and patching infrastructure if the system was joined to the domain and is configured to do so.

> **NOTE**
>
> When selecting the Download and Install Updates link for the very first time, if updates are not being installed automatically, you will be prompted with the option to turn on automatic updates. In addition, it is possible to select the Find Out More link to obtain updates for other Microsoft products installed on the server.

The final section on the Initial Configuration Tasks Wizard is called Customize This Server. The options are covered in the following sections.

### Adding Roles

Using the Add Roles link on the Initial Configuration Tasks Wizard, you can quickly install server roles, such as Active Directory Domain Services, Active Directory Rights Management Services, DNS Server, and much more to your server. The process also adds dependent services and components as needed (alerting you along the way). This ensures that as you are setting up your system, all the necessary components are installed—alleviating the need to use multiple tools to install, secure, and manage a given server role—and that the roles are set up securely. Although it's critical to understand dependencies for whatever role or function the server might hold, getting the system set up quickly, efficiently, and accurately is always paramount, and these setup tools help accomplish just that.

### Adding Features

You can use the Add Features link to help configure useful tools and system features installed on the server. Features such as RPC over HTTP Proxy for Exchange, Remote Assistance, .NET Framework 3.0 Features, Background Intelligent Transfer Service (BITS), and SMTP Server can be installed and configured. Backup and other management tools can also be installed using this tool.

### Enabling Remote Desktop

By enabling Remote Desktop, you can connect to either a remote console or an RDP session while not physically at the server. Using Remote Desktop to manage systems greatly eases administration of servers but does open another door into each system; therefore, you should consider restricting access via Remote Desktop to users who have a need to access those systems. The two options for allowing Remote Desktop access include Allow Connections From Computers Running Any Version of Remote Desktop (Less Secure) and Allow Connections From Computers Running Remote Desktop with Network Level Authentication (More Secure).

### Configuring Windows Firewall

By default, Windows Firewall is turned on when the base OS is first installed. Although the firewall only protects the server from inbound and outbound access (as opposed to compromises from within the OS, such as a virus or other malware), this is typically adequate protection on a newly built machine until the system is patched and loaded with antivirus software or any other protective systems. Unless you configure exceptions to the firewall, users will not be able to access resources or services on the server. Exceptions to this are services or resources that are made available using the Initial Configuration Tasks Wizard or other GUI-based tools, such as Server Manager, that automatically create the exceptions, enabling you to leave the firewall on while enabling access to specific functions on the server, if desired. With Windows Server 2008 R2, it is possible to configure incoming and outgoing firewall rules on each network connection.

# Upgrading to Windows Server 2008 R2

When upgrading an existing server to Windows Server 2008 R2, all configuration settings, files, and programs are retained from the previous installation. However, there are still several important prerequisite tasks that you perform before the upgrade, as discussed in the following sections.

> **NOTE**
>
> When upgrading a system to Windows Server 2008 R2, you need to have at least 834MB of free space on the system partition; otherwise, the upgrade will come to a halt.

## Backing Up the Server

When making a major change on a server, something could go wrong. A complete backup of your operating system and data, including the System State, can make the difference between confidently telling the boss you had a setback so you conducted a rollback or quivering while you try to find a way to tell your boss a complete disaster has taken place.

## Verifying System Compatibility

In the past, you could check system compatibility before starting an upgrade. Now, it is a best practice to use the Microsoft Application Compatibility Toolkit to verify Windows Server 2008 R2 compatibility before an installation. The tool can be accessed from the following Microsoft link: http://technet.microsoft.com/en-us/windows/aa905066.aspx.

### Running the Windows Memory Diagnostics Tool

As a prerequisite task, it is also beneficial to test the physical memory in the server before conducting the upgrade. Do the test by running the Windows Memory Diagnostics tool. The tool can be obtained from the following Microsoft link: http://go.microsoft.com/fwlink/?LinkId=50362.

## Ensuring the Drivers Are Digitally Signed

Microsoft started certifying drivers for plug-and-play devices during the release of Windows 2000 Server to stabilize the operating system. When installing drivers, an administrator had the opportunity to choose from digitally signed drivers or unsigned drivers. Digitally signed drivers ensure stability; however, it was also possible to install unsigned drivers. The unsigned drivers were not blessed or certified by Microsoft.

When upgrading to Windows Server 2008 R2, an error message is displayed when unsigned drivers are detected. In addition, the unsigned driver will not be loaded when the operating system is upgraded and finally rebooted. Based on these issues, it is a best practice to obtain only digitally signed drivers, upgrade unsigned drivers, or disable the signature requirement for a driver if you cannot boot your computer after the upgrade.

The following procedures should be used to disable the signature requirement on Windows Server 2008 R2:

1. Reboot the server and press F8 during startup.
2. Select Advanced Boot Options.
3. Select Disable Driver Signature Enforcement.
4. Boot into Windows.
5. Uninstall the unsigned driver.

## Performing Additional Tasks

It is also beneficial to perform the following additional tasks before proceeding with the installation upgrade. Disconnect UPS devices as they negatively affect installation when detecting devices on serial ports, disable antivirus software as it might affect this installation process, and obtain drivers for the mass storage devices from the manufacturers.

> **CAUTION**
>
> It is worth noting when upgrading to Windows Server 2008 R2, the Windows Firewall will be automatically enabled once the upgrade is complete. Therefore, you will have to either disable the firewall or configure the appropriate inbound and outbound firewall rules after the upgrade is complete.

## Performing the Upgrade

At this point, your data is backed up, you have verified compatibility with the new operating system, and you have read the release notes. It's time to upgrade, so conduct the following steps:

1. Log on to the server and insert the Windows Server 2008 R2 media. The Install Windows page should automatically launch; otherwise, click on Setup.exe.

2. Click Install Now to begin the upgrade process.

3. On the Get Important Updates for Installation page, first select the I Want to Help Make Windows Installation Better option. By doing this, you will participate in the Windows Installation Customer Experience Improvement Program that allows Microsoft to collect information about the hardware configuration, installation settings, and errors received. This information helps Microsoft determine if updates are needed and identify areas of improvement.

4. On the same page, select either Go Online to Get the Latest Updates for Installation or Do Not Get the Latest Updates for Installation, as shown in Figure 3.7.

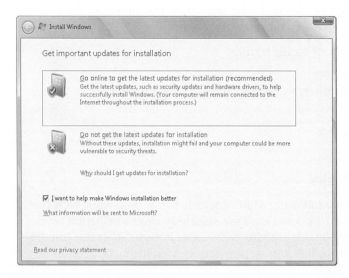

FIGURE 3.7    Getting important updates for the Windows Server 2008 R2 installation.

**NOTE**

If the server is connected to the Internet, it is a best practice to select the first option. Obtaining the latest updates ensures a successful installation as the latest hardware drivers and Windows code are utilized.

5. On the Select the Operating System You Want to Install page, select the desired operating system, such as Windows Server 2008 R2 Enterprise (Full Installation). Click Next to continue, as illustrated in Figure 3.8.

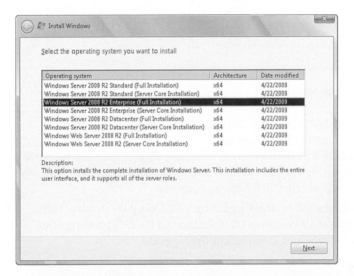

FIGURE 3.8    Selecting the operating system to install.

**NOTE**

Just as a reminder, as stated earlier in this chapter, you cannot upgrade a Windows Server 2003 system or Windows Server 2008 full installation to Server 2008 R2 Server Core. If Server Core is selected, the compatibility check on the subsequent page will produce an error and require a different edition to be selected.

6. Review the license terms and select the I Accept the License Terms option, and then click Next.

7. On the Which Type of Installation Do You Want page, select the Upgrade option, as illustrated in Figure 3.9. Upgrading the system will maintain existing files, settings, and programs.

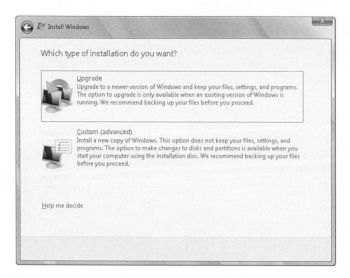

FIGURE 3.9    Selecting the Upgrade option.

**8.** The Compatibility Report page is invoked. This screen includes a warning that it is a best practice to visit the following Microsoft link, http://go.microsoft.com/fwlink/?LinkID=85172, to ensure all programs are supported and can remain installed during the installation. It is recommended to uninstall any applications that are not supported. Click Next to continue.

**9.** The upgrade process commences and the Upgrading Windows page displays status on the following items: Copying Windows Files, Gathering Files, Expanding Files, Installing Features and Updates, and Completing the Upgrade.

> **NOTE**
>
> During this process, Windows will automatically reboot the machine a few times, complete the installation process, and prepare the server for its first use.

The process for completing the installation and conducting postinstallation tasks is the same for both an upgrade and initial installation except that some settings may have been preserved during the upgrade process. In addition, after the upgrade is complete, it is a best practice to open Server Manager and verify events, determine if system services are operational, and ensure the upgraded server roles were, in fact, installed and configured correctly. In addition, review the Resources and Support section in Server Manager for recommended configurations, tasks, and best practices.

> **NOTE**
>
> After the Windows Server 2008 R2 upgrade is complete, the Windows Firewall included with the operating system is enabled by default. It is a best practice to review and change firewall rules and settings to ensure server functionality.

# Understanding Server Core Installation

Windows Server Core, an installation option, was one of the most innovative and anticipated features of Windows Server 2008. The Windows Server Core installation provides a minimal environment for running a specific server role, including, but not limited to, a domain controller, web server, or DHCP server. In this situation, only a subset of the Windows Server 2008 R2 binaries is utilized. The Server Core installation is so stripped that traditional installation components, such as a desktop shell, graphical user interface, Windows Explorer, Microsoft Internet Explorer, and the MMC, are not included. Therefore, the server must be fully managed and configured via the command prompt or by using remote administration tools from another server.

By maintaining a minimized installation footprint by only stripping out the typical components and only supporting specific roles, the Server Core installation reduces maintenance, attack surface, management, and disk space required to support the installation.

Another great feature, particularly for administrators who do not understand scripting commands and who heavily rely on the GUI tools to manage a server, is the ability to remotely manage the Server Core installation through MMC.

Windows Server 2008 R2 includes the following new features and functionality for Server Core:

▶ **.NET Framework**—A highly desired feature to be supported on Windows Server 2008 R2 was the .NET Framework. Versions 2.0, 3.0, 3.5.1, and 4.0 are now supported on a Server Core R2 installation.

▶ **ASP.NET**—Because the .NET Framework is now supported, ASP.NET can now be enabled on Server Core R2.

▶ **PowerShell**—Another highly desired feature to be supported on Server Core R2 is PowerShell. Administrators can use a wide range of PowerShell cmdlets on Server Core R2.

▶ **Active Directory Certificate Services**—The Active Directory Certificate Services role can be installed on a Server Core R2 system.

▶ **SCONFIG**—By typing SCONFIG at the command prompt, administrators can easily configure Server Core deployments. Some of the simplified tasks include Domain Join, Rename Computer, Configure Remote Management, Network Settings, and Download and Install Updates.

## Performing a Server Core Installation

When installing Windows Server 2008 R2 Server Core, the actual installation process is very similar to a regular server install, which was conducted in the earlier sections of this chapter. To recap, an administrator agrees to the licensing terms, supplies configuration responses, and the Windows Server 2008 R2 Install Windows Wizard copies the files and configures the server. However, unlike a traditional installation of Windows, when the installation is complete and you log on, there isn't a GUI to configure the server. The server can only be configured and managed via the command prompt.

The Server Core installation will reboot your machine or virtual server a couple of times when device detection and the installation takes place. Eventually, you'll be presented with the logon screen.

Follow these steps to conduct a Windows Server 2008 R2 Server Core installation:

1. Insert the Windows Server 2008 R2 media. The Install Windows page will automatically be launched; otherwise, click on Setup.exe.

2. Specify the Language to Install, Time and Currency Format, and Keyboard or Input Method, and then click Next.

3. Click Install Now to begin the installation process.

4. On the Select the Operating System You Want to Install page, select the Windows Server 2008 R2 Server Core, as shown in Figure 3.10. Click Next to continue.

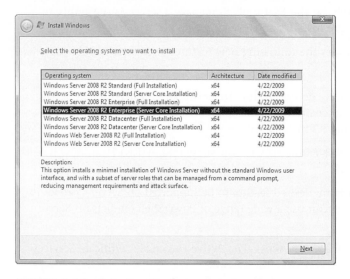

FIGURE 3.10    Selecting the Server Core installation.

5. Review the license terms and select the I Accept the License Terms option, and then click Next.

6. On the Which Type of Installation Do You Want page, select Custom (Advanced), as shown in Figure 3.11. Because you cannot upgrade a legacy Windows operating system to Server Core, the Upgrade option will not work.

7. On the Where Do You Want to Install Windows page, select the disk where you plan to install the Windows system files. Alternatively, you can click on the Drive (Options) to create, delete, extend, or format partitions. In addition, click Load Driver to install drivers for the Windows Server 2008 R2 installation that are not available on the media.

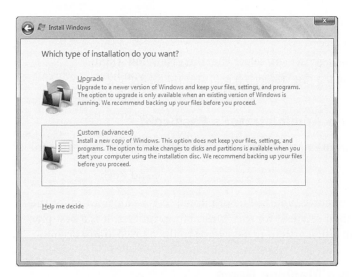

FIGURE 3.11   Selecting a custom installation.

**NOTE**

If the only drive available is Unallocated Space, Windows Server 2008 R2 will automatically create a partition based on the largest size and format the partition with NTFS.

The installation process will commence by copying the files, installing the Windows operating system, and configuring features. After this process is complete, the server will automatically reboot itself and require the installer to change the administrator password for the system. Enter and confirm the administrator password to change the password and log on. You will now be presented with a Command Prompt window, the only GUI available in Server Core.

# Managing and Configuring a Server Core Installation

The following sections cover general tasks associated with managing and configuring a Server Core system after the installation is complete via the command prompt. As an alternative, an administrator can use the SCONFIG utility to configure general settings.

## Launching the Command Prompt in a Server Core Installation

Remember, the Start menu does not exist. Because of this, one of the most important tasks an administrator must understand when managing a Server Core installation is how to launch the command prompt. The following steps will assist you:

1. Press Ctrl+Alt+Delete.
2. Select Start Task Manager.
3. On the Windows Task Manager screen, select File, then New Task (Run).
4. In the Create New Task dialog box, type cmd.exe, and then click OK.

## Changing the Server Core Administrator's Password

After the initial password has been set, the syntax to change the administrator password is:

```
Net user administrator *
```

After the command has been executed, you will be prompted to type a password for the user. Enter the password and then retype it for the confirmation process. It is a best practice to use a complex password when assigning passwords to the administrator account.

## Changing the Server Core Machine Name

After the Server Core installation is complete, another common task is to change the machine name of the server. By default, Windows automatically generates and assigns a server name starting with WIN and followed by a string of characters. The syntax to change the Server Core machine name follows:

```
netdom renamecomputer <ExistingComputerName> /newname:<NewComputerName>
```

When manipulating this syntax, replace the <ExistingComputerName> argument with the existing hostname (which can be found using the hostname command) and the <NewComputerName> argument with the new machine name for the Server Core installation. Changing the server name from Win-123 to "ServerCore" is depicted in the following example:

```
netdom renamecomputer Win-123 /newname:ServerCore
```

## Assigning a Static IPV4 IP Address and DNS Settings

Another common Server Core management task is assigning an IP address, including the primary and secondary DNS settings. Before this task can be executed, you must run the following command to obtain and identify the names of the network interfaces installed on the server. This includes capturing the unique ID associated with each network interface. To display a list of network interfaces, including their respective unique IDs, run the following command:

```
netsh interface ipv4 show interfaces
```

The next step is to make a note of the network interface name and unique ID that you must change. The ID is located in the leftmost column and is referred to as Idx. This is depicted in the output of the netsh interface ipv4 show interfaces command, as displayed in Figure 3.12.

FIGURE 3.12    Reviewing the Idx ID for a network interface.

**NOTE**

If you plan to change the IP address settings on more than one interface, take note of all the interface names and Idx unique IDs.

Now that you have captured the names and IDs, utilize the following syntax to change the IP address for a desired interface.

```
netsh interface ipv4 set address name="<ID>" source=static address=<StaticIP>
mask=<SubnetMask> gateway=<DefaultGateway>
```

Replace the ID argument with the network interface name or ID. In addition, enter the static IP address, subnet mask, and default gateway in subsequent arguments. An example is `netsh interface ipv4 set address name="1" source=static address=192.168.115.10 mask=255.255.255.0 gateway=192.168.115.1`.

The final step when configuring the network interface is to enter a primary and secondary DNS entry for the interface. Do this by using the following syntax:

```
netsh interface ipv4 add dnsserver name="<ID>" address=<DNSIP>index=1
```

The same command is utilized and repeated when entering more than one DNS entry. However, increment the index each time. When finalized, run IP Config /all to verify the IP address settings.

## Adding the Server Core System to a Domain

The following script illustrates the basic syntax of how to add a Server Core system to a Windows domain:

```
Netdom join <computername> /domain:<domain> /userd:<domain>\<username> /password:*
```

Input the domain name and supply the user account and password for an account that has permissions to add computers to the domain.

## Activating the Server Core System

Activating a Server Core system can be achieved in two easy steps. The first step includes entering a product key and the second step requires you to activate the server. The syntax for entering a product key is as follows:

```
slmgr.vbs -ipk<productkey>
```

Once the product key has been successfully entered, you activate the server by typing in the following command:

```
slmgr.vbs -ato
```

## Server Core Roles and Feature Installations

The typical Windows server roles can be configured on a Server Core installation. The following bullets list the server roles that are currently supported on a Server Core installation:

- Active Directory Domain Services (AD DS)
- Active Directory Lightweight Directory Services (AD LDS)
- Active Directory Certificate Services
- Dynamic Host Configuration Protocol (DHCP) Server
- DNS Server
- File Services
- Print Server
- Streaming Media Services
- Web Server (IIS)
- Hyper-V

The following are optional features that are also supported on a Server Core installation:

- Microsoft Failover Cluster
- Network Load Balancing
- Subsystem for UNIX-based Applications
- Windows Backup
- Multipath I/O
- Removable Storage Management
- Windows Bitlocker Drive Encryption
- Simple Network Management Protocol (SNMP)

- ▶ Windows Internet Naming Service (WINS)

- ▶ Telnet Client

- ▶ Quality of Service (QoS)

- ▶ .NET Framework

- ▶ PowerShell

---

**NOTE**

The following command lists all of the potential server roles and associated features:

```
Dism /online /get-features /format:table
```

---

The OCSetup command-line program is responsible for setting up and configuring the server roles and features on a Server Core installation. You can configure the OCSetup command-line options using the following syntax:

```
ocsetup.exe [/?] [/h] [/help] component [/log:file] [/norestart] [/passive]
[/quiet] [/unattendfile:file] [/uninstall] [/x: parameter]
```

Use Table 3.3 to understand each of the options that are available when using the OCSetup command-line program.

TABLE 3.3   Available Command Options for OCSetup

| Parameter | Description |
|---|---|
| /?, /h, /help | Explains all the options available for OCSetup |
| component | Represents the name of the component you plan on installing, such as DNS, DHCP, Web Server (IIS), and more |
| /log:file | Specifies the log file location if you do not want to take advantage of the default location |
| /norestart | Does not reboot the computer after the installation |
| /passive | Suppresses unnecessary noise and only includes progress status |
| /quiet | Does not require user interaction |
| /unattendfile:file | Requires additional configurations |
| /uninstall | Removes server components |
| /x: parameter | Supplies additional configuration parameters |

**Performing a Server Role Installation on a Server Core Installation**

Table 3.4 outlines basic server role installation examples based on the use of the OCSetup command-line tool.

TABLE 3.4    Server Role Installation Command Lines with OCSetup

| Server Role | Command |
|---|---|
| DNS Server role | `ocsetup DNS-Server-Core-Role` |
| DHCP Server role | `ocsetup DHCPServerCore` |
| File Server role | `ocsetup FRS-Infrastructure` |
| Print Server role | `ocsetup Printing-ServerCore-Role` |
| Active Directory Lightweight Directory Server role | `ocsetup DirectoryServices-ADAM-ServerCore` |
| Windows Deployment Server (Windows DS) role | `ocsetup Microsoft-Windows-Deployment-Services` |
| Web Server (IIS) role | `ocsetup IIS-WebServerRole` |
| Streaming Media Services role | `ocsetup MediaServer` |
| Hyper-V role | `ocsetup Microsoft-Hyper-V` |

The previous sections are a prelude to some of the common Server Core command-line arguments for installing and configuring elements on a Windows Server 2008 R2 Server Core installation. For a full list of command-line arguments, visit the Microsoft website and conduct a search for Windows Server 2008 R2 Server Core.

## Installing the Active Directory Domain Services Role

Even though Active Directory Domain Services is just another server role, you cannot install it with ocsetup on Server Core. You must use the dcpromo utility. The problem is that dcpromo normally starts a wizard with a graphical user interface and Server Core does not support GUIs. You have to provide the input for dcpromo by supplying the operation parameters or by using an answer file.

There are 40 different operation parameters that the dcpromo utility can accept. While this may seem like a dizzying array of options, few command lines will utilize all of them. Please refer to the TechNet dcpromo command reference at http://technet.microsoft.com/en-us/library/cc732887(WS.10).aspx for a complete list and explanation of each parameter. You can use this reference to build the correct dcpromo command line or create an unattend file suitable for your core domain controller.

The following example creates a domain controller for a new Active Directory forest. It installs and configures the DNS Server service and configures the forest and domain functional levels to Windows Server 2008 R2:

```
[DCInstall]
; New forest promotion
ReplicaOrNewDomain=Domain
NewDomain=Forest
```

```
NewDomainDNSName=companyabc.com
ForestLevel=4
DomainNetbiosName=COMPANYABC
DomainLevel=4
InstallDNS=Yes
ConfirmGc=Yes
CreateDNSDelegation=No
DatabasePath="C:\Windows\NTDS"
LogPath="C:\Windows\NTDS"
SYSVOLPath="C:\Windows\SYSVOL"
; Set SafeModeAdminPassword to the correct value prior to using the unattend file
SafeModeAdminPassword=
; Run-time flags (optional)
RebootOnCompletion=Yes
```

Use the following steps to run dcpromo with an unattend file:

1. Copy or create the unattend.txt file to the root of the C: drive.
2. Enter the command dcpromo.exe /unattend:C:\unattend.txt and press Enter. The installation will proceed.
3. At the end of the installation, the server will automatically reboot.

# Performing an Unattended Windows Server 2008 R2 Installation

In many large enterprise environments, it is necessary to automate the installation of Windows Server 2008 R2. This is because there might be more than 10,000 servers within the organization and installing each server manually is not a practical or efficient way of utilizing resources or capital expenditures. Windows Deployment Services is a great tool offered by Microsoft to automate the installation process of Windows Server 2008 R2 when trying to achieve economies of scale.

For more information on Windows Deployment Services and performing an unattended installation of Windows Server 2008 R2, see Chapter 26, "Windows Server 2008 R2 Administration Tools for Desktops."

# Summary

The Windows Server 2008 R2 installation process and deployment tools bear similarities to those found in previous versions of Windows. However, feature and performance enhancements have improved the installation experience—whether you are installing a single system by hand or deploying thousands of systems across your corporate environment with Windows Deployment Services.

The new Windows Server Core supported roles and features such as Hyper-V and PowerShell have been a much anticipated feature set for the Windows Server 2008 R2 family of operating systems. Server Core installations can further meet today's administrators' and organizations' needs by providing a mechanism of utilizing the Windows Server 2008 R2 operating system with the fewest amount of binaries, in the most highly secured fashion, while also reducing management overhead.

## Best Practices

The following are best practices from this chapter:

► Verify that your hardware, devices, and drivers are supported by Windows Server 2008 R2.

► Stick to using the recommended or optimal hardware and software requirements.

► Make sure you document your server configuration information and perform a backup of any data that you want to keep.

► Use the Windows Server 2008 R2 Initial Configuration Tasks Wizard to conduct postinstallation tasks.

► Utilize Windows Server Core installations when the highest level of security is warranted.

► Use a consistent naming convention to name the servers and client machines.

► Use only Internet-standard characters in your computer name. This includes the letters A–Z (upper- and lowercase), the numbers 0–9, and the hyphen (-).

► Periodically verify that system backups can be used to recover a system in a lab environment.

► As soon as you complete the installation, rename the administrator account and assign a strong password, for the sake of security.

► Automate installation by using Windows Deployment Services.

► Choose and install Windows Server 2008 R2 roles and features to a server to take advantage of new capabilities built in to Windows Server 2008 R2.

# Active Directory Domain Services Primer

Microsoft's Active Directory technologies have come a long way since their original release with Windows 2000 Server. From a single product referred to simply as Active Directory (AD), Windows Server 2008 R2 now encompasses a total of five separate Active Directory technologies. Each of these technologies is similar—they all exist to supply directory services and to serve as a platform for future integration of Microsoft technologies. The additional four Active Directory services roles in Windows Server 2008 R2 include Active Directory Lightweight Directory Services (AD LDS), Active Directory Federation Services (AD FS), Active Directory Certificate Services (AD CS), and Active Directory Rights Management Services (AD RMS).

The focus of this chapter is on the traditional Active Directory service, Active Directory Domain Services (AD DS), and touches upon the information needed to understand what AD DS is and how it has become the most common enterprise directory platform in use today. This chapter initially focuses on describing a history of directory services in general. It then proceeds to give a primer on AD DS itself as a technology. Finally, specific changes made to Active Directory technologies in general are outlined at the end of the chapter, including all new improvements introduced in the Windows Server 2008 R2 version of AD DS. The additional Active Directory services outside of AD DS are covered in subsequent chapters, primarily in Chapter 8, "Creating Federated Forests and Lightweight Directories."

# Examining the Evolution of Directory Services

Directory services have existed in one form or another since the early days of computing to provide basic lookup and authentication functionality for enterprise network implementations. A directory service provides detailed information about a user or object in a network, much in the same way that a phone book is used to look up a telephone number for a provided name. For example, a user object in a directory service can store the phone number, email address, department name, and as many other attributes as an administrator desires.

Directory services are commonly referred to as the white pages of a network. They provide user and object definition and administration. Early electronic directories were developed soon after the invention of the digital computer and were used for user authentication and to control access to resources. With the growth of the Internet and the increase in the use of computers for collaboration, the use of directories expanded to include basic contact information about users. Examples of early directories included MVS PROFS (IBM), Grapevine's Registration Database, and WHOIS.

Application-specific directory services soon arose to address the specific addressing and contact-lookup needs of each product. These directories were accessible only via proprietary access methods and were limited in scope. Applications utilizing these types of directories were programs such as Novell GroupWise, Lotus Notes, and the UNIX sendmail /etc/aliases file.

The further development of large-scale enterprise directory services was spearheaded by Novell with the release of Novell Directory Services (NDS) in the early 1990s. It was adopted by NetWare organizations and eventually was expanded to include support for mixed NetWare/NT environments. The flat, unwieldy structure of NT domains and the lack of synchronization and collaboration between the two environments led many organizations to adopt NDS as a directory service implementation. It was these specific deficiencies in NT that Microsoft addressed with the introduction of AD DS.

The development of the Lightweight Directory Access Protocol (LDAP) corresponded with the growth of the Internet and a need for greater collaboration and standardization. This nonproprietary method of accessing and modifying directory information that fully utilized TCP/IP was determined to be robust and functional, and new directory services implementations were written to utilize this protocol. AD DS itself was specifically designed to conform to the LDAP standard.

## Reviewing the Original Microsoft Directory Systems

Exchange Server 5.5 ran its own directory service as part of its email environment. In fact, AD DS took many of its key design components from the original Exchange directory service. For example, the AD DS database uses the same Jet database format as Exchange 5.5 and the site replication topology is similar in many ways.

Several other Microsoft applications ran their own directory services, namely Internet Information Server and Site Server. However, each directory service was separate from the others, and integration was not very tight between the different implementations.

## Examining the Key Features of Active Directory Domain Services

Five key components are central to AD DS's functionality. As compatibility with Internet standards has become required for new directory services, the existing implementations have adjusted and focused on these areas:

▶ **TCP/IP compatibility**—Unlike some of the original proprietary protocols such as IPX/SPX and NetBEUI, the Transmission Control Protocol/Internet Protocol (TCP/IP) was designed to be cross-platform. The subsequent adoption of TCP/IP as an Internet standard for computer communications has propelled it to the forefront of the protocol world and essentially made it a requirement for enterprise operating systems. AD DS and Windows Server 2008 R2 utilize the TCP/IP protocol stack as their primary method of communications.

▶ **Lightweight Directory Access Protocol support**—The Lightweight Directory Access Protocol (LDAP) has emerged as the standard Internet directory protocol and is used to update and query data within the directory. AD DS directly supports LDAP.

▶ **Domain name system (DNS) support**—DNS was created out of a need to translate simplified names that can be understood by humans (such as www.cco.com) into an IP address that is understood by a computer (such as 12.155.166.151). The AD DS structure supports and effectively requires DNS to function properly.

▶ **Security support**—Internet standards-based security support is vital to the smooth functioning of an environment that is essentially connected to millions of computers around the world. Lack of strong security is an invitation to be hacked, and Windows Server 2008 R2 and AD DS have taken security to greater levels. Support for IP Security (IPSec), Kerberos, Certificate Authorities, and Secure Sockets Layer (SSL) encryption is built in to Windows Server 2008 R2 and AD DS.

▶ **Ease of administration**—Although often overlooked in powerful directory services implementations, the ease in which the environment is administered and configured directly affects the overall costs associated with its use. AD DS and Windows Server 2008 R2 are specifically designed for ease of use to lessen the learning curve associated with the use of a new environment. Windows Server 2008 R2 also enhanced AD DS administration with the introduction of the Active Directory Administration Center, Active Directory Web Services, and an Active Directory module for Windows PowerShell command-line administration.

# Understanding the Development of AD DS

Introduced with Windows 2000 Server as a replacement to Windows NT 4.0 domains, AD DS (then known simply as AD) was later greatly improved in Windows Server 2003 and Windows Server 2003 R2 Edition. AD DS has achieved wide industry recognition and acceptance and has proven itself in reliability, scalability, and performance. The introduction of AD DS served to address some limitations in the legacy NT 4.0 domain structure design and also allowed for future Microsoft and third-party products to tie into a common interface.

## Detailing Microsoft's Adoption of Internet Standards

Since the early development of Windows 2000/2003 and continuing with Windows Server 2008 R2, Microsoft has strived to make all its products embrace the Internet. Standards that before had been options or previously incompatible were subsequently woven into the software as primary methods of communication and operability. All applications and operating systems became TCP/IP compliant, and proprietary protocols such as NetBEUI were phased out.

With the introduction of Windows Server 2008 R2, the Internet readiness of the Microsoft environment reaches new levels of functionality, with enhancements such as the ability to restore deleted objects using the Active Directory Recycle Bin, Offline Domain Join, Managed Service Accounts, the ability to use multiple password policies per domain, Read-Only Domain Controller (RODC) support, the ability to start/stop AD on a domain controller (DC), and the ability to audit changes made to AD objects.

# Examining AD DS's Structure

The logical structure of AD DS enables it to scale from small offices to large, multinational organizations. Administrative granularity is built in to allow delegation of control to groups or specific users. No longer is the assigning of administrative rights an all-or-nothing scenario.

AD DS loosely follows an X.500 directory model but takes on several characteristics of its own. Many of us are already getting used to the forests and trees of AD DS, and some limitations that existed before in Windows 2000 and Windows Server 2003 have been lifted. To understand AD DS, we must first take a good look at its core structural components.

## Understanding the AD DS Domain

An AD DS domain, traditionally represented by a triangle, as shown in Figure 4.1, is the initial logical boundary of AD DS. In a standalone sense, an AD DS domain acts very much like the legacy Windows NT 4.0 domain structure that it replaced. Users and computers are all stored and managed from within the boundaries of the domain. However, several major changes have been made to the structure of the domain and how it relates to other domains within the AD DS structure.

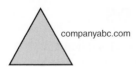
companyabc.com

FIGURE 4.1    Examining a sample domain in AD DS.

Domains in AD DS serve as administrative security boundaries for objects and contain their own security policies. It is important to keep in mind that domains are a logical organization of objects, and can easily span multiple physical locations. Consequently, it is no longer necessary to set up multiple domains for different remote offices or sites as replication concerns and security concerns are more properly addressed with the use of AD DS sites or Read-Only Domain Controllers, which will be described in greater detail in the following sections.

## Describing AD DS Domain Trees

An AD DS tree is composed of multiple domains connected by two-way transitive trusts. Each domain in an AD DS tree shares a common schema and global catalog. In Figure 4.2, the root domain of the AD DS tree is companyabc.com and the subdomains are asia.companyabc.com and europe.companyabc.com.

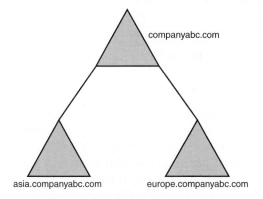

FIGURE 4.2    Viewing a sample Windows Server 2008 R2 AD DS tree with subdomains.

The transitive trust relationship is automatic. The transitive trust relationship means that because the Asia domain trusts the root companyabc domain, and the Europe domain trusts the companyabc domain, the Asia domain trusts the Europe domain as well. The trusts flow through the domain structure.

> **NOTE**
>
> Although trusts are transitive in an AD DS environment, that does not mean that permissions are fully accessible to all users or even to administrators between domains. The trust only provides a pathway from one domain to another. By default, no access rights are granted from one transitive domain to another. The administrator of a domain must issue rights for users or administrators in another domain to access resources within their domain.

All domains within a tree share the same namespace, in this example companyabc.com, but have security mechanisms in place to segregate access from other domains. In other words, an administrator in the Europe domain could have relative control over his entire domain, without users from the Asia or companyabc domains having privileges to resources. Conversely, the administrators in Europe can allow groups of users from other domains access if they so want. The administration is granular and configurable.

## Describing Forests in AD DS

Forests are a group of interconnected domain trees. Implicit trusts connect the roots of each tree together into a common forest.

The overlying characteristics that tie together all domains and domain trees into a common forest are the existence of a common schema and a common global catalog. However, domains and domain trees in a forest do not need to share a common namespace. For example, the domains microsoft.com and msnbc.com could theoretically be part of the same forest but maintain their own separate namespaces.

Forests are the main organizational security boundary for AD DS, and it is assumed that all domain administrators within a forest are trusted to some degree. If a domain administrator is not trusted, that domain administrator should be placed in a separate forest.

## Understanding AD DS Authentication Modes

Windows NT 4.0 used a system of authentication known as NT LAN Manager (NTLM). This form of authentication sent the encrypted password across the network in the form of a hash. The problem with this method of authentication was that anyone could monitor the network for passing hashes, collect them, and then use third-party decryption tools that effectively decrypt the password using dictionary and brute-force techniques.

All versions of Windows Server beyond Windows 2000 utilize a form of authentication known as Kerberos, which is described in greater detail in the following sections of this chapter. In essence, Kerberos does not send password information over the network and is inherently more secure than NTLM.

## Outlining Functional Levels in Windows Server 2008 R2 AD DS

Just as Windows 2000 and Windows 2003 had their own functional levels that ensured down-level compatibility with legacy domain versions, Windows Server 2008 R2 has its own functional levels that are used to maintain compatibility. The following functional levels exist in Windows Server 2008 R2:

- **Windows 2000 Native functional level**—This functional level allows Windows Server 2008 R2 domain controllers to coexist with both Windows 2000 SP3+ and Windows 2003 domain controllers within a forest.

- **Windows Server 2003 functional level**—This functional level allows Windows 2003 and Windows Server 2008 R2 domain controllers to coexist. Additional functionality is added to the forest, including cross-forest transitive trust capabilities and replication enhancements.

- **Windows Server 2008 functional level**—In this functional level, all domain controllers must be running Windows Server 2008 or later. Changing the domain and forest functional level to Windows Server 2008 adds additional functionality, such as fine-grained password policies.

▶ **Windows Server 2008 R2 functional level**—In this functional level, all domain controllers must be running Windows Server 2008 R2. Changing the forest functional level to this latest AD DS level grants Windows Server 2008 R2 feature functionality, such as access to the Active Directory Recycle Bin.

By default, a fresh installation of Active Directory on Windows Server 2008 R2 domain controllers allows you to choose which functional level you want to start the forest in. If an existing forest is in place, it can be brought to Windows Server 2008 R2 functional level by performing the following steps:

1.  Ensure that all domain controllers in the forest are upgraded to Windows Server 2008 R2 or replaced with new Windows Server 2008 R2 DCs.

2.  Open Active Directory Domains and Trusts from the Administrative Tools menu on a domain controller.

3.  In the left scope pane, right-click on the domain name, and then click Raise Domain Functional Level.

4.  In the box labeled Raise Domain Functional Level, select Windows Server 2008 R2, and then click Raise.

5.  Click OK and then click OK again to complete the task.

6.  Repeat steps 1–5 for all domains in the forest.

7.  Perform the same steps on the root node of Active Directory Domains and Trusts, except this time choose Raise Forest Functional Level and follow the prompts.

When all domains and the forest level have been raised to Windows Server 2008 R2 functionality, the forest can take advantage of the latest AD DS functionality, such as the Active Directory Recycle Bin, outlined in more detail later in this chapter. Remember, before you accomplish this task, Windows Server 2008 R2 essentially operates in a downgraded mode of compatibility.

# Outlining AD DS's Components

The main components of AD DS were designed to be highly configurable and secure. AD DS and all it contains are physically located in a database file but are composed of a wide assortment of objects and their attributes. Many of these characteristics are familiar to those acquainted with other directory services products, but there are some new additions as well.

## Understanding AD DS's X.500 Roots

AD DS loosely follows, but does not exactly conform to, the X.500 directory services information model. In a nutshell, X.500 defines a directory service through a distributed approach defined by a Directory Information Tree (DIT). This logically divides a directory service structure into the now familiar servername.subdomainname.domainname.com layout. In X.500, directory information is stored across the hierarchical layout in what are called Directory System Agents (DSAs). Microsoft designed AD DS around many of the basic principles of the X.500 definition, but AD DS itself is not compatible with X.500 implementations, as X.500 follows an OSI model that is inefficient under the TCP/IP implementation that AD DS follows.

## Conceptualizing the AD DS Schema

The AD DS schema is a set of definitions for all object types in the directory and their related attributes. The schema determines the way that all user, computer, and other object data are stored in AD DS and configured to be standard across the entire AD DS structure. Secured by the use of discretionary access control lists (DACLs), the schema controls the possible attributes to each object within AD DS. In a nutshell, the schema is the basic definition of the directory itself and is central to the functionality of a domain environment. Care should be taken to delegate schema control to a highly selective group of administrators because schema modification affects the entire AD DS environment.

### Schema Objects

Objects within the AD DS structure such as users, printers, computers, and sites are defined in the schema as objects. Each object has a list of attributes that define it and that can be used to search for that object. For example, a user object for the employee named Weyland Wong will have a FirstName attribute of Weyland and a LastName attribute of Wong. In addition, there might be other attributes assigned, such as departmental name, email address, and an entire range of possibilities. Users looking up information in AD DS can make queries based on this information, for example, searching for all users in the Sales department.

### Extending the Schema

One of the major advantages to the AD DS structure is the ability to directly modify and extend the schema to provide for custom attributes. A common attribute extension occurs with the installation of Microsoft Exchange Server, which extends the schema, more than doubling it in size. An upgrade from Windows Server 2003 or Windows Server 2008 AD to Windows Server 2008 R2 AD DS also extends the schema to include attributes specific to Windows Server 2008 R2. Many third-party products have their own schema extensions as well, each providing for different types of directory information to be displayed.

### Performing Schema Modifications with the AD DS Service Interfaces

An interesting method of actually viewing the nuts and bolts of the AD DS schema is by using the AD DS Service Interfaces (ADSI) utility. This utility was developed to simplify access to the AD DS and can also view any compatible foreign LDAP directory. The ADSIEdit utility, shown in Figure 4.3, enables an administrator to view, delete, and modify schema attributes. Great care should be taken before schema modifications are undertaken because problems in the schema can be difficult to fix.

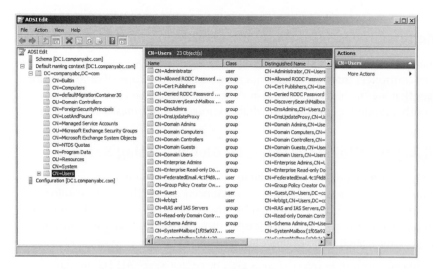

FIGURE 4.3    Viewing and editing the Active Directory schema using the ADSIEdit utility.

## Defining the Lightweight Directory Access Protocol (LDAP)

The Directory Service Protocol that is utilized by AD DS is based on the Internet-standard Lightweight Directory Access Protocol defined by RFC-3377. LDAP allows queries and updates to take place in AD DS. Objects in an LDAP-compliant directory must be uniquely identified by a naming path to the object. These naming paths take two forms: distinguished names and relative distinguished names.

### Explaining Distinguished Names in AD

The distinguished name of an object in AD DS is represented by the entire naming path that the object occupies in AD DS. For example, the user named Brian McElhinney can be represented by the following distinguished name:

```
CN=Brian McElhinney,OU=Sydney,DC=Companyabc,DC=com
```

The CN component of the distinguished name is the common name, which defines an object within the directory. The OU portion is the organizational unit in which the object belongs. The DC components define the DNS name of the Active Directory domain.

### Outlining Relative Distinguished Names

The relative distinguished name of an object is basically a truncated distinguished name that defines the object's place within a set container. For example, take a look at the following object:

```
OU=Sydney,DC=companyabc,DC=com
```

This object would have a relative distinguished name of OU=Sydney. The relative distinguished name in this case defines itself as an organizational unit within its current domain container.

## Detailing Multimaster Replication with AD DS Domain Controllers

AD DS uses domain controllers (DCs) to authenticate users. These DCs use the concept of multiple domain controllers that each contain a master read/write copy of domain information. Changes that are made on any domain controller within the environment are replicated to all other domain controllers in what is known as multimaster replication.

## Conceptualizing the Global Catalog and Global Catalog Servers

The global catalog is an index of the AD DS database that contains a partial copy of its contents. All objects within the AD DS forest are referenced within the global catalog, which allows users to search for objects located in other domains. Not every attribute of each object is replicated to the global catalogs, only those attributes that are commonly used in search operations, such as first name, last name, and so on.

Global catalog servers, commonly referred to as GCs or GC/DCs, are AD DS domain controllers that contain a copy of the global catalog. It is wise to either locate a minimum of one global catalog server in each physical location or utilize Read-Only Domain Controllers (RODCs) in remote sites as the global catalog must be referenced often by clients and the traffic across slower wide area network (WAN) links would limit this traffic. In addition, technologies such as Microsoft Exchange Server need fast access to global catalog servers for all user transactions, making it very important to have a global catalog server nearby. Note that Exchange cannot make use of RODCs or Read-Only Global Catalog (ROGC) servers.

Often, a larger organization will employ the use of multiple domain controllers and multiple global catalog servers in each large location, which distributes load, provides redundancy, and locates resources where they are needed. Choosing the right blend of global catalog servers and domain controllers is vital to the proper functionality of your AD DS environment.

## Numbering the Operations Master (OM) Roles

Most domain controller functionality in Windows Server 2000, Windows Server 2003, Windows Server 2008, and Windows Server 2008 R2 was designed to be distributed, multimaster-based. This effectively eliminated the single point of failure that was present with Windows NT primary domain controllers (PDCs). However, five functions still require the use of a single server because their functionality makes it impossible to follow a distributed approach. These Operations Master (OM) roles (previously referred to as FSMO roles) are outlined as follows:

▶ **Schema master**—There is only one writable master copy of the AD DS schema in a single AD DS forest. It was deliberately designed this way to limit access to the schema and to minimize potential replication conflicts. There can be only one schema master in the entire AD DS forest.

▶ **Domain naming master**—The domain naming master is responsible for the addition of domains into the AD DS forest. This OM role must be placed on a global catalog server because it must have a record of all domains and objects to perform its function. There can be only one domain naming master in a forest.

▶ **PDC emulator**—This role used to exist to emulate the legacy Windows NT 4.0 primary domain controller (PDC) for down-level clients. With Windows Server 2008 R2, the PDC emulator still performs certain roles, such as acting as the primary time sync server for the domain. There is one PDC emulator FSMO role per AD DS domain.

▶ **RID master**—All objects within AD DS that can be assigned permissions are uniquely identified through the use of a security identifier (SID). Each SID is composed of a domain SID, which is the same for each object in a single domain, and a relative identifier (RID), which is unique for each object within that domain. When assigning SIDs, a domain controller must be able to assign a corresponding RID from a pool that it obtains from the RID master. When that pool is exhausted, it requests another pool from the RID master. If the RID master is down, you might not be able to create new objects in your domain if a specific domain controller runs out of its allocated pool of RIDs. There is one RID master per AD DS domain.

▶ **Infrastructure master**—The infrastructure master manages references to domain objects not within its own domain. In other words, a DC in one domain contains a list of all objects within its own domain, plus a list of references to other objects in other domains in the forest. If a referenced object changes, the infrastructure master handles this change. Because it deals with only referenced objects and not copies of the object itself, the infrastructure master must not reside on a global catalog server in multiple domain environments. The only exceptions to this are if every domain controller in your domain is a global catalog server or if you are in a single-domain environment. In the first case, there is no need to reference objects in other domains because full copies are available. In the second case, the infrastructure master role is not utilized because all copies of objects are local to the domain.

Transfer of an OM role to another domain controller can be performed as part of regular maintenance, or in the case of a disaster recovery situation where an OM server is brought offline, the OM can be seized to be brought back online. This is true for conditions where the schema master, domain naming master, PDC emulator, infrastructure master, or RID master either needs to be moved to another system (transfer) or has gone down and no backup is available (seized). The transfer and seizure of an OM role is done through the use of a command-line tool called ntdsutil, shown in Figure 4.4. Keep in mind that you should use this utility only in emergency situations and should never bring the old OM server that has had its role seized back online into the domain at risk of some serious system conflicts. More information on the use of this tool can be found in Chapter 7, "Active Directory Infrastructure."

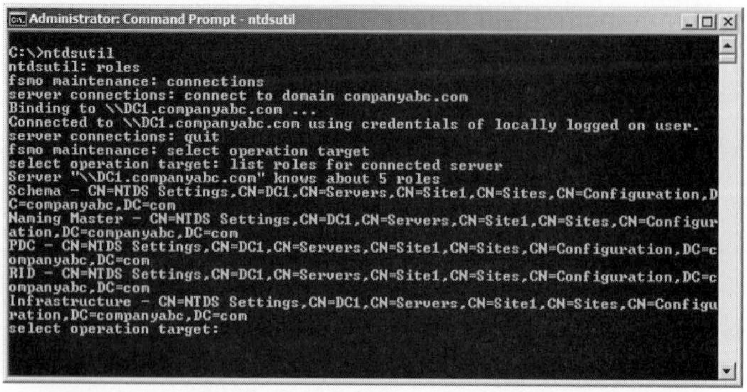

```
Administrator: Command Prompt - ntdsutil                          _ | □ | x |
C:\>ntdsutil
ntdsutil: roles
fsmo maintenance: connections
server connections: connect to domain companyabc.com
Binding to \\DC1.companyabc.com ...
Connected to \\DC1.companyabc.com using credentials of locally logged on user.
server connections: quit
fsmo maintenance: select operation target
select operation target: list roles for connected server
Server "\\DC1.companyabc.com" knows about 5 roles
Schema - CN=NTDS Settings,CN=DC1,CN=Servers,CN=Site1,CN=Sites,CN=Configuration,D
C=companyabc,DC=com
Naming Master - CN=NTDS Settings,CN=DC1,CN=Servers,CN=Site1,CN=Sites,CN=Configur
ation,DC=com
PDC - CN=NTDS Settings,CN=DC1,CN=Servers,CN=Site1,CN=Sites,CN=Configuration,DC=c
ompanyabc,DC=com
RID - CN=NTDS Settings,CN=DC1,CN=Servers,CN=Site1,CN=Sites,CN=Configuration,DC=c
ompanyabc,DC=com
Infrastructure - CN=NTDS Settings,CN=DC1,CN=Servers,CN=Site1,CN=Sites,CN=Configu
ration,DC=companyabc,DC=com
select operation target:
```

FIGURE 4.4    Viewing the ntdsutil utility for AD DS management.

# Understanding Domain Trusts

Domain trusts across forests used to require individual, explicitly defined trusts for each domain. This created an exponential trust relationship, which was difficult, to say the least, to manage. Windows 2003 took the trust relationship to a new level of functionality, with transitive trusts supplying automatic paths "up and down the forest tree." These trusts are implicitly easier to understand and troubleshoot, and have greatly improved the manageability of Windows networks.

## Conceptualizing Transitive Trusts

Two-way transitive trusts are automatically established upon the creation of a subdomain or with the addition of a domain tree into an AD DS forest. Transitive trusts are normally two-way, with each domain trusting the other domain. In other words, users in each domain can access resources such as printers or servers in the other domain if they are explicitly given rights in those domains. Bear in mind that just because two domains have a trust relationship does not mean that users from one domain can automatically access all the resources in the other domain; it is simply the first step in accessing those resources. The proper permissions still need to be applied.

## Understanding Explicit Trusts

Explicit trusts are those that are set up manually, similar to the way that Windows NT trusts were constructed. A trust can be set up to join two unrelated domain trees into a shared security framework, for example. Explicit trusts are one-way, but two explicit trusts can be established to create a two-way trust. In Figure 4.5, an explicit trust has been established between the companyabc domain and the companyxyz domain to join them into the same structure. Explicit trusts to down-level (pre-Windows 2003 Functional mode) forests are required as cross-forest transitive trusts are not available until the forest is in Windows Server 2003, Windows Server 2008, or Windows Server 2008 R2 Functional modes.

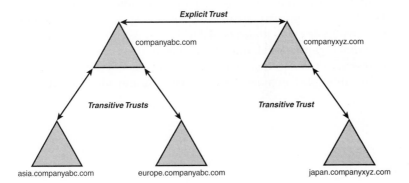

FIGURE 4.5   Sample explicit trust between two domain trees.

When an explicit trust is set up to expedite the flow of trusts from one subdomain to another, it is known as a shortcut trust. Shortcut trusts simply allow authentication verifications to be processed faster, as opposed to having to move up and down a domain tree. In Figure 4.6, while a transitive trust exists between the asia.companyabc.com and the europe.companyabc.com domains, a shortcut trust has been created to minimize authentication time for access between the two subdomains of this organization.

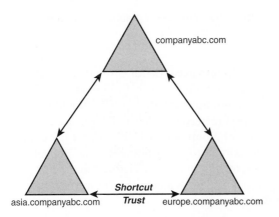

FIGURE 4.6   Sample shortcut trust between two subdomains in a forest.

Another possible use for explicit trusts is to allow connectivity between an AD DS forest and an external domain. These types of explicitly defined trusts are known as external trusts, and they allow different forests to share information without actually merging schema information or global catalogs.

# Defining Organizational Units

As defined in the RFC for the LDAP standard, organizational units (OUs) are containers that logically store directory information and provide a method of addressing AD DS through LDAP. In AD DS, OUs are the primary method for organizing user, computer, and other object information into a more easily understandable layout. As shown in Figure 4.7, the organization has a root organizational unit where three nested organizational units (marketing, IT, and research) have been placed. This nesting enables the organization to distribute users across multiple containers for easier viewing and administration of network resources.

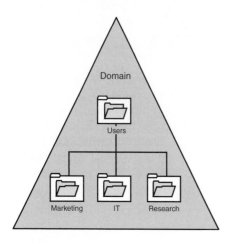

FIGURE 4.7    Viewing an organizational unit structure that provides a graphical view of network resource distribution.

As you can see, OUs can be further subdivided into resource OUs for easy organization and delegation of administration. Far-flung offices could have their own OUs for local administration as well. It is important to understand, however, that an OU should be created typically when the organization has a specific need to delegate administration to another set of administrators. If the same person or group of people administer the entire domain, there is no need to increase the complexity of the environment by adding OUs. In fact, too many OUs can affect group policies, logons, and other factors. Chapter 6, "Designing Organizational Unit and Group Structure," gives a detailed rundown of the design considerations encountered with organizational units.

## Determining Domain Usage Versus OU Usage

As previously mentioned, some administrators tend to start applying the AD DS domain structure to political boundaries within the organization. The dry-erase markers come out and, very soon, well-meaning managers get involved, organizing the AD DS structure based on political boundaries. Subdomains start to become multiple layers deep, with each department taking its own subdomain. The AD DS structure allows for this type of administrative granularity without division into multiple domains. In fact, the rule of thumb when designing domains is to start with a single domain and add additional domains only when necessary. In a nutshell, the type of administrative control required by many organizations can be realized by division of groups into separate organizational units rather than into separate domains.

OUs can, therefore, be structured to allow for separate departments to have various levels of administrative control over their own users. For example, a secretary in the Engineering department can be delegated control of resetting passwords for users within his own OU. Another advantage of OU use in these situations is that users can be easily dragged and dropped from one OU to another. For example, if users are moved from one department to another, moving them into their new department's OU is extremely simple.

It is important to keep in mind that OU structure can be modified on the fly any time an administrator feels fit to make structural changes. This gives AD DS the added advantage of being forgiving for OU design flaws because changes can be made at any time.

## Outlining the Role of Groups in an AD DS Environment

The AD DS group structure, although not new in AD DS, provides an efficient mechanism for managing security on large numbers of users. Without groups to logically organize users, permissions on each object in a network would have to be set up manually on a per-user basis. This means that if an entire department needed access to a printer, each user would need to be manually entered into the permissions list of that printer. These tasks would make administration of security daunting.

The concept of groups was therefore devised to ease administration. If a large department needed access to that same printer, the department's group need only be supplied the necessary permissions. This greatly eases security-based administration and has the added advantage of providing for ease of transition if specific users leave the company or are transferred to a different department. For example, imagine an administrator in charge of printing and her user account is a member of a group named Printer Admins, which has full administrative privilege to the printers. Now, if this user transfers to become an email administrator, for example, reassigning permissions to a new print administrator is as simple as adding that new user to the Printer Admins group. This capability greatly simplifies these types of situations.

Groups in AD DS work in the way that previous group structures, particularly in Windows NT, have worked, but with a few modifications to their design. Groups are divided into two categories: group type and group scope. There are two group types in AD DS: security and distribution. Essentially, a security group can be used to apply permissions to objects for the members of the group. A distribution group, on the other hand, cannot be used for permissions but is used instead to send mail to members of the group. Group scope in AD DS is likewise divided into several components, defined as follows:

► **Machine local groups**—Machine local groups, also known as simply "local groups," can theoretically contain members from any trusted location. Users and groups in the local domain, as well as in other trusted domains and forests, can be included in this type of group. However, it is important to note that local groups allow resources to be accessed only on the machine where they are located, which greatly reduces their usability.

▶ **Domain local groups**—Domain local groups are essentially the same thing as local groups in Windows NT, and are used to administer resources located only on their own domain. They can contain users and groups from any other trusted domain. Most typically, these types of groups are used to grant access to resources for groups in different domains.

▶ **Global groups**—Global groups are on the opposite side from domain local groups. They can contain users only in the domain in which they exist but are used to grant access to resources in other trusted domains. These types of groups are best used to supply security membership to user accounts that share a similar function, such as the sales global group.

▶ **Universal groups**—Universal groups can contain users and groups from any domain in the forest and can grant access to any resource in the forest. Along with this added power come a few caveats. First, universal groups are available only in domains with a functional level of Windows 2000 Native or later. Second, all members of each universal group are stored in the global catalog, increasing the replication load. It is important to note, however, that universal group membership replication has been noticeably streamlined and optimized in Windows Server 2008 R2 because the membership is incrementally replicated.

## Types of Groups

Although groups are covered in more detail in Chapter 6, the type of group used (domain local, global, or universal) has significant impact on replication of group objects for large, multidomain organizations as well as organizations with sites connected through slow links.

For a single-domain organization with high-speed connections to all sites, domain local, global, and universal groups are effectively the same because the organization has only one domain, and replication occurs at high speeds to all domain controllers.

However, in a multidomain environment, by default, only the group name of a global group replicates between domains, not the membership names. Therefore, if a user in one domain wants to view the member list of a global group in another domain, the user's request will have to query across a WAN to the other domain to view the membership of the global group.

Universal groups, on the other hand, do replicate group membership information between domains, so a user query of a universal group membership list will be immediately available in the user's local domain. However, because universal group membership replicates between domains, if a list of group members is not needed to replicate between domains, traffic can be minimized by simply making the group a global group.

## Choosing Between OUs and Groups

Whereas OUs are primarily used to segregate administrative function, groups are useful for logical organization of security functions. Translated, OUs are created if there is a need for a department or physical location to have some certain type of administrative control over its own environment. For example, an organization with offices in Japan could organize its Japanese users into a separate OU and give a local administrator password-change and account-creation privileges for that OU. Groups, however, can be used to organize users to more easily apply security permissions. For example, you can create a group named Japanese Office Users that contains all the users from the office in Japan. Security permissions can then be established on objects in AD DS using that group. They could, for example, be given privileges to folders in the main corporate location, something that could not be done at the OU level.

To summarize, the basic differences between OUs and groups is that groups can be used when applying security to objects, whereas OUs exist when certain administrative functionality needs to be delegated. Chapter 6 gives a more thorough explanation of groups and OU design.

# Explaining AD DS Replication

Replication in AD DS is a critical function that is necessary to fulfill the functionality of a multimaster environment. The ability to make changes on any domain controller in a forest and then have those changes replicate to the other domain controllers is key. Consequently, a robust method of distributing this information was a major consideration for the development team at Microsoft. AD DS replication is independent of the forest, tree, or domain structure, and it is this flexibility that is central to AD's success.

## Sites, Site Links, and Site Link Bridgeheads

For purposes of replication, AD DS logically organizes groups of servers into a concept known as sites. Typically speaking, a single site should be composed of servers that are connected to each other via high-speed connections. The links that are established to connect two or more locations connected potentially through slower-speed connections are known as site links. Sites are created with site links connecting the locations together to enable the administrator to specify the bandwidth used to replicate information between sites.

Rather than having information replicated immediately between servers within a high-speed connected site, the administrator can specify to replicate information between two sites only once per night or at a time when network demands are low, allowing more bandwidth availability to replicate AD DS information.

Servers that funnel intersite replication through themselves are known as site link bridgeheads.

Figure 4.8 shows a potential Windows Server 2008 R2 AD DS site structure. Site links exist between offices, and a domain controller in each site acts as the site link bridgehead. The site structure is completely modifiable, and should roughly follow the WAN structure of an organization. By default, only a single site is created in AD DS, and administrators must manually create additional sites to be able to optimize replication. More on these concepts can be found in Chapter 7.

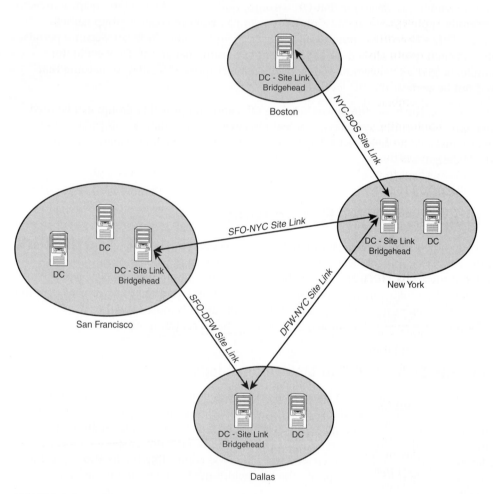

FIGURE 4.8    Sample site structure where locations are connected by site links.

## Understanding Originating Writes

Replication of objects between domain controllers is accomplished through the use of a property known as Originating Writes. As changes are made to an object, this property is incrementally increased in value. A domain controller compares its own version of this value with the one received during a replication request. If it is lower, the change is applied; if not, it is discarded. This simplistic approach to replication is also extremely reliable and efficient and allows for effective object synchronization. For more information on replication, including a detailed analysis of Originating Writes and its other key components, refer to Chapter 7.

# Outlining the Role of DNS in AD DS

When Microsoft began development on AD DS, full compatibility with the domain name system (DNS) was a critical priority. AD DS was built from the ground up not just to be fully compatible with DNS but to be so integrated with it that one cannot exist without the other. Microsoft's direction in this case did not just happen by chance, but because of the central role that DNS plays in Internet name resolution and Microsoft's desire to make its product lines embrace the Internet.

While fully conforming to the standards established for DNS, AD DS can expand upon the standard feature set of DNS and offer some new capabilities such as AD-integrated DNS, which greatly eases the administration required for DNS environments. In addition, AD DS can easily adapt to exist in a foreign DNS environment, such as UNIX BIND, as long as the BIND version is 8.2.x or higher.

Given the importance of DNS in Windows Server 2008 R2's AD DS, a thorough understanding of DNS is a must. Chapter 10, "Domain Name System and IPv6," goes into greater detail on DNS in Windows Server 2008 R2.

## Examining DNS Namespace Concepts

A DNS namespace, simply defined, is the bounded logical area formed by a DNS name and its subdomains. For example, europe.companyabc.com, asia.companyabc.com, and companyabc.com are all part of the same contiguous DNS namespace. A DNS namespace in AD DS can be published on the Internet, such as microsoft.com or msn.com, or it can be hidden from public exposure, depending on the strategy and security needs of its implementers.

▶ **External (published) namespaces**—A DNS name that can be resolved from anywhere on the Internet is known as a published or external namespace. This type of namespace was previously common for organizations that wanted the full convenience of having their commonly used Internet domain name represent their AD DS structure. Best practices have evolved to make this model less attractive, however, as security becomes a concern and DNS must be set up as "split brain" because it is generally ill-advised to have internal AD DNS zones accessible from the Internet.

▶ **Internal (hidden) namespaces**—For many organizations, publication of their internal domain structure is too high a security risk. These organizations can easily define their AD DS with an internal namespace that is not readable from the Internet. For example, a company might have an external DNS namespace of cco.com but decide that its AD DS structure will correspond to cco.internal or any namespace it wants. Bear in mind that any combination will work for internal namespaces because there is no limitation on using .com, .net, .gov, and so on when dealing with a namespace that is not published. For all intents and purposes, you could name your domain ilovemydomain.verymuch if you want (although it's not recommended, of course). For practical reasons, however, the .internal namespace has been specifically reserved for private name addressing, and using it is a best-practice approach in many cases.

---

**NOTE**

If deciding to use a domain namespace that theoretically could be bought and used on the Internet either now or in the future, it is wise to purchase the rights to that domain name to prevent potential conflicts with name resolution in the future. For example, if you choose the internal namespace companyabc.com, you might want to first verify that it is not taken and buy it if possible. If you find the domain name is already owned by another company, you might choose a different domain name for your AD DS namespace. Even though your domain might not be published on the Internet, home or laptop users who need dial-in or VPN access to your domain might experience conflicts because they would be incorrectly routed to the wrong DNS name on the Internet instead of your company's namespace.

---

## Comprehending Dynamic DNS

Dynamic DNS (DDNS) was developed as an answer to the problem of DNS tables having to be manually updated when changes were made. DDNS in Windows Server 2008 R2 automatically updates the DNS table based on registrations, and can work in conjunction with DHCP to automatically process DNS changes as clients are added and removed from the network infrastructure. DDNS is not required for AD DS to function properly, but it makes administration much easier than previous manual methods.

---

**NOTE**

Although DDNS is fully supported by Windows Server 2008 R2 and is typically enabled for all Windows AD DS domain-to-domain name replication, DDNS is still sometimes not implemented at the enterprise level. Organizations with UNIX-based DNS servers tend to manually or statically update DNS tables rather than dynamically update DNS tables. This is solely the choice of the DNS administrator in an organization to enable DDNS.

---

## Comparing Standard DNS Zones and AD-Integrated DNS Zones

Standard DNS essentially stores all name records in a text file and keeps it updated via dynamic updates. If you are accustomed to using UNIX BIND DNS or other standard forms of DNS, this is essentially what Standard DNS is in Windows Server 2008 R2.

AD DS expands upon other implementations of DNS by allowing administrators to integrate DNS into AD DS. By doing this, the DNS zones themselves exist as objects in the AD DS, which allows for automatic zone transfers to be accomplished. DNS replication traffic piggybacks off AD DS traffic, and the DNS records are stored as objects in the directory. In Windows Server 2008 R2's implementation of AD DS, AD-integrated DNS zones are optimized by being stored in the application partition, thus reducing replication traffic and improving performance. For more information on DNS, see Chapter 9, "Integrating Active Directory in a UNIX Environment."

### Understanding How AD DS DNS Works with Foreign DNS

Often, some local administrators might be hesitant to deploy AD DS because of their desire to maintain their own foreign DNS implementation, usually UNIX BIND. If this is the case, it is possible for Windows Server 2008 R2 DNS to coexist in this type of environment, as long as the DNS supports dynamic updates and SRV records (BIND 8.2.x or higher). These situations occur more often than not, as political situations within IT departments are often divided into pro-Microsoft and pro-UNIX groups, each of which has its own ideology and plans. The ability of Windows Server 2008 R2 to coexist peacefully in these types of environments is, therefore, key.

For a more detailed analysis of DNS in Windows Server 2008 R2, see Chapter 9.

## Outlining AD DS Security

The security built around Active Directory was designed to protect valuable network assets. Development of Windows Server 2008 R2 security has also been affected by the Trustworthy Computing initiative by Microsoft, which changed the primary focus of Microsoft products to security. In a nutshell, Microsoft is more focused than ever before on the security of its products, and all new features must pass a security litmus test before they can be released. This initiative has affected the development of Windows Server 2008 R2 and is evident in the security features.

### Understanding Kerberos Authentication

Kerberos was originally designed at MIT as a secure method of authenticating users without actually sending a user password across the network, encrypted or not. Being able to send a password this way greatly reduces the threat of password theft because malicious users are no longer able to seize a copy of the password as it crosses the network and run brute-force attacks on the information to decrypt it.

The actual functionality of Kerberos is complicated, but essentially what happens is the computer sends an information packet to the client that requires authentication. This packet contains a "riddle" of sorts that can be answered only by the user's proper credentials. The user applies the "answer" to the riddle and sends it back to the server. If the proper password was applied to the answer, the user is authenticated. Although used in Windows Server 2008 R2, this form of authentication is not proprietary to Microsoft, and is available as an Internet standard. For a greater understanding of Kerberos security, see Chapter 13, "Server-Level Security."

## Taking Additional Security Precautions

AD DS implementations are, in essence, as secure as the Windows Server 2008 R2 environment in which they run. The security of the AD DS structure can be increased through the utilization of additional security precautions, such as secured server-to-server communications using IPSec or the use of smart cards or other encryption techniques. In addition, the user environment can be secured through the use of group policies that can set parameter changes such as user password restrictions, domain security, and logon access privileges.

# Outlining AD DS Changes in Windows Server 2008 R2

Improvements in the functionality and reliability of AD DS are of key importance to the development team at Microsoft. It is, therefore, no small surprise that Windows Server 2008 R2 introduces improvements in AD DS. From the ability to have multiple password policies in a domain to improvements in domain controller deployment with the RODC role, the changes made to the structure of AD DS warrant a closer look.

Windows Server 2008 itself introduced multiple changes to AD DS functionality above and beyond the Windows Server 2003 and Windows Server 2003 R2 Active Directory versions. Windows Server 2008 R2 then introduced additional features and functionalities above those introduced with the RTM version of Windows Server 2008. The Windows Server 2008 R2 enhancements include the following:

- **Active Directory Recycle Bin**—Provides for the ability to restore deleted AD DS objects

- **Offline Domain Join**—Allows for prestaging of the act of joining a workstation to the AD DS domain

- **Managed Service Accounts**—Provides a mechanism for controlling and managing AD DS service accounts

- **Authentication Mechanism Assurance**—Allows for administrators to grant access to resources differently based on whether a user logs on with a smart card or multi-factor authentication source or whether they log on via traditional techniques

- **Enhanced Administrative Tools**—Includes newly designed and powerful utilities such as Active Directory Web Services, Active Directory Administrative Center, Active Directory Best Practice Analyzer, a new AD DS Management Pack, and an Active Directory Module for Windows PowerShell

The previous version of AD DS introduced with the release of Windows Server 2008 included the following key features that are still available with Windows Server 2008 R2. If upgrading from any of the Windows Server 2003 versions of Active Directory or Windows 2000 Active Directory, all of these new features will be made available:

- **Ability to create multiple fine-grained password policies per domain**—Lifts the restrictions of a single password policy per domain

- **Ability to restart AD DS on a domain controller**—Allows for maintenance of an AD DS database without shutting the machine down

▶ **Enhanced AD DS auditing capabilities**—Provides useful and detailed item-level auditing capabilities in AD DS without an overwhelming number of logs generated

## Restoring Deleted AD DS Objects Using the Active Directory Recycle Bin

One of the most significant additions to Windows Server 2008 R2's implementation of AD DS is the Active Directory Recycle Bin. A Windows Server 2008 R2 Active Directory forest and domain now allows for the recovery of deleted OUs, users, groups, or other AD objects. There are a few prerequisites that must be satisfied, however, before the AD Recycle Bin can be enabled:

▶ The AD DS forest and domain must be in Windows Server 2008 R2 functional level.

▶ When restoring objects, the OU in which they previously existed must first be restored. If the object resided in a nested OU structure, the top-level OU must first be restored, followed by the next-highest child OU, and so on.

▶ Membership in the Enterprise Administrators group is required to enable the AD Recycle Bin.

▶ The process of enabling the AD Recycle Bin is nonreversible.

### Enabling the AD Recycle Bin

To enable the Active Directory Recycle Bin, perform the following steps:

1. Click Start, All Programs, Administrative Tools. Right-click on Active Directory Module for Windows PowerShell and then click Run As Administrator.

2. From the PowerShell prompt, type the following command, as shown in Figure 4.9.

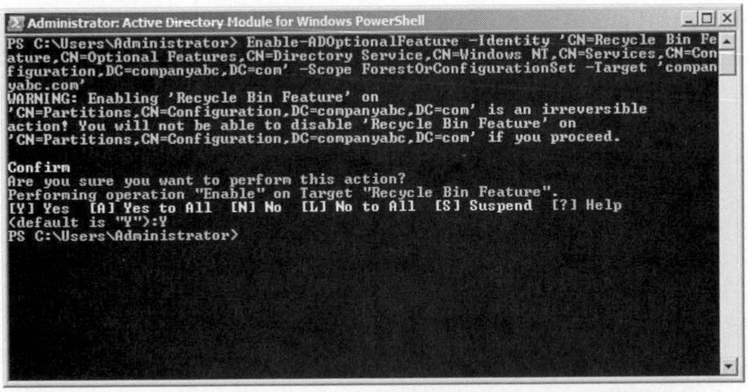

FIGURE 4.9    Enabling the AD Recycle Bin.

```
Enable-ADOptionalFeature –Identity 'CN=Recycle Bin Feature,CN=Optional
Features,CN=Directory Service,CN=Windows
```

```
NT,CN=Services,CN=Configuration,DC=companyabc,DC=com' -Scope
ForestOrConfigurationSet -Target 'companyabc.com'
```

Replace companyabc.com and DC=companyabc,DC=com with the appropriate name of the domain where the AD Recycle Bin will be enabled.

3. When prompted, type Y to confirm and press Enter.

4. To validate that the Recycle Bin is enabled, go to the CN=Partitions container, using an editor such as ADSIEdit. In the details pane, find the `msDS-EnabledFeature` attribute, and confirm that the value includes the Recycle Bin target domain name that you typed in step 2.

## Recovering Deleted Items Using the AD Recycle Bin

Deleted objects can be restored using the `LDP.exe` utility, or they can be recovered using Windows PowerShell. PowerShell offers a much more straightforward approach to recovery of deleted items, and is recommended in most cases.

To recover a deleted object, use the Get-ADObject cmdlet from the Active Directory Module for Windows PowerShell, being sure to open the module using the Run As Administrator option. Get-ADObject can be used to find objects, which can then be recovered using the Restore-ADObject cmdlet. For example, the following syntax, shown in Figure 4.10, recovers a deleted user account for user Zachary Sefanov:

```
Get-ADObject -Filter {displayName -eq "Zachary Sefanov"} -IncludeDeletedObjects ¦
Restore-ADObject
```

For more information about these cmdlets, type `Get-Help Get-AdObject` of `Get-Help Restore-ADObject` from PowerShell.

## Restarting AD DS on a Domain Controller

Windows Server 2008 originally introduced new capabilities to start or stop directory services running on a domain controller without having to shut it down. This allows administrators to perform maintenance or recovery on the Active Directory database without having to reboot into Directory Services Restore Mode.

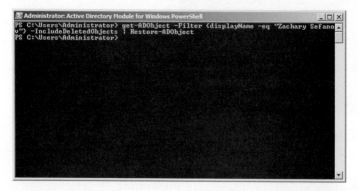

FIGURE 4.10   Restoring a deleted AD object from the AD Recycle Bin.

In addition to allowing for maintenance and recovery, turning off the domain controller functionality on an AD DC essentially turns that domain controller into a member server, allowing for a server to be quickly brought out of DC mode if necessary. Microsoft has also removed the need for local Administrators on the DC to have Domain Admin rights as well, which improves overall security in places where administration of the DC server is required, but full Domain Admin rights are not needed.

To take a Windows Server 2008 R2 DC offline, perform the following steps:

1. Open up the Services MMC (Start, All Programs, Administrative Tools, Services).

2. From the Services MMC, select the Active Directory Domain Services service, as shown in Figure 4.11. Right-click it and choose Stop.

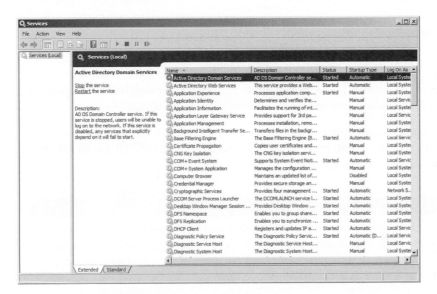

FIGURE 4.11    Applying a PSO to a group.

3. When prompted that stopping AD DS will stop other associated services such as DNS, DFS, Kerberos, and Intersite Messaging, choose Yes to continue.

4. To restart AD DS, right-click the AD DS service and choose Start. Start the Intersite Messaging Service and Kerberos Key Distribution Center service as well.

## Implementing Multiple Password Policies per Domain

Another Windows Server 2008 addition to AD DS is the ability to implement granular password policies across a single domain. Previously, this was only an option with third-party password change utilities installed on the domain controllers in a forest. With

Windows Server 2008 or Windows Server 2008 R2, administrators can define which users have more complex password policies, and which will be able to use more lenient policies.

There are a few key points to this technology that must be understood before implementing it. These points are listed as follows:

- Domain mode must be set to Windows Server 2008 or Windows Server 2008 R2 level, which means that all DCs in the domain must be running Windows Server 2008 R2 or RTM.

- Fine-grained password policies always win over a domain password policy.

- Password policies can be applied to groups, but they must be global security groups.

- Fine-grained password policies applied to a user always win over settings applied to a group.

- The Password Settings Objects (PSOs) are stored in the Password Settings Container in AD (that is, CN=Password Settings Container,CN=System,DC=companyabc,DC=com).

- Only one set of password policies can apply to a user. If multiple password policies are applied, the policy with the lower number precedence wins.

To create a custom password policy for a specific user, a Password Settings Object (PSO) must be created using the ADSIEdit tool, which is used for low-level changes to AD DS or AD LDS directory objects and attributes.

---

**CAUTION**

ADSIEdit is a very powerful, low-level directory editor, and great care should be taken when using it. Be extremely cautious using the editor, especially when deleting objects, as ADSIEdit could easily delete entire portions of an AD tree with a single keystroke if care is not taken.

---

The version of ADSIEdit included with Windows Server 2008 RTM/R2 provides for a crude wizard that allows for PSOs to be created. The wizard automates the creation of a PSO, and allows for specific attributes to be set on the PSO that are related to password policies. Table 4.1 displays the attributes that are prompted for creation by the wizard. All attributes in this table must be entered in the proper format for a PSO to be created. Note that only the final attribute in this list msDS-PSOAppliesTo is not prompted by the wizard, and must be entered in manually.

TABLE 4.1   PSO Attributes

| Attribute | Description | Sample Value |
|---|---|---|
| Cn | The unique name of the password policy. | PasswordPolicyforAdmins |
| msDS-PasswordSettings Precedence | The priority of the policy. Lower number "wins." Leave space on both sides of the number to reprioritize if necessary. | 20 |
| msDS-PasswordReversible EncryptionEnabled | The policy used for specific circumstances where a user's password needs to be able to be decrypted. Normally set to False. | FALSE |
| msDS-PasswordHistory Length | The number of passwords "remembered" by the system. | 10 |
| msDS-PasswordComplexity Enabled | The policy that sets whether or not password complexity is enabled. Password complexity enforces whether users should be forced to include a combination of numbers, uppercase letters, lowercase letters, and special characters as part of their password. Enabling complexity forces them to include at least three of the four types in their passwords. | TRUE |
| msDS-MinimumPassword Length | The policy setting that enforces the minimum password character length. | 8 |
| msDS-MinimumPasswordAge | The minimum number of days that must be waited before resetting the password to something different. This disallows users from simply "cycling through" password changes to keep the same password. Expressed in a format of Days:Hours:Minutes:Seconds. For example, 3:00:00:00 equals 3 days. | 3:00:00:00 |
| msDS-MaximumPasswordAge | The maximum number of days that a password is valid for. Expressed in a format of Days:Hours:Minutes:Seconds. | 60:00:00:00 |
| msDS-LockoutThreshold | The number of invalid password attempts that can be made before locking out the account. | 5 |

4

TABLE 4.1    PSO Attributes

| Attribute | Description | Sample Value |
| --- | --- | --- |
| `msDS-LockoutObservation Window` | The length of time (expressed in Days:Hours:Minutes:Seconds format) before the invalid password attempt counter is reset. Cannot exceed the msDS-LockoutDuration value. | 0:00:10:00 |
| `msDS-LockoutDuration` | The length of time (expressed in Days:Hours:Minutes:Seconds format) an account remains locked out. | 0:00:15:00 |
| `msDS-PSOAppliesTo` | The user or group of users to which the PSO applies. Note that this field is not displayed as part of the default wizard; you must click the More Attributes button at the end of the wizard and enter the distinguished name (DN) of the group or user object. Enter the group using its full DN. Read the previous sections of this chapter for more information on how to format a DN. In this example, the policy will apply to the Global Security named Admins in the Resources—Admins OU in companyabc.com. | CN=Admins, OU=Admins, OU=Resources, DC=companyabc, DC=com |

To create a new PSO, open ADSIEdit from the Administrative Tools menu and point it to the fully qualified domain name (FQDN) of the domain where the PSO will be created. After ADSIEdit has been invoked, perform the following steps to create a PSO:

1. Under the container for the domain, navigate to CN=System, CN=Password Settings Container.
2. Right-click on the CN=Password Settings Container, and choose New, Object.
3. Select msDS-PasswordSettings, and click Next to continue.
4. From the Create Object dialog box, shown in Figure 4.12, enter in the attributes, using Table 4.1 as a guide.
5. When on the final screen of the wizard, click the More Attributes button.
6. Click the Select a Property to View drop-down list arrow, and then select msDS-PSOAppliesTo.
7. In the Edit Attribute field, enter the DN of the group or user to which the PSO will apply. Be sure to click the Add button, or the setting will not be applied. The value should be displayed, similar to what is shown in Figure 4.13.
8. Click OK and then click Finish.

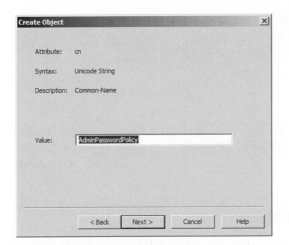

FIGURE 4.12   Creating a PSO.

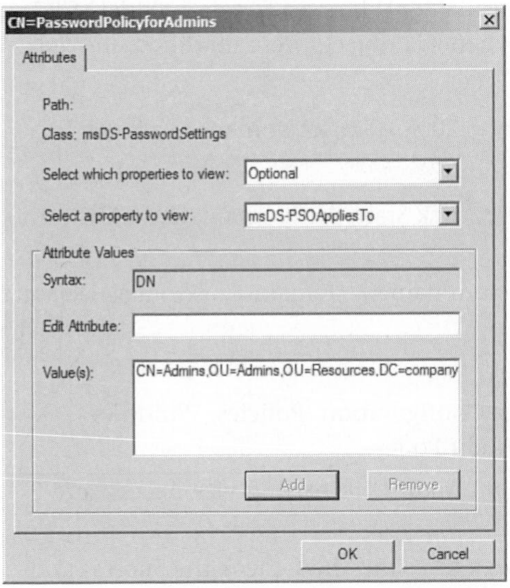

FIGURE 4.13   Applying a PSO to a group.

After creation, the PSO policy will appear in the details pane, as shown in Figure 4.14. Any of the attributes listed in Table 4.1 can be subsequently modified using ADSIEdit by right-clicking the individual PSO and choosing Properties. This includes changing the scope of which users the policy applies to.

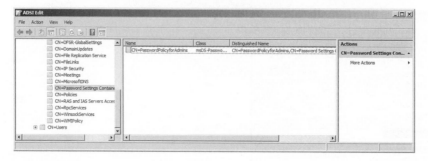

FIGURE 4.14    Viewing the PSO object.

## Auditing Changes Made to AD Objects

Another important change to Active Directory that can be enabled in a Windows Server 2008 or Windows Server 2008 R2 functional domain is the concept of auditing changes made to Active Directory objects. Previously, it was difficult to tell when changes were made, and AD-specific auditing logs were not available. Windows Server 2008 RTM/R2 allows administrators to be able to determine when AD objects were modified, moved, or deleted.

To enable AD object auditing on a Windows Server 2008 RTM/R2 domain controller, perform the following steps:

1. From a member server or domain controller, click Start, All Programs, Administrative Tools, Group Policy Management.

2. Navigate to <forest name>, Domains, <domain name>, Domain Controllers, Default Domain Controllers Policy.

3. Click Edit.

4. In the GPO window, navigate to Computer Configuration, Policies, Windows Settings, Security Settings, Local Policies, Audit Policy.

5. Under the Audit Policy setting, right-click on Audit Directory Service Access, and click Properties.

6. Check the Define These Policy Settings check box, and then check the Success and Failure check boxes, as shown in Figure 4.15.

7. Click OK to save the settings.

Global AD DS auditing on all DCs will subsequently be turned on. Audit event IDs will be displayed as Event ID 5136, 5137, 5138, 5139, or 5141, depending on if the operation is a modify, create, undelete, move, or delete respectively.

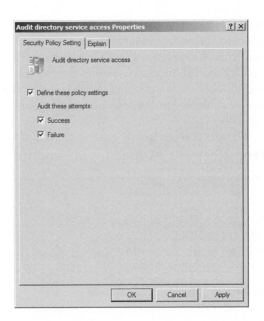

FIGURE 4.15   Enabling AD DS object auditing.

## Reviewing Additional Active Directory Services

Five separate technologies in Windows Server 2008 R2 now contain the Active Directory moniker in their title. Some of the technologies previously existed as separate products, but they have all come under the global AD umbrella. These technologies are as follows:

▶ **Active Directory Lightweight Directory Services (AD LDS)**—AD LDS, previously referred to as Active Directory in Application Mode (ADAM), is a smaller-scale directory service that can be used by applications that require a separate directory. It can be used in situations when a separate directory is needed, but the overhead and cost of setting up a separate AD DS forest is not warranted. Detailed information on AD LDS can be found in Chapter 8.

▶ **Active Directory Federation Services (AD FS)**—AD FS in Windows Server 2008 R2 is an improvement to the older standalone versions of the ADFS product previously offered by Microsoft. AD FS provides for Single Sign-On technology to allow for a user logon to be passed to multiple web applications within a single session. Information on AD FS can also be found in Chapter 8.

▶ **Active Directory Certificate Services (AD CS)**—AD CS refers to the latest version of Windows Certificate Services. AD CS provides for the ability to create a Public Key Infrastructure (PKI) environment and assign PKI certificates to AD users and machines. These certificates can be used for encryption of traffic, content, or logon credentials. More information on deploying AD CS can be found in Chapter 14, "Transport-Level Security."

▶ **Active Directory Rights Management Services (AD RMS)**—AD RMS is the evolution of the older Windows Rights Management Server technology. AD RMS is a service that protects confidential information from data leakage by controlling what can be done to that data. For example, restrictions can be placed on documents, disallowing them from being printed or programmatically accessed (such as by cutting/pasting of content). Chapter 13 covers this Active Directory technology in more detail.

## Examining Additional Windows Server 2008 R2 AD DS Improvements

In addition to the changes listed in the preceding sections, AD DS in Windows Server 2008 R2 supports the following features:

▶ **Read-Only Domain Controller (RODC) support**—Windows Server 2008 R2 includes the ability to deploy domain controllers with read-only copies of the domain. This is useful for remote branch office scenarios where security might not be tight. This scenario is covered in detail in Chapter 7.

▶ **Group Policy central store**—Administrative templates for group policies are stored in the SYSVOL on the PDC emulator in Windows Server 2008 R2, resulting in reduced replication and reduced SYSVOL size.

▶ **DFS-R Replication of the SYSVOL**—A Windows Server 2008 RTM/R2 functional domain uses the improved Distributed File System Replication (DFS-R) technology rather than the older, problematic File Replication Service (FRS) to replicate the SYSVOL.

▶ **Active Directory database mounting tool (DSAMain)**—The Active Directory database mounting tool (DSAMain.exe) allows administrators to view snapshots of data within an AD DS or AD LDS database. This can be used to compare data within databases, which can be useful when performing AD DS data restores. More information on using this tool can be found in Chapter 7.

▶ **GlobalNames DNS zone**—Windows Server 2008 R2 DNS allows for creation of the concept of the GlobalNames DNS zone. This type of DNS zone allows for a global namespace to be spread across multiple subdomains. For example, a client in the asia.companyabc.com subdomain would resolve the DNS name portal.asia.companyabc.com to the same IP address as a client in a different subdomain resolving portal.europe.companyabc.com. This can improve DNS resolution in multizone environments. More information on this technology can be found in Chapter 10.

## Reviewing Legacy Windows Server 2003 Active Directory Improvements

It is important to understand that AD DS is a product in constant development since its release with Windows 2000. From humble beginnings, Active Directory as a product has developed and improved over the years. The first major set of improvements to AD was released with the Windows Server 2003 product. Many of the improvements made with Windows Server 2003 AD still exist today in Windows Server 2008 R2 AD DS. It is subsequently important to understand what functionality in AD was born from Windows Server 2003. The following key improvements were made in this time frame:

▶ **Windows Server 2003 Active Directory Domain Rename Tool**—Windows Server 2003 originally introduced the concept of Domain Rename, which has continued to be supported in Windows Server 2008 R2. This gives administrators the ability to prune, splice, and rename AD DS domains. Given the nature of corporations, with restructuring, acquisitions, and name changes occurring constantly, the ability of AD DS to be flexible in naming and structure is of utmost importance. The Active Directory Domain Rename Tool was devised to address this very need.

Before AD DS domains can be renamed, several key prerequisites must be in place before the domain structure can be modified. First, and probably the most important, all domain controllers in the entire forest must be upgraded to Windows Server 2003 or 2008 in advance. In addition, the domains and the forest must be upgraded to at least Windows Server 2003 functional level. Finally, comprehensive backups of the environment should be performed before undertaking the rename.

The domain rename process is complex and should never be considered as routine. After the process, each domain controller must be rebooted and each member computer across the entire forest must also be rebooted (twice). For a greater understanding of the Domain Rename Tool and process, see Chapter 5, "Designing a Windows Server 2008 R2 Active Directory."

▶ **Cross-forest transitive trust capabilities**—Windows Server 2003 Active Directory introduced the capability to establish cross-forest transitive trusts between two disparate AD DS forests. This capability allows two companies to share resources more easily, without actually merging the forests. Note that both forests must be running at least at Windows Server 2003 functional levels for the transitive portion of this trust to function properly.

▶ **AD DS replication compression disable support**—Another feature introduced in Windows Server 2003 AD was the ability to turn off replication compression to increase domain controller performance. This would normally be an option only for organizations with very fast connections between all their domain controllers.

▶ **Schema attribute deactivation**—Developers who write applications for AD DS continue to have the ability, introduced in Windows Server 2003, to deactivate schema attributes, allowing custom-built applications to utilize custom attributes without fear of conflict. In addition, attributes can be deactivated to reduce replication traffic.

▶ **Incremental universal group membership replication**—Before Windows Server 2003, Windows 2000 Active Directory had a major drawback in the use of universal groups. Membership in those groups was stored in a single, multivalued attribute in AD DS. Essentially, what this meant was that any changes to membership in a universal group required a complete re-replication of all membership. In other words, if you had a universal group with 5,000 users, adding number 5,001 would require a major replication effort because all 5,001 users would be re-replicated across the forest. Windows Server 2003 and 2008 simplify this process and allow for incremental replication of universal group membership. In essence, only the 5,001st member is replicated in Windows Server 2003/2008.

▸ **AD–integrated DNS zones in application partitions**—Windows Server 2003 improved DNS replication by storing DNS zones in the application partition. This basically meant that fewer objects needed to be stored in AD, reducing replication concerns with DNS.

▸ **AD lingering objects removal**—Another major improvement originally introduced with Windows Server 2003 and still supported in 2008 is the ability to remove lingering objects from the directory that no longer exist.

# Summary

Microsoft has worked to continue development of Active Directory Domain Services, which has become a common framework to tie in the various applications and frameworks. The success of Windows 2000 and 2003 Active Directory supplied Microsoft with the medium into that common framework. Along with the addition of new capabilities such as the AD Recycle Bin, fine-grained password policy support, RODCs, object auditing, and other enhancements, the newest version of Active Directory builds on its "road worthiness" and the real-world experience it gained with Windows 2000, Windows Server 2003, and Windows Server 2008 to bring a robust, secure environment for networking services and functionality.

# Best Practices

The following are best practices from this chapter:

▸ Design domains sparingly: Don't necessarily set up multiple domains for different remote offices or sites.

▸ Turn on the Active Directory Recycle Bin after upgrading to Windows Server 2008 R2 forest functional level to take advantage of the ability to do a full-fidelity restore of domain objects that have been deleted.

▸ Purchase any internal or external domain namespaces that theoretically could be bought and used on the Internet.

▸ Use RODCs in remote sites where security is not as strong.

▸ Strongly consider using Dynamic DNS in an AD DS domain environment.

▸ Turn on global AD DS auditing to gain a better understanding of what changes are made to Active Directory objects.

▶ Consider using cross-forest transitive trusts between two disparate AD DS forests when merging the forests is not an option.

▶ Place the infrastructure master role on a domain controller that isn't also a global catalog unless all domain controllers in the domain are global catalog servers or you are in a single domain environment.

▶ Properly plan fine-grained password policies to avoid conflicting policies being applied to users. Leave enough numerical space between the precedence numbers of individual PSOs so as to allow for new PSOs to be placed above and below the PSO in order of priority.

▶ Switch to Windows Server 2008 R2 Functional mode as early as possible, to be able to take advantage of the numerous improvements, including AD Recycle Bin support, fine-grained password policies, Kerberos improvements, last interactive logon information, and the use of DFS-R for the SYSVOL replication.

▶ Use the ntdsutil command-line utility to transfer or seize OM roles in disaster recovery situations.

▶ Use global groups to contain users in the domain in which they exist but also to grant access to resources in other trusted domains.

▶ Use universal groups to contain users from any domain in the forest and to grant access to any resource in the forest.

# CHAPTER 5

# Designing a Windows Server 2008 R2 Active Directory

Proper design of a Windows Server 2008 R2 Active Directory Domain Services (AD DS) structure is a critical component in the successful deployment of the technology. Mistakes made in the design portion of AD DS can prove to be costly and difficult to correct. Many assumptions about basic AD DS domain and functional structure have been made, and many of them have been incorrect or based on erroneous information. Solid understanding of these components is vital, however, and anyone looking at Windows Server 2008 R2 should keep this point in mind.

AD DS was specifically designed to be scalable. This means that, theoretically, organizations of every shape and size should be able to implement the technology. For obvious reasons, this means that the structure of the AD DS forest will vary from organization to organization.

This chapter focuses on best practices for AD DS design, including a discussion of the specific elements that compose AD DS, such as feature upgrades added in this latest version, Windows Server 2008 R2. Various domain design models for AD DS are presented and identified with specific real-world scenarios. The domain rename procedure is outlined as well, to provide for an understanding of how the concept affects domain design decisions.

## Understanding AD DS Domain Design

Before any domain design decisions can be made, it is important to have a good grasp of AD DS's domain structure and functionality. Some fairly major changes have been made in Windows Server 2008 R2 that require a reintroduction to the domain design process. In addition, real-world experience with AD domain design has changed some of the assumptions that were made previously.

## Examining Domain Trusts

Windows Server 2008 R2's AD DS domains can be linked to each other through the use of a concept known as trusts. A trust is essentially a mechanism that allows resources in one domain to be accessible by authenticated users from another domain. AD trusts take on many forms but typically fall into one of the four categories described in the following sections.

### Transitive Trusts

Transitive trusts are automatic two-way trusts that exist between domains in the same forest in AD DS. These trusts connect resources between domains in AD DS and are different from explicit trusts in that the trusts flow through from one domain to the other. In other words, if Domain A trusts Domain B, and Domain B trusts Domain C, Domain A trusts Domain C. This flow greatly simplifies the trust relationships between Windows domains because it forgoes the need for multiple exponential trusts between each domain.

### Explicit Trusts

An explicit trust is one that is set up manually between domains to provide for a specific path for authentication sharing between domains. This type of trust relationship can be one-way or two-way, depending on the needs of the environment. In other words, all trusts in legacy Windows NT 4.0 could have been defined as explicit trusts because they all are manually created and do not allow permissions to flow in the same way as transitive trusts do. The use of explicit trusts in AD DS allows designers to have more flexibility and to be able to establish trusts with external and down-level domains. All trusts between AD DS domains and other forest domains that aren't in Windows Server 2003, Windows Server 2003 R2, Windows Server 2008, or Windows Server 2008 R2 forest functional level are explicit trusts.

### Shortcut Trusts

A shortcut trust is essentially an explicit trust that creates a shortcut between any two domains in a domain structure. For example, if a domain tree has multiple subdomains that are many layers deep, a shortcut trust can exist between two domains deep within the tree, similar to the shortcut trust shown in Figure 5.1. This relationship allows for increased connectivity between those two domains and decreases the number of hops required for authentication requests. Normally, those requests would have to travel up the transitive trust tree and back down again, thus increasing overhead.

The example in Figure 5.1 shows how a shortcut trust could theoretically be used to reduce the overhead involved in sharing resources between the two sales subdomains in the companyabc.com tree. More information on these trusts can be found in the individual design model sections later in this chapter.

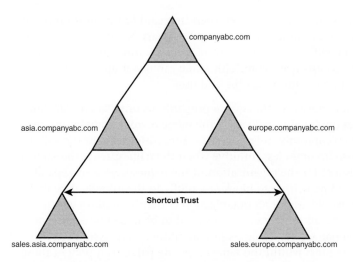

FIGURE 5.1     Shortcut trusts minimize hops between domains.

### Cross-Forest Transitive Trusts

Cross-forest transitive trusts are essentially two-way transitive trusts that exist between two disparate AD DS forests. Although explicit trusts between separate AD domains in separate forests were possible in Windows 2000 Server, the cross-forest trusts in all versions of Windows Server beyond the 2003 release allow for two-way transitive trusts to exist between two separate forests. More information about these trusts can be found later in this chapter in the section "Understanding the Federated Forests Design Model."

# Choosing a Domain Namespace

The first step in the actual design of the AD DS structure is the decision on a common Domain Name System (DNS) namespace that AD DS will occupy. AD DS revolves around, and is inseparable from, DNS, and this decision is one of the most important ones to make. The namespace chosen can be as straightforward as microsoft.com, for example, or it can be more complex. Multiple factors must be considered, however, before this decision can be made. Is it better to register an AD namespace on the Internet and potentially expose it to intruders, or is it better to choose an unregistered internal namespace? Is it necessary to tie in multiple namespaces into the same forest? These and other questions must be answered before the design process can proceed.

## Choosing an External (Published) Namespace

The simplest method of implementing an AD DS structure is through the use of a single, common DNS namespace that reflects the company's name and is registered on the Internet. Microsoft.com is an obvious example, and a myriad of other possibilities exist as well. Several advantages to a published namespace are that it is readily accessible from the

Internet and there is less confusion on the end user's part in regard to the location on the network and on the Internet. For example, a user named Rosemary Nahrvar working for the CompanyABC Corporation will be represented in the network through the user principal name (UPN) as Rosemary@companyabc.com. This name can be set up to exactly match her email address, limiting confusion for the end user.

The limitations to this type of namespace strategy are primarily security based. Publishing your AD DS namespace leaves potential hackers with the name of your domain system and part of what is needed to compromise user accounts. Administering your firewall to block internal DNS queries also becomes less intuitive when the namespace is the same as the published Internet namespace for the organization. If the namespaces were separate, for example, a simple rule could be written to block any traffic to the internal domain structure. Another limitation would arise if an organization currently employs multiple namespaces to identify itself, and all those namespaces need to be joined into the same forest; in this case, a common namespace design is not an option. Mergers and acquisitions or even multiple business units within the same corporate parent can present these types of problems.

## Choosing an Internal Namespace

If desired or required by your organization, the namespace that the AD DS structure inhabits can be internal, or not published to the Internet. Using internal namespaces adds a layer of complexity to your network because users' UPNs are different from their email addresses. However, the increase in security that is realized from this design is also a factor that leads organizations to choose this route. Another factor that might influence your decision to choose an Internet namespace is that you are no longer limited to the InterNIC standard namespaces of .com, .net, .biz, .info, and so on. For example, many organizations use the .internal namespace, or some other namespace that is not used on the Internet.

Keep in mind that it is important to secure an internal namespace from registration anywhere on the Internet other than in your own network. In other words, if an organization registers internalnetwork.net, and another organization on the Internet registers the same domain name for its network, there could be naming conflicts with applications and other systems that perform DNS lookups against your forest. For example, if an application on a laptop usually attempts to access an internal namespace but then tries to access it remotely through an Internet service provider (ISP), the ISP's DNS will forward you to the registered DNS name on the Internet. In a nutshell, if you are going to design your domain with an unpublished namespace but use a standard such as .net or .org that someone else could theoretically register, it is best to register and reserve that domain but not point it anywhere. Another common tactic is to name your domain something that will never be published, such as a root with your company's stock ticker symbol (for example, network.msft), or by utilizing the .internal suffix, which has been specifically reserved for internal use only.

# Examining Domain Design Features

AD DS has evolved over the years and has added additional functionality with Windows Server 2003, Windows Server 2003 R2, Windows Server 2008, and, finally, Windows Server 2008 R2. Some of these functionality improvements have changed some of the design concepts associated with Windows Server 2008 R2. These functionality changes are as follows:

▶ **Active Directory Recycle Bin**—The ability to do a full-fidelity recovery of deleted objects in AD DS was introduced in this latest version of AD DS included with Windows Server 2008 R2. By adding this critical functionality, there is less worry that accidental deletion of user accounts, groups, or even entire OUs will cause major havoc, and there is subsequently less reason to create multiple domains in a forest simply to spread the risk of domain object deletion. Note that this capability is only available when the forest functional level is raised to Windows Server 2008 R2 functional level and when it is subsequently turned on in a domain. More information about this topic can be found in Chapter 4, "Active Directory Domain Services Primer."

▶ **Fine-grained password policies**—The ability to have multiple password policies within a single domain was originally released in Windows Server 2008 and is still supported with Windows Server 2008 R2. The addition of this functionality means that many organizations that previously implemented additional domains because of the restriction of a single password policy per domain might be able to collapse those domains. Note that this functionality is only available in either Windows Server 2008 or Windows Server 2008 R2 domain functional levels. For more information on using fine-grained password policies, see Chapter 4.

▶ **Domain rename function**—The capability to rename a domain in a Windows Server 2003/2008 forest has opened up a new field of possibilities for the design and potential redesign of AD DS domain structures. Previously, stern caveats were issued about the inability to rename domains or change the overall structure of an AD DS forest. With the domain rename functionality present in AD DS implementation, these limitations are lifted, and designers can take heart in the fact that design changes can be made after implementation. Having this ability does not change the fact that it is still wise to plan out your domain design thoroughly, however. Not having to make changes to domain names or reposition domains in a forest is much easier than having to go through the domain rename process. Just knowing that such functionality exists, however, is a breath of fresh air for designers.

▶ **Cross-forest transitive trusts**—Introduced in Windows Server 2003, the concept of cross-forest transitive trusts lessens domain designers' connectivity worries. In the past, some administrators balked at the limitations of collaboration within Windows 2000 AD DS structures. The cross-forest transitive trust capability of AD DS negates those concerns because multiple AD DS forests can now be joined via cross-forest trusts that are transitive, rather than explicit, in nature. The combination of these forests is known in the Microsoft world as federated forests. Note that both forests

5

must be at Windows Server 2003 or Windows Server 2008 R2 functional levels for this feature to work.

▶ **Domain controller promotion from media**—The capability to promote remote servers to domain controllers via a CD image of the global catalog helps to limit replication traffic and the time associated with establishing remote domain controllers. Windows Server 2003/2008 solves the issue of replication over the wide area network (WAN) by providing you with the ability to save the global catalog to media (like a CD-ROM), ship it to a remote site, and, finally, run domain controller promotion (dcpromo) and insert the data disk with the directory on it for restoration. Only the deltas, or changes made since media creation, are then replicated, saving time and bandwidth. The effect of this on domain design creation is reflected in reduced setup times, less network bandwidth consumption, and increased flexibility of global catalog domain controller placement.

# Choosing a Domain Structure

There is a basic tenet to consider when designing the AD DS domain structure. Start simple, and then expand only if expansion is necessary to address a specific need. This concept is, by and large, the most important concept to remember when you're designing AD DS components. In regard to domain design, this means you should always start the design process with a single domain and then add on to your design if your organizational concerns dictate that you do so. Following this basic philosophy during the design process will reduce headaches down the road.

When you're designing the AD DS, you must contemplate a common framework for diagrams. In AD DS, for example, domains are often pictorially represented by triangles, as shown in Figure 5.2. So, when beginning your design, start with a single triangle.

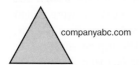

FIGURE 5.2    Domain diagram representation as a triangle.

In this example, the fictional company named CompanyABC has begun the process of domain design. Depending on its unique needs, CompanyABC might decide to expand upon that model or keep it simplistic. These decisions should be made with a detailed knowledge of the different domain design models and the environments in which they work best.

Active Directory was designed to be a flexible, forgiving directory services implementation. This is even more true with Windows Server 2008 R2's AD DS implementation. Consequently, there are multiple design models available to choose from, depending on the individual needs of organizations. The major design models are as follows:

- Single domain model

- Multiple domain model

- Multiple trees in a single forest model

- Federated forests design model

- Peer-root model

- Placeholder domain model

- Special-purpose domain model

In reality, not all AD structures fall underneath these categories because the possibilities exist for numerous variations and mutations of AD structure. However, most domain structures either fall into these categories or are a hybrid model, possessing traits of two different models. Out of all these models, however, the single domain model is the most common design model and also happens to be the easiest to deploy.

# Understanding the Single Domain Model

The most basic of all AD DS structures is the single domain model; this type of domain structure comes with one major advantage over the other models: simplicity. A single security boundary defines the borders of the domain, and all objects are located within that boundary. The establishment of trust relationships between other domains is not necessary, and implementation of technologies such as Group Policies is made easier by the simple structure. More organizations than not can take advantage of this design because AD DS has been simplified, and its capability to span multiple physical boundaries has been enhanced.

## Choosing the Single Domain Model

The single domain model is ideal for many organizations and can be modified to fit many more. A single domain structure possesses multiple advantages, first and foremost being simplicity. As any administrator or engineer who has done work in the trenches can confirm, often the simplest design works the best. Adding unnecessary complexity to the system's architecture introduces potential risk and makes troubleshooting these systems more difficult. Consequently, consolidating complex domain structures into a simpler single domain AD DS structure can reduce the costs of administration and minimize headaches in the process.

Another advantage realized by the creation of a single domain is the attainment of centralized administration. Many organizations with a strong central IT structure want the capability to consolidate control over the entire IT and user structure. AD DS and, specifically, the single domain model allows for a high level of administrative control and the ability to delegate tasks to lower sets of administrators. This has proven to be a strong draw to AD DS.

Not all AD DS structures can be composed of a single domain, however, and some factors might limit an organization's ability to adopt a single domain structure. If these factors affect your organization, you might need to begin expanding your domain model to include other domains in the forest and a different domain design. For example, the single security boundary formed by a single domain might not be exactly what your organization needs. Organizational units (OUs) can be used to delegate administration of security elements, but members of the Domain Admins group can still override permissions within different OUs. If the security lines within your organization need to follow exact boundaries, a single domain might not be for you. For example, if your HR department requires that no users from IT have access to resources within its environment, you will need to expand your domain structure to accommodate the additional security concerns.

Another disadvantage of the single domain model is that a single domain in a forest necessitates that the computer with the role of schema master is located in that domain. This places the schema master within the domain that contains all the user accounts. Although access to the schema master can be strictly controlled through proper administration, your risk of schema exposure is greater when the schema master role resides in a user domain. For example, members of the domain administrators group could override the security of the schema administrators group and add their account to that group. If this design model poses problems for you as an organization, design models that separate the schema master into a placeholder domain can do the trick. The placeholder domain model is described in more detail later in this chapter in the section "Understanding the Placeholder Domain Model."

## Exploring a Single Domain Real-World Design Example

To illustrate a good example of an organization that would logically choose a single domain model, let's consider fictional CompanyA. CompanyA is a 500-user organization with a central office located in Minneapolis. A few smaller branch offices are scattered throughout the Midwest, but all help desk administration is centralized at the company headquarters. CompanyA currently utilizes a single user domain and has multiple resource domains in various locations across the country.

The IT team in Minneapolis is designing an AD DS structure and wants to centralize administration at corporate headquarters. Branch offices should have the capability to change passwords and clear print jobs locally, but should have no other form of administrative privilege on the network.

During the AD DS design process, CompanyA started with a single AD DS forest, domain, and namespace named companya.net. Organizational units for each branch office were added to delegate password-change control and print administration to those offices.

Current legacy Windows 2000 AD and Windows Server 2003 forests and domains were consolidated into the AD DS structure, as shown in Figure 5.3. CompanyA could not justify the existence of additional domains because their security model was centralized, and it did not have any far-flung geographical locations with slow link speeds to the main office or any other similar constraints that required additional domains.

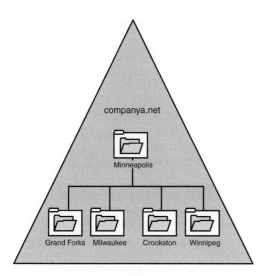

FIGURE 5.3   AD DS structure with organizational unit structure.

Delegation of password-change control and other local administrative functions was granted to individuals in each specific geographical OU, which gave those administrators permissions specific to only resources within their own group but maintained central administrative control in Minneapolis. A detailed discussion of organizational unit design is covered in Chapter 6, "Designing Organizational Unit and Group Structure."

Several AD DS sites were created to control the frequency of replication. A site was positioned to correspond with each separate geographical area, creating a site structure similar to the one shown in Figure 5.4.

Creating the separate sites helped to throttle replication traffic and reduce the load placed on the WAN links between the sites. For more details about site links and replication, see Chapter 7, "Active Directory Infrastructure."

This type of single domain design is ideal for the type of organization described in this section and actually can be used for many other types of organizations, large and small. Because delegation of administration is now accomplished through the use of OUs and Group Policy Objects, and the throttling of replication is accomplished through AD sites, the number of reasons for organizations to use multiple domains has been reduced.

# Understanding the Multiple Domain Model

For various reasons, organizations might need to add more than one domain to their environment but preserve the functionality that is inherent in a single forest. When this occurs, the addition of one or multiple domains into the forest is warranted. Domain addition should not be taken lightly, however, and proper consideration must be given to the particular characteristics of multiple domain models.

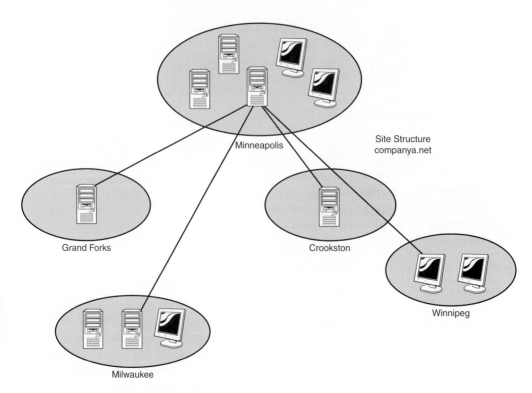

FIGURE 5.4    Site structure created by geographical locations.

By default, two-way transitive trusts exist between subdomains and domains in AD DS. Bear in mind, however, that this does not mean that resource access is automatically granted to members of other domains. A user in subdomain B is not automatically granted any rights in domain A; the rights need to be explicitly defined through the use of groups. Understanding this concept will help to determine the logistics of domain addition.

## Choosing When to Add Additional Domains

As previously mentioned, it is advisable to begin your Windows Server 2008 R2 AD DS design with a single domain and then add domains only when absolutely necessary. Adding child domains to an existing domain structure might become necessary if the following traits exist within an infrastructure:

▶ **Decentralized administration**—If different branches of an organization generally manage their own IT structure and there are no future plans to consolidate them into a centralized model, multiple interconnected domains might be ideal. Each domain acts as a security boundary for most types of activity and can be set up to disallow administration from escaping the boundaries of domains. This approach, however, exposes many of the limitations associated with a multiple domain environment. In other words, it is better to try to centralize administration before deploying AD DS because you will gain more of AD's advantages. It is also much better to organize administration along organizational unit boundaries than by domains, so consider this option first.

▶ **Geographic limitations**—If extremely slow or unreliable links or great geographical distances separate different parts of your company, it might be wise to segment the user population into separate domains. This will help to limit replication activity between domains and also make it easier to provide support during business hours for distant time zones. Keep in mind that slow links by themselves do not necessitate the creation of multiple domains, as Windows Server 2008 R2 AD DS uses the concept of AD DS sites to throttle replication across slow links. The main reason that might exist for domain creation for geographical reasons is administrative flexibility. In other words, if there is a problem with the network in Japan, a Japanese administrator will have more power to administer the Asia domain and will not need to call the North American administrator in the middle of the night.

▶ **Unique DNS namespace considerations**—If two organizational entities want to use their Internet-registered namespace for AD DS but use a common forest, such as hotmail.com or microsoft.com, those domains must be added as separate domains. This type of domain model is described more fully in the "Understanding the Multiple Trees in a Single Forest Model" section later in this chapter.

▶ **Enhanced security concerns**—Depending on the needs of your organization, separating the schema master role into a domain separate from your users might be applicable. In this case, the single domain model would not be applicable, and a model such as the peer-root or placeholder domain would be more appropriate.

When contemplating additional domains, remember the mantra, "Simplicity is best." However, if during the design process, the specific need arises to add domains, proper design is still warranted, or your environment will run the risk of becoming more inefficient than it could be.

## Exploring a Multiple Domain Real-World Design Example

The following example illustrates an organization that would have grounds to establish multiple domains. CompanyB is an engineering company based in York, Pennsylvania. Administration for all branch locations is currently centralized in the home office, and OUs and group policies are used for delegation of lower-level tasks. Recently, the company acquired two separate companies named Subsidiary A and Subsidiary B; each contains its own IT department and operates in separate geographical areas. CompanyB decided to implement AD DS as part of a Windows Server 2008 R2 implementation and wanted to include the two acquired companies into a single common forest.

Because each acquired company possesses its own IT department and there was no agreement on the ownership of the Domain Admins accounts, CompanyB decided to deploy an AD DS structure with two subdomains for Subsidiary A and Subsidiary B, as shown in Figure 5.5.

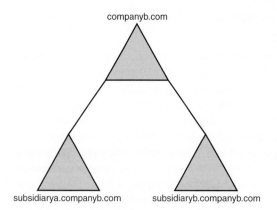

FIGURE 5.5    AD DS with two subdomains.

This design model allowed for a certain degree of administrative freedom with the newly acquired subsidiaries but also allowed for a common forest and schema to be used and kept the domains within the same DNS namespace.

This design model has the particular advantage of being politically easier to implement than consolidation of existing domains. Branch offices and subsidiary companies can keep their own domain structure and security boundaries, and their IT teams can retain a greater deal of administrative autonomy.

Be warned, however, that consolidation of a larger number of domains into fewer domains is a key feature of AD DS, so the addition of domains purely for political reasons adds complexity and potentially unnecessary infrastructure. It is, therefore, very important to consider the alternatives before deciding on this design model.

## Understanding the Multiple Trees in a Single Forest Model

Let's say that your organization wants to look at AD DS and wants to use an external namespace for your design. However, your environment currently uses multiple DNS namespaces and needs to integrate them into the same design. Contrary to popular misconception, integration of these namespaces into a single AD forest can be done through the use of multiple trees that exist in one forest. One of the most misunderstood characteristics of AD DS is the difference between a contiguous forest and a contiguous DNS namespace. Many people do not realize that multiple DNS namespaces can be integrated into a single AD DS forest as separate trees in the forest. For example, Figure 5.6 shows how Microsoft could theoretically organize several AD DS domains that share the same forest but reside in different DNS namespaces.

Only one domain in this design is the forest root—in this case, microsoft.com—and only this domain controls access to the forest schema. All other domains, including subdomains of microsoft.com and the other domains that occupy different DNS structures, are

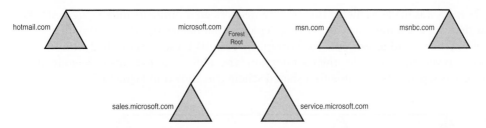

**FIGURE 5.6** Sample AD DS forest with multiple unique trees within the same forest.

members of the same forest. All trust relationships between the domains are transitive, and trusts flow from one domain to another.

## Choosing When to Deploy a Multiple Tree Domain Model

If an organization currently operates multiple units under separate DNS namespaces, one option might be to consider a design such as this one. It is important to understand, however, that simply using multiple DNS namespaces does not automatically qualify you as a candidate for this domain design. For example, you could own five separate DNS namespaces and instead decide to create an AD DS structure based on a new namespace that is contiguous throughout your organization. Consolidating your AD DS under this single domain could simplify the logical structure of your environment while keeping your DNS namespaces separate from AD DS.

If your organization makes extensive use of its separate namespaces, you might want to consider a design like this. Each domain tree in the forest can then maintain a certain degree of autonomy, both perceived and real. Often, this type of design will seek to satisfy even the most paranoid of branch office administrators who demand complete control over their entire IT structure.

## Examining a Multiple Tree Domain Real-World Design Example

To gain a greater understanding of the times an organization might use this particular design model, examine the following AD structure. CityA is a local county governmental organization with a loose-knit network of semi-independent city offices, such as the police and fire departments that are spread out around the city. Each department currently uses a DNS namespace for name resolution to all hosts and user accounts local to itself, which provides different email addresses for users located in the fire department, police department, and other branches. The following namespaces are used within the city's infrastructure:

- ▶ citya.org
- ▶ firedeptcitya.org
- ▶ policeofcitya.org
- ▶ cityalibrary.org

The decision was made to merge the existing network environments into a single AD DS forest that will accommodate the existing departmental namespaces but maintain a common schema and forest root. To accomplish this, AD DS was established with citya.gov as the namespace for the root domain. The additional domains were added to the forest as separate trees but with a shared schema, as shown in Figure 5.7.

FIGURE 5.7    Single AD DS forest with separate directory trees for departments..

The individual departments were able to maintain control over their individual security and are disallowed from making changes in domains outside their control. The common forest schema and global catalog helped to increase collaboration between the varying organizations and allow for a certain amount of central administration.

This type of domain design is logically a bit messier but technically carries the same functionality as any other single forest design model. All the domains are set up with two-way transitive trusts to the root domain and share a common schema and global catalog. The difference lies in the fact that they all utilize separate DNS namespaces, a fact that must also be reflected in the zones that exist in DNS.

## Understanding the Federated Forests Design Model

A feature of Windows Server 2008 R2's AD DS implementation is the concept of cross-forest transitive trusts. In essence, this enables you to establish transitive trusts between two forests with completely separate schemas that allow users between the forests to share information and to authenticate users.

The capability to perform cross-forest trusts and synchronization is not automatic, however, because the forest functionality of each forest must be brought up to at least Windows Server 2003 (or higher) functional levels.

The federated forest design model is ideal for two different situations. One is to unite two disparate AD DS structures in situations that arise from corporate acquisitions, mergers, and other forms of organizational restructuring. In these cases, two AD forests need to be linked to exchange information. For example, a corporate merger between two large organizations with fully populated AD DS forests could take advantage of this capability and link their two environments, as shown in Figure 5.8, without the need for complex domain migration tools.

In this example, users in both forests now can access information in each other's forests through the two-way cross-forest trust set up between each forest's root.

The second type of scenario in which this form of forest design could be chosen is one in which absolute security and ownership of IT structure are required by different divisions

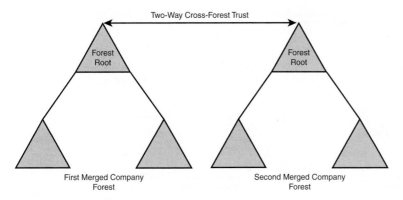

Two-Way Cross-Forest Trust

Forest Root

Forest Root

First Merged Company Forest

Second Merged Company Forest

FIGURE 5.8    Cross-forest trust between two completely different organizations needing to share resources.

or subsidiaries within an organization, but exchange of information is also required. For example, an aeronautics organization could set up two AD forests, one for the civilian branch of its operations and one for the military branch. This would effectively segregate the two environments, giving each department complete control over its environment. A one- or two-way cross-forest trust could then be set up to exchange and synchronize information between the two forests to facilitate communication exchange.

This type of design is sometimes precipitated by a need for the complete isolation of security between different branches of an organization. Since the release of Active Directory in Windows 2000, several interdomain security vulnerabilities have been uncovered that effectively set the true security boundary at the forest level. One in particular takes advantage of the SIDHistory attribute to allow a domain administrator in a trusted domain in the forest to mimic and effectively seize the Schema Admin or Enterprise Admin roles. With these vulnerabilities in mind, some organizations might choose separate forests, and simply set up trusts between the forests that are specifically designed to strip off the SIDHistory of a user.

In Figure 5.9, a one-way cross-forest transitive trust with SIDHistory-filtering enabled was set up between the civilian branch and the military branch of the sample aeronautics organization. In this example, this setup would allow only accounts from the military branch to be trusted in the civilian branch, in essence giving the military branch users the ability to access files in both forests. As with other types of trusts, cross-forest trusts are one-way by default. Unlike explicit trusts, however, cross-forest trusts are transitive. To set up two-way transitive trusts, you must establish two one-way trusts between the two forest roots.

## Determining When to Choose Federated Forests

The concept of federated forests greatly enhances the abilities of AD DS forests to exchange information with other environments. In addition, organizations that were reluctant to implement AD because of the lack of a solid security boundary between domains can now take heart in the capability of the federated forest design to allow

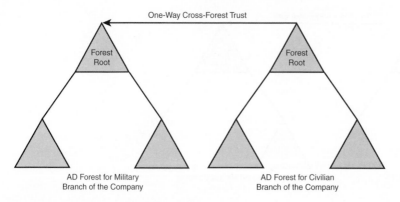

FIGURE 5.9    One-way cross-forest trust.

specific departments or areas to have complete control over their own forests, while allowing for the transfer of information between the domains.

## Exploring a Federated Forests Real-World Design Example

To illustrate a good example of an organization that would choose a federated forest design model, let's consider fictional ConglomerateA, which is a food distributor with multiple sites worldwide. It currently operates a Windows Server 2008 R2 AD DS implementation across its entire organization. All computers are members of the forest with a namespace of companyb.net. A root domain exists for conglomeratea.net, but it is not populated because all users exist in one of three subdomains: asia, europe, and na.

ConglomerateA has recently entered into a joint venture with SupplierA and wants to facilitate the sharing of information between the two companies. SupplierA also currently operates in a Windows Server 2008 R2 AD DS environment and keeps all user and computer accounts in an AD DS forest that is composed of two domains in the suppliera.com namespace and a separate tree with a DNS namespace of supplierabranch.org that reflects a certain function of one of its branches.

The decision was made to create a cross-forest trust between the two forests so that credentials from one forest are trusted by the other forest and information can be exchanged. The cross-forest trust was put into place between the root domains in each forest, as shown in Figure 5.10.

Remember, a trust does not automatically grant any permissions in other domains or forests; it simply allows for resources to be implicitly shared. Administrators from the trusting domain still need to manually grant access. In our example, administrators in both forests can decide what resources will be shared and can configure their environment as such.

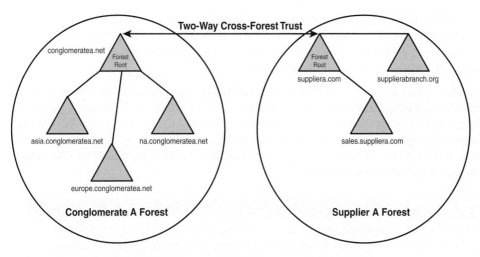

FIGURE 5.10   Cross-forest trust between root domains in each forest.

# Understanding the Empty-Root Domain Model

The schema is the most critical component of AD DS and should, therefore, be protected and guarded closely. Unauthorized access to the schema master domain controller for a forest can cause some serious problems and is probably the best way to corrupt the entire directory. Needless to say, segregation of the keys to the schema from the user base is a wise option to consider. From this concept was born the empty-root domain model, shown in Figure 5.11.

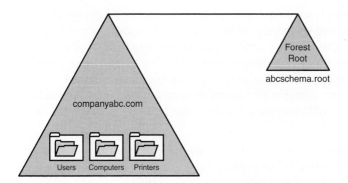

FIGURE 5.11   Empty-root domain model with an unpopulated forest root.

In short, the peer-root domain model makes use of an unpopulated forest root domain that exists solely to segregate the schema master function from the rest of the network.

In Figure 5.11, the companyabc.com domain is used for all user and computer accounts, whereas the abcschema.root domain is the peer-root domain that holds the schema master role for the company. Most users would not even be aware of the fact that this domain exists, which makes it even more secure.

The one major disadvantage to this design model lies in the hardware costs. Because a separate domain is necessary, at least one extra domain controller will be needed as part of the design plan, and preferably two for redundancy issues. This domain controller for the empty-root domain will not need to be the speediest machine because it will not perform much work, but it should definitely be made redundant, because the forest-specific FSMO roles will be handled by the machine.

> **NOTE**
>
> Instead of using a physical hardware system for the schema master, an organization could choose to use Windows Server 2008 R2 Hyper-V virtualization and create virtual domain controllers for the empty-root domain. This would help to reduce the costs of deploying the empty-root model. Do be sure to treat these virtual machines with the same respect as you would any other domain controller, with regular maintenance and backups, as losing the forest root would be disastrous for the other domains in the forest.

## Determining When to Choose the Empty-Root Model

Security needs vary from organization to organization. A company that performs top-secret work for the military is going to have drastically different security issues than a company that manufactures toys. Consequently, if the needs of your organization require a greater amount of security, the peer-root domain model might be the right one for you.

An additional advantage that this type of environment gives you is the flexibility to rename domains, add domains, and essentially move in and out of subdomains without the need to rename the forest. Although the domain rename tool exists in Windows Server 2008 R2, undertaking this task is still complicated, and using the peer-root model can help to simplify changes. In a merger, for example, if your peer root is named root.network and all your resource domains are located in companyabc.com in the same forest, it becomes much easier to add companya.net into your forest by joining it to the root.network domain.

The beauty of the peer-root domain model is that it can be incorporated into any one of the previously defined domain models. For example, a large grouping of trees with published namespaces can have a forest root with any name desired.

The example shown in Figure 5.12 demonstrates how this type of environment could conceivably be configured. The flexibility of AD DS is not limited by this design model because the options available for multiple configurations still exist.

Of course, many organizations often cannot justify the increased hardware costs, and this type of design model can prove to be more costly. Realistically, at least two domain controllers need to be established in the root domain to handle authentication requests

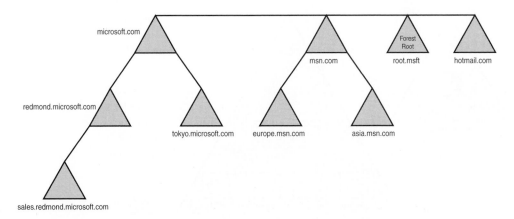

**FIGURE 5.12**  The empty-root domain model using different domain tree names throughout the forest.

and to provide for redundancy within the domain. Keeping these costs in mind, it is important to align your organization's security requirements with the cost-benefit ratio of this design model.

## Examining a Real-World Empty-Root Domain Design Example

CompanyD is a biomedical corporation centered in the San Francisco Bay area. Infrastructure security is highly important for the organization, and the company needs to ensure that directory information is safe and secure in the network environment. The IT organization is centralized, and most employees are located at the main headquarters building.

The administrators of CompanyD originally chose AD DS and Windows Server 2008 R2 to provide for robust security for their environment and to take advantage of the increased functionality. However, management was concerned about limiting access to vital components of the directory service, such as the schema. Further investigation into the varying domain design models for AD DS uncovered the peer-root domain model as a fully functional substitute to the single domain model, but with the added schema security that they desired. This resulted in a forest structure similar to the one shown in Figure 5.13.

Organizational units were created for each department and placed in the companyd.com domain. The only user account in the rootd.peer domain is the Administrator account for the forest. Access to this account was limited to a choice group of high-level administrators. This helped to control access to the schema root for the security-conscious organization and provided for the simplicity of a single domain environment for its users.

# Understanding the Placeholder Domain Model

The placeholder domain model, also known as the sterile parent domain model, deserves special mention because of its combination of a single namespace/multiple domain model and the peer-root model. Simply put, the placeholder domain model,

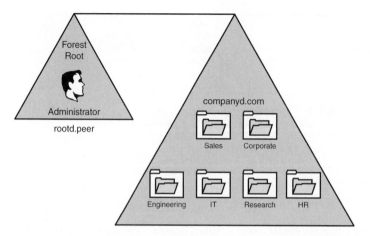

FIGURE 5.13    Peer-root domain with schema security for added protection and integrity.

shown in Figure 5.14, is composed of an unoccupied domain as the forest root, with multiple subdomains populated with user accounts and other objects.

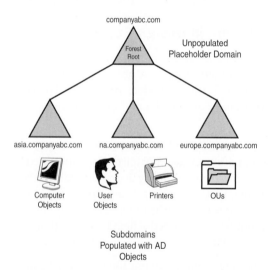

FIGURE 5.14    Unpopulated placeholder domain.

There are two distinct advantages to this design. First, as with the peer-root model, the schema is separate from the user domains, thus limiting their exposure and helping to protect the schema. Second, the namespace for the user accounts is consistent in the namespace, thus mitigating any potential political issues. In other words, because all users in all locations are at the same logical level in the domain structure, no one group will feel superior or inferior to another. This issue might seem trite, but the psychological nature of humans is finicky, and you might find that this design offers advantages for certain organizations.

### Examining a Placeholder Domain Real-World Design Example

CompanyE is an architectural firm with major offices located in New York, Chicago, Los Angeles, San Paulo, Rio de Janeiro, Berlin, Paris, London, Tokyo, Singapore, and Hong Kong. Administration is centralized in New York, but regional administration takes place in Rio de Janeiro, London, and Tokyo. The company has recently migrated to AD DS and has chosen to deploy a placeholder domain model for its organization that looks similar to Figure 5.15.

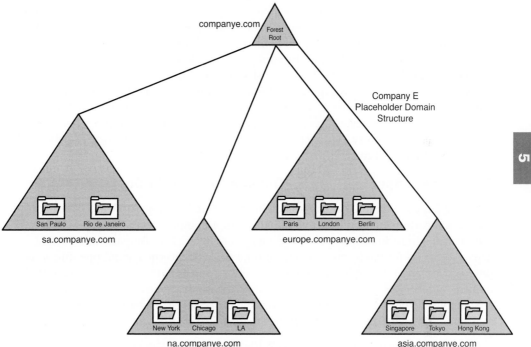

FIGURE 5.15    Complex AD DS placeholder domain structure.

All users authenticate to geographically centric subdomains. In addition, the administrators in New York have segregated the schema master function into the placeholder domain, limiting its exposure and have limited access to this domain to a small group of high-level administrators. Each domain is logically oriented as well, to give the impression of autonomy to each geographical unit.

## Understanding the Special-Purpose Domain Design Model

A special-purpose domain or forest is one that is set up to serve a specific need. For example, your organization might set up a special-purpose domain to house outside contractors or temporary workers to limit their exposure to the main AD DS forest. In addition, trust relationships could be established between this domain or other domains to allow for resource access.

Generally, there has to be a good reason before additional domains are deployed in AD DS. Overhead is increased with each domain that is added to an environment, and your logical network structure begins to look convoluted. However, in some unique cases, a special-purpose domain might become necessary.

Another possible use for a separate special-purpose domain structure is to house a directory service–capable application that requires itself, for security or other reasons, to have exclusive access to the schema. In other words, if your HR department runs an application that stores confidential employee information in an application that utilizes an LDAP-compliant directory, such as AD DS, a domain could be set up for that application alone. A cross-forest trust relationship can be established to allow for the sharing of information between the two environments. This type of situation is rare because most of these applications make use of their own directory, but it is possible. Because the AD DS schema must be unique across the forest, this would preclude the use of a single forest if these applications require exclusive access or utilize common schema attributes. This concept, known as Active Directory Lightweight Domain Services (AD LDS), is further elaborated in Chapter 8, "Creating Federated Forests and Lightweight Directories."

### Examining a Special-Purpose Domain Real-World Design Example

CompanyE is a computer consulting firm headquartered in Morioka, Japan. Most consulting work is performed by full-time CompanyE employees; however, some outside contractors are brought in from time to time to help on projects. The company had already deployed AD DS for the internal organization, but was concerned about opening access to the forest for any nonemployees of the company. Consequently, a single domain AD DS implementation was created for the nonemployees to use. A cross-forest transitive trust was established between this domain and the internal forest, and access to resources such as file and print services were delegated and controlled by the central IT organization.

Users in the contractor domain can access resources in the main companye.com domain, but only those to which they are specifically granted access. In addition, the exposure that the main companye.com domain receives from nonemployees is greatly reduced.

# Renaming an AD DS Domain

AD DS in Windows Server 2008 R2 gives domain designers the flexibility to rename their domain namespace and/or splice domains in a forest to different locations within a forest. This capability gives AD DS great new functionality because design changes can be made because of corporate mergers or organizational changes.

Domain rename supports renaming either the AD DS namespace (for example, companyabc.com) or the NetBIOS (legacy NT) domain name or both. The procedure is a rather brute-force process, however, and should not be considered to be a routine operation.

The domain rename functionality in Windows Server 2008 R2 is mainly a psychological factor because the prerequisites for deploying domain rename make it unlikely to be widely performed, at least in the initial stages of Windows Server 2008 R2 adoption. Domain rename offers long-term answers to the previous barriers to AD DS adoption, which revolved around the fact that organizations did not want to be locked in to any decisions that could not be changed. Because a Windows 2000 AD DS namespace decision was irreversible, this effectively put many decision makers on edge, as they did not want to "paint themselves into a corner," so to speak. Domain rename removes this stipulation and makes AD DS adoption much more palatable to decision makers within an organization.

## Domain Rename Limitations

Domain rename has several limitations. It is important to understand the following restrictions before considering a domain rename operation:

▶ **Cannot reduce the number of domains in a forest**—The domain rename tool cannot be used to drop additional domains from a forest. For example, if a forest is composed of four domains, there must be four domains remaining after the procedure is complete. This type of domain consolidation role can be performed only through the use of other tools, such as the Active Directory Migration Tool.

▶ **The current root domain cannot be demoted**—Although the domain rename tool can splice and transplant domains from one portion of an AD DS namespace to another, it cannot fundamentally change the root domain in a tree. A root domain can be renamed, however.

▶ **Cannot transfer current domain names in one cycle**—A production domain cannot be named the same as another production domain that exists in a forest. You need to run the domain rename procedure twice to achieve this type of desired functionality.

## Outlining Domain Rename Prerequisites

In addition to the limitations of the domain rename tool, specific prerequisites for domain rename must be met before a domain can be renamed. These prerequisites are as follows:

▶ **The entire forest must be at least Windows Server 2003 functional level**—All domain controllers in the domain must be first upgraded or replaced with Windows Server 2003, 2003 R2, 2008, or 2008 R2 and the forest functional level raised to at least Windows Server 2003 functional level.

▶ **New DNS zones must be created**—The DNS server(s) for a domain must have a zone added for the new domain namespace to which the domain will be renamed. The exception is if the domain rename procedure will be renaming only the NetBIOS domain name.

▶ **Domain rename must run from a console server**—A member Windows Server 2008 R2 computer (not a domain controller) must serve as the console server for the domain rename procedure. All domain rename operations are run from this one box.

▶ **Shortcut trust relationships might need to be created**—Any domains that will be "spliced" into a new location in the AD DS forest will need to have a shortcut trust established between itself and the parent domain where it will be transplanted.

## Renaming a Domain

The domain rename procedure, from the back end, is not extremely complex. Most of the barriers to domain renaming, aside from the limitations and prerequisites listed in the preceding section, come in the form of the disruption to the forest that is caused by the reboots applied to all the computers in the forest.

After the prerequisites have been satisfied, the domain rename process can proceed. The entire domain rename process is accomplished through six basic steps. As previously mentioned, however, this routine is rather harsh on the network because it causes downtime to a network infrastructure and should not be considered to be a common operation.

### Step 1: List Current Forest Description

The tool used for domain rename is known as Rendom. Rendom has several flags that are used in import and export operations. The first procedure run from the console server is rendom /list, which locates the domain controllers for a domain and parses all domain-naming information into an XML document named Domainlist.xml.

This XML document can easily be modified by any text editor such as Notepad and, as will become evident, is central to the domain rename procedure.

### Step 2: Modify Forest Description with New Domain Name(s)

The XML file generated by the /list flag must be modified with the new domain-naming information. For example, if CompanyABC is changing its name to CompanyXYZ, all references to companyabc in the XML list are changed to companyxyz. This includes the NetBIOS and DNS names.

### Step 3: Upload Rename Script to DCs

After the XML document is updated with the new domain information, it can be uploaded to all domain controllers in a forest through the use of the rendom /upload command. This procedure copies the instructions and new domain information up to all domain controllers within a forest.

### Step 4: Prepare DCs for Domain Rename

Domain rename is a thorough process because it is absolutely necessary that all domain controllers in a forest receive the update information. It is, therefore, necessary to run rendom /prepare to initiate a preparation process that checks to see if every single domain controller listed in AD DS responds and signifies that it is ready for the migration. If every single domain controller does not respond, the prepare function fails and must be restarted. This precaution exists to keep domain controllers that are powered down, or not accessible across the network, from coming up at a later time and attempting to service clients on the old domain name.

### Step 5: Execute Domain Rename Procedure

After all domain controllers respond positively to the prepare operation, you can initiate the actual domain rename by running the rendom /execute command from the console server. Before the execute command is run, there are actually no changes made to the production environment. However, as the command is run, all domain controllers execute the changes and automatically reboot. You then must establish a method of rebooting all member servers, workstations, and other client machines and then reboot them all a second time to ensure that all services receive the domain-naming change.

### Step 6: Post-Rename Tasks

The final step in the Rendom task is to run the rendom /clean operation, which will remove temporary files created on the domain controller and return the domain to a normal operating state.

In addition to the cleanup tasks, you need to effectively rename each domain controller, to change its primary DNS suffix. Each domain controller needs to go through this operation, which you run via the netdom command-line utility. The following steps outline the renaming of a domain controller:

1. Open a Command Prompt window (choose Start, Run, and then type `cmd.exe`).
2. Type `netdom computername OldServerName /add:NewServerName`.
3. Type `netdom computername OldServerName /makeprimary:NewServerName`.
4. Restart the server.
5. Type `netdom computername NewServerName /remove:OldServerName`.

You run all the preceding commands from the command line. Replace the generic designators OldServerName and NewServerName with the entire DNS name of the old server and the new server, such as server1.companyabc.com and server1.companyxyz.com.

# Summary

With the advent of technologies such as domain rename, fine-grained password policies, and cross-forest trusts, mistakes in AD DS design have become more forgiving than they were in the past. However, it is still important to thoroughly examine the political and technical aspects of any organization to design an infrastructure that aligns with its needs. AD DS is very flexible in these regards and can be matched with the needs of almost any organization.

# Best Practices

The following are best practices from this chapter:

▶ Fully understand the structure of AD DS before designing.

▶ Implement fine-grained password policies and the Active Directory Recycle Bin to reduce the need for additional domains.

▶ Secure any external namespace chosen by registering it so that it cannot be used anywhere on the Internet.

▶ Start a domain design by considering the single domain model first.

▶ Consider using multiple domains for specific reasons only.

▶ Consider using the federated forest design model when uniting two disparate AD DS structures.

▶ Control and optimize replication traffic by using sites.

▶ Upgrade any down-level clients to reduce administration and maintenance.

▶ Use domain rename sparingly, and only when faced with no other alternative.

CHAPTER 6

# Designing Organizational Unit and Group Structure

The organization of users, computers, and other objects within the Windows Server 2008 R2 Active Directory Domain Services (AD DS) structure gives administrators great flexibility and control over their environments. Both organizational unit (OU) and group structure design can be tailored to fit virtually any business need. There is, however, a great bit of confusion among administrators in the design and use of OUs and groups. Often, OUs are indiscriminately used without reason, and group structure is ineffectual and confusing. With the proper preparation and advance knowledge of their use, however, a functional OU and group design can do wonders to simplify a Windows Server 2008 R2 AD DS environment.

In addition to the lessons learned from OU and group use in Windows 2000 Server and Windows Server 2003, Windows Server 2008 R2 introduced functionality such as the Active Directory Recycle Bin, which reduces the risk of OU deletion, and Active Directory Web Services and an Active Directory Module for Windows PowerShell, which makes it easier to administer OUs. In addition, AD DS builds upon the improvements to OU structure and design introduced with the release of Windows Server 2008, such as OU Deletion Protection, universal group membership caching, incremental group replication, and other enhancements that have increased the flexibility of OU and group design and have given administrators greater tools to work with.

This chapter defines organizational units and groups within Windows Server 2008 R2's AD DS and describes methods of integrating them into various AD DS designs. Specific step-by-step instructions and "best practice" design advice are given as well. In addition, functional OU and group design models are detailed and compared.

# Defining Organizational Units in AD DS

An organizational unit is an administrative-level container, depicted in Figure 6.1, that is used to logically organize objects in AD DS. The concept of the organizational unit is derived from the Lightweight Directory Access Protocol (LDAP) standard upon which AD DS was built, although there are some conceptual differences between pure LDAP and AD DS.

FIGURE 6.1   Examining AD DS organizational unit structure.

Objects within Active Directory can be logically placed into OUs as defined by the administrator. Although all user objects are placed in the Users container by default and computer objects are placed in the Computers container, they can be moved at any time.

> **NOTE**
>
> The default Users and Computers folders in AD DS are not technically organizational units. Rather, they are technically defined as Container class objects. It is important to understand this point because these Container class objects do not behave in the same way as organizational units. To be able to properly utilize services such as Group Policies, which depend on the functionality of OUs, it is recommended that you move your user and computer objects from their default container locations into an OU structure.

Each object in the AD DS structure can be referenced via LDAP queries that point to its specific location in the OU structure. You will often see objects referenced in this format when you're writing scripts to modify or create users in AD DS or simply running LDAP queries against AD DS. For example, in Figure 6.2, a user named Paul Cochrane in the SF sub-OU of the Locations OU would be represented by the following LDAP string:

```
CN=Paul Cochrane,OU=SF,OU=Locations,DC=companyabc,DC=com
```

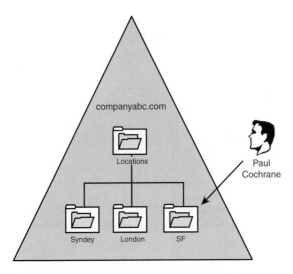

FIGURE 6.2   Viewing the LDAP structure of a user object in AD.

NOTE

The OU structure can be nested, or include sub-OUs that are many layers deep. Keep in mind, however, that the more complex the OU structure, the more difficult it becomes to administer and the more time consuming directory queries become. Microsoft recommends not nesting more than 10 layers deep. However, it would be wise to keep the complexity significantly shorter than that number to maintain the responsiveness of directory queries.

OUs primarily satisfy the need to delegate administration to separate groups of administrators. Although there are other possibilities for the use of OUs, this type of administration delegation is, in reality, the primary factor that exists for the creation of OUs in an AD environment. See the "Starting an OU Design" section of this chapter for more details on this concept.

## THE NEED FOR ORGANIZATIONAL UNITS

Although there is a tendency to use organizational units to structure the design of AD DS, OUs should not be created to just document the organizational chart of the company. The fact that the organization has a Sales department, a Manufacturing department, and a Marketing department doesn't suggest that there should be these three AD DS OUs. An administrator should create OUs if the departments will be administered separately and/or policies will be applied differently to the various departments. However, if the departments will all be administered by the same IT team, and the policies being applied will also be the same, having multiple OUs is not necessary.

Additionally, OUs are not exposed to the directory, meaning that if a user wants to send an email to the members of an OU, he would not see the OU structure nor the members in the OU grouping.

To see members of an organizational structure, AD DS groups should be created. Groups are exposed to the directory and will be seen when a user wants to list members and groups in the organization.

# Defining AD Groups

The idea of groups has been around in the Microsoft world for much longer than OUs have been. As with the OU concept, groups serve to logically organize users into an easily identifiable structure. However, there are some major differences in the way that groups function as opposed to OUs. Among these differences are the following:

▶ **Group membership is viewable by users**—Whereas OU visibility is restricted to administrators using special administrative tools, groups can be viewed by all users engaged in domain activities. For example, users who are setting security on a local share can apply permissions to security groups that have been set up on the domain level.

▶ **Membership in multiple groups**—OUs are similar to a file system's folder structure. In other words, a file can reside in only one folder or OU at a time. Group membership, however, is not exclusive. A user can become a member of any one of a number of groups, and her membership in that group can be changed at any time.

▶ **Groups as security principles**—Each security group in AD DS has a unique security identifier (SID) associated with it upon creation. OUs do not have associated access control entries (ACEs) and consequently cannot be applied to object-level security. This is one of the most significant differences because security groups allow users to grant or deny security access to resources based on group membership. Note, however, that the exception to this is distribution groups, which are not used for security.

▶ **Mail-enabled group functionality**—Through distribution groups and (with the latest version of Microsoft Exchange) mail-enabled security groups, users can send a single email to a group and have that email distributed to all the members of that group. The groups themselves become distribution lists, while at the same time being available for security-based applications. This concept is elaborated further in the "Designing Distribution Groups" section later in this chapter.

## Outlining Group Types: Security or Distribution

Groups in Windows Server 2008 R2 come in two flavors: security and distribution. In addition, groups can be organized into different scopes: machine local, domain local, global, and universal.

### Security Groups

The type of group that administrators are most familiar with is the security group. This type of group is used to apply permissions to resources en masse so that large groups of users can be administered more easily. Security groups can be established for each department in an organization. For example, users in the Marketing department can be given membership in a Marketing security group, as shown in Figure 6.3. This group is then allowed to have permissions on specific directories in the environment.

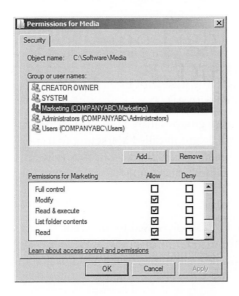

FIGURE 6.3   Examining security group permission sharing.

As previously mentioned, security groups have a unique security identifier (SID) associated with them, much in the same way that individual users in AD DS have an SID. The uniqueness of the SID is utilized to apply security to objects and resources in the domain. This concept also explains why you cannot simply delete and rename a group to have the same permissions that the old group previously maintained.

**Distribution Groups**

The concept of distribution groups in Windows Server 2008 R2 was introduced in Windows 2000 Server along with its implementation of Active Directory. Essentially, a distribution group is a group whose members are able to receive Simple Mail Transfer Protocol (SMTP) mail messages that are sent to the group. Any application that can use AD DS for address book lookups (essentially LDAP lookups) can utilize this functionality in Windows Server 2008 R2.

Distribution groups are often confused with mail-enabled groups, a concept in environments with Exchange 2000/2003/2007/2010. In addition, in most cases distribution groups are not utilized in environments without Exchange Server because their functionality is limited to infrastructures that can support them.

> **NOTE**
>
> In environments with Exchange Server, distribution groups can be used to create email distribution lists that cannot be used to apply security. However, if separation of security and email functionality is not required, you can make security groups mail-enabled.

### Mail-Enabled Groups

AD DS includes a concept called mail-enabled groups. These groups are essentially security groups that are referenced by an email address, and can be used to send SMTP messages to the members of the group. This type of group is primarily used with Exchange Server, but can also be used with foreign mail systems integrated with AD DS.

Most organizations will find that mail-enabled security groups satisfy most of their needs, both security-wise and email-wise. For example, a single group called Marketing that contains all users in that department could also be mail-enabled to allow Exchange users to send emails to everyone in the department.

## Understanding Group Scope

There are four primary scopes of groups in AD DS. Each scope is used for different purposes, but they simply serve to ease administration and provide a way to view or perform functions on large groups of users at a time. The group scopes are as follows:

- ▶ Machine local groups
- ▶ Domain local groups
- ▶ Global groups
- ▶ Universal groups

Group scope can become one of the most confusing aspects of AD DS. However, if certain design criteria are applied to group membership and creation, the concept becomes more palatable.

### Machine Local Groups

Machine local groups are essentially groups that are built in to the operating system and can be applied only to objects local to the machine in which they exist. In other words, they are the default local groups such as Power Users, Administrators, and the like created on a stand-alone system. Before networking simplified administration, local groups were used to control access to the resources on a server. The downside to this approach was that users needed to have a separate user account on each machine that they wanted to access. In a domain environment, using these groups for permissions is not recommended because the administrative overhead would be overwhelming.

### Domain Local Groups

Domain local groups, a term that might seem contradictory at first, are domain-level groups that can be used to establish permissions on resources in the domain in which they reside. Essentially, domain local groups are the evolution of the old Windows NT local groups.

Domain local groups can contain members from anywhere in an AD DS forest or any trusted domain outside the forest. A domain local group can contain members from any of the following:

▶ Global groups

▶ User accounts

▶ Universal groups

▶ Other domain local groups

Domain local groups are primarily used for access to resources because different domain local groups are created for each resource and then other accounts and/or groups are added to them. This helps to readily determine which users and groups have access to a resource.

### Global Groups

Global groups are the reincarnation of the legacy Windows NT global group, but with slightly different characteristics. These groups can contain the following types of objects:

▶ User accounts

▶ Global groups from their own domain

Global groups are primarily useful in sorting users into easily identifiable groupings and using them to apply permissions to resources. What separates global groups from universal groups, however, is that global groups stop their membership replication at the domain boundary, limiting replication outside the domain.

### Universal Groups

The concept of universal groups was new with the release of Windows 2000 and is still useful in Windows Server 2008 R2. Universal groups are just that—universal. They can contain objects from any trusted domain and can be used to apply permissions to any resource in the domain.

Although simply making all groups within a domain into universal groups might seem practical, the limiting factor has always been that membership in universal groups is replicated across the entire forest. To make matters worse, Windows 2000 AD DS universal group objects contained a single multi-entry attribute that defined membership. This meant that any time membership was changed in a universal group, the entire group membership was re-replicated across the forest. Consequently, universal groups were limited in functionality.

Windows Server 2003 introduced the concept of incremental universal group membership replication, which accomplishes replication of membership in universal groups on a member-by-member basis. This drastically reduced the replication effects that universal groups had on an environment and made the concept of universal groups more feasible for distributed environments. This functionality is available in any domain functional level at or beyond Windows Server 2003 functional level.

# Examining OU and Group Design

Understanding the concepts used with Windows Server 2008 R2 design is only part of the battle. The application of those concepts into a best-practice design is the tricky part. You can take heart in the fact that of all the design elements in AD DS, OU and group structure is the most flexible and forgiving. Although care should be taken when moving objects between OUs that have group policies enabled, the operation is not visible to end users and has no effect. That said, care should be taken to ensure that group policies that might be in place on OUs are moved in before user or computer accounts move. Not taking this into account can lead to the application of unwanted group policies to various computer or user objects, often with adverse effects. Group membership is also readily changeable, although thought should be given to the deletion of security groups that are already in use.

> **NOTE**
>
> Because each group SID is unique, you must take care not to simply delete and re-create groups as you go. As with user accounts, even if you give a new group the same name as a deleted group and add the same users into it, permissions set on the old group will not be applied to the new group. If a group is deleted, it can be recovered, but only if the Active Directory Recycle Bin is enabled, as outlined in Chapter 4, "Active Directory Domain Services Primer."

While keeping these factors in mind and after successfully completing your forest and domain design (see Chapters 4, "Active Directory Domain Services Primer," and 5, "Designing a Windows Server 2008 R2 Active Directory"), it's now time to start designing an OU and group structure.

# Starting an OU Design

As with AD DS domain design, OU design should be kept simple and expanded only if a specific need makes the creation of an OU necessary. As you will see, compelling reasons for creation of OUs are generally limited to delegation of administration, in most cases.

As with domain design, it is important to establish a frame of reference and common design criteria when beginning design of the OU structure. Organizational units are often graphically represented by a folder that looks like the icon in Figure 6.4.

OU

FIGURE 6.4    Folder icon in AD DS.

Another common method of displaying OU structure is represented by simple text hierarchy, as shown in Figure 6.5.

FIGURE 6.5    Simple text hierarchy for an OU structure.

Whichever method is chosen, it is important to establish a standard method of illustrating the OU design chosen for an organization.

The first step in the design process is to determine the best method of organizing users, computers, and other domain objects within an OU structure. It is, in a way, too easy to create OUs, and often domain designers create a complex structure of nested OUs, with three or more for every department. Although this approach will work, the fact is that it gives no technical advantages, and instead complicates LDAP directory queries and requires a large amount of administrative overhead. Consequently, it is better to start an OU design with a single OU and expand the number of OUs only if absolutely necessary.

## Examining Overuse of OUs in Domain Design

Administrators have heard conflicting reports for years about the use of organizational units in AD DS. Books and resource guides and pure conjecture have fueled the confusion and befuddled many administrators over best practices for their OU structure.

The basic truth about OUs, however, is that you likely do not need as many as you think you need. Add an OU to a domain if a completely separate group needs special administrative access to a segment of users. If this condition does not exist, and a single group of people administers the entire environment, there is often no need to create more than one OU.

This is not to say that there might not be other reasons to create OUs. Application of Group Policy, for example, is a potential candidate for OU creation. However, even this type of functionality is better accomplished through other means. It is a little-known fact that Group Policy can be applied to groups of users, thus limiting the need to create an OU for this express purpose. For more information on how to accomplish this, see the section "Group Policies and OU Design" later in this chapter.

## OU Flexibility

Domain designers are in no way locked in to an OU structure. Users can be moved back and forth between OUs during normal business hours without affecting domain functionality. This fact also helps designers easily correct any design flaws that might have been made to the OU structure.

OUs were introduced as part of Active Directory with the release of Windows 2000 and continued with later releases of Active Directory. There are essentially no real technical differences between the functionality of OUs in Windows 2000/2003 and the functionality of OUs in Windows Server 2008 R2, although there is one important update. By default, Windows Server 2008 or Windows Server 2008 R2 allows for OUs to be created with Delete Protection turned on, making it much more difficult for them to be accidentally deleted. In addition, real-world experience with OU design has changed some of the major design assumptions that were previously made in Windows 2000.

# Using OUs to Delegate Administration

As previously mentioned, one of the most important reasons for creating an OU structure in AD DS is for the purpose of delegating administration to a separate administrator or administrative group. AD DS allows for this level of administrative granularity in a single domain. This concept is further illustrated in this section.

A group of users can be easily granted specific levels of administrative access to a subset of users. For example, a remote IT group can be granted standard user creation/deletion/password-change privileges to its own OU. The process of delegating this type of access is quite simple and involves the following steps:

1. In Active Directory Users and Computers, right-click the OU where you want to delegate permissions, and choose Delegate Control.
2. Click Next at the Welcome screen.
3. Click Add to select the group to which you want to give access.
4. Type in the name of the group, and click OK.
5. Click Next to continue.
6. Under Delegate the Following Common Tasks, choose the permissions you want—in the example shown in Figure 6.6—and click Next to continue.

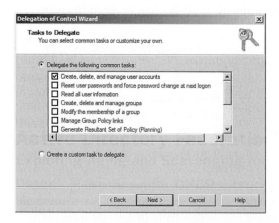

FIGURE 6.6    Choosing delegation of common tasks.

7. For example, select Create, Delete, and Manage User Accounts, and then click Next.

8. Click Finish to finalize the changes.

In fact, the Delegation of Control Wizard allows for an extremely specific degree of administrative granularity. If desired, an administrator can delegate a group of users to be able to modify only phone numbers or similar functionality for users in a specific OU. Custom tasks can be created and enabled on OUs to accomplish this and many other administrative tasks. For the most part, a very large percentage of all the types of administration that could possibly be required for delegation can work in this way. To use the phone administration example, follow these steps to set up custom delegation:

1. In Active Directory Users and Computers, right-click the OU where you want to delegate permissions, and choose Delegate Control.

2. Click Next at the Welcome screen.

3. Click Add to select the group to which you want to give access.

4. Type in the name of the group, and click OK.

5. Click Next to continue.

6. Select Create a Custom Task to Delegate, and click Next.

7. Under Delegate Control Of, choose Only the Following Objects in the Folder.

8. Check Users Objects and click Next.

9. Under Permissions, check Read and Write Phone and Mail Options, as shown in Figure 6.7, and click Next.

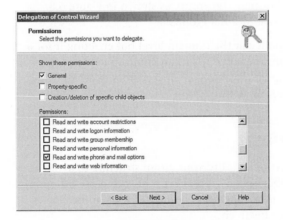

FIGURE 6.7    Selecting permissions to delegate.

10. Click Finish to finalize the changes.

The possible variations are enormous, but the concept is sound. AD DS's capability to delegate administrative functionality to this degree of granularity is one of the major advantages inherent in Windows Server 2008 R2.

# Group Policies and OU Design

Administrators create group policies to limit users from performing certain tasks or to automatically set up specific functionality. For example, a group policy can be established to display a legal disclosure to all users who attempt to log on to a system, or it can be set up to limit access to the command prompt. Group policies can be set on AD DS sites, domains, and OUs but can also be configured to apply specifically to groups. This functionality increases the domain designer's flexibility to apply group policies.

As previously mentioned in this chapter, creating additional OUs simply to apply multiple group policies is not an efficient use of OU structure and can lead to overuse of OUs in general. Rather, you can achieve a more straightforward approach to group policies by applying them directly to groups of users. The following procedure illustrates how you can apply a specific group policy at the domain level but enact it only on a specific group:

1. Open the Group Policy Management Console (Start, All Programs, Administrative Tools, Group Policy Management).

2. Navigate to the OU where the group policy is linked, then select the group policy that you want to apply to a group.

3. In the Details pane, under Security Filtering, select the Authenticated Users group, click Remove, and then click OK to acknowledge removal.

4. In the Details pane, under Security Filtering, click the Add button to select a group to which you want to apply the policy.

5. Type the name of the group into the text box, and click OK.

6. The Security Filtering settings should display the group, as shown in Figure 6.8. Repeat steps 4-5 to apply the policy to additional groups.

This concept of applying a specific group policy at the domain level but enacting it for a specific group can reduce the number of unnecessary OUs in an environment and help simplify administration. In addition, Group Policy enforcement becomes easier to troubleshoot as complex OU structures need not be scrutinized.

# Understanding Group Design

As with organizational unit design, it is best to simplify your group structure to avoid unnecessary administrative overhead. Establishing a set policy on how to deal with groups and which groups can be created will help to manage large groups of users more effectively and help troubleshoot security more effectively.

## Detailing Best Practice for Groups

In the days before Windows Server 2003 and Exchange Server 2007, it was common to use domain local groups to control access to resources and use global groups to organize similar groups of users. When this is done, the global groups created are then applied to the domain local groups as members, allowing those users permissions to those resources and limiting the effect that replication has on an environment.

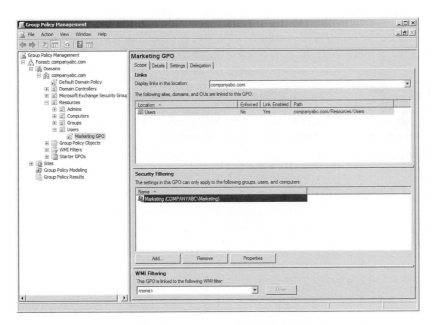

FIGURE 6.8    Adding Read and Apply Group Policy security properties.

To illustrate this type of use, consider the example shown in Figure 6.9. Users in the Marketing and Finance departments need access to the same shared printer on the network. Two global groups named Marketing and Finance, respectively, were created and all user accounts from each respective group were added. A single domain local group called Printer1 was created and granted sole access to the shared printer. The Marketing and Finance groups were then added as members of the Printer1 group. Although this is still feasible, current best practice holds that universal groups can be used instead of domain local and global groups in an AD DS environment.

The concept of the universal group is also coming of age in Windows Server 2008 R2. Now that the replication issue has been solved through incremental membership replication in Windows 2003, it is more likely that this form of group will be possible in an environment. When necessary, a universal group can take the place of global groups or can potentially include global groups as members. Universal groups are most useful in consolidating group membership across domain boundaries, and this should be their primary function if utilized in Windows Server 2008 R2.

## Establishing Group Naming Standards

As with all objects in AD DS, a group should be easily identifiable so that there is less ambiguity for both end users and administrators. Consequently, it is important to establish some form of naming convention for all groups to have and to communicate those naming conventions to the administrators who will create those groups. Using such conventions will help to alleviate headaches involved with determining what a certain group is used for, who owns it, and similar issues.

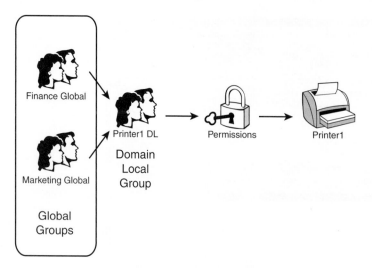

FIGURE 6.9   Best-practice group design example.

## Group Nesting

Groups can be nested, or included as members in other groups, to easily add multiple members of known groups as members of other groups. This added flexibility reduces the total number of groups necessary and helps to reduce administrative overhead.

## Designing Distribution Groups

If required by your organization, distribution groups can be set up to allow for SMTP mail to be sent to multiple recipients. Bear in mind that these groups do not have SIDs associated with them and consequently cannot be used for security permission assignments. In reality, it is rare that distribution groups will be designed in an organization that is not running a version of Microsoft Exchange Server. However, understanding their role and potential is important in determining proper group design.

# Exploring Sample Design Models

Although the possibilities for OU and group design are virtually unlimited, often the same designs unfold because business needs are similar for many organizations. Over time, two distinctive models that influence OU and group design have emerged. The first model is based on a business function design, where varying departments dictate the existence of OUs and groups. The second model is geographically based, where remote sites are granted separate OUs and groups.

## Examining a Business Function–Based Design

CompanyA is a clothing manufacturer based in St. Louis, Missouri. Facilities for the company are limited to a small group of locations in Dayton that are connected by T1 lines. A central IT department directly manages approximately 50% of the computer infrastructure within the company. The rest of the company is remotely managed by the following independent groups within the company:

- ▶ Sales

- ▶ Manufacturing

- ▶ Design

- ▶ Management

### Detailing OU Design for a Business Function–Based Design

Although the culture of the company revolves around a decentralized business approach, the IT department wanted to consolidate into a single AD domain, while at the same time preserving the administrative autonomy that the various departments had with the old environment. The result was a single AD DS domain named companya.com that used five separate OUs, one for each department, similar to the structure shown in Figure 6.10.

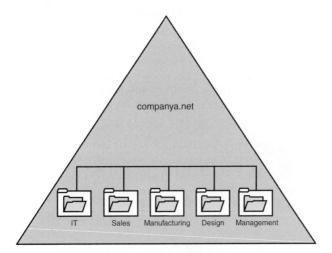

FIGURE 6.10    Organizational unit design.

To create this structure, resources were created in the single AD domain. Administrative rights were assigned to each OU by creating special global groups whose members included the local administrators for each department. These groups were then delegated password change, user creation/deletion, and other typical administrative capabilities on their respective department's OUs through use of the Delegation of Control Wizard (see the "Using OUs to Delegate Administration" section earlier in this chapter).

### Detailing Group Design for a Business Function–Based Design

A group structure was created with five separate global groups that contained users from each department. The global groups were named as follows:

- ▶ IT Global

- ▶ Sales Global

- ▶ Manufacturing Global

- ▶ Design Global

- ▶ Management Global

Resources were assigned domain local groups that followed a standard naming scheme, such as that represented in the following examples:

- ▶ Printer1 DL

- ▶ FileServer3 DL

- ▶ VidConfServer1 DL

- ▶ Printer3 DL

Security rights for all resources were then given to the appropriate domain local groups that were set up. The global groups were added as members to those groups as appropriate. For example, the printer named Printer3 was physically located in an area between both the Design and the Sales departments. It was determined that this printer should be accessible from both groups. Consequently, printing access was given to the Printer3 DL group, and both the Design Global and Sales Global groups were added as members to the Printer3 DL group, as shown in Figure 6.11.

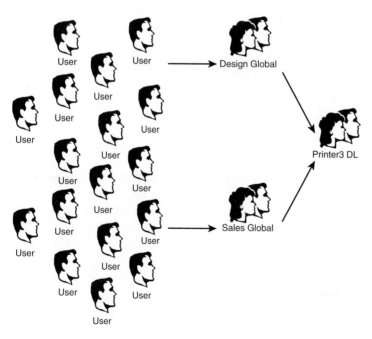

FIGURE 6.11    Nesting groups to assign permissions.

This type of resource security allowed for the greatest amount of flexibility and reduced the replication of group membership needed in the domain. If, at a later time, the decision is made to allow the IT department to print off Printer3 as well, simply adding the IT Global group into the Printer3 DL group will do the trick. This flexibility is the main goal of this type of design.

## Understanding Geographically Based Design

As was the case with the business function–based design model, domain structures can easily be tailored to the needs of organizations with geographically dispersed locations, each with its own set of administrators. It is important to understand that simply having sites in remote locations does not immediately warrant creation of an OU for each site. Some type of special local administration is required in those remote sites before OU creation should be considered.

Keeping this point in mind, consider the example of CompanyB. It is an international semiconductor producer that is centralized in Sacramento, California, but has worldwide remote branches in Malaysia, Costa Rica, Tokyo, Australia, Berlin, and Kiev, as shown in Figure 6.12.

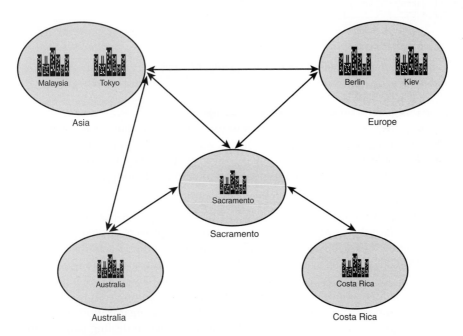

FIGURE 6.12   Sample administrative structure.

Administration takes place on a continent-by-continent basis. In other words, Berlin and Kiev are both managed by the same team, and Tokyo and Malaysia use the same administrators. Australia administers its own users, as does Costa Rica.

### Outlining OU Design for a Geographically Based Design

The AD designers at CompanyB determined that the local administrative requirements of the branch offices were best served through the creation of OUs for each administrative region. A Europe OU was created for users in Berlin and Kiev, and an Asia OU was created for Tokyo and Malaysia. The three other sites were given individual OUs, as shown in Figure 6.13.

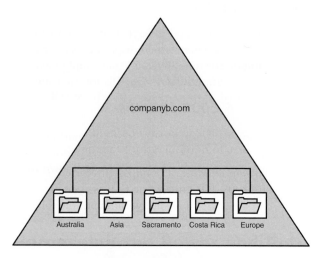

**FIGURE 6.13**    Redesign using organizational units instead of domains.

### Examining Group Design for a Geographically Based Design

Domain local groups were created to grant access to each OU on a resource basis. For example, a domain local group named Europe OU DL was created for application of security to the Europe organizational unit. To apply this security, the Delegation of Control Wizard was run on each OU, and each corresponding domain local group was granted administrative access to its own respective OUs.

Membership in the domain local groups was only the first step for allowing CompanyB's administrators to manage their own environments. Global groups were created for each IT team, corresponding with their physical location. For example, Berlin IT Admins Global and Kiev IT Admins Global groups were created, and each IT admin user account for the remote locations was added as a member of its respective groups. The two global groups were then added as members of the Europe OU DL domain local group, as shown in Figure 6.14. The same process was applied to the other OUs in the organization. This solution allowed for the greatest degree of administrative flexibility when dealing with permissions set on the OUs.

Each administrative team was consequently granted a broad range of administrative powers over its own environment, allowing each team to create users, change passwords, and effectively administer its own environments without the need for broad, sweeping administrative powers over the entire domain.

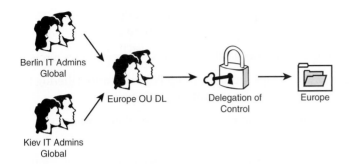

FIGURE 6.14   Nested delegation of control.

The added advantage of this design is that it is completely flexible, and administrative control can be redelegated on the fly, so to speak. For example, if a branch office opens in Paris, and IT administrators in that location need to have equivalent administrative control over the Europe OU, a simple global group can be created and added as a member to the Europe OU DL domain local group. Removing permissions is subsequently straightforward. In addition, entire OU memberships can effectively be collapsed into a different OU structure, as required by the changing needs of different organizations.

## Summary

Without some form of logical organization of users within your network environment, chaos reigns and administration grinds to a halt. Administrators need some way to lasso groups of users together into logically identifiable groupings so that changes, security privileges, and administration can be accomplished en masse. AD DS was specifically designed to be extremely scalable in regard to administrative functionality, and the flexibility of organizational unit and group design is a testament to this strength. Proper design of both OU and group structure will go a long way toward helping gain control and reduce overhead in a domain environment.

## Best Practices

The following are best practices from this chapter:

> ▶ Move your user and computer objects into an OU structure, as opposed to the default Users and Computers containers, as Group Policy Objects cannot be applied to the container objects.

> ▶ Create critical OUs with Deletion Protection enabled, to avoid accidental deletion. Enable the Active Directory Recycle Bin to be able to recover OUs and their objects if they have been deleted.

> ▶ Keep the OU structure as simple as possible, and only expand on the design if there is a specific reason to do so.

▶ Do not nest OUs more than 10 layers deep, and preferably keep them less than 3 layers deep if possible.

▶ Use the principles of role-based access control (RBAC) to control access to resources.

▶ Apply Group Policy to members of groups through Group Policy Security Filtering to avoid the creation of OUs simply for the sake of creating group policies.

▶ Use domain local groups to control access to resources, and use global groups to organize similar groups of users.

▶ Use distribution groups or mail-enabled security groups to create email distribution lists in environments with Exchange Server.

▶ Mail-enable security groups if separation of security and email functionality is not required. Alternately, use distribution groups if separation is required.

▶ Don't simply delete and re-create groups on the fly because each group SID is unique.

▶ Don't use local groups for permissions in a domain environment.

# CHAPTER 7

# Active Directory Infrastructure

In an ideal world, all areas of your network would be connected with high-capacity links, and every server would communicate with each other without latency or congestion. Alas, no real networks work this way, and traffic concerns must be taken into consideration in all but the smallest, single-server Active Directory Domain Services (AD DS) structure. Windows Server 2008 R2 expands upon the AD DS replication capabilities introduced with the original Active Directory implementation in Windows 2000 Server with a range of new features and functionality. Consequently, the introduction of these new capabilities greatly increases the capabilities of AD DS and also changes some of the fundamental design elements of Active Directory (AD) replication.

This chapter focuses on the definition of the components of Windows Server 2008 R2's AD DS that make up its replication topology. It details design strategies for AD DS sites and provides real-world examples to illustrate the principles behind them. The concept of Read-Only Domain Controllers (RODCs) and how they can be deployed in remote sites is covered. In addition, Windows Server 2008 R2's support for IPv6 (Internet Protocol version 6) is outlined and described.

## Understanding AD DS Replication in Depth

Windows Server 2008 R2 improvements in AD DS replication are directly drawn from lessons learned in Windows 2000, Windows Server 2003, and Windows Server 2008.

Read-Only Domain Controllers (RODCs) can be created in remote sites to reduce replication and increase security. Replication compression can now be disabled in well-connected sites, enabling designers to sacrifice bandwidth for processor utilization in domain controllers (DCs). In addition, concepts such as DC promotion from media allow global catalog servers to be created from CDs or other media, which greatly increases DC placement flexibility. Other improvements, such as universal group caching on domain controllers, allow remote domain controllers to function as global catalog servers by caching frequently used universal group membership locally.

Many of these improvements to AD DS replication were introduced with Windows Server 2008 and, although there are few new replication-specific improvements in Windows Server 2008 R2, this latest version cements these new features and fixes design limitations that have thwarted replication plans in the past. Problems with replication design can potentially cripple a network; therefore, it is wise to put some serious thought into the proper layout and design of an effective replication scheme.

## Understanding the Role of Replication in AD DS

All enterprise directory environments must include mechanisms to synchronize and update directory information across the entire directory structure. In Windows Server 2008 R2 AD DS, this means that every domain controller must be updated with the most recent information so that users can log on, access resources, and interact with the directory accurately.

AD DS differs from many directory services implementations in that the replication of directory information is accomplished independently from the actual logical directory design. The concept of AD DS sites is completely independent from the logical structure of AD DS forests, trees, and domains. In fact, a single site in AD DS can actually host domain controllers from different domains or different trees within the same forest. This allows for the creation of a replication topology based on a wide area network (WAN) structure, while the directory topology can mirror the organization's structure.

## Outlining Multimaster Topology Concepts

AD DS was specifically written to allow for the creation, modification, and deletion of directory information from multiple domain controllers. This concept, known as multimaster replication, allows no one domain controller to be authoritative. If any domain controllers go out of service, any one of the rest of the writable domain controllers can make changes to directory information. Those changes are then replicated across the domain infrastructure. Of course, there needs to be some level of control on this type of replication so that only the most recent changes take precedence. This type of control is realized in AD DS through the concept of Update Sequence Numbers (USNs).

## Explaining Update Sequence Numbers (USNs)

All enterprise directory services implementations require a mechanism to handle the incremental storage of changes made to directory objects. In other words, whenever a password is changed, that information must be accurately passed to all domain controllers in the domain. This mechanism must also be able to apply only those changes that occurred at the most recent intervals.

Many directory services implementations relied on exact time synchronization on all domain controllers to synchronize information. However, keeping the clocks of multiple servers in sync has been proven to be extremely difficult, and even slight variations in time could affect replication results.

Thus was born the concept of the Update Sequence Number. AD DS utilizes USNs to provide for accurate application of directory changes. A USN is a 64-bit number that is maintained by each domain controller in AD DS. The USN is sequentially advanced upon each change that is made to the directory on that specific server. Each additional domain controller also contains a copy of the last-known USN from its peers. Updates are subsequently made to be more straightforward. For example, when requesting a replication update from Server2, Server1 will reference its internal table for the most recent USN that it received from Server2 and request only those changes that were made since that specific number. The simplicity of this design also ensures accuracy of replication across the domain environment.

The integrity of replication is ensured with USNs because the USN number is updated only upon confirmation that the change has been written to the specific domain controller. This way, if a server failure interrupts the replication cycle, the server in question will still seek an update based on its USN number, ensuring the integrity of the transaction.

## Describing Replication Collisions

The concept of USNs does not completely eliminate the role of proper time synchronization in AD DS. It is still important to maintain accurate time across a domain environment because of the possibility of replication collisions. A replication collision is an inaccuracy in replicated information that takes place because of changes that are enacted on the same object, but before that change has been replicated to all domain controllers. For example, if an administrator resets a user's password on Server1, and another administrator resets the same user's password on Server2 before Server1 has had a chance to replicate that change, a replication collision will occur. Replication collisions are resolved through the use of property version numbers.

## Understanding Property Version Numbers

Property version numbers are applied as an attribute to all objects within AD DS. These numbers are sequentially updated and time-stamped whenever a change is made to that object. If a replication collision occurs, the property version number with the latest time stamp will be enacted, and the older change will be discarded. In the example from the preceding section, the password change with the latest time stamp will be applied to the user.

This concept subsequently requires accurate time synchronization to be a priority for an AD DS domain—although it is not as critical as in other directory services implementations that rely on it for all replication activity.

### WINDOWS TIME

Time is an important aspect in AD DS. Kerberos is the native authentication mechanism used by Windows AD DS and bases its ticketing system on an accurate time source. If two machines in the same domain differ by more than five minutes, authentication will break. As such, accurate time must be shared among domain members.

Windows Server 2008 R2 utilizes the Windows Time Service and the domain hierarchy to maintain a consistent source of time among all the domain controllers throughout the domain.

One server, the PDC emulator, is responsible for getting accurate time from a manual trusted source, such as NIST, time.windows.com, pool.ntp.org, or a GPS clock. This trusted source is known as stratum 0. The PDC emulator is stratum 1. Stratum 2 goes to all other DCs in the same site as the PDC emulator. The bridgehead server in remote sites is stratum 3 and all other DCs in the same remote site are stratum 4.

Member computers will try to get time from the lowest stratum DC in their own site. If that DC is not serving time, they will use the next highest stratum.

Domain computers always honor this system, which explains why the clock will reset to the domain time automatically, even if you change the local clock. Time normally syncs at startup and every 45 minutes thereafter for three consecutive, successful times, and then the interval check period is increased to 8 hours.

It is important that administrators configure and test the manually configured external time source on the PDC emulator.

## Describing Connection Objects

Connection objects are automatically generated by the AD DS Knowledge Consistency Checker (KCC) to act as pathways for replication communication. They can be manually established, as well, and essentially provide a replication path between one domain controller and another. If, for example, an organization wants to have all replication pushed to a primary domain controller (PDC) before it is disseminated elsewhere, direct connection objects can be established between the two domain controllers.

Creating a connection object is a straightforward process. After one is created, Windows Server 2008 R2 does not attempt to automatically generate a new one across the same route unless that connection object is deleted. To manually set a connection object to replicate between domain controllers, perform the following steps:

1. Open Active Directory Sites and Services.
2. Expand Sites\<Sitename>\Servers\<Servername>\NTDS Settings, where Servername is the source server for the connection object.
3. Right-click NTDS Settings and choose New Active Directory Domain Services Connection.
4. Select the target domain controller, and click OK.
5. Name the connection object, and click OK.

6. Right-click the newly created connection object, and select Properties to open a properties page for the object. You can then modify the connection object to fit any specific schedule, transport, and so on.

---

**NOTE**

The connection objects that appear as automatically generated were created by the KCC component of AD DS to provide for the most efficient replication pathways. You must, therefore, have a good reason to manually create these pathways because the automatically generated ones usually do the trick.

---

## Understanding Replication Latency

Administrators who are not accustomed to AD DS's replication topology might become confused when they make a change in AD and find that the change is not replicated immediately across their environment. For example, an administrator might reset a password on a user's account, only to have that user complain that the new password does not immediately work. The reason for these types of discrepancies simply lies in the fact that not all AD changes are replicated immediately. This concept is known as replication latency. Because the overhead required in replicating change information to all domain controllers immediately is large, the default schedule for replication is not as often as might be desired. Replication of critical information can be forced through the following procedure:

1. Open Active Directory Sites and Services.
2. Drill down to Sites\<Sitename>\Servers\<Servername>\ NTDS Settings, where Servername is the server that you are connected to and that the desired change should be replicated from.
3. Right-click each connection object, and choose Replicate Now.

Another useful tool that can be used to force replication is the repadmin command-line tool. This tool is installed as part of a default Windows Server 2008 R2 domain controller install. After being installed, repadmin can be used to force replication for the entire directory, specific portions of the directory, or to sync domain controllers across site boundaries. If the bandwidth is available, a batch file can be effectively written to force replication between domain controllers, converging the directory as quickly as possible.

The default replication schedule can be modified to fit the needs of your organization. For example, you might decide to change the default schedule of 180 minutes to a schedule as low as every 15 minutes. To make this change, perform the following steps:

1. Open Active Directory Sites and Services.
2. Drill down to Sites\Inter-Site Transports\IP.
3. Right-click the site link that requires schedule changes and choose Properties.
4. Change the Replicate every field to the new replication interval, as shown in Figure 7.1.

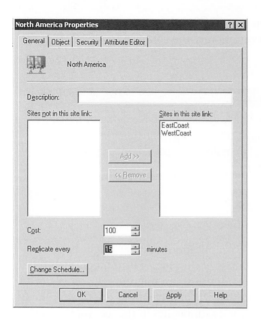

FIGURE 7.1    Setting the intersite replication interval.

**5.** Click OK to save any schedule changes.

Of course, changing this schedule comes with some caveats, namely watching for increased frequency of high network bandwidth utilization. You should match the trade-off of your organization's needs with the increased resource consumption levels required.

# Understanding Active Directory Sites

The basic unit of AD DS replication is known as the site. Not to be confused with actual physical sites, the AD site is simply a group of highly connected computers and domain controllers. Each site is established to more effectively replicate directory information across the network. In a nutshell, domain controllers within a single site will, by default, replicate more often than those that exist in other sites. The concept of the site consti-tutes the centerpiece of replication design in AD DS.

> **NOTE**
>
> Intrasite replication is approximately 15 seconds when the forest functional level is set to Windows Server 2003 or higher. The intrasite replication is set to 5 minutes for Windows 2000 Server forest functional level.

### Outlining Windows Server 2008 R2 Site Improvements

Specific functionality that affects sites has evolved since the early days of Active Directory. Windows Server 2003 introduced numerous replication enhancements that directly affect the functionality of sites and allow for greater design flexibility in regard to site design.

These changes continue to exist in Windows Server 2008 R2 and have been further improved. These enhancements include the following:

► Read-Only Domain Controllers (RODCs) and Read-Only Global Catalogs (ROGCs)

► AD DS optionally installed on Server Core

► GC universal group membership caching

► Media-based domain controller creation

► Linked-value replication

► ISTG algorithm improvements

► No global catalog full synchronization with schema changes

► Ability to disable replication packet compression

► Lingering object detection

These concepts are elaborated more fully in later sections of this chapter.

## Associating Subnets with Sites

In most cases, a specific site in AD DS physically resides in a specific subnet. This idea stems from the fact that the site topology most often mimics, or should mimic, the physical network infrastructure of an environment.

In AD DS, sites are associated with their respective subnets to allow for the intelligent assignment of hosts to their respective domain controllers. For example, consider the design shown in Figure 7.2.

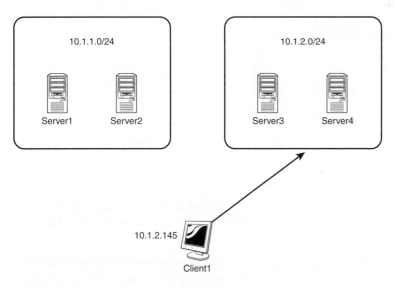

FIGURE 7.2  Sample client site assignment.

Server1 and Server2, both members of Site1, are both physically members of the 10.1.1.x subnet. Server3 and Server4 are both members of the 10.1.2.x subnet. Client1, which has a physical IP address of 10.1.2.145, will be automatically assigned Server3 and Server4 as its default domain controllers by AD DS because the subnets have been assigned to the sites in advance. Making this type of assignment is fairly straightforward. The following procedure details how to associate a subnet with a site:

1. Open Active Directory Sites and Services.

2. Drill down to Sites\Subnets.

3. Right-click Subnets and choose New Subnet.

4. Enter the network portion of the IP range that the site will encompass. In our example, we use the 10.1.2.0/24 (subnet mask of 255.255.255.0), as shown in Figure 7.3. Select a site for the subnet, and click OK.

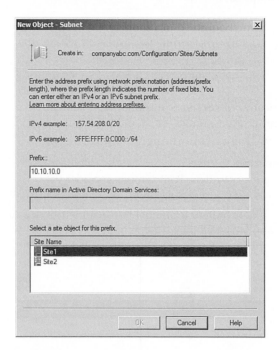

FIGURE 7.3    Associating a subnet with a site.

## Using Site Links

By default, the creation of two sites in AD DS does not automatically create a connection linking the two sites. This type of functionality must be manually created, in the form of a site link.

A site link is essentially a type of connection that joins together two sites and allows for replication traffic to flow from one site to another. Multiple site links can be set up and should normally follow the WAN lines that your organization uses. Multiple site links also ensure redundancy so that if one link goes down, replication traffic follows the second link.

Creation of site links is another straightforward process, although you should establish in advance which type of traffic will be utilized by your site link: SMTP or IP (refer to the "Choosing SMTP or IP Replication" section).

Site link replication schedules can be modified to fit the existing requirements of your organization. If, for example, the WAN link is saturated during the day, a schedule can be established to replicate information at night. This functionality enables you to easily adjust site links to the needs of any WAN link.

With the assumption that a default IP site link is required, the following steps will create a simple site link to connect Site1 to Site2. In addition, the replication schedule will be modified to allow replication traffic to occur only from 6:00 p.m. to 6:00 a.m. at one-hour intervals:

1. Open Active Directory Sites and Services.

2. Drill down to Sites\Inter-Site Transports\IP.

3. Right-click IP and choose New Site Link to open a properties page similar to the one shown in Figure 7.4.

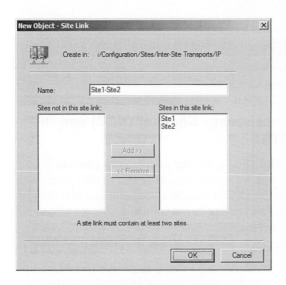

FIGURE 7.4   Site link creation properties page.

4. Give a name to the site link that will easily identify what it is. In our example, we named it Site1-Site2.

5. Ensure that the sites you want to connect are located in the Sites in This Site Link box.

6. Click OK to create the site link.

7. Right-click the newly created site link, and choose Properties.

8. Click Change Schedule.

9. Select the appropriate time for replication to occur.

10. Click OK twice to save all settings to the site link.

## Defining Site Link Bridging

By default, all site links are bridged, which means that all domain controllers in every site can communicate directly with any other domain controller through any of a series of site links. Such a bridge has the advantage of introducing redundancy into an environment; for example, if Site A has a link with Site B, and Site B is linked to Site C, servers in Site C can communicate directly with Site A.

On some occasions, it is preferable to turn off this type of replication. For example, your organization might require that certain domain controllers never communicate directly with other domain controllers. In this case, site bridging can be turned off through the following procedure:

1. Open Active Directory Sites and Services.

2. Navigate to Sites\Inter-Site Transports\IP (or SMTP, if appropriate).

3. Right-click the IP (or SMTP) folder, and choose Properties.

4. Uncheck the Bridge All Site Links check box.

5. Click OK to save the changes.

> **NOTE**
>
> Turning off site link bridging will effectively make your domain controller replication dependent on the explicit site links you have established.

## Understanding the Knowledge Consistency Checker (KCC) and the Intersite Topology Generator (ISTG)

Every domain controller contains a role called the Knowledge Consistency Checker (KCC) that automatically generates the most efficient replication topology at a default interval of every 15 minutes. The KCC creates connection objects that link domain controllers into a common replication topology. The KCC has two components: an intrasite KCC, which deals with replication within the site, and an intersite topology generator (ISTG), which establishes connection objects between sites.

In Windows Server 2003, the Active Directory design team vastly improved the algorithm used by the ISTG, which resulted in a several-fold increase in the number of sites that can effectively be managed in AD DS. The number of sites that can be effectively managed in AD DS now exceeds 5,000, particularly if 64-bit domain controllers are installed.

> **NOTE**
>
> Because all domain controllers in a forest must agree on the ISTG algorithm, the improvements to the ISTG are not realized until the forest is in Windows Server 2003 or higher forest functional level.

## Detailing Site Cost

An AD replication mechanism allows designers and administrators to establish preferred routes for replication to follow. This mechanism is known as site cost, and every site link in AD DS has a cost associated with it. The concept of site cost, which might be familiar to many administrators, follows a fairly simple formula. The lowest-cost site link becomes the preferred site link for communications to a site. Higher-cost site links are established mainly for redundancy or to reduce traffic on a specific segment. In this way, administrators can "shape" the flow of traffic between and among sites. Figure 7.5 illustrates a sample AD site structure that utilizes different costs on specific site links.

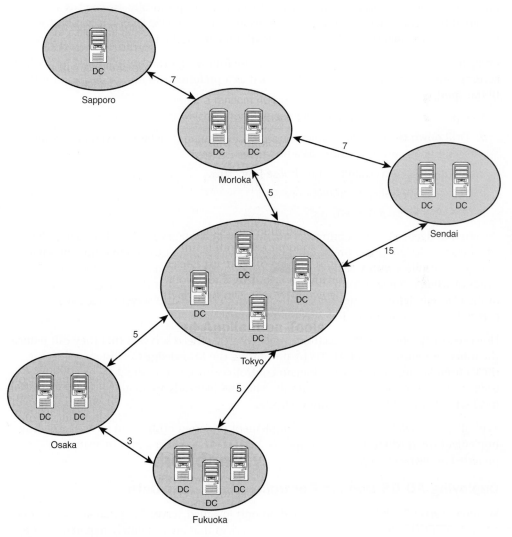

FIGURE 7.5   Understanding site costs.

In this example, traffic between the Morioka and Fukuoka sites follow the two Tokyo links for a total cost of 10. However, if there is a problem with the connection between Morioka and Tokyo or it is saturated, replication traffic will be routed through the Sendai-Morioka and then through the Sendai-Tokyo and Tokyo-Fukuoka site links because the total cost (all site link costs added together) for this route is 27. This type of situation illustrates the advantage of utilizing multiple routes in an AD DS site topology.

## Utilizing Preferred Bridgehead Servers

Often, it becomes necessary to segregate all outgoing or incoming intersite traffic to a single domain controller, thus controlling the flow of traffic and off-loading the special processor requirements that are required for this functionality. This concept gave rise to preferred bridgehead servers, domain controllers that are specifically assigned as a preferred bridgehead server for a specific transport (IP or SMTP). The preferred bridgehead servers will subsequently be the handler for all intersite traffic for that specific transport.

Bridgeheads can be easily defined in AD DS. The following example illustrates how this is accomplished. In these steps, Server2 is added as a preferred site link bridgehead for the IP transport:

1. Open Active Directory Sites and Services.
2. Drill down to Sites\<Sitename>\Servers\<Servername>, where Servername is the server you want to establish as a bridgehead server.
3. Right-click <Servername> and choose Properties.
4. Select the IP transport and choose Add.
5. Click OK to save the settings.

Preferred bridgehead servers bring with them both advantages and disadvantages. The advantage of designating a preferred bridgehead server is that in an environment where domain controllers with weaker processors need to be excluded as designated site bridgeheads or when a domain controller holds an Operations Master (OM) role, especially that of the PDC emulator, having a designated preferred bridgehead server can allow for controlled communications to a specific bridgehead server.

However, the problem with selecting a preferred bridgehead server is that they can reduce the inherent redundancy of AD DS by preventing the Knowledge Consistency Checker (KCC) from failing over to other domain controllers in the same site if the preferred bridgehead server goes offline. As a result, when bridgeheads are required, multiple bridgehead servers should be used within each site.

Typically, organizations choose to not implement preferred bridgehead servers, and only implement them when they have a specific need to designate a server in a site as a preferred bridgehead server.

## Deploying AD DS Domain Controllers on Server Core

Windows Server 2008 R2 has an installation option called Server Core that allows the operating system to be deployed with only those services that are absolutely required for the role that the server holds. For domain controllers, this includes only those services that are needed for a DC to operate. Server Core is configured to run at a command prompt, without a graphical user interface (GUI) to further reduce the security profile of the box.

Deploying dedicated domain controllers using Server Core is ideal in many situations where security is a strong requirement. By doing so, only the necessary functionality is deployed, and no auxiliary services are required.

# Planning Replication Topology

Network traffic patterns are an important consideration when implementing AD DS, and a firm understanding of the "pipes" that exist in an organization's network is warranted. If all remote sites are connected by T1 lines, for example, there will be fewer replication concerns than if network traffic passes through a slower link.

With this point in mind, mapping out network topology is one of the first steps in creating a functional and reliable replication topology.

## Mapping Site Design into Network Design

Site structure in Windows Server 2008 R2 is completely independent from the domain, tree, and forest structure of the directory. This type of flexibility allows domain designers to structure domain environments without needing to consider replication constraints. Consequently, domain designers can focus solely on the replication topology when designing their site structure, enabling them to create the most efficient replication environment.

Essentially, a site diagram in Windows Server 2008 R2 should look similar to a WAN diagram of your environment. In fact, site topology in AD DS was specifically designed to be flexible and adhere to normal WAN traffic and layout. This concept helps to define where to create sites, site links, and preferred site link bridgeheads.

Figure 7.6 illustrates how a sample site structure in AD overlays easily onto a WAN diagram from the same organization. Consequently, it is a very good idea to involve the WAN personnel in a site design discussion. Because WAN environments change in structure as well, WAN personnel will subsequently be more inclined to inform the operating system group of changes that could affect the efficiency of your site design as well.

## Establishing Sites

Each "island" of high connectivity should normally be configured as a site. This not only assists in domain controller replication, but also ensures that clients receive the closest domain controller and global catalog server to themselves.

> **NOTE**
>
> If your DNS records are inaccurate for a site, clients could be potentially redirected to a domain controller or global catalog server other than the one that is closest to them. Consequently, it is important to ensure that all your sites listed in DNS contain the appropriate server host records. This concept is explained more thoroughly in Chapter 10, "Domain Name System and IPv6."

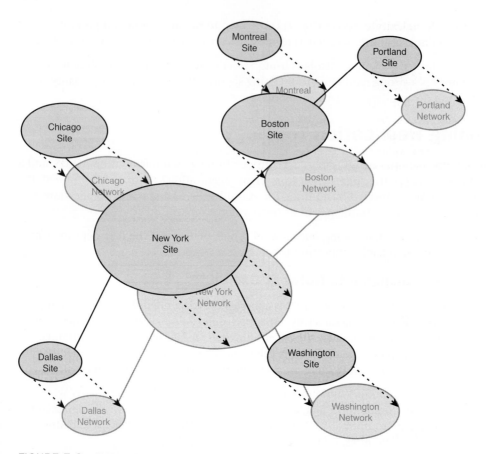

FIGURE 7.6    Site and WAN structure.

## Choosing Between One Site or Many Sites

In some cases, multiple LAN segments might be consolidated into a single site, given that the appropriate bandwidth exists between the two segments. This might be the case for a corporate campus, with various buildings that are associated with LAN "islands" but that are all joined by high-speed backbones. However, there might also be reasons to break these segments into sites themselves. Before the decision is made to consolidate sites or separate into individual sites, all factors must be taken into account.

Single-site design is simpler to configure and administer, but also introduces an increase in intersegment traffic, as all computers in all buildings must traverse the network for domain authentication, lookups, frequent replication, and so on.

A multiple-site design addresses the problems of the intersegment traffic because all local client requests are handled by domain controllers or global catalog servers locally.

However, the complexity of the environment is more significant and the resources required increase.

> **NOTE**
>
> It is no longer a firm recommendation that all sites contain at least one global catalog domain controller server. The introduction of the universal group caching capability and Read-Only Domain Controllers (RODCs) can reduce the number of global catalog servers in your environment and significantly reduce the amount of replication activity that occurs. This recommendation still stands, however, for sites with a local Exchange server, as one or more local full global catalog servers are still critical for these environments.

The requirements of an organization with the resources available should be mapped to determine the best-case scenario for site design. Proper site layout helps to logically organize traffic, increase network responsiveness, and introduce redundancy into an environment.

## Associating Subnets with Sites

It is critical to establish the physical boundaries of your AD sites because this information utilizes the most efficient logon and directory requests from clients and helps to determine where new domain controllers should be located. Multiple subnets can be associated with a single site, and all potential subnets within an organization should be associated with their respective sites to realize the greatest benefit.

## Determining Site Links and Site Link Costs

As previously mentioned, site links should normally be designed to overlay the WAN link structure of an organization. If multiple WAN routes exist throughout an organization, it is wise to establish multiple site links to correspond with those routes.

Organizations with a meshed WAN topology need not establish site links for every connection, however. Logically consolidating the potential traffic routes into a series of pathways is a more effective approach and helps to make your environment easier to understand and troubleshoot.

## Choosing Replication Scheduling

Replication traffic can potentially consume all available bandwidth on small or saturated WAN links. By changing the site link replication schedule for off-hours, you can easily force this type of traffic to occur during times when the link is not utilized as heavily. Of course, the drawback to this approach is that changes made on one side of the site link would not be replicated until the replication schedule dictates. Weighing the needs of the WAN with the consistency needs of your directory is, therefore, important. Throttling the replication schedule is just another tool that can help to achieve these goals.

## Choosing SMTP or IP Replication

By default, most connections between sites in AD DS utilize IP for replication because the default protocol used, RPC, is more efficient and faster. However, in some cases, it might be wiser to utilize SMTP-based replication. For example, if the physical links on which the replication traffic passes are not always on (or intermittent), SMTP traffic might be more ideal because RPC has a much lower retry threshold.

A second common use for SMTP connections is in cases where replication needs to be encrypted so as to cross unsecured physical links, such as the Internet. SMTP can be encrypted through the use of a Certificate Authority (CA) so that an organization that requires replication across an unsecured connection can implement certificate-based encryption.

> **NOTE**
>
> SMTP replication cannot be used as the only method of replicating to a remote site. It can only be used as a supplemental replication transport, as only certain aspects of domain replication are supported over SMTP. Subsequently, the use of SMTP replication as a transport is limited to scenarios where this form of replication is used in addition to RPC-based replication.

## Windows Server 2008 R2 Replication Enhancements

The introduction of Windows 2000 provided a strong replication topology that was adaptive to multiple environments and allowed for efficient, site-based dissemination of directory information. Real-world experience with the product has uncovered several areas in replication that required improvement. Windows Server 2008 R2 addressed these areas by including replication enhancements in AD DS that can help to increase the value of an organization's investment in AD.

## Domain Controller Promotion from Media

An ingenious mechanism in Windows Server 2008 R2 allows for the creation of a domain controller directly from media such as a burnt CD/DVD, USB drives, or tape. The upshot of this technique is that it is now possible to remotely build a domain controller or global catalog server across a slow WAN link by shipping the media to the remote site ahead of time, effectively eliminating the common practice of building a domain controller in the central site and then shipping it to a remote site after the fact.

The concept behind the media-based GC/DC replication is straightforward. A current, running domain controller backs up the directory through a normal backup process. The backup files are then copied to a backup media, such as a CD/DVD, USB drive, or tape, and shipped off to the remote destination. Upon their arrival, the dcpromo command can be run, and Advanced mode can be chosen from the wizard. In the Advanced mode of the wizard, the dialog box shown in Figure 7.7 allows for dcpromo to be performed against a local media source.

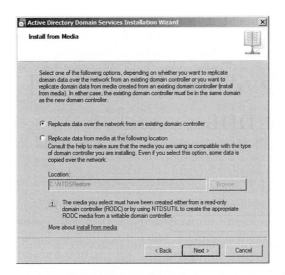

FIGURE 7.7   Dcpromo from media.

After the dcpromo command restores the directory information from the backup, an incremental update of the changes made since the media was created will be performed. Because of this, there still needs to be network connectivity throughout the dcpromo process, although the amount of replication required is significantly less. Because some dcpromo operations across slow WAN links have been known to take days and even weeks, this concept can dramatically help to deploy remote domain controllers.

> **NOTE**
>
> If the copy of the global catalog that has been backed up is older than the tombstone date for objects in the AD DS (by default, 60 days from when an object was last validated as being active), this type of dcpromo will fail. This built-in safety mechanism prevents the introduction of lingering objects and also ensures that the information is relatively up to date and no significant incremental replication is required.

### Identifying Linked-Value Replication/Universal Group Membership Caching

Previously, all groups in AD DS had their membership listed as a multivalued attribute. This meant that any time the group membership was changed, the entire group membership needed to be rereplicated across the entire forest. Windows Server 2008 R2 includes an incremental replication approach to these objects, known as linked-value replication. This approach significantly reduces replication traffic associated with AD DS.

Directly associated with this concept, Windows Server 2008 R2 allows for the creation of domain controllers that cache universal group membership. This means that it is no longer necessary to place a global catalog server in each site. Any time a user utilizes a universal group, the membership of that group is cached on the local domain controller and is utilized when the next request comes for that group's membership. This also lessens the replication traffic that would occur if a global catalog was placed in remote sites.

One of the main sources of replication traffic was discovered to be group membership queries—hence, the focus on fixing this problem. In Windows 2000 Active Directory, every time a client logged on, the client's universal group membership was queried, requiring a global catalog to be contacted. This significantly increased logon and query time for clients who did not have local global catalog servers. Consequently, many organizations stipulated that every site, no matter the size, must have a local global catalog server to ensure quick authentication and directory lookups. The downside of this was that replication across the directory was increased because every site received a copy of every item in the entire AD, even though only a small portion of those items was referenced by an average site.

Universal group caching solved this problem because only those groups that are commonly referenced by a site are stored locally, and requests for group replication are limited to the items in the cache. This helps to limit replication and keep domain logons speedy.

Universal group caching capability is established on a per-site basis through the following technique:

1. Open Active Directory Sites and Services.
2. Navigate to Sites\<Site Name>.
3. Right-click NTDS Site Settings and choose Properties.
4. Check the Enable Universal Group Membership Caching check box, as shown in Figure 7.8.

   Optionally, you can specify from which site to refresh the cache.
5. Click OK to save the changes.

## Removing Lingering Objects

Lingering objects, also known as zombies, are created when a domain controller is down for a period of time that is longer than the tombstone date for the deletion of items. When the domain controller is brought back online, it never receives the tombstone request and those objects always exist on the downed server. These objects could then be rereplicated to other domain controllers, arising from the dead as "zombies." Windows Server 2008 R2 has a mechanism for detecting lingering objects, isolating them, and marking them for cleanup.

## Disabling Replication Compression

By default, intersite AD replication is compressed so as to reduce the bandwidth consumption required. The drawback to this technique is that extra CPU cycles are required on the domain controllers to properly compress and decompress this data. Windows Server 2008 R2 allows designers the flexibility to turn off this compression, if an organization is short on processor time and long on bandwidth, so to speak.

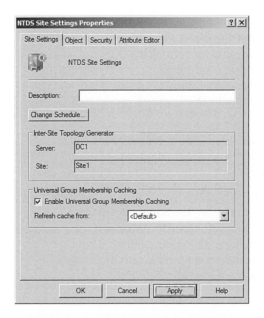

FIGURE 7.8    Enabling universal group caching in a site.

## Understanding How AD Avoids Full Synchronization of Global Catalog with Schema Changes

In the original version of Active Directory, any schema modifications would force a complete resynchronization of the global catalog with all domain controllers across an enterprise. This made it extremely ominous to institute any type of schema modifications because replication modifications would increase significantly following schema modifications. Windows Server 2003 or 2008 environments do not have this limitation, however, and schema modifications are incrementally updated in the global catalog.

## Intersite Topology Generator Algorithm Improvements

The intersite topology generator (ISTG) portion of the Knowledge Consistency Checker (KCC) has been updated to allow AD environments to scale to site structures of up to 5,000 sites. Previous limitations to the Windows 2000 ISTG essentially kept AD implementations effectively limited to 1,000 sites. This improvement, however, is available only when all domain controllers in your AD DS environment are at least Windows Server 2003 systems and the forest functional level has been raised to Windows Server 2003 or 2008 level.

# Outlining Windows Server 2008 R2 IPv6 Support

When the original structure of the Internet was taking shape, an addressing scheme was formulated to scale to a large number of hosts. From this thinking came the original design of the Internet Protocol, which included theoretical support for around 4 billion addresses, or $2^{32}$. The thinking at the time was that this would be more than enough addresses for all hosts on the Internet. This original design gave birth to the IP address structure that is common today, known as dotted-decimal format (such as 12.155.166.151). At the time, this address space filled the addressing needs of the Internet. However, it was quickly discovered that the range of addresses was inadequate, and stopgap measures such as Network Address Translation (NAT) were required to make more efficient use of the available addresses.

In addition to an inadequate supply of available addresses, the Internet Protocol version 4 (IPv4), as it is known, did not handle routing, IPSec, and QoS support very efficiently. The need for a replacement to IPv4 was evident.

In the early '90s, a new version of the Internet Protocol, known as Internet Protocol version 6 (IPv6), was formulated. This design had several functional advantages to IPv4, namely a much larger pool of addresses from which to choose by allowing for $2^{128}$ theoretical IP addresses, or over 340 undecillion, which gives more than enough IP addresses for every square centimeter on the earth. This protocol is the future of Internet addressing, and it's vitally important that an operating system support it.

Windows Server 2008 R2 comes with a version of IPv6 installed, and is fully supported as part of the operating system. Given the complexity of IPv6, it will undoubtedly take some time before it is adopted widely, but understanding that the support exists is the first step toward deploying it widely.

## Defining the Structure of IPv6

To say that IPv6 is complicated is an understatement. Attempting to understand IPv4 has been difficult enough for network engineers; throw in hexadecimal 128-bit addresses, and life becomes much more interesting. At a minimum, however, the basics of IPv6 must be understood as future networks will use the protocol more and more as time goes by.

IPv6 was written to solve many of the problems that persist on the modern Internet today. The most notable areas that IPv6 improved upon are the following:

▶ **Vastly improved address space**—The differences between the available addresses from IPv4 to IPv6 are literally exponential. Without taking into account loss because of subnetting and other factors, IPv4 could support up to 4,294,967,296 nodes. IPv6, on the other hand, supports up to 340,282,366,920,938,463,463,374,607,431, 768,211,456 nodes. Even taking into account IP addresses reserved for overhead, IPv6 authors were obviously thinking ahead and wanted to make sure that they wouldn't run out of space again.

▶ **Improved network headers**—The header for IPv6 packets has been streamlined, standardized in size, and optimized. To illustrate, even though the address is four times as long as an IPv4 address, the header is only twice the size. In addition, by having a standardized header size, routers can more efficiently handle IPv6 traffic than they could with IPv4.

▶ **Native support for automatic address configuration**—In environments where manual addressing of clients is not supported or desired, automatic configuration of IPv6 addresses on clients is natively built in to the protocol. This technology is the IPv6 equivalent to the Automatic Private Internet Protocol Addressing (APIPA) feature added to Windows for IPv4 addresses.

▶ **Integrated support for IPSec and QoS**—IPv6 contains native support for IPSec encryption technologies and Quality of Service (QoS) network traffic optimization approaches, improving their functionality and expanding their capabilities.

## Understanding IPv6 Addressing

An IPv6 address, as previously mentioned, is 128 bits long, as compared with IPv4's 32-bit addresses. The address itself uses hexadecimal format to shorten the nonbinary written form. Take, for example, the following 128-bit IPv6 address written in binary:

11111110100000000000000000000000000000000000000000000000000000000
0000100000011000010100111111111111111001000100011111000111111

The first step in creating the nonbinary form of the address is to divide the number in 16-bit values, as follows:

1111111010000000 0000000000000000

0000000000000000 0000000000000000

0000001000001100 0010100111111111

1111111001000100 0111111000111111

Each 16-bit value is then converted to hexadecimal format to produce the IPv6 address:

FE80:0000:0000:0000:020C:29FF:FE44:7E3F

Luckily, the authors of IPv6 included ways of writing IPv6 addresses in shorthand by allowing for the removal of zero values that come before other values. For example, in the address listed previously, the 020C value becomes simply 20C when abbreviated. In addition to this form of shorthand, IPv6 allows continuous fields of zeros to be abbreviated by using a double colon. This can only occur once in an address, but can greatly simplify the overall address. The example used previously then becomes the following:

FE80:::20C:29FF:FE44:7E3F

> **NOTE**
>
> It is futile to attempt to memorize IPv6 addresses, and converting hexadecimal to decimal format is often best accomplished via a calculator for most people. This has proven to be one of the disadvantages of IPv6 addressing for many administrators.

IPv6 addresses operate much in the same way as IPv4 addresses, with the larger network nodes indicated by the first string of values and the individual interfaces illustrated by the numbers on the right. By following the same principles as IPv4, a better understanding of IPv6 can be achieved.

## Migrating to IPv6

The migration to IPv6 has been, and will continue to be, a slow and gradual process. In addition, support for IPv4 during and after a migration must still be considered for a considerable period of time. It is consequently important to understand the tools and techniques available to maintain both IPv4 and IPv6 infrastructure in place during a migration process.

Even though IPv6 is installed by default on Windows Server 2008 R2, IPv4 support remains. This allows for a period of time in which both protocols are supported. After migrating completely to IPv6, however, connectivity to IPv4 nodes that exist outside of the network (on the Internet, for example) must still be maintained. This support can be accomplished through the deployment of IPv6 tunneling technologies.

Windows Server 2008 R2 tunneling technology consists of two separate technologies. The first technology, the Intrasite Automatic Tunnel Addressing Protocol (ISATAP), allows for intrasite tunnels to be created between pools of IPv6 connectivity internally in an organization. The second technology is known as 6to4, which provides for automatic intersite tunnels between IPv6 nodes on disparate networks, such as across the Internet. Deploying one or both of these technologies is a must in the initial stages of IPv6 industry adoption.

## Making the Leap to IPv6

Understanding a new protocol implementation is not at the top of most people's wish lists. In many cases, improvements such as improved routing, support for IPSec, no NAT requirements, and so on are not enough to convince organizations to make the change. The process of change is inevitable, however, as the number of available nodes on the IPv4 model decreases. Consequently, it's good to know that Windows Server 2008 R2 is well prepared for the eventual adoption of IPv6.

# Detailing Real-World Replication Designs

Site topology in Windows Server 2008 R2's AD DS has been engineered in a way to be adaptable to network environments of all shapes and sizes. Because so many WAN topologies exist, a subsequently large number of site topologies can be designed to match the WAN environment. Despite the variations, several common site topologies are implemented, roughly following the two design models detailed in the following sections.

These real-world models detail how the Windows Server 2008 R2 AD site topology can be used effectively.

## Viewing a Hub-and-Spoke Replication Design

CompanyA is a glass manufacturer with a central factory and headquarters located in Leuven, Belgium. Four smaller manufacturing facilities are located in Marseille, Brussels, Amsterdam, and Krakow. WAN traffic follows a typical hub-and-spoke pattern, as diagrammed in Figure 7.9.

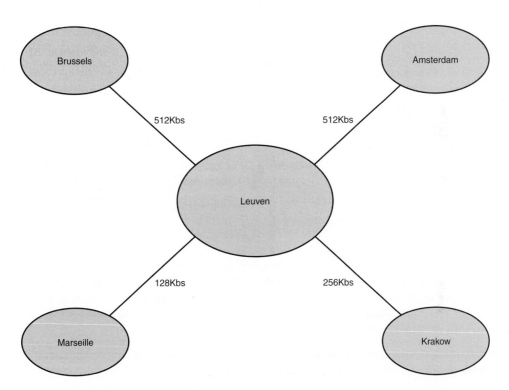

FIGURE 7.9    CompanyA WAN diagram.

CompanyA decided to deploy Windows Server 2008 R2 to all its branch locations and allocated several domain controllers for each location. Sites in AD DS were designated for each major location within the company and given names to match their physical location. Site links were created to correspond with the WAN link locations, and their replication schedules were closely tied with WAN utilization levels on the links themselves. The result was a Windows Server 2008 R2 AD DS site diagram that looks similar to Figure 7.10.

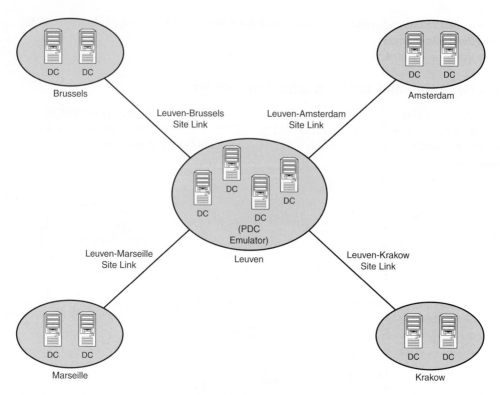

FIGURE 7.10    CompanyA site topology.

Both domain controllers in each site were designated as a preferred bridgehead server to lessen the replication load on the global catalog servers in the remote sites. However, the PDC emulator in the main site was left off the list of preferred bridgehead servers to lessen the load on that server. Site link bridging was kept activated because there was no specific need to turn off this functionality.

This design left CompanyA with a relatively simple but robust replication model that it can easily modify at a future time as WAN infrastructure changes.

## Outlining Decentralized Replication Design

CompanyB is a mining and mineral extraction corporation that has central locations in Duluth, Charleston, and Cheyenne. Several branch locations are distributed across the continental United States. Its WAN diagram utilizes multiple WAN links, with various connection speeds, as diagrammed in Figure 7.11.

CompanyB recently implemented Windows Server 2008 R2 AD DS across its infrastructure. The three main locations consist of five AD DS domain controllers and two global catalog servers. The smaller sites utilize one or two domain controllers for each site, depending on the size. Each server setup in the remote sites was installed using the Install from Media

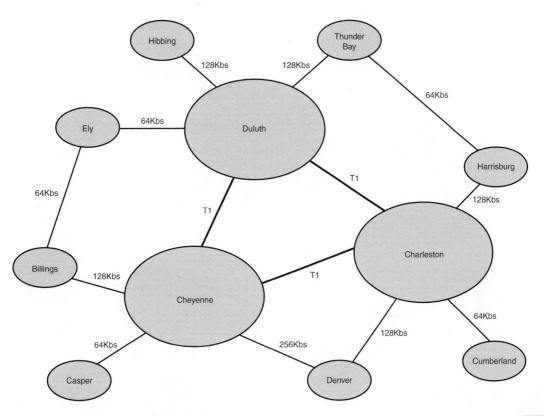

FIGURE 7.11   CompanyB WAN diagram.

option because the WAN links were not robust enough to handle the site traffic that a full
dcpromo operation would involve.

A site link design scheme, like the one shown in Figure 7.12, was chosen to take into
account the multiple routes that the WAN topology provides. This design scheme provides
for a degree of redundancy as well, because replication traffic could continue to succeed
even if one of the major WAN links was down.

Each smaller site was designated to cache universal group membership because bandwidth
was at a minimum and CompanyB wanted to reduce replication traffic to the lowest levels
possible, while keeping user logons and directory access prompt. In addition, traffic on the
site links to the smaller sites was scheduled to occur only at hour intervals in the evening
so that it did not interfere with regular WAN traffic during business hours.

Each domain controller in the smaller sites was designated as a preferred bridgehead
server. In the larger sites, three domain controllers with extra processor capacity were
designated as the preferred bridgehead servers for their respective sites to off-load the extra
processing load from the other domain controllers in those sites.

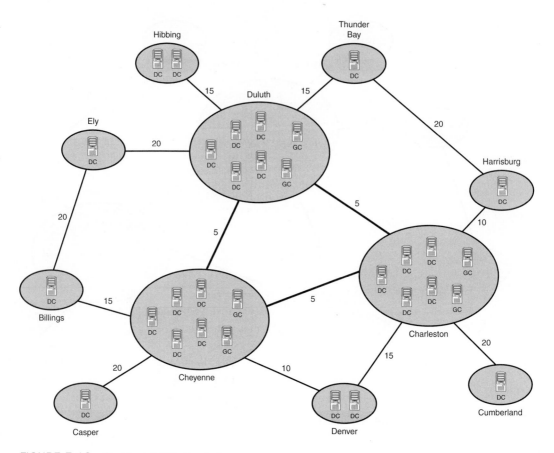

FIGURE 7.12    CompanyB site topology.

This design left CompanyB with a robust method of throttling replication traffic to its slower WAN links, but at the same time maintaining a distributed directory service environment that AD provides.

# Deploying Read-Only Domain Controllers (RODCs)

A new concept in Windows Server 2008 R2 is the Read-Only Domain Controller (RODC) Server role. RODCs, as their name implies, hold read-only copies of forest objects in their directory partitions. This role was created to fill the need of branch office or remote site locations, where physical security might not be optimal, and storing a read/write copy of directory information is ill-advised.

## Understanding the Need for RODCs

Before Windows Server 2008 R2, domain controllers could only be deployed with full read/write replicas of domain objects. Any change initiated at a domain controller would eventually replicate to all DCs in the forest. This would occur even if the change was undesirable, such as in the case of accidental deletion of OUs.

In remote sites, physical security was an issue for these DCs. Although organizations didn't want to deploy DCs to these sites for security reasons, in many cases slow WAN links would dictate that the remote office would need a local DC, or run the risk of diminished performance in those sites.

In response to these issues, Microsoft built the concept of RODCs into Windows Server 2008 R2. They also built functionality in RODCs that allowed only specific passwords to be replicated to these RODCs. This greatly reduces the security risk of deploying domain controllers to remote sites.

## Outlining the Features of RODCs

Several key features of RODCs must be understood before they are deployed in an organization. These features and functionality are listed as follows:

▶ RODCs can be installed on a server with Server Core, to further reduce the security risk by reducing the number of services running on the server.

▶ RODCs can be configured as global catalog servers, which effectively makes them ROGCs.

▶ Domain and forest functional levels must be set to Windows Server 2003 or higher levels to install RODCs.

▶ Replication to RODCs is unidirectional, as there is nothing to replicate back from the RODCs.

▶ RODCs that run the DNS service will maintain a read-only copy of DNS partitions as well. Clients who need to write their records into DNS will be issued a referral to a writable DNS server. The record that they write will be quickly replicated back to the RODC.

▶ An existing Windows Server 2008 R2 forest must be prepared to use RODCs by running dcpromo /rodcprep from the Windows Server 2008 R2 media. This allows for the proper permissions to be set for the Read-only DNS Server partitions. This can be run manually, but is run automatically during the dcpromo process for an RODC.

## Deploying an RODC

The process for deploying an RODC is similar to the process of deploying a regular domain controller. In both scenarios, the dcpromo command is used to initiate the wizard. The wizard is greatly improved over Windows Server 2003, however, and includes the ability to make that server an RODC. To configure a server as an RODC, do the following:

1. From the domain controller, choose Start, Run.

2. Type dcpromo to initiate the wizard.

3. From the wizard welcome screen, check the Use Advanced Mode Installation check box, and click Next to continue.

4. Read the warning about Operating System Compatibility and click Next to continue.

5. Choose Existing Forest and Existing Domain because RODCs can only be installed in domains with existing domain controllers. Click Next to continue.

6. Enter the name of the domain the RODC will be installed into and enter Domain Admin credentials into the Alternate Credentials field, as shown in Figure 7.13. Click Next to continue.

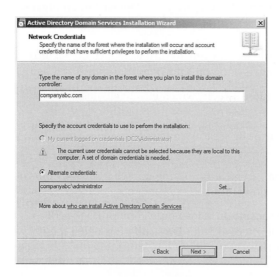

FIGURE 7.13    Installing an RODC.

7. Select the domain again from the list, and click Next to continue.

8. Select a site to install the DC into from the list, and click Next to continue.

9. On the Additional Domain Controller Options page, check the box for RODC, as shown in Figure 7.14; you can also define if the RODC is a global catalog server and/or a DNS server. Click Next to continue.

10. On the Password Replication Policy page, specify if the passwords of any specific accounts will be replicated to the RODC. Often, local users and passwords in the

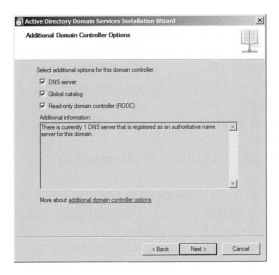

FIGURE 7.14    Choosing to make a server into an RODC.

remote location could be added here to allow for them to be replicated and to improve logon times. After adding groups and/or users, click Next to continue.

11. On the Delegation of RODC Installation and Administration page, shown in Figure 7.15, specify any accounts or groups that will be local administrators on the box. Windows Server 2008 R2 removes the requirement that local administrators of RODCs be domain-level built-in administrators, which gives greater flexibility for remote administration of the server. Enter a group (preferred) or user account into the Group or User field, and click Next to continue.

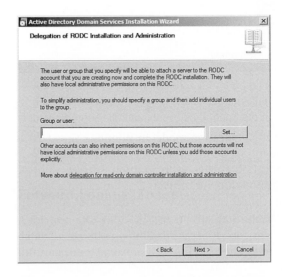

FIGURE 7.15    Setting local administrator rights on the RODC.

12. On the Install from Media page, choose to replicate either from an existing domain controller or from local media. By storing the DC information on a burnt CD or other media and shipping it to the remote location, replication time can be greatly reduced. In this case, we are replicating from an existing DC, so click Next to continue.

13. On the Source Domain Controller page, choose to either let the wizard pick a DC, or specify one yourself. Click Next to continue.

14. The next dialog box on database location, set the location for the SYSVOL, logs file, and database, and click Next to continue.

15. Set a Directory Services Restore Mode password on the next page, and click Next to continue.

16. On the summary page, review the options chosen, and click Next to continue.

17. Because new domain controllers require a reboot, it can be convenient to check the Reboot on Completion check box, as shown in Figure 7.16, which is displayed when the DC is being provisioned. By doing so, the RODC will automatically reboot when complete.

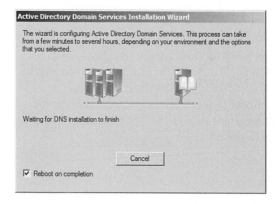

FIGURE 7.16    Setting the DC to reboot after provisioning.

# Summary

The separation of the directory model from the replication model in Windows Server 2008 R2 AD DS enables domain designers to have full flexibility when designing replication topology and enables them to focus on replication efficiency. In addition, several features in Windows Server 2008 R2, such as RODCs, IPv6 support, universal group caching, and Install from Media DC promotion, give the replication topology an even greater edge and allow for the realization of improved replication times and reduced bandwidth.

# Best Practices

The following are best practices from this chapter:

▶ Utilize RODCs to allow for local DC functionality in sites with lesser physical security.

▶ Consider installing dedicated domain controllers using Server Core, to reduce the overall security profile that a server presents.

▶ Use the automatically generated connection objects that are created by the KCC, unless a specific reason exists to hard-code replication pathways.

▶ Ensure that all your sites listed in DNS contain the appropriate SRV records.

▶ Ensure that the schema version has been upgraded to R2 levels before preparing to install Windows Server 2008 R2 on any domain controllers.

▶ Use the repadmin tool to troubleshoot and validate AD DS replication.

▶ Consider using IPv6 for environments consisting of Windows 7/Vista and Windows Server 2008 R2 and other IPv6-compliant devices.

▶ Use IPv6 tunneling mechanisms such as ISATAP and 6to4 to provide long-term compatibility between IPv4 and IPv6.

▶ Don't turn off site link bridging unless you want to make your domain controller replication dependent on the explicit site links that you have established.

7

# CHAPTER 8

# Creating Federated Forests and Lightweight Directories

Windows Server 2008 R2 not only contains the traditional directory services known as Active Directory Domain Services (AD DS), but it also includes a version of directory services meant for specific applications and smaller, more lightweight applications. This directory services version is known as Active Directory Lightweight Directory Services (AD LDS).

Keeping information and identities synchronized across these directories can be a challenge, so Microsoft also included Active Directory Federation Services (AD FS) and supports a metadirectory synchronization tool known as Forefront Identity Manager (FIM) to help with federation. This chapter addresses the creation of federated forests and lightweight directories for enterprise directory and application use.

## Keeping a Distributed Environment in Sync

When Microsoft originally developed Active Directory in Windows 2000 Server, it was designed to be the only directory an organization would ever need. The idea was that all services would be centralized within an organization's Active Directory environment, and applications would use it as their own directory.

As information technology developed, the exact opposite effect happened; a proliferation of directories within organizations occurred. Not only were multiple directories created within applications, but many organizations deployed multiple Active Directory forests for security reasons.

As Active Directory matured, Microsoft saw a need to tie these directories together into a single, federated metadirectory. In addition, they also saw an opportunity to supply applications with their own directories that were based on the AD model.

This chapter covers these technologies, covering how multiple AD DS forests can be unified into a single federated forest, and how that structure can be synchronized with other foreign directory platforms. Microsoft's Forefront Identity Manager, which provides for these capabilities, is covered in detail. In addition, Active Directory Lightweight Directory Services (AD LDS) and Active Directory Federation Services (AD FS) is explained.

## Active Directory Lightweight Directory Services

A feature of the Active Directory technologies in Windows Server 2008 R2 is the Active Directory Lightweight Directory Services (AD LDS). AD LDS, previously known as Active Directory in Application Mode (ADAM), is a directory technology that is very similar to the full Active Directory Domain Services (AD DS), but has the capability to run separate instances of itself as unique services. AD LDS allows specialized applications to utilize AD LDS as their own directory service, negating the need for a new form of directory service for every critical application within an organization.

AD LDS uses the same replication engine as AD DS, follows the same X.500 structure, and is close enough to real AD DS functionality to allow it to be installed as a test bed for developers who design AD DS applications. Despite the similarities, however, AD LDS runs as a separate service from the operating system, with its own schema and structure.

The real value to an AD LDS implementation comes from its capability to utilize the security structure of the production domain(s), while maintaining its own directory structure.

## Understanding the Need for AD LDS

AD LDS functionality was developed in direct response to one of the main limitations in using Microsoft's AD DS: the fact that the directory was so intrinsically tied to the NOS that applications that did not require the extra NOS-related functionality of AD DS were restricted in their particular directory needs. AD LDS allows each application to have its own separate AD DS directory forest and allows for personalized modification of the directory, such as schema extensions, tailored replication (or lack of replication) needs, and other key directory needs.

One of the major advantages to AD LDS also lies in the fact that multiple instances of AD LDS can run on a single machine, each with its own unique name, port number, and separate binaries. In addition, AD LDS can run on any version of Windows Server 2008 R2 or even on Windows 7 or Vista Professional for development purposes. Each instance of AD LDS can utilize a separate, tailored schema.

AD LDS is virtually indistinguishable from a normal NOS instance of AD DS and consequently can be administered using the standard tools used for AD, such as ADSIEdit, LDP.exe, and the Microsoft Management Console (MMC) tools. In addition, user accounts can be created, unique replication topologies can be created, and all normal AD DS functionality can be performed on a tailored copy of an AD LDS forest.

In short, AD LDS provides applications with the advantages of the AD DS environment, but without the NOS limitations that previously forced the implementation of multiple, cost-ineffective directories. Developers now can exploit the full functionality of Windows Server 2008 R2 AD DS without limitation, while at the same time assuming the numerous advantages of integration into a common security structure.

## Outlining the Features of AD LDS

The following key points about AD LDS should be understood before installing it into an organization:

- ▶ Unlike AD DS, AD LDS does not support global catalogs, Group Policy, domains, forests, or domain trusts.

- ▶ AD LDS does not need to be installed on domain controllers. In fact, it's completely independent of the operating system, and more than one AD LDS entity can exist on each server.

- ▶ Management of AD LDS cannot be performed using the familiar AD DS tools such as Active Directory Users and Computers. Tools such as ADSIEdit or LDP.exe or a custom front end need to be used instead.

## Installing AD LDS

Multiple AD LDS instances can be installed on the same server, or a single AD LDS instance can be replicated to multiple servers for redundancy. If installing the first AD LDS instance, follow these steps:

1. From the server, open the Server Manager application (Start, All Programs, Administrative Tools, Server Manager).

2. Navigate to the Roles node, and then click the link for Add Roles.

3. On the Before You Begin page, review the notes provided, and click Next to continue.

4. From the list of server roles, shown in Figure 8.1, choose Active Directory Lightweight Directory Services by checking the box next to it. Click Next to continue.

5. On the Introduction to Active Directory Lightweight Directory Services page, review the information provided, and click Next to continue.

6. Note the additional informational messages about needing to run the setup wizard and click the Install button.

7. Click Close when the Add Roles Wizard is complete.

8. Launch the Active Directory Lightweight Directory Services Setup Wizard from the Administrative Tools menu.

9. Click Next at the Welcome screen.

10. From the dialog box shown in Figure 8.2, choose whether to create a new unique instance or a replica of an existing instance. In this example, we are creating a new instance from scratch. Click Next to continue.

11. Type a name for the instance. This name should reflect what the AD LDS instance will be used for. Click Next to continue.

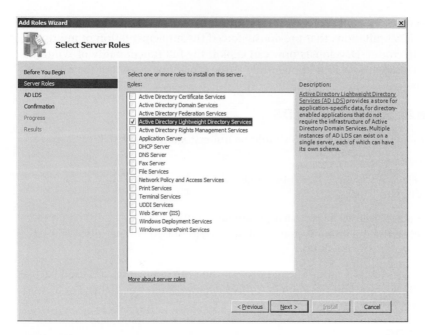

FIGURE 8.1    Installing the AD LDS role on a server.

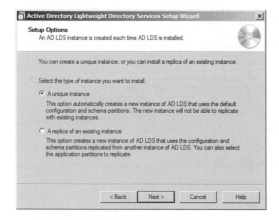

FIGURE 8.2    Installing AD LDS.

12. Enter the LDAP and LDAP port that will be used for this instance. If the default
    LDAP port of 389 or LDAP port of 636 is already in use (for example, if the server is
    already running AD DS or if another instance of AD LDS is running), choose a
    unique port. In this example, we choose port 50000 for LDAP and 50001 for LDAPS.
    Click Next to continue.

13. On the Application Directory Partition page, shown in Figure 8.3, choose whether to
    create an application directory partition. If the application you will be installing
    creates its own partition, leave it as No. If it does not, and you need to create a parti-

tion manually to store objects in, enter it in distinguished name format (that is, CN=PartitionName,DC=domain,DC=com). Click Next to continue.

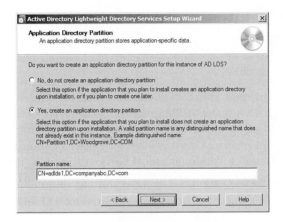

FIGURE 8.3    Configuring the application directory partition for AD LDS.

14. Select where to store the data and data recovery files for AD LDS on the File Locations page, and click Next.

15. On the Service Account Selection page, select whether to use the network service account (the default) as the service account for this instance of AD LDS. Click Next to continue.

16. The subsequent page allows for a specific user or group to be defined as administrators for the AD LDS instance. A group account is recommended. After choosing This Account and adding the group, click Next to continue.

17. The Importing LDIF Files page, shown in Figure 8.4, allows for custom LDIF files to be imported. These LDIF files were created for specific scenarios that required AD LDS, such as when users will be created in AD LDS. In this example, we import the MS-User.LDF file, so we can create user class objects in the AD LDS instance. Check the boxes required and click Next to continue.

18. On the summary page, review the selections and click Next to start the creation of the AD LDS instance.

19. Click Finish when the wizard is complete.

After being created, the AD LDS instance can be administered using ADSIEdit, a low-level directory tool available in the Administrative Tools menu. From ADSIEdit, choose Action, Connect To, and enter a name for the connection (in this example, ADLDS1). Then enter the naming context for the connection point that was created for the instance during the wizard (in our example, CN=adlds1,DC=companyabc,DC=com) and the local server name and custom port created for the computer (in this example, dc2:50000), as shown in Figure 8.5.

Although it is a much cruder tool to use than the full AD Users and Computers tool, ADSIEdit is very powerful, and full administration of the naming context for the AD LDS

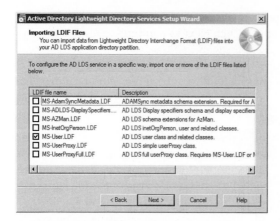

FIGURE 8.4    Importing LDIF files into the AD LDS instance.

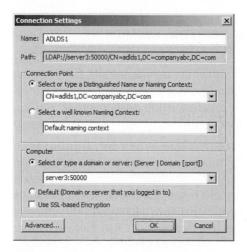

FIGURE 8.5    Connecting to the AD LDS instance.

instance can be performed. In addition, some custom applications might have their own front end for AD LDS, allowing for eased administration of the instance.

# Active Directory Federation Services

Active Directory Federation Services (AD FS) provides for Single Sign-On (SSO) capabilities across multiple platforms, including non-Microsoft environments. By managing web-based logon identities and tying them together, through Windows logon authentication, organizations can more easily manage customer access to web-based applications without compromising internal security infrastructure.

AD FS is managed from an MMC administrative tool, shown in Figure 8.6, which can be installed on a Windows Server 2008 R2 Enterprise Edition or Datacenter Edition system.

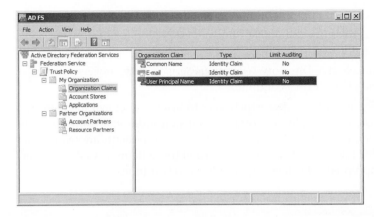

FIGURE 8.6   Viewing the AD FS MMC administrative tool.

AD FS is not a replacement for technologies such as Forefront Identity Manager (FIM), a directory sync product introduced later in this chapter. Instead of synchronizing identities across various directories as FIM does, AD FS manages logon attempts to web applications made from disparate directories. It is important to understand this concept because AD FS and FIM perform different roles in an organization's environment.

## Understanding the Key Components of AD FS

AD FS is composed of three different server components, as follows:

▶ **Federation server**—A federation server is the main AD FS component, which holds the Federation Service role. These servers route authentication requests between connected directories.

▶ **Federation proxy server**—A federation proxy server acts as a reverse proxy for AD FS authentication requests. This type of server normally resides in the demilitarized zone (DMZ) of a firewall, and is used to protect the back-end AD FS server from direct exposure to the untrusted Internet.

▶ **AD FS Web Agents**—The Web Agents component of AD FS hosts the claims-aware agent and the Windows token-based agent components that manage authentication cookies sent to web server applications.

Each one of these components can be individually installed in an AD FS structure, or they can be all installed on the same system.

## Installing AD FS with Windows Server 2008 R2

Installation of the AD FS role on a server can be performed via the following process:

1. From the server, open the Server Manager Application (Start, All Programs, Administrative Tools, Server Manager).

2. Navigate to the Roles node, and then click the Add Roles link.

3. On the Before You Begin page, review the notes provided, and click Next to continue.

4. From the list of server roles, choose Active Directory Federation Services by checking the box next to it. Click Next to continue.

5. On the Introduction to Active Directory Federations Services page, review the information provided, and click Next to continue.

6. On the Select Role Services page, select which roles to install, as shown in Figure 8.7. By clicking on the roles, you might be prompted to install additional components to make those roles work. For example, IIS and a few other components are required for the Federation Service role. If necessary, click to install those items as well. After you have selected the appropriate check boxes, click Next to continue.

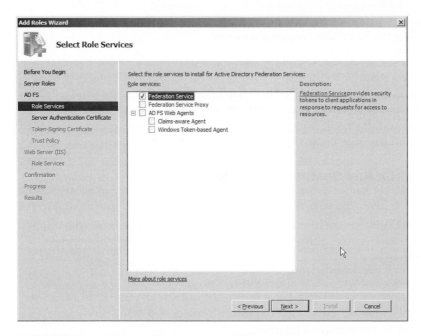

FIGURE 8.7    Installing the Active Directory Federation Services role.

7. Select whether to create a server authentication certificate or to choose an existing certificate installed on the server. Because SSL encryption is required for AD FS, a certificate from either a trusted internal Certificate Authority or an external trusted authority (most common scenario) must be used to install ADFS. Click Import if a certificate is available, but it must be installed locally on the server. After making your selection, click Next. If you are only installing AD FS for testing purposes, select to create a self-signed certificate, and click Next to continue.

8. On the subsequent page, choose a token-signing certificate, using the same process outlined in the previous step. This certificate can be created from an internal CA (if available) or imported from an external certificate provider. If using AD FS for testing, you can select to create a self-signed token-signing certificate. Click Next to continue.

9. On the Select Trust Policy page, select to either create a new trust policy for the type of claims used by your organization or to use an existing one, as shown in Figure 8.8. Click Next to continue.

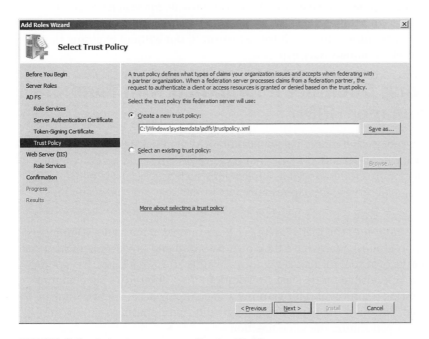

FIGURE 8.8    Selecting a trust policy for AD FS.

10. If additional components such as IIS were selected for installation, the Add Roles Wizard will continue with selections for those roles. Follow through the wizard for these roles, if necessary, until the Install button becomes available in the wizard. Click the Install button to begin configuration of AD FS.

11. Click Close when the Add Roles Wizard is complete.

## Working with AD FS

AD FS works by inputting information about connected partners, such as AD forests or AD LDS organizations, and inputting specific partner and application information. Each set of information can be inputted by running the various wizards installed by AD FS, as follows:

▶ **Add Resource Partner Wizard**—This wizard allows for resource partners to be manually created or automatically imported by using an Extensible Markup Language (XML) file. Resource partners contain information about the specific web-based applications that users can access.

▶ **Add Account Partner Wizard**—This wizard adds the information about specific account partners, which are connected security token issuers, such as domain controllers.

▸ **Add Applications Wizard**—This wizard adds specific claims-aware applications to AD FS.

By entering in the information about the various web-based applications, and which directories and identities are to be granted access, AD FS can provide for seamless sign-on capabilities between various directories. It can be a valuable asset for an organization that wants to share corporate information with trusted partners, but without exposing their valuable internal assets to unnecessary exposure.

# Synchronizing Directory Information with Forefront Identity Manager (FIM)

In most enterprises today, each individual application or system has its own user database or directory to track who is permitted to use that resource. Identity and access control data reside in different directories as well as applications such as specialized network resource directories, mail servers, human resource, voice mail, payroll, and many other applications.

Each has its own definition of the user's "identity" (for example, name, title, ID numbers, roles, membership in groups). Many have their own password and process for authenticating users. Each has its own tool for managing user accounts and, sometimes, its own dedicated administrator responsible for this task. In addition, most enterprises have multiple processes for requesting resources and for granting and changing access rights. Some of these are automated, but many are paper-based. Many differ from business unit to business unit, even when performing the same function.

Administration of these multiple repositories often leads to time-consuming and redundant efforts in administration and provisioning. It also causes frustration for users, requiring them to remember multiple IDs and passwords for different applications and systems. The larger the organization, the greater the potential variety of these repositories and the effort required to keep them updated.

In response to this problem, Microsoft developed Microsoft Metadirectory Services (MMS) to provide for identity synchronization between different directories. As the product improved, it was rereleased under the new name Microsoft Identity Integration Server (MIIS). For a third time, the tool was renamed, this time as Identity Lifecycle Manager (ILM) 2007. The latest and fourth rename of this tool took place shortly before the release of Exchange Server 2010—Microsoft has now incorporated this tool into their Forefront security line, and named it Forefront Identity Manager (FIM).

The use of FIM for Exchange Server 2010 is particularly useful because it can synchronize information between the AD forest that contains Exchange and the other messaging systems in use within the organization.

## Understanding FIM

FIM is a system that manages and coordinates identity information from multiple data sources in an organization, enabling you to combine that information into a single logical view that represents all of the identity information for a given user or resource.

FIM enables a company to synchronize identity information across a wide variety of heterogeneous directory and identity stores. This enables customers to automate the process of updating identity information across heterogeneous platforms while maintaining the integrity and ownership of that data across the enterprise.

Password management capabilities enable end users or help desk staff to easily reset passwords across multiple systems from one easy-to-use web interface. End users and help desk staff no longer have to use multiple tools to change their passwords across multiple systems.

## Understanding FIM Concepts

It is important to understand some key terms used with FIM before comprehending how it can be used to integrate various directories. Keep in mind that the following terms are used to describe FIM concepts but might also help give you a broader understanding of how metadirectories function in general:

- ▶ **Management agent (MA)**—A FIM MA is a tool used to communicate with a specific type of directory. For example, an Active Directory MA enables FIM to import or export data and perform tasks within Active Directory.

- ▶ **Connected directory (CD)**—A connected directory is a directory that FIM communicates with using a configured MA. An example of a connected directory is an Active Directory forest.

- ▶ **Connector namespace (CS)**—The connector namespace is the replicated information and container hierarchy extracted from or destined to the respective connected directory.

- ▶ **Metaverse namespace (MV)**—The metaverse namespace is the authoritative directory data created from the information gathered from each of the respective connector namespaces.

- ▶ **Metadirectory**—Within FIM, the metadirectory is made up of all the connector namespaces plus the authoritative metaverse namespace.

- ▶ **Attributes**—Attributes are the fields of information that are exported from or imported to directory entries. Common directory entry attributes are name, alias, email address, phone number, employee ID, or other information.

FIM can be used for many tasks, but is most commonly used for managing directory entry identity information. The intention here is to manage user accounts by synchronizing attributes, such as logon ID, first name, last name, telephone number, title, and department. For example, if a user named Jane Doe is promoted and her title is changed from manager to vice president, the title change could first be entered in the HR or Payroll databases; then through FIM MAs, the change could be replicated to other directories within the organization. This ensures that when someone looks up the title attribute for Jane Doe, it is the same in all the directories synchronized with FIM. This is a common and basic use of FIM referred to as identity management. Other common uses of FIM include account provisioning and group management.

> **NOTE**
>
> FIM is a versatile and powerful directory synchronization tool that can be used to simplify and automate some directory management tasks. Because of the nature of FIM, it can also be a very dangerous tool because MAs can have full access to the connected directories. Misconfiguration of FIM MAs could result in data loss, so careful planning and extensive lab testing should be performed before FIM is released to the production directories of any organization. In many cases, it might be prudent to contact Microsoft consulting services and certified Microsoft solution provider/partners to help an organization decide whether FIM is right for its environment, or even to design and facilitate the implementation.

## Exploring FIM Account Provisioning

FIM enables administrators to easily provision and deprovision users' accounts and identity information, such as distribution, email and security groups across systems, and platforms. Administrators will be able to quickly create new accounts for employees based on events or changes in authoritative stores such as the human resources system. In addition, as employees leave a company, they can be immediately deprovisioned from those same systems.

Account provisioning in FIM enables advanced configurations of directory MAs, along with special provisioning agents, to be used to automate account creation and deletion in several directories. For example, if a new user account is created in Active Directory, the Active Directory MA could tag this account. Then, when the respective MAs are run for other connected directories, a new user account could be automatically generated.

One enhancement of FIM over previous versions is that password synchronization is now supported for specific directories that manage passwords within the directory. FIM provides an application programming interface (API) accessed through the Windows Management Instrumentation (WMI). For connected directories that manage passwords in the directory's store, password management is activated when an MA is configured in MA Designer. In addition to enabling password management for each MA, Management Agent Designer returns a system name attribute using the WMI interface for each connector space object.

## Outlining the Role of Management Agents (MAs) in FIM

An MA links a specific connected data source to the metadirectory. The MA is responsible for moving data from the connected data source and the metadirectory. When data in the metadirectory is modified, the MA can also export the data to the connected data source to keep the connected data source synchronized with the metadirectory. Generally, there is at least one MA for each connected directory. FIM includes MAs for multiple directory sources, as shown in Figure 8.9.

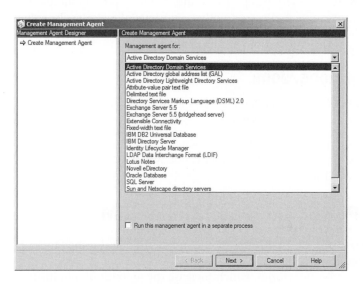

FIGURE 8.9    Potential management agents for FIM.

> **NOTE**
>
> FIM includes integrated support for synchronization with additional directories such as SAP, Oracle, IBM, and Sun. In addition, it also introduced the ability for end users to reset their own passwords via a web management interface.

MAs contain rules that govern how an object's attributes are mapped, how connected directory objects are found in the metaverse, and when connected directory objects should be created or deleted.

These agents are used to configure how FIM will communicate and interact with the connected directories when the agent is run. When an MA is first created, all the configuration of that agent can be performed during that instance. The elements that can be configured include which type of directory objects will be replicated to the connector namespace, which attributes will be replicated, directory entry join and projection rules, attribute flow rules between the connector namespace and the metaverse namespace, plus more. If a necessary configuration is unknown during the MA creation, it can be revisited and modified later.

### Defining FIM and Group Management

Just as FIM can perform identity management for user accounts, it also can perform management tasks for groups. When a group is projected into the metaverse namespace, the group membership attribute can be replicated to other connected directories through their MAs. This enables a group membership change to occur in one directory and be replicated to other directories automatically.

### Installing FIM with SQL 2005/2008

FIM requires a licensed version of SQL Server 2005 or 2008 to run, and an install of the product will prompt for the location of a SQL server.

It is not necessarily required to install a new instance of SQL because an existing SQL farm can be used as well. If an existing SQL 2005/2008 server is not available, SQL can be installed on the same system as FIM.

## Harnessing the Power and Potential of FIM

FIM is a very capable and powerful tool. With the right configuration and some fancy scripting, it can be configured to perform an incredible variety of automatic tasks. Today's environments are rife with directories, which increase the amount of administration required to create accounts, delete accounts, and update user information manually. FIM can greatly ease these requirements, improving administration and security. The next section focuses on some of the most valuable capabilities of FIM and how to effectively use them.

### Managing Identities with FIM

FIM can be used for the most basic and easiest configurations. For example, FIM can be used to synchronize identity information between accounts in different directories. Identity information could include names, email and physical addresses, titles, department affiliations, and much more. Generally speaking, identity information is the type of data commonly found in corporate phone books or intranets. To use FIM for identity management between Active Directory and an LDAP directory server, follow these high-level steps:

1. Install the Metadirectory services component of FIM.
2. Create a management agent for each of the directories, including an Active Directory management agent and an LDAP agent.
3. Configure the management agents to import directory object types into their respective connector namespaces.

4. Configure one of the management agents—for example, the Active Directory MA—to project the connector space directory objects and directory hierarchy into the metaverse namespace.

5. Within each of the management agents, a function can be configured called attribute flow to define which directory object attributes from each directory will be projected into the respective metaverse directory objects. Configure the attribute flow rules for each management agent.

6. Configure the account-joining properties for directory objects. This is the most crucial step because it will determine how the objects in each directory are related to one another within the metaverse namespace. To configure the account join, certain criteria such as an employee ID or first name and last name combination can be used. The key is to find the most unique combination to avoid problems when two objects with similar names are located—for example, if two users named Tom Jones exist in Active Directory.

7. After completely configuring the MAs and account joins, configure management agent run profiles to tell the management agent what to perform with the connected directory and connector namespace. For example, perform a full import or an export of data. The first time the MA is run, the connected directory information is imported to create the initial connector namespace.

8. After running the MAs once, they can be run a second time to propagate the authoritative metaverse data to the respective connector namespaces and out to the connected directories.

These steps can be used to simplify account maintenance tasks when several directories need to be managed simultaneously. In addition to performing identity management for user accounts, FIM can also be used to perform management tasks for groups. When a group is projected into the metaverse namespace, the group membership attribute can be replicated out to other connected directories through their management agents. This allows a group membership change to occur in one directory and be replicated to other directories automatically.

## Provisioning and Deprovisioning Accounts with FIM

Account provisioning in FIM allows advanced configurations of directory management agents, along with special provisioning agents, to be used to automate account creation and deletion in several directories. For example, if a new user account is created in Active Directory, the Active Directory MA could tag this account. Then, when the respective MAs are run for other connected directories, a new user account can be automatically generated in those other accounts.

The provisioning and deprovisioning process in FIM can be an extremely useful tool in situations where automatic creation and deletion of user accounts is required. For example, a single user account can be created in an HR Oracle database, which can initiate a chain-event of account creations, as illustrated in Figure 8.10.

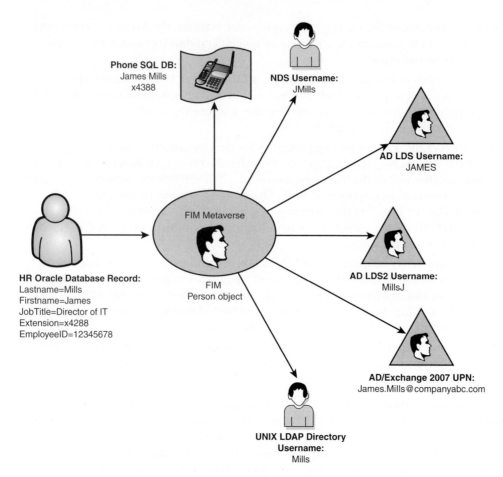

**FIGURE 8.10**    Synchronizing multiple identities with FIM.

In addition to creating these accounts, all associated accounts can be automatically deleted or disabled through a deprovisioning process in FIM. By automating this process, administration of the multitude of user accounts in an organization can be simplified and the risk of accidentally leaving a user account enabled after an employee has been terminated can be minimized.

The following high-level example demonstrates the steps required to set up simple account provisioning. In this example, a connected AD DS domain is connected to FIM. Any user accounts created in that domain have corresponding Exchange mailboxes created in a separate Active Directory resource forest:

1. Install FIM.

2. Configure a management agent for the connected AD DS domain.

3. Configure the AD DS MA so that the attributes necessary to create a resource mailbox flow into the metaverse.

4. Configure the attribute flow between the AD DS MA attributes and the FIM metaverse.

5. Configure an additional MA for the AD DS Exchange Resource domain.

6. Ensure that the AD DS Exchange Resource MA attributes that FIM will need to create the mailbox are set. These include the object types container, group, `inetOrgPerson`, `organizationUnit`, and user.

7. Using Visual Studio, configure a custom Rules Extension DLL to provide for the automatic creation of a mailbox-enabled user account in the resource forest. In this case, the DLL must use the `MVExtensionExchange` class in the script.

8. Install this rules extension DLL into the metaverse.

9. Configure run profiles to import the information and automatically create the mailboxes.

The example described previously, although complex, is useful in situations in which a single Exchange Server forest is used by multiple organizations. The security identifier (SID) of the AD DS account is imported into the metaverse and used to create a mailbox in the resource forest that has the external domain account listed as the Associated External Account. Through a centralized FIM implementation, the Exchange resource forest can support the automatic creation of resource mailboxes for a large number of connected domains.

# Summary

Active Directory as a platform provides for powerful tools to enable organizations to centralize and store information about users and other objects in an organization. The efficiencies built in to having a centralized directory platform are greatly diminished if multiple directory platforms, each with their own disparate users and attributes, are maintained. Tools from Microsoft such as the Forefront Identity Manager (FIM) product give administrators the ability to synchronize across these directories and to keep organizational information standardized across multiple platforms.

In addition to directory sync technologies such as FIM, Microsoft offers support for products such as AD FS and AD LDS, which enable organizations to streamline identity logons and create personalized directories for applications. Through proper use of these technologies, organizations can take greater advantage of the knowledge that is traditionally distributed across multiple technologies.

# Best Practices

The following are best practices from this chapter:

▶ Use FIM to keep disparate directories synchronized together.

▶ Use AD LDS for applications that require custom schema changes, and keep the information in those AD LDS instances synchronized to a central AD DS farm with the use of FIM.

- ▶ Use the Server Manager application to add AD FS and AD LDS roles to a server.

- ▶ Use AD FS for Single Sign-On support across multiple platforms.

- ▶ Consider using FIM for automatic provisioning/provisioning of user accounts across multiple directories. By establishing a firm policy on deprovisioning accounts that are no longer active, greater overall security can be achieved.

- ▶ Consider deploying AD LDS on Windows Server 2008 R2 Server Core to reduce the attack surface area of the server.

# CHAPTER 9

# Integrating Active Directory in a UNIX Environment

In the past, Microsoft had a bad reputation for giving the impression that its technologies would be the only ones deployed at organizations. The toolsets available to coexist in cross-platform environments were often weak and were provided mostly as a direct means to migrate from those environments to Microsoft environments. The introduction of Windows Server 2008 R2, however, coincides with the maturation of technologies from Microsoft that simplify and expand the ability to integrate with UNIX environments.

This chapter focuses on those technologies, and pays considerable attention to the Services for NFS role in Windows Server 2008 R2. In addition to explaining the features in Services for NFS, this chapter introduces the Subsystem for UNIX-based Applications (SUA), a tool used to allow UNIX applications to run on Windows.

## Understanding and Using Windows Server 2008 R2 UNIX Integration Components

Microsoft has a long history of not "playing well" with other technologies. With Windows Server 2008 R2, Microsoft provides native support for Windows Server 2008 R2 UNIX Integration, a series of technologies that was previously included in a product line called Windows Services for UNIX (SFU). With Windows Server 2008 R2, each of the components of the old SFU product is included as integrated services in the Windows Server 2008 R2 OS.

For many years, UNIX and Windows systems were viewed as separate, incompatible environments that were physically, technically, and ideologically different. Over the years, however, organizations found that supporting two completely separate topologies within their environments was inefficient and expensive; a great deal of redundant work was also required to maintain multiple sets of user accounts, passwords, environments, and so on.

Slowly, the means to interoperate between these environments was developed. At first, most of the interoperability tools were written to join UNIX with Windows, as evidenced by Samba, a method for Linux/UNIX platforms to be able to access Windows file shares. Microsoft's tools always seemed a step behind those available elsewhere. With Windows Server 2008 R2 UNIX Integration tools, Microsoft leapfrogs traditional solutions, like Samba, and becomes a leader for cross-platform integration. Password synchronization, the capability to run UNIX scripts on Windows, joint security credentials, and the like were presented as viable options and can now be considered as part of a migration to or interoperability scenario with Windows Server 2008 R2.

## The Development of Windows Server 2008 R2 UNIX Integration Components

Windows Server 2008 R2 UNIX Integration has made large strides in its development since the original attempts Microsoft made in this area. Originally released as a package of products called Services for UNIX (SFU), it received initial skepticism. Since then, the line of technologies has developed into a formidable integration and migration utility that allows for a great deal of interenvironmental flexibility. The first versions of the software, 1.x and 2.x, were limited in many ways, however. Subsequent updates to the software vastly improved its capabilities and further integrated it with the core operating system.

A watershed advancement in the development of Services for UNIX was the introduction of the 3.0 version of the software. This version enhanced support for UNIX through the addition or enhancement of nearly all components. Included was the Interix product, as well as an extension to the POSIX infrastructure of Windows to support UNIX scripting and applications natively on a Windows server.

Later, version 3.5 of Services for UNIX was released, which included several functionality improvements over Windows Server for UNIX 3.0. The following components and improvements were made in the 3.5 release:

▶ Greater support for Active Directory Directory Services (AD DS) authentication

▶ Improved utilities for international language support

▶ Threaded application support in Interix (separated into a separate application in Windows Server 2008 R2 named the Subsystem for UNIX-based Applications)

▶ Support for the Volume Shadow Copy Service of Windows Server 2008 R2

Finally, we come to the Windows Server 2008 version of Services for UNIX, which was broken into several components that became embedded into the operating system. No longer were the components a part of a separate package. Instead, the components were built in to the various server roles on the operating system for the first time.

Here is the structure of major improvements for the Windows Server 2008 UNIX Integration:

- ▶ x64-bit Windows Server OS support

- ▶ AD lookup capabilities through the inclusion of Group ID (GID) and User ID (UID) fields in the AD schema

- ▶ Enhanced UNIX support with multiple versions supported, including Solaris v9, Red Hat Linux v9, IBM AIX version 5L 5.2, and Hewlett Packard HP-UX version 11i

- ▶ Ability for the Telnet Server component to accept both Windows and UNIX clients

- ▶ Extended Network Information Service (NIS) interoperability, including allowing a Windows Server 2008 R2 system to act as a NIS master in a mixed environment

- ▶ Removal of the User Mapping component and transfer of the functionality directly into the AD DS schema

- ▶ NFS server functionality expanded to Mac OS X and higher clients

- ▶ Subsystem for UNIX-based Applications (SUA), which allows POSIX-compliant UNIX application to be run on Windows Server 2008 R2, including many common UNIX tools and scripts

- ▶ Easier porting of native UNIX and Linux scripts to the SUA environment

Finally, some minor changes were added to the UNIX support in this latest release, Windows Server 2008 R2. These include the following, all related to the Services for NFS component:

- ▶ Netgroup support provides the ability to create and manage networkwide named groups of hosts.

- ▶ The Unmapped UNIX User Access functionality allows NFS data to be stored on Windows servers without first creating UNIX to Windows account mapping.

- ▶ RPCSEC_GSS support provides for native support of this RPC security feature. Windows Server 2008 R2 does not provide support for the RPCSEC_GSS privacy security service, however.

- ▶ WMI Management support provides extendibility of management to NFS servers.

- ▶ Kerberos Authentication (Krb5 and Krb5i) on Shares improves standards for secured information access.

## Understanding the UNIX Interoperability Components in Windows Server 2008 R2

Windows Server 2008 R2 UNIX Integration is composed of several key components, each of which provides a specific integration task with different UNIX environments. Any or all of these components can be used as part of Windows Server 2008 R2 UNIX Integration as the installation of the suite can be customized, depending on an organization's needs. The major components of Windows Server 2008 R2 UNIX Integration are as follows:

- Services for NFS (includes Server for NFS and Client for NFS)
- Telnet Server (supports Windows and UNIX clients)
- Identity Management for UNIX (includes the Server for Network Information Services and Password Synchronization components)
- Subsystem for UNIX-based Applications (SUA)

Each component can be installed as part of a server role. For example, the Services for NFS component is installed as part of the File Services role in Windows Server 2008 R2. Each component is described in more detail in the following sections.

## Prerequisites for Windows Server 2008 R2 UNIX Integration

Windows Server 2008 R2 UNIX services interoperate with various flavors of UNIX, but were tested and specifically written for use with the following UNIX versions:

- Sun Solaris 7.x, 8.x, 9.x, or 10
- Red Hat Linux 8.0 and later
- Hewlett-Packard HP-UX 11i
- IBM AIX 5L 5.2
- Apple Macintosh OS X

**NOTE**

Windows Server 2008 R2 UNIX Integration is not limited to these versions of Sun Solaris, Red Hat Linux, HP-UX, IBM AIX, and Apple OS X. It actually performs quite well in various other similar versions and implementations of UNIX, Linux, and Mac OS X.

## Installing Services for Network File System (NFS)

The installation of Windows Server 2008 R2 UNIX Integration for Windows Server 2008 R2 is as simple as adding specific server roles to a server using the Add Roles Wizard. The individual components can be installed as part of different roles added to the server. For example, to add the Services for NFS role, simply add the File Services role to a server via the following process:

1. Open Server Manager (Start, All Programs, Administrative Tools, Server Manager).
2. Click on the Roles node in the tasks pane, and then click the Add Roles link.
3. On the Add Roles Wizard welcome page, click Next to continue.
4. From the list of roles to install, check the box for File Services, and click Next to continue.
5. On the Introduction to File Services page, click Next to continue.
6. On the Select Role Services page, shown in Figure 9.1, keep the File Server box checked and check the box for Services for Network File System. Click Next to continue.

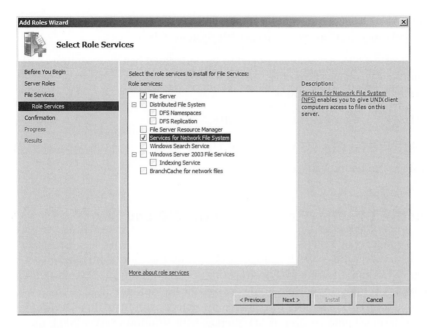

FIGURE 9.1   Installing Services for NFS.

7. On the Confirmation page, review the settings and click the Install button.

8. Click Close when the wizard completes.

**NOTE**

If the File Services role has already been installed, you can add the Services for Network File System by right-clicking the File Services role and selecting Add Role Services.

Services for NFS streamlines the sharing of information between UNIX and Windows Server 2008 R2, allowing users from both environments to seamlessly access data from each separate environment, without the need for specialized client software. Utilizing the Services for NFS and NFS Client allows for this level of functionality and provides for a more integrated environment.

## Using and Administering Services for NFS

The Services for NFS component acts as a UNIX-standard NFS server by providing disk space from any Windows-based computer on a network to NFS clients, translating their NFS requests to Windows SMB-based requests. No additional client software is necessary, and the Windows Server 2008 R2 server acts and functions like a normal NFS-based UNIX server for these clients. This is a great way to bring a standardized share format to a heterogeneous network as UNIX and Apple clients might have difficulties using standard Windows file protocols such as Common Internet File System (CIFS).

After installing Services for NFS, several tasks need to be performed before accepting UNIX clients to the Windows file shares. These tasks include the following, covered in more detail in the following sections of this book:

- ▶ Configure AD DS lookup for UNIX GID and UID
- ▶ Configure the Server for NFS and Client for NFS components
- ▶ Create NFS shared network resources

## Configuring Active Directory Lookup for UNIX GID and UID Information

So that NTFS permissions can be properly mapped to UNIX user accounts, integration with Active Directory Domain Services (AD DS) must be set up between AD DS and UNIX. This requires the proper schema extensions to be enabled in the domain. By default, Windows Server 2008 R2 AD DS includes these schema extensions. If installing Services for NFS into a down-level schema version of AD, such as with Windows Server 2003, the schema must be extended first to Windows Server 2008 R2 levels.

To enable AD DS lookup for Services for NFS, do the following:

1. Open the Services for Network File System MMC (Start, All Programs, Administrative Tools, Services for Network File System).
2. Right-click on the Services for NFS node in the node pane, and choose Properties.
3. In the Identity Mapping Source section, check the Active Directory domain name check box, and enter the name of the domain in which identity mapping will be enabled, as shown in Figure 9.2.
4. Click OK to save the changes.

> **NOTE**
>
> Windows Server 2008 R2 Services for NFS still supports the legacy User Name Mapping service, although installation of the User Name Mapping service itself cannot be done on a Windows Server 2008 R2 server. It is preferable to use the AD DS integration, however, rather than the User Name Mapping service.

## Configuring Client for NFS and Server for NFS Settings

After enabling the lookup method used for Services for NFS, you can configure the individual Server for NFS and Client for NFS settings by right-clicking the individual nodes and choosing Properties. This allows you to change default file permissions levels, TCP and UDP settings, mount types, new Windows Server 2008 R2 Kerberos settings, and file-name support levels. For example, in Figure 9.3, the screen for customizing Client for NFS settings is displayed.

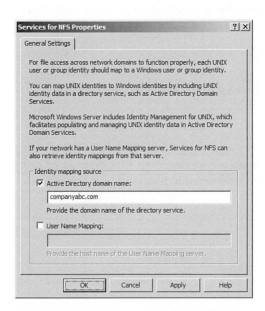

FIGURE 9.2    Enabling AD DS mapping for Services for NFS.

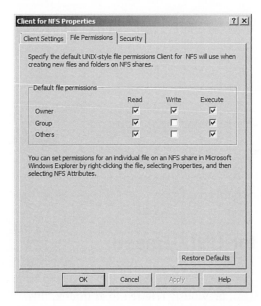

FIGURE 9.3    Customizing Client for NFS settings.

## Creating NFS Shared Network Resources

Configuring a shared resource with Server for NFS requires opening the Command Prompt window with elevated privileges (Start, All Programs, Accessories, right-click Command Prompt, Run As Administrator) and then creating the share using the nfsshare command-line utility. Type nfsshare /? for the exact syntax.

To create an NFS shared network resource using the GUI interface, perform the following tasks:

1. From Windows Explorer on the server, navigate to the folder that will be shared, right-click it, and choose Properties.
2. Select the NFS Sharing tab.
3. Click the Manage NFS Sharing button.
4. Check the Share This Folder check box, as shown in Figure 9.4. Configure if anonymous access will be allowed (not normally recommended) or configure any special permissions by clicking Permissions.

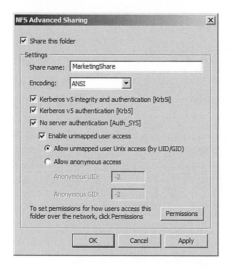

FIGURE 9.4    Creating a shared resource for NFS.

5. Click OK and then click Close to save the changes.

# Reviewing the Subsystem for UNIX-Based Applications (SUA)

The Subsystem for UNIX-based Applications (SUA), previously referred to as Interix, fills the gap between development on UNIX platforms and development in Windows. It was written to allow programmers familiar with UNIX to continue to use the most familiar programming tools and scripts, such as grep, tar, cut, awk, vi, and many others. In addition, with limited reprogramming efforts, applications that run on UNIX-based systems can be ported over to the Wintel platform, building on the low cost of ownership of Windows while retaining software investments from UNIX.

Windows Server 2008 R2 UNIX Integration further enhances the capabilities of the UNIX subsystem. Performance increases for file I/O, pipe bandwidth, and overall response time have been noticeable, in some cases doubling in speed.

## Installing the Subsystem for UNIX-Based Applications

The SUA component is available as a feature on Windows Server 2008 R2. It can be installed via the following process:

1. Open Server Manager (Start, All Programs, Administrative Tools, Server Manager).
2. Click on the Features node in the tasks pane, and then click the Add Features link.
3. On the Add Roles Wizard welcome page, click Next to continue.
4. Check the Subsystem for UNIX-based Applications check box, and click Next to continue.
5. Click Install.
6. Click Close when the install wizard completes. Click Yes to reboot the server if prompted.

## Subsystem for UNIX-Based Applications Scripting

Administrators familiar with UNIX environments will feel at home working with Interix as both the Korn and C shells are available, and both behave exactly as they would in UNIX. Windows Server 2008 R2 UNIX Integration also supports the single-rooted file system through these shells, which negates the need to convert scripts to support drive letters. The single-rooted file system allows for a great deal of functionality, allowing scripts written for UNIX to more natively port over to a Windows environment.

## Subsystem for UNIX-Based Application Tools and Programming Languages

SUA supports all common UNIX tools and utilities, with all the familiar commands such as grep, man, env, pr, nice, ps, kill, and many others. Each tool was built to respond exactly the way it is expected to behave in UNIX, and SUA users can build or import their own customizable tools using the same procedures that they would in a UNIX environment.

# Understanding the Identity Management for UNIX Components

The goal of Single Sign-On (SSO), in which users on a network log on once and then have access to multiple resources and environments, is still a long way off. It is common for a regular user to maintain and use three or more separate usernames and associated sets of passwords. Windows Server 2008 R2 UNIX Integration goes a long way toward making SSO a reality, however, with the Identity Management for UNIX role service.

Identity Management for UNIX is an additional role service on a Windows Server 2008 R2 machine that includes three major components, as follows:

- ▶ **Server for Network Information Services (SNIS)**—Server for NIS allows a Windows AD DS environment to integrate directly with a UNIX NIS environment by exporting NIS domain maps to AD entries. This allows an AD domain controller to act as the master NIS server.

- ▶ **Password Synchronization**—Installing the Password Synchronization role on a server allows for passwords to be changed once, and to have that change propagated to both the UNIX and AD DS environment.

- ▶ **Administrative Tools**—Installing this role service gives administrators the tools necessary to administer the SNIS and Password Synchronization components.

The Identity Management for UNIX components have some other important prerequisites and limitations that must be taken into account before considering them for use in an environment. These factors include the following:

- ▶ Server for Network Information Services (SNIS) must be installed on an Active Directory domain controller. In addition, all domain controllers in the domain must be running Server for NIS.

- ▶ SNIS must not be subservient to a UNIX NIS server—it can only be subservient to another Windows-based server running Server for NIS. This requirement can be a politically sensitive one and should be broached carefully, as some UNIX administrators will be hesitant to make the Windows-based NIS the primary NIS server.

- ▶ The SNIS authentication component must be installed on all domain controllers in the domain in which security credentials will be utilized.

## Installing Identity Management for UNIX Components

To install one or all of the Identity Management for UNIX components on a Windows Server 2008 R2 server, perform the following steps from a domain controller:

1. Open Server Manager (Start, All Programs, Administrative Tools, Server Manager).

2. Expand the Roles node in the tasks pane, and select Active Directory Domain Services.

3. Right-click the Active Directory Domain Services role, and select Add Role Services. Check the box next to Identity Management for UNIX, which should automatically check the remaining boxes as well, as shown in Figure 9.5. Click Next to continue.

4. Review the installation options, and click Install to begin the process.

5. Click Close when complete, and choose Yes to restart the server.

6. After restart, the server should continue with the configuration of the server before allowing you to log on. Let it finish and click Close when the process is complete.

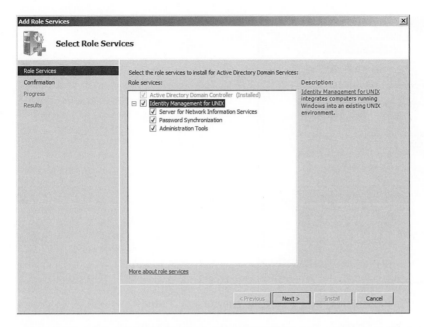

FIGURE 9.5    Installing the Identity Management for UNIX components.

## Configuring Password Change Capabilities

To enable password change functionality, a connection to a UNIX server must be enabled. To set up this connection, perform the following steps:

1. Open the MMC Admin console (Start, All Programs, Microsoft Identity Management for UNIX, Microsoft Identity Management for UNIX).

2. In the node pane, navigate to Password Synchronization, UNIX-Based Computers.

3. Right-click on UNIX-based Computers, and choose Add Computer.

4. Enter a name in the Computer Name text box, and specify whether to sync passwords to/from UNIX. Enter the port required for password sync and an encryption key that is mutually agreed upon by the UNIX server, similar to what is shown in Figure 9.6. Click OK.

5. Click OK to confirm the addition of the UNIX system.

## Adding NIS Users to Active Directory

For users who want their existing NIS servers to continue to provide authentication for UNIX and Linux servers, the SNIS component might not be the best choice. Instead, there is a package of Korn shell scripts downloadable from Microsoft.com that simplifies adding existing NIS users to AD. The getusers.ksh script retrieves a list of all users in a NIS database, including the comment field. This script must be run with an account with the permission to run ypcat passwd. The makeusers.ksh script imports these users to Active Directory. The makeusers.ksh script must be run by a user with domain admin privileges. The –e flag enables accounts—by default, the accounts are created in a disabled state. This

9

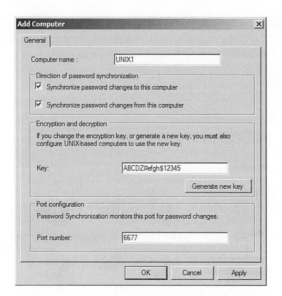

FIGURE 9.6    Configuring password sync to UNIX systems.

is a perfect solution for migrations that will require the existing NIS servers to remain intact indefinitely.

---

**NOTE**

For more advanced scenarios that involve automatic synchronization between UNIX NIS accounts and AD DS user accounts, including automatic provisioning/deprovisioning and attribute synchronization, consider using the Forefront Identity Manager (FIM) product from Microsoft. FIM's predecessor, ILM 2007, is covered in more detail in Chapter 8, "Creating Federated Forests and Lightweight Directories."

---

# Administrative Improvements with Windows Server 2008 R2

One of the main focuses of Windows Server 2008 R2 UNIX Integration was the ability to gain a better measure of centralized control over multiple environments. Tools such as an enhanced Telnet server and client, ActivePerl 5.6 for scripting, and a centralized MMC Admin console make the administration of the Windows Server 2008 R2 UNIX Integration components easier than ever. Combined with the improved MMC interface in Windows Server 2008 R2, it is easier than ever to manage mixed environments from the Windows platform.

## Performing Remote Administration with Telnet Server and Client

Windows Server 2008 R2 UNIX Integration uses a single Telnet service to provide for Telnet functionality to both Windows and UNIX clients. This was a change over the way that it previously was, as two separate components were installed. This version of Windows Server 2008 R2 Telnet Server supports NT LAN Manager (NTLM) authentication in addition to the basic logon that supports UNIX users.

To install the Telnet Server component, perform the following steps:

1. Open Server Manager (Start, All Programs, Administrative Tools, Server Manager).

2. Click on the Features node in the tasks pane, and then click the Add Features link.

3. Check the box next to the Telnet Server role, as shown in Figure 9.7. Click Next to continue.

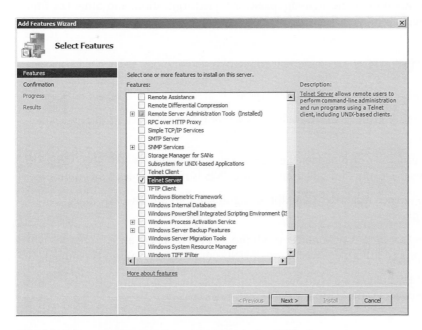

FIGURE 9.7    Installing the Telnet Server role for UNIX clients.

4. Review the settings and click Install.

5. When the wizard is finished, click Close.

## Scripting with ActivePerl

With Windows Server 2008 R2 UNIX Integration tools, you can write scripts using the ActivePerl tool, which was fully ported from UNIX Perl. Perl scripts can be used in a Windows environment, and ActivePerl directly supports use of the Windows Scripting Host (WSH), which enables Perl scripts to be executed on WSH server systems.

## Summary

Integration of key Microsoft technology with non-Microsoft environments is no longer an afterthought with the maturation of the three major products detailed in this chapter. No longer a separate product, integration with UNIX is built in to the OS with components such as Services for NFS, the Subsystem for UNIX-based Applications, and the Identity Management for UNIX components. Proper utilization of Windows UNIX integration components can help to lower the total cost of ownership associated with maintaining multiple platform environments. In addition, these technologies bring closer the lofty ideal of bringing multiple directory environments under a single directory umbrella through the realization of Single Sign-On, password synchronization, and other key functionality that integrates directories with Windows Server 2008 R2.

## Best Practices

The following are best practices from this chapter:

- ▶ Only install Server for NIS if the Windows server is not subservient to any UNIX NIS servers.

- ▶ Consider using the downloadable `getusers.ksh` and `makeusers.ksh` Korn scripts to create AD user accounts for NIS users if using SNIS is not possible in an environment.

- ▶ Use SUA to replace legacy UNIX scripts and run them in a native Windows environment.

- ▶ Use the ForeFront Identity Manager (FIM) product for more advanced scenarios where automatic provisioning/deprovisioning of UNIX and AD DS accounts is required.

- ▶ Use the AD DS Integration with Services for NFS, rather than the legacy User Name Mapping service, as integration is tighter with AD DS.

# Domain Name System and IPv6

Name resolution is a key component in any network operating system (NOS) implementation. The capability of any one resource to locate other resources is the centerpiece of a functional network. Consequently, the name-resolution strategy chosen for a particular NOS must be robust and reliable, and it ideally will conform to industry standards.

Windows Server 2008 R2 utilizes the domain name system (DNS) as its primary method of name resolution, and DNS is a vital component of any Active Directory implementation. Windows Server 2008 R2's DNS implementation was designed to be compliant with the key Request for Comments (RFCs) that define the nature of how DNS should function. This makes it particularly beneficial for existing network implementations, as it allows Windows Server 2008 R2 to interoperate with other types of RFC-compliant DNS implementations.

IPv6 is rapidly gaining traction in the IT world and is an integral feature of the Windows Server 2008 R2 operating system. Windows Server 2008 R2 supports IPv4 fully in roles such as DNS, Dynamic Host Configuration Protocol (DHCP), and Internet Information Services (IIS). Windows Server 2008 R2 even includes additional features such as the GlobalNames zone to support single-label names with IPv6.

This chapter details the key components of DNS in general and provides an overview of Windows Server 2008 R2's specific implementation of DNS. A particular emphasis is placed on the role of DNS in Active Directory Domain Services and the way it fits in standard and nonstandard configurations. Step-by-step instructions outline how to install and configure specific DNS components on Windows Server 2008 R2. In addition, troubleshooting DNS issues and specific Active Directory design scenarios helps to give a hands-on approach to your understanding of DNS.

# Understanding the Need for DNS

Computers and humans conceptualize in drastically different ways. In terms of understanding locations, humans are much better at grasping the concept of names rather than numbers. For example, most people think of cities by their names, not by their ZIP codes. Computers, however, work in binary, and subsequently prefer to work with numbers. For example, computers at the post office translate the city and address names into specific ZIP codes for that region, helping each letter reach its destination.

Name resolution for computer systems works in a similar way. A user-friendly name is translated into a computer-identifiable number. TCP/IP uses a number scheme that uniquely identifies each computer interface on a network by a series of numbers, such as 10.1.2.145, known as an IP address. Because most humans are not interested in memorizing several of these types of numbers, they must be easily resolvable into user-friendly names such as www.microsoft.com.

DNS, in its simplest form, provides for name resolution in a distributed fashion, with each server or set of servers controlling a specified zone and with entries for each resource called resource records (RRs) that indicate the location of a particular object.

A good analogy for DNS can be found in telephone books. Each city or metropolitan area (namespace) publishes a separate phone book (zone) that contains many listings (resource records) that map people's names to their phone numbers (IP addresses). This simple example illustrates the basic principle behind DNS. When you understand these basics, further drilling down into the specifics, especially with regard to Windows Server 2008 R2's DNS, is possible.

## Detailing the History of DNS

The Internet, as originally implemented, utilized a simple text file called a HOSTS file that contained a simple list of all servers on the Internet and their corresponding IP addresses. This file was copied manually from the master server to multiple secondary HOSTS servers. As more and more servers were added to the Internet, however, updating this file became unmanageable, and a new system became necessary.

In 1983, in direct response to this problem, the RFCs for the DNS were drawn up, and this form of name resolution was implemented on a large scale across the Internet. Instead of a small number of static HOSTS files, DNS servers formed a hierarchical method of name resolution, in which servers resolved only a certain segment of hosts on the Internet and delegated requests that it did not manage. This allowed the number of records held in DNS to scale enormously, without a subsequently large performance decrease.

Microsoft developed its own implementation of DNS in Windows NT 4.0, which was based on the RFC standards on which DNS was founded. With the introduction of Windows 2000, Microsoft adopted DNS as the principle name-resolution strategy for

Microsoft products. Older, legacy name-resolution systems such as Windows Internet Naming Service (WINS) are slowly being phased out. Since that time, the DNS implementation used by Microsoft has evolved to include a number of key benefits that distinguish it from standard DNS implementations—for example, UNIX BIND. To understand these improvements, however, you first need a basic understanding of DNS functionality.

## Establishing a Framework for DNS

DNS structure is closely tied to the structure of the Internet and often is confused with the Internet itself. The structure of DNS is highly useful, and the fact that it has thrived for so long is a tribute to its functionality. A closer examination of what constitutes DNS and how it is logically structured is important in understanding the bigger picture of how DNS fits into Windows Server 2008 R2.

## Explaining the DNS Hierarchy

DNS uses a hierarchical approach to name resolution in which resolution is passed up and down a hierarchy of domain names until a particular computer is located. Each level of the hierarchy is divided by dots (.), which symbolize the division. A fully qualified domain name (FQDN), such as server1.sales.companyabc.com, uniquely identifies a resource's space in the DNS hierarchy. Figure 10.1 shows how the fictional CompanyABC fits into the DNS hierarchy.

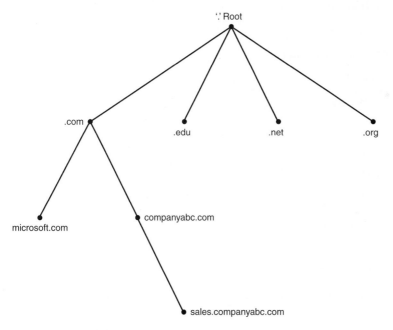

FIGURE 10.1    DNS hierarchy.

The top of the hierarchy is known as the root, and is represented by a single . (dot). Moving down the DNS hierarchy, the next layer in the model is made up of top-level domain (TLD) names, which are .com, .net, .gov, .fr, and similar domain namespaces that loosely define the particular category that a domain namespace fits into. The Internet Assigned Numbers Authority (IANA) oversees the global root zone management and management of the TLDs. The IANA is operated by the Internet Corporation for Assigned Names and Numbers (ICANN). The official list of all generic TLDs maintained by IANA is given in Table 10.1.

TABLE 10.1    List of Generic Top-Level Domain Names

| TLD | Purpose |
| --- | --- |
| .aero | Air Travel Industry |
| .asia | Asia-Pacific Region |
| .biz | Businesses |
| .cat | Catalan Language |
| .com | Commercial |
| .coop | Cooperatives |
| .edu | Educational Institutions |
| .gov | U.S. Government |
| .info | Informational |
| .int | International Organizations |
| .jobs | Companies (Job Postings) |
| .mil | U.S. Military |
| .mobi | Mobile Devices |
| .museum | Museums |
| .name | Individuals |
| .net | Network |
| .org | Organization |
| .pro | Professions |
| .tel | Internet Communications |
| .travel | Travel and Tourism Industry |

For example, educational institutions are commonly given .edu extensions, and commercial businesses are given .com extensions. These extensions form the first set of branches to the DNS tree. The .biz, .com, .info, .name, .net, and .org are all open TLDs, meaning any individual or entity can register the domains. Other TLDs have restrictions based on the intended use.

In addition to the generic TLDs, the IANA maintains country-code TLDs. These country codes are the two-letter codes specified in International Organization for Standardization (ISO) 3166 standard. For example, .co is maintained for Colombia and .fr is maintained for France. Interestingly, all the country-code TLDs listed in ISO 3166 are maintained, but some are unused, such as the Saint Martin (.mf). There are also a handful of exceptions, such as the listing for United Kingdom, which is listed in the ISO 3166 standard as .gb, but .uk is used instead.

The second level in the DNS hierarchy commonly contains the business name of an organization, such as companyabc in Figure 10.1. This level is normally the first area in the DNS hierarchy where an organization has control over the records within the domain and where it can be authoritative.

Subdomains can easily be, and often are, created in the DNS hierarchy for various reasons. For example, sales.microsoft.com is a potential domain that could exist as a sublevel of the microsoft.com domain. The DNS hierarchy works in this way, with multiple levels possible.

## Outlining the DNS Namespace

The bounded area that is defined by the DNS name is known as the DNS namespace. Microsoft.com is a namespace, as is marketing.companyabc.com. Namespaces can be either public or private. Public namespaces are published on the Internet and are defined by a set of standards. All the .com, .net, .org, and similar namespaces are external, or public. An internal namespace is not published to the Internet, but is also not restricted by extension name. In other words, an internal, unpublished namespace can occupy any conceivable namespace, such as dnsname.local or companyabc.internal. Internal namespaces are most often used with Active Directory because they give increased security to a namespace. Because such namespaces are not published, they cannot be directly accessed from the Internet.

# Getting Started with DNS on Windows Server 2008 R2

To fully understand the capabilities that Windows Server 2008 R2 offers for DNS, the product should be installed in a lab environment. This helps to conceptualize the various components of DNS that are presented in this chapter.

## Installing DNS Using the Add Roles Wizard

Although there are various ways to install and configure DNS, the most straightforward and complete process involves invoking the Add Roles Wizard and the subsequent Configure a DNS Server Wizard. The process detailed in this section illustrates the installation of a standard zone. Multiple variations of the installation are possible, but this particular scenario is illustrated to show the basics of DNS installation.

**NOTE**

It is recommended that DNS servers are configured with static IPv4 addresses because if the IP address changes, clients might be unable to contact the DNS server.

Installation of DNS on Windows Server 2008 R2 is straightforward, and no reboot is necessary. To install and configure the DNS service on a Windows Server 2008 R2 computer, follow these steps:

1. Launch Server Manager.
2. Select the Roles node and click the Add Roles link.
3. Click Next on the Before You Begin page.
4. Select the DNS Server role check box and click Next.
5. Click Next on the Introduction to DNS Server page.
6. Click Install on the Confirmation page to install the DNS role.
7. Click Close to exit the Add Roles Wizard.

The DNS role has been installed on the Windows Server 2008 R2 server, but has not been configured. To configure the role, execute the following steps:

1. Launch Server Manager.
2. Expand the Roles, DNS Server, DNS nodes, and then select the DNS server name.
3. Select Action, Configure a DNS Server.
4. On the Welcome page for the Configure a DNS Server Wizard, click Next to continue.
5. Select Create Forward and Reverse Lookup Zones (Recommended for Large Networks), and click Next.
6. Select Yes, Create a Forward Lookup Zone Now (Recommended), and click Next.
7. Select the type of zone to be created—in this case, choose Primary Zone—and click Next. If the server is a writable domain controller, the Store the Zone in Active Directory check box is available.
8. If storing the zone in Active Directory, select the replication scope and click Next.
9. Type the FQDN of the zone in the Zone Name box, and click Next.
10. At this point, if creating a non-AD-integrated zone, you can create a new zone text file or import one from an existing zone file. In this case, choose Create a New File with This File Name, and accept the default. Click Next to continue.
11. The subsequent page allows a zone to either accept or decline dynamic updates. For this example, enable dynamic updates by selecting the Allow Both Nonsecure and Secure Updates option button and clicking Next.

**NOTE**

Dynamic updates allow DNS clients to register and update their own resource records in the DNS zone. When enabling dynamic updates to be accepted by your DNS server, be sure you know the sources of dynamic updated information. If the sources are not reliable, you can potentially receive corrupt or invalid information from a dynamic update.

12. The next page allows for the creation of a reverse lookup zone. Here, select Yes, Create a Reverse Lookup Zone Now, and click Next.

13. Select Primary Zone for the reverse lookup zone type, and click Next.

14. If storing the zone in Active Directory, select the replication scope and click Next.

15. Accept the default IPv4 Reverse Lookup Zone, and click Next.

16. Type in the network ID of the reverse lookup zone, and click Next. (The network ID is typically the first set of octets from an IP address in the zone. If a Class C IP range of 192.168.3.0/24 is in use on a network, you would enter the values 192.168.3, as illustrated in Figure 10.2.)

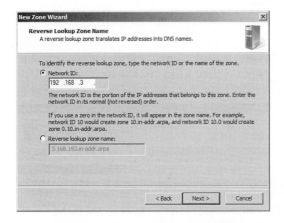

FIGURE 10.2    Reverse lookup zone creation.

17. Again, if creating a non-AD-integrated zone, you are offered the option to create a new zone file or to utilize an existing file. For this example, choose Create a New File with This File Name, and click Next to continue.

18. Again, you are presented the option for dynamic updates. For this example, select Allow Both Nonsecure and Secure Updates, and click Next to continue.

19. The next page deals with the setup of forwarders, which is described in more detail in the "Understanding DNS Zones" section later in this chapter. In this example, choose No, It Should Not Forward Queries, and click Next to continue.

10

20. The final window displays a summary of the changes that will be made and the zones that will be added to the DNS database. Click Finish to finalize the changes and create the zones.

---

**NOTE**

Depending on network connectivity, there might be a pop-up dialog box between the two clicks to finish the DNS changes in step 20. If you are not connected to a local area network (LAN), an error dialog box is displayed regarding searching for root hints. Although the dialog box notes the root hint error, clicking OK will still configure DNS successfully.

---

### Configuring DNS Server to Point to Itself

One subtask that should be accomplished after the installation is configuring the DNS server address in the TCP/IP settings to point to itself for DNS resolution, unless there is a specific reason not to do so. To accomplish this task, perform the following steps:

1. Launch Server Manager.
2. Click the View Network Connections link.
3. While in Network Connections, right-click the Local Area Connection icon and select Properties.
4. Double-click Internet Protocol Version 4 (TCP/IPv4).
5. In the DNS Server boxes, make sure that Use the Following DNS Server Addresses is selected and then type the IP address of the DNS server into the Preferred DNS Server box.
6. If you have another DNS server, you can enter it into the Alternate DNS Server box.
7. Click OK twice to complete the changes.

---

**NOTE**

Previous recommendations for Windows 2000 stipulated that a root DNS server point to another DNS server as the primary name server. This recommendation was made in response to what is known as the "island" problem in Windows DNS. Administrators will take heart in the fact that Windows Server 2003 and higher (including Windows Server 2008 R2) are no longer subject to this problem, and it is now recommended that you configure a DNS server to point to itself in most cases. You can find more information on this concept later in this chapter.

---

# Resource Records

In the DNS hierarchy, objects are identified through the use of resource records (RRs). These records are used for basic lookups of users and resources within the specified domain and are unique for the domain in which they are located. Because DNS is not a flat namespace, however, multiple identical RRs can exist at different levels in a DNS hierarchy. The distributed nature of the DNS hierarchy allows such levels.

Several key resource records exist in most DNS implementations, especially in those associated with Windows Server 2008 R2 Active Directory Domain Services. A general familiarity with these specific types of RRs is required to gain a better understanding of DNS.

## Start of Authority (SOA) Records

The Start of Authority (SOA) record in a DNS database indicates which server is authoritative for that particular zone. The server referenced by the SOA records is subsequently the server that is assumed to be the authoritative source of information about a particular zone and is in charge of processing zone updates. The SOA record contains information such as the Time to Live (TTL) interval, the contact person responsible for DNS, and other critical information, as illustrated in Figure 10.3.

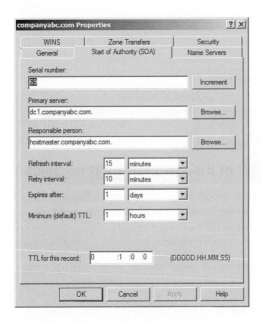

FIGURE 10.3   A sample SOA record.

An SOA record is automatically created when DNS is installed for Active Directory Domain Services in Windows Server 2008 R2 and is populated with the default TTL, primary server, and other pertinent information for the zone. After installation, however, these values can be modified to fit the specific needs of an organization.

## Host (A) Records

The most common type of RR in DNS is the host record, also known as an A record. This type of RR simply contains the name of the host and its corresponding IP address, as illustrated in Figure 10.4.

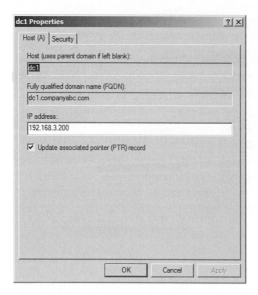

FIGURE 10.4    Sample host record.

The vast majority of RRs in DNS are A records because they are used to identify the IP addresses of most resources within a domain.

---

**NOTE**

Most resource records also contain advanced information about the record, which includes the Time to Live (TTL) and, optionally, the record time stamp. To view or update this information, select Advanced from the View menu of the DNS Management console.

---

## Name Server (NS) Records

Name Server (NS) records identify which computers in a DNS database are the name servers, essentially the DNS servers for a particular zone. Although there can be only one SOA record for a zone, there can be multiple NS records for the zone, which indicate to clients which machines are available to run DNS queries against for that zone.

---

**NOTE**

Name Server records, or NS records, do not actually contain the IP information of a particular resource. In fact, in most cases, only A records contain this information. NS records and other similar records simply point to a server's A record. For example, an NS record will simply point to server1.companyabc.com, which will then direct the query to the server1 A record in the companyabc.com zone.

---

## Service (SRV) Records

Service (SRV) records are RRs that indicate which resources perform a particular service. Domain controllers in Active Directory Domain Services are referenced by SRV records that define specific services, such as the global catalog (GC), Lightweight Directory Access Protocol (LDAP), and Kerberos. SRV records are a relatively new addition to DNS, and did not exist in the original implementation of the standard. Each SRV record contains information about a particular functionality that a resource provides. For example, an LDAP server can add an SRV record, indicating that it can handle LDAP requests for a particular zone. SRV records can be very useful for Active Directory Domain Services because domain controllers can advertise that they handle global catalog requests, as illustrated in Figure 10.5.

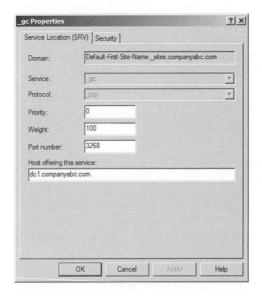

FIGURE 10.5   Sample SRV record for an AD GC entry.

**NOTE**

Because SRV records are a relatively new addition to DNS, they are not supported by several down-level DNS implementations, such as UNIX BIND 4.1.x and NT 4.0 DNS. It is, therefore, critical that the DNS environment that is used for Windows Server 2008 R2's Active Directory Domain Services has the capability to create SRV records. For UNIX BIND servers, version 8.1.2 or higher is recommended.

## Mail Exchanger (MX) Records

A Mail Exchanger (MX) record indicates which resources are available for Simple Mail Transfer Protocol (SMTP) mail reception. MX records can be set on a domain basis so that mail sent to a particular domain will be forwarded to the server or servers indicated by the MX record. For example, if an MX record is set for the domain companyabc.com, all mail sent to user@companyabc.com will be automatically directed to the server indicated by the MX record.

### Pointer (PTR) Records

Reverse queries to DNS are accomplished through the use of Pointer (PTR) records. In other words, if a user wants to look up the name of a resource that is associated with a specific IP address, he would do a reverse lookup using that IP address. A DNS server would reply using a PTR record that would indicate the name associated with that IP address. PTR records are most commonly found in reverse lookup zones.

### Canonical Name (CNAME) Records

A Canonical Name (CNAME) record represents a server alias, and allows any one of a number of servers to be referred to by multiple names in DNS. The record essentially redirects queries to the A record for that particular host. CNAME records are useful when migrating servers and for situations in which friendly names, such as mail.companyabc.com, are required to point to more complex server-naming conventions, such as sfoexch01.companyabc.com.

### Other DNS Record Types

Other, less common forms of records that might exist in DNS have specific purposes, and there might be cause to create them. The following is a sample list, but is by no means exhaustive:

▶ **AAAA**—Maps a standard IP address into a 128-bit IPv6 address. This type of record will become more prevalent as IPv6 is adopted and is discussed later in the chapter.

▶ **ISDN**—Maps a specific DNS name to an ISDN telephone number.

▶ **KEY**—Stores a public key used for encryption for a particular domain.

▶ **RP**—Specifies the Responsible Person for a domain.

▶ **WKS**—Designates a particular Well-Known Service.

▶ **MB**—Indicates which host contains a specific mailbox.

# Understanding DNS Zones

A zone in DNS is a portion of a DNS namespace that is controlled by a particular DNS server or group of servers. The zone is the primary delegation mechanism in DNS and is used to establish boundaries over which a particular server can resolve requests. Any server that hosts a particular zone is said to be authoritative for that zone, with the exception of stub zones, which are defined later in the chapter in the "Stub Zones" section. Figure 10.6 illustrates how different portions of the DNS namespace can be divided into zones, each of which can be hosted on a DNS server or group of servers.

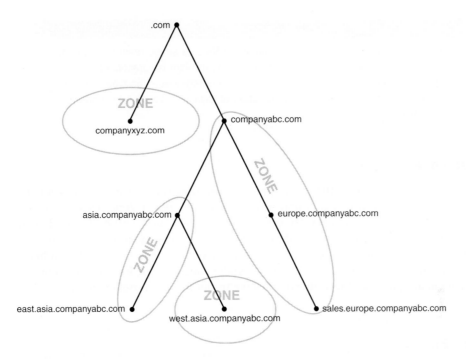

FIGURE 10.6    DNS zones.

It is important to understand that any section or subsection of DNS can exist within a single zone. For example, an organization might decide to place an entire namespace of a domain, subdomains, and subsubdomains into a single zone. Or specific sections of that namespace can be divided up into separate zones. In fact, the entire Internet namespace can be envisioned as a single namespace with . as the root, which is divided into a multitude of different zones.

> **NOTE**
>
> A server that is installed with DNS but does not have any zones configured is known as a caching-only server. Establishing a caching-only server can be useful in some branch office situations because it can help to alleviate large amounts of client query traffic across the network and eliminate the need to replicate entire DNS zones to remote locations.

## Forward Lookup Zones

A forward lookup zone is created to, as the name suggests, forward lookups to the DNS database. In other words, this type of zone resolves names to IP addresses and resource information. For example, if a user wants to reach dc1.companyabc.com and queries for its IP address through a forward lookup zone, DNS returns 172.16.1.11, the IP address for that resource.

10

> **NOTE**
>
> There is nothing to stop the assignment of multiple RRs to a single resource. In fact, this practice is common and useful in many situations. It might be practical to have a server respond to more than one name in specific circumstances. This type of functionality is normally accomplished through the creation of CNAME records, which create aliases for a particular resource.

## Reverse Lookup Zones

A reverse lookup zone performs the exact opposite operation as a forward lookup zone. IP addresses are matched up with a common name in a reverse lookup zone. This is similar to knowing a phone number but not knowing the name associated with it. Reverse lookup zones are usually manually created and do not always exist in every implementation. Creating a new zone using the Configure a DNS Server Wizard, as in the example earlier in this chapter, can automatically create a reverse lookup zone. Reverse lookup zones are primarily populated with PTR records, which serve to point the reverse lookup query to the appropriate name.

## Primary Zones

In traditional (non–Active Directory–integrated) DNS, a single server serves as the master DNS server for a zone, and all changes made to that particular zone are done on that particular server. A single DNS server can host multiple zones, and can be primary for one and secondary for another. If a zone is primary, however, all requested changes for that particular zone must be performed on the server that holds the master copy of the zone.

## Secondary Zones

A secondary zone is established to provide redundancy and load balancing for the primary zone. Each copy of the DNS database is read-only, however, because all record keeping is done on the primary zone copy. A single DNS server can contain several zones that are primary and several that are secondary. The zone creation process is similar to the one outlined in the preceding section on primary zones, but with the difference being that the zone is transferred from an existing primary server.

## Stub Zones

The concept of stub zones is unique to Microsoft DNS. A stub zone is essentially a zone that contains no information about the members in a domain but simply serves to forward queries to a list of designated name servers for different domains. A stub zone subsequently contains only NS, SOA, and glue records. Glue records are essentially A records that work in conjunction with a particular NS record to resolve the IP address of a particular name server. A server that hosts a stub zone for a namespace is not authoritative for that zone.

As illustrated in Figure 10.7, the stub zone effectively serves as a placeholder for a zone that is authoritative on another server. It allows a server to forward queries that are made to a specific zone to the list of name servers in that zone.

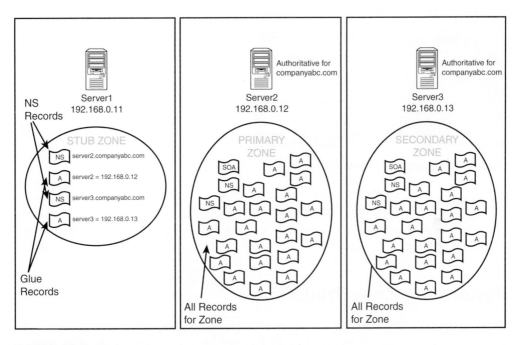

FIGURE 10.7    Stub zones.

You can easily create a stub zone in Windows Server 2008 R2 after the need has been established for this particular type of functionality. To create a stub zone, follow these steps:

1. Launch Server Manager.
2. Expand the Roles, DNS Server, and DNS nodes, and then select the server name.
3. Select the Forward Lookup Zones node.
4. Select Action, New Zone.
5. Click Next on the Welcome page.
6. Select Stub Zone from the list of zone types. Because this zone will not be AD-integrated, uncheck the Store the Zone in Active Directory check box if it is checked, and then click Next to continue.
7. Type in the name of the zone that will be created, and click Next to continue.
8. Select Create a New File with This File Name and accept the defaults, unless migrating from an existing zone file. Then click Next to continue.
9. Type in the IP address of the server or servers from which the zone records will be copied. Press Enter for each server entered, and they will be validated, as shown in Figure 10.8. Click Next to continue.

10

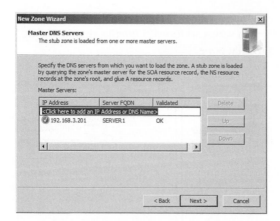

FIGURE 10.8    Entering stub master servers.

**10.** Click Finish on the Summary page to create the zone.

The newly created stub zone will hold only the SOA, NS, and glue records for the domain at which it is pointed.

# Performing Zone Transfers

Copying the DNS database from one server to another is accomplished through a process known as a zone transfer. Zone transfers are required for any non-Active Directory-integrated zone that has more than one name server responsible for the contents of that zone. The mechanism for zone transfers varies, however, depending on the version of DNS. Zone transfers are always pulled by the secondary servers from the primary servers.

Primary DNS servers can be configured to notify secondary DNS servers of changes to a zone and to begin a zone transfer. They can also be configured to perform a zone transfer on a scheduled basis. To set up a secondary server to pull zone transfers from a forward lookup zone, follow this procedure:

1. Launch Server Manager on the DNS server with the primary zone.
2. Expand the Roles, DNS Server, DNS nodes, and then select the server name.
3. Select the Forward Lookup Zones node.
4. Right-click the name of the zone and choose Properties.
5. Choose the Zone Transfers tab.
6. Check Allow Zone Transfers and select Only to the Following Servers.
7. Click Edit, type in the IP address of the server that will receive the update, and press Enter. The server will be validated, as shown in Figure 10.9. Because the server is not yet an authoritative server for the zone, the error message "The server with this IP address is not authoritative for the required zone" appears. This will be done in the next section. The error can be safely ignored. Click OK to save.

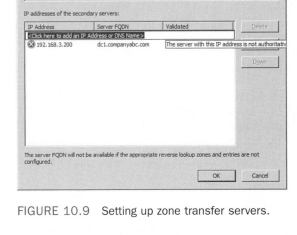

FIGURE 10.9    Setting up zone transfer servers.

8. To ensure that updates will be processed correctly, click the Notify button, enter the name of the secondary server, and press Enter. Click OK to save changes.

9. Click OK to save the changes.

> **NOTE**
>
> In addition to specifically defining recipients of zone transfer notifications by IP address, you can select the Only to Servers Listed on the Name Servers Tab option button as well, assuming that the recipient server or servers are listed on the Name Servers tab.

Now that the primary zone on the primary DNS server has been configured to allow transfers, the secondary zone has to be configured on the secondary DNS server. To create the secondary zone and begin zone transfers, execute the following steps:

1. Launch Server Manager.

2. Expand the Roles, DNS Server, DNS nodes, and then select the server name.

3. Select the Forward Lookup Zones node.

4. Select Action, New Zone.

5. Click Next on the Welcome page.

6. Select Secondary Zone from the list of zone types. Secondary zones cannot be AD-integrated and the options will be grayed out. Click Next to continue.

7. Type in the name of the zone that will be created (this should match the primary zone name), and click Next to continue.

8. Type in the IP address of the server or servers from which the zone records will be transferred. Press Enter for each server entered, and they will be validated. Click Next to continue.

**9.** Click Finish on the Summary page to create the zone.

After the last step, the zone will automatically transfer from the primary DNS server to the secondary DNS server.

## Performing Full Zone Transfers

The standard method for zone transfers, which transfers the entire contents of a DNS zone from the primary server to the secondary server, is known as asynchronous zone transfer (AXFR), or full zone transfer. This type of zone transfer copies every item in the DNS database to the secondary server, regardless of whether the server already has some of the items in the database. Older implementations of DNS utilized AXFR exclusively, and it is still utilized for specific purposes today.

## Initiating Incremental Zone Transfers

An incremental zone transfer (IXFR) is a process by which all incremental changes to a DNS database are replicated to the secondary DNS server. This saves bandwidth over AXFR replication changes because only the deltas, or changes made to the database since the last zone transfer, are replicated.

IXFR zone transfers are accomplished by referencing a serial number that is stored on the SOA of the DNS server that holds the primary zone. This number is incremented upon each change to a zone. If the server requesting the zone transfer has a serial number of 45, for example, and the primary zone server has a serial number of 55, only those changes made during the period of time between 45 and 55 will be incrementally sent to the requesting server via an IXFR transfer. However, if the difference in index numbers is too great, the information on the requesting server is assumed to be stale, and a full AXFR transfer will be initiated. For example, if a requesting server has an index of 25, and the primary zone server's index is 55, an AXFR zone transfer will be initiated, as illustrated in Figure 10.10.

# Understanding DNS Queries

The primary function of DNS is to provide name resolution for requesting clients, so the query mechanism is subsequently one of the most important elements in the system. Two types of queries are commonly made to a DNS database: recursive and iterative.

## Performing Recursive Queries

Recursive queries are most often performed by resolvers, or clients, that need a specific name resolved by a DNS server. Recursive queries are also accomplished by a DNS server if forwarders are configured to be used on a particular name server. A recursive query essentially asks whether a particular record can be resolved by a particular name server. The

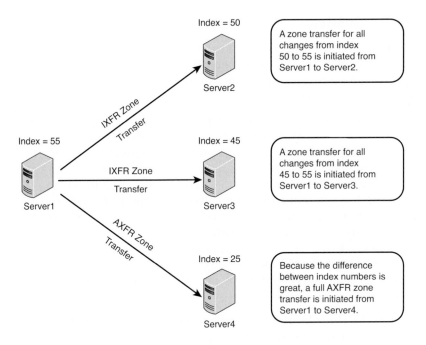

FIGURE 10.10   IXFR zone transfers.

response to a recursive query is either negative or positive. A common recursive query scenario is illustrated in Figure 10.11.

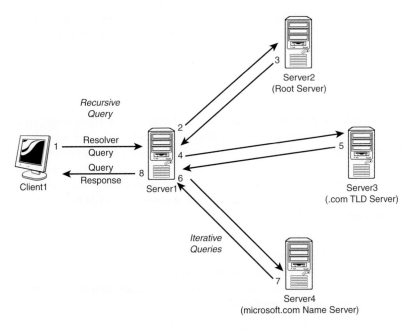

FIGURE 10.11   Recursive and iterative queries.

## Performing Iterative Queries

Iterative queries ask a DNS server to either resolve the query or make a best-guess referral to a DNS server that might contain more accurate information about where the query can be resolved. Another iterative query is then performed to the referred server and so on until a result, positive or negative, is obtained.

In the example shown in Figure 10.11, Client1 in CompanyABC opens a web browser and attempts to browse to the website for www.microsoft.com. A recursive query is initiated to the default name server; in this case, Server1 is contacted. Because Server1 is authoritative only for the companyabc.com namespace, and no entries exist for microsoft.com, the query is sent to an "upstream" DNS server that is listed in the root hints of the DNS server. That server, Server2, is not authoritative for microsoft.com but sends a referral back to Server1 for Server3, which is a name server for the .com namespace. Server3 knows that Server4 handles name-resolution requests for microsoft.com and sends that information back to Server1. A final iterative query is then sent from Server1 to Server4, and Server4 successfully resolves www to the proper IP address. Server1, with this information in hand, returns Client1's original recursive query with the proper IP address and Client1's browser successfully resolves www.microsoft.com.

This type of functionality lies at the heart of the distributed nature of DNS and allows DNS lookups to function as efficiently as they do.

# Other DNS Components

Several other key components lie at the heart of DNS and are necessary for it to function properly. In addition, you need to fully understand the functionality of several key components of DNS that are utilized heavily by Microsoft DNS.

## Dynamic DNS

Older versions of DNS relied on administrators manually updating all the records within a DNS database. Every time a resource was added or information about a resource was changed, the DNS database was updated manually, normally via a simple text editor, to reflect the changes. Dynamic DNS was developed as a direct response to the increasing administrative overhead that was required to keep DNS databases functional and up to date. With Dynamic DNS, clients can automatically update their own records in DNS, depending on the security settings of the zone.

It is important to note that only Windows 2000/XP and higher clients support dynamic updates and that down-level (NT/9x) clients must have DHCP configured properly for them to be updated in DNS. There are, however, security issues associated with this functionality that are detailed in subsequent sections of this chapter and are described further in Chapter 11, "DHCP/WINS/Domain Controllers."

## The Time to Live Value

The Time to Live (TTL) value for a RR is the amount of time (in seconds) that a resolver or name server will keep a cached DNS request before requesting it again from the original name server. This value helps to keep the information in the DNS database relevant. Setting TTL levels is essentially a balancing act between the need for updated information and the need to reduce DNS query traffic across the network.

In the example from the "Performing Iterative Queries" section, if Client1 already requested the IP address of www.microsoft.com, and the information was returned to the DNS server that showed the IP address, it would make sense that that IP address would not change often and could, therefore, be cached for future queries. The next time another client requests the same information, the local DNS server will give that client the IP address it received from the original Client1 query as long as the TTL has not expired. This helps to reduce network traffic and improve DNS query response time.

The TTL for a response is set by the name server that successfully resolves a query. In other words, you might have different TTLs set for items in a cache, based on where they were resolved and the TTL for the particular zone they originated from.

> **NOTE**
>
> The default TTL for manually created records in Windows Server 2008 R2 DNS is one hour. Records created dynamically via Dynamic DNS have a 20-minute default TTL.

The TTL setting for a zone is modified via the SOA record. The procedure for doing this in Windows Server 2008 R2 is as follows:

1. Launch Server Manager.
2. Expand the Roles, DNS Server, DNS, server name, and Forward Lookup Zones nodes.
3. Select the zone node.
4. Find the SOA record for the zone and double-click it.
5. Modify the Minimum (Default) TTL entry to match the TTL you want, as shown in Figure 10.12.
6. Click OK to accept the changes.

## Performing Secure Updates

One of the main problems with a Dynamic DNS implementation lies with the security of the update mechanism. If no security is enforced, nothing will prevent malicious users from updating a record for a server, for example, to redirect it to another IP address. This is known as DNS poisoning. For this reason, dynamic updates are, by default, turned off on new standard zones that are created in Windows Server 2008 R2. However, with AD-integrated DNS zones, a mechanism exists that allows clients to perform secure dynamic

10

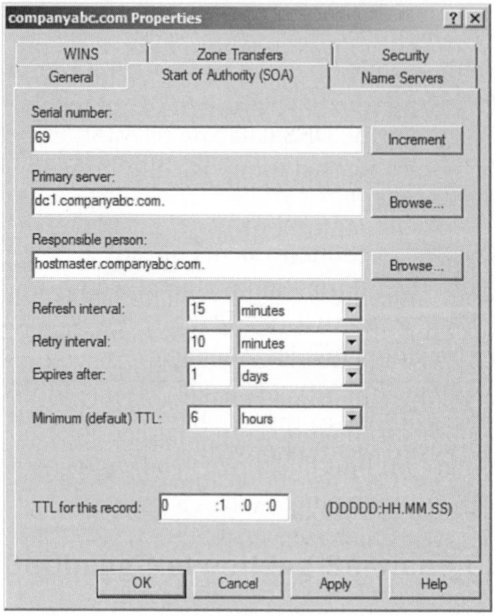

FIGURE 10.12   Changing the TTL.

updates. Secure updates utilize Kerberos to authenticate computers and ensure that only those clients that created a record can subsequently update the same record.

If you're using DHCP to provide secure updates on behalf of DHCP clients, one important caveat is that DHCP servers should not be located on the domain controller, if possible, because of specific issues in regard to secure updates. The reason for this recommendation is that all DHCP servers are placed in a group known as DNSUpdateProxy. Any members of this group do not take ownership of items that are published in DNS. This group was created because DHCP servers can dynamically publish updates for clients automatically, and the clients would need to modify their entries themselves. Subsequently, the first client to access a newly created entry would take ownership of that entry. Because domain controllers create sensitive SRV records and the like, it is not wise to use a domain controller as a member of this group, and it is subsequently not wise to have DHCP on domain controllers for this reason. If establishing DHCP on a domain controller is unavoidable, it is recommended to disable this functionality by not adding the server into this group.

## Exploring Aging and Scavenging for DNS

DNS RRs often become stale, or no longer relevant, as computers are disconnected from the network or IP addresses are changed without first notifying the DNS server. The process of scavenging those records removes them from a database after their original owners do not update them. Scavenging is not turned on, by default, but this feature can be enabled in Windows Server 2008 R2 by following these steps:

1. Launch Server Manager.

2. Expand the Roles, DNS Server, and DNS nodes, and then select the DNS server name.

3. Right-click the server name and choose Properties.

4. Select the Advanced tab.

5. Check the Enable Automatic Scavenging of Stale Records check box.

6. Select a scavenging period, as shown in Figure 10.13, and click OK to save your changes.

FIGURE 10.13    Turning on scavenging.

Scavenging makes a DNS database cleaner, but overly aggressive scavenging can also remove valid entries. Therefore, if you're using scavenging, it is wise to strike a balance between a clean database and a valid one.

## Examining Root Hints

By default, a DNS installation includes a listing of Internet-level name servers that can be used for name resolution of the .com, .net, .uk, and like domain names on the Internet. When a DNS server cannot resolve a query locally in its cache or in local zones, it consults the Root Hints list, which indicates which servers to begin iterative queries with.

The Hints file should be updated on a regular basis to ensure that the servers listed are still relevant. This file is located in \%systemroot%\system32\DNS\cache.dns and can be updated on the Internet at the following address:

ftp://ftp.rs.internic.net/domain/named.cache.

10

At the time of writing, the latest root hints file, or root name servers, was dated December 12, 2008. The contents are shown in Listing 10.1. You can see the root server names (such as "A.ROOT-SERVER.NET") and their A records (such as "192.41.0.4").

LISTING 10.1   Root Hints File Contents

```
;       This file holds the information on root name servers needed to
;       initialize cache of Internet domain name servers
;       (e.g. reference this file in the "cache  .  <file>"
;       configuration file of BIND domain name servers).
;
;       This file is made available by InterNIC
;       under anonymous FTP as
;           file                /domain/named.cache
;           on server           FTP.INTERNIC.NET
;       -OR-                    RS.INTERNIC.NET
;
;       last update:    Dec 12, 2008
;       related version of root zone:    2008121200
;
; formerly NS.INTERNIC.NET
;
.                           3600000  IN  NS   A.ROOT-SERVERS.NET.
A.ROOT-SERVERS.NET.         3600000      A    198.41.0.4
A.ROOT-SERVERS.NET.         3600000      AAAA 2001:503:BA3E::2:30
;
; FORMERLY NS1.ISI.EDU
;
.                           3600000      NS   B.ROOT-SERVERS.NET.
B.ROOT-SERVERS.NET.         3600000      A    192.228.79.201
;
; FORMERLY C.PSI.NET
;
.                           3600000      NS   C.ROOT-SERVERS.NET.
C.ROOT-SERVERS.NET.         3600000      A    192.33.4.12
;
; FORMERLY TERP.UMD.EDU
;
.                           3600000      NS   D.ROOT-SERVERS.NET.
D.ROOT-SERVERS.NET.         3600000      A    128.8.10.90
;
; FORMERLY NS.NASA.GOV
;
.                           3600000      NS   E.ROOT-SERVERS.NET.
E.ROOT-SERVERS.NET.         3600000      A    192.203.230.10
;
```

```
; FORMERLY NS.ISC.ORG
;
.                           3600000         NS      F.ROOT-SERVERS.NET.
F.ROOT-SERVERS.NET.         3600000         A       192.5.5.241
F.ROOT-SERVERS.NET.         3600000         AAAA    2001:500:2F::F
;
; FORMERLY NS.NIC.DDN.MIL
;
.                           3600000         NS      G.ROOT-SERVERS.NET.
G.ROOT-SERVERS.NET.         3600000         A       192.112.36.4
;
; FORMERLY AOS.ARL.ARMY.MIL
;
.                           3600000         NS      H.ROOT-SERVERS.NET.
H.ROOT-SERVERS.NET.         3600000         A       128.63.2.53
H.ROOT-SERVERS.NET.         3600000         AAAA    2001:500:1::803F:235
;
; FORMERLY NIC.NORDU.NET
;
.                           3600000         NS      I.ROOT-SERVERS.NET.
I.ROOT-SERVERS.NET.         3600000         A       192.36.148.17
;
; OPERATED BY VERISIGN, INC.
;
.                           3600000         NS      J.ROOT-SERVERS.NET.
J.ROOT-SERVERS.NET.         3600000         A       192.58.128.30
J.ROOT-SERVERS.NET.         3600000         AAAA    2001:503:C27::2:30
;
; OPERATED BY RIPE NCC
;
.                           3600000         NS      K.ROOT-SERVERS.NET.
K.ROOT-SERVERS.NET.         3600000         A       193.0.14.129
K.ROOT-SERVERS.NET.         3600000         AAAA    2001:7FD::1
;
; OPERATED BY ICANN
;
.                           3600000         NS      L.ROOT-SERVERS.NET.
L.ROOT-SERVERS.NET.         3600000         A       199.7.83.42
L.ROOT-SERVERS.NET.         3600000         AAAA    2001:500:3::42
;
; OPERATED BY WIDE
;
.                           3600000         NS      M.ROOT-SERVERS.NET.
M.ROOT-SERVERS.NET.         3600000         A       202.12.27.33
M.ROOT-SERVERS.NET.         3600000         AAAA    2001:DC3::35
; End of File
```

You can see the root hints for a Windows Server 2008 R2 DNS server by doing the following:

1. Launch Server Manager.
2. Expand the Roles, DNS Server, and DNS nodes, and then select the DNS server name.
3. Right-click the server name and choose Properties.
4. Select the Root Hints tab.

The name servers should match those in the root hints file retrieved from the Internic FTP site.

## Understanding the Role of Forwarders

Forwarders are name servers that handle all iterative queries for a name server. In other words, if a server cannot answer a query from a client resolver, servers that have forwarders simply forward the request to an upstream forwarder that will process the iterative queries to the Internet root name servers. Forwarders are often used in situations in which an organization utilizes the DNS servers of an Internet service provider (ISP) to handle all name-resolution traffic. Another common situation occurs when Active Directory's DNS servers handle all internal AD DNS resolution but forward outbound DNS requests to another DNS environment within an organization, such as a legacy UNIX BIND server.

In conditional forwarding, queries that are made to a specific domain or set of domains are sent to a specifically defined forwarder DNS server. This type of scenario is normally used to define routes that internal domain resolution traffic will follow. For example, if an organization controls the companyabc.com domain namespace and the companyxyz.com namespace, it might want queries between domains to be resolved on local DNS servers, as opposed to being sent out to the Internet just to be sent back again so that they are resolved internally.

Forward-only servers are never meant to do iterative queries, but rather to forward all requests that cannot be answered locally to a forwarder or set of forwarders. If those forwarders do not respond, a failure message is generated.

If you plan to use forwarders in a Windows Server 2008 R2 DNS environment, you can establish them by following these steps:

1. Launch Server Manager.
2. Expand the Roles, DNS Server, and DNS nodes, and then select the DNS server name.
3. Right-click the server name and choose Properties.
4. Select the Forwarders tab.
5. Click Edit to create forwarders.

6. Type in the IP address of the server or servers that will be forwarders. Press Enter for each server entered, and they will be validated. Click OK when you are finished.

7. If this server will be configured only to forward, and to otherwise fail if forwarding does not work, uncheck the Use Root Hints If No Forwarders Are Available check box.

8. Click OK to save the changes.

### Using WINS for Lookups

In environments with a significant investment in WINS, the WINS database can be used in conjunction with DNS to provide for DNS name resolution. If a DNS query has exhausted all DNS methods of resolving a name, a WINS server can be queried to provide for resolution. This method creates WINS RRs in DNS that are established to support this approach.

To enable WINS to assist with DNS lookups, follow these steps:

1. Launch Server Manager.

2. Expand the Roles, DNS Server, DNS, server name, and Forward Lookup Zones nodes.

3. Select the zone node.

4. Right-click the zone in question and choose Properties.

5. Choose the WINS tab.

6. Check the Use WINS Forward Lookup check box.

7. Enter the IP address of the WINS server(s), click the Add button, and then click OK to save the changes.

# Understanding the Evolution of Microsoft DNS

Windows Server 2008 R2's implementation of Active Directory Domain Services expands upon the advanced feature set that Windows 2000 DNS introduced and was expanded again in Windows Server 2003. Several key functional improvements were added, but the overall design and functionality changes have not been significant enough to change any Windows 2003 design decisions that were previously made regarding DNS. The following sections describe the functionality introduced in Windows 2000/2003/2008 DNS that has been carried over to Windows Server 2008 R2 DNS and helps to distinguish it from other DNS implementations.

## Active Directory-Integrated Zones

The most dramatic change in Windows 2000's DNS implementation was the concept of directory-integrated DNS zones, known as AD-integrated zones. These zones were stored in Active Directory, as opposed to a text file as in standard DNS. When the Active Directory was replicated, the DNS zone was replicated as well. This also allowed for secure updates, using Kerberos authentication, as well as the concept of multimaster DNS, in which no one server is the master server and all DNS servers contain a writable copy of the zone.

Windows Server 2008 R2, like Windows Server 2008, utilizes AD-integrated zones, but with one major change to the design. Instead of storing the zone information directly in the naming contexts of Active Directory, it is stored in the application partition to reduce replication overhead. You can find more information on this concept in the following sections.

## Dynamic Updates

As previously mentioned, dynamic updates, using Dynamic DNS (DDNS), allow clients to automatically register, update, and unregister their own host records as they are connected to the network. This concept was a new feature introduced with Windows 2000 DNS and is carried over to Windows Server 2008 R2.

## Unicode Character Support

Introduced in Windows 2000 and supported in Windows Server 2008 R2, Unicode support of extended character sets enables DNS to store records written in Unicode, or essentially multiple character sets from many different languages. This functionality essentially allows the DNS server to utilize and perform lookups on records that are written with nonstandard characters, such as underscores, foreign letters, and so on.

> **NOTE**
>
> Although Microsoft DNS supports Unicode characters, it is a best practice that you make any DNS implementation compliant with the standard DNS character set so that you can support zone transfers to and from non-Unicode-compliant DNS implementations, such as UNIX BIND servers. This character set includes a–z, A–Z, 0–9, and the hyphen (-) character.

# DNS in Windows Server 2008 R2

The Windows Server 2008 R2 improvements on the basic BIND version of DNS help to further establish DNS as a reliable, robust name-resolution strategy for Microsoft and non-Microsoft environments. An overall knowledge of the increased functionality and the structural changes will help you to further understand the capabilities of DNS in Windows Server 2008 R2.

## Application Partition

Perhaps the most significant feature in Windows Server 2008 R2 DNS implementation, Active Directory-integrated zones are stored in the application partition of the AD. For every domain in a forest, a separate application partition is created and is used to store all records that exist in each AD-integrated zone. Because the application partition is not included as part of the global catalog, DNS entries are no longer included as part of global catalog replication.

With the application partition concept, replication loads are now reduced while important zone information is delegated to areas of the network where they are needed.

## Automatic Creation of DNS Zones

The Configure a DNS Server Wizard, as demonstrated in "Installing DNS Using the Add Roles Wizard" section, allows for the automatic creation of a DNS zone through a step-by-step wizard. This feature greatly eases the process of creating a zone, especially for Active Directory. The wizard can be invoked by right-clicking on the server name in the DNS MMC and choosing Configure a DNS Server.

## Fix to the "Island" Problem

Earlier versions of the Microsoft DNS had a well-documented issue that was known as the "island" problem, which was manifested by a DNS server that pointed to itself as a DNS server. If the IP address of that server changed, the DNS server updated its own entry in DNS, but then other DNS servers within the domain were unable to successfully retrieve updates from the original server because they were requesting from the old IP address. This effectively left the original DNS server in an "island" by itself, hence the term.

Microsoft DNS fixed this problem in Windows Server 2003 and above. Windows Server 2008 R2 DNS first changes its host records on a sufficient number of other authoritative servers within DNS so that the IP changes made will be successfully replicated, thus eliminating this "island" problem. As a result, it is no longer necessary to point a root DNS server to another DNS server for updates, as was previously recommended as a method of resolving this issue.

## Forest Root Zone for _msdcs

In Active Directory, all client logons and lookups are directed to local domain controllers and global catalog servers through references to the SRV records in DNS. These SRV records were stored in a subdomain to an Active Directory domain that is known as the _msdcs subdomain.

In Windows Server 2008 R2, _msdcs is a separate zone in DNS, as shown in Figure 10.14. This zone, stored in the application partition, is replicated to every domain controller that is a DNS server. This listing of SRV records was moved mainly to satisfy the requirements of remote sites. In Windows 2000, these remote sites had to replicate the entire DNS database locally to access the _msdcs records, which led to increased replication time and

10

reduced responsiveness. If you delegate the SRV records to their own zone, only this specific zone can be designated for replication to remote site DNS servers, saving replication throughput and increasing the response time for clients.

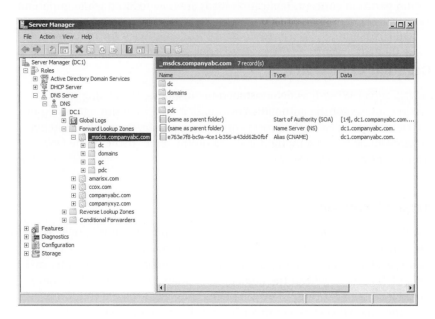

FIGURE 10.14    _msdcs zone.

# DNS in an Active Directory Domain Services Environment

DNS is inseparable from Active Directory. In fact, the two are often confused for one another because of the similarities in their logical structures.

Active Directory uses a hierarchical X.500-based structure that was designed to map into the DNS hierarchy, hence the similarities. In addition, Active Directory utilizes DNS for all internal lookups, from client logons to global catalog lookups. Subsequently, strong consideration into how DNS integrates with Active Directory is required for those considering deploying or upgrading AD.

## The Impact of DNS on Active Directory Domain Services

Problems with DNS can spell disaster for an Active Directory environment. Because all servers and clients are constantly performing lookups on one another, a break in name-resolution service can severely affect Active Directory functionality.

For this and other reasons, installing a redundant DNS infrastructure in any Active Directory Domain Services implementation is strongly recommended. Even smaller environments should consider duplication of the primary DNS zone, and nearly as much emphasis as is put into protecting the global catalog AD index should be put into protecting DNS.

Security considerations for the DNS database should not be taken for granted. Secure updates to AD-integrated zones are highly recommended, and keeping DHCP servers off a domain controller can also help to secure DNS (see previous sections of this chapter for more details on this concept). In addition, limiting administrative access to DNS will help to mitigate problems with unauthorized "monkeying around" with DNS.

## Active Directory Domain Services in Non-Microsoft DNS Implementations

Active Directory Domain Services was specifically written to be able to coexist and, in fact, utilize a non-Microsoft DNS implementation as long as that implementation supports dynamic updates and SRV records. For example, AD will function in all versions of UNIX BIND 8.1.2 or higher. With this point in mind, however, it is still recommended that an organization with a significant investment in Microsoft technologies consider hosting Active Directory DNS on Windows Server 2008 R2 systems because functionality and security enhancements provide for the best fit in these situations.

For environments that use older versions of DNS or are not able (or willing) to host Active Directory clients directly in their databases, Active Directory DNS can simply be delegated to a separate zone in which it can be authoritative. The Windows Server 2008 R2 systems can simply set up forwarders to the foreign DNS implementations to provide for resolution of resources in the original zone.

## Using Secondary Zones in an AD DS Environment

Certain situations in Active Directory require the use of secondary zones to handle specific name resolution. For example, in peer-root domain models, where two separate trees form different namespaces within the same forest, secondaries of each DNS root were required in Windows 2000 to maintain proper forestwide synchronization.

Because each tree in a peer-root model is composed of independent domains that might not have security privileges in the other domains, a mechanism will need to be in place to allow for lookups to occur between the two trees. The creation of secondary zones in each DNS environment will provide a solution to this scenario, as illustrated in Figure 10.15. Windows Server 2008 R2 now has the option of replicating these separate trees to all DNS servers in the forest, reducing the need for secondary zones. Replicating secondary zones outside of a forest is still sometimes necessary, however. Conditional forwarding and stub zones can also be used in certain cases to achieve a similar result without the need for data replication.

## SRV Records and Site Resolution

All Active Directory Domain Services clients use DNS for any type of domain-based lookups. Logons, for example, require lookups into the Active Directory for specific SRV records that indicate the location of domain controllers and global catalog servers.

10

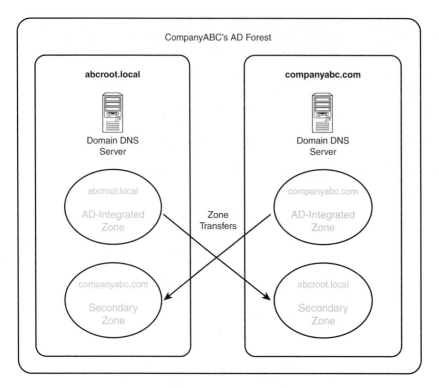

FIGURE 10.15    Peer-root domain DNS secondary zones.

Windows Server 2008 R2, as previously mentioned, divides the location of the SRV records into a separate zone, which is replicated to all domain controllers that have DNS installed on them.

Subdomains for each site are created in this zone; they indicate which resource is available in those specific sites, as shown in Figure 10.16. In a nutshell, if an SRV record in the specific site subdomain is incorrect, or another server from a different site is listed, all clients in that site are forced to authenticate in other sites. This concept is important because a common problem is that when Active Directory sites are created before they are populated with servers, an SRV record from the hub location is added to that site subdomain in DNS. When a new server is added to those sites, their SRV records join the other SRV records that were placed there when the site was created. These records are not automatically deleted, and they consequently direct clients to servers across slow wide area network (WAN) links, often making logon times very slow.

In addition to the site containers, the root of these containers contains a list of all domain controllers in a specific domain. These lists are used for name resolution when a particular site server does not respond. If a site domain controller is down, clients randomly choose a domain controller in this site.

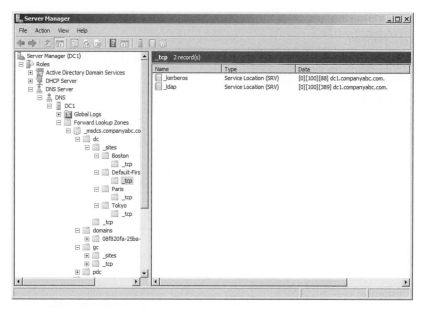

FIGURE 10.16    Site-level SRV records.

## GlobalNames Zone

In some cases, using a fully qualified domain name (FQDN) is not convenient for the end users. This is especially true for novice users or in the case of very long domain names. A user entering the uniform resource locator (URL) http://intranet.convergentcomputing. com is quite likely to make a mistake in the typing. The WINS name resolution provides relief from this, in that single-label names can be used instead. This allows the user to type the URL http://intranet and still reach the desired resource.

However, with the advent of IPv6, WINS will no longer be supported as the new address-ing is deployed throughout the organization. There are also many advantages of DNS over WINS, including reducing administrative overhead, single name resolution repository, security, and open standards.

Windows Server 2008 R2 provides a feature that was introduced in Windows Server 2008 to address this problem, specifically the GlobalNames zone (GNZ). This zone provides single-label name resolution via a DNS zone, similar to WINS. The zone is a normal forward lookup zone, albeit with a special name (GlobalNames), and is used by the DNS server in a special way. If the DNS server is unable to resolve an address in its local zones, it will then resolve the single-label address against the GlobalNames zone.

The GNZ holds out the promise of finally doing away with WINS and NetBIOS naming.

10

To configure the GlobalNames zone, execute the following steps:

1. Launch Server Manager.

2. Expand the Roles, DNS Server, and DNS nodes, and then select the server name.

3. Select the Forward Lookup Zones node.

4. Select Action, New Zone.

5. Click Next on the Welcome page.

6. Select Primary Zone and make sure that the Store the Zone in Active Directory check box is checked. Click Next.

7. Select To All DNS Servers in This Forest, and click Next.

8. Enter the Zone name GlobalNames and click Next.

9. Leave the default Dynamic Update setting and click Next.

10. Click Finish to create the zone.

11. Open a command prompt and enter the command `dnscmd /config /EnableGlobalNamesSupport 1`. The message "Registry property EnableGlobalNamesSupport successfully reset" should be returned. This command must be run on each DNS server that is expected to resolve GlobalNames, regardless of if the zone is replicated to them already.

Now the GlobalNames zone is ready to respond to queries. For any server that needs to respond to single-label queries, enter a CNAME record in the GlobalNames zone with the appropriate FQDN for the resource. The DNS server will try the GlobalNames zone after trying other local zones.

# Troubleshooting DNS

Much has been written about the complexity of DNS, and even more confusion and misconceptions have been written about it. In truth, however, DNS structure is logical, so you can easily troubleshoot it, if you use the proper tools and techniques. A good grasp of these tools and their functionality is a must for proper name-resolution troubleshooting with DNS.

## Using the DNS Event Viewer to Diagnose Problems

As any good administrator will know, Event Viewer is the first place to look when troubleshooting. Windows Server 2008 R2 makes it even more straightforward to use because DNS events compiled from Event Viewer are immediately accessible from the DNS Manager Console. Parsing this set of logs can help you troubleshoot DNS replication issues, query problems, and other issues.

For more advanced event log diagnosis, you can turn on Debug Logging on a per-server basis. It is recommended that this functionality be turned on only as required, however, as this can affect server performance and the log files can fill up fast. To enable Debug Logging, follow these steps:

1. Launch Server Manager.

2. Expand the Roles, DNS Server, DNS nodes, and then select the DNS server name.

3. Right-click the server name and choose Properties.

4. Select the Debug Logging tab.

5. Check the Log Packets for Debugging check box.

6. Configure any additional settings as required, and click OK.

By default, the log file is named dns.log and is saved in the c:\windows\system32\dns\ directory. Listing 10.2 shows the debug of the DNS server dc1.companyabc.com of a lookup of the record www.cco.com from the server at 192.168.3.201. You can see from the log that the request was forwarded to the DNS server at 192.168.2.5 and that the results were then sent to the requesting server at 192.168.3.201.

LISTING 10.2     DNS Log File

```
9/27/2009 11:52:03 AM 0388 PACKET  0000000002425D80 UDP Rcv 192.168.3.201    0002
Q [0001   D   NOERROR] A      (3)www(3)cco(3)com(10)companyabc(3)com(0)
9/27/2009 11:52:03 AM 0388 PACKET  0000000002425D80 UDP Snd 192.168.3.201    0002 R
Q [8385 A DR NXDOMAIN] A      (3)www(3)cco(3)com(10)companyabc(3)com(0)
9/27/2009 11:52:03 AM 0388 PACKET  000000000381E940 UDP Rcv 192.168.3.201    0003
Q [0001   D   NOERROR] AAAA   (3)www(3)cco(3)com(10)companyabc(3)com(0)
9/27/2009 11:52:03 AM 0388 PACKET  000000000381E940 UDP Snd 192.168.3.201    0003 R
Q [8385 A DR NXDOMAIN] AAAA   (3)www(3)cco(3)com(10)companyabc(3)com(0)
9/27/2009 11:52:03 AM 0388 PACKET  00000000032FF460 UDP Rcv 192.168.3.201    0004
Q [0001   D   NOERROR] A      (3)www(3)cco(3)com(0)
9/27/2009 11:52:03 AM 0388 PACKET  0000000003C74A00 UDP Snd 192.168.2.5      95b5
Q [1001   D   NOERROR] A      (3)www(3)cco(3)com(0)
9/27/2009 11:52:04 AM 0388 PACKET  0000000003138020 UDP Rcv 192.168.2.5      95b5 R
Q [8081   DR  NOERROR] A      (3)www(3)cco(3)com(0)
9/27/2009 11:52:04 AM 0388 PACKET  00000000032FF460 UDP Snd 192.168.3.201    0004 R
Q [8081   DR  NOERROR] A      (3)www(3)cco(3)com(0)
9/27/2009 11:52:04 AM 0388 PACKET  0000000002425D80 UDP Rcv 192.168.3.201    0005
Q [0001   D   NOERROR] AAAA   (3)www(3)cco(3)com(0)
9/27/2009 11:52:04 AM 0388 PACKET  00000000032FF460 UDP Snd 192.168.2.5      1240
Q [1001   D   NOERROR] AAAA   (3)www(3)cco(3)com(0)
9/27/2009 11:52:04 AM 0388 PACKET  0000000002F30BE0 UDP Rcv 192.168.2.5      1240 R
Q [8081   DR  NOERROR] AAAA   (3)www(3)cco(3)com(0)
9/27/2009 11:52:04 AM 0388 PACKET  0000000002425D80 UDP Snd 192.168.3.201    0005 R
Q [8081   DR  NOERROR] AAAA   (3)www(3)cco(3)com(0)
```

The DNS log can be very detailed and tedious to read, but provides a wealth of information about exactly what the DNS server is doing. You can get even more detail by selecting the Details check box on the Debug Logging tab, which also enables you to see the data

**10**

that was returned. Logging does add significantly to the load of the DNS server, so it should only be enabled when troubleshooting and disabled immediately afterwards.

## Using Performance Monitor to Monitor DNS

Performance Monitor is a built-in, often-overlooked utility that allows for a great deal of insight into issues in a network. In regard to DNS, many critical DNS counters can be monitored relating to queries, zone transfers, memory utilization, and other important factors.

## Client-Side Cache and HOST Resolution Problems

Windows 2000 and higher clients have a built-in client cache for name resolution that caches all information retrieved from name servers. When requesting lookups, the client resolver parses this cache first, before contacting the name server. Items remain in this cache until the TTL expires, the machine is rebooted, or the cache is flushed. In cases where erroneous information has been entered into the client cache, it can be flushed by typing `ipconfig /flushdns` at the command prompt.

By default, all clients have a file named HOSTS that provides for a simple line-by-line resolution of names to IP addresses. This file is normally located in `\%systemroot%\system32\drivers\etc`. Problems can occur when these manual entries conflict with DNS, and it is, therefore, wise to ensure that there are not conflicts with this HOSTS file and the DNS database when troubleshooting.

## Using the NSLOOKUP Command-Line Utility

The NSLOOKUP command-line utility is perhaps the most useful tool for DNS client troubleshooting. Its functionality is basic, but the information obtained can do wonders for helping to understand DNS problems. NSLOOKUP, in its most basic operation, contacts the default DNS server of a client and attempts to resolve a name that is inputted. For example, to test a lookup on www.companyabc.com, type `nslookup www.companyabc.com` at the command prompt. Different query types can also be input into NSLOOKUP. For example, you can create simple queries to view the MX and SOA records associated with a specific domain by following these steps, which are illustrated in Figure 10.17:

1. Open a command-prompt instance by choosing Start, All Programs, Accessories, Command Prompt.

2. Type `nslookup` and press Enter.

3. Type `set query=mx` and press Enter.

4. Type `<domainname>` and press Enter.

5. Type `set query=soa` and press Enter.

6. Type `<domainname>` and press Enter.

NSLOOKUP's functionality is not limited to these simple lookups. Performing an `nslookup /?` lists the many functions it is capable of. NSLOOKUP is a tool of choice for many name-resolution problems and is a must in any troubleshooter's arsenal.

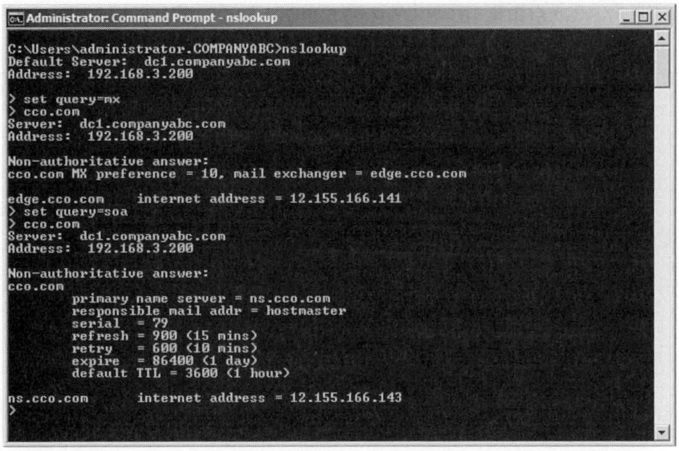

FIGURE 10.17    NSLOOKUP of an MX and an SOA record.

## Using the IPCONFIG Command-Line Utility

Another important tool for DNS resolution problems is the IPCONFIG utility, the same utility used for common TCP/IP issues. There are several key functions that IPCONFIG offers in regard to DNS. These functions can be invoked from the command prompt with the right parameter, detailed as follows:

- ▶ `ipconfig /flushdns`—If you experience problems with the client-side cache, the cache itself can be "flushed" through the invocation of the `flushdns` flag. This removes all previously cached queries that a client might be storing and is particularly useful if a server name has just changed IP addresses and particular clients have trouble connecting to it.

- ▶ `ipconfig /registerdns`—The `registerdns` flag forces the client to dynamically reregister itself in DNS, if the particular zone supports dynamic updates.

- ▶ `ipconfig /displaydns`—An interesting but not well-known parameter is `displaydns`. This flag displays the contents of the client-side cache and is useful for troubleshooting specific issues with individual records.

## Using the TRACERT Command-Line Utility

The TRACERT utility is a valuable resource that gives you an idea of the path that a DNS query takes when being sent over a network. By directing TRACERT at www.microsoft. com, for example, you can get an idea of how many routers and DNS servers the packet is crossing. The way that TRACERT works is simple, but actually quite interesting. A DNS query that has a TTL of 1 is sent out. Because all routers are supposed to drop the TTL by 1 on each packet that they process, this means that the first router will refuse to forward the packet and send that refusal back to the originator. The originating machine then increments the TTL by 1 and resends the packet. This time the packet will make it past the first router and get refused by the second. This process continues until the destination is met. Needless to say, using this command-line utility is a simple yet effective way of viewing the path that a DNS query takes as it crosses the Internet.

## Using the DNSCMD Command-Line Utility

The DNSCMD utility is essentially a command-line version of the MMC DNS console. Installed as part of the Windows Server 2008 R2 DNS Server role, this utility allows administrators to create zones, modify records, and perform other vital administrative functions via the command line. You can view the full functionality of this utility by typing DNSCMD /? at the command line, as illustrated in Listing 10.3.

LISTING 10.3    DNSCMD Command Options

```
Usage: DnsCmd <ServerName> <Command> [<Command Parameters>]


<ServerName>:
  IP address or host name      — remote or local DNS server
  .                            — DNS server on local machine
<Command>:
  /Info                        — Get server information
  /Config                      — Reset server or zone configuration
  /EnumZones                   — Enumerate zones
  /Statistics                  — Query/clear server statistics data
  /ClearCache                  — Clear DNS server cache
  /WriteBackFiles              — Write back all zone or root-hint datafile(s)
  /StartScavenging             — Initiates server scavenging
  /IpValidate                  — Validate remote DNS servers
  /ResetListenAddresses        — Set server IP address(es) to serve DNS requests
  /ResetForwarders             — Set DNS servers to forward recursive queries to
  /ZoneInfo                    — View zone information
  /ZoneAdd                     — Create a new zone on the DNS server
  /ZoneDelete                  — Delete a zone from DNS server or DS
  /ZonePause                   — Pause a zone
  /ZoneResume                  — Resume a zone
  /ZoneReload                  — Reload zone from its database (file or DS)
  /ZoneWriteBack               — Write back zone to file
  /ZoneRefresh                 — Force refresh of secondary zone from master
  /ZoneUpdateFromDs            — Update a DS integrated zone by data from DS
  /ZonePrint                   — Display all records in the zone
  /ZoneResetType               — Change zone type
  /ZoneResetSecondaries        — Reset secondary\notify information for a zone
  /ZoneResetScavengeServers    — Reset scavenging servers for a zone
  /ZoneResetMasters            — Reset secondary zone's master servers
  /ZoneExport                  — Export a zone to file
  /ZoneChangeDirectoryPartition — Move a zone to another directory partition
  /TrustAnchorsResetType       — Change zone type for a trust anchor zone
```

```
/EnumRecords              — Enumerate records at a name
/RecordAdd                — Create a record in zone or RootHints
/RecordDelete             — Delete a record from zone, RootHints, or cache
/NodeDelete               — Delete all records at a name
/AgeAllRecords            — Force aging on node(s) in zone
/TrustAnchorAdd           — Create a new trust anchor zone on the DNS server
/TrustAnchorDelete        — Delete a trust anchor zone from DNS server or DS
/EnumTrustAnchors         — Enumerate records at a name
/EnumDirectoryPartitions  — Enumerate directory partitions
/DirectoryPartitionInfo   — Get info on a directory partition
/CreateDirectoryPartition — Create a directory partition
/DeleteDirectoryPartition — Delete a directory partition
/EnlistDirectoryPartition — Add DNS server to partition replication scope
/UnenlistDirectoryPartition — Remove DNS server from replication scope
/CreateBuiltinDirectoryPartitions — Create built-in partitions
/ExportSettings           — Output settings to DnsSettings.txt in the DNS
server database directory
/OfflineSign              — Offline signing zone files, including key genera-
tion/deletion

<Command Parameters>:
 DnsCmd <CommandName> /? — For help info on specific Command
```

The /config option of the DNSCMD was used to set the Global Names option of the DNS server earlier in the chapter. There is no option in the DNS console to set this value.

# IPv6 Introduction

The Internet is running out of IP addresses. To resolve this problem, a relatively new technology is being deployed to give us more addresses. This technology is IPv6 and is completely integrated into Windows Server 2008 R2.

You might wonder why there is need for more address space when good old IPv4 provides somewhere in the range of four billion addresses. Unfortunately, there are over 6 billion people on the planet and, thus, not enough IP addresses for each and every person. In this age of ever-advancing technologies and Internet-enabled devices, it isn't uncommon for a single individual to utilize more than one IP address. For example, an individual might have an Internet connection at home, a workstation in the office, an Internet-enabled phone, and a laptop to use in a cafe. This problem will only become more exacerbated as devices such as refrigerators and coffeemakers become part of the wired world.

IPv6, Internet Protocol Version 6, not only brings a number of new features, as reviewed in Chapter 7, "Active Directory Infrastructure," such as integrated IPSec, QoS, stateless

10

configuration, and so on, but, more important, it will also provide over 340,000,000,000,000,000,000,000,000,000,000,000,000 unique addresses—that's 3.4 x $10^{38}$!

As mentioned in an earlier chapter, IPv6 provides a number of new features over IPv4: vastly improved address space, improved network headers, native support for auto address configuration, and integrated support for IPSec and QoS.

Windows Server 2008 R2's networking advances are mostly due to the new TCP/IP stack introduced with IPv6 in Windows Server 2008. Highlighted in the following list are a few of the features that are included with Windows Server 2008 R2, derived from the new TCP/IP stack:

> ▶ **Dual IP layer architecture for IPv6**—Windows 2003 required a separate protocol to be installed to enable IPv6 support; whereas in Windows Server 2008 R2, IPv6 is enabled and supported by default. Windows Server 2008 R2 supports the new stack that integrates IPv4 and IPv6, leveraging the fact that IPv4 and IPv6 share common layers (transport and framing).

> ▶ **Windows Filtering Platform**—All layers of the TCP/IP stack can be filtered, enabling Windows Filtering Platform to be more secure, stack integration.

> ▶ **Protocol stack off-load**—By off-loading TCP and/or other protocols to the Network Driver Interface Specification (NDIS) miniport and/or network interface adapters, performance improvements can occur on traffic-intensive servers.

> ▶ **Restart-less configuration changes**—Leveraging the new TCP/IP stack's ability to retain configuration settings, server restarts to enable configuration changes are no longer necessary.

In the United States, IPv6 is quietly making its way into the mainstream by starting at the edge. Broadband providers in California such as Comcast have already implemented IPv6 for their customers. Countries like China with their recent implementations have opted to move to IPv6 as a default.

---

**NOTE**

From an implementation perspective, Microsoft Internet Acceleration Server (ISA) 2006 does not support IPv6. As a matter of fact, installing the IPv6 protocol stack on an ISA 2006 server is a security risk as it exposes the server directly to the Internet. This has made it difficult for many organizations to start deploying IPv6 in a meaningful way.

One of the few IPv6 ready applications is the DirectAccess technology introduced in Windows Server 2008 R2. See Chapter 24, "Server-to-Client Remote Access and DirectAccess," for more details.

Going forward, Microsoft Forefront Threat Management Gateway 2010 (TMG) fully supports IPv6 and allows many organizations to step into the IPv6 world.

---

## IPv6 Addressing

With the increased address space, there is a change in the addressing. IPv6 is 128 bits, normally displayed in eight sets of four 16-bit hexadecimal digits. Hexadecimal digits range from A through F and 0 through 9 (see Table 10.2).

TABLE 10.2  Number Conversion

| Decimal | Hexadecimal | Binary |
| --- | --- | --- |
| 0 | 0 | 0000 |
| 1 | 1 | 0001 |
| 2 | 2 | 0010 |
| 3 | 3 | 0011 |
| 4 | 4 | 0100 |
| 5 | 5 | 0101 |
| 6 | 6 | 0110 |
| 7 | 7 | 0111 |
| 8 | 8 | 1000 |
| 9 | 9 | 1001 |
| 10 | A | 1010 |
| 11 | B | 1011 |
| 12 | C | 1100 |
| 13 | D | 1101 |
| 14 | E | 1110 |
| 15 | F | 1111 |

The reason for displaying the digits in hexadecimal is to cut down on the length of the address. For example, an IPv6 address in binary form would be as follows:

```
0010000000000001 0000110110111000
1111101110010010 0000000000000000
0000000000000000 0000000000000000
1001000111000010 0000000000010010
```

10

This makes for a very long address to have to type in. However, displayed in hexadecimal, the same address would be as follows:

`FC00:0db8:fb92:0000:0000:0000:91c2:0012`

This is much shorter. This can be abbreviated even more as the following:

`FC00:db8:fb92::91c2:12`

These methods of shortening the IPv6 address, such as the abbreviated form (more on this later in the chapter), help make the IPv6 addressing more manageable.

Still, this is a huge change from the 32-bit IPv4 addressing, where an address would be something like 172.16.1.11. Trying to remember 32 hexadecimal digits versus 4 decimal numbers is a significant change, when DNS itself was created so that users would not have to remember the 4 decimal numbers.

## Comprehending IPv6 Addressing

Comprehending IPv6 addressing can become a steep uphill challenge, as well as hard on the fingers due to all the typing. The addresses are so long that abbreviation mechanisms and conventions are used to ease the burden. However, this makes learning the addressing that much more difficult.

Here are a few rules and tips to assist with the future IPv6 change, as well as some conventions that reduce the typing needed to enter the addresses:

▶ IPv6 DNS records show as AAAA records (or quad A).

▶ With IPv6 prefixes, a / slash in IPv6 defines the network with addresses (for example, fc00:db8:1234::/48 is fc00:1234:5678:0000:0000:0000:0000:0000 through FC00:0db8:1234:FFFF: FFFF: FFFF: FFFF: FFFF). Thus, FC00:db8:1234::/48 implies that the first 48 bits are assigned to the network portion of the address—4 bits for each hexadecimal digit, visible or not, totaling 16 bits for each segment and 48 bits for three segments. This leaves 80 bits remaining out of a total of 128 bits in the address. 80 bits translates into five groups of four hexadecimal digits. Because each hexadecimal digit represents 4 bits, four multiplied by four, and then by five (for the five groupings), makes 80. After you get the hang of it, it is similar to dealing with "/24" being three groups of eight represented as 255.255.255.0 in IPv4.

▶ With IPv6 zero compression, consecutive groups of zeros can be subbed with a double ":" (colon). This means that FC00:db8:bc92:0000:0000:1293:91c2:0012 would be the same as FC00:db8:fb92::1293:91c2:0012.

---

**NOTE**

The caveat is that there can be only one double colon used in an IPv6 address to compress consecutive groups of zeros. Otherwise, it would not be possible to determine how many zeros were compressed.

---

► RFC 2732 dictates that IPv6 address can be used in a URL syntax. As an example, FBAC:FA9A:B6A54:3910:A81C:C1A8:B6A4:A2BB can be literally used in a URL as long as it is enclosed in brackets [ and ], as seen in this example: http://[FBAC:FA9A:B6A54:3910:A81C:C1A8:B6A4:A2BB].

► Loopback for IPv6 is ::1. This might be the only case where an IPv6 address is shorter than the equivalent IPv4 address.

These conventions make it much easier to enter the addresses, if not quite as easy as IPv4 addresses.

> **NOTE**
>
> The fc00::/7 prefix is the private reserved IPv6 address range. The private ranges in IPv6 are called the unique local addresses (ULA) and are not globally routable. This is equivalent to the 10.x.x.x, 172.16-31.x.x, and 192.168.x.x IPv4 private addresses.
>
> The unique local address range (fc00::/7) is further divided into 2 /8 address ranges. The first is the fc00::/8 range, which is available for private use. The second is the fd00::/8 range, which is to include a random 40-bit string. The local link address is assigned the fe80::/10 range, which is from the second range.

## IPv6 Transition Technologies

IPv6 is most likely to be deployed in an IPv4 world today, given the prevalence of IPv4 in the Internet today. This creates an IPv4 gap across which IPv6 devices need to communicate. Figure 10.18 shows the gap between IPv6 devices.

FIGURE 10.18    The IPv4 gap between IPv6 devices.

Most organizations will need to use IPv6 transition technologies to bridge the IPv4 gap from their IPv6-enlightened devices to communicate. Figure 10.19 shows the IPv4/IPv6 protocol stacks in place of the devices shown in the previous figure.

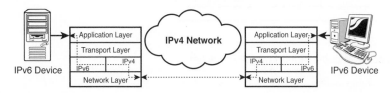

FIGURE 10.19    Bridging the IPv4 gap with transition technologies.

Communications between IPv6 devices (either hosts or routers) over IPv4 networks is accomplished with IPv6 over IPv4 tunneling. In tunneling, the IPv6 packets are encapsulated in an IPv4 packet by the source device and routed through the IPv4 network. When the encapsulated packet arrives at the boundary between the IPv4 and IPv6 networks, the IPv4 encapsulation is stripped off and the IPv6 packet continues on its way.

Older operating systems such as Windows 2003 and Windows XP implemented a dual protocol stack to support IPv6. This essentially duplicates the Transport layer, including the TCP and UDP protocols. These are the workhorse protocols of the Internet, and the dual-stack architecture is very inefficient and introduces a lot of overhead. Windows 2008 R2, Windows 2008, Windows 7, and Windows Vista have a modern protocol dual IP layer architecture that is designed from the ground up to support IPv6. This architecture is much more efficient and performs much better. Figure 10.20 shows the two architectures.

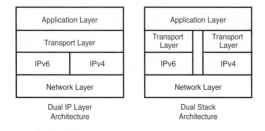

FIGURE 10.20    Dual IP layer and dual-stack architectures.

These transition protocols provide tunneling of IPv6 traffic through IPv4 network by encapsulating the IPv6 packet in an IPv4 packet, as shown in Figure 10.21.

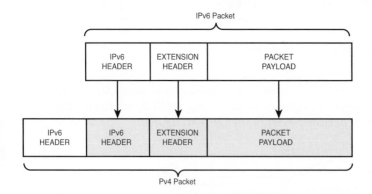

FIGURE 10.21    IPv6 packet encapsulation in an IPv4 packet.

The IETF RFC2893, "Transition Mechanisms for IPv6 Hosts and Routers," defines the IPv4 compatibility mechanisms for tunneling IPv6 over IPv4. The RFC defines two types of tunnels, specifically:

▶ **Configured tunnels**—These are tunnels that are manually configured with the static routes through the IPv4 network.

▶ **Automatic tunnels**—These tunnels don't require manual configuration, as they are derived from the IPv4 addresses of the devices. Windows supports the ISATAP, 6to4, and Teredo automatic tunneling protocols.

**NOTE**

In Windows, static tunneling routes can be added with the `netsh interface ipv6 add v6v4tunnel` command.

Most IPv6 tunnels are automatic tunnels, due to the ease of configuration. ISATAP and 6to4 are enabled by default on Windows Server 2008, Windows Server 2008 R2, Windows Vista, and Windows 7.

## The ISATAP Tunneling Protocol

The Intra-Site Automatic Tunnel Addressing Protocol (ISATAP) is an IPv6 transition protocol. It provides for the automatic conversion of an IPv4 address to an IPv6 address, as well as a mechanism for setting up a virtual IPv6 network that transmits over an IPv4 network. The protocol does not require any manual configuration.

**NOTE**

Link-local addresses are network addresses that are only designed to communicate on a segment and basically allow communications with neighboring devices without needing a globally routable address. They are mandatory in IPv6 and are automatically assigned with the FE80::/10 prefix.

The components of ISATAP are the following:

▶ **ISATAP host**—The ISATAP host communicates IPv6 over IPv4 networks with other ISATAP hosts and with ISATAP routers.

▶ **ISATAP router**—The ISATAP router advertises address prefixes to the local ISATAP subnet, forwards ISATAP traffic to IPv6 networks, and acts as the default route for ISATAP hosts.

This is useful for deploying IPv6 without having to explicitly define and configure a IPv6 network addressing scheme because it allows IPv6 devices to communicate over IPv4 networks. Figure 10.22 illustrates the ISATAP network.

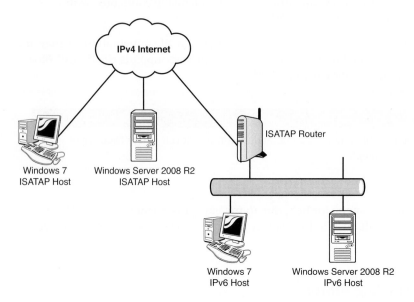

FIGURE 10.22    ISATAP network.

The Windows Vista RTM, Windows Server 2003, and Windows XP all automatically enable and configure the ISATAP tunneling adapter if the IPv6 protocol is installed. These operating systems use the name Automatic Tunneling Pseudo-Interface rather than ISATAP to identify the adapter.

The Windows Server 2008 R2, Windows 2008, Windows 7, and Windows Vista SP1 operating systems do not enable the ISATAP tunneling adapter unless they can resolve the name "ISATAP" in to an IPv4 address. The ISATAP address is the IPv4 address of the local ISATAP router. The name resolution can use any of the standard methods to resolve, including DNS, WINS, NetBIOS broadcast, or the LMHOSTS file. When these operating systems are able to resolve the ISATAP address, they configure the ISATAP tunneling adapter and add a default route of ::/0 to the link-local address of the ISATAP router.

ISATAP address IPv4 to IPv6 address translation is done by concatenating a 64-bit prefix with :0000:5EFE:w.x.y.z, where w.x.y.z is the IPv4 address in dotted decimal format. The prefix can be a link-local prefix (that is, FE80::/64), a global prefix (for example, FC00:1234:5678:9abc::/64), or even a global 6to4 prefix (for example, 2002:c9b:a602:1:0::/64), discussed in the next section. Table 10.3 lists some example values for IP address conversions in ISATAP.

TABLE 10.3    Example ISATAP IP Address Conversions

| IPv4 Address | IPv6 ISATAP Address |
|---|---|
| 12.155.166.101 | 2002:c9b:a602:1:0:5EFE:12.155.166.101 |
| 192.168.2.5 | FE80::5EFE:192.168.2.5 |
| 10.12.1.1 | FC00:1234:5678:9abc:5EFE:10.12.1.1 |

**NOTE**

The format FE80::5EFE:w.x.y.z is functionally equivalent to the format FE80::5EFE:WWXX:YYZZ, where the dotted decimal IPv4 address format is converted to hexadecimal format. Each decimal number (for example, w) is converted to a two-digit hexadecimal number (for example, WW). In the first example above, the IPv6 address FE80::5EFE:12.155.166.101 would be expressed as FE80::5EFE:0C9B:A665. This format is known as the colon hexadecimal format.

## The 6to4 Tunneling Protocol

The 6to4 protocol provides for automatic address assignment and tunneling of IPv6 across the IPv4 Internet. The protocol is detailed in IETF RFC3056. The 6to4 protocol uses the prefix 2002::/16—otherwise known as a 6to4 address.

The global address prefix for a given organization takes the form 2002:WWXX:YYZZ::/48, where WWXX:YYZZ is the colon hexadecimal format of the organization's public IPv4 dotted decimal address w.x.y.z assigned to the router.

**NOTE**

The 6to4 protocol only supports IPv6 computer to IPv6 computer communications. It does not support communications between IPv6 and IPv4 computers. Both endpoints must support IPv6.

The 6to4 protocol allows organizations to assign globally routable IPv6 address without needing to connect to the IPv6 Internet or to request an assigned range of IPv6 addresses. Because the IPv6 address is derived from the public assigned IPv4 address, it is guaranteed to be unique.

In addition, the 6to4 address supports a subnet field for organizations with IPv4 subnet address ranges. The format of the 6to4 IPv6 address is shown in Figure 10.23. For example, the public IPv4 address 12.155.166.101 with subnet 255.255.255.128 would automatically generate the global IPv6 prefix 2002:C9B:A665:80::/64.

10

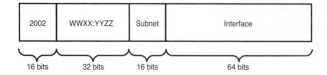

FIGURE 10.23    6to4 IPv6 address format.

Table 10.4 lists some example values for IP address conversions in 6to4.

TABLE 10.4    Example 6to4 IP Address Conversions

| IPv4 Address | IPv6 6to4 Address |
| --- | --- |
| 12.155.166.101 | 2002:C9B:A665:1:: C9B:A665 |
| 65.55.12.249 | 2002:4137:CF9:1: :4137:CF9 |
| 144.48.9.14 | 2002:9030:90E:1::9030:90E |

The 6to4 protocol defines several components that participate in the transmission of packets. These are as follows:

▶ **6to4 host**—A IPv6 device that is configured with a 6to4 address (that is, a 2002::/16 prefix).

▶ **6to4 router**—Routes IPv6 traffic over the IPv4 Internet using 6to4 tunneling.

▶ **6to4 host/router**—An IPv6 device that is configured with a 6to4 address and can also use 6to4 tunneling to communicate with other 6to4 devices over the IPv4 Internet. However, it does not route traffic to other devices.

▶ **6to4 relay**—Forwards 6to4 traffic between the IPv4 Internet and pure IPv6 devices.

Essentially, 6to4 and its components allow IPv6 devices to communicate while residing in the IPv4 world. Figure 10.24 shows the components of 6to4.

Windows Server 2008 R2, Windows 2008, Windows 7, and Windows Vista can function as a 6to4 host/router or a 6to4 router. By default, these operating systems operate as 6to4 host/router components. The Windows IPv6 protocol automatically does the following if there is a public IPv4 address assigned to a network interface:

1. Creates a 6to4 tunnel adapter and assigns it a 6to4 address in the form 2002:WWXX:YYZZ::WWXX:YYZZ for each of the public addresses.

2. Creates a 2002::/16 route to forward all 6to4 addresses to the tunnel adapter.

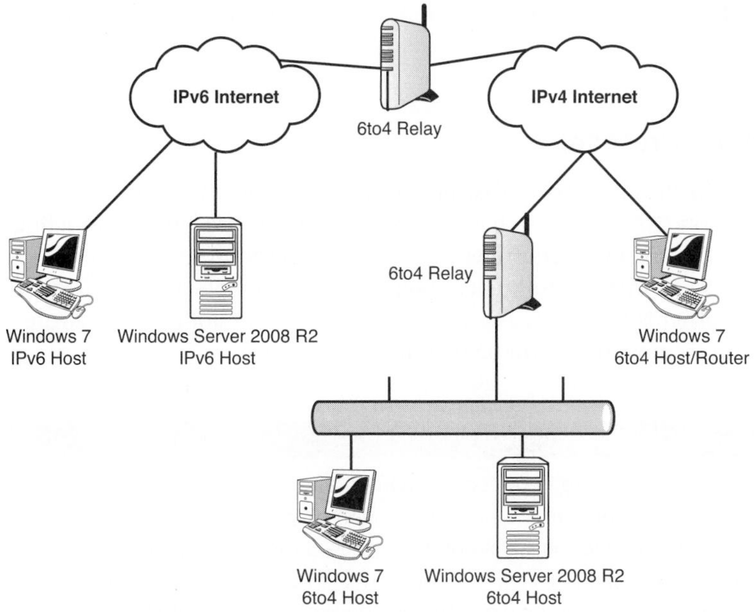

FIGURE 10.24    6to4 network.

3. Does a lookup of the FQDN 6to4.ipv6.microsoft.com will give a 6to4 relay address. That address is set as the next hop for the 6to4 tunnel adapter.

---

**NOTE**

The FQDN 6to4.ipv6.microsoft.com is the address of the 6to4 relay that is operated by Microsoft and allows 6to4 access to the IPv6 Internet. This is a service that Microsoft provides to help with the integration of Microsoft operating systems with IPv6.

---

To have a system operate as a 6to4 router component, the Internet Connection Sharing (ICS) feature must be enabled. If ICS is enabled on network interface with an IPv4 address, the IPv6 protocol automatically does the following:

1. Enables IPv6 forwarding on the 6to4 tunneling adapter and on any private network interfaces.
2. Assigns a 6to4 subnet prefix of the form 2002:WWXX:YYZZ:I::/64, where WWXX:YYZZ is the colon hexadecimal form of the IPv4 public IP address and I is the interface index of the private network interface.
3. Sends router advertisements on the private network interface.

For any traffic forwarded to other 6to4 sites, the Windows 6to4 router uses the default 2002::/16 route.

## The Teredo Tunneling Protocol

The Teredo tunneling protocol is a protocol that provides IPv6 connectivity through Network Address Translation (NAT) devices that are not IPv6 aware. The Teredo tunneling protocol is described in IETF RFC4380. The Teredo protocol gets around the requirement of the 6to4 tunneling protocol that the tunnel endpoint be a public IPv4 address. The reality of today's IPv4 Internet is that there is a scarcity of public IPv4 address (the entire rational behind IPv6) and so most hosts will be behind a NAT device.

> **NOTE**
>
> Perhaps less than fortuitously, the Teredo protocol is named after the shipworm "Teredo navalis," which tunneled through the hulls of wooden ships and sank many a vessel back in the day. These marine mollusks continue to be a threat today to any wood structure in seawater, like dikes, docks, and piers. The Teredo protocol tunnels through NAT firewalls in much the same fashion. The Teredo protocol was initially named the "Shipworm" protocol, but that made it seem too much like malicious software, and it was renamed to Teredo.

Teredo encapsulates the IPv6 packets twice: once to encapsulate the IPv6 packet in an IPv4 packet with the IPv4 protocol field set to 41, and a second time to put the resulting IPv4 packet in the message of a IPv4 UDP packet. This double encapsulation gets through the NAT but comes at a heavy cost in protocol overhead. In addition, the Teredo tunnel also exposes the host to scanning attacks because the Teredo tunneling adapter in effect opens a port on the host to entities through the firewall. This port can be discovered and attacked. Thus, due to the overhead and security concerns, the Teredo tunneling protocol is really a tunneling protocol of last resort.

Microsoft's implementation of the Teredo protocol includes additional measures against IPv6 scanning attacks, including an option of which traffic to accept: from anywhere except the Teredo tunnel (the default), from anywhere including the Teredo tunnel, or only from the local Intranet. The default option prevents scanning of the Teredo tunnel interface. Of course, the host can initiate traffic through the tunnel.

Teredo clients use IPv6 addresses that start with the prefix 2001::/32, otherwise known as the Teredo prefix. The address is somewhat more complicated than the addressing for the other tunneling protocols. The elements of the Teredo address are the following:

▶ **Teredo prefix (32 bits)**—This is 2001 for all Teredo addresses, per IETF RFC4380.

▶ **Teredo server IPv4 address (32 bits)**—The IPv4 address of the Teredo Server in colon hexadecimal format.

▶ **Flags (16 bits)**—This includes a bit for the type of NAT. Microsoft uses two of the bits to set the Universal/Local flag and the Individual/Group flag for the enhanced security. The remaining bits are set to a random number to make scanning attacks more difficult.

▶ **Obscured external port (16 bits)**—This is the external UDP port that is assigned by the NAT, but is obscured by an XOR it with FFFF.

▶ **Obscured external address (32 bits)**—This is the IPv4 external address of the NAT, but it is obscured by an XOR with FFFFFFFF.

Figure 10.25 shows the structure of a Teredo address.

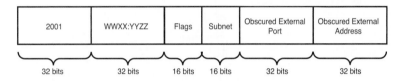

| 2001 | WWXX:YYZZ | Flags | Subnet | Obscured External Port | Obscured External Address |
|---|---|---|---|---|---|
| 32 bits | 32 bits | 16 bits | 16 bits | 32 bits | 32 bits |

FIGURE 10.25    Teredo IPv6 address format.

Because of the flag randomization, UDP port assignment, and the obscuring, the final Teredo addresses will vary considerably even within the same Teredo client.

Teredo tunneling components include the following:

▶ **Teredo client**—This is an IPv6/IPv4 device that has a Teredo tunneling adapter and communicates with other Teredo clients or IPv6 networks via a Teredo Relay. The Teredo client is typically behind a NAT.

▶ **Teredo server**—This is an IPv6/IPv4 device that is connected to both the IPv6 and IPv4 networks. The Teredo server assists with the configuration of Teredo clients.

▶ **Teredo relay**—This is an IPv6/IPv4 device that is connected to IPv6 and IPv4 networks. The Teredo relay routes between Teredo clients and IPv6 hosts in the IPv6 network.

▶ **Teredo host-specific relay**—This is an IPv6/IPv4 device that is connected to IPv6 and IPv4 networks. It can communicate with the IPv6 network, the IPv4 network, and Teredo clients without a Teredo relay.

Figure 10.26 shows the components of Teredo.

10

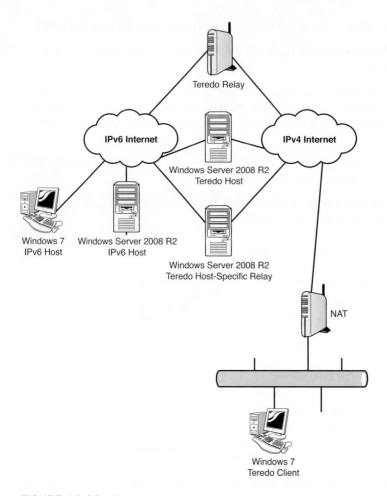

FIGURE 10.26    Teredo network.

Windows Server 2008 R2, Windows Server 2008, Windows 7, and Windows Vista can all operate as Teredo clients and Teredo host-specific relays.

The Windows Teredo clients send Router Solicitation messages to Teredo servers. These responses to the router solicitation messages are used to build the Teredo address and what type of NAT is in place.

> **NOTE**
>
> The command `netsh interface ipv6 show teredo` can be used to see how the Teredo client configured itself.

Once the Teredo address has been determined, the Teredo client can then communicate with Teredo clients. This is facilitated by the Teredo server, which brokers communications between the two Teredo clients during the initial start of communications. Following the initial setup of communications, the two Teredo clients communicate directly.

## NAT-PT Devices

Internally, IPv6 devices can use Network Address Translation-Protocol Translation (NAT-PT) devices, which can be used to provide access to IPv4 resources. Resources that don't support IPv6 natively can be accessed through the use of a Network Address Translation-Protocol Translation (NAT-PT) device. Microsoft Windows Server 2008 R2 does not currently include that capability, so a third-party device would be needed for this functionality.

> **NOTE**
>
> NAT-PT is covered in IETF RFC-2766 (http://tools.ietf.org/html/rfc2766), but was reclassified from a Proposed Standard to Historic due to issues with the standard. RFC4966 (http://tools.ietf.org/html/rfc4966) contains the details of these issues. These include difficulty with integrity mechanisms, inability to redirect protocols that lack demultiplexing capabilities, premature state timeouts, loss of information due to IPv4 and IPv6 header incompatibilities, packet fragmentation issues, and an inability to handle multicast traffic. NAT-PT devices are only recommended as a stop-gap measure due to these issues.

As long as all Intranet resources that IPv6 clients need to reach support IPv6, then there should be no need for NAT-PT devices.

# How to Configure IPv6 on Windows Server 2008 R2

Many of the tasks for configuring IPv6 are exactly the same as those for IPv4 addresses, albeit with longer addresses to type. This includes manually setting IP addressing, creating DHCP scopes, and creating DNS host records. The steps in this section walk through some of the administrator tasks for configuring IPv6 on Windows Server 2008 R2.

## Manually Setting the IPv6 Address

On many occasions, it is necessary to set the IP addresses manually. This is normally the case for servers, routers, and other devices that have static IP addresses.

To set the IPv6 addressing of a Windows Server 2008 R2 server, execute the following steps:

1. Launch Server Manager.
2. Click on View Network Connections from the options in the left pane of the window.
3. Right-click on the desired Local Area Connection, and select Properties.
4. Click Internet Protocol Version 6 (TCP/IPv6), and select Properties. If the item is not enabled, check the box first.

10

5. Click the Use the Following IPv6 Address option button.

6. In the IPv6 Address field, type in Fc00:1234:5678:9abc::2, and then press Tab. Notice that the Subnet Prefix Length field auto-populates with "64." Leave that in place and press Tab to move to the Default Gateway input field.

7. Enter Fc00:1234:5678:9abc::1 for the default gateway.

8. Press Tab again to move to the Use the Following DNS Server Address field. Then press Tab to move to the Preferred DNS Server input field. For this example, use the IPv6 address for this server. In the Preferred DNS Server field, type in the sample IPv6 address Fc00:1234:5678:9abc::2 and leave the Alternate DNS Server field blank. The settings should match those shown in Figure 10.27.

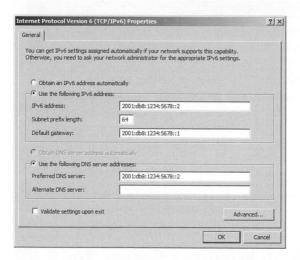

FIGURE 10.27    IPv6 settings.

9. Click OK to close the IPv6 Properties window. Click Close to close the Local Area Connection Properties window.

**NOTE**

The IPv6 prefix Fc00:1234:5678:9abc::/64 for the address Fc00:1234:5678:9abc::2 is a ULA—that is, a private non-globally routable address.

The DNS server also needs to have a reverse lookup zone created to allow computers to register their IPv6 addresses. This is separate from the IPv4 reverse lookup zone created earlier in the chapter, although it serves the same purpose. To create the IPv6 reverse lookup zone, perform the following steps:

1. Launch Server Manager on the DNS server.

2. Expand the Roles node, DNS Server node, DNS node, and the server node, and select the Reverse Lookup Zones node.

3. Right-click the Reverse Lookup Zones node and select New Zone.

4. Click Next at the Welcome screen.

5. Ensure that Primary Zone and Store the Zone in Active Directory are selected, and then click Next.

6. Select to replicate to all domain controllers in the forest, and then click Next.

7. Select the IPv6 Reverse Lookup Zone option and click Next.

8. Enter FC00:1234:5678:9abc::/64 for the IPv6 address prefix. The reverse lookup zone name will be created automatically. Click Next.

9. Allow only secure updates and click Next.

10. Click Finish to complete the task.

## Setting Up a DHCPv6 Server on Windows Server 2008 R2

IPv6 is installed and enabled by default in Windows Server 2008 R2, and native IPv6 functionality is already included into Windows Server 2008 R2 DHCP by way of DHCPv6.

In this example, we assume that the Windows Server 2008 R2 server is assigned with the IPv6 address from the previous example: Fc00:1234:5678:9abc::2. To set up the DHCP role, execute the following steps:

1. Launch Server Manager and click the Add Roles link.

2. Read the Before You Begin page and ensure that you have followed the bulleted items. Click Next if you are ready to continue.

3. On the Server Roles page, click the check box to enter a check mark next to DHCP Server (as shown in Figure 10.28), and click Next.

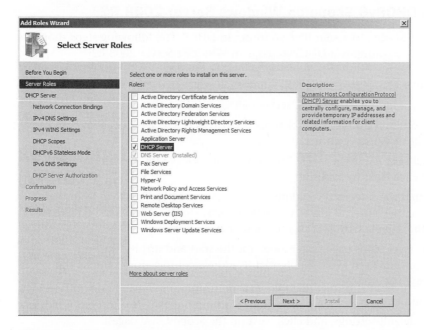

FIGURE 10.28    Selecting the DHCP server role.

4. A warning message might appear, asking for confirmation to "Install DHCP Server Without a Static IP Address." For this example, we have not assigned a static IPv4 address. The wizard is detecting this, and this can be ignored during this example. If this message appears, click Install DHCP Server Anyway (Not Recommended).

5. Be sure to take the time to read the "Introduction to DHCP Server," and click Next when you are ready to continue.

6. The next three sections for IPv4—IPv4 DNS Settings, IPv4 WINS Settings, and DHCP Scopes—can be bypassed by clicking Next.

7. On the DHCPv6 Stateless Mode page, two options are available. For the Windows Server 2008 R2 server to issue IPv6 addresses, select Disable DHCPv6 Stateless Mode for This Server, and click Next.

8. On the DHCP Server Authorization page, specify the account that will be used to authorize this DHCP server on the network, and click Next.

9. On the Confirmation page, review the settings, and click Install when you are ready to continue.

10. It is important to not disrupt the installation progress, and allow the installation to complete.

11. Confirm the installation on the Results page, and click Close.

The DHCPv6 server is set up, but an IPv6 scope still needs to be configured for the server to begin assigning addresses.

## Setting Up a DHCPv6 Scope on Windows Server 2008 R2

A separate scope is needed to assign IPv6 addresses in DHCP. The following steps show the administrator how to configure a DHCPv6 scope in Windows Server 2008 R2:

1. Launch Server Manager, expand Roles, and then select DHCP Server.

2. In the DHCP window, expand the server name, and then click IPv6.

3. Right-click on IPv6, and click on New Scope. This opens a New Scope Wizard window. Click Next to continue.

4. For this example, name the scope "Test IPv6 Scope," leave the Description field blank, and click Next to continue.

5. Assuming that the server's IPv6 address is still Fc00:1234:5678:9abc::2 from the previous example, enter in a prefix of Fc00:1234:5678:9abc::, leave the Preference setting at the default setting of 0, and click Next.

6. On the Add Exclusions page, enter :0000 for the start and :ffff for the end. Exclusions are added to avoid a potential IP address conflict (for example, the server issuing its own address).

7. Click the Add button, and click Next to continue. See Figure 10.29 for more detail.

8. Review the default settings, and click Next on the Scope Lease page.

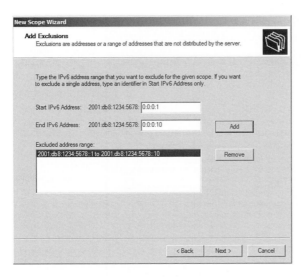

FIGURE 10.29    Adding exclusions.

9. Confirm the settings, ensure that the Yes option button under Activate Scope Now is selected, and then click Finish.

Now the DHCP server will begin to assign IPv6 addresses from the scope.

## Adding an IPv6 Host Record in Windows Server 2008 R2 DNS

Configuring IPv6 host records in DNS is very similar to configuring IPv4 records. When configuring IPv6 records in Windows Server 2008 R2 DNS, it is possible to provide the abbreviated IPv6 addressing, meaning that you are able to use double "::". The following steps walk through configuring an AAAA host record for IPv6:

1. Launch the Server Manager, expand the Roles, expand DNS Server, expand DNS, and select the DNS server name.

2. Expand the server, expand Forward Lookup Zones, and select the zone.

3. Right-click on the zone, and select New Host (A or AAAA). See Figure 10.30 for more detail.

4. Type the short name of the host (hostname without the FQDN) and populate the IPv6 address. Ensure that the Create Associated Pointer (PTR) Record check box is checked, and then click Add Host.

5. Click OK on the The Host Record Was Successfully Created message box. Add additional host records, and click Done when you are finished.

As noted earlier in the chapter, IPv6 host records are displayed as AAAA (quad A) records in DNS. Other records associated to an IPv6 address will reflect the full IPv6 address in the Data column.

10

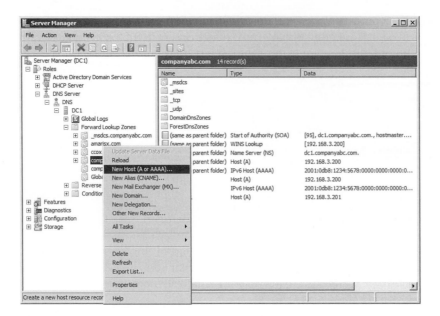

FIGURE 10.30    Adding IPv6 AAAA DNS records.

The new record can be tested by pinging the FQDN, as follows:

1. Launch a command prompt.

2. Enter the command `ping -6 <fqdn>` where <fqdn> is the host name.

3. The command should return a series of four pings to the IPv6 address.

> **NOTE**
>
> The `ping` command defaults to IPv4, so a ping to a hostname by default will not let you test the IPv6 address. You can force IPv6 by using the syntax `ping -6 <hostname>`. You can also force IPv4 by using the syntax `ping -4 <hostname>`.

# Secure DNS with DNSSEC

Because DNS does not offer any form of security natively, it is vulnerable to spoofing, man-in-the-middle, and cache poisoning attacks. For this reason, it has become critical to develop a means for securing DNS. DNSSEC was developed to do just that.

There are a series of IETF RFCs that specify the DNSSEC extensions to DNS. These include the following:

▶ **RFC 4033**—DNS Security Introduction and Requirements

▶ **RFC 4034**—Resource Records for the DNS Security Extensions

▶ **RFC 4035**—Protocol Modifications for the DNS Security Extensions

There are also several other supporting IETF RFCs. Together, these RFCs modify and extend the DNS protocol. The DNSSEC extensions provide the following:

▶ Origin authority

▶ Data integrity

▶ Authenticated denial of existence

In a nutshell, DNSSEC allows clients to know that the DNS information is coming from a valid server, wasn't changed, and that a given host exists or doesn't exist.

Windows Server 2008 R2 and Windows 7 fully support the latest DNSSEC RFCs 4033 through 4035.

### NOTE

Interestingly, Windows Server 2003 and Windows Server 2008 do not support the latest RFCs, as their implementation of DNSSEC was based on the now obsolete RFC 2535. That RFC required secondary zones and, thus, they cannot interoperate with the Windows Server 2008 R2 DNSSEC.

## DNSSEC Components

The DNSSEC relies on signed zones, which is a zone whose records are signed as defined by RFC 4035. A signed zone contains one or more of the new DNSEC record types, which are DNSKEY, NSEC, RRSIG, and DS records. These records allow DNS data to be validated by resolvers.

Zone Signing Key (ZSK) is the encryption key used to sign the zone, essentially a public and private key combination stored in a certificate. The Key Signing Key (KSK) is the key used to sign the ZSK to validate it, essentially a public and private key combination as well.

The DNSKEY record is a DNSSEC record type used to store a public key. The KSK and the ZSK public keys are stored in the DNSKEY records to allow the zone signatures to be validated.

Next Secure (NSEC) record is a DNSSEC record type used to prove non-existence of a DNS name. This allows DNS clients to be sure that if a record is not retrieved in a DNS lookup, the record does not exist in the DNSSEC zone.

The Resource Record Signature (RRSIG) record is used to hold the signature for a DNS record. For each A record, there will be a corresponding RRSIG record. For each NSEC record, there will also be a corresponding RRSIG record.

The Delegation Signer (DS) record is used to secure delegations to other DNS servers and confirm their validity. This prevents man-in-the-middle DNS servers from breaking the security chain during recursive lookups.

A nonvalidating security-aware stub resolver is a security-aware stub resolver that trusts one or more security-aware DNS servers to perform DNSSEC validation on its behalf. All Windows DNS clients are nonvalidating security-aware stub resolvers, meaning they do not actually do the DNSSEC validation.

The Windows DNS client is nonvalidating, meaning that the Windows DNS client does not check to see if the DNS records are secured but instead implicitly trusts the DNS server. The Windows DNS client flags the DNS request based on the NRPT table and expects the DNS server to perform the check for it. The DNS server returns the results regardless and indicates if the check for DNSSEC was successful or not. If the check was successful, the Windows DNS client passes the results to the application requesting the DNS lookup.

> **NOTE**
>
> To really ensure the security of the DNS requests, the DNS client must be able to validate the DNS server. The method of doing this for Windows systems is to use IPSec. To really, really secure DNS, IPSec must be deployed as well.

## Requirements

In the Windows Server 2008 R2 implementation of DNSSEC, the zones are signed offline—that is, the zone file for the DNS zone is signed and then loaded into the DNS server. Thus, you cannot have dynamic zones with Windows Server 2008. They must be static.

The signed zones can be Active Directory-integrated zones but must be file backed up. The records are all text based, so Active Directory integrated zones do not pose a problem.

To request DNSSEC security for a lookup, the DNS client must have a Name Resolution Policy Table (NRPT) entry. This then forces the DNS client to flag the request as a secure request, which causes the DNS server to check the security of the lookup and return the records with the secure flag set. If the client does not request security, the DNS server simply returns the records.

Finally, to fully secure the DNS lookups, IPSec should be deployed.

## Configuring a DNSSEC Zone

In this scenario, the zone secure.companyabc.com will be encrypted. The zone is unsecured to start and contains several records, shown in Figure 10.31. The zone is a file-based zone, with the DNS zone stored in the default directory c:\windows\system32\dns\ in a file named secure.companyabc.com.dns.

The DNSSEC configuration and management is done using the dnscmd.exe utility.

The first step is to generate the signing certificates for the secured zone; that is, generate the ZSK and KSK certificates. The steps to generate the KSK and ZSK certificates are the following:

1. On the DNS server, select Start, Command Prompt, and Run As Administrator.

2. Type the command cd \windows\system32\dns.

3. To generate the KSK, run the command dnscmd /OfflineSign /GenKey /Alg rsasha1 /Flags KSK /Length 1024 /Zone secure.companyabc.com /SSCert /FriendlyName KSK-secure.companyabc.com.

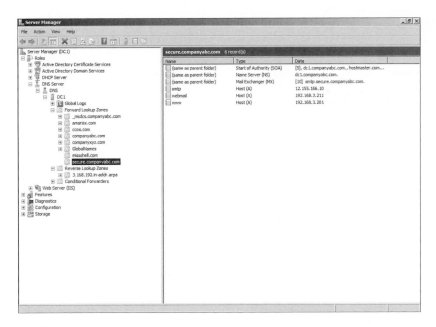

FIGURE 10.31   Unsecured DNS zone.

4. To generate the ZSK, run the command dnscmd /OfflineSign /GenKey /Alg
   rsasha1 /Length 1024 /Zone secure.companyabc.com /SSCert /FriendlyName
   ZSK-secure.companyabc.com.

The keys are stored in the Local Computer certificate store of the DNS server in the MS-
DNSSEC folder. The certificates are shown in Figure 10.32 from the MMC certificates
snap-in for the Local Computer. The validity period of the signing certificates is five years
by default.

The next step is to sign the zone file and the records. This takes the existing zone file
(secure.companyabc.com.dns), signs the zone and records, and saves it to another zone
file (signed.secure.companyabc.com.dns). The certificates generated in the previous steps
will be used for the signing. The steps to sign the zone are the following:

1. On the DNS server, launch Server Manager.

2. Expand Roles, DNS Server, DNS, DC1, Forward Lookup Zones, and select
   secure.companyabc.com.

3. Right-click on secure.companyabc.com and select Update Server Data File. This
   ensures that the latest updates are saved in the file.

4. Select Start, Command Prompt, and Run As Administrator.

5. Type the command cd \windows\system32\dns.

6. To sign the zone file, run the command DnsCmd /OfflineSign /SignZone /input
   secure.companyabc.com.dns /output signed.secure.companyabc.com.dns /zone
   secure.companyabc.com /signkey /cert /friendlyname KSK-secure.compa-
   nyabc.com /signkey /cert /friendlyname ZSK-secure.companyabc.com.

10

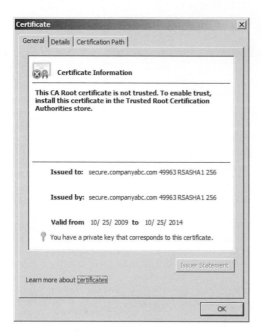

FIGURE 10.32    KSK and ZSK certificates.

The signed zone file is now ready to be loaded into the DNS server.

The last step in signing the zone is to reload the zone file into the DNS server. The unsigned zone must be deleted first; then the signed zone file (signed.secure.companyabc.com.dns) is loaded. The steps to reload the zone are the following:

1. On the DNS server, select Start, Command Prompt, and Run As Administrator.

2. Type the command `cd \windows\system32\dns`.

3. Type `dnscmd /ZoneDelete secure.companyabc.com /f`. This deletes the zone from the DNS server.

4. Type `dnscmd /ZoneAdd secure.companyabc.com /primary /file signed.secure.companyabc.com /load`. This loads the signed zone file.

The zone secure.companyabc.com is now encrypted. Also, if saved, the zone file will save to the new signed.secure.companyabc.com.dns if updates are made. Figure 10.33 shows the zone records after encryption.

> **NOTE**
>
> The records show an inception date of 10/26/2009 and an expiration date of 11/25/2009. The default validity date is 30 days from the date of the signing of the zone. This means that the zone file will need to be resigned within 30 days. If a longer validity period is needed, the optional /ValidFrom and /ValidTo parameters can be specified on the dnscmd.exe command when signing the zone file.

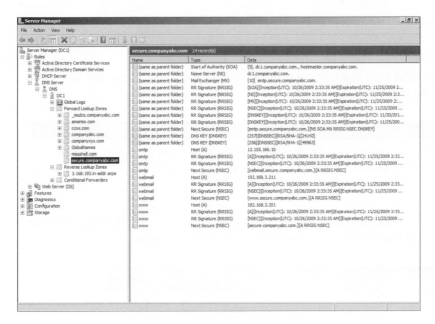

FIGURE 10.33   Encrypted zone records.

There are four records for each previous entry now, which are the following:

▶ Standard A Record

▶ RR Signature (RRSIG) Record for the Standard Record

▶ Next Secure (NSEC) Record

▶ RR Signature (RRSIG) Record for the Next Secure Record

Without any additional configuration, the DNS clients blissfully ignore the DNSSEC for the zone. To have the clients use the DNSSEC properties of the DNS zone, they must be configured to request secure DNS entries. This is done by configuring a Name Resolution Policy Table (NRPT) policy for clients.

The NRPT policy can be configured through group policy. The steps to create a NRPT group policy for the secure.companyabc.com zone are the following:

1. On the domain controller DC1, launch Server Manager.

2. Expand Features, Group Policy Management, Forest: companyabc.com, Domains, and select companyabc.com.

3. Right-click on companyabc.com and select Create a GPO in This Domain, and Link It Here.

4. Enter NRPT Group Policy Object and click OK.

5. Right-click the NRPT Group Policy Object link and select Edit.

6. Expand Policies, Windows Settings, and select Name Resolution Policy.

10

7. In the field "To which part of the namespace does this rule apply?" select Suffix and enter `secure.companyabc.com`.

8. In the DNSSEC tab, check the Enable DNSSEC in This Rule.

9. Check the Validation box Require DNS Clients to Check That Name and Address Data Has Been Validated.

**NOTE**

The wording of this option is precise. The Windows DNS client will check that the DNS server has validated the data, but will NOT do the validation itself.

10. Click the Create button to create the record in the Name Resolution Policy Table at the bottom of the screen. Figure 10.34 shows how the record should look.

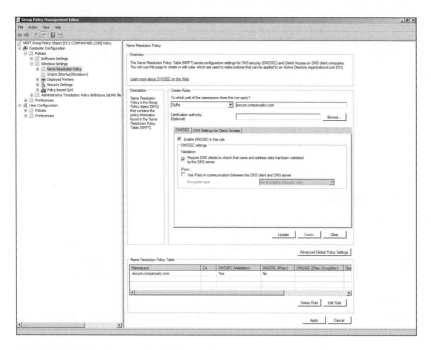

FIGURE 10.34   Name resolution policy.

11. Close the GPMC editor to save the changes.

Now, all domain DNS clients will request that DNS servers check the validity of the lookups for domain secure.companyabc.com using DNSSEC.

Additional steps that might be needed to maintain the secured DNS zone include the following:

> ▶ Back up the KSK and ZSK certificates.

> ▶ Back up the secured and unsecured zone files.

> ▶ Establish a maintenance schedule to refresh the zone signatures.

## Summary

DNS has proven itself over time to be a robust, dependable, and extremely scalable solution to name resolution. Windows Server 2008 R2 takes DNS to the next level and builds on the enhancements introduced with Windows 2000/2003 DNS. Windows Server 2008 R2 also incorporates IPv6 fully into the DNS and protocol stack to allow administrators to deploy IPv6 immediately.

Whether using DNS for a full-fledged Active Directory Domain Services implementation or simply setting up an Internet DNS presence, Windows Server 2008 R2's DNS builds on a successful, road-tested base to provide for a functional, reliable, enterprise name-resolution strategy.

## Best Practices

The following are best practices from this chapter:

> ▶ Use Windows Server 2008 R2 DNS whenever possible to support Active Directory Domain Services. If you must use a non-Windows DNS to host the AD zone, ensure that it supports SRV records, such as with BIND version 8.1.2 or higher.

> ▶ Establish a caching-only server in small branch office situations to alleviate large amounts of client query traffic across the network and to eliminate the need to replicate entire DNS zones to remote locations.

> ▶ Configure DHCP to dynamically update DNS information for down-level clients if dynamic records are necessary.

> ▶ Identify the sources of dynamically updated information to prevent problems with reliability.

> ▶ Configure a DNS server to point to itself for DNS queries rather than to another DNS server.

> ▶ Make any DNS implementation compliant with the standard DNS character set so that you can support zone transfers to and from non-Unicode-compliant DNS implementations such as UNIX BIND servers. This includes a–z, A–Z, 0–9, and the hyphen (-) character.

> ▶ Use the GlobalNames zone (GNZ) to reduce the reliance on WINS in the enterprise.

> ▶ Turn on Debug Logging on a per-server basis for more advanced DNS event log diagnosis only when required, and turn off this functionality when it's no longer necessary.

> ▶ Begin to deploy IPv6 to gain familiarity with the new addressing.

10

# CHAPTER 11

# DHCP/WINS/Domain Controllers

Often, some of the more important components of a network are overlooked because they consistently do their job and keep a low profile. It's only when a problem erupts with one of these components that their true value arises and attention is paid to them. The Dynamic Host Configuration Protocol (DHCP) and the Windows Internet Naming Service (WINS) are two such services, faithfully performing their functions day in and day out, while often delegated to a beat-up old server.

Although not glamorous, the functionality in DHCP and WINS is critical in a network environment, and a good deal of thought should be put into their design, administration, and functional requirements. This chapter explores these oft-forgotten services and provides best-practice design and configuration information for utilizing them.

In addition to information on DHCP and WINS, this chapter explores the functionality of global catalog domain controllers in a Windows Server 2008 R2 Active Directory infrastructure, specifically focusing on server placement issues. In addition, a new type of domain controller released with Windows Server 2008, Read-Only Domain Controller, is explored. Finally, this chapter includes step-by-step installation instructions for these services and best-practice migration scenarios.

# Understanding the Key Components of an Enterprise Network

Although an enterprise network has many functional layers, this chapter focuses on three key concepts that are critical to the functionality of a Windows Server 2008 R2 environment. These three concepts—network addressing, name resolution, and directory integration—provide for the base-level functionality expected of any modern enterprise or even a small business network, and they provide the backbone for the Windows Server 2008 R2 infrastructure.

## Detailing the Importance of Network Addressing

The first concept of a network is network addressing. Network addressing allows for systems to be attached to a network, and it lays the foundation to allow for communication between network systems. Network addressing was historically configured by proprietary network protocols, one for each network operating system (NOS). This gave NOS designers a great deal of flexibility in tailoring the communications components of their network to their specific design needs but made it difficult to exchange information between networks or systems running different network operating systems.

One of the first common network protocols developed was the Transmission Control Protocol/Internet Protocol (TCP/IP). TCP/IP was designed to interoperate between a different variety of networks and network operating systems, allowing network clients to speak a common language. The rise of this protocol coincided with the widespread adoption of the Internet itself, and it was this popularity and ubiquitous use of this protocol that led Microsoft to choose it as the standard protocol for Windows 2000. Windows Server 2008 R2 continues to use TCP/IP as the default network protocol, fortifying its position within the Microsoft NOS world. And to be frank, any company that develops an operating system that does not support TCP/IP or the next-generation version, IPv6, will never have widespread adoption in the business or consumer computer, network, and Internet market.

TCP/IP requires that each node or device on the network be assigned a unique IP address, such as 192.168.206.10. One way to look at this is to consider that each computer IP address is just like a phone number. Each household with a phone has a unique number, but the neighbors may share a common area code and prefix. TCP/IP networking works similarly in that each node's IP address on a common network will share some common number, called the network number, and the unique portion is called the host number.

Each node that is connected and desires to communicate on the network must be assigned an IP address manually or by an automatic method. The automatic method is provided by a service known as Dynamic Host Configuration Protocol or DHCP. Of course with DHCP, proper planning and management of addresses and configuration options is essential and, historically, many DHCP services lacked functionality. This is where the Windows Server 2008 R2 DHCP service really shines with new features that will enable better management and higher reliability. You can find more details on DHCP in the "Exploring DHCP Changes in Windows Server 2008 R2" section later in this chapter.

## Understanding Name Resolution

The second concept or desired function on a network is name resolution. Because humans understand and remember names better than they do phone numbers, for example—or for this chapter, IP addresses—the need for name resolution was realized early in the development phases of computer networking. Name resolution can be described as matching a name to an IP address for the purposes of establishing network communication.

Windows Server 2008 R2 provides two services that provide computer networking name resolution. These two services are the domain name system (DNS) and the Windows Internet Naming Service (WINS), which is detailed in this chapter.

The first type, the domain name system (DNS), translates fully qualified domain names (FQDNs) into IP addresses, which allows them to be addressed in an Active Directory or Internet DNS infrastructure. DNS name resolution is the standard for all Internet name resolution and it is required in all Microsoft Active Directory environments. The DNS service is covered in more detail in Chapter 10, "Domain Name System and IPv6."

The second type of name resolution, mapping legacy Microsoft NetBIOS names into IP addresses, is provided by WINS. Although it is technically possible (and ideal) to create a Windows Server 2008 R2 environment free of NetBIOS name resolution, the truth is that divorcing a network from WINS dependency is very difficult, so it will likely remain an active part of network services in most organizations, at least for a few more years. You can find more information on WINS in the "Reviewing the Windows Internet Naming Service (WINS)" section later in this chapter.

> **NOTE**
>
> When Windows Server 2008 DNS service was released, it introduced a new feature, known as the GlobalNames zone. The GlobalNames zone provided single-label name resolution for large enterprise networks that do not deploy WINS and for which using DNS name suffixes to provide single-label name resolution was not practical. See Chapter 10 for more information on DNS GlobalNames.

## Examining Directory Integration

The third concept that is critical to a functional Active Directory networking infrastructure is Directory Integration. Having a centralized directory that contains a database of all network clients, their services, user accounts, and security groups that can be used to define security and permissions is vital to any centrally managed modern computer network. Microsoft provides the Active Directory Domain Services role to serve this purpose. Active Directory Domain Services is detailed in Chapter 7, "Active Directory Infrastructure."

The Active Directory Domain Services role, included with Windows Server 2008 R2, is a core service that is depended upon by many other roles and services hosted on the network. As an example of this, the servers that host the Active Directory Domain Services role, also known as domain controllers, are accessed by other servers and workstations to verify authentication to resources and to also locate resources on the network. Domain controllers contain the full set of directory data used for many networking functions, but certain domain controllers also host a role known as the global catalog. The global catalog hosts a compact subset of the entire Active Directory domain controller database that is indexed, read-only, and used to provide faster results to directory lookups and searches. Global catalog domain controllers are explained in more detail in the "Understanding the Role of the Active Directory Global Catalog" section later in this chapter.

Subsequently, choosing where to place domain controllers and domain controllers that are also global catalog servers is critical to the design and operation of the Windows Server 2008 R2 Active Directory infrastructure. Special considerations must be made regarding this concept because access to directory lookup and registration are crucial functions for Active Directory clients on the network. Of course, before an Active Directory client can locate or register with a domain controller or do a search of the global catalog, they must first get on the network and find the right systems hosting these services, through network addressing and name resolution.

## Outlining Networking Services Changes in Windows Server 2008 R2

Windows Server 2008 R2 introduces several functional improvements to networking services. These improvements allow for increased administrative functionality, greater reliability, and an overall increase in value for an organization's network infrastructure.

DHCP improvements such as DHCP MAC address filtering for leases, DHCP delay in address distribution for redundant DHCP architectures, and DHCP migration improvements using the new Windows Server Migration Tools feature of Windows Server 2008 R2 provide the functionality that many DHCP administrators desired. WINS improvements include advanced database searches and filtering in the WINS console, but the architecture and functionality has not changed too much in this release. You can find more information about these capabilities later in this chapter.

# Exploring the Dynamic Host Configuration Protocol (DHCP)

Amazingly little is known about the DHCP service, although it is used in virtually all organizations and networks. The service itself has simple beginnings but has evolved to become an important component in a network environment. If you have ever connected a computer to a network, such as a Wi-Fi hot spot at the local café, the computer was given a network address from a DHCP service running on that network.

## Detailing the Need for DHCP

Aside from just assigning a network device a unique IP address on the network, there needs to be a network architecture that manages how network devices communicate, and, particularly, which devices can communicate and when. This network communication management is provided by the TCP/IP networking protocol. TCP/IP is too complex and not necessary to define in this chapter but one thing that is certain is that each device connected to a TCP/IP network requires a unique address. This unique address defines the node's network affiliation and provides for a means of sending and receiving network information between itself and the destination network device(s). This address, or IP address, must be assigned to each device on the network to allow for communication using TCP/IP. In the past, many IP addresses were manually distributed as new clients were added to a network. This required a large amount of administrative overhead to maintain, and often resulted in problems in configuration caused by simple typographical errors and basic human error. Also, manually adding IP addresses to devices, without a well-managed and up-to-date address table or database, resulted in multiple machines on the network using the same address. When multiple devices were configured with the same IP address on a single network, the result usually included failed networking on both devices. As an example of this, if two people in the same household picked up different phones to dial simultaneously, they would both hear the dial tone but when they dialed the number, most likely an incorrect number would be dialed that did not match either of the desired numbers.

Aside from building in checks to deal with duplicate IP addressed devices on a single TCP/IP network, administrators quickly realized that automating address distribution was the way to go. The search for such a system led to the predecessors of DHCP: RARP and BOOTP.

## Outlining DHCP Predecessors: RARP and BOOTP

The need for dynamic allocation of IP addresses to clients was first addressed by the Reverse Address Resolution Protocol (RARP). RARP simply allocated an IP address to a client after that client requested it through a network broadcast. This protocol was quickly discovered to be ineffective for communicating between different networks.

The successor to RARP was the Bootstrap Protocol (BOOTP), which improved the dynamic assignment of IP addresses by allowing for routing through different networks and used a concept called a magic cookie, a 64-byte portion of the BOOTP packet that contained configuration information such as subnet mask, DNS server designations, and so on. This protocol was a drastic improvement over RARP but was still limited in a few functional areas—namely, the fact that the database was not dynamic and was stored in a static text file, which limited its usability. BOOTP is still used today to deliver IP addresses to systems that need to connect to a network to locate the necessary files to load an application or operating system, such as is the case in a diskless computer.

## Exploring the DHCP Server Service

DHCP was developed as an improvement to BOOTP. In fact, a DHCP packet is almost identical to a BOOTP packet, except for the modification of the magic cookie portion of a packet, which was expanded in size to accommodate additional options such as DNS server, WINS server, and so on.

The DHCP process is straightforward. A client boots up, and a broadcast request is sent out to all nodes on the network to which the client is connected. If a DHCP service is active and listening for these broadcasts, it will respond to the client request by issuing an available IP address from a predefined range or pool, as illustrated in Figure 11.1.

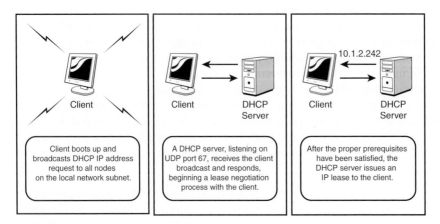

FIGURE 11.1  The DHCP IP request process.

In addition to an IP address, all options that are defined on the server scope are issued to a client. This includes DNS servers, WINS servers, gateways, subnet masks, and many other settings. If these options are issued automatically, the chance for errors is lessened and the entire IP address assignment becomes automated, decreasing administrative overhead.

## Examining the DHCP Client Service

The server portion of DHCP is only half of the equation in a DHCP transaction. The request for an IP address comes from a specific interface known as the DHCP client. The DHCP Client service is included in all versions of TCP/IP deployed with Microsoft Windows, but on some of the older clients, TCP/IP would need to be installed separately.

The DHCP client, as previously mentioned, interacts with the DHCP Server service, in terms of requesting, accepting, and releasing IP addresses. Each version of the Windows TCP/IP protocol included with each operating system includes a different DHCP client, and there are slight variations in the functionality of each of them. However, the overall function—to apply for and receive an IP address from a DHCP server—remains the same in each.

## Understanding Automatic Private IP Addressing (APIPA)

The TCP/IP DHCP Client/Server service was updated with the release of Windows 2000 to enable Windows clients to automatically assign themselves an IP address if no BOOTP or DHCP server was available; it does so through a process called Automatic Private IP

Addressing (APIPA). APIPA clients automatically assign themselves an IP address in the 169.254.0.0/16 range in this situation, which allows them to have basic TCP/IP connectivity in small networks. So, in essence, a small workgroup network can be built with Windows 2000, XP, Vista, or Windows 7 workstations, and without too much work, these systems would be able to communicate with each other using addresses self-assigned by the APIPA service.

APIPA might be problematic in larger networks because it forces clients to assign themselves addresses in a range that is normally not part of a local company subnet. If a DHCP server is down, clients that are attempting to renew a lease or obtain a new IP address from a DHCP server will fail and automatically assign themselves an APIPA address. When the server comes back online, these clients will not immediately get a legitimate IP address from the DHCP server because they are no longer broadcasting for an IP address, and will essentially remain cut off from the network. In a case like this, the client workstation will need to initiate a new DHCP address request by rebooting the system or forcing a manual address request using a command such as `Ipconfig /renew` from a command prompt. This can be quite troublesome for corporate network administrators and help desk support staff if the DHCP services on their network are slow to respond or fail often. In certain situations, network administrators might want to disable the APIPA functionality, and Microsoft supplies a Registry key that will perform this function for Windows 2000 and later systems. A Registry key can be manually created on the systems in the following location:

```
HKLM\SYSTEM\CurrentControlSet\Services\Tcpip\Parameters\Interfaces\<AdapterName>\
IPAutoconfigurationEnabled:REG_DWORD=0
```

You can create this key by following these steps on the client:

1. Open Registry Editor (choose Start, Run, and then enter `regedit`).
2. Navigate to HKEY_LOCAL_MACHINE\SYSTEM\CurrentControlSet\Services\ Tcpip\Parameters\_Interfaces\<AdapterName> (where AdapterName is the hexadecimal representation of the network adapter in question).
3. Right-click on the <AdapterName> key and choose New, DWORD Value.
4. Enter `IPAutoconfigurationEnabled` to rename the DWORD value.
5. Double-click the new value and ensure that 0 is entered as the value data.
6. Click OK and close the Registry Editor.

To validate that APIPA is disabled, an administrator should run IPCONFIG /ALL from the command prompt and then check that the Autoconfiguration Enabled option is set to No.

> **NOTE**
>
> APIPA can also be effectively disabled in Windows XP clients through an alternate IP configuration, which allows for the designation of a static IP address if DHCP is unavailable. You can find more information on this concept in the section "Understanding DHCP Client Alternate Network Capability," later in this chapter.

## Detailing DHCP Relay Agents

Because DHCP clients use network broadcasts to seek out DHCP servers, it is important that there is a DHCP server on each network. To send and receive network traffic between separate networks, a device known as a network router is used. By default, network routers do not forward any broadcast network traffic between networks. On complex networks that include network routers, if network clients on each network require the automatic IP address assignment functionality of a DHCP service, there will either need to be a DHCP server on each network or a service known as a DHCP Relay Agent must be deployed. DHCP Relay Agents can be servers, a service hosted by a network router, or, in some cases, a network switch. DHCP agents will listen for DHCP broadcast requests and forward them to previously designated DHCP servers on another network. As an example of this, Cisco routers provide a service called ip-helper, which is defined with the DHCP server to forward broadcast requests to. If this type of router configuration is not utilized, a Windows server running the Routing and Remote Access Service must be configured as a DHCP Relay Agent, as illustrated in Figure 11.2.

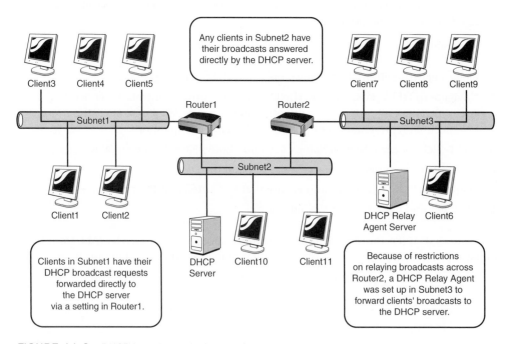

FIGURE 11.2    DHCP broadcast packet routing.

> **NOTE**
>
> In most real-world implementations of DHCP, the routers between network segments are configured to forward client DHCP broadcast packets directly to the DHCP server. Therefore, in large organizations, it is important to include the network architecture team in any discussions on DHCP design.

## Examining DHCP and Dynamic DNS

Using the DNS service in Windows Server 2008 R2, clients can automatically register themselves in the DNS database through a mechanism called Dynamic DNS (DDNS). For more information on this concept, refer to Chapter 10.

DHCP in Windows Server 2008 R2 integrates directly with DDNS to provide for automatic registration of clients into DNS. By default, all Windows 2000 or higher clients will perform this function by themselves, but DHCP servers can perform Dynamic DNS registration for DHCP clients that are not able to register themselves. Also, DHCP servers can be configured to always register the Dynamic DNS entry on behalf of the client. In many cases, this is ideal because the DHCP service will own the record and can remove it from the DNS zone when the lease expires. These settings can be configured at the DHCP server level and within each DHCP scope properties, through the DHCP administrative console. A DHCP scope is a set of included and excluded IP addresses and networking options that define the configuration that DHCP clients will be sent. How to plan and configure DHCP scopes is detailed in the next section.

## Installing DHCP and Creating New Scopes

DHCP installation historically has been two parts: Install the service and then later configure the service. In Windows Server 2008 R2, DHCP Server role installation has been streamlined through the use of the Add Roles Wizard. This wizard installs the DHCP Server service and automatically invokes the New Scope Wizard, which can be used to establish and configure DHCP scopes. To install and configure a Windows Server 2008 R2 system as a DHCP server, follow these steps:

1. Click Start, click All Programs, click Administrative Tools, and select Server Manager. If prompted for User Account Control verification, click Continue to confirm the action.

2. In Server Manager, click the Roles node in the left pane to display the Roles Summary information in the right pane. Then click the Add Roles link in the right pane to initiate the Add Roles Wizard.

3. After reading the Before You Begin information, click Next to continue.

4. On the Select Server Roles page, select the check box next to DHCP Server, and then click Next to continue.

5. On the Introduction to DHCP Server page, helpful information is displayed to learn more about the DHCP server. Click on any of the informative links as desired and after reading the information, click Next to continue the installation.

6. On the Select Network Connection Bindings page, check the box next to the desired network connections that will host the DHCP Server service, as illustrated in Figure 11.3, and click Next to continue.

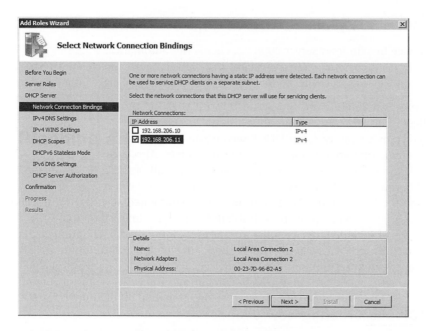

FIGURE 11.3   Verifying Binding options for the DHCP install.

7. At this point, the Add Roles Wizard displays the Specify IPv4 DNS Server Settings page. Enter the name of the parent domain that clients will use for name resolution. Enter the name of the preferred DNS server IPv4 IP address and the alternate DNS server IPv4 IP address. Click the Validate button to check the IP addresses of the preferred and alternate DNS servers. Once the DNS server IP addresses are validated, click Next to continue.

8. On the Specify IPv4 WINS Server Settings page, click the option button to indicate whether WINS is required on the network. If required, specify the IP addresses for the primary and, if needed, alternate server. Click Next to continue.

9. On the Add or Edit DHCP Scopes page, click Add and then type a descriptive name for the scope such as Headquarters Network DHCP Scope. Type in the starting IP address and ending IP address. Select whether the subnet is a wired or wireless network, which will set the DHCP address lease duration to either eight days or eight hours. In addition, type in a subnet mask for the subnet in question, and a default gateway if the DHCP client needs to communicate with separate networks, as

illustrated in Figure 11.4. Also if the DHCP server will be used immediately, check the Activate this Scope check box and click OK to complete the creation of the scope. If no additional scopes will be created, click Next to continue.

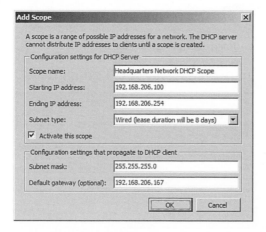

FIGURE 11.4    Defining the address in the Add or Edit DHCP Scopes page of the Add Roles Wizard.

10.  If DHCPv6 is required, select Enable DHCPv6 Stateless Mode for This Server to configure the server for DHCPv6 stateless operation; otherwise, select Disable DHCPv6 Stateless Mode for This Server. If Disable is selected, DHCPv6 can manually be configured later from the DHCP server MMC snap-in. Click Next to continue.

11.  If you enabled DHCPv6 Stateless mode in the preceding step, you must configure the IPV6 DNS Server settings. On the Specify IPv6 DNS Server Settings page, enter the parent domain and the necessary IPv6 addresses into the Preferred DNS and Alternate DNS server information fields and click Next when finished.

12.  On the Authorize DHCP Server page, select whether to use the current or alternate credentials used to authorize the DHCP server in the domain. DHCP servers must be authorized by Active Directory before they can be used to manage and distribute IP addresses. If the account used to install the DHCP Server service has the necessary group membership, select the Use Current Credentials option button and click Next to continue. If you are not sure, click the Skip Authorization of this DHCP Server in AD DS option and click Next to continue. Ask the Active Directory domain administrator to authorize the DHCP server later.

13.  On the Confirm Installation Selections page, review the information for accuracy and click Install to continue the DHCP server installation and configuration process.

14.  The Add Roles Wizard then indicates that the server has successfully become a DHCP server, as indicated in Figure 11.5. Click Close to close the wizard.

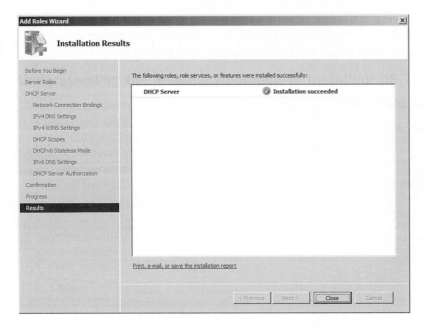

FIGURE 11.5    Completion of the Add Roles Wizard for the DHCP server.

Administrators will now be able to see the newly created DHCP server reflected in Server Manager. It will be located beneath the Roles node in the Server Manager tree in the left pane. The Roles Summary section will also reflect the newly created DHCP server in the right pane.

---

**NOTE**

It is recommended that all tests utilizing DHCP be conducted in a lab environment. In addition, testing in production will be difficult because the Authorization Component of DHCP will also make it impossible to enable scopes on a Windows Server 2008 R2 DHCP server, as described in the "Examining DHCP Authorization" section later in this chapter.

---

# Exploring DHCP Changes in Windows Server 2008 R2

As previously discussed, two improvements have been made to the functionality of DHCP in Windows Server 2008 R2. These improvements allow for an increased level of functionality beyond the major improvements made in Windows 2000, Windows Server 2003, and Windows Server 2008. Even though there are new improvements, the architecture and design decisions that might have been made in previous Windows Server versions will still remain valid, but the new functionality will enhance these best-practice designs.

## Automating DHCP Database Backup and Restore

The process of backing up all DHCP settings and restoring them onto the same (or a different) server has been streamlined in Windows Server 2008 R2. No longer do administrators need to export Registry keys and manually move databases between servers or use the DHCP import/export tool from Microsoft to migrate DHCP. The backup and restore process can be accomplished directly from the MMC, and the migration of DHCP server data can be performed using tools included with the Windows Server 2008 R2 operating system.

The DHCP Server service on Windows Server 2008 R2 will back itself up automatically each hour to the %systemroot%\system32\dhcp\backup. Of course, only the most recent backup is maintained in this folder; if historic backup is required, an administrator should enable Volume Shadow Copy on the drive that contains the system root and also perform periodic backups of the DHCP server using Windows Backup or another backup solution, such as Microsoft Data Protection Manager. When a DHCP administrator is going to make changes to a DHCP server, it is a best practice to manually perform a backup of the DHCP database and configuration by performing the following steps:

1. Open the DHCP management console (Start, All Programs, Administrative Tools, DHCP). If prompted, click Continue to confirm the action.

2. Right-click the server name and choose Backup, as illustrated in Figure 11.6.

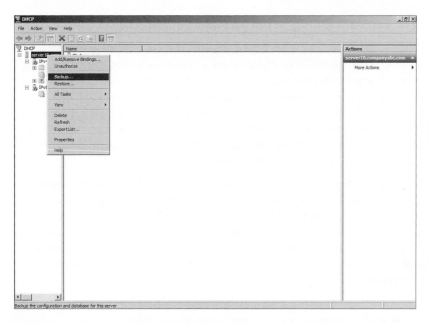

FIGURE 11.6   Backing up a DHCP database.

3. Specify a location for the backup file, and click OK. The backup files will then be saved into the location you chose.

To restore a previously backed up DHCP server configuration and database to the same or an alternate server, perform the following steps:

1. Open the DHCP management console on the server to which you want to restore the scope (Start, All Programs, Administrative Tools, DHCP). If prompted, click Continue to confirm the action.

2. Right-click the server name and choose Restore. Select the location where the backup files can be found, and click OK.

3. When you see a dialog box asking whether the service can be stopped and restarted, click Yes to continue. The service will be restarted, and the entire database and Registry will be restored.

> **NOTE**
>
> The DHCP backup and restore process is extremely useful in migrating existing DHCP server configurations, scopes, and up-to-date lease information to new DHCP servers. However, because down-level (pre–Windows Server 2008 R2) DHCP servers do not support automatic backup and restore, you will need to migrate from these servers by either the DHCP import/export tool between Windows 2003 systems or the Windows Server Migration Tools can be used to migrate the Windows Server 2003 DHCP server configuration and database to a Windows Server 2008 R2 system.

## Migrating DHCP Servers Using Windows Server Migration Tools

Windows Server 2008 R2 includes a new set of PowerShell cmdlets called the Windows Server Migration Tools. These tools can be installed on a Windows Server 2008 R2 system from the Add Features Wizard in Server Manager. The Windows Server Migration Tools can be used to migrate services between source servers running Windows Server 2003, Windows Server 2008, and Windows Server 2008 R2 to destination Windows Server 2008 R2 systems. DHCP is one of the services that can be migrated with these tools. One of the major advantages of this tool is the fact that it will migrate not only scope information, but it will also migrate the existing leases on the source server scope.

Before the Windows Server Migration Tools can be used to migrate DHCP services from one server to another, the tools will need to be installed on both the source and destination servers. Because the Windows Server Migration Tools are included with Windows Server 2008 R2, the tool must be packaged and installed on Windows Server 2003 or Windows Server 2008 systems if the source servers are running either of these operating systems. The overall process of using the Windows Server Migration Tools to migrate DHCP services is as follows:

1. Verify that the DHCP server settings, scopes, and scope options on the source DHCP server are the desired settings to migrate, and adjust as necessary.

2. Install the Windows Server Migration Tools on a Windows Server 2008 R2 system.

3. Create a deployment folder for the correct operating system (Windows Server 2003 or Windows Server 2008) and platform (x86 or amd64) from a command prompt on the Windows Server 2008 R2 system with the Window Server Migration Tools installed.

4. Install or verify that the Windows Server Migration Tools prerequisites are installed on the source and destination servers, which include the latest Windows PowerShell for the specific operating system and platform.

5. Install the Windows Server Migration Tools package on the desired source and destination DHCP servers.

6. Run the Windows Server Migration Tools export cmdlet, locally, on the source DHCP server and copy the export files to the destination DHCP server.

7. Unauthorize the source DHCP server and change the IP address or remove the system from the network permanently.

8. Add the original source DHCP server IP address to the destination server as a primary IPv4 address on a network adapter.

9. Run the Windows Server Migration Tools import cmdlet, locally, on the destination DHCP server.

10. Enable the DHCP Server service, start it, and verify the imported settings.

11. Authorize the DHCP server.

**Installing the Windows Server Migration Tools on Windows Server 2008 R2**
Before the Windows Server Migration Tools can be used to migrate DHCP services between servers, it must be installed on a Windows Server 2008 R2 system. To install the Windows Server Migration Tools, perform the following steps:

1. Choose Start, All Programs, Administrative Tools, Server Manager. In the console tree, right-click on Features and then click Add Features to start the Add Features Wizard.

2. On the Select Features page, scroll down the list of features and select the check box next to Windows Server Migration Tools; then click Next to continue.

3. On the Confirm Installation Selections page, click Install to begin installing the Windows Server Migration Tools.

4. On the Installation Results page, review the results and click Close to complete the installation.

**Creating the Deployment Folder Package of the Windows Server Migration Tools for Down-Level Operating System Installation**
When DHCP services will be migrated to a Windows Server 2008 R2 DHCP server from a source Windows Server 2003 or Windows Server 2008 system, the Windows Server Migration Tools will need to be packaged for deployment and installation on those down-level operating systems. To build the deployment folder package, perform the following steps:

1. Using an account with administrator permissions, log on to the Windows Server 2008 R2 system that has the Windows Server Migration Tools installed.

2. Open an elevated command prompt by clicking Start, All Programs, Accessories; locate and right-click Command Prompt and choose Run As Administrator. If prompted for confirmation, click Continue.

3. In the Command Prompt window, change the directory to %systemroot%\system32\ServerMigrationTools.

4. Type the command `SmigDeploy.exe /package /architecture x86 /os ws03 /path c:\downloads` and press Enter. This command creates the installation package for a Windows Server 2003 x86 system and places the files in the c:\downloads\SMT_ws03_x86 folder. If the downloads folder is not already created, the command creates it automatically.

5. Type the command `SmigDeploy.exe /package /architecture amd64 /os ws08 /path c:\downloads` and press Enter. This command creates the installation package for a Windows Server 2008 x64 system and places the files in the c:\downloads\SMT_ws08_amd64 folder. If the downloads folder is not already created, the command creates it automatically.

6. Repeat the last command for any additional operating systems that will be used as either source or destination DHCP servers.

7. Close the command prompt and, if necessary, share the c:\downloads folder so that it can be accessed across the network.

**Installing the Windows Server Migration Tools on Windows Server 2003 DHCP Server**
Before the Windows Server Migration Tools can be installed on a Windows Server 2003 system, the .NET Framework 2.0 must be installed as well as the latest Windows PowerShell. Download and install these two prerequisites and also download any security updates for these add-ons. Once those steps are completed, perform the following steps before the Windows Server Migration Tools can be used:

1. Using an account with administrator permissions, log on to the Windows Server 2003 x86 DHCP server.

2. Click Start and select Run.

3. Type in the location where the Server Migration Tools package for this operating system is stored (for this example, \\server20\downloads\).

4. Locate the "SMT_ws03_x86" folder that was created previously, right-click the folder, and choose Copy.

5. Click Start and select Run.

6. Type c:\ and click OK.

7. On the root of the C: drive, right-click on a blank space and click Paste to create the c:\SMT_ws03_x86 folder on the Windows Server 2003 system. Close the window.

8. Click Start and select Run.

9. Type cmd and click OK to open a command prompt.

10. In the Command Prompt window, change the directory to c:\SMT_ws03_x86\.

11. Type `SmigDeploy.exe` and press Enter to register the Windows Server Migration Tools cmdlets into Windows PowerShell.

12. After the command completes, the original Command Prompt window will be open, as well as a separate PowerShell window. Type exit in each of the Command Prompt windows to close them.

The Windows Server Migration Tools are now installed and registered with Windows PowerShell on the Windows Server 2003 x86 system and can be used in a PowerShell window.

### Installing the Windows Server Migration Tools on Windows Server 2008 64-Bit Edition DHCP Server

Before the Windows Server Migration Tools can be installed on a Windows Server 2008 64-bit system, install Windows PowerShell from the Add Features link in Server Manager if it is not already installed. Once Windows PowerShell is installed, perform the following steps before the Windows Server Migration Tools can be used:

1. Using an account with administrator permissions, log on to the Windows Server 2008 64-bit DHCP server.

2. Click Start. In the search pane, enter the path to the location where the Server Migration Tools package for this operating system is stored and press Enter (for this example, \\server20\downloads\).

3. Locate the "SMT_ws08_amd64" folder that was created previously, right-click the folder, and choose Copy.

4. Click Start. In the search pane, type c:\ and press Enter.

5. On the root of the C: drive, right-click on a blank space and click Paste to create the c:\SMT_ws08_amd64 folder on the Windows Server 2008 system. Close the window.

6. Click Start, and in the search pane, type cmd. When the command prompt is listed, right-click the shortcut and choose Run As Administrator. If prompted, click Continue to open an elevated Command Prompt window.

7. In the Command Prompt window, change the directory to c:\SMT_ws08_amd64\.

8. Type SmigDeploy.exe and press Enter to register the Windows Server Migration Tools cmdlets into Windows PowerShell.

9. After the command completes, the original Command Prompt window will be open, as well as a separate PowerShell window. Type exit in each of the Command Prompt windows to close them.

The Windows Server Migration Tools are now installed and registered with Windows PowerShell on the Windows Server 2008 64-bit and can be used in a PowerShell window.

## Migrating DHCP Services from Windows Server 2003 x86 to Windows Server 2008 R2

The proceeding steps can be used to migrate DHCP services from a Windows Server 2003 x86 DHCP server to a Windows Server 2008 R2 system. Migrating the DHCP services includes several steps, which are outlined in the following sections.

**Exporting DHCP Servers Setting from a Windows Server 2003 DHCP Server**

Exporting the DHCP server settings and scopes must be performed on the source DHCP server. Before this task can be performed, the .NET framework, Windows PowerShell, and the Server Migration Tools need to be installed. Once these tools are installed, follow these steps to export the DHCP settings from a Windows Server 2003 x86-based system.

1. Using an account with administrator permissions, log on to the Windows Server 2003 x86 DHCP server that has the Windows Server Migration Tools installed and registered with Windows PowerShell.

2. Click Start, click All Programs, click Administrative Tools, and select DHCP.

3. In the DHCP Server console, select and expand the DHCP server. Right-click the DHCP server, and select Properties.

4. In the DHCP Server Properties window, select the Advanced tab and click the Bindings button. Note the IP address the DHCP server is using because we will need this IP address later during the import process on the destination DHCP server. Close the DHCP Server Properties window.

5. In the DHCP Server console, select and expand the DHCP server. Right-click the DHCP server and select Backup.

6. Select the backup location and click OK to perform the backup.

7. In the DHCP console window, right-click the DHCP server, select All Tasks, and select Stop to stop the DHCP Server service. Close the DHCP console window.

8. Click Start, click All Programs, click Administrative Tools, click Windows Server Migration Tools, and click the PowerShell shortcut for Windows Server Migration Tools. When the PowerShell window opens, it should default to the c:\SMT_ws03_x86\ folder.

9. In the PowerShell window, type `.\Servermigration.psc1` and press Enter to open a separate PowerShell window with the Windows Server Migration Tools module loaded.

10. In the PowerShell window, type the command `Export-SmigServerSetting –FeatureID DHCP` and press Enter.

11. When prompted for the path, enter c:\DHCPExport and press Enter.

12. When prompted for a password that will be used to secure the exported data, enter a password that is six characters or longer and press Enter to export the settings. Please note this password as it will be used to import the settings.

13. Close any open Command Prompt and PowerShell windows.

14. Copy the exported folder to the C:\ drive on the destination DHCP server.

15. Change the IP address of the server or remove it from the network permanently.

The original DHCP server IP address will be added to the destination server to ensure full functionality after the migration. The IP address change is required to ensure that clients with existing leases will be able to contact the DHCP server by the original DHCP server IP address. If this step is not performed, most clients will fail a DHCP renew and may need to have help desk staff assist with an Ipconfig /release and Ipconfig /renew on each machine that fails a DHCP renew.

**Importing DHCP Server Settings to a Windows Server 2008 R2 DHCP Server**

To import the previously exported Windows Server 2003 x86 DHCP server settings, install the Windows Server Migration Tools from the Add Feature link in Server Manager. Windows PowerShell is already installed on a Windows Server 2008 R2 system so this task is not necessary. The DHCP import function will overwrite all DHCP settings if imported onto an existing DHCP server, so it is a best practice to not install the DHCP Server role before running the import. To import the DHCP server settings and information from the original Windows Server 2003 system, perform the following steps:

1. Using an account with administrator permissions, log on to the Windows Server 2008 R2 system that has the Windows Server Migration Tools installed.

2. Open an elevated command prompt by clicking Start, All Programs, Accessories; locate and right-click on Command Prompt and choose Run As Administrator. If prompted for confirmation, click Continue.

3. Ping the original IP address of the Windows Server 2003 DHCP server to ensure that it is no longer in use.

4. Click Start, click All Programs, click Administrative Tools, click Windows Server Migration Tools, and click the PowerShell shortcut for Windows Server Migration Tools.

5. In the PowerShell window, type the command `Import-SmigServerSettings -FeatureID DHCP -Verbose` and press Enter.

6. When prompted for the path, type `c:\DHCPexport` and press Enter.

7. When prompted, enter the password used to secure the exported DHCP settings and press Enter. If the DHCP service had been installed previously, this import will fail. If the import failed due to the DHCP role being previously installed, the –Force option can be appended to the command; however, all existing DHCP server settings will be overwritten.

8. Once the import completes and reports successful, type `exit` and press Enter to close the Windows PowerShell window.

9. Click Start, click All Programs, click Administrative Tools, and select Services.

10. Scroll down in the left pane to locate the DHCP Server service, right-click the service, and choose Properties.

11. Change the DHCP Server service startup to Automatic and click OK to save the settings.

12. Right-click the DHCP Server service and select Start to start the service and then close the Services console window.

13. Click Start, click All Programs, click Administrative Tools, and select DHCP.

14. In the DHCP console window, the local server should be listed, expand the server, and expand the IPv4 node to reveal the imported scope. Review the scope settings, leases, and other information.

15. In the console pane, right-click the IPv4 node and select Properties.

16. Select the Advanced tab and click the Bindings button. Verify that the original DHCP server IP address is listed and checked. Click OK to close the Bindings window and click OK again to close the IPv4 Properties window.

17. In the console pane, right-click the local server node and select Authorize.

18. Refresh the window and verify the server is operational.

19. In the console pane, right-click DHCP at the top and select Manage Authorized Servers.

20. If the original server is listed, select it and click Unauthorize.

21. Verify that a new lease can be obtained and close the DHCP console.

This completes the DHCP server migration process.

## Understanding DHCP Client Alternate Network Capability

The DHCP client that is included in client systems running Windows 7, Windows Vista, Windows XP, and Windows 2000 can have a static IP address assigned to clients when a DHCP server is unavailable. This static IP address takes the place of the APIPA address that would normally be configured in these cases.

> **NOTE**
>
> If the Registry key to disable APIPA has been created, it will also disable the alternate IP configuration settings.

This type of functionality could be used on remote network systems that run into issues with DHCP Relay Agents not responding in a timely fashion. This setting should be used with extreme caution as a machine that is taken to a foreign network without a DHCP server might end up adding itself to the network with an IP address that is already in use. If the network administrator wants to configure this setting, the following steps can be executed on a Windows 7 client as an example:

1. Click Start and select Control Panel.

2. Click on Network and Internet.

3. Click on View Network Status and Tasks.

4. Click on Change Adapter Settings in the left pane.

5. Right-click the adapter in question, and choose Properties. If prompted for authorization, enter the credentials, if required, and click Yes or click Continue.

6. Select Internet Protocol Version 4 (TCP/IPv4) and choose Properties.

7. Select the Alternate Configuration tab.

8. Select the User Configured option button, enter the appropriate static IP information, and click OK.

9. Click the Close button to close the property page.

# Enhancing DHCP Reliability

The importance of DHCP cannot be understated. Unscheduled downtime of DHCP services can be very disruptive to a network, especially if the service is not available when users arrive and connect their notebooks to the network or turn their desktops on. It is extremely important for any organization to build redundancy into the DHCP infrastructure, when possible, and to document and test disaster recovery procedures for the DHCP services.

Multiple Windows Server 2008 R2 DHCP servers can be deployed on a network to provide redundancy and a greater level of administrative and management functionality than offered in previous versions of the Windows Server operating systems. New DHCP features that can be used to increase DHCP reliability and network security for the DHCP service in Windows Server 2008 R2 include, but are not limited to, the following:

- ▶ Link layer filtering or MAC address filtering for DHCP leases

- ▶ Generating Link Layer address filter lists from existing address leases

- ▶ Generating reservations from existing DHCP leases

- ▶ Configuring unique DHCP options for reservations

- ▶ DHCP Name Protection

- ▶ DHCP Network Access Protection Integration

- ▶ DHCP activity logging

- ▶ DHCP Split-Scope Configuration Wizard

- ▶ Delayed DHCP server response setting

## Link Layer Filtering

Link layer filtering is not necessarily a new feature, but it is a new feature to Windows Server 2008 R2 DHCP services. Link Layer or MAC address filtering was historically used on wireless networks to restrict access to only known wireless adapters. With Windows Server 2008 R2 DHCP for IPv4 networks, link layer filtering can be enabled to restrict which devices will be assigned an IP address from the DHCP server, and which will be denied an IP address. This filtering is not scope specific, and if enabled, it will apply to all IPv4 scopes on the particular server. Before this feature is enabled, it is a best-practice recommendation to first add all valid clients who have already obtained a lease to the allow list before enabling this feature. To prepopulate the Link Layer Filter Allow list, perform the following steps:

1. Open the DHCP console on the server to which you want to add devices to a Link Layer Filtering list by clicking Start and clicking on All Programs, Administrative Tools, DHCP. If prompted, click Continue to confirm the action.

2. When the DHCP console loads, expand the server to reveal the IPv4 node.

3. Expand the IPv4 node to reveal the Filters node and expand it.

4. Beneath the Filters node are Allow and Deny nodes, which will include the allowed and denied MAC addresses for the filter to process.

5. To add a particular MAC address to the Allow list, right-click on the Allow node beneath the Filter node, and click New Filter.

6. Enter the MAC address of a known network interface card, enter a description as desired, and click Add to complete this task. The same procedure can be followed to add a MAC address to the Deny list by right-clicking on the Deny node and choosing New Filter.

In most cases, DHCP administrators will choose to add MAC addresses to either the Allow or Deny Link Layer Filter list by reviewing existing DHCP leases. To add one or more MAC addresses to the Link Layer Filter lists from existing leases, perform the following steps:

1. Open the DHCP console on the server to which you want to add devices to a Link Layer Filter list by clicking Start, All Programs, Administrative Tools, DHCP. If prompted, click Continue to confirm the action.

2. When the DHCP console loads, expand the server to reveal the IPv4 node.

3. Expand the IPv4 node to reveal the Scope nodes for any existing scopes.

4. Select and expand the desired scope, and select the Address Leases node.

5. In the Center pane, select the Address lease entry or select multiple entries.

6. Right-click the selected lease(s), click Add to Filter, and click on the desired Filter, either Allow or Deny.

7. In the confirmation dialog box, click Yes to add the leases to the selected filter.

8. Click OK to close the resulting dialog box.

9. Under the IPv4 node in the left pane, select and expand the Filters node and select the Allow or Deny node to show the list of the existing MAC addresses already added to the Link Layer Filter list.

After the desired MAC addresses have been added to the Allow or Deny Link Layer Filter lists, a DHCP administrator might be inclined to enable link layer filter functionality on the server. To enable link layer filtering functionality on all existing and future IPv4 scopes on a Window Server 2008 R2 DHCP server, perform the following steps:

1. Open the DHCP console on the server to which you want to enable link layer filtering by clicking Start, All Programs, Administrative Tools, DHCP. If prompted, click Continue to confirm the action.

2. When the DHCP console loads, expand the server to reveal the IPv4 node.

3. Right-click the IPv4 node and select Properties.

4. Select the Filters tab, check the Enable Allow List check box and/or the Enable Deny List check box, and click OK when completed, as shown in Figure 11.7.

## DHCP Reservations

A DHCP reservation is a configuration on a DHCP server that will match a MAC address to a specific IP address in the DHCP Scope Address pool. This enables DHCP administrators to leave systems enabled for DHCP but to predefine which IP address the system will

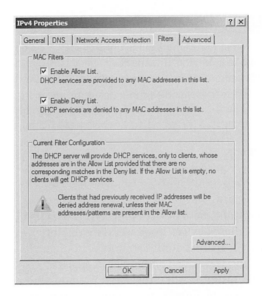

FIGURE 11.7    Enabled link layer filtering.

obtain when requesting an IP address from the particular DHCP scope on that server. This is especially handy for network printers and network workstations that need to be accessed remotely by mobile users. In many cases, setting static IP configuration on printers or end-user computers can cause problems when these devices are moved to other networks so a DHCP reservation is desirable when this device needs to be reliably contacted when on the organization's network. DHCP reservations can be created manually or they can be created from existing leases on the DHCP server. To create a DHCP reservation, perform the following steps:

1. Open the DHCP console on the server to which you want to create DHCP reservations by clicking Start, All Programs, Administrative Tools, DHCP. If prompted, click Continue to confirm the action.

2. When the DHCP console loads, expand the server to reveal the IPv4 node.

3. Expand an existing scope to reveal the Reservations node and select it to show any existing reservations in the center or right pane.

4. Right-click the Reservations node and select New Reservation.

5. Enter a friendly name for the reservation, the specific MAC address of the network adapter, and the desired IP address that is within the DHCP address pool range. Also enter a description as desired and click the Add button to create the reservation.

Alternately, a reservation can be created from an existing lease by right-clicking on the lease and selecting Add to Reservation.

**NOTE**

Reservations can be assigned to IP addresses within either the included or excluded IP address ranges defined within a scope's address pool. This is especially handy when split scopes are used on redundant DHCP servers to ensure that a system will get the same IP address regardless of which DHCP server handles the request for an IP address.

**Configuring Reservation-Specific DHCP Scope Options**

In some networking situations, there might be a requirement to provide specific DHCP options to a subset of devices—for example, Voice over IP phones or mobile devices. These devices might need to be segmented for security or functionality requirements. As an example, a network administrator might not want these devices to receive a default router or gateway scope option setting, to block these devices from accessing the Internet or other networks. Windows Server 2008 R2 DHCP enables administrators to configure specific DHCP options for specific systems, but they must be configured on a DHCP scope reservation. So, essentially, the DHCP administrator will either need to know the MAC address of the device, or take the lease and create a reservation before specific options can be set. Setting reservation-specific DHCP options can be created by performing the following steps:

1. Open the DHCP console on the server to which you want to define reservation-specific DHCP options by clicking Start, All Programs, Administrative Tools, DHCP. If prompted, click Continue to confirm the action.

2. When the DHCP console loads, expand the server to reveal the IPv4 node.

3. Expand an existing scope to reveal the Reservations node and select it to show any existing reservations in the center or right pane.

4. Right-click an existing reservation in the center or right pane and select Configure Options.

5. Select the desired DHCP options and configure the desired settings by checking on the option and either entering the values or leaving the value blank. Click OK when completed. If no options are checked, the reservation will maintain the options defined in the scope or global DHCP server options settings.

## DHCP Name Protection

Another new feature of the Windows Server 2008 R2 DHCP service is DHCP Name Protection. DHCP Name Protection is a feature that ties in directly with DNS service to prevent a system from registering or overwriting an existing name in the DNS zone for a particular DNS domain. DHCP Name Protection is based on a new DNS resource record type name DHCID. For more information on DHCID, review the RFC on DHCID. To enable DHCP Name Protection on a Windows Server 2008 R2 system, perform the following steps:

1. Open the DHCP console on the server to which you want to enable DHCP Name Protection by clicking Start, All Programs, Administrative Tools, DHCP. If prompted, click Continue to confirm the action.

2. When the DHCP console loads, expand the server to reveal the IPv4 node.

3. To enable DHCP Name Protection on all IPv4 scopes, right-click the IPv4 node in the tree pane and select Properties.

4. Select the DNS tab, and near the bottom of the window, click the Configure button in the Name Protection section.

5. In the Name Protection window, check Enable Name Protection check box and click OK.

6. Click OK again to save the settings to the IPv4 node. This will only enable Name Protection on new scopes.

7. To enable Name Protection on existing scopes, expand the IPv4 node in the tree pane to reveal all the IPv4 DHCP scopes.

8. Right-click the desired scope and select Properties.

9. Select the DNS tab, and near the bottom of the window, click the Configure button in the Name Protection section.

10. In the Name Protection window, check the Enable Name Protection check box and click OK.

11. Click OK again to save the settings to the IPv4 scope.

## DHCP Network Access Protection Integration

Windows Server 2008 R2 DHCP includes support for Network Access Protection (NAP). NAP is a service that can be implemented on a network that will define a policy that clients must adhere to before they can be fully connected to the network. Network Access Protection is configured within a Windows Network Policy Server, which is detailed in Chapter 15, "Security Policies, Network Policy Server, and Network Access Protection." To enable DHCP Network Access Protection Integration on a Windows Server 2008 R2 DHCP server, perform the following steps:

1. Open the DHCP console on the server to which you want to enable DHCP Network Access Protection by clicking Start, All Programs, Administrative Tools, DHCP. If prompted, click Continue to confirm the action.

2. When the DHCP console loads, expand the server to reveal the IPv4 node.

3. Right-click the IPv4 node and select Properties.

4. Select the Network Access Protection tab and click the Enable on All Scopes button.

5. Click Yes to confirm that the Network Access Protection settings will be overwritten on all existing scopes.

6. In the lower section of the IPv4 Network Access Protection page, select the option button that is appropriate to determine the action the DHCP server will perform when a Network Policy Server is unreachable, such as Restricted Access, and click OK to save the settings.

7. If Network Access Protection will only be enabled on a single IPv4 scope, right-click the desired scope and select Properties.

8. In the Scope Properties window, select the Network Access Protection tab and click the Enable for This Scope option button. If necessary, specify the NAP profile that will be used, if the default profile will not be used. Click OK to complete this task.

## Access DHCP Activity Logs

Windows Server 2008 R2 DHCP service includes much more logging than in previous versions. All configuration changes to a DHCP server will be logged on the system's event logs, under the DHCP logs. Also, there is a new DHCP activity log that is stored in the %systemroot%\system32\DHCP folder by default. This location can be changed on a scope-by-scope basis by configuring the audit log file path location from the protocol Properties Advanced page of the desired protocol (IPv4 or IPv6). One log will be created for each day of the week and will be named DhcpSrvLog-Mon.log for Monday for IPv4 activity and DhcpV6SrvLog-Mon.log for IPv6 activity. This log can be accessed on the local DHCP server by opening the desired file with Notepad, although the Microsoft DHCP Server team has created a DHCP Server Events Tool MMC snap-in, which can be downloaded and installed, that will allow for simple and quick review of the DHCP activity logs. For more information on this tool and to locate the download, review the information located on the DHCP Server team site at http://blogs.technet.com/teamdhcp. To access the DHCP event logs, open the Event Viewer from the Administrative Tools menu, expand Applications and Services Logs, expand Microsoft, expand Windows, and select the DHCP-Server node. Within this folder is the FilterNotifications log, which logs entries for any action that was taken, based on an enabled link layer filter. The other log in the DHCP-Server node is the operational log, which logs any and all changes to the DHCP configuration of the server.

# Implementing Redundant DHCP Services

The previous sections of this chapter detailed features that provide Windows Server 2008 R2 DHCP administrators with the ability to gain tighter control over DHCP address resources and DHCP client configurations, as well as tighter monitoring through increased logging. The next few sections of this chapter present some important information for DHCP administrators to consider when deploying DHCP services when a redundant configuration is required.

DHCP administrators who recognize the need to provide redundancy for DHCP have been challenged for many years and have had to implement manual configurations to provide any level of redundancy. Many of these implementations lacked certain functionality and required network resources that were not always readily available, such as a suitable second server to deploy DHCP services on. DHCP services redundancy can be achieved by either deploying multiple DHCP servers running overlapping or split scopes or by deploying clustered DHCP services. Many organizations do not have the administrative support or budget to deploy clustered DHCP services, so the more common approach to providing DHCP redundancy is to deploy multiple DHCP servers running split scopes.

## DHCP Split Scope

A DHCP scope is primarily defined by an address pool that contains the IP addresses that will be made available to DHCP clients. Within a scope, there is usually an included and excluded IP address list as well as DHCP scope options, such as default gateway and DNS server options, which will be delivered to clients receiving a DHCP IP address lease. A scope also contains IP address reservations and other general scope properties that enable administrators to define how the DHCP server will deal with Dynamic DNS registration for DHCP leases, audit log path settings, Name Protection settings, and much more. When redundancy is required for DHCP services, and deploying DHCP services on a cluster is not a viable option, DHCP administrators will deploy multiple DHCP servers set up in a split-scope configuration.

A DHCP split scope is a range of IP addresses available for DHCP IP address leases that are logically split between two or more DHCP servers. The IP address pool is the same on both servers, and the defining configuration for a split scope is the excluded IP range. For example, suppose a DHCP administrator was given an address pool of 192.168.1.1 to 192.168.1.254. On a split-scope configuration, both DHCP servers would have this range defined in the scope, but on the first DHCP server, there would be an excluded address range of 192.168.1.1 to 192.168.1.100; this means that the first DHCP server would lease addresses 192.168.1.101 to 192.168.1.254. The second DHCP server would also have 192.168.1.1 to 192.168.1.254 defined in the included address pool, but the excluded address range would be 192.168.1.101 to 192.168.1.254. With this configuration, the second DHCP server would lease addresses from 192.168.1.1 to 192.168.1.100. With a split-scope configuration, if a single DHCP server becomes unavailable, the secondary DHCP server can still provide DHCP leases on the network to which the split scope applies.

Historically, a split-scope configuration needed to be manually created by DHCP administrators, but starting with Windows Server 2008 R2, Microsoft now includes a DHCP Split-Scope Configuration Wizard. This wizard allows a DHCP administrator to take an existing scope on the primary DHCP server and run the wizard to duplicate the scope on a designated secondary DHCP server and define how the addresses will be split among the two servers. This wizard will make the necessary changes to both of the DHCP servers, leaving less room for user error. But before the DHCP Split-Scope Configuration Wizard can be run, a DHCP administrator must consider how the scope will be split, and the following section describes three common split-scope configurations that should be considered. The process of splitting an existing DHCP scope is detailed later in this chapter.

### Examining the 50/50 Split-Scope Configuration

The 50/50 split-scope configuration includes two DHCP servers, in which each DHCP server is configured with the same address range for the address pool, but each must have a different excluded IP address and the total number of addresses is split in half or 50/50.

Figure 11.8 illustrates the 50/50 split-scope configuration. As indicated in the diagram, the network has 200 clients defined by 192.168.1.0/24. Each DHCP server contains a scope to cover the entire specific client subnet. Server1's scope is configured with exclusions for all IP addresses except for the range of 192.168.1.1–192.168.1.125. Server2's scope is configured with exclusions for the first half and a client lease range of 192.168.1.126–192.168.1.254.

**192.168.1.0/24 Subnet**

200 Clients

Server1
**Scope Name:** First Scope
**Scope Range:** 192.168.1.1-192.168.1.254
**Exclusions:** 192.168.1.126-192.168.1.254

Server2
**Scope Name:** Second Scope
**Scope Range:** 192.168.1.1-192.168.1.254
**Exclusions:** 192.168.1.1-192.168.1.126

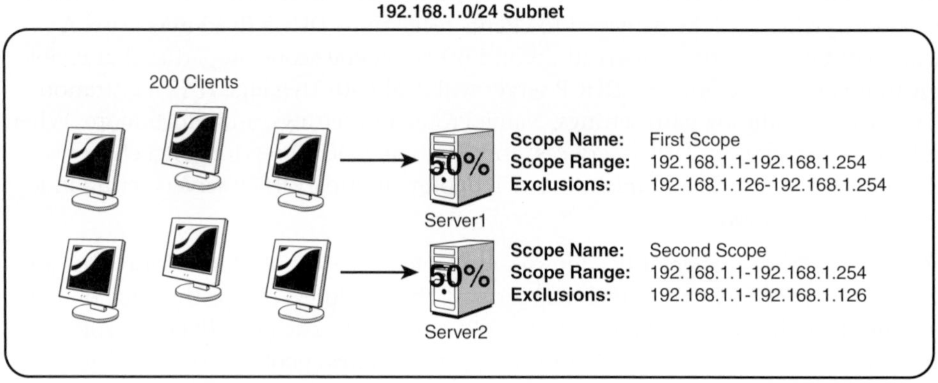

FIGURE 11.8    Examining the 50/50 failover approach.

Upon requesting a client IP address, the first server to respond to a request will be accepted, thus roughly balancing the load between the two servers, except for one thing: There is no way to determine which DHCP server will respond first and serve the client requests, so there is a chance that one DHCP server will run out of IP addresses before all IP addresses are used. Also, another issue with this configuration is that both DHCP servers would respond to lease requests and a DHCP administrator would need to review both servers to troubleshoot and determine what the true number of available IP addresses are, when clients are having issues getting an IP address lease.

### Exploring the 80/20 Failover Approach to DHCP Fault Tolerance

The 80/20 failover approach is similar to the 50/50 approach, except that the effective scope range on the server designated as the backup DHCP server contains only 20% of the available client IP range. The server with 80% of the range would be considered the primary DHCP server, and the 20% server would be considered the secondary. In the event of primary server failure, the secondary server would have enough IP addresses to provide leases until the primary server could be fixed and returned to operation. This is the best-practice split-scope configuration, but until Windows Server 2008 R2, this configuration frequently resulted in the secondary server running out of IP addresses during regular operation because it can respond to client requests as fast as the primary server—and the first server to respond wins!

### Understanding the 100/100 Failover Approach to DHCP Fault Tolerance

The 100/100 split-scope configuration in Windows Server 2008 R2 DHCP can be the most effective means of achieving high availability out of a DHCP environment. The 100/100 split-scope configuration, in its simplest form, is the same as the 50/50 except that the total scope range contains at least twice the number of total DHCP clients.

In Figure 11.9, the 10.2.0.0/16 subnet has a total of 750 clients. This subnet is serviced by two DHCP servers, each of which has a scope for the subnet. Each server has a scope with addresses from 10.2.1.1 through 10.2.8.254. The scope on Server1 excludes all IP addresses except those in the range of 10.2.1.1 through 10.2.4.254. The scope on Server2 excludes all IP addresses except those in the range from 10.2.5.1 through 10.2.8.254. Each effective range is subsequently large enough to handle 1,000 clients, which is more than enough for every machine on the network.

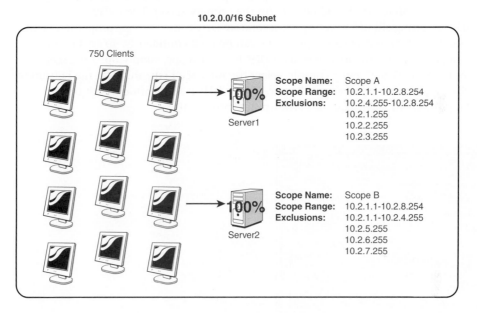

FIGURE 11.9    The 100/100 failover approach.

If one of the DHCP servers experiences an interruption in service, and it no longer responds, the second server will take over, responding to clients and enabling them to change their IP addresses to the IP addresses available in the separate range. With this configuration, extended downtime of a single DHCP server can be tolerated without much loss of functionality.

The main caveat to this approach is that a large number of IP addresses must be available for clients, more than twice the number than would normally be available. This might prove to be difficult, if not impossible, in many networks that have a limited IP range to work with, and is especially true when deploying new DHCP services on existing or established networks. However, in organizations with a larger IP range, such as those offered by private Class A network configurations (10.x.x.x and so on), this type of configuration might be ideal.

As you can see in Figure 11.9, both servers are configured with the same IP address range but even with the exclusion range, each server individually contains enough IP addresses to serve the entire DHCP client base.

### Windows Server 2008 R2 Delay Configuration Setting

Starting with Windows Server 2008 R2, the DHCP Server service now includes an IPv4 scope setting named Delay Configuration. The Delay Configuration setting is configured on the Advanced Scope Properties page and allows a DHCP administrator to delay the response from a DHCP server, to ensure that the desired primary DHCP server answers all DHCP lease requests, unless it is out of service. With this new setting alone, DHCP administrators can simplify the management of a split-scope DHCP configuration; as during normal operation, all leases should be only on the primary server. The Delay Configuration setting should be set up on secondary DHCP server scope properties. With this setting, the 80/20 best-practice split scope can be used confidently. To enable the Delay Configuration setting on a secondary DHCP server scope, simply open the scope properties from the DHCP server console, select the Advanced tab, and near the bottom of the window, type in the number of milliseconds the DHCP server should wait before responding to a client lease request, as shown in Figure 11.10.

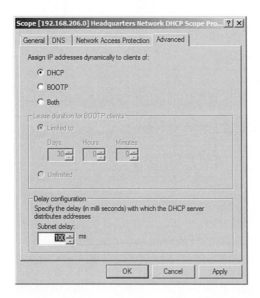

FIGURE 11.10    Setting the DHCP scope Delay Configuration setting.

### DHCP Split-Scope Configuration Wizard

When deploying multiple DHCP servers in a split-scope configuration is desired, it is recommended to use the new DHCP Split-Scope Configuration Wizard. The DHCP Split-Scope Configuration Wizard will create the new scope on the secondary DHCP server and will even copy client scope reservations that are already defined. Link Layer Filter Allow and Deny lists, however, will not be copied over. As a best practice, before running the

DHCP Split-Scope Configuration Wizard, create all the necessary reservations on the primary DHCP server scope and manually copy over any Link Layer Filter lists. Ensure that if Link Layer Filtering for either Allow or Deny or both is enabled on the primary server, that the Link Layer Filtering configuration on the secondary DHCP server matches this configuration. To deploy a split-scope configuration—for this example, in an 80/20 split— follow these steps:

1. Install the DHCP service on two servers. For this example, we will use Server10 as the primary and Server60 as the secondary.

2. On the primary server, create a new DHCP scope that contains the entire scope range and DHCP options for that scope.

3. On the secondary server, do not create any scopes.

4. Open the DHCP server console on the primary server, and expand the server node in the tree pane to reveal the IPv4 and IPv6 nodes.

5. Add the secondary server to the console by right-clicking on the DHCP node at the top of the tree pane and selecting Add Server.

6. In the Add Server window, type in the secondary server name or choose it from the managed authorized server list and click OK to complete this task.

7. After both servers are listed in the console, select and expand the primary server IPv4 node to display the desired IPv4 scope that will be split for this example.

8. Select and right-click the desired IPv4 scope on the primary DHCP server, select Advanced, and then click on Split-Scope, as shown in Figure 11.11.

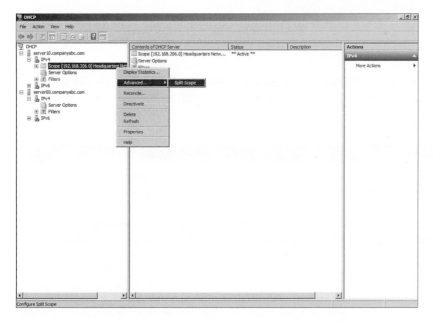

FIGURE 11.11   Initiating the DHCP Split-Scope Configuration Wizard.

9. In the DHCP Split-Scope Configuration Wizard, click Next on the Introduction to DHCP Split-Scope page to continue.

10. On the Additional DHCP Server page, type in the name of the secondary DHCP server (for this example, Server60), and click Next to continue.

11. On the Percentage of Split page, the wizard will default to the 80/20 split, which will configure the primary server with 80% of the addresses for lease and exclude the remaining 20%. The secondary server will be configured with 20% of the addresses available for lease and the other 80% will be excluded. Accept the defaults or move the slider to the desired percentage split, and click Next to continue, as shown in Figure 11.12.

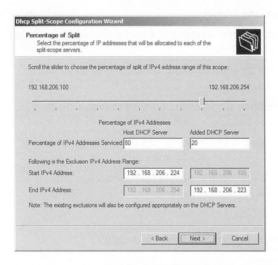

FIGURE 11.12    Defining the percentage split of addresses.

12. On the Delay in DHCP Offer page, define the delay in milliseconds on the secondary server to ensure that the bulk of clients will be serviced by the primary server, and click Next to continue.

**NOTE**

Determining how long to delay the secondary DHCP server must be concluded by performing tests on the actual network that will serve the DHCP clients. It is key that the primary server is given ample time to respond and the delay on the secondary is short enough that when the primary server is down, DHCP clients will be acknowledged and serviced by the secondary DHCP server. For our test network, 100 milliseconds was suitable, but on some larger networks, this number might need to be increased.

13. On the Summary of Split-Scope Configuration page, review the chosen settings and click Finish to configure both of the DHCP servers.

14. Once the process completes, the status of the configuration changes on both servers is displayed in the window. Review the results and click Close to close the wizard.

15. Once the wizard is closed, in the tree pane, select and expand the secondary server to expose the IPv4 node.

16. Expand the IPv4 node to reveal the new scope. Review the scope settings, and if things look good, right-click the scope and click Activate to finalize the split-scope configuration, as shown in Figure 11.13.

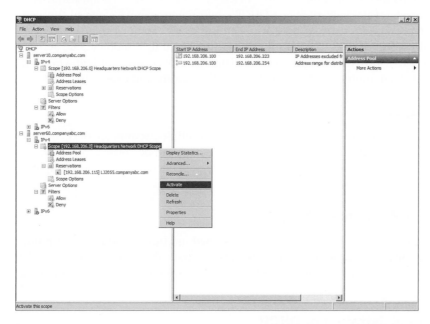

FIGURE 11.13    Activating the new split scope on the secondary DHCP server.

Both the primary and secondary DHCP servers configured in a split-scope configuration will honor client scope address reservations, even if the reservation IP address falls within the excluded IP address range. For this to be 100% effective, the reservation will need to be defined on both servers, and the wizard will copy any existing reservations defined on the primary server. Link Layer Filter lists will not be copied over, and any new reservations created on the primary server will need to be manually created on the secondary server scope.

## Clustering DHCP Servers

The final redundancy option, and frankly the easiest to configure and maintain, if resources allow, is to deploy a clustered DHCP service. In this configuration, if a single server goes down, the second server in a cluster will take over DHCP operations. This option requires a greater investment in hardware and should be considered only in specific cases in which it is necessary. The biggest benefit for this configuration is that all leases, Link Layer Filter lists, and reservations will be contained with the configuration of the single clustered DHCP server. For more information on clustering servers, see Chapter 29, "System-Level Fault Tolerance (Clustering/Network Load Balancing)."

# Exploring Advanced DHCP Concepts

DHCP has been an unassuming network service as of late. The simplicity of the protocol is another reason for its success because it is not cursed by a high degree of administrative complexity. However, greater control over a DHCP environment can be achieved through the understanding of some advanced concepts regarding its use. Some of these concepts are new to Windows Server 2008 R2, and some were introduced in Windows 2000 Server, Windows Server 2003, and Windows Server 2008. These improvements can help you gain control over a DHCP environment and provide for more security and ease of use.

## Understanding DHCP Superscopes

A DHCP superscope is used for environments in which multiple network subnets encompass a single scope environment. In these cases, a superscope can be created to contain multiple scopes. The individual scopes are subsequently dependent on the master superscope. If it is turned off, they will also be deactivated.

## Examining DHCP Multicast Scopes

A multicast scope is created to allow clients to be assigned multicast IP addresses. A multicast IP address is one in which destination hosts can each have the same IP address, which is useful in one-to-many forms of communications, such as webcasts and videoconferencing sessions.

## Delegating Administration of DHCP

It is never wise to hand over full administrative privileges to individuals who need to perform only a specific network function. If a small group of administrators needs control over the DHCP environment, Windows Server 2008 R2 makes it easy to delegate administrative capabilities to them through the inclusion of a group called DHCP Administrators. Adding users or, preferably, groups to this security group will enable those users to administer the DHCP servers in an environment. If the DHCP server is a member server, this will be a local security group. If DHCP is deployed on a domain controller, this will be a domain security group and membership in this group will apply to all DHCP servers in the domain that are running on domain controllers. There is also another group named DHCP Users that can be used to grant read-only view rights to the DHCP system. This is a good group for desktop or Network Operations Center administrators to be members of.

## Using the Netsh Command-Line Utility

Windows Server 2008 R2 has made great strides in allowing virtually all administrative functions to be performed through the command line. This not only helps those users who are used to command-line administration, such as that in UNIX operating systems, but also allows for the execution of scripts and batch files, which can automate administrative processes. The Netsh command-line utility is one such utility that effectively allows administrators to accomplish virtually all DHCP tasks that can be run through the MMC GUI interface. For a full listing of potential functions with Netsh, run `netsh /?` from the command line, as illustrated in Figure 11.14.

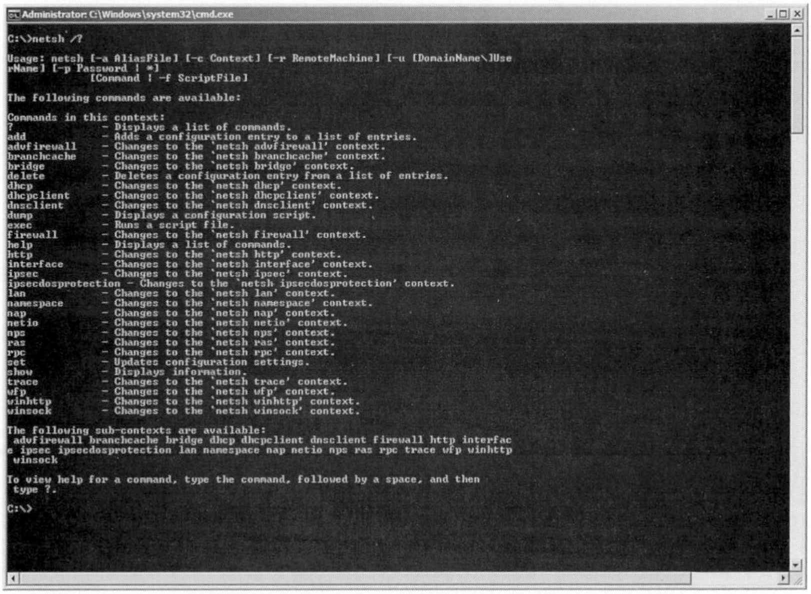

FIGURE 11.14    `Netsh` command-line options.

# Securing DHCP

The DHCP protocol is effectively insecure. There is no way to determine if a request from a client is legitimate or is malicious. Users who have evil intentions can conduct denial-of-service attacks against the DHCP server by simply requesting all available IP addresses in a range, effectively disallowing legitimate users from being granted IP addresses. For this and other reasons, it is important to keep wired security as a high priority. Although this point might seem obvious, keeping potential intruders physically off a network is a must, not only for DHCP but for other network services prone to denial-of-service attacks. This includes auditing the security of wireless networks, such as 802.11b, which can (and often do) provide unrestricted access to malicious users.

When securing DHCP services is required, link layer filtering should be enabled for both Allow and Deny lists. This will ensure that only the desired and approved clients can receive an IP address and all others will be ignored. Also, deploying a Network Policy Server (NPS) and configuring an appropriate health policy can be performed, and the DHCP server can be configured to check a client's health information with the NPS server and deny a lease if the system does not meet the health policy. More information on Network Policy Servers can be found in Chapter 15.

## Examining DHCP Authorization

DHCP is an unauthenticated service, which means that anyone can deploy a DHCP server on a network and start to accept clients and assign them erroneous addresses or redirect them for malicious purposes. Consequently, since Windows 2000, it has become necessary to authorize a DHCP server that is running in an Active Directory domain. After the DHCP server is authorized by the proper domain administrative authority, that server can then accept client leases.

The downside to this approach is that a Windows NT 4.0 or Linux server could still be added, unauthenticated, to a network. In this situation, it would become necessary to use a network analyzer to determine the location of rogue DHCP servers.

Authorization of a Windows Server 2008 R2 DHCP server is straightforward, as long as the server is a member of an AD DS domain and the logged-on user has proper DHCP privileges in the domain. Normally authorization occurs during the installation of the DHCP Server role. However, a domain DHCP server that has been unauthorized or a workgroup DHCP server that is joined to the domain will need to be authorized. This can be accomplished by following these steps:

1. Open the DHCP console (Start, All Programs, Administrative Tools, DHCP).
2. Right-click DHCP in the console tree, and then click Manage Authorized Servers to display the Manage Authorized Servers dialog box.
3. In the Manage Authorized Servers dialog box, click the Authorize button, as shown in Figure 11.15.

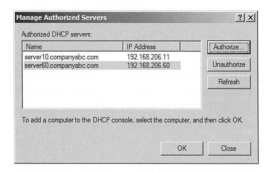

FIGURE 11.15   Authorizing a DHCP server.

4. When prompted, type the IP address or name of the DHCP server to be authorized, and then click OK.
5. Confirm the DHCP server to be authorized in the Confirm Authorization dialog box, and then click OK. In a few minutes, the DHCP should be authorized, and the scopes can be activated. Click OK to close any remaining dialog boxes.

## Understanding DHCP and Domain Controller Security

If at all possible, the DHCP service should not be run on an Active Directory domain controller because the security of the SRV records generated is lost. The reasons for this are as follows.

DNS entries in an Active Directory–integrated DNS zone are "secure," which means that only the client that originally created the record can subsequently update that same record. This can cause problems if the DHCP server is automatically updating client records, however, as the client no longer performs this function and cannot have security applied to a record.

DHCP in Windows Server 2008 R2 overcomes this limitation by providing a special group in Active Directory, called DNSUpdateProxy. Members of this group do not have any security applied to objects that they create in the DNS database. The theory is that the first client to "touch" the record will then take over security for that record.

The problem with this concept is that the records created by DHCP servers possess no immediate security and are consequently subject to takeover by hostile clients. Because domain controllers are responsible for publishing SRV DNS records, which indicate the location of domain controllers, Kerberos servers, and the like, this leaves a gaping security hole that users could exploit. Consequently, it is preferable to keep DHCP off domain controllers. If this cannot be avoided, it is recommended to not place the DHCP server into the DNSUpdateProxy group so as to avoid the security problems associated with it or to ensure that each scope on the DHCP server is configured with a user account to use for Dynamic DNS updates. To add a designated user account to perform Dynamic DNS registration for the DHCP server, open the DHCP server console, and on the desired DHCP server, expand and right-click the IPv4 node, select the Advanced tab, and click the Credentials button. Enter the name, domain, and password of the user account that will update and own the Dynamic DNS entries related to DHCP leases. Ensure that this account is just a standard user and not a domain administrator to ensure that it can only manage records that it creates and will be denied the ability to update or replace any existing records created by Windows clients or DNS administrators.

# Reviewing the Windows Internet Naming Service (WINS)

The Windows Internet Naming Service (WINS) has a long history in Microsoft networks. In the beginning, Microsoft networks were primarily broadcast-based, using protocols such as NetBEUI to identify local computers. If a user on a Windows client wanted to find a system by name, the Windows client would send out a broadcast message by name, and if the system was on the same network, it would respond so the two systems could establish a connection and begin communication. The problem with this type of name resolution was that it did not scale beyond multiple subnets, and with today's networks, broadcast messages can be blocked by local server and workstation firewalls and anti-malware software. With the adoption of TCP/IP as an easily routable protocol, the need to translate

NetBIOS or Windows computer names to IP addresses became a reality. This need gave rise to the development of the Windows Internet Naming Service (WINS).

WINS provided a central database that can be referenced when a client system is looking up another system by hostname, and that is the key difference between WINS and DNS, hostname versus fully qualified name. As an example of this, a server named SERVER10 in the companyabc.com domain would have a WINS record named "SERVER10" and a DNS record in the companyabc.com DNS zone named "server10.companyabc.com."

## Understanding the Need for Legacy Microsoft NetBIOS Resolution

WINS is effectively a simple database of NetBIOS names and their corresponding IP addresses. Some additional information, such as domain name, server type or service type, and so on, can be determined as well, from the 16th byte in a NetBIOS name stored in WINS.

WINS is considered legacy in the Microsoft world because NetBIOS resolution is being phased out in favor of the domain name system (DNS) form of name resolution. However, it is difficult to divorce WINS from modern networks because of the reliance on WINS by down-level (pre-Windows 2000) clients, legacy applications, and even some Microsoft services, such as the Distributed File System (DFS), that utilize NetBIOS resolution by default. Also, many Independent Software Vendors, or ISVs, develop their software for Microsoft networks, but their test networks sometimes only include a single network with no firewalling between systems. When these software applications are deployed on enterprise networks, they can fall short in name resolution results, and deploying WINS might be the only viable solution.

As mentioned previously, the new DNS GlobalNames feature is designed to remove the need for WINS. See Chapter 10 for more information on DNS GlobalNames.

## Exploring WINS and DNS Integration

DNS can use the WINS database to provide for quasi-DNS resolution of WINS clients. This means that if a name resolution request is sent to a DNS server to resolve client1.companyabc.com, for example, the DNS server will first look in the companyabc.com zone. If no record exists for client1.companyabc.com, the DNS server will perform a lookup on the WINS database for CLIENT1; if a WINS record exists, the DNS server will take this IP address and send it back to the DNS client as client1.companyabc.com, as illustrated in Figure 11.16.

This functionality must be enabled on the DNS server because it is not configured by default. This feature is configured on a zone-by-zone basis; however, if the forward lookup zone is an Active Directory–integrated zone, each Windows Server 2008 R2 DNS server hosting this zone will copy this WINS setting. To enable WINS resolution on a DNS server, follow these steps:

1. On a server running DNS, open the DNS MMC snap-in (Start, Administrative Tools, DNS).
2. Navigate to DNS\<Servername>\Forward Lookup Zones.

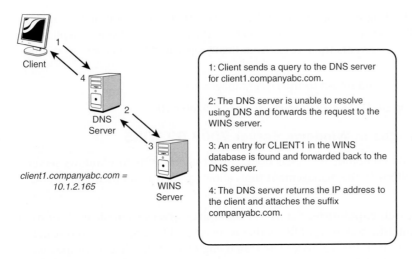

1: Client sends a query to the DNS server for client1.companyabc.com.

2: The DNS server is unable to resolve using DNS and forwards the request to the WINS server.

3: An entry for CLIENT1 in the WINS database is found and forwarded back to the DNS server.

4: The DNS server returns the IP address to the client and attaches the suffix companyabc.com.

FIGURE 11.16    WINS integration with DNS.

3. Right-click the zone in question and click Properties.

4. Choose the WINS tab.

5. Select the Use WINS Forward Lookup check box.

6. Enter the IP address of the WINS server(s) to be used for resolution of names not found in DNS, and click Add to save the changes, as illustrated in Figure 11.17.

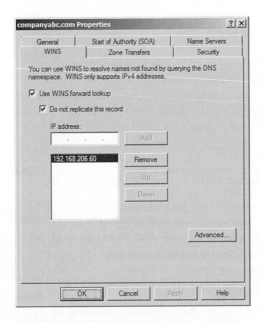

FIGURE 11.17    Configuring WINS resolution in DNS.

7. If you are replicating this zone between DNS servers that are not running Windows Server 2008 R2 DNS services, make sure to check the box labeled Do Not Replicate This Record. This prevents the records from being replicated to other servers during zone transfers.

8. Click OK to finish and return to the DNS Manager page.

For more information on DNS configuration, refer to Chapter 10.

## Reviewing Changes in Windows Server 2008 R2 WINS

Although the overall function of WINS has not changed significantly in Windows Server 2008 R2, some additions to the management tools allow for increased functionality and capabilities:

▶ **Advanced search capabilities for WINS databases**—Previous implementations of WINS had simplistic search capabilities that were limited to simple keyword searches of NetBIOS records in the database. The search engine for WINS has been updated in Windows Server 2008 R2 to support more advanced search parameters, thus giving administrators more flexibility in searching for specific records.

▶ **WINS pull record filtering and replication partner acceptance**—Instead of entire transfers of all records on other servers, replication can be limited to only those records owned by a specific server, thus excluding extraneous records from littering a WINS database.

In addition to these advances in Windows Server 2008 R2, Windows 2000 introduced enhancements to WINS, such as an updated database engine, persistent connections, manual tombstoning, and other improvements.

# Installing and Configuring WINS

As with many services in Windows Server 2008 R2, the installation and configuration process of a WINS server is streamlined through the Add Features Wizard. This wizard automatically installs all necessary services and databases and configures other settings pertinent to a particular service. Although other methods of installation still exist, this method is the preferred approach in Windows Server 2008 R2.

## Installing WINS

To install WINS on a server using the Server Manager Add Features Wizard, follow these steps:

1. Choose Start, All Programs, Administrative Tools, Server Manager. In the console tree, right-click on Features, and then click Add Features to start the Add Features Wizard.

2. On the Select Features page, scroll down the list of features and select the check box next to WINS Server. Then click Next to continue.

3. Verify that WINS Server is displayed in the selections window.

4. Click Install on the Confirm Installation Selections page to begin installing the WINS server.

5. It will take a few minutes for the installation to begin and the basic configuration of the WINS server to complete.

6. If desired, click the Print, E-mail, or Save the Installation Report link to archive the installation results.

7. Click Close on the Installation Results page to finish setup.

## Configuring Push/Pull Partners

If a WINS server in an environment is the sole WINS server for that network, no additional configuration is required other than ensuring that clients will be pointing to the WINS server in their IP configuration. However, if it has been decided that WINS is required, it is a best-practice recommendation to deploy a secondary WINS server to provide redundancy. Unlike DHCP, however, WINS replication partners will replicate their registered entries between each other. WINS replication is established through the designation of WINS push/pull partners.

A push partner for a particular WINS server is the server that pushes WINS database information to a receiving or pull partner. A pull partner is a WINS server from which changes are "pulled." In a nutshell, if Server1 has Server2 configured as a push partner, Server2 must have Server1 configured as a pull partner, and vice versa.

A WINS push/pull topology should roughly map to an organization's network topology. For example, if an organization is composed of two main offices that serve as network hubs, and several branch offices, each with its own WINS servers, the WINS push/pull topology could look something like Figure 11.18. In many organizations, however, if network connectivity is reliable between locations, it is a best practice to deploy only two WINS servers for the entire organization. This reduces WINS database replication and administration. Remote or branch office WINS servers should only be deployed on networks where network and/or firewall administrators block WINS traffic from remote networks.

## Examining WINS Replication

WINS replicates database changes on a set schedule, which can be modified on a per-connection basis. Just as with any network communications, the replication schedule should be modified to fit the particular needs of an organization. If a wide area network (WAN) link is saturated with traffic, it might be wise to throttle back the WINS replication schedule. However, if a link between push/pull partners is robust, a shorter schedule can be established. To establish WINS replication between two WINS servers, complete the following steps:

1. Install WINS on two designated servers as previously outlined. For our example, we will use SERVER10 and SERVER60.

2. On one of the servers, log in and open the WINS console (Start, All Programs, Administrative Tools, WINS). If prompted, click Continue to confirm the action.

3. Expand the WINS server in the console tree, and then choose Replication Partners. The right pane will display any existing replication partners.

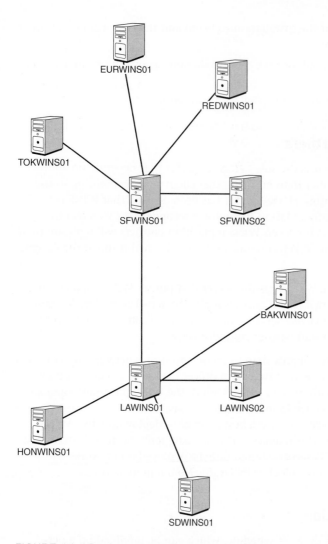

FIGURE 11.18    Sample WINS push/pull topology.

4. If the desired replication partner is not already defined, in the console tree, right-click Replication Partners and select New Replication Partner.

5. Enter the name of the desired WINS server and click OK. This adds the designated WINS server as a push/pull partner, meaning that these servers will replicate and synchronize their database with one another.

6. In the WINS console tree, right-click the WINS node and choose Add Server.

7. Type in the name of the WINS server previously defined as a replication partner.

8. Once the second WINS server is added to the console, repeat the preceding steps to add the first server as a replication partner.

WINS replication partners need to be defined on both systems before replication will function.

WINS replication partners will replicate their database information with one another every 30 minutes by default. If you, the WINS administrator, want to change this replication schedule, complete the following steps:

1. Open the WINS console (Start, All Programs, Administrative Tools, WINS). If prompted, click Continue to confirm the action.
2. Expand the WINS server in the console tree, and then choose Replication Partners.
3. Right-click Push/Pull Partner (if one does not exist, it will have to be created), and choose Properties.
4. In the replication partner property pages, select the Advanced tab, and change the Replication Interval time to the desired length, as indicated in Figure 11.19, and click OK to save the settings.

FIGURE 11.19   WINS replication settings.

5. Repeat this process on the other replication partner.

This can also be used to change other partner replication settings, such as number of retries, start replication at service startup, persistent connections, and other pertinent replication information.

## Understanding NetBIOS Client Resolution and the LMHOSTS File

A Windows client does not immediately resort to a WINS server to determine the IP address of a NetBIOS name. This knowledge is essential in the troubleshooting of name resolution on a Windows client. Instead, a client first accesses its local NetBIOS cache for resolution. If an IP address changes, this cache might report the old address, impeding troubleshooting. To flush this cache, run nbtstat -R (with uppercase R) at the command line.

In addition to the local cache, clients by default always parse an LMHOSTS file, if one exists, before contacting a WINS server. If the LMHOSTS file contains erroneous information, it will impede proper name resolution. Always check to see whether this file is populated (it is usually located in %systemroot%\system32\drivers\etc on clients) before beginning to troubleshoot the WINS server.

# Planning, Migrating, and Maintaining WINS

As previously mentioned, WINS is necessary in most production environments because the overriding dependencies on NetBIOS that were built in to Windows have not entirely been shaken out. In fresh installations of Windows Server 2008 R2, WINS might not be necessary, but for older, upgraded environments, plans should be made for WINS being around for a few years.

## Upgrading a WINS Environment

The WINS service itself is one of the more straightforward services to migrate to a separate set of servers as part of an upgrade to Windows Server 2008 R2. A simple upgrade of the existing WINS server will do the trick for many environments; however, migrating to a separate server or set of servers might be beneficial if changing topology or hardware.

Migration of an existing WINS environment is most easily accomplished through the procedure described in this section. This procedure allows for the migration of an entire WINS database to a new set of servers, but without affecting any clients or changing WINS server settings. Figure 11.20 illustrates a WINS migration using this procedure.

In Figure 11.20, the existing servers, OldServer1 and OldServer2, handle WINS traffic for the entire network of fictional CompanyABC. They are configured with IP addresses 10.1.1.11 and 10.1.1.12, which are configured in all clients' IP settings as Primary and Secondary WINS, respectively. OldServer1 and OldServer2 are configured as push/pull partners.

The new servers, NewServer1 and NewServer2, are added to the network with the WINS service installed and configured as push/pull partners for each other. Their initial IP addresses are 10.1.1.21 and 10.1.1.22. OldServer1 and NewServer1 are then connected as push/pull partners for the network. Because the servers are connected this way, all database information from the old WINS database is replicated to the new servers, as illustrated in step 1, shown in Figure 11.20.

After the entire WINS database is replicated to the new servers, the old servers are shut down (on a weekend or evening to minimize impact), and NewServer1 and NewServer2

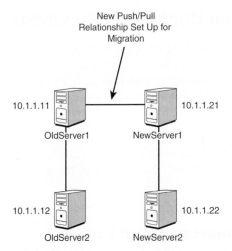

FIGURE 11.20   The first step in the WINS migration procedure.

are immediately reconfigured to take the IP addresses of the old servers, as illustrated in step 2, shown in Figure 11.21.

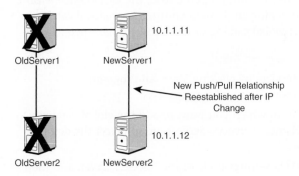

FIGURE 11.21   The second step in the WINS migration procedure.

The push/pull partner relationship between NewServer1 and NewServer2 is then reestablished because the IP addresses of the servers changed. The entire downtime of the WINS environment can be measured in mere minutes, and the old database is migrated intact. In addition, because the new servers assume the old IP addresses, no client settings need to be reconfigured.

There are a few caveats with this approach, however. If the IP addresses cannot be changed, WINS servers must be changed on the client side. If you're using DHCP, you can do this by leaving all old and new servers up in an environment until the WINS change can be automatically updated through DHCP. Effectively, however, WINS migrations can be made very straightforward through this technique, and they can be modified to fit any WINS topology.

# Exploring Global Catalog Domain Controller Placement

The placement of domain controllers in Windows Server 2008 R2 is a critical factor in providing quality communication between Active Directory clients and domain controllers. Without prompt response from a domain controller, a user might have to wait several seconds to several minutes to merely log on to the network or a computer to complete booting up.

This section deals with specific server placement issues for Active Directory domain controllers and global catalog servers. For more in-depth coverage of these concepts, refer to Chapter 4, "Active Directory Domain Services Primer," and Chapter 5, "Designing a Windows Server 2008 R2 Active Directory."

## Understanding the Role of the Active Directory Global Catalog

The global catalog in Active Directory holds an indexed subset of frequently queried or accessed objects in an Active Directory forest. Not all domain controllers in the Windows Server 2008 R2 Active Directory are global catalog servers by default. That being said, when installing a new Windows Server 2008 R2 forest, the first Windows Server 2008 R2 domain controller in the forest will be configured as a global catalog server because this is a necessary service for Active Directory to function properly. Also, the DCPROMO Wizard on Windows Server 2008 R2 defaults to deploy all domain controllers as global catalog servers. Domain controllers that are not global catalog servers can be established as such through the following procedure:

1. Open Active Directory Sites and Services by clicking Start, All Programs, Administrative Tools, Active Directory Sites and Services.
2. In the console tree, click the server to which you want to add the global catalog. Do this by navigating to Sites\<SiteName>\Servers\<ServerName>. Select the desired server in the console or tree pane.
3. In the Details pane, right-click NTDS Settings node of the selected server, and then click Properties.
4. Select the Global Catalog check box on the General tab.
5. Click OK to finish.

---

**NOTE**

To complete this process, the administrator must be a member of the Enterprise Admins group in the forest or a member of the Domain Admins group in the domain of the selected domain controller or equivalent permissions. Security best practices dictate that this process be performed with the lowest-level user account and using the Run As Administrator option to manage Active Directory Domain Services.

---

## Placing Global Catalog/Domain Controllers

It is important to understand that global catalog objects must be physically located close to all objects in a network that require prompt logon times and fast connectivity. Because a global catalog entry is parsed for universal group membership every time a user logs on, this effectively means that this information must be close at hand. This can be accomplished by placing global catalog and domain controller (GC/DC) servers on the same WAN site or by using a process called universal group caching.

## Exploring Universal Group Caching

Universal group caching is a process by which an Active Directory site caches all universal group membership locally so that the next time clients log on, information is more quickly provided to the clients and they are able to log on faster.

Universal group caching can be more effective than placing a GC/DC server locally because only those universal groups that are relevant to a local site's members are replicated and are cached on the local domain controller. The downside to this approach, however, is that the first logon for clients will still be longer than if a local GC/DC were provided, and the cache eventually expires, requiring another sync with a GC/DC.

## Examining Global Catalog and Domain Controller Placement

As illustrated in the preceding sections, decisions must be made regarding the most efficient placement of DCs and GC/DCs in an environment. Determining the placement of GC/DCs and universal group caching sites must be done with an eye toward determining how important fast logons are for users in a site compared with higher replication throughput. For many Windows Server 2008 R2 environments, the following guidelines apply:

▶ **Sites with fewer than 50 users**—Use a single DC configured with universal group caching.

▶ **Sites with 50–100 users**—Use two DCs configured for universal group caching.

▶ **Sites with 100–200 users**—Use a single GC server and single DC server.

▶ **Sites with 200+ users**—Alternate adding additional DCs and GC/DCs for every 100 users.

The recommendations listed here are generalized and should not be construed as relevant to every environment. Some scenarios might call for variations to these approaches, such as when using Microsoft Exchange Server in a site where Exchange requires close connection to a global catalog server (not a caching controller) or in single domain/single forest environments with limited sites where all domain controllers can be global catalog servers. However, these general guidelines can help to size an Active Directory environment for domain controller placement.

## Examining Read-Only Domain Controllers

A concept similar to universal group caching, one of the new features for Active Directory Domain Services in Windows Server 2008 and Windows Server 2008 R2 is the Read-Only Domain Controller (RODC). An RODC server is a new type of domain controller that contains read-only replicas of the domain Active Directory database. As shown in Figure 11.22, this is well suited for branch offices or other locations where physical security of the domain controller can be compromised, where excessive wide area networking activity might have a negative impact on productivity, or where other applications must run on a domain controller and be maintained by an understaffed technical department or an IT department with little technical knowledge. The benefits of RODCs are a read-only Active Directory Domain Services database, inbound-only replication, credential caching, administrator role separation, and read-only DNS.

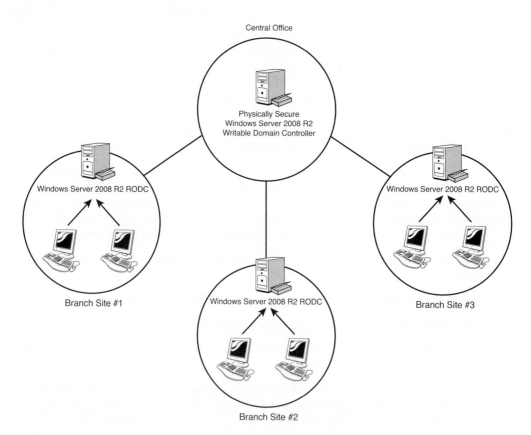

FIGURE 11.22    Sample deployment of a Read-Only Domain Controller in a Windows Server 2008 R2 environment.

Although an RODC can replicate data from domain controllers running Windows Server 2003, it can only replicate updates of the domain partition from a Windows Server 2008 or Windows Server 2008 R2 domain controller running within the same domain. Because RODCs cannot perform outbound replication, they cannot be a source domain controller for any other domain controller. In contrast, writable Windows Server 2008 R2 domain controllers and Windows Server 2008 domain controllers can perform inbound and outbound replication of all available partitions. Thus, they do not require the same placement considerations required by RODCs.

Because an RODC can replicate the domain partition only from a writable Windows Server 2008 R2 or Windows Server 2008 domain controller, careful planning is required. The placement of an RODC and writable Windows Server 2008 R2 domain controllers is important as their deployment might be affected by the site topology and network constraints; each RODC requires a writable Windows Server 2008 R2 domain controller for the same domain from which the RODC directly replicates. This requires a writable Windows Server 2008 R2 domain controller be placed in the nearest site that contains a direct site link to the site in the topology that includes the RODC, as illustrated in Figure 11.22.

An RODC server contains the same objects and attributes as a writable domain controller with the exception of user passwords. The difference between an RODC server and the writable domain controller is that changes that originate locally are not made to the RODC replica itself but are forwarded to a writable domain controller and then replicated back to the RODC server. Also, the Active Directory administrator can determine or limit which user account password or credentials can be cached on a remote RODC. This improves security by reducing the risk or exposure of the read-only Active Directory database on the RODC.

Active Directory administrators might also specifically configure an RODC to cache user credentials. The first time a user attempts to authenticate to an RODC, the RODC forwards the request to a writable domain controller. When authentication is successful, the RODC requests a copy of the user credentials. By default, the RODC does not cache the passwords of any domain users so administrators must modify the default password replication policy for the RODC to allow the RODC to authenticate users and their computers when the WAN link to the hub site is unavailable. The active Password Replication Policy determines if the credentials are allowed to be replicated and cached on the RODC. The next time that user attempts to log on, the request is directly serviced by the RODC. This occurs until the RODC is informed by the writable domain controller that a user credential change has occurred. In the scenario, end-user productivity is vastly improved because of the efficient logon process. Connectivity issues commonly experienced by branch offices such as poor network bandwidth or WAN latency are mitigated because the user is authenticated on the locally deployed RODC. Because the RODC only performs inbound replication, network traffic is also reduced. To allow a user account's password to be cached on a Read-Only Domain Controller, the user will need to be added to the default "Allowed RODC Password Replication Group" or the user can be added specifically to the Password Replication Policy on the specific Read-Only Domain Controllers.

RODCs also help reduce security risks and administration tasks associated with branch office servers. Because Active Directory Domain Services also manages a list of all credentials stored on RODCs, if an RODC is compromised, administrators can force a password reset for all user credentials stored on that RODC. To further mitigate security risks,

RODCs cannot operate as an operation role holder (Flexible Single Master Operations [FSMO]) because this role requires writing of information to the Active Directory database. Also, RODCs cannot act as a bridgehead server because bridgehead servers are designed to replicate changes from other sites.

Another feature of RODCs is delegation of installation and management task to non-administrative personnel at a branch office. Nontechnical branch office personnel can perform an installation by attaching a server to the RODC account that a domain administrator has previously created. This eliminates the need to use a home office staging site for branch office domain controllers. This feature also eliminates the need to send installation media and a domain administrator to branch locations, which reduces the cost of server setup and improves setup time at branch locations.

For more information on domain controller and Active Directory, see Chapter 7, "Active Directory Infrastructure."

## Summary

Although often overlooked, the services of DHCP and WINS are some of the most critical components of a functional Windows Server 2008 R2 environment. In addition, global catalog domain controller placement and related issues are integral to the functionality of an Active Directory environment. A new feature, the Read-Only Domain Controller, provides a secure and effective way to set up branch locations. Because end-user credentials can be cached locally on the RODC and inbound-only replication occurs, end users experience improvements in productivity. As a result, it is important to have a strong understanding of these components and their related design, migration, and maintenance procedures to ensure the high availability, reliability, and resilience of a network infrastructure.

## Best Practices

The following are best practices from this chapter:

- ▶ Perform all tests with DHCP, WINS, and RODC in a lab environment.

- ▶ Implement redundancy in a DHCP using split scopes or clustered DHCP services.

- ▶ Manually perform a backup of the DHCP database before making any configuration changes to the server.

- ▶ Before enabling link layer filters, first add all of the approved clients to the Allowed list on all DHCP servers that may service the clients.

- ▶ When deploying DHCP in a split-scope configuration, split the scope in an 80/20 split and configure the delay setting on the secondary server scope.

- ▶ Before running the DHCP Split-Scope Configuration Wizard, create all of the necessary reservations on the primary DHCP server scope so these can be copied over to the secondary server by the wizard.

▶ Implement redundant WINS servers by configuring servers as push/pull partners.

▶ Limit the number of WINS servers on the network to reduce WINS server replication and administration and to simplify WINS troubleshooting.

▶ When migrating DHCP services from one server to another, use the Windows Server Migration Tools to assist in transferring DHCP scopes and leases.

▶ Properly plan the most efficient placement of DCs and GC/DCs in an environment.

▶ Use a single DC configured with universal group caching for Active Directory sites with fewer than 50 users that do not need a local GC for services such as Exchange.

▶ Use at least two DCs in Active Directory sites with between 50 and 100 users.

▶ Deploy RODCs in branch offices to reduce security risks, reduce network traffic, and improve end-user logon times.

▶ When RODCs are deployed, create a new security group and add this group to the Password Replication Policy of that specific RODC, and add members to this group as necessary to reduce security exposure.

11

# Internet Information Services

Internet Information Services (IIS) has been going through continuous change for years, so it isn't surprising that the most current version of IIS is Microsoft's most powerful, most reliable, and most secure web server. Without a doubt, the fundamental capabilities of IIS 7.5 are exhilarating. The new web server includes a plethora of new features and functionality that provide numerous benefits to organizations hosting applications and developers creating web applications with the latest .NET Framework. Among other things, organizations can also simplify management, reduce surface area attacks, benefit from improved diagnostic and troubleshooting capabilities, and enjoy greater scalability.

To reap the full benefits of IIS 7.5, this chapter gives web administrators the knowledge base necessary to understand the improvements and new management user interface in IIS 7.5. The first sections of the chapter focus on planning an IIS 7.5 infrastructure and installing or upgrading to IIS 7.5. The second sections focus on creating both web and File Transfer Protocol (FTP) sites, and discuss how to configure the new settings. The final sections of the chapter discuss how to secure IIS 7.5.

## Understanding Internet Information Services (IIS) 7.5

Organizations and web administrators must fully understand IIS 7.5 before installing, upgrading, or creating sites with the product. Specifically, they should be familiar with the new improvements, the new look and feel of the management tools and user interface, and be comfortable with the new working panes associated with administration. The next few sections examine these areas of interest.

## Improvements in Internet Information Services (IIS) 7.5

Several key enhancements and structural changes have been made to the new IIS 7.5 web and application platform. These enhancements are designed not only to build upon the latest version of .NET, but also to increase overall reliability, performance, security, and administration. Some of the major IIS 7.5 improvements that IT professionals, web hosters, and developers will take pleasure in having include the following:

▶ **Modular-based installation**—Unlike previous versions, IIS 7.5 is no longer monolithic. The installation process offers more than 40 different features/components. Although some of these features are installed by default, they can be selectively removed and others can be independently installed to produce a customized IIS 7.5. Ultimately, the system is made more secure and easier to manage as you only install and manage the features you need.

▶ **Improved management tools**—Microsoft has completely rewritten the Internet Information Services (IIS) Manager toolset, including the user interface. The new user interface can manage both IIS and ASP.NET settings from one utility, increasing administrators' productivity through centralized management. IIS 7.5 also introduces a new command-line tool called appcmd.exe to help automate common IIS 7.5 management tasks and configuration changes, which does away with all the administration scripts as you knew them in IIS 6.0. Finally, IIS 7.5 is tightly integrated with Windows PowerShell, meaning greater productivity can be achieved by scripting management and administration tasks.

▶ **Diagnostics and troubleshooting**—IIS 7.5 introduces enhancements to IIS logs, automatic failures, and error codes to reduce overall IIS downtime. By providing detailed error messages and trace events, troubleshooting has become a whole lot easier in IIS 7.5. For example, the IIS logs are much more detailed and include more status codes to help troubleshoot, diagnose, and repair an error much more efficiently and effectively. In addition, the Runtime Status and Control API (RSCA) further improves IIS 7.5 troubleshooting abilities as it provides detailed runtime diagnostics about the server. It can also be used to examine and manage other things, including, but not limited to, sites and .NET application domains.

▶ **A contemporary FTP server that supports SSL**—A much-desired and requested feature was to have a secure FTP solution for streamlined content publishing based on today's industry standards. The FTP server component has been completely rewritten and now not only supports Secure Sockets Layer (SSL) for enhanced security, but also includes virtual hostname support and user isolation. This FTP server will support UTF8, IPv6, COM, and .NET extensibility, and .NET membership integration with SQL Server and other repositories. The FTP component is an out-of-band offering; however, it is fully integrated into IIS 7.5. Unlike IIS 7.0, which needed to be downloaded and installed as an out-of-band offering from Microsoft, IIS 7.5 is fully integrated and included with Windows Server 2008 R2.

▶ **Delegated and remote administration**—A new role-based administration concept has been introduced into IIS 7.5 to maximize administration efficiently and securely. Administrators can log on to the same IIS management console and manage only their particular site. In addition, administrators, along with a few other designated people, can remotely manage IIS over the web using HTTP/SSL.

▶ **Improved server farm support**—Now, it is possible to share both the .config and applicationHost.config files on a central Universal Naming Convention (UNC) share. This improves server farm support when running more than one node in a Network Load Balancing (NLB) cluster as all nodes can access the same .config file, which means management of server farms is much easier. In addition, the configuration settings are stored within the .config files; therefore, they can be easily copied from one server to another without the need for replication programs, which tend to be error prone.

▶ **Enhanced developer experience**—The all-new server application programming interface (API) allows tight ASP.NET integration utilizing the latest .NET Framework. Hands down, developers are provided with the best experience and extensibility ever with this version of IIS. Classic ASP and other commercial frameworks are still supported.

▶ **Best Practices Analyzer (BPA)**—By leveraging BPA via Windows Server 2008 R2's Server Manager and/or Windows PowerShell, it is now possible to scan the IIS 7.5 Web Server role to ensure that there aren't any best-practice compliance or configuration violations.

▶ **.NET on Server Core**—The .NET Framework is an installation option now available on Server Core. This means that the full use of PowerShell cmdlets can be leveraged because ASP.NET applications on IIS installations can be enabled by administrators on Server Core. In addition, this also allows for greater support for remote management tasks. The versions of the .NET Framework include 2.0, 3.0, 3.51, and 4.0.

▶ **Windows PowerShell Provider**—Common IIS administrative tasks can be automated via the Windows PowerShell Provider for IIS. A collection of task-oriented cmdlets provides an easier way to manage websites, applications, and servers.

## Understanding the New IIS Manager Tools

The centerpiece of IIS 7.5 is the new Internet Information Services (IIS) Manager user interface. The user interface is used to manage IIS and ASP.NET, health and diagnostics, and security. It is, however, the Internet Information Services (IIS) Manager snap-in tool that reigns supreme as it contains the majority of the features and tools that are necessary for configuring and managing various functions of IIS 7.5.

IIS is configured through the IIS Manager snap-in, which can be accessed by selecting Start, Administration Tools, and Internet Information Services (IIS) Manager. Because understanding the console is a must to comprehend how to administer IIS and where to conduct the task, the next sections examine the layout of the new user interface.

## Exploring the IIS Manager Administration Panes

Each area within the IIS Manager console is referenced by a descriptive word, as shown in Figure 12.1. For example, the descriptive words associated with the areas or panes such as the Connections pane make it easier to identify the location of the IIS features. The following is a list of the panes included in the IIS Manager console and their respective functions:

▶ **The Connections pane**—The Connections pane is located on the left side of the console and displays the IIS console tree, which is also known as the node tree. Web administrators can conduct the following tasks from within this pane:

  ▶ View the Start Page

  ▶ Connect to a server, site, or application

  ▶ Manage server settings

  ▶ Configure IIS, application pools, FTP, and websites

▶ **Central Details pane**—Also known as the "workspace," this large pane is located in the center of the IIS 7.5 management console. This pane displays the configuration options for each IIS feature installed. Each feature is represented by a new icon and replaces the legacy property sheets and tabs that most administrators in the industry were not too fond of in the past. The feature icons can be grouped by category or area; otherwise, grouping can be turned off.

▶ **Actions pane**—The Actions pane is located on the right side of the console and displays common actions, including wizards associated with each task. This pane also

FIGURE 12.1    Examining Internet Information Services (IIS) Manager.

typically contains multiple tabs for the different options available based on the node chosen.

## Examining the IIS Manager Administration Nodes in the Connections Pane

Many web services components need to be configured to optimize IIS for security, functionality, and redundancy. The IIS snap-in is the interface used to administer IIS services. In the left pane of the snap-in, as shown in Figure 12.2, you will see folders or nodes similar to the following:

▶ **Start Page**—The Start Page is the first item within the Connections pane and is ultimately a digital dashboard for IIS. It provides users with a wealth of information by displaying IIS newsfeeds and links to online resources. In addition, the Start Page includes recent connection information and connection tasks.

▶ **IIS Server**—The main place to administer and manage server properties and features is the server node. After being selected, the IIS feature icons are displayed in the central pane. An administrator must double-click a feature to configure property settings specific to that feature. Examples of feature icons include Feature Delegation, Logging, and Machine Key.

▶ **Application Pools**—Application pools are actually sections of physical memory dedicated to the applications running within a pool. Application pools segment applications from the rest of the memory resources used by other IIS services. This promotes higher reliability and security, but it also requires more memory to be

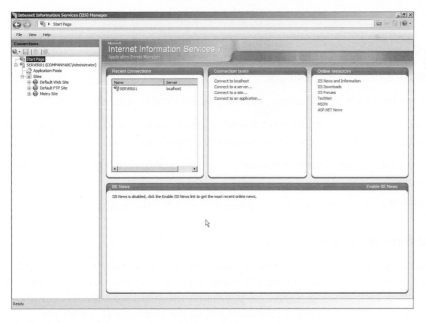

FIGURE 12.2   Examining the IIS 7.5 Connections pane.

configured on the web server. The application pool elements can be sorted based on Name, Status, .NET Framework Version, Managed Pipeline Mode, Identify, and Applications.

▶ **Web Sites**—This folder contains all the websites being hosted on the web server. The Default Web Site is created during the installation of IIS 7.5.

▶ **FTP Sites**—This folder contains all the FTP sites being hosted on the web server. Note that FTP services are not installed by default.

---

**NOTE**

An Internet Information Services (7.5) Manager can be started by typing `"start inet-mgr"` at the command prompt.

---

# Planning and Designing Internet Information Services 7.5

Two of the most important tasks to accomplish before implementing IIS 7.5 are thorough planning and designing. Planning and designing are the beginning phases to properly implementing IIS, and they can consist of the following:

▶ Defining goals and objectives of the IIS 7.5 project

▶ Identifying and reviewing IIS application types and requirements

▶ Designing the IIS infrastructure to support the goals and objectives

▶ Deciding on which IIS 7.5 features will be utilized during the installation process to meet the goals of the organization

▶ Defining fault-tolerance requirements

▶ Designing the back-end infrastructure, such as the database or application tier

▶ Defining security requirements to meet the goals and objectives and balancing the security methodologies between risks and end-user experience

▶ Examining and designing disaster recovery plans, and monitoring requirements and maintenance practices

▶ Documenting the current or new IIS infrastructure and the IIS design decisions

## Determining Server Requirements

Hardware and software requirements are typically based on the information gathered and the requirements set forth in the design and planning stages of a project. The necessary hardware and software requirements should always match the goals and objectives of the project. This information is very detailed and describes all the resources necessary for hardware and software.

IIS 7.5 does not have specific minimum server requirements tailored toward running IIS on Windows Server 2008 R2. The minimum server requirements are based on Windows Server 2008 R2. It is a best practice, however, to stick with multiple dual- or quad-core processors, fault-tolerant disks such as RAID 1 running at 15K rpm, and use as much RAM as needed, depending on how many sites and users you will be hosting. For more information on recommended Windows Server requirements, review Chapter 1, "Windows Server 2008 R2 Technology Primer," or for server performance tuning, network optimization, and SSL off-loading, see Chapter 34, "Capacity Analysis and Performance Optimization."

### Determining Fault-Tolerance Requirements

Fault tolerance is a key aspect of any web infrastructure and should be addressed during planning and designing phases, regardless of whether an organization can afford downtime of its websites or requires 99.999% uptime. In view of this, service-level agreements (SLAs) are highly recommended and should be determined from the operational goals during the design and planning phase. After an SLA is in place, it will be easy to apply the appropriate fault tolerance to the web infrastructure because expectations and tolerances are clearly defined and previously agreed upon by everyone involved in the process.

Various technologies can be applied to a Windows Server 2008 R2 web infrastructure to support even the most demanding SLAs. For example, Windows Server 2008 R2 web servers can use Network Load Balancing (NLB) to distribute the load and client requests among multiple web servers, and provide fault tolerance. This is also known as scaling IIS by creating a web server farm. NLB is more suited for scaling web servers than Microsoft Cluster Service in a failover cluster scenario to provide fault tolerance as the IIS components are not cluster aware.

NLB on Windows Server 2008 R2 also offers many new features and functionality, which makes it more appealing. For instance, NLB offers support for multiple dedicated IP addresses per node. For a complete list of NLB features, benefits, and step-by-step procedures, see Chapter 29, "System-Level Fault Tolerance (Clustering/Network Load Balancing)."

# Installing and Upgrading IIS 7.5

The installation process and architecture for many of Microsoft's new products that have been or will be released in the upcoming years are completely modularized like Internet Information Services 7.5 on Windows Server 2008 R2. By providing a modularized approach, web administrators have complete control over the footprint of IIS when customizing the installation. This results in the surface area being reduced, which, in turn, drastically minimizes the chances of a security compromise.

**NOTE**

As part of the Microsoft Trustworthy security campaign, IIS is not installed on Windows Server 2008 R2 by default. You have to add the Web Server (IIS) role via Server Manager if you want IIS installed.

Before installing or upgrading Internet Information Services, it is a best practice to fully understand the new modular installation process, including the features associated with the installation.

## Understanding the Modular Approach to Installing IIS 7.5

The new buzzword for Internet Information Services 7.5 modularized installation process is "slim and efficient." The modular setup is made up of more than 40 separate feature modules allowing for complete customization when deploying IIS 7.5. This typically results in minimal surface area and more granularity compared with older editions of IIS. In addition, even patching is based on a component level. All of this translates to a customized footprint for each organization running IIS 7.5.

As illustrated in Figure 12.3, the modules, also known as "role services" or "components," that can be selected during the installation process of the Web Server (IIS) role consist of the following:

▶ Web Server

▶ Management Tools

▶ FTP Server

The following sections depict the modular role services, including an explanation for each.

### Web Server Modular/Role Service

The Web Server modular is the main service role within IIS 7.5. It can be considered the chief functionality for a web server because it provides the foundation for supporting

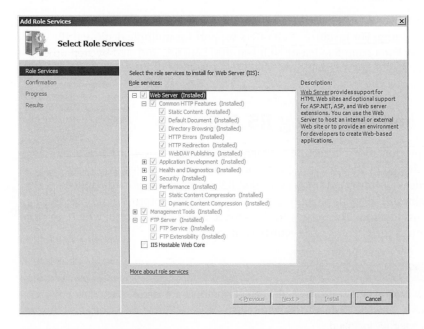

FIGURE 12.3   Reviewing the role services and feature installation options.

websites and provides developers with a foundation for development. The Web Server role is further broken down into more types of features, which can be independently installed, which promotes further customization of the installation:

▶ **Common HTTP Features**—A set of features that allow for static content to be delivered, the creation of customized HTTP errors, directory browsing, and selection of default documents are enabled by default. The HTTP Redirection and WebDAV publishing features are disabled by default.

▶ **Application Development**—This feature set is not enabled by default during the installation. If selected, the Application Development role service makes available features for creating and hosting web applications. These features include ASP.NET, .NET Extensibility, ASP, CGI, ISAPI Extensions, ISAPI Filters, and Server-Side Includes.

▶ **Health and Diagnostics**—Select this feature to install the tools associated with monitoring, managing, and troubleshooting an IIS installation. The independent features include HTTP Logging, Logging Tools, Request Monitor, Tracing, Custom Logging, and ODBC Logging.

▶ **Security**—The Security role service includes security features for controlling website authorization based on authentication alternatives. In addition, it provides the infrastructure for securing IIS and the websites associated with the installation. The features that can be selected include Basic Authentication, Windows Authentication, Digest Authentication, Client Certificate Mapping Authentication, IIS Client Certificate Mapping Authentications, URL Authorization, Request Filtering, and IP and Domain Restrictions.

▶ **Performance**—Performance features such as Static Content Compression and Dynamic Content Compression bolster website performance by managing bandwidth and compression.

### Management Tools Modular/Role Service

The next role service associated with the Web Server (IIS) role installation is Management Tools. The management tools provide the means of managing and administering the IIS 7.5 infrastructure. The following bullets explain the different management tools available for installation:

▶ **IIS Management Console**—If selected, the IIS Management Console feature installs the latest User Interface tool for managing, administering, monitoring, and securing IIS 7.5. The tool has been much improved and provides support for both IIS and ASP.NET.

▶ **IIS Management Scripts and Tools**—It is now possible to manage all of the IIS settings and configurations based on automated script commands. This feature provides the infrastructure that allows IIS to be managed by scripts. This is great when there is a need to manage many IIS 7.5 servers within an infrastructure.

▶ **Management Service**—This feature provides the foundation within the IIS 7.5 infrastructure for remote management.

▶ **IIS 6 Management Compatibility**—This feature provides the tools for backward compatibility when managing an IIS 6.0 infrastructure from a Windows Server 2008 system running IIS 7.5. In addition, it lets IIS 6.0 management scripts run on IIS 7.5.

### FTP Server Modular/Role Service

The next role service is known as the FTP Server. It provides a reliable method for making files available for download and also offers a reliable place for users to upload files if needed. The three FTP features that can be installed are as follows:

▶ **FTP Service**—The FTP Service feature provides the infrastructure for creating and hosting FTP sites within IIS.

▶ **FTP Extensibility**—This features enables support for custom providers and ASP.NET/IIS Manager users.

▶ **IIS Hostable Web Core Role Service**—The last role service allows an administrator the potential to write custom code that will host core IIS functionality in your own application.

## Installing the Web Server (IIS) Role

Now that you understand the installation process, including the modules, the next step is to install the Web Server (IIS) role. You must have Local User Administrator (LUA) security privileges on the Windows Server 2008 R2 system to be able to install IIS. There are two ways to begin the installation: adding the Web Server (IIS) role via Server Manager or installing the services via the command line.

To install the Web Server (IIS) server role using Server Manager, follow these steps:

1. Click Start, Administrative Tools, Server Manager. The Server Manager tools appear.

2. Right-click Roles in the left pane of Server Manager, then select Add Roles.

3. On the Select Server Roles page, install IIS 7.5 by selecting Web Server (IIS) in the Roles section, as shown in Figure 12.4. A dialog box pops up, informing you about additional features required for Web Server (IIS). Click Add Required Features, and then click Next.

4. Review the introduction messages and notes on the Web Server (IIS) page, and click Next.

5. Select the desired Web Server IIS role services and features to install. The default settings include Static Content, Default Document, Directory Browsing, HTTP Errors, HTTP Logging, Request Monitor, Request Filtering, Static Content Compression, and the IIS Management Console Management Tool. Click Next. The Confirm Installation Selections page appears.

> **NOTE**
>
> When installing some of the IIS components, the wizard warns you that additional services and features are required as dependencies. Click Add Required Role Services in the Add Roles Wizard to install the dependencies. These dependencies might include components of the new Windows Process Activation service.

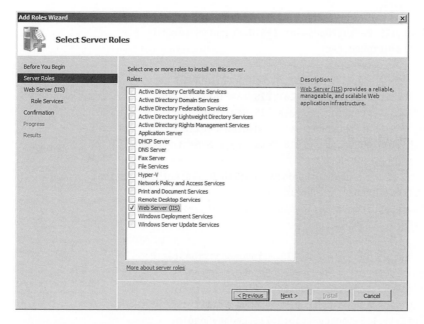

FIGURE 12.4   Selecting the Web Server (IIS) role during the installation process.

6. On the Confirm Installation Selections page, review the roles, services, and features that have been selected for installation, and then click Install to commence the installation process.

7. Ensure the installation succeeded by reviewing the messages on the Installation Results page, and click Close.

**NOTE**

After the installation is complete, additional IIS role services and features can be added or removed by clicking either Add Role Services or Remove Role Services within Server Manager based on the Web Server (IIS) role.

**Installing the Web Server (IIS) Role via the Command Line**

Windows features and roles such as IIS 7.5 can be installed using the command line. To install a default installation of IIS 7.5, run the following script from a command-line window:

```
start /w pkgmgr /iu:IIS-WebServerRole;WAS-WindowsActivationService;
➥WAS-ProcessModel;WAS-NetFxEnvironment;WAS-ConfigurationAPI
```

Alternatively, the following syntax can be used to install all of the IIS 7.5 features and functionality:

```
start /w pkgmgr /iu:IIS-WebServerRole;IIS-WebServer;IIS-CommonHttpFeatures;
➥IIS-StaticContent;IIS-DefaultDocument;IIS-DirectoryBrowsing;
➥IIS-HttpErrors;IIS-HttpRedirect

start /w pkgmgr /iu:IIS-ApplicationDevelopment;IIS-ASPNET;
➥IIS-NetFxExtensibility;IIS-ASP;IIS-CGI;IIS-ISAPIExtensions;
➥IIS-ISAPIFilter;IIS-ServerSideIncludes;IIS-HealthAndDiagnostics;
➥IIS-HttpLogging;IIS-LoggingLibraries;IIS-RequestMonitor;IIS-HttpTracing;
➥IIS-CustomLogging;IIS-ODBCLogging;IIS-Security;IIS-BasicAuthentication

start /w pkgmgr /iu:IIS-WindowsAuthentication;IIS-DigestAuthentication;
➥IIS-ClientCertificateMappingAuthentication;
➥IIS-IISCertificateMappingAuthentication;IIS-URLAuthorization;
➥IIS-RequestFiltering;IIS-IPSecurity

start /w pkgmgr /iu:IIS-Performance;IIS-HttpCompressionStatic;
➥IIS-HttpCompressionDynamic;IIS-WebServerManagementTools;
➥IIS-ManagementConsole;IIS-ManagementScriptingTools;
➥IIS-ManagementService;IIS-IIS6ManagementCompatibility;IIS-Metabase;
➥IIS-WMICompatibility;IIS-LegacyScripts;IIS-LegacySnapIn;
➥IIS-FTPPublishingService;IIS-FTPServer;IIS-FTPManagement;
➥WAS-WindowsActivationService;WAS-ProcessModel;WAS-NetFxEnvironment;
➥WAS-ConfigurationAPI
```

## Upgrading from Other Versions of IIS

In many situations, a fresh installation of IIS 7.5 and Windows Server 2008 R2 will not occur because organizations might want to preserve the existing IIS settings and content. Therefore, organizations must upgrade their existing IIS infrastructure to IIS 7.5. With the upgrade of the previous version of Windows to Windows Server 2008 R2, IIS is also automatically upgraded, allowing web content to be preserved, translated, and, finally, transitioned. However, you should note early in the process that Windows Server 2008 R2 only supports a direct upgrade path from Windows Server 2008 and Windows Server 2003, which means only an in-place upgrade from IIS 6.0 or IIS 7.0 is supported. Likewise, if legacy versions of IIS need upgrading such as IIS 5.0, you must first upgrade the operating system to Windows Server 2003 and then to Windows Server 2008.

> **NOTE**
>
> IIS 7.5 no longer uses a metabase as in IIS 6.0. The IIS 7.5 XML configuration files replace the legacy IIS 6.0 metabase.

The upgrade process for IIS is conducted in three major phases. In the first phase, the new operating system detects and performs an inventory of IIS components and features already installed on the operating system. The second phase of the upgrade process involves upgrading the legacy operating system to Windows Server 2008 R2. After the Windows Server 2008 R2 upgrade is complete, the final phase kicks in and automatically translates the IIS 6.0 metabase information gathered in the first step, upgrades the legacy IIS metabase to IIS 7.5, and installs the appropriate IIS 7.5 features.

> **NOTE**
>
> For more information on how to upgrade a system to Windows Server 2008 R2, see Chapter 3, "Installing Windows Server 2008 R2 and Server Core."

As is typically the case with most revised products, Windows Server 2008 R2 IIS is inherently superior to its previous versions. In particular, it lays claim to being more secure. This is witnessed during upgrades of websites to IIS 7.5. Website services are stopped after the upgrade and must be manually restarted, thus minimizing IIS security vulnerabilities due to previous Windows defaults. To allow for more clarity, suppose you have a Windows server with IIS installed, but it isn't supposed to be serving as a web server; the server will be more secure by default after you upgrade to IIS 7.5 because it will not be turned on automatically and made a subject for attacks.

Another appealing reason for upgrading from previous versions of IIS is that the IIS 7.5 installation process is granular and modularized. After upgrading, it is best to only install the features you require to reduce the surface area utilized. With that said, be aware that after upgrading to IIS 7.5, a majority of the web server features are installed right out of the gate as many legacy versions were not granular.

# Installing and Configuring Websites

As mentioned earlier, IIS can support thousands of websites on a single web server. The number of websites that you have depends on the way the system is configured, including the number of processors, the amount of RAM, bandwidth, and more. For every website that the system supports for the Internet, there must be a public IP address and registered domain name. However, if you have only one public IP address and you want to support other websites, you can also create virtual directories or leverage host headers to have those sites serving users on the Internet.

## Creating a Website with IIS 7.5

The Default Web Site is located within the Web Sites folder in the IIS snap-in. You can use the Default Web Site to publish content, but it is possible to create and configure a separate website.

To begin creating a new website, do the following:

1. In Internet Information Services (IIS) Manager, right-click on the Sites node in the Connections pane, and click Add Web Site.

2. The Add Web Site page is opened; enter a website name such as NewWebSite.

3. If desired, click the Select button in the Application Pool section to modify the Application Pool settings for this new site. The default application pool drop-down option available is DefaultAppPool.

4. In the Content Directory section, enter the physical path to where the Web Sites folder resides. Alternatively, navigate to the folder by clicking the ellipses button.

**NOTE**

A user can also choose a remote share when providing the location of the content directory's physical path. If a remote share is used, you must ensure IIS has access to that folder by clicking the Connect As button and specifying connectivity to the remote share by choosing a specific user account that has appropriate permissions or you can select the Pass-Through Authentication option.

5. You must now specify whether this new site will use HTTP or HTTPS, provide an IP address to the new site or leave the IP Address setting unassigned, and indicate which port this new site will listen on. These settings are configured in the Binding section of the Add Web Site page.

6. An optional setting can be configured before completing the page. A user can enter a host header for the new site, such as www.companyabc.com.

7. Check the option to start the website immediately.

8. Review all the configuration settings inputted, as illustrated in Figure 12.5, and then click OK to finalize the creation of the new website.

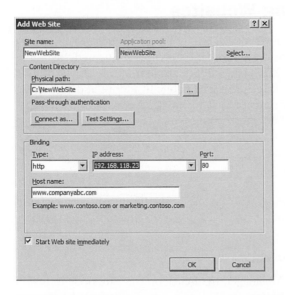

FIGURE 12.5    Reviewing the settings in the Add Web Site dialog box.

## Creating a Virtual Directory

Virtual directories extend the home directory of your website by providing an alias linking another directory not contained within the home directory. This alias will appear to users as simply a subfolder to the website even though it might be located on an entirely different server.

The virtual directory can contain documents and other information for the website as well as a new website. For example, if CompanyABC's website (www.companyabc.com) wants to host a temporary website for another organization, it could use a virtual directory to contain the website. In this scenario, CompanyXYZ would have its own website located at www.companyabc.com/companyxyz/. You must have Web Server Administrator, Web Site Administrator, or Web Applications Administrator privileges to create a virtual directory.

To create a virtual directory using the IIS Manager, do the following:

1. Select Start, All Programs, Administrative Tools, Internet Information Services (IIS) Manager.

2. In the Connections pane, expand the IIS server, and then expand the Sites node within the tree.

3. Select the desired website that will contain the new virtual directory. Right-click the website, and select Add Virtual Directory.

4. Enter the virtual directory's alias, such as Images.

5. Enter the physical path to the content folder of the virtual directory, or alternatively, navigate to the folder by clicking the ellipses button.

6. Review the settings, as displayed in Figure 12.6, and click OK to finalize the creation of the virtual directory.

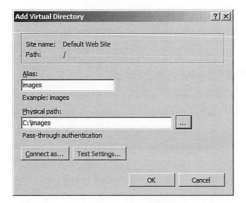

FIGURE 12.6    Add Virtual Directory dialog box.

> **NOTE**
>
> If the content folder specified is a remote share, click Connect As and enter credentials for an account that has permissions to access the remote share. Alternatively, select the application user (Pass-Through Authentication) option.

## Configuring IIS 7.5 Website Properties

In the not-so-distant past, right-clicking a website or default website in IIS Manager and then selecting Properties gave you options for modifying the default settings and properties for a website. This is no longer the case as the property pages and tabs have been overhauled in IIS 7.5. In their place are feature icons in the central pane and tasks in the Actions pane. For simplicity, this section describes only the feature icons–associated properties pages in IIS 7.5.

The Features View tab is located in the Central Details pane. Some of the feature icons are connected to this tab for the purpose of configuring properties associated with a website. From here, you can control everything associated with application development, HTTP features, health, diagnostics, performance, and security. These options are as follows:

▶ IIS 7.5 Features Associated with ASP.NET

▶ IIS 7.5 Features Associated with IIS

▶ Management Features

### IIS 7.5 Features Associated with ASP.NET

The following bullets highlight the feature icons and respective configuration pages associated with an ASP.NET configuration:

▶ **.NET Authorization Rules feature page**—Use this page to control access to a website and application by configuring Allow and Deny rules and specifying users, roles, and user groups.

▶ **.NET Compilation feature page**—Use this page to configure ASP.NET configuration settings. Settings are configured based on the following high-level elements: Batch, Behavior, General, and Assemblies.

▶ **.NET Error Pages feature page**—This page is used to configure HTTP error responses for when an error occurs on a website or application.

▶ **.NET Globalization feature page**—This page controls international settings tailored toward local language and cultural environments. As the world converges and the global climate is getting smaller, this is a great feature to leverage to translate and format content by reutilizing the existing code and automatically presenting it to different geographical locations.

▶ **.NET Profile feature page**—A list of profile properties is used to track custom data about an application with this feature page.

▶ **.NET Roles feature page**—This page is used to create predefined roles for managing groups of users' authorization access. This concept is also known as role-based security. To leverage this feature, a default provider must be configured. The two options available are `AspNetWindowsTokenRoleProvider` and `AspNetSqlRoleProvider`.

▶ **.NET Trust Levels feature page**—This page is used to specify the trust level for managed objects, such as modules, handlers, and applications in the Web.config file.

▶ **.NET Users feature page**—This feature page identifies and manages the identities of users for an application. The feature controls the identity management behavior for users defined for an application. When a user is created, the page displays name, email addresses, data created, and last logon.

▶ **.NET Application Settings feature page**—To manage the variables associated with key/value pairs stored in the website's .config file, this feature page is recommended. The application setting variables and value elements are created by selecting Add Task from the Actions pane. These settings can be accessed from anywhere within the application.

▶ **Connections Strings feature page**—This page is dedicated to creating and managing connections strings for managed web applications. By selecting Add Task in the Actions pane, you can create connections strings to SQL Server for database access. Typically, the credentials used to access the database are Windows Integrated; however, it is possible to specify a SQL Server account as well.

▶ **Machine Key feature page**—Because IIS 7.5 is tightly integrated with .NET web services and there is a major push for security, this page is used to manage encryption. You can enter encryption and decryption methods, including key generations to secure forms-based authentication, cookie, and page-level view state data.

▶ **Pages and Controls feature page**—This page manages how the setting of ASP.NET pages and controls are compiled on the web server. New controls can be registered by selecting the task from the Actions pane. Additional elements can be configured, such as the behavior, user interface, view state, compilation, general, and services.

▶ **Providers feature page**—When you want to manage and administer a list of providers the web server can take advantage of, use this features page. Default examples include `AspNetSqlRoleProvider` and `AspNetWindowsTokenRoleProvider`. Additionally, providers can be added by users by selecting Add from the Actions pane.

▶ **Session State feature page**—This page, as displayed in Figure 12.7, is leveraged when it is necessary to control the behavior of information across browser sessions. It is possible to enable or disable a session state or store a session state in the web browser or in a SQL Server database. Additional elements include defining how cookies are processed when managing session states. Options include Auto Detect, Use Cookies, Use Device Profile, or Use URI.

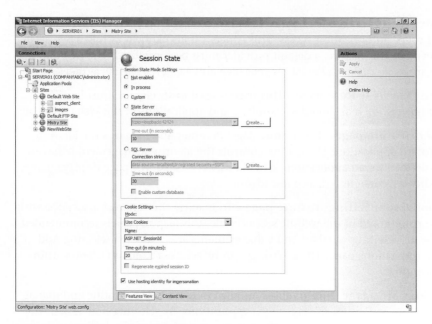

FIGURE 12.7    Viewing the Session State feature page.

▶ **SMTP E-Mail feature page**—The final ASP.NET feature is SMTP E-Mail that uses the System.Net.Mail API. The feature page, as illustrated in Figure 12.8, includes properties that need to be specified, such as email address, SMTP server name, and port to control message sending functionality from the web server.

### IIS 7.5 Features Associated with IIS

The following bullets highlight the feature icons and respective configuration pages associated with IIS configurations:

▶ **ASP feature page**—The first IIS feature page in the list is ASP. This page is meant for managing classic ASP settings, such as the following elements: Behavior, Compilation, Services, Caching Properties, Com Plus Properties, and Sessions Properties.

▶ **Authentication feature page**—The Authentication page is synonymous to the legacy Security tab in IIS. This page is used to configure security authentication. Security can be administered for a web server, website, or a specific page. Authentication such as Anonymous, ASP.NET Impersonation, Basic Authentication, Digest Authentication, Forms Authentication, and Windows Authentication can be configured. Take note as Anonymous authentication is enabled by default and might have to be disabled before a different authentication method can be used. In the past, these authentication types existed out of the box. However, with the modularized installation approach, each element now needs to be selected separately during the installation process.

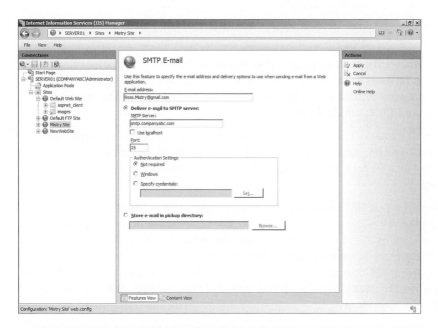

FIGURE 12.8    Viewing the SMTP E-Mail feature page.

▶ **Authentication Rules feature page**—Use this page to enforce control of web content access by utilizing Allow or Deny rules. Other IIS features such as Users and Roles are associated with this feature as you can specify Allow and Deny rules to already created users and roles.

▶ **CGI feature page**—IIS 7.5 supports CGI applications. This page is used to configure CGI properties, which allows these applications to run on an IIS 7.5 web server. Additional elements on this page control other aspects of CGI applications, including CGI timeout values, whether or not a CGI application runs in its own console, and, finally, the security context the application will utilize.

▶ **Compression feature page**—There are two options available on this page that enhance transmission times between the server and browsers. The compression elements that can be configured consist of compressing static content and compressing dynamic content.

> **NOTE**
>
> For clients to leverage this feature, they must use a web browser that supports compression, such as Microsoft Internet Explorer 7.0. In addition, the use of dynamic compression can increase processor utilization.

▶ **Default Document feature page**—Similar to the concept in earlier versions of IIS, the Default Document page is used to select the default web page that appears when a user connects to a site. An example is default.htm. This feature can be enabled or disabled via the Actions pane.

▶ **Directory Browsing feature page**—This feature is disabled out of the box. By selecting the Enable task in the Actions pane, this page can be used to configure directory browsing functionality. The elements that can be selected include Time, Size, Extension, Date, and Long Date.

▶ **Errors feature page**—The Errors feature page is similar to the Cluster Errors tab on earlier versions of IIS. An administrator can use this page to create custom error messages for web server clients. It is possible to edit a default error or create a new error page.

▶ **Failed Request Tracing Rules feature page**—This setting is used to manage a list of tracing rules for failed requests. The Failed Request Tracing Rules Wizard is invoked by clicking Add in the Actions pane. The wizard walks you through the creation of the trace by first requesting information on what will be traced. The options include All Content, ASP.NET, ASP, and Custom Creation. Trace Conditions are defined on the next page. Conditions include Event Severity, Status Codes, or Time Taken in Seconds. The final page is utilized to select the trace providers.

**NOTE**

When configuring Failed Request Tracing Rules for a site, logging of failed requests must be enabled for the site at the server scope. If it is not, Failed Request Tracing Rules will not be available for a site.

▶ **Handler Mappings feature page**—Use this page to specify resources that will handle responses for specific request types. Actions include Add Managed Handler, Add Script Map, and Add Module Mapping.

▶ **HTTP Redirect feature page**—There will be times when there is a need to redirect incoming requests to an alternate uniform resource locator (URL) or website file. To achieve this goal, the HTTP Redirect page can be used to redirect requests to a specific destination.

▶ **HTTP Response Headers feature page**—This feature should be used to configure HTTP headers based on entering name and values to responses from the web server.

▶ **IP Address and Domain Restrictions feature page**—This page is used to create and manage rules that allow computer networks and IP addresses the opportunity to either gain access or be denied to specific web content. The rules available consist of Allow or Deny and it is possible to enter a single IP address, range of IP addresses, or domain name. Finally, rules can be added to a page, site, or inherited from the parent.

▶ **ISAPI Filters feature page**—ISAPI filters are programs that respond to certain events during HTTP request processing. You can add, enable, and disable filters for a website on this page.

▶ **Logging feature page**—The Logging feature page configures how IIS log requests will be handled for the web server. For more information on logging, see the section "Using IIS Logging" toward the end of the chapter.

▶ **MIME Types feature page**—The MIME Types feature page is utilized for managing a list of Multipurpose Internet Mail Extensions (MIME) types for the web server or website. When creating or managing MIME types, the following elements need to be entered: Extension, MIME Type, and Entry Type.

▶ **Modules feature page**—This feature should be used when managing or adding managed modules and adding native modules to a web server or website. Authentication and compression are examples of native code modules.

▶ **Output Caching feature page**—The Output Caching features page is leveraged when defining a set of rules associated with caching content. Some of the cache settings include defining file extensions, maximum cache response sizes, and cache size limit in MB.

▶ **Request Filtering feature page**—The page is used to configure filtering rules for a website or application.

▶ **SSL Settings feature page**—This page helps an administrator create, manage, and assign certificates for the web server. For more information on creating certificates and assigning them to a website, review the section "Using SSL Certificates."

▶ **WebDav Authoring Rules feature page**—This feature page is used for managing a list of authoring rules that control access to content.

### IIS 7.5 Features Associated with Management

The following bullets highlight the feature icons and respective configuration pages associated with Management configurations:

▶ **Configuration Editor feature page**—This new page allows an administrator to access and manage configuration files affiliated with sections such as server, site, or application within IIS Manager.

▶ **IIS Manager Permissions feature page**—This feature page is used for managing and provisioning IIS Manager users, Windows users, and members of Windows groups that require access to a website or application.

# Installing and Configuring FTP Services

It's hard to find a person today who hasn't used File Transfer Protocol (FTP). FTP can be considered the backbone for transferring files to and from a website. The basic premise of an FTP server is based on placing files in directories and allowing users to access or publish information with an FTP client or an FTP-enabled web browser, such as Microsoft Internet

Explorer 7.0. Depending on the placement of the FTP server, amateurs and professionals alike can either upload or download data from the Internet or intranet.

In the past few releases of IIS, Microsoft did not place a tremendous amount of emphasis on revamping the FTP service. As a result, the Windows FTP service has not been heavily used by the IT community as organizations require strong security and native encryption; however, things are about to change. With Windows Server 2008 R2, Microsoft listened to the needs of its IT community and accordingly reengineered the FTP service for IIS. It is now more robust, dependable, and it supports SSL for data encryption.

Now that we know that FTP has been revamped and enriched with many new features, here comes the confusing stuff. Windows Server 2008 had two FTP servers. The first FTP server was included with the installation of IIS 7.0 on Windows Server 2008. It was, however, not installed by default and could be added as an FTP role service in Server Manager. The FTP service offered here was "out of the box" and is essentially the exact same FTP solution included with IIS 6.0. Essentially, this means it did not include any new features and functionality. In addition, the Internet Information Services IIS (6.0) Manager legacy tools were required to administer the FTP components, service, and properties.

The second FTP server was a new and improved secure FTP service, which included all the new bells and whistles. Unfortunately, Microsoft ran out of time and did not have the opportunity to finalize the new FTP service before going live with Windows Server 2008. Therefore, the product was stripped from the official release of Windows Server 2008 and was considered "out-of-band," meaning it can be obtained as a separate download from Microsoft.

With Windows Server 2008 R2, a new version of FTP Server services is included with the product as an optional component to be installed with IIS 7.5. It is fully integrated and can be managed with the same IIS 7.5 administrative interface. FTP Server Services with IIS 7.5 includes extended support for new Internet standards, such as FTP over Secure Sockets Layer (SSL), support for extended character sets by including UTF-8 support, and support for IPv6.

## Examining the New FTP 7.5 Server Service Features

Microsoft has made many improvements to the FTP 7.5 Service. First, the FTP 7.5 Service has been completely rewritten from scratch. As a result, it is more secure and meets today's industry standards for publishing content in a secure fashion. The following is a list of new features for the FTP 7.5 Service running on Windows Server 2008 R2:

▶ There is now tight integration with IIS 7.5 websites and IIS Manager.

▶ It supports today's demanding security needs by supporting FTP over SSL.

▶ Organizations can now host multiple FTP sites with the same IP address, as the bindings support host headers.

▶ Both web and FTP content can be hosted from the same site.

▶ UTF8, IPv6, and integration with other repositories such as SQL Server are supported.

▶ Improved logging and diagnostics are now available.

Microsoft certainly realizes FTP is not going away and is still the preferred method for publishing content and exchanging large pieces of data between organizations. By rewriting the FTP service, utilizing Extensible Markup Language (XML) configuration files, and providing secured FTP, the product now meets today's industry FTP requirements out of the box without the need to purchase third-party plug-ins.

## Installing the FTP Server

Similar to the previous version of IIS, the FTP publishing service is not installed by default. To add the FTP role service included with IIS 7.5 running on Windows Server 2008 R2, perform the following steps in Server Manager:

1. Assuming the Web Server is already installed from the previous steps in this chapter, in Server Manager, first expand the Roles node and then select Web Server (IIS).

2. Right-click the Web Server (IIS) node, and then select Add Role Services.

3. Select the following Web Server role services and subcomponents: FTP Server, FTP Service, and FTP Extensibility, as displayed in Figure 12.9, and then click Next.

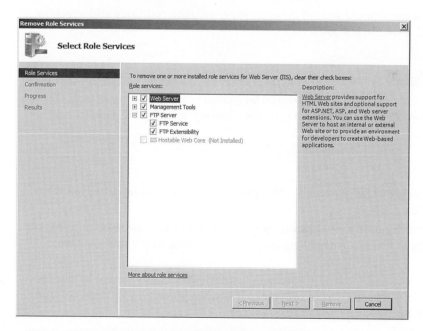

FIGURE 12.9   Selecting the FTP 7.5 features to install.

4. On the Confirm Installation Selections page, review the FTP roles, services, and features selected for installation, and then click Install to initiate the installation process.

5. Ensure the installation succeeded by reviewing the messages on the Installation Results page, and then click Close.

## Creating a Secure FTP 7.5 Site Using SSL

With IIS 7.5, it is not only possible to create a new FTP site or add FTP publishing to an existing website, but it is also possible to have both FTP and HTTP coexist. To create a new FTP site, in addition to the Default FTP Site, do the following:

1. Select Start, All Programs, Administrative Tools, Internet Information Services (IIS) Manager.

2. In the Connections pane, expand the IIS server, and then expand the Sites node within the tree.

3. Right-Click Sites and select Add FTP Site.

4. Enter the FTP site name and specify the physical path for the FTP site you will use. If needed, click the Connect As button to provide path credentials.

5. In the Binding section of the Binding and SSL Settings page, enter the IP address and port of the FTP server.

6. From within the Binding and SSL Settings page, specify a certificate and select the Require SSL option in the SSL section.

> **NOTE**
>
> When using SSL, an IIS 7.5 certificate should be created prior to these procedures. For more information on creating an IIS 7.5 certificate, review the "Using SSL Certificates" later in this chapter.

7. Select the Start FTP Site Automatically option, and click Next, as displayed in Figure 12.10.

8. On the Authentication and Authorization Information page, specify how users will authenticate to the site by choosing Anonymous or Basic in the Authentication section.

9. In the Authorization section, specify who has authorization to the site by selecting from the following: All Users, Anonymous Users, Specified Roles or Users Groups, and, finally, Specified Users.

10. The final setting on the Authentication and Authorization Information page is the Permissions section. Specify the permissions for the FTP site. You can choose from Read and/or Write.

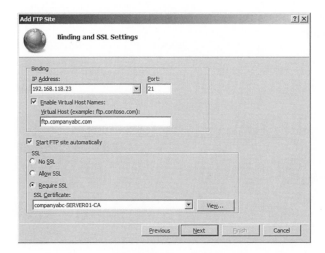

FIGURE 12.10    Setting the binding and SSL settings for FTP.

**11.** Review the settings, as illustrated in Figure 12.11, and then click Finish to finalize the FTP site creation.

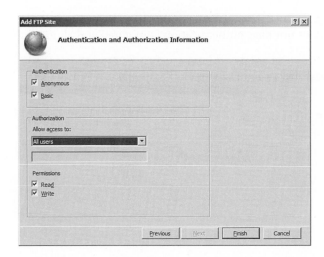

FIGURE 12.11    Specifying authentication and authorization settings for an FTP site.

## Configuring the FTP 7.5 Features and Properties

The FTP Site Creation Wizard configures the basic settings for an FTP server; however, there is still a need to configure more advanced settings or refine the original ones. Similar to managing websites, you no longer manage property pages by right-clicking the site. The new FTP feature icons have replaced the old style property FTP pages. The FTP feature icons are installed during the installation process and are located in the Central Details pane, as shown in Figure 12.12. The new FTP features for configuring basic and advanced FTP properties consist of the following:

▶ FTP Authentication

▶ FTP Authorization Rules

▶ FTP Current Sessions

▶ FTP Directory Browsing

▶ FTP Firewall Support

▶ FTP IPv4 and Domain Restrictions

▶ FTP Logging

▶ FTP Messages

▶ FTP Request Filtering

▶ FTP SSL Settings

▶ FTP User Isolation

### FTP Authentication Feature Page

The FTP Authentication feature page is utilized to configure authentication methods for FTP clients. By default, an FTP site does not have authentication configured and all mecha-

FIGURE 12.12    The FTP feature icons.

nisms are disabled out of the box. An administrator must grant the desired authentication to the FTP site. The authentication mechanisms for FTP consist of the following items:

▶ **Anonymous Authentication**—This built-in authentication mechanism should be selected when you want to provide public access to an FTP site without having end users pass credentials.

▶ **Basic Authentication**—It is another built-in authentication mechanism for FTP sites. Basic authentication requires the FTP clients to enter a valid Windows user account and password when gaining access to the FTP site. Basic Authentication sends password credentials in clear text, which is a security hazard. As such, implement SSL when using this mechanism to encrypt passwords in transit.

▶ **ASP.NET Authentication**—The FTP site will provide authorization to FTP clients by having them enter a valid ASP.NET user account and password. This is a custom authentication mechanism that requires a provider and connection string to an ASP.NET user database.

▶ **IIS Manager Authentication**—This is another custom authentication mechanism similar to ASP.NET. An FTP client must provide a legitimate IIS Manager username and password to gain access to FTP content. Similar to Basic Authentication, the credentials are not encrypted, so it is recommended for this authentication to be used in conjunction with SSL.

> **NOTE**
>
> Don't forget that to utilize these authentication mechanisms, the appropriate authentication role services must be installed prior to configuration.

### FTP Authorization Rules Feature Page

This page should be used to manage Allow and Deny authorization rules that control access to FTP sites. The Actions pane options Add Allow Rule and Add Deny Rule should be selected to invoke the Allow or Deny Authorization Rule page. After the page is invoked, rules can be applied to All Users, All Anonymous Users, Specified Roles or User Groups, and Specified Users. In addition, the rules are based on Read or Write permissions.

### FTP Current Sessions Feature Page

This page should be used to monitor current sessions for an FTP site. The following elements are displayed: User Name, Session Start Time, Current Command, Previous Command, Command Start Time, Bytes Sent, Bytes Received, Session ID, and Client IP.

### FTP Directory Browsing Feature Page

The FTP Directory Browsing page illustrated in Figure 12.13 is broken out into two sections. The first section is called Directory Listing Style. The format presentation options

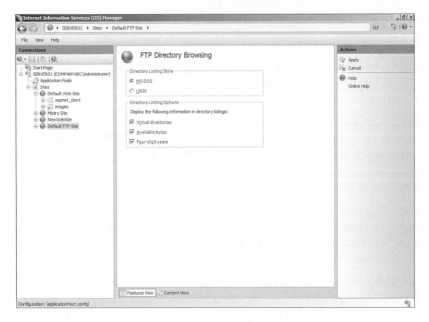

FIGURE 12.13    The FTP Directory Browsing feature page.

include MS-DOS and UNIX. The second section, Directory Listing Options, controls how directory information is displayed. The display options include the following:

▶ **Virtual Directories**—This option allows you to specify whether to include virtual directories.

▶ **Available Bytes**—This setting controls the display behavior of the available bytes remaining when a disk quota is enabled.

▶ **Four-Digit Years**—When enabled, this setting displays the last modified date for a file based on the four-year date, such as 1974, and not a two-year date format, such as 74.

### FTP Firewall Support Feature Page
A new FTP feature associated with IIS 7.5 is the FTP Firewall Support. This feature allows the server to accept passive connections when the FTP client is behind a firewall. An administrator must enter the Data Channel Port Range and External IP Address of the Firewall settings and then click Apply in the Actions pane.

### FTP IPv4 and Domain Restrictions Feature Page
The exact same settings are associated with the FTP IPv4 and Domain Restrictions as for a website in IIS 7.5. The FTP IPv4 and Domain Restrictions feature page should be used to create and manage rules that allow computer networks and IP addresses the opportunity to either gain access or be denied to specific web content. You can either allow or deny access. It is also possible to enter a single IP address, a range of IP addresses, or a domain name. Finally, rules can be added to a page, site, or inherited from the parent.

## FTP Logging Feature Page

The FTP Logging feature page includes the exact same logging settings as for a website. This page controls the type of log file to use, the location to be stored, and the log file rollover settings.

## FTP Messages Feature Page

The FTP Messages feature page illustrated in Figure 12.14 is a great way to create a banner, or welcome and exit message that will be displayed to FTP users. The message behavior is controlled by the following elements:

▶ **Suppress Default Banner**—If enabled, this option displays a default welcome banner. Otherwise, a customizable banner is displayed.

▶ **Support User Variables in Messages**—By enabling this setting, user variables such as BytesReceived, BytesSent, SessionID, SiteName, and UserName are included in the message banner.

▶ **Show Detailed Messages for Local Requests**—This setting controls the behavior for displaying FTP error messages. If enabled, FTP error messages are displayed to the local host.

The next section on the FTP Messages feature page is called Message Text. The administrator enters message text in the various text boxes. The message boxes include Banner, Welcome, Exit, and Maximum Connections.

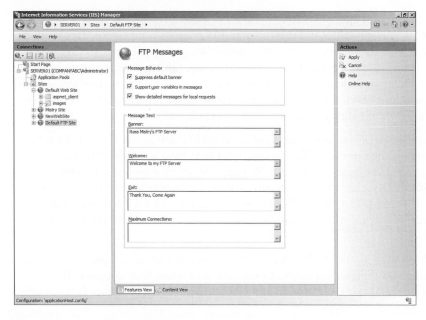

FIGURE 12.14    The FTP Messages feature page.

### FTP Request Filtering

The FTP Request Filtering feature page should be used to define the list of Allow or Deny rules based on the specific elements:

▶ **File Name Extensions**—This tab allows for the creation of filename extensions for which the FTP service will either allow or deny access to the site. For example, an administrator can prevent Internet clients from uploading any files with the extension of *.txt or *.com.

▶ **Hidden Segments**—The Hidden Segments tab should be used if you want to hide specific areas of your FTP site. If hidden, the specific section will not be displayed in the directory listings.

▶ **Defined URL Sequences**—This setting should be used to define the list of URL sequences for which the FTP service will deny access.

▶ **Commands**—The final tab Commands defines the list of commands for which the FTP service will either allow or deny access to further tighten security.

### FTP SSL Settings Feature Page

This page should be utilized for enabling and configuring SSL settings for an FTP site. The options include a drop-down menu for selecting the SSL certificate you will use and SSL policy. The SSL Policy options include Allow SSL Connections, Require SSL Connections, and Advanced Custom Settings. You will also have the chance to choose whether to use 128-bit encryption for SSL connections.

### FTP User Isolation Feature Page

Similar to IIS 6.0, IIS 7.5 can still isolate FTP users so FTP content is protected. This is an especially useful feature for Internet service providers (ISPs) and application service providers (ASPs) servicing a large number of users. FTP users can have their own separate directory to upload and download files to the web or FTP server. Users who connect see only their directory as the top-level directory and can't browse other FTP directories. Permissions can be set on the FTP home directory to allow create, modify, or delete operations.

It is worth noting that FTP user isolation is based on an FTP site rather than at the server level and is either enabled or disabled. However, sites that need to enable FTP user isolation aren't forced to strictly use this feature. You can enable anonymous access in conjunction with FTP user isolation by creating a virtual directory within the FTP site and allowing read-only access. The only limitation to mixing the FTP user isolation and anonymous access is that information can be downloaded only from the public or read-only virtual directory.

The configuration settings on the FTP User Isolation page, as shown in Figure 12.15, consist of the following options for where to start the user when they connect. The options include the FTP Root Directory or User Name Directory. In addition, it is possible

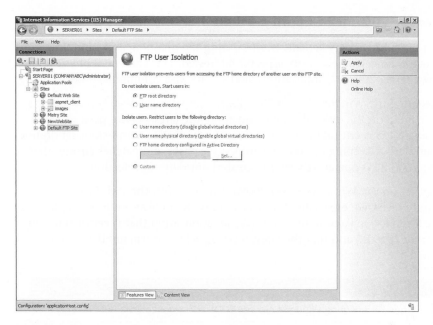

FIGURE 12.15    The FTP User Isolation feature page.

to isolate users by restricting them to following directories. The Isolate Users options consist of the following:

▶ User Name Directory (Disable Global Virtual Directories)

▶ User Name Physical Directory (Enable Global Virtual Directories)

▶ FTP Home Directory Configured in Active Directory

# Securing Internet Information Services 7.5

There shouldn't be any question that IIS is significantly more secure than its predecessors. Several key enhancements such as a reduced attack surface, minimum install by default, and enhanced application isolation deliver a robust and secure web platform. IIS also is enabled by default to present only static information (that is, to use applications or other dynamic content, you must manually enable them).

However, Microsoft products are also the most popular products to try to hack. For this reason, it's important to secure the web server as much as possible. The more barriers there are, the less inclined a hacker would be to try to gain unauthorized access. Each component on the web server must be secure; the server is only as secure as its weakest point.

## Windows Server 2008 R2 Security

Windows Server 2008 R2 security actually begins during the planning and designing phases so that every conceivable security aspect is addressed. This can entail physical, logical (Windows Server 2008 R2, applications, and so on), and communications security.

When you're securing the Windows Server 2008 R2 system with the Web Server role, it's important to use NTFS on the disk subsystem and apply the latest service pack and security patches. Using NTFS is critical because it can have appropriate permissions set on files, folders, and shares. Also, keeping up to date with service packs and patches ensures that Windows Server 2008 R2 is operating with the greatest amount of protection.

Application security on the Windows Server 2008 R2 system with the Web Server role should be carefully reviewed, especially if it's a custom-built application. If the application is developed by a vendor, make sure that you have an application that is certified to run on Windows Server 2008 R2 and that the latest service packs and patches have been applied and tested.

> **NOTE**
>
> For more information on securing Windows Server 2008 R2, refer to Part IV, "Security."

## IIS Authentication

Authentication is a process that verifies that users are who they say they are. IIS supports a multitude of authentication methods, including the following:

- **Anonymous Authentication**—Users can establish a connection to the website without providing credentials.

- **Active Directory Client Certificate Authentication**—Users can establish a connection by using their Active Directory client certificate for authentication.

- **ASP.NET Impersonation**—Users can utilize an impersonation context other than the ASP.NET account.

- **Windows Authentication**—This authentication method can be integrated with Active Directory. As users log on, the hash value of the password is sent across the wire instead of the actual password.

- **Digest Authentication**—Similar to Integrated Windows authentication, a hash value of the password is transmitted. Digest authentication requires a Windows Server domain controller to validate the hash value.

- **Basic Authentication**—Basic authentication sends the username and password over the wire in clear text format. This authentication method offers little security to protect against unauthorized access.

- **Forms Authentication**—Users are redirected to a page where they enter their credentials. After they have been authenticated, they are redirected back to the page they originally requested.

These authentication methods can be enabled under the Authentication feature page, as illustrated in Figure 12.16. You can view this window by clicking the Edit button located on the Directory Security tab of a website properties page.

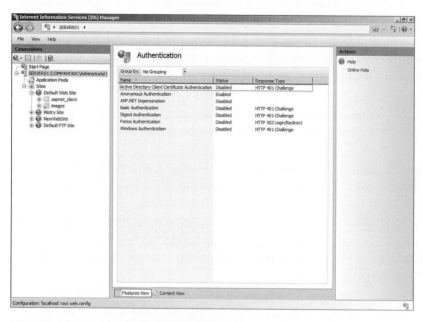

FIGURE 12.16   Authentication feature page.

## Auditing Web Services

Windows Server 2008 R2 auditing can be applied to web and FTP sites to document attempts to log on (successful and unsuccessful), to gain unauthorized access to service accounts, to modify or delete files, and to execute restricted commands. These events can be viewed through Event Viewer. It's also important to monitor IIS logs in conjunction with audited events to determine how, when, and if external users were trying to gain unauthorized access.

## Using SSL Certificates

Secure Sockets Layer (SSL) encryption preserves user and content integrity as well as confidentiality so that communications from a client and the web server, containing sensitive data such as passwords or credit card information, are protected. SSL is based on the public key security protocol that protects communication by encrypting data before being transmitted.

Previous versions of IIS could use SSL, and IIS 7.5 is no different. The exception to this, though, is now it is possible to secure FTP sites by implementing SSL for FTP when using the FTP Server included with version 7.5.

SSL certificates serve three primary purposes, although they are typically used to encrypt connections. These purposes include the following:

▶ **SSL server authentication**—This allows a client to validate a server's identity. SSL-enabled client software can use a Public Key Infrastructure (PKI) to check whether a server's certificate is valid. It can also check whether the certificate has been issued by a trusted certificate authority (CA).

▶ **SSL client authentication**—This allows a server to validate a client's identity. SSL can validate that a client's certificate is valid as well as check whether the certificate is from a trusted CA.

▶ **Encrypting SSL connections**—The most common application of SSL is encrypting all traffic on a given connection. This provides a high degree of confidentiality and security.

From an IIS perspective, SSL can be applied to an entire website, directories, or specific files within the website. SSL configuration can be done through Internet Information Services (IIS) Manager.

The high-level steps for utilizing certificates and SSL consist of the following: The first step is to obtain a certificate. The second step is to create an HTTPS binding for a specific site that needs to be encrypted. The final step is to configure SSL settings for a site, application, or physical directory.

To use SSL on a website, a certificate must first be requested and then installed. The request can be created to obtain a certificate either from an external, trusted CA or from an internal PKI. The types of server requests available in Internet Information Services include the following:

▶ **Create Certificate Request**—This option is typically used for creating a certificate request, which will be submitted to a third-party public CA. The certificate's distinguished name properties, cryptographic service provider, and bit-length information are entered into a file and then submitted to a public CA for approval.

**TIP**

When creating the certificate request to a public CA, it is recommended to use 1024 (the default) or higher as the bit length. Keep in mind that higher bit lengths enforce stronger security; however, a greater length can decrease performance.

▶ **Create Domain Certificate Request**—A domain certificate request is used when providing a request to an internal certificate authority. Typically, the internal certificate authority would be an enterprise certificate authority associated with the company's Active Directory domain. This approach reduces the cost of purchasing third-party certificates and also simplifies the certificate deployment.

▶ **Create Self-Signed Certificate Request**—The final option available when creating a certificate request is to use a self-signed certificate. Typically, this method is only used for maintaining certificates for a testing environment because the certificates are not from a trusted CA.

This example illustrates the procedures to create a domain-based certificate request. To complete this task, this example requires an internal certificate authority running within your domain. For more information on creating an internal CA, refer to Chapter 15, "Security Policies, Network Policy Server, and Network Access Protection."

To create a domain-based certificate request, do the following:

1. Launch Internet Information Services (IIS) Manager.

2. In the Connections pane, highlight the IIS server that will request an Internet Server Certificate.

3. In the Feature view, double-click the Server Certificates element.

4. In the Actions pane, select Create Domain Certificate Request.

5. On the Distinguished Name Properties page, specify the required information for the certificate, as displayed in Figure 12.17. The common name is typically the fully qualified domain name (FQDN) of the URL users will use to connect to the website (for example, www.companyabc.com). Click Next to continue.

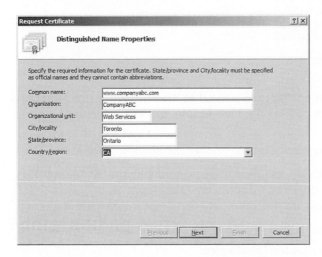

FIGURE 12.17   Creating a domain-based certificate request.

6. Because this is a domain-based certificate request, the next page presented is the Online Certificate Authority. Specify the online certificate authority that will accept the request by selecting the CA from a list. In addition, a friendly name is also required. Click Finish to finalize the request.

After the create certificate process has been completed, either the administrator of the CA must approve the request or it can be automatically approved based on the autoenrollment feature of the domain-based CA. The CA in this example automatically fulfilled the request; therefore, the certificate resides on the Server Certificates page and can be viewed by selecting it and clicking View Task in the Actions pane. Otherwise, an additional procedure is required to install the certificate.

Because the certificate is already installed, the next step in the process is to bind the Internet Server Certificate for the desired website and enable SSL. To do this, follow these steps:

1. Open the IIS Manager snap-in and select the website for which the binding will be created.

2. In the Actions Pane, select Bindings to launch the Site Binding utility.

3. In the Web Site Bindings dialog box, click Add.

4. In the Add Site Binding dialog box, select the HTTPS option from the Type drop-down menu, assign an IP address, and verify the port is 443, as shown in Figure 12.18.

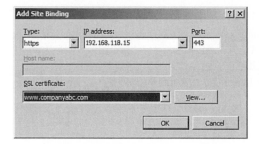

FIGURE 12.18    Adding SSL site binding.

5. Select a certificate, such as the one that was created in the previous section. You can view the certificate selected by clicking the View button. Click OK to return to the Site Bindings dialog box.

6. Click Close in the Site Bindings dialog box to finalize the binding process.

The final process when configuring a site to utilize SSL is to configure the SSL settings for the site application or the physical directory. To configure SSL settings on the new website that was created in the previous steps, do the following:

1. In IIS Manager, navigate to the desired site for which you will configure SSL settings.

2. Double-Click the SSL Settings icon in Features view.

3. On the SSL Settings page, enable the Require SSL option. Alternatively, select the Require 128-bit SSL option to force 128-bit encryption.

4. The final setting is to configure whether to accept, ignore, or require client certificates. Choose the appropriate Client Certificates option, and click Apply in the Actions pane to save the changes, as shown in Figure 12.19.

## Administering IIS 7.5 Administrator and User Security

Several built-in administrator roles exist for managing Internet Information Services (IIS) 7.5. This is a new approach to IIS administration as users can be assigned to these administrative roles to conduct specific administrative tasks on the web server, website,

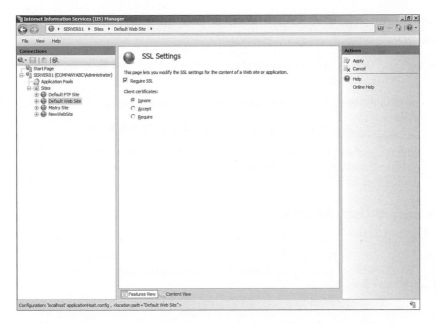

FIGURE 12.19   Configuring the properties on the SSL Settings feature page.

or web application. There are three IIS administrative roles: Web Server Administrator, Web Site Administrator, and Web Application Administrator. Each role dictates the settings that can be configured. Table 12.1 lists each IIS administrative role and permissions associated with it.

TABLE 12.1   Server-Level Roles

| IIS Administrative Role | Configuration Tasks |
| --- | --- |
| Web Server Administrator | Complete and unrestricted access to the web server, including all sites and applications |
| | Web server |
| | Application pools |
| | Websites |
| | Virtual directories |
| | Physical directories in the websites and web applications |
| | Web server security |
| Web Site Administrator | Full control over the web to which they have been delegated |
| | Web application within the delegation |
| | Virtual directories within the delegation |
| | Physical directory within the delegation |

TABLE 12.1    Server-Level Roles

| IIS Administrative Role | Configuration Tasks |
| --- | --- |
| Web Application Administrator | Configure web application settings to which they have been delegated |
| | Virtual directories within the web application delegation |
| | Physical directory within the web application delegation |
| | Files in the virtual and physical directory within the web application delegation |

## Creating an IIS 7.5 User Account

There might be situations when you need to provide a non-Windows user IIS 7.5 management capabilities. You need to create an IIS 7.5 user account; therefore, this non-Windows user has management privileges to delegate features and IIS functionality. Follow these steps to create an IIS 7.5 user account:

1. In Internet Information Services (IIS) Manager, navigate to the Connections pane and select the IIS server.

2. Select the IIS Manager Users feature icon, which is located in the central details pane.

3. On the IIS Manager Users feature page, click the Add User task, which is located in the Actions pane.

4. In the Add User dialog box, enter the new user account name and password, and then click OK.

> **NOTE**
>
> When entering a password, the password policy will be governed by the local Windows Server 2008 R2 group policy. Therefore, the password will need to be strong to meet the default complexity password policy.

For ongoing user account management, after the user account is created, use the additional tasks on the Actions pane to change the password, disable, or remove the account.

## Assigning Permissions to an IIS 7.5 User Account

The next step in the user creation process is to assign the appropriate permissions to the newly created user account. This process allows the user to configure delegated features for a specific website or application. Follow these steps to authorize a user account to connect to a site or an application:

1. In Internet Information Services (IIS) Manager, navigate to the Connections pane, expand the IIS server, and then expand the Sites node.

2. Specify the site to which the user account will be granted authorization, and then select the IIS Manager Permissions feature icon, which is located in the Central Details pane.

3. On the IIS Manager Permissions feature page, click the Allow User task, which is located in the Actions pane.

4. In the Allow User dialog box, first select the IIS Manager option, then enter the account that was created in the previous steps, and then click OK.

**NOTE**

If the IIS Manager option is not available in the Allow User dialog box, the management service is not set to accept connections from IIS users. To do so, use the Management Service page to enable remote connections and select the identify option, Windows Credentials or IIS Manager Credentials.

## Configuring Feature Delegation

Follow these steps to configure feature delegation for a newly created website:

1. In Internet Information Services (IIS) Manager, navigate to the Connections pane and select the IIS server.

2. Select the Feature Delegation feature icon, which is located in the Central Details pane.

3. On the Features Delegation page, select the Custom Web Site Delegation task from the Actions pane. Alternatively, select the Customer Web Application Delegation if you want to delegate an application.

4. Select the site to be delegated from the Sites drop-down menu on the Custom Website page.

5. Select the appropriate feature in the list and then set the desired feature delegation from the Actions pane. The delegations include: Read/Write, Read Only, Not Delegated, and Reset to Inherited.

**NOTE**

There might be circumstances when there is a need to reset delegation or restore the defaults. When necessary, click the Reset All Delegation or Default Delegation in the Actions pane.

## Using IIS Logging

IIS logging should be viewed as a necessity rather than an optional feature of IIS because it helps to ensure IIS security and is also extremely useful for maintenance and troubleshooting. For example, in the event of a system compromise, logs can be used and a forensic review performed on the intimate details contained in them. This information can then be used to review maintenance procedures and identify problems in the system. Equally important, many organizations now require logging because of regulatory compliance so it seems logging is here to stay.

IIS text-based logging, such as the W3C Extended Log File Format, Microsoft IIS Log File Format, and NCSA Common Log File Format, is controlled by Http.sys, which is a kernel-mode process. This is a significant change from previous versions where logging was a user-mode process. The only other log file format that comes close to previous versions is ODBC as it is implemented using a user mode worker process.

Another bonus about logging is its ability to be implemented at the server, site, web application, file, and directory level. For organizations wanting to configure IIS 7.5 logging for a specific website, follow these procedures:

1. Launch Internet Information Services (IIS) Manager.

2. In the Connections pane, select the desired website for which you want to configure logging.

3. Double-click the Logging feature in the Actions pane.

4. On the Logging page, select the desired logging format to be utilized.

5. Specify the location of the log file by typing a log path into the Directory text box. Alternatively, click the Browse button and select a directory to store the files.

6. In the Log File Rollover section, select the method to create the new log file. The options include specifying an Hourly, Daily, Weekly, or Monthly schedule, entering a maximum file size (in bytes), or selecting the option that puts a stop to the creation of new log files.

7. The final option requires you to determine whether to use local time for file naming and rollover.

8. After all the log file settings have been inputted, select Apply in the Actions pane to commit the changes.

---

**NOTE**

It is possible to either enable or disable a log file for a specific site by selecting Enable or Disable in the Actions pane of the Logging feature page. To enable logging for IIS 7.5, the HTTP Logging Module must be installed.

---

# Summary

IIS 7.5 is a major improvement over previous versions in terms of security, reliability, availability, and performance. These facets have been a top priority for Microsoft. Microsoft has incorporated both internal and customer-based feedback to provide a robust platform for providing web, application, and FTP services.

Key points in this chapter covered the planning and design of the new IIS 7.5 capabilities built in to Windows Server 2008 R2. The features have been greatly enhanced to provide better management, scalability, modification, and reporting of web services operations.

Instead of having IIS installed on every installation of Windows server, an administrator now needs to "add" the IIS server role to the system and then go through a process of enabling functionality and configuring the web services function to meet the needs of the organization. This change (from having web services installed automatically to now requiring specific services to be enabled) provides better security for server systems but also requires a better understanding of which services should be added or modified to meet the needs of the organization's applications.

And even with IIS requiring manual installation and configuration, there are still key security practices that need to be performed to ensure that web services are not attacked and compromised, thus creating a security hole in the organization's network security.

The IIS 7.5 server role is a significant improvement in Windows Server 2008 R2, and one that administrators from early adopter organizations have found to be a welcome change in ongoing operations.

# Best Practices

The following are best practices from this chapter:

- ▶ Use IIS 7.5 to improve performance and strengthen security.

- ▶ Thoroughly design and plan the IIS 7.5 environment.

- ▶ Define the goals and objectives of the IIS 7.5 project.

- ▶ Identify and review IIS application types and requirements.

- ▶ Define security requirements to meet the goals and objectives.

- ▶ Balance the security methodologies to be used with the associated risks and end-user experience.

- ▶ Examine and design disaster recovery plans, and monitor requirements and maintenance practices.

- ▶ Document the current IIS infrastructure and the IIS design decisions.

- ▶ Build fault tolerance into the web infrastructure based on how much downtime can be afforded and existing SLAs.

- ▶ Use IIS to monitor applications such as pinging worker processes after a specified period of time, monitoring for failed applications, and disabling the application pool after a certain number of failures or a set number of failures within a given time frame.

- ▶ Isolate FTP users so that FTP content is protected.

- ▶ Provide search capabilities for Adobe Acrobat PDF file content on a website by using the iFilter driver.

- ▶ Use NTFS on the disk subsystem, and apply the latest service pack and security patches to begin securing the IIS system.

418    CHAPTER 12    Internet Information Services

► Carefully review application security on the Windows Server 2008 web server, especially if using a custom-built application.

► Choose an authentication method carefully depending on business and technical requirements.

► Apply auditing to web and FTP sites to document attempts to log on (successful and unsuccessful), to gain unauthorized access to service accounts, to modify or delete files, and to execute restricted commands.

► Use SSL to ensure confidentiality.

► Use local folders to share downloads, and secure them with NTFS. The folder should be located on a separate partition from Windows Server 2008 R2 system files.

► Monitor disk space and IIS logs to ensure that a hacker isn't attempting to gain unauthorized access.

► Use logging not only to review IIS security, but also to assist with maintenance and troubleshooting.

# CHAPTER 13

# Server-Level Security

The term Microsoft security was long considered, whether fairly or unfairly, to be an oxymoron. High-profile vulnerabilities and viruses that were exploited in the legacy Windows NT 4.0 and Windows 2000 Server operating systems often made organizations wary of the security, or lack of security, that was built in to Microsoft technologies. In direct response to this criticism, security since the development of Windows Server 2003 has become the major, if not the most important, priority for the development team. Windows Server 2008 R2 continues this trend, with improvements in functionality such as Server Core and a built-in intelligent firewall.

This chapter focuses on the server-side security mechanisms in Windows Server 2008 R2. Improved features such as the intelligent integrated firewall are explained in detail. Particular emphasis is placed on the importance of keeping servers up to date with security patches through such utilities as Windows Server Update Services, a major improvement to Windows security. In addition, file-level security, physical security, and other critical server security considerations are presented.

## Defining Windows Server 2008 R2 Security

Security on the server level is one of the most important considerations for a network environment. Servers in an infrastructure not only handle critical network services, such as domain name system (DNS), Dynamic Host Configuration Protocol (DHCP), directory lookups, and authentication, but they also serve as a central location for most, if not all, critical files in an organization's network. Subsequently, it is important to establish a server-level security plan and to gain a full understanding of the security capabilities of Windows Server 2008 R2.

## Outlining Microsoft's Trustworthy Computing Initiative

On the heels of several high-profile viruses and security holes, Bill Gates developed what became known as the Trustworthy Computing initiative. The basics of the initiative boiled down to an increased emphasis on security in all Microsoft technologies. Every line of code in Windows Server was combed for potential vulnerabilities, and the emphasis was shifted from new functionality to security. What the initiative means to users of Microsoft technology is the fact that security has become a major priority for Microsoft, and Windows Server 2008 R2 is the third major server release after Windows Server 2003 that uses this concept.

## Common Language Runtime

All Microsoft code is verified through a process called common language runtime. It processes application code and automatically checks for security holes that can be caused by mistakes in programming. In addition, it scrutinizes security credentials that are used by specific pieces of code, making sure that they perform only those actions that they are supposed to. Through these techniques, the common language runtime effectively reduces the overall threat posed to Windows Server 2008 R2 by limiting the potential for exploitations and vulnerabilities.

## Understanding the Layered Approach to Server Security

Security works best when it is applied in layers. It is much more difficult to rob a house, for example, if a thief not only has to break through the front door, but also has to fend off an attack dog and disable a home security system. The same concept applies to server security: Multiple layers of security should be applied so that the difficulty in hacking into a system becomes exponentially greater.

Windows Server 2008 R2 seamlessly handles many of the security layers that are required, utilizing Kerberos authentication, NTFS file security, and built-in security tools to provide for a great deal of security right out of the box. Additional security components require that you understand their functionality and install and configure their components. Windows Server 2008 R2 makes the addition of extra layers of security a possibility, and positions organizations for increased security without sacrificing functionality.

# Deploying Physical Security

One of the most overlooked but perhaps most critical components of server security is the actual physical security of the server itself. The most secure, unbreakable web server is powerless if a malicious user can simply unplug it. Worse yet, someone logging on to a critical file server could potentially copy critical data or sabotage the machine directly.

Physical security is a must for any organization because it is the most common cause of security breaches. Despite this fact, many organizations have loose levels, or no levels, of physical security for their mission-critical servers. An understanding of what is required to secure the physical and logon access to a server is, consequently, a must.

## Restricting Physical Access

Servers should be physically secured behind locked doors, in a controlled-access environment. It is unwise to place mission-critical servers at the feet of administrators or in similar, unsecure locations. Rather, a dedicated server room or server closet that is locked at all times is the most ideal environment for the purposes of server security.

Most hardware manufacturers also include mechanisms for locking out some or all of the components of a server. Depending on the other layers of security deployed, it might be wise to utilize these mechanisms to secure a server environment.

## Restricting Logon Access

All servers should be configured to allow only administrators to physically log on to the console. By default, such use is restricted on domain controllers, but other servers such as file servers, utility servers, and the like must specifically forbid these types of logons. To restrict logon access, follow these steps:

1. Click Start, All Programs, Administrative Tools, Local Security Policy.
2. In the node pane, navigate to Security Settings, Local Policies, User Rights Assignment.
3. Double-click Allow Log On Locally.
4. Remove any users or groups that do not need access to the server, as illustrated in Figure 13.1. (Keep in mind that, on web servers, the IUSR_SERVERNAME account needs to have Log On Locally access to properly display web pages.) Click OK when you are finished.

> **NOTE**
>
> If you replace Local Security Policy in the restriction lockdown instructions in step 1 with the Domain Controllers Security Policy, you will be able to carry out these same instructions on a Windows Server 2008 R2 domain controller.

> **NOTE**
>
> A group policy set at an OU level can be applied to all servers, simplifying this task and negating the need to perform it manually on every server. For more information on setting up these types of group policies, refer to Chapter 27, "Group Policy Management for Network Clients."

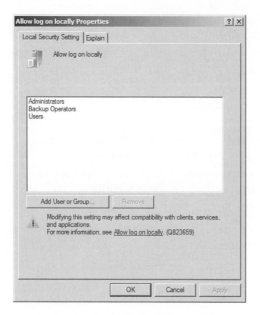

FIGURE 13.1    Restricting logon access.

## Using the Run As Administrator Command for Administrative Access

Logging off administrators after using any and all workstations and servers on a network is often the most difficult and tedious security precaution. If an administrator forgets, or simply steps away from a workstation temporarily without logging off, any persons passing by can muck around with the network infrastructure as they please.

For this reason, it is wise to consider a logon strategy that incorporates the Run As Administrator command that is embedded in Windows Server 2008 R2. Essentially, this means that all users, including IT staff, log on with restricted, standard user accounts. When administrative functionality is required, IT support personnel can invoke the tool or executable by using the Run As Administrator command, which effectively gives that tool administrative capabilities. If an administrator leaves a workstation console without logging off, the situation is not critical because the console will not grant a passerby full administrator access to the network.

The following example illustrates how to invoke the Computer Management MMC snap-in using the Run As command from the GUI interface:

1. Navigate to (but do not select) Start, All Programs, Administrative Tools, Computer Management.
2. Hold down the Shift key, right-click Computer Management in the program list, and then choose Run As Different User.
3. In the Run As dialog box, choose the credentials under which you want to run the program, and click OK.

In addition to the manual method of using Run As, an administrator's desktop can be configured to have each shortcut automatically run as a computer administrator. For example, the Active Directory Users and Computers MMC snap-in can be set to permanently run with elevated privileges by following these steps:

1. Click Start, All Programs, Administrative Tools.
2. Right-click Computer Management and choose Properties.
3. On the Shortcut tab, click the Advanced button.
4. Check the Run As Administrator check box, as shown in Figure 13.2, and click OK twice to save the settings.

FIGURE 13.2    Running a shortcut with Administrator privileges.

**NOTE**

Ironically, administrative access is sometimes required to be able to change some of the shortcut properties. Consequently, you might need to log on as a user with higher privileges to set up the shortcuts on other users' profiles.

## Using Smart Cards for Logon Access

The ultimate in secured infrastructures utilize so-called smart cards for logon access; these smart cards are fully supported in Windows Server 2008 R2. A smart card can exist in multiple forms, commonly as a credit card-sized piece of plastic with an encrypted microchip embedded within or as a USB key. Each user is assigned a unique smart card and an associated PIN. Logging on to a workstation is as straightforward as inserting the smart card into a smart card reader and entering in the PIN, which can be a combination of numbers and letters, similar to a password.

Security can be raised even higher by stipulating that when the smart card is removed, the user is automatically logged off the console. In this scenario, users insert into the smart card reader a smart card that is physically attached to their person via a chain or string. After entering their PIN, they log on and perform all necessary functions. Upon leaving, they simply remove the smart card from the reader, which automatically logs them off the workstation. In this scenario, it is nearly impossible for users to forget to log off because they must physically detach themselves from the computer to leave.

## Securing Wireless Networks

Wireless security has always been an issue, but recent trends toward wireless networks have made it even more so. Most organizations are shocked to see what kind of damage can be done to a network simply by a person being able to connect via a network port. The addition of wireless networks makes access even easier; for example, an unsavory individual can simply pull up in the parking lot and access an organization's local area network (LAN) via a laptop computer and a standard wireless card. The standard security employed by wireless networks, Wireless Encryption Protocol (WEP), is effectively worthless because it can be cracked in several minutes.

Controlling the network ports and securing network switches are part of the securing strategy. For organizations with wireless networks, more stringent precautions must be taken. Deployment of wireless networks using the 802.1x protocol vastly increases the security of the mechanism. Microsoft uses 802.1x to secure its vast wireless network, and Windows Server 2008 R2 fully supports the protocol.

For those organizations without the time or resources to deploy 802.1x, the simple step of placing wireless access points outside the firewall and requiring virtual private network (VPN) access through the firewall can effectively secure the wireless network. Even if trespassers were to break the WEP key, they would be connected only to an orphaned network, with no place to go.

### Firewall Security

Deployment of an enterprise firewall configuration is a must in any environment that is connected to the Internet. Servers or workstations directly connected to the Internet are prime candidates for hacking. Modern firewall implementations such as Microsoft's Internet Security and Acceleration (ISA) 2006 offer advanced configurations, such as web proxying and demilitarized zone (DMZ) configuration, as well. Proper setup and configuration of a firewall in between a Windows Server 2008 R2 network and the Internet are a must.

# Using the Integrated Windows Firewall with Advanced Security

Windows Server 2008 R2 includes a vastly improved integrated firewall that is turned on by default in all installations of the product. The firewall, administered from an MMC snap-in shown in Figure 13.3 (Start, All Programs, Administrative Tools, Windows Firewall with Advanced Security), gives unprecedented control and security to a server.

## Understanding Windows Firewall Integration with Server Manager

The firewall with advanced security is fully integrated with the Server Manager utility and the Server Roles Wizard. For example, if an administrator runs the Server Roles Wizard and chooses to make the server a file server, only then are those ports and protocols that are required for file server access opened on the server.

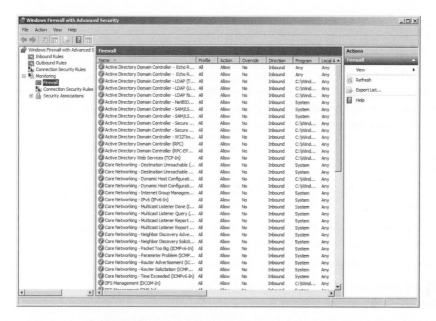

FIGURE 13.3    Using the integrated Windows Firewall with Advanced Security.

---

**NOTE**

It is instinctual for most administrators to disable software firewalls on servers, as they have caused problems with functionality in the past. This is not recommended in Windows Server 2008 R2, however, as the product itself is tightly integrated with its firewall, and the firewall itself provides for a much greater degree of security than previous versions of Windows Server provided.

---

## Creating Inbound and Outbound Rules on the Windows Firewall

In certain cases, when a third-party application is not integrated with Server Manager, or when needing to open specific individual ports, it might become necessary to create firewall rules for individual services to run properly. Both inbound rules, addressing traffic to the server, and outbound rules, addressing how the server can communicate out, can be created. Rules can be created based on the following factors:

▶ **Program**—A rule can be created that allows a specific program executable access. For example, you can specify that the c:\Program Files\Custom Program\myprogram.exe file has full outbound access when running. The Windows Firewall program will then allow any type of connections made by that program full access. This can be useful in scenarios when a specific application server uses multiple varied ports, but the overall security that the firewall provides is still desired.

▶ **Port**—Entering a traditional UDP or TCP port into the Add Rules Wizard is supported. This covers traditional scenarios such as "We need to open Port 8787 on the server."

▶ **Predefined**—Windows Server also has built-in, predefined rules, such as those that allow AD DS, DFS, BITS, HTTP, and many more. The advantage to using a predefined rule is that Microsoft has done all the legwork in advance, and it becomes much easier to allow a specific service.

▶ **Custom**—The creation of custom rule types not covered in the other categories is also supported.

For example, the following procedure details the creation of an inbound rule to allow a custom application to use TCP Port 8787 for inbound communication:

1. Open the Windows Firewall MMC (Start, All Programs, Administrative Tools, Windows Firewall with Advanced Security).

2. Click on the Inbound Rules node in the node pane.

3. In the Actions pane, click the New Rule link.

4. On the Rule Type page of the New Inbound Rule Wizard, shown in Figure 13.4, select Port to create a rule based on the port, and click Next to continue.

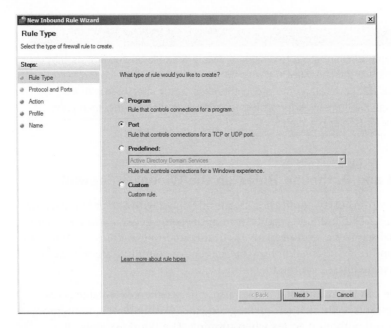

FIGURE 13.4    Creating a rule on the Windows Firewall.

5. On the Protocol and Ports page, shown in Figure 13.5, select TCP, and enter 8787 in the Specific Local Ports field. Click Next to continue.

6. On the Action page, select Allow to enable the connection.

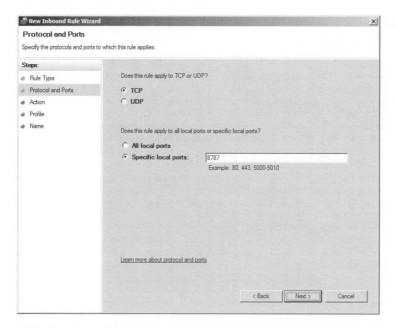

FIGURE 13.5    Entering port information for the firewall rule.

> **NOTE**
>
> The Action page of the New Inbound Rule Wizard also allows for a rule to be configured that only allows the connection if it is secured using IPSec technologies. For more on IPSec, see Chapter 14, "Transport-Level Security."

7. On the Profile page, shown in Figure 13.6, select all three check boxes. This enables an administrator to specify that a rule only applies when connected to specific networks. Click Next to continue.

8. Enter a descriptive name for the rule, and click Finish.

Review the rule settings in the Inbound Rules node, shown in Figure 13.7. This allows for a quick-glance view of the rule settings. You can also include a rule in a rule group, which allows for multiple rules to be tied together for easy on/off application.

Using the integrated Windows Firewall is no longer just a good idea; it's a vital part of the security of the product. The addition of the ability to define rules based on factors such as scope, profile, IPSec status, and the like further positions the Server OS as one with high levels of integrated security.

# Hardening Server Security

Previous versions of Windows Server required a great deal of configuration after installation to "harden" the security of the server and ensure that viruses and exploits would not overwhelm or disable the server. The good news with Windows Server 2008 R2 is that, by

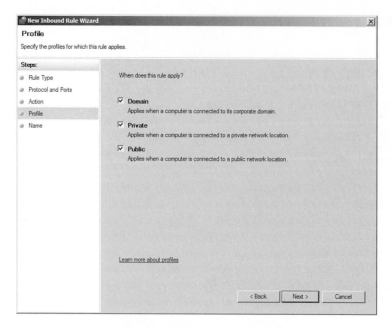

FIGURE 13.6    Specifying the profile of a firewall rule.

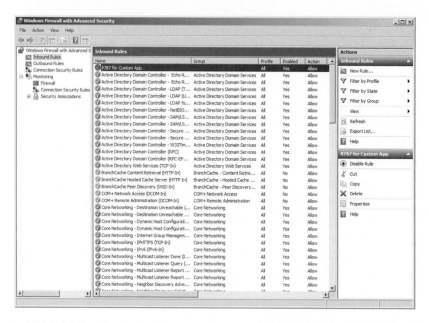

FIGURE 13.7    Viewing the firewall rules.

default, many less commonly used services are turned off. In fact, a fresh installation of Windows Server 2008 R2 only has those services enabled that are vital for the OS to run properly, and everything else must be enabled by running Server Manager. In addition, by default an intelligent firewall is enabled, and only those services that absolutely need to run are allowed through the firewall.

Subsequently, in Windows Server 2008 R2, it is important to first define which roles a server will utilize and then to turn on only those services that are necessary, with the use of Server Manager, which automates the deployment of server roles.

## Defining Server Roles

Depending on the size of an organization, a server might be designated for one or multiple network roles. In an ideal world, a separate server or servers would be designated to handle a single role, such as DHCP server or DNS server. Even smaller organizations can take advantage of virtualization technology such as Windows Server 2008 R2's Hyper-V server virtualization platform to provision multiple dedicated guests on a smaller number of physical hosts.

Because any service that is activated increases the overall risk, it is important to fully define which roles a server will take on so that those services can be properly configured. Although these components can be set up manually, the process of turning on these services is streamlined through the use of the Configure Your Server Wizard.

### Securing a Server Using Server Manager

With the list of roles that a server will perform in hand, the ideal utility for turning on these roles and securing them is the newly renovated Server Manager. By default, if a server is a DNS server but does not do file and print services, Server Manager not only opens the ports required for DNS, but also blocks any file and print access to the server.

Windows Server 2008 R2 Server Manager, shown in Figure 13.8, allows for individual roles to be enabled on a server. After being enabled, those roles are turned on and the proper ports to run those roles are opened on the server.

# Examining File-Level Security

Files secured on Windows Server 2008 R2 are only as secure as the permissions that are set on them. Subsequently, it is good to know that Windows Server 2008 R2 does not grant the Everyone group full control over share-level and NTFS-level permissions. In addition, critical operating system files and directories are secured to disallow their unauthorized use.

Despite the overall improvements made, a complete understanding of file-level security is recommended to ensure that the file-level security of a server is not neglected.

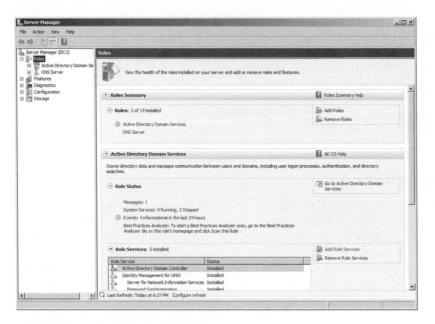

FIGURE 13.8    Viewing Server Manager.

## Understanding NT File System (NTFS) Security

The latest revision of the NT File System (NTFS) is used in Windows Server 2008 R2 to provide for file-level security in the operating system. Each object that is referenced in NTFS, which includes files and folders, is marked by an access control entry (ACE) that physically limits who can and cannot access a resource. NTFS permissions utilize this concept to strictly control read, write, and other types of access on files.

File servers should make judicious use of NTFS-level permissions, and all directories should have the file-level permissions audited to determine if there are any holes in the NTFS permission set. Changing NTFS permissions in Windows Server 2008 R2 is a straightforward process; simply follow these steps:

1. Right-click the folder or file onto which the security will be applied, and choose Properties.

2. Select the Security tab.

3. Click the Advanced button.

4. Click the Change Permissions button.

5. Uncheck the Include Inheritable Permissions from This Object's Parent check box.

6. Click Remove when prompted about the application of parent permissions.

7. While you're in the Advanced dialog box, use the Add button to give access to the groups and/or users who need access to the files or folders.

8. Check the Replace All Child Object Permissions with Inheritable Permissions from This Object check box, as shown in Figure 13.9, and click OK.

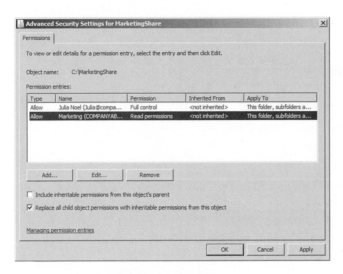

## 13

FIGURE 13.9   Setting NTFS permissions.

9. When prompted about replacing security on child objects, click Yes to replace child object security and continue.

10. Click OK and then click OK again to close the property pages.

## Examining Share-Level Security Versus NTFS Security

Previous Windows security used share-level permissions, which were independently set. A share is a file server entry point, such as \\sfofs01\marketing, that enables users to have access to a specific directory on a file server. Older file systems such as FAT, HPFS, and FAT32 did not include file-level security, so the security was set instead on the share level. Although share-level security can still be set on files, it is preferable to use NTFS-level security, where possible. Share-level security is not very secure because it cannot secure the contents of subdirectories easily.

## Auditing File Access

A good practice for file-level security is to set up auditing on a particular server, directory, or file. Auditing on NTFS volumes enables administrators to be notified of who is accessing, or attempting to access, a particular directory. For example, it might be wise to audit access to a critical network share, such as a finance folder, to determine whether anyone is attempting to access restricted information.

**NOTE**

Audit entries are another example of security settings that can be automatically set via security templates in Windows Server 2008 R2. It is wise to consider the use of security templates to more effectively control audit settings.

The following steps illustrate how to set up simple auditing on a folder in Windows Server 2008 R2:

1. Right-click the folder or file onto which the auditing will be applied, and choose Properties.

2. Select the Security tab.

3. Click the Advanced button.

4. Select the Auditing tab.

5. Click the Edit button.

6. Using the Add button, enter all users and groups that will be audited. If you're auditing all users, enter the Everyone group.

7. On the Auditing property page, select all types of access that will be audited. If you're auditing for all success and failure attempts, select all the options, as indicated in Figure 13.10.

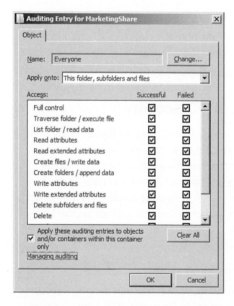

FIGURE 13.10    Selecting what to audit.

8. Click OK to apply the settings.

9. Click OK twice to save the settings.

> **NOTE**
>
> An effective way of catching "snoops" in the act is to create serious-looking shares on the network, such as Financial Statements, Root Info, or similar such shares, and audit access to those folders. This mechanism, known as a honeypot, has been successfully used to identify internal (or external) saboteurs before they could do some serious damage.

## Encrypting Files with the Encrypting File System

Windows Server 2008 R2 continues support for the Encrypting File System (EFS), a method of scrambling the contents of files to make them unintelligible to unauthorized users. EFS has proven to be valuable for organizations that desire to keep proprietary data, especially those stored on laptops, out of the wrong hands. A more comprehensive approach to client encryption is with Windows 7/Vista BitLocker Drive Encryption, which encrypts all files on the entire hard drive, with the exception of a few files required for startup.

# Additional Security Mechanisms

In an insecure world, a server is only as secure as the software that runs on it. Windows Server 2008 R2 is the most secure Windows yet, and includes many built-in mechanisms to keep a server secure. Additional security considerations such as antivirus options and backup should be taken into account, however, as they directly affect the overall security of the operating system itself.

## Antivirus Precautions

Viruses might be one of the most dangerous threats faced by servers. Many viruses are written to specifically exploit key vulnerabilities that are present in server infrastructure. Others infect files that might be held on a server, spreading the infection to clients who download files. Consequently, it is extremely important to consider the use of an enterprise antivirus solution on all file servers in a network. All the major antivirus manufacturers include robust file-level scanners, and administrators should consider using them.

Microsoft itself has released a line of antivirus products with tight integration with the Windows Server line. This is part of the Forefront line of security products. An advantage to using the Forefront product suite is that it uses five antivirus engines all running at the same time. This way, if one of the engines doesn't catch a virus or isn't updated quickly enough, there is a good chance that one of the other vendors' engines will detect the virus. More information on the Forefront line can be found at www.microsoft.com/forefront.

An aggressive plan should be in place to keep antivirus patterns and engines up to date. Because virus outbreaks can wreak havoc worldwide in a matter of hours, rather than days, it is wise to have servers check for updates at least daily.

## Deploying Backup Security

Although the need for a backup strategy might seem obvious to most people, it is often surprising to find out how inadequately prepared many organizations are in regard to their backups. All too often, a company will discover that it is very easy to back up a server but often more difficult to restore. In addition to disaster recovery issues, the issue of backup security is often neglected.

File server backups require that an authenticated user account with the proper privileges copy data to a storage mechanism. This requirement ensures that not just anyone can back up an environment and run off with the tape. Keeping this point in mind, the tapes that contain server backups should be protected with the same caution given to the server itself. All too often, a big pile of server backup tapes is left out on unsecured desks, and there is often no mechanism in place to account for how many tapes are in which location. Implementing a strict tape retention and verification procedure is, subsequently, a must.

# Using Windows Server Update Services

One of the main drawbacks to Windows security has been the difficulty in keeping servers and workstations up to date with the latest security fixes. For example, the security fix for the Index Server component of IIS was available for more than a month before the Code Red and Nimbda viruses erupted onto the scene. If the deployed web servers had downloaded the patch, they would not have been affected. The main reason that the vast majority of the deployed servers were not updated was that keeping servers and workstations up to date with the latest security patches was an extremely manual and time-consuming process. For this reason, a streamlined approach to security patch application was required and realized with the formulation of Windows Server Update Services (WSUS).

## Understanding the Background of WSUS: Windows Update

In response to the original concerns regarding the difficulty in keeping computers properly patched, Microsoft made available a centralized website called Windows Update to which clients could connect, download security patches, and install those patches. Invoking the Windows Update web page remotely installed an executable, which ran a test to see which hotfixes had been applied and which were needed, based on the Microsoft components installed on the machine. Those that were not applied were offered up for download, and users could easily install these patches.

Windows Update streamlined the security patch verification and installation process, but the major drawback was that it required a manual effort to go up to the server every few days or weeks and check for updates. A more efficient, automated process was required.

## Deploying the Automatic Updates Client

The Automatic Updates client was developed to automate the installation of security fixes and patches and to give users the option to automatically "drizzle" patches across the Internet to the local computer for installation. Drizzling, also known as Background

Intelligent Transfer Service (BITS), is a process in which a computer intelligently utilizes unused network bandwidth to download files to the machine. Because only unused bandwidth is used, there is no perceived effect on the network client itself.

All currently supported versions of Microsoft clients include the Automatic Updates client built in to the OS.

## Understanding the Development of Windows Server Update Services

The Windows Update website and the associated client provided for the needs of most home users and some small offices. However, large organizations, concerned about the bandwidth effects of hundreds of machines downloading large numbers of updates over the Internet, often disabled this service or discouraged its use. These organizations often had a serious need for Windows Update's capabilities. This fact led to the development of Software Update Services (SUS), which was later improved into the new product, Windows Server Update Services (WSUS).

WSUS started as a free download from Microsoft that effectively gives organizations their own, independent version of the Windows Update server. The latest version of WSUS runs on either a Windows Server 2003 SP1 or greater machine that is running Internet Information Services. Clients connect to a central intranet WSUS server for all their security patches and updates.

WSUS is not considered to be a replacement technology for existing software deployment solutions such as System Center Configuration Manager (SCCM), but rather it is envisioned as a solution for mid- to large-size businesses to take control over the fast deployment of security patches as they become available. It also offers a myriad of reports for administrators.

## Examining WSUS Prerequisites

Deploying WSUS on a dedicated server is preferable, but it can also be deployed on a Windows Server 2008 R2 server that is running other tasks, as long as that server is running Internet Information Services. The following list details the minimum levels of hardware on which WSUS will operate:

- ▶ Windows Server 2003 SP1/SP2 or greater

- ▶ Internet Information Services (IIS)

- ▶ Background Intelligent Transfer Service (BITS)

- ▶ Windows Internal Database role or SQL Server 2005 installed locally or on a remote server

- ▶ Microsoft .NET Framework 2.0 or greater

## Installing WSUS on a Windows Server 2008 R2 Server

The installation of WSUS is very easy, as it is installed as a server role from Server Manager. The guided setup will install WSUS and any required components.

To complete the initial installation of WSUS, follow these steps:

1. Launch Server Manager.

2. In the Roles Summary pane, select Add Roles to start the wizard.

3. Click Next.

4. Select Windows Server Update Services, and click Next.

5. The Add Role Services and Features Required for Windows Server Update Services window prompts for additional components to install, if necessary. Required components are the Web Server (IIS) web server and management tools, the Windows Process Activation Service Process Model, and the .NET environment. Click Add Required Role Services to continue.

6. Click Next.

7. Read the Introduction to Web Server (IIS) overview, and click Next.

8. Click Next to select the default role services to install for Web Server (IIS).

9. Read the Introduction to Windows Server Update Services overview, and click Next.

10. Read the summary of installation selections, and click Install.

11. Server Manager shows "Searching for Updates" and "Downloading" while it connects to the Microsoft download site and downloads the most recent version of WSUS. It also installs Web Services (IIS) and the Windows Process Activation Service, if needed.

12. The Windows Server Update Services Setup Wizard displays during the installation progress. Click Next.

13. Read and accept the license agreement, and click Next.

14. If prompted that Report Viewer 2005 is not installed, click Next to continue (certain reports will be unavailable without this downloadable add-on).

15. Check the Store Updates Locally check box, and enter a location in which to store them, as shown in Figure 13.11. This location must be large enough to hold a large number of downloadable patches. Click Next to continue.

16. Select Install the Windows Internal Database on This Computer or Use an Existing Database Server on a Remote Computer if you want to use an external SQL server.

17. Select to Use the Existing IIS Web Site. Click Next to continue.

18. Click Next after reviewing the settings on the Ready to Install page.

19. The installation completes in Server Manager and, after the Finish button is clicked, the WSUS Configuration Wizard is displayed. Read the information and click Next.

20. Click Next to join the Microsoft Update Improvement Program.

21. Select Synchronize from Microsoft Update, and click Next.

22. Configure your proxy server settings, if necessary, and click Next.

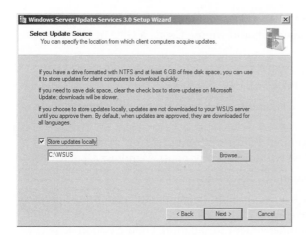

FIGURE 13.11   Installing WSUS.

23. Click Start Connecting to save settings and download update information. This might take several minutes. Click Next.

24. Select the update language(s), and click Next.

25. Select the products for which you want updates, and click Next.

26. Select the classifications of updates you want to download, and click Next.

27. Configure the schedule that you want WSUS to synchronize with the Microsoft Update servers or select Synchronize Manually. Click Next.

28. Ensure that Begin Initial Synchronization is selected, and click Finish.

29. Review the installation results, click Close, and close Server Manager.

WSUS administration is performed from the WSUS MMC. This console is the main location for all configuration settings for WSUS and is the sole administrative console. It can be accessed from Administrative Tools, Microsoft Windows Server Update Services 3.0 SP1, or directly from Server Manager.

## Automatically Configuring Clients via Group Policy

The configuration of the Automatic Updates client included with all current versions of Windows can be streamlined by using a group policy in an Active Directory environment. Windows Server 2008 R2 domain controllers automatically contain the proper Windows Update Group Policy extension, and a group policy can be defined by following these steps:

1. Open Group Policy Management (Start, All Programs, Administrative Tools, Group Policy Management).

2. Navigate to the organizational unit that will have the group policy applied, right-click the name of the organizational unit, and choose Create a GPO in This Domain, and Link It Here.

3. Enter a name for the GPO, such as WSUS GPO. You also have the option to start from the settings of an existing GPO. Click OK.

4. Right-click on the newly created GPO, and select Edit to invoke the Group Policy Management Editor.

5. Expand the Group Policy Management Editor to Computer Configuration\Policies\Administrative Templates\Windows Components\Windows Update.

6. Double-click the Configure Automatic Updates setting.

7. Set the group policy to be enabled, and configure the automatic updating sequence as desired. The three options given—2, 3, and 4—allow for specific degrees of client intervention. For seamless, client-independent installation, choose option 4, as shown in Figure 13.12.

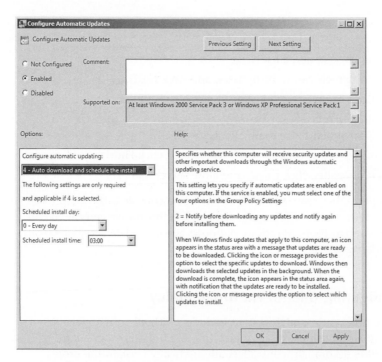

FIGURE 13.12    Configuring Windows Update Group Policy settings.

8. Schedule the interval that updates will be installed, bearing in mind that some updates require reboots.

9. Click Next Setting to configure more options.

10. Click Enabled to specify the web location of the WSUS server. Entering the fully qualified domain name of the server is recommended. Enter both settings (usually the same server), and click OK to save the Group Policy settings. Click Next Setting.

> **NOTE**
>
> Organizations that choose to use a custom web IIS website are required to use Port 8530 for client access to WSUS. In this case, enter the web location with the port number, such as http://sfwsus.companyabc.com:8530, for both settings.

11. Enter how often the client checks for updates, and then click Next Setting.

12. Review the remaining option settings and configure as desired. Click OK when you are finished.

13. Repeat the procedure for any additional organizational units. (The same group policy can be linked in more than one location.)

> **NOTE**
>
> Organizations that do not use Active Directory or group policies have to manually configure each client's settings to include the location of the WSUS server. This can be done through a local policy or manually through Registry settings, as defined in the WSUS Help.

## Deploying Security Patches with WSUS

Depending on the settings chosen by the group policy or the Registry, the clients that are managed by WSUS automatically download updates throughout the day and install them at a specified time. Some computers might be configured to allow for local interaction, scheduling proper times for the installation to take place and prompting for "drizzle" downloading.

Clients that are configured to use WSUS are not prompted to configure their Automatic Update settings, and they are grayed out to prevent any changes from occurring. Users without local administrative access cannot make any changes to the installation schedule, although local admin users can postpone forced installs.

> **NOTE**
>
> Generally, it is good practice to allow servers to control the download and installation schedule, but to force clients to do both automatically. Depending on the political climate of an organization, this might or might not be a possibility.

# Summary

Out of the box, Windows Server 2008 R2 is by far the most secure Windows yet. Increased security emphasis through the Trustworthy Computing initiative helps to increase overall server security by disabling unnecessary services and locking out file-level permissions by default. In addition to the standard features, advanced options in Windows Server 2008 R2, such as the integrated intelligent firewall, enable administrators to add multiple layers of security to servers, further protecting them from attacks and vulnerabilities. In addition, the automatic updating capabilities of tools such as Windows Server Update Services give organizations an edge in protecting servers and workstations from constantly changing security threats.

# Best Practices

The following are best practices from this chapter:

- ▶ Physically secure servers behind locked doors, in a controlled-access environment.

- ▶ Apply security in layers.

- ▶ Use the Server Roles Wizard for turning on server roles and having them automatically secured.

- ▶ Use the integrated Windows Firewall for enhanced security, and only open ports or allow protocols when necessary.

- ▶ Use both inbound and outbound firewall rules to limit the exposure a compromised server would have.

- ▶ Use the Run As Administrator command when administrative access is required instead of logging on as an administrator.

- ▶ Consider a honeypot solution using auditing to identify internal (or external) saboteurs before they can do some serious damage by creating serious-looking shares on the network, such as Financial Statements, Root Info, or similar such shares, and audit access to those folders.

- ▶ Plan to run the initial synchronization of WSUS over a weekend, beginning the download on Friday evening.

- ▶ Test and approve WSUS patches before deploying them to production, either manually or through a process of setting up a pilot WSUS server and a production WSUS server.

CHAPTER 14

# Transport-Level Security

In the past, networks were closed environments, insulated from each other and accessible only on internal segments. Over time, a need developed to share information between these networks, and connections were established to transmit data from network to network. The transmission of this information was originally insecure, however, and, if intercepted, could easily be read by unauthorized persons. The need to secure this information was subsequently made a priority, and became a critical component of network infrastructure.

Over time, the technology used to keep this information safe evolved along with the technology available to exploit and obtain unauthorized access to data. Despite these threats, intelligent design and configuration of secure transport solutions using Windows Server 2008 R2 greatly increase the security of a network. In many cases, they are absolutely required, especially for data sent across uncontrolled network segments, such as the Internet.

This chapter focuses on the mechanisms that exist to protect and encrypt information sent between computers on a network. New and improved transport security features in Windows Server 2008 R2 are highlighted, and sample situations are detailed. IPSec, Public Key Infrastructure (PKI), and virtual private network (VPN) use is outlined and illustrated. In addition, specific server functionality, such as that provided by Windows Server 2008 R2 Active Directory Certificate Services (AD CS) and Active Directory Rights Management Services (AD RMS), is outlined.

# Introduction to Transport-Level Security in Windows Server 2008 R2

Transport-level security is the securing of communications between client and server, and between servers. Although some organizations put in firewalls or encrypt files, the implementation of security at the transport-level is yet another level of security important in the design and implementation of a protected network environment.

## The Need for Transport-Level Security

The very nature of interconnected networks requires that all information be sent in a format that can easily be intercepted by any client on a physical network segment. The data must be organized in a structured, common way so that the destination server can translate it into the proper information. This simplicity also gives rise to security problems, however, because intercepted data can easily be misused if it falls into the wrong hands.

The need to make information unusable if intercepted is the basis for all transport-level encryption. Considerable effort goes into both sides of this equation: Security specialists develop schemes to encrypt and disguise data, and hackers and other security specialists develop ways to forcefully decrypt and intercept data. The good news is that encryption technology has developed to the point that properly configured environments can secure their data with a great deal of success, as long as the proper tools are used. Windows Server 2008 R2 offers much in the realm of transport-level security, and deploying some or many of the technologies available is highly recommended to properly secure important data.

## Deploying Security Through Multiple Layers of Defense

Because even the most secure infrastructures are subject to vulnerabilities, deploying multiple layers of security on critical network data is recommended. If a single layer of security is compromised, the intruder will have to bypass the second or even third level of security to gain access to the vital data. For example, relying on a complex 128-bit "unbreakable" encryption scheme is worthless if an intruder simply uses social engineering to acquire the password or PIN from a validated user. Putting in a second or third layer of security, in addition to the first one, will make it that much more difficult for intruders to break through all layers.

Transport-level security in Windows Server 2008 R2 uses multiple levels of authentication, encryption, and authorization to provide for an enhanced degree of security on a network. The configuration capabilities supplied with Windows Server 2008 R2 allow for the establishment of several layers of transport-level security.

> **NOTE**
>
> Security through multiple layers of defense is not a new concept, but is rather adapted from military strategy, which rightly holds that multiple lines of defense are better than one.

## Understanding Encryption Basics

Encryption, simply defined, is the process of taking intelligible information and scrambling it so as to make it unintelligible for anyone except the user or computer that is the destination of this information. Without going into too much detail on the exact methods of encrypting data, the important point to understand is that proper encryption allows this data to travel across unsecured networks, such as the Internet, and be translated only by the designated destination. If packets of properly encrypted information are intercepted, they are worthless because the information is garbled. All mechanisms described in this chapter use some form of encryption to secure the contents of the data sent.

# Deploying a Public Key Infrastructure with Windows Server 2008 R2

The term Public Key Infrastructure (PKI) is often loosely thrown around, but is not often thoroughly explained. PKI, in a nutshell, is the collection of digital certificates, registration authorities, and certificate authorities that verify the validity of each participant in an encrypted network. Effectively, a PKI itself is simply a concept that defines the mechanisms that ensure that the user who is communicating with another user or computer on a network is who he says he is. PKI implementations are widespread and are becoming a critical component of modern network implementations. Windows Server 2008 R2 fully supports the deployment of multiple PKI configurations, as defined in the following sections.

PKI deployments can range from simple to complex, with some PKI implementations utilizing an array of smart cards and certificates to verify the identity of all users with a great degree of certainty. Understanding the capabilities of PKI and choosing the proper deployment for an organization are subsequently a must.

## Defining Private Key versus Public Key Encryption

Encryption techniques can primarily be classified as either symmetrical or asymmetrical. Symmetrical encryption requires that each party in an encryption scheme hold a copy of a private key, which is used to encrypt and decrypt information sent between the two parties. The problem with private key encryption is that the private key must somehow be transmitted to the other party without it being intercepted and used to decrypt the information.

Public key, or asymmetrical, encryption uses a combination of two keys, which are mathematically related to each other. The first key, the private key, is kept closely guarded and is used to encrypt the information. The second key, the public key, can be used to decrypt the information. The integrity of the public key is ensured through certificates, which will be explained in depth in the following sections of this chapter. The asymmetric approach to encryption ensures that the private key does not fall into the wrong hands and only the intended recipient will be able to decrypt the data.

## Exploring Digital Certificates

A certificate is essentially a digital document that is issued by a trusted central authority and is used by the authority to validate a user's identity. Central, trusted authorities such as VeriSign are widely used on the Internet to ensure that software from Microsoft, for example, is really from Microsoft, and not a virus in disguise.

Certificates are used for multiple functions, such as the following:

- ▶ Secure email
- ▶ Web-based authentication
- ▶ IP Security (IPSec)
- ▶ Code signing
- ▶ Certification hierarchies

Certificates are signed using information from the subject's public key, along with identifying information, such as name, email address, and so on, and a digital signature of the certificate issuer, known as the Certificate Authority (CA).

# Understanding Active Directory Certificate Services (AD CS) in Windows Server 2008 R2

Windows Server 2008 R2 includes a built-in Certificate Authority (CA) technology that is known as Active Directory Certificate Services (AD CS). The first iteration of AD CS emerged with Windows Server 2008, though previous versions of the technology were simply known as Certificate Services. AD CS can be used to create certificates and subsequently manage them; it is responsible for ensuring their validity. AD CS is often used in Windows Server 2008 R2 if there is no particular need to have a third-party verify an organization's certificates. It is common practice to set up a standalone CA for network encryption that requires certificates only for internal parties. Third-party certificate authorities such as VeriSign are also extensively used but require an investment in individual certificates.

> **NOTE**
>
> Although the term Active Directory has been incorporated into the name of the Windows Certificate Services function, it should be understood that AD CS does not necessarily require integration with an existing Active Directory Domain Services (AD DS) forest environment. Although this is commonly the case, it is important to understand that AD CS has independence over AD DS forest design. For more information on AD DS, see Chapter 4, "Active Directory Domain Services Primer," and Chapter 5, "Designing a Windows Server 2008 R2 Active Directory."

Windows Server 2008 R2 introduced a few additions to AD CS features, including the following:

▶ **Certificate Enrollment Web Service and Certificate Enrollment Policy Web Service**—This is the most significant improvement, essentially allowing certificates to be enrolled directly over HTTP, enabling non-domain or Internet-connected clients to connect and request certificates from a CA server.

▶ **Improved support for high-volume CAs used for NAP**—AD CS in Windows Server 2008 R2 improves the database performance when high-volume scenarios such as NAP are utilized.

▶ **Support for cross-forest certificate enrollment**—AD CS in Windows Server 2008 R2 allows for CA consolidation across multiple forests.

## Reviewing the Certificate Authority Roles in AD CS

AD CS for Windows Server 2008 R2 can be installed as one of the following CA types:

▶ **Enterprise root certification authority**—The enterprise root CA is the most trusted CA in an organization and should be installed before any other CA. All other CAs are subordinate to an enterprise root CA. This CA should be highly physically secured, as a compromise of the enterprise CA effectively makes the entire chain compromised.

▶ **Enterprise subordinate certification authority**—An enterprise subordinate CA must get a CA certificate from an enterprise root CA but can then issue certificates to all users and computers in the enterprise. These types of CAs are often used for load balancing of an enterprise root CA.

▶ **Standalone root certification authority**—A standalone root CA is the root of a hierarchy that is not related to the enterprise domain information. Multiple standalone CAs can be established for particular purposes. A standalone root CA is often used as the root for other enterprise subordinate CAs to improve security in an environment. In other words, the root is configured as standalone, and subordinate enterprise domain integrated CAs are set up within the domains in a forest to provide for autoenrollment across the enterprise.

▶ **Standalone subordinate certification authority**—A standalone subordinate CA receives its certificate from a standalone root CA and can then be used to distribute certificates to users and computers associated with that standalone CA.

> **CAUTION**
>
> Making decisions about the structure of AD CS architecture is no small task, and should not be taken lightly. Simply throwing AD CS on a server as an enterprise CA and letting it run is not the best approach from a security perspective, as compromise of that server can have a disastrous effect. Subsequently, it is wise to carefully consider AD CS design before deployment. For example, one common best practice is to deploy a standalone root CA, then several enterprise subordinate CAs, and then to take the standalone root CA physically offline and secure it in a very safe location, only turning it on again when the subordinate CAs need to have their certificates renewed.

## Detailing the Role Services in AD CS

AD CS is composed of several role services that perform different tasks for clients. One or more of these role services can be installed on a server as required. These role services are as follows:

- ▶ **Certification Authority**—This role service installs the core CA component, which allows a server to issue, revoke, and manage certificates for clients. This role can be installed on multiple servers within the same root CA chain.

- ▶ **Certification Authority Web Enrollment**—This role service handles the web-based distribution of certificates to clients. It requires Internet Information Services (IIS) to be installed on the server.

- ▶ **Online Responder**—The role service responds to individual client requests regarding information about the validity of specific certificates. It is used for complex or large networks, when the network needs to handle large peaks of revocation activity, or when large certificate revocation lists (CRLs) need to be downloaded.

- ▶ **Certificate Enrollment Web Service**—This new service enables users and computers to enroll for certificates remotely or from nondomain systems via HTTP.

- ▶ **Certificate Enrollment Web Policy Service**—This service works with the related Certificate Enrollment Web Service but simply provides policy information rather than certificates.

- ▶ **Network Device Enrollment Service**—This role service streamlines the way that network devices such as routers receive certificates.

## Installing AD CS

To install AD CS on Windows Server 2008 R2, determine which server will serve as the root CA, keeping in mind that it is highly recommended that this be a dedicated server and also recommended that it be physically secured and shut off for most of the time to ensure integrity of the certificate chain. It is important to note that an enterprise CA cannot be shut down; however, a standalone root with a subordinate enterprise CA can be shut down. If the strategy of having a standalone root with a subordinate enterprise CA is taken, the root CA must first be created and configured, and then an enterprise subordinate CA must then be created.

In smaller scenarios, an enterprise root CA can be provisioned, though in many cases, those smaller organizations might still want to consider a standalone root and a subordinate enterprise CA. For the single enterprise root CA scenario, however, the following steps can be taken to provision the CA server:

> **CAUTION**
>
> After AD CS is installed onto a server, the name of that server and the domain status of that server cannot change. For example, you cannot demote it from being a domain controller, or you cannot promote it to one if it is not. Also, the server name must not change while it is a CA.

1. Open Server Manager (Start, All Programs, Administrative Tools, Server Manager).
2. In the Nodes pane, select Roles, and then click the Add Roles link in the tasks pane.
3. Click Next at the welcome page.
4. On the Select Server Roles page, check the box for Active Directory Certificate Services, and then click Next.
5. Review the information about AD CS on the Introduction page, and click Next to continue.
6. On the Select Role Services page, shown in Figure 14.1, choose which role services will be required. A base install will need only the Certificate Authority role. Click Next to continue.

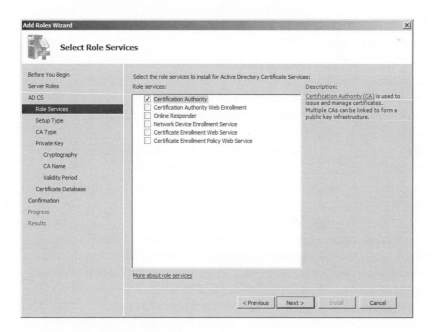

FIGURE 14.1   Installing AD CS.

7. Select whether to install an Enterprise (integrated with AD DS) CA or a Stand-alone CA on the subsequent page. In this example, we are installing a domain-based enterprise root CA. Click Next to continue.

8. On the Specify CA Type page, specify the CA type, as shown in Figure 14.2. In this case, we are installing a root CA on the server. Click Next to continue.

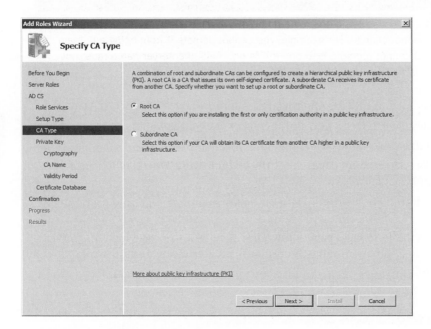

FIGURE 14.2    Specifying a CA type.

9. On the following Set Up Private Key page, you can choose whether to create a new private key from scratch or reuse an existing private key from a previous CA implementation. In this example, we create a new key. Click Next to continue.

10. On the Configure Cryptography for CA page, enter the private key encryption settings, as shown in Figure 14.3. Normally, the defaults are fine, but there might be specific needs to change the CSP, key length, or other settings. Click Next to continue.

11. Choose a common name that will be used to identify the CA. Bear in mind that this name will appear on all certificates issued by the CA. In this example, we enter the common name CompanyABC-CorpCA. Click Next to continue.

12. Set the validity period for the certificate that will be installed on this CA server. If this is a root CA, the server will have to reissue the certificate chain after the expiration period has expired. In this example, we choose a 5-year validity period, though many production scenarios will have a 20-year CA created for the root. Click Next to continue.

13. Specify a location for the certificate database and log locations, and click Next to continue.

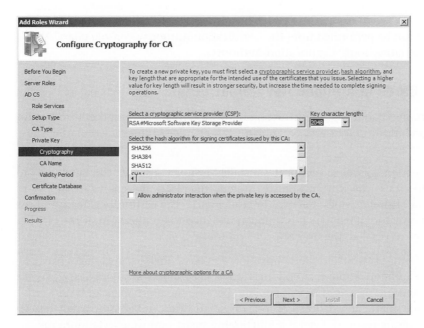

FIGURE 14.3   Choosing cryptography settings.

**14.** Review the installation selections on the confirmation page, as shown in Figure 14.4, and click Install.

**15.** Click Close when the wizard is complete.

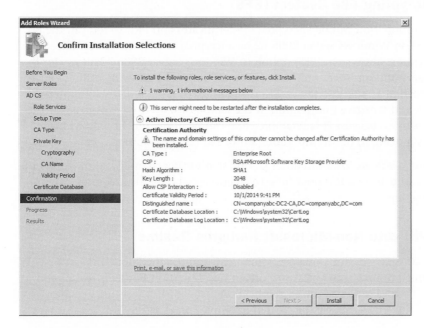

FIGURE 14.4   Reviewing AD CS installation options.

After you install AD CS, additional CAs can be installed as subordinate CAs and administration of the PKI can be performed from the Certification Authority console (Start, All Programs, Administrative Tools, Certification Authority).

## Using Smart Cards in a Public Key Infrastructure

A robust solution for a Public Key Infrastructure network can be found in the introduction of smart card authentication for users. Smart cards can be microchip enabled plastic cards, USB keys, or other devices.

User logon information, as well as certificates installed from a CA server, can be placed on a smart card. When a user needs to log on to a system, she places the smart card in a smart card reader or simply swipes it across the reader itself. The certificate is read, and the user is prompted only for a PIN, which is uniquely assigned to each user. After the PIN and the certificate are verified, the user is logged on to the domain.

Smart cards are a form of two-factor authentication and have obvious advantages over standard forms of authentication. It is no longer possible to simply steal or guess someone's username and password in this scenario because the username can be entered only via the unique smart card. If stolen or lost, the smart card can be immediately deactivated and the certificate revoked. Even if a functioning smart card were to fall into the wrong hands, the PIN would still need to be used to properly access the system. Smart cards are fast becoming a more accepted way to integrate the security of certificates and PKI into organizations.

## Using the Encrypting File System (EFS)

Just as transport information can be encrypted via certificates and PKI, so too can the NT File System (NTFS) on Windows Server 2008 R2 be encrypted to prevent unauthorized access. The Encrypting File System (EFS) option in Windows Server 2008 R2 allows for this type of functionality and improves on the previous EFS model by allowing offline folders to maintain encryption sets on the server. EFS is advantageous, particularly for laptop users who tote around sensitive information. If the laptop or hard drive is stolen, the file information is worthless because it is scrambled and can be unscrambled only with the proper key. EFS is proving to be an important part of PKI implementations.

Windows 7 and/or Windows Vista BitLocker go one step further than EFS, allowing for the entire hard drive, aside from a few boot files, to be encrypted. This also requires PKI certificates to be set up.

## Integrating PKI with Non-Microsoft Kerberos Realms

Windows Server 2008 R2's Active Directory component can use the Public Key Infrastructure, which utilizes trusts between foreign non-Microsoft Kerberos realms and Active Directory. The PKI serves as the authentication mechanism for security requests across the cross-realm trusts that can be created in Active Directory.

# Active Directory Rights Management Services

Active Directory Rights Management Services (AD RMS) is a Digital Rights Management (DRM) technology that allows for restrictions to be placed on how content is managed, transmitted, and viewed. RMS uses PKI technology to encrypt content such as documents and email messages, and only allows access to view said content if restrictions are placed on the content, such as disabling the ability to print, cut/paste, and/or forward information.

AD RMS in Windows Server 2008 R2 is the next iteration of the Windows Rights Management Server technology that has been developed over a period of several years. In addition to retaining existing functionality, it adds tighter integration with Active Directory Domain Services (AD DS) and greater scalability.

## Understanding the Need for AD RMS

Many organizations are faced with the problem of defining how their intellectual property can be managed after it has been distributed. Several high-profile leaks of sensitive internal emails from major corporations have exposed the need to manage and restrict how email that contains sensitive corporate information is disseminated.

The problem stems from the fact that computer systems have historically been good at restricting information to unauthorized individuals, but as soon as an authorized individual gains access to that data, those organizations have traditionally lost control over what is done with the content. Authorized individuals have copied documents offsite, emailed sensitive information, had their laptops stolen, and have found a myriad of other ways to lose control of an organization's confidential information.

Active Directory RMS was designed to give the control back to an organization. It allows enforcement personnel the ability to restrict how a document is transmitted, printed, copied, or when it expires. Integration with Active Directory Domain Services allows the content to be only decrypted by individuals stipulated in the policies as well.

> **NOTE**
>
> Changes to RMS-protected documents are not reflected unless the document itself is "republished" and the client does not have the use license cached in conjunction with a local copy of the RMS-protected document. If the original use license has not expired, users will continue to have access to protected documents that have either not been republished or have been moved from the location of the newly published document.

AD RMS also includes a role service known as Identity Federation. Installing this service allows an organization to share rights-protected content with other organizations.

## Understanding AD RMS Prerequisites

Before installing AD RMS, the following prerequisites must be satisfied:

▶ Create a service account for RMS within AD DS. The service account must be different from the account that is used to install RMS.

▶ The AD RMS server must be a domain member within the domain of the user accounts that will use the service.

▶ An AD RMS root cluster for certification and licensing must be created.

▶ A fully qualified domain name resolvable from the locations where RMS files will be consumed needs to be set up. For example, rms.companyabc.com can be set up for clients to be able to connect to the AD RMS server to validate their RMS rights.

▶ A server running SQL Server must be available to store the AD RMS databases. It is highly recommended to use an alternate server than the one where AD RMS is installed.

## Installing AD RMS

Installation of AD RMS can be performed using the Server Manager utility, by adding the AD RMS role to the server. The process of adding the AD RMS role is as follows:

1. Open Server Manager (Start, All Programs, Administrative Tools, Server Manager).

2. In the Nodes pane, select Roles, and then click the Add Roles link in the tasks pane.

3. Click Next at the welcome page.

4. On the Select Server Roles page, check the box for Active Directory Rights Management Services. If prompted to add additional services and features such as IIS or the Message Queuing Service, choose to add the Required Role Services, and then click Next to continue.

5. Review the Introduction page, and click Next to continue.

6. On the Select Role Services page, shown in Figure 14.5, select which components to install. In this case, only the core AD RMS role service is installed. Click Next to continue.

7. On the AD RMS Cluster page, choose to Create a New AD RMS Cluster, and click Next to continue.

8. On the Select Configuration Database page, choose whether to install the limited Windows Internal Database service (not recommended) or to create an RMS database on a separate server running SQL Server 200x.

9. On the Specify Service Account page, shown in Figure 14.6, choose which service account will be used for RMS by using the Specify button. It cannot be the same account that is used to install AD RMS.

10. On the subsequent page, select Use AD RMS Centrally Managed Key Storage, and click Next.

11. Enter a strong password when prompted, and click Next to continue.

12. Confirm which IIS website (Default Web Site for a dedicated build) will hold the AD RMS web services, and click Next to continue.

13. Type the FQDN that will be used for the AD RMS service. For this example, enter `rms.companyabc.com`, and then click the Validate button. The FQDN must already be set up to resolve to the IP address of the IIS website on the RMS server. Click Next to continue.

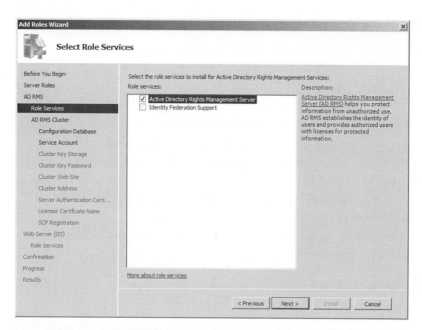

FIGURE 14.5   Installing AD RMS.

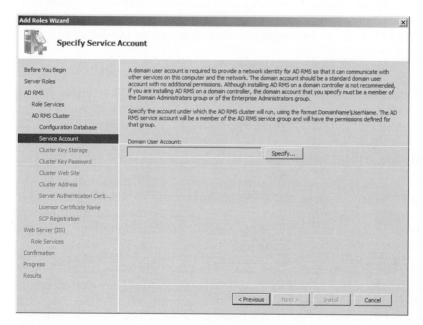

FIGURE 14.6   Specifying the RMS Service Account.

> **NOTE**
>
> Using an SSL certificate for an HTTPS connection to the RMS server is recommended, and can be enabled from this wizard.

14. If using SSL to protect the IIS website, select the certificate.

15. Enter a descriptive name for the RMS cluster, and click Next to continue.

16. On the AD RMS Service Connection Point Registration page, click Next to register the Service Connection Point (SCP) in AD DS.

17. If installing IIS at the same time, accept the defaults for setup by clicking Next, and then clicking Next again.

18. Click Install to finalize the installation wizard. It might take a while for the installation to complete.

19. Click Finish when the wizard is complete. Restart the server and log back on to complete the install.

# Using IPSec Encryption with Windows Server 2008 R2

IP Security (IPSec), mentioned briefly in previous sections, is essentially a mechanism for establishing end-to-end encryption of all data packets sent between computers. IPSec operates at Layer 3 of the OSI model and subsequently uses encrypted packets for all traffic between members.

IPSec is often considered to be one of the best ways to secure the traffic generated in an environment, and is useful for securing servers and workstations both in high-risk Internet access scenarios and also in private network configurations for an enhanced layer of security.

## Understanding the IPSec Principle

The basic principle of IPSec is this: All traffic between clients—whether initiated by applications, the operating system, services, and so on—is entirely encrypted by IPSec, which then puts its own header on each packet and sends the packets to the destination server to be decrypted. Because every piece of data is encrypted, this prevents electronic eavesdropping, or listening in on a network in an attempt to gain unauthorized access to data.

Several functional IPSec deployments are available, and some of the more promising ones are actually built in to the network interface cards (NICs) of each computer, performing encryption and decryption without the operating system knowing what is going on. Aside from these alternatives, Windows Server 2008 R2 includes a robust IPSec implementation by default, which can be configured to use a PKI certificate network.

## Detailing Key IPSec Functionality

IPSec in Windows Server 2008 R2 provides for the following key functionality that, when combined, provides for one of the most secure solutions available for client/server encryption:

▶ **Data privacy**—All information sent from one IPSec machine to another is thoroughly encrypted by such algorithms as 3DES, which effectively prevents the unauthorized viewing of sensitive data.

▶ **Data integrity**—The integrity of IPSec packets is enforced through ESP headers, which verify that the information contained within an IPSec packet has not been tampered with.

▶ **Anti-replay capability**—IPSec prevents streams of captured packets from being re-sent, known as a "replay" attack, blocking such methods of obtaining unauthorized access to a system by mimicking a valid user's response to server requests.

▶ **Per-packet authenticity**—IPSec utilizes certificates or Kerberos authentication to ensure that the sender of an IPSec packet is actually an authorized user.

▶ **NAT Traversal**—Windows Server 2008 R2's implementation of IPSec now allows for IPSec to be routed through current Network Address Translation (NAT) implementations, a concept that will be defined more thoroughly in the following sections.

▶ **Diffie-Hellman 2048-bit key support**—Virtually unbreakable Diffie-Hellman 2048-bit key lengths are supported in Windows Server 2008 R2's IPSec implementation, essentially ensuring that the IPSec key cannot be broken.

## Exploring IPSec NAT Traversal

As previously mentioned, IPSec in Windows Server 2008 R2 supports the concept of Network Address Translation Traversal (NAT-T). Understanding how NAT-T works first requires a full understanding of the need for NAT itself.

Network Address Translation (NAT) was developed simply because not enough IP addresses were available for all the clients on the Internet. Because of this, private IP ranges were established (10.x.x.x, 192.168.x.x, and so on) to allow all clients in an organization to have a unique IP address in their own private space. These IP addresses were designed to not route through the public IP address space, and a mechanism was needed to translate them into a valid, unique public IP address.

NAT was developed to fill this role. It normally resides on firewall servers or routers to provide for NAT capabilities between private and public networks. Routing and Remote Access Service (RRAS) for Windows Server 2008 R2 provides NAT capabilities as well.

Because the construction of the IPSec packet does not allow for NAT addresses, IPSec traffic has, in the past, simply been dropped at NAT servers, as there is no way to physically route the information to the proper destination. This posed major barriers to the widespread implementation of IPSec because many of the clients on the Internet today are addressed via NAT.

NAT Traversal (or NAT-T), which was introduced in Windows Server 2008 and is available in Windows Server 2008 R2's IPSec implementation, was jointly developed as an Internet standard by Microsoft and Cisco Systems. NAT-T works by sensing that a NAT connection will need to be traversed and subsequently encapsulating the entire IPSec packet into a UDP packet with a normal UDP header. NAT-T handles UDP packets flawlessly, and they are subsequently routed to the proper address on the other side of the NAT.

NAT Traversal works well but requires that both ends of the IPSec transaction understand the protocol so as to properly pull the IPSec packet out of the UDP encapsulation. With the latest IPSec client and server, NAT-T becomes a reality and is positioned to make IPSec into a much bigger success than it is today.

> **NOTE**
>
> NAT-T was developed to keep current NAT technologies in place without changes. However, some implementations of NAT have attempted to make IPSec work natively across the translation without NAT-T. Disabling this functionality with NAT-T might not be wise, however—it might interfere with IPSec because both NAT-T and the NAT firewall will be attempting to overcome the NAT barrier.

# Summary

In today's interconnected networks, transport-level security is a major, if not one of the most important, security consideration for any organization. Securing the communications between users and computers on a network is vital, and in some cases required by law. Windows Server 2008 R2 builds on the strong security base of Windows Server 2003 and Windows Server 2008 to include support for transport-level security mechanisms, such as IPSec and PKI, using technologies such as AD CS and AD RMS. Proper configuration and utilization of these tools can effectively lock down an organization's transmission of data and ensure that it is used only by the proper individuals.

# Best Practices

The following are best practices from this chapter:

▶ To secure a networking environment, deploy some or many of the transport-level security technologies available.

▶ Because even the most secure infrastructures are subject to vulnerabilities, it is recommended to deploy multiple layers of security on critical network data.

▶ It is highly recommended to avoid installing the AD RMS database locally on the RMS server. Instead, use a remote full SQL Server instance.

▶ Take strong care to secure the Active Directory Certificate Services root CA server, as a security breach of this server would compromise the entire CA chain.

▶ Store a standalone root CA server in a physically locked location and shut it down when not in use. This best practice does not apply to enterprise root CAs, which cannot be shut down for long periods of time.

▶ Implement IPSec to secure the traffic generated in an environment and for securing servers and workstations both in high-risk Internet access scenarios and also in private network configurations.

14

CHAPTER 15

# Security Policies, Network Policy Server, and Network Access Protection

Windows Server 2008 R2 contains built-in support for a new set of services and an application programming interface (API) known as Network Access Protection (NAP). NAP supports the ability to restrict network clients based on the overall health of their systems. If, for example, the client attempting to connect to the network does not have the latest security patches or antivirus definitions installed, the technology disallows those clients from connecting to the network.

The Windows Server 2008 R2 NAP enforcement server role is known as a Network Policy Server (NPS). An NPS system controls and manages a series of defined health policies, and enforces those policies on clients that have their own local Windows System Health Agent. This chapter covers this technology in Windows Server 2008 R2. Particular attention is focused on the Network Policy Server role, and how it can be used to restrict Dynamic Host Configuration Protocol (DHCP), IPSec, 802.1X, and virtual private network (VPN) access to an environment.

## Understanding Network Access Protection (NAP) in Windows Server 2008 R2

NAP in Windows Server 2008 R2 is composed of a series of components that provide for the ability to restrict client access to networks through various mechanisms such as controlling who gets an IP address from a DHCP server or who issues an IPSec certificate. NAP itself was developed as an industry-independent technology, and was made with a published set of APIs that allow third-party vendors, such as

network device makers and other software companies, to develop their own set of devices
that integrate together with Windows Server 2008 R2 devices.

## Exploring the Reasons for Deploying NAP

Network Access Protection was developed as a technology in response to the threats faced
by computers that are not up to date with the latest security patches or do not have other
security controls in place, such as up-to-date versions of antivirus software or the lack of a
local software firewall. These systems are often the first to be compromised, and are often
the target of spyware attacks and are, subsequently, especially vulnerable.

Simply allowing these clients unfettered access to a network is no longer an option.
Compromised systems inside an internal network pose an especially strong security risk, as
they could easily be controlled by malicious entities and could compromise sensitive data.
Identifying a method for controlling these clients is becoming critical, which is why
Microsoft developed the NAP concept in Windows Server 2008 R2.

## Outlining NAP Components

There are three main characteristics of NAP, all of which are included within Windows
Server 2008 R2 functionality. These characteristics are as follows:

- ▶ **Health policy compliance**—The ability to fix the problem is central to a NAP platform. Subsequently, compliance mechanisms, such as Windows Server Update
  Services (WSUS) servers, System Center Configuration Manager 2007 agents, and
  other remediation services fill the health policy compliance space of a NAP platform.
  Windows Server 2008 R2 can automatically refer clients to a remediation server
  before granting full network access. For example, a client that is out of date with
  patches can be referred to a WSUS server to have their patches installed.

- ▶ **Health state validation**—Through agents on the client systems, the specific state
  of an individual client can be monitored and logged. The administrator of a NAP
  platform will be able to tell how many systems on the network are out of date with
  patches, don't have their firewalls turned on, and many other health state statistics.
  In some cases, health status is simply noted; in others, it is used to block access to
  clients.

- ▶ **Access limitation**—The cornerstone to an effective NAP platform is the ability to
  restrict access to networks based on the results of the health state validation. The
  type of access granted can be very granular. For example, clients can have access to
  specific systems for patching, but not to other clients. Windows Server 2008 R2
  includes custom access limitation capabilities in NAP, allowing administrators to create flexible policies.

## Understanding Windows Server 2008 R2 NAP Terminology

The following terms are useful to understand NAP concepts used in Windows Server 2008 R2:

▶ **Enforcement Client (EC)**—A client that takes part in a NAP infrastructure. Windows 7, Windows Vista, and Windows XP SP3 support NAP and can be an EC in a NAP topology, as they all contain the System Health Agent component.

▶ **Enforcement Server (ES)**—A server that takes part in a NAP infrastructure and enforces the policies. In Windows Server 2008 R2, this is the Network Policy Server (NPS) role.

▶ **System Health Agent (SHA)**—The actual agent that sends health information to the NAP ES servers. In Windows 7, Windows Vista, and Windows XP SP3, this is the Windows System Health Validator SHA, which is a service that runs on each client and monitors the local Windows Security Center on the machines.

▶ **System Health Validator (SHV)**—An SHV is the server-side component of NAP that processes the information received from the SHAs and enforces policies. The Windows Server 2008 R2 SHV can be fully integrated into NAP products from other vendors, as it is based on open standards.

▶ **Remediation Server**—A server that is made accessible to clients that have failed the NAP policy tests. These servers generally provide for services that clients can use to comply with policies, such as WSUS servers, DNS servers, and System Center Configuration Manager servers.

## Changes in NAP and NPS in Windows Server 2008 R2

NAP and NPS concepts were originally built in to the original Windows Server 2008 operating system. Windows Server 2008 R2 adds a few changes and improvements to both technologies, including the following:

▶ **Multiconfiguration Service Health Validators**—The biggest change to NAP in Windows Server 2008 R2 is the ability to create multiple SHVs across a single set of NAP health policy servers. This allows for multiple policies, creating some which might be more or less restrictive and providing for the creation of exceptions.

▶ **NPS templates**—Templates are now provided for elements such as RADIUS clients or shared secrets. These templates can be exported for use on other NPS servers.

▶ **Accounting improvements in NPS**—RADIUS accounting improvements have been added to NPS along with full support for international character sets providing better logging and tracking capabilities.

# Deploying a Windows Server 2008 R2 Network Policy Server

The Windows Server 2008 R2 server role that handles NAP is the Network Policy Server role. Installing this role on a server effectively makes it an SHV and an Enforcement Server. The specific role added to the Server Role Wizard is called the Network Policy and Access Services role, and includes the following components:

▶ **Routing and Remote Access Service (RRAS)**—The server role that provides for virtual private network (VPN) capabilities, allowing for clients to "tunnel" their communications in an encrypted fashion across an insecure network such as the Internet. The role services included with this role include the Remote Access Service, which provides VPN support, and the Routing service, which provides software-based routing capabilities on the server itself.

▶ **Host Credential Authorization Protocol (HCAP)**—An industry-standard protocol that is used when integrating Microsoft NAP with the Cisco Network Access Control Server. This allows the Windows NPS role to examine Cisco 802.1X access client health.

▶ **Health Registration Authority (HRA)**—A server that distributes health certificates to clients that pass health policy checks. The HRA is only used in Microsoft's NAP implementation for IPSec enforcement.

▶ **Network Policy Server**—The Windows Server 2008 R2 role that acts as a NAP Health Policy Server and a Remote Authentication Dial-In User Service (RADIUS) server for authentication and authorization.

## Exploring NPS Concepts

The Network Policy Server role in Windows Server 2008 R2 allows for the creation of enforcement policies that apply to the following types of network access:

▶ **Internet Protocol Security (IPSec)**—IPSec encryption allows for all communications, even those that would normally be unencrypted, to be highly secured through PKI-based encryption. IPSec can be configured to be required between servers, and a system configured with the NPS role can regulate which clients are allowed as IPSec clients based on their local health.

▶ **802.1X authentication**—802.1X is a network-based authentication method that uses PKI-based certificates to authenticate that the user who attaches to the network is who he claims to be. 802.1X authentication is often used on wireless fidelity (Wi-Fi) networks. A system with the NPS role in Windows Server 2008 R2 can add clients to the 802.1X network based on their health status.

▶ **Virtual private network (VPN) connections**—A VPN connection allows for traffic to be sent in an encrypted tunnel across an untrusted network such as the Internet. VPNs are often used by roaming users to connect to the internal local area network

(LAN) of an organization. The NPS role includes support for restricting client VPN access based on system health.

▶ **Dynamic Host Configuration Protocol (DHCP) addresses**—One very useful NPS enforcement method is the ability to restrict which clients get DHCP addresses based on their system health. Although this is the easiest NAP policy to set up, this is also the easiest to circumvent as clients could set their own IP addresses.

## Understanding RADIUS Support on a Network Policy Server

As previously mentioned, installing the Network Policy and Access Services role adds support for the RADIUS protocol, an industry-standard authentication mechanism supported by a wide range of clients.

> **NOTE**
>
> The NPS role in Windows Server 2008 R2 is the replacement for the legacy Internet Authentication Service (IAS) role. The old IAS role provided simple RADIUS authentication support to Active Directory sources.

RADIUS authentication allows for Active Directory users to be authenticated using RADIUS authentication, rather than AD DS authentication. This is commonly used in scenarios where VPN access requires RADIUS authentication, or when other devices cannot use AD-based authentication.

RADIUS client support is limited to a maximum of 50 clients and two remote RADIUS server groups with the Standard Edition of Windows Server 2008 R2. Enterprise and Datacenter Editions offer unlimited support. Windows Web Server 2008 R2 does not support NPS.

## Installing a Network Policy Server

Installation of the Network Policy and Access Services role installs the Network Policy Server component and the RADIUS role. To install, perform the following steps:

1. Open Server Manager (Start, All Programs, Administrative Tools, Server Manager).
2. Click the Add Roles link in the Actions pane.
3. On the Welcome page, click Next to continue.
4. From the list of roles to install, select Network Policy and Access Services from the list, and click Next to continue.
5. Review the information provided on the Welcome page, and click Next to continue.
6. On the Select Role Services page, shown in Figure 15.1, select which role services to install on the server, using the information provided in the previous section of this chapter. Click Next to continue.

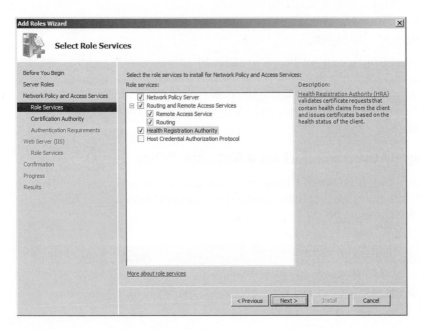

FIGURE 15.1    Installing the Network Policy and Access Services roles.

---

**NOTE**

Adding the Health Registration Authority role service requires the IIS Web Server Role
to be installed on the server. Selecting the role service might prompt you to install
these services as well.

---

7. On the Certificate Authority page, choose whether to install a local CA for issuing
   health certificates or to use an existing remote CA. If using a remote CA, make sure it
   is dedicated to issuing only health certificates. In this example, we install a local CA;
   this will install AD Certificate Services (AD CS) on the system. Click Next to continue.

8. Select whether to configure the HRA to allow only domain-authenticated users to get
   health certificates, as shown in Figure 15.2. This can improve security, but might not
   be wanted in environments with untrusted domains or with workgroup members.
   Click Next to continue.

9. If installing AD CS on the server, the wizard will lead you through the AD CS installation process. For information on this process, reference Chapter 14, "Transport-
   Level Security."

10. If installing the IIS role on the server, the wizard will lead you through the IIS instal-
    lation process. For more information on this installation routine, reference Chapter
    12, "Internet Information Services."

11. On the Confirmation page, click Install.

12. Click Close when the wizard completes.

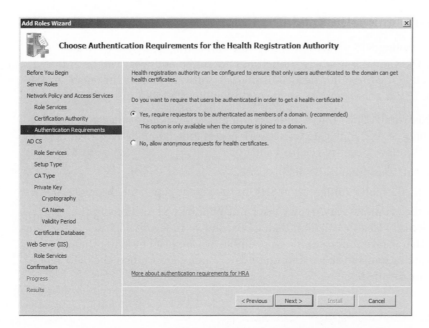

FIGURE 15.2    Choosing HRA client authentication requirements.

# Enforcing Policy Settings with a Network Policy Server

The goal of a Network Policy Server is to enforce policy settings defined by the administrator, for example, to configure the NPS role to block clients from connecting if they don't have an antivirus application installed. There are multiple variations on this theme, but the same principles apply to each of the variations.

This section of the chapter focuses on describing a scenario where NPS is configured to block DHCP clients from receiving IP addresses if they do not have an antivirus application installed and if their antivirus definitions are out of date. The same overall process can be used for 802.1X validation, VPN validation, or IPSec validation.

The process to set up this type of validation on an NPS system consists of the following five high-level steps:

1. Create a System Health Validator.
2. Create a health policy for compliant clients.
3. Create a health policy for noncompliant clients.
4. Create a network policy for compliant clients.
5. Create a network policy for noncompliant clients.

Each of these five steps is explained in more detail in the following sections of this chapter.

## Creating a System Health Validator

The first step to enabling NPS validation is to create and configure a System Health
Validator (SHV). The validator is where the settings are stored and what will be enforced
on the client, such as if a firewall is needed, if spyware software must be installed, and so
on. To create the SHV for the example we are outlining, do the following:

1. From the Network Policy MMC tool (Start, All Programs, Administrative Tools,
   Network Policy Server), navigate to Network Access Protection, System Health
   Validators, Windows Security Health Validator.

2. Click on the Settings link in the details pane.

3. Right-click the Default Configuration SHV in the details pane and choose Properties.

4. From both the Windows 7/Windows Vista and Windows XP sections in the
   Windows Security Health Validator dialog box, shown in Figure 15.3, select the type
   of policies that will be enforced. In our example, we are just enforcing that an
   antivirus application is installed and up to date. Click OK and then click OK again
   when you are finished.

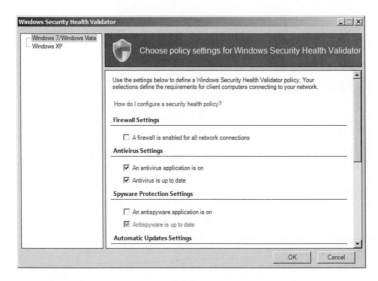

FIGURE 15.3    Configuring a Security Health Validator.

## Creating a Health Policy for Compliant Clients

After the System Health Validator has been configured, a health policy for clients that are
compliant must be created. Any client that complies with the SHV will have this policy
applied. To create this policy, do the following:

1. Open the Network Policy Server MMC tool (Start, All Programs, Administrative
   Tools, Network Policy Server).

2. In the node pane, navigate to Policies, Health Policies.

3. Right-click Health Policies, and choose New.

4. Enter a name for the policy, such as Compliant-Clients, and then select which SHV checks the client must pass, as shown in Figure 15.4. In this case, we create a health policy where clients must pass all checks. Check the box next to the Windows Security Health Validator, choose the setting (typically the default configuration, though R2 allows for multiple configurations), and click OK to save the policy.

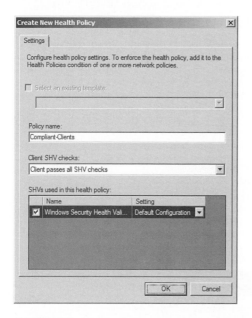

FIGURE 15.4   Creating a compliant health policy.

## Creating a Health Policy for Noncompliant Clients

In addition to creating a health policy for compliant clients, there must be a policy for clients who fail one or more of the checks in the SHV. To create this policy, do the following:

1. Open the Network Policy Server MMC tool (Start, All Programs, Administrative Tools, Network Policy Server).

2. In the node pane, navigate to Policies, Health Policies.

3. Right-click Health Policies and choose New.

4. Enter a name for the policy, such as NonCompliant-Clients. In this example, we select that the client fails one or more SHV checks setting from the dialog box. Check the box next to the Windows System Health Validator, and click OK to save the policy.

## Creating a Network Policy for Compliant Clients

After the SHV and two health policies have been created, network policies for both compliant and noncompliant clients need to be created. These network policies will define what type of access a compliant or a noncompliant client will have. To create the compliant network policy for this example, do the following:

1. From the Network Policy MMC tool, navigate to Policies, Network Policies from the node pane.

2. Right-click the Network Policies node, and choose New.

3. On the Specify Network Policy Name and Connection Type page, enter a descriptive policy name, such as `Compliant-Network-Full-Access`, and click Next (leave the type of server as Unspecified).

4. On the Specify Conditions page, click the Add button.

5. Select Health Policies from the list, as shown in Figure 15.5, and click the Add button.

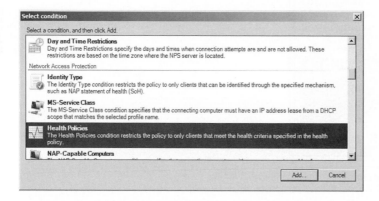

FIGURE 15.5   Creating a network policy for compliant clients.

6. From the list of health policies, choose the Compliant-Clients policy previously created, and click OK.

7. Click Next to continue.

8. On the Specify Access Permission page, select the Access Granted option button, and click Next to continue.

9. On the Configure Authentication Methods page, select only the Perform Machine Health Check Only check box and deselect any other ones, as shown in Figure 15.6. Click Next to continue.

10. On the Configure Constraints page, leave the defaults in place, and click Next.

11. On the Configure Settings page, ensure that Allow Full Network Access is selected under NAP Enforcement, as shown in Figure 15.7. Click Next to continue.

12. Click Finish to complete the wizard.

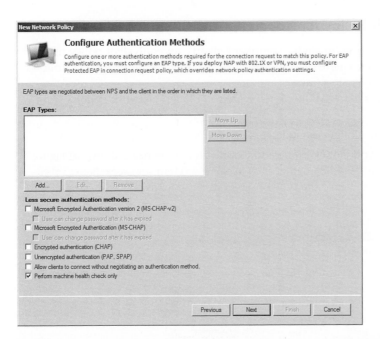

FIGURE 15.6   Configuring authentication methods for the compliant network policy.

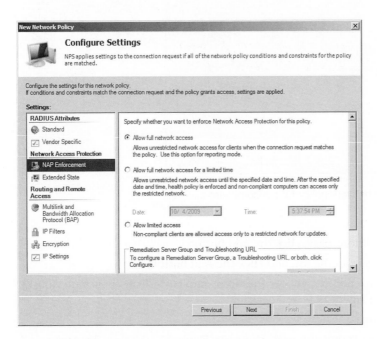

FIGURE 15.7   Validating NAP Enforcement settings.

## Creating a Network Policy for Noncompliant Clients

After a network policy has been made for compliant clients, an equivalent policy needs to
be created for noncompliant clients. The process is similar, with a few changes as follows:

1. From the Network Policy MMC tool, navigate to Policies, Network Policies from
   the node pane.
2. Right-click the Network Policies node, and choose New.
3. On the Specify Network Policy Name and Connection Type page, shown in Figure
   15.8, enter a descriptive policy name, such as NonCompliant-Network-Restricted-
   Access, and click Next (leave the type of server as Unspecified).

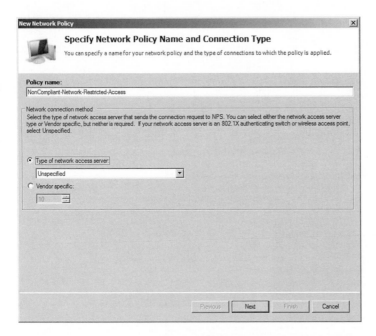

FIGURE 15.8    Creating a network policy for noncompliant clients.

4. On the Specify Conditions page, click the Add button.
5. Select Health Policies from the list, and click the Add button.
6. From the list of health policies, choose the NonCompliant-Clients policy previously
   created, as shown in Figure 15.9, and click OK.
7. Click Next to continue.
8. On the Specify Access Permission page, shown in Figure 15.10, select the Access
   Granted option button, and click Next to continue.

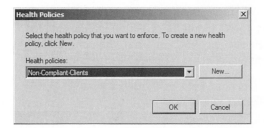

FIGURE 15.9   Adding the noncompliant client's health policy to the network policy.

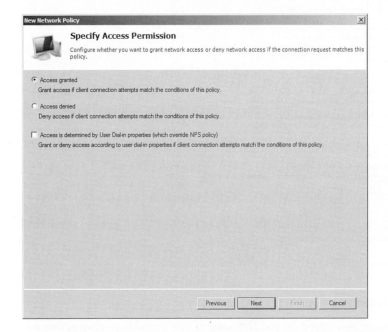

FIGURE 15.10   Specifying access permission to the network policy.

**NOTE**

It might seem counterintuitive to select the Access Granted option button for a non-compliant network policy. It's important to note, however, that this simply means that the access is granted to the policy itself, not to the network. If the Access Granted option is not selected, the policy will not work.

9. On the Configure Authentication Methods page, select only the Perform Machine Health Check Only check box and deselect any other ones. Click Next to continue.

10. On the Configure Constraints page, leave the defaults in place, and click Next.

11. On the Configure Settings page, select NAP Enforcement and select the Allow Limited
    Access option button, as shown in Figure 15.11. If auto remediation will be enabled
    (allowing the server to access other servers such as WSUS or DNS), then check the
    Enable Auto-remediation of Client Computers check box. Click Next to continue.

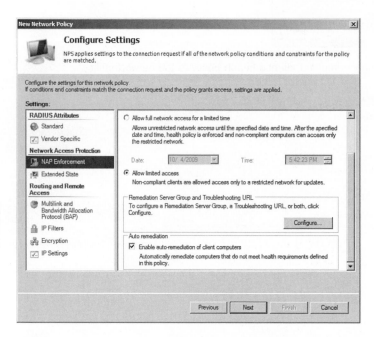

FIGURE 15.11    Configuration Settings options for NAP Enforcement.

12. Click Finish to complete the wizard.

After all five steps have been performed on the NPS system, the individual services can be
integrated with the NPS system to restrict clients based on the health and network policies
that were created. This includes the DHCP Server role and the services that control 802.1X
and RRAS for VPN. In this example, we will configure the DHCP role to block clients
based on the SHV that we created in the earlier steps.

## Configuring a DHCP Server to Restrict Client Leases Based on the NPS Policy

After the NPS policies have been created, the DHCP server and DHCP scope used can be
configured to use NAP settings to validate the client health before granting IP addresses.
In the example we've been using so far, this would restrict only those clients with a valid
and up-to-date antivirus application from getting a DHCP address.

To configure the DHCP scope for NPS, do the following:

1. On the DHCP server, open the DHCP MMC tool (Start, All Programs, Administrative
   Tools, DHCP).

2. Navigate to SERVERNAME, IPv4, Scope Name.

3. Right-click Scope Name, and choose Properties.

4. Select the Network Access Protection tab, and click the Enable for This Scope option button, as shown in Figure 15.12. Click OK to save the changes.

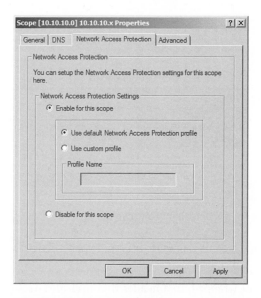

FIGURE 15.12    Enabling NAP on a DHCP scope.

After enabling NAP on a Scope, individual scope options can be configured for noncompliant clients. These scope options appear under the User Class named Default Network Access Protection Class, as shown in Figure 15.13. By not configuring any scope options, the clients effectively have no DHCP access to resources. Or, in a different example, you could configure the clients to use an alternate DNS server for remediation. Scope options can be configured by right-clicking on the Scope Options node under the Scope Name and choosing Configure Options. Click the Advanced tab to view the classes and options.

> **NOTE**
>
> The default User Class is used for compliant NAP clients—the Default Network Access Protection Class is used for noncompliant clients.

# Deploying and Enforcing a Virtual Private Network (VPN) Using an RRAS Server

A common method of securing information sent across unsecured networks is to create a virtual private network (VPN), which is effectively a connection between two private nodes or networks that is secured and encrypted to prevent unauthorized snooping of the traffic between the two connections. From the client perspective, a VPN looks and feels

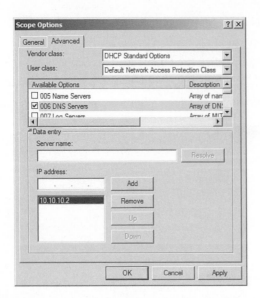

FIGURE 15.13    Configuring DHCP scope options for noncompliant NAP clients.

just like a normal network connection between different segments on a network—hence
the term virtual private network.

Data that is sent across a VPN is encapsulated, or wrapped, in a header that indicates its
destination. The information in the packet is then encrypted to secure its contents. The
encrypted packets are then sent across the network to the destination server, using what is
known as a VPN tunnel.

The Windows Server 2008 R2 RRAS role allows for the creation of VPNs, and integrates
with the NPS role to provide for validation of client health before creating a VPN session.

> **NOTE**
>
> Virtual private network support in Windows Server 2008 R2 provides for simple VPN
> tunnels to be created. For more complex scenarios where specific rules need to be cre-
> ated and application-layer filtering of the VPN traffic is needed, look at Microsoft's
> Forefront Edge line of products, which includes the Forefront Threat Management
> Gateway (previously called Internet Security and Acceleration or ISA Server) and the
> Forefront Unified Access Gateway products.

## Exploring VPN Tunnels

The connection made by VPN clients across an unsecured network is known as a VPN
tunnel. It is named as such because of the way it "tunnels" underneath the regular traffic
of the unsecured network.

VPN tunnels are logically established on a point-to-point basis but can be used to connect
two private networks into a common network infrastructure. In many cases, for example,

a VPN tunnel serves as a virtual wide area network (WAN) link between two physical locations in an organization, all while sending the private information across the Internet. VPN tunnels are also widely used by remote users who log on to the Internet from multiple locations and establish VPN tunnels to a centralized VPN server in the organization's home office. These reasons make VPN solutions a valuable asset for organizations, and one that can be easily established with the technologies available in Windows Server 2008 R2.

> **NOTE**
>
> VPN tunnels can either be voluntary or compulsory. In short, voluntary VPN tunnels are created when a client, usually out somewhere on the Internet, asks for a VPN tunnel to be established. Compulsory VPN tunnels are automatically created for clients from specific locations on the unsecured network, and are less common in real-life situations than are voluntary tunnels.

## Tunneling Protocols

The tunneling protocol is the specific technology that defines how data is encapsulated, transmitted, and unencapsulated across a VPN connection. Varying implementations of tunneling protocols exist, and correspond with different layers of the Open System Interconnection (OSI) standards-based reference model. The OSI model is composed of seven layers, and VPN tunneling protocols use either Layer 2 or Layer 3 as their unit of exchange. Layer 2, a more fundamental network layer, uses a frame as the unit of exchange, and Layer 3 protocols use a packet as a unit of exchange.

The most common Layer 2 VPN protocols are the Point-to-Point Tunneling Protocol (PPTP) and the Layer 2 Tunneling Protocol (L2TP), both of which are fully supported protocols in Windows Server 2008 R2.

## PPTP and L2TP Protocols

Both PPTP and L2TP are based on the well-defined Point-to-Point Protocol (PPP) and are consequently accepted and widely used in VPN implementations. L2TP is the preferred protocol for use with VPNs in Windows Server 2008 R2 because it incorporates the best of PPTP, with a technology known as Layer 2 Forwarding. L2TP allows for the encapsulation of data over multiple network protocols, including IP, and can be used to tunnel over the Internet. The payload, or data to be transmitted, of each L2TP frame can be compressed, as well as encrypted, to save network bandwidth.

Both PPTP and L2TP build on a suite of useful functionality that was introduced in PPP, such as user authentication, data compression and encryption, and token card support. These features, which have all been ported over to the newer implementations, provide for a rich set of VPN functionality.

## L2TP/IPSec Secure Protocol

Windows Server 2008 R2 uses an additional layer of encryption and security by utilizing IP Security (IPSec), a Layer 3 encryption protocol, in concert with L2TP in what is known, not surprisingly, as L2TP/IPSec. IPSec allows for the encryption of the L2TP header and trailer information, which is normally sent in clear text. This also has the added advantage of dual-encrypting the payload, adding an additional level of security into the mix.

L2TP/IPSec has some distinct advantages over standard L2TP, namely the following:

▶ L2TP/IPSec allows for data authentication on a packet level, allowing for verification that the payload was not modified in transit, as well as the data confidentiality that is provided by L2TP.

▶ Dual-authentication mechanisms stipulate that both computer-level and user-level authentication must take place with L2TP/IPSec.

▶ L2TP packets intercepted during the initial user-level authentication cannot be copied for use in offline dictionary attacks to determine the L2TP key because IPSec encrypts this procedure.

An L2TP/IPSec packet contains multiple, encrypted header information and the payload itself is deeply nested within the structure. This allows for a great deal of transport-level security on the packet itself.

## Enabling VPN Functionality on an RRAS Server

By installing the Routing and Remote Access Service (RRAS) on the server, the ability to allow VPN connections to and/or from the server is enabled. The following type of VPN connections can be created:

▶ **VPN gateway for clients**—The most common scenario, this involves the RRAS server being the gateway into a network for VPN clients. This scenario requires the server to have two network cards installed.

▶ **Site-to-site VPN**—In this scenario, the RRAS server creates a VPN tunnel between another RRAS server in a remote site, allowing for traffic to pass unimpeded between the networks, but in an encrypted state.

▶ **Dial-up RAS server**—In this layout, the server is installed with a modem or pool of modems and provides for dial-in capabilities.

▶ **NAT between networks**—On an RRAS server installed in Routing mode, this deployment option provides for Network Address Translation (NAT) between network segments. For example, on one network, the IP addresses might be public, such as 12.155.166.x, while on the internal network they might be 10.10.10.x. The NAT capability translates the addresses from public to private and vice versa.

▶ **Routing between networks**—On an RRAS server installed in Routing mode, this deployment option allows for direct routing of the traffic between network segments.

▶ **Basic firewall**—The RRAS server can act as a simple Layer 3 router, blocking traffic by port. For more secure scenarios, use of an advanced Layer 7 firewall such as Microsoft's Forefront Threat Management Gateway (previously called Internet Security and Acceleration or ISA Server) is recommended.

> **NOTE**
>
> Setting up a VPN connection requires the server to have at least two network cards installed on the system. This is because the VPN connections must be coming from one network and subsequently passed into a second network, such as from the demilitarized zone (DMZ) network into the internal network.

To set up the RRAS server for the most common scenario, VPN gateway, perform the following tasks:

1. Open the Routing and Remote Access MMC tool (Start, All Programs, Administrative Tools, Routing and Remote Access).

2. Select the local server name or connect to a remote RRAS server by right-clicking Routing and Remote Access and selecting Add Server.

3. Click Action, Configure and Enable Routing and Remote Access.

4. Click Next at the Welcome page.

5. Choose from the list of configuration settings, as shown in Figure 15.14. Different scenarios would require different settings. For example, if setting up a site-to-site VPN, you should select the Secure Connection Between Two Private Networks option. In this case, we are setting up a simple VPN, so we select Remote Access (Dial-up or VPN).

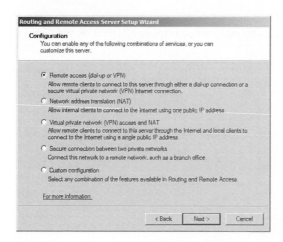

FIGURE 15.14   Enabling VPN functionality.

6. On the Remote Access page, check the box next to VPN. If enabling dial-up, such as in scenarios when the VPN box has a modem attached to it, the Dial-up box can be checked as well. Click Next to continue.

7. On the VPN Connection page, shown in Figure 15.15, select which network card is connected to the network where VPN clients will be coming from. This might be

the Internet, or it might be a secured perimeter network such as a DMZ. Click Next
to continue.

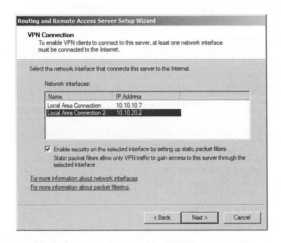

FIGURE 15.15    Specifying the network card for VPN clients.

8. On the IP Address Assignment page, select how VPN clients will get their IP
   addresses (typically Automatically). In addition, a manual range can be specified.
   Click Next to continue.

9. On the Managing Multiple Remote Access Servers page, shown in Figure 15.16, select
   whether to use RRAS to authenticate locally or to use a remote RADIUS server. Click
   Next to continue.

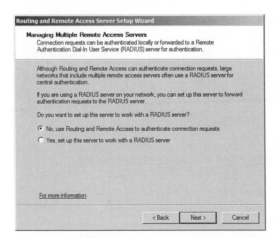

FIGURE 15.16    Specifying RADIUS settings for the VPN server.

10. Review the wizard settings and click Finish when complete.

11. Click OK when prompted about the default connection request policy being created and click OK again if prompted about the DHCP Relay Agent.

12. Click Finish when the wizard is complete.

The wizard will enable RRAS on the server and allow for administration of the VPN settings and client from the Routing and Remote Access dialog box, shown in Figure 15.17. Review the settings within this tool to familiarize yourself with how the system is configured.

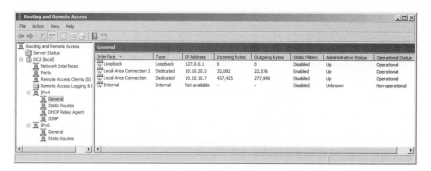

FIGURE 15.17    Administering the server from the RRAS MMC tool.

## Modifying the RRAS Network Policy

After installing and configuring RRAS, the NPS system will deny access by default to the RRAS server for clients, unless the network policy generated is modified. The network policy, which is labeled Connections to Microsoft Routing and Remote Access server, can be found under the Network Policies node of the Network Policy Server.

The policy must be set to Grant Access in the Access Permission section of the dialog box, as shown in Figure 15.18. This dialog box can be invoked by right-clicking the policy and choosing Properties. After enabling, the NPS system will allow client connections.

> **NOTE**
>
> VPN clients can be controlled and monitored using the NPS role just like the IPSec, 802.1X, and DHCP clients can. Use the NPS Admin tool and the techniques described earlier in this chapter to enable client health monitoring.

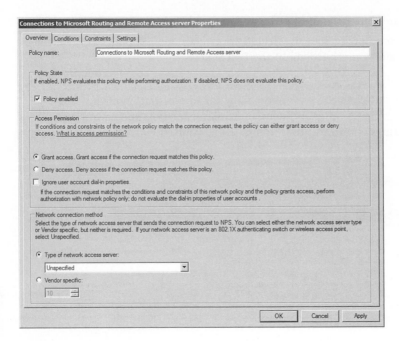

FIGURE 15.18     Modifying the RRAS network policy on the NPS server.

# Summary

Network Access Protection in Windows Server 2008 R2 provides for much-needed capabilities to isolate and control clients that don't conform to an organization's policies. By limiting the type of network access these clients can obtain, organizations can greatly reduce their overall security risk. NAP support in Windows Server 2008 R2 is built in to the operating system on both the server and the Windows 7, Windows Vista, and Windows XP SP3 operating systems.

Windows Server 2008 R2's NAP implementation provides for a robust set of tools in the Network Policy Server role that can be used to restrict clients using NAP. The NPS role contains built-in support for abilities to limit DHCP, IPSec, 802.1x, and VPN clients if they do not pass system health checks. In addition, Windows Server 2008 R2 has improved VPN capabilities, allowing administrators to control and encrypt the connections clients make to the internal network. Using a combination of these technologies can greatly improve the security in an environment.

# Best Practices

The following are best practices from this chapter:

▶ Install the Network Policy Server role to restrict client access to networks and services.

▶ Use a dedicated Certificate Authority server for generation of health certificates for IPSec.

▶ Ensure that the server certificate used for the Network Policy Server is issued from a certificate authority that is trusted by the clients that will be connecting.

▶ Install at least two network cards in a server that will handle VPN client connections.

▶ Although Windows Server 2008 R2 VPN functionality is strong, consider the use of an advanced firewall/VPN solution, such as the Forefront Edge line, consisting of Forefront Threat Management Gateway and/or Forefront Unified Access Gateway to further improve VPN security.

▶ Use L2TP over IPSec encryption for VPN connections when possible. Avoid using the less-secure PPTP VPN connection type.

15

# CHAPTER 16

# Migrating from Windows Server 2003/2008 to Windows Server 2008 R2

In many ways, a migration from Windows Server 2003/2008 Active Directory to Windows Server 2008 R2 Active Directory Domain Services is more of a service pack upgrade than a major migration. The architectures are fundamentally the same and require mainly upgrades to the schema and domains. The differences between the operating systems are more evolutionary than revolutionary, and, subsequently, there are fewer design considerations than in upgrades from the NT 4.0 operating system.

That said, several immediate improvements to the operating system can be realized through migration to Windows Server 2008 R2, whether by migrating all servers immediately or by using a slow, phased approach. Improvements to Active Directory Domain Services (AD DS), such as the ability to use Read-Only Domain Controllers as global catalog servers, the Recycle Bin for AD, and greater scalability, provide incentive for Windows Server 2003/2008 Active Directory environments to begin migration. Standalone server improvements such as Hyper-V, Remote Desktop Services, File and Print Server improvements, Automated Server Recovery, and many more also serve to encourage migrations.

This chapter focuses on the planning, strategy, and logistics of migration from Windows Server 2003/2008 Active Directory to Windows Server 2008 R2 Active Directory Domain Services. Several scenarios for migration are considered, including a Big Bang upgrade, a phased upgrade, and a consolidation migration.

# Beginning the Migration Process

Any migration procedure should define the reasons for migration, steps involved, fallback precautions, and other important factors that can influence the migration process. After finalizing these items, the migration can begin.

## Identifying Migration Objectives

Two underlying philosophies influence technology upgrades, each philosophy working against the other. The first is the expression "If it ain't broke, don't fix it." Obviously, if an organization has a functional, easy-to-use, and well-designed Windows Server 2003/2008 infrastructure, popping in that Windows Server 2008 R2 DVD and upgrading might not be so appealing. The second philosophy is something along the lines of "Those who fail to upgrade their technologies perish." Eventually, all technologies become outdated and unsupported.

Choosing a pragmatic middle ground between these two philosophies effectively depends on the factors that drive an organization to upgrade. If the organization has critical business needs that can be satisfied by an upgrade, such an upgrade might be a good idea. If, however, no critical need exists, it might be wise to wait until the next iteration of Windows or a future service pack for Windows Server 2008 R2.

## Establishing Migration Project Phases

After the decision is made to upgrade, a detailed plan of the resources, timeline, scope, and objectives of the project should be outlined. Part of any migration plan requires establishing either an ad-hoc project plan or a professionally drawn-up project plan. The migration plan assists the project managers of the migration project to accomplish the planned objectives in a timely manner with the correct application of resources.

The following is a condensed description of the standard phases for a migration project:

▶ **Discovery**—The first portion of a design project should be a discovery, or fact-finding, portion. This section focuses on the analysis of the current environment and documentation of the analysis results. Current network diagrams, server locations, wide area network (WAN) throughputs, server application dependencies, and all other networking components should be detailed as part of the Discovery phase.

▶ **Design**—The Design portion of a project is straightforward. All key components of the actual migration plan should be documented, and key data from the Discovery phase should be used to draw up design and migration documents. The project plan itself would normally be drafted during this phase. Because Windows Server 2008 R2 Active Directory is not dramatically different from Windows Server 2003 or 2008, significant reengineering of an existing Active Directory environment is not necessary. However, other issues such as server placement, new feature utilization, and changes in AD DS replication models should be outlined.

▶ **Prototype**—The Prototype phase of a project involves the essential lab work to test the design assumptions made during the Design phase. The ideal prototype would involve a mock production environment that is migrated from Windows Server 2003/2008 to Windows Server 2008 R2. For Active Directory, this means creating a production domain controller (DC) and then isolating it in the lab and seizing the Flexible Single Master Operations (FSMO) roles with a server in the lab. The Active Directory migration can then be performed without affecting the production environment. Step-by-step procedures for the migration can also be outlined and produced as deliverables for this phase.

▶ **Pilot**—The Pilot phase, or Proof-of-Concept phase, involves a production "test" of the migration steps, on a limited scale. For example, a noncritical server could be upgraded to Windows Server 2008 R2 in advance of the migration of all other critical network servers. In a slow, phased migration, the Pilot phase would essentially transition into Implementation, as upgrades are performed slowly, one by one.

▶ **Implementation**—The Implementation portion of the project is the full-blown migration of network functionality or upgrades to the operating system. As previously mentioned, this process can be performed quickly or slowly over time, depending on an organization's needs. It is, subsequently, important to make the timeline decisions in the Design phase and incorporate them into the project plan.

▶ **Training and support**—Learning the ins and outs of the new functionality that Windows Server 2008 R2 can bring to an environment is essential in realizing the increased productivity and reduced administration that the OS can bring to the environment. Consequently, it is important to include a Training portion into a migration project so that the design objectives can be fully realized.

For more detailed information on the project plan phases of a Windows Server 2008 R2 migration, refer to Chapter 2, "Planning, Prototyping, Migrating, and Deploying Windows Server 2008 R2 Best Practices."

## Comparing the In-Place Upgrade Versus New Hardware Migration Methods

Due to the changes in Windows Server 2008 R2, the in-place upgrade path is limited to servers using the 64-bit version of Windows Server 2003 and Windows Server 2008. Depending on the type of hardware currently in use in a Windows Server 2003/2008 network, this type of migration strategy might be an option. Often, however, it is more appealing to simply introduce newer systems into an existing environment and retire the current servers from production. This technique normally has less impact on current environments and can also support fallback more easily.

> **NOTE**
>
> Because Windows Server 2008 R2 is a 64-bit only operating system, upgrades from 32-bit versions of older operating systems are not supported. Upgrades from Windows 2000 Server are also not supported.

Determining which migration strategy to use depends on one additional factor: the condition of the current hardware environment. If Windows Server 2003/2008 is taxing the limitations of the hardware in use, it might be preferable to introduce new servers into an environment and simply retire the old Windows Server 2003/2008 servers. This is particularly true if the existing servers are veterans of previous upgrades, maybe transitioning from Windows 2000 Server to Windows Server 2003 to Windows Server 2008. If, however, the hardware in use for Windows Server 2003/2008 is newer and more robust, and could conceivably last for another two to three years, it might be easier to simply perform in-place upgrades of the systems in an environment.

In most cases, organizations take a hybrid approach to migration. Older hardware, 32-bit systems, or Windows Server 2003 domain controllers are replaced by new hardware running Windows Server 2008 R2. Newer Windows Server 2008 64-bit systems are instead upgraded in place to Windows Server 2008 R2. Consequently, auditing all systems to be migrated and determining which ones will be upgraded and which ones will be retired are important steps in the migration process.

## Identifying Migration Strategies: "Big Bang" Versus Phased Coexistence

As with most technology implementations, there are essentially two approaches in regard to deployment: a quick "Big Bang" approach or a slower phased coexistence approach. The Big Bang option involves the entire Windows Server 2003/2008 infrastructure being quickly replaced, often over the course of a weekend, with the new Windows Server 2008 R2 environment; whereas the phased approach involves a slow, server-by-server replacement of Windows Server 2003/2008.

Each approach has its particular advantages and disadvantages, and key factors to Windows Server 2008 R2 should be taken into account before a decision is made. Few Windows Server 2008 R2 components require a redesign of current Windows Server 2003/2008 design elements. Because the arguments for the Big Bang approach largely revolve around not maintaining two conflicting systems for long periods of time, the similarities between Windows Server 2003/2008 and Windows Server 2008 R2 make many of these arguments moot. Windows Server 2008 R2 domain controllers can easily coexist with Windows Server 2003/2008 domain controllers. With this point in mind, it is more likely that most organizations will choose to ease into Windows Server 2008 R2, opting for the phased coexistence approach to the upgrade. Because Windows Server 2008 R2 readily fits into a Windows Server 2003/2008 environment, and vice versa, this option is easily supported.

## Exploring Migration Options

As previously mentioned, the Windows Server 2008 R2 and Windows Server 2003/2008 Active Directory domain controllers coexist together very well. The added advantage to this fact is that there is greater flexibility for different migration options. Unlike migrations from NT 4.0 or non-Microsoft environments such as Novell NDS/eDirectory, the migration path between these two systems is not rigid, and different approaches can be used successfully to achieve the final objectives desired.

In this chapter, three Windows Server 2008 R2 migration scenarios are explored:

▶ **Big Bang migration**—This scenario upgrades all domain controllers in a short span of time. This is typically suitable only for single domain and small organizations.

▶ **Phased migration**—This scenario takes a phased coexistence approach and upgrades the domain controllers in phases over an extended period of time. During this time, there is coexistence between the existing versions of Active Directory and the new Windows Server 2008 R2 Active Directory Domain Services. This is typically the approach used when there are multiple domains or for large organizations.

▶ **Multiple domain consolidation migration**—A variation on the phased upgrade, the multiple domain consolidation migrates the existing domains to a new Windows Server 2008 R2 Active Directory domain. This is the typical approach when there are problems with the existing domains, too many domains, or when merging organizations.

The remainder of this chapter walks through each of these scenarios step-by-step.

# Big Bang Migration

The Big Bang approach to migrate from Windows Server 2008 to Windows Server 2008 R2 is the most straightforward approach to migration. An upgrade simply takes any and all settings on the domain controllers and upgrades them to Windows Server 2008 R2. If a Windows Server 2008 server handles Windows Internet Naming Service (WINS), domain name system (DNS), and Dynamic Host Configuration Protocol (DHCP), the upgrade process will upgrade all WINS, DNS, and DHCP components, as well as the base operating system. This makes this type of migration very tempting, and it can be extremely effective, as long as all prerequisites described in the following sections are satisfied.

The prerequisites are as follows:

▶ The operating system on the domain controllers is Windows Server 2003 SP2 or higher.

▶ The domain controller hardware exceeds the Windows Server 2008 R2 requirements and all software is compatible with Windows Server 2008 R2, including antivirus software and drivers.

▶ There is enough disk space free to perform the operating system and Active Directory upgrade. Specifically, verify that your free space is at least twice the size of your Active Directory database plus the minimum 32GB needed to install the operating system.

▶ The current domain functional level is Windows 2000 Native or Windows Server 2003. You cannot upgrade directly from Windows NT 4.0, Windows 2000 Mixed, or Windows Server 2003 interim domain functional levels.

Often, upgrading any given server can be a project in itself. The standalone member servers in an environment are often the workhorses of the network, loaded with a myriad of different applications and critical tools. Performing an upgrade on these servers would be simple if they were used only for file or print duties and if their hardware systems were all up to date. Because this is not always the case, it is important to detail the specifics of each server that is marked for migration.

## Verifying Hardware Compatibility

It is critical to test the hardware compatibility of any server that will be directly upgraded to Windows Server 2008 R2. The middle of the installation process is not the most ideal time to be notified of problems with compatibility between older system components and the drivers required for Windows Server 2008 R2. Subsequently, the hardware in a server should be verified for Windows Server 2008 R2 on the manufacturer's website or on Microsoft's Hardware Compatibility List (HCL), currently located at http://www.microsoft.com/whdc/hcl/default.mspx.

Microsoft suggests minimum hardware levels on which Windows Server 2008 R2 will run, but it is highly recommended that you install the OS on systems of a much higher caliber because these recommendations do not take into account any application loads, domain controller duties, and so on. The following is a list of Microsoft's minimum hardware levels for Windows Server 2008 R2:

- ▶ 1.4GHz 64-bit processor
- ▶ 512MB of RAM
- ▶ 32GB free disk space

That said, it cannot be stressed enough that it is almost always recommended that you exceed these levels to provide for a robust computing environment. See Chapter 3, "Installing Windows Server 2008 R2 and Server Core," for additional details on hardware requirements.

> **NOTE**
>
> One of the most important features that mission-critical servers can have is redundancy. Putting the operating system on a mirrored array of disks, for example, is a simple yet effective way of increasing redundancy in an environment.

## Verifying Application Readiness

Nothing ruins a migration process like discovering a mission-critical application that is installed on the current Windows Server 2003 server will not work in the new environment. Subsequently, it is very important to identify and list all applications on a server that will be required in the new environment. Applications that will not be used or whose functionality is replaced in Windows Server 2008 R2 can be retired and removed from consideration. Likewise, applications that have been verified for Windows Server 2008 R2 can be designated as safe for upgrade. For any other applications that might not be compatible but are necessary, you either need to move them to another Windows Server 2003 server or delay the upgrade of that specific server.

In addition to the applications, the version of the operating system that will be upgraded is an important consideration in the process. A Windows Server 2003 SP2 or R2, Standard Edition domain controller can be upgraded to either Windows Server 2008 R2, Standard Edition or Windows Server 2008 R2, Enterprise Edition. However, a Windows Server 2003 SP2 or R2, Enterprise Edition installation can only be upgraded to Windows Server 2008 R2, Enterprise Edition.

## Backing Up and Creating a Recovery Process

It is critical that a migration does not cause more harm than good to an environment. Subsequently, we cannot stress enough that a good backup system is essential for quick recovery in the event of upgrade failure. Often, especially with the in-place upgrade scenario, a full system backup might be the only way to recover; consequently, it is very important to detail fallback steps in the event of problems. The backup should include the boot and system partitions as well as the System State.

## Virtual Domain Controller Rollback Option

It is always good to have several fallback options, in case one of the options is unsuccessful. Another option to consider, in addition to a full backup, is to create a virtual domain controller. Using a virtual server platform such as Hyper-V or VMware Server, you can create a domain controller for little or no cost.

A virtual machine is created on the host, which can be an existing installation or even on a desktop with Virtual PC or VMware Workstation. This virtual machine is then joined to the domain and promoted to be a domain controller.

Prior to the upgrade, the virtual domain controller is shut down. Backup copies of the virtual domain controller files can even be made for safekeeping.

In the event of a major failure in the upgrade process, the virtual domain controller can be used to rebuild the domain from scratch. If the upgrade is successful, the virtual domain controller can either be turned back on and demoted, or simply be deleted and cleaned from the domain.

## Performing an Upgrade on a Single Domain Controller Server

After all various considerations regarding applications and hardware compatibility have been thoroughly validated, a standalone server can be upgraded.

The health of the domain controllers should be verified prior to upgrading the domain controllers. In particular, the Domain Controller Diagnostics (DCDIAG) utility should be run and any errors fixed before the upgrade. The Windows Server 2003 DCDIAG utility is

part of the Support Tools, which can be found on the installation media under
\support\tools\. The Support Tools are installed via an MSI package named
SUPTOOLS.MSI in Windows Server 2003. After installing the tools, the DCDIAG utility
can be run. The same utility is included in Windows Server 2008 with no additional
installs required. Execute the tool and verify that all tests passed.

The Active Directory Domain Services forest and the domain need to be prepared prior to
the upgrade. This installs the schema updates that are new to Windows Server 2008 R2
Active Directory. The following steps should be run on the Flexible Single Master
Operations (FSMO) role holder(s), specifically the schema master for forestprep and the
infrastructure master for domainprep. In a small environment or a single domain, all these
roles are typically on the same domain controller. To prepare the forest and domain,
execute the following steps on the domain controller with the roles:

1. Insert the Windows Server 2008 R2 DVD into the drive. If the Install Windows
   autorun page appears, close the window.

> **NOTE**
>
> When preparing the forest, be sure to log on to the schema master as a member of
> the Schema, Enterprise, and Domain Admins group.

2. Select Start, Run.

3. Enter d:\support\adprep\adprep.exe /forestprep and click OK, where d: is the
   DVD drive.

4. A warning appears to verify that all Windows 2000 domain controllers are at Service
   Pack 4 or later. Enter C and press Enter to start the forest preparation.

5. Enter d:\support\adprep\adprep.exe /domainprep /gpprep and click OK.

6. Enter d:\support\adprep\adprep.exe /rodcprep and click OK. This update allows
   Read-Only Domain Controllers.

Now that the schema updates have been installed and the domain preparation is done,
the domain is ready to be upgraded. The FSMO role holder should be the first Windows
Server 2003/2008 domain controller to be upgraded. Follow these steps to upgrade:

1. Insert the Windows Server 2008 R2 DVD into the DVD drive of the server to be
   upgraded.

2. The Install Windows page should appear automatically. If not, choose Start, Run and
   then type d:\Setup, where d: is the drive letter for the DVD drive.

3. Click Install Now.

4. Click the large Go Online to Get the Latest Updates button. This ensures that the
   installation has the latest information for the upgrade.

5. Enter your product key and click Next.

6. Select the I Accept the License Terms option on the License page, and click Next
   to continue.

7. Click the large Upgrade button.

8. Review the compatibility report and verify that all issues have been addressed. Click Next to continue.

9. The system then copies files and reboots as a Windows Server 2008 R2 server, continuing the upgrade process. After all files are copied, the system is then upgraded to a fully functional install of Windows Server 2008 R2 (see Figure 16.1) and will then reboot again. All this can take some time to complete.

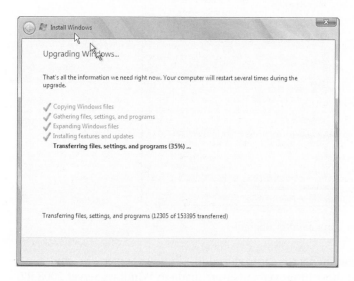

FIGURE 16.1    Big Bang upgrade.

10. After the final reboot, the domain controller will be at the familiar Ctrl+Alt+Del screen. After logon, the domain controller will open to the Server Manager console, as shown in Figure 16.2. The domain controller upgrade is complete.

The upgrade process shown in steps 1 through 10 is then repeated for each of the remaining Windows Server 2003/2008 domain controllers.

## Phased Migration

In many cases, the Windows Server 2003/2008 environment that will be migrated includes one or many Active Directory domains and forests. Because Active Directory is one of the most important portions of a Microsoft network, it is subsequently one of the most important areas to focus on in a migration process. In addition, many of the improvements made to Windows Server 2008 R2 are directly related to Active Directory, making it even more appealing to migrate this portion of an environment.

The decision to upgrade Active Directory should focus on these key improvement areas. If one or more of the improvements to Active Directory Domain Services justifies an upgrade,

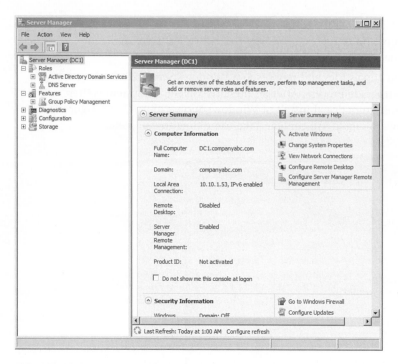

FIGURE 16.2    Server Manager console after upgrade.

it should be considered. Improvements were introduced in Windows Server 2003 and
Windows Server 2008, and yet more improvements were made in Windows Server 2008 R2.

The following list details some of the many changes made to Active Directory in Windows
Server 2003 that improved on the original Windows 2000 Server Active Directory:

▶ **Domain rename capability**—Windows Server 2003 Active Directory supported the
  renaming of either the NetBIOS name or the LDAP/DNS name of an Active Directory
  domain. The Active Directory domain rename tool can be used for this purpose, but
  only in domains that have completely upgraded to Windows Server 2003 or later
  domain controllers.

▶ **Cross-forest transitive trusts**—Windows Server 2003 supports the implementation
  of transitive trusts that can be established between separate Active Directory forests.
  Windows 2000 supported only explicit cross-forest trusts, and the trust structure did
  not allow for permissions to flow between separate domains in a forest. This limitation has been lifted in Windows Server 2003 or later.

▶ **Universal group caching**—One of the main structural limitations of Active
  Directory was the need to establish very "chatty" global catalog servers in every site
  established in a replication topology, or run the risk of extremely slow client logon
  times and directory queries. Windows Server 2003 or later enables remote domain
  controllers to cache universal group memberships for users so that each logon
  request does not require the use of a local global catalog server.

▶ **Intersite topology generator (ISTG) improvements**—The ISTG in Windows Server 2003 was improved to support configurations with extremely large numbers of sites. In addition, the time required to determine site topology has been noticeably improved through the use of a more efficient ISTG algorithm.

▶ **Multivalued attribute replication improvements**—In Windows 2000 Server, if a universal group changed its membership from 5,000 users to 5,001 users, the entire group membership had to be rereplicated across the entire forest. Windows Server 2003 addressed this problem and allowed incremental membership changes to be replicated.

▶ **Lingering objects (zombies) detection**—Domain controllers that have been out of service for a longer period of time than the Time to Live (TTL) of a deleted object could theoretically "resurrect" those objects, forcing them to come back to life as zombies, or lingering objects. Windows Server 2003 properly identified these zombies and prevented them from being replicated to other domain controllers.

▶ **AD-integrated DNS zones in application partitions**—Replication of DNS zones was improved and made more flexible in Windows Server 2003 by storing AD-integrated zones in the application partition of a forest, thus limiting their need to be replicated to all domain controllers and reducing network traffic. Conversely, the DNS zones could be configured to replicate them to the entire forest if that was appropriate.

The Windows Server 2008 Active Directory retained all the new features of Windows Server 2003 Active Directory and adds several key new features, as follows:

▶ **Fine-grained password policies**—Password policies can be customized to different users within the same Active Directory domain.

▶ **Read-Only Domain Controllers**—These domain controllers are designed for branch offices and for extranet scenarios, in that they allow directory information to be accessed but not changed. This adds an element of security to scenarios that require directory services but are not as secure as the corporate data center.

▶ **Granular auditing**—The Active Directory auditing is much more granular and allows tracking of some objects but not others. This reduces the volume of security logs; however, it provides less information for the auditor or analyst to review during an audit or information acquisition process.

▶ **Distributed File System Replication (DFSR)**—DFSR is now used for SYSVOL replication, replacing the File Replication Service (FRS) that is used to replicate SYSVOL in Windows 2000 Server and Windows Server 2003. This feature provides more robust and detailed replication of SYSVOL contents and is available when the domain functional level is raised to Windows Server 2008.

Features introduced with the upgrade to Windows Server 2008 R2 include the following:

▶ **Active Directory Module for Windows PowerShell**—The Active Directory Module for Windows PowerShell is a consolidated group of Windows PowerShell cmdlets you can use to manage Active Directory.

**16**

▶ **Active Directory Administrative Center**—The Active Directory Administrative Center is a task-oriented AD management console that allows for the management of users, groups, computers, sites, and domains from one console.

▶ **Recycle Bin for AD**—Previously deleted objects can now be restored from the Recycle Bin.

▶ **Offline Domain Join**—Join Windows machines to the domain, while offline, via an XML file.

▶ **Managed Service Accounts**—This feature greatly improves the daunting task of managing service account passwords by automatically updating all services when the service account password is changed.

---

**NOTE**

For more information on the improvements to Active Directory and the ways they can be used to determine whether your organization should upgrade, refer to Chapter 4, "Active Directory Domain Services Primer," Chapter 5, "Designing a Windows Server 2008 R2 Active Directory," Chapter 6, "Designing Organizational Unit and Group Structure," and Chapter 7, "Active Directory Infrastructure."

---

In the scenario in this section, there are two domains (companyabc.com and asia.companyabc.com), which are members of the same forest (shown in Figure 16.3). The companyabc.com domain has all Windows 2000 Server SP4 domain controllers and the asia.companyabc.com domain has all Windows Server 2003 SP2 domain controllers. The entire forest will be upgraded to Windows Server 2008 R2, but they need to be migrated over time. Thus, a phased migration will be used.

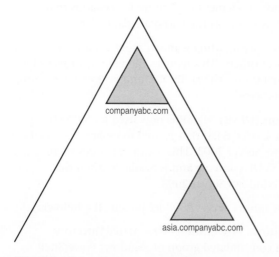

FIGURE 16.3    Company ABC forest.

## Migrating Domain Controllers

There are two approaches to migrating domain controllers, similar to the logic used in the "Performing an Upgrade on a Single Domain Controller Server" section. The domain controllers can either be directly upgraded to Windows Server 2008 R2 or replaced by newly introduced Windows Server 2008 R2 domain controllers. The decision to upgrade an existing server largely depends on the hardware of the server in question. The rule of thumb is, if the hardware will support Windows Server 2008 R2 now and for the next two to three years, a server can be directly upgraded. If this is not the case, using new hardware for the migration is preferable.

The prerequisites for upgrading an Active Directory forest and domain discussed earlier still apply. The prerequisites to upgrade to Windows Server 2008 R2 Active Directory are as follows:

▶ The operating system on the domain controllers is Windows Server 2003 SP2 or higher.

▶ The current domain functional level is Windows 2000 Native or Windows Server 2003. You cannot upgrade directly from Windows NT 4.0, Windows 2000 Mixed, or Windows Server 2003 interim domain functional levels.

These prerequisites are required to upgrade to Windows Server 2008 R2.

> **NOTE**
>
> A combined approach can be and is quite commonly used, as indicated in Figure 16.4, to support a scenario in which some hardware is current but other hardware is out of date and will be replaced. Either way, the decisions applied to a proper project plan can help to ensure the success of the migration.

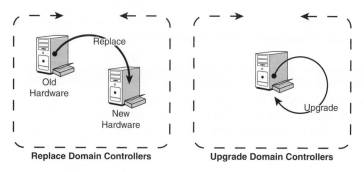

Replace

Old
Hardware

New
Hardware

**Replace Domain Controllers**

Upgrade

**Upgrade Domain Controllers**

FIGURE 16.4   Combined approach to the upgrade process.

The scenario in this section will use the combined approach to the upgrade, replacing the Windows 2000 SP4 companyabc.com domain controllers and upgrading the Windows Server 2003 asia.companyabc.com domain controllers.

The health of the domain controllers should be verified prior to upgrading the domain controllers. In particular, the Domain Controller Diagnostics (DCDIAG) utility should be run and any errors fixed before the upgrade. The Windows Server 2003 DCDIAG utility is part of the Support Tools, which can be found on the installation media under \support\tools\. The Support Tools are installed via an MSI package named SUPTOOLS.MSI in Windows Server 2003. After installing the tools, the DCDIAG utility can be run. The dcdiag /e option should be used to check all domain controllers in the enterprise. Verify that all tests passed.

## Preparing the Forest and Domains Using adprep

The introduction of Windows Server 2008 R2 domain controllers into a Windows Server 2003/2008 Active Directory requires that the core AD database structure, the schema, be updated to support the increased functionality. In addition, several other security changes need to be made to prepare a forest for inclusion of Windows Server 2008 R2. The Windows Server 2008 R2 DVD includes a command-line utility called adprep that will extend the schema to include the extensions required and modify security as needed. Adprep requires that both forestprep and domainprep be run before the first Windows Server 2008 R2 domain controller can be added.

The adprep utility must be run from the Windows Server 2008 R2 DVD or copied from its location in the \support\adprep\ folder. This installs the schema updates that are new to Windows Server 2008 R2 Active Directory. The following steps should be run on the Flexible Single Master Operations (FSMO) role holder, specifically the Schema Master role holder:

1. Insert the Windows Server 2008 R2 DVD into the drive. If the Install Windows autorun page appears, close the window.

2. Select Start, Run.

3. Enter d:\support\adprep\adprep.exe /forestprep and click OK, where d: is the DVD drive.

4. A warning appears to verify that all Windows 2000 Server domain controllers are at Service Pack 4 or later. Enter C and press Enter to start the forest preparation.

### NOTE

Any previous extensions made to the Active Directory schema, such as those made with Exchange Server 2003 or Exchange Server 2007, are not affected by the adprep procedure. This procedure simply adds additional attributes and does not change those that currently exist.

Now that the schema updates have been installed, the domain is ready to be prepared. The operation must be run once in every domain in a forest. It must be physically invoked on the server that holds the infrastructure master Operations Master (OM) role. The steps for executing the domainprep procedure are as follows:

1. On the Operations Master domain controller, insert the Windows Server 2008 R2 DVD into the drive. If the Install Windows autorun page appears, close the window.

2. Select Start, Run.

3. Enter `d:\support\adprep\adprep.exe /domainprep /gpprep` and click OK, where d: is the DVD drive.

4. Enter `d:\support\adprep\adprep.exe /rodcprep` and click OK. This update allows Read-Only Domain Controllers by updating the permissions on all the DNS application directory partitions in the forest and allows them to be replicated by all RODCs that are also DNS servers.

Repeat steps 1 through 4 for each domain that will be upgraded.

After the forestprep and domainprep operations are run, the Active Directory forest will be ready for the introduction or upgrade of Windows Server 2008 R2 domain controllers. The schema is extended and includes support for Active Directory Recycle Bin and other enhancements. After these updates have had sufficient time to replicate across all domains, the process of upgrading the domain controllers to Windows Server 2008 R2 can commence.

## Upgrading Existing Domain Controllers

If the decision has been made to upgrade all or some existing hardware to Windows Server 2008 R2, the process for accomplishing this is straightforward. However, as with the standalone server, you need to ensure that the hardware and any additional software components are compatible with Windows Server 2008 R2. The requirements for the server to upgrade are as follows:

▶ The operating system on the domain controllers must be a 64-bit operating system.

▶ The operating system on the domain controllers is Windows Server 2003 SP2. The domain controller hardware exceeds the Windows Server 2008 R2 requirements and all software is compatible with Windows Server 2008 R2, including antivirus software and drivers.

▶ There is enough disk space free to perform the operating system and Active Directory upgrade. Specifically, verify that your free space is at least twice the size of your Active Directory database plus the minimum 32GB needed to install the operating system.

After establishing this, the actual migration can occur. The procedure for upgrading a domain controller to Windows Server 2008 R2 is nearly identical to the procedure outlined in the previous section "Performing an Upgrade on a Single Domain Controller Server." Essentially, simply insert the DVD and upgrade, and an hour or so later the machine will be updated and functioning as a Windows Server 2008 R2 domain controller.

The specific steps are as follows:

1. Insert the Windows Server 2008 R2 DVD into the DVD drive of the server to be upgraded.

2. The Install Windows page should appear automatically. If not, choose Start, Run and then type `d:\Setup`, where d: is the drive letter for the DVD drive.

3. Click Install Now.

4. Click the large Go Online to Get the Latest Updates button. This ensures that the installation has the latest information for the upgrade.

5. Select the operating system you want to install and click Next.

6. Select the I Accept the License Terms option on the License page, and click Next to continue.

7. Click the large Upgrade button.

8. Review the compatibility report and verify that all issues have been addressed. Click Next to continue.

9. The system then copies files and reboots as a Windows Server 2008 R2 server, continuing the upgrade process. After all files are copied, the system is then upgraded to a fully functional install of Windows Server 2008 R2 and then reboots again. All this can take some time to complete.

10. After the final reboot, the domain controller will be at the familiar Ctrl+Alt+Del screen. After logon, the domain controller opens to the Server Manager console. The domain controller upgrade is complete.

Repeat for all domain controllers that will be upgraded.

## Replacing Existing Domain Controllers

If you need to migrate specific domain controller functionality to the new Active Directory environment but plan to use new hardware, you need to bring new domain controllers into the environment before retiring the old servers.

Windows Server 2008 R2 uses a roles-based model. To make a Windows Server 2008 R2 server a domain controller, the Active Directory Domain Services role is added. This is the most thorough approach, and the following steps show how to accomplish this to establish a new Windows Server 2008 R2 domain controller in a Windows Server 2003/2008 Active Directory domain:

> **NOTE**
>
> This procedure assumes that the Windows Server 2008 R2 operating system has been installed on the server. See Chapter 3 for steps to do this. The server does not need to be a domain member.

1. Log on to the new server as an administrator.

2. Launch Server Manager.

3. Select the Roles node.

4. Click Add Roles.

5. Click Next.

6. Select the Active Directory Domain Services check box, and click Next.

> **NOTE**
>
> The .NET Framework 3.5.1 features are required; if prompted to install, click Add Required Features.

7. Click Next on the Introduction page.

8. Click Install to install the role. This installs the binaries necessary for the server to become a domain controller.

9. Click Close on the Installation Results page.

10. In the Server Manager console, expand the Roles node and select the Active Directory Domain Services node.

11. In the Summary section, click the Run the Active Directory Domain Services Installation Wizard (dcpromo.exe) link.

12. Click Next on the Welcome page.

13. Select the Existing Forest option button.

14. Select the Add a Domain Controller to an Existing Domain option button, and click Next.

15. Enter the name of the domain.

16. Click Set to specify alternate credentials to use for the operation.

17. Enter the credentials of a domain administrator in the target domain, and click OK.

18. Click Next to continue.

19. Select the appropriate domain for the new domain controller, and click Next. In this example, the companyabc.com domain is used.

20. Select a site for the domain, and click Next.

21. Select the Additional Domain Controller Options, which are DNS Server and Global Catalog by default. The Read-Only Domain Controller option is not available if this is the first Windows Server 2008 R2 domain controller in the domain. Click Next.

22. Click Yes if presented with a DNS Delegation warning dialog box.

23. Select locations for the database, log files, and the SYSVOL, and then click Next.

24. Enter the Directory Services Restore mode administrator password, and then click Next.

25. Review the summary, and then click Next. The installation wizard will create the domain controller and replicate the Active Directory database, which might take some time depending on the network and the size of the Active Directory database.

16

26. After the wizard completes the installation, click Finish.

27. Click Restart Now to reboot the new domain controller.

This process should be repeated for each new replacement domain controller.

## Moving Operation Master Roles

Active Directory Domain Services uses a multimaster replication model, in which any one server can take over directory functionality, and each full domain controller contains a read/write copy of directory objects (with the exception of Read-Only Domain Controllers, which hold, as their name suggests, a read-only copy). There are, however, a few key exceptions to this, in which certain forestwide and domainwide functionality must be held by a single domain controller in the forest and in each domain respectively. These exceptions are known as Operation Master (OM) roles, also known as Flexible Single Master Operations (FSMO) roles. There are five OM roles, as shown in Table 16.1.

TABLE 16.1    FSMO Roles and Their Scope

| FSMO Roles | Scope |
| --- | --- |
| Schema master | Forest |
| Domain naming master | Forest |
| Infrastructure master | Domain |
| RID master | Domain |
| PDC emulator | Domain |

If the server or servers that hold the OM roles are not directly upgraded to Windows Server 2008 R2 but will instead be retired, these OM roles will need to be moved to another server. The best tool for this type of move is the NTDSUTIL command-line utility.

Follow these steps using NTDSUTIL to move the forestwide OM roles (schema master and domain naming master) to a single Windows Server 2008 R2 domain controller:

1. Open a command prompt on the Windows Server 2008 R2 domain controller (choose Start, type cmd, and press Enter).

2. Type ntdsutil and press Enter. The prompt will display "ntdsutil:".

3. Type roles and press Enter. The prompt will display "fsmo maintenance:".

4. Type connections and press Enter. The prompt will display "server connections:".

5. Type connect to server <Servername>, where <Servername> is the name of the target Windows Server 2008 R2 domain controller that will hold the OM roles, and press Enter.

6. Type quit and press Enter. The prompt will display "fsmo maintenance:".

7. Type transfer schema master and press Enter.

8. Click Yes at the prompt asking to confirm the OM change. The display will show the location for each of the five FSMO roles after the operation.

9. Type `transfer naming master` and press Enter.

10. Click Yes at the prompt asking to confirm the OM change.

11. Type `quit` and press Enter, then type `quit` and press Enter again to exit the NTDSUTIL.

12. Type `exit` to close the Command Prompt window.

Now the forestwide FSMO roles will be on a single Windows Server 2008 R2 domain controller.

The domainwide FSMO roles (infrastructure master, RID master, and PDC emulator) will need to be moved for each domain to a domain controller within the domain. The steps to do this are as follows:

1. Open a command prompt on the Windows Server 2008 R2 domain controller (choose Start, click Run, type `cmd`, and press Enter).

2. Type `ntdsutil` and press Enter.

3. Type `roles` and press Enter.

4. Type `connections` and press Enter.

5. Type `connect to server <Servername>`, where `<Servername>` is the name of the target Windows Server 2008 R2 domain controller that will hold the OM roles, and press Enter.

6. Type `quit` and press Enter.

7. Type `transfer pdc` and press Enter.

8. Click Yes at the prompt asking to confirm the OM change.

9. Type `transfer rid master` and press Enter.

10. Click Yes at the prompt asking to confirm the OM change.

11. Type `transfer infrastructure master` and press Enter.

12. Click Yes at the prompt asking to confirm the OM change.

13. Type `quit` and press Enter, then type `quit` and press Enter again to exit the NTDSUTIL.

14. Type `exit` to close the Command Prompt window.

The preceding steps need to be repeated for each domain.

## Retiring Existing Windows Server 2003/2008 Domain Controllers

After the entire Windows Server 2003/2008 domain controller infrastructure is replaced by Windows Server 2008 R2 equivalents and the OM roles are migrated, the process of demoting and removing all down-level domain controllers can begin. The most straightforward and thorough way of removing a domain controller is by demoting it using the dcpromo utility, per the standard Windows Server 2003/2008 demotion process. After you run the dcpromo command, the domain controller becomes a member server in the domain. After disjoining it from the domain, it can safely be disconnected from the network.

16

## Retiring "Phantom" Domain Controllers

As is often the case in Active Directory, domain controllers might have been removed from the forest without first being demoted. They become phantom domain controllers and basically haunt the Active Directory, causing strange errors to pop up every so often. This is because of a couple remnants in the Active Directory, specifically the NTDS Settings object and the SYSVOL replication object. These phantom DCs might come about because of server failure or problems in the administrative process, but you should remove those servers and remnant objects from the directory to complete the upgrade to Windows Server 2008 R2. Not doing so will result in errors in the event logs and in the DCDIAG output as well as potentially prevent raising the domain and forest to the latest functional level.

Simply deleting the computer object from Active Directory Sites and Services does not work. Instead, you need to use a low-level directory tool, ADSIEdit, to remove these servers properly. The following steps outline how to use ADSIEdit to remove these phantom domain controllers:

1. Launch Server Manager.
2. Expand the Roles node and select the Active Directory Domain Services node.
3. Scroll down to the Advanced Tools section of the page and click on the ADSI Edit link.
4. In the ADSIEdit window, select Action, Connect To.
5. In the Select a Well Known Naming Context drop-down menu, select Configuration, and click OK.
6. Select the Configuration node.
7. Navigate to `Configuration\CN=Configuration\CN=Sites\CN=<Sitename>\`
   `CN=Servers\CN=<Servername>`, where <Sitename> and <Servername> correspond to the location of the phantom domain controller.
8. Right-click the CN=NTDS Settings, and click Delete, as shown in Figure 16.5.
9. At the prompt, click Yes to delete the object.
10. In the ADSIEdit window, select the top-level ADSIEdit node, and then select Action, Connect To.
11. In the Select a Well Known Naming Context drop-down menu, select Default Naming Context, and click OK.
12. Select the Default Naming Context node.
13. Navigate to `Default naming context\CN=System\CN=File Replication`
    `Service\CN=Domain System Volume(SYSVOL share)\CN=<Servername>`, where <Servername> corresponds to the name of the phantom domain controller.
14. Right-click the CN=<Servername>, and select Delete.
15. At the prompt, click Yes to delete the object.
16. Close ADSIEdit.

At this point, after the NTDS Settings are deleted, the server can be normally deleted from the Active Directory Sites and Services snap-in.

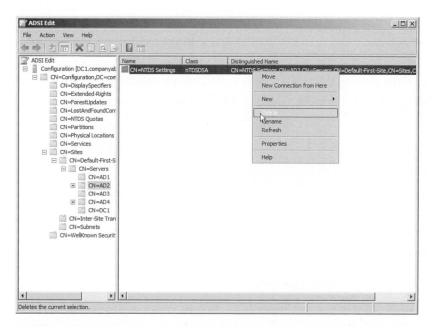

FIGURE 16.5   Deleting phantom domain controllers.

> **NOTE**
>
> ADSIEdit was included in the Support Tools in Windows Server 2003, but is now included in the AD DS Tools that are installed automatically with the Active Directory Domain Services role in Windows Server 2008 R2.

## Upgrading Domain and Forest Functional Levels

Windows Server 2008 R2 Active Directory Domain Services does not immediately begin functioning at a new functional level, even when all domain controllers have been migrated. The domains and forest will be at the original functional levels. You first need to upgrade the functional level of the domain to Windows Server 2008 R2 before you can realize the full advantages of the upgrade. See Chapter 4 for a detailed discussion of the forest and domain functional levels.

> **NOTE**
>
> The act of raising the forest or domain functional levels is irreversible. Be sure that any Windows Server 2003/2008 domain controllers do not need to be added anywhere in the forest before performing this procedure.

After all domain controllers are upgraded or replaced with Windows Server 2008 R2 domain controllers, you can raise the domain level by following these steps:

1. Ensure that all domain controllers in the forest are upgraded to Windows Server 2008 R2.

2. Launch Server Manager on a domain controller.

3. Expand the Roles node and then expand the Active Directory Domain Services node.

4. Select the Active Directory Users and Computers snap-in.

5. Right-click on the domain name, and select Raise Domain Functional Level.

6. In the Select an Available Domain Functional Level drop-down menu, select Windows Server 2008 R2, and then select Raise, as shown in Figure 16.6.

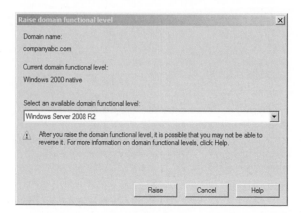

FIGURE 16.6    Raising the domain functional level.

7. Click OK at the warning and then click OK again to complete the task.

Repeat steps 1 through 7 for each domain in the forest. Now the forest functional level can be raised. Depending on the current forest functional level, this change might not add any new features, but it does prevent non-Windows Server 2008 R2 domain controllers from being added in the future. To raise the forest functional level, execute the following steps:

1. Launch Server Manager.

2. Expand the Roles node and select the Active Directory Domain Services node.

3. Scroll down to the Advanced Tools section of the page, and click on the AD Domains and Trusts link.

4. With the topmost Active Directory Domains and Trusts node selected, select Action, Raise Forest Functional Level.

5. In the Select an Available Forest Functional Level drop-down menu, select Windows Server 2008 R2, and then select Raise.

6. Click OK at the warning and then click OK again to complete the task.

After each domain functional level is raised, as well as the forest functional level, the Active Directory environment is completely upgraded and fully compliant with all the AD DS improvements made in Windows Server 2008 R2.

## Moving AD-Integrated DNS Zones to Application Partitions

The final step in a Windows Server 2008 R2 Active Directory upgrade is to move any AD-integrated DNS zones into the newly created application partitions that Windows Server 2008 R2 uses to store DNS information. To accomplish this, follow these steps:

1. Launch Server Manager on a domain controller.
2. Expand the Roles node and then expand the DNS Server node.
3. Select the DNS snap-in.
4. Navigate to DNS\<Servername>\Forward Lookup Zones and select the zone to be moved.
5. Right-click the zone to be moved, and click Properties.
6. Click the Change button to the right of the Replication description.
7. Select either To All DNS Servers Running on Domain Controllers in This Forest or To All DNS Servers Running on Domain Controllers in This Domain, depending on the level of replication you want, as shown in Figure 16.7. Click OK when you are finished and click OK again to save the changes.

FIGURE 16.7   Moving AD-integrated zones.

Repeat the process for any other AD-integrated zones.

# Multiple Domain Consolidation Migration

There are cases when it is better to migrate to a new forest and domain, rather than bring along the baggage of a legacy Active Directory. This includes needing to consolidate names, concerns with the legacy Active Directory schema, or simply to consolidate Active Directory services. The consolidation migration allows an administrator to, in effect, start fresh with a clean installation of Active Directory. Figure 16.8 shows an example of the migration scenario used in this section, where the companyabc.com and asia.companyabc.com will be consolidated to a new forest with the domain companyxyz.com.

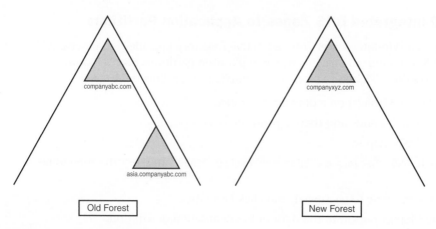

FIGURE 16.8    CompanyXYZ forest.

However, this can be disruptive to the users and applications if not handled carefully. Migrating to a new domain and forest results in changes to the security identifiers, which can impact access. It can also result in password changes, making it difficult for users. However, there are tools and techniques, which are explored in this section, to mitigate the impact to the users and applications.

The introduction of Windows Server 2008 coincided with improvements in the Active Directory Migration Tool, a fully functional domain migration utility. ADMT version 3.1 allows Active Directory users, computers, and groups to be consolidated, collapsed, or restructured to fit the design needs of an organization. In regard to Windows Server 2003/2008 migrations, ADMT v3.1 provides for the flexibility to restructure existing domain environments into new Windows Server 2008 R2 Active Directory environments, keeping security settings, user passwords, and other settings.

## Understanding ADMT v3.1 Functionality

ADMT is an effective way to migrate users, groups, and computers from one domain to another. It is robust enough to migrate security permissions and Exchange mailbox domain settings. ADMT is composed of the following components and functionality:

▶ **ADMT migration wizards**—ADMT includes a series of wizards, each designed to migrate specific components. You can use different wizards to migrate users, groups, computers, service accounts, and trusts.

▶ **Low client impact**—ADMT automatically installs a service on source clients negating the need to manually install client software for the migration. In addition, after the migration is complete, these services are automatically uninstalled.

▶ **SID History and security migrated**—Users can continue to maintain network access to file shares, applications, and other secured network services through migration of the SID History attributes to the new domain. This preserves the extensive security structure of the source domain.

> **NOTE**
>
> One unfortunate change in ADMT v3.1 is the removal of the test migration and rollback functionality that was present in ADMT v2. Microsoft had numerous difficulties with it and chose to deprecate the feature rather than resolve the issues.

ADMT v3.1 installs very easily but requires a thorough knowledge of the various wizards to be used properly. In addition, best-practice processes should be used when migrating from one domain to another.

The migration example in the following sections describes the most common use of the Active Directory Migration Tool: an interforest migration of domain users, groups, and computers into another domain. This procedure is by no means exclusive, and many other migration techniques can be used to achieve proper results. Subsequently, matching the capabilities of ADMT with the migration needs of an organization is important.

## Using ADMT in a Lab Environment

You can develop the most effective lab by creating new domain controllers in the source and target domains and then physically segregating them into a lab network, where they cannot contact the production domain environment. The Operations Master (OM) roles for each domain can then be seized for each domain using the NTDSUTIL utility, which effectively creates exact replicas of all user, group, and computer accounts that can be tested with the ADMT.

## ADMT v3.1 Installation Procedure

Install the ADMT component on a Windows Server 2008 domain controller in the target domain, where the accounts will be migrated to. To install, follow these steps:

> **NOTE**
>
> As of the writing of this book, ADMT 3.1 does not support installation on Windows Server 2008 R2. To utilize the tool, install it on a Windows Server 2008 server. After migration, decommission the Windows Server 2008 server.

1. Download ADMT 3.1 from the Microsoft Download site.
2. Choose Start, Run. Then browse to the download location, select `admtsetup31.exe`, and click Open. Click OK.
3. Click Run to launch the setup.
4. On the Welcome page, click Next to continue.
5. Accept the end-user license agreement (EULA), and click Next to continue.
6. On the Customer Improvement Program page, click Next
7. Accept the default database selection, and click Next to continue.

16

8. Leave the default No, Do Not Import Data from an Existing Database (Default). Click Next to continue.

9. After installation, click Finish to close the wizard.

## ADMT Domain Migration Prerequisites

As previously mentioned, the most important prerequisite for migration with ADMT is lab verification. Testing as many aspects of a migration as possible can help to establish the procedures required and identify potential problems before they occur in the production environment.

That said, several technical prerequisites must be met before the ADMT can function properly. These are as follows:

▶ **Create two-way trusts between source and target domains**—The source and target domains must each be able to communicate with each other and share security credentials. Consequently, it is important to establish trusts between the two domains before running the ADMT.

▶ **Assign proper permissions on source domain and source domain workstations**—The account that will run the ADMT in the target domain must be added into the Builtin\Administrators group in the source domain. In addition, each workstation must include this user as a member of the local Administrators group for the computer migration services to be able to function properly. Domain group changes can be easily accomplished, but a large workstation group change must be scripted, or manually accomplished, prior to migration.

▶ **Create the target OU structure**—The destination for user accounts from the source domain must be designated at several points during the ADMT migration process. Establishing an organizational unit (OU) for the source domain accounts can help to simplify and logically organize the new objects. These objects can be moved to other OUs after the migration and this OU collapsed, if you want.

## Exporting Password Key Information

The Password Export Server (PES) service is used to migrate passwords during interforest migrations. This service must be installed on the source domain and uses a password key generated previously.

A 128-bit encrypted password key must be installed from the target domain on a server in the source domain. This key allows for the migration of password and SID History information from one domain to the next.

To create this key, follow these steps from the command prompt of the ADMT server in the target domain:

1. Insert a USB drive to store the key. (The key can be directed to the network but, for security reasons, directing to a USB drive is better.)

2. Open a command prompt.

3. Type `admt key /option:create /sourcedomain:<SourceDomainName> /keyfile:f:\domain.pes /keypassword:*`, where `<SourceDomainName>` is the NetBIOS or DNS name of the source domain, `f:` is the destination drive for the key, and `domain.pes` is the password encryption filename. Then press Enter.

4. The utility prompts for the password and confirmation of the password. Then the utility creates the password onto the destination drive.

5. Upon successful creation of the key, remove the USB drive and keep it in a safe place.

This needs to be repeated for each domain to be migrated.

## Installing PES on the Source Domain

After exporting the password key from the target domain, the encrypted password key needs to be installed on a domain controller in the source domain. The procedure uses the key generated previously. The following procedure outlines this installation:

1. Insert the USB drive with the exported key from the target domain into the server's disk drive.

2. The installation source is a separate download from Microsoft with a version for 32-bit servers and one for 64-bit servers. This should be downloaded to the source domain controller.

3. Start the Password Migration Installer by browsing to find the downloaded file, `PwdMig.msi`, and running it.

4. On the Welcome page, click Next.

5. Accept the license agreement, and then click Next.

6. Enter the location of the key that was created on the target domain; normally, this is the USB drive that was used to transfer the key. Click Next to continue.

7. Enter and confirm the password that was set on the key file, and click Next.

8. On the Verification page, click Next to continue.

9. Select an administrator account in the target domain for the service in the form domain\account and the password, and then click OK.

10. Click Finish after the installation is complete.

11. Open the Services console (Start, Administrative Tools, Services). Select the Password Export Server service and change its startup type to Automatic.

12. The system must be restarted, so click Yes when prompted to automatically restart. Upon restarting, the proper settings will be in place to make this server a Password Export Server.

The account used for the service will be granted the Logon As a Service right. This needs to be installed on at least one source domain controller in each domain to be migrated.

## Setting Proper Registry Permissions

The installation of the proper components creates special Registry keys, but leaves them disabled by default for security reasons. One of these is the AllowPasswordExport value. You need to enable this Registry key on the source domain to allow passwords to be

**16**

exported from the Password Export Server. The following procedure outlines the use of the Registry Editor to perform this function:

1. On the PES domain controller in the source domain, open the Registry Editor (Start, Regedit).

2. Navigate to `HKEY_LOCAL_MACHINE\SYSTEM\CurrentControlSet\Control\Lsa`.

3. Double-click the AllowPasswordExport DWORD value.

4. Change the properties from 0 to 1 (Hexadecimal).

5. Click OK and close the Registry Editor.

6. Reboot the machine for the Registry changes to be enacted.

This allows passwords to be exported from the source domain to the target domain.

## Configuring Domains for SID Migration

Migration of the source security identifiers (SIDs) into the target domain SID History allows the security assigned in access control lists (ACLs) to work transparently after the migration. This gives the administrator time to reset ACLs on a gradual basis or even after all objects are migrated.

There are several settings that need to be configured to allow for the SIDs to be transferred. These settings include creating a local group in the source domain for auditing, enabling TCP/IP client support on the source PDC emulator, and, finally, enabling auditing on both the source and target domains.

To create the local group on the source domain for auditing, execute the following steps:

1. Log on to a domain controller on the source domain.

2. Launch Active Directory Users and Computers.

3. Create a domain local group named SourceDomain$$$, where SourceDomain is the NetBIOS name of the source domain. For example, the local group for the companyabc.com domain would be companyabc$$$.

Do not add any members to the group, or the migration process will fail.

To enable TCP/IP client support, execute the following steps:

1. Log on to the PDC emulator domain controller in the source domain.

2. Launch the Registry Editor.

3. Navigate to `\HKEY\LocalMachine\System\CurrentControlSet\Control\LSA`.

4. Create the value TcpipClientSupport REG_DWORD and assign it a value of 1.

5. Exit the Registry Editor and restart the computer.

To enable auditing in Windows Server 2008 R2 domains, execute the following steps:

1. Select Start, Administrative Tools, Group Policy Management.

2. Drill Down to Forest, Domains, Domain, Domain Controllers, Default Domain Controller Policy, and then right-click and select Edit.

3. Drill down to Computer Configuration, Policies, Windows Settings, Security Settings, Local Policies, and select the Audit Policy node.

4. Double-click on the Audit Account Management policy.

5. Check the Define These Policy Settings and select both Success and Failure.

6. Click OK to save the changes.

7. Exit the Group Policy Management Editor.

8. Repeat the preceding steps for all source and target domains.

Now the source and target domains will be prepared to transfer SIDs into the SID History.

## Migrating Groups

In most cases, the first objects to be migrated into a new domain should be groups. If users are migrated first, their group membership will not transfer over. However, if the groups exist before the users are migrated, they will automatically find their place in the group structure. To migrate groups using ADMT v3.1, use the Group Account Migration Wizard, as follows:

1. Open the ADMT MMC snap-in (Start, Administrative Tools, Active Directory Migration Tool).

2. Right-click Active Directory Migration Tool in the left pane, and choose Group Account Migration Wizard.

3. Click Next to continue.

4. Type the source and destination domains, select the source and destination domain controllers, and click Next to continue.

5. Choose the Select Groups from Domain option, and click Next.

6. On the subsequent page, you can select the group accounts from the source domain. Select all the groups required by using the Add button and selecting the objects. After you select the groups, click Next to continue.

7. Enter the destination OU for the accounts from the source domain by clicking Browse and selecting the OU created in the steps outlined previously. Click Next to continue.

8. On the following page, there are several options to choose from that determine the nature of the migrated groups. Clicking the Help button details the nature of each setting. In the sample migration, choose the settings shown in Figure 16.9. After choosing the appropriate settings, click Next to continue.

16

FIGURE 16.9    Setting group options.

9. Enter a user account with proper administrative rights on the source domain on the following page. Then click Next to continue.

10. The subsequent page allows for the exclusion of specific directory-level attributes from migration. If you need to exclude any attributes, they can be set here. In this example, no exclusions are set. Click Next to continue.

11. Naming conflicts often arise during domain migrations. In addition, different naming conventions might apply in the new environment. Objects will not be migrated if conflicts occur. Click Next.

12. The verification page is the last wizard page you see before any changes are made. Once again, make sure that the procedure has been tested before running it because ADMT will henceforth write changes to the target Windows Server 2008 R2 Active Directory environment. Click Finish when you're ready to begin group migration.

13. The group migration process then commences. The window shows the migration progress. Click Close when it completes.

The group(s) is (are) now migrated to the new domain.

## Migrating User Accounts

User accounts are the "bread and butter" of domain objects and are among the most important components. The biggest shortcoming of older versions of ADMT was their inability to migrate passwords of user objects, which effectively limited its use. However, ADMT v3.1 does an excellent job of migrating users, their passwords, and the security associated with them. To migrate users, follow these steps:

1. Open the ADMT MMC snap-in (Start, Administrative Tools, Active Directory Migration Tool).

2. Right-click the Active Directory Migration Tool, and choose User Account Migration Wizard.

3. Click Next on the Welcome page.

4. Select the source and target domains on the subsequent page, and click Next to continue.

5. Choose the Select Users from Domain option, and click Next.

6. The following page allows you to choose user accounts for migration. Just click the Add button and select the user accounts to be migrated. After you select all the user accounts, click Next to continue.

7. The next page allows you to choose a target OU for all created users. Choose the OU by clicking the Browse button. After you select it, click Next to continue.

8. Select Migrate Passwords and then select the server in the source domain in which the Password Export Server (PES) service was installed, as covered in the "Installing PES on the Source Domain" section. Click Next to continue.

9. On the Account Transition Options page, leave the default transition options, and click Next.

10. Enter the account to use when adding SID History, which has to have administrative rights on the source domain. Then click Next.

11. The subsequent page deals with User Options settings. Click Help for an overview of each option. Select Translate Roaming Profiles. Then click Next to continue.

12. The next page is for setting exclusions. Specify any property of the user object that should not be migrated here. In this example, no exclusions are set. Click Next to continue.

13. Naming conflicts for user accounts are common. Designate a procedure for dealing with duplicate accounts in advance and enter such information on the next wizard page. Select the appropriate options for duplicate accounts and click Next to continue.

14. The following verification page presents a summary of the procedure that will take place. This is the last page before changes are written to the target domain. Verify the settings and click Finish to continue.

15. The Migration Progress status box displays the migration process as it occurs, indicating the number of successful and unsuccessful accounts created. When the process is complete, review the log by clicking View Log and verify the integrity of the procedure. Click Close when you are finished.

**NOTE**

Depending on if other wizards have already been run, there might be additional steps at this point that happen one time only to set up proper Registry settings, reboot DCs, and create special groups.

## Migrating Computer Accounts

Another important set of objects that must be migrated is also one of the trickier ones. Computer objects must not only be migrated in AD, but they must also be updated at the workstations themselves so that users will be able to log on effectively from their consoles. ADMT seamlessly installs agents on all migrated computer accounts and reboots them, forcing them into their new domain structures.

The account running the ADMT must have local administrator rights to the computers being migrated. The agents must also be accessible over the network, so any firewalls should be disabled for the migration or grant exceptions.

Follow these steps to migrate computer accounts:

1. Open the ADMT MMC snap-in (Start, Administrative Tools, Active Directory Migration Tool).

2. Right-click the Active Directory Migration Tool, and choose Computer Migration Wizard.

3. Click Next on the Welcome page.

4. Type the names of the source and destination domains in the drop-down boxes on the next page, and click Next to continue.

5. Choose the Select Computers from Domain option, and click Next.

6. On the following page, select the computer accounts that will be migrated by clicking the Add button and selecting the appropriate accounts. Click Next to continue.

7. Select the OU the computer accounts will be migrated to, and click Next to continue.

8. The next Translate Objects page allows for the option to specify which settings on the local clients will be migrated. Click the Help button for a detailed description of each item. In this example, select all items, as shown in Figure 16.10. Click Next to continue.

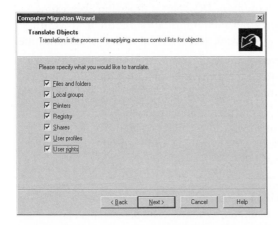

FIGURE 16.10 Specifying objects that will be translated.

9. The subsequent page prompts to choose whether existing security will be replaced, removed, or added to. In this example, replace the security. Click Next to continue.

10. A prompt then informs you that the user rights translation will be performed in Add mode only. Click OK to continue.

11. The next page is important, as it allows an administrator to specify how many minutes a computer will wait before restarting itself (the default is 5 minutes). Click Next to continue.

12. Just as in the previous wizards, exclusions can be set for specific attributes in the following wizard page. Select any exclusions needed and click Next to continue.

13. Naming conflicts are addressed on the subsequent page. If any specific naming conventions or conflict resolution settings are required, enter them here. Click Next to continue.

14. The Completion page lists a summary of the changes that will be made. Review the list and click Finish when you are ready. All clients that will be upgraded are subsequently rebooted.

15. When the migration process is complete, you can view the Migration log by clicking the View Log button. After verifying all settings, click Close.

16. The ADMT Agent Dialog window opens. This tool allows the administrator to control the agent operations. Click Start to run pre-check. This identifies any potential issues with the agent migration. The results of the pre-check will be displayed in the Pre-check column. Verify that all computers passed.

17. In the Agent Actions box, select the Run Pre-check and Agent Operations option button. Then click Start to perform the migration operations.

18. The client agents are subsequently distributed to all clients that have been migrated. Click Close on the ADMT MMC snap-in to end the wizard.

Each agent is installed automatically and counts down until the designated time limit set during the configuration of the Computer Migration Wizard. Then the migrated computers reboot into the new domain with the designated settings migrated.

## Migrating Other Domain Functionality

In addition to the Group, User, and Computer Migration Wizards, several other wizards can be used to migrate specific domain-critical components. These wizards operate using the same principles as those described in the preceding sections and are straightforward in their operation. The following is a list of the additional wizards included in ADMT v3.1:

▶ Security Translation Wizard

▶ Reporting Wizard

▶ Service Account Migration Wizard

▶ Exchange 5.5 Mailbox Translation Wizard

▶ Retry Task Wizard

▶ Password Migration Wizard

Virtually all necessary functionality that needs replacing when migrating from one domain to another can be transferred by using ADMT v3.1. It has proven to be a valuable tool that gives administrators an additional option to consider when migrating and restructuring Active Directory environments.

### Migrating Server Roles to Windows Server 2008 R2

Migrating server roles, system settings, and data from your 32-bit and older Windows operating systems to Windows Server 2008 R2 has been made easier with the introduction of the Windows Server Migration Tools, the Printer Migration Wizard, and the printbrm.exe command-line utility. The following sections go over the installation, setup, and usage of these tools.

### Windows Server Migration Tools

The Windows Server Migration Tools are a Windows Server 2008 R2 feature, installed via the Add Feature Wizard, that uses PowerShell cmdlets to facilitate the migration of server roles, system settings, and data from older versions of Windows and 32-bit versions of Windows to Windows Server 2008 R2. Before the Windows Server Migration Tools can be used to migrate services from one server to another, the tools need to be installed on both the source and destination servers. Because the Windows Server Migration Tools are included with Windows Server 2008 R2, the tool must be packaged and installed on Windows Server 2003 or Windows Server 2008 systems if the source servers are running either of these operating systems.

Windows Server Migration Tools source server requirements are as follows:

- Windows Server 2003 SP2 or later

- 25MB of free space to store the Windows Server Migration Tools folder

- Microsoft .NET Framework 2.0

- Windows PowerShell 1.0 or later

As with any migration, a backup of the system or data being migrated is recommended prior to using the Windows Server Migration Tools. Prior to decommissioning any migrated server, confirm the new server is functioning properly.

To prepare the target Windows Server 2008 R2 server for migration, perform the following steps:

1. On the target server, go to Add Features, click Windows Server Migration Tools, and then click Next.

2. Click Install and then click Close when installation is complete.

3. On the target server, open a command prompt as an administrator.

4. Type CD %windir%\system32\servermigrationtools, and then press Enter.

5. Type smigdeploy /package /architecture x86 /os ws03 /path <folderpath>.

---

**NOTE**

If the source server is 64-bit, change x86 to amd64, and if the source server is Windows Server 2008, change WS03 to WS08. The previous command will create an appropriately named folder in the path specified.

---

To prepare the source server for migration, perform the following steps:

1. Copy <folderpath>\SMT_WS03_x86 from the target server to the source server.

2. Open a command prompt, type cd  <folderpath>\SMT_WS03_x86, and then press Enter.

3. Type .\smigdeploy.exe, and then press Enter.

You have now installed the Windows Server Migration Tools and are ready to start migrating.

### Migrating AD and DNS

An Active Directory Domain Services and DNS migration to Windows Server 2008 R2 can be accomplished quickly and easily. In the following example, we migrate AD Domain Services and DNS from a legacy domain controller to a Windows Server 2008 R2 system. These procedures assume the Windows Server 2008 R2 system is a member server and that you have used adprep.exe to prepare both the forest and domain. If this is not the case, follow the steps earlier in this chapter before continuing on.

To migrate AD and DNS:

1. On the destination server, click Start, click Run, type DCPROMO, and then click OK.

2. On the Welcome page, check Use Advanced Mode Installation, and then click Next.

3. On the Operating System Compatibility page, click Next.

4. Click Existing Forest, confirm that the Add a Domain Controller to an Existing Domain option is selected, and then click Next.

5. Type the domain name, and set the administrative credentials that will be used to perform the installation if you are not already logged on as a domain admin.

6. Select or confirm the correct domain, and then click Next.

7. Select or confirm the correct site, and then click Next.

8. If the source server is a DNS server and a global catalog, leave DNS Server and Global Catalog checked. If it is not a DNS server or a global catalog, uncheck the corresponding role(s).

9. If prompted regarding delegation for this DNS server cannot be found, click Yes.

10. On the Install from Media page, click Next.

11. Select Use This Specific Domain Controller, select the source domain controller, and then click Next.

12. Change or accept the default location for the system folders, and click Next.

13. Provide your Directory Service Restore mode administrator password, and click Next.

14. Review the summary and click Next.

15. Click Finish and restart the domain controller when complete.

16. On the source server, open a command prompt and type dnscmd /enumdirectory-partitions. Note the partitions, as we will be using them on the target server in the next step.

17. On the target server, open a command prompt and type dnscmd /enumdirectory-partitions to confirm the same directory partitions exist and are enlisted.

16

18. If either or both partitions are not listed, type dnscmd /enlistdirectorypartition `<FullyQualifiedDirectoryPartition>`, for example, dnscmd /enlistdirectorypartition DomainDNSZones.companyabc.com.

19. On the source server, type net stop "dns server".

20. Export the following Registry keys: HKLM\System\CurrentControlSet\Services\DNS\Parameters and HKLM\Software\Microsoft\WindowsNT\CurrentVersion\DNS Server.

21. From a command prompt, type xcopy %windir%\system32\dns C:\export /s.

22. If C:\export does not exist, type d when prompted to create the directory.

23. Delete the Samples folder that was just copied to C:\export as it's not needed.

24. From a command prompt, type net start "dns server".

25. On the target server, type Net stop "dns server". Copy both exported Registry keys to the target server, and then double-click them both to complete the import.

26. Copy the content of C:\Export from the source server to %windir%\system32\dns.

27. Type net start "dns server".

> **NOTE**
>
> At this point, both domain controllers are online and servicing client authentication and DNS requests. If the source domain controller is holding any FSMO roles, follow the steps earlier in this chapter to move them to another DC.

> **NOTE**
>
> The next steps, which include migrating the IP configuration, can be done manually or be done using the Windows Server Migration Tools. The process for installing and configuring the tools on both servers is described in detail previously in this chapter.

28. On the source server, click Start, Administrative Tools, Windows Server Migration Tools, right-click Windows Server Migration Tools, and click Run as Administrator.

29. Type Export-smigserversetting –ipconfig –path C:\export -verbose.

30. Provide a password when prompted.

31. Type ipconfig /all > C:\export\sourceIP.txt.

32. Copy the export file and sourceip.txt to your destination server.

33. Change the source server's IP address to a different static IP.

34. On the destination server, click Start, Administrative Tools, Windows Server Migration Tools, right-click Windows Server Migration Tools, and click Run As Administrator.

35. Type import-smigserversetting –ipconfig ALL -sourcephysicaladdress "<sourcephysicaladdress1>" -targetphysicaladdress "<targetphysicaladdress1>" -path <datapath> -verbose.

> **NOTE**
>
> This example assumes one network adapter on the source domain controller. For multiple NICs, add a source and target physical address reference for each. This process is described in more detail later in the chapter.

> **NOTE**
>
> Use `sourceip.txt` to get the physical address information from the source server and use `ipconfig /all` in a separate command prompt to get it from the destination server.

36. Provide the password set during export when prompted.

37. Rename the source DC using the following command: `netdom renamecomputer %computername% /newname:<NewName>`.

38. Rename the target DC using the same command, but change the `<NewName>` to that of the source DC's old name.

39. Restart to complete the migration.

**Migrating DHCP**

DHCP server migration to Windows Server 2008 R2 can be accomplished quickly and easily using the Windows Server Migration Tools. In the following example, we use the Windows Server 2008 R2 Migration Tools to migrate DHCP server settings from a 32-bit Windows Server 2003 SP2 server. The following steps assume you have already followed the procedures for installing the Windows Server Migration Tools and have configured both source and target servers. The overall process of using the Windows Server Migration Tools to migrate DHCP services is as follows:

1. Verify the DHCP configuration on the source server is current and working correctly.

2. Click Start, Administrative Tools, Windows Server Migration Tools, right-click Windows Server Migration Tools, and click Run As Administrator.

3. Type `stop-service dhcpserver`, and press Enter.

4. Type `get-smigserverfeature`, and press Enter.

> **NOTE**
>
> `Get-SmigServerFeature` is the command that scans the source computer for roles or features supported for migration using the Windows Server Migration Tools.

5. Type `export-smigserversetting -featureid dhcp –ipconfig –user ALL -group -path <folderpath> -verbose`.

> **NOTE**
>
> The –user and –group switches are optional and only used when migrating the DHCP Administrators group membership. The –user switch is only used if there are local user accounts listed as members.

6. Type a password when prompted, and press Enter to start the export.

7. After the export completes, move the export created in <folderpath> to the target server.

8. Unauthorize the source DHCP server.

9. On the target server, click Start, Administrative Tools, Windows Server Migration Tools.

10. Type import-smigserversetting –featureid dhcp –path <folderpath> -verbose.

11. Type the password used to create the migration file earlier.

> **NOTE**
>
> The Windows Server Migration Tools installs the required roles and features to complete the migration. In this case, the DHCP server role has been installed.

12. Confirm Success is marked as True to confirm migration is complete.

13. Type start-service dhcpserver.

14. Authorize the new DHCP server to complete the server migration.

### Migrating IP Configuration

The Windows Server Migration Tools can be used to migrate the IP configuration from your source Windows Server 2003, Windows Server 2008, or Windows Server 2008 R2 server to your target Windows Server 2008 R2 system. The IP configuration migration can be included in any other service migration by simply adding the –ipconfig switch to the export-smigserversetting command.

The overall process of using the Windows Server Migration Tools to migrate DHCP services is as follows:

1. On the source server, click Start, Administrative Tools, Windows Server Migration Tools, right-click Windows Server Migration Tools, and click Run As Administrator.

2. Type Export-smigserversetting –ipconfig –path <datapath> -verbose.

3. Provide a password when prompted.

4. When the export is complete, you can copy the export file to your destination server and then start the import process.

> **NOTE**
>
> Take a snapshot of your current IPConfig by typing ipconfig /all > C:\ipconfig.txt. This can be used to verify settings postmigration if needed.

5. On the source server, change the IP address or disconnect it from the network.

6. On the target server, click Start, Administrative Tools, Windows Server Migration Tools, right-click Windows Server Migration Tools, and click Run As Administrator.

7. Type `import-smigserversetting –ipconfig ALL -sourcephysicaladdress` `"<sourcephysicaladdress1>","<sourcephysicaladdress2>" -targetphysicalad-` `dress "<targetphysicaladdress1>","<targetphysicaladdress2>" -path <data-` `path> -verbose.`

8. When prompted, provide the password set during export.

> **NOTE**
>
> You must specify the physical mapping for each adapter indicated by `<sourcephysicaladdress1>` and `<targetphysicaladdress1>`. Use the physical address for each adapter where indicated.

9. A restart is required for some of the settings to take effect.

### Migrating Print Services

Migrating printer settings from an older environment can be accomplished by first exporting print queues, printer ports, and settings before importing them to Windows Server 2008 R2. The tools at your disposal for this job are the Printer Migration Wizard or the `printbrm.exe` command-line utility.

> **NOTE**
>
> Migrating printer settings directly from Windows 2000 servers and older using the Printer Migration Wizard or the `printbrm.exe` command-line tool is not supported. An interim migration to Windows Server 2003 or 2008 is required before migrating to Windows Server 2008 R2.

The Printer Migration Wizard gives you the graphical user interface that walks you through the migration process. This is the easiest method of migrating printers. The steps to migrate print servers are as follows:

1. Open Print Management (Start, Administrative Tools).

2. If not already there, add the remote print server using add/remove servers.

3. Right-click on the remote server and select Export Printers to a File to launch the Printer Migration Wizard.

4. Review the list of items to be exported, and then click Next.

5. Browse to the location on the local server to save the export file, and click Next.

6. Click Finish when the export is complete.

7. Still in Print Management, right-click on the target server, and click Import Printers from a File to launch the Printer Migration Wizard.

8. Browse to the export file location on the local server, click Open, and click Next.

9. Review the list of items to be imported, and click Next.

10. Select Import mode, specifying if you want to overwrite or keep existing printers.

11. Select List in the Directory to specify your preferences for listing the imported printers in the Active Directory.

12. Check Convert LPR Ports to Standard Port Monitors if you want to take advantage of the faster Standard Port Monitor.

13. Click Next to start the import.

14. When the import has completed, click Finish.

---

**NOTE**

For in-place-upgrades, use the Printer Migration Wizard to export printer settings before the upgrade and then import printer settings back to the same server after the upgrade has completed.

---

An alternative method of migrating the printer servers is to use the command-line utility `printbrm.exe`. This utility is not as "pretty" to use as the Printer Migration Wizard, but it allows you to automate the migration process and reduces the number of steps. The steps to migrate using the command line are as follows:

1. On the target server, click Start, All Programs, Accessories, then right-click Command Prompt and select Run As Administrator.

2. Type `CD %Windir%\system 32\spool\tools` and then press Enter.

3. Type `printbrm -s \\<SourceServer>\ -b -f <filename>.printerexport` and then press Enter.

4. Type `printbrm -s \\<TargetServer>\ -r -f <filename>.printerexport` and then press Enter.

# Summary

Although Windows Server 2003/2008 and Windows Server 2008 R2 are close cousins in the operating system family tree, there are some compelling reasons to upgrade to Windows Server 2008 R2 Active Directory Domain Services. The evolutionary nature of Windows Server 2008 R2 makes performing this procedure more straightforward because the upgrade does not require major changes to Active Directory architecture or the operating system design.

In addition, advanced tools such as ADMT v3.1 provide for a broad range of options to bring organizations to Windows Server 2008 R2 functionality and closer to realizing the benefits that can be obtained through a migration.

# Best Practices

The following are best practices from this chapter:

▶ Ensure that one of the postupgrade tasks performed is an audit of all services so that servers that need IIS have the service reenabled after migration.

▶ Because prototype phases of a project are essential to test the design assumptions for a migration or implementation, create a production domain controller and then isolate it in the lab for testing.

▶ Test the hardware compatibility of any server that will be directly upgraded to Windows Server 2008 R2 against the published Hardware Compatibility List from Microsoft.

▶ Keep in mind that Windows Server 2008 R2 is only available as 64-bit when developing migration plans. Older 32-bit hardware will need to be decommissioned or repurposed.

▶ Because the decision to raise the forest or domain functional levels is irreversible, ensure that there is no additional need to add Windows Server 2003/2008 domain controllers anywhere in the forest and that there are no other compatibility issues before performing this procedure.

▶ If the server or servers that hold the OM roles are not directly upgraded to Windows Server 2008 R2 but will instead be retired, move these OM roles to another server.

▶ When using ADMT, migrate groups into a new domain first to keep users' group membership intact.

▶ Use the new Windows Server Migration Tools to migrate server roles to Windows Server 2008 R2.

# Compatibility Testing

At this point in the book, the new features of Windows Server 2008 R2 have been presented and discussed in depth, as have the essential design considerations and migration processes. The goal of this chapter is to examine the process of testing the actual applications that rely on the Windows Server 2008 R2 infrastructure.

This chapter provides insight into the steps necessary to gather information before the testing process begins, how to actually test the applications and document the results, and how to determine whether a more extensive prototype testing process is needed. Going through this process is vital to ensure the success of the project and to avoid a displeased end-user community. The application testing process is intended as a quick way to validate the compatibility and functionality of the proposed end state for the upgrade.

Currently, many companies are seeking to "right-size" their network environment, and might be using the upgrade to Windows Server 2008 R2 as a chance to actually reduce the number of servers within the network infrastructure. At the end of the process, fewer servers will handle the same tasks as before, and new functionality might have been added, making the configurations of the individual servers that much more complex, and making it even more important to thoroughly test the mission-critical networking applications on the server. For example, Windows Server 2008 R2 introduces a tremendous amount of new technologies that enhance failover clustering, web applications, virtualization, security, Remote Desktop Services, improved branch office deployments, and much more, prompting some organizations to replace existing Windows systems with Windows Server 2008 R2. Thus, it's even more important to test this configuration to ensure that the hardware and software are compatible, the performance meets user expectations, and the everyday features used by the employees to share knowledge and collaborate are in place.

The results of the application compatibility testing process will validate the goals of the project or reveal goals that need to be modified because of application incompatibility or instability. If one key application simply won't work reliably on Windows Server 2008 R2, the legacy Windows system might need to be kept as part of the networking environment, which changes the overall design. As discussed in Part II of this book, "Windows Server 2008 R2 Active Directory," a variety of different combinations of Windows Server system configurations can be combined in the end configuration, so the chances that there will be a way to keep the troublesome applications working in the new environment are good.

> **NOTE**
>
> Many legacy systems running old applications and operating systems cannot be upgraded to Windows Server 2008 R2. This is because the application is not compatible with Windows Server 2008 R2, a direct upgrade from the legacy operating system is not supported, and/or the hardware is not compatible with Windows Server 2008 R2. When these circumstances exist, it is common for organizations to utilize virtualization technologies such as Hyper-V Server or VMware to emulate and maintain these legacy applications and operating systems.

# The Importance of Compatibility Testing

The process presented in this chapter is an essential step to take in validating the design for the end state of the migration or upgrade. The size of the organization and the breadth and scope of the upgrade are important factors to consider in determining the level of testing needed, and whether a full prototype should be conducted.

The differences between a prototype phase and an application testing phase can be dramatic or negligible based on the nature of the upgrade. A prototype phase replicates the end state as completely as possible, often using the same hardware in the test lab that will be used in the production rollout.

> **CAUTION**
>
> Application testing can be performed on different hardware with different configurations than the end state, but be aware that the more differences there are between the testing environment and the actual upgraded environment, the greater the risk for unexpected results. Essentially, you can do an application testing phase without a complete prototype phase, but you shouldn't do a prototype phase without a thorough application testing process. This recommendation also applies when planning to use virtual technologies such as Hyper-V.

Most network users don't know or care which server or how many servers perform which task or house which application, but they will be unhappy if an application no longer works after a migration to Windows Server 2008 R2. If the organization already has Active Directory in place and is running Windows Server 2003 systems, the risk of application incompatibility is likely to be less than if the organization is migrating from an older operating system, such as NT 4.0 Server, Windows 2000, or a competing operating system, such as Novell NetWare. It is possible to conduct an in-place upgrade from Windows Server 2003 or Windows Server 2008 to Windows Server 2008 R2. However, a direct upgrade from Windows NT 4.0 or Windows 2000 is not supported.

> **NOTE**
>
> If there is a need to preserve settings by upgrading a legacy operating system such as Windows NT 4.0 or Windows 2000, the system should first be upgraded to Windows Server 2003 and then again to Windows Server 2008 R2. Typically, this is not the recommended approach because the hardware is typically outdated; however, the multiple upgrade approach is doable.

# Preparing for Compatibility Testing

Although the amount of preparation needed will vary based on a number of factors, certain steps should be followed in any organization—the scope of the testing should be identified (what's in and what's out), the goals of the testing process should be clarified, and the process should be mapped out.

A significant advantage of following a phased design methodology, as presented in Chapter 2, "Planning, Prototyping, Migrating, and Deploying Windows Server 2008 R2 Best Practices," is in the planning discussions that take place and in the resulting statements of work, design, and migration documents that are created as deliverables. Often, companies contract with migration experts or Microsoft partners—such as Convergent Computing, also known as CCO—to help companies avoid classic mistakes in the upgrade process. By the end of this planning process, it will be very clear why the project is happening, which departments need which features and capabilities, and what budget is available to perform the work. The timeline and key milestones also will be defined.

If a phased discovery and design process hasn't been followed, this information needs to be gathered to ensure that the testing process addresses the goals of the project stakeholders, and that the right applications are in fact tested and verified by the appropriate people.

## Determining the Scope for Application Testing

At this point in the process, a list should be put together that clarifies which Windows Server 2008 R2 version is to be used, which version of server software will be used, which add-in features are required, and which third-party applications are needed. As discussed previously, Windows Server 2008 R2 comes in Web, Standard, Enterprise, and Datacenter Editions. New in Windows Server 2008 R2, the server comes in 64-bit version only, eliminating the 32-bit version of the server operating system. Smaller companies might choose to use the Standard Edition of Windows Server 2008 R2 operating system, whereas larger organizations might require Enterprise Edition on their server systems for more advanced scalability and fault tolerance.

A key issue to discuss at this point is whether it is acceptable to have multiple versions of the Windows Server operating system in the final solution. Some organizations want to control standards on both software and support services, and require just a single network operating system such as Windows Server 2008 R2 across the board.

**NOTE**

Although the Standard Edition of Windows Server 2008 R2 is significantly less expensive than the Enterprise Edition of the license, cost should not be the primary reason for choosing one version over another. It is a daunting task to upgrade from the Standard to Enterprise Edition, not as simple as just changing a software license key. It requires either setting up a brand-new server with the Windows Server 2008 R2, Enterprise Edition and migrating applications from server to server, or a full upgrade of the Enterprise Edition over an existing Standard Edition license. An organization should seriously consider whether it needs the functionality of the Enterprise Edition before choosing to buy and install the Standard Edition and attempting to upgrade later.

Third-party applications should be identified as well. The applications most often used include tape-backup software modules or agents, antivirus software, fax software, and voicemail integration products. Additional third-party add-on products might include the following:

▶ Administration

▶ Antispam

▶ Backup and storage

▶ Customer relationship management (CRM)

▶ Log monitoring

▶ Line-of-business applications

▶ Migration

▶ Reporting

▶ Security and encryption

The hardware to be used should be listed as well, to ensure that it is available when needed. Ideally, the exact hardware to be used in the upgrade will be ordered for the application testing process, but if that is not possible, hardware with specifications similar to that of the servers that will eventually be used should be allocated. Although processor speed and amount of RAM will most likely not make a difference to whether the application functions properly on the server platform, certain hardware devices should be as similar as possible. Tape drives, for example, should have the same features as the ones to be used in the production environment because this is one of the most critical components. If an autoloader will be used in the production environment, one should be made available for the application testing process. If faxing from the Outlook Inbox is required, the same faxing hardware should be allocated as well. Another example is implementing clustering with a storage area network (SAN) back end. If a SAN will be utilized in production and the test criteria of the lab is to validate clustering functionality, the same production SAN should be utilized in the test environment. By using the same SAN solution, clustering test criteria and clustering functionality can be validated and guaranteed.

Some applications require clients to be present for the testing process, so at least one workstation class system should be available for this purpose. Connectivity to the Internet might also be necessary for testing the functionality of remote access products and antivirus software.

Table 17.1 shows a sample checklist of requirements for summarizing the scope of the application testing phase.

TABLE 17.1     Checklist for Application Testing

**Server #1 Details (Include Version Numbers)**

Server specs required:

> Processor
> RAM
> Hard drive configuration
> Other

Network OS and service packs:

Tape backup software version and agents:

Additional third-party apps required:

Virtualization? Yes/No

Additional hardware required:

> SAN device
> Tape drive
> UPS
> Switch/hub
> Other

Internet access required? Yes/No

This process should not take a great deal of time if previous planning has taken place. If the planning phase was skipped, some brainstorming will be required to ensure that the scope includes all the key ingredients required for the application testing. The goals for the application testing process will also affect the scope, which is covered in the following section.

## Defining the Goals for Compatibility Testing

As with the previous step of defining the scope of the testing process, defining the goals might be a very quick process, or could require some discussions with the stakeholders involved in the project.

One useful way of looking at the goals for the project is to treat them as the checklist for successful completion of the testing. What conditions need to be met for the organization to confidently move forward with the next step in the Windows migration? The next step might be a more complete prototype testing phase. For smaller organizations, it might be a pilot rollout, where the new networking environment is offered to a select group of savvy users.

These goals are separate from the business goals the company might have, such as a more reliable network infrastructure or improved security. A more complete prototype phase could seek to address these goals, while the application testing process stays focused on the performance of the specific combinations of the operating system and embedded and connected applications.

A convenient way to differentiate the goals of the project is to split them into key areas, as described in the following sections.

### Time Frame for the Testing

This goal can be defined with the statement: "The testing must be completed in X days/weeks."

If there is very little time available to perform the testing, this limits how much time can be spent on each application and how many end users can put each through its paces. It also necessitates a lesser degree of documentation. Remember to include time for researching the applications' compatibility with the vendors as part of the timeline. A quick project plan might be useful in this process as a way of verifying the assumptions and selling the timeline to the decision makers.

Contingency time should ideally be built in to this goal. Resources assigned to the testing can get sick or might be pulled back into the office for production support, or applications might require additional testing when problems are encountered. Vendors might not provide trial versions of the software as quickly as desired, or new versions of software or even the hardware itself can be delayed. With many companies seeking to consolidate the number of servers in use, it is not uncommon to see labs evolve through the testing process. Different versions of the Windows operating system are used, as are different versions of various application software programs.

## Estimating the Duration of the Application Testing Process

A good rule of thumb is to allow four hours per application to be tested for basic testing, and eight hours for a more thorough testing process. This allows time for the initial research with the vendors, configuration of the Windows Server 2008 R2 operating system, and testing of the applications. Of course, the total time required will vary based on the types of applications to be tested.

For example, a Windows Server 2008 R2 system with a line-of-business application, such as an enterprise resource planning (ERP) program with a front-end web application, would take an estimated one or two days to test for basic compatibility and functionality, and potentially a week for more rigorous testing.

Note that if more than one resource is available to perform the testing, these configurations can be tested in parallel, shortening the *duration* of the process, but not the *work effort*.

It's always better to have some extra time during the testing phase. This time can be used for more extensive user testing, training, or documentation.

### Budget for the Testing

This goal can be defined with the statement: "The testing must be completed within a budget of $X."

Of course, there might be no budget allocated for testing, but it's better to know this as soon as possible. A lack of budget means that no new hardware can be ordered, evaluation copies of the software (both Microsoft and the third-party applications) need to be used, and no external resources will be brought in. If the budget is available or can be accessed in advance of the production upgrade, a subset of the production hardware should be ordered for this phase. Testing on the exact hardware that will be used in the actual upgrade rather than a cast-off server will yield more valuable results.

More and more virtualization technology is being utilized in test labs for reducing costs associated with hardware procurement. Virtualization is an excellent way to reduce capital expenditures. Keep in mind that hardware-specific prototype testing cannot be achieved when using virtualization as the guest operating system. In addition, performance metrics might get skewed when running more than one guest operating system on a virtual server.

### Resources to Be Used

This goal can be defined with the statement: "The testing will be completed by in-house resources and/or external consultants."

Often, the internal network administration staff is too busy with daily tasks or tackling emergencies that spring up (which might be the reason for the upgrade in the first place), and staff personnel should not be expected to dedicate 100% of their time to the testing process.

If an outside consulting firm with expertise in Windows Server 2008 R2 is going to be used in the testing process, it can be a good leverage point to have already created and decided upon an internal budget for the testing process. This cuts down on the time it takes to debate the approaches from competing firms.

### Extent of the Testing

The extent of compatibility testing can be defined with the statement: "Each application will be tested for basic, midlevel, or complete compatibility and feature sets."

This goal might be set for different types of applications where some mission-critical applications would need to have extensive testing, whereas less-critical applications might have more basic testing performed. A short time frame with a tightly limited budget won't allow for extensive testing, so basic compatibility will most likely be the goal.

---

**Defining the Different Levels of Compatibility Testing**

*Basic compatibility testing*, as used in this chapter, essentially means that the mission-critical applications are tested to verify that they load without errors and perform their primary functions properly with Windows Server 2008 R2. Often the goal with basic testing is to simply see whether the application works, without spending a lot of time or money on hardware and resources, and with a minimum amount of documentation and training. Note that this level of testing reduces but does not eliminate the risks involved in the production rollout.

*Midlevel testing* is defined as a process whereby Windows Server 2008 R2 is configured with all the applications that will be present in the eventual implementation, so that the test configuration matches the production configuration as closely as possible to reduce the chance of surprise behavior during the rollout. This level of testing requires more preparation to understand the configuration and more involvement from testing resources, and should include end users. Some training should take place during the process, and documentation is created to record the server configurations and details of the testing process. Although this level of testing greatly reduces the risks of problems during the production migration or upgrade, the migration process of moving data between servers and training the resources on this process hasn't been covered, so some uncertainty still exists.

*Complete testing* adds additional resource training and possibly end-user training during the process, and should include testing of the actual migration process. Complete training requires more documentation to record the processes required to build or image servers and perform the migration steps. Complete testing is what is typically defined as a prototype phase.

---

### Training Requirements During Testing

This goal can be defined with the statement: "Company IT resources will/will not receive training during the application testing process."

Although the IT resources performing the testing will learn a great deal by going through the testing process, the organization might want to provide additional training to these individuals, especially if new functionality and applications are being tested. If external consultants are brought in, it is important that the organization's own resources are still involved in the testing process for training and validation purposes. The application testing phase might be an excellent time to have help desk personnel or departmental managers in the user community learn more about new features that will soon be offered so they can help support the user community and generate excitement for the project.

### Documentation Required

This goal can be defined with the statement: "Documentation will/will not be generated to summarize the process and results."

Again, the budget and timeline for the testing will affect the answer to this question. Many organizations require a paper trail for all testing procedures, especially when the Windows infrastructure will have an impact on the viability of the business itself. For other organizations, the networking environment is not as critical, so less or no documentation might be required.

The application testing phase is a great opportunity to document the steps required for application installations or upgrades if time permits, and this level of instruction can greatly facilitate the production rollout of the upgraded networking components.

### Extent of User Community Involvement

This goal can be defined with the statement: "End users will be included/will not be included in the testing process."

If there are applications such as customer relationship management (CRM), document routing, voicemail or paging add-ons, or connectivity to PDAs and mobile devices, a higher level of user testing (at least from the power users and executives) should be considered.

### Fate of the Testing Lab

This goal can be defined with the statement: "The application testing lab will/will not remain in place after the testing is complete."

There are a number of reasons that organizations decide to keep labs in place after their primary purpose has been served. Whenever a patch or upgrade to Windows Server 2008 R2 or to a third-party application integrates with Windows Server 2008 R2, it is advisable to test it in a nonproduction environment. Even seemingly innocent patches to antivirus products can crash a production server. Other items might require user testing to see whether they should be rolled out to the production servers.

## Documenting the Compatibility Testing Plan

The information discussed and gathered through the previous exercises needs to be gathered and distributed to the stakeholders to ensure that the members of the team are working toward the same goals. These components are the scope and the goals of the application testing process, and should include the timeline, budget, extent of the testing (basic, midlevel, complete), training requirements, documentation requirements, and fate of the testing lab. This step is even more important if a formal discovery and design phase was not completed.

By taking the time to document these constraints, the testing process will be more structured and less likely to miss a key step or get bogged down on one application. The individuals performing the testing will essentially have a checklist of the exact testing process, and are less likely to spend an inordinate amount of time on one application, or "get creative" and try products that are not within the scope of work. After the testing is complete, the stakeholders will also have made it clear what is expected in terms of documentation so the results of the testing can be presented and reviewed efficiently.

This summary document should be presented to the stakeholders of the project for review and approval. The organization will then be ready to proceed with the research and testing process for Windows Server 2008 R2 compatibility.

# Researching Products and Applications

The next step in the compatibility testing process is to actually begin research on the products and applications being tested. With the documented goals and expectations of the necessary compatibility testing process, the organization can proceed with information gathering.

## Taking Inventory of Network Systems

The first step of the information-gathering process is to take inventory of the network systems that will be part of the Windows Server 2008 R2 environment. These systems include domain controllers, application servers, gateway systems, and utility servers.

> **NOTE**
>
> When you're identifying the systems that are part of the Windows Server 2008 R2 environment, you should create separate lists that note whether a server is a domain controller or member server of the environment, or whether the server is standalone and does not directly interact with the domain. Usually, standalone servers that are not integrated into the domain are significantly less likely to require a parallel upgrade to Windows Server 2008 R2. Because the system is operating as a standalone, it will typically continue to operate in that manner and can be removed from the scope of testing and migration during the initial migration phase. Removing this server can also greatly minimize the scope of the project by limiting the number of servers that need to be included in the testing and migration process.

For systems that are part of the network domain, the devices should be identified by which network operating system they are running. Another item that should be captured is whether the server is physical or virtual. Table 17.2 shows a sample system device inventory sheet.

TABLE 17.2   System Device Inventory Table

| Server Name | Member of Domain (Y/N) | Domain Controller (Y/N) | Virtual Server (Y/N) | General Functions | Operating System |
|---|---|---|---|---|---|
| SERVER-A | Y | Y | Y | DC, DNS, DHCP | Windows 2003 R2 |
| SERVER-B | Y | N | N | Exchange Server | Windows 2000 SP3 |
| SERVER-C | Y | N | Y | File/Print Server | Windows NT 4.0 |
| SERVER-D | N | N | N | WWW Web Server | Windows 2003 SP1 |

## Taking Inventory of Applications on Existing Servers

Now that you have a list of the server systems on your network, the next step is to take inventory of the applications running on the systems. Care should be taken to identify all applications running on a system, including tape software, antivirus software, and network monitoring and management utilities.

The primary applications that need to be upgraded will be obvious, as well as the standard services such as data backup and antivirus software. However, in most organizations, additional applications hiding on the network need to be identified. If System Center Configuration Manager 2007 (ConfigMgr) is in use, or another network management tool with inventory capabilities, it should also be able to provide this basic information.

> **NOTE**
>
> Another angle to validating that all applications are tested before a migration is to simply ask all departmental managers to provide a list of applications that are essential for them and their employees. This takes the opposite angle of looking not at the servers and the applications, but looking at what the managers or employees in the organization say they use as part of their job responsibilities. From these lists, you can put together a master list.

## Understanding the Differences Between Applications and Windows Services

We need to make a distinction as it pertains to the Windows Server 2008 R2 operating environment. Applications are programs that run on top of Windows Server 2008 R2, such as application tools or front-end services, and services are programs that integrate with the

17

operating system, such as SQL, Exchange, antivirus applications, and so on. As discussed previously, in the .NET Framework, applications are designed to sit on top of the Windows platform, so the more embedded the legacy application is in the NOS, the greater the potential for problems.

It is also helpful to separate the Microsoft and non-Microsoft applications and services. The Microsoft applications that are to be upgraded to the new Windows Server 2008 R2 environment are likely to have been thoroughly tested by Microsoft. Possible incompatibilities should have been identified, and a great deal of information will be available on Microsoft TechNet or on the Microsoft product page of its website. On the other hand, for non-Microsoft applications and services, weeks could pass after a product's release before information regarding any compatibility problems with the Microsoft operating system surfaces. This is also true for service packs and product updates where problems might be made public weeks or months after the release of the update.

Furthermore, many organizations that create custom applications will find that little information is available on Windows Server 2008 R2 compatibility, so they could require more complex lab tests to validate compatibility.

## Completing an Inventory Sheet per Application

An organization should create an inventory sheet for each application being validated. Having an inventory sheet per application can result in dozens, if not hundreds, of sheets of paper. However, each application needs to go through extensive verification for compatibility, so the information gathered will be helpful.

A sample product inventory sheet includes the following categories:

- ▶ Vendor name
- ▶ Product name
- ▶ Version number
- ▶ Application or service?
- ▶ Mission-critical?
- ▶ Compatible with Windows Server 2008 R2 (Y/N)?
- ▶ Vendor-stated requirements to make compatible
- ▶ Decision to migrate (update, upgrade, replace, remain on existing OS, stop using, proceed without vendor support)

Additional items that might be relevant could include which offices or departments use the application, how many users need it, and so on.

Any notes from the vendor, such as whitepapers for migration, tip/trick migration steps, upgrade utilities, and any other documentation should be printed, downloaded, and kept on file. Although a vendor might state that a product is compatible on its website today, you might find that by the time an upgrade occurs, the vendor has changed its statement on compatibility. Any backup information that led to the decision to proceed with the migration might also be useful in the future.

## Prioritizing the Applications on the List

After you complete and review the list, you will have specific information showing the consensus of which applications are critical and which are not.

There is no need to treat all applications and utilities with equal importance because a simple utility that does not work and is not identified as a critical application can be easily upgraded or replaced later and should not hold up the migration. On the other hand, problems with a mission-critical business application should be reviewed in detail because they might affect the whole upgrade process.

Remember that certain utility applications should be considered critical to any network environment. These include tape backup (with the appropriate agents) and virus-protection software. In organizations that perform network and systems management, management tools and agents are also essential.

# Verifying Compatibility with Vendors

Armed with the full list of applications that need to be tested for compatibility, the application testing team can now start hitting the phones and delving into the vendors' websites for the compatibility information.

For early adopters of certain application software programs, more research might be necessary because vendors tend to lag behind in publishing statements of compatibility with new products. Past experience has shown that simply using the search feature on the vendor's site can be a frustrating process, so having an actual contact who has a vested interest in providing the latest and greatest information (such as the company's sales representative) can be a great time-saver.

Each vendor tends to use its own terminology when discussing Windows Server 2008 R2 compatibility (especially when it isn't 100% tested); a functional way to define the level of compatibility is with the following four areas:

- ▶ Compatible

- ▶ Compatible with patches or updates

- ▶ Not compatible (requires version upgrade)

- ▶ Not compatible and no compatible version available (requires new product)

When possible, it is also a good practice to gather information about the specifics of the testing environment, such as the version and SP level of the Windows operating system the application was tested with, along with the hardware devices (if applicable, such as tape drives, specific PDAs and mobile devices, and so forth) tested.

## Tracking Sheets for Application Compatibility Research

For organizational purposes, a tracking sheet should be created for each application to record the information discovered from the vendors. A sample product inventory sheet includes the following categories:

▶ Vendor name

▶ Product name and version number

▶ Vendor contact name and contact information

▶ Level of criticality: Critical, near-critical, or nice to have

▶ Compatible with Windows Server 2008 R2: Yes/no/did not say

▶ Vendor-stated requirements to upgrade or make application compatible

▶ Recommended action: None, patch/fix/update, version upgrade, replace with new product, stop using product, continue using product without vendor support

▶ Operating system compatibility: Windows Server 2008 R2, Windows Server 2008, Windows Server 2003 R2, Windows Server 2003, Windows 2000 Server, Windows NT Server, other

▶ Processor architecture compatibility: 64-bit compatible?

▶ Notes: Conversation notes, URLs used, copies of printed compatibility statements, or hard copy provided by vendor

It is a matter of judgment as to the extent of the notes from discussions with the vendors and materials printed from websites that are retained and included with the inventory sheet and kept on file. Remember that URLs change frequently, so it makes sense to print the information when it is located.

In cases where product upgrades are required, information can be recorded on the part numbers, cost, and other pertinent information.

## Six States of Compatibility

There are essentially six possible states of compatibility that can be defined, based on the input from the vendors, and that need to be verified during the testing process. These levels of compatibility roughly equate to levels of risk of unanticipated behavior and issues during the upgrade process:

1. The application version currently in use is compatible with Windows Server 2008 R2.

2. The application version currently in use is compatible with Windows Server 2008 R2, with a minor update or service patch.

3. The application currently in use is compatible with Windows Server 2008 R2, with a version upgrade of the application.

4. The application currently in use is not compatible with Windows Server 2008 R2 and no upgrade is available, but it will be kept running as is on an older version of

Windows Server (or other network operating system) in the upgraded Windows Server 2008 R2 networking environment.

5. The application currently in use is not compatible with Windows Server 2008 R2, and will be phased out and not used after the upgrade is complete.

6. The application currently in use is not compatible with Windows Server 2008 R2 per the vendor, or no information on compatibility was available, but it apparently runs on Windows Server 2008 R2 so the organization needs to determine if it will run the application on an operating system potentially not supported by the application vendor.

Each of these states is discussed in more detail in the following sections.

### Using a Windows Server 2008 R2–Compatible Application

Although most applications require some sort of upgrade, the vendor might simply state that the version currently in use will work properly with Windows Server 2008 R2 and provide supporting documentation or specify a URL with more information on the topic. This is more likely to be the case with applications that don't integrate with the Windows Server components, but instead interface with certain components, and might even be installed on separate servers.

It is up to the organization to determine whether testing is necessary to verify the vendor's compatibility statement. If the application in question is critical to the integrity or security of the Windows Server 2008 R2 operating system, or provides the users with features and capabilities that enhance their business activities and transactions, testing is definitely recommended. For upgrades that have short time frames and limited budgets available for testing (basic testing as defined earlier in the chapter), these applications might be demoted to the bottom of the list of priorities and would be tested only after the applications requiring updates or upgrades had been tested.

A clear benefit of the applications that the vendor verifies as being Windows Server 2008 R2–compatible is that the administrative staff will already know how to install and support the product and how it interfaces with Windows Server 2008 R2 and the help desk; end users won't need to be trained or endure the learning curves required by new versions of the products.

17

**NOTE**

As mentioned previously, make sure to clarify what NOS and which specific version of Windows operating system was used in the testing process, including the processor architecture version, because seemingly insignificant changes, such as security patches to the OS, can influence the product's performance in your upgraded environment. Tape backup software is notorious for being very sensitive to minor changes in the version of Windows, and tape backups can appear to be working when they aren't. If devices such as text pagers or mobile devices are involved in the process, the specific operating systems tested and the details of the hardware models should be verified if possible to make sure that the vendor testing included the models in use by the organization.

If a number of applications are being installed on one Windows Server 2008 R2 system, unpredictable conflicts are possible. Therefore, testing is still recommended for mission-critical Windows Server 2008 R2 applications, even for applications the vendor asserts are fully compatible with Windows Server 2008 R2.

### Requiring a Minor Update or Service Patch for Compatibility

When upgrading from Windows Server 2008 or Windows Server 2003, many applications simply need a relatively minor service update or patch for compatibility with Windows Server 2008 R2. This is less likely to be the case when migrating from Windows NT 4.0 or Windows 2000 Server or a completely different operating system, such as Novell NetWare or Linux. This is also evident when running web applications because IIS 7.5 has evolved and been completely rewritten.

During the testing process, the service updates and patches are typically quick and easy to install, are available over the Internet, and are often free of charge. It is important to read any notes or readme files that come with the update because specific settings in the Windows Server 2008 R2 configuration might need to be modified for them to work. These updates and patches tend to change and be updated themselves after they are released, so it is worth checking periodically to see whether new revisions have become available.

These types of updates generally do not affect the core features or functionality of the products in most cases, although some new features might be introduced; so they have little training and support ramifications because the help desk and support staff will already be experienced in supporting the products.

### Applications That Require a Version Upgrade for Compatibility

In other cases, especially when migrating from Windows NT 4.0 or another network operating system, a complete migration strategy is required, and this tends to be a more complex process than downloading a patch or installing a minor update to the product. The process will vary by product, with some allowing an in-place upgrade, where the software is not on the Windows Server 2008 R2 server itself, and others simply installing from scratch.

The amount of time required to install and test these upgrades is greater and the learning curve steeper, and the danger of technical complexities and issues increases. Thus, additional time should be allowed for testing the installation process of the new products, configuring them for optimal Windows connectivity, and fine-tuning for performance factors. Training for the IT resources and help desk staff will be important because of the probability of significant differences between the new and old versions.

Compatibility with all hardware devices should not be taken for granted, whether it's the server itself, tape backup devices, or SAN hardware.

If a new version of the product is required, it can be difficult to avoid paying for the upgrade, so budget can become a factor. Some vendors can be persuaded to provide evaluation copies that expire after 30–120 days.

### Handling an Incompatible Application That Will Remain "As Is"

As discussed earlier in this chapter, Windows Server 2008 R2 can coexist with previous versions of the Windows operating system, so a Windows Server 2008 R2 migration does not require that every server be upgraded. In larger organizations, for example, smaller offices might choose to remain on legacy versions for a period of time, if there are legitimate business reasons or cost concerns with upgrading expensive applications. If custom scripts or applications have been written that integrate and add functionality to Windows NT 4.0, Windows 2000, or Windows Server 2003, it might make more sense to simply keep those servers intact on the network.

Although it might sound like an opportunity to skip any testing because the server configurations aren't changing, connectivity to the new Windows Server 2008 R2 configurations still needs to be tested, to ensure that the functionality between the servers is stable.

Again, in this scenario, the application itself is not upgraded, modified, or changed, so there won't be a requirement for administrative or end-user training.

### Incompatible Applications That Won't Be Used

An organization might decide that because an application is incompatible with Windows Server 2008 R2, no upgrade is available, or the cost is prohibitive, so it will simply retire it. Windows Server 2008 R2 includes a variety of new features, as discussed throughout the book, which might make certain utilities and management tools unnecessary. For example, a disaster recovery module for a tape backup product might no longer be necessary after clustering is implemented.

Care should be taken during the testing process to note the differences that the administrative staff, help desk, and end users will notice in the day-to-day interactions with the networking system. If features are disappearing, a survey to assess the impact can be very helpful. Many users will raise a fuss if a feature suddenly goes away, even if it was rarely used, whereas the complaints could be avoided if they had been informed in advance.

17

### Officially Incompatible Applications That Seem to Work Fine

The final category applies to situations in which no information can be found about compatibility. Some vendors choose to provide no information and take no stance on compatibility with Windows Server 2008 R2. This puts the organization in a precarious situation, as it has to rely on internal testing results to make a decision. Even if the application seems to work properly, the decision might be made to phase out or retire the product if its failure could harm the business process. If the application performs a valuable function, it is probably time to look for or create a replacement, or at least to allocate time for this process at a later time.

If the organization chooses to keep the application, it might be kept in place on an older version of Windows or moved to the new Windows Server 2008 R2 environment. In either case, the administrative staff, help desk, and end users should be warned that the application is not officially supported or officially compatible and might behave erratically.

## Creating an Upgrade Decision Matrix

Although each application will have its own inventory sheet, it is helpful to put together a brief summary document outlining the final results of the vendor research process and the ramifications to the network upgrade project. As with all documents that affect the scope and end state of the network infrastructure, this document should be reviewed and approved by the project stakeholders.

This document can be expanded to summarize which applications will be installed on which network server if there are going to be multiple Windows Server 2008 R2 servers in the final configuration. In this way, the document can serve as a checklist to follow during the actual testing process.

## Assessing the Effects of the Compatibility Results on the Compatibility Testing Plan

After all the data has been collected on the compatibility, lack of compatibility, or lack of information, the compatibility testing plan should be revisited to see whether changes need to be made. As discussed earlier in the chapter, the components of the compatibility testing plan are the scope of the application testing process and the goals of the process (timeline, budget, extent of the testing, training requirements, documentation requirements, and fate of the testing lab).

Some of the goals might now be more difficult to meet, and require additional budget, time, and resources. If essential network applications need to be replaced with version upgrades or a solution from a different vendor, additional time for testing and training might also be required. Certain key end users might also need to roll up their sleeves and perform hands-on testing to make sure that the new products perform to their expectations.

This might be the point in the application testing process at which a decision is made that a more complete prototype testing phase is needed, and the lab would be expanded to more closely, or exactly, resemble the end state of the migration.

# Microsoft Assessment and Planning (MAP) Toolkit

As mentioned throughout the chapter, it is important to conduct compatibility testing when upgrading or migrating to Windows Server 2008 R2. It is essential to have specific knowledge about each server within the infrastructure and whether or not the server and associated hardware and software are ready for Windows Server 2008 R2. Microsoft has a free toolkit that will help accelerate your migration to Windows Server 2008 R2.

The MAP toolkit can assist with a migration or upgrade to Windows Server 2008 R2 by conducting inventory, assessments, and reporting on servers throughout the infrastructure. In addition, unlike other tools, it can gather information without installing agents on servers.

The following prerequisites are required for installing the toolkit on Windows Server 2008 R2:

▶ Microsoft Word 2007 or Word 2003 SP2

▶ Microsoft Word Primary Interop Assemblies

▶ Microsoft Excel 2007 or Excel 2003 SP2

▶ Microsoft Excel Primary Interop Assemblies

▶ Microsoft Office Compatibility Pack for Office 2007

▶ Microsoft Windows Server Installer

▶ .NET Framework 3.5 Service Pack 1 or higher

▶ SQL Server 2008 Express

▶ Computer is not a domain controller

After the prerequisites have been installed, the toolkit can be downloaded from http://technet.microsoft.com/en-us/solutionaccelerators/dd537573.aspx. Once the toolkit is installed, you can create a server inventory report, which will identify currently installed operating systems. The report will also include detailed analysis of software and hardware readiness and compatibility with Windows Server 2008 R2.

# Lab-Testing Existing Applications

With the preparation and research completed and the compatibility testing plan verified as needed, the actual testing can begin. The testing process should be fairly anticlimactic at this point because the process has been discussed at length, and it will be clear what the testing goals are and which applications will be tested. Due diligence in terms of vendor research should be complete, and now it is just a matter of building the test server or servers and documenting the results.

The testing process can yield unforeseen results because the exact combination of hardware and software might affect the performance of a key application; but far better to have this occur in a nonproduction environment in which failures won't affect the organization's ability to deliver its services.

During the testing process, valuable experience with the installation and upgrade process will be gained and will contribute to the success of the production migration. The migration team will be familiar with—or possibly experts at—the installation and application migration processes when it counts, and are more likely to avoid configuration mistakes and resolve technical issues.

## Allocating and Configuring Hardware

Ideally, the budget will be available to purchase the same server hardware and related peripherals (such as tape drives, UPSs, mobile devices, and applications) that will be used in the production migration. This is preferable to using a server machine that has been sitting in a closet for an undetermined period of time, which might respond differently than the eventual hardware that will be used. Using old hardware can actually generate more work in the long run and adds more variables to an already complex process.

If the testing process is to exactly mirror the production environment, this would be considered to be a prototype phase, which is generally broader in scope than compatibility testing, and requires additional hardware, software, and time to complete. A prototype phase is recommended for more complex networks in which the upgrade process is riskier and more involved and in which the budget, time, and resources are available.

Don't forget to allocate a representative workstation for each desktop operating system that is supported by the organization and a sample remote access system, such as a typical laptop or mobile device that is used by the sales force or traveling executive.

## Allocating and Configuring Windows Server 2008 R2

By this point, the software has been ordered, allocated, downloaded, and set aside for easy access, along with any notes taken or installation procedures downloaded in the research phase. If some time has elapsed since the compatibility research with the vendors, it is worth checking to see whether any new patches have been released. The upgrade decision matrix discussed earlier in the chapter is an excellent checklist to have on hand during this process to make sure that nothing is missed that could cause delays during the testing process.

When configuring the servers with the appropriate operating systems, the company standards for configurations, based on industry best practices, should be adhered to, if they have been documented. Standards can include the level of hard drive redundancy, separation of the application files and data files, naming conventions, roles of the servers, approved and tested security updates, and security configurations.

Next, Windows Server 2008 R2 should be configured to also meet company standards and then for the essential utilities that will protect the integrity of the data and the operating system, which typically include the backup software, antivirus software, and management utilities and applications. After this base configuration is completed, it can be worth performing a complete backup of the system or taking a snapshot of the server configuration, using an application such as Ghost, in case the subsequent testing is problematic and a rollback is necessary.

## Loading the Remaining Applications

With Windows Server 2008 R2 configured with the core operating system and essential utilities, the value-added applications can be tested. Value-added applications enhance the functionality of Windows and enable the users to perform their jobs more efficiently and drive the business more effectively. It's helpful to provide a project plan calendar or schedule to the end users who will be assisting in the testing process at this point so they know when their services will be needed.

There are so many different combinations of applications that might be installed and tested at this point that the different permutations can't all be covered in this chapter. As a basic guideline, first test the most essential applications and the applications that were not identified previously as being compatible. By tackling the applications that are more likely to be problematic early on in the process, the testing resources will be fresh and any flags can be raised to the stakeholders while there is still time left in the testing process for remediation.

Thorough testing by the end users is recommended, as is inclusion of the help desk staff in the process. Notes taken during the testing process will be valuable in creating any configuration guides or migration processes for the production implementation.

> **NOTE**
>
> Beyond basic functionality, data entry, and access to application-specific data, some additional tests that indicate an application has been successfully installed in the test environment include printing to different standard printers, running standard reports, exporting and importing data, and exchanging information with other systems or devices. Testing should be done by end users of the application and administrative IT staff who support, maintain, and manage the application. Notes should be taken on the process and the results because they can be very useful during the production migration.

## Certified for Windows Server 2008 R2

Microsoft offers a program that enables vendors to innovate on the Windows Server 2008 R2 platform and related technologies. This program is called Innovate on Windows Server, and it allows vendors, organizations, and partners to build, test, and certify that their applications and products are compatible with Windows Server 2008 R2. Once certified, a logo will be placed on the product stating Certified for Windows Server 2008 R2.

During the analysis phase of whether existing applications will be compatible with Windows Server 2008 R2, it is a best practice to validate that the applications do carry the Certified for Windows Server 2008 R2 logo by contacting the manufacturer. By having the logo, application testing and additional analysis of a specific application is minimized when upgrading to Windows Server 2008 R2.

The Innovate on Windows Server partner program can be found at the following hyperlink: www.innovateonwindowsserver.com/Default.aspx.

## Testing the Migration and Upgrade Process

This section touches on the next logical step in the testing process. After it has been verified that the final configuration agreed upon in the planning process is stable and which applications and utilities will be installed on which server, the actual upgrade process can be tested. The upgrade process is covered in Chapter 16, "Migrating from Windows Server 2003/2008 to Windows Server 2008 R2."

# Documenting the Results of the Compatibility Testing

A number of documents can be produced during the compatibility testing process. Understanding the expectations of the stakeholders and what the documents will be used for is important. For example, more detailed budgetary information might need to be compiled based on the information, or go-no-go decisions might need to be reached. Thus, a summary of the improvements offered by Windows Server 2008 R2 in the areas of reliability, performance visible to the user community, and features improved and added might need to be presented in a convincing fashion.

At a minimum, a summary of the testing process should be created, and a final recommendation for the applications to be included in the production upgrade or migration should be provided to the stakeholders. This can be as simple as the upgrade decision matrix discussed earlier in the chapter, or it can be more thorough, including detailed notes of the exact testing procedures followed. Notes can be made available summarizing the results of end-user testing, validating the applications, and describing results—both positive and negative.

If the testing hardware is the same as the hardware that will be used in the production upgrade, server configuration documents that list the details of the hardware and software configurations can be created; they will ensure that the servers built in the production environment will have the same fundamental configuration as was tested in the lab.

A more detailed build document can be created that walks the technician through the exact steps required to build the Windows Server 2008 R2 system, in cases where many network servers need to be created in a short period of time.

The level of effort or the amount of time to actually perform the upgrade or the migration of a sample subdirectory can be recorded as part of the documentation, and this information can be very helpful in planning the total amount of time that will be required to perform the upgrade or migration.

# Determining Whether a Prototype Phase Is Required

The issue of whether a more complete prototype phase is needed or if a more limited application compatibility testing phase is sufficient has come up several times in this chapter. The essential difference between the two is that the prototype phase duplicates as exactly as possible the actual end state of the upgrade, from server hardware to peripherals and software, so that the entire upgrade process can be tested to reduce the chance of surprises during the production upgrade. The application testing phase can be less extensive, involve a single server or virtual servers, and be designed to verify that the applications required will work reliably on the Windows Server 2008 R2 configuration. Compatibility testing can take as little time as a week—from goal definition, to research, to actual testing. A prototype phase takes considerably longer because of the additional steps required.

The following is a checklist that will help your organization make the decision:

- ▶ Is sufficient budget available for a subset of the actual hardware that will be used in the upgrade?

- ▶ Is sufficient time available for the configuration of the prototype lab and testing of the software?

- ▶ Are the internal resources available for a period of time long enough to finish the prototype testing? Is the budget available to pay for external consulting resources to complete the work?

- ▶ Is the Windows networking environment mission-critical to the business' capability to go about its daily activities and generate revenues, and will interruption of Windows services cost the company an unacceptable amount of money?

- ▶ Does the actual migration process need to be tested and documented to ensure the success of the upgrade?

- ▶ Do resources need to be trained on the upgrade process (building the servers, and configuring the network operating system and related applications)?

- ▶ Do the applications that will be tested need to be compatible with 64-bit processor architecture?

If you find that the answer to more than half of these questions is yes, it's likely that a prototype phase will be required.

# Summary

Windows Server 2008 R2 compatibility testing should be performed before any upgrade or migration. The process can be completed very quickly for smaller networks (basic testing) or for larger networks with fairly simple networking environments.

The first steps include identifying the scope and goals of the project to make sure that the stakeholders are involved in determining the success factors for the project. Then research needs to be performed, internal to the company, on which in-place applications are network-related. This includes not only Windows Server, but tape backup software, antivirus software, network management and monitoring tools, add-ons, and inventory sheets created summarizing this information. Decisions as to which applications are critical, near-critical, or just nice to have should also be made. Research should then be performed with the vendors of the products, tracking sheets should be created to record this information, and the application should be categorized in one of six states of compatibility. Next, the testing begins, with the configuration of the lab environment that is isolated from the production network, and the applications are loaded and tested by both administrative and end user or help desk staff. The results are then documented, and the final decisions of whether to proceed are made.

17

With this process, the production upgrade or migration is smoother, and the likelihood of technical problems that can harm the business' ability to transact or provide its services is greatly reduced. The problems are identified beforehand and resolved, and the resources who will perform the work gain familiarity with all the products and processes involved.

## Best Practices

The following are best practices from this chapter:

- ▶ Take the time to understand the goals of the project (What will the organization gain by doing the upgrade?), as well as the scope of the project (What is included and what is excluded from the project?).

- ▶ Understand all the applications that connect with Windows Server 2008 R2 and whether they are critical, near-critical, or simply nice to have.

- ▶ Accelerate a migration to Windows Server 2008 R2 by using the MAP toolkit.

- ▶ Document the research process for each application because this will prove to be very valuable if problems are encountered during the testing process.

- ▶ Create a lab environment that is as close to the final end state of the upgrade as possible. This reduces the variables that can cause problems at the least opportune time.

- ▶ Test applications for compatibility with both typical end users of the application and application administrators who support, maintain, and manage the application.

- ▶ Leverage Virtual Server technology to minimize the cost associated with procuring hardware for a test lab.

- ▶ Ensure that applications have been tested for compatibility with a 64-bit operating system, such as Windows Server 2008 R2.

# Windows Server 2008 R2 Administration

Administrators can administer a Windows Server 2008 R2 infrastructure by learning only a few simple tasks and applying them at different levels and to different objects. This enables the administrator to easily scale the administration of the infrastructure without proportionally increasing the work. However, this requires defining and enforcing an administrative model.

The overall management of an environment is composed of administrative tasks that touch almost every aspect of the network, including user administration, server and workstation administration, and network administration. For example, in a single day, an administrator might check for a successful server backup, reset a user's password, add users to or remove them from existing groups, or manage local area network (LAN) and wide area network (WAN) hardware. Although each of these tasks can independently be very simple or difficult in nature, administrators should at least understand their portion of the overall enterprise network and understand how the different components that make up the network communicate and rely on one another.

Active Directory forms the basis for the administrative model in Windows Server 2008 R2. The Active Directory structure is used to control the authorization and access to other technologies such as Microsoft Exchange 2007, System Center Operations Manager 2007, and SharePoint 2007. This chapter focuses on the common Windows Server 2008 R2 Active Directory (AD) user and group administrative tasks and touches on the management of Active Directory sites to optimize user access and replication performance.

# Defining the Administrative Model

Before the computer and networking environment can be managed effectively, an organization and its IT group must first define how the tasks will be assigned and managed. The job of delegating responsibility for the network defines the organization's administrative model. Three different types of administrative models can be used to logically break up the management of the enterprise network between several IT specialists or departments within the organization's IT division. These models are as follows:

- Centralized
- Distributed
- Mixed

When there is no administrative model, the environment is managed chaotically, and the bulk of work is usually made up of firefighting. Server updates and modifications must more frequently be performed on the spot without proper testing. Also, when administrative or maintenance tasks are not performed correctly or consistently, securing the environment and auditing administrative events are nearly impossible. Environments that do not follow an administrative model are administered reactively rather than proactively.

To choose or define the correct administrative model, the organization must discover what services are needed in each location and where the administrators with the skills to manage these services are located. Placing administrators in remote offices that require very little IT administration might be a waste of money, but when the small group is composed of VIPs in the company, it might be a good idea to give these elite users the highest level of service available.

## The Centralized Administration Model

The centralized administration model is simple in concept: All the IT-related administration is controlled by one group, usually located at one physical location. In the centralized model, all the critical servers are housed in one or a few locations instead of distributed at each location. This arrangement allows for a central backup and always having the correct IT staff member available when a server fails. For example, if an organization uses the Microsoft Exchange 2010 messaging server and a server is located at each site, a qualified staff member might not be available at each location if data or the entire server must be recovered from backup. In such a scenario, administration would need to be handled remotely if possible, but in a centralized administration model, both the Exchange Server 2010 administrator and the servers would be located in the same location, enabling recovery and administration to be handled as efficiently and effectively as possible.

## The Distributed Administration Model

The distributed administration model is the opposite of the centralized model in that tasks can be divided among IT and non-IT staff members in various locations. The rights to perform administrative tasks can be granted based on geography, department, or job function. Also, administrative control can be granted for a specific network service such as domain name system (DNS) or Dynamic Host Configuration Protocol (DHCP). This allows separation of server and workstation administration without giving unqualified administrators the rights to modify network settings or security.

Windows Server 2008 R2 systems allow for granular administrative rights and permissions, giving enterprise administrators more flexibility when assigning tasks to staff members. Distributed administration based only on geographical proximity is commonly found among organizations. After all, if a physical visit to the server, workstation, or network device is needed, having the closest qualified administrator responsible for it might prove more effective.

## The Mixed Administration Model

The mixed administration model is a mix of administrative responsibilities, using both centralized and distributed administration. One example could be that all security policies and standard server configurations are defined from a central site or headquarters, but the implementation and management of servers are defined by physical location, limiting administrators from changing configurations on servers in other locations. Also, the rights to manage only specified user accounts can be granted to provide even more distributed administration on a per-site or per-department basis.

# Examining Active Directory Site Administration

Sites can be different things, depending on whom you ask. If you ask an operations manager, she might describe a site as any physical location from which the organization operates business. Within the scope of Active Directory, a site defines the internal and external replication boundaries and helps users locate the closest servers for authentication and network resource access. It can also serve as a boundary of administrative control, such as delegating authority to a local administrator to their AD site. This section discusses Active Directory site administration.

## Sites

A site is made up of a site name; subnets within that site; links and bridges to other sites; site-based policies; and, of course, the servers, workstations, and services provided within that site. Some of the components, such as the servers and workstations, are dynamically configured to a site based on their network configuration. Domain controller services and Distributed File System (DFS) targets are also located within sites by the network configuration of the server on which the resources are hosted.

AD sites can be configured to match a single or many locations that have high-bandwidth connectivity between them. They can be optimized for replication and, during regular daily operations, require very little network bandwidth. After an AD site is defined, servers and client workstations use the information stored in the site configuration to locate the closest domain controllers, global catalog servers, and distributed file shares. Configuring a site can be a simple task, but if the site topology is not defined correctly, network access speed might suffer because servers and users might connect to resources across the WAN instead of using local resources.

As mentioned previously, configuring a site should take only a short time because there are very few components to manipulate. In most cases, defining and setting up an Active Directory site configuration might take only a few hours of work. After initial setup, AD sites rarely need to be modified unless changes are made to network addressing, domain controllers are added to or removed from a site, or new sites are added and old ones are decommissioned.

Examples of sites might include the name of the city where the company locations are, airport codes for the cities, or the office identifier if the company already has one.

## Subnets

Subnets define the network boundaries of a site and limit WAN traffic by allowing clients to find local services before searching across a WAN link. Many administrators do not define subnets for locations that do not have local servers; instead, they relate site subnets only to Active Directory domain controller replication.

If a user workstation subnet is not defined within Active Directory, the workstation picks another domain controller essentially at random. The domain controller could be one from the same physical location or it could be one on another continent across multiple WAN links. The user workstation might authenticate and download policies or run services from a domain controller that is not directly connected to a LAN. This authentication and download across a WAN could create excessive traffic and unacceptable response times.

In looking at the Active Directory infrastructure, it might seem that branch offices with no domain controller could simply be lumped with their central office site by adding the branch office subnets to the main office site. This would save a lot of configuration time needed to create those branch office sites.

This is somewhat shortsighted, as many other applications are Active Directory-aware and leverage the Active Directory site architecture to control the behavior of their application. This includes the Distributed File System (DFS) and System Center Configuration Manager (SCCM) 2007. Thus, it is important to fully define the Active Directory site architecture, including the subnets to mirror the WAN architecture of the organization.

All subnets should be defined in Active Directory Sites and Services to ensure that the proper domain controller assignments are made to workstations. And all locations should have their own sites and subnets defined, even if there is no domain controller currently in the location. This ensures that resources are allocated correctly by the Active Directory infrastructure not only for domain services, but other services as well.

## Site Links

Site links control Active Directory replication and connect individual sites directly together. A site link is configured for a particular type of protocol (namely, IP or SMTP) and the frequency and schedule of replication is configured within the link. Site links are used by the Active Directory Knowledge Consistency Checker (KCC) to build the proper connections to ensure that replication occurs in the most efficient manner.

Once again, some administrators do not fully define the site architecture and don't create sites for locations that do not have a domain controller. The reasoning is that the sites are used by Active Directory for replication, and so domain controller-challenged locations don't need a site defined.

Just like with subnet design, this is also shortsighted, as many other applications are Active Directory-aware and leverage the Active Directory site architecture to control the behavior of their application. Site links are also used by Active Directory-aware applications to understand the physical topology to optimize WAN communications. This includes DFS and SCCM 2007.

Thus, it is important to fully define the Active Directory site architecture, including both subnets and site links to mirror the WAN architecture of the organization.

Examples of site links include a site link for every WAN link, such as from the main office to each of the branch offices. For fully meshed offices, a single site link can be used. This can be done for just a subset of offices if needed.

## Site Group Policies

Site group policies allow computer and user configurations and permissions to be defined in one location and applied to all the computers and/or users within the site. Because the scope of a site can span all the domains and domain controllers in a forest, site policies should be used with caution. Therefore, site policies are not commonly used except to define custom network security settings for sites with higher requirements or to delegate administrative rights when administration is performed on a mostly geographic basis.

> **NOTE**
>
> Because sites are usually defined according to high-bandwidth connectivity, some design best practices should be followed when you're defining the requirements for a site. If possible, sites should contain local network services, such as domain controllers, global catalog servers, DNS servers, DHCP servers, and, if necessary, Windows Internet Naming Service (WINS) servers. This way, if network connectivity between sites is disrupted, the local site network will remain functional for authentication, Group Policy, name resolution, and resource lookup. Placing file servers at each site might also make sense unless files are housed centrally for security or backup considerations.

18

That said, there are some specific applications where site group policies can prove to be very useful. For example, it is a best practice to have VPN users assigned to a site in Active Directory. This is accomplished by creating a VPN site in Active Directory Sites and Services and assigning the VPN subnet to that site. Then, group policies that add additional controls can be assigned to the VPN site using a Site Group Policy Object. That way, when users use their laptop to connect in the office, they receive the standard set of group policies. However, when they use the same laptop to connect to the office via the VPN, they get the additional policies needed for VPN access.

# Configuring Sites

The job of configuring and creating sites belongs to the administrators who manage Active Directory, but those who manage the network must be well informed and possibly involved in the design. Whether Active Directory and the network are handled by the same or different groups, they affect each other, and undesired network utilization or failed network connectivity might result. For example, if the Active Directory administrator defines the entire enterprise as a single site, and several Active Directory changes happen each day, replication connections would exist across the enterprise, and replication traffic might be heavy, causing poor network performance for other networking services. On the other side, if the network administrator allows only specific ports to communicate between certain subnets, adding Active Directory might require that additional ports be opened or involve specific network requirements on the servers at each location.

For these examples, the company locations and IP addresses in Table 18.1 will be used. The company has a hub-and-spoke topology, with each branch office connected to the main office. The main office has an IPv4 and an IPv6 subnet.

TABLE 18.1    Common Subnet Mask to Prefix Length

| Location | Role | Subnets | WAN Link |
|----------|------|---------|----------|
| Oakland, USA | Main Office | 192.168.3.0/24 | |
| | | 2001:db8:1234:5678::/64 | |
| Boston, USA | Branch Office | 192.168.10.0/24 | T3 |
| Paris, France | Branch Office | 192.168.11.0/24 | T1 |
| Tokyo, Japan | Branch Office | 192.168.12.0/24 | T1 |

## Creating a Site

When creating a site, Active Directory and network administrators must decide how often AD will replicate between sites. They also must share certain information such as the line speed between the sites and the IP addresses of the servers that will be replicating. Knowing the line speed helps determine the correct cost of a site link. For the network administrator, knowing which IP addresses to expect network traffic from on certain ports is helpful when troubleshooting or monitoring the network. To create a site, the AD administrator needs a site name and subnet and also needs to know which other sites will replicate to the new site.

To create a site, follow these steps:

1. Launch Server Manager on a domain controller.
2. Expand the Roles folder.

> **NOTE**
>
> The Server Manager console is used extensively throughout this chapter and is often the central point of administration. See Chapter 20, "Windows Server 2008 R2 Management and Maintenance Practices," for details on the Server Manager console.

3. Expand the Active Directory Domain Services folder.

4. Expand the Active Directory Sites and Services snap-in.

5. Right-click the Sites container and choose New Site.

6. Type in the name of the site and select any existing site link, as shown in Figure 18.1. Then click OK to create the site.

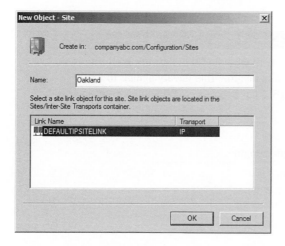

FIGURE 18.1   Creating a new site.

7. A pop-up window might appear, stating what tasks still need to be completed to properly create a site. Read the information, take notes if necessary, and click OK.

Repeat this for each site that needs to be created. For the sample company, Table 18.2 lists the sites that will be created.

TABLE 18.2   Company ABC Sites

| Location | Site Name |
| --- | --- |
| Oakland, USA | Oakland |
| Boston, USA | Boston |

TABLE 18.2    Company ABC Sites

| Location | Site Name |
| --- | --- |
| Paris, France | Paris |
| Tokyo, Japan | Tokyo |

**Creating Site Subnets**

After you create a site, it should be listed in the console window. To complete the site creation process, follow these steps:

1. Within the Active Directory Sites and Services snap-in, right-click the Subnets container, and choose New Subnet.

2. Type in the address prefix in the Prefix field—for example, 192.168.3.0/24 for the Oakland site IPv4 subnet.

> **NOTE**
>
> The address prefix is the IP address and the mask entered in network prefix notation. This is the format "IP network address/prefix length." This is very similar to the IP address and subnet mask format. Table 18.3 lists some common subnet masks and their prefix length values.

TABLE 18.3    Common Subnet Mask to Prefix Length

| Subnet Mask | Prefix Length |
| --- | --- |
| 255.0.0.0 | 8 |
| 255.255.0.0 | 16 |
| 255.255.255.0 | 24 |

3. Select the appropriate site from the list at the bottom of the window to associate it with the new subnet.

4. Click OK to create the new subnet.

Repeat this for each subnet in the locations. Table 18.4 lists the resulting entries for the sample Company ABC.

TABLE 18.4    Company ABC Sites and Subnets

| Location | Site Name | Subnets |
| --- | --- | --- |
| Oakland, USA | Oakland | 192.168.3.0/24<br>2001:db8:1234:5678::/64 |
| Boston, USA | Boston | 192.168.10.0/24 |

TABLE 18.4    Company ABC Sites and Subnets

| Location | Site Name | Subnets |
|---|---|---|
| Paris, France | Paris | 192.168.11.0/24 |
| Tokyo, Japan | Tokyo | 192.168.12.0/24 |

### Adding Domain Controllers to Sites

If a new domain controller is added to a forest, it will dynamically join a site with a matching subnet if the site topology is already configured and subnets have been previously defined. However, a preexisting domain controller will not change sites automatically, unlike workstations and member servers. A domain controller has to be moved manually if the topology changes. If an existing domain controller is being moved to a new site or the site topology or replication strategy has changed, you can follow these steps to move a domain controller to a different site:

1. Launch Server Manager on a domain controller.

2. Expand the Roles folder.

3. Expand the Active Directory Domain Services folder.

4. Expand the Active Directory Sites and Services snap-in.

5. Expand the Sites folder.

6. Locate the site that contains the desired domain controller to move. You can browse the site servers by expanding the site and selecting the Servers container of the site, as shown in Figure 18.2.

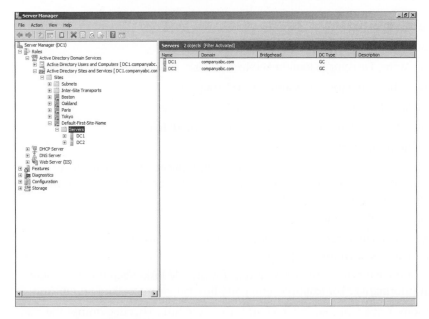

FIGURE 18.2    Browsing for site servers.

18

7. When you locate the desired server, take note of the source site, right-click the server name, and choose Move.

8. When a window opens listing all the sites in the forest, select the destination site, and click OK to initiate the server move.

9. When the move is complete, verify that the domain controller has been placed in the correct Servers container of the desired site.

---

**NOTE**

Although you can manually create replication connections if the desired connections are not automatically created by the intersite topology generator (ISTG) within 15 minutes after moving the server, the fact that the automatic creation did not happen usually indicates a problem with site configuration and replication. For more information on the ISTG and replication connections, refer to Chapter 7, "Active Directory Infrastructure."

---

## Establishing Site Links

Site links establish connectivity between domain controllers to allow Active Directory replication to be managed and scheduled. The Active Directory database, global catalog, group policies, and the domain controller SYSVOL directory replicate according to the replication schedule configured in a site link. For more information on site links, refer to Chapter 7.

To create an IP-based site link, follow these steps:

1. Launch Server Manager on a domain controller.

2. Expand the Roles folder.

3. Expand the Active Directory Domain Services folder.

4. Expand the Active Directory Sites and Services snap-in.

5. Expand the Sites folder.

6. Expand the Inter-Site Transports folder, and select the IP folder.

7. Right-click the IP container and select New Site Link.

8. Enter a name for the site link, select a site that will replicate Active Directory using this site link, and click Add. Repeat this step until all the desired sites are in the right pane, as shown in Figure 18.3 for Oakland and Boston sites.

9. Click OK to create the site link.

10. Back in the Active Directory Sites and Services console, right-click the new site link in the right pane, and choose Properties.

11. At the top of the window, enter a description for the site link. Keep the description simple but informative. For example, enter Site link between Oakland and Boston.

12. At the bottom of the window, enter a cost for the site link. This determines the preferred link if more than one is available. See the text following these steps for a

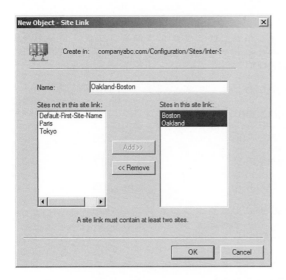

FIGURE 18.3   Adding sites to a site link.

discussion of site link costs and Table 18.5 for some typical costs. In this example, the connection between Oakland and Boston is a T3 and the cost is set to 220.

TABLE 18.5   Typical Link Types, Speeds, and Site Link Costs

| Link Type | Link Speed (bps) | Cost |
| --- | --- | --- |
| Dial-up 9600 | 9,600 | 1042 |
| Dial-up 14.4 | 14,400 | 884 |
| Dial-up 28.8 | 28,800 | 702 |
| Dial-up 33.6 | 33,600 | 671 |
| Leased 56 | 56,000 | 586 |
| ISDN Single | 64,000 | 567 |
| Fractional T1 - 1 Ch | 64,000 | 567 |
| DS0 | 64,000 | 567 |
| ISDN Dual | 128,000 | 486 |
| Fractional T1 - 2 Ch | 128,000 | 486 |
| Fractional T1 - 4 Ch | 256,000 | 425 |
| Fractional T1 - 8 Ch | 512,000 | 378 |

18

TABLE 18.5    Typical Link Types, Speeds, and Site Link Costs

| Link Type | Link Speed (bps) | Cost |
| --- | --- | --- |
| DS1/T1 | 1,544,000 | 321 |
| DS2/T2 | 6,312,000 | 269 |
| 10BaseT | 10,000,000 | 256 |
| DS3/T3 | 44,736,000 | 220 |
| OC1 | 51,840,000 | 217 |
| 100BaseT | 100,000,000 | 205 |
| FDDI | 100,000,000 | 205 |
| OC3/STM1 | 155,520,000 | 197 |
| OC12/STM4 | 622,080,000 | 177 |
| 1000BaseT | 1,000,000,000 | 171 |
| OC48/STM16 | 2,488,320,000 | 160 |
| OC192/STM64 | 9,953,280,000 | 146 |

13. Enter the replication frequency. This number indicates how often Active Directory will attempt to replicate during the allowed replication schedule. The default is 180 minutes. The lowest this can be set to between sites is 15 minutes. In most well-connected organizations, the frequency is usually set to 15.

14. Click the Change Schedule button to configure specific intervals when Active Directory should not replicate. This is not typically used in modern well-connected networks. Click OK to leave unchanged.

15. Click OK on the Site Link property page to complete the site link configuration.

After the site link is configured, the Active Directory connections between domain controllers in different sites will generate new connections to optimize replication when the KCC runs. The cost of a site link is an arbitrary value that is selected by the administrator to reflect the speed and reliability of the physical connection between the sites. When you lower the cost value on the link, the priority is increased. Site links have a replication interval and a schedule that are independent of the cost. The cost is used by the KCC to prefer one site link path over another.

Cost values determine which connector is preferred for data transfer. Costs are associated with address spaces and connected routing group information. When costs are assigned to the links, the KCC will compute the replication topology automatically and clients will automatically go to the cheapest link. Link costs can be based on the following formula:

```
Cost = 1024/log(bw/1000)
Where
    bw = Bandwidth of the link between the two sites in bits per second (bps)
    Cost = Site link cost setting
```

Table 18.5 lists the cost values for some typical bandwidths. The values in the cost column would be entered into the Cost field of the site link properties.

Of course, in a simple network with only a single WAN connection between locations, the site link cost value can be left at the default value of 100 with little impact. In this configuration, all links are considered equal by the KCC.

In general, a site link topology serves to provide an Active Directory-integrated method for defining preferred routes between physically remote sites connected by WAN links.

The site links created for Company ABC are shown in Table 18.6. The site links represent the hub-and-spoke topology on the Company ABC WAN, with the appropriate costs based on the link speeds.

TABLE 18.6   Company ABC Site Links and Sites

| Site Link Name | Cost | Replication Interval | Sites |
| --- | --- | --- | --- |
| Oakland-Boston | 220 | 15 | Oakland, Boston |
| Oakland-Paris | 321 | 15 | Oakland, Paris |
| Oakland-Tokyo | 321 | 15 | Oakland, Tokyo |

> **NOTE**
>
> Once the Active Directory site topology has been defined, it is important to remove all the sites from the default site link (DEFAULTIPSITELINK). This prevents replication connections from being generated by the KCC automatically. It is also a best practice to delete the default site and site link—that is, Default-First-Site-Name and DEFAULTIP-SITELINK. This ensures that they don't get mistakenly used.

## Delegating Control at the Site Level

Control is sometimes delegated at the site level to give network administrators the rights to manage Active Directory replication without giving them the rights to manage any additional Active Directory objects. Site delegation can also do just the opposite, effectively denying network administrators the right to access Active Directory objects on a per-site basis. Specific administrative rights can be granted using the built-in Delegate Control Wizard, whereas others can be set for all the site objects using a site's group policies.

To delegate control at the site level, follow these steps:

1. Launch Server Manager on a domain controller.
2. Expand the Roles folder.

18

3. Expand the Active Directory Domain Services folder.

4. Expand the Active Directory Sites and Services snap-in.

5. Expand the Sites folder.

6. Right-click the Sites container and select Delegate Control.

7. Click Next on the Delegate Control Wizard Welcome screen.

8. Using the Add button, select the user, users, or groups that will delegate control over the site, and click OK. You can choose an Active Directory group created for the organization's networking team or the default group named Network Configuration Operators.

9. Click Next to continue.

10. On the Active Directory Object Type page, select This Folder, Existing Objects in This Folder, and Creation of New Objects in This Folder, which is the default option to delegate control. The permissions granted will trickle down to each of the containers below the initial Sites container. If you don't want this outcome, return to step 6 and select the appropriate site or subnet container.

11. Click Next to continue.

12. On the Permissions page, check the desired permissions type check boxes and choose each permission the administrator or, in this case, the networking group should have.

13. Click Next and then click Finish to complete the Delegate Control Wizard.

# Examining Windows Server 2008 R2 Active Directory Groups

An Active Directory group is made up of a collection of objects (users and computers and other groups used to simplify resource access and for emailing purposes). Groups can be used for granting administrative rights, granting access to network resources, or distributing email. There are many flavors of groups, and depending on which mode the domain is running in, certain group functionality might not be available.

## Group Types

Windows Server 2008 R2 Active Directory supports two distinct types of groups: distribution and security. Both have their own particular uses and advantages if they are used properly and their characteristics are understood.

### Distribution Groups

Distribution groups allow for the grouping of contacts, users, or groups primarily for emailing purposes. These types of groups cannot be used for granting or denying access to domain-based resources. Discretionary access control lists (DACLs), which are used to grant or deny access to resources or define user rights, are made up of access control entries (ACEs). Distribution groups are not security enabled and cannot be used within a DACL. In some cases, this might simplify security management when outside vendors need to be located in address books but will never need access to resources in the domain or forest.

### Security Groups

Security groups are security enabled and can be used for assigning user rights and resource permissions or for applying computer and Active Directory-based group policies. Using a security group instead of individual users simplifies administration. Groups can be created for particular resources or tasks, and when changes are made to the list of users who require access, only the group membership must be modified to reflect the changes throughout each resource that uses this group.

To perform administrative tasks, security groups can be defined for different levels of responsibility. For example, a level 1 server administrator might have the right to reset user passwords and manage workstations, whereas a level 2 administrator might have those permissions plus the right to add or remove objects from a particular organizational unit or domain. The level of granularity granted is immense, so creating a functional security group structure can be one way to simplify administration across the enterprise. This is sometimes referred to as role-based access control or RBAC.

Security groups can also be used for emailing purposes, so they can serve a dual purpose.

## Group Scopes in Active Directory

To complicate the group issue somewhat more, after the type of group is determined, the scope of the group must also be chosen. The scope, simply put, defines the boundaries of who can be a member of the group and where the group can be used. Because only security groups can be used to delegate control or grant resource access, security group types are implied for the rest of this chapter.

### Domain Local Groups

Domain local groups can be used to assign permissions to perform domain-based administrative tasks and to access resources hosted on domain controllers. These groups can contain members from any domain in the forest and can also contain other groups as members. Domain local groups can be assigned permissions only in the domain in which they are hosted.

### Global Groups

Global groups are somewhat more functional than domain local groups. These groups can contain members only from the domain in which they are hosted, but they can be assigned permissions to resources or delegated control to perform administrative tasks or manage services across multiple domains when the proper domain trusts are in place.

### Universal Groups

Universal groups can contain users, groups, contacts, or computers from any domain in the forest. This simplifies the need to have single-domain groups that have members in multiple forests. Universal group memberships in large, multidomain environments should be kept low or should not be changed frequently because group membership is replicated across domains and populated in the global catalog. As a best practice in these environments, create a universal group to span domains but have only a global group from each domain as a member. This practice reduces cross-domain replication.

> **NOTE**
>
> Universal security groups can be created only in domains running in Windows 2000 Native, Windows Server 2003, Windows Server 2008, or Windows Server 2008 R2 domain functional level. If this level cannot be reached, use global groups from each domain when setting permissions on resources that need to be accessed from users in many domains.

# Creating Groups

When it comes to creating groups, understanding the characteristics and limitations of each different type and scope is only half the battle. Other points to consider for group creation are how the group will be used and who will need to be a member of the group. A group is commonly used for three separate functions, including delegating administrative rights, distributing email, and securing network resources such as file shares and printer devices. To help clarify group usage, the following examples show how the different groups can be used in different administrative scenarios.

## User Administration in a Single Domain

If a group is needed to simplify the process of granting rights to reset user passwords in a single domain, either a domain local or global security group would suffice. The actual domain user rights should have local groups applied only to their access control lists or settings, but these local groups should have global groups as members. For a single-domain model, if the specific user rights need to be granted only at the domain level, a domain local group with users as members would be fine. However, if you need to add the same group of users to an access control list on a member server resource or you need to create a completely new domain, the domain local group cannot be used. This is the main reason it is recommended to place users only into global groups and assign permissions to resources using local groups that have global groups as members. After you use this strategy and use global groups over and over, saving administration time, the reasoning will be validated.

> **NOTE**
>
> With current group management mechanisms including most domains moving out of "Mixed mode" into at least Windows 2003 Native mode, the use of universal groups is more common. Also with Exchange 2007 and Exchange 2010 effectively requiring universal groups as distribution lists, the default group in an enterprise tends to be the de facto group in place of global groups in the past.

## User Administration Across a Forest of Domains

When multiple domains need to be supported by the same IT staff, even if the domain levels are set to Windows 2000 Mixed mode, each domain's Domain Admins group should be added to each domain's Administrators group. For example, domain A's Administrators group would have Domain A Domain Admins, Domain B Domain Admins, and Domain C Domain Admins groups as members. You would need to add these domains whenever a resource or administrative task needs to grant or deny groups from each domain access to a resource in the forest.

If all the domains in the forest run in Windows 2000 Native, Windows Server 2003, or Windows Server 2008 R2 functional level, you could create a universal security group named "Forest Admins" with each of the domain's Domain Admin groups as members. Then you would need to configure only a single entry to allow all the administrators access forestwide for a particular resource or user right. Universal security groups are preferred because they can have members from each domain, but if the group strategy necessitates their use, domain local and domain global groups could still handle most situations.

## Domain Functional Level and Groups

There are many different domain functional levels, with each level adding more functionality. The reason for all the different levels is to provide backward compatibility to support domain controllers running on different platforms. This allows a phased migration of the domain controllers. The four domain functional levels are as follows:

▶ **Windows 2000 Native**—This domain level allows only Windows 2000, Windows Server 2003, Windows Server 2008, and Windows Server 2008 R2 domain controllers in the domain. Universal security groups can be leveraged, along with universal and global security group nesting. This level can be raised to Windows Server 2003 Native level, which also enables you to change some existing groups' scopes and types on the fly.

▶ **Windows Server 2003**—This level allows only Windows Server 2003, Windows Server 2008, and Windows Server 2008 R2 domain controllers. It provides all the features of the Windows 2000 Native domain level, plus additional security and functionality features, such as domain rename, logon time stamp updates, and selective authentication.

▶ **Windows Server 2008**—The Windows Server 2008 functional level allows only Windows Server 2008 and Windows Server 2008 R2 domain controllers. This level supports all the features of the Windows Server 2003 functional level plus additional features such as AES 128 and AES 256 encryption support for Kerberos, last interactive logon information to provide visibility into true logon activity by the user, fine-grained password policies to allow policies to be set on a per-group and per-user basis, and uses DFSR for Active Directory replication.

▶ **Windows Server 2008 R2**—The Windows Server 2008 R2 functional level adds Authentication Mechanism Assurance. This essentially inserts the type of logon method into the Kerberos token and allows applications to determine authorization or access based on the logon method. For example, an application could only allow logon type 2 (interactive) and not type 3 (network) to ensure that the user was actually at a workstation.

The most important note is that all of the domain functional levels supported by Windows Server 2008 R2 allow universal security groups.

## Creating AD Groups

Now that you understand what kinds of groups you can create and what they can be used for, you are ready to create a group. To do so, follow these steps:

1. Launch Server Manager on a domain controller.
2. Expand the Roles folder.
3. Expand the Active Directory Domain Services folder.
4. Expand the Active Directory Users and Computers snap-in.
5. Expand the domain folder (in this example, the companyabc.com folder).
6. Select a container—for example, the Users container. Right-click it and select New, Group.
7. Enter the group name and select the appropriate group type and scope, as shown in Figure 18.4.

FIGURE 18.4    Creating a group.

8. Click OK to finish creating the group.

## Populating Groups

After you create a group, you can add members to it. The domain level that the domain is running in determines whether this group can have other groups as members.

To add members to an existing group, follow these steps:

1. Launch Server Manager on a domain controller.
2. Expand the Roles folder.
3. Expand the Active Directory Domain Services folder.
4. Expand the Active Directory Users and Computers snap-in.
5. Expand the domain folder (in this example, the companyabc.com folder).
6. Select the Users container that was used in the previous section. In the right pane, right-click the group that was created earlier, and select Properties.
7. Enter a description for the group on the General tab and then click the Members tab.
8. Click Add to add members to the group.
9. In the Select Users, Contacts, Computers, or Groups window, type in the name of each group member separated by a semicolon and click OK to add these users to the group. If you don't know the names, clicking the Advanced button opens a window where you can perform a search to locate the desired members.
10. When all the members are listed on the Members tab of the group's property page, click OK to complete the operation.

## Group Management

After a group is created, it needs to be managed by an administrator, users, or a combination of both, depending on the dynamics of the group.

To delegate control of a group to a particular user, follow these steps:

1. Launch Server Manager on a domain controller.
2. Expand the Roles folder.
3. Expand the Active Directory Domain Services folder.
4. Select Active Directory Users and Computers and select Advanced Features from the View menu.
5. Expand the Active Directory Users and Computers snap-in.
6. Expand the domain folder (in this example, the companyabc.com folder).
7. Select the Users container that was used in the previous section. In the right pane, right-click the group that was created earlier, and select Properties.
8. Select the Security tab.
9. At the bottom of the page, click the Advanced button.
10. In the Advanced Security Settings for Group dialog box, select the Permissions tab.

11.  Click Add. In the Select User, Computer, or Group window, type in the name of the account for which you want to grant permissions, and click OK.

12.  When the Permissions Entry for Group window appears, select the Properties tab.

13.  Click the Apply To drop-down list arrow, and then select This Object Only.

14.  In the Permissions section, check the Allow boxes for Read Members and Write Members, as shown in Figure 18.5. Then click OK.

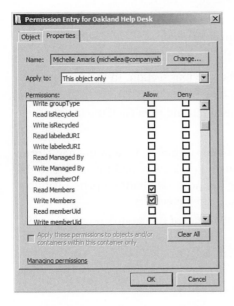

FIGURE 18.5    Granting permissions to modify group membership.

15.  Click OK to close the Advanced Security Settings for Group dialog box.

16.  Click OK to close the group's property pages.

# Managing Users with Local Security and Group Policies

Windows Server 2008 R2 systems provide local security policies to manage user and group administrative access on a per-server basis. Within Active Directory, you can use group policies to set configurations and security on a specified collection of computers, users, or groups of users from a single policy. These policies can be used to deliver standard desktop configurations and security settings for server access and application functionality. Also, policies can set user configurations to deliver software on demand, redirect desktop folders, plus affect many more settings. Many settings within each policy explain what the setting controls and whether computer-based settings apply to only Windows XP, Windows Vista, or Windows 7 workstations. Chapter 15, "Security Policies, Network Policy

Server, and Network Access Protection," describes security policy in more depth, but the best way to discover and learn about all the Group Policy settings is to open an actual Group Policy Object and start browsing each section.

## Viewing Policies with the Group Policy Management Console

You can view Active Directory-based group policies or server and workstation local security policies with very little effort by using a single console, the Group Policy Management Console (GPMC). This tool is added to the Server Manager console when the Active Directory Domain Services role is added to a server. The GPMC enables administrators to view group policies, edit group policies, and model the effects of combinations of group policies (that is, model the resulting configuration).

To open an existing policy, follow these steps:

1. Launch Server Manager on a domain controller.
2. Expand the Features folder.
3. Expand the Group Policy Management Console.
4. Expand the Forest folder.
5. Expand the Domains folder.
6. Expand the specific domain, such as companyabc.com.
7. Select a Group Policy Object, such as the Default Domain Policy. Click OK to close the linked policy warning window.
8. Select the Settings tab to review the settings. Or right-click the Group Policy Object, and select Edit to change the settings.

After you access the policy, you can view each setting or settings container to determine the default value and, in some cases, learn what the setting controls. Keep in mind that, with the correct level of permissions, any changes you make to this policy are live changes; there is no undo other than reversing the individual setting changes or performing an authoritative restore of Active Directory.

## Creating New Group Policies

When changes need to be made or tested using group policies, the administrator should leave the production environment untouched and create test policies in isolated test lab environments. When test labs are not available or cannot replicate the production environment, the administrator can test policies in isolated organizational units within a domain. Also, if domain- or site-based policies need to be created for testing, security filtering could be modified to apply the policy only to a specific set of test users or groups.

The preceding section described how to locate a group policy. Using the Group Policy Management Console, you can also create, configure, and open site, domain, and organizational unit (OU) group policies for editing.

In some cases, it will be necessary to prevent a GPO from being applied to a user or computer. That is, there might be a GPO that applies to all members of a department, but it is necessary to make a single exception to the rule. Rather than create a specific OU to apply the GPO, security filtering can be used to allow or deny the application of the Group Policy Object.

The following steps outline how to create a new domain-based policy and configure its security filtering to apply to a single user:

1. Launch Server Manager on a domain controller.
2. Expand the Features folder.
3. Expand the Group Policy Management Console.
4. Expand the Forest folder.
5. Expand the Domains folder.
6. Select the specific domain, such as companyabc.com.
7. Right-click on the domain and select Create a GPO in This Domain, and Link It Here.
8. Type in a descriptive policy name, leave the source starter GPO set to None, and click OK to create the policy.

> **NOTE**
>
> Source starter GPOs are GPO templates that can be used to prepopulate settings in GPOs. If there are common settings that will go into GPOs, they can be created in starter GPOs and then seeded into new GPOs as they are created.
>
> The starter GPOs are stored in a common folder named StarterGPOs. Any GPOs created in this folder are available for seeding GPOs. There are no starter GPOs in a domain by default.

9. The new policy will be displayed in the right pane. Right-click the new policy and select Edit to launch the Group Policy Management Editor snap-in.
10. Right-click the GPO name in the Group Policy Management Editor, and select Properties.
11. Select the Security tab and highlight the Authenticated Users entry.
12. In the Permissions section, scroll down and uncheck the Allow check box for Apply Group Policy. This means that the GPO will not take effect on any user or computer.
13. Select each entry in the Group Policy access control list and verify that no existing groups are allowed to apply Group Policy.
14. Click Add and type in the name of a user or group. To find a list of users and groups within the current domain, click the Advanced button, and in the search window, click Find Now to return the complete list. Scroll down and select the users or groups you want, and click OK.
15. Click OK to add the entries to the policy.
16. Back in the security window, select the respective entry and check the Allow check box for Apply Group Policy, as shown in Figure 18.6. This means that the GPO will

take effect on the members of this group, which could include both users and computers. Click OK when you're finished.

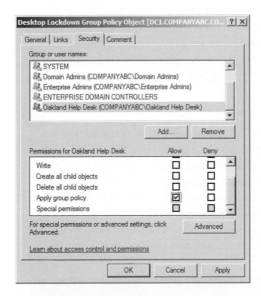

FIGURE 18.6    Modifying a group policy's application scope.

**17.** Close the Group Policy Management Editor snap-in.

Now the group policies set in the GPO will affect only the users or computers that were specified—in this case, members of the Oakland Help Desk. This allows for fine-grained application of group policies to targeted groups.

## Configuring and Optimizing Group Policy

After a Group Policy Object is created, a few steps should be taken to configure how the policy will be applied and to optimize the time to apply the policy. Group policies can be limited to computer- or user-specific settings. To determine whether either type of setting can be disabled, the administrator should determine which settings are necessary to provide the desired policy settings. In many cases, a policy uses settings for both types. To disable either user or computer policy settings, open the properties as described in the section "Viewing Policies with the Group Policy Management Console" earlier in this chapter. When the policy is listed, select the Details tab. Adjust the GPO status field to disable computer or user settings as required.

When multiple group policies exist, they are applied in a predefined order. For a particular user or computer, the order can be derived using the Resultant Set of Policies snap-in. The results of standard policies are that if setting X is enabled on a top-level policy and disabled on the last policy to apply to an object, the resulting setting will disable setting X. Many policy settings have three states: enabled, disabled, and the default of not configured.

You can limit group policies to apply to specific users or computers by modifying the security entries. In addition to disabling portions of each GPO, policy inheritance can be blocked at the domain or OU container level using a setting called Block Policy Inheritance. When blocking or precedence rules need to be ignored for the settings of a particular group policy, the group policy can be configured as Enforced.

### Group Policy Objects and Logon Performance

It is important that policies be effectively placed to avoid slow logon performance. For each level in the OU structure where a group policy is linked, the download and application of the policies at that level can cause 15–30 seconds of additional logon or startup delay. This is because the Group Policy Objects at a particular OU level are evaluated at one time, which takes a few seconds. The process is repeated for each OU level where there are GPOs, and that processing time can really stack up, leading to longer logon delays for the users and complaints to the help desk. Interestingly, the same applies for the computer startup as the policies are applied, but users don't notice that as much.

> **NOTE**
>
> The logon delay is something that can develop over time as the Active Directory infrastructure matures. When initially deployed, the Active Directory will have relatively few GPOs and, consequently, logon delays will be short. As time progresses, more GPOs are added and more OU levels with GPOs are added, with an increase in the logon times that users experience. This creeping logon time can be directly traced to the proliferation of GPOs.

The general guidelines to reduce the logon performance impact are as follows:

▶ **Reduce the number of OU levels**—By reducing the number of OU levels, there will be fewer levels to link GPOs to and, thus, better performance. The best practice is to have a maximum of three levels, if possible. If more are needed, prohibit the linking of GPOs to some of the levels.

▶ **Reduce the number of GPOs**—By consolidating settings into fewer GPOs, less processing time is needed to read the GPOs. A single GPO at the same OU level will perform faster than 10 GPOs at the same level.

▶ **Use security filtering**—If a GPO is security filtered to not apply to a user or computer, the settings do not need to be read or processed. This speeds up logon and startup performance.

▶ **Disable user or computer settings in GPOs**—Each GPO consists of a user and a computer section. If there are no settings in either of those sections, that section can be disabled and will be ignored. For example, if a GPO only has computer settings and the user settings are disabled, that GPO will be skipped at logon (which only deals with user settings).

These guidelines can dramatically improve logon and startup performance.

The last guideline suggested disabling the user setting or computer settings, as processing a GPO takes a certain amount of time for a computer at startup and for a user at logon. To enable or disable the entire GPO or the user/computer portion of the GPO, run the following steps:

1. Open the Group Policy Management console.
2. Expand the Forest folder, expand the Domains folder, select the specific domain, and select the Group Policy Objects.
3. Select the GPO to enable or disable it.
4. Right-click the GPO and select GPO Status.
5. Select the appropriate option: Enable, User Configuration Settings Disabled, Computer Configuration Settings Disabled, or All Settings Disabled.

This will take effect immediately. The All Setting Disabled option is useful for troubleshooting when you want to completely disable a GPO without changing the ACLs or the settings.

### Block Policy Inheritance

The Block Policy Inheritance option enables an administrator to prevent higher-level policies from applying to users and computers within a certain domain or OU. This capability can be useful to optimize Group Policy applications and protect sensitive user and/or computer accounts from organization-wide policy settings.

To block policy inheritance, follow these steps:

1. Launch Server Manager on a domain controller.
2. Expand the Features folder.
3. Expand the Group Policy Management Console.
4. Expand the Forest folder.
5. Expand the Domains folder.
6. Select the specific domain, such as companyabc.com.
7. Locate and right-click the OU for which you want to block inheritance, and select Block Inheritance, as shown in Figure 18.7.

18

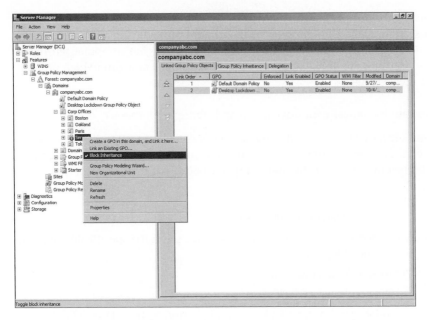

FIGURE 18.7    Blocking policy inheritance for an OU.

In this example, policy inheritance was blocked on the Servers OU. Group policies created above the OU will not affect objects within the OU (unless the group policy is enforced; see the next section). Note the blue exclamation mark icon on the OU to alert the administrator that policy inheritance is blocked.

### The Enforce Option

Configuring the Enforce option prevents lower-level policies from blocking policy inheritance and from changing the parameters or configured settings in a policy. This option should be used only if a policy needs to be enforced on AD objects in every container and subcontainer with a link or inheritance to this policy object.

To configure the Enforce option for a policy, follow these steps:

1. Launch Server Manager on a domain controller.

2. Expand the Features folder.

3. Expand the Group Policy Management Console.

4. Expand the Forest folder.

5. Expand the Domains folder.

6. Select the specific domain, such as companyabc.com.

7. Right-click the group policy to enforce, and select Enforce.

Now the group policy will be enforced even if the Block Policy Inheritance option is set on down-level OUs. Note that the group policy will now have a small lock icon associated with it to show that it is enforced.

## Troubleshooting Group Policy Applications

When policies are used throughout an organization, sometimes the policy settings do not apply to a user or computer as originally intended. To begin basic troubleshooting of Group Policy application issues, you need to understand the policy application hierarchy. First, any local server or workstation policies are applied to the user or computer, followed by site group policies, domain group policies, and, finally, the organizational unit group policies. If nested OUs have group policies, the parent OU policies are processed first, followed by the child OUs, and, finally, the OU containing the Active Directory object (user or computer). You might find it easier to remember "LSD-OU"—the acronym for local, site, domain, and then OU.

Now that you know the order in which policies are applied, you can proceed to use the Group Policy testing and troubleshooting tools provided with Windows Server 2008 R2—namely the Group Policy Modeling tool in the Group Policy Management Console and the command-line utility GPResult.exe, which is the command-line version of the RSoP snap-in.

### The Group Policy Modeling Tool

The Group Policy Modeling snap-in can be used to show the effective policy settings for a user who logs on to a server or workstation after all the respective policies have been applied. This tool is good for identifying which policies are being applied and what the effective setting is.

To simulate the policies for a user, use the Group Policy Modeling snap-in as follows:

1. Launch Server Manager on a domain controller.
2. Expand the Features folder.
3. Expand the Group Policy Management Console.
4. Expand the Forest folder.
5. Select the Group Policy Modeling snap-in.
6. Select Action, Group Policy Modeling Wizard to launch the wizard.
7. Click Next.
8. Leave the default domain controller selection, which chooses any available domain controller. The domain controller must be running Windows Server 2003, Windows Server 2008, or Windows Server 2008 R2. Click Next.
9. Select the User option button in the User Information box, and click Browse.
10. Enter the name of a user to check, and click OK. Click Next to accept the user and computer selection.

> **NOTE**
>
> In the Group Policy Modeling Wizard, the net effect of the group policies can be modeled for specific users, computers, or entire containers for either object. This enables an administrator to see the effects for individual objects or for objects placed within the containers, making the tool very flexible.

11. Click Next on the Advanced Simulation Options page. The advanced simulation options enable you to model slow network connections or specific sites.

12. Click Next to skip the Alternate AD Paths.

13. The User Security Groups page shows the groups that the user is a member of. You can add additional groups to see the effects of changes. Leave as is and click Next.

14. Click Next to skip the WMI Filters for Users page.

15. Click Next to run the simulation.

16. Click Finish to view the results.

17. Click the Show link next to Group Policy Objects.

18. Click the Show link next to Denied GPOs.

Within the console, you can review each particular setting to see whether a setting was applied or the desired setting was overwritten by a higher-level policy. The report shows why specific GPOs were denied. Figure 18.8 shows that one GPO was denied to the user object "michellea." The Desktop Lockdown Group Policy Object was denied due to security filtering. This is the GPO created earlier in the chapter, which was applied only to members of the Oakland Help Desk group. The user michellea is not a member of this group and, hence, does not have the GPO applied.

## Managing Printers with the Print Management Console

The Print Management console in Windows Server 2008 R2 helps organizations better manage and administer printers on an enterprise basis. Prior to the Print Management console, a network administrator would have to point to each network printer or printer server individually to manage and administer the device. For a large enterprise with hundreds of printers and dozens of printer servers, this was a very tedious task to select print servers each and every time a printer needed to be managed. Furthermore, if the administrator didn't remember which printer was attached to which print server, it could take a while to eventually find the printer and print server that needed management.

The Print Management console provides a single interface where an administrator can open the Print Management console, and view all printers and print servers in the enterprise. Furthermore, it could be configured to group printers together so that certain administrators could manage and administer only certain printers. As an example, if an organization has an administrator for a particular building, the Print Management inter-

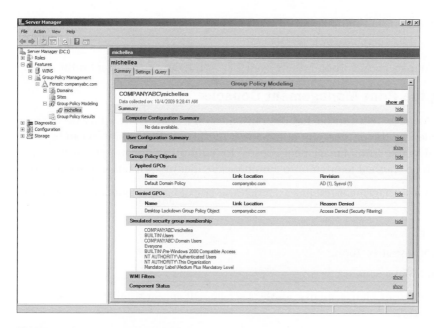

FIGURE 18.8    The Group Policy Modeling report.

face could be filtered to only list printers within the building. This would allow the administrator to only see certain printers they are responsible for, as well as consolidate multiple print server groups of printers into a single interface for management and administration.

The Print Management component only needs to be installed on the system that the administrator is managing from—it does not need to be installed on all print servers or systems in the enterprise. Functionally, Print Management could be installed on just one system. However, it is automatically installed on Windows Server 2008 R2 servers with the Print Service role installed.

## Installing the Print Management Console

The Print Management console is installed as one of the Remote Server Administration Tools in the features or as part of the Print Server role of Windows Server 2008 R2. To install the Print Management console on a management server that is not a print server, complete the following steps:

1. Launch Server Manager.

2. Select the Features folder and click the Add Features link.

3. Expand the Remote Server Administration Tools.

4. Expand the Role Administration Tools.

5. Select the Print and Document Services Tools check box.

6. Click Next.

7. Click Install to install the snap-in.

8. Click Close to close the wizard.

Now the Print Management console will be available within Server Manager on the server.

## Configuring the Print Management Console

After the Print Management console has been installed on a system, the utility needs to be configured to identify the printers and print servers in the enterprise. Printers can be manually added to the Print Management console for administration and management, or the network can be scanned to attempt to automatically identify printers in the enterprise.

To configure print management resources, launch the Print Management console by doing the following:

1. Select Start.

2. Select Administrative Tools.

3. Select Print Management.

Upon opening the Print Management console, a screen will appear similar to the one shown in Figure 18.9.

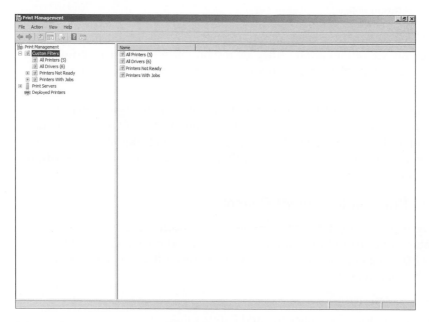

FIGURE 18.9    Print Management console.

## Adding New Printers as Network Shared Resources

There are two ways to add new printers to a Windows Server 2008 R2 network. One way is the standard Windows printer installation method of using the Add Printer option. The other option is using the new Print Management console and adding a printer within the utility. Both methods return the same result, so the main reason to use the Print Management console method is to simplify all print management tasks of adding, modifying, and managing printers from a single utility.

### Using the Add Printer Option in Windows to Add a Local Printer

To add a new printer that is locally attached to a print server using the standard Windows Add Printer option method, do the following:

1. Select Start, Control Panel, and double-click on Devices and Printers.

2. Click on the Add a Printer button to launch the Add Printer Wizard.

3. Because the printer is locally attached to the print server, click Add a Local Printer.

4. Choose the port (LPT1, LPT2, COM1, COM2, and so on) to which the printer is attached, and then click Next.

5. Choose the manufacturer and the printer type of the printer being added (such as HP for manufacturer, and LaserJet P2015 PCL6 for printer type), and then click Next.

6. When prompted, give the printer a name (such as HP LaserJet P2015 PCL6 in the Marketing Dept), and then click Next.

7. When prompted whether you want to share the printer, select the Share Name option and type in a name that will describe the printer (such as HP20016MKTG), and then click Next.

8. If you want to print a test page, click the Print a Test Page button; otherwise, click Finish to complete the addition of the printer.

### Using the Add Printer Option in the Print Management Console

Another method of adding a printer to the network is to use the Print Management console to add the printer. This process is identical to adding the printer using the Windows Add Printer option addressed in the previous section; however, rather than using two separate interfaces for adding and managing printers, using the Print Management console can centralize the tasks into a single interface.

To start the Network Printer Installation Wizard within the Print Management console, do the following:

1. Expand the Print Servers section of the Print Management console.

2. Right-click on one of the print servers listed in the Print Servers section of the interface, and choose Add Printer.

3. If the printer is attached directly to the print server, choose Add a New Printer Using an Existing Port and follow the instructions in the "Using the Add Printer Option in Windows to Add a Local Printer" section of this chapter.

## Adding Print Servers to the Print Management Console

After printers and print servers have been added to the network as noted in the previous sections, an administrator can now begin to add print servers to the Print Management console to centrally view, manage, and maintain the printers on the network.

Adding a print server to the Print Management console allows the administrator to manage the print server and all the printers the print server hosts. To add a print server to the Print Management console, do the following:

1. Right-click on the Print Servers item in the Print Management console, and choose Add/Remove Servers.

2. Type in the name of the print server you want to add, or click on Browse and search the Microsoft Windows network to view the various servers in the environment.

3. Click OK to add the print server.

## Using the Print Management Console

With printers added to the network, and print servers added to the Print Management console, an administrator can now begin to centrally view, manage, and administer the printers and print servers. Some of the tasks that an administrator can perform from the Print Management console are tasks that an administrator would normally do right on the print server, such as change printer ports, add or modify forms, or view the status of printers whether the printers are online or not. Other tasks are new to the Print Management console, such as creating custom printer filters that allow multiple administrators to view and manage selected printers based on their site, rights, and roles.

### Performing General Printer Administration Tasks

From within the Print Management console, the administrator can perform general printer administration tasks. Some of these tasks include the following:

▶ **Updating printer drivers**—By right-clicking the Drivers item in the Print Server section of the Print Management console and choosing Manage Drivers, an administrator can update or change the printer driver of a printer. This is rarely done in a network environment, but there are times when a new printer add-on, such as an envelope feeder or expansion paper feeder or sorter, is added, and a new printer driver is needed to support the new add-on.

▶ **Managing forms**—By right-clicking on the Forms item in the Print Server section and choosing Manage Forms, an administrator can create and delete new forms to support different size paper or to specify a custom letterhead paper form. Additionally within this interface, an administrator can change the printer port that a printer is attached to on a print server, define log settings, and enable the function to have users notified when a print job has successfully completed printing.

---

**NOTE**

You might wonder when someone would ever create a new printer form or worry about being notified when a print job has been completed, especially when most print jobs are simple 1-page emails or a handful of pages of a Microsoft Word document. However, a creative use of this feature is used by accounting departments, publishers, or other individuals who print large print jobs. For example, you would want to know when a 400-page document has finished printing, or when 100 sets of a 15-page document has completed being printed, collated, and stapled by the printer.

By creating a custom form—which might just be a simple 8-1/2 x 11 form, but with advanced notifications enabled to notify the user that the job has been completed—a user who chooses that form instead of the normal 8-1/2 x 11 form will be notified when the print job has been completed.

### Creating Custom Filters

A unique function of the Print Management console is the Custom Filters function that enables administrators to group printers typically for the purpose of distributing the administration of printers in the environment. For large organizations that might have multiple buildings, sites, and administration boundaries of devices such as printers, the administrators can perform a filter view to see only the printers that fit within their administrative responsibilities.

First, to view all printers in the environment, an administrator can click on the All Printers section of the Custom Filters section of the Print Management console. All of the printers for the network will be listed here.

> **NOTE**
>
> If printers on the network are not listed in the All Printers view, refer to the section "Adding Print Servers to the Print Management Console."

To create a custom printers view, do the following:

1. Right-click on the Custom Filters View in the Print Management console, and choose Add New Printer Filter.

2. Type in a descriptive name for this filter view, such as All Printers in the Oakland Site.

3. Check the Display the Total Number of Printers Next to the Name of the Printer Filter check box. Click Next.

4. In the Field drop-down list, choose a field that will contain information that can be filtered. In many cases, the print servers can be filtered because a print server frequently services printers in a specific geography. Alternately, organizations that entered in location information for printers such as Building 11 would be able to filter for that designation in a custom printer filter filtered by name. An example might be Field=Location, Condition=Contains, Value=Oakland. Click Next to continue.

5. On the Set Notification Options page, an administrator can note an email address where the administrator would be notified on the status of events related to the printers in the filter. You can also run a script. This might include being emailed every time a printer is offline, or every time a printer is out of paper. Enter in the appropriate email information (email address, SMTP mail server to be used, and message desired), or leave this section unchecked, and then click Finish.

By clicking on the newly created filter, the filter rule is applied and the printers noted in the filter will be displayed, as shown in Figure 18.10. In this figure, you will notice that

18

there are five printers in the environment; however, the filter is searching only for print-ers in Oakland, and, thus, only three printers are displayed for this administrator to view and manage.

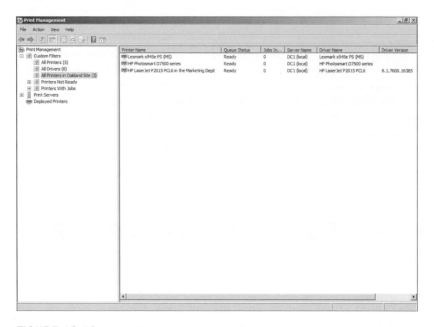

FIGURE 18.10    Sample custom printer filter.

Virtually an unlimited number of printer filters can be created to show different groupings of printers to be managed or administered. Organizations have created custom printer filters by printer manufacturer such as HP, Xerox, and Sharp or by printer type such as laser, color laser, and plotter to be able to view assets by make, model, or configuration. Printer filters can even be created based on queue length and to run an automatic script to take action in addition to notifying the administrator.

# Summary

Managing Active Directory sites, groups, users, and printers in Windows Server 2008 R2 can be daunting if some of these tasks cannot be automated or simplified. This chapter outlined ways and tools to create these objects and included the information necessary to manage these objects from a standalone and enterprise level.

This chapter addressed options for administration that included centralized, decentralized, and mixed administration, which provides a model that fits pretty much all organizations. Some of the key criteria in administration are addressed when sites and groups are created that identify administration boundaries and define the role of administration within and across the boundaries.

In addition, policies better clarify how management and administration will be handled, which ultimately trickle down to profiles and configuration settings to create a managed and administered Windows Server 2008 R2 environment.

# Best Practices

The following are best practices from this chapter:

- ▶ Clearly understand your roles and responsibilities in the enterprise network and understand how the different components that make up the network communicate and rely on one another.

- ▶ Choose the appropriate administrative model (central, distributed, or mixed) for the organization based on required services and skill sets in each location.

- ▶ Always define the site for physical locations to accurately model the WAN and LAN architecture, even if those locations don't contain domain controllers.

- ▶ Always define all subnets in the Active Directory Sites and Services to ensure that all domain computers can be located to their closest Active Directory resources.

- ▶ Use site links to accurately reflect the WAN and LAN topology.

- ▶ Use site policies to define custom network security settings for sites with higher requirements or to delegate administrative rights when administration is performed on a mostly geographic basis.

- ▶ Ensure that sites contain local network services, such as domain controllers, global catalog servers, DNS servers, DHCP servers, and, if necessary, WINS servers.

- ▶ Use security groups to create distribution lists.

- ▶ Create a universal group to span domains, but have only a global group from each domain as a member.

- ▶ Use local and group policies to manage users and desktops.

- ▶ Modify Group Policy security entries to limit Group Policy application to specific users or computers.

- ▶ Reduce the OU levels and the number of GPOs by consolidating multiple GPOs into a single GPO where possible to improve logon and startup performance.

- ▶ Use Group Policy Modeling to view and troubleshoot the way group policies are applied.

- ▶ Use the Print Management console added in to Windows Server 2008 R2 to centrally view, manage, and administer printers in the network environment.

# CHAPTER 19

# Windows Server 2008 R2 Group Policies and Policy Management

Since the inception of computer networks, there has been a need and a desire to centrally administer and configure devices on the network. As small campus and corporate networks evolved and became connected with other institutions, security concerns prompted the requirement to secure access to resources and to limit administration of connected devices.

With Microsoft networks, the solution to the security concern was first addressed with the Windows NT file system (NTFS) and with Windows domains, system policies addressed the centralized security and configuration requirements. Starting with Windows 2000 Server and the introduction of Active Directory, system policies have now evolved into what we now know as group policies, which are discussed in this chapter.

This chapter presents an overview of the concepts and application of the newly revised Windows Server 2008 R2 Group Policy infrastructure used to manage Windows Active Directory networks.

## Group Policy Overview

The Microsoft Group Policy infrastructure is a complex system that utilizes several features and services included in the Windows server and client operating systems and the IP networks that these systems reside on.

In its simplest concept, Group Policy is a mechanism used to centrally secure, configure, and deploy a common set of computer and user configurations, security settings, and, in some cases, software, to Windows servers, Windows workstations, and users in an Active Directory forest.

The Group Policy infrastructure enables organizations to enforce configurations, simplify desktop administration, secure access to network resources, and, in some cases, meet regulatory compliance requirements. As an example of this, group policies can be configured to apply and enforce an end-user password policy that requires complex passwords that must exceed seven characters and that must also be changed every 30 days. Another sample policy can be configured to enable the Windows Firewall on client workstations, remove an end user's ability to disable it, including local administrators, and allow the corporate desktop support team to remotely administer these workstations while they are connected to the corporate network or virtual private network (VPN).

Group Policy settings and reliability have changed tremendously since they were first introduced in Windows 2000 Server. In the Windows 2000 Server version, Group Policy Objects (GPOs) lacked many features and basically were not as resilient to network changes and many of the advanced functions just did not work. With Windows XP and Windows Server 2003, many features were fixed and new settings were introduced. With Windows Server 2008 and Windows Vista, many of the pain points realized in the previous versions were resolved and the infrastructure was in many ways rebuilt from the ground up to improve network performance and add functionality. Now with the release of Windows Server 2008 R2 and Windows 7, many of the new Group Policy features of the Windows Vista and Windows Server 2008 infrastructure have been further improved and extended to provide more out-of-the-box functionality.

This chapter addresses the administration and management of GPOs for Windows XP, Windows Vista, and Windows 7 client operating systems as well as Windows Server 2003, Windows Server 2008, and Windows Server 2008 R2 server operating systems.

# Group Policy Processing—How Does It Work?

The way a group policy is processed is determined by a number of different settings and criteria. Computers and users process policies differently; furthermore, each policy also can contain specific settings to define how and when a policy will be processed.

GPOs contain a revision number for both the computer and user configuration section of the policy. By default, if the revision number has not changed since the last application of the GPO, most of the GPO processing is skipped. Certain portions, however, such as the computer startup and shutdown scripts and the user logon and logoff scripts, are processed each time a GPO is processed during that cycle.

## Computer GPO Processing

Computers process policies in a predetermined order and during certain events. Group policies are applied to computer objects during startup, shutdown, and periodically during the background refresh interval. By default, the refresh interval is every 90 minutes on member servers and workstations with an offset of 0 to 30 minutes. On domain controllers, group policies are refreshed every 5 minutes. The offset ensures that not all domain computers refresh or process group policies simultaneously. When a computer starts up, if the computer can successfully locate and communicate with an authenticating domain controller, GPO processing will occur. During GPO processing, the system checks each linked or inherited GPO to verify if the policy has changed since the last processing cycle, to run any startup scripts and check for any other requirement to reapply policy. During the shutdown and refresh interval, the GPOs are processed again to check for any updates or changes since the last application cycle.

Computer GPO processing is determined by GPO links, security filtering, and Windows Management Instrumentation (WMI) filters.

## User GPO Processing

GPO processing for users is very similar to GPO processing for computers. The main differences are that GPO processing for users occurs at user logon, logoff, and periodically. The default refresh interval for user GPO processing is 90 minutes plus a 0- to 30-minute offset.

User GPO processing is determined by GPO links and security filtering.

## Network Location Awareness

Network Location Awareness (NLA) is a service built in to Windows that is used to determine when the computer has connectivity to the Active Directory infrastructure. The Group Policy infrastructure utilizes NLA to determine whether to attempt to download and apply GPOs. This Group Policy function is called slow link detection.

In previous versions, Group Policy processing used slow link detection to determine if the network was reliable enough to process and apply policies. Slow link detection relied on the Internet Control Message Protocol (ICMP) or Ping to test for network connectivity and was not very reliable. Due to this specification, Group Policy processing on mobile and remote client workstations was very unreliable. When a mobile client workstation connected to the corporate network through a VPN connection or after waking from hibernation or sleep mode, the change in network connectivity usually passed by unnoticed and GPOs were not applied or refreshed. In these cases, the only way to get these clients to apply their GPOs was to have them manually run a Group Policy update from the command line or have these machines reboot while connected to the corporate network via wired Ethernet connections.

Group Policy processing on Windows Vista, Windows 7, Windows Server 2008, and Windows Server 2008 R2 now utilize the rebuilt Network Location Awareness (NLA) service to detect network changes. The new NLA service is much better at detecting changes to network connections, and when a connection is established, NLA checks for domain controller connectivity. If a domain controller can be contacted, the NLA service notifies the computer Group Policy service, which, in turn, triggers Group Policy processing for both computer- and user-based Group Policy settings. The NLA service is not dependent on ICMP or Ping, which on its own makes it more reliable. The NLA service should run on most networks without any special configuration on the network devices or network firewalls, even if ICMP communication is disabled or blocked by the firewall.

19

## Managing Group Policy Processing with GPO Settings

Within the Policies\Administrative Templates\System\GroupPolicy section of both the Computer Configuration and User Configuration nodes of a GPO, as shown in Figure 19.1, an administrator can review and control how group policies will be processed. These sections contain the Group Policy settings that will determine how often a policy will be refreshed, if a policy will be reapplied even if the revision number has not changed since the last cycle, and if the policy will be applied across slow links or if any local computer policies will be processed by a computer or a user.

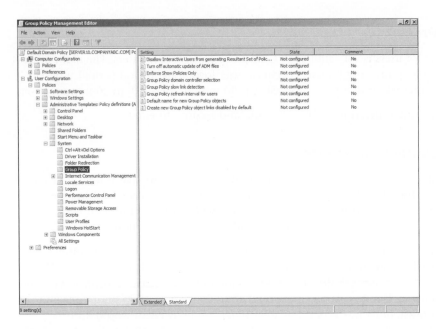

FIGURE 19.1 Examining Group Policy settings.

# Local Group Policies

Two different types of policies can be applied to Windows systems and Windows system user accounts: local group policies and Active Directory group policies. Local group policies exist on all Windows systems, but Active Directory group policies are only available in an Active Directory forest. Until the release of Windows Vista and Windows Server 2008, servers and workstations could contain and apply only a single local computer and user policy. This policy contained the settings that could be applied to the local computer and the user objects to control the security and configuration settings.

In many environments, usually due to legacy or line-of-business application requirements, end users were frequently granted local Administrators group membership on workstations and essentially excluded from the application of many security settings applied by both the local and group policies. End users with local Administrators group membership have the ability to override settings and make configuration changes that could compro-mise the security, or more frequently, reduce the reliability of the system.

Starting with Windows Vista and Windows Server 2008, administrators now have the ability to create multiple local group policies. One of the new features is that specific user group policies can be created for all users, for users who are not administrators, and for users who are members of the local Administrators group on the computers. This new feature can be especially valuable for computers configured in workgroup or standalone configurations to increase the security and reliability of the computer. In domain configu-rations, computer security policies are usually specified using group policies and applied to the Active Directory computers.

## Local Computer Policy

The default local computer policy contains out-of-the-box policy settings, as shown in Figure 19.2, which are available to configure the computer and user environment. This policy will be applied first for both computer and user objects logging on to the worksta-tion in workgroups or domains.

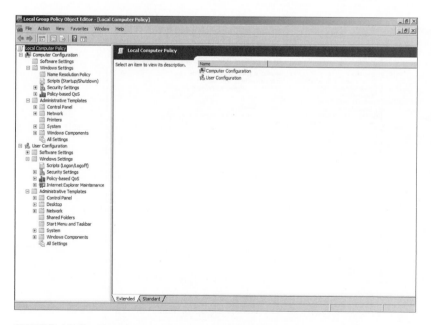

FIGURE 19.2     Examining local computer policy settings.

## Local User Policies for Non-Administrators and Administrators

Starting with Windows Vista and Windows Server 2008, and continuing with Windows 7 and Windows Server 2008 R2, administrators now have the option to create multiple local user group policies on a single machine. In previous versions, the single local computer policy allowed administrators to apply the single policy settings to all users logging on to a workstation that is part of a workgroup. Now, workgroup computers and domain computers can have additional policies applied to specific local users. Also, policies can be applied to local computer administrators or nonadministrators. This allows the workstation administrator to leave the user section of the default local computer policy blank, and create a more-restrictive policy for local users and a less-restrictive policy for members of the local workstation Administrators security group.

## Security Templates

Within each local computer policy and within a GPO Computer Configuration node, there is a section named Security Settings, as shown in Figure 19.3. This section includes settings for computer audit policies, account management settings, and user rights assignments. This section of the policy is unique because it can be imported and exported individually. In previous versions of Windows, several security templates were provided out of the box to give administrators the ability to quickly load a set of best-practice security configuration settings. These templates included basic workstation and server templates along with high security, compatible security, and domain controller security templates.

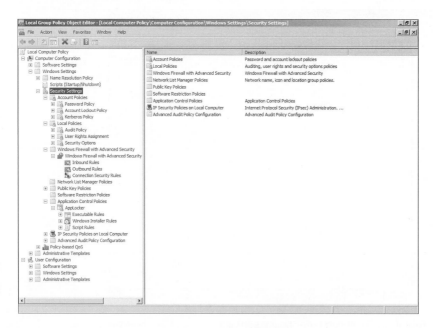

FIGURE 19.3 Examining the computer security section.

To manage and apply a standard set of security configurations to workgroup or standalone systems, administrators can leverage the management functions of security templates. Either using the Group Policy Object Editor, the Local Security Policy editor, or the Security Configuration and Analysis MMC snap-in, administrators can import a base template, configure or adjust settings to meet the desired security settings, and export and save the settings to a custom template file. This custom template file could then be imported or applied to all the desired systems using the tools referenced previously.

Security templates exist for Windows Vista, Windows 7, Windows Server 2008, and Windows Server 2008 R2. These base security templates are located in the %systemroot%\inf folder or on a default install, c:\windows\inf. The default security templates all start with the name `deflt` and end with an `.inf` extension. For example, on Windows Server 2008 R2, the templates that exist are named `defltbase.inf`, `defltsv.inf`, and `defltdc.inf`. These files can be used to configure a system's security settings to a standard set of security configurations.

> **CAUTION**
>
> Importing security templates to servers or workstations already deployed can cause several issues, including losing the ability to log on or access the system from the network. Please make sure to test any changes to security settings when working with the import and application of security templates.

# Elements of Group Policy

This section of the chapter provides an overview of the concepts and terminology of the elements of Group Policy to provide system administrators with the information required to understand, support, and deploy group policies in an Active Directory forest. As a follow-up to this chapter, Chapter 27, "Group Policy Management for Network Clients," provides useful best-practice examples of how Group Policy can be deployed to simplify the management and configuration of your Active Directory servers, workstations, and users. Although some administrators might be inclined to skip the remainder of this chapter and jump right to Chapter 27, it is highly recommended that you review this chapter to understand how to manage the Group Policy infrastructure before attempting to manage the devices in the Active Directory forest.

## Group Policy Objects

The elements of Group Policy start with the Group Policy Objects (GPOs) themselves. GPOs are a predefined set of available settings that can be applied to Active Directory computer and/or user objects. The settings available within a particular GPO are created using a combination of administrative template files included or referenced within that GPO. As the particular computer or user management needs change, additional administrative templates can be imported into a particular GPO to extend its functionality.

## Group Policy Object Storage and Replication

GPOs are stored in both the file system and the Active Directory database. Each domain in an Active Directory forest stores a complete copy of that particular domain's GPOs.

Within Active Directory, the GPO links and version information are stored within the domain naming context partition of the database. Because this partition is only replicated within a single domain, processing GPOs linked across domains, either using sites or just a cross-domain GPO link, can take longer to load and process.

The GPO settings are stored in the file system of all domain controllers within the sysvol folder. The sysvol folder is shared on all domain controllers. Each domain GPO has a corresponding folder located within the sysvol\companyabc.com\Policies subfolder, as shown in Figure 19.4 as an example of the companyabc.com domain. The GPO folder is named after the globally unique identifier (GUID) assigned to that GPO during creation. The GUID of a GPO is listed when viewing the properties of a domain GPO using the Group Policy Management Console. Within the GPO folder are a common set of subfolders and files, including the User folder, Machine folder, sometimes the ADM folder, and the gpt.ini file.

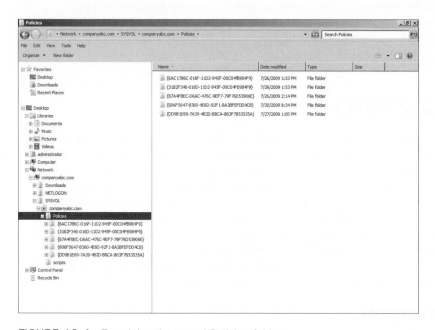

FIGURE 19.4    Examining the sysvol Policies folder.

### Group Policy Object Replication

Because GPOs are stored within the Active Directory database and on the domain controller file system, all GPO information is replicated by the domain controllers. The file system portion of the domain GPOs is replicated within the Domain System Volume Distributed File System Replication group by the Distributed File System Replication service.

The Domain System Volume replication schedule is controlled by the DFSR schedule, which, by default, follows the same replication cycle as the Active Directory database. Replication occurs every 5 minutes or immediately between domain controllers in a single Active Directory site and follows the site link schedule between domain controllers in separate sites. Legacy domains will use the File Replication Service instead of DFSR.

### User Subfolder

The User subfolder contains the files and folders used to store the settings, software, scripts, and any other policy settings specific to user and user object policies configured within a particular GPO.

### Machine Subfolder

The Machine subfolder contains the files and folders used to store the settings, software, scripts, and any other policy settings specific to machine or computer object policies configured within a particular GPO.

### ADM Subfolder

The ADM subfolder is created on new GPOs when legacy administrative template files are imported into a GPO. Any GPOs created using Windows 2000 and Windows XP client software, or Windows 2000 Server and Windows Server 2003 system software, will contain an ADM subfolder to store all the legacy administrative template files referenced and imported into the GPO.

### registry.pol Files

Within a particular group policy, the settings are segmented into several sections. Many settings with the GPO configure keys and values within the Registry. The configuration status and value of these settings are stored within the registry.pol files in either the User or Machine subfolders. The registry.pol file contains only the configured settings within the GPO to improve processing.

### gpt.ini File

When a GPO is created, a folder for the GPO is created within the connected domain controller's sysvol folder. At the root of that GPO folder is a file named gpt.ini. This file contains the revision number of the GPO. The revision number is used when a GPO is processed by a computer or user object. When a GPO is first processed, the revision number is stored on the system and when subsequent GPO processing occurs, the reference number in the gpt.ini file is compared with the stored value on the local system cache. If the number has not changed, certain portions of the GPO are not processed. There are, however, certain portions of a GPO that are always processed, like scripts.

Each time a GPO is changed, the reference or revision number is increased, and even though the gpt.ini file contains a single number, it actually represents a separate revision number for the computer and user section of the GPO.

The default configuration of not processing certain GPO sections if the revision number has not changed can be overridden. In some cases, even though the GPO has not changed, the intended settings could have been changed by the user or a program and sometimes forcing the entire GPO to always be processed is required.

This configuration setting is available in both the Computer Configuration and User Configuration nodes of the GPO and is discussed later in Chapter 27.

## Group Policy Administrative Templates

GPO administrative templates are, in most cases, a set of text or Extensible Markup Language (XML)–based files that include clearly defined settings that can be set to a number of different values.

Administrative templates are provided to give administrators easy access to many configurable settings commonly used to manage server and workstation computers and end users.

When a new GPO is created, a base set of administrative templates are imported or referenced within that policy. Additional administrative templates can be imported to a particular policy to add functionality as required.

## Windows 7 and Windows Server 2008 R2 Central Store

As stated earlier in this chapter, each GPO in the Active Directory forest will have a corresponding folder stored in the sysvol folder on each domain controller in the domain in which the GPO is created. If the domain controllers in the particular domain are running Windows Server 2003, each of these GPO folders would contain a copy of each of the administrative templates loaded in that particular GPO. This created many duplicated administrative template files and required additional storage space and increased replication traffic.

Starting with the new Group Policy infrastructure included with Windows Vista and Windows Server 2008 and continuing with Windows 7 and Windows Server 2008 R2, newly created GPOs only store the files and folders required to store the configured settings, scripts, registry.pol, and other GPO-related files. When the GPO is opened for editing or processed by a Windows Vista, Windows 7, Windows Server 2008, or Windows Server 2008 R2 computer, the local copy of the administrative templates is referenced but not copied to the new GPO folder in sysvol. Instead, the administrative templates are referenced from files stored on the local workstations or the domain central store.

The GPO central store is a file repository that houses each of the next generation administrative templates. The central store would contain all of the new ADMX and ADML administrative templates and each workstation would reference the files on the domain controller they are using to process group policies. With a central store created, when a GPO is opened or processed, the system first checks for the existence of the central store and then only uses the templates stored in the central store.

The GPO central store can be created within Active Directory infrastructures running any version of Windows Server 2003, Windows Server 2008, or Windows Server 2008 R2 domain controllers.

## Starter GPOs

Windows Server 2008 and Windows Server 2008 R2 Group Policy Management Console provide a new feature of GPO management called starter GPOs. Starter GPOs are similar to regular GPOs, but they only contain settings available from administrative templates. Just as security templates can be used to import and export the configured settings within the security section of a policy, starter GPOs can be used to prepopulate configured settings in the Administrative Templates sections of the Computer Configuration and User Configuration nodes within a GPO. After the release of Windows Server 2008 and included in Windows Server 2008 R2, Microsoft released a set of predefined starter GPOs for Windows Vista and Windows XP. The predefined settings in these starter GPOs are based on information that can be found in the Windows XP and Windows client security guide published by Microsoft. These particular starter GPOs are read-only policies, but administrators can create their own starter GPOs as needed by the organization.

How to enable starter GPO functionality and how to create and manage starter GPOs are covered later in this chapter in the section, "Creating and Utilizing Starter GPOs."

## Policy Settings

Policy settings are simply the configurable options made available within a particular GPO. These settings are provided from the base administrative templates, security settings, scripts, policy-based QOS, and, in some cases, software deployment packages. Many policy settings correspond one to one with a particular Registry key and value. Depending on the particular settings, different values, including free-form text, might be acceptable as a legitimate value.

GPO policy settings are usually configurable to one of three values: not configured, enabled, or disabled. It is very important for administrators to understand not only the difference among these three values, but to also understand what the particular policy setting controls. For example, a policy setting that disables access to Control Panel will block access to Control Panel when enabled but will allow access when disabled.

GPO policy settings apply to either a computer or a user object. Within a particular GPO, an administrator might find the same policy setting within both the Computer Configuration and User Configuration nodes. In cases like this, if the policy setting is configured for both objects, the computer setting will override the user setting if the policy is linked to the user object and the workstation to which the user is logged on.

## Preference Settings

Group Policies have two main setting nodes, including the Computer and User Configuration nodes. Each of these contains two main nodes as well, the Policies and Preferences setting nodes. The group policy extensions presented in the Preferences node provide administrators with the ability to configure many default or initial configuration and environmental settings for users and computers. One really great feature of GPO Preferences is Item-Level Targeting, which only applies a certain preference, such as setting the Start menu on Windows 7 workstations to configure the power button to perform a logoff instead of a computer shutdown, to only defined users or groups within the Item-Level Target definition of that GPO. When a user logs on to a workstation and has that preference applied, this will be the initial setting, but users would be able to change that setting if they desire. One important distinction that all GPO administrators must make is that policies set and enforce settings, whereas preferences configure initial settings but do not block the settings from changes. More information on GPO preferences is detailed in Chapter 27.

## Group Policy Object Links

GPO links are the key to deploying GPOs to a predetermined set of Active Directory computers and/or users. GPO links define where the particular policy or policies will be applied in terms of the Active Directory domain and site hierarchy design.

GPOs can be linked to Active Directory sites, domains, and organizational units (OUs). Also, a single GPO can be linked to multiple sites, domains, and OUs in a single forest. This gives administrators the flexibility to create a single policy and apply it to several different sets of computers and users within an Active Directory forest.

The design of the Active Directory infrastructure, including site design, domain and tree design, and OU hierarchy, is critical to streamlining targeted GPO application. Careful planning and consideration should be taken into account during the Active Directory design phase with regard to how GPOs will be used and how user, group, and computer objects will be organized.

GPO links can also be disabled as required, to assist with troubleshooting GPO application or processing.

## Group Policy Link Enforcement

Microsoft provides administrators with many ways to manage their infrastructure, including forcing configurations down from the top. GPO link "enforcement," historically known as "No Override," is an option of a GPO link that can be set to ensure that the settings in a particular policy will be applied and maintained even if another GPO has the same setting configured with a different value. GPO link enforcement is shown in Figure 19.5.

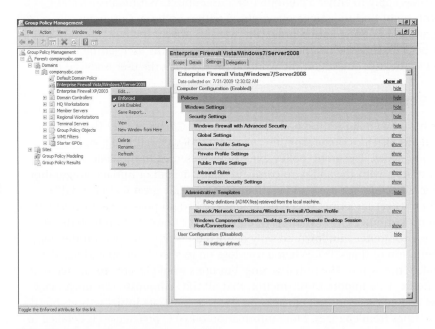

FIGURE 19.5    Enforcing a group policy.

This function should be used with caution because it might result in undesired functionality or a different level of security than what is required to run a particular service or application or manage a system. Before enabling GPO enforcement on any policy, carefully research and test to ensure that this will not break any functionality or violate an organization's IT or regulatory policy.

## Group Policy Inheritance

GPOs can be linked at the site, domain, and multiple OU levels. When an Active Directory infrastructure contains GPOs linked at the domain level, as an example, every container and OU beneath the domain root container inherits any linked policies. As a default example, the "Domain Controllers" OU inherits the default domain policy from the domain.

GPO inheritance allows administrators to set a common base policy across an Active Directory infrastructure while allowing other administrators to apply more granular policies at a lower level that apply to subsets of users or computers. As an example of this, a GPO can be created and linked at the domain level that restricts all users from running Windows Update, while an OU representing a branch office in the domain can have a GPO linked that enables the branch office desktop administrators security group to run Windows Update.

GPO links inherited from parent containers are processed before GPO links at the container itself, and the last applied policy setting value is the resulting value, if multiple GPOs have the same configured setting with different values. This Group Policy inheritance is also known as GPO precedence and is shown in Figure 19.6.

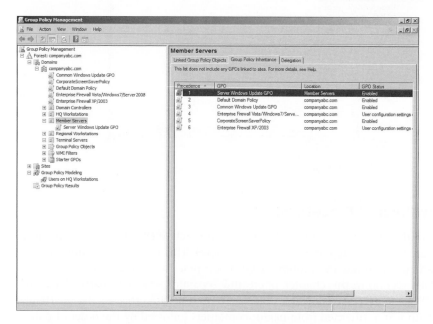

FIGURE 19.6    Examining Group Policy precedence.

## Group Policy Block Inheritance

Just as GPOs can be inherited, Active Directory also provides the option to block inheritance, as shown in Figure 19.7, of all GPOs from parent containers. This is actually an option applied to an Active Directory domain or organizational unit within the Group Policy Management Console and not on a GPO. This option can be useful if the container contains users and/or computer objects that are very security sensitive or business critical. As an example of this option in use, an OU can be created to contain the Remote Desktop Services host systems, which would not function correctly if domain-level GPOs were applied. The OU can be configured to block inheritance to ensure that only the policies linked to the particular OU were applied. If GPOs need to be applied to this container, links would need to be created at that particular container level, or the GPO link from the parent container would need to be enforced, which would override the block inheritance setting.

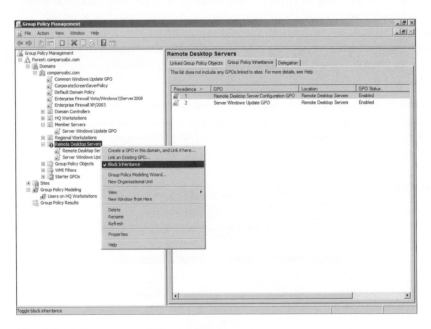

FIGURE 19.7    Blocking GPO inheritance.

## Group Policy Order of Processing

GPOs can be linked at many different levels and in many Active Directory infrastructures; multiple GPOs are linked at the same OU or domain level. This is a very common practice because this particular configuration follows a GPO best-practice recommendation, included in a later section in this chapter, of creating separate GPOs for a particular set of functions. As GPOs are processed one at a time, the GPO links are processed in a particular order starting with GPOs inherited from parent containers followed by the order of policies that were linked to that container. The resulting impact of this processing order is that when multiple GPOs contain the same configured setting, the last GPO applied provides the resulting setting value. As an example of this, if two GPOs are linked at the domain level, named GPO1 and GPO2, and GPO1 has a configured setting of "Remove Task Manager" set to disabled and GPO2 has the same setting set to enabled, the end result is enabled for that setting. To fully understand what the end resulting policy will be in a container that has multiple GPOs linked and inherited, the Resultant Set of Policy tool should be run in Planning mode from the Active Directory Users and Computers console or Group Policy Modeling can be run from the GPMC console. Resultant Set of Policies will provide a console showing the final applied policy settings. Group Policy Modeling will go further and provide a report detailing which policies were applied, in which order the policies were applied, and the resulting policy settings. The steps required to run Group Policy Modeling are detailed in Chapter 27. One easy way to understand this is to know that when looking at a particular Active Directory container in GPMC, the group policy link order and the group policy precedence order are processed from the highest number down. This means that the group policy that has a link order of 1 will always be processed last by objects within that container.

## GPO Filtering

Applying GPOs can be tricky and the design of the Active Directory forest, domains, sites, and OU hierarchy play a major part in this. One of the most important considerations when designing the Active Directory OU hierarchy within a domain is to understand how the domain administrators plan to manage the domain computers and users with group policies. Designing the Active Directory infrastructure is discussed in detail in Chapters 5 and 6, "Designing a Windows Server 2008 R2 Active Directory" and "Designing Organizational Unit and Group Structure," respectively.

In many cases, even with the most careful planning of the Active Directory infrastructure, GPOs will be applied to computers and/or users that do not necessarily need the settings contained within that GPO. To better target which computer and user objects a particular GPO applies to, Microsoft has built in a few different mechanisms to help filter out or include only the necessary objects to ensure that only the desired computers or users actually apply the policy. The mechanisms that control or filter how a policy will be applied are as follows:

▶ GPO security filtering

▶ GPO WMI filtering

▶ GPO status for the Computer Configuration or User Configuration nodes

### GPO Security Filtering

GPO security filtering is the "group" in Group Policy. Many administrators can get frustrated when having to explain the fact that Group Policy applies to computers and users but not to groups. In fact, the GPO security filtering is where administrators can define which users, computers, or members of security groups will actually apply the group policy.

By default, GPOs apply to the Authenticated Users security group, which includes all users and computers in the domain. The scope of GPO application is then segmented based on the location of the Group Policy links. It can be segmented even further by removing the Authenticated Users group from the GPO security filtering, as shown in Figure 19.8, and replacing it with a custom security group.

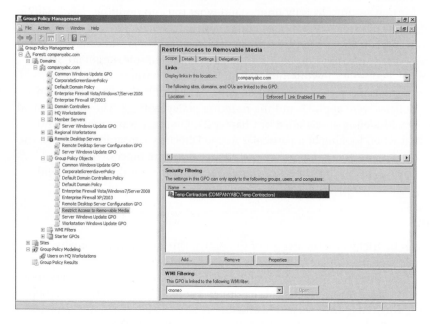

FIGURE 19.8    Examining GPO security filtering.

When the security filtering of a GPO is configured to apply to a custom security group, only the members of that group, whether users, other groups, or computer objects, will actually apply that particular policy. Last but not least, it is most important to always keep the group membership current; otherwise, the application of Group Policy might be incomplete or incorrect.

### GPO WMI Filtering

GPO WMI filtering is a Group Policy concept introduced in Windows XP and Windows Server 2003. A WMI filter is a query that is processed by computer objects only and can be used to include or exclude particular computer objects from applying a GPO that includes the WMI filter. An example of a WMI filter could be a query that includes only computer objects with an operating system version of "6.1*," which includes all Windows 7 and Windows Server 2008 R2 systems. Of course, it is important to state that WMI filters will not be processed by legacy Windows 2000 or older systems. The security filtering must also meet the criteria for the GPO to be processed. WMI filters work great when the Active

Directory hierarchy is relatively flat, but maintaining computer group membership can be tedious. How to create WMI filters, including a few examples, is included in Chapter 27.

### GPO Status

As mentioned previously in this chapter, GPOs are applied to computer and user objects. Within a particular GPO, the settings available are segmented into two distinct nodes, including the Computer Configuration node and the User Configuration node.

Configuring or changing the GPO status, shown in Figure 19.9, enables administrators to change the GPO as follows:

▶ Enabled (Default)

▶ User Configuration Settings Disabled

▶ Computer Configuration Settings Disabled

▶ All Settings Disabled

This function of a GPO can be a very effective tool in troubleshooting GPOs as well as optimizing GPO processing. As an example, if a GPO only contains configured settings in the Computer Configuration node, if any user objects are located in containers linked to that particular GPO, the GPO will still be processed by the user to check for any configured settings. This simple check can add a few seconds to the entire GPO processing time for that user, and if many GPOs are processed, it could increase the logon, logoff, or refresh interval by minutes or more. As a troubleshooting tool, if a user or computer is

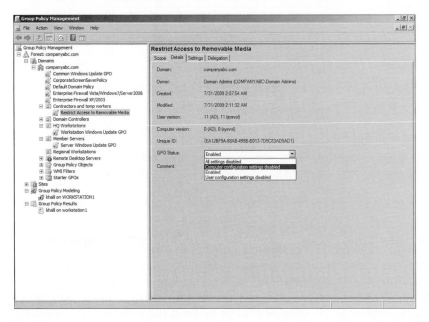

FIGURE 19.9    Examining GPO status.

not receiving the desired end result of a set of applied policies, disabling a node or the entire policy can aid an administrator in identifying the suspect GPO causing the undesired result.

## Group Policy Loopback Processing

Group Policy loopback processing, shown in Figure 19.10, allows for the processing of both the Computer Configuration and User Configuration nodes within a policy even if the user object is not in the same container as the computer that the group policy is linked to. As an example, this function would be useful with a Remote Desktop Session Host deployment where you want to apply computer configuration policies to configure the Remote Desktop server settings but you also want to control the user settings of any user who logs on to the server, regardless of where the actual user account is stored in Active Directory.

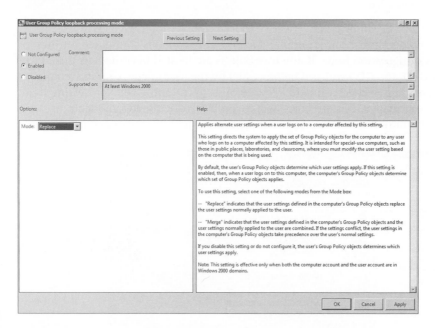

FIGURE 19.10    Examining Group Policy loopback processing.

## Group Policy Slow Link Detection and Network Location Awareness

Group Policy uses several mechanisms to determine whether a policy should be processed. One of the mechanisms used by the Group Policy client computer is called slow link detection. By default, network tests are performed between the client computer and the domain controller to determine the speed of the link between the systems. If the speed is determined to be less than 500kbit/sec, the Group Policy does not process any policies. Slow link detection default settings, along with the ability to disable slow link detection, are configurable with each policy.

In previous versions, Group Policy utilized the ICMP protocol or Ping to detect slow links; this setting is shown in Figure 19.11. With Windows Vista, Windows 7, Windows Server 2008, and Windows Server 2008 R2, Group Policy now uses the Windows Network Location Awareness service to determine network status. The slow link detection settings are controlled within the Policies\Administrative Templates\System\Group Policy sections of the GPO.

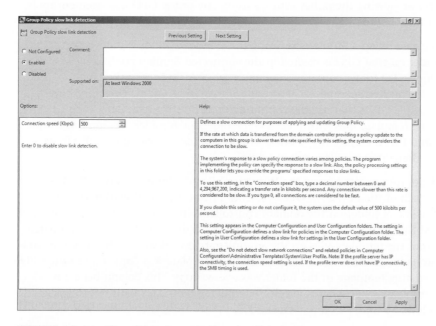

FIGURE 19.11    Examining Group Policy slow link detection.

# Group Policy Administrative Templates Explained

Administrative templates are the core elements that make up a GPO. Most settings available within an administrative template are used to configure a corresponding Registry value for the computer or a user account, usually defined within the HKEY_Local_Machine or the HKEY_Current_User Registry hive. Other settings are provided to run computer- and user-based scripts and, in some instances, install or make software packages available to subsets of users or computers.

Administrative templates come in three basic types:

▶ ADM files for Windows 2000 client and server, Windows XP, and Windows Server 2003

▶ ADMX and ADML files for Windows Vista, Windows 7, Windows Server 2008, and Windows Server 2008 R2

▶ Custom ADM, ADMX, and ADML files used to extend GPO functionality beyond what is already included in the Microsoft provided templates

## Administrative Templates for Windows 2000, Windows XP, and Windows Server 2003

Administrative templates for Windows 2000, Windows XP, and Windows Server 2003 have a file extension of .adm. ADM file formats are unlike any other file format and are not the easiest to interpret and create. ADM files include not only the policy settings and their possible values, but they also include the friendly language used to represent the settings to the administrator viewing the policy settings using any of the GPO management tools, detailed later in this chapter.

For each GPO created by an administrator using the Windows XP or Windows Server 2003 GPO tools, a folder for that GPO is created in the connected domain controller's sysvol folder. This unique GPO folder contains a common set of ADM files in the language used on the administrative client computer. As a result of this, in an Active Directory infrastructure that has multiple GPOs that use the common administrative templates, each GPO has copies of the same template files within each GPO folder. Each folder is commonly 3MB to 5MB in size and this is commonly referred to as sysvol bloat because the GPO folders are stored in the domain controller's sysvol folder.

When new policies were created using the Windows XP and Windows Server 2003 GPO tools, a copy of each of the of the ADM template files from the client workstation was pushed up to the sysvol folder on the domain controller. When an existing GPO was edited or opened for viewing, the copy of the templates in the GPO folder was compared with the version of the template files on the administrative workstation. If the administrative workstation had a newer version, the workstation template was copied up to the GPO folder and the existing template in the folder was overwritten. This default behavior caused several problems when Microsoft released updated templates with service pack releases of Windows XP and Windows Server 2003.

A common issue related to this feature, as an example, is that if an administrator working on a Windows XP SP2 administrative workstation opened an existing GPO that was created with a Windows XP SP1 workstation, the template files would be updated to the new version, causing a replication of the updated templates across all domain controllers. Another implication of the template file is that the template files included the friendly language of the administrative workstation the GPO was created on and administrators across the globe would be unable to manage the same GPO in their local operating system language. This, of course, caused several administration issues and, in some cases, regional Active Directory domains were created to allow regional administrators to manage their client workstations and users with GPOs written and managed in their local language. To support global administration, Active Directory infrastructures have become unnecessarily complicated and moved away from the original reason GPOs were created, to simplify the management, standardize security, and centrally administer and configure companywide resources.

As a means of avoiding the administrative- and infrastructure-related issues associated with this GPO infrastructure, a common best practice for managing GPOs for XP or later operating systems is to only manage GPOs from workstations or servers that meet a single specification for operating system version, service pack level, and language. Another means of controlling this is to follow a common practice of configuring all GPOs to not automatically update GPO templates when a GPO is opened for editing. Automatic updates of ADM files, shown in Figure 19.12, is located in the User Configuration\Policies\Administrative Templates\System\Group Policy\ section and is named Turn off automatic updates of ADM Files. As a best practice, many administrators enable this setting to improve GPO reliability and to keep GPO replication traffic at a minimum.

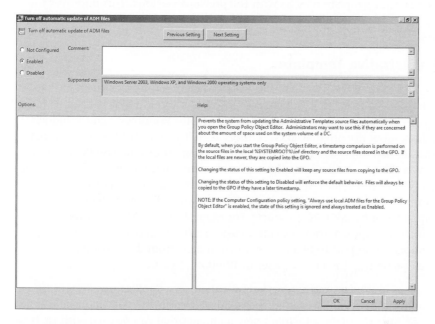

FIGURE 19.12    Examining automatic updates of ADM files.

## Group Policy Administrative Templates for Windows Vista, Windows 7, Windows Server 2008, and Windows Server 2008 R2

Group Policy for Windows Vista and Windows Server 2008 have been completely revised and rebuilt from the previous versions, but they still support Windows 2000 client and server, Windows XP, and Windows Server 2003. Windows 7 and Windows Server 2008 R2 build upon this new revision, adding new settings to support the features of the latest operating systems. The original ADM files have been replaced or split into two files:

▶ ADMX administrative template settings file

▶ ADML administrative template language file

The original GPO single administrative template ADM file format was replaced to overcome many of the original issues with this file format, including the unique ADM format as well as the inclusive local language of the particular ADM files contained on the administrative workstation.

With the separation of the ADM file into a settings and local language file, the new templates enable the administration of a single GPO using different local languages.

19

In previous versions, when an administrator viewed or edited a GPO, the local template files from the administrative workstation were pushed up to the server GPO folder. With the new Windows Vista/Windows Server 2008 R2 GPO infrastructure, when the GPO is opened for viewing or editing, the template files located on the local hard drive are loaded to view the GPO. The GPO folder created with the Windows Vista or Windows Server 2008 R2 GPO tools contains only the files and folders that provide the specifics of the GPO and not the general template files, as with the previous versions. This improves the GPO processing time as well as reduces the amount of data stored in the sysvol folder on each domain controller.

## Custom Administrative Templates

Microsoft has provided, in previous versions as well as the current release, the ability for administrators and independent software vendors (ISVs) to create their own administrative templates. The current administrative templates released with Windows 7 and Windows Server 2008 R2 have all of the original ADM settings as well as many of the settings that administrators either had to create custom templates to support or purchase ISV-created templates. But even though the new templates provide many more settings, there will still be custom Registry keys and values, specific application services, and other functions that organizations want to manage with GPOs. These settings will still need to be provided with custom templates or by ISV GPO products. For example, when Microsoft releases a new version of Internet Explorer, they provide a custom administrative template Group Policy administrators can import to block domain computers from downloading, installing, or even presenting the new browser in Windows Updates.

Many ISVs now provide administrative templates for their own applications. Microsoft also provides administrative templates to further manage their own applications and suites; for example, Microsoft Office includes new templates that can be used with each new version of the Office suites.

Custom administrative templates can be created in both the ADM and ADMX/ADML file formats. To support the amount of time and effort administrators and ISVs have put into creating custom templates and to support legacy applications, new GPOs will continue to support administrative templates created in the original ADM file format as well as the new ADMX/ADML formats.

Although Microsoft has provided the steps to create custom ADMX and ADML files, the current GPO management tools only allow adding custom ADM templates to specific GPOs. To leverage the settings in a new custom ADM file, the file must be added to each GPO that will use it. ADM files that are added to a GPO are made available beneath the respective Administrative Templates\Classic Administrative Templates (ADM) section of the computer or user configuration Policies node.

**NOTE**

When a Group Policy administrator needs to extend Group Policy settings using ADMX/ADML templates, they should consider using a central store and simply add these templates to the store, as explained in Chapter 27.

# Policy Management Tools

Microsoft provides several different tools administrators can use to create and manage local and domain group policies. The operating system version the administrator is using to manage policies determines the functionality the tools provide. As an example, when new group policies are created using the Windows Server 2008 or Windows Server 2008 R2 Group Policy Management Console, the GPO folder utilizes the new ADMX/ADML templates, whereas the Windows XP and Windows Server 2003 tool uploads the original ADM template files into the GPO folder.

This section of the chapter details the tools provided with Windows Vista, Windows 7, Windows Server 2008, and Windows Server 2008 R2 to manage local and group policies.

## Group Policy Management Console (GPMC)

The most functional and useful tool provided to create and manage Active Directory group policies is the Group Policy Management Console (GPMC), shown in Figure 19.13. The GPMC was introduced after the release of Windows Server 2003; the functionality included with different operating systems produces different options and resulting operations when creating and managing Active Directory group policies.

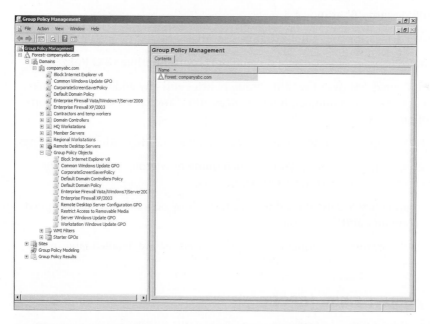

FIGURE 19.13   Examining the Group Policy Management Console.

The GPMC is a Microsoft Management Console (MMC) snap-in and can be added to a custom console. The GPMC snap-in provides the most functionality for administrators who want to manage domain group policies. The GPMC provided with Windows Server 2008 R2 can perform the following Group Policy administrative functions:

- Enable starter GPO functionality and create new starter GPOs.
- Create new domain group policies.
- Create new group policies using starter GPOs as templates.
- Create and configure GPO links to sites, domains, and organizational units.
- View and manage GPOs in domains in the local and trusted Active Directory forests.
- Back up and restore a single or all GPOs in a domain.
- Back up and restore a single or all starter GPOs in a domain.
- Import group policies from external domains and migrate security settings using migration tables to ensure proper import functionality.
- Manage GPO link enforcement, enable links, and disable links.
- Configure the block inheritance settings for sites, domains, and organizational units.
- Manage GPO status to control which nodes in a GPO are enabled or disabled.
- Create and link WMI filters for GPOs.
- Manage GPO security filtering.
- Manage GPO delegation and administrative security.
- Manage the GPO order of processing on containers with multiple GPO links.
- View all configured settings of existing group policies and any additional information, such as the revision number, filtering, delegation, and create exported reports of the configuration.
- Generate HTML reports used to summarize Group Policy configurations and settings.
- Run the Group Policy Modeling Wizard to determine how group policies will be applied to users or computers in specific containers.
- Run the Group Policy Results Wizard to investigate how policies have been applied to specific computer and/or user objects.

Many of the GPMC administrative functions in the previous list are detailed later in this chapter.

## Group Policy Object Editor (GPOE)

The Group Policy Object Editor (GPOE), shown in Figure 19.14, is the tool used to edit local group computer and user policies. Each server and workstation computer has a default local security policy. This policy is accessed through the shortcut to the specific Local Security Policy MMC snap-in located in the Administrative Tools program folder. Now that Windows Vista, Windows 7, Windows Server 2008, and Windows Server 2008

R2 support multiple local group policies, the GPOE must be used to manage or create any local group policies other than the default.

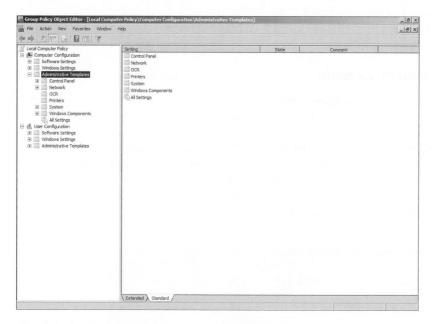

FIGURE 19.14    Examining the Group Policy Object Editor.

The GPOE is used to edit all of the configuration settings of a policy. This includes configuring security settings, installing software packages, creating restriction policies, defining the scripts used by computers and users, and many other functions.

## Group Policy Management Editor (GPME)

To manage domain group policies, the Group Policy Management Editor (GPME) is used and provides the same functionality as the GPOE plus additional functionality only available with this tool. One of the biggest differences is that the GPME includes not only the Policy Settings node, but it also includes the Preferences Settings node, which is only available in domains. GPME is installed on Windows Vista and Windows 7 by downloading and installing the RSAT tools for the particular service pack and operating system. On Windows Server 2008 and Windows Server 2008 R2 operating systems, the group policy tools can be installed from the Add Features applet of Server Manager.

## Group Policy Starter GPO Editor

The Group Policy Starter GPO Editor is used to edit starter GPOs created by Group Policy administrators. This console only shows the Administrative Templates nodes under the Computer Configuration and User Configuration sections of a starter GPO. By default, the settings available in the Administrative Templates sections are all that can be set in a starter GPO; however, Microsoft provides read-only starter GPOs for Windows Vista and Windows XP and will later release starter GPOs for Windows 7 that can be downloaded and imported into the domain starter GPO repository that includes additional settings, including security- and firewall-related settings. The Group Policy Starter GPO Editor is included with the Windows Vista, Windows 7, Windows Server 2008, and Windows Server 2008 R2 Remote Server Administration Tools.

## Print Management Console

First introduced with Windows Server 2003 R2 edition, the Print Management console is used to manage Active Directory and local server and workstation printers. The Print Management console, shown in Figure 19.15, can be used to view settings, configure drivers and options, and manage printer and print jobs on a particular system or Active Directory–wide. The Print Management console can also be used to deploy printers to computers or users using the Deployed Printers node. Deploying printers is a function that extends Group Policy functionality to allow printers to be deployed to a predetermined set of users or computer objects to which a GPO is linked.

FIGURE 19.15    Examining the Print Management console.

The GPOE and the GPME on Windows Vista and Windows 7 will include the Deployed Printers node beneath the Windows Settings node in both the Computer Configuration and User Configuration settings nodes. On Windows Server 2008 and Windows Server 2008 R2, the Print Management console will need to be installed from the Server Manager Features, Add Features link before the Deployed Printers node will be available in the Group Policy Editor consoles. If a policy contains printers defined in the Deployed

Printers nodes, and the policy is viewed using the GPMC or GPME on Windows XP, the deployed printers will not be viewed. Furthermore, if the policy is opened on a Windows Server 2003 R2 server, and if the Print Management console is not installed from Windows components, the Deployed Printers node will not be shown. As a best practice, only create GPOs to deploy printers using the GPMC and GPME on Windows Vista, Windows 7, and Windows Server 2008 R2 systems. To install the Print Management console on Windows Server 2008 R2, run the Add Features applet from Server Manager and select the Print and Document Services Tools from the Remote Administration Tools submenu.

## gpupdate.exe

The gpupdate.exe tool is a command-line tool that assists administrators in troubleshooting GPO processing and initiating GPO processing on demand. Certain sections of group policies will only be applied at computer startup and user logon, whereas others will be applied during these intervals as well as during the periodic refresh interval. For the settings that apply during the computer startup and user logon intervals, if network connectivity to the domain controllers is not available during this interval, these settings might not ever be applied. Also, remote or mobile workstations, systems that are put to sleep or hibernated, and users logging on using cached credentials usually do not get these policies applied. This is where the new Network Location Awareness service for Windows Vista, Window 7, Windows Server 2008, and Windows Server 2008 R2 comes into play as it will notify the system that a domain controller is available and that will trigger a group policy refresh cycle.

The gpupdate.exe tool provides the ability for user and computer policies to be applied immediately. One common use of this tool was to add the gpupdate.exe to a VPN post connection script to allow these settings to be applied to remote workstations that belong to the Active Directory infrastructure. This tool provides the following options:

- ▶ gpupdate.exe /Target:{Computer|user}—This function allows the tool to process only the specified node of the group policy.

- ▶ gpupdate.exe /Force—This option reapplies all policy settings. This option does not automatically reboot the computer or log off the users.

- ▶ gpupdate.exe /Wait—This option defines how many seconds to allow GPO processing to complete. The default is 600 seconds, or 10 minutes.

- ▶ gpupdate.exe /Logoff—This option logs off the user account after GPO processing has completed.

- ▶ gpupdate.exe /Boot—This option reboots the computer after Group Policy processing completes. This is to apply the GPO settings that are only applied during computer startup.

- ▶ gpupdate.exe /Sync—This option processes GPO settings that normally only occur during computer startup and user logon. This option requires that the administrator designate whether the system can restart the computer or log off the user.

## PowerShell Management of Group Policies

With the release of Windows 7 and Windows Server 2008 R2, Microsoft has now added functionality to manage group policies with PowerShell. This functionality will be automatically enabled once the Group Policy Management feature is installed on a Windows 7 or Windows Server 2008 R2 system. Microsoft has included 25 out-of-the-box PowerShell cmdlets for Group Policy. The cmdlets allow a Group Policy administrator to perform a number of different functions from within PowerShell, including, but not limited to, the following:

▶ Create new GPOs and create new starter GPOs.

▶ Create new GPO links.

▶ Restore or import GPOs.

▶ Remove GPOs and GPO links.

▶ Read and/or set the properties of an OU to inherit parent GPO links or to block inheritance.

▶ Rename a GPO.

▶ Generate a report of GPO settings and configurations.

▶ Generate a Resultant Set of Policies report.

▶ Set GPO administrative permissions and delegation.

▶ Set GPO policy and preference settings that are stored in the Registry.

Two important points that need to be stated about managing GPOs though PowerShell is that in order to manage or report on any existing GPO, the Group Policy administrator must know the GUID ID of the GPO or the exact spelling of the name. The second point is that currently there is no PowerShell GPO cmdlet that can configure or report on the GPO link precedence of a particular domain or organizational unit.

## Microsoft Desktop Optimization Pack for Software Assurance

The Microsoft Desktop Optimization Pack for Software Assurance contains several functions and features that administrators can leverage to assist with the management of the organization's desktops. One feature included with this kit is called Microsoft Advanced Group Policy Management (AGPM), which provides extended functionality not available in the GPMC and GPME. This feature provides several functions to improve GPO management, including GPO change control, GPO archiving, offline editing of GPOs, granular GPO administrative delegation, integration of policy changes, and auditing and GPO difference and comparison functionality. AGPM can even enable administrators to reject changes to GPOs or roll back a GPO to a previous version stored in the archive. AGPM 3.0

is supported on Windows Vista and Windows Server 2008, but provides only partial support for Windows 7 and Windows Server 2008 R2.

The Desktop Optimization Pack is only available for software assurance customers and your Microsoft reseller should be contacted to determine how to qualify for or download the pack.

## ADMX Migrator

The ADMX Migrator tool, shown in Figure 19.16, allows administrators to take existing ADM templates and migrate those settings to the new ADMX and ADML template format. This tool is fully supported by www.fullarmor.com, the company that makes ADMX Migrator. The tool creates both the ADMX and ADML files, and after they are created, they can be copied to the PolicyDefinitions folder of a Windows Vista, Windows 7, Windows Server 2008, or Windows Server 2008 R2 system or GPO central store in a test Active Directory infrastructure for testing. Any ADMX/ADML files created using this tool should be tested thoroughly before releasing to a pilot group or users or computers in production.

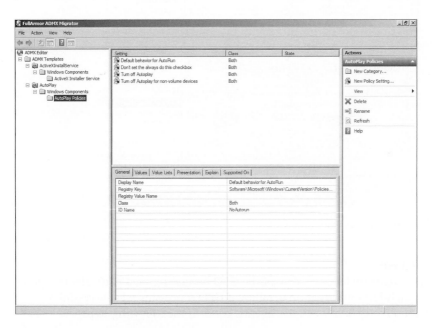

FIGURE 19.16   Examining the ADMX Migrator tool.

## Group Policy Log View (GPLogView)

GPLogview is a downloadable tool from Microsoft that allows administrators to monitor or generate reports of GPO administrative and operational events in text, XML, and HTML format. The tool can be run in monitor mode during a Group Policy refresh interval to

19

watch a live view of what the GPO processing is logging. GPLogView is available for download but is not supported by Microsoft.

## Event Viewer

Event Viewer for Windows 7 and Windows Server 2008 R2 includes several new event logs, which now provide additional GPO logging events, similar to those shown in Figure 19.17. GPO logging now includes administrative GPO events, stored in the system log with a source of "Group Policy," and GPO operational events, stored in the "Applications and Services Logs," which is stored in Microsoft/Windows/GroupPolicy/Operational.

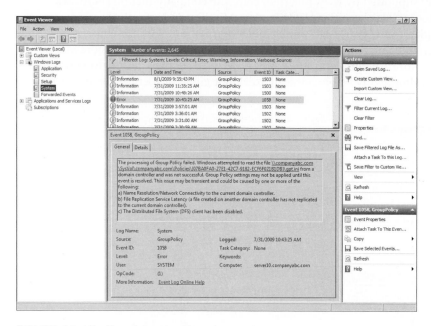

FIGURE 19.17    Examining the filtered event log.

### GPO Administrative Events

The administrative events include the state of the GPO processing on a particular computer or user, including high-level information detailing if GPO processing was successful or failed. To view Group Policy administrative events, perform the following steps:

1. Log on to a designated administrative workstation running Windows Server 2008 R2.

2. Click the Start button.

3. Select All Programs.

4. Select Administrative Tools.

5. Double-click the shortcut for Event Viewer.

6. When Event Viewer opens, expand Windows Logs.

7. Right-click the System log and select Filter Current Log.

8. In the middle of the filter windows, click the Event Sources drop-down list arrow.

9. Scroll down and check Group Policy and click back on the filter window to close the menu.

10. Click OK at the bottom of the window to apply the filter.

11. Review the group policy events.

12. If the task is complete, close Event Viewer to clear the filter; otherwise, clear the filter by right-clicking on the system log and selecting Clear Filter.

13. Close Event Viewer when you are finished.

### GPO Operational Events

The GPO operational events include very granular detail of GPO processing. When GPO processing occurs, the operational events are created almost one for one with each task included within the GPO processing. This new logging functionality simplifies troubleshooting GPO processing tremendously. To view the GPO operational events on a Windows Server 2008 R2 system, perform the following steps:

1. Log on to a designated administrative workstation running Windows Server 2008 R2.

2. Click the Start button.

3. Select All Programs.

4. Select Administrative Tools.

5. Double-click the shortcut for Event Viewer.

6. When Event Viewer opens, expand Applications and Services Logs.

7. Expand Microsoft.

8. Expand Windows.

9. Expand Group Policy.

10. Select the Operational log beneath the Group Policy container and view the events in the right pane.

11. Click on particular events to see the details.

12. Close Event Viewer when you are finished.

## DFS Management

GPO files are stored in the Active Directory domain sysvol folder. GPO files in the sysvol folder are replicated by the Distributed File System Replication service. The DFS Management console enabled administrators to configure the replication options, including scheduling and other DFS management tasks. The sysvol share is known as the domain system volume and the replication of this volume follows the site link replication schedule. More details about the DFSR service can be found in Chapter 28, "File System Management and Fault Tolerance." Changing or managing the domain system volume replication schedule between domain controllers in the same Active Directory site is not an option.

# Designing a Group Policy Infrastructure

Designing a Group Policy infrastructure requires a detailed understanding of the available configuration settings available in Group Policy Objects. Chapter 27 details the available settings administrators can configure with group policies and also covers some best-practice configurations. This section of the chapter covers the high-level steps required to successfully plan and deploy a reliable Group Policy infrastructure.

## Active Directory Design and Group Policy

A key to determining how to best design the Group Policy infrastructure is to first understand how the Active Directory infrastructure is configured. The site, domain, and OU design of an Active Directory infrastructure usually follows a few key elements, including physical office locations, network connectivity, and delegation of administration, including branch office management, separation of Active Directory management tasks, desktop and server administration, and, of course, security and reliability.

### Site Group Policy Links

Group policies can be linked to Active Directory site objects. There is no default site policy created when Active Directory is first deployed. In the past, common uses of site-linked group policies included settings related to networking and security configurations. Some considerations for determining whether a GPO should be linked at a site should include the following:

▶ Every object in a site, determined by the associated site subnet, will process the policy, regardless of the domain the user or computer account is located in. Is this the desired configuration?

▶ Does the site contain a domain controller in the domain in which the group policy is created?

▶ Do any of the associated site subnets include networks across slow links or virtual private networks? If so, changing the default values or disabling slow link detection on the site policy might be required for proper processing.

▶ Is there a particular security requirement for the site that required a higher level of enforced security or a required configuration or application?

Before a GPO can be linked to a site, the site will need to be added into the GPMC. To add an Active Directory site to the GPMC and add a GPO link, perform the following steps:

1. Log on to a designated Windows Server 2008 R2 administrative server.

2. Open the Group Policy Management Console.

3. Right-click the Sites container and select Show Sites.

4. In the Show Sites window, click the Select All button or check the box next to the site you want to add to the GPMC. Click OK to add the site(s) to the console.

5. In the tree pane, expand the Sites container, and right-click the desired site.

6. Select the Link an Existing GPO option.

7. In the Select GPO window, select the source domain from which you want to link the GPO.

8. In the Group Policy Objects section of the window, select the desired GPO or GPOs, and then click OK to create the link.

9. If necessary, configure the link settings for each new site link and then close the GPMC.

### Domain GPO Links

When Active Directory is deployed, two preconfigured, default group policies are created. One is linked to the domain named the Default Domain Policy and the other is linked to the Domain Controllers OU named the Default Domain Controllers Policy.

The Default Domain Policy contains the default security settings for the entire domain, including account policies. As a best practice, use this policy only for managing the default account policies for the entire domain. Any additional GPO settings that an organization would desire to apply to all users and/or computers, including domain controllers, member servers, and client workstations, should be added to new Group Policy Objects and linked at the domain level. The number of policies linked at the domain level should be kept to a minimum to ensure quality Group Policy processing performance for the organization.

### Organizational Unit Links

Linking GPOs to organizational units is the most common use of GPO links. OU GPO links provide the most targeted GPO application and granular administrative control of the OU GPO–related tasks as well as the configuration and management of the objects contained in the OU. The only way to get more granular on an OU GPO link is to apply a security filter or a WMI filter on that particular GPO, but that would affect each GPO link related to that particular policy.

## Separation of GPO Functions

Determining which features and settings of a GPO will be utilized is one consideration; another is determining how to deploy those settings. There is one major consideration with GPO management that should be considered: Should a single GPO be created to contain all the necessary settings, or should separate GPOs be created for a particular set of features or functions?

As a best practice, separating GPO functions across multiple GPOs provides more flexibility but also adds time to GPO processing and increases the amount of GPO administration that needs to be performed. Separating GPOs for specific functions provides additional troubleshooting options and greater flexibility for how GPOs can be linked and filtered. As an example of how to separate GPO functions, the following list of GPOs can be applied to a Branch Office OU that contains user objects, group objects, and computer objects:

▶ **Branch Office Help Desk GPO**—This GPO would configure settings to allow help desk administrators to manually run Windows Update, access all Control Panel applets, and run all software with unrestricted access. This would be the last GPO applied and would override any conflicting settings. This GPO status would be set to Computer Configuration Settings Disabled and the security filtering would be configured to use a security group called Branch Office Help Desk, which would include the help desk support staff.

▶ **Branch Office Server GPO**—This GPO can contain the default security settings and software packages specific for branch office servers. Also this policy would configure specific audit settings, account management settings, and user rights assignments for servers. The GPO status would be configured for User Configuration Settings Disabled and would have a WMI filter linked that includes computers with an operating system name that includes the word server.

▶ **Branch Office User GPO**—This GPO can contain the default security and configuration settings to configure the end-user desktop environment, including managing Microsoft Internet Explorer settings, redirecting folders to the branch office DFSR shares, enabling offline files, mapping network drives, installing network printers, and configuring settings to hide or restrict access to specific Control Panel applets. The GPO status of this GPO would be configured to Computer Configuration Settings Disabled.

▶ **Branch Office Workstation GPO**—This GPO can contain the default security settings used to manage the services, install corporate software packages and VPN clients, configure workstation security, and enable remote access. This GPO would be filtered using a WMI filter that includes only computer objects whose operating system name value contained Windows 7. The GPO status would be set to User Configuration Settings Disabled. This GPO would be applied first to the workstations after local and inherited GPOs.

## Separation of GPO by Targeted Operating System

With each release of a Microsoft client or server operating system, Microsoft provides new Group Policy settings and functionality. The release of Windows 7 and Windows Server 2008 R2 is no different as there are several new Group Policy settings that will not apply to any other operating systems. These include both policy and preference settings to manage. Some of the preferences include managing power settings on Windows Vista and newer operating systems as well as adding scheduled tasks and immediately scheduled tasks that will run at the next Group Policy refresh cycle. These preferences are detailed in Chapter 27.

When operating system–specific Group Policy settings will be used, a best practice is to filter out all other operating systems the GPO applies to. The best way to do this is with the use of a WMI filter for computers. Security filtering can also be used but if a security group is used, a computer will only pick up group changes during startup, so getting application of a new policy adopted is less successful. A WMI filter will be processed by all

Windows XP, Windows Vista, Windows 7, Windows Server 2003, or Windows Server 2008 systems. How to create a WMI filter is detailed later in this chapter in the section "Creating and Linking WMI Filters to GPOs."

# GPO Administrative Tasks

This section of the chapter includes detailed steps an administrator can perform to execute GPO-related administrative tasks.

## Installing the Group Policy Management Tools

Before Group Policy can be managed, the Group Policy Management Tools must be installed. These tools are installed by default on Windows Server 2008 R2 domain controllers, but for other systems, they must be manually installed. The following sections detail installation steps for Windows Server 2008 R2 and Windows 7 systems.

### Installing the Group Policy Management Tools on Windows Server 2008 R2

Before group policies can be managed from a Windows Server 2008 R2 system, the Group Policy Management feature must be installed, as detailed in the following steps:

1. Log on to a designated administrative system running Windows Server 2008 R2.

2. Open Server Manager from the Administrative Tools menu.

3. After Server Manager loads, click on the Features node in the tree pane.

4. Select Add Features in the right pane.

5. Scroll down and check the box next to Group Policy Management and click Next.

6. Confirm the selection and click Install to begin the process.

7. After the process completes, click Close to complete the installation.

### Installing the Group Policy Management Tools on Windows 7

To manage domain group policies from a Windows 7 system, the administrator must download the "Remote Server Administration Tools for Windows 7" from the Microsoft download site. After the tool is downloaded, it must be installed on the Windows 7 system by an administrator. Once the tool is installed, the Group Policy Management feature can be installed from Control Panel, as detailed in the following steps:

1. Log on to a designated administrative system running Windows 7 after the Remote Server Administration Tools for Windows 7 are installed.

2. Open Control Panel from the Start menu.

3. Select Programs and click on the Turn Windows Features On or Off link.

4. Scroll down and expand Remote Server Administration Tools.

5. Expand Feature Administration Tools and check the box next to Group Policy Management Tools.

6. Click OK on the Windows Features window to begin the installation.

7. Once the installation completes, close Control Panel.

After these steps are completed, the Group Policy Management feature can be accessed from the Administrative Tools menu. Installing these tools also installs the Group Policy module for PowerShell.

## Managing Group Policy with Windows PowerShell

From a Windows 7 or a Windows Server 2008 R2 system with the Group Policy Management Tools installed, several new Windows PowerShell cmdlets can be leveraged to manage Group Policy. To access these Group Policy cmdlets, follow these steps:

1. Log on to a designated administrative system running Windows 7 or Windows Server 2008 R2.

2. Click the Start or Windows button on the taskbar and in the search pane type in PowerShell.

3. When the results are shown, right-click Windows PowerShell and select Run as Administrator.

4. In the PowerShell window, type `Import-module grouppolicy` and press Enter to enable Group Policy management.

5. Now in the window, type `Get-command *GP* -commandtype cmdlet` and press Enter to see a list of the 25 different Group Policy cmdlets available.

6. To get help information on a specific Group Policy cmdlet, such as "get-gporeport", type `Get-help get-gporeport` and press Enter.

7. And to see syntax usage of a specific cmdlet such as "get-gporeport", type `Get-help get-gporeport -example` and press Enter to see several different examples.

## Creating a GPO Central Store

Starting with Windows Vista and Windows Server 2008, administrators now have the ability to manually create a folder on the Active Directory domain controller that contains all of the necessary ADMX and ADML files. This folder is referred to as the GPO central store and will need to be created and managed manually. The GPO central store can be created in a domain that contains at least Windows Server 2003 domain controllers or greater.

By default, with Windows Vista, Windows 7, Windows Server 2008, and Windows Server 2008 R2, when a GPO is opened for editing on one of these operating systems, the system first checks the domain controller to which the GPO management tool is connected for the existence of a GPO central store. If the folder exists, the GPO loads the templates stored in the folder. If the central store does not exist, the local copies of the ADMX and ADML files are loaded to view the GPO.

The creation of the GPO central store provides a simple, yet effective way for administrators to manage administrative templates from the server. To create the GPO central store, perform the following steps:

1. Log on to a designated administrative system running Windows Vista, Windows 7, Windows Server 2008, or Windows Server 2008 R2.

2. Browse to the C:\Windows\ folder and copy the PolicyDefinitions folder to the Clipboard.

3. In a domain named companyabc.com, open the following folder: \\companyabc.com\sysvol\companyabc.com\policies.

4. Paste the PolicyDefinitions folder from the Clipboard to the folder referenced in the preceding step.

5. Close any open folder windows.

The preceding steps create the central store and populate the store with the ADML language files of the administrative workstation. If additional language files are required, the language subfolder within the PolicyDefinitions folder of the administrative workstation can be copied into the domain's central store now located at \\companyabc.com\sysvol\companyabc.com\policies\PolicyDefinitions.

## Verifying the Usage of the GPO Central Store

To verify whether the central store is actually being used, perform the following steps:

1. Log on to a designated administrative system.

2. Open the Group Policy Management Console.

3. Expand the domain to expose the Group Policy Objects container and expand it.

4. Select any existing GPO that contains at least one configured setting within the Administrative Templates section of either the Computer Configuration or User Configuration node.

5. In the right pane, select the Settings tab to view the settings of the GPO, similar to the settings shown in Figure 19.18.

19

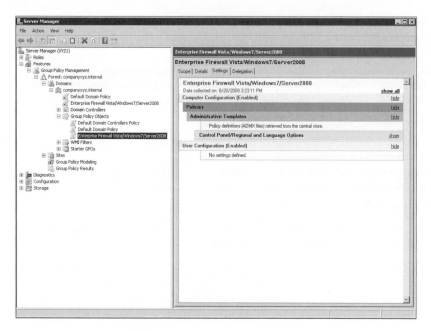

FIGURE 19.18    Examining Group Policy settings.

6. Under Administrative Templates, it will state whether policy definitions (ADMX) files were retrieved from the local machine or from the central store.

7. Close the Group Policy Management Console.

## Creating and Utilizing Starter GPOs

The Windows 7 and Windows Server 2008 R2 GPMC includes a feature and GPO function named starter GPOs. This function allows administrators to create or load base GPOs with preconfigured administrative template settings and values, which can be used to prepopulate new GPOs. If any starter GPOs exist, an administrator creating a new GPO from a Windows 7 or a Windows Server 2008 R2 GPMC console will have the option of using any existing starter GPO to prepopulate newly created GPOs with a number of setting values. Once the starter GPO functionality is enabled, Group Policy administrators can create new starter GPOs customized for their organization's needs.

Starter GPOs can be viewed within the GPMC and can be edited using the Group Policy Starter GPO Editor, but the files are stored within the domain controller sysvol folders. As an example, starter GPOs for the companyabc.com domain would be located at the \\companyabc.com\SYSVOL\companyabc.com\StarterGPOs folder. Microsoft provides some starter GPOs that will be automatically installed when starter GPO functionality is enabled. These currently include templates for two environments as described in the Windows client security guides. These are the Enterprise Client (EC) environment scenario and the Specialized Security Limited Functionality (SSLF) client environment scenario.

The Enterprise Client (EC) environment, as described in the Windows client security guide, is an Active Directory domain infrastructure that runs Windows Server 2003 and Windows Server 2008 servers and Windows Vista and Windows XP client workstations where functionality is as important as security. The preconfigured settings in the EC starter GPOs have been designed to enable the necessary functionality to allow businesses to function with centrally managed user and computer configuration management as well as security management and audit settings.

The Specialized Security Limited Functionality (SSLF) environment, as described in the Windows client security guide, is designed to provide security configurations and guidelines for environments that require higher security, which outweighs the importance of smoother user experiences and manageability. As an example of this, the Windows Vista SSLF Computer starter GPO would deny logon through Terminal Services functionality, whereas the Windows Vista EC Computer policy leaves this setting undefined. This policy setting allows Administrators and/or members of the Remote Desktop Users groups to connect using Remote Desktop Connection or Terminal Services clients.

> **CAUTION**
>
> Any Group Policy administrator must take the highest precautions to ensure that no group policies deployed on a network are released without thorough testing in an isolated lab environment. This is especially true when considering deploying policies built on the EC or SSLF starter GPO policies.

The starter GPOs included with Windows Server 2008 R2 GPCM include the following policies:

- ▶ Windows Vista EC Computer
- ▶ Windows Vista EC User
- ▶ Windows Vista SSLF Computer
- ▶ Windows Vista SSLF User
- ▶ Windows XP EC Computer
- ▶ Windows XP EC User
- ▶ Windows XP SSLF Computer
- ▶ Windows XP SSLF User

For more information about the EC and SSLF starter GPOs, refer to the Windows client security guides online.

### Enabling Starter GPOs

Before starter GPOs can be put to use, the functionality must first be enabled in the domain. Enabling this function is about as simple as pushing a button. To enable the starter GPO feature, perform the following steps:

1. Log on to a designated Windows 7 or Windows Server 2008 R2 administrative system.
2. Open the Group Policy Management Console.
3. Expand the domain to expose the Starter GPOs container and select it.
4. In the right pane, click the Create Starter GPOs Folder button.

Once the task is completed, the eight out-of-the-box starter GPOs will be available for review in the GPMC. Also, the Group Policy administrator can now create new starter GPOs from scratch and can also create new GPOs by using starter GPOs as templates.

> **NOTE**
>
> The starter GPOs included with Windows 7 and Windows Server 2008 R2 are read-only and cannot be edited directly. Copies of the built-in starter GPOs can be edited.

### Creating a Starter GPO

Starter GPOs can be created or added to a domain in a few ways. A starter GPO can be created from scratch using a blank template, it can be created by restoring from a starter GPO backup folder, or it can be imported from a provided starter GPO cabinet file. Before the release of the Windows 7 and Windows Server 2008 R2 Group Policy Management tools, the Microsoft EC and SSLF starter GPO policies were provided as separate downloads, stored in cabinet backup files. If an organization has not yet adopted Windows Server 2008 R2 domain controllers, this is the only way to import these starter GPO policies. To create a starter GPO from a backup, please refer to the "Backing Up and Restoring Starter GPOs" section. To create a new starter GPO, perform the following steps:

1. Log on to a designated Windows Server 2008 R2 administrative system.
2. Open the Group Policy Management Console.
3. Expand the domain to expose the Starter GPOs container and select it.
4. Verify that the starter GPO functionality is enabled by viewing the right pane.
5. Right-click the Starter GPOs container in the tree pane, and select New.
6. In the New Starter GPO dialog box, type in a name for the new starter GPO, and enter a comment to describe what will be included in this starter GPO and when and where it should be applied as a template.
7. Click OK to create the new starter GPO.
8. To configure settings in the new starter GPO, right-click the GPO and select Edit to open the GPO in the Group Policy Starter GPO Editor.
9. When the GPO is configured as desired, close the Group Policy Starter GPO Editor.
10. In the GPMC, right-click the newly configured starter GPO, and select Backup to back up this individual starter GPO.
11. Specify a destination folder to back up the GPO, enter a description for this backup, and click Back Up to back up the starter GPO.
12. When the backup completes, review the backup results and click OK to close the window.
13. Close the GPMC tool.

### Creating Starter GPOs from Cabinet Files

To create a new starter GPO from a cabinet file (*.cab), perform the following steps:

1. Log on to a designated Windows Server 2008 R2 administrative system.
2. Open the Group Policy Management Console.
3. Expand the domain to expose the Starter GPOs container and select it.
4. Verify that the starter GPO functionality is enabled by viewing the right pane.
5. In the right pane, near the bottom, select the Load Cabinet button.
6. In the Load Starter GPO dialog box, click the Browse for CAB button to specify the folder location of the starter GPO cabinet file.
7. Locate the cab file, select it, and click Open to return to the Load Starter GPO dialog box.
8. Back in the Load Starter GPO dialog box, the dialog box will display the version information of the cab file in comparison with any existing starter GPOs. Also, the comment will be displayed and the administrator can view the settings. Click OK to load or import the cab file to the domain starter GPO repository.
9. If an existing starter GPO has the same name, it will be overwritten and a confirmation dialog box will require the administrator to click OK to accept this change.
10. Once the cab file is imported, close the GPMC.

## Backing Up and Restoring Starter GPOs

Backing up and restoring starter GPOs is a simple operation that can be performed using the Windows 7 or the Windows Server 2008 R2 GPMC. Starter GPOs can be backed up individually or all of the starter GPOs can be backed up together.

Starting with Windows Vista and Windows Server 2008, the backup functionality of the GPMC allows for the backup of multiple versions of the same GPOs. In previous versions, if an organization wanted historical backups of GPOs, or revisions, the GPOs would need to be backed up to separate folder locations. Now, the backups can all be stored in a single folder.

### Backing Up All Starter GPOs

To back up all of the starter GPOs in a domain, perform the following steps:

1. Log on to a designated Windows Server 2008 R2 administrative system.
2. Open the Group Policy Management Console.
3. Expand the domain to expose the Starter GPOs container and select it.
4. Right-click the starter GPOs and select the Back Up All button.
5. Specify the folder location to store the backup, enter a description of the backup, and click the Back Up button to back up the starter GPOs.

**NOTE**

We recommend that the designated backup folder and the description of the backup specify or make it very easy to differentiate between starter GPO backups and domain GPO backups.

6. In the Backup window, review the status of the backup, and click OK when the backup completes.

### Backing Up a Single Starter GPO

Backing up a starter GPO can only be performed from the Windows 7 or the Windows Server 2008 R2 GPMC. Starter GPOs can be backed up using the original GPMC backup method, which includes version or revision history, but a single starter GPO can also be backed up as a cabinet file. To back up a single starter GPO, perform the following steps:

1. Log on to a designated Windows Server 2008 R2 administrative system.
2. Open the Group Policy Management Console.
3. Expand the domain to expose the Starter GPOs container and expand it.
4. Select the desired starter GPO, right-click it, and then select the Back Up button.
5. Specify the folder location to store the backup, enter a description of the backup, and click the Back Up button to back up the starter GPO.
6. In the Backup window, review the status of the backup, and click OK when the backup completes.

### Saving a Starter GPO as a Cabinet File

Starter GPOs can be exported or saved as individual cabinet (*.cab) files. Starter GPO cabinet files can be used to create new starter GPOs or can be used to move starter GPOs between isolated test and production Active Directory environments. To save an individual starter GPO as a cabinet file, perform the following steps:

1. Log on to a designated Windows Server 2008 R2 administrative system.
2. Open the Group Policy Management Console.
3. Expand the domain to expose the Starter GPOs container and select it.
4. In the right pane, select a single starter GPO, and at the bottom of the pane, click the Save as Cabinet button. This option will only be available if the Starter GPOs container is selected in the tree pane and a single starter GPO is selected in the right pane when the contents page is selected.
5. Browse or type in the location in which to save the cabinet file, specify a name for the cabinet file, and click the Save button to save the starter GPO.

### Restoring a Starter GPO from Backup

Restoring a starter GPO can be performed to revert a GPO to a previously backed-up state or to recover from a starter GPO deletion.

To restore a deleted starter GPO, perform the following steps:

1. Log on to a designated Windows Server 2008 R2 administrative system.
2. Open the Group Policy Management Console.
3. Expand the domain to expose the Starter GPOs container and select it.
4. Right-click the Starter GPO container and select Manage Backups.
5. Browse to or specify the starter GPO backup location to load the starter GPO backup set.
6. In the window, select the desired GPO object.
7. If a filtered view is desired, check the Show Only the Latest Version of Each Starter GPO check box.
8. To view the settings of a particular backed-up GPO, select the desired GPO, and click the View Settings button. Close the browser window after the settings are reviewed.
9. After the desired starter GPO is determined, select the GPO and click the Restore button.
10. Click OK in the Restore confirmation dialog box to restore the starter GPO.
11. Review the GPO restore progress, and click OK when it completes.
12. After all the necessary GPOs are restored, close the Manage Backups window.

To change an existing starter GPO to a previously backed-up version, perform the following steps:

1. Log on to a designated Windows Server 2008 R2 administrative system.
2. Open the Group Policy Management Console.
3. Expand the domain to expose the Starter GPOs container, select and expand it.
4. Locate and right-click the desired starter GPO, and select Restore from Backup.
5. In the Restore Starter GPO Wizard window, click next on the Welcome page.
6. On the next page, browse to or specify the starter GPO backup location, and click Next.
7. If a filtered view is desired, select the Show Only the Latest Version of Each Starter GPO check box.
8. To view the settings of a particular backed-up GPO, select the desired GPO, and click the View Settings button. Close the browser window after the settings are reviewed.
9. After the desired starter GPO is determined, select the GPO, and click Next.
10. Review the settings summary on the Completing the Restore Starter GPO Wizard page, and click Finish to start the restore process.
11. Review the GPO restore progress, and click OK when it completes.

19

### Disabling Starter GPO Functionality

An organization may determine that starter GPO functionality should be removed. In those situations, it is quite easy to disable starter GPO functionality. If starter GPO functionality needs to be removed from a domain, perform the following steps:

1. Log on to a designated Windows Server 2008 R2 administrative system.
2. Open the Group Policy Management Console.
3. Expand the domain to expose the Starter GPOs container and select it.
4. Verify that the starter GPO functionality is enabled by viewing the right pane.
5. If the functionality is enabled, close the GPMC.
6. Click Start and in the search field, type \\companyabc.com\sysvol\companyabc.com\ and press Enter. This example is for the companyabc.com domain; you should substitute your Active Directory DNS domain name.
7. When the explorer window opens, one of the folders shown is the StarterGPOs folder. Right-click and delete that entire folder.
8. Close the explorer windows.
9. Open the Group Policy Management Console again.
10. Expand the domain to expose the Starter GPO container and select it.
11. Verify that the starter GPO functionality is now disabled by viewing the right pane. If starter GPOs are now disabled, there will be a button labeled Create Starter GPO Folder.
12. The task is now complete; close the GPMC.

Removing starter GPO functionality will not affect any domain group policies that were previously creating using any starter GPOs.

## Creating New Domain Group Policies

To create a new domain Group Policy Object, perform the following steps:

1. Log on to a designated Windows Server 2008 R2 administrative system.
2. Open the Group Policy Management Console.
3. Expand the domain to expose the Group Policy Objects container and select it.
4. Right-click the Group Policy Objects container and select New.
5. Type in a name for the new GPO.
6. If the starter GPO functionality in the domain is enabled and if a suitable starter GPO exists, click the Source Starter GPO menu and select either (None) or the desired starter GPO.
7. Click OK to create the GPO.
8. As necessary, edit the security filtering, configure delegation, configure the GPO status, and edit the settings. These steps are detailed in the section "Managing GPO Security Filtering."

9. After the GPO is configured, back up the GPO.

10. Create GPO links and configure advanced link options, as required.

11. Close the GPMC tool.

## Creating and Configuring GPO Links

After a GPO is created and configured, the next step is to link the GPOs to the desired Active Directory containers. To link an existing GPO to an Active Directory container, perform the following steps:

1. Log on to a designated Windows Server 2008 R2 administrative system.

2. Open the Group Policy Management Console.

3. Add the necessary domains or sites to the GPMC, as required.

4. Expand the Domains or Sites node to expose the container to which the GPO will be linked.

5. Right-click the desired site, domain, or organizational unit, and select Link an Existing GPO.

6. In the Select GPO window, select the desired GPO or select multiple GPOs and click OK to link.

### Advanced GPO Link Configuration

After a GPO link is created, it is enabled by default. Each link has its own configuration options, which include link enforcement and the ability to enable and disable the link. To change the default configuration of a GPO link, perform the following steps:

1. Log on to a designated Windows Server 2008 R2 administrative system.

2. Open the Group Policy Management Console.

3. Add the necessary domains or sites to the GPMC, as required.

4. Expand the Domains or Sites node to expose the GPO-linked container.

5. If the GPO link is to be enforced, right-click on the desired GPO link, and select Enforced to enforce the link.

6. If the GPO link will be changed from enabled to disabled, right-click on the desired GPO link and select Link Enabled to check the link (enabled) or uncheck the link (disabled).

## Managing GPO Status

GPO status controls whether the entire GPO is enabled, disabled, or if only the Computer Configuration or User Configuration node is enabled. GPO status is applied to the GPO itself, so all links will be affected by any changes to the GPO status. To view or modify the status of a GPO, perform the following steps:

1. Log on to a designated Windows Server 2008 R2 administrative system.

2. Open the Group Policy Management Console.

3. Expand the domain to expose the Group Policy Objects container and expand it.

4. Select the desired GPO and select the Details tab in the right pane.

5. On the Details tab, in the GPO Status drop-down menu, note the current status of the GPO.

6. If the GPO status needs to be changed, click the drop-down list arrow and select one of the following options:

   ▶ Enabled

   ▶ User Configuration Settings Disabled

   ▶ Computer Configuration Settings Disabled

   ▶ All Settings Disabled

7. After you select the desired GPO status, a confirmation window opens; click OK to complete the status change.

## Creating and Linking WMI Filters to GPOs

When applying security filtering to a GPO is not granular enough to target a specific set of computers, a WMI filter can be linked to the GPO. For this example, we will create a WMI filter that includes a computer with an operating system name of Windows 7. To create the example WMI filter, perform the following steps:

1. Log on to a designated Windows Server 2008 R2 administrative system.

2. Open the Group Policy Management Console.

3. Expand the domain and select the WMI Filters container.

4. Right-click on the WMI Filters container and select New.

5. In the Name section, type in `Windows 7 WMI Filter`.

6. In the Description section, type in `WMI filter to include only Windows 7 workstations`.

7. Click the Add button to create the WMI filter query.

8. In the Query section, type `Select * from Win32_OperatingSystem Where (Name LIKE "%Windows 7%")` to show a GPO WMI filter similar to the one shown in Figure 19.19.

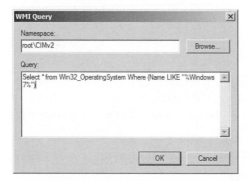

FIGURE 19.19    Examining a GPO WMI filter.

9. Click OK to save the query and return to the WMI Filter window.

10. Click Save to create the WMI filter in the domain.

To link an existing WMI filter to a GPO, perform the following steps:

1. Log on to a designated Windows Server 2008 R2 administrative workstation.

2. Open the Group Policy Management Console.

3. Expand the domain to expose the Group Policy Objects container and expand it.

4. Select the desired GPO and select the Scope tab in the right pane.

5. At the bottom of the Scope tab, in the WMI Filter section, click the WMI Filter drop-down list arrow, and select the desired filter.

6. A confirmation dialog box will open; click Yes to apply the WMI filter to this GPO.

## Managing GPO Security Filtering

Managing security filtering is one of the best ways to target a specific group of users and computers for GPO application. Security filtering can be set to a specific user, computer, or security group object or a combination of all three object types. To change the security filtering of a GPO from the default of Authenticated Users, perform the following steps:

1. Log on to a designated Windows Server 2008 R2 administrative system.

2. Open the Group Policy Management Console.

3. Expand the domain to expose the Group Policy Objects container and expand it.

4. Select the desired GPO and select the Scope tab in the right pane.

5. In the Security Filtering section of the Scope tab, select the Authenticated Users group, and click the Remove button.

6. Click OK in the confirmation dialog box to remove the security group from the GPO security filtering.

7. In the Security Filtering section of the Scope tab, click the Add button to add an Active Directory object to the security filter for the GPO.

8. Type in the name of the user or security group that will be applied to the GPO security filtering, and click OK.

9. If multiple objects need to be added, repeat this process until all of the objects are added to the security filter.

10. If a specific computer object needs to be added, in the Select Users and Group window, click the Object Types button, check the Computers object, and click OK. Type the computer object name or browse for the object, and then click OK.

## Managing GPO Link Order of Processing

When an Active Directory container has multiple GPOs linked to it, a specific order of processing will occur. In many instances, the set of linked GPOs will have some conflicting settings and the order of GPO processing must be modified to produce the desired result. When reviewing both the Linked Group Policy Objects Link order on a container or the Group Policy Inheritance Precedence order, the Group Policies will be applied in a countdown sequence ending with the number 1 policy being applied last. Group Policy Link Order is inherited down from any parent or domain container and can only be adjusted on the actual domain or container the GPO is linked to. To change the GPO link order of processing, perform the following steps:

1. Log on to a designated Windows Server 2008 R2 administrative system.

2. Open the Group Policy Management Console.

3. Add the necessary domains or sites to the GPMC, as required.

4. Expand the Domains or Sites node to expose the container with multiple GPOs linked.

5. Select the desired container.

6. In the right pane, select the Linked Group Policy Objects tab.

> **NOTE**
>
> When the order is presented, the policy with the highest numeric value is applied first and the remainder of the policies are applied sequentially and numerically. The GPO listed as number 1 in the link order is processed last.

7. If the placement or order of a particular GPO needs to be changed, select the GPO and click one of the following buttons on the left:

   ▶ Move Link to Top is a double up arrow

   ▶ Move Link Up is a single up arrow

   ▶ Move Link Down is single down arrow

   ▶ Move Link to Bottom is a double down arrow

8. After the GPO links are in the correct order, the task is complete.

## Viewing GPO Settings and Creating Reports

One of the great features of the GPMC is the ability to view GPO settings from within the window, and to save the settings to share with others as HTML files. To view the settings of a particular GPO, perform the following steps:

1. Log on to a designated Windows Server 2008 R2 administrative system.

2. Open the Group Policy Management Console.

3. Expand the domain to expose the Group Policy Objects container and expand it.

4. Select the desired GPO in the tree pane and select the Settings tab in the right pane.

5. Browse the settings by expanding the sections using the Hide and Show hyperlinks.

6. To save the settings to an XML or HTML file, right-click on the desired GPO in the left pane, and click Save Report.

7. Specify the location in which to save the GPO report, choose Save the File as an HTML or an XML File, and click Save to save the file.

# Backing Up and Restoring Domain GPOs

Backing up GPOs is a task that should be performed regularly. This section contains step-by-step instructions to back up and restore domain group policies.

### Backing Up All Domain GPOs

To back up all of the domain GPOs, perform the following steps:

1. Log on to a designated Windows Server 2008 R2 administrative system.

2. Open the Group Policy Management Console.

3. Expand the domain to expose the Group Policy Objects container and select it.

4. Right-click the Group Policy Objects container and select the Back Up All button.

5. Specify the folder location in which to store the backup, enter a description of the backup, and click the Back Up button to back up the domain group policies.

6. In the Backup window, review the status of the backup and click OK when the back-up completes.

### Backing Up a Single Domain GPO

To back up a single domain GPO, perform the following steps:

1. Log on to a designated Windows Server 2008 R2 administrative system.

2. Open the Group Policy Management Console.

3. Expand the domain to expose the Group Policy Objects container and expand it.

4. Select the desired GPO, right-click it, and click the Back Up button.

5. Specify the folder location in which to store the backup, enter a description of the backup, and click the Back Up button to back up the domain group policy.

6. In the Backup window, review the status of the backup and click OK when the back-up completes.

### Restoring a Domain GPO

Restoring a domain GPO can be performed to revert a GPO to a previously backed-up state or to recover from a domain GPO deletion.

To restore a deleted domain GPO, perform the following steps:

1. Log on to a designated Windows Server 2008 R2 administrative workstation.

2. Open the Group Policy Management Console.

3. Expand the domain to expose the Group Policy Objects container and select it.

4. Right-click the Group Policy Objects container, and select Manage Backups.

5. Browse to or specify the domain GPO backup location to load the GPO backup set.

6. Select the desired GPO object.

7. If a filtered view is desired, select the Show Only the Latest Version of Each GPO check box.

8. To view the settings of a particular backed-up GPO, select the desired GPO, and click the View Settings button. Close the browser window after the settings are reviewed.

9. After the desired GPO is determined, select the GPO and click the Restore button.

10. Click OK in the Restore confirmation dialog box to restore the GPO.

11. Review the GPO restore progress, and click OK when it is finished.

12. After all the necessary GPOs are restored, close the Manage Backups window.

> **NOTE**
>
> Restoring a domain GPO from a backup does not re-create or restore any links previously associated with that GPO. GPO links must be re-created and reconfigured manually.

To change an existing domain GPO to a previously backed-up version, perform the following steps:

1. Log on to a designated Windows Server 2008 R2 administrative system.

2. Open the Group Policy Management Console.

3. Expand the domain to expose the Group Policy Objects container and select it.

4. Locate and right-click the desired domain GPO, and select Restore from Backup.

5. In the Restore Group Policy Object Wizard window, click Next on the Welcome page.

6. On the next page, browse to or specify the domain GPO backup location and click Next.

7. To view the settings of a particular backed-up GPO, select the desired GPO, and click the View Settings button. Close the browser window after the settings are reviewed.

8. After the desired GPO is determined, select the GPO, and click Next.

9. Review the settings summary on the Completing the Restore GPO Wizard page, and click Finish to start the restore process.

10. Review the GPO restore progress, and click OK when it is finished.

## Group Policy Modeling Operations

The GPMC has a function called Group Policy Modeling that allows administrators to run tests to determine the projected outcome of GPO processing. Group Policy Modeling allows administrators to test the outcome of applying new GPOs, changing the status of GPOs, changing the location of a computer or user object, or changing the group membership of a computer or users. Detailed Group Policy Modeling is covered in Chapter 27.

## Group Policy Results

Group Policy Results provides administrators with an additional tool to investigate the history of GPO processing on a particular computer and user object. This function requires access to the remote computer to evaluate and summarize the logged results of historical GPO processing. Starting with Windows Vista and Windows Server 2008 R2, the operational event logs for Group Policy provide much of the same functionality. This tool is useful as a troubleshooting tool to assist administrators who need to investigate GPO processing on computers running previous version operating systems. Group Policy Results is covered in Chapter 27.

## GPO Administrative Delegation

GPO administrative delegation is a process that administrators can utilize to delegate permissions to specific users or configure security rights across all GPOs, specific GPOs, and GPO-related tasks on specific Active Directory containers, such as sites, domains, and organizational units.

GPO delegation or delegation of administration within Active Directory should only be used in organizations that have separate IT groups that manage the infrastructure and servers and other groups that manage the desktop and support the end user. If the IT group of an organization contains administrators who all perform GPO and Active Directory administration, adding a delegation model might not be necessary and can add unnecessary complexity.

All GPO administrative delegation tasks detailed in the following sections are performed using the Group Policy Management Console.

### Delegating GPO Creation Rights

The right to create GPOs can only be delegated at the domain's Group Policy Objects container and the Starter GPOs container. After a policy is created, though, the right to completely edit, modify security, and even delete the GPO can be granted on a per GPO basis. To grant the right to create GPOs in a domain, perform the following steps:

1. Log on to a designated administrative system running Windows Server 2008 R2.
2. Open the Group Policy Management Console.
3. Expand the domain to expose the Group Policy Objects Container and select it.
4. In the right pane, select the Delegation tab.
5. Click the Add button at the bottom of the pane.
6. Type in the name of the user account or security group, and click OK to apply the changes.

Alternately, the specific user or security group could be added as a member of the Group Policy Creator Owners security group.

### Delegating GPO Management Rights on Existing GPOs

After a group policy is created, it will inherit a base set of administrative rights to completely edit the settings and modify the security of the policy. By default, administrative rights are granted to the Domain Admins, Enterprise Admins, and System objects. If the policy was created by a separate group or user that had been granted GPO creation rights, that object would also have these rights. If additional users or security groups need to be granted the right to edit the settings, manage the security, or delete a specific policy, perform the following steps:

19

1. Log on to a designated administrative system running Windows Server 2008 R2.

2. Open the Group Policy Management Console.

3. Expand the domain to expose the Group Policy Objects Container and select it.

4. Expand the Group Policy Objects container to expose the domain GPOs.

5. Select the desired GPO and select the Delegation tab in the right pane.

6. At the bottom of the pane, click the Add button.

7. Type in the name of the specific user account or security group, and click OK.

8. In the Add Group or User window, click the Permissions drop-down list arrow, and select the appropriate permission of Read, Edit Settings, or Edit Settings, Delete, Modify Security, and click OK to apply the changes.

### Delegating GPO Administrative Tasks on Active Directory Containers

The GPMC allows administrators to delegate the rights to manage GPO links and perform testing and troubleshooting tasks at the site, domain, and organizational unit container levels. To delegate GPO administrative rights over an Active Directory container, perform the following steps:

1. Log on to a designated administrative workstation running Windows Server 2008 R2.

2. Open the Group Policy Management Console.

3. Expand the Active Directory Forest container.

4. Select either the Domains or Sites node and expand it.

5. If the desired domain or site is not listed, right-click the node and select Show Domains or Show Sites and add the object as required.

6. Expand the Domains or Sites node to expose the container that will have the GPO delegation rights applied to it and select it.

7. In the right pane, select the Delegation tab.

8. On the Delegation tab, near the top of the pane, select the desired permission that will be delegated from the following options:

    ▶ Link GPOs

    ▶ Perform Group Policy Modeling Analyses

    ▶ Read Group Policy Results Data

9. At the bottom of the pane, click the Add button.

10. Type in the name of the specific user account or security group and click OK.

11. In the Add Group or User window, click the Permissions drop-down list arrow, and select the appropriate permission of This Container Only or This Container and All Child Containers, and click OK.

**NOTE**

Even though the right to perform Group Policy Modeling and view results data can be delegated at a container level, if the task is not performed on the domain controller, the user or group will also need to be a member of the domain's Distributed COM Users security group.

# Summary

This chapter detailed the Group Policy infrastructure of the Windows 7 and Windows Server 2008 R2 operating systems. For an administrator to successfully design and support a Group Policy infrastructure, a thorough understanding of the general GPO functions and how to use the GPO management tools is a necessity.

This chapter introduced how policies work, the difference between local group policies and domain policies, and the elements of a group policy. For administrators who are creating multiple policies for their environment, rather than creating individual policies for each user, site, or domain, the concept of creating a starter GPO to use as a template or baseline policy was discussed.

Windows Server 2008 R2 also introduced improvements in the Group Policy Management Console tool that is used for the creation and management of policies throughout the Windows Server 2008 R2 environment. The GPMC provides the ability to create policies, edit policies, and generate reports to determine specifically what a policy is doing in the environment.

After the administrator is familiar with the tools available for the creation and management of group policies, this chapter provided guidance on the policy management tasks and best practices an administrator could follow in leveraging the capabilities of policies within the Windows Server 2008 R2 environment.

# Best Practices

The following are best practices from this chapter:

- Use common sense naming conventions for GPOs.

- Don't use the same name for two different GPOs.

- When you are working with Group Policy Objects, disable unused Computer and User Configuration nodes of the policy when possible.

- When you delegate the creation of GPOs to nonadministrators, also consider delegating the capability to manage the links for a specific OU and to allow these administrators to run modeling and to read Group Policy results data.

▶ Use the Enforced and Block Inheritance settings in GPOs sparingly.

▶ Only configure the default account policies for the entire domain in the default domain policy. Leave all other settings to separate policies.

▶ Use fully qualified (UNC) paths—for example, \\server.companyabc.com\share.

▶ Only create GPOs to deploy printers using the GPMC and GPME on Windows Vista, Windows 7, and Windows Server 2008 R2 systems.

▶ Keep from applying group policies to sites and instead apply them to domains and organizational units.

▶ Use starter GPOs to set baseline standards for administrators to create subsequent policies in the environment.

▶ Try to separate GPO functions across multiple policies to provide more flexibility with regard to targeting GPO application, delegation, and troubleshooting.

▶ When creating operating system–specific Group Policy settings, create separate policies and apply WMI filters for the desired operating systems.

▶ Use Group Policy security and WMI filters to gain more granular control of policies and the application of policies on users and computers.

▶ Delegate administration to key individuals instead of allowing the individuals or security groups rights to create, edit, or manage policies across the entire domain.

▶ Leverage the backup and restore capabilities of the Group Policy Management Console as a method to create a copy of the policies so that if a policy is accidentally edited, deleted, or corrupted, the policy can be restored to its original state.

# CHAPTER 20

# Windows Server 2008 R2 Management and Maintenance Practices

Windows Server systems are the heart of the IT infrastructure that supports businesses. These servers need to be managed and maintained to keep the businesses running optimally. Server management and maintenance help maximize investment in infrastructure and productivity. They also keep the IT infrastructure running effectively and efficiently to boost availability and reliability.

Windows Server 2008 R2 brings many new tools and features to help keep the servers managed and maintained. These tools include the new Server Manager, better auditing, improved configuration of servers through the roles and features, better remote management, and a slew of other capabilities. Many formerly manual tasks are automated in Windows Server 2008 R2 using the enhanced Task Scheduler. These include tasks such as defragmentation and backup.

Server management entails many different tasks; they include, but are not limited to, administering and supervising servers based on functional roles, proactively monitoring the network environment, keeping track of activity, and implementing solid change-control practices. These management functions for Windows Server 2008 R2 can be performed both locally and remotely.

As systems' workloads, capacities, and usage change in the environment, the systems need to be maintained so that they operate as efficiently as possible. Without such maintenance, systems become more susceptible to causing slower response times and decreased reliability. Efforts to maintain those systems should be made periodically to avoid any inefficiency. This chapter covers best practices on ways an organization can maintain and manage its Windows Server 2008 R2 environment.

# Going Green with Windows Server 2008 R2

A big part of server management and maintenance practices is planning for resources, including reducing the environmental impact of servers. Power consumption of servers is a huge environmental concern today. Not only is there the expense of power, but there is the environmental impact in the form of the carbon footprint of anything that consumes power.

Windows Server 2008 R2 was developed with green concerns in mind and specifically with reducing the power consumption, carbon footprint, and, thus, environmental impact of running a server. This includes server-level improvements and data center-level improvements.

Windows Server 2008 R2 reduces the power consumption of individual servers through several new technologies, as follows:

▶ **A new Processor Power Management (PPM) engine**—The new PPM engine adjusts the processor speed and, thus, power consumption, in response to demand. Windows Server 2008 R2 also introduces the core parking feature, which idles processor cores that are not being used and, thus, their power consumption is reduced.

▶ **Storage power management**—The ATA Slumber feature allows for new power states for a more nuanced power utilization. Windows Server 2008 R2 will recognize solid state drives and power them down when not in use, to reduce their power consumption. And Windows Server 2008 R2 supports boot to SANs, eliminating the need for direct attached drives and, thus, reducing power consumption.

▶ **Intelligent Timer Tick Distribution**—This allows processors to skip activation if not needed for work, reducing the power consumption of underutilized systems.

▶ **Reduced background work**—The Windows Server 2008 R2 also has reduced operating system background work requirements, reducing power draw even further especially in idle states.

Windows Server 2008 R2 also enables administrators to better manage power consumption across servers through the following:

▶ **Remote manageability of power policy**—Windows Server 2008 R2 has new Group Policy features for controlling power options across a number of servers. Power policy can also be configured remotely with PowerShell and with WMI scripting via the new root\cimv2\power namespace. These allow for much more sophisticated programmatic control of power consumption.

▶ **In-band power metering and budgeting**—Power consumption can be displayed as a performance counter in the new Power Meter object. This object allows manufacturers to instrument their platform power consumption live. This can be consumed by management applications such as Operations Manager 2007 R2 with thresholds and alerts. There is also a budget counter in the Power Meter object, which allows power budgets to be set on a server-by-server basis.

▶ **New additional qualifier designed for Windows Server 2008 R2 Logo program**—This Power Management AQ addition to the program allows manufacturers to distinguish themselves and identify power-saving features in their products, enabling IT managers to purchase power-saving hardware to complement the power-saving Windows Server 2008 R2 operating system.

Many of these features require no specific action on the part of an administrator, but management and maintenance practices can be adjusted to account for these green power features. For example, the power consumption at 100% utilization for Windows Server 2003 SP2 and for Windows Server 2008 R2 servers is roughly the same. However, the power consumption at 30% utilization is approximately 20% higher for Windows Server 2003 SP2 than for Windows Server 2008 R2. At lower workloads, Windows Server 2008 R2 consumes less power. Most servers operate at lower workloads, so the power savings for a Windows Server 2008 R2 server can be significant.

These Windows Server 2008 R2 features help organization move toward greener servers and data centers and protect the environment.

## Initial Configuration Tasks

One of the features of Windows Server 2008 R2 is the Initial Configuration Tasks tool, shown in Figure 20.1. Windows Server 2008 R2 streamlines the typical installation steps, enabling an administrator to quickly set up a new server without having to answer an endless stream of questions.

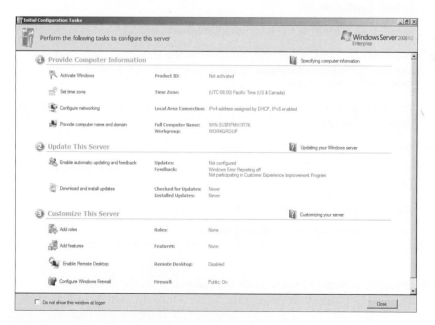

FIGURE 20.1   Initial Configuration Tasks tool.

This helps separate the tasks of installing the base operating system and configuring the server, making the best use of the administrator's time. This will be a welcome relief to all the administrators who have sat through a prior Windows version install, watching files get copied from CD to the hard drive.

After the server operating system has been installed, it will boot up into a secure state and be ready for the initial configuration tasks. The initial configuration tasks are broken into three general categories, as follows:

▶ **Provide Computer Information**—This section is where computer-specific information such as the administrator password, time zone, network configuration, and computer name are set.

▶ **Update This Server**—This section of tasks is where the automatic update options are set and the updates are manually installed.

▶ **Customize This Server**—This section is where the roles and features for the computer are added, as well as configuring the remote desktop and the firewall.

The initial configuration settings are stripped down and basic (as shown in Table 20.1), with little or no security. For example, the latest security updates have not been applied and the system is not configured to download them automatically. Thus, the Windows Firewall is enabled by default to protect the server from network access until the initial configuration is completed and the Remote Desktop feature is turned off.

TABLE 20.1    Default Configuration Settings

| Setting | Default Configuration |
| --- | --- |
| Time zone | Pacific Time (GMT-8) is the time zone set by default. |
| Computer name | The computer name is randomly assigned during installation. Administrators can modify the computer name by using commands in the Initial Configuration Tasks Wizard. |
| Domain membership | The computer is not joined to a domain by default; it is joined to a workgroup named WORKGROUP. |
| Windows Update | Windows Update is turned off by default. |
| Network connections | All network connections are set to obtain IP addresses automatically by using DHCP. |
| Windows Firewall | Windows Firewall is turned on by default. |
| Roles installed | No role or features are installed by default. |

Each of the settings can be configured via wizards that launch from the Initial Configuration Tasks, making it easy to configure the server. Once the initial configuration is completed, there is a check box in the Initial Configuration Tasks console that will prevent it from launching automatically.

**NOTE**

Once the Initial Configuration Tasks console is closed, there is no menu option to launch it again. If you need to use the console again (for example, if it was closed accidentally), the tool can be launched manually by opening a command prompt and running the command oobe.exe. The "oobe" stands for Out-Of-Box Experience.

# Managing Windows Server 2008 R2 Roles and Features

To help organize and manage the expanded functionality of Windows Server 2008 R2, the platform continues to use the roles and features paradigm. The roles and features enable administrators to add and manage functionality in coherent blocks. This includes tools to summarize, manage, and maintain the installed roles and features.

## Roles in Windows Server 2008 R2

Server roles in Windows Server 2008 R2 are used to organize the functionality of the operating system. The server roles are an expansion of the server roles of previous versions of Windows, with significant enhancements. Roles usually include a number of related functions or services that make up the capabilities that the server will offer. A role designates a primary function of the server, although a given server can have multiple roles.

Windows Server 2008 R2 includes the following roles:

▶ Active Directory Certificate Services

▶ Active Directory Domain Services

▶ Active Directory Federation Services

▶ Active Directory Lightweight Directory Services

▶ Active Directory Rights Management Services

▶ Application Server

▶ DHCP Server

▶ DNS Server

▶ Fax Server

▶ File Services

▶ Hyper-V

▶ Network Policy and Access Services

▶ Print and Document Services

▶ Remote Desktop Services

20

▶ Web Server (IIS)

▶ Windows Deployment Services

▶ Windows Server Update Services

Within each role, a number of role services make up the role. The role services allow the administrator to load only the specific services that are needed for a particular server instance. In some cases, such as for the DHCP Server or DNS Server roles, the role and the role service are one and the same. In other cases, the role will contain multiple services that can be chosen. For example, the File Services role contains the following role services:

▶ File Server

▶ Distributed File System

▶ DFS Namespaces

▶ DFS Replication

▶ File Server Resource Manager

▶ Services for Network File System

▶ Windows Search Service

▶ Windows Server 2003 File Services

▶ Indexing Service

▶ BranchCache for Network Files

Adding a role and role services installs the binaries (that is, the code) that allow the services to function. There is typically additional installation and configuration that needs to be done after the roles are installed, such as for the Active Directory Domain Services role.

Only loading the roles required for each server and, thus, only the appropriate binaries, reduces the complexity, the attack surface, and the patch surface of the server. This results in a more secure, less complex, and more efficient server—in short, resulting in fewer headaches for the administrator who has to manage the server!

**NOTE**

The patch surface of a server is the code in the server that requires patches to be applied. This can increase the need for patches and, thus, downtime, as well as administrative overhead. If code is installed on a server, it needs to be patched even if that particular code is not in use on a server. This is analogous to the attack surface of the server.

A good example of this is the Web Server role. If a domain controller has the Web Server role added, any patches that apply to the code base of the Web Server role need to be installed. This is true even if the services are disabled or just not used. Thus, the patch surface of the domain controller has been increased.

However, if the domain controller only has the roles (and, thus, the code) for the roles it needs, the patches for other roles will not need to be applied to the domain controller. Thus, the patch surface of the domain controller has been reduced.

## Features in Windows Server 2008 R2

In addition to the roles and role services, Windows Server 2008 R2 also has the ability to add features. Features are typically supporting components that are independent of the server role, but might provide support for a role or role service. For example, a domain controller is configured with the Active Directory Domain Services role. However, in some organizations, the domain controller will also serve as a Windows Internet Naming Service (WINS) server. WINS is a feature in Windows Server 2008 R2.

There are many different features in Windows Server 2008 R2, including the following:

- ▶ NET Framework 3.5.1 Features
- ▶ Background Intelligent Transfer Service (BITS)
- ▶ BitLocker Drive Encryption
- ▶ BranchCache
- ▶ Connection Manager Administration Kit
- ▶ Desktop Experience
- ▶ DirectAccess Management Console
- ▶ Failover Clustering
- ▶ Group Policy Management
- ▶ Ink and Handwriting Services
- ▶ Internet Printing Client
- ▶ Internet Storage Name Server
- ▶ LPR Port Monitor
- ▶ Message Queuing
- ▶ Multipath I/O
- ▶ Network Load Balancing
- ▶ Peer Name Resolution Protocol
- ▶ Quality Windows Audio Video Experience
- ▶ Remote Assistance

20

▶ Remote Differential Compression

▶ Remote Server Administration Tools

▶ RPC over HTTP Proxy

▶ Simple TCP/IP Services

▶ SMTP Server

▶ SNMP Services

▶ Storage Manager for SANs

▶ Subsystem for UNIX-Based Applications

▶ Telnet Client

▶ Telnet Server

▶ TFTP Client

▶ Windows Biometric Framework

▶ Windows Internal Database

▶ Windows PowerShell Integrated Scripting Environment (ISE)

▶ Windows Process Activation Service

▶ Windows Server Backup Features

▶ Windows Server Migration Tools

▶ Windows System Resource Manager

▶ Windows TIFF IFilter

▶ WinRM IIS Extension

▶ WINS Server

▶ Wireless LAN Service

▶ XPS Viewer

The features are installed with the Server Manager Add Features Wizard. To add a feature, execute the following steps:

1. In the Initial Configuration Tasks Wizard or Server Manager, click the Add Features link.

2. Select a feature or set of features.

3. Click Next to accept the selected features.

4. Click Install to install the selected features.

5. Click Close to exit the wizard.

6. Close the Server Manager window.

The feature will now be installed.

---

**NOTE**

Unlike previous versions of Windows, all the binaries for Windows Server 2008, Windows Vista, Windows 7, and Windows Server 2008 R2 are installed in the C:\WINDOWS\WINSXS directory. All the components—that is, roles and features—are stored in the WINSXS directory. This eliminates the need to use the original DVD installation media when adding roles or features.

However, the trade-off is that the WINSXS folder is more than 5GB, as it contains the entirety of the operating system. In addition, it will grow over time as updates and service packs are installed. For a physical machine, the additional disk space is not much of an issue. However, for virtual machines, it means that there is an additional 5GB of additional disk space that has to be allocated for each and every Windows server.

---

# Server Manager

Server Manager is a new tool that provides a central location for managing all the roles and features that Windows Server 2008 R2 provides. This console gives an administrator access to the complete operational status, monitoring tools, and configuration tools for the entire server in a convenient single console.

Server Manager enables the administrator to do the following:

▶ Add and remove roles and features from the server

▶ Monitor and manage the server

▶ Administer the roles and features on the server

In effect, Server Manager is a one-stop shop for all the administrator management and monitoring needs. The features of Server Manager are available via the Server Manager console.

Selecting the server name in the folder tree will show the Server Manager main window in the Details pane. This consists of several section windows. The Server Summary window (shown in Figure 20.2) shows computer information such as the computer name, networking information, and if Remote Desktop is enabled. It also shows security information, such as if Windows Firewall is enabled and the Windows Updates status. The window also has active links that enable the administrator to launch wizards to change the configuration or get help.

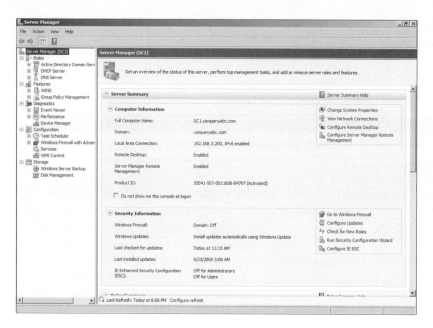

FIGURE 20.2    Server Manager Server Summary window.

Server Manager launches automatically when the Initial Configuration Wizard is closed and each time a user logs on to the server.

The next sections discuss the components and features of Server Manager.

## Server Manager Roles and Features

The Roles Summary and Feature Summary windows, shown in Figure 20.3, show which roles and features are installed. In the Roles Summary window, the status of the roles can be seen as well. As can be seen in the figure, the Active Directory Domain Services role and the DNS Server role have information icons, indicating that there are informational messages. If there were problems with the roles, these would change to warning or critical icons. The summary windows also include links to add or remove roles and features, as well as to access context-sensitive help.

## Server Manager Roles Page

The Server Manager console has a folder tree dedicated to the roles of the server. Selecting the Roles folder in the console tree shows a summary of the roles installed on the server, as well as a summary page for each of the roles. The summary page for each role shows the role status, such as the status of the system services and the events for the role.

However, selecting the folder for a specific role shows the Server Manager role-specific page for that role. The role-specific pages are dedicated to the role and contain operational information about the role. The following sections discuss the sections included in the role-specific page.

FIGURE 20.3    Server Manager Roles and Features Summary windows.

### Events Section

There is a problem with going to the full Event Viewer and seeing all the events for all roles, services, and the operating system. There is usually so much information that it ends up overloading the administrator, making it difficult to see real problems. The Events section in the role-specific page addresses this by only presenting the role-specific events.

From the Events section, the administrator can see a summary of the events that pertain to the role, review the details of the events, and filter the events as needed. The default filter shows only events in the last 24 hours, but this can be adjusted via the Filter Events control.

The full Event Viewer can also be launched from this section.

### System Services Section

The System Services section lists the services that the role depends on and their status. It also describes each service and includes control links to Stop, Start, Restart, and configure Preferences.

The Preferences control enables the administrator to adjust the monitored services. For example, if an administrator determines that the Windows Time service is essential to the role of the Active Directory Domain Services server (that is, the domain controller), that service can be monitored by checking it in the Preferences section.

### Role Services Section

The Role Services section shows which of the role services that are available for the role have been installed. There are also links to add or remove the role services.

A nice feature of this section is that when a role service is selected, a brief description is shown of what the role service is for. This includes a link to get more information on the role service.

### Advanced Tools Section

In the case of some roles, there will be an Advanced Tools section with a list of tools that help support the role. This includes both command-line tools and MMC consoles with brief explanations of their functions.

In the case of the Active Directory Domain Services role (which, by far, has the most advanced tools of any role), there are 21 different tools in the section, including the following:

- ▶ **AD DS Tools**—These are tools such as the AD Domains and Trusts console, the ADSI Edit console, and the NTDSUTIL tool.

- ▶ **Directory Services Tools**—These include DSADD, DSGET, and DSMGMT tools.

- ▶ **Networking and Other Tools**—These include such tools as NSLOOKUP and W32TM.

The tools can be launched by clicking on the active links. In the case of console tools, the console will be launched. In the case of command-line tools, the tool will be launched with the help option to display the options for the tool.

For example, after installing the Active Directory Domain Services role on a server, you can use the Advanced Tools section to launch DCPROMO to complete the configuration of the domain services.

### Resources and Support Section

The Resources and Support section is an extremely useful section. It provides a brief recommendation on configurations, best practices, and links to resources.

The recommendations are listed in a window; highlighting the recommendation shows a brief explanation of the recommendation with a link to a more detailed explanation. This is great for researching the recommendations. The section also includes links to online resources, such as the appropriate TechCenter and Community Center for the role.

For example, the Resources and Support section for the Active Directory Domain Services role (shown in Figure 20.4) includes over 18 different recommendations on installation. One of the recommendations is Improve Active Directory Redundancy by Adding Another Domain Controller. Highlighting this recommendation shows a brief paragraph explaining the recommendation and includes a link to get more detailed information on the recommendation.

An important note is that these recommendations are static and don't adjust to changes in the environment.

### Tools Folders

For each of the role folders in the Server Manager folder tree, there are subfolders that are the MMC snap-ins for the role. This is a cool feature that makes it easy to access the tools

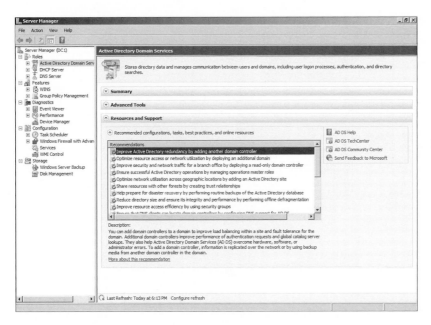

FIGURE 20.4    Resources and Support section.

from within Server Manager without having to search for the tools in the Administrative Tools folder.

For example, the Active Directory Domain Services role has two tools folders: the Active Directory Users and Computers snap-in and the Active Directory Sites and Services snap-in, shown in Figure 20.5.

As can be seen in the figure, these are the same full-featured snap-ins that can be launched from the Administrative Tools folder. The Users container is selected in the figure, and contents of the container can be seen.

For the other roles on the server (the DHCP Server role and DNS Server role), the respective tools can be seen as well.

## Server Manager Features Page

The Features page shows a summary of the installed features. There are active links to add and remove features, as well as a link to get help.

In the case of some features, there will be a folder under the Features folder that is the MMC snap-in for the feature. For example, the Active Directory Domain Services role automatically installs the Group Policy Management feature. This places the Group Policy Management Console under the Features folder.

FIGURE 20.5   Role tools folders.

# Server Manager Diagnostics Page

The Diagnostics page in Server Manager consolidates three different consoles into a convenient location. The three consoles are as follows:

▶ Event Viewer

▶ Performance

▶ Device Manager

The next sections review the various features of the three consoles on the Diagnostics page.

## Event Viewer

The Windows Server 2008 R2 Event Viewer functionality has been improved over the Windows Server 2003 version. The version in Windows Server 2008 R2 is the version that released in Windows Vista. The event logs can contain an overwhelming volume of information, which the new Event Viewer summarizes and drills into very effectively.

Selecting the Event Viewer folder under Diagnostics shows the Overview and Summary page. The Summary of Administrative Events section on this page shows a high-level summary of the administrative events, organized by level:

▶ Critical

▶ Error

▶ Warning

▶ Information

▶ Audit Success

▶ Audit Failure

The view shows the total number of events in the last hour, 24 hours, 7 days, and the total. Each of these nodes can be expanded to show the counts of particular event IDs within each level. Double-clicking on the event ID count shows a detailed list of the events with the matching event ID. This is very useful for drilling on the specific events to see when they are occurring.

The Overview and Summary page also has a Log Summary section, which shows a list of all the various logs on the server. This is important, as there are now over 100 different logs in Windows Server 2008 R2. In addition to the standard system, security, and application logs, there is a setup log and a forwarded events log. Then there are the numerous application and services logs, which include logs for each application, service, and a huge number of diagnostic and debugging logs. For each of the logs, the Log Summary section shows the log name, current size, maximum size, last modification, if it is enabled, and what the retention policy for the log is. This allows the administrator to quickly see the status of all the logs, which would be a daunting task otherwise.

Of course, the logs can be viewed directly by expanding the Windows Logs folder or the Applications and Services Logs folder. The Windows Logs folder contains all the standard application, security, setup, system, and forwarded events logs. The applications and services logs contain all the other ones.

Custom views can be created to filter events and combine logs into a coherent view. There is a default Administrative Events view, which combines the critical, error, and warning events from all the administrative logs. There is also a custom view created for each role that is installed on the server. New ones can be created by the administrator as needed.

Subscriptions can collect events from remote computers and store them in the forwarded events log. The events to be collected are specified in the subscription. The functionality depends on the Windows Remote Management (WinRM) and the Windows Event Collector (Wecsvc) services, and they must be running on both the collecting and forwarding servers.

## Server Manager Performance Monitor

The Performance monitor is incorporated into Server Manager as well. This diagnostic tool enables the administrator to monitor the performance of the server in real time, generate reports, and also save the performance data to logs for analysis.

The top-level folder of the Performance Monitor displays the System Summary. This gives a comprehensive overview of the memory, network interface, physical disk, and processor utilization during the past 60 seconds (shown in Figure 20.6). The System Summary is organized in a matrix, with a column for each instance of the network interface, disk, and processor. The information is updated every second. Unfortunately, the pane is a fixed height, so it is hard to see all the information at once, and excessive scrolling is needed.

20

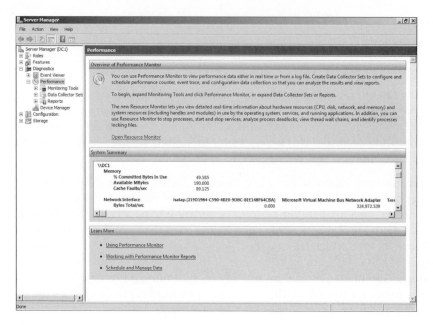

FIGURE 20.6    System Summary in Performance Monitor.

The Monitoring Tools contains the Performance Monitor tool. This tool allows you to monitor the performance of the server in more detail. The Performance Monitor has not really changed from previous versions of Windows. It allows you to select performance counters and add them to a graph view for real-time monitoring. The graph can be configured to be a line graph, a bar graph, or even a simple text report of the counters being monitored. The monitor shows the last, average, minimum, maximum, and duration of the windows (1 minute 40 seconds by default).

For longer-term tracking, the Data Collector Sets can be used. Data Collector Sets can log data from the following data sources:

- ▶ Performance counters

- ▶ Event traces

- ▶ Registry key values

This data can be logged over an extended period of time and then reviewed. The data collected will also be analyzed and presented in reports that are very useful. There are two reports defined by default, the System Diagnostics and System Performance. When roles are added, such as the Active Directory Domain Services role, there might be additional Data Collector Sets defined. These data sets gather data that is presented in reports, which is new to Windows Server 2008 R2. There is a new reports folder in the Performance Monitor where the reports are saved.

To generate data for a Performance Monitor report, execute the following steps:

1. Launch Server Manager.

2. Expand the Diagnostics node.

3. Expand the Performance node.

4. Expand the Data Collector Sets node.

5. Expand the System node and select the System Performance Data Collector Set. Note that the Data Collector Set includes an NT Kernel trace and performance counters.

6. Right-click on the NT Kernel trace object and select Properties. Note the events that will be collected. Click Cancel to exit without saving.

7. Right-click on the Performance Counter object and select Properties. Note the performance counters that will be collected. Click Cancel to exit without saving.

8. Right-click on the System Performance Data Collector Set and select Start. The Data Collector Set will start collecting data.

9. Right-click on the System Performance Data Collector Set and select Latest Report.

The report will show a detailed analysis of the system performance. The Summary and the Diagnostic Results are shown in Figure 20.7. The Diagnostic Results indicate that memory is the busy component on the DC1 server. The report contains a wealth of details on the CPU, Network, Disk, Memory, and overall report statistics.

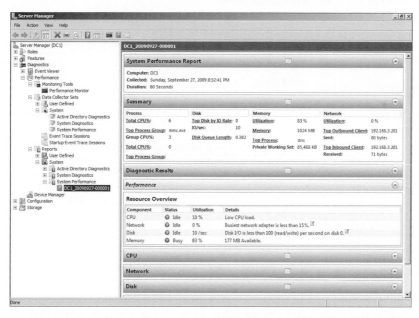

FIGURE 20.7   System Performance Report in Performance Monitor Data Collector Sets.

You can also view the performance data that the report is based on directly. This can be done by right-clicking the specific report and selecting View, Performance Monitor. This shows the graph of all the counters selected during the data collection. You can select which counters to show in the graph.

The System Performance Data Collector Set only collects for 1 minute, which is not long enough for detailed trend analysis. New Data Collector Sets can be defined in the User Defined folder. For example, to create a duplicate of the System Performance Data Collector Set that will run for an hour instead of a minute, do the following:

1. Launch Server Manager.

2. Expand the Diagnostics node.

3. Expand the Performance node.

4. Expand the Data Collector Sets node.

5. Select the User Defined node.

6. Right-click on the User Defined node and select New, Data Collector Set.

7. Enter `System Performance 1 Hour` for the name and make sure that the Create from a Template is selected. Click Next.

8. Select System Performance and Click Next.

9. Click Next to keep the default root directory.

10. Select the Open properties for this Data Collector Set and click Finish.

11. Click on the Stop Condition tab.

12. Change the Overall Duration setting to 1 hour.

13. Click OK to save.

This Data Collector Set can now be run and will collect the same data as the default System Performance, but for 1 hour instead of just 1 minute.

## Device Manager

The Device Manager node shows the hardware that is installed on the server. It shows the hardware grouped by type of device, such as Disk Drives, Display Adapters, and Network Adapters. Each instance of the device type is listed in a node underneath the device type.

The Device Manager can be used to update the device drivers of the hardware, to change settings, and to troubleshoot issues with the hardware. Specifically, you can perform the following tasks:

▶ Scan for new hardware

▶ Identify hardware problems

▶ Adjust configurations

▶ View device driver versions

▶ Update the device drivers

▶ Roll back device driver upgrades

▶ Enable or disable hardware

For example, sometimes older video drivers or network card drivers will cause problems with the system. It is easy to check the Microsoft online driver repository using Device

Manager. To check for an update to the device driver for the network adapter, follow these steps:

1. Expand the Network Adapters node in Device Manager.
2. Select the network adapter to check.
3. Select Action, Update Driver Software from the menu.
4. Click on Search Automatically for Updated Driver Software.
5. Click on Yes, Always Search Online (Recommended).
6. Install the update if found.
7. Click Close to exit the wizard.

> **NOTE**
>
> Many times, the latest version of the driver will already be installed. In these cases, the message "The best driver for your device is already installed" will be shown.

# Server Manager Configuration Page

The Configuration page in Server Manager is somewhat misleading. This is not the page from which you would configure the server. The Configuration node in Server Manager is simply a container for the following four snap-ins:

▶ Task Scheduler

▶ Windows Firewall with Advanced Security

▶ Services

▶ WMI Control

These snap-ins enable the administrator to control some elements of the server configuration and are covered in the next four sections.

## Task Scheduler

One of the greatly expanded features of Windows Server 2008 R2 is the Task Scheduler. In previous versions of Windows, this was an anemic service with limited options and auditing features. The Task Scheduler features in Windows Server 2008 R2 have been expanded into a more sophisticated tool. The scheduler can start based on a variety of triggers, can take a number of predefined actions, and can even be mitigated by conditions and the settings.

Appropriately, there are expanded elements to the Task Scheduler, as follows:

▶ **Triggers**—Tasks run when the trigger criteria are met. This could be a scheduled time, logon, startup, idle, log event, user session connect or disconnect, or workstation lock or unlock. These various triggers give the administrator a wide range of options on when to start a task.

20

▶ **Actions**—The actions are the work that the task will perform. This can be executing a program, sending an email via SMTP, or displaying a message on the desktop.

▶ **Conditions**—Conditions allow the task trigger criteria to be filtered. Conditions include if the computer is idle, on battery power, or connected to a network. This allows administrators to prevent tasks from running if the computer is busy, on battery, or disconnected from the network.

▶ **Settings**—The settings control how a task can be executed, stopped, or deleted. In the settings of a task, the administrator can control if the task can be launched manually, if it runs after a missed schedule start, if it needs to restart after a failure, if it needs to run multiple tasks in parallel, or to delete it if it is not set to run in the future.

Another big improvement is the Task Scheduler Library, which includes approximately 40 different predefined tasks. These tasks include the following:

▶ **ScheduledDefrag**—This task runs every week and uses the command `defrag.exe -c` to defragment all the volumes on the server. This is a major improvement of previous versions of Windows, which required this command to be run manually. The task runs at 1:00 a.m. every Wednesday of every week by default.

▶ **ServerManager**—This task runs at user logon and runs the ServerManagerLauncher to launch the Server Manager console whenever a user logs on.

Both these tasks demonstrate the capabilities of the Task Scheduler to automate routine tasks or to ensure that certain tasks run at logon.

The Task Scheduler has a new feature that goes hand in hand with the library, namely the ability to create folders to store the tasks. This helps organize the tasks that are created. The scheduler includes a Microsoft folder for the tasks that ship with the operating system. Administrators can create other folders to organize and store their tasks.

Selecting the Task Scheduler folder in the Server Manager configuration shows the Task Scheduler Summary (shown in Figure 20.8). This window has two sections: Task Status and Active Tasks. The Task Status section shows the status of tasks within a time frame (by default, the last 24 hours). The time frame can be set to the last hour, last 24 hours, last 7 days, or last 30 days. For each task that has run within the time frame, it shows the Task Name, Run Result, Run Start, and Run End. The section also summarizes the task status; Figure 20.8 shows that 13 total tasks have run with 1 running and 12 succeeded. The figure also shows that it is the System Performance 1 Hour data collector task that was created earlier that is running.

The Active Tasks name is somewhat misleading because it shows tasks that are enabled and their triggers. It does not show tasks that are running. For the scheduled tasks, it shows the Next Run Time. This section is very useful for seeing which tasks will run on a given server in response to a trigger, either a schedule or an event. If the task does not appear in this section, it will only be run if executed manually.

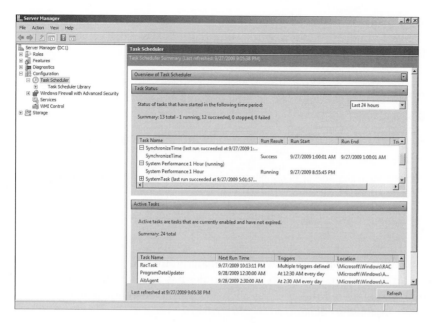

FIGURE 20.8    Task Scheduler Summary window.

## Windows Firewall with Advanced Security

The Windows Firewall with Advanced Security feature provides access to the combined Windows Firewall and Connection Security features of Windows Server 2008 R2. These technologies work in tandem to provide protection from network-based attacks to the server. The firewall rules determine what network traffic is allowed or blocked to the server. The connection security rules determine how the allowed traffic is secured.

The Windows Firewall and the Connection Security features are covered in detail in Chapter 13, "Server-Level Security," and Chapter 14, "Transport-Level Security."

The Windows Firewall with Advanced Security folder shows a summary of which profile is active (Domain, Private, or Public), the profile's high-level configuration, and links to the other components of the snap-in.

The other components of the Windows Firewall with Advanced Security snap-in are for configuration and monitoring the features. These components are as follows:

▶ Inbound rules

▶ Outbound rules

▶ Connection Security rules

▶ Monitoring

20

The inbound and outbound rules control what traffic is allowed in to and out of the server. There are several hundred rules governing what traffic is allowed. These are organized into profiles for ease of application. Table 20.2 shows these profiles.

TABLE 20.2    Firewall Profiles

| Profile | Description |
| --- | --- |
| Domain Profile | Applied when the server is connected to its Active Directory domain. |
| Private Profile | Applied when the server is connected to a private network but not to the Active Directory domain. |
| Public Profile | Applied when the server is connected to a public network. |

Clearly, the vast majority of services will have the Domain Profile active, as they will likely be on a network with Active Directory. Each of the profiles has a set of rules associated with it. In addition, a number of rules apply to all profiles, which are designated as "Any." Some of the rules are disabled by default.

Connection Security rules are stored in the likewise named folder. The rules specify how the computers on either side of a permitted connection authenticate and secure the network traffic. This is essentially the IPSec policy from previous versions of Windows, albeit with a much improved interface. By default, there are no Connection Security rules created in Windows Server 2008 R2. Rules can be created and reviewed in this portion of the snap-in.

The Monitoring folder is somewhat limited in scope. It has a Firewall folder and a Connection Security Rules folder. These two folders simply show what rules are active, but show no traffic details or if the rules have blocked or allowed anything. In effect, they show the net result of the profile that is active.

## Services

The Services snap-in in the Configuration container in Server Manager is essentially unchanged from the previous version of Windows. All the services are listed, along with their status, startup type, and logon credentials.

From the Services snap-in, administrators can control services on the server, including the following:

▶ Start or stop the services.

▶ Change the startup type to set the service to start automatically, be started manually, or even prevent the service from starting at all.

▶ Change the account the service runs under.

▶ Set up recovery actions if the service stops, such as restarting the service or even restarting the server.

▶ View the configuration details of the service, such as what the executable is, what the service name is (which is shown in the Task Manager window), and what dependencies it has.

A feature that was added in Windows Server 2008 and still available in Windows Server 2008 R2 is the Automatic (Delayed Start) startup type. This is a setting used to reduce the crunch of services starting all at once during bootup of the server. All the services with the Automatic (Delayed Start) setting will be started after the services with the automatic setting. This allows all the services to come up automatically, but allows essential services to start first.

## WMI Control

The last snap-in in the Configuration container of the Server Manager is the WMI Control tool. This is a new tool that enables administrators to maintain the Windows Management Instrumentation (WMI) configuration on the server. Interestingly, the tool is not an integrated snap-in, but rather a separate tool.

With the WMI Control tool, an administrator can do the following:

▶ Back up and restore the WMI repository.

▶ Change the default scripting namespace (`root\cimv2`).

▶ Manage access to the WMI via the Security tab.

Before the introduction of the WMI Control tool, these tasks were difficult to accomplish.

For example, to back up the WMI repository, perform these steps:

1. Open the Server Manager console.
2. Expand the Configuration folder.
3. Select the WMI Control folder.
4. Select the Action menu and then Properties.
5. Select the Backup/Restore tab.
6. Select the Back Up Now option.
7. Enter a filename with a full path. The file type will be a WMI Recovery File (`.rec`).
8. Click Save to save the file.
9. Click OK to exit the tool.

# Server Manager Storage Page

The Storage folder in the Server Manager has two tools to support storage in Windows Server 2008 R2. These pages allow the administrator to see the status of storage and the backups of the storage.

20

## Windows Server Backup

The Windows Server Backup page shows a summary of the backup state of the server. This includes information on the status of backups, how much disk space the backups are using, and what the oldest and newest backups are. This allows an administrator to understand how recoverable the server is at a glance. The backup subsystem in Windows Server 2008 R2 has fundamentally changed from a backup-to-tape job paradigm to a backup-to-disk state paradigm, requiring a different understanding of where backup stands. It is not enough to know that the latest backup job completed, but rather the span of the backups and how much space they take up.

For the Windows Server Backup folder to be active, you need to install the Windows Server Backup feature. To do this, perform the following steps:

1. Open the Server Manager console.

2. Select the Features folder.

3. Click on the Add Features link.

4. Select the Windows Server Backup Features check box.

5. Click Next and then click Install to install the new features.

6. Click Close to close the wizard.

Now the Server Manager Windows Server Backup folder will be active. Selecting the folder shows the Windows Server Backup summary page, shown in Figure 20.9. This figure shows the latest active backup messages, status, scheduled backup, and disk usage. From this page, the administrator can also click on links to set the backup schedules, run an immediate backup, start a recovery, or perform other backup-related tasks.

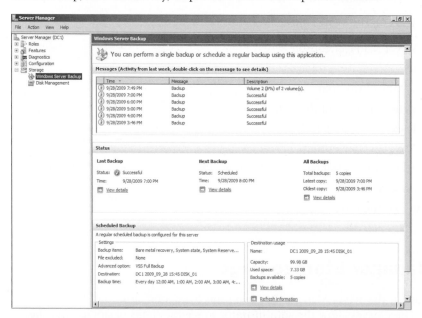

FIGURE 20.9    Windows Server Backup summary page.

The Messages section shows the active messages. You can see in the figure that a backup is running and that Volume 2 is 8% complete. You can also see that backups completed successfully at 3:46 p.m., 4:00 p.m., 5:00 p.m., 6:00 p.m., and 7:00 p.m., and that the current one started at 7:49 p.m.

The Status section shows a summary of the backups, including the last backup, the next scheduled backup, and for all backups. For each of these categories, you can click on the View Details link to get additional information. This helps the administrator quickly understand what backups are available for recovery.

The Scheduled Backup section shows a summary of the scheduled backups for the server and the disk usage of the backups. The Settings box shows what is being backed up (backup item), where it is being backed up to (the target disk), and when it is being backed up (the backup time). The backup time can be modified using the Action, Backup Schedule option.

The Destination Usage box shows the capacity, the used space, and the number of backups that are available on the target. You can click on the View Details link to see the disk usage and details of the backups. Figure 20.10 shows the disk usage after the backup in the previous figure completed.

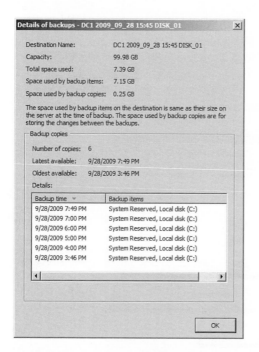

FIGURE 20.10   Windows Server Backup disk usage.

Chapter 30, "Backing Up the Windows Server 2008 R2 Environment," covers the use of Windows Server Backup in more detail.

## Disk Management

The Disk Management snap-in is used to conduct storage disk-related tasks. The Disk Management snap-in has not changed substantially from previous versions, and most administrators will find it to be quite familiar. The snap-in allows administrators to manage disks by doing the following:

▶ Creating and formatting partitions

▶ Creating and formatting volumes

▶ Extending, shrinking, and mirroring volumes

▶ Assigning drive letters

▶ Viewing the status of disks, partitions, and volumes

As shown in Figure 20.11, the snap-in shows volumes in the top window with capacity, free space, and status information. This is a logical representation and is independent of the physical media. The bottom window shows the physical disks as recognized by Windows Server 2008 R2 and the position of the partitions and volumes within the disks—that is, the layout of the partitions and volumes. The bottom window also shows the status and the type of disks.

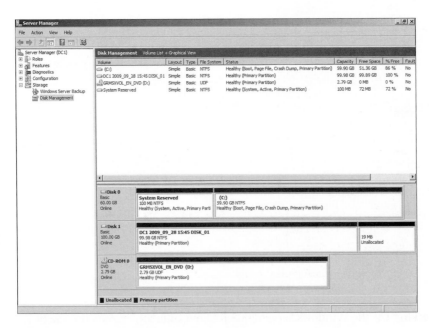

FIGURE 20.11   Disk Management console.

> **NOTE**
>
> It should be stated that the physical disks shown in the Disk Management snap-in are the disk configurations as recognized by Windows Server 2008 R2. The actual hardware configuration of the disks might be very different, as it is abstracted by the hardware controller.
>
> For example, what the operating system recognizes as Disk 0 with 32.00 GB might actually be a fault-tolerant RAID-1 configuration of two 32-GB physical disks that the hard drive controller presents as one disk to the operating system.

# Auditing the Environment

Auditing is a way to gather and keep track of activity on the network, devices, and entire systems. By default, Windows Server 2008 R2 enables some auditing, whereas many other auditing functions must be manually turned on. This allows for easy customization of the features the system should have monitored.

Auditing is typically used for identifying security breaches or suspicious activity. However, auditing is also important to gain insight into how the network, network devices, and systems are accessed. Windows Server 2008 greatly expanded auditing as compared with previous versions of Windows. As it pertains to Windows Server 2008 R2, auditing can be used to monitor successful and unsuccessful events on the system. Windows Server 2008 R2 auditing policies must first be enabled before activity can be monitored.

## Audit Policies

Audit policies are the basis for auditing events on a Windows Server 2008 R2 system. Depending on the policies set, auditing might require a substantial amount of server resources in addition to those resources supporting the server's functionality. Otherwise, it could potentially slow server performance. Also, collecting lots of information is only as good as the evaluation of the audit logs. In other words, if a lot of information is captured and a significant amount of effort is required to evaluate those audit logs, the whole purpose of auditing is not as effective. As a result, it's important to take the time to properly plan how the system will be audited. This allows the administrator to determine what needs to be audited, and why, without creating an abundance of overhead.

Audit policies can track successful or unsuccessful event activity in a Windows Server 2008 R2 environment. These policies can audit the success and failure of events. The policies that can be monitored consist of the following:

▶ **Audit account logon events**—Each time a user attempts to log on, the successful or unsuccessful event can be recorded. Failed logon attempts can include logon failures for unknown user accounts, time restriction violations, expired user accounts, insufficient rights for the user to log on locally, expired account passwords, and locked-out accounts.

20

▶ **Audit account management**—When an account is changed, an event can be logged and later examined.

▶ **Audit directory service access**—Any time a user attempts to access an Active Directory object that has its own system access control list (SACL), the event is logged.

▶ **Audit logon events**—Logons over the network or by services are logged.

▶ **Audit object access**—The object access policy logs an event when a user attempts to access a resource (for example, a printer or shared folder).

▶ **Audit policy change**—Each time an attempt to change a policy (user rights, account audit policies, trust policies) is made, the event is recorded.

▶ **Audit privilege use**—Privileged use is a security setting and can include a user employing a user right, changing the system time, and more. Successful or unsuccessful attempts can be logged.

▶ **Audit process tracking**—An event can be logged for each program or process that a user launches while accessing a system. This information can be very detailed and take a significant amount of resources.

▶ **Audit system events**—The system events policy logs specific system events such as a computer restart or shutdown.

The audit policies can be enabled or disabled through the local system policy, domain controller security policy, or Group Policy Objects. Audit policies are located within the Computer Configuration\Policies\Windows Settings\Security Settings\Local Policies\Audit Policy folder of the Group Policy Management Editor, as shown in Figure 20.12.

For the audit policies, the recommended settings are given in Table 20.3. These should be set on the Default Domain and Default Domain Controller GPOs. By default, all the policies are Not Defined. Figure 20.12 shows the recommended settings.

TABLE 20.3   Matching Audit Policies Recommended Settings

| Audit Policy | Recommended Setting |
| --- | --- |
| Audit account logon events | Success and Failure |
| Audit account management | Success and Failure |
| Audit directory service access | Success |
| Audit logon events | Success and Failure |
| Audit object access | Not Defined |
| Audit policy change | Success |
| Audit privilege use | Not Defined |
| Audit process tracking | Success |
| Audit system events | Success |

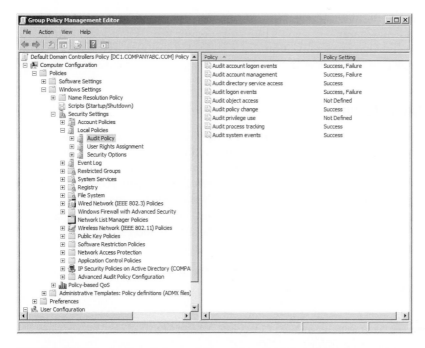

FIGURE 20.12   Audit policies and the recommended settings.

The recommended settings are designed to address specific threats. These threats are primarily password attacks and misuse of privilege. Table 20.4 matches the threats to the specific audit policies.

TABLE 20.4   Matching Specific Threats to Audit Policy Recommended Settings

| Threat Addressed | Audit Policy |
| --- | --- |
| Random password attacks | Audit account logon events (failures) |
| | Audit logon events (failures) |
| Stolen password attacks | Audit account logon events (successes) |
| | Audit logon events (successes) |
| Misuse of privileges | Audit account management |
| | Audit directory service access |
| | Audit policy change |
| | Audit process tracking |
| | Audit system events |

20

These recommended settings are sufficient for the majority of organizations. However, they can generate a heavy volume of events in a large organization. Or, there might be a subset of security events that an organization needs to track. In those cases, the next section discusses how to fine-tune the audit policy using audit policy subcategories.

## Audit Policy Subcategories

Windows Server 2008 R2 allows more granularity in the setting of the audit policies. In previous versions of the Windows Server platform, the audit policies could only be set on the general categories. This usually resulted in a large number of security events, many of which are not of interest to the administrator. System management software was usually needed to help parse all the security events to find and report on the relevant entries. Windows Server 2008 R2 exposes additional subcategories under each of the general categories, which can each be set to No Auditing, Success, Failure, or Success and Failure. These subcategories allow administrators to fine-tune the audited events.

Unfortunately, the audit categories do not quite match the audit policies. Table 20.5 shows how the categories match the policies.

TABLE 20.5    Matching Audit Policies to Audit Categories

| Audit Policy | Audit Category |
| --- | --- |
| Audit account logon events | Account Logon |
| Audit account management | Account Management |
| Audit directory service access | DS Access |
| Audit logon events | Logon/Logoff |
| Audit object access | Object Access |
| Audit policy change | Policy Change |
| Audit privilege use | Privilege Use |
| Audit process tracking | Detailed Tracking |
| Audit system events | System |

There are over 50 different subcategories that can be individually set. These give the administrator and security professionals unprecedented control over the events that will generate security log entries. Table 20.6 lists the categories and the subcategories of audit policies.

TABLE 20.6   Audit Subcategories

| Audit Category | Audit Subcategory |
| --- | --- |
| System | Security State Change |
| | Security System Extension |
| | System Integrity |
| | IPSec Driver |
| | Other System Events |
| Logon/Logoff | Logon |
| | Logoff |
| | Account Lockout |
| | IPSec Main Mode |
| | IPSec Quick Mode |
| | IPSec Extended Mode |
| | Special Logon |
| | Network Policy Server |
| | Other Logon/Logoff Events |
| Object Access | File System |
| | Registry |
| | Kernel Object |
| | SAM |
| | Certification Services |
| | Application Generated |
| | Handle Manipulation |
| | File Share |
| | Filtering Platform Packet Drop |
| | Detailed File Share |
| | Filtering Platform Connection |
| | Other Object Access Events |
| Privilege Use | Sensitive Privilege Use |
| | Non-Sensitive Privilege Use |
| | Other Privilege Use Events |
| Detailed Tracking | Process Creation |
| | Process Termination |
| | DPAPI Activity |
| | RPC Events |

20

TABLE 20.6    Audit Subcategories

| Audit Category | Audit Subcategory |
| --- | --- |
| Policy Change | Audit Policy Change |
| | Authentication Policy Change |
| | Authorization Policy Change |
| | MPSSVC Rule-Level Policy Change |
| | Filtering Platform Policy Change |
| | Other Policy Change Events |
| Account Management | User Account Management |
| | Computer Account Management |
| | Security Group Management |
| | Distribution Group Management |
| | Application Group Management |
| | Other Account Management Event |
| DS Access | Directory Service Access |
| | Directory Service Changes |
| | Directory Service Replication |
| | Detailed Directory Service Replication |
| Account Logon | Kerberos Service Ticket Operations |
| | Credential Validation |
| | Kerberos Authentication Service |
| | Other Account Logon Events |

You can use the AUDITPOL command to get and set the audit categories and subcategories. To retrieve a list of all the settings for the audit categories and subcategories, use the following command:

```
auditpol /get /category:*
```

To enable auditing of the Distribution Group Management subcategory of the Account Management category for both success and failure events, the following command can be used:

```
auditpol /set /subcategory:"Distribution Group Management"
 /success:enable /failure:enable
```

This command would need to be run on each domain controller for the policy to have a uniform effect. To get all the options for the Audit Policy command, use the following command:

```
auditpol /?
```

## Auditing Resource Access

Object access can be audited, although it is not one of the recommended settings. Auditing object access can place a significant load on the servers, so it should only be enabled when it is specifically needed. Auditing object access is a two-step process: Step one is enabling "Audit object access" and step two is selecting the objects to be audited. When enabling Audit object access, you need to decide if both failure and success events will be logged. The two options are as follows:

▶ Audit object access failure enables you to see if users are attempting to access objects to which they have no rights. This shows unauthorized attempts.

▶ Audit object access success enables you to see usage patterns. This shows misuse of privilege.

Enable the appropriate policy setting in the Group Policy Object. It is a best practice to apply the GPO as close to the monitored system as possible, so avoid enabling the auditing on too wide a set of systems.

> **NOTE**
>
> Monitoring both success and failure resource access can place additional strain on the system. Success events can generate a large volume of events.

After enabling the object access policy, the administrator can make auditing changes through the property pages of a file, folder, or a Registry key. If the object access policy is enabled for both success and failure, the administrator will be able to audit both successes and failures for a file, folder, or Registry key.

After object access auditing is enabled, you can easily monitor access to resources such as folders, files, and printers.

### Auditing Files and Folders

The network administrator can tailor the way Windows Server 2008 R2 audits files and folders through the property pages for those files or folders. Keep in mind that the more files and folders that are audited, the more events that can be generated, which can increase administrative overhead and system resource requirements. Therefore, choose wisely which files and folders to audit. To audit a file or folder, do the following:

1. In Windows Explorer, right-click the file or folder to audit and select Properties.
2. Select the Security tab and then click the Advanced button.
3. In the Advanced Security Settings window, select the Auditing tab and click the Edit button.
4. Click the Add button to display the Select User or Group window.
5. Enter the name of the user or group to audit when accessing the file or folder. Click the Check Names button to verify the name.

**20**

6. Click OK to open the Auditing Entries window.

7. In the Auditing Entry window, shown in Figure 20.13, select which events to audit for successes or failures.

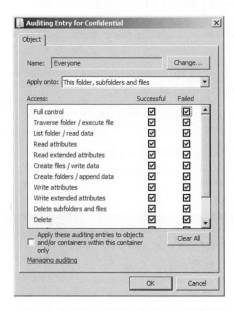

FIGURE 20.13    The Auditing Entry window.

8. Click OK four times to exit.

**NOTE**

This step assumes that the audit object access policy has been enabled.

When the file or folder is accessed, an event is written to Event Viewer's security log. The category for the event is Object Access. An Object Access event is shown in the following security log message:

```
Log Name:      Security
Source:        Microsoft-Windows-Security-Auditing
Date:          9/28/2009 6:22:56 PM
Event ID:      4663
Task Category: File System
Level:         Information
Keywords:      Audit Success
User:          N/A
Computer:      DC1.companyabc.com
```

```
Description:
An attempt was made to access an object.

Subject:
        Security ID:            COMPANYABC\Administrator
        Account Name:           Administrator
        Account Domain:         COMPANYABC
        Logon ID:               0x2586e

Object:
        Object Server:  Security
        Object Type:    File
        Object Name:    C:\Confidential\Secret.txt
        Handle ID:      0xec

Process Information:
        Process ID:     0xfd8
        Process Name:   C:\Windows\System32\notepad.exe

Access Request Information:
        Accesses:       WriteData (or AddFile)
                        AppendData (or AddSubdirectory or CreatePipeInstance)

        Access Mask:    0x6
```

The event is well organized into Subject (whom attempted the access), Object (what was acted on), Process Information (what program was used), and Access Request Information (what was done). If the event was Audit Success, the attempt was successful. If the event was Audit Failure, the attempt failed. You can see from the event that the administrator wrote to the file Secret.txt at 6:22:56 p.m. and even that the program Notepad was used.

### Auditing Printers

Printer auditing operates on the same basic principles as file and folder auditing. In fact, the same step-by-step procedures for configuring file and folder auditing apply to printers. The difference lies in what successes and failures can be audited. These events include the following:

▶ Print

▶ Manage printers

▶ Manage documents

▶ Read permissions

▶ Change permissions

▶ Take ownership

These events are stored in Event Viewer's security log, as are all audit events.

20

To audit a printer, do the following:

1. In the Printers Control Panel applet, right-click the printer to audit, and select Properties.

2. Select the Security tab and then click the Advanced button.

3. In the Advanced Security Settings window, select the Auditing tab, and click the Edit button.

4. Click the Add button to display the Select User or Group window.

5. Enter the name of the user or group to audit when accessing the file or folder. Click the Check Names button to verify the name.

6. Click OK to open the Auditing Entries window.

7. In the Auditing Entry window, select which events to audit for successes or failures. The objects to audit will be different than the auditing available for files and folders, as the printer is a different class of object.

8. Click OK three times to exit.

Now access to the printer will generate security log events, depending on the events that were selected to be audited.

# Managing Windows Server 2008 R2 Remotely

Windows Server 2008 R2's built-in feature set allows it to be easily managed remotely. This capability reduces administration time, expenses, and energy by allowing administrators to manage systems from remote locations rather than having to be physically at the system.

## Server Manager Remote Management

New to Windows Server 2008 R2 is the Server Manager Remote Management, which allows the Server Manager console to remotely manage another server. This makes available all the features of Server Manager to the remote computer, allowing administrators to easily manage Windows Server 2008 R2 servers from a central location.

Server Manager Remote Management is disabled by default. This is a security feature, much like Remote Desktop, and so Windows Server 2008 R2 defaults to a more secure state out of the box. To enable the Server Manager Remote Management, execute the following steps:

1. Launch Server Manager.

2. Click on the Configure Server Manager Remote Management link.

3. Select the Enable Remote Management of This Server from Other Computers check box.

4. Click OK.

Now the system is ready to accept connections from remote Server Manager consoles. To connect to a remote computer with the Server Manager console, right-click on the Server

Manager root and select Connect to Another Computer. Enter the remote computer name and click OK.

## Remote Server Administration Tools

The Remote Server Administration Tools include a number of tools to manage Windows Server 2008 R2 remotely. This set of tools replaced the `Adminpack.msi` set of tools that shipped with Windows Server 2003.

There are different tools for the roles (see Table 20.7) and for the features (see Table 20.8).

TABLE 20.7    Remote Server Administration Tools for Roles

| Tool | Description |
| --- | --- |
| Active Directory Certificate Services Tools | Active Directory Certificate Services Tools include the Certification Authority, Certificate Templates, Enterprise PKI, and Online Responder Management snap-ins. |
| Active Directory Domain Services (AD DS) Tools | Active Directory Domain Services Tools include Active Directory Users and Computers, Active Directory Domains and Trusts, Active Directory Sites and Services, and other snap-ins and command-line tools for remotely managing Active Directory Domain Services. |
| Active Directory Lightweight Directory Services (AD LDS) Tools | Active Directory Lightweight Directory Services Tools include Active Directory Sites and Services, ADSI Edit, Schema Manager, and other snap-ins and command-line tools for managing Active Directory Lightweight Directory Services. |
| Active Directory Rights Management Services (AD RMS) Tools | Active Directory Rights Management Services (AD RMS) Tools includes the Active Directory Rights Management Services (AD RMS) snap-in. |
| DHCP Server Tools | DHCP Server Tools include the DHCP snap-in. |
| DNS Server Tools | DNS Server Tools include the DNS Manager snap-in and `dnscmd.exe` command-line tool. |
| Fax Server Tools | Fax Server Tools include the Fax Service Manager snap-in. |
| File Services Tools | File Services Tools include the following: Distributed File System Tools, which include the DFS Management snap-in, and the `dfsradmin.exe`, `dfscmd.exe`, `dfsdiag.exe`, and `dfsutil.exe` command-line tools. File Server Resource Manager Tools include the File Server Resource Manager snap-in, and the `filescrn.exe` and `storrept.exe` command-line tools. Services for Network File System Tools include the Network File System snap-in, and the `nfsadmin.exe`, `showmount.exe`, and `rpcinfo.exe` command-line tools. |

**20**

TABLE 20.7    Remote Server Administration Tools for Roles

| Tool | Description |
| --- | --- |
| Hyper-V Tools | Hyper-V Tools include the snap-ins and tools for managing the Hyper-V role. |
| Network Policy and Access Services Tools | Network Policy and Access Services Tools include the Routing and Remote Access and Health Registration Authority snap-ins. |
| Print and Document Services Tools | Print Services Tools include the Print Management snap-in. |
| Remote Desktop Services Tools | Remote Desktop Services Tools include the TS RemoteApp Manager, TS Gateway Manager, and TS Licensing Manager snap-ins. |
| Web Server (IIS) Tools | Web Server (IIS) Tools include the Internet Information Services (IIS) 6.0 Manager and IIS Manager snap-ins. |
| Windows Deployment Services Tools | Windows Deployment Services Tools include the Windows Deployment Services snap-in, `wdsutil.exe` command-line tool, and Remote Install extension for the Active Directory Users and Computers snap-in. |

TABLE 20.8    Remote Server Administration Tools for Features

| Tool | Description |
| --- | --- |
| BitLocker Drive Encryption Tools | BitLocker Drive Encryption Tools include the `manage-bde.wsf` script. |
| BITS Server Extensions Tools | BITS Server Extensions Tools include the Internet Information Services (IIS) 6.0 Manager and IIS Manager snap-ins. |
| Failover Clustering Tools | Failover Clustering Tools include the Failover Cluster Manager snap-in and the `cluster.exe` command-line tool. |
| Network Load Balancing Tools | Network Load Balancing Tools include the Network Load Balancing Manager snap-in and the `nlb.exe` and `wlbs.exe` command-line tools. |
| SMTP Server Tools | SMTP Server Tools include the Internet Information Services (IIS) 6.0 Manager snap-in. |
| WINS Server Tools | Windows Internet Naming Service (WINS) Server Tools include the WINS snap-in. |

The tools are installed as a feature. You can install all the tools or only the specific ones that you need. To install the Remote Server Administration Tools, execute the following steps:

1. Launch Server Manager.

2. Select the Features folder.

3. Click the Add Features link.

4. Locate the Remote Server Administration Tools feature.

5. Select the desired tools (more than one can be selected).

6. Click Next to accept the selected tools.

7. Click Install to install the selected tools.

8. Click Close to exit the wizard.

9. Close the Server Manager window.

After the tools are installed, you can manage remote computers by selecting the Connect to Another Computer command from the Action menu.

## Windows Remote Management

Windows Remote Management (WinRM) enables an administrator to run command lines remotely on a target server. When WinRM is used to execute the command remotely, the command executes on the target server and the output of the command is piped to the local server. This allows administrators to see the output of those commands.

The commands run securely, as the WinRM requires authentication and also encrypts the network traffic in both directions.

WinRM is both a service and a command-line interface for remote and local management of servers. The service implements the WS-Management protocol on Windows Server 2008 R2. WS-Management is a standard web services protocol for management of software and hardware remotely.

In Windows Server 2008 R2, the WinRM service establishes a Listener on the HTTP and HTTPS ports. It can coexist with Internet Information Services (IIS) and share the ports, but uses the /wsman URL to avoid conflicts. The IIS role does not have to be installed for this to work.

The WinRM service must be configured to allow remote management of the target server and the Windows Firewall must be configured to allow Windows Remote Management traffic inbound. The WinRM service can be configured through GPO or via the WinRM command line. To have the WinRM service listen on port 80 for all IP addresses on the server and to configure the Windows Firewall, execute the following commands on the target server:

1. Select Start, Run.

2. Enter the command `winrm quickconfig`.

3. Click OK to run the command.

4. Read the output from WinRM. Answer y to the prompt that asks: "Make These Changes [y/n]?"

Now the target server is ready to accept commands. For example, suppose an administrator is logged on to a server dc1.companyabc.com and needs to remotely execute a command on branch office server dc3.companyabc.com. These steps assume that WinRM has been configured and the firewall rule has been enabled. Use the following steps to remotely execute the command:

1. Open a command prompt on DC1.

2. Enter the command `winrs -r: dc3.companyabc.com ipconfig /all`.

The output of the command will be shown on the local server (DC1)—in this case, the IP configuration of the target server (DC3).

This is particularly useful when executing a command or a set of commands on numerous servers. Rather than having to log on to an RDP session on each server and execute the command, the command can be remotely executed in a batch file against all the target servers.

## PowerShell

The powerful new command-line shell is now integrated into Windows Server 2008 R2. PowerShell 2.0 is an administrator-focused shell and scripting language that has a consistent syntax that makes it easy to use. It operates on a cmdlet paradigm, which is, in effect, mini command-line tools. The syntax for the cmdlets is the same as for the PowerShell scripting language, reducing the learning curve of the administrator. In the Windows Server 2008 R2, the PowerShell 2.0 allows for shells to run against remote systems. This enables administrators to execute cmdlets and scripts across the organization from a central console.

PowerShell can run its own scripts and cmdlets, as well as legacy scripts such as VBScript (`.vbs`), batch files (`.bat`), and Perl scripts (`.perl`). The shell can even run Windows-based command-line tools. Many of Microsoft's new applications, such as Microsoft Exchange 2010 and System Center Operations Manager 2007 R2, are integrated with PowerShell and add a host of cmdlets to help automate administration.

PowerShell is added as a feature in Windows Server 2008 R2. See Chapter 21, "Automating Tasks Using PowerShell Scripting," for more details on PowerShell and Windows Server 2008 R2.

## Print Management Console

The Print Management console enables administrators to manage printers across the enterprise from a single console. It shows the status of printers on the network. It also allows the control of those printers, such as the following:

▶ Pausing or resuming printing

▶ Canceling jobs

▶ Listing printers in Active Directory

▶ Deleting printers

▶ Managing printer drivers

Many of the operational controls support multiselecting printers, so that the commands can be run against many printers at once.

The Print Management console is available within the Server Manager console or as a standalone tool. Server Manager is the preferred method of accessing the Print Management console, as it will also manage the role and provide event messages and other operational information.

The Print Management console supports printers running on a wide variety of operating systems, including Windows Server 2008 R2, Windows 7, Windows Server 2008, Windows Vista, Windows Server 2003, Windows XP, and even Windows 2000.

# Using Common Practices for Securing and Managing Windows Server 2008 R2

There are a handful of practices used to secure and manage a Windows Server 2008 R2 environment. The first is to identify security risks to determine what the organization needs to be concerned about when applying a security policy. The second is that the organization can implement a tool like Microsoft System Center Operations Manager to monitor the network and simplify management tasks on a day-to-day basis. And the third is to use maintenance practices to improve the ability of keeping the network environment stable and operational.

## Identifying Security Risks

A network's security is only as good as the security mechanisms put into place and the review and identification process. Strong security entails employing Windows Server 2008 R2 security measures, such as authentication, auditing, and authorization controls, but it also means that security information is properly and promptly reviewed. Information that can be reviewed includes, but isn't limited to, Event Viewer logs, service-specific logs, application logs, and performance data.

All the security information for Windows Server 2008 R2 can be logged, but without a formal review and identification process, the information is useless. Also, security-related information can be complex and unwieldy depending on what information is being recorded. For this reason, manually reviewing the security information might be tedious but can prevent system or network compromise.

The formal review and identification process should be performed daily. Any identified activity that is suspicious or could be potentially risky should be reported and dealt with appropriately. For instance, an administrator reviewing a particular security log might run across some data that might alert him of suspicious activity. This incident would then be reported to the security administrator to take the appropriate action. Whatever the course of action might be in the organization, there should be points of escalation and remediation.

## Using System Center Operations Manager 2007 R2 to Simplify Management

Many of the recommendations in this chapter focus on reviewing event logs, monitoring the configuration, and monitoring the operations of the Windows Server 2008 R2 system. This can be difficult to do for an administrator on a daily basis and the problem is proportional to the number of servers that an administrator is responsible for. Microsoft has developed a product to make these tasks easier and more manageable, namely System Center Operations Manager 2007 R2.

System Center Operations Manager 2007 R2 is an enterprise-class monitoring and management solution for Windows environments. It is designed to simplify Windows management by consolidating events, performance data, alerts, and more into a centralized repository. Reports on this information can then be tailored depending on the environment and on the level of detail that is needed and extrapolated. This information can assist administrators and decision makers in proactively addressing Windows Server 2008 R2 operation and any problems that exist or might occur.

Many other intrinsic benefits are gained by using System Center Operation Manager 2007 R2, including, but not limited to, the following:

▶ Event log monitoring and consolidation

▶ Monitoring of various applications, including those provided by third parties

▶ Enhanced alerting capabilities

▶ Assistance with capacity-planning efforts

▶ A customizable knowledge base of Microsoft product knowledge and best practices

▶ Web-based interfaces for reporting and monitoring

See Chapter 23, "Integrating System Center Operations Manager 2007 R2 with Windows Server 2008 R2," for more details on System Center Operations Manager 2007 R2.

## Leveraging Windows Server 2008 R2 Maintenance Practices

Administrators face the often-daunting task of maintaining the Windows Server 2008 R2 environment in the midst of daily administration and firefighting. Little time is spent identifying and then organizing maintenance processes and procedures.

To decrease the number of administrative inefficiencies and the amount of firefighting an administrator must go through, it's important to identify those tasks that are important to the system's overall health and security. After they've been identified, routines should be set to ensure that the Windows Server 2008 R2 environment is stable and reliable. Many of the maintenance processes and procedures described in the following sections are the most opportune areas to maintain.

# Keeping Up with Service Packs and Updates

Service packs (SPs) and updates for both the operating system and applications are vital parts to maintaining availability, reliability, performance, and security. Microsoft packages these updates into SPs or individually.

An administrator can update a system with the latest SP or update in several ways: Automatic Windows Updates, CD-ROM, manually entered commands, or Microsoft Windows Server Update Services (WSUS).

> **NOTE**
>
> Thoroughly test and evaluate SPs and updates in a lab environment before installing them on production servers and client machines. Also, install the appropriate SPs and updates on each production server and client machine to keep all systems consistent.

## Manual Update or CD-ROM Update

Manual updating is typically done when applying service packs, rather than hotfixes. Service packs tend to be significantly larger than updates or hotfixes, so many administrators will download the service pack once and then apply it manually to their servers, or the service pack can be obtained on CD-ROM.

When a Service Pack CD-ROM is inserted into the drive of the server, it will typically launch an interface to install the service pack.

In the case of downloaded service packs or of CD-ROM-based service packs, the service pack can also be applied manually via a command line. This allows greater control over the install (see Table 20.9), such as by preventing a reboot or to not back up files to conserve space.

TABLE 20.9    Update.exe Command-Line Parameters

| Update.exe Parameter | Description |
| --- | --- |
| -f | Forces applications to close at shutdown. |
| -n | Prevents the system files from being backed up. This keeps SPs from being uninstalled. |
| -o | Overwrites OEM files. |
| -q | Indicates Quiet mode; no user interaction is required. |
| -s | Integrates the SP in a Windows Server 2008 R2 share. |
| -u | Installs SP in Unattended mode. |
| -z | Keeps the system from rebooting after installation. |

20

## Automatic Updates

Windows Server 2008 R2 can be configured to download and install updates automatically using Automatic Windows Updates. With this option enabled, Windows Server 2008 R2 checks for updates, downloads them, and applies them automatically on a schedule. The administrator can just have the updates downloaded, but not installed, to give the administrator more control over when they are installed. Windows Update can also download and install recommended updates, which is new for Windows Server 2008 R2.

When the Windows Server 2008 R2 operating system is installed, Windows Update is not configured and, as shown in Figure 20.14, the Server Manager Security Information section shows the Windows Update as Not Configured. This can be an insecure configuration, as security updates will not be applied.

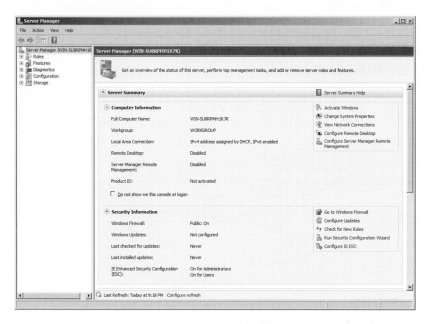

FIGURE 20.14    Windows Updates Not Configured error.

Windows Updates can be configured using the following steps:

1. Launch Server Manager.

2. Click on the Configure Updates link in the Security Information section.

3. Click on the Have Windows Install Updates Automatically to have the updates downloaded and installed.

4. The Windows Updates status will change to Install Updates Automatically Using Windows Updates.

The configuration of Windows Update can be reviewed by clicking on the Configure Updates link again. The Windows Update console appears (shown in Figure 20.15). The figure shows that updates will be installed automatically at 3:00 a.m. every day. The console also shows when updates were checked for last. In the console, the administrator can also do the following:

▶ Manually check for updates.

▶ Change the Windows Updates settings.

▶ View the update history.

▶ See installed updates.

▶ Get updates for more products.

The link to get updates for more products allows the administrator to check for updates not just for the Windows Server 2008 R2 platform, but also for other products, such as Microsoft Exchange and Microsoft SQL. Clicking the link launches a web page to authorize the server to check for the broader range of updates.

Clicking the Change Settings link allows the Windows Update setting to be changed. The Change Settings window, shown in Figure 20.16, enables the administrator to adjust the time of installs, to install or just download, and whether to install recommended updates.

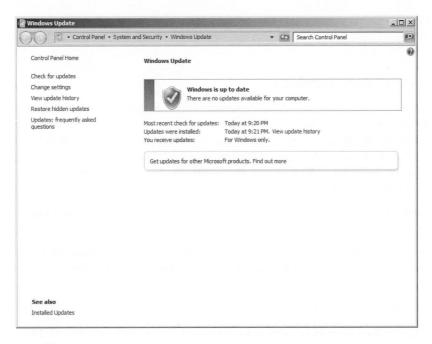

FIGURE 20.15   Windows Update console.

20

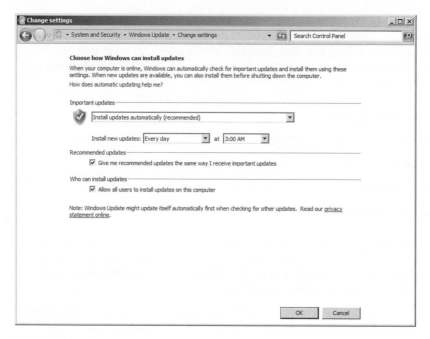

FIGURE 20.16    Windows Update console.

The Windows Updates functionality is a great tool for keeping servers updated with very little administrative overhead, albeit with some loss of control.

## Windows Server Update Services

Realizing the increased administration and management efforts administrators must face when using Windows Update to keep up with SPs and updates for anything other than small environments, Microsoft has created the Windows Server Update Services (WSUS) client and server versions to minimize administration, management, and maintenance of mid- to large-sized organizations. WSUS 3.0 SP1 communicates directly and securely with Microsoft to gather the latest SPs and updates.

Microsoft Windows Server Update Services provides a number of features to support organizations, such as the following:

▶ Support for a broad range of products such as Windows operating system family, Exchange messaging, SQL Server, Office, System Center family, and Windows Defender.

▶ Automatic download of updates.

▶ Administrative control over which updates are approved, removed, or declined; the remove option permits updates to be rolled back.

▶ Email notification of updates and deployment status reports.

- ▶ Targeting of updates to specific groups of computers for testing and for control of the update process.

- ▶ Scalability to multiple WSUS servers controlled from a single console.

- ▶ Reporting on all aspects of the WSUS operations and status.

- ▶ Integration with Automatic Windows Updates.

The SPs and updates downloaded onto WSUS can then be distributed to either a lab server for testing (recommended) or to a production server for distribution. After these updates are tested, WSUS can automatically update systems inside the network.

The following steps install the Windows Server Update Services role:

1. Open the Server Manager console.
2. Select the Roles folder and click Add Roles.
3. In the Add Roles Wizard, select Windows Server Update Services and follow the instructions onscreen. The wizard will install WSUS 3.0 SP1 and any required components, including Web Server (IIS), if needed.

Unlike other server roles, the binaries for WSUS 3.0 SP1 are downloaded from Microsoft. This ensures that any time WSUS is installed, you will always be installing the most current version.

# Maintaining Windows Server 2008 R2

Maintaining Windows Server 2008 R2 systems isn't an easy task for administrators. They must find time in their firefighting efforts to focus and plan for maintenance on the server systems. When maintenance tasks are commonplace in an environment, they can alleviate many of the common firefighting tasks.

The processes and procedures for maintaining Windows Server 2008 R2 systems can be separated based on the appropriate time to maintain a particular aspect of Windows Server 2008 R2. Some maintenance procedures require daily attention, whereas others might require only quarterly checkups. The maintenance processes and procedures that an organization follows depend strictly on the organization; however, the categories described in the following sections and their corresponding procedures are best practices for organizations of all sizes and varying IT infrastructures.

## Daily Maintenance

Certain maintenance procedures require more attention than others. The procedures that require the most attention are categorized into the daily procedures. Therefore, it is recommended that an administrator take on these procedures each day to ensure system reliability, availability, performance, and security. These procedures are examined in the following three sections.

### Checking Overall Server Functionality

Although checking the overall server health and functionality might seem redundant or elementary, this procedure is critical to keeping the system environment and users working productively.

Some questions that should be addressed during the checking and verification process are the following:

▶ Can users access data on file servers?

▶ Are printers printing properly? Are there long queues for certain printers?

▶ Is there an exceptionally long wait to log on (that is, longer than normal)?

▶ Can users access messaging systems?

▶ Can users access external resources?

### Verifying That Backups Are Successful

To provide a secure and fault-tolerant organization, it is imperative that a successful backup be performed each night. In the event of a server failure, the administrator might be required to perform a restore from tape. Without a backup each night, the IT organization will be forced to rely on rebuilding the server without the data. Therefore, the administrator should always back up servers so that the IT organization can restore them with minimum downtime in the event of a disaster. Because of the importance of the backups, the first priority of the administrator each day needs to be verifying and maintaining the backup sets.

If disaster ever strikes, the administrators want to be confident that a system or entire site can be recovered as quickly as possible. Successful backup mechanisms are imperative to the recovery operation; recoveries are only as good as the most recent backups.

### Monitoring Event Viewer

Event Viewer is used to check the system, security, application, and other logs on a local or remote system. These logs are an invaluable source of information regarding the system. The Event Viewer Overview and Summary page in Server Manager is shown in Figure 20.17.

> **NOTE**
>
> Checking these logs often helps your understanding of them. There are some events that constantly appear but aren't significant. Events will begin to look familiar, so you will notice when something is new or amiss in your event logs.

All Event Viewer events are categorized either as informational, warning, or error. Some best practices for monitoring event logs include the following:

▶ Understanding the events that are being reported

▶ Setting up a database for archived event logs

▶ Archiving event logs frequently

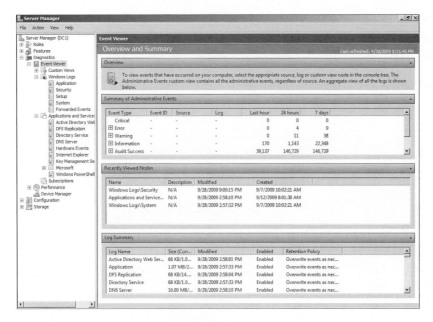

FIGURE 20.17    The Event Viewer snap-in.

To simplify monitoring hundreds or thousands of generated events each day, the administrator should use the filtering mechanism provided in Event Viewer. Although warnings and errors should take priority, the informational events should be reviewed to track what was happening before the problem occurred. After the administrator reviews the informational events, she can filter out the informational events and view only the warnings and errors.

To filter events, do the following:

1. Expand the Event View folder in Server Manager.
2. Select the log from which you want to filter events.
3. Right-click the log and select Filter Current Log.
4. In the log properties window, select the types of events to filter. In this case, select the Critical, Error, and Warning check boxes.
5. Click OK when you're done.

Figure 20.18 shows the results of filtering on the system log. You can see in the figure that there are a total of 8,006 events. In the message above the log, the filter is noted and also the 92 resulting number of events. The filter reduced the events by a factor of over 80 to 1. This really helps reduce the volume of data that an administrator needs to review.

20

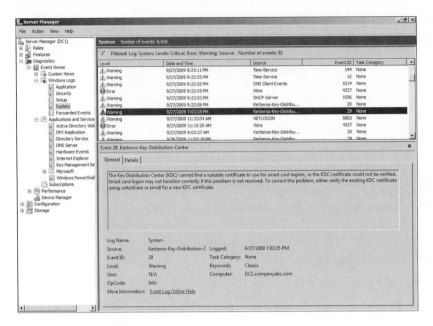

FIGURE 20.18    The Event Viewer filter.

Some warnings and errors are normal because of bandwidth constraints or other environmental issues. The more you monitor the logs, the more familiar you will become with the messages and, therefore, the more likely you will be able to spot a problem before it affects the user community.

> **TIP**
>
> You might need to increase the size of the log files in Event Viewer to accommodate an increase in logging activity. The default log sizes are larger in Windows Server 2008 R2 than in previous versions of Windows, which were notorious for running out of space.

## Weekly Maintenance

Maintenance procedures that require slightly less attention than daily checking are categorized in a weekly routine and are examined in the following sections.

### Checking Disk Space

Disk space is a precious commodity. Although the disk capacity of a Windows Server 2008 R2 system can be virtually endless, the amount of free space on all drives should be checked at least weekly if not more frequently. Serious problems can occur if there isn't enough disk space.

One of the most common disk space problems occurs on data drives where end users save and modify information. Other volumes such as the system drive and partitions with logging data can also quickly fill up.

As mentioned earlier, lack of free disk space can cause a multitude of problems, including, but not limited to, the following:

▶ Application failures

▶ System crashes

▶ Unsuccessful backup jobs

▶ Service failures

▶ The inability to audit

▶ Degradation in performance

To prevent these problems from occurring, administrators should keep the amount of free space to at least 25%.

### CAUTION

If you need to free disk space, you should move or delete files and folders with caution. System files are automatically protected by Windows Server 2008 R2, but data is not.

### Verifying Hardware

Hardware components supported by Windows Server 2008 R2 are reliable, but this doesn't mean that they'll always run continuously without failure. Hardware availability is measured in terms of mean time between failures (MTBF) and mean time to repair (MTTR). This includes downtime for both planned and unplanned events. These measurements provided by the manufacturer are good guidelines to follow; however, mechanical parts are bound to fail at one time or another. As a result, hardware should be monitored weekly to ensure efficient operation.

Hardware can be monitored in many different ways. For example, server systems might have internal checks and logging functionality to warn against possible failure, Windows Server 2008 R2's System Monitor might bring light to a hardware failure, and a physical hardware check can help to determine whether the system is about to experience a problem with the hardware.

If a failure has occurred or is about to occur, having an inventory of spare hardware can significantly improve the chances and timing of recoverability. Checking system hardware on a weekly basis provides the opportunity to correct the issue before it becomes a problem.

### Running Disk Defragmenter

Whenever files are created, deleted, or modified, Windows Server 2008 R2 assigns a group of clusters depending on the size of the file. As file size requirements fluctuate over time, so does the number of groups of clusters assigned to the file. Even though this process is efficient when using NTFS, the files and volumes become fragmented because the file doesn't reside in a contiguous location on the disk.

As fragmentation levels increase, disk access slows. The system must take additional resources and time to find all the cluster groups to use the file. To minimize the amount

20

of fragmentation and give performance a boost, the administrator should use the Disk Defragmenter to defragment all volumes. As mentioned earlier in the chapter, the Disk Defragmenter is a built-in utility that can analyze and defragment volume fragmentation. Fragmentation negatively affects performance because files aren't efficiently read from disk. There is a command-line version of the tool and a graphical user interface version of the tool.

To use the graphical user interface version of the Disk Defragmenter, do the following:

1.  Start Disk Defragmenter by choosing Start, Run.

2.  Enter dfrgui and click OK.

3.  The tool automatically analyzes all the drives and suggests whether to defragment. This only happens if disk defragmentation is not scheduled to run automatically.

4.  Select the volumes to defragment.

5.  Click Defragment Disk to defragment immediately.

6.  The defragmentation runs independently of the Disk Defragmenter GUI, so you can exit the tool while the defragmentation is running by clicking Close.

Unlike previous versions of the software, the Windows Server 2008 R2 Disk Defragmenter does not show a graphical view of the Disk Defragmenter.

The Disk Defragmenter also enables the administrator to set up a schedule for the backup. This modifies the ScheduledDefrag task in the Task Scheduler (located in Task Scheduler\Task Scheduler Library\Microsoft\Windows\Defrag\). After selecting the Run on a Schedule option, the schedule can be set by clicking the Modify Schedule button and the volumes to be defragmented can be selected by clicking the Select Volumes button. New volumes will automatically be defragmented by the task.

### Running the Domain Controller Diagnosis Utility

The Domain Controller Diagnosis (DCDIAG) utility is installed with the Active Directory Domain Services roles in Windows Server 2008 R2 and is used to analyze the state of a domain controller (DC) and the domain services. It runs a series of tests, analyzes the state of the DC, and verifies different areas of the system, such as the following:

- ▶ Connectivity

- ▶ Replication

- ▶ Topology integrity

- ▶ Security descriptors

- ▶ Netlogon rights

- ▶ Intersite health

- ▶ Roles

- ▶ Trust verification

DCDIAG should be run on each DC on a weekly basis or as problems arise. DCDIAG's syntax is as follows:

```
dcdiag.exe /s:<Directory Server>[:<LDAP Port>] [/u:<Domain>\<Username>
/p:*¦<Password>¦""]
[/hqv] [/n:<Naming Context>] [/f:<Log>] [/x:XMLLog.xml]
[/skip:<Test>] [/test:<Test>]
```

Parameters for this utility are as follows:

- ▸ /h—Display this help screen.

- ▸ /s—Use <Domain Controller> as the home server. This is ignored for DCPromo and RegisterInDNS tests, which can only be run locally.

- ▸ /n—Use <Naming Context> as the naming context to test. Domains can be specified in NetBIOS, DNS, or distinguished name (DN) format.

- ▸ /u—Use domain\username credentials for binding with a password. Must also use the /p option.

- ▸ /p—Use <Password> as the password. Must also use the /u option.

- ▸ /a—Test all the servers in this site.

- ▸ /e—Test all the servers in the entire enterprise. This parameter overrides the /a parameter.

- ▸ /q—Quiet; print only error messages.

- ▸ /v—Verbose; print extended information.

- ▸ /i—Ignore; ignore superfluous error messages.

- ▸ /fix—Fix; make safe repairs.

- ▸ /f—Redirect all output to a file <Log>; /ferr will redirect error output separately.

- ▸ /ferr:<ErrLog>—Redirect fatal error output to a separate file <ErrLog>.

- ▸ /c—Comprehensive; run all tests, including nondefault tests but excluding DCPromo and RegisterInDNS. Can use with /skip.

- ▸ /skip:<Test>—Skip the named test. Do not use in a command with /test.

- ▸ /test:<Test>—Test only the specified test. Required tests will still be run. Do not use with the /skip parameter.

- ▸ /x:<XMLLog.xml>—Redirect XML output to <XMLLog.xml>. Currently works with the /test:dns option only.

- ▸ /xsl:<xslfile.xsl or xsltfile.xslt>—Add the processing instructions that reference a specified style sheet. Works with the /test:dns /x:<XMLLog.xml> option only.

20

The command supports a variety of tests, which can be selected. Some tests are run by default and others need to be requested specifically. The command line supports selecting tests explicitly (/test) and skipping tests (/skip). Table 20.10 shows valid tests that can be run consistently.

TABLE 20.10    DCDIAG Tests

| Test Name | Description |
|---|---|
| Advertising | Checks whether each DC is advertising itself and whether it is advertising itself as having the capabilities of a DC. |
| CheckSDRefDom | Checks that all application directory partitions have appropriate security descriptor reference domains. |
| CheckSecurityError | Locates security errors and performs the initial diagnosis of the problem. This test is not run by default and has to be requested with the /test option. |
| Connectivity | Tests whether DCs are DNS registered, pingable, and have LDAP/RPC connectivity. This is a required test and cannot be skipped with the /skip option. |
| CrossRefValidation | This test looks for cross-references that are in some way invalid. |
| CutoffServers | Checks for servers that won't receive replications because their partners are down. This test is not run by default and has to be requested with the /test option. |
| DCPromo | Tests the existing DNS infrastructure for promotion to the domain controller. |
| DNS | Checks the health of DNS settings for the whole enterprise. This test is not run by default and has to be requested with the /test option. |
| FrsEvent | Checks to see if there are any operation errors in the file replication server (FRS). Failing replication of the sysvol share can cause policy problems. |
| DFSREvent | Checks to see if there are any operation errors in the DFS. |
| DFSREvent | Checks to see if there are any operation errors in the DFS. |
| LocatorCheck | Checks that global role holders are known, can be located, and are responding. |
| Intersite | Checks for failures that would prevent or temporarily hold up inter-site replication. |
| Kccevent | Checks that the Knowledge Consistency Checker is completing without errors. |
| KnowsOfRoleHolders | Checks whether the DC thinks it knows the role holders of the five FSMO roles. |

TABLE 20.10   DCDIAG Tests

| Test Name | Description |
| --- | --- |
| MachineAccount | Checks to see whether the machine account has the proper information. Use the `/RecreateMachineAccount` parameter to attempt a repair if the local machine account is missing. Use `/FixMachineAccount` if the machine's account flags are incorrect. |
| NCSecDesc | Checks that the security descriptors on the naming context heads have appropriate permissions for replication. |
| NetLogons | Checks that the appropriate logon privileges allow replication to proceed. |
| ObjectsReplicated | Checks that machine account and DSA objects have replicated. You can use `/objectdn:<dn>` with `/n:<nc>` to specify an additional object to check. |
| OutboundSecureChannels | Verifies that secure channels exist from all the DCs in the domain to the domains specified by `/testdomain`. The `/nositerestriction` parameter prevents the test from being limited to the DCs in the site. This test is not run by default and has to be requested with the `/test` option. |
| RegisterInDNS | Tests whether this domain controller can register the Domain Controller Locator DNS records. These records must be present in DNS for other computers to locate this domain controller for the `<Active_Directory_Domain_DNS_Name>` domain. Reports whether any modifications to the existing DNS infrastructure are required. Requires the `/DnsDomain:<Active_Directory_Domain_DNS_Name>` argument. |
| Replications | Checks for timely replication between domain controllers. |
| RidManager | Checks to see whether RID master is accessible and whether it contains the proper information. |
| Services | Checks to see whether DC services are running on a system. |
| Systemlog | Checks that the system is running without errors. |
| Topology | Checks that the generated topology is fully connected for all DCs. This test is not run by default and has to be requested with the `/test` option. |
| VerifyEnterpriseReferences | Verifies that certain system references are intact for the FRS and replication infrastructure across all objects in the enterprise. This test is not run by default and has to be requested with the `/test` option. |
| VerifyReferences | Verifies that certain system references are intact for the FRS and replication infrastructure. |

20

TABLE 20.10    DCDIAG Tests

| Test Name | Description |
| --- | --- |
| VerifyReplicas | Verifies that all application directory partitions are fully instantiated on all replica servers. This test is not run by default and has to be requested with the /test option. |

## Monthly Maintenance

It is recommended that you perform the tasks examined in the following sections on a monthly basis.

### Maintaining File System Integrity

CHKDSK scans for file system integrity and can check for lost clusters, cross-linked files, and more. If Windows Server 2008 R2 senses a problem, it will run CHKDSK automatically at startup.

Administrators can maintain FAT, FAT32, and NTFS file system integrity by running CHKDSK once a month. To run CHKDSK, do the following:

1. At the command prompt, change to the partition that you want to check.

2. Type CHKDSK without any parameters to check only for file system errors. No changes will be made.

3. If any errors are found, run the CHKDSK utility with the /f parameter to attempt to correct the errors found.

### Testing the UPS

An uninterruptible power supply (UPS) can be used to protect the system or group of systems from power failures (such as spikes and surges) and keep the system running long enough after a power outage so that an administrator can gracefully shut down the system. It is recommended that an administrator follow the UPS guidelines provided by the manufacturer at least once a month. Also, monthly scheduled battery tests should be performed.

### Validating Backups

Once a month, an administrator should validate backups by restoring the backups to a server located in a lab environment. This is in addition to verifying that backups were successful from log files or the backup program's management interface. A restore gives the administrator the opportunity to verify the backups and to practice the restore procedures that would be used when recovering the server during a real disaster. In addition, this procedure tests the state of the backup media to ensure that they are in working order and builds administrator confidence for recovering from a true disaster.

### Updating Documentation

An integral part of managing and maintaining any IT environment is to document the network infrastructure and procedures. The following are just a few of the documents you should consider having on hand:

- Server build guides
- Disaster recovery guides and procedures
- Checklists
- Configuration settings
- Change configuration logs
- Historical performance data
- Special user rights assignments
- Special application settings

As systems and services are built and procedures are ascertained, document these facts to reduce learning curves, administration, and maintenance.

It is not only important to adequately document the IT environment, but it's often even more important to keep those documents up to date. Otherwise, documents can quickly become outdated as the environment, processes, and procedures change as the business changes.

## Quarterly Maintenance

As the name implies, quarterly maintenance is performed four times a year. Areas to maintain and manage on a quarterly basis are typically fairly self-sufficient and self-sustaining. Infrequent maintenance is required to keep the system healthy. This doesn't mean, however, that the tasks are simple or that they aren't as critical as those tasks that require more frequent maintenance.

### Checking Storage Limits

Storage capacity on all volumes should be checked to ensure that all volumes have ample free space. Keep approximately 25% free space on all volumes.

Running low or completely out of disk space creates unnecessary risk for any system. Services can fail, applications can stop responding, and systems can even crash if there isn't plenty of disk space.

### Changing Administrator Passwords

Administrator passwords should, at a minimum, be changed every quarter (90 days). Changing these passwords strengthens security measures so that systems can't easily be compromised. In addition to changing passwords, other password requirements such as password age, history, length, and strength should be reviewed.

20

# Summary

Although administrators can easily get caught up in daily administration and firefighting, it's important to structure system management and maintenance of Windows Server 2008 R2 to help prevent unnecessary amounts of effort. Windows Server 2008 R2 provides many tools, such as the server roles and Server Manager, to enable administrators to more effectively manage their servers.

Server Manager is a one-stop shop for the management and monitoring of most of the functions of a Windows Server 2008 R2 server. The operating system automatically adds the appropriate snap-ins to manage the features and the roles that are installed on the server as they are installed. This makes it the home base for administrators and simplifies their tasks by placing the tools and techniques in a single location.

Systems management and maintenance is not just about the cool technologies, but also about how those technologies are used. Following a management and maintenance regimen reduces administration, maintenance, and business expenses, while at the same time increasing reliability, stability, and security.

# Best Practices

The following are best practices from this chapter:

▶ Use System Manager as the central point of administration for Windows Server 2008 R2 servers.

▶ Manage servers based on their roles.

▶ Try to maintain the network environment's systems periodically to avoid any inefficiency.

▶ Audit not only to identify security breaches or suspicious activity, but also to gain insight into how the network, network devices, and systems are accessed.

▶ Enable audit policies through the local system policy or Group Policy Objects.

▶ Remotely manage systems using Role and Feature tools, Remote Desktop for Administration, scripting, Windows Remote Management, and command-line utilities.

▶ Use System Center Operations Manager 2007 to proactively manage Windows Server 2008 R2.

▶ Identify tasks that are important to the system's overall health and security.

▶ Install the appropriate service packs and updates on each production server and client machine to keep all systems consistent.

▶ Thoroughly test and evaluate service packs and updates in a lab environment before installing them on production servers.

▶ Use Windows Software Update Services to minimize administration, management, and maintenance associated with keeping up with the latest service packs and updates.

▶ Distribute the service packs and hotfixes downloaded from WSUS to a lab server for testing.

▶ Categorize and document daily maintenance activities, such as checking server functionality, verifying that backups were successful, and monitoring Event Viewer events.

▶ Categorize and document weekly maintenance processes and procedures, such as checking disk space, verifying hardware operation, archiving event logs, defragmenting volumes, and diagnosing domain controllers with DCDIAG.

▶ Categorize and document monthly maintenance processes and procedures, such as maintaining file system integrity, testing UPS functionality, validating backups, updating ASR sets, and updating documentation.

▶ Use the Data Collector Sets and reports to analyze server performance and pinpoint problems and resource issues.

▶ Categorize and document quarterly maintenance processes and procedures, such as checking storage limits and changing administrative passwords.

# Automating Tasks Using PowerShell Scripting

Shells are a necessity in using operating systems. They give the ability to execute arbitrary commands as a user and the ability to traverse the file system. Anybody who has used a computer has dealt with a shell by either typing commands at a prompt or clicking an icon to start a word processing application. A shell is something that every user uses in some fashion. It's inescapable in whatever form when working on a computer system.

Until now, Windows users and administrators primarily have used the Windows Explorer or cmd command prompt (both shells) to interact with most versions of the Window operating systems. With Microsoft's release of PowerShell, both a new shell and scripting language, the current standard for interacting with and managing Windows is rapidly changing. This change became very evident with the release of Microsoft Exchange Server 2007, which used PowerShell as its management backbone, the addition of PowerShell as a feature within Windows Server 2008, and now the inclusion of PowerShell as part of the Windows 7 and Windows Server 2008 R2 operating systems.

In this chapter, we take a closer look at what shells are and how they have developed. Next, we review Microsoft's past attempts at providing an automation interface (WSH) and then introduce PowerShell. From there, we step into understanding the PowerShell features and how to use it to manage Windows 2008. Finally, we review some best practices for using PowerShell.

# Understanding Shells

A shell is an interface that enables users to interact with the operating system. A shell isn't considered an application because of its inescapable nature, but it's the same

as any other process running on a system. The difference between a shell and an application is that a shell's purpose is to enable users to run other applications. In some operating systems (such as UNIX, Linux, and VMS), the shell is a command-line interface (CLI); in other operating systems (such as Windows and Mac OS X), the shell is a graphical user interface (GUI).

Both CLI and GUI shells have benefits and drawbacks. For example, most CLI shells allow powerful command chaining (using commands that feed their output into other commands for further processing; this is commonly referred to as the pipeline). GUI shells, however, require commands to be completely self-contained. Furthermore, most GUI shells are easy to navigate, whereas CLI shells require a preexisting knowledge of the system to avoid attempting several commands to discern the location and direction to head in when completing an automation task. Therefore, choosing which shell to use depends on your comfort level and what's best suited to perform the task at hand.

> **NOTE**
>
> Even though GUI shells exist, the term "shell" is used almost exclusively to describe a command-line environment, not a task that is performed with a GUI application, such as Windows Explorer. Likewise, shell scripting refers to collecting commands normally entered on the command line or into an executable file.

## A Short History of Shells

The first shell in wide use was the Bourne shell, the standard user interface for the UNIX operating system; UNIX systems still require it for booting. This robust shell provided pipelines and conditional and recursive command execution. It was developed by C programmers for C programmers.

Oddly, however, despite being written by and for C programmers, the Bourne shell didn't have a C-like coding style. This lack of similarity to the C language drove the invention of the C shell, which introduced more C-like programming structures. While the C shell inventors were building a better mousetrap, they decided to add command-line editing and command aliasing (defining command shortcuts), which eased the bane of every UNIX user's existence: typing. The less a UNIX user has to type to get results, the better.

Although most UNIX users liked the C shell, learning a completely new shell was a challenge for some. So, the Korn shell was invented, which added a number of the C shell features to the Bourne shell. Because the Korn shell is a commercially licensed product, the open source software movement needed a shell for Linux and FreeBSD. The collaborative result was the Bourne Again shell, or Bash, invented by the Free Software Foundation.

Throughout the evolution of UNIX and the birth of Linux and FreeBSD, other operating systems were introduced along with their own shells. Digital Equipment Corporation (DEC) introduced Virtual Memory System (VMS) to compete with UNIX on its VAX systems. VMS had a shell called Digital Command Language (DCL) with a verbose syntax, unlike that of its UNIX counterparts. Also, unlike its UNIX counterparts, it wasn't case sensitive, nor did it provide pipelines.

Somewhere along the way, the PC was born. IBM took the PC to the business market, and Apple rebranded roughly the same hardware technology and focused on consumers. Microsoft made DOS run on the IBM PC, acting as both kernel and shell and including some features of other shells. (The pipeline syntax was inspired by UNIX shells.)

Following DOS was Windows, which went from application to operating system quickly. Windows introduced a GUI shell, which has become the basis for Microsoft shells ever since. Unfortunately, GUI shells are notoriously difficult to script, so Windows provided a DOSShell-like environment. It was improved with a new executable, cmd.exe instead of command.com, and a more robust set of command-line editing features. Regrettably, this change also meant that shell scripts in Windows had to be written in the DOSShell syntax for collecting and executing command groupings.

Over time, Microsoft realized its folly and decided systems administrators should have better ways to manage Windows systems. Windows Script Host (WSH) was introduced in Windows 98, providing a native scripting solution with access to the underpinnings of Windows. It was a library that allowed scripting languages to use Windows in a powerful and efficient manner. WSH is not its own language, however, so a WSH-compliant scripting language was required to take advantage of it, such as JScript, VBScript, Perl, Python, Kixstart, or Object REXX. Some of these languages are quite powerful in performing complex processing, so WSH seemed like a blessing to Windows systems administrators.

However, the rejoicing was short-lived because there was no guarantee that the WSH-compliant scripting language you chose would be readily available or a viable option for everyone. The lack of a standard language and environment for writing scripts made it difficult for users and administrators to incorporate automation by using WSH. The only way to be sure the scripting language or WSH version would be compatible on the system being managed was to use a native scripting language, which meant using DOSShell and enduring the problems that accompanied it. In addition, WSH opened a large attack vector for malicious code to run on Windows systems. This vulnerability gave rise to a stream of viruses, worms, and other malicious programs that have wreaked havoc on computer systems, thanks to WSH's focus on automation without user intervention.

The end result was that systems administrators viewed WSH as both a blessing and a curse. Although WSH presented a good object model and access to a number of automation interfaces, it wasn't a shell. It required using Wscript.exe and Cscript.exe, scripts had to be written in a compatible scripting language, and its attack vulnerabilities posed a security challenge. Clearly, a different approach was needed for systems management; over time, Microsoft reached the same conclusion.

# Introduction to PowerShell

The introduction of WSH as a standard in the Windows operating system offered a robust alternative to DOSShell scripting. Unfortunately, WSH presented a number of challenges, discussed in the preceding section. Furthermore, WSH didn't offer the CLI shell experience that UNIX and Linux administrators had enjoyed for years, resulting in Windows administrators being made fun of by the other chaps for the lack of a CLI shell and its benefits.

Luckily, Jeffrey Snover (the architect of PowerShell) and others on the PowerShell team realized that Windows needed a strong, secure, and robust CLI shell for systems management. Enter PowerShell. PowerShell was designed as a shell with full access to the underpinnings of Windows via the .NET Framework, Component Object Model (COM) objects, and other methods. It also provided an execution environment that's familiar, easy, and secure. PowerShell is aptly named, as it puts the power into the Windows shell. For users wanting to automate their Windows systems, the introduction of PowerShell was exciting because it combined "the power of WSH with the warm-fuzzy familiarity of a CLI shell."

PowerShell provides a powerful native scripting language, so scripts can be ported to all Windows systems without worrying about whether a particular language interpreter is installed. In the past, an administrator might have gone through the rigmarole of scripting a solution with WSH in Perl, Python, VBScript, JScript, or another language, only to find that the next system that they worked on didn't have that interpreter installed. At home, users can put whatever they want on their systems and maintain them however they see fit, but in a workplace, that option isn't always viable. PowerShell solves that problem by removing the need for nonnative interpreters. It also solves the problem of wading through websites to find command-line equivalents for simple GUI shell operations and coding them into .cmd files. Last, PowerShell addresses the WSH security problem by providing a platform for secure Windows scripting. It focuses on security features such as script signing, lack of executable extensions, and execution policies (which are restricted by default).

For anyone who needs to automate administration tasks on a Windows system or a Microsoft platform, PowerShell provides a much-needed injection of power. As such, for Windows systems administrators or scripters, becoming a PowerShell expert is highly recommended. After all, PowerShell can now be used to efficiently automate management tasks for Windows, Active Directory, Terminal Services, SQL Server, Exchange Server, Internet Information Services (IIS), and even a number of different third-party products.

As such, PowerShell is the approach Microsoft had been seeking as the automation and management interface for their products. Thus, PowerShell is now the endorsed solution for the management of Windows-based systems and server products. Over time, PowerShell could even possibly replace the current management interfaces, such as cmd.exe, WSH, CLI tools, and so on, while becoming even further integrated into the Windows operating system. The trend toward this direction can be seen with the release of Windows Server 2008 R2 and Windows 7, in which PowerShell is part of the operating system.

## PowerShell Uses

In Windows, an administrator can complete a number of tasks using PowerShell. The following list is a sampling of these tasks:

▶ **Manage the file system**—To create, delete, modify, and set permissions for files and folders.

▶ **Manage services**—To list, stop, start, restart, and even modify services.

▶ **Manage processes**—To list (monitor), stop, and start processes.

▶ **Manage the Registry**—To list (monitor), stop, and start processes.

▶ **Use Windows Management Instrumentation (WMI)**—To manage not only Windows, but also other platforms such as IIS and Terminal Services.

▶ **Use existing Component Object Model (COM) objects**—To complete a wide range of automation tasks.

▶ **Manage a number of Windows roles and features**—To add or remove roles and features.

## PowerShell Features

PowerShell is a departure from the current management interfaces in Windows. As such, it has been built from the ground up to include a number of features that make CLI and script-based administration easier. Some of PowerShell's more key features are as follows:

▶ It has 240 built-in command-line tools (referred to as cmdlets).

▶ The scripting language is designed to be readable and easy to use.

▶ PowerShell supports existing scripts, command-line tools, and automation interfaces, such as WMI, ADSI, .NET Framework, ActiveX Data Objects (ADO), and so on.

▶ It follows a strict naming convention for commands based on a verb-noun format.

▶ It supports a number of different Windows operating systems: Windows XP SP2 or later, Windows Server 2003 SP1 or later, Windows Vista, Windows Server 2008, and now Windows Server 2008 R2 and Windows 7.

▶ It provides direct "access to and navigation of" the Windows Registry, certificate store, and file system using a common set of commands.

▶ PowerShell is object based, which allows data (objects) to be piped between commands.

▶ It is extensible, which allows third parties (as noted earlier) to build upon and extend PowerShell's already rich interfaces for managing Windows and other Microsoft platforms.

## PowerShell 2.0 Enhancements

Windows Server 2008 R2 has the Windows PowerShell 2.0 version built in to the operating system. In this version of PowerShell, a number of enhancements have been made to both PowerShell itself and the ability for managing Windows Server 2008 R2's roles and features. The following is a summary for some of the improvements in PowerShell 2.0 (these features are talked about in greater detail later in this chapter and throughout this book):

▶ The number of built-in cmdlets has nearly doubled from 130 to 240.

▶ PowerShell 2.0 now includes the ability to manage a number of roles and features such as the Active Directory Domain Services, Active Directory Rights Management Services, AppLocker, Background Intelligent Transfer Service [BITS], Best Practices Analyzer, Failover Clustering [WSFC], Group Policy, Internet Information Services [IIS], Network Load Balancing [NLB], Remote Desktop Services [RDS], Server Manager, Server Migration, and Windows Diagnostics roles and features.

▶ PowerShell 2.0 also includes the introduction of the Windows PowerShell debugger. Using this feature, an administrator can identify errors or inefficiencies in scripts, functions, commands, and expressions while they are being executed through a set of debugging cmdlets or the Integrated Scripting Environment (ISE).

▶ The PowerShell Integrated Scripting Environment (ISE) is a multi-tabbed GUI-based PowerShell development interface. Using the ISE, an administrator can write, test, and debug scripts. The ISE includes such features as multiline editing, tab completion, syntax coloring, selective execution, context-sensitive help, and support for right-to-left languages.

▶ Background jobs enable administrators to execute commands and scripts asynchronously.

▶ Also through the inclusion of script functions, administrators can now create their own cmdlets without having to write and compile the cmdlet using a managed-code language like C#.

▶ PowerShell 2.0 also includes a new powerful feature, called modules, which allows packages of cmdlets, providers, functions, variables, and aliases to be bundled and then easily shared with others.

▶ The lack of remote command support has also been addressed in PowerShell 2.0 with the introduction of remoting. This feature enables an administrator to automate the management of many remote systems through a single PowerShell console.

However, with all of these features, the most important advancement that is found in PowerShell 2.0 is the focus on what is called the Universal Code Execution model. The core concept in this model is flexibility over how expressions, commands, and script-blocks are executed across one or more machines.

# Understanding the PowerShell Basics

To begin working with PowerShell, some of the basics like accessing PowerShell, working from the command-line interface, and understanding the basic commands are covered in this section of the book.

## Accessing PowerShell

After logging in to your Windows interactive session, there are several methods to access and use PowerShell. The first method is from the Start menu, as shown in the following steps:

1. Click Start, All Programs, Accessories, Windows PowerShell.

2. Choose either Windows PowerShell (x86) or Windows PowerShell.

To use the second method, follow these steps:

1. Click Start.

2. Type PowerShell in the Search Programs and Files text box and press Enter.

Both these methods open the PowerShell console, whereas the third method launches PowerShell from a cmd command prompt:

1. Click Start, Run.

2. Type cmd and click OK to open a cmd command prompt.

3. At the command prompt, type powershell and press Enter.

## Command-Line Interface (CLI)

The syntax for using PowerShell from the CLI is similar to the syntax for other CLI shells. The fundamental component of a PowerShell command is, of course, the name of the command to be executed. In addition, the command can be made more specific by using parameters and arguments for parameters. Therefore, a PowerShell command can have the following formats:

▶ [command name]

▶ [command name] -[parameter]

▶ [command name] -[parameter] -[parameter] [argument1]

▶ [command name] -[parameter] -[parameter] [argument1],[argument2]

When using PowerShell, a parameter is a variable that can be accepted by a command, script, or function. An argument is a value assigned to a parameter. Although these terms are often used interchangeably, remembering these definitions is helpful when discussing their use in PowerShell.

## Navigating the CLI

As with all CLI-based shells, an understanding is needed in how to effectively navigate and use the PowerShell CLI. Table 21.1 lists the editing operations associated with various keys when using the PowerShell console.

TABLE 21.1    PowerShell Console Editing Features

| Keys | Editing Operation |
| --- | --- |
| Left and right arrows | Move the cursor left and right through the current command line. |
| Up and down arrows | Moves up and down through the list of recently typed commands. |
| PgUp | Displays the first command in the command history. |
| PgDn | Displays the last command in the command history. |
| Home | Moves the cursor to the beginning of the command line. |
| End | Moves the cursor to the end of the command line. |
| Insert | Switches between insert and overstrike text-entry modes. |
| Delete | Deletes the character at the current cursor position. |
| Backspace | Deletes the character immediately preceding the current cursor position. |
| F3 | Displays the previous command. |
| F4 | Deletes up to the specified number of characters from the current cursor. |
| F5 | Moves backward through the command history. |
| F7 | Displays a list of recently typed commands in a pop-up window in the command shell. Use the up and down arrows to select a previously typed command, and then press Enter to execute the selected command. |
| F8 | Moves backward through the command history with commands that match the text that has been entered at the command prompt. |
| F9 | Prompts for a command number and executes the specified command from the command history (command numbers refer to the F7 command list). |
| Tab | Auto-completes command-line sequences. Use the Shift+Tab sequence to move backward through a list of potential matches. |

Luckily, most of the features in Table 21.1 are native to the cmd command prompt, which makes PowerShell adoption easier for administrators already familiar with the Windows command line. The only major difference is that the Tab key auto-completion is enhanced in PowerShell beyond what's available with the cmd command prompt.

As with the cmd command prompt, PowerShell performs auto-completion for file and directory names. So, if you enter a partial file or directory name and press Tab, PowerShell returns the first matching file or directory name in the current directory. Pressing Tab again returns a second possible match and enables you to cycle through the list of results. Like the cmd command prompt, PowerShell's Tab key auto-completion can also auto-complete with wildcards. The difference between Tab key auto-completion in cmd and PowerShell is that PowerShell can auto-complete commands. For example, you can enter a partial command name and press the Tab key, and PowerShell steps through a list of possible command matches.

PowerShell can also auto-complete parameter names associated with a particular command. Simply enter a command and partial parameter name and press the Tab key, and PowerShell cycles through the parameters for the command that has been specified. This method also works for variables associated with a command. In addition, PowerShell performs auto-completion for methods and properties of variables and objects.

## Command Types

When a command is executed in PowerShell, the command interpreter looks at the command name to figure out what task to perform. This process includes determining the type of command and how to process that command. There are four types of PowerShell commands: cmdlets, shell function commands, script commands, and native commands.

### cmdlet

The first command type is a cmdlet (pronounced "command-let"), which is similar to the built-in commands in other CLI-based shells. The difference is that cmdlets are implemented by using .NET classes compiled into a dynamic link library (DLL) and loaded into PowerShell at runtime. This difference means there's no fixed class of built-in cmdlets; anyone can use the PowerShell Software Developers Kit (SDK) to write a custom cmdlet, thus extending PowerShell's functionality.

A cmdlet is always named as a verb and noun pair separated by a "-" (hyphen). The verb specifies the action the cmdlet performs, and the noun specifies the object being operated on. An example of a cmdlet being executed is shown as follows:

```
PS C:\> Get-Process
```

| Handles | NPM(K) | PM(K) | WS(K) | VM(M) | CPU(s) | Id | ProcessName |
|--------:|-------:|------:|------:|------:|-------:|-----:|-------------|
| 425 | 5 | 1608 | 1736 | 90 | 3.09 | 428 | csrss |
| 79 | 4 | 1292 | 540 | 86 | 1.00 | 468 | csrss |
| 193 | 4 | 2540 | 6528 | 94 | 2.16 | 2316 | csrss |
| 66 | 3 | 1128 | 3736 | 34 | 0.06 | 3192 | dwm |

```
    412        11     13636      20832    125      3.52    1408 explorer
...
```

While executing cmdlets in PowerShell, you should take a couple of considerations into account. Overall, PowerShell was created such that it is both forgiving and easy when it comes to syntax. In addition, PowerShell also always attempts to fill in the blanks for a user. Examples of this are illustrated in the following items:

▶ Cmdlets are always structured in a nonplural verb-noun format.

▶ Parameters and arguments are positional: `Get-Process winword`.

▶ Many arguments can use wildcards: `Get-Process w*`.

▶ Partial parameter names are also allowed: `Get-Process -P w*`.

> **NOTE**
>
> When executed, a cmdlet only processes a single record at a time.

### Functions

The next type of command is a function. These commands provide a way to assign a name to a list of commands. Functions are similar to subroutines and procedures in other programming languages. The main difference between a script and a function is that a new instance of the shell is started for each shell script, and functions run in the current instance of the same shell.

> **NOTE**
>
> Functions defined at the command line remain in effect only during the current PowerShell session. They are also local in scope and don't apply to new PowerShell sessions.

Although a function defined at the command line is a useful way to create a series of commands dynamically in the PowerShell environment, these functions reside only in memory and are erased when PowerShell is closed and restarted. Therefore, although creating complex functions dynamically is possible, writing these functions as script commands might be more practical. An example of a shell function command is as follows:

```
PS C:\> function showFiles {Get-ChildItem}
PS C:\> showfiles


Directory: Microsoft.PowerShell.Core\FileSystem::C:\
```

```
Mode                LastWriteTime      Length Name
----                -------------      ------ ----
d----        9/4/2007   10:36 PM             inetpub
d----        4/17/2007  11:02 PM             PerfLogs
d-r--        9/5/2007   12:19 AM             Program Files
d-r--        9/5/2007   11:01 PM             Users
d----        9/14/2007  11:42 PM             Windows
-a---        3/26/2007   8:43 PM          24 autoexec.bat
-ar-s        8/13/2007  11:57 PM        8192 BOOTSECT.BAK
-a---        3/26/2007   8:43 PM          10 config.sys
```

## Advanced Functions

Advanced functions are a new feature that was introduced in PowerShell v2.0. The basic premise behind advanced functions is to enable administrators and developers access to the same type of functionality as a compiled cmdlet, but directly through the PowerShell scripting language. An example of an advanced function is as follows:

```
function SuperFunction {
        <#
        .SYNOPSIS
                Superduper Advanced Function.
        .DESCRIPTION
                This is my Superduper Advanced Function.
        .PARAMETER Message
                Message to write.
        #>
        param(
                [Parameter(Position=0, Mandatory=$True, ValueFromPipeline=$True)]
                        [String] $Message
                )
        Write-Host $Message
        }
```

In the previous example, you will see that one of the major identifying aspects of an advanced function is the use of the CmdletBinding attribute. Usage of this attribute in an advanced function allows PowerShell to bind the parameters in the same manner that it binds parameters in a compiled cmdlet. For the SuperFunction example, CmdletBinding is used to define the $Message parameter with position 0, as mandatory, and is able to accept values from the pipeline. For example, the following shows the SuperFunction being executed, which then prompts for a message string. That message string is then written to the console:

```
PS C:\Users\tyson> SuperFunction
```

```
cmdlet SuperFunction at command pipeline position 1
Supply values for the following parameters:
Message: yo!
yo!
```

Finally, advanced functions can also use all of the methods and properties of the PSCmdlet class, for example:

▶ Usage of all the input processing methods (Begin, Process, and End)

▶ Usage of the ShouldProcess and ShouldContinue methods, which can be used to get user feedback before performing an action

▶ Usage of the ThrowTerminatingError method, which can be used to generate error records

▶ Usage of a various number of Write methods

### Scripts

Scripts, the third command type, are PowerShell commands stored in a .ps1 file. The main difference from functions is that scripts are stored on disk and can be accessed any time, unlike functions that don't persist across PowerShell sessions.

Scripts can be run in a PowerShell session or at the cmd command prompt. To run a script in a PowerShell session, type the script name without the extension. The script name can be followed by any parameters. The shell then executes the first .ps1 file matching the typed name in any of the paths located in the PowerShell $ENV:PATH variable.

To run a PowerShell script from a cmd command prompt, first use the CD command to change to the directory where the script is located. Then run the PowerShell executable with the command parameter and specifying which script to be run, as shown here:

```
C:\Scripts>powershell -command .\myscript.ps1
```

If you don't want to change to the script's directory with the cd command, you can also run it by using an absolute path, as shown in this example:

```
C:\>powershell -command C:\Scripts\myscript.ps1
```

An important detail about scripts in PowerShell concerns their default security restrictions. By default, scripts are not enabled to run as a method of protection against malicious scripts. You can control this policy with the Set-ExecutionPolicy cmdlet, which is explained later in this chapter.

### Native Commands

The last type of command, a native command, consists of external programs that the operating system can run. Because a new process must be created to run native commands, they are less efficient than other types of PowerShell commands. Native commands also have their own parameters for processing commands, which are usually different from PowerShell parameters.

## .NET Framework Integration

Most shells operate in a text-based environment, which means you typically have to manipulate the output for automation purposes. For example, if you need to pipe data from one command to the next, the output from the first command usually must be reformatted to meet the second command's requirements. Although this method has worked for years, dealing with text-based data can be difficult and frustrating.

Often, a lot of work is necessary to transform text data into a usable format. Microsoft has set out to change the standard with PowerShell, however. Instead of transporting data as plain text, PowerShell retrieves data in the form of .NET Framework objects, which makes it possible for commands (or cmdlets) to access object properties and methods directly. This change has simplified shell use. Instead of modifying text data, you can just refer to the required data by name. Similarly, instead of writing code to transform data into a usable format, you can simply refer to objects and manipulate them as needed.

### Reflection

Reflection is a feature in the .NET Framework that enables developers to examine objects and retrieve their supported methods, properties, fields, and so on. Because PowerShell is built on the .NET Framework, it provides this feature, too, with the Get-Member cmdlet. This cmdlet analyzes an object or collection of objects you pass to it via the pipeline. For example, the following command analyzes the objects returned from the Get-Process cmdlet and displays their associated properties and methods:

```
PS C:\> get-process | get-member
```

Developers often refer to this process as "interrogating" an object. This method of accessing and retrieving information about an object can be very useful in understanding its methods and properties without referring to MSDN documentation or searching the Internet.

### Extended Type System (ETS)

You might think that scripting in PowerShell is typeless because you rarely need to specify the type for a variable. PowerShell is actually type driven, however, because it interfaces with different types of objects from the less-than-perfect .NET to Windows Management Instrumentation (WMI), Component Object Model (COM), ActiveX Data Objects (ADO), Active Directory Service Interfaces (ADSI), Extensible Markup Language (XML), and even custom objects. However, you don't need to be concerned about object types because PowerShell adapts to different object types and displays its interpretation of an object for you.

In a sense, PowerShell tries to provide a common abstraction layer that makes all object interaction consistent, despite the type. This abstraction layer is called the PSObject, a common object used for all object access in PowerShell. It can encapsulate any base object (.NET, custom, and so on), any instance members, and implicit or explicit access to adapted and type-based extended members, depending on the type of base object.

Furthermore, it can state its type and add members dynamically. To do this, PowerShell uses the Extended Type System (ETS), which provides an interface that allows PowerShell cmdlet and script developers to manipulate and change objects as needed.

> **NOTE**
>
> When you use the Get-Member cmdlet, the information returned is from PSObject. Sometimes PSObject blocks members, methods, and properties from the original object. If you want to view the blocked information, use the `BaseObject` property with the PSBase standard name. For example, you could use the `$Procs.PSBase ¦ get-member` command to view blocked information for the $Procs object collection.

Needless to say, this topic is fairly advanced, as PSBase is hidden from view. The only time you should need to use it is when the PSObject doesn't interpret an object correctly or you're digging around for hidden jewels in PowerShell.

### Static Classes and Methods

Certain .NET Framework classes cannot be used to create new objects. For example, if you try to create a `System.Math` typed object using the New-Object cmdlet, the following error occurs:

```
PS C:\> New-Object System.Math
New-Object : Constructor not found. Cannot find an appropriate constructor for type
System.Math.
At line:1 char:11
+ New-Object <<<<  System.Math
    + CategoryInfo          : ObjectNotFound: (:) [New-Object], PSArgumentException
    + FullyQualifiedErrorId : CannotFindAppropriateCtor,Microsoft.PowerShell.
Commands.NewObjectCommand

PS C:\>
```

The reason this occurs is because static members are shared across all instances of a class and don't require a typed object to be created before being used. Instead, static members are accessed simply by referring to the class name as if it were the name of the object followed by the static operator (::), as follows:

```
PS > [System.DirectoryServices.ActiveDirectory.Forest]::GetCurrentForest()
```

In the previous example, the `DirectoryServices.ActiveDirectory.Forest` class is used to retrieve information about the current forest. To complete this task, the class name is enclosed within the two square brackets ([...]). Then, the `GetCurrentForest` method is invoked by using the static operator (::).

> **NOTE**
>
> To retrieve a list of static members for a class, use the Get-Member cmdlet: `Get-Member -inputObject ([System.String]) -Static`.

### Type Accelerators

A type accelerator is simply an alias for specifying a .NET type. Without a type accelerator, defining a variable type requires entering a fully qualified class name, as shown here:

```
PS C:\> $User = [System.DirectoryServices.DirectoryEntry]"LDAP:
//CN=Fujio Saitoh,OU=Accounts,OU=Managed Objects,DC=companyabc,DC=com"
PS C:\> $User


distinguishedname:{CN=Fujio Saitoh,OU=Accounts,OU=Managed
Objects,DC=companyabc,DC=com}
path            : LDAP:
//CN=Fujio Saitoh,OU=Accounts,OU=Managed Objects,DC=companyabc,DC=com


PS C:\>
```

Instead of typing the entire class name, you just use the [ADSI] type accelerator to define the variable type, as in the following example:

```
PS C:\> $User = [ADSI]"LDAP://CN=Fujio Saitoh,OU=Accounts, OU=Managed
Objects,DC=companyabc,DC=com"
PS C:\> $User


distinguishedname:{CN=Fujio Saitoh,OU=Accounts,OU=Managed
Objects,DC=companyabc,DC=com}
path            : LDAP:
//CN=Fujio Saitoh,OU=Accounts,OU=Managed Objects,DC=companyabc,DC=com


PS C:\>
```

Type accelerators have been included in PowerShell mainly to cut down on the amount of typing to define an object type. However, for some reason, type accelerators aren't covered in the PowerShell documentation, even though the [WMI], [ADSI], and other common type accelerators are referenced on many web blogs.

Regardless of the lack of documentation, type accelerators are a fairly useful feature of PowerShell. Table 21.2 lists some of the more commonly used type accelerators.

TABLE 21.2    Important Type Accelerators in PowerShell

| Name | Type |
| --- | --- |
| Int | System.Int32 |
| Long | System.Int64 |
| String | System.String |
| Char | System.Char |

TABLE 21.2    Important Type Accelerators in PowerShell

| Name | Type |
| --- | --- |
| Byte | System.Byte |
| Double | System.Double |
| Decimal | System.Decimal |
| Float | System.Float |
| Single | System.Single |
| Regex | System.Text.RegularExpressions.Regex |
| Array | System.Array |
| Xml | System.Xml.XmlDocument |
| Scriptblock | System.Management.Automation.ScriptBlock |
| Switch | System.Management.Automation.SwitchParameter |
| Hashtable | System.Collections.Hashtable |
| Type | System.Type |
| Ref | System.Management.Automation.PSReference |
| Psobject | System.Management.Automation.PSObject |
| pscustomobject | System.Management.Automation.PSCustomObject |
| Psmoduleinfo | System.Management.Automation.PSModuleInfo |
| Powershell | System.Management.Automation.PowerShell |
| runspacefactory | System.Management.Automation.Runspaces.RunspaceFactory |
| Runspace | System.Management.Automation.Runspaces.Runspace |
| Ipaddress | System.Net.IPAddress |
| Wmi | System.Management.ManagementObject |
| Wmisearcher | System.Management.ManagementObjectSearcher |
| Wmiclass | System.Management.ManagementClass |
| Adsi | System.DirectoryServices.DirectoryEntry |
| Adsisearcher | System.DirectoryServices.DirectorySearcher |

## The Pipeline

In the past, data was transferred from one command to the next by using the pipeline, which makes it possible to string a series of commands together to gather information from a system. However, as mentioned previously, most shells have a major disadvantage: The information gathered from commands is text based. Raw text needs to be parsed (transformed) into a format the next command can understand before being piped.

The point is that although most UNIX and Linux shell commands are powerful, using them can be complicated and frustrating. Because these shells are text based, often commands lack functionality or require using additional commands or tools to perform tasks. To address the differences in text output from shell commands, many utilities and scripting languages have been developed to parse text.

The result of all this parsing is a tree of commands and tools that make working with shells unwieldy and time consuming, which is one reason for the proliferation of management interfaces that rely on GUIs. This trend can be seen among tools Windows administrators use, too; as Microsoft has focused on enhancing the management GUI at the expense of the CLI.

Windows administrators now have access to the same automation capabilities as their UNIX and Linux counterparts. However, PowerShell and its use of objects fill the automation need Windows administrators have had since the days of batch scripting and WSH in a more usable and less parsing-intense manner. To see how the PowerShell pipeline works, take a look at the following PowerShell example:

```
PS C:\> get-process powershell ¦ format-table id -autosize


 Id
 --
3628


PS C:\>
```

> **NOTE**
>
> All pipelines end with the Out-Default cmdlet. This cmdlet selects a set of properties and their values and then displays those values in a list or table.

## Modules and Snap-Ins

One of the main design goals behind PowerShell was to make extending the default functionality in PowerShell and sharing those extensions easy enough that anyone could do it. In PowerShell 1.0, part of this design goal was realized through the use of snap-ins.

PowerShell snap-ins (PSSnapins) are dynamic-link library (DLL) files that can be used to provide access to additional cmdlets or providers. By default, a number of PSSnapins are loaded into every PowerShell session. These default sets of PSSnapins contain the built-in cmdlets and providers that are used by PowerShell. You can display a list of these cmdlets by entering the command `Get-PSSnapin` at the PowerShell command prompt, as follows:

```
PS C:\> get-pssnapin
```

```
Name        : Microsoft.PowerShell.Core
PSVersion   : 2.0
Description : This Windows PowerShell snap-in contains Windows PowerShell manage-
ment cmdlets used to manage components
              of Windows PowerShell.

Name        : Microsoft.PowerShell.Host
PSVersion   : 2.0
Description : This Windows PowerShell snap-in contains cmdlets used by the Windows
PowerShell host.
...
```

```
PS C:\>
```

In theory, PowerShell snap-ins were a great way to share and reuse a set of cmdlets and providers. However, snap-ins by definition must be written and then compiled, which often placed snap-in creation out of reach for many IT professionals. Additionally, snap-ins can conflict, which meant that attempting to run a set of snap-ins within the same PowerShell session might not always be feasible.

That is why in PowerShell 2.0, the product team decided to introduce a new feature, called modules, which are designed to make extending PowerShell and sharing those extensions significantly easier. In its simplest form, a module is just a collection of items that can be used in a PowerShell session. These items can be cmdlets, providers, functions, aliases, utilities, and so on. The intent with modules, however, was to allow "anyone" (developers and administrators) to take and bundle together a collection of items. These items can then be executed in a self-contained context, which will not affect the state outside of the module, thus increasing portability when being shared across disparate environments.

## Remoting

With PowerShell 1.0, one of its major disadvantages was the lack of an interface to execute commands on a remote machine. Granted, you could use Windows Management Instrumentation (WMI) to accomplish this and some cmdlets like Get-Process and Get-Service, which enable you to connect to remote machines. But, the concept of a native-based "remoting" interface was sorely missing when PowerShell was first released. In fact, the lack of remote command execution was a glaring lack of functionality that needed to be addressed. Naturally, the PowerShell product team took this functionality limitation to heart and addressed it by introducing a new feature in PowerShell 2.0, called "remoting."

Remoting, as its name suggests, is a new feature that is designed to facilitate command (or script) execution on remote machines. This could mean execution of a command or commands on one remote machine or thousands of remote machines (provided you have the infrastructure to support this). Additionally, commands can be issued synchronously or asynchronously, one at time or through a persistent connection called a runspace, and even scheduled or throttled.

To use remoting, you must have the appropriate permissions to connect to a remote machine, execute PowerShell, and execute the desired command(s). In addition, the remote machine must have PowerShell 2.0 and Windows Remote Management (WinRM) installed, and PowerShell must be configured for remoting.

Additionally, when using remoting, the remote PowerShell session that is used to execute commands determines execution environment. As such, the commands you attempt to execute are subject to a remote machine's execution policies, profiles, and preferences.

**WARNING**

Commands that are executed against a remote machine do not have access to information defined within your local profile. As such, commands that use a function or alias defined in your local profile will fail unless they are defined on the remote machine as well.

### How Remoting Works

In its most basic form, PowerShell remoting works using the following conversation flow between "a client" (most likely the machine with your PowerShell session) and "a server" (remote host) that you want to execute command(s) against:

1. A command is executed on the client.
2. That command is transmitted to the server.
3. The server executes the command and then returns the output to the client.
4. The client displays or uses the returned output.

At a deeper level, PowerShell remoting is very dependent on WinRM for facilitating the command and output exchange between a "client" and "server." WinRM, which is a component of Windows Hardware Management, is a web-based service that enables administrators to enumerate information on and manipulate a remote machine. To handle remote sessions, WinRM was built around a SOAP-based standards protocol called WS-Management. This protocol is firewall-friendly, and was primarily developed for the exchange of management information between systems that might be based on a variety of operating systems on various hardware platforms.

When PowerShell uses WinRM to ship commands and output between a client and server, that exchange is done using a series of XML messages. The first XML message that is exchanged is a request to the server, which contains the desired command to be executed. This message is submitted to the server using the SOAP protocol. The server, in return, executes the command using a new instance of PowerShell called a runspace. Once execution of the command is complete, the output from the command is returned to the requesting client as the second XML message. This second message, like the first, is also communicated using the SOAP protocol.

This translation into an XML message is performed because you cannot ship "live" .NET objects (how PowerShell relates to programs or system components) across the network. So, to perform the transmission, objects are serialized into a series of XML (CliXML) data elements. When the server or client receives the transmission, it converts the received XML message into a deserialized object type. The resulting object is no longer live. Instead, it is a record of properties based on a point in time and, as such, no longer possesses any methods.

### Remoting Requirements
To use remoting, both the local and remote computers must have the following:

- ▶ Windows PowerShell 2.0 or later
- ▶ Microsoft .NET Framework 2.0 or later
- ▶ Windows Remote Management 2.0

---

**NOTE**

Windows Remote Management 2.0 is part of Windows 7 and Windows Server 2008 R2. For down-level versions of Windows, an integrated installation package must be installed, which includes PowerShell 2.0.

---

### Configuring Remoting
By default, WinRM is installed on all Windows Server 2008 R2 machines as part of the default operating system installation. However, for security purposes, PowerShell remoting and WinRM are, by default, configured to not allow remote connections. You can use several methods to configure remoting, as described in the following sections.

**Method One**    The first and easiest method to enable PowerShell remoting is to execute the Enable-PSRemoting cmdlet. For example:

```
PS C:\> enable-pssremoting
```

Once executed, the following tasks are performed by the Enable-PSRemoting cmdlet:

- ▶ Runs the Set-WSManQuickConfig cmdlet, which performs the following tasks:
  - ▶ Starts the WinRM service.
  - ▶ Sets the startup type on the WinRM service to Automatic.

► Creates a listener to accept requests on any IP address.

► Enables a firewall exception for WS-Management communications.

► Enables all registered Windows PowerShell session configurations to receive instructions from a remote computer.

► Registers the "Microsoft.PowerShell" session configuration, if it is not already registered.

► Registers the "Microsoft.PowerShell32" session configuration on 64-bit computers, if it is not already registered.

► Removes the "Deny Everyone" setting from the security descriptor for all the registered session configurations.

► Restarts the WinRM service to make the preceding changes effective.

> **NOTE**
>
> To configure PowerShell remoting, the Enable-PSRemoting cmdlet must be executed using the Run As Administrator option.

**Method Two**    The second method to configure remoting is to use Server Manager. Use the following steps to use this method:

1. Open Server Manager.
2. In the Server Summary area of the Server Manager home page, click Configure Server Manager Remote Management.
3. Next, select Enable Remote Management of This Server from Other Computers.
4. Click OK.

**Method Three**    Finally, the third method to configure remoting is to use GPO. Use the following steps to use this method:

1. Create a new GPO, or edit an existing one.
2. Expand Computer Configuration, Policies, Administrative Templates, Windows Components, Windows Remote Management, and then select WinRM Service.
3. Open the Allow Automatic Configuration of Listeners Policy, select Enabled, and then define the IPv4 filter and IPv6 filter as *.
4. Click OK.
5. Next, expand Computer Configuration, Policies, Windows Settings, Security Settings, Windows Firewall with Advanced Security, Windows Firewall with Advanced Security, and then Inbound Rules.
6. Right-click Inbound Rules, and then click New Rule.
7. In the New Inbound Rule Wizard, on the Rule Type page, select Predefined.
8. On the Predefined pull-down menu, select Remote Event Log Management. Click Next.

9. On the Predefined Rules page, click Next to accept the new rules.

10. On the Action page, select Allow the Connection, and then click Finish. Allow the Connection is the default selection.

11. Repeat steps 6 through 10 and create inbound rules for the following predefined rule types:

   ▸ Remote Service Management

   ▸ Windows Firewall Remote Management

### Background Jobs

Another new feature that was introduced in PowerShell 2.0 is the ability to use background jobs. By definition, a background job is a command that is executed asynchronously without interacting with the current PowerShell session. However, once the background job has finished execution, the results from these jobs can then be retrieved and manipulated based on the task at hand. In other words, by using a background job, you can complete automation tasks that take an extended period of time to run without impacting the usability of your PowerShell session.

By default, background jobs can be executed on the local computer. But, background jobs can also be used in conjunction with remoting to execute jobs on a remote machine.

> **NOTE**
>
> To use background jobs (local or remote), PowerShell must be configured for remoting.

## PowerShell ISE

Another new feature that was introduced in PowerShell 2.0 is called the Integrated Scripting Environment (ISE). The ISE, as shown in Figure 21.1, is a Windows Presentation Foundation (WPF)–based host application for Windows PowerShell. Using the ISE, an IT professional can both run commands and write, test, and debug scripts.

Additional features of the ISE include the following:

▸ A Command pane for running interactive commands.

▸ A Script pane for writing, editing, and running scripts. You can run the entire script or selected lines from the script.

▸ A scrollable Output pane that displays a transcript of commands from the Command and Script panes and their results.

▸ Up to eight independent PowerShell execution environments in the same window, each with its own Command, Script, and Output panes.

▸ Multiline editing in the Command pane, which lets you paste multiple lines of code, run them, and then recall them as a unit.

▸ A built-in debugger for debugging commands, functions, and scripts.

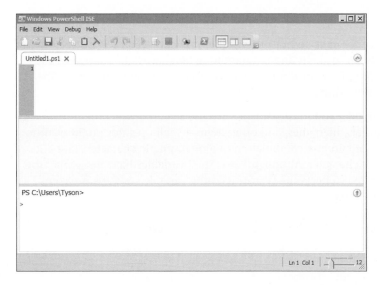

FIGURE 21.1    The PowerShell ISE.

▶ Customizable features that let you adjust the colors, font, and layout.

▶ A scriptable object model that lets you further customize and extend the PowerShell ISE.

▶ Line and column numbers, keyboard shortcuts, tab completion, context-sensitive Help, and Unicode support.

The PowerShell ISE is an optional feature in Windows Server 2008 R2. To use the ISE, it first must be installed using the Add Features Wizard. Because the ISE requires the .NET Framework 3.5 with Service Pack 1, the Server Manager will also install this version of the .NET Framework if it is not already installed. Once installed, use either of the following methods to start it:

1. Start Windows PowerShell ISE by clicking Start, All Programs, Accessories, Windows PowerShell, and then click Windows PowerShell ISE or Windows PowerShell ISE (x86).

2. Or execute the `powershell_ise.exe` executable.

### ISE Requirements

The following requirements must be met to use the ISE:

▶ Windows XP and later versions of Windows

▶ Microsoft .NET Framework 3.5 with Service Pack 1

> **NOTE**
>
> Being a GUI-based application, the PowerShell ISE does not work on Server Core installations of Windows Server.

## Variables

A variable is a storage place for data. In most shells, the only data that can be stored in a variable is text data. In advanced shells and programming languages, data stored in variables can be almost anything, from strings to sequences to objects. Similarly, PowerShell variables can be just about anything.

To define a PowerShell variable, you must name it with the $ prefix, which helps delineate variables from aliases, cmdlets, filenames, and other items a shell operator might want to use. A variable name can contain any combination of alphanumeric characters (a–z and 0–9) and the underscore (_) character. Although PowerShell variables have no set naming convention, using a name that reflects the type of data the variable contains is recommended, as shown in this example:

```
PS C:\> $Stopped = get-service | where {$_.status -eq "stopped"}
PS C:\> $Stopped

Status    Name                DisplayName
------    ----                -----------
Stopped   ALG                 Application Layer Gateway Service
Stopped   Appinfo             Application Information
Stopped   AppMgmt             Application Management
Stopped   aspnet_state        ASP.NET State Service
Stopped   AudioEndpointBu...  Windows Audio Endpoint Builder
Stopped   Audiosrv            Windows Audio
...
```

As you can see from the previous example, the information that is contained within the $Stopped variable is a collection of services that are currently stopped.

> **NOTE**
>
> A variable name can consist of any characters, including spaces, provided the name is enclosed in curly braces ({ and } symbols).

## Aliases

Like most existing command-line shells, command aliases can be defined in PowerShell. Aliasing is a method that is used to execute existing shell commands (cmdlets) using a different name. In many cases, the main reason aliases are used is to establish abbreviated command names in an effort to reduce typing. For example:

```
PS C:\> gps | ? {$_.Company -match ".*Microsoft*"} | ft Name, ID, Path –Autosize
```

The preceding example shows the default aliases for the Get-Process, Where-Object, and Format-Table cmdlets.

### Alias cmdlets

In PowerShell, several alias cmdlets enable an administrator to define new aliases, export aliases, import aliases, and display existing aliases. By using the following command, an administrator can get a list of all the related alias cmdlets:

```
PS C:\> get-command *-Alias
```

```
CommandType     Name                            Definition
- - - - - - - - - -   - - - -                           - - - - - - - - - -
Cmdlet          Export-Alias                    Export-Alias [-Path] <String...
Cmdlet          Get-Alias                       Get-Alias [[-Name] <String[]...
Cmdlet          Import-Alias                    Import-Alias [-Path] <String...
Cmdlet          New-Alias                       New-Alias [-Name] <String> [...
Cmdlet          Set-Alias                       Set-Alias [-Name] <String> [...
```

Use the Get-Alias cmdlet to produce a list of aliases available in the current PowerShell session. The Export-Alias and Import-Alias cmdlets are used to export and import alias lists from one PowerShell session to another. Finally, the New-Alias and Set-Alias cmdlets allow an administrator to define new aliases for the current PowerShell session.

### Creating Persistent Aliases

The aliases created when using the New-Alias and Set-Alias cmdlets are valid only in the current PowerShell session. Exiting a PowerShell session discards any existing aliases. To have aliases persist across PowerShell sessions, they can be defined in a profile file, as shown in this example:

```
set-alias new new-object
set-alias time get-date
...
```

Although command shortening is appealing, the extensive use of aliases isn't recommended. One reason is that aliases aren't very portable in relation to scripts. For example, if a lot of aliases are used in a script, each alias must be included via a Set-Aliases sequence at the start of the script to make sure those aliases are present, regardless of machine or session profile, when the script runs.

However, a bigger concern than portability is that aliases can often confuse or obscure the true meaning of commands or scripts. The aliases that are defined might make sense to a scripter, but not everyone shares the logic in defining aliases. So if a scripter wants others to understand their scripts, they shouldn't use too many aliases.

---

**NOTE**

If aliases will be used in a script, use names that other people can understand. For example, there's no reason, other than to encode a script, to create aliases consisting of only two letters.

## Scopes

A scope is a logical boundary in PowerShell that isolates the use of functions and variables. Scopes can be defined as global, local, script, and private. They function in a hierarchy in which scope information is inherited downward. For example, the local scope can read the global scope, but the global scope can't read information from the local scope. Scopes and their use are described in the following sections.

### Global

As the name indicates, a global scope applies to an entire PowerShell instance. Global scope data is inherited by all child scopes, so any commands, functions, or scripts that run make use of variables defined in the global scope. However, global scopes are not shared between different instances of PowerShell.

The following example shows the $Processes variable being defined as a global variable in the ListProcesses function. Because the $Processes variable is being defined globally, checking $Processes.Count after ListProcesses completes returns a count of the number of active processes at the time ListProcesses was executed:

```
PS C:\> function ListProcesses {$Global:Processes = get-process}
PS C:\> ListProcesses
PS C:\> $Processes.Count
37
```

> **NOTE**
>
> In PowerShell, an explicit scope indicator can be used to determine the scope a variable resides in. For instance, if a variable is to reside in the global scope, it should be defined as $Global:variablename. If an explicit scope indicator isn't used, a variable resides in the current scope for which it's defined.

### Local

A local scope is created dynamically each time a function, filter, or script runs. After a local scope has finished running, information in it is discarded. A local scope can read information from the global scope but can't make changes to it.

The following example shows the locally scoped variable $Processes being defined in the ListProcesses function. After ListProcesses finishes running, the $Processes variable no longer contains any data because it was defined only in the ListProcesses function. Notice how checking $Processes.Count after the ListProcesses function is finished produces no results:

```
PS C:\> function ListProcesses {$Processes = get-process}
PS C:\> ListProcesses
PS C:\> $Processes.Count
PS C:\>
```

## Script

A script scope is created whenever a script file runs and is discarded when the script finishes running. To see an example of how a script scope works, create the following script and save it as ListProcesses.ps1:

```
$Processes = get-process
write-host "Here is the first process:" -Foregroundcolor Yellow
$Processes[0]
```

After creating the script file, run it from a PowerShell session. The output should look similar to this example:

```
PS C:\> .\ListProcesses.ps1
Here is the first process:

Handles  NPM(K)    PM(K)     WS(K) VM(M)   CPU(s)      Id ProcessName
-------  ------    -----     ----- -----   ------      -- -----------
    105       5     1992      4128    32              916 alg

PS C:\> $Processes[0]
Cannot index into a null array.
At line:1 char:12
+ $Processes[0 <<<< ]
PS C:\>
```

Notice that when the ListProcesses.ps1 script runs, information about the first process object in the $Processes variable is written to the console. However, when you try to access information in the $Processes variable from the console, an error is returned because the $Processes variable is valid only in the script scope. When the script finishes running, that scope and all its contents are discarded.

What if an administrator wants to use a script in a pipeline or access it as a library file for common functions? Normally, this isn't possible because PowerShell discards a script scope whenever a script finishes running. Luckily, PowerShell supports the dot-sourcing technique, a term that originally came from UNIX. Dot sourcing a script file tells PowerShell to load a script scope into the calling parent's scope.

To dot source a script file, simply prefix the script name with a period (dot) when running the script, as shown here:

```
PS C:\> . .\coolscript.ps1
```

## Private

A private scope is similar to a local scope, with one key difference: Definitions in the private scope aren't inherited by any child scopes.

The following example shows the privately scoped variable $Processes defined in the ListProcesses function. Notice that during execution of the ListProcesses function, the

$Processes variable isn't available to the child scope represented by the script block enclosed by { and } in lines 6–9.

```
PS C:\> function ListProcesses {$Private:Processes = get-process
>>       write-host "Here is the first process:" -Foregroundcolor Yellow
>>       $Processes[0]
>>       write-host
>>>>     &{
>>           write-host "Here it is again:" -Foregroundcolor Yellow
>>           $Processes[0]
>>       }
>> }
>>PS C:\> ListProcesses
Here is the first process:


Handles  NPM(K)    PM(K)      WS(K) VM(M)   CPU(s)     Id ProcessName
-------  ------    -----      ----- -----   ------     -- -----------
    105       5     1992       4128    32               916 alg


Here it is again:
Cannot index into a null array.
At line:7 char:20
+           $Processes[0 <<<< ]
PS C:\>
```

This example works because it uses the & call operator. With this call operator, you can execute fragments of script code in an isolated local scope. This technique is helpful for isolating a script block and its variables from a parent scope or, as in this example, isolating a privately scoped variable from a script block.

## Providers and Drives

Most computer systems are used to store data, often in a structure such as a file system. Because of the amount of data stored in these structures, processing and finding information can be unwieldy. Most shells have interfaces, or providers, for interacting with data stores in a predictable, set manner. PowerShell also has a set of providers for presenting the contents of data stores through a core set of cmdlets. You can then use these cmdlets to browse, navigate, and manipulate data from stores through a common interface. To get a list of the core cmdlets, use the following command:

```
PS C:\> help about_core_commands
...
    ChildItem CMDLETS
    Get-ChildItem

    CONTENT CMDLETS
    Add-Content
    Clear-Content
```

```
    Get-Content
    Set-Content
...
```

To view built-in PowerShell providers, use the following command:

```
PS C:\> get-psprovider
```

```
Name              Capabilities                      Drives
----              ------------                      ------
WSMan             Credentials                       {WSMan}
Alias             ShouldProcess                     {Alias}
Environment       ShouldProcess                     {Env}
FileSystem        Filter, ShouldProcess             {C, D, E}
Function          ShouldProcess                     {Function}
Registry          ShouldProcess, Transactions       {HKLM, HKCU}
Variable          ShouldProcess                     {Variable}
Certificate       ShouldProcess                     {cert}
```

```
PS C:\>
```

The preceding list displays not only built-in providers, but also the drives each provider currently supports. A drive is an entity that a provider uses to represent a data store through which data is made available to the PowerShell session. For example, the Registry provider creates a PowerShell drive for the HKEY_LOCAL_MACHINE and HKEY_CURRENT_USER Registry hives.

To see a list of all current PowerShell drives, use the following command:

```
PS C:\> get-psdrive
```

```
Name        Used (GB)     Free (GB) Provider      Root
----        ---------     --------- --------      ----
Alias                               Alias
C               68.50        107.00 FileSystem    C:\
cert                                Certificate   \
D                8.98          1.83 FileSystem    D:\
E                                   FileSystem    E:\
Env                                 Environment
Function                            Function
HKCU                                Registry      HKEY_CURRENT_USER
HKLM                                Registry      HKEY_LOCAL_MACHINE
Variable                            Variable
WSMan                               WSMan
```

```
PS C:\>
```

## Profiles

A PowerShell profile is a saved collection of settings for customizing the PowerShell environment. There are four types of profiles, loaded in a specific order each time PowerShell starts. The following sections explain these profile types, where they should be located, and the order in which they are loaded.

### The All Users Profile

This profile is located in `%windir%\system32\windowspowershell\v1.0\profile.ps1`. Settings in the All Users profile are applied to all PowerShell users on the current machine. If you plan to configure PowerShell settings across the board for users on a machine, this is the profile to use.

### The All Users Host-Specific Profile

This profile is located in `%windir%\system32\windowspowershell\v1.0\ShellID_ profile.ps1`. Settings in the All Users host-specific profile are applied to all users of the current shell (by default, the PowerShell console). PowerShell supports the concept of multiple shells or hosts. For example, the PowerShell console is a host and the one most users use exclusively. However, other applications can call an instance of the PowerShell runtime to access and run PowerShell commands and scripts. An application that does this is called a hosting application and uses a host-specific profile to control the PowerShell configuration. The host-specific profile name is reflected by the host's ShellID. In the PowerShell console, the ShellID is the following:

```
PS C:\ $ShellId
Microsoft.PowerShell
PS C:\
```

Putting this together, the PowerShell console's All Users host-specific profile is named Microsoft.PowerShell_profile.ps1. For other hosts, the ShellID and All Users host-specific profile names are different. For example, the PowerShell Analyzer (www.powershellana-lyzer.com) is a PowerShell host that acts as a rich graphical interface for the PowerShell environment. Its ShellID is PowerShellAnalyzer.PSA, and its All Users host-specific profile name is `PowerShellAnalyzer.PSA_profile.ps1`.

### The Current User's Profile

This profile is located in `%userprofile%\My Documents\WindowsPowerShell\profile.ps1`. Users who want to control their own profile settings can use the current user's profile. Settings in this profile are applied only to the user's current PowerShell session and don't affect any other users.

### The Current User's Host-Specific Profile

This profile is located in `%userprofile%\My Documents\WindowsPowerShell\ShellID_ profile.ps1`. Like the All Users host-specific profile, this profile type loads settings for the current shell. However, the settings are user specific.

**NOTE**

When PowerShell is started for the first time, you might see a message indicating that scripts are disabled and no profiles are loaded. This behavior can be modified by changing the PowerShell execution policy.

## Security

When WSH was released with Windows 98, it was a godsend for Windows administrators who wanted the same automation capabilities as their UNIX brethren. At the same time, virus writers quickly discovered that WSH also opened up a large attack vector against Windows systems.

Almost anything on a Windows system can be automated and controlled by using WSH, which is an advantage for administrators. However, WSH doesn't provide any security in script execution. If given a script, WSH runs it. Where the script comes from or its purpose doesn't matter. With this behavior, WSH became known more as a security vulnerability than an automation tool.

### Execution Policies

Because of past criticisms of WSH's security, when the PowerShell team set out to build a Microsoft shell, the team decided to include an execution policy to mitigate the security threats posed by malicious code. An execution policy defines restrictions on how PowerShell allows scripts to run or what configuration files can be loaded. PowerShell has four primary execution policies, discussed in more detail in the following sections: Restricted, AllSigned, RemoteSigned, and Unrestricted.

**NOTE**

Execution policies can be circumvented by a user who manually executes commands found in a script file. Therefore, execution policies are not meant to replace a security system that restricts a user's actions and instead should be viewed as a restriction that attempts to prevent malicious code from being executed.

**Restricted**   By default, PowerShell is configured to run under the Restricted execution policy. This execution policy is the most secure because it allows PowerShell to operate only in an interactive mode. This means no scripts can be run, and only configuration files digitally signed by a trusted publisher are allowed to run or load.

**AllSigned**   The AllSigned execution policy is a notch under Restricted. When this policy is enabled, only scripts or configuration files that are digitally signed by a publisher you trust can be run or loaded. Here's an example of what you might see if the AllSigned policy has been enabled:

```
PS C:\Scripts> .\evilscript.ps1
The file C:\Scripts\evilscript.ps1 cannot be loaded. The file
C:\Scripts\evilscript.ps1 is not digitally signed. The script will not
execute on the system. Please see "get-help about_signing" for more
details.
At line:1 char:16
+ .\evilscript.ps1 <<<<
PS C:\Scripts>
```

Signing a script or configuration file requires a code-signing certificate. This certificate can come from a trusted certificate authority (CA), or you can generate one with the Certificate Creation Tool (Makecert.exe). Usually, however, you want a valid code-signing certificate from a well-known trusted CA, such as VeriSign, Thawte, or your corporation's internal Public Key Infrastructure (PKI). Otherwise, sharing your scripts or configuration files with others might be difficult because your computer isn't a trusted CA by default.

**RemoteSigned**    The RemoteSigned execution policy is designed to prevent remote PowerShell scripts and configuration files that aren't digitally signed by a trusted publisher from running or loading automatically. Scripts and configuration files that are locally created can be loaded and run without being digitally signed, however.

A remote script or configuration file can be obtained from a communication application, such as Microsoft Outlook, Internet Explorer, Outlook Express, or Windows Messenger. Running or loading a file downloaded from any of these applications results in the following error message:

```
PS C:\Scripts> .\interscript.ps1
The file C:\Scripts\interscript.ps1 cannot be loaded. The file
C:\Scripts\interscript.ps1 is not digitally signed. The script will not execute on
the system. Please see "get-help about_signing" for more details..
At line:1 char:17
+ .\interscript.ps1 <<<<
PS C:\Scripts>
```

To run or load an unsigned remote script or configuration file, you must specify whether to trust the file. To do this, right-click the file in Windows Explorer and click Properties. On the General tab, click the Unblock button (see Figure 21.2).

After you trust the file, the script or configuration file can be run or loaded. If it's digitally signed but the publisher isn't trusted, however, PowerShell displays the following prompt:

```
PS C:\Scripts> .\signed.ps1
```

```
Do you want to run software from this untrusted publisher?
```

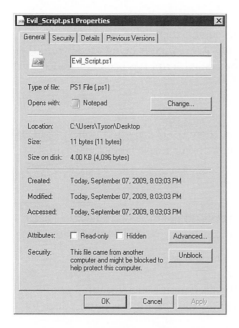

FIGURE 21.2   Trusting a remote script or configuration file.

```
File C:\Scripts\signed.ps1 is published by CN=companyabc.com, OU=IT,
O=companyabc.com, L=Oakland, S=California, C=US and is not trusted on your
system. Only run scripts from trusted publishers.
[V] Never run   [D] Do not run   [R] Run once   [A] Always run   [?] Help
(default is "D"):
```

In this case, you must choose whether to trust the file content.

**Unrestricted**   As the name suggests, the Unrestricted execution policy removes almost all restrictions for running scripts or loading configuration files. All local or signed trusted files can run or load, but for remote files, PowerShell prompts you to choose an option for running or loading that file, as shown here:

```
PS C:\Scripts> .\remotescript.ps1
```

```
Security Warning
Run only scripts that you trust. While scripts from the Internet can be useful,
 this script can potentially harm your computer. Do you want to run
C:\Scripts\remotescript.ps1?
[D] Do not run   [R] Run once   [S] Suspend   [?] Help (default is "D"):
```

In addition to the primary execution policies, two new execution policies were introduced in PowerShell 2.0, as discussed in the following sections.

### Bypass

When this execution policy is used, nothing is blocked and there is no warning or prompts. This execution policy is typically used when PowerShell is being used by another application that has its own security model or a PowerShell script has been embedded into another application.

### Undefined

When this execution policy is defined, it means that there is no execution policy set in the current scope. If Undefined is the execution policy for all scopes, the effective execution policy is Restricted.

### Setting the Execution Policy

By default, when PowerShell is first installed, the execution policy is set to Restricted. To change the execution policy, you use the Set-ExecutionPolicy cmdlet, shown here:

```
PS C:\> set-executionpolicy AllSigned
```

Or, you can also use a Group Policy setting to set the execution policy for number of computers. In a PowerShell session, if you want to know the current execution policy for a machine, use the Get-ExecutionPolicy cmdlet:

```
PS C:\> get-executionpolicy
AllSigned
PS C:\>
```

Execution policies can not only be defined for the local machine, but can also be defined for the current user or a particular process. These boundaries between where an execution policy resides is called an execution policy scope. To define the execution policy for a scope, you would use the Scope parameter for the Set-ExecutionPolicy cmdlet. Additionally, if you wanted to know the execution policy for a particular scope, you would use the Scope parameter for the Get-ExecutionPolicy cmdlet. The valid arguments for the Scope parameter for both cmdlets are Machine Policy, User Policy, Process, CurrentUser, and LocalMachine.

> **NOTE**
>
> The order of precedence for the execution policy scopes is Machine Policy, User Policy, Process, CurrentUser, and LocalMachine.

# Using Windows PowerShell

PowerShell is a powerful tool that enables administrators to manage Windows platform applications and to complete automation tasks. This section sheds some light on how PowerShell's many uses can be discovered and how it can be used to manage Windows Server 2008 R2.

# Exploring PowerShell

Before using PowerShell, you might want to become more familiar with its cmdlets and features. To assist administrators with exploring PowerShell, the PowerShell team decided to do two things. First, they included a cmdlet that functions very similarly to how the UNIX man pages function. Second, they also included a cmdlet that returns information about commands available in the current session. Together, these cmdlets allow a novice to tap into and understand PowerShell without secondary reference materials; explanations of these cmdlets are discussed in the following sections.

## Getting Help

The Get-Help cmdlet is used to retrieve help information about cmdlets, aliases, and from help files. To display a list of all help topics this cmdlet supports, enter Get-Help * at the PowerShell command prompt, as shown here:

```
PS C:\> get-help *

Name                    Category            Synopsis
----                    --------            --------
ac                      Alias               Add-Content
asnp                    Alias               Add-PSSnapin
clc                     Alias               Clear-Content
cli                     Alias               Clear-Item
clp                     Alias               Clear-ItemProperty
clv                     Alias               Clear-Variable
cpi                     Alias               Copy-Item
cpp                     Alias               Copy-ItemProperty
cvpa                    Alias               Convert-Path
...
```

If that list seems too large to work with, it can be shortened by filtering on topic name and category. For example, to get a list of all cmdlets starting with the verb Get, try the command shown in the following example:

```
PS C:\> get-help -Name get-* -Category cmdlet

Name                    Category            Synopsis
----                    --------            --------
Get-Command             Cmdlet              Gets basic information...
Get-Help                Cmdlet              Displays information a...
Get-History             Cmdlet              Gets a list of the com...
Get-PSSnapin            Cmdlet              Gets the Windows Power...
Get-EventLog            Cmdlet              Gets information about...
Get-ChildItem           Cmdlet              Gets the items and chi...
Get-Content             Cmdlet              Gets the content of th...
...

PS C:\>
```

After selecting a help topic, that topic can be retrieved by using the topic name as the parameter to the Get-Help cmdlet. For example, to retrieve help for the Get-Content cmdlet, enter the following command:

```
PS C:\> get-help get-content
```

After executing this command, a shortened view of the help content for the Get-Content cmdlet is displayed. To view the full help content, include the full switch parameter with the command:

```
PS C:\> get-help get-content –full
```

After executing the command with the full switch parameter, you will find that the full help content is divided into several sections. Table 21.3 describes each of these sections.

TABLE 21.3   PowerShell Help Sections

| Help Section | Description |
| --- | --- |
| Name | The name of the cmdlet |
| Synopsis | A brief description of what the cmdlet does |
| Description | A detailed description of the cmdlet's behavior, usually including usage examples |
| Syntax | Specific usage details for entering commands with the cmdlet |
| Parameters | Valid parameters that can be used with this cmdlet |
| Inputs | The type of input this cmdlet accepts |
| Outputs | The type of data that the cmdlet returns |
| Notes | Additional detailed information on using the cmdlet, including specific scenarios and possible limitations or idiosyncrasies |
| Examples | Common usage examples for the cmdlet |
| Related Links | References other cmdlets that perform similar tasks |

**Get-Command**

The Get-Command is used to gather basic information about cmdlets and other commands that are available. For example, when executed, the Get-Command lists all the cmdlets available to the PowerShell session:

```
PS C:\> get-command
```

```
CommandType     Name                         Definition
-----------     ----                         ----------
Cmdlet          Add-Content                  Add-Content [-Path] <String[...
Cmdlet          Add-History                  Add-History [[-InputObject] ...
Cmdlet          Add-Member                   Add-Member [-MemberType] <PS...
Cmdlet          Add-PSSnapin                 Add-PSSnapin [-Name] <String...
Cmdlet          Clear-Content                Clear-Content [-Path] <Strin...
Cmdlet          Clear-Item                   Clear-Item [-Path] <String[]...
Cmdlet          Clear-ItemProperty           Clear-ItemProperty [-Path] <...
Cmdlet          Clear-Variable               Clear-Variable [-Name] <Stri...
Cmdlet          Compare-Object               Compare-Object [-ReferenceOb...
...
```

```
PS C:\>
```

Next, to retrieve basic information about a particular cmdlet, you would then include that cmdlet's name and argument. For example:

```
PS C:\> Get-Command Get-Process
```

```
CommandType     Name                         Definition
-----------     ----                         ----------
Cmdlet          Get-Process                  Get-Process [[-Name] <String...
```

```
PS C:\>
```

The Get-Command cmdlet is more powerful than Get-Help because it lists all available commands (cmdlets, scripts, aliases, functions, and native applications) in a PowerShell session, as shown in this example:

```
PS C:\> get-command note*
```

```
CommandType     Name                         Definition
-----------     ----                         ----------
Application     NOTEPAD.EXE                   C:\WINDOWS\NOTEPAD.EXE
Application     notepad.exe                   C:\WINDOWS\system32\notepad.exe
```

```
PS C:\>
```

When using Get-Command with elements other than cmdlets, the information returned is a little different from information you see for a cmdlet. For example, with an existing application, the value of the Definition property is the path to the application. However, other information about the application is also available, as shown here:

```
PS C:\> get-command ipconfig | format-list *
FileVersionInfo : File:              C:\WINDOWS\system32\ipconfig.exe
                  InternalName:      ipconfig.exe
                  OriginalFilename:  ipconfig.exe
                  FileVersion:       5.1.2600.2180 (xpsp_sp2_rtm.040803-2158)
                  FileDescription:   IP Configuration Utility
                  Product:           Microsoftr Windowsr Operating System
                  ProductVersion:    5.1.2600.2180
                  Debug:             False
                  Patched:           False
                  PreRelease:        False
                  PrivateBuild:      False
                  SpecialBuild:      False
                  Language:          English (United States)

Path          : C:\WINDOWS\system32\ipconfig.exe
Extension     : .exe
Definition    : C:\WINDOWS\system32\ipconfig.exe
Name          : ipconfig.exe
CommandType   : Application
```

With a function, the Definition property is the body of the function:

```
PS C:\> get-command Prompt


CommandType     Name                          Definition
-----------     ----                          ----------
Function        prompt                        Write-Host ("PS " + $(Get-Lo...

PS C:\>
```

With an alias, the Definition property is the aliased command:

```
PS C:\> get-command write


CommandType     Name                          Definition
-----------     ----                          ----------
Alias           write                         Write-Output
PS C:\>
```

With a script file, the Definition property is the path to the script. With a non-PowerShell script (such as a .bat or .vbs file), the information returned is the same as other existing applications.

## Managing Services

In PowerShell, a number of cmdlets can be used to manage services on a local machine. A list of these cmdlets is as follows:

- ▶ **Get-Service**—Used to gather service information from Windows.

- ▶ **New-Service**—Used to create a new service in Windows.

- ▶ **Restart-Service**—Used to restart services.

- ▶ **Resume-Service**—Used to resume suspended services.

- ▶ **Set-Service**—Used to modify service configurations.

- ▶ **Start-Service**—Used to start services.

- ▶ **Stop-Service**—Used to stop services.

- ▶ **Suspend-Service**—Used to suspend services.

### Getting Service Information

When the Get-Service cmdlet is executed, it returns a collection of objects that contains information about all the services that are present on a Windows system. A representation of that object collection is then outputted into a formatted table, as shown in the following example:

```
PS C:\> get-service


Status    Name              DisplayName
------    ----              -----------
Running   AeLookupSvc       Application Experience
Stopped   ALG               Application Layer Gateway Service
Running   AppHostSvc        Application Host Helper Service
Stopped   Appinfo           Application Information
Stopped   AppMgmt           Application Management
Stopped   aspnet_state      ASP.NET State Service
Stopped   AudioEndpointBu... Windows Audio Endpoint Builder
Stopped   AudioSrv          Windows Audio
...
```

To filter the information returned based on the service status, the object collection can be piped to the Where-Object cmdlet, as shown in the following example:

```
PS C:\> get-service | where-object {$_.Status -eq "Stopped"}


Status    Name              DisplayName
------    ----              -----------
Stopped   ALG               Application Layer Gateway Service
Stopped   Appinfo           Application Information
```

```
Stopped  AppMgmt             Application Management
Stopped  aspnet_state        ASP.NET State Service
Stopped  AudioEndpointBu...   Windows Audio Endpoint Builder
Stopped  AudioSrv            Windows Audio
...
```

As shown in the preceding example, the Where-Object object cmdlet is used in conjunction with a code block {...}, which is executed as the filter. In this case, the code block contained an expression that filtered the object collection based on services that were "Stopped." The same type of logic can also be applied to return information about a particular service. For example:

```
PS C:\> get-service ¦ where-object {$_.Name -eq "DNS"} ¦ fl
```

```
Name                 : DNS
DisplayName          : DNS Server
Status               : Running
DependentServices    : {}
ServicesDependedOn   : {Afd, Tcpip, RpcSs, NTDS}
CanPauseAndContinue  : True
CanShutdown          : True
CanStop              : True
ServiceType          : Win32OwnProcess
```

```
PS C:\>
```

In the preceding example, the object collection from the Get-Service cmdlet is piped to the Where-Object cmdlet. The filter statement defined script block then instructs the Where-Object cmdlet to return an object for the DNS service. The object that is returned by this cmdlet is then piped to the Format-List cmdlet, which writes a formatted list (containing information about the object) back to the console session.

> **NOTE**
>
> A shorter method for performing the preceding action is to use the name switch, as shown in the following command: get-service –name DNS.

**Managing Service Statuses**

To stop a service in PowerShell, the Stop-Service cmdlet is used, as shown in this example:

```
PS C:\> stop-service -name dns
```

Notice that when the cmdlet has finished executing, no status information about the service's status is returned. To gather that information, the passthru switch parameter can be used to pass the object created by a cmdlet through to the pipeline. For example:

```
PS C:\> start-service -name dns -pass ¦ ft
```

```
Status    Name              DisplayName
------    ----              -----------
Running   DNS               DNS Server
```

In the preceding example, the passthru switch parameter is used in conjunction with the Start-Service cmdlet. When the cmdlet has finished executing, thus starting the DNS service, the object is piped to the Format-Table cmdlet, which then displays status information about the DNS service.

### Modifying Services

The Set-Service cmdlet is used to change a service's properties (such as its description, display name, and start mode). To use this cmdlet, either pass it a service object or specify the name of the service to be modified, plus the property to be modified. For example, to modify the startup type of the DNS service, use the following command:

```
PS C:\> set-service -name DNS -start "manual"
```

A startup type can be defined as Automatic, Manual, or Disabled. To change a service's description, a command might look as follows:

```
PS C:\> set-service -name DNS -description "My Important DNS Service"
```

> **NOTE**
>
> The service management cmdlets in PowerShell are not end-alls for managing Windows services. There are a number of areas in which these cmdlets are lacking—for example, not being able to define a service's logon account or report on its startup type. Luckily, if a more in-depth interface is needed, an administrator can always fall back onto WMI.

## Gathering Event Log Information

In PowerShell, the Get-EventLog cmdlet can be used to gather information from a Windows event log and list the event logs that are present on a system. To gather event log information, the name of the event log must be specified, as shown in the following example:

```
PS C:\> get-eventlog -logname application
```

```
Index Time            Type Source              EventID Message
----- ----            ---- ------              ------- -------
 1778 Oct 05 19:44    Info MSExchangeFBPublish    8280 When initializing ses...
 1777 Oct 05 19:38    Info MSExchangeIS           9826 Starting from 10/5/20...
 1776 Oct 05 19:38    Info MSExchange ADAccess    2080 Process MSEXCHANGEADT...
 1775 Oct 05 19:16    Info MSExchange ADAccess    2080 Process MAD.EXE (PID=...
...
```

To create a list of all the event logs on the local system, use the list switch parameter, as shown in the following command:

```
PS C:\> get-eventlog -list


 Max(K) Retain OverflowAction        Entries Name
 ------ ------ -------------        ------- ----
 20,480      0 OverwriteAsNeeded      1,778 Application
 15,168      0 OverwriteAsNeeded         44 DFS Replication
    512      0 OverwriteAsNeeded      1,826 Directory Service
 16,384      0 OverwriteAsNeeded         38 DNS Server
 20,480      0 OverwriteAsNeeded          0 Hardware Events
    512      7 OverwriteOlder             0 Internet Explorer
 20,480      0 OverwriteAsNeeded          0 Key Management Service
    512      7 OverwriteOlder           155 PowerShell
131,072      0 OverwriteAsNeeded      9,596 Security
 20,480      0 OverwriteAsNeeded      3,986 System
 15,360      0 OverwriteAsNeeded        278 Windows PowerShell


PS C:\>
```

To gather in-depth information about a particular set of events or event, the information returned from the Get-EventLog cmdlet can be further filtered. For example:

```
PS C:\> $Errors = get-eventLog -logname application ¦ where {$_.eventid -eq 8196}
PS C:\> $Errors[0]  ¦ fl -Property *


EventID           : 8196
MachineName       : dc01.companyabc.com
Data              : {}
Index             : 1772
Category          : (0)
CategoryNumber    : 0
EntryType         : Information
Message           : License Activation Scheduler (SLUINotify.dll) was not able
                      to automatically activate. Error code:
                    0x8007232B
```

```
Source               : Software Protection Platform Service
ReplacementStrings   : {0x8007232B}
InstanceId           : 1073750020
TimeGenerated        : 10/5/2009 6:56:36 PM
TimeWritten          : 10/5/2009 6:56:36 PM
UserName             :
Site                 :
Container            :
```

PS C:\>

In the preceding example, the Get-EventLog cmdlet is used in conjunction with the Where-Object cmdlet to create a collection of objects that all have an EventID equal to 8196. This collection is then defined as the variable $Errors. In the next command, the first object in the $Errors variable is passed to the Format-List cmdlet, which then writes a list of all the object's properties to the console.

## Managing the Files and Directories

As mentioned earlier in this chapter, specifically in the section "Providers and Drives," a set of core cmdlets can be used to access and manipulate PowerShell data stores. Because the Windows file system is just another PowerShell data store, it is accessed through the FileSystem provider. Each mounted drive or defined location is represented by a PSDrive and can be managed by using the core cmdlets. Details about how these core cmdlets are used are discussed in the following sections.

### Listing Directories of Files

In PowerShell, you can use several cmdlets to explore the file system. The first cmdlet, Get-Location, is used to display the current working location:

```
PS C:\> get-location


Path
----
C:\


PS C:\>
```

To get information about a specified directory or file, you can use the Get-Item cmdlet:

```
PS C:\temp> get-item autorun.inf


    Directory: C:\temp
```

```
Mode                LastWriteTime     Length Name
----                -------------     ------ ----
-a---          8/7/2007  10:06 PM         63 autorun.inf

PS C:\temp>
```

To get information about directories or files under a specified directory, you can use the Get-ChildItem cmdlet:

```
PS C:\> get-childitem c:\inetpub\wwwroot


    Directory: C:\inetpub\wwwroot


Mode                LastWriteTime     Length Name
----                -------------     ------ ----
d----         10/4/2009  11:09 PM            aspnet_client
-a---         10/4/2009   2:10 PM        689 iisstart.htm
-a---         10/4/2009   2:10 PM     184946 welcome.png

PS C:\>
```

### Creating Directories or Files

Creating a directory or file in PowerShell is a simple process and just involves the use of the New-Item cmdlet:

```
PS C:\> new-item -path c:\ -name work -type dir


    Directory: C:\


Mode                LastWriteTime     Length Name
----                -------------     ------ ----
d----         10/7/2009  11:44 AM            work

PS C:\>
```

In the preceding example, it should be noted that the itemtype parameter is a parameter that must be defined. If this parameter is not defined, PowerShell prompts you for the type of item to be created. An example of this is shown here:

```
PS C:\work> new-item -path c:\work -name script.log
Type: file


    Directory: C:\work
```

```
Mode                LastWriteTime     Length Name
----                -------------     ------ ----
-a---           10/7/2009   8:58 PM        0 script.log
```

PS C:\work>

In the previous example, PowerShell prompts you to define the value for the itemtype parameter. However, because you wanted to create a file, the value is defined as "file."

---

**NOTE**

With files, in addition to using the New-Item cmdlet, you can use several other cmdlets to create files. Examples of these are Add-Content, Set-Content, Out-Csv, and Out-File. However, the main purpose of these cmdlets is for adding or appending content within a file.

---

### Deleting Directories and Files

To delete directories and files in PowerShell, the Remote-Item cmdlet is used. Usage of this cmdlet is shown in the next example:

PS C:\work> remove-item script.log

Notice how PowerShell doesn't prompt you for any type of confirmation. Considering that the deletion of an item is a very permanent action, you might want to use one of the PowerShell common parameters to confirm the action before executing the command. For example:

PS C:\work> remove-item test.txt -confirm

```
Confirm
Are you sure you want to perform this action?
Performing operation "Remove File" on Target "C:\work\test.txt".
[Y] Yes  [A] Yes to All  [N] No  [L] No to All  [S] Suspend  [?] Help
(default is "Y"):
```

In the prior example, the confirm common parameter is used to verify the deletion of the test.txt file. Usage of this parameter can help prevent you from making mistakes when executing commands that might or might not be intended actions.

---

**NOTE**

In addition to the Remove-Item cmdlet, you can use the Clear-Content cmdlet to wipe content from a file instead of deleting it.

---

**Renaming Directories and Files**

To rename directories and files in PowerShell, use the Rename-Item cmdlet:

```
PS C:\> rename-item c:\work scripts
```

When using the Rename-Item cmdlet, the argument for the first parameter named path is defined as the path to the directory or file being renamed. The secondary parameter, newName, is then defined as the new name for the directory or file.

**Moving or Copying Directories and Files**

To move and copy directories or files in PowerShell, you can use either the Move-Item or Copy-Item cmdlets. An example of using the Move-Item cmdlet is as follows:

```
PS C:\> move-item -path c:\scripts -dest c:\work
PS C:\> get-childitem c:\work


    Directory: C:\work


Mode                LastWriteTime     Length Name
----                -------------     ------ ----
d----         10/7/2009   9:20 PM            scripts


PS C:\>
```

The syntax for using the Copy-Item cmdlet is very similar, as shown in the next example:

```
PS C:\work> copy-item 4444.log .\logs
PS C:\work> gci .\logs
    Directory: C:\work\logs


Mode                LastWriteTime     Length Name
----                -------------     ------ ----
-a---         10/7/2009  10:41 PM          6 4444.log


PS C:\work>
```

**Reading Information from Files**

To read information from a file, you can use the Get-Content cmdlet. An example of using this cmdlet is as follows:

```
PS C:\work\logs> get-content 4444.log
PowerShell was here!
```

When the Get-Content cmdlet is executed, it reads content from the specified file line-by-line and returns an object for each line that is read. For example:

```
PS C:\work\logs> $logs = get-content 4444.log
PS C:\work\logs> $logs[0]
PowerShell was here!
PS C:\work\logs>
```

## Managing the Registry

PowerShell has a built-in provider, Registry, for accessing and manipulating the Registry on a local machine. The Registry hives available in this provider are HKEY_LOCAL_MACHINE (HKLM) and HKEY_CURRENT_USER (HKCU). These hives are represented in a PowerShell session as two additional PSDrive objects named HKLM: and HKCU:.

> **NOTE**
>
> The WshShell object has access to not only the HKLM: and HKCU: hives, but also HKEY_CLASSES_ROOT (HKCR), HKEY_USERS, and HKEY_CURRENT_CONFIG. To access these additional Registry hives in PowerShell, you use the Set-Location cmdlet to change the location to the root of the Registry provider.

Because the Windows Registry is treated as a hierarchy data store, like the Windows file system, it can also be managed by the PowerShell core cmdlets. For example, to read a Registry value, you use the Get-ItemProperty cmdlet:

```
PS C:\> $Path = "HKLM:\Software\Microsoft\Windows NT\CurrentVersion"
PS C:\> $Key = get-itemproperty $Path
PS C:\> $Key.ProductName
Windows Server 2008 R2 Enterprise
PS C:\>
```

To create or modify a Registry value, you use the Set-ItemProperty cmdlet:

```
PS C:\> $Path = "HKCU:\Software"
PS C:\> set-itemproperty -path $Path -name "PSinfo" –type "String" –value "Power-
Shell_Was_Here"
PS C:\>
PS C:\> $Key = get-itemproperty $Path
PS C:\> $Key.PSinfo
PowerShell_Was_Here
PS C:\>
```

Remember that the Windows Registry has different types of Registry values. You use the Set-ItemProperty cmdlet to define the Type parameter when creating or modifying Registry values. As a best practice, you should always define Registry values when using the Set-ItemProperty cmdlet. Otherwise, the cmdlet defines the Registry value with the default type, which is String. Other possible types are as follows:

- ▶ ExpandString

- ▶ Binary

- ▶ DWord

- ▶ MultiString

- ▶ Qword

> **NOTE**
>
> Depending on the Registry value you're creating or modifying, the data value you set the named value to needs to be in the correct format. So, if the Registry value is type REG_BINARY, you use a binary value, such as $Bin = 101, 118, 105.

To delete a Registry value, you use the Remove-ItemProperty cmdlet, as shown here:

```
PS C:\> $Path = "HKCU:\Software"
PS C:\> remove-itemproperty -path $Path -name "PSinfo"
PS C:\>
```

## Managing Processes

In PowerShell, you can use two cmdlets to manage processes. The first cmdlet, Get-Process, is used to get information about the current processes that are running on the local Windows system:

```
PS C:\> get-process
```

| Handles | NPM(K) | PM(K) | WS(K) | VM(M) | CPU(s) | Id | ProcessName |
|---|---|---|---|---|---|---|---|
| 782 | 12 | 2500 | 4456 | 113 | 4.02 | 448 | csrss |
| 237 | 10 | 3064 | 6228 | 113 | 76.70 | 488 | csrss |
| 292 | 26 | 20180 | 14632 | 356 | 12.94 | 1496 | dfsrs |
| 160 | 13 | 3020 | 5536 | 55 | 0.34 | 2696 | dfssvc |
| 203 | 24 | 6368 | 5888 | 64 | 1.75 | 3220 | dns |

...

To filter the object collection that is returned by the Get-Process cmdlet to a particular process, you can specify the process name or ID, as shown in the following example:

```
PS C:\> get-process dns
```

| Handles | NPM(K) | PM(K) | WS(K) | VM(M) | CPU(s) | Id | ProcessName |
|---|---|---|---|---|---|---|---|
| 203 | 24 | 6368 | 5888 | 64 | 1.77 | 3220 | dns |

21

```
PS C:\> get-process -id 3220

Handles  NPM(K)    PM(K)      WS(K) VM(M)   CPU(s)     Id ProcessName
-------  ------    -----      ----- -----   ------     -- -----------
    203      24     6368       5888    64     1.77   3220 dns

PS C:\>
```

In addition to the preceding examples, you could also combine the Get-Process cmdlet with the Where-Object cmdlet. For example:

```
PS C:\> get-process ¦ ? {$_.workingset -gt 100000000} ¦ sort ws -descending

Handles  NPM(K)    PM(K)      WS(K) VM(M)   CPU(s)     Id ProcessName
-------  ------    -----      ----- -----   ------     -- -----------
    471      29   108608     104972   658    95.88   4208 mmc
    629      39   130716     104208   705   108.58   4332 mmc

PS C:\>
```

By using these cmdlets together, a more robust view of the current running processes based on a specified filter statement can be created. In the previous example, the resulting object collection includes processes that only have a working set greater than 100,000,000 bytes. In addition, the Sort-Object cmdlet is used to sort the formatted table's WS(K) column in descending order.

The second cmdlet that is used to manage processes is the Stop-Process cmdlet. Usage of this cmdlet is as follows:

```
PS C:\work\logs> stop-process -name notepad
```

The process that is being stopped can either be defined by its name, ID, or as an object that is passed to the Stop-Process cmdlet via the pipeline.

## Using WMI

Using WMI in PowerShell has similar conceptual logic as in WSH. The main difference is that the PowerShell methods are based on WMI .NET instead of the WMI Scripting API. You have three methods for using WMI in PowerShell: WMI .NET (which is the .NET System.Management and System.Management.Instrumentation namespaces), the Get-WmiObject cmdlet, or the PowerShell WMI type accelerators: [WMI], [WMIClass], and [WMISearcher].

The first method, using the System.Management and System.Management.Instrumentation namespaces, isn't discussed in this chapter because it's not as practical as the other methods. It should be only a fallback method in case PowerShell isn't correctly encapsulating an object within a PSObject object when using the other two methods.

The second method, the Get-WmiObject cmdlet, retrieves WMI objects and gathers information about WMI classes. This cmdlet is fairly simple. For example, getting an instance of the local `Win32_ComputerSystem` class just requires the name of the class, as shown here:

```
PS C:\> get-wmiobject "Win32_ComputerSystem"


Domain              : companyabc.com
Manufacturer        : Hewlett-Packard
Model               : Pavilion dv8000 (ES184AV)
Name                : Wii
PrimaryOwnerName    : Damon Cortesi
TotalPhysicalMemory : 2145566720

PS C:\>
```

The next example, which is more robust, connects to the remote machine named Jupiter and gets an instance of the `Win32_Service` class in which the instance's name equals Virtual Server. The result is an object containing information about the Virtual Server service on Jupiter:

```
PS C:\> get-wmiobject -class "Win32_Service" -computerName "Jupiter" -filter
"Name='Virtual Server'"


ExitCode  : 0
Name      : Virtual Server
ProcessId : 656
StartMode : Auto
State     : Running
Status    : OK

PS C:\>
```

The following command returns the same information as the previous one but makes use of a WQL query:

```
PS C:\> get-wmiobject -computerName "Jupiter" -query "Select *From Win32_Service
Where Name='Virtual Server'"


ExitCode  : 0
Name      : Virtual Server
ProcessId : 656
StartMode : Auto
State     : Running
Status    : OK

PS C:\>
```

Finally, here's an example of using Get-WmiObject to gather information about a WMI class:

```
PS C:\> get-wmiobject -namespace "root/cimv2" -list ¦ where {$_.Name
 -eq "Win32_Product"} ¦ format-list *


Name               : Win32_Product
__GENUS            : 1
__CLASS            : Win32_Product
__SUPERCLASS       : CIM_Product
__DYNASTY          : CIM_Product
__RELPATH          : Win32_Product
__PROPERTY_COUNT   : 12
__DERIVATION       : {CIM_Product}
__SERVER           : PLANX
__NAMESPACE        : ROOT\cimv2
__PATH             : \\PLANX\ROOT\cimv2:Win32_Product
...


PS C:\>
```

Although using Get-WmiObject is simple, using it almost always requires typing a long command string. This drawback brings you to the third method for using WMI in PowerShell: the WMI type accelerators.

### [WMI] Type Accelerator

This type accelerator for the ManagementObject class takes a WMI object path as a string and gets a WMI object bound to an instance of the specified WMI class, as shown in this example:

```
PS C:\> $CompInfo = [WMI]"root\cimv2:Win32_ComputerSystem.Name='PLANX'"
PS C:\> $CompInfo


Domain              : companyabc.com
Manufacturer        : Hewlett-Packard
Model               : Pavilion dv8000 (ES184AV)
Name                : PLANX
PrimaryOwnerName    : Frank Miller
TotalPhysicalMemory : 2145566720


PS C:\>
```

> **NOTE**
>
> To bind to an instance of a WMI object directly, you must include the key property in the WMI object path. For the preceding example, the key property is Name.

### [WMIClass] Type Accelerator

This type accelerator for the ManagementClass class takes a WMI object path as a string and gets a WMI object bound to the specified WMI class, as shown in the following example:

```
PS C:\> $CompClass = [WMICLASS]"\\.\root\cimv2:Win32_ComputerSystem"
PS C:\> $CompClass


   NameSpace: ROOT\cimv2


Name                             Methods            Properties
----                             -------            ----------
Win32_ComputerSystem             {SetPowerState, R... {AdminPasswordSt...
PS C:\> $CompClass | format-list *


Name           : Win32_ComputerSystem
__GENUS        : 1
__CLASS        : Win32_ComputerSystem
__SUPERCLASS   : CIM_UnitaryComputerSystem
__DYNASTY      : CIM_ManagedSystemElement
__RELPATH      : Win32_ComputerSystem
__PROPERTY_COUNT : 54
__DERIVATION   : {CIM_UnitaryComputerSystem, CIM_ComputerSystem, CIM_System,
                 CIM_LogicalElement...}
__SERVER       : PLANX
__NAMESPACE    : ROOT\cimv2
__PATH         : \\PLANX\ROOT\cimv2:Win32_ComputerSystem
...


PS C:\>
```

### [WMISearcher] Type Accelerator

This type accelerator for the ManagementObjectSearcher class takes a WQL string and creates a WMI searcher object. After the searcher object is created, you use the Get() method to get a WMI object bound to an instance of the specified WMI class, as shown here:

```
PS C:\> $CompInfo = [WMISearcher]"Select * From Win32_ComputerSystem"
PS C:\> $CompInfo.Get()


Domain           : companyabc.com
Manufacturer     : Hewlett-Packard
Model            : Pavilion dv8000 (ES184AV)
Name             : PLANX
PrimaryOwnerName : Miro
```

```
TotalPhysicalMemory : 2145566720
```

```
PS C:\>
```

### AuthenticationLevel and ImpersonationLevel

When using the Get-WmiObject cmdlet in PowerShell 1.0 in conjunction with the IIsWebService class to manage the W3SVC service on a remote machine, the following error would be encountered:

```
PS > get-wmiobject -class IIsWebService -namespace "root\microsoftiisv2" -Computer
sc1-app01
Get-WmiObject : Access denied
At line:1 char:14
+ Get-WMIObject <<<<  -class IIsWebService -namespace "root\microsoftiisv2" -com-
puter sc1-app01
```

This is normal behavior for any of the IIS WMI classes because they require the AuthenticationLevel property defined as PacketPrivacy. The AuthenticationLevel property is an integer, which defines the COM authentication level that is assigned to an object and in the end determines how DCOM will protect information sent from WMI. In this case, the IIS WMI classes require that data is encrypted, which is not the default behavior of WMI.

Although defining the AuthenticationLevel property in WSH was a simple line of code, in PowerShell 1.0's version of the Get-WmiObject cmdlet, there was no method to define this property. Additionally, there wasn't a way to change either the ImpersonationLevel property or enable all privileges, both of which are often requirements when working with WMI. To correct this problem, the product team has updated the Get-WmiObject cmdlet in PowerShell 2.0 to include new parameters to define the AuthenticationLevel and ImpersonationLevel properties, as well as enable all privileges. Additionally, these parameters also work with the new WMI cmdlets (Invoke-WMIMethod, Remove-WMIObject, and Set-WMIInstance), which were also introduced in PowerShell 2.0. For example:

```
PS > get-wmiobject -class IIsWebService -namespace "root\microsoftiisv2" -Computer
sc1-app01 –Authentication 6
```

In the previous example, the Authentication parameter is used to define the AuthenticationLevel property. In this case, the value is defined as 6 (PacketPrivacy).

### Set-WMIInstance Cmdlet

The Set-WMIInstance cmdlet was developed to reduce the number of steps needed to change a read-write WMI property (or property that allows direct modification). For example, in PowerShell 1.0, the following set of commands might be used to change the LoggingLevel for the WMI service:

```
PS C:\> $WMISetting = Get-WMIObject Win32_WMISetting
PS C:\> $WMISetting.LoggingLevel = 2
PS C:\> $WMISetting.Put()
```

By using the Set-WMIInstance cmdlet, you can complete the same task using a single command:

```
PS > set-wmiinstance –class "Win32_WMISetting" –argument @{LoggingLevel=2}
```

In the previous example, the class parameter is defined as a Win32_WMISetting, whereas the argument parameter is defined as a HashTable that contains the property and the value the property will be set to. Additionally, because this parameter requires an argument that is a HashTable, then to define multiple property and value pairs, you would separate the pairs with a semicolon, as shown here:

```
–argument @{LoggingLevel=1;MaxLogFileSize=1000}
```

However, the true power of this cmdlet is to use the computername parameter to change read-write WMI properties on multiple machines at once. For example:

```
PS > set-wmiinstance –class "Win32_WMISetting" –argument @{LoggingLevel=1} –comput-
ername sc1-app01,sc1-app02
```

The arguments for the computername parameter can be either a NetBIOS name, fully qualified domain name (FQDN), or IP address. Additionally, each argument must be separated by a comma.

### Invoke-WMIMethod Cmdlet

With WMI, there are two different types of methods: instance or static. With static methods, you must invoke the method from the class itself, whereas instance methods are invoked on specific instances of a class. In PowerShell 1.0, working with instance methods were fairly straightforward and only involved creating an object of a particular instance of a WMI class. However, to work with a static method required a fairly complex and unintuitive WQL statement, as shown in the following example:

```
PS > $ProcFac = get-wmiobject -query "SELECT * FROM Meta_Class WHERE __Class =
'Win32_Process'" -namespace "root\cimv2"
PS > $ProcFac.Create("notepad.exe")
```

Granted, you could also use the [WMIClass] type accelerator, as shown here:

```
PS > $ProcFac = [wmiclass]"Win32_Process"
PS > $ProcFac.Create("notepad.exe")
```

But, if you wanted to use the Get-WMIObject cmdlet or were having problems with the [WMIClass] type accelerator, employing the use of the noted WQL statement wasn't very command-line friendly. To fill this noted gap, the PowerShell product team has introduced the Invoke-WMIMethod cmdlet in PowerShell 2.0.

As its name suggests, the purpose of the Invoke-WMIMethod cmdlet is to make it easier to directly invoke WMI methods. To use this cmdlet to invoke a static method, you use the following command:

```
PS > invoke-wmimethod -path "Win32_Process" -name "create" -argumentList
"notepad.exe"
```

In the previous command example, the path parameter requires the name of the WMI class from which the method is to be invoked. In this case, the method being invoked is the Create method as defined for the name parameter. If you were invoking an instance method, the argument for the path parameter would need to be the complete path to an existing WMI instance. For example:

```
PS > invoke-wmimethod -path "Win32_Process.Handle='42144'" -name terminate
```

Finally, the argumentList parameter is used to define any arguments that a method requires when it is invoked. In cases where the method requires multiple values or you want to pass multiple values, you must assign those values into an array. Then, the array must be defined as the argument for the argumentList parameter.

> **NOTE**
>
> Values for methods are not in the same order as used with the WMI's scripting API. Instead, values are ordered such as they appear in Wbemtest.exe.

### Remove-WMIObject Cmdlet

The last new cmdlet to be introduced in PowerShell 2.0 is the Remove-WMIObject cmdlet. This cmdlet is used to remove instances of WMI objects. For example, to terminate a process using WMI in PowerShell 1.0, you might use the following set of commands:

```
PS > $Proc = get-wmiobject -class "Win32_Process" -filter "Name='wordpad.exe'"
PS > $Proc.Terminate()
```

However, depending on the type of WMI object that you are trying to remove, there can be any number of methods that would need to be used. For instance, to delete a folder using WMI in PowerShell 1.0, you would use the following command:

```
PS > $Folder = get-wmiobject -query "Select * From Win32_Directory Where Name
='C:\\Scripts'"
PS > $Folder.Delete()
```

Conversely, using the Remove-WMIObject cmdlet, you can remove instances of any type of WMI object. For example, to remove an instance of the Win32_Process class, you would use the following commands:

```
PS > $Proc = get-wmiobject -class "Win32_Process" -filter "Name='wordpad.exe'"
```

21

```
PS > $Proc ¦ remove-wmiobject
```

Whereas the following commands are used to remove a directory:

```
PS > $Folder = get-wmiobject -query "Select * From Win32_Directory Where Name
='C:\\Scripts'"
PS > $Folder ¦ remove-wmiobject
```

## Using Snap-Ins

Snap-ins are used to show a list of all the registered PSSnapins outside of the default snap-ins that come with PowerShell. Entering the command Get-PSSnapin  -Registered on a newly installed PowerShell system will return nothing, as shown in the following example:

```
PS C:\> get-pssnapin -registered
```

In most cases, a setup program will accompany a PowerShell snap-in and ensure that it becomes correctly registered for use. However, if this is not the case, the .NET utility InstallUtil.exe is used to complete the registration process. In the following example, InstallUtil.exe is being used to install a third-party library file called freshtastic-automation.dll:

```
PS C:\> & "$env:windir\Microsoft.NET\Framework\v2.0.50727\InstallUtil.exe" fresh-
tastic-automation.dll
```

Once the DLL library file has been registered with PowerShell, the next step is to register the DLL's snap-in with PowerShell so that the cmdlets contained in the DLL are made available to PowerShell. In the case of the freshtastic-automation library, the snap-in is registered by using the command Add-PSSnapin freshtastic, as follows:

```
PS C:\> add-pssnapin freshtastic
```

Now that the freshtastic snap-in has been registered, you can enter the following command Get-Help freshtastic to review the usage information for the freshtastic cmdlets:

```
PS C:\> get-help freshtastic
```

Now that the registration of the freshtastic library DLL is complete and the associated snap-in has been added to the console, you can enter the command Get-PSSnapin –registered again and see that the freshtastic snap-in has been added to the console:

```
PS C:\> get-pssnapin -registered


Name       : freshtastic
PSVersion  : 2.0
```

Description : Used to automate freshness.

```
PS C:\>
```

Now that you have registered the third-party library file and added its snap-in to the console, you might find that the library does not meet your needs, and you want to remove it. The removal process is basically a reversal of the installation steps listed previously. First, you remove the snap-in from the console using the command `Remove-PSSnapin freshtastic`, as follows:

```
PS C:\> Remove-PSSnapin freshtastic
```

Once the third-party snap-in has been unregistered, you will once again use `InstallUtil.exe` with a `/U` switch to unregister the DLL, as follows:

```
PS C:\> & "$env:windir\Microsoft.NET\Framework\v2.0.50727\InstallUtil.exe" /U
freshtastic-automation.dll
```

Once the uninstall has completed, you can verify that the library file was successfully unregistered by entering the command `Get-PSSnapin -registered` and verifying that no third-party libraries are listed.

## Using Modules

In Windows Server 2008 R2, a set of base modules are loaded when the operating system is installed. Additionally, modules can be added or removed using the Add Features Wizard in Server Manager.

### Default Module Locations

There are two default locations for modules. The first location is for the machine, as follows:

```
$pshome\Modules (C:\Windows\system32\WindowsPowerShell\v1.0\Modules)
```

The second location is for the current user:

```
$home\Documents\WindowsPowerShell\Modules
(UserProfile%\Documents\WindowsPowerShell\Modules)
```

### Installing New Modules

As mentioned previously, new modules can be added using the Add Features Wizard in Server Manager. Additionally, other modules should come with an installation program that will install the module for you. However, if need be, you can also manually install a new module. To do this, use the following steps:

1. Create a new folder for the module that is being installed. For example:

```
PS C:\> New-Item -type directory -path
$home\Documents\WindowsPowerShell\Modules\Spammer1000
```

2. Copy the contents of the module into the newly created folder.

### Using Installed Modules

After a module has been installed on a machine, it can then be imported into a PowerShell session for usage. To find out what modules are available for use, use the Get-Module cmdlet:

```
PS C:\> Get-Module -listAvailable
```

Or, to list modules that have already been imported into the current PowerShell session, just use the Get-Module cmdlet without the listAvailable switch parameter:

```
PS C:\> Get-Module
```

Next, to import a module into a PowerShell session, use the Import-Module cmdlet. For example, if the ActiveDirectory module has been installed, the following command would be used:

```
PS C:\> Import-Module ActiveDirectory
```

> **NOTE**
>
> A complete path to the module folder must be provided for modules that are not located in one of the default modules locations or any additional module locations that have been defined for the current PowerShell session. This is required when using the Import-Module cmdlet to define the module location used by the cmdlet.

Additionally, if you want to import all modules that are available on a machine into a PowerShell session, one of two methods can be used. The first method is to execute the following command, which lists all modules and then pipes that to the Import-Module cmdlet:

```
PS C:\> Get-Module -listAvailable | Import-Module
```

The second method is to right-click the Windows PowerShell icon in the taskbar, and then select Import System Modules. Additionally, you can also use the Windows PowerShell Modules shortcut, which is found in Control Panel, System and Security, Administrative Tools.

> **NOTE**
>
> By default, modules are not loaded into any PowerShell session. To load modules by default, the Import-Module cmdlet should be used in conjunction with a PowerShell profile configuration script.

### Removing a Module

The act of removing a module causes all the commands added by a module to be deleted from the current PowerShell session. When a module is removed, the operation only reverses the Import-Module cmdlet's actions and does not uninstall the module from a machine. To remove a module, use the Remove-Module cmdlet, as shown here:

```
PS C:\> Remove-Module ActiveDirectory
```

## Using Remoting

When using remoting, three different modes can be used to execute commands. These modes are as follows:

- ▶ **1 to 1**—Referred to as Interactive mode. This mode enables you to remotely manage a machine similar to using an SSH session.

- ▶ **Many to 1**—Referred to as the Fan-In mode. This mode allows multiple administrators to manage a single host using an interactive session.

- ▶ **1 to Many**—Referred to as the Fan-Out mode. This mode allows a command to execute across a large number of machines.

More information about each mode is provided in the following sections.

### Interactive Remoting

With interactive remoting, the PowerShell session you are executing commands within looks and feels very much like an SSH session, as shown in the following example:

```
PS C:\> enter-pssession abc-util01
[abc-util01]: PS C:\Users\administrator.COMPANYABC\Documents>
```

The key to achieving this mode of remoting is a PowerShell feature called a runspace. Runspaces by definition are instances of the System.Management.Automation class, which defines the PowerShell session and its host program (Windows PowerShell host, cmd.exe, and so on). In other words, a runspace is an execution environment in which PowerShell runs.

Not widely discussed in PowerShell 1.0, runspaces in PowerShell 2.0 are the method by which commands are executed on local and remote machines. When a runspace is created, it resides in the global scope and it is an environment upon itself, which includes its own properties, execution polices, and profiles. This environment persists for the lifetime of the runspace, regardless of the volatility of the host machine's environment.

Being tied to the host program that created it, a runspace ceases to exist when the host program is closed. When this happens, all aspects of the runspace are gone, and you can no longer retrieve or use the runspace. However, when created on a remote machine, a runspace will remain until it is stopped.

To create a runspace on a machine, you can use two cmdlets. The first cmdlet, Enter-PSSession, is used to create an interactive PowerShell session. This is the cmdlet that was shown in the previous example. When this cmdlet is used against a remote machine, a new runspace (PowerShell process) is created and a connection is established from the local machine to the runspace on the remote computer. If executed against the local machine, a new runspace (PowerShell process) is created and connection is established back to the local machine. To close the interactive session, you would use the Exit-PSSession cmdlet or the exit alias.

### Fan-In Remoting

Fan-In remoting is named in reference to the ability for multiple administrators to open their own runspaces at the same time. In other words, many administrators can "Fan-In" from many machines into a single machine. When connected, each administrator is then limited to the scope of their own runspace. This partitioning of access can be achieved thanks to the new PowerShell 2.0 security model, which allows for the creation of restricted shells and cmdlets.

However, the steps needed to fully utilize the new security model require a degree of software development using the .NET Framework. The ability of being able to provide secure partitioned remote management access on a single host to a number of different administrators is a very powerful feature. Usage could range from a web hosting company wanting to partition remote management access to each customer for each of their websites to internal IT departments wanting to consolidate their management consoles on a single server.

### Fan-Out Remoting

Fan-Out remoting is named in reference to the ability to issue commands to a number of remote machines at once. When using this method of remoting, command(s) are issued on your machine. These commands then "Fan-Out" and are executed on each of the remote machines that have been specified. The results from each remote machine are then returned to your machine in the form of an object, which you can then review or further work with—in other words, the basic definition for how remoting was defined earlier in this chapter.

Ironically enough, PowerShell has always supported the concept of Fan-Out remoting. In PowerShell 1.0, Fan-Out remoting was achieved using WMI. For example, you could always import a list of machine names and then use WMI to remotely manage those machines:

```
PS C:\> import-csv machineList.csv | foreach {Get-WmiObject Win32_
➥NetworkAdapterConfiguration -computer $_.MachineName}
```

Although the ability to perform Fan-Out remoting in PowerShell 1.0 using WMI was a powerful feature, this form of remoting suffered in usability because it was synchronous in nature. In other words, once a command had been issued, it was executed on each remote machine one at a time. While this happened, further command execution had to wait until the command issued had finished being executed on all the specified remote machines.

Needless to say, attempting to synchronously manage a large number of remote machines can prove to be a challenging task. To address this challenge in PowerShell 2.0, the product team tweaked the remoting experience such that Fan-Out remoting could be done asynchronously. With these changes, you could still perform remote WMI management, as shown in the previous example. However, you can also asynchronously execute remote commands using the following methods:

▶ Executing the command as a background job

▶ Using the Invoke-Command cmdlet

▶ Using the Invoke-Command cmdlet with a reusable runspace

The first method, a background job, as its name might suggest, allows commands to be executed in the background. Although not truly asynchronous, a command that is executed as a background job enables you to continue executing additional commands while the job is being completed. For example, to run the previously shown WMI example as a background job, you can simply add the AsJob parameter for the Get-WmiObject cmdlet:

```
PS C:\> import-csv machineList.csv | foreach {Get-WmiObject Win32_
➥NetworkAdapterConfiguration -computer $_.MachineName -asjob}
```

With the AsJob parameter (new in PowerShell 2.0) being used, each time the Get-WmiObject cmdet is called in the foreach loop, a new background job is created to complete execution of the cmdlet. Although more details about background jobs are provided later in this chapter, this example shows how background jobs can be used to achieve asynchronous remote command execution when using WMI.

The second method to asynchronously execute remote commands is by using the new cmdlet called Invoke-Command. This cmdlet is new in PowerShell 2.0, and it enables you to execute commands both locally and remotely on machines—unlike WMI, which uses remote procedure calls (RPC) connections to remotely manage machines. The Invoke-Command cmdlet utilizes WinRM to push the commands out to each of the specified "targets" in an asynchronous manner.

To use the cmdlet, two primary parameters need to be defined. The first parameter, ScriptBlock, is used to specify a scriptblock, which contains the command to be executed. The second parameter, ComputerName (NetBIOS name or IP address), is used to specify the machine or machines to execute the command that is defined in the script-block. For example:

```
PS C:\> invoke-command -scriptblock {get-process} -computer sc1-infra01,sc1-infra02
```

Additionally, the Invoke-Command cmdlet also supports a set of parameters that make it an even more powerful vehicle to conduct remote automation tasks with. These parameters are described in Table 21.4.

TABLE 21.4    Important Invoke-Command Cmdlet Parameters

| Parameter | Details |
| --- | --- |
| AsJob | Used to execute the command as a background job |
| Credential | Used to specify alternate credentials that are used to execute the specified command(s) |
| ThrottleLimit | Used to specify the maximum number of connections that can be established by the Invoke-Command cmdlet |
| Session | Used to execute the command in the specified PSSessions |

As discussed previously, the AsJob parameter is used to execute the specified command as a background job. However, unlike the Get-WmiObject cmdlet, when the AsJob parameter is used with the Invoke-Command cmdlet, a background job is created on the client machine, which then spawns a number of child background job(s) on each of the specified remote machine(s). Once execution of a child background job is finished, the result(s) are returned to the parent background job on the client machine.

Needless to say, if there are a large number of remote machines defined using the ComputerName parameter, the client machine might become overwhelmed. To help prevent the client machine or your network from drowning in an asynchronous connection storm, the Invoke-Command cmdlet will, by default, limit the number of concurrent remote connections for an issued command to 32. If you want to tweak the number of concurrent connections allowed, you would use the ThrottleLimit parameter.

**NOTE**

The ThrottleLimit parameter can also be used with the New-PSSession cmdlet.

An important concept to understand when using the Invoke-Command cmdlet is how it actually executes commands on a remote machine. By default, this cmdlet will set up temporary runspace for each of the targeted remote machine(s). Once execution of the specified command has finished, both the runspace and the connection resulting from that runspace are closed. This means, irrespective of how the ThrottleLimit parameter is used, if you are executing a number of different commands using the Invoke-Command cmdlet at the same time, the actual number of concurrent connections to a remote machine is the total number of times you invoked the Invoke-Command cmdlet.

Needless to say, if you want to reuse the same existing connection and runspace, you need to use the Invoke-Command cmdlet's Session parameter. However, to make use of the parameter requires an already existing runspace on the targeted remote machine(s). To create a persistent runspace on a remote machine, you would use the New-PSSession cmdlet, as shown in the following example:

```
PS C:\> new-pssession -computer "sc1-infra01","sc1-ad01"
```

After executing the previous command, two persistent runspaces on each of the specified targets will have been created. These runspaces can then be used to complete multiple commands and even share data between those commands. To use these runspaces, you need to retrieve the resulting runspace object(s) using the Get-PSSession cmdlet and then pass it into the Invoke-Command cmdlet. For example:

```
PS C:\> $Sessions = new-pssession -computer "sc1-infra01","sc1-ad01"
PS C:\> invoke-command -scriptblock {get-service "W32Time"} -session $Sessions ¦ ft
PSComputerName, Name, Status
```

| PSComputerName | Name | Status |
| --- | --- | --- |
| sc1-ad01 | W32Time | Running |
| sc1-infra01 | W32Time | Running |

First, the `$Sessions` variable is used to store the two resulting runspace objects that are created using the New-PSSession cmdlet. Next, the `$Sessions` variable is then defined as the argument for the `Session` parameter of the Invoke-Command cmdlet. By doing this, the command that is defined as the argument for the `ScriptBlock` parameter is executed within each of the runspaces represented by the `$Sessions` variable. Finally, the results from the command executed within each of the runspaces is returned and piped into the Format-Table cmdlet to format the output. In this case, the output shows the current status of the W32Time service on each of the specified remote machines.

After you have finished executing commands, it's important to understand that the runspaces that were created will remain open until you close the current PowerShell console. To free up the resources being consumed by a runspace, you need to delete it using the Remove-PSSession cmdlet. For example, to remove the runspaces contained in the $Sessions variable, you would pass that variable into the Remove-PSSession cmdlet:

```
PS C:\> $Sessions ¦ remove-pssession
```

## Using the New-Object Cmdlet

The New-Object cmdlet is used to create both .NET and COM objects. To create an instance of a .NET object, you simply provide the fully qualified name of the .NET class you want to use, as shown here:

```
PS C:\> $Ping = new-object Net.NetworkInformation.Ping
```

By using the New-Object cmdlet, you now have an instance of the Ping class that enables you to detect whether a remote computer can be reached via Internet Control

Message Protocol (ICMP). Therefore, you have an object-based version of the Ping.exe command-line tool.

To an instance of a COM object, the comObject parameter is used. To use this parameter, define its argument as the COM object's programmatic identifier (ProgID), as shown here:

```
PS C:\> $IE = new-object -comObject InternetExplorer.Application
PS C:\> $IE.Visible=$True
PS C:\> $IE.Navigate("www.cnn.com")
```

# Summary

In this chapter, you have been introduced to PowerShell, its features, concepts, and how it can be used to manage Windows. Of all the topics and items covered in this chapter, the most important concept that should be remembered is that PowerShell should not be feared—rather, it should be used. The PowerShell team has produced a CLI shell that is easy and fun to use. With practice, using PowerShell should become second nature.

After all, the writing is on the wall. With the inclusion of PowerShell in the Windows Server 2008 R2 operating system and with the integration into its next generation of products, Microsoft's direction is toward embracing PowerShell. This trend toward all things PowerShell is even clearer when looking at all the community-based projects and third-party products being developed and released that use or enhance PowerShell. After all, PowerShell is the answer that Microsoft has been seeking as the management interface for Windows and its platform products. Thanks to a good feature set, which includes being built around the .NET Framework, being object based, being developed with security in mind, and so on, PowerShell is a powerful tool that should be part of any administrator's arsenal.

# Best Practices

The following are best practices from this chapter:

- ▶ If a function needs to persist across PowerShell sessions, define that function within your profile.ps1 file.

- ▶ To access block information about a base, use the BaseObject property with the PSBase standard name.

- ▶ When naming a variable, don't use special characters or spaces.

- ▶ When using aliases and variables in a script, use names that other people can understand.

- ▶ If possible, try not to use aliases in a script.

- ▶ In a production environment, don't configure the PowerShell execution policy as unrestricted and always digitally sign your scripts.

- ▶ If built-in PowerShell cmdlets don't meet your needs, always remember that you can fall back onto existing automation interfaces (ADSI, WMI, COM, and so forth).

# CHAPTER 22

# Documenting a Windows Server 2008 R2 Environment

As technology advances, we, as implementers, work to learn it, understand it, and figure out how to use it to make our environments more reliable, more secure, and help end users be more productive. We upgrade from one version of an application to the next, and although some of the technology becomes obsolete, the need for accurate documentation remains the same.

Documentation serves several purposes throughout the life cycle of the Windows Server 2008 R2 operating system and is especially important for the planning and execution of a Windows Server 2008 R2 implementation project. In the initial stages of a project, it serves to provide a historical record of the options and decisions made during the design process. During the testing and implementation phases, documents such as step-by-step procedures and checklists guide project team members and help ensure that all steps are completed. When the implementation portion of the project is complete, support documentation plays a key role in maintaining the health of the new environment. Support documents include administration and maintenance procedures, checklists, detailed configuration settings, and monitoring procedures.

This chapter is dedicated to providing the breadth and scope of documentation for a Windows Server 2008 R2 environment. Equally important, it provides considerations and best practices for keeping your messaging environment well documented, maintained, and manageable.

# Benefits of Documentation

Documentation that is developed with specific goals, and goes through a review or approval process, is typically well organized, complete, and contributes to the overall professionalism of the organization and its knowledge base. The following sections examine some of the other benefits of professional documentation in the Windows Server 2008 R2 environment.

## Organizational Benefits

Many of the benefits of documenting your Windows Server 2008 R2 environment are obvious and tangible. Documentation is an integral part of the installation or design of a Windows Server 2008 R2 environment as well as the maintenance, support, and recovery of new or existing environments.

Other benefits can be harder to identify. For example, the process of putting the information down on paper encourages a higher level of analysis and review of the topic at hand. The process also encourages teamwork and collaboration within an organization and interdepartmental exchange of ideas.

In today's world of doing more with less, the intangible benefits of good documentation can become a challenge to justify to upper management. Some key benefits of documentation include the following:

▶ **Collaboration**—Producing the documentation to support a good Windows Server 2008 R2 implementation requires input from departments across the organization. This teamwork encourages deeper analysis and more careful review of the project goals. With better base information, the project team can make more informed decisions and avoid having to go back to the drawing board to address missed objectives.

▶ **Historical records**—Implementation projects are composed of several different stages during which goals are identified and key decisions are made to support them. It is important to make sure these decisions and their supporting arguments are recorded for future reference. As the project moves forward, it is not uncommon for details to get changed because of incomplete information being passed from the design stage onto the implementation stage.

▶ **Training**—Life is ever changing. That might sound a bit philosophical for a book on technology, but when it comes to people, we know that some of them move on to other challenges. And that is when good documentation becomes an invaluable tool to provide information to their replacement. This is equally true for the executive sponsor, the project manager, or the engineer building the Windows server.

## Financial Benefits

Proper Windows Server 2008 R2 documentation can be time consuming and adds to the cost of a project. In addition, ongoing costs can come up for maintenance and disaster recovery documents. In lean economic times for a company or organization, it is often difficult to justify the expense of project documentation. However, when looking at documents for maintenance or disaster recovery scenarios, it is easy to see that creating this documentation makes financial sense. For example, in an organization where downtime can cost thousands of dollars per minute, the return on investment (ROI) in disaster recovery and maintenance documentation is easy to calculate. In a company that is growing rapidly and adding staff and new servers on a regular basis, tested documentation on server builds and administration training can also have immediate and visible benefits.

Financial benefits are not limited to maintenance and disaster recovery documentation. Well-developed and professional design and planning documentation helps the organization avoid costly mistakes in the implementation or migration process, such as buying too many server licenses or purchasing too many servers.

## Types of Documents

Each document should be created with a specific goal in mind and knowledge of the target audience. The following list specifies the main document categories that are used to implement a Windows Server 2008 R2 project and maintain the environment:

- ▶ Historical/planning (who made which decision and how we will manage the project)

- ▶ Support and maintenance (to assist with maintaining the hardware and software on the network)

- ▶ Policy (service-level agreements)

- ▶ Training (for end users or administrators)

It is important that any documentation produced be reviewed by other stakeholders in the organization to make sure that it meets their needs as well, and to simply get input from other sources. For technical procedures, the document must be tested and validated. Ideally, the procedures are written by one resource and validated by one of the target users, be it an end user or one of the administrators. With a review process of this sort, the document will be more useful and more accurate. For example, a server build document that has gone through this process is more likely to be complete and useful in the event the server in question needs to be rebuilt in an emergency.

Documentation that is not historical and that is intended to be used for supporting the network environment or to educate on company policies should be reviewed periodically to make sure that it is still accurate and reflects current corporate policies and processes.

The discipline of creating effective documentation that satisfies the requirements of the appropriate support personnel as well as management is also an asset to the company and can have dramatic effects. The material in this chapter gives a sense of the range of different documents that can have value to an organization and should help in the process of deciding which ones are critical in the organization.

# Planning to Document the Windows Server 2008 R2 Environment

When planning documentation (whether for general purposes, specific aspects such as disaster recovery, or a particular project), several factors should be considered:

▶ The business requirements of the organization

▶ The technical requirements of the organization

▶ The audience that will be using the documents

▶ How and when the documents will be produced and maintained

The extent of the documentation depends on the business and technical requirements of the organization. Some organizations require that each step be documented, and other organizations require that only the configuration be recorded. Careful consideration should be given to any regulatory requirements or existing internal organization policies.

After the specific documentation requirements have been determined, it is important to consider who the audience for each document will be. Who will use each document, in what setting, and for what purpose? It would be impractical to develop a 300-page user guide when all the user wants to do is log on to the messaging system. In that case, all that would be required is a quick reference guide. Properly analyzing the purpose and goals of each document aids in the development of clear and useful documentation.

Planning the schedule for document production often requires a separate project timeline or plan. The plan should include checkpoints, sponsorship or management review, and a clear schedule. Tools such as Microsoft Project facilitate the creation of a documentation project plan. The project plan can also provide an initial estimate of the number of hours required and the associated costs. For instance, based on previous documentation projects, there is an estimate that one to two pages per hour will be produced.

# Knowledge Sharing and Knowledge Management

Knowledge sharing is about making the enterprise documentation available to the people who are going to use it. The right documentation enables an organization to organize and manage its data and intellectual property. Company policies and procedures are typically located across multiple locations that include individual files for various departments. Consolidating this information into logical groupings makes it easier to locate for day-to-day usage as well as updating the documents in a timely manner.

> **TIP**
>
> Place documentation in at least two different locations where it is easily accessible for authorized users, such as on the intranet, in a public folder, or in hard-copy format. Also consider using a document management system such as Microsoft Office SharePoint Server 2007.

A complete design document consolidates and summarizes key discussions and decisions, budgetary concerns, and timing issues. This consolidation provides a single source of information for questions that might emerge at a later date. In addition, a document that describes the specific configuration details of the Windows server might prove very valuable to a manager in another company office when making a purchasing decision.

Knowledge management is about keeping the information contained in the documents updated and relevant to the most current environment as well as archiving the historical documentation. All of the documents should be readily available at all times. This is especially critical regarding disaster recovery documents. Centralizing the documentation and communicating the location helps reduce the use of out-of-date documentation and reduce confusion during disaster recovery. It is also recommended that documentation be available in a number of formats, such as hard copy, the appropriate place on the network, and even via an intranet.

**TIP**

Add review and updating of configuration and procedural documents into the recurring maintenance tasks list. This will help keep the task at the forefront of the administrator's responsibilities and ensure the documents are up to date when the time comes to use them.

# Windows Server 2008 R2 Project Documents

A Windows Server 2008 R2 implementation is a complex endeavor that should be approached in phases. First and foremost, a decision should be made on how the project will be tracked. This can be done using a simple Microsoft Excel spreadsheet, but a tool like Microsoft Project will make mapping out the tasks much easier. Also, the first round of mapping out a project will most likely have at most 15 to 20 lines of tasks. Using a tool like Microsoft Project makes it easier to fill in more line items as you progress in the design and planning stages.

With the tracking method in place, you can move on to address the documents that are typically created for a Windows Server 2008 R2 implementation:

- Project plan
- Design and planning document
- Communication plan
- Migration plan
- Training plan
- Test plan

- ▶ Pilot test plan

- ▶ Support and project completion document

This chapter discusses each of these documents individually and outlines their key elements.

## Project Plan

A project plan is essential for more complex migrations and can be useful for managing smaller projects, even single-server migrations. Tasks should be laid out in the order in which they will occur and be roughly half-day durations or more because a project plan that tries to track a project hour by hour can be overwhelmingly hard to keep up to date.

Tools such as Microsoft Project facilitate the creation of project plans and enable the assignment of one or more resources per task and the assignment of durations and links to key predecessors. The project plan can also provide an initial estimate of the number of hours required from each resource and the associated costs if outside resources are to be used. "What-if" scenarios are easy to create by simply adding resources to more complex tasks or cutting out optional steps to see the effect on the budget.

> **NOTE**
>
> It's a great idea to revisit the original project plan after everything is completed (the baseline) to see how accurate it was. Many organizations fail to take this step and miss the opportunity to learn from the planning process to better prepare for the next time.

## Design and Planning Document

The first step in the implementation of the Windows Server 2008 R2 environment is the development and approval of a design. Documenting this design contributes to the success of the project. The design document records the decisions made during the design process and provides a reference for testing, implementation, and support. The key components to a design document include the following:

- ▶ The goals and objectives of the project

- ▶ The background or what led up to the design

- ▶ The approach that will be used to implement the solution

- ▶ The details of the end state of the project

Goals and objectives can be surprisingly hard to pin down. They need to be detailed and concrete enough to define the results that you want while staying at a high level. For instance, "reduce downtime" is too vague to be considered a functional goal, whereas "implement server clustering with Windows Server 2008 R2 Enterprise Server to reduce downtime to less than five minutes in the case of a single-server failure" is much more specific.

Including the background of meetings and brainstorming sessions that led up to the decisions for the end state of the project provides the groundwork for the detailed designs provided later in the document. For example, a decision might have been made "because the CEO wants it that way," which affects the postmigration environment. Other decisions might have come about after many hours of debates over the particulars and required technical research to come up with the "right" answer. Recording this level of information can be extremely useful in the future if performance issues are encountered or additional changes to the network are being considered.

The description of the end state to be implemented can be very high level or can drill down to more specific configurations of each server, depending on the document's audience. However, it is recommended that the design document not include step-by-step procedures or other details of how the process will be accomplished. This level of detail is better handled, in most cases, in dedicated configuration or training documents as discussed later in this chapter.

The Windows Server 2008 R2 design and planning document is the outcome of the design sessions held with the subject matter expert (SME) and the technical staff within the organization. A standard Windows Server 2008 R2 design and planning document will contain the following information:

- ▶ Executive Summary
  - ▶ Project Overview
- ▶ Project Organization
  - ▶ Resources
  - ▶ Costs
- ▶ Risk Assessment
- ▶ Goals and Objectives
- ▶ Active Directory Architecture
  - ▶ Design
  - ▶ Domain Design
  - ▶ Placeholder Root
  - ▶ Namespace
  - ▶ Organizational Unit Design
  - ▶ Group Design
  - ▶ Site Design
  - ▶ Group Policy Design
- ▶ Mixed Mode Versus Native Mode
- ▶ AD Services Design
  - ▶ Domain Controller (DC) Placement
  - ▶ Global Catalog (GC) Placement

- ▶ DNS, DDNS, and Integration

- ▶ Platform Selection and Alternatives

- ▶ Autosite Coverage

- ▶ WINS Placement

- ▶ Flexible Single Master Operations (FSMO) Role Placement

- ▶ DC Sizing

- ▶ Client Performance

- ▶ Service-Level Agreements

▶ Replication Topology

   - ▶ Site Link Topology

   - ▶ Site Link Bridges

   - ▶ Costs

   - ▶ Cost Formula = 1024/log (bw)

   - ▶ Schedule

   - ▶ Latency/Convergence Time

   - ▶ Traffic

▶ Transport: IP/RPC Versus SMTP

   - ▶ Knowledge Consistency Checker (KCC) and Complexity Equation

   - ▶ Connection Creation—Automatic Versus Scripted Versus Manual

▶ Active Directory Database Sizing

   - ▶ Domain Database

   - ▶ Global Catalog

   - ▶ Attributes

   - ▶ Exchange 2007/2010 Extensions

▶ Security Model

   - ▶ Groups

   - ▶ Administrators

   - ▶ Domain Administrators

   - ▶ Schema Administrators

   - ▶ Enterprise Administrators

   - ▶ DNS Administrators

- ▶ Administrative Model
  - ▶ Delegation
  - ▶ Group Policy
  - ▶ Default Domain
  - ▶ Default Domain Controller
  - ▶ Security Templates
- ▶ Directory Integration
  - ▶ Existing Windows Environments
  - ▶ LDAP
  - ▶ NDS
  - ▶ AD
- ▶ Application Integration
- ▶ Desktop Clients
  - ▶ Existing Windows Clients
  - ▶ UNIX
  - ▶ Apple Mac
  - ▶ PDAs
  - ▶ Group Policy and Lockdown
  - ▶ Group Policy Application
  - ▶ Templates

## Communication Plan

The detail of the communication plan depends on the size of the organization and management requirements. From the project management perspective, the more communication the better! This is especially important when a project touches all aspects of the server environment.

Mapping out the how, when, and who to communicate with allows the project team to prepare well-thought-out reports and plan productive meetings and presentations. This also provides the recipients of the reports the chance to review the plan and set their expectations. Once again, there are no surprises for the project team or the project sponsors.

A good communication plan should include the following topics:

- ▶ Audience
- ▶ Content

▶ Delivery method

▶ Timing and frequency

Table 22.1 gives an example of a communication plan. To make the plan more detailed, columns can be added to list who is responsible for the communication and specific dates for when the communication is delivered.

TABLE 22.1    Communication Plan

| Audience | Content (Message) | Delivery Method | Timing Stage/Frequency |
|----------|-------------------|-----------------|------------------------|
| Executive sponsor | Project status | Written report | Weekly in email |
| Project team | Project status | Verbal updates | Weekly in meeting |
| IT department | Project overview | Presentation | Quarterly meeting |

## Migration Plan

After the design and planning document has been mapped out, the project team can begin planning the logistics of implementing Windows Server 2008 R2. This document will be a guide that contains the technical steps needed to implement Windows Server 2008 R2 from the ground up. This document will go into great detail on the specific steps for migration. Depending on how the migration team is set up, it might also include logistical instructions, such as the following:

▶ Communication templates

▶ Location maps

▶ Team roles and responsibilities during the implementation

In a large organization, a session or sessions will be held to develop the migration plan. An agenda for the development of the plan will look something like this:

▶ Goals and Objectives

▶ Project Management

    ▶ Phase I—Design/Planning

    ▶ Phase II—Prototype

    ▶ Phase III—Pilot

    ▶ Phase IV—Implement

    ▶ Phase V—Support

    ▶ Timeline

    ▶ Resource Requirements

- ▶ Risk Management

- ▶ Iterative Refinement of Plan

▶ Migration Planning—Active Directory

- ▶ In-Place Versus Restructuring

- ▶ Account Domains

- ▶ Resource Domains

- ▶ Active Directory Migration Tool (ADMT)

- ▶ DNS Integration

▶ Deployment Tools

- ▶ Scripting

- ▶ Built-in

- ▶ Third-party

▶ Building

- ▶ Normalize Environment

- ▶ Data Center First

- ▶ Deployment Strategies

- ▶ Staged Versus Scripted Versus Manual

▶ Documentation

- ▶ Design

- ▶ Plan

- ▶ Build Guides

- ▶ Migration Guides

- ▶ Administration Guides

- ▶ Maintenance Guides

- ▶ As Builts

- ▶ Disaster Recovery Guides

- ▶ User Guides

▶ Training

- ▶ Users

- ▶ Administrators

▸ Migration Team

▸ Technical Experts

▸ Communications

  ▸ Migration Team

  ▸ Executives and Management

  ▸ Administrators

  ▸ Users

  ▸ Methods

  ▸ Frequency

  ▸ Detail Level

▸ Administration and Maintenance

  ▸ Administration

  ▸ Maintenance

  ▸ Disaster Recovery

  ▸ Guides

  ▸ Periodic Schedules

  ▸ Daily/Weekly/Monthly

  ▸ Planned Downtime

  ▸ Checklists

▸ Testing

Note that many of the agenda topics are stated in a way that facilitates discussion. This is a great way to organize discussion points and at the same time keep them on track.

**NOTE**

The results of testing the design in a prototype or pilot might alter the actual migration steps and procedures. In this case, the migration plan document should be modified to take these changes into account.

### Server Migration Procedures

High-level migration procedures should be decided on during a design and planning process and confirmed during a prototype/testing phase. The initial migration document also should focus on the tools that will be used to migrate data, users, and applications, as well as the division of labor for these processes.

A draft of the document can be put together, and when the process is tested again, it can be verified for accuracy. When complete, this information can save you a great deal of time if a number of servers need to be migrated.

> **TIP**
>
> Server migration procedures should be written in such a way so that even less-experienced staff members can use the procedures for the actual migrations.

The procedures covered can include the following:

- ▶ Server hardware configuration details
- ▶ Windows Server 2008 R2 version for each server
- ▶ Service pack (SP) and hotfixes to install on each server
- ▶ Services (such as DNS and DHCP) to enable or disable and appropriate settings
- ▶ Applications (such as antivirus and SQL Server) to install and appropriate settings
- ▶ Security settings
- ▶ Steps required to migrate services and data to the new server(s)
- ▶ Steps required to test the new configuration to ensure full functionality
- ▶ Steps required to remove old servers from production

### Desktop Migration Procedures

As with the documented server migration process, the desktop migration process should be discussed in the design and planning phase and documented in the migration document. In some migrations, the changes might be minimal, whereas other migrations might require dramatic upgrades. For instance, a desktop machine might qualify for an in-place upgrade to Windows 7, whereas another might require hardware or system replacement.

What specifically is documented will vary among organizations; however, the recommended areas to consider documenting are as follows:

- ▶ Hardware inventory
- ▶ Installation method(s), such as Remote Installation Services, third-party imaging software, and network-based installations
- ▶ Base installation applications
- ▶ Security configuration
- ▶ Templates being used
- ▶ Language options
- ▶ Accessibility considerations

### User Migration Procedures

Users and their related information (username, password, and contact information) in other systems or directories need to be migrated to take advantage of Windows Server 2008 R2. The procedures to migrate the users should be examined during the design and planning phases of the project.

User information can exist in many different places such as an Active Directory (AD) domain, an application, and more. The user information might be inconsistent depending on where it exists and how it is stored. Procedures should be documented for migrating the user information from each different location. For example, if some users will be migrated from another operating system or from multiple forests, separate procedures should be documented for each process.

Another scenario to document is the migration of user profiles and desktops. Although some of this information might be redundant with desktop migration scenarios, it is nonetheless important to capture the procedures for making sure that, when clients log on after the migration, all their settings still exist and they won't have any problems with the applications they use. This is a very important consideration for mobile users. For instance, will mobile users need to come back into the office to have settings changed or migrated? Will these changes be performed the next time they log on?

## Checklists

The migration process can often be a long process, based on the amount of data that must be migrated. It is very helpful to develop both high-level and detailed checklists to guide the migration process. High-level checklists determine the status of the migration at any given point in the process. Detailed checklists ensure that all steps are performed in a consistent manner. This is extremely important if the process is being repeated for multiple sites.

## Training Plan

When creating a training plan for a Windows Server 2008 R2 implementation, the first thing that needs to be identified is the target audience. That will determine what type of training needs to be developed. Some of the user groups that need to be targeted for training are as follows:

▶ **End users**—If the implementation is going to change the desktop client, the end user will have to receive some level of training.

▶ **Systems administrators**—The personnel involved in the administration of the messaging systems will need to be trained.

▶ **Help desk**—In organizations where the support is divided among different teams, each one will have to be trained on the tasks they will be carrying out.

▶ **Implementation team**—If the implementation is spread across multiple locations, some project teams choose to create implementation teams. These teams will need to be trained on the implementation process.

After the different groups have been identified, the training plan for each one can be created. The advantage of creating a training plan in-house is the ability to tailor the training to the organization's unique Windows environment. The trainees will not have to go over configurations or settings that do not apply to their network.

As a special note, if the systems administrators and implementation team members can be identified ahead of time, it is wise to have them participate in the prototype stage.

The implementation team can assist by validating procedures and, through the repetitive process, can become more familiar with the procedures. After the prototype environment is set up, administrators and help desk personnel can come in to do the same for the administrative procedures.

This provides the necessary validation process and also allows the systems groups to become more comfortable with the new tools and technology.

## Test Plan

Thorough testing is critical in the success of any implementation project. A test plan details the resources required for testing (hardware, software, and lab personnel), the tests or procedures to perform, and the purpose of the test or procedure.

It is important to include representatives of every aspect of the network in the development of the test plan. This ensures that all aspects of the Windows Server 2008 R2 environment or project and its impact will be included in the test plan.

### Prototype Test Plan

Going in to the prototype stage, experienced engineers and project managers are aware that the initial plan will probably have to be modified because of reasons such as application incompatibility, administrative requirements, or undocumented aspects of the current environment.

So, if it was important to start out this stage with a well-documented plan, the most important documentation goal for the prototype is to track these changes to ensure that the project still meets all goals and objectives of the implementation.

The document tool the project team will use to do this is the test plan. A well-developed test plan will contain a master test plan and provide the ability to document the test results for reference at a later date. This is necessary because the implementation procedures will likely have changes from the first round of testing to the next and the project team will need to refer to the outcome to compare results.

A test plan outline will contain the following:

- ▶ Summary of what is being tested and the overall technical goals of the implementation
- ▶ Scope of what will be tested
- ▶ Resources Needed
    - ▶ Hardware
    - ▶ Software
    - ▶ Personnel

▶ Documentation

  ▶ What will be recorded

  ▶ Test Plan Outline

▶ Operating System

  ▶ Hardware Compatibility

  ▶ Install First Domain Controller

  ▶ Test Replication

  ▶ Install Additional Domain Controllers

  ▶ Client Access

  ▶ Role-Based Configuration

  ▶ DNS

  ▶ DHCP

  ▶ IIS

  ▶ Domain Controller

  ▶ Exchange

  ▶ Group Policy

  ▶ New Settings

  ▶ Group Policy Management Console

  ▶ Resultant Set of Policies

  ▶ Antivirus

  ▶ Password Policy

  ▶ Security Templates

  ▶ File Migration

  ▶ Print Migration

  ▶ Distributed File System

  ▶ Volume Shadow Copy

  ▶ Remote Assistance

  ▶ UPS Battery Backup Software

  ▶ Applications Testing

  ▶ Backup and Restore

    ▶ Monitoring Software (Systems Center Operations Manager 2007)

    ▶ Administrative Rights

Each individual test should be documented in a test form listing the expected outcome and the actual outcome. This becomes part of the original test plan and is used to validate the implementation procedure or document a change.

Table 22.2 shows a sample test form.

TABLE 22.2    Sample Test Form

| **Test Name** |
| --- |
| Hardware requirements: |
| Software requirements: |
| Other requirements: |
| Expected outcome: |
| Actual outcome: |
| Tester: |
| Date: |

At the end of the stage, it should be clearly documented what, if anything, has changed. The documentation deliverables of this stage are as follows:

    ▶ Pilot implementation plan

    ▶ Implementation plan

    ▶ Rollback plan

## Pilot Test Plan

Documenting a pilot implementation has special requirements because it is the first time the implementation will touch the production environment. If the environment is a complex one where multiple applications are affected by the implementation, all details should be documented along with the outcome of the pilot.

This is done by having a document similar in content to the test plan form and tracking any issues that come up.

In extreme cases, the project team will have to put into effect the rollback plan. Before starting the pilot implementation, the team should have an escalation process along with contact names and numbers of the personnel with the authority to make the go-no-go decision in a given situation.

## Support and Project Completion Document

A Windows Server 2008 R2 implementation should include a plan for handing off administration to the personnel who will be supporting the environment after the implementation is complete. This is especially true if the subject matter experts are brought in to implement the Windows Server 2008 R2 infrastructure and will not be remaining onsite to support it.

The handoff plan should be included in the original project plan and have a timeline for delivery of the administrative documentation as well as training sessions if needed.

# Administration and Maintenance Documents

Administration and maintenance documentation can be critical in maintaining a reliable network environment. These documents help the administrator of a particular server or set of servers organize and keep track of the different steps that need to be taken to ensure the health of the systems under his or her care. They also facilitate the training of new resources and reduce the variables and risks involved in these transitions.

Windows Server 2008 R2 systems can serve several different functions on the network, such as file servers, print servers, web servers, messaging servers, terminal servers, and remote access servers. The necessary maintenance procedures might be slightly different for each one based on its function and importance in the network.

One key component to administration or maintenance documentation is a timeline detailing when certain procedures should be followed. As Chapter 20, "Windows Server 2008 R2 Management and Maintenance Practices," discusses, certain daily, weekly, monthly, and quarterly procedures should be followed. These procedures, such as weekly event log archiving, should be documented to make sure that there are clearly defined procedures and frequency in which they should be performed.

## Step-by-Step Procedure Documents

Administration and maintenance documentation contains a significant amount of procedural documentation. These documents can be very helpful for complex processes, or for processes that are not performed on a regular basis. Procedures range from technical processes that outline each step to administrative processes that help clarify roles and responsibilities.

Flowcharts from Microsoft Visio or a similar product are often sufficient for the administrative processes, such as when testing a new patch to a key software application, approving the addition of a new server to the network, or scheduling network downtime.

## Policies

Although policy documents might not be exciting reading, they can be an administrator's best friend in touchy situations. A well-thought-out, complete, and approved policy document makes it very clear who is responsible for what in specific situations. It's also important to be realistic about which policies need to be documented and what is excessive—for example, document policies concerning when and how the servers can be updated with patches, newer hardware, or software.

## Documented Checklists

Administration and maintenance documentation can be extensive, and checklists can be quick reminders for those processes and procedures. Develop comprehensive checklists that will help administrators perform their scheduled and unscheduled tasks. A timeline checklist highlighting the daily, weekly, monthly, and quarterly tasks helps keep the Windows Server 2008 R2 environment healthy. In addition, these checklists function as excellent auditing tools.

## Active Directory Infrastructure

Active Directory is one of the core services for a Windows Server 2008 R2 environment. As such, documenting the AD infrastructure is a critical component to the environment. There are many aspects to documents as they relate to AD, including, but not limited to, the following:

- ▶ Forest and domain structure, such as DNS names, NetBIOS names, mode of operation, and trust relationships
- ▶ Names and placement of domain controllers (DCs) and global catalog (GC) servers
- ▶ Flexible Single Master Operations (FSMO) locations on DCs or GCs
- ▶ Sites, site links, link costs, and site link bridges
- ▶ Organizational unit (OU) topology
- ▶ Special schema entries (such as those made by applications)
- ▶ Security groups and distribution lists
- ▶ AD-integrated DNS information
- ▶ AD security
- ▶ Group Policy Object (GPO) configurations and structure

This information can be extremely useful in day-to-day operations, as well as when you're troubleshooting AD issues, such as replication latency or logon problems.

## Server Build Procedures

The server build procedure is a detailed set of instructions for building the Windows Server 2008 R2 system. This document can be used for troubleshooting and adding new servers, and is a critical resource in the event of a disaster.

The following is an example of a table of contents from a server build procedure document:

Windows Server 2008 R2 Build Procedures

- System Configuration Parameters
- Configure the Server Hardware
    - Install Vendor Drivers
    - Configure RAID
- Install and Configure Windows Server 2008 R2
    - Using Images
    - Scripted Installations
- Applying Windows Server 2008 R2 Security
    - Using a Security Template
    - Using GPOs
    - Configuring Antivirus
    - Installing Service Packs and Critical Updates
- Backup Client Configuration

## Configuration (As Built) Documentation

The configuration document, often referred to as an as built, details a snapshot configuration of the Windows Server 2008 R2 system as it is built. This document contains essential information required to rebuild a server.

The following is a Windows Server 2008 R2 as built document template:

**Introduction**

The purpose of this Windows Server 2008 R2 as built document is to assist an experienced network administrator or engineer in restoring the server in the event of a hardware failure. This document contains screenshots and configuration settings for the server at the time it was built. If settings are not implicitly defined in this document, they are assumed to be set to defaults. It is not intended to be a comprehensive disaster recovery with step-by-step procedures for rebuilding the server. For this document to remain useful as a recovery aid, it must be updated as configuration settings change.

- System Configuration
    - Hardware Summary
    - Disk Configuration
    - Logical Disk Configuration
    - System Summary

- ▶ Device Manager

- ▶ RAID Configuration

- ▶ Windows Server 2008 R2 TCP/IP Configuration

- ▶ Network Adapter Local Area Connections

- ▶ Security Configuration

  - ▶ Services

  - ▶ Lockdown Procedures (Checklist)

  - ▶ Antivirus Configuration

- ▶ Share List

- ▶ Applications and Configurations

## Topology Diagrams

Network configuration diagrams and related documentation generally include local area network (LAN) connectivity, wide area network (WAN) infrastructure connectivity, IP subnet information, critical servers, network devices, and more. Having accurate diagrams of the new environment can be invaluable when troubleshooting connectivity issues. For topology diagrams that can be used for troubleshooting connectivity issues, consider documenting the following:

- ▶ Internet service provider contact names, including technical support contact information

- ▶ Connection type (such as frame relay, ISDN, OC-12)

- ▶ Link speed

- ▶ Committed Information Rate (CIR)

- ▶ Endpoint configurations, including routers used

- ▶ Message flow and routing

## Administration Manual

The administration manual is the main tool for the administrative group. All of the Windows tasks are documented with details specific to the organization. A well-prepared administration manual can also be used for training new administrators.

## Using Documentation for Troubleshooting Purposes

Troubleshooting documentation is helpful both in terms of the processes that the company recommends for resolving technical issues, as well as documenting the results of actual troubleshooting challenges. Often, companies have database and trouble-ticket processes in place to record the time a request was made for assistance, the process followed, and the results. This information should then be available to the appropriate support staff so they know the appropriate resolution if the problem comes up again.

Organizations might also choose to document troubleshooting methodologies to use as training aids and also to ensure that specific steps are taken as a standard practice for quality of service to the user community.

## Procedural Documents

Although security policies and guidelines comprise the majority of security documentation, procedures are equally as important. Procedures include not only the initial configuration steps, but also maintenance procedures and more important procedures that are to be followed in the event of a security breach.

Additional areas regarding security that can be documented include, but are not limited to, the following:

- ▶ Auditing policies, including review
- ▶ Service packs (SPs) and hotfixes
- ▶ Certificates and certificates of authority
- ▶ Antivirus configurations
- ▶ BitLocker
- ▶ Password policies (such as length, strength, age)
- ▶ GPO security-related policies
- ▶ Registry security
- ▶ Lockdown procedures

# Network Infrastructure

Network configuration documentation is essential when you're designing technologies that might be integrated into the network, when managing network-related services such as DNS, when administering various locations, and when troubleshooting. Network environments usually don't change as much as a server infrastructure. Nonetheless, it's important to keep this information current and accurate through periodic reviews and analysis.

## Documenting the WAN Infrastructure

Network configuration documentation also includes WAN infrastructure connectivity. Consider documenting the following:

- ▶ Internet service provider contact names, including technical support contact information
- ▶ Connection type (such as frame relay, ISDN, OC-12)

- ▶ Link speed

- ▶ Committed Information Rate (CIR)

- ▶ Endpoint configurations, including routers used

Enterprise networks can have many different types of WAN links, each varying in speed and CIR. This documentation is useful not only for understanding the environment, but also for troubleshooting connectivity, replication issues, and more.

## Network Device Documentation

Network devices such as firewalls, routers, and switches use a proprietary operating system. Also, depending on the device, the configuration should be documented. Some devices permit configuration dumps to a text file that can be used in the overall documentation, whereas others support web-based retrieval methods. In worst-case scenarios, administrators must manually document the configurations.

Network device configurations, with possibly the exception of a firewall, rarely change. If a change does occur, it should be documented in a change log and updated in the network infrastructure documentation. This allows administrators to keep accurate records of the environment and also provides a quick, documented way to rebuild the proper configurations in case of a failure.

> **NOTE**
>
> Step-by-step procedures for rebuilding each network device are recommended. This information can minimize downtime and administration.

# Disaster Recovery Documentation

Creating and maintaining a disaster recovery plan for the Windows Server 2008 R2 infrastructure requires the commitment of IT managers as well as the systems administrators in charge of the messaging systems. This is because creating a disaster recovery plan is a complex process and, after it is developed, the only way of maintaining it is by practicing the procedures on a regular schedule. This will, of course, involve the administrative personnel and should be worked into their scheduled tasks.

The initial steps of creating the DR plan will involve determining what the desired recovery times are. Then, the team will move on to discuss possible disaster scenarios and map out a plan for each one. The following table of contents outlines the different topics that are addressed when creating the DR plan.

- ▶ Executive Summary or Introduction

- ▶ Disaster Recovery Scenarios

- ▶ Disaster Recovery Best Practices

    - ▶ Planning and Designing for Disaster

▶ Business Continuity and Response

    ▶ Business Hours Response to Emergencies

    ▶ Recovery Team Members

    ▶ Recovery Team Responsibilities

    ▶ Damage Assessment

    ▶ Off-hours Response to an Emergency

    ▶ Recovery Team Responsibilities

    ▶ Recovery Strategy

    ▶ Coordinate Equipment Needs

▶ Disaster Recovery Decision Tree

▶ Software Recovery

▶ Hardware Recovery

▶ Server Disaster Recovery

▶ Preparation

    ▶ Documentation

    ▶ Software Management

    ▶ Knowledge Management

▶ Server Backup

    ▶ Client Software Configuration

▶ Restoring the Server

    ▶ Build the Server Hardware

    ▶ Post Restore

▶ Active Directory Disaster Recovery

    ▶ Disaster Recovery Service-Level Agreements

    ▶ Windows Server 2008 R2 Disaster Recovery Plan

    ▶ Complete RAID-5 Failure

    ▶ Complete RAID-1 Failure

    ▶ Complete System Failure

    ▶ NIC, RAID Controller Failures

▶ Train Personnel and Practice Disaster Recovery

Every organization should go through the process of contemplating various disaster scenarios. For instance, organizations on the West Coast might be more concerned with earthquakes than those on the East Coast. Each disaster can pose a different threat. Therefore, it's important to determine every possible scenario and begin planning ways to minimize those disasters.

Equally important is analyzing how downtime resulting from a disaster might affect the company (reputation, time, productivity, expenses, loss in profit or revenue) and determine how much should be invested in remedies to avoid or minimize the effects.

A number of different components make up disaster recovery documentation. Without this documentation, full recovery is difficult at best.

## Disaster Recovery Planning

The first step of the disaster recovery process is to develop a formal disaster recovery plan. This plan, while time consuming to develop, serves as a guide for the entire organization in the event of an emergency. Disaster scenarios, such as power outages, hard drive failures, and even earthquakes, should be addressed. Although it is impossible to develop a scenario for every potential disaster, it is still helpful to develop a plan to recover for different levels of disaster. It is recommended that organizations encourage open discussions of possible scenarios and the steps required to recover from each one. Include representatives from each department because each department will have its own priorities in the event of a disaster. The disaster recovery plan should encompass the organization as a whole and focus on determining what it will take to resume normal business function after a disaster.

## Backup and Recovery Development

Another important component of a disaster recovery development process is the evaluation of the organization's current backup policies and procedures. Without sound backup policies and procedures, a disaster recovery plan is useless. It is not possible to recover a system if the backup is not valid.

Backup procedures encompass not only backing up data to tape or other media, but also a variety of other tasks, including advanced system recovery, offsite storage, and retention. These tasks should be carefully documented to accurately represent what backup methodologies are implemented and how they are carried out. Step-by-step procedures, guidelines, policies, and more can be documented.

Periodically, the backup documents should be reviewed and tested, especially after any configuration changes. Otherwise, backup documents can become stale and can only add more work and add to the problems during recovery attempts.

Recovery documentation complements backup documentation. This documentation should include where the backup data resides and how to recover from various types of failures (such as hard drive failure, system failure, and natural disaster). As with backup documentation, recovery documentation can take the form of step-by-step guides, policies, frequently asked questions (FAQs), and checklists. Moreover, recovery documents should be reviewed for validity and revised if necessary.

### Monitoring and Performance Documentation

Monitoring is not typically considered a part of disaster recovery documentation. However, alerting mechanisms can detect and bring attention to issues that might arise. Alerting mechanisms can provide a proactive means to determining whether a disaster might strike. Documenting alerting mechanisms and the actions to take when an alert is received can reduce downtime and administration.

### Windows System Failover Documentation

Organizations using failover technologies or techniques such as clustering or network load balancing (NLB) can benefit from having documentation regarding failover. When a system fails over, knowing the procedures to get the system back up and running quickly can help you avoid unnecessary risk. These documented procedures must be thoroughly tested and reviewed in a lab setting so that they accurately reflect the process to recover each system.

## Change Management Procedures

Changes to the environment occur all the time in an organization, yet often those changes are either rarely documented or no set procedures are in place for making those changes. IT personnel not responsible for the change might be oblivious to those changes, and other administration or maintenance might be adversely affected.

Documented change management seeks to bring knowledge consistency throughout IT, control when and how changes are made, and minimize disruption from incorrect or unplanned changes. As a result, documenting change procedures should entail the processes to request and approve changes, the high-level testing procedures, the actual change procedures, and any rollback procedures in case problems arise.

## Performance Documentation

Documenting performance-related information is a continuous process because of the ever-changing metrics of business. This type of documentation begins by aligning with the goals, existing policies, and service-level agreements (SLAs) for the organization. When these areas are clearly defined and detailed, baseline performance values can be established using System Monitor, System Center Operations Manager (SCOM), or third-party tools (such as PerfMon and BMC Patrol). Performance baselines capture performance-related metrics, such as how much memory is being used, the average processor utilization, and more; they also illustrate how the Windows Server 2008 R2 environment is performing under various workloads.

After the baseline performance values are documented and understood, the performance-related information that the monitoring solution is still capturing should be analyzed periodically. More specifically, pattern and trend analysis needs to be examined on a weekly basis if not on a daily basis. This analysis can uncover current and potential bottlenecks and proactively ensure that the system operates as efficiently and effectively as possible.

# Baselining Records for Documentation Comparisons

Baselining is a process of recording the state of a Windows Server 2008 R2 system so that any changes in its performance can be identified at a later date. Complete baselining also pertains to the overall network performance, including WAN links, but in those cases it might require special software and tools (such as sniffers) to record the information.

A Windows Server 2008 R2 system baseline document records the state of the server after it is implemented in a production environment and can include statistics such as memory use, paging, disk subsystem throughput, and more. This information then allows the administrator or appropriate IT resource to determine at a later date how the system is performing in comparison to its initial operation.

# Routine Reporting

Although System Monitor can log performance data and provide reporting when used with other products such as Microsoft Excel, it behooves administrators to use products such as SCOM for monitoring and reporting functionality. For example, SCOM can manage and monitor multiple systems and provide graphical reports with customizable levels of detail.

## Management-Level Reporting

Management-level reporting on performance data should be concise and direct but still at a high level. Stakeholders don't require an ample amount of performance data, but it's important to show trends, patterns, and any potential problem areas. This extremely useful information provides a certain level of insight to management so that decisions can be made as to what is required to keep the systems operating in top-notch condition. For instance, administrators identify and report to management that, if current trends on Windows Server 2008 R2 server processor utilization continue at the current rate of a 5% increase per month, this will require additional processors in 10 months or less. Management can then take this report, follow the issue more closely over the next few months, and then determine whether to allocate funds to purchase additional processors. If the decision is made to buy more processors, management has more time to negotiate quantity, processing power, and cost instead of having to potentially pay higher costs for the processors on short notice.

## Technical Reporting

Technical performance information reporting is much more detailed than management-level reporting. Details are given on many different components and facets of the system. For example, many specific counter values can be given to determine disk subsystem utilization. In addition, trend and pattern analysis should also be included to show historical information and determine how to plan for future requirements.

# Security Documentation

Administrators can easily feel that documenting security settings and other configurations is important but that this documentation might lessen security mechanisms in the Windows Server 2008 R2 environment. Nevertheless, documenting security mechanisms and corresponding configurations is vital to administration, maintenance, and any potential security compromise.

As with many of the documents about the network environment, they can do a lot of good for someone either externally or internally trying to gain unauthorized access. So, security documentation and many other forms of documentation, including network diagrams, configurations, and more, should be well guarded to minimize any security risk.

Some areas regarding security that should be documented include, but aren't limited to, the following:

- ▶ Auditing policies including review
- ▶ Service packs (SPs) and hotfixes
- ▶ Certificates and certificates of authority
- ▶ Firewall and proxy configurations
- ▶ Antivirus configurations
- ▶ Access control policies, including NTFS-related permissions
- ▶ BitLocker
- ▶ Password policies (such as length, strength, and age)
- ▶ GPO security-related policies
- ▶ Registry security
- ▶ Security breach identification procedures
- ▶ Lockdown procedures

## Change Control

Although the documentation of policies and procedures to protect the system from external security risks is of utmost importance, internal procedures and documents should also be established. Developing, documenting, and enforcing a change-control process helps protect the system from well-intentioned internal changes.

In environments with multiple administrators, it is very common to have the interests of one administrator affect those of another. For instance, an administrator might make a configuration change to limit volume size for a specific department. If this change is not documented, a second administrator might spend a significant amount of time trying to troubleshoot a user complaint from that department. Establishing a change-control process that documents these types of changes eliminates confusion and wasted resources. The change-control process should include an extensive testing process to reduce the risk of production problems.

### Reviewing Reports

A network environment might have many security mechanisms in place, but if the information such as logs and events obtained from them isn't reviewed, security is more relaxed. Monitoring and management solutions (such as SCOM) can help consolidate this information into a report that can be generated on a periodic basis. This report can be invaluable to continuously evaluating the network's security.

The reports should be reviewed daily and should include many details for the administrators to analyze. SCOM, for example, can be customized to report on only the most pertinent events for keeping the environment secure.

### Management-Level Reporting for Security Assessments

Management should be informed of any unauthorized access or attempts to compromise security. The technical details that an administrator appreciates are usually too detailed for management. Therefore, management-level reporting on security issues should contain only vital statistics and any risks that might be present. Business policy and budget-related decisions can then be made to strengthen the environment's security.

## Summary

Most, if not all, aspects of a Windows Server 2008 R2 network environment can be documented. However, the type of documentation that can benefit the environment depends on each organization. Overall, documenting the environment is an important aspect of the network and can assist all aspects of administration, maintenance, support, troubleshooting, testing, and design.

## Best Practices

The following are best practices from this chapter:

- ▶ Create documents that target a specific audience and meet a particular goal.

- ▶ Have documentation reviewed and approved by other stakeholders in the organization to make sure that it meets their needs as well, and to simply get input from another source. For technical procedures, the document also must be tested and walked through.

▶ Consolidate and centralize documentation for the organization.

▶ Document the company's policies and procedures for securing and maintaining the Windows environment.

▶ Create well-thought-out and professional planning and design documentation to avoid costly mistakes in the implementation or migration process, such as buying too many server licenses or purchasing too many servers.

▶ Baseline and document the state of a Windows Server 2008 R2 server so that any changes in its performance can be identified at a later date.

▶ Use tools such as Microsoft Project to facilitate the creation of project plans, enable the assignment of one or more resources per task, and enable the assignment of durations and links to key predecessors.

▶ Create disaster recovery documentation that includes step-by-step procedures for rebuilding each server and network device to minimize downtime and administration.

▶ Document daily, weekly, monthly, and quarterly maintenance tasks to ensure the health of the systems.

▶ Use documentation to facilitate training.

▶ Document business and technical policies for the organization.

▶ Establish a plan for reviewing and updating documents and make it a part of routine maintenance.

# CHAPTER 23

# Integrating System Center Operations Manager 2007 R2 with Windows Server 2008 R2

System Center Operations Manager (OpsMgr) 2007 R2 provides the best-of-breed approach to monitoring and managing Windows Server 2008 R2 within the environment. OpsMgr helps to identify specific environmental conditions before they evolve into problems through the use of monitoring and alerting components.

OpsMgr provides a timely view of important Windows Server 2008 R2 conditions and intelligently links problems to knowledge provided within the monitoring rules. Critical events and known issues are identified and matched to technical reference articles in the Microsoft Knowledge Base for troubleshooting and quick problem resolution.

The monitoring is accomplished using standard operating system components such as Windows Management Instrumentation (WMI), Windows event logs, and Windows performance counters, along with Windows Server 2008 R2 specific API calls and scripts. OpsMgr-specific components are also designed to perform synthetic transaction and track the health and availability of network services. In addition, OpsMgr provides a reporting feature that allows administrators to track problems and trends occurring on the network. Reports can be generated automatically, providing network administrators, managers, and decision makers with a current and long-term historical view of environmental trends. These reports can be delivered via email or stored on file shares for archive to power web pages.

The following sections focus on defining OpsMgr as a monitoring system for Windows Server 2008 R2. This chapter provides specific analysis of the way OpsMgr

operates and presents OpsMgr design best practices, specific to deployment for Windows
Server 2008 R2 monitoring.

# Windows Server 2008 R2 Monitoring

The Operations Manager 2007 R2 monitoring is organized into management packs (MPs)
for ease of installation and versioning. The Operations Manager 2007 R2 includes some of
the best management packs for monitoring and maintaining Windows Server 2008 R2.
These include the following:

- Windows Server Operating System MPs

- Active Directory Server MPs

- Windows Cluster Management MPs

- Microsoft Windows DNS Server MPs

- Microsoft Windows DHCP Server MPs

- Microsoft Windows Group Policy MPs

- Microsoft Windows Hyper-V MPs

- Windows Server Internet Information Services MPs

- Windows Server Network Load Balancing MPs

- Windows Server Print Server MPs

- Windows Terminal Services MPs

Each of the preceding categories includes several different management packs to support
monitoring, discovery, and libraries. These management packs were developed by the
product groups and include deep knowledge about the product.

The features of the management packs for the following major systems are as follows:

- **Windows Operating System Management Pack**—Monitors and alerts all the
  major elements that Windows Server 2008 R2 runs on, including processor, memory,
  network, disk, and event logs. It gathers performance metrics and alerts on thresholds, as well as critical events.

- **Active Directory Management Pack**—Monitors and alerts on Active Directory key
  metrics, such as replication latency, domain controller response times, and critical
  events. The management pack generates synthetic transactions to test the response
  time of the PDC, LDAP, and other domain services.

- **DNS Management Pack**—Monitors and alerts on DNS servers for resolution failures and latency as well as critical events.

- **IIS Management Pack**—Monitors and alerts on IIS services, application pools, performance, and critical events.

On all these elements, administrators can generate Availability reports to ensure that the servers and systems are meeting the service-level agreements (SLAs) set by the organization.

The management pack includes a comprehensive set of reports that are specific to Windows Server 2008 R2. These include reports on performance, availability, events, and even configuration for the various Windows Server 2008 R2 roles. These reports can be generated ad hoc, scheduled for email delivery on a regular basis, or even generated into web pages for portal viewing. Figure 23.1 shows a Performance report for a server. The report shows that processor utilization is low and that memory utilization is steady, with regular skips of activity in the pages per sec, which correspond to available memory dips.

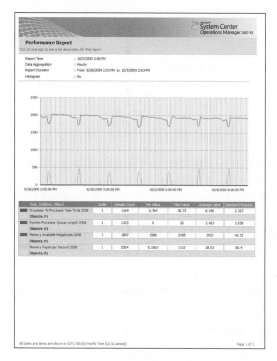

FIGURE 23.1    Sample Performance report.

This kind of summary Performance report is invaluable to reporting on the Windows Server 2008 R2 infrastructure and really ties together the low-level technical monitoring into a high-level view that support personnel can use.

# What's New in OpsMgr R2

System Center Operations Manager 2007 R2 was released in the spring of 2009 and includes many new improvements on the previous version, Operations Manager 2007 Service Pack 1. Some of these improvements include the following:

- **Cross-platform support**—This is support for non-Microsoft platforms, such as UNIX and Linux. This allows administrators to have a single-pane view of their entire IT environment in OpsMgr.

- **Integration with System Center Virtual Machine Manager 2008**—This integrates with the VMM 2008 and allows synergies such as Performance Resource and Optimization (PRO) Tips, which provides virtual machine recommendations based on observed performance and the ability to implement the recommendation at the click of a button.

- **Notifications**—The notification system has been revamped and now sports an Outlook rule style interface. Notifications can be generated for specific alerts and can be sent out as high-priority emails.

- **Overrides view**—Rather than hunt for overrides within all the management packs, OpsMgr R2 has an authoring view that shows all the overrides defined in the system.

- **Improved Management Pack maintenance**—OpsMgr 2007 R2 allows Microsoft management packs to be browsed, downloaded, and imported directly from the console. It even includes versioning and dependency checks, as well as the ability to search from management pack updates.

- **Service-level monitoring**—Applications can be defined from various monitored objects and the service level of the application can be monitored and reported on against defined target SLAs.

- **Better scaling of URL monitoring**—The URL monitor will now scale to thousands of websites without undue performance impact.

- **Improved database performance**—The overall performance of the database and console has been dramatically improved.

These improvements bring the platform to a new level of performance and interoperability, while retaining the look and feel of the original Operations Manager 2007 tool.

# Explaining How OpsMgr Works

OpsMgr is a sophisticated monitoring system that effectively allows for large-scale management of mission-critical servers. Organizations with a medium to large investment in Microsoft technologies will find that OpsMgr allows for an unprecedented ability to keep on top of the tens of thousands of event log messages that occur on a daily basis. In its simplest form, OpsMgr performs two functions: processing monitored data and issuing alerts and automatic responses based on that data.

The model-based architecture of OpsMgr presents a fundamental shift in the way a network is monitored. The entire environment can be monitored as groups of hierarchical services with interdependent components. Microsoft, in addition to third-party vendors and a large development community, can leverage the functionality of OpsMgr components through customizable monitoring rules.

OpsMgr provides for several major pieces of functionality, as follows:

▶ **Management packs**—Application-specific monitoring rules are provided within individual files called management packs. For example, Microsoft provides management packs for Windows Server systems, Exchange Server, SQL Server, SharePoint, DNS, DHCP, along with many other Microsoft technologies. Management packs are loaded with the intelligence and information necessary to properly troubleshoot and identify problems. The rules are dynamically applied to agents based on a custom discovery process provided within the management pack. Only applicable rules are applied to each managed server.

▶ **Event monitoring rules**—Management pack rules can monitor for specific event log data. This is one of the key methods of responding to conditions within the environment.

▶ **Performance monitoring rules**—Management pack rules can monitor for specific performance counters. This data is used for alerting based on thresholds or archived for trending and capacity planning. A performance graph shown in Figure 23.2 shows Client GC Search Time data for a couple of domain controllers. There was a brief spike in latency at about 11:00 p.m., but the latency is normally less than 0.1.

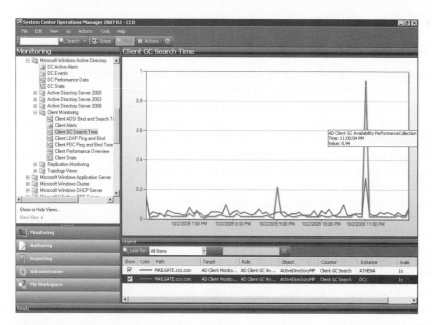

FIGURE 23.2    Operations Manager 2007 R2 performance charts.

▶ **State-based monitors**—Management packs contain monitors, which allow for advanced state-based monitoring and aggregated health rollup of services. Monitors also provide self-tuning performance threshold monitoring based on a two- or three-state configuration.

▶ **Alerting**—OpsMgr provides advanced alerting functionality by enabling email alerts, paging, short message service (SMS), instant messaging (IM), and functional alerting roles to be defined. Alerts are highly customizable, with the ability to define alert rules for all monitored components.

▶ **Reporting**—Monitoring rules can be configured to send monitored data to both the operations database for alerting and the reporting database for archiving.

▶ **End-to-end service monitoring**—OpsMgr provides service-oriented monitoring based on System Definition Model (SDM) technologies. This includes advanced object discovery and hierarchical monitoring of systems.

## Processing Operational Data

OpsMgr manages Windows Server 2008 R2 infrastructures through monitoring rules used for object discovery, Windows event log monitoring, performance data gathering, and application-specific synthetic transactions. Monitoring rules define how OpsMgr collects, handles, and responds to the information gathered. OpsMgr monitoring rules handle incoming event data and allow OpsMgr to react automatically, either to respond to a predetermined problem scenario, such as a failed hard drive, with predefined corrective and diagnostics actions (for example, trigger an alert, execute a command or script) to provide the operator with additional details based on what was happening at the time the condition occurred.

## Generating Alerts and Responses

OpsMgr monitoring rules can generate alerts based on critical events, synthetic transactions, or performance thresholds and variances found through self-tuning performance trending. An alert can be generated by a single event or by a combination of events or performance thresholds. Alerts can also be configured to trigger responses such as email, pages, Simple Network Management Protocol (SNMP) traps, and scripts to notify you of potential problems. In brief, OpsMgr is completely customizable in this respect and can be modified to fit most alert requirements. A sample alert is shown in Figure 23.3. The alert indicates that the domain controller's DNS is incorrectly configured. Also note that there are two information alerts shown, indicating that the domain controller stopped and started.

# Outlining OpsMgr Architecture

OpsMgr is primarily composed of five basic components: the operations database, reporting database, Root Management Server, management agents, and Operations Console. These components make up a basic deployment scenario. Several optional components are

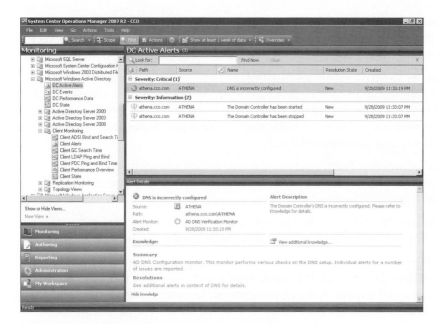

FIGURE 23.3   Operations Manager 2007 R2 alert.

also described in the following bulleted list; these components provide functionality for advanced deployment scenarios.

OpsMgr was specifically designed to be scalable and can subsequently be configured to meet the needs of any size company. This flexibility stems from the fact that all OpsMgr components can either reside on one server or can be distributed across multiple servers.

Each of these various components provides specific OpsMgr functionality. OpsMgr design scenarios often involve the separation of parts of these components onto multiple servers. For example, the database components can be delegated to a dedicated server, and the management server can reside on a second server.

The following list describes the different OpsMgr components:

▶ **Operations database**—The operations database stores the monitoring rules and the active data collected from monitored systems. This database has a 7-day default retention period.

▶ **Reporting database**—The reporting database stores archived data for reporting purposes. This database has a 400-day default retention period.

▶ **Root Management Server**—This is the first management server in the management group. This server runs the software development kit (SDK) and Configuration service and is responsible for handling console communication, calculating the health of the environment, and determining what rules should be applied to each agent.

▶ **Management server**—Optionally, an additional management server can be added for redundancy and scalability. Agents communicate with the management server to deliver operational data and pull down new monitoring rules.

▶ **Management agents**—Agents are installed on each managed system to provide efficient monitoring of local components. Almost all communication is initiated from the agent with the exception of the actual agent installation and specific tasks run from the Operations Console. Agentless monitoring is also available with a reduction of functionality and environmental scalability.

▶ **Operations Console**—The Operations Console is used to monitor systems, run tasks, configure environmental settings, set author rules, subscribe to alerts, and generate and subscribe to reports.

▶ **Web console**—The Web console is an optional component used to monitor systems, run tasks, and manage Maintenance mode from a web browser.

▶ **Audit Collection Services**—This is an optional component used to collect security events from managed systems; this component is composed of a forwarder on the agent that sends all security events, a collector on the management server that receives events from managed systems, and a special database used to store the collected security data for auditing, reporting, and forensic analysis.

▶ **Gateway server**—This optional component provides mutual authentication through certificates for nontrusted systems in remote domains or workgroups.

▶ **Command shell**—This optional component is built on PowerShell and provides full command-line management of the OpsMgr environment.

▶ **Agentless Exception Monitoring**—This component can be used to monitor Windows and application crash data throughout the environment and provides insight into the health of the productivity applications across workstations and servers.

▶ **Connector Framework**—This optional component provides a bidirectional web service for communicating, extending, and integrating the environment with third-party or custom systems.

The Operations Manager 2007 architecture is shown in Figure 23.4, with all the major components and their data paths.

## Understanding How OpsMgr Stores Captured Data

OpsMgr itself utilizes two Microsoft SQL Server databases for all collected data. Both databases are automatically maintained through OpsMgr-specific scheduled maintenance tasks.

The operations database stores all the monitoring rules and is imported by management packs and operational data collected from each monitored system. Data in this database is retained for 7 days by default. Data retention for the operations database is lower than the reporting database to improve efficiency of the environment. This database must be

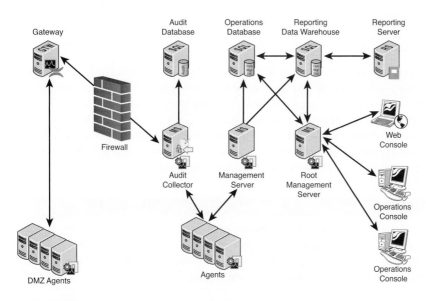

**FIGURE 23.4**   Operations Manager 2007 R2 architecture.

installed as a separate component from OpsMgr but can physically reside on the same server, if needed.

The reporting database stores data for long-term trend analysis and is designed to grow much larger than the operations database. Data in the reporting database is stored in three states: raw data, hourly summary, and daily summary. The raw data is only stored for 14 days, whereas both daily and hourly data are stored for 400 days. This automatic summarization of data allows for reports that span days or months to be generated very quickly.

## Determining the Role of Agents in System Monitoring

The agents are the monitoring components installed on each managed computer. They monitor the system based on the rules and business logic defined in each of the management packs. Management packs are dynamically applied to agents based on the different discovery rules included with each management pack.

## Defining Management Groups

OpsMgr utilizes the concept of management groups to logically separate geographical and organizational boundaries. Management groups allow you to scale the size of OpsMgr architecture or politically organize the administration of OpsMgr.

At a minimum, each management group consists of the following components:

- ▶ An operations database
- ▶ An optional reporting database
- ▶ A Root Management Server

▸ Management agents

▸ Management consoles

OpsMgr can be scaled to meet the needs of different sized organizations. For small organizations, all the OpsMgr components can be installed on one server with a single management group. In large organizations, on the other hand, the distribution of OpsMgr components to separate servers allows the organizations to customize and scale their OpsMgr architecture. Multiple management groups provide load balancing and fault tolerance within the OpsMgr infrastructure. Organizations can set up multiple management servers at strategic locations, to distribute the workload among them.

> **NOTE**
>
> The general rule of thumb with management groups is to start with a single management group and add on more management groups only if they are absolutely necessary. Administrative overhead is reduced, and there is less need to re-create rules and perform other redundant tasks with fewer management groups.

# Understanding How to Use OpsMgr

Using OpsMgr is relatively straightforward. The OpsMgr monitoring environment can be accessed through three sets of consoles: an Operations Console, a Web console, and a command shell. The Operations Console provides full monitoring of agent systems and administration of the OpsMgr environment, whereas the Web console provides access only to the monitoring functionality. The command shell provides command-line access to administer the OpsMgr environment.

## Managing and Monitoring with OpsMgr

As mentioned in the preceding section, two methods are provided to configure and view OpsMgr settings. The first approach is through the Operations Console and the second is through the command shell.

Within the Administration section of the Operations Console, you can easily configure the security roles, notifications, and configuration settings. Within the Monitoring section of the Operations Console, you can easily monitor a quick "up/down" status, active and closed alerts, and confirm overall environment health.

In addition, a web-based monitoring console can be run on any system that supports Microsoft Internet Explorer 6.0 or higher. This console can be used to view the health of systems, view and respond to alerts, view events, view performance graphs, run tasks, and manage Maintenance mode of monitored objects. New to OpsMgr 2007 R2 is the ability to display the Health Explorer in the Web console.

## Reporting from OpsMgr

OpsMgr management packs commonly include a variety of preconfigured reports to show information about the operating system or the specific application they were designed to work with. These reports are run in SQL Reporting Services. The reports provide an effective view of systems and services on the network over a custom period, such as weekly, monthly, or quarterly. They can also help you monitor your networks based on performance data, which can include critical pattern analysis, trend analysis, capacity planning, and security auditing. Reports also provide availability statistics for distributed applications, servers, and specific components within a server.

Availability reports are particularly useful for executives, managers, and application owners. These reports can show the availability of any object within OpsMgr, including a server (shown in Figure 23.5), a database, or even a service such as Windows Server 2008 R2 that includes a multitude of servers and components. The Availability report shown in Figure 23.5 indicates that the SP server was down on 9/29/2009 for about 4.17% of the time or just slightly over 1 hour. The rest of the time it had been up.

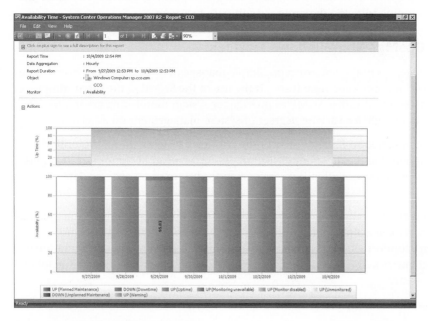

FIGURE 23.5   Availability report.

The reports can be run on demand or at scheduled times and delivered via email. OpsMgr can also generate HTML-based reports that can be published to a web server and viewed from any web browser. Vendors can also create additional reports as part of their management packs.

## Using Performance Monitoring

Another key feature of OpsMgr is the capability to monitor and track server performance. OpsMgr can be configured to monitor key performance thresholds through rules that are set to collect predefined performance data, such as memory and CPU usage over time. Rules can be configured to trigger alerts and actions when specified performance thresholds have been met or exceeded, allowing network administrators to act on potential performance issues. Performance data can be viewed from the OpsMgr Operations Console.

In addition, performance monitors can establish baselines for the environment and then alert the administrator when the counter subsequently falls outside the defined baseline envelope.

## Using Active Directory Integration

Active Directory integration provides a way to install management agents on systems without environmental-specific settings. When the agent starts, the correct environmental settings, such as the primary and failover management servers, are stored in Active Directory. The configuration of Active Directory integration provides advanced search and filter capabilities to fine-tune the dynamic assignment of systems.

## Integrating OpsMgr Non-Windows Devices

Network management is not a new concept. Simple management of various network nodes has been handled for quite some time through the use of the SNMP. Quite often, simple or even complex systems that utilize SNMP to provide for system monitoring are in place in an organization to provide for varying degrees of system management on a network.

OpsMgr can be configured to integrate with non-Windows systems through monitoring of syslog information, log file data, and SNMP traps. OpsMgr can also monitor TCP port communication and website transaction sequencing for information-specific data management.

New to OpsMgr 2007 R2 is the ability to monitor non-Microsoft operating systems such as Linux and UNIX, as well as the applications that run on them such as Apache and MySQL. OpsMgr monitors the file systems, network interfaces, daemons, configurations, and performance metrics. Operations Manager 2007 R2 supports monitoring of the following operating systems:

- ▶ HP-UX 11i v2 and v3 (PA-RISC and IA64)

- ▶ Sun Solaris 8 and 9 (SPARC) and Solaris 10 (SPARC and x86)

- ▶ Red Hat Enterprise Linux 4 (x86/x64) and 5 (x86/x64) Server

- ▶ Novell SUSE Linux Enterprise Server 9 (x86) and 10 SP1 (x86/x64)

- ▶ IBM AIX v5.3 and v6.1

These operating systems are "first-class citizens" in Microsoft's parlance, meaning they are treated as equals with the Windows operating systems. Agents can be pushed from the console, operations data is collected automatically, tasks can run against the agents, and all major functions are supported.

Special connectors can be created to provide bidirectional information flows to other management products. OpsMgr can monitor SNMP traps from SNMP-supported devices as well as generate SNMP traps to be delivered to third-party network management infrastructures.

### Exploring Third-Party Management Packs

Software and hardware developers can subsequently create their own management packs to extend OpsMgr's management capabilities. These management packs extend OpsMgr's management capabilities beyond Microsoft-specific applications. Each management pack is designed to contain a set of rules and product knowledge required to support its respective products. Currently, management packs have been developed for APC, Cisco, Citrix, Dell, F5, HP, IBM, Linux, Oracle, Solaris, UNIX, and VMware to name a few. A complete list of management packs can be found at the following Microsoft site: http://technet. microsoft.com/en-us/opsmgr/cc539535.aspx.

# Understanding OpsMgr Component Requirements

Each OpsMgr component has specific design requirements, and a good knowledge of these factors is required before beginning the design of OpsMgr. Hardware and software requirements must be taken into account, as well as factors involving specific OpsMgr components, such as the Root Management Server, gateway servers, service accounts, mutual authentication, and backup requirements.

### Exploring Hardware Requirements

Having the proper hardware for OpsMgr to operate on is a critical component of OpsMgr functionality, reliability, and overall performance. Nothing is worse than overloading a brand-new server only a few short months after its implementation. The industry standard generally holds that any production servers deployed should remain relevant for three to four years following deployment. Stretching beyond this time frame might be possible, but the ugly truth is that hardware investments are typically short term and need to be replaced often to ensure relevance. Buying a less-expensive server might save money in the short term but could potentially increase costs associated with downtime, troubleshooting, and administration. That said, the following are the Microsoft-recommended minimums for any server running an OpsMgr 2007 server component:

- ▶ 2.8GHz processor or faster
- ▶ 20GB of free disk space
- ▶ 2GB of random access memory (RAM)

These recommendations apply only to the smallest OpsMgr deployments and should be seen as minimum levels for OpsMgr hardware. More realistic deployments would have the following minimums:

- ▶ 2–4 2.8GHz cores
- ▶ 64-bit Windows operating system
- ▶ 64-bit SQL Server
- ▶ 60GB free disk space on RAID 1+0 for performance
- ▶ 4–8GB RAM

Operations Manager 2007 R2 is one of Microsoft's most resource-intensive applications, so generous processor, disk, and memory are important for optimal performance. Future expansion and relevance of hardware should be taken into account when sizing servers for OpsMgr deployment, to ensure that the system has room to grow as agents are added and the databases grow.

## Determining Software Requirements

OpsMgr components can be installed on either 32-bit or 64-bit versions of Windows Server 2003, Windows Server 2008, or Windows Server 2008 R2. The database for OpsMgr must be run on a Microsoft SQL Server 2005 or Microsoft SQL Server 2008 server. The database can be installed on the same server as OpsMgr or on a separate server, a concept that is discussed in more detail in following sections.

OpsMgr itself must be installed on a member server in a Windows Active Directory domain. It is commonly recommended to keep the installation of OpsMgr on a separate server or set of dedicated member servers that do not run any other applications that could interfere in the monitoring and alerting process.

A few other requirements critical to the success of OpsMgr implementations are as follows:

- ▶ Microsoft .NET Framework 2.0 and 3.0 must be installed on the management server and the reporting server.
- ▶ Windows PowerShell.
- ▶ Microsoft Core XML Services (MSXML) 6.0.
- ▶ WS-MAN v1.1 (for UNIX/Linux clients).
- ▶ Client certificates must be installed in environments to facilitate mutual authentication between nondomain members and management servers.
- ▶ SQL Reporting Services must be installed for an organization to be able to view and produce custom reports using OpsMgr's reporting feature.

## OpsMgr Backup Considerations

The most critical piece of OpsMgr, the SQL databases, should be regularly backed up using standard backup software that can effectively perform online backups of SQL databases. If integrating these specialized backup utilities into an OpsMgr deployment is not possible, it becomes necessary to leverage built-in backup functionality found in SQL Server.

# Understanding Advanced OpsMgr Concepts

OpsMgr's simple installation and relative ease of use often belie the potential complexity of its underlying components. This complexity can be managed with the right amount of knowledge of some of the advanced concepts of OpsMgr design and implementation.

## Understanding OpsMgr Deployment Scenarios

As previously mentioned, OpsMgr components can be divided across multiple servers to distribute load and ensure balanced functionality. This separation allows OpsMgr servers to come in four potential "flavors," depending on the OpsMgr components held by those servers. The four OpsMgr server types are as follows:

▶ **Operations database server**—An operations database server is simply a member server with SQL Server installed for the OpsMgr operations database. No other OpsMgr components are installed on this server. The SQL Server component can be installed with default options and with the system account used for authentication. Data in this database is kept for 7 days by default.

▶ **Reporting database server**—A reporting database server is simply a member server with SQL Server and SQL Server Reporting Services installed. This database stores data collected through the monitoring rules for a much longer period than the operations database and is used for reporting and trend analysis. This database requires significantly more drive space than the operations database server. Data in this database is kept for 13 months by default.

▶ **Management server**—A management server is the communication point for both management consoles and agents. Effectively, a management server does not have a database and is often used in large OpsMgr implementations that have a dedicated database server. Often, in these configurations, multiple management servers are used in a single management group to provide for scalability and to address multiple managed nodes.

▶ **All-in-one server**—An all-in-one server is effectively an OpsMgr server that holds all OpsMgr roles, including that of the databases. Subsequently, single-server OpsMgr configurations use one server for all OpsMgr operations.

## Multiple Configuration Groups

As previously defined, an OpsMgr management group is a logical grouping of monitored servers that are managed by a single OpsMgr SQL database, one or more management servers, and a unique management group name. Each management group established operates completely separately from other management groups, although they can be configured in a hierarchical structure with a top-level management group able to see "connected" lower-level management groups.

The concept of connected management groups allows OpsMgr to scale beyond artificial boundaries and also gives a great deal of flexibility when combining OpsMgr environments. However, certain caveats must be taken into account. Because each management group is an island in itself, each must subsequently be manually configured with individual settings. In environments with a large number of customized rules, for example, such manual configuration would create a great deal of redundant work in the creation, administration, and troubleshooting of multiple management groups.

## Deploying Geographic-Based Configuration Groups

Based on the factors outlined in the preceding section, it is preferable to deploy OpsMgr in a single management group. However, in some situations, an organization needs to divide its OpsMgr environment into multiple management groups. The most common reason for division of OpsMgr management groups is division along geographic lines. In situations in which wide area network (WAN) links are saturated or unreliable, it might be wise to separate large "islands" of WAN connectivity into separate management groups.

Simply being separated across slow WAN links is not enough reason to warrant a separate management group, however. For example, small sites with few servers would not warrant the creation of a separate OpsMgr management group, with the associated hardware, software, and administrative costs. However, if many servers exist in a distributed, generally well-connected geographical area, that might be a case for the creation of a management group. For example, an organization could be divided into several sites across the United States but decide to divide the OpsMgr environment into separate management groups for East Coast and West Coast, to roughly approximate their WAN infrastructure.

Smaller sites that are not well connected but are not large enough to warrant their own management group should have their event monitoring throttled to avoid being sent across the WAN during peak usage times. The downside to this approach, however, is that the reaction time to critical event response is increased.

## Deploying Political or Security-Based Configuration Groups

The less-common method of dividing OpsMgr management groups is by political or security lines. For example, it might become necessary to separate financial servers into a separate management group to maintain the security of the finance environment and allow for a separate set of administrators.

Politically, if administration is not centralized within an organization, management groups can be established to separate OpsMgr management into separate spheres of control. This would keep each OpsMgr management zone under separate security models.

As previously mentioned, a single management group is the most efficient OpsMgr environment and provides for the least amount of redundant setup, administration, and troubleshooting work. Consequently, artificial OpsMgr division along political or security lines should be avoided, if possible.

## Sizing the OpsMgr Database

Depending on several factors, such as the type of data collected, the length of time that collected data will be kept, or the amount of database grooming that is scheduled, the size of the OpsMgr database will grow or shrink accordingly. It is important to monitor the size of the database to ensure that it does not increase well beyond the bounds of acceptable size. OpsMgr can be configured to monitor itself, supplying advance notice of database problems and capacity thresholds. This type of strategy is highly recommended because OpsMgr could easily collect event information faster than it could get rid of it.

The size of the operations database can be estimated through the following formula:

```
Number of agents x 5MB x retention days + 1024 overhead = estimated database size
```

For example, an OpsMgr environment monitoring 1,000 servers with the default 7-day retention period will have an estimated 35GB operations database:

```
(1000 * 5 * 7) + 1024 = 36024 MB
```

The size of the reporting database can be estimated through the following formula:

```
Number of agents x 3MB x retention days + 1024 overhead = estimated database size
```

The same environment monitoring 1,000 servers with the default 400-day retention period will have an estimated 1.1TB reporting database:

```
(1000 * 3 * 400) + 1024 = 1201024 MB
```

It is important to understand that these estimates are rough guidelines only and can vary widely depending on the types of servers monitored, the monitoring configuration, the degree of customization, and other factors.

## Defining Capacity Limits

As with any system, OpsMgr includes some hard limits that should be taken into account before deployment begins. Surpassing these limits could be cause for the creation of new management groups and should subsequently be included in a design plan. These limits are as follows:

▶ **Operations database**—OpsMgr operates through a principle of centralized, rather than distributed, collection of data. All event logs, performance counters, and alerts are sent to a single, centralized database, and there can subsequently be only a single operations database per management group. Considering the use of a backup and high-availability strategy for the OpsMgr database is, therefore, highly recommended, to protect it from outage. It is recommended to keep this database with a 50GB limit to improve efficiency and reduce alert latency.

▶ **Management servers**—OpsMgr does not have a hard-coded limit of management servers per management group. However, it is recommended to keep the environment between three to five management servers. Each management server can support approximately 2,000 managed agents.

▶ **Gateway servers**—OpsMgr does not have a hard-coded limit of gateway servers per management group. However, it is recommended to deploy a gateway server for every 200 nontrusted domain members.

▶ **Agents**—Each management server can theoretically support up to 2,000 monitored agents. In most configurations, however, it is wise to limit the number of agents per management server, although the levels can be scaled upward with more robust hardware, if necessary.

▶ **Administrative consoles**—OpsMgr does not limit the number of instances of the Web and Operations Console; however, going beyond the suggested limit might introduce performance and scalability problems.

## Defining System Redundancy

In addition to the scalability built in to OpsMgr, redundancy is built in to the components of the environment. Proper knowledge of how to deploy OpsMgr redundancy and place OpsMgr components correctly is important to the understanding of OpsMgr redundancy. The main components of OpsMgr can be made redundant through the following methods:

▶ **Management servers**—Management servers are automatically redundant and agents will failover and failback automatically between them. Simply install additional management servers for redundancy. In addition, the RMS system acts as a management server and participates in the fault tolerance.

▶ **SQL databases**—The SQL database servers hosting the databases can be made redundant using SQL clustering, which is based on Windows clustering. This supports failover and failback.

▶ **Root Management Server**—The RMS can be made redundant using Windows clustering. This supports failover and failback.

Having multiple management servers deployed across a management group allows an environment to achieve a certain level of redundancy. If a single management server experiences downtime, another management server within the management group will take over the responsibilities for the monitored servers in the environment. For this reason, it might be wise to include multiple management servers in an environment to achieve a certain level of redundancy if high uptime is a priority.

The first management server in the management group is called the Root Management Server. Only one Root Management Server can exist in a management group and it hosts the software development kit (SDK) and Configuration service. All OpsMgr consoles communicate with the management server so its availability is critical. In large-scale environments, the Root Management Server should leverage Microsoft Cluster technology to provide high availability for this component.

Because there can be only a single OpsMgr database per management group, the database is subsequently a single point of failure and should be protected from downtime. Utilizing Windows Server 2008 R2 clustering or third-party fault-tolerance solutions for SQL databases helps to mitigate the risk involved with the OpsMgr database.

## Monitoring Nondomain Member Considerations

DMZ, Workgroup, and Nontrusted Domain Agents require special configuration; in particular, they require certificates to establish mutual authentication. Operations Manager 2007 R2 requires mutual authentication, that is, the server authenticates to the client and the client authenticates to the server, to ensure that the monitoring communications are not hacked. Without mutual authentication, it is possible for a hacker to execute a man-in-the-middle attack and impersonate either the client or the server. Thus, mutual authentication is a security measure designed to protect clients, servers, and sensitive Active Directory domain information, which is exposed to potential hacking attempts by the all-powerful management infrastructure. However, OpsMgr relies on Active Directory Kerberos for mutual authentication, which is not available to nondomain members.

> **NOTE**
>
> Workgroup servers, public web servers, and Microsoft Exchange Edge Transport role servers are commonly placed in the DMZ and are for security reasons not domain members, so almost every Windows Server 2008 R2 environment will need to deploy certificate-based authentication.

In the absence of Active Directory, trusts, and Kerberos, OpsMgr 2007 R2 can use X.509 certificates to establish the mutual authentication. These can be issued by any PKI, such as Microsoft Windows Server 2008 Enterprise CA. See Chapter 14, "Transport-Level Security," for details on PKI and Windows Server 2008 R2.

Installing agents on DMZ servers is discussed later in this chapter in the section "Monitoring DMZ Servers with Certificates."

# Securing OpsMgr

Security has evolved into a primary concern that can no longer be taken for granted. The inherent security in Windows Server 2008 R2 is only as good as the services that have access to it; therefore, it is wise to perform a security audit of all systems that access information from servers. This concept holds true for management systems as well because

they collect sensitive information from every server in an enterprise. This includes potentially sensitive event logs that could be used to compromise a system. Consequently,
securing the OpsMgr infrastructure should not be taken lightly.

## Securing OpsMgr Agents

Each server that contains an OpsMgr agent and forwards events to management servers
has specific security requirements. Server-level security should be established and should
include provisions for OpsMgr data collection. All traffic between OpsMgr components,
such as the agents, management servers, and database, is encrypted automatically for security, so the traffic is inherently secured.

In addition, environments with high-security requirements should investigate the use of
encryption technologies such as IPSec to scramble the event IDs that are sent between
agents and OpsMgr servers, to protect against eavesdropping of OpsMgr packets.

OpsMgr uses mutual authentication between agents and management servers. This means
that the agent must reside in the same forest as the management server. If the agent is
located in a different forest or workgroup, client certificates can be used to establish
mutual authentication. If an entire nontrusted domain must be monitored, the gateway
server can be installed in the nontrusted domain, agents can establish mutual authentication to the gateway server, and certificates on the gateway and management server are
used to establish mutual authentication. In this scenario, you can avoid needing to place a
certificate on each nontrusted domain member.

## Understanding Firewall Requirements

OpsMgr servers that are deployed across a firewall have special considerations that must
be taken into account. Port 5723, the default port for OpsMgr communications, must
specifically be opened on a firewall to allow OpsMgr to communicate across it.

Table 23.1 describes communication for this and other OpsMgr components.

TABLE 23.1    OpsMgr Communication Ports

| From | To | Port |
| --- | --- | --- |
| Agent | Root Management Server | 5723 |
| Agent | Management server | 5723 |
| Agent | Gateway server | 5723 |
| Agent (ACS forwarder) | Management server ACS collector | 51909 |
| Gateway server | Root Management Server | 5723 |
| Gateway server | Management server | 5723 |
| Management or Gateway server | UNIX or Linux computer | 1270 |
| Management or Gateway server | UNIX or Linux computer | 22 |

TABLE 23.1    OpsMgr Communication Ports

| From | To | Port |
|------|------|------|
| Management server | Operations Manager database | 1433 |
| Management server | Root Management Server | 5723, 5724 |
| Management server | Reporting data warehouse | 1433 |
| Management server ACS collector | ACS database | 1433 |
| Operations Console | Root Management Server | 5724 |
| Operations Console (reports) | SQL Server Reporting Services | 80 |
| Reporting server | Root Management Server | 5723, 5724 |
| Reporting server | Reporting data warehouse | 1433 |
| Root Management Server | Operations Manager database | 1433 |
| Root Management Server | Reporting data warehouse | 1433 |
| Web console browser | Web console server | 51908 |
| Web console server | Root Management Server | 5724 |

The firewall port for the agents is the port that needs to be opened most often, which is only port 5723 from the agent to the management servers for monitoring. Other ports, such as 51909 for ACS, are more rarely needed. Figure 23.6 shows the major communications paths and ports between OpsMgr components.

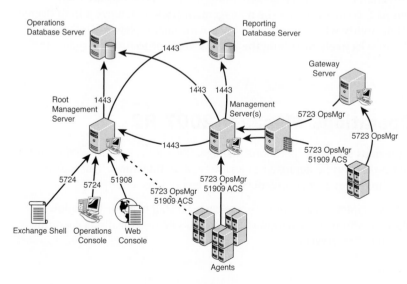

FIGURE 23.6    Communications ports.

## Outlining Service Account Security

In addition to the aforementioned security measures, security of an OpsMgr environment can be strengthened by the addition of multiple service accounts to handle the different OpsMgr components. For example, the Management Server Action account and the SDK/Configuration service account should be configured to use separate credentials, to provide for an extra layer of protection in the event that one account is compromised.

▶ **Management Server Action account**—The account responsible for collecting data and running responses from management servers.

▶ **SDK and Configuration service account**—The account that writes data to the operations database; this service is also used for all console communication.

▶ **Local Administrator account**—The account used during the agent push installation process. To install the agent, local administrative rights are required.

▶ **Agent Action account**—The credentials the agent will run as. This account can run under a built-in system account, such as Local System, or a limited domain user account for high-security environments.

▶ **Data Warehouse Write Action account**—The account used by the management server to write data to the reporting data warehouse.

▶ **Data Warehouse Reader account**—The account used to read data from the data warehouse when reports are executed.

▶ **Run As accounts**—The specific accounts used by management packs to facilitate monitoring. These accounts must be manually created and delegated specific rights as defined in the management pack documentation. These accounts are then assigned as Run As accounts used by the management pack to achieve a high degree of security and flexibility when monitoring the environment. New to OpsMgr 2007 R2 is the ability to selectively distribute the Run As Account to just the agents that need them.

# Installing Operations Manager 2007 R2

As discussed in the previous section, Operations Manager 2007 R2 is a multitier and multi-component application that can be deployed in a variety of architectures. This allows OpsMgr to support scaling from a small organization to a very large enterprise.

For the purposes of this chapter, an all-in-one single-server install is used. This allows for monitoring of small- to medium-sized Windows Server 2008 R2 organizations spanning a handful of servers to up to 250 servers.

## Single-Server OpsMgr 2007 R2 Install

This section steps through the install of OpsMgr and Reporting on a single-server configuration. The specification for a single-server configuration to support up to 250 agent systems is as follows:

- ▶ 2 x 2.8GHz Cores

- ▶ 8GB RAM

- ▶ 4 Drive RAID 0+1 Disk (200+GB Space)

These hardware requirements ensure that the system can perform to specification.

**NOTE**

If the configuration were to be virtualized on a Windows Server 2008 Hyper-V host or a VMware ESX host, a single-server configuration is not recommended. Instead, a two-server configuration is recommended and SQL Server 2008 should be installed on the second server to balance the load.

The steps in this section assume that the single server has been prepared with the following:

- ▶ Windows Server 2008 R2 operating system installed

- ▶ Web role with the appropriate features installed

**NOTE**

To install SQL Reporting Services and the Web components of OpsMgr 2007 R2, the following Windows Server 2008 Web role features need to be installed: Static Content, Default Document, HTTP Redirection, Directory Browsing, ASP, ASP.NET, ISAPI Extension, ISAPI Filters, Windows Authentication, IIS Metabase, and IIS 6 WMI.

- ▶ SQL Server 2008 with Reporting Services installed

- ▶ An OpsMgr service account with local administrator rights to the server and system administrator rights to SQL Server 2008

This prepares the system for the install of OpsMgr 2007 R2. See the following prerequisite checker information for additional requirements and how to check them.

Before installing, it is important to run the built-in prerequisite checker. This utility is available on the OpsMgr installation media and confirms a host of software prerequisites before attempting the actual installation. This gives the administrator time to download and install the necessary software, rather than have the installation bomb out in the middle after entering a lot of configuration information.

This section assumes a Windows Server 2008 and SQL Server 2008 server will be used for the single-server installation, but the prerequisite checker looks at more general requirements based on the OpsMgr supported platforms. The prerequisite checker looks for the following software on a single-server configuration:

▶ Windows Server 2003 Service Pack 1 or Windows Server 2008 Service Pack 1

▶ Microsoft SQL Server 2005 Service Pack 1 or SQL Server 2008 Service Pack 1

▶ Microsoft SQL Server 2005 Reporting Services Service Pack 1 or SQL Server 2008 Reporting Services Service Pack 1

▶ World Wide Web Service is running and set for automatic startup

▶ WS-Management v1.1

▶ MDAC version 2.80.1022.0 or higher

▶ ASP.NET AJAX Extensions 1.0

▶ .NET Framework 2.0 and .NET Framework 3.0 components

▶ Windows PowerShell

▶ Key hotfixes

To use the Prerequisite Viewer for a single-server configuration, run the following steps:

1. Log on with an account that has administrator rights.
2. Insert the Operations Manager 2007 R2 installation media.
3. The setup will start automatically or launch the SetupOM.exe.
4. Click Check Prerequisites to start the Prerequisite Viewer.
5. Select Operational Database, Server, Console, PowerShell, Web Console, Reporting, and Data Warehouse, and then click Check.

> **NOTE**
>
> The prerequisite checker findings will be displayed and will have active links that can be clicked to get specific guidance, as well as links to download software and hotfixes.

6. When you are finished with the Prerequisite Viewer, click Close.

Follow the corrections in the prerequisite checker to resolve any problems before proceeding to the installation. Some of the guidance will be warnings, particularly with some of the hotfixes. Leaving out hotfixes might allow the installation to proceed, but might make the OpsMgr application less stable. It is highly recommended that all the recommendations be applied to ensure the most stable platform possible. If any of the installations require a reboot, it is recommended to run the prerequisite checker again.

Once the server meets all the prerequisites and is ready for installation, the steps to run the install are as follows:

1. Logon with the OpsMgr service account.
2. Launch SetupOM.exe from the OpsMgr installation media.
3. Click Install Operations Manager 2007 R2.
4. Click Next.
5. Accept the license agreement and click Next.
6. Enter the CD key if required and then click Next.
7. When the Custom Setup page displays, leave the components set to their defaults, and then click Next.
8. Type the management group name in the Management Group text box and click Next.
9. Select the instance of SQL Server on which to install the Operations Manager 2007 R2 database (the local system because this is a single-server install), and then click Next.
10. Leave the default database size of 1,000 MB, and then click Next.
11. Select Domain or Local Computer Account, type the user account and password, select the domain or local computer from the list, and then click Next.
12. On the SDK and Config Service Account page, select Domain or Local Account, type the user account and password, select the domain or local computer from the list, and then click Next.
13. On the Web Console Authentication Configuration page, select Use Windows Authentication and click Next.
14. On the Operations Manager Error Reports page, leave the Do You Want to Send Error Reports to Microsoft option cleared and click Next to not send Operations Manager 2007 R2 error reports to Microsoft.
15. On the Customer Experience Improvement Program page, leave the default option of I Don't Want to Join the Program Selected, and then click Next.
16. On the Ready to Install page, click Install.
17. When the Completing the System Center Operations Manager 2007 R2 Setup Wizard page appears, leave the Backup Encryption Key check box selected to back up the encryption key.

**NOTE**

A copy of the encryption key is needed to promote a management server to the role of the Root Management Server in the event of a failure of the RMS.

18. Leave Start the Console selected to open the Operations Console.
19. Click Finish.

Operations Manager 2007 R2 is now installed in a single-server configuration. This configuration can manage up to 250 servers.

## Importing Management Packs

After the initial installation, OpsMgr only includes a few management packs. The management packs contain all the discoveries, monitors, rules, knowledge, reports, and views that OpsMgr needs to be able to effectively monitor servers and applications. One of the first tasks after installing OpsMgr 2007 is to import management packs into the system.

There are a large number of management packs in the Internet catalog on the Microsoft website. These include updated management packs, management packs for new products, and third-party management packs. It is important to load only those management packs that are going to be used, as each additional management pack increases the database size, adds discoveries that impact the performance of agents, and, in general, clutters up the interface.

The key management packs for a Windows Server 2008 R2 environment are as follows:

- ▶ Windows Server Operating System MPs
- ▶ Active Directory Server MPs
- ▶ Windows Cluster Management MPs
- ▶ Microsoft Windows DNS Server MPs
- ▶ Microsoft Windows DHCP Server MPs
- ▶ Microsoft Windows Group Policy MPs
- ▶ Microsoft Windows Hyper-V MPs
- ▶ Windows Server Internet Information Services MPs
- ▶ Windows Server Network Load Balancing MPs
- ▶ Windows Server Print Server MPs
- ▶ Windows Terminal Services MPs
- ▶ SQL Server MPs (to monitor the OpsMgr database roles)

There might be other management packs that are appropriate for the environment, depending on the applications that are installed. For example, if the organization has deployed Exchange Server 2010 and HP Proliant server hardware, it would be good for the organization to deploy the Exchange management packs and the HP Proliant management packs.

For each of these management packs, it is important to load the relevant versions only. For example, if the environment includes Windows Server 2008 only, only load the Windows Server Core OS 2008 management pack. If the environment includes both Windows Server 2003 and Windows Server 2008, load both the Windows Server Core OS

2003 and the Windows Server Core OS 2008. In addition, a number of language packs don't need to be loaded unless those particular languages are supported by the organization at the server level.

Some collections of management packs require that all versions be loaded, but the Management Pack Import Wizard will check and warn if that's the case.

In versions of OpsMgr prior to R2, the management packs had to be downloaded from the Microsoft website one by one, the MSI installed one by one, and the management packs imported one by one. Dependencies would not be checked unless additional steps were taken to consolidate the management pack files prior to importing. This was a very labor-intensive process. Also, there was no easy way for checking for updates to already installed management packs.

In OpsMgr 2007 R2, a new Management Pack Import Wizard was introduced. This wizard connects directly to the Microsoft management pack catalog and will download, check, and import management packs. It even does version checks to ensure that the management packs are the latest versions. This is a huge improvement over the old method of importing management packs.

To import the key management packs, use the following steps:

1. Launch the Operations Console.
2. Select the Administration section.
3. Select the Management Packs folder.
4. Right-click the Management Packs folder and select Import Management Packs.
5. Click the Add button and select Add from Catalog.
6. Click the Search button to search the entire catalog.

**NOTE**

The View pull-down menu in the Management Pack Import Wizard includes four options, which are All Management Packs in the Catalog, Updates Available for Installed Management Packs, All Management Packs Released in the Last 3 Months, and All Management Packs Released in the Last 6 Months. The Updates option checks against the already installed management packs and allows the download of updated versions of those.

7. Select the key management packs from the previous bulleted list and click the Add button for each of them. Each of the major management packs might include a number of submanagement packs for discovery, monitoring, and other breakdowns of functionality.
8. When done adding management packs, click OK.
9. The wizard now validates the added management packs, checking for versions, dependencies, and security risks. It allows problem management packs to be removed and dependencies to be added to the list.

10. Click Install to begin the download and import process. Progress will be shown for each of the management packs being imported.

11. After all the management packs are imported, click Close to exit the wizard.

After the import completes, the management packs take effect immediately. Agents will begin discovering based on the schedule specified in the management packs and monitors and rules will begin deploying.

## Deploying OpsMgr Agents

OpsMgr agents are deployed to all managed servers through the OpsMgr Discovery Wizard, or by using software distribution mechanisms such as Active Directory GPOs or System Center Configuration Manager 2007. Installation through the Operations Console uses the fully qualified domain name (FQDN) of the computer. When searching for systems through the Operations Console, you can use wildcards to locate a broad range of computers for agent installation. Certain situations, such as monitoring across firewalls, can require the manual installation of these components.

The Discovery Wizard can discover and configure monitoring for Windows computers, UNIX/Linux computers, and for network devices. It will push agents to Windows and UNIX/Linux computers, as long as the proper rights are provided, such as an account with local administrator rights or a root account.

To install domain member agents using the Discovery Wizard, run the following steps:

1. Launch the Operations Console and select the Administration section.

2. Right-click the top-level Administration folder and select Discovery Wizard.

3. Select the Windows computers and click Next.

4. Select Automatic Computer Discovery and click Next. This scans the entire Active Directory domain for computers.

5. Leave the Use Selected Management Server Action Account and click Discover. This starts the discovery process.

6. After the discovery process runs (this might take a few minutes), the list of discovered computers is displayed. Select the devices that should have agents deployed to them, as shown in Figure 23.7.

> **NOTE**
>
> The list only includes systems that do not already have agents installed. If a computer has an agent installed, the wizard excludes it from the list of devices.

7. Click Next.

8. Leave the Agent Installation Directory and the Agent Action Account at the defaults, and then click Finish.

9. The Agent Management Task Status window appears, listing all the computers selected and the progress of each installation. As shown in Figure 23.8, the agent installation task started for the selected computers.

10. Click Close when the installation completes.

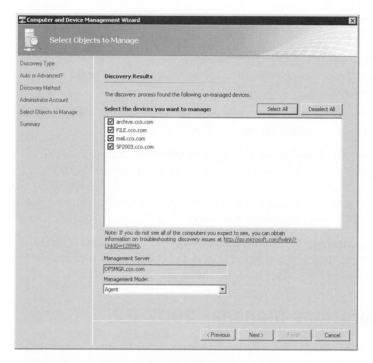

FIGURE 23.7    Discovered computers.

FIGURE 23.8    Agent installation progress.

Even if the window is closed before the installs complete, the results of the installs can be viewed in Task Status view in the Monitoring section of the Operations Console.

The agent deployment is very efficient and a large number of computers can be selected for deployment without any issues. The agents will start automatically and begin to be monitored as they are discovered.

After installation, it might be necessary to wait a few minutes before the information from the agents will be sent to the management server.

During the next few minutes after installation, the agent contacts the management server and establishes a mutually authenticated, encrypted communication channel with the assigned management server. If the agent was pushed through a software delivery system such as System Center Configuration Manager 2007 R2, the agent determines the management server through Active Directory–integrated discovery.

The agent downloads rules to discover the various applications and components it's hosting, allowing the correct application-specific management packs to be applied. This discovery process runs periodically to ensure the correct rules are always applied to the server.

# Configuring Operations Manager 2007 R2

After installing the Operations Manager 2007 R2 infrastructure, several configuration steps should be taken to have the system monitor properly, generate Active Directory synthetic transactions, and send out email notifications of alerts.

## Agent Proxy Configuration

Operations Manager 2007 R2 has a variety of security measures built in to the product to prevent security breaches. One measure in particular is the prevention of impersonation of one agent by another. That is, an agent SERVER1 cannot insert operations data into the database about a domain controller DC1. This could constitute a security violation, where SERVER1 could maliciously generate fraudulent emergencies by making it appear that DC1 was having operational issues.

Although this is normally a good feature, this can be a problem if, in fact, SERVER1 is monitoring DC1 from a client perspective. The Operations Manager infrastructure would reject any information presented about DC1 by SERVER1. When this occurs, the system generates an alert to indicate that an attempt to proxy operations data has occurred. Figure 23.9 shows an example of the alert. In the normal course of events, this alert is not an indication of an attack but rather a configuration problem.

To get around this problem, Agent Proxy can be selectively enabled for agents that need to be able to present operational data about other agents. To enable Agent Proxy for a computer, run the following steps:

1. Open the Operations Manager 2007 R2 console.
2. Select the Administration section.
3. Select the Agent Managed node.

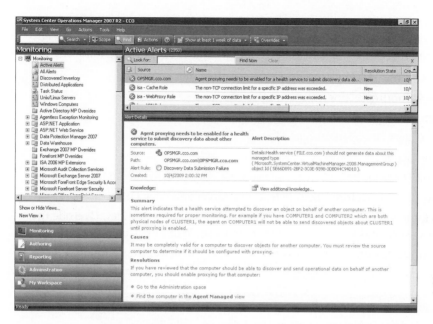

FIGURE 23.9    Agent Proxy alert.

4. Right-click the agent in the right pane and select Properties.

5. Click the Security tab.

6. Check the Allow This Agent to Act as a Proxy and Discover Managed Objects on Other Computers check box.

7. Click OK to save.

Repeat this for all agents that need to act as proxy agents.

---

**NOTE**

Because the alerts generated by this condition are rule-based and not monitor-based, the alert needs to be manually resolved by right-clicking on it and selecting Close Alert.

---

## Active Directory Client Monitoring Configuration

Although monitoring performance of Active Directory services is done by the domain controllers using a variety of measures, sometimes what really matters is how clients perceive the performance of the domain services. To measure that, the Windows Server 2008 Active Directory management pack can generate synthetic transactions from selected client systems. These transactions include ADSI bind and search times, LDAP ping and bind times, global catalog search times, and PDC ping and bind times. The clients execute tests and log the results, as well as alert on slow performance.

The Active Directory Server Client object discovery is disabled by default. The object discovery has to be overridden to discover objects that will then run the rules. To selectively override the Active Directory Server Client object discovery, run the following steps:

1. Open the Operations Manager 2007 R2 console.
2. Select the Authoring section.
3. Expand the Management Pack Object node.
4. Select the Object Discoveries node.
5. Select View, Scope.
6. In the Look For field, type Client Perspective. This narrows down the selections.
7. Check the Active Directory Client Perspective target and click OK.
8. Right-click the AD Client Monitoring Discovery and select Overrides, Override the Object Discovery, and For a Specific Object of Class: Windows Computer.
9. A list of Windows Computer objects will be displayed. Select the computer that will act as an Active Directory client and click OK.

> **NOTE**
>
> The selected Windows Computer should not be a domain controller.

10. Check the Override box next to Enabled and set the value to True.
11. In the Select Destination Management Pack pull-down menu, select the appropriate override management pack. If none exists, create one for the Active Directory management pack by clicking New.

> **NOTE**
>
> Never use the Default Management Pack for overrides. Always create an override management pack that corresponds to each imported management pack.

12. Click OK to save the override.
13. Repeat for each Windows computer that will be an Active Directory Server Client agent.

After a period of time, the selected agents will begin to generate Active Directory client perspective data and alerts. As a best practice, key Exchange servers are often selected as Active Directory Server Client agents. It is also a best practice to select at least one agent in each location to be an Active Directory Server Client agent as well.

## Active Directory Replication Monitoring Configuration

The Active Directory management pack can monitor the replication latency between domain controllers in Active Directory. It uses sources and targets domain controllers, where the source domain controllers create objects in the OpsMgrLatencyMonitors container. These objects are read by the targets, which log performance data in the OpsMgr databases. There will be a replication counter for each domain partition, for the DomainDNSZones partition, and for the ForestDNSZones partition between each source and target pair. There will also be a counter for minimum replication latency and average replication latency.

The Active Directory management pack has the sources and targets disabled by default due to the number of counters that can potentially be created. Overrides need to be created for each source and each target domain controller to get the replication monitoring to function.

It is a best practice to reduce the number of sources and targets to a minimum, due to the number of counters that get created. An example of a source-target model might be to make all branch offices sources and a single central office DC as the target. Another example might be to pick a single DC in each site to be in both the source and target groups, assuming there are a limited number of sites.

The steps to set the source overrides are as follows:

1. Launch the Operations Manager 2007 R2 console.
2. Select the Authoring section.
3. Expand the Management Pack Objects node.
4. Ensure that the console is not scoped for any objects.
5. Select the Rules node.
6. In the Look For field, enter sources and click Find Now.
7. Select the rule "AD Replication Monitoring Performance Collection (Sources)" in the "Type: Active Directory Domain Controller Server 2008 Computer Role".
8. Right-click the rule and select Overrides, Override the Rule, and For a Specific Object of Class: Active Directory Domain Controller Server 2008 Computer Role.
9. The Select Object window opens and shows matching objects. Select the domain controller that will be the source and click OK.
10. Check the Override box next to Enabled and set the value to True.
11. In the Select Destination Management Pack pull-down menu, select the appropriate override management pack. If none exists, create a new management pack named "Active Directory MP Overrides" by clicking New.

> **NOTE**
>
> Never use the Default Management Pack for overrides. Always create an override management pack that corresponds to each imported management pack.

12. Click OK to save the override.
13. Repeat for each domain controller that will be a source.

The steps to set the target overrides are as follows:

1. Launch the Operations Manager 2007 R2 console.

2. Select the Authoring section.

3. Expand the Management Pack Objects node.

4. Ensure that the console is not scoped for any objects.

5. Select the Rules node.

6. In the Look For field, enter targets and click Find Now.

7. Select the rule "AD Replication Monitoring Performance Collection (Targets)" in the "Type: Active Directory Domain Controller Server 2008 Computer Role".

8. Right-click the rule and select Overrides, Override the Rule, and For a Specific Object of Class: Active Directory Domain Controller Server 2008 Computer Role.

9. The Select Object window opens and shows matching objects. Select the domain controller that will be the source and click OK.

10. Check the Override box next to Enabled and set the value to True.

11. In the Select Destination Management Pack pull-down menu, select the appropriate override management pack. Use the same one from the previous steps when selecting the sources.

12. Click OK to save the override.

13. Repeat for each domain controller that will be a target.

After a period of time, monitoring will begin. Counters will be measuring the replication latency between the partitions. In addition, replication latency alerts will be triggered if latency falls below the predefined thresholds.

This sets the sources and targets for Windows Server 2008 domain controllers. For other versions such as Windows Server 2003 and Windows 2000 Server domain controllers, the overrides need to be created for those domain controllers separately. Also, the replication latency mechanism does not support cross-version replication latency measurement.

---

**NOTE**

It might be tempting to make all domain controllers both sources and targets. Each domain controller would then be connected to every other domain controller. This is also known as a full mesh. However, the problem is that the number of connections grows as a power of 2. The general function for the number of connection in a full mesh is:

$f(x) = (x^2 - x)/2$

where x is the number of domain controllers and f(x) is the number of connections.

This means that 2 DCs will have 1 connection, 3 DCs will have 3 connections, 4 DCs will have 6 connections, and so on. By the time you get to 20 domain controllers, you have 190 connections. The connections are bidirectional and there are at least 5 counters that are collected per source-target pair, so for 20 DCs in a full mesh, there would be 1,900 performance counters (190 connections x 2 bidirectional x 5 counters) gathering data. Full mesh is bad!

## Agent Restart Recovery

Agents will heartbeat every 60 seconds by default, contacting their management server to check for new rules and upload data. On the Root Management Server, there is a Health Service Watcher corresponding to each managed agent. If the Health Service Watcher for an agent detects three missed heartbeats in a row (that is, 3 minutes without a heartbeat), the Health Service Watcher executes a pair of diagnostics:

▶ First, the Health Service Watcher attempts to ping the agent.

▶ Second, the Health Service Watcher checks to see if the Health Service is running on the agent.

An alert is then generated for each of the diagnostics if they failed. If the agent is reachable via ping but the Health Service is stopped, there is a recovery to restart the Health Service. This allows the agent to recover automatically from stopped agent conditions.

The Restart Health Service Recovery is disabled by default. To enable the functionality, an override can be created for the Health Service Watcher objects. To enable the recovery, execute the following steps:

1. Open the Operations Manager 2007 R2 console.

2. Select the Authoring space.

3. Expand the Management Pack Objects node.

4. Select the Monitors node.

5. Select View, Scope.

6. Type health service watcher in the Look For field and click the View All Targets option button.

7. Select the Health Service Watcher target. Don't pick the ones with additional information in parentheses.

8. Click OK.

9. Type Heartbeat Failure in the Look For field and click Find Now.

10. Right-click the Health Service Heartbeat Failure aggregate rollup node and select Overrides, Override Recovery, Restart Health Service, and For All Objects of Class: Health Service Watcher.

11. Check the Override box next to Enabled and set the value to True.

12. In the Select Destination Management Pack pull-down menu, select the appropriate override management pack. If none exists, create a new management pack named "Operations Manager MP Overrides" by clicking New.

> **NOTE**
>
> Never use the Default Management Pack for overrides. Always create an override management pack that corresponds to each imported management pack.

13. Click OK to save the override.

Now if the Health Service is stopped on an agent, the Root Management Server will automatically attempt to restart it.

## Notifications and Subscriptions

When alerts are generated in the console, there is a wealth of information available about the nature of the problem and how to troubleshoot and resolve it. However, most administrators will not be watching the console at all times. Operations Manager has a sophisticated notification mechanism that allows alerts to be forwarded to email, SMS, IM, or even a command-line interface. The most common method of alert notification is email.

However, Operations Manager generates a lot of alerts. If each one of these alerts were forwarded, this would overwhelm the average administrator's Inbox and prove totally useless. Operations Manager has two alert parameters to help categorize the alerts. Each alert has two parameters that help guide the notification process, severity and priority.

Alert Severity is the first and main parameter. There are three severity levels:

▶ **Critical (2)**—These alerts indicate that there is a problem that needs to be fixed immediately and is directly actionable (that is, there is something that can be done).

▶ **Warning (1)**—These alerts indicate that there is a problem, but that it might not be immediately impacting the environment or might not be directly actionable.

▶ **Information (0)**—These alerts indicate that there is something that is good to know, but might not be a problem nor is actionable.

By the nature of things, there are a lot more warning alerts generated than critical alerts. In general, notifications should only be sent out for critical alerts. That is, there should never be an email sent for a warning or informational alert.

Alert Priority is the second parameter that qualifies the alert status. The priority allows management pack authors to make some alerts more important than others. There are three levels of priority as well:

▶ High

▶ Medium

▶ Low

In general, a high-priority, critical severity alert is very important. This includes events like an agent down or a security breach. A medium-priority, critical severity alert is important. Both are generally actionable.

The best practice is to create two SMTP channels to deliver the alert notification emails, which are as follows:

▶ **SMTP (High Priority)**—High-priority email to an SMTP gateway

▶ **SMTP (Regular Priority)**—Regular email to an SMTP gateway

Then, create two notification subscriptions that use the Severity and the Priority to select the emails to be sent:

▶ Notification for All Critical Severity High-Priority Alerts

▶ Notification for All Critical Severity Medium-Priority Alerts

This provides a configuration that will deliver the very important alerts (high-priority critical severity alerts) via high-priority email and important alerts (medium-priority critical severity alerts) via regular email. All other alerts will be available in the console and no emails will be sent to notify of them.

The next sections will set up the notification infrastructure described previously.

The first step is to set up a channel, that is, how the emails will be sent. The steps are as follows:

1. Launch the Operations Manager 2007 R2 console.
2. Select the Administration space.
3. Select the Channels node.
4. Right-click the Channels node and select New Channel, E-Mail (SMTP).
5. Enter `SMTP Channel (High Priority)` for the channel name and click Next.
6. Click the Add button, enter the FQDN of the SMTP server, and click OK.
7. Enter a return SMTP address and click Next.
8. Change the Importance to High and click Finish. Click Close to close wizard.
9. Right-click the Channels node and select New Channel, E-Mail (SMTP).
10. Enter `SMTP Channel (Normal Priority)` for the channel name and click Next.
11. Click the Add button, enter the FQDN of the SMTP server, and click OK.
12. Enter a return SMTP address and click Next.
13. Leave the Importance at Normal and click Finish. Click Close to close wizard.

The second step is to set up the subscriber, that is, to whom the emails will be sent. The steps are as follows:

1. Launch the Operations Manager 2007 R2 console.
2. Select the Administration space.
3. Select the Subscribers node.
4. Right-click the Subscribers node and select New Subscriber.
5. Click the "..." button and select a user or distribution group. Click OK.
6. Click Next.
7. Click Next to always send notifications.
8. Click the Add button.
9. Type `Email` for the address name and click Next.
10. Select the Channel Type as E-Mail (SMTP) and enter the delivery email address.
11. Click Finish.
12. Click Finish again to save the subscriber. Click Close to exit the wizard.

23

**NOTE**

It is a best practice to use distribution lists rather than user email addresses for subscribers.

---

The last step is to set up the subscriptions, that is, what to notify on. The steps are as follows:

1. Launch the Operations Manager 2007 R2 console.
2. Select the Administration space.
3. Select the Subscriptions node.
4. Right-click the Subscriptions node and select New Subscription.
5. Enter `Notification for All Critical Severity High Priority Alerts` for the subscription name and click Next.
6. Check the Of a Specific Severity and the Of a Specific Priority check boxes.
7. In the Criteria Description pane, click the "Specific Severity" link, check the Critical check box, and click OK.
8. In the Criteria Description pane, click the "Specific Priority" link, check the High check box, and click OK.
9. Click Next.
10. Click the Add button, click Search, select the subscriber, click the Add button, and click OK.
11. Click Next.
12. Click the Add button, click Search, select the SMTP Channel (High Priority) channel, click the Add button, and click OK.
13. Click Next and then click Finish.
14. Right-click the Subscriptions node and select New Subscription.
15. Enter `Notification for All Critical Severity Medium Priority Alerts` for the subscription name and click Next.
16. Check the Of a Specific Severity and the Of a Specific Priority check boxes.
17. In the Criteria Description pane, click the "Specific Severity" link, check the Critical check box, and click OK.
18. In the Criteria Description pane, click the "Specific Priority" link, check the Medium check box, and click OK.
19. Click Next.
20. Click the Add button, click Search, select the subscriber, click the Add button, and click OK.
21. Click Next.
22. Click the Add button, click Search, select the SMTP Channel (Normal Priority) channel, click the Add button, and click OK.
23. Click Next and then click Finish.

Now, the subscribers will get email notifications for alerts based on the severity and priority. These severities and priorities are based on the judgments of the authors of the management packs, which might or might not be optimal for any given organization. Later in the chapter, the priority and severity of alerts will be used to tune the management packs to reduce alert noise.

# Monitoring DMZ Servers with Certificates

Servers in an organization's demilitarized zone (DMZ) are usually not domain members and, thus, cannot do automatic mutual authentication with the OpsMgr server. However, these servers are the most exposed in the organization and, thus, critical to be monitored. Thankfully, there is a well-defined process for using certificates to handle the mutual authentication.

> **NOTE**
>
> This topic also applies to machines that are workgroup servers or servers that are members of domains where there is no trust to the OpsMgr domain.

Monitoring servers in the DMZ requires an install of certificate-based mutual authentication. This process has a lot of steps, but is straightforward. To install and configure certificates to allow the DMZ servers to use mutual authentication, the following five major tasks need to be completed:

1. Create a certificate template to issue the correct format of X.509 certificates for Operations Manager to use for mutual authentication.

2. Request the root CA certificate to trust the CA and the certificates it issues. This is done for each DMZ server and possibly for the management servers if not using an enterprise CA.

3. Request a certificate from the root CA to use for mutual authentication. This is done for each DMZ server and for each management server.

4. Install the Operations Manager agent manually. This is done for each DMZ server.

5. Configure the agent to use the certificate. This is done for each DMZ server and for each management server.

These various X.509 certificates are issued from a certificate authority, which could be a Windows Server 2008 R2 CA.

## Creating a Certificate Template

This step creates a certificate template named Operations Manager that can be issued from the Windows Server 2008 R2 certification authority web enrollment page. The certificate template will support Server Authentication (OID 1.3.6.1.5.5.7.3.1) and Client Authentication (OID 1.3.6.1.5.5.7.3.2) as well as allow the name to be manually entered rather than autogenerated from Active Directory because the DMZ server will not be an Active Directory domain member.

The steps to create the security template are as follows:

1. Log on to the CA, which is DC1.companyabc.com in this example.
2. Launch Server Manager.
3. Expand Roles, Active Directory Certificate Services, and select Certificate Templates (*fqdn*).
4. Right-click the Computer template and select Duplicate Template.
5. Leave the version at Windows 2003 Server, Enterprise Edition and click OK.
6. On the General tab in the Template Display Name field, enter Operation Manager.
7. Select the Request Handling tab and mark the Allow Private Key to Be Exported option.
8. Select the Subject Name tab and select Supply in the Request option. Click OK at the warning.
9. Select the Security tab, select Authenticated Users, and check the Enroll right.
10. Click OK to save the template.
11. Select the Enterprise PKI to expose the CA.
12. Right-click the CA and select Manage CA.
13. In the certsrv console, expand the CA, right-click Certificates Templates, then select New, Certificate Template to Issue.
14. Select the Operations Manager certificate template and click OK.

The new Operations Manager template will now be available in the Windows Server 2008 R2 web enrollment page.

## Requesting the Root CA Server Certificate

This allows the DMZ server to trust the Windows Server 2008 R2 CA. This does not need to be done on the OpsMgr management servers, as the Windows Server 2008 R2 CA is an enterprise CA and all domain members automatically trust it. If the CA is not an enterprise CA, the steps need to be completed for the management servers as well.

To request and install the root CA certificate on the DMZ server, execute the following steps:

1. Log on to a DMZ server with local administrator rights.
2. Open a web browser and point it to the certificate server, in this case https://dc1.companyabc.com/certsrv. Enter credentials if prompted.
3. Click the Download a CA Certificate, Certificate Chain, or CRL link (shown in Figure 23.10).
4. Click the Download CA Certificate link. Note: If the certificate does not download, add the site to the Local Intranet list of sites in Internet Explorer.
5. Click Open to open the CA certificate.
6. Click Install Certificate to install the CA certificate.

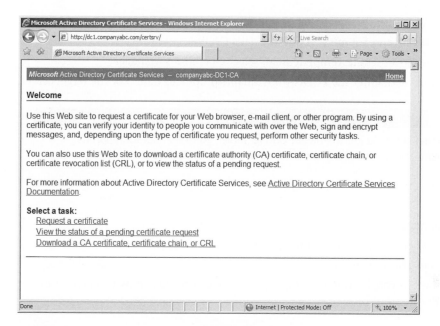

FIGURE 23.10    Downloading a root CA certificate.

7. At the Certificate Import Wizard screen, click Next.

8. Select Place All Certificates in the Following Store option button.

9. Click Browse.

10. Click the Show Physical Stores check box.

11. Expand the Trusted Root Certification Authorities folder and select the local computer store.

12. Click OK.

13. Click Next, Finish, and OK to install the CA certificate.

14. Close any open windows.

Repeat for all DMZ servers. Now the DMZ servers will trust certificates issued by the certification authority. The next step is to request the certificates to use for the mutual authentication for all servers.

## Requesting a Certificate from the Root CA Server

Each of the management servers and the servers in the DMZ will need to be issued certificates to use for communication.

The steps to request a certificate are as follows:

1. Log on as an administrator, then open a web browser and point it to the certificate server (in this case, https://dc1.companyabc.com/certsrv).

2. Click the Request a Certificate link.

3. Click the Advanced Certificate Request link.

4. Click the Create and Submit a Request to This CA link.

5. In the Type of Certificate Template field, select Operations Manager.

6. In the Name field, enter the FQDN (fully qualified domain name) of the target server.

---

**NOTE**

Go to the actual server to get the name! On the server, go to Computer Properties, Computer Name. Copy the full computer name and paste it into the Name field of the form.

---

7. Click Submit.

8. Click Yes when you get the warning pop-up.

9. Click Install This Certificate.

10. Click Yes when you see the warning pop-up. The certificate is now installed in the user certificate store.

---

**NOTE**

The certificate was installed in the user certificate store, but needs to be in the local computer store for Operations Manager. The ability to use web enrollment to directly place the certificate into the local computer store was removed from the Windows Server 2008 web enrollment, so the certificate needs to be moved manually.

---

11. Select Start, Run and then enter mmc to launch an MMC console.

12. Select File and Add/Remove Snap-In.

13. Select Certificates and click the Add button.

14. Select My User Account and click Finish.

15. Select Certificates again and click the Add button.

16. Select Computer Account and click Next.

17. Select the local computer, click Finish, and then click OK.

18. Expand the Certificates – Current User, Personal, and select the Certificates folder.

19. In the right pane, right-click the certificate issued earlier and select All Tasks, Export. The certificate can be recognized by the certificate template name Operations Manager.

20. At the Certificate Export Wizard, click Next.

21. Select Yes, Export the Private Key. Click Next.

22. Click Next.

23. Enter in a password and click Next.

24. Enter in a directory and filename and click Next.

25. Click Finish to export the certificate. Click OK at the pop-up.

26. Expand the Certificates (Local Computer), Personal, and select the Certificates folder.

> **NOTE**
>
> If this is the first certificate in the local computer store, the Certificates folder will not exist. Simply select the Personal folder instead and the Certificates folder will be created automatically.

27. Right-click in the right pane and select All Tasks, Import.

28. At the Certificate Import Wizard, select Next.

29. Click Browse to locate the certificate file saved earlier. Change the file type to Personal Information Exchange (.pfx) to see the file. Click Next.

30. Enter in the password used earlier, select the Mark This Key as Exportable, and click Next.

31. Click Next.

32. Click Finish and then click OK at the pop-up to complete the import.

The preceding steps need to be completed for each DMZ server and for each management server.

## Installing the Agent on the DMZ Server

The agent needs to be installed manually on each DMZ server. Normally, agents would be pushed by the Operations Manager console, but DMZ servers typically reside in the DMZ and are not members of the domain.

The steps to manually install the agent are as follows:

1. Log on as an administrator and insert the OpsMgr 2007 R2 installation media.

2. At the AutoPlay menu, select Run SetupOM.exe.

3. Select Install Operations Manager 2007 R2 Agent from the menu.

4. Click Next.

5. Click Next to accept the default directory.

6. Click Next to specify management group information.

7. Type in the management group name and FQDN of the management server. Keep the default management server port as 5723. The example shown in Figure 23.11 has COMPANYABC as the management group name and omr2.companyabc.com as the management server.

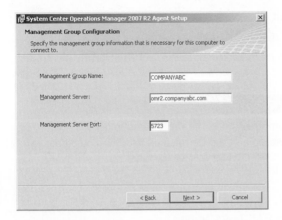

FIGURE 23.11    Manually entered management group information.

8. Click Next.

9. Click Next at the Agent Action Account page to leave the local system as the
   action account.

10. Click Install to complete the installation.

11. When the installer is finished, click Finish.

The preceding steps need to be completed for each DMZ server.

The agent is installed, but will not communicate correctly with the management server.
This is because the agent has not been configured to use the certificate for mutual authentication. This will be done in the next section.

## Configuring the Agent to Use the Certificate

After the agent is installed, the agent still needs to be configured to use the correct certificate. The OpsMgr installation includes a utility called MOMCertImport.exe that configures
the agent to use certificates for authentication and specifies which certificate in the local
computer store to use. The tool does not do any validation checking of the certificate
itself, so care needs to be taken that the correct certificate is selected.

The steps to configure the agent to use a certificate are as follows:

1. Log on as an administrator on the DMZ server and insert the OpsMgr 2007 R2 installation media.

2. At the AutoPlay menu, select Run SetupOM.exe.

3. Select Browse This CD from the menu.

4. Select the SupportTools directory and then the AMD64 directory.

> **NOTE**
>
> Windows Server 2008 R2 is a 64-bit operating system, so the AMD64 is the correct folder for the 64-bit binaries. If the procedure is being run for 32-bit servers, select the appropriate directory for the binaries such as i386.

5. In the directory, double-click MOMCertImport.exe.

6. In the pop-up window, select the certificate issued previously and click OK. The View Certificate button can be used to view the certificate details if the correct certificate is not obvious.

The Operation Manager service will restart automatically to have the certificate selection take effect. The preceding steps need to be repeated for each DMZ server and for each management server.

The Operations Manager event log can be viewed with the Windows Event Viewer. It is named Operations Manager and is located in the Applications and Services Logs folder in the tool. Any problems with the certificate will be shown in the log immediately following the start of the System Center Management service.

# Using Operations Manager 2007 R2

After Operations Manager 2007 R2 has been installed and configured, ongoing work needs to be done to ensure that the product performs as expected. The two primary activities are to, first, tune the management packs to ensure that alerts are valid for the environment and that alert noise is reduced and, second, produce reports of the information that Operations Manager 2007 R2 is collecting.

## Alert Tuning

After deploying Operations Manager 2007 R2, there are frequently complaints about the number of alert notifications that get generated. This can cause organizations to decommission the product, ignore the emails, or generally complain about what a bad product it is. In reality, the Operations Manager alert notifications just need to be tuned.

The following process will help you tune the management packs quickly and effectively to reduce alert and email noise. This is done by adjusting parameters on the rules (Enable/Disable, Severity, and Priority) using overrides.

Alert Severity is the first parameter to be tuned. There are three levels:

▶ Critical (2)

▶ Warning (1)

▶ Information (0)

The numeric value of the severity is given as well, as some rules and monitors will show the severity as a value rather than as text.

Alert Priority is the second parameter to be tuned. There are three levels of priority as well:

▶ High

▶ Medium

▶ Low

These tuning procedures assume that the notification subscriptions were created that were outlined in the "Notifications and Subscriptions" section earlier in the chapter. These notification subscriptions are as follows:

▶ Notification for All Critical Severity High-Priority Alerts

▶ Notification for All Critical Severity Medium-Priority Alerts

When you get an email from an alert that you don't want, you need to tune the management pack monitor or rule. The basic decision tree is as follows:

A. **Disable the Alert?**   If yes, create an override to disable the rule for either the instance of the object, the class of objects, or a group of the objects. This prevents the alert from being generated, so no console alerts and definitely no emails are generated. This would be done if the alert does not reflect a real problem.

B. **Change Severity?**   If yes, create an override to change the alert severity to Warning. This keeps the alert in the console as a warning, but does not generate an email. This would be done if the alert is real, but is not actionable.

C. **Change Priority?**   If yes, create an override to change the alert priority to low. This keeps the alert as a critical alert, but prevents an email from being generated. This would be done if the alert is real, but is not resolvable in the immediate future.

D. **Change Threshold?**   For performance-based alerts, there is the option to change the trigger threshold to a different value. This would be done if the problem is real and actionable, but the alert is firing too soon.

These options can be taken for all objects of the target class, for just the specific instance that generated the alert, or for a group. The group would have to be created in advance and would have to contain objects of the type targeted by the monitor or rule generating the alert.

For example, let's say there is an Application of Group Policy critical alert that is occurring frequently in the environment. It is occurring on a number of Windows Server 2008 R2 servers and is generating a lot of email notifications. This alert is valid, but does not require immediate action. The alert needs to be tuned to change the severity from critical to warning. The steps to tune the alert are as follows:

1. Open the Operations Manager 2007 R2 console.

2. Select the Monitoring space.

3. Select the Active Alerts view.

4. Locate and select the Application of Group Policy alert that is to be tuned.

5. Right-click the alert and select Overrides, Override the Monitor, and For All Objects of Class: Group Policy 2008 Runtime. This overrides the alert for all objects of that class.

> **NOTE**
>
> The alert is to be tuned for all objects, rather than any specific instances. If the alert is to be tuned for the specific instance that raised the alert, the For the Object option should be chosen. If it is a group of the objects, the For a Group option should be chosen. The group would have to be precreated and be a group of the target objects.

6. Check the Override box next to Alert Severity and set the value to Warning.

7. In the Select Destination Management Pack pull-down menu, select the appropriate override management pack. If none exists, create a new override management pack named "Group Policy MP Overrides" by clicking New.

> **NOTE**
>
> Never use the Default Management Pack for overrides. Always create an override management pack that corresponds to each imported management pack.

8. Click OK to save the override.

Now the next time the monitor triggers an alert, it will be of warning severity and will not generate a notification email. However, the alert can still be reviewed in the console.

This approach to tuning will address 90% of the noisy alerts that you get. To target the noisiest alerts, see the report Most Common Alerts in the next section. This helps identify the alerts that are responsible for the most noise. You'll frequently find that 50% of your alerts are coming from less than five rules or monitors. Tuning those will give you the most bang for your buck.

## Scheduling Reports

The Operations Manager 2007 R2 infrastructure collects many Windows Server 2008 R2 data points. This information can be presented in reports, which can be generated ad hoc or scheduled. The scheduling option is very useful, as it reduces the need to actively open the console and instead the reports are delivered via email.

### Performance Reports

When managing a number of agents, it can be difficult to pinpoint the problem systems. For example, which systems are the most heavily utilized? A report showing a graph of all the resources would be very messy and difficult to read even in a medium-sized organization with a number of servers. Operations Manager 2007 R2 has a set of reports that address this specific concern, the Performance Top Objects and Performance Top

Instances. These reports take data from performance collection rules, perform some statistical analysis, and list the top systems.

For example, Figure 23.12 shows the top five systems with the most processor utilization. It is based on the "Processor % Processor Time Total 2008" rule. It shows the top five heaviest processor utilization systems for the previous week.

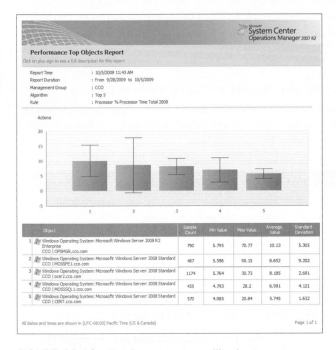

FIGURE 23.12    Top five processor utilization report.

This report is one of the reports in the Microsoft Generic Report Library and can be used against any performance counter. The report can pick the top (the default) or bottom objects, as well as vary the number of objects to return (the default is five).

The best-practice recommendation is to generate daily reports spanning the previous week for the following rules:

▶ Processor % Processor Time Total 2008

▶ Page File Percentage Use 2008

▶ Memory % Committed Bytes in Use 2008

▶ Network Adapter Bytes Total per Second 2008

▶ % Logical Disk Free Space 2008

The Performance Top Objects report for each of these rules gives a good overview of the performance issues (or lack thereof) over the collection of all the monitored systems. These should be delivered on a daily basis in an email or to a share.

To schedule a report for email delivery, use the following steps:

1. Launch the Operations Manager 2007 R2 console.
2. Select the Reporting space.
3. Select the Microsoft Generic Report Library node.
4. Right-click the Performance Top Objects report and select Open.
5. In the From field, select Advanced.
6. Change the Offset to minus and the number of days to 7. Click the green check mark (OK) to save the selections. The From field will show "Today -7 day(s)".
7. Change both the From and the To times to 12:00 AM.
8. In the Rule field, click the Browse button.
9. In the Rule Name field, enter `Processor % Processor Time Total 2008` and click the Search button.
10. In the Available Items pane, select the rule and click OK.
11. Click Run and confirm that the report looks good.
12. Select File, Schedule.
13. In the Description, enter `Processor % Processor Time Total 2008 Report`.
14. In the Delivery Method field, select Email.
15. In the To field, enter the SMTP address of the recipient.
16. In the Subject field, replace @ReportName with `Processor % Processor Time Total 2008 Report`. The variable name is unfortunately very long and ugly, so it's best to replace it.
17. Click Next.
18. Change the schedule to Daily.
19. Change the time to be the time that the report should be generated on a daily basis, for example 6:00 a.m. Click Next.
20. Because the report was generated and all the parameters were selected initially, no parameters need to be changed. This method ensures that the email report will match expectations.
21. Click Finish to save the scheduled report.

The report will now be automatically generated every morning at 6:00 a.m. and delivered via email to the recipients. Additional reports can be created in exactly the same way for the recommended rules and any others that are needed. To review the schedules, go to the Scheduled Reports node in the Reporting space. The schedules can be adjusted as well.

---

**NOTE**

The performance rules are generally specific to each operating system. Thus, the reports are specific to each operating system. The rules in this section reflect Windows Server 2008 and Windows Server 2008 R2 performance data. If there are other operating systems such as Windows Server 2003, additional reports using those rules would need to be created.

---

### OpsMgr 2007 R2 Maintenance Reports

There are also reports on Operations Manager 2007 R2 that should be generated to ensure that the health and performance of the infrastructure is good. The reports to generate are as follows:

▶ **Most Common Alerts**—This report is useful for determining what alerts are the noisiest and might be spamming the Inboxes of notification subscribers. The report shows which alerts are most common and gives additional statistical analysis.

▶ **Alert Logging Latency**—This report is useful for determining the health of the OpsMgr infrastructure, as measured by the time an event occurs on a managed computer to the time an alert is raised. If this is too long (that is, greater than 30 seconds), it indicates that there is a problem.

▶ **SQL Database Space report**—This report shows the database space and growth of SQL databases. This is generated against the OpsMgr databases to monitor the growth.

These reports should be generated on a weekly basis (for example, Monday at 6:00 a.m.) spanning the previous week and be sent to the Operations Manager administrators.

The Most Common Alerts report is based on the management packs that are installed. By default, the report selects all the installed management packs and shows the top five most common alerts. To schedule the Most Common Alerts report, execute the following steps:

1. Launch the Operations Manager 2007 R2 console.

2. Select the Reporting space.

3. Select the Microsoft Generic Report Library node.

4. Right-click the Most Common Alerts report and select Open.

5. In the From field, select Advanced.

6. Change the Offset to minus and the number of days to 7. Click the green check mark (OK) to save the selections. The From field will show "Today -7 day(s)".

7. Change both the From and the To times to 12:00 AM.

8. Click Run and confirm that the report looks good.

9. Select File, Schedule.

10. In the Description, enter `Most Common Alerts Report`.

11. In the Delivery Method field, select Email.

12. In the To field, enter the SMTP address of the recipient.

13. In the Subject field, replace @ReportName with `Most Common Alerts Report`.

14. Click Next.

15. Change the schedule to Weekly and ensure that only Mon is checked.

16. Change the time to be the time that the report should be generated on a daily basis, for example 6:00 a.m. Click Next.

17. Because the report was generated and all the parameters were selected initially, no parameters need to be changed. This method ensures that the email report will match expectations.

18. Click Finish to save the scheduled report.

Figure 23.13 shows an example of the Most Common Alerts report. The most common alert for the previous week was the Disk Transfer Latency Is Too High, with 16.67% of alerts. This alert could be tuned to reduce the volume of alerts or the problem resolved.

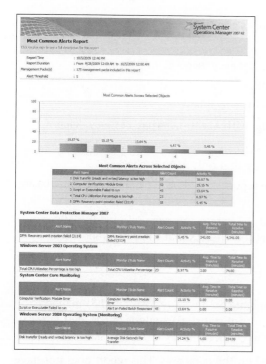

FIGURE 23.13   Most Common Alerts report.

The Alert Logging Latency report is based on the objects selected. The report does not include any objects by default, so the objects must be selected. It is a best practice to select the groups of agents, agentless, and agent watchers objects. To schedule the Alert Logging Latency report, execute the following steps:

1. Launch the Operations Manager 2007 R2 console.

2. Select the Reporting space.

3. Select the Microsoft Generic Report Library node.

4. Right-click the Alert Logging Latency report and select Open.

5. In the From field, select Advanced.

6. Change the Offset to minus and the number of days to 7. Click the green check mark (OK) to save the selections. The From field will show "Today -7 day(s)".

7. Change both the From and the To times to 12:00 AM.

8. Click the Add Group button.

9. In the Group Name field, enter agent and click the Search button.

10. Select the Agent Managed Computer Group, the Agentless Managed Computer Group, and the Microsoft.SystemCenter.AgentWatchersGroup and click the Add button.

11. Click OK to save the selections.

12. Click Run and confirm that the report looks good.

13. Select File, Schedule.

14. In the Description, enter Alert Logging Latency Report.

15. In the Delivery Method field, select Email.

16. In the To field, enter the SMTP address of the recipient.

17. In the Subject field, replace @ReportName with Alert Logging Latency Report.

18. Click Next.

19. Change the schedule to Weekly and ensure that only Mon is checked.

20. Change the time to be the time that the report should be generated on a daily basis, for example 6:00 a.m. Click Next.

21. Because the report was generated and all the parameters were selected initially, no parameters need to be changed. This method ensures that the email report will match expectations.

22. Click Finish to save the scheduled report.

The Alert Logging Latency report will now generate on a weekly basis and be emailed to the recipients. The report has two pages with lots of statistical analysis of the alert latency. It is one of the more complicated reports in the OpsMgr library of reports.

Finally, the SQL Database Space report is based on the databases. This report does not have any objects selected by default, so the Operations Manager database objects will need to be selected. To schedule the SQL Database Space report, run the following steps:

1. Launch the Operations Manager 2007 R2 console.

2. Select the Reporting space.

3. Select the SQL Server 2008 (Monitoring) node.

4. Right-click the SQL Database Space report and select Open.

5. In the From field, select Advanced.

6. Change the Offset to minus and the number of days to 7. Click the green check mark (OK) to save the selections. The From field will show "Today -7 day(s)".

7. Change both the From and the To times to 12:00 AM.

8. Click the Add Object button.

**NOTE**

When the Add Object window appears, note that there is a caution triangle with the text "Filter Options Have Been Applied." The objects returned will only be those that match the report criteria, in the case of SQL database objects. This is new to Operations Manager 2007 R2. Before this, all object classes would be returned and it was difficult to ensure that the correct objects were included in the report. Many times, reports would be returned without any data at all due to the incorrect objects being selected. This is a huge improvement in OpsMgr 2007 R2.

9. In the Object Name field, enter Operations and click the Search button.

10. Select all the OperationsManager databases and click the Add button.

11. Click OK to save the selections.

12. Click Run and confirm that the report looks good.

13. Select File, Schedule.

14. In the Description, enter Operations Manager Database Space Report.

15. In the Delivery Method field, select Email.

16. In the To field, enter the SMTP address of the recipient.

17. In the Subject field, replace @ReportName with Operations Manager Database Space Report.

18. Click Next.

19. Change the schedule to Weekly and ensure that only Mon is checked.

20. Change the time to be the time that the report should be generated on a daily basis, for example 6:00 a.m. Click Next.

21. Because the report was generated and all the parameters were selected initially, no parameters need to be changed. This method ensures that the email report will match expectations.

22. Click Finish to save the scheduled report.

The SQL Database Space report will be delivered every week on Monday at 6:00 a.m.

These three reports help ensure that the Operations Manager 2007 R2 infrastructure is healthy and performing well.

# Summary

System Center Operations Manager 2007 is key to managing Windows Server 2008 R2. It can also be used in Windows 2003/2008 or mixed environments to provide for automated monitoring of all vital operating system, application, and network functionality. This type of functionality is instrumental in reducing downtime and getting the most out of a Windows Server 2008 R2 investment. In a nutshell, OpsMgr is an effective way to gain proactive, rather than reactive, control over the entire environment.

# Best Practices

The following are best practices from this chapter:

▶ Deploy System Center Operations Manager 2007 R2 for monitoring Windows Server 2008 R2.

▶ Install the Windows Operating System, Active Directory, DNS, IIS, and Windows Server 2008 R2 management packs into OpsMgr to monitor network systems and applications that Windows Server 2008 R2 depends on.

▶ Deploy Operations Manager components on Windows 64-bit and SQL 64-bit for optimal performance.

▶ Create override management packs for each application management pack, such as the Windows Server 2008 R2 management pack. Don't use the Default Management Pack.

▶ Take future expansion and relevance of hardware into account when sizing servers for OpsMgr deployment.

▶ Keep the installation of OpsMgr on a separate server or set of separate dedicated member servers that do not run any other separate applications.

▶ Use SQL Server Reporting Services to produce custom reports using OpsMgr's reporting feature.

▶ Start with a single management group and add on additional management groups only if they are absolutely necessary.

▶ Use a dedicated service account for OpsMgr.

▶ Allocate adequate space for the databases depending on the length of time needed to store events and the number of managed systems.

▶ Monitor the size of the OpsMgr database to ensure that it does not increase beyond the bounds of acceptable size.

▶ Leverage the reporting database to store and report on data over a long period.

▶ Modify the grooming interval to aggressively address environmental requirements.

▶ When tuning, err on the side of fewer alerts. If nothing will be done about an alert, make sure it doesn't send a notification email.

▶ When tuning, use the Most Common Alerts report to see which alerts are the most valuable targets for tuning.

▶ Configure OpsMgr to monitor itself.

23

# CHAPTER 24

# Server-to-Client Remote Access and DirectAccess

As the Internet grows year after year, so does the need to work productively away from the office. Companies are always looking for alternative cost-effective methods of connecting their remote and mobile users without sacrificing performance or security. Although Windows Server 2008 offered Routing and Remote Access Service (RRAS) in the form of virtual private network (VPN) or dial-up services, Windows Server 2008 R2 adds DirectAccess as an alternative method of remote connectivity.

As the Internet has evolved and become ubiquitous, the vast majority of users have high-speed Internet connections at home, while on the road at hotels, and even while sipping a latte in a coffee shop. The Internet to which they are connecting is full of hackers, worms, and viruses, from which the connections need to be protected. These users use remote access in the form of tunnels (shown in Figure 24.1) that connect from their workstation in the coffee shop through the dangerous Internet to the corporate resources. This chapter discusses the traditional VPN components of server-to-client remote and mobile access. This chapter also discusses the new DirectAccess, which makes this process even simpler for the remote worker, allowing application-level access without requiring a traditional VPN.

A huge problem is ensuring that the resources that are connecting to the internal network are healthy and will not infect internal resources. When the remote and mobile clients are connected to the internal network, they have direct network connectivity to internal resources, such as the database server, file servers, and directory server. This can present a huge risk if not managed and mitigated properly. Windows Server 2003 offered some features, but they were difficult to use. Windows Server 2008 provided a vastly improved access control mechanism for validating and controlling access to sensitive network resources via the Network Policy Server (NPS). Network Policy Server introduced key features to detect unhealthy systems, control what internal resources they can access, and even remediate the problems on the remote clients. Windows Server 2008 R2 extends NPS functionality with templates for NPS configuration, SQL logging for RADIUS, and support for non-English languages.

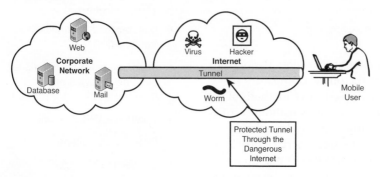

FIGURE 24.1    Connecting securely over the Internet.

DirectAccess, a new feature introduced in Windows Server 2008 R2, seamlessly connects users to the corporate network anywhere they have Internet access. DirectAccess loads as the system boots, extending access into the "office." Remote systems are treated just as if they are on the local network and can be managed in a similar manner with the added quarantine and remediation functionality of the NPS system.

This chapter focuses on client-to-server connectivity in Windows Server 2008 R2, rather than server-to-server security or site-to-site connectivity. Please refer to Chapter 14, "Transport-Level Security," for a detailed discussion on the server-to-server and site-to-site connectivity features of Windows Server 2008 R2.

# VPN in Windows Server 2008 R2

A virtual private network (VPN) is the extension of a private network that encompasses links across shared or public networks like the Internet. A VPN allows data to be sent between two computers across the Internet in a manner that emulates a point-to-point private link. With a virtual private network, illustrated in Figure 24.2, a private link is created between the client and the VPN server by encrypting the data for confidentiality; data packets that are intercepted while traveling through the Internet are unreadable without the proper encryption keys.

VPN technology provides corporations with a scalable and low-cost solution for remote access to corporate resources, such as database, file, and directory servers. VPN connections allow remote users to securely connect to their corporate networks across the

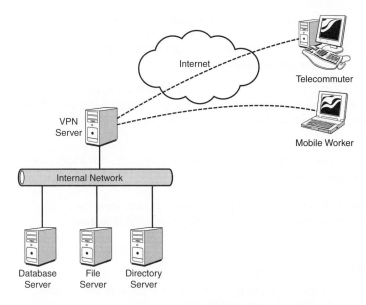

FIGURE 24.2   Virtual private networking across the Internet.

Internet. Remote users would access resources as if they were physically connected to the corporate local area network (LAN).

Later in the chapter, a new technology introduced with Windows Server 2008 R2 called DirectAccess is discussed. Microsoft has positioned DirectAccess as being different from a traditional VPN. This positioning is based mainly on the automated nature of DirectAccess, rather than on technical or architectural differences. DirectAccess is technically a VPN, but we'll focus on key differences from traditional VPNs later in this chapter.

## Windows Server 2008 R2 RRAS Features and Services

Windows Server 2008 R2 builds on the Routing and Remote Access features that were provided by Windows NT 4.0, Windows 2000 Server, Windows Server 2003, and Windows Server 2008. Routing and Remote Access in Windows Server 2008 R2 includes all of the VPN features and services from previous versions of the Windows Server product and adds several key features.

The following VPN features were provided by Windows NT 4.0:

- ▶ IP packet filtering

- ▶ Point-to-Point Tunneling Protocol (PPTP) support for router-to-router VPN connections

- ▶ Routing and Remote Access administrative tool and the Routemon command-line utility

The following additional VPN features were provided by Windows 2000 Server:

▶ Layer 2 Tunneling Protocol (L2TP) over Internet Protocol Security (IPSec) support for router-to-router VPN connections and remote access.

▶ Demand-dial routing that can route IP and Internetwork Packet Exchange (IPX) over on-demand or persistent wide area network (WAN) links, such as analog phone lines, Integrated Services Digital Network (ISDN), or over VPN connections that use either PPTP or L2TP over IPSec.

▶ RRAS integration that provides the capability to integrate a firewall with RRAS and Network Address Translation (NAT) functions.

Windows Server 2003 continued the evolution of RRAS by adding some new features. Some of the Routing and Remote Access Service for Windows Server 2003 features included the following:

▶ Quarantine Policy Check.

▶ Improved administration and management tools that use a Microsoft Management Console (MMC) snap-in or the Netsh command-line tool.

Windows Server 2008 added new VPN functionality and improved on some of the existing functionality. The features new in Windows Server 2008 included the following:

▶ Network Policy Server (NPS) to provide access control and to assess, validate, and remediate the health of clients; this replaces the Windows Server 2003 Quarantine Policy Check.

▶ Secure Socket Tunneling Protocol (SSTP) to provide for HTTPS VPN tunnels over port 443 to seamlessly provide connectivity over firewalls, NAT, and web proxies.

▶ Point-to-Point Protocol (PPP), which now supports the use of Protected EAP (PEAP) with PEAP-MS-CHAP v2 and PEAP-TLS for better security.

▶ Full IPv6 support in addition to IPv4 support, both of which coexist completely.

▶ New Connection Manager Administration Kit (CMAK) features, such as multiple language support.

▶ Connection Manager, which now supports Dynamic DNS client registration.

▶ Network Diagnostics Framework Client-based connections to support basic diagnostics capabilities with the Network Diagnostics Framework.

▶ New cryptographic L2TP/IPSec-based VPN connections, which now support the Advanced Encryption Standard (AES) with 128- and 256-bit keys.

▶ Windows Server 2008 R2 shows evolutionary progress in the area of remote access.

▶ VPN Reconnect enables users to transparently reconnect to traditional VPN connections even when roaming or changing networks, which is made possible through the implementation the IKEv2 mobility function, MOBIKE.

## Components Needed to Create a Traditional VPN Connection

A point-to-point link, or tunnel, is created by encapsulating or wrapping the data with a header that provides routing information that allows the data to travel through the Internet. A virtual private network connection requires a VPN client and a VPN server or infrastructure. A secured connection is created between the client and server through encryption that establishes the tunnel, as shown in Figure 24.3.

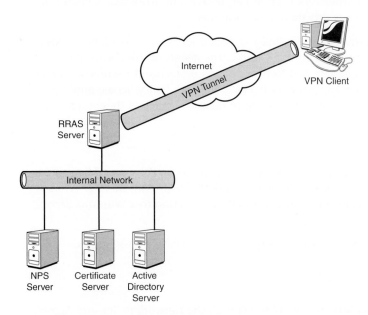

FIGURE 24.3    Establishing a VPN tunnel between a client and server.

The tunnel is the portion of the connection in which data is encapsulated. The VPN connection is the portion of the connection where the data is encrypted. The data encapsulation, along with the encryption, provides a secure VPN connection.

**NOTE**

A tunnel that is created without the encryption is not a VPN connection because the private data is sent across the Internet unencrypted and can be easily read. This violates the "P" for Private in a Virtual Private Network (VPN).

The figure also depicts the roles in a typical Windows 2008 VPN infrastructure. The roles in Windows Server 2008 R2 consist of the following:

▶ VPN client

▶ RRAS server

- ▶ NPS server

- ▶ Certificate server

- ▶ Active Directory server

These roles work together to provide the VPN functionality.

A shared or public internetwork is required to establish a VPN connection. For Windows Server 2008 R2, the transit internetwork is always an IP-based network that includes the Internet as well as a corporation's private IP-based intranet.

The topics and examples in this chapter utilize Certificate Services, Network Policy Server, and Network Access Protection to secure VPN access. The details of the Certificate Authority, the Network Policy Server, and Network Access Protection in Windows Server 2008 R2 are covered in Chapter 15, "Security Policies, Network Policy Server, and Network Access Protection." Please refer to that chapter for in-depth coverage of these topics.

## The VPN Client

A VPN client is a computer that initiates a VPN connection to a VPN server. Microsoft clients, including Windows NT 4.0, Windows 9x, Windows 2000, Windows XP, Windows Vista, and Windows 7, can create a remote access VPN connection to a Windows Server 2008 R2 system.

VPN clients can also be any non-Microsoft PPTP client or L2TP client using IPSec.

## The RRAS Server

An RRAS server is a Windows Server 2008 R2 server with the Network Policy and Access Services role installed and the Routing and Remote Access Service role services installed. This is the server that accepts VPN connections from VPN clients. The RRAS server name or IP address must be resolvable as well as accessible through corporate firewalls, which could be by either having a network interface connected to the demilitarized zone (DMZ) or by providing the appropriate access rule on the firewall.

## The NPS System

The Network Policy Server (NPS) provides the authentication, authorization, auditing, and accounting for the VPN clients. The NPS system has the Network Policy and Access Services role installed with the Network Policy Server role service installed. In Windows Server 2008, NPS was an English-only solution. In Windows Server 2008 R2, support is added for non-English character sets.

The Network Policy Server (NPS) is used to enforce network access policies for client health, client authentication, and client authorization. NPS works with Network Access Protection (NAP), which is a technology to manage, enforce, and remediate client health. The NPS service provides the policies for NAP to validate against. NPS also has multiple templates for larger-scale deployments or configuring multiple NPS servers identically.

In NAP, System Health Agents (SHAs) are used to inspect and assess the health of clients according to policies. System Health Validators (SHVs) are the policies that the agents validate against.

The Windows Security Health Agent is the SHA in Windows 7 and the Windows Security Health Validator is the SHA in Windows Server 2008 R2. These provide the following features in their SHVs:

▶ Firewall software installed and enabled

▶ Antivirus software installed and running

▶ Current antivirus updates installed

▶ Antispyware installed and running

▶ Current antispyware updates installed

▶ Microsoft Update Service enabled

These are configured in the client health policies or SHVs on the NPS. When a client attempts a connection, the client SHA will send a Statement of Health (SoH) to the NPS system. The SoH is compared with the health policy, resulting in a pass or a fail. Based on that result, the NPS does one of four actions. In the case of a pass (that is, the client is healthy), it just allows the client to connect. In the case where the SoH fails the policy comparison (that is, the client is unhealthy), the NPS can prevent the client from connecting, connect the client to a restricted network, or even allow the client to connect even though it is unhealthy, as shown in Table 24.1.

TABLE 24.1    NPS Actions

| SoH Versus Policy | NPS Action |
| --- | --- |
| Passes | Client is allowed to connect. |
| Fails | Client is not allowed to connect; client is connected to a restricted network; or client is allowed to connect even if it is deemed unhealthy. |

When a client fails and is not allowed to connect, that is straightforward. When the client fails and is connected to a restricted network, this allows the client to connect to secured remediation servers to download software, patches, and/or updates to be remediated. The SHA can even conduct remediation automatically and then allow the client to connect. Interestingly, in some cases, the client might fail and yet the policy still allows it to connect. This might be for reporting purposes.

Additionally, third-party SHVs and SHAs can be written that access the NAP application programming interface (API).

Remediation server groups can be configured to restrict noncompliant VPN clients to just those servers where software and updates are stored. After the appropriate software and updates are applied that bring the client into compliance, the NPS will allow the clients full access to the network.

This server handles VPN client authentication requests for the RRAS server and validates those requests against its policies. This allows for a centralized policy and access control, while allowing the RRAS server role to be scaled out as needed.

See Chapter 15 for more details on the NPS system and NAP technologies.

## Certificate Server

The certificate server is a Certificate Authority (CA) that issues certificates for the servers and clients to use in the authentication and encryption of tunnels. In Windows Server 2008 R2, this is a Windows Server 2008 R2 server with the Active Directory Certificate Services role installed with the Certification Authority and the Certification Authority Web Enrollment role services installed. These roles also require some other supporting roles to be installed, such as the Web Server (IIS) role and the File Services role.

Using Windows Server 2008 R2 allows the administrator to issue and control certificates for the VPN infrastructure. This could also be handled by a third-party CA such as VeriSign, thereby not requiring a server albeit at an annual cost.

Although not a requirement for all configurations of the VPN infrastructure, certificates are considered a best practice to enhance the security of the VPN infrastructure. An AD certificate server is always required for DirectAccess deployment. Later in the chapter, we review the various VPN protocols and the role that certificates play in them.

Chapter 15 provides more details on the certificate server.

## Active Directory Server

The Active Directory server provides the authentication database for the VPN client users. In Windows Server 2008 R2, this is a server with the Active Directory Domain Services role installed.

# Authentication Options to an RRAS System

Authentication in any networking environment is critical for validating whether the individual wanting access should be allowed access to network resources. Authentication is an important component in the Windows Server 2008 R2 security initiative. Windows Server 2008 R2 can authenticate a remote access user connection through a variety of PPP authentication protocols, including the following:

- Password Authentication Protocol (PAP)
- Challenge-Handshake Authentication Protocol (CHAP)
- Microsoft Challenge Handshake Authentication Protocol (MS-CHAP)
- MS-CHAP version 2 (MS-CHAP v2)

- ▶ Extensible Authentication Protocol (EAP)

- ▶ Protected Extensible Authentication Protocol (PEAP)

## Authentication Protocols for PPTP Connections

For PPTP connections, only four authentication protocols (MS-CHAP, MS-CHAP v2, EAP, and PEAP) provide a mechanism to generate the same encryption key on both the VPN client and VPN server. Microsoft Point-to-Point Encryption (MPPE) uses this encryption key to encrypt all PPTP data sent on the VPN connection. MS-CHAP and MS-CHAP v2 are password-based authentication protocols.

Without a Certificate Authority (CA) server or smart cards, MS-CHAP v2 is highly recommended because it provides a stronger authentication protocol than MS-CHAP. MS-CHAP v2 also provides mutual authentication, which allows the VPN client to be authenticated by the VPN server and the VPN server to be authenticated by the VPN client.

If a password-based authentication protocol must be used, it is good practice to enforce the use of strong passwords (passwords greater than eight characters) that contain a random mixture of upper- and lowercase letters, numbers, and punctuation. Group policies can be used in Active Directory to enforce strong user passwords.

## EAP and PEAP Authentication Protocols

Extensible Authentication Protocol (EAP) and Protected Extensible Authentication Protocol (PEAP) are designed to be used along with a certificate infrastructure that uses user certificates or smart cards.

With EAP, the VPN client sends its user certificate for authentication, and the VPN server sends a computer certificate for authentication. This is the strongest authentication method because it does not rely on passwords. Third-party CAs can be used as long as the certificate in the computer store of the Network Policy Server (NPS) server contains the Server Authentication certificate purpose (also known as a certificate usage or certificate issuance policy). A certificate purpose is identified using an object identifier (OID). If the OID for Server Authentication is 1.3.6.1.5.5.7.3.1, the user certificate installed on the Windows remote access client must contain the Client Authentication certificate purpose (OID 1.3.6.1.5.5.7.3.2).

PEAP does not specify an authentication method, but rather secures EAP by creating an encrypted channel between the client and the server. As such, it provides additional security on top of EAP. PEAP can even be used with MS-CHAP v2 to provide additional security to the password authentication protocol.

## Authentication Protocols for L2TP/IPSec Connections

For L2TP/IPSec connections, any authentication protocol can be used because the authentication occurs after the VPN client and VPN server have established a secure connection known as an IPSec security association (SA). The use of a strong authentication protocol such as MS-CHAP v2, EAP, or PEAP is recommended to provide strong user authentication.

## Choosing the Best Authentication Protocol

Organizations spend very little time choosing the most appropriate authentication protocol to use with their VPN connections. In many cases, the lack of knowledge about the differences between the various authentication protocols is the reason a selection is not made. In other cases, the desire for simplicity is the reason heightened security is not chosen as part of the organization's authentication protocol decisions. Whatever the case, we make the following suggestions to assist you in selecting the best authentication protocol for VPN connections:

▶ Using the EAP or PEAP authentication protocol for PPTP, L2TP, and SSTP connections is highly recommended if the following conditions exist in an organization. If a smart card will be used, or if a certificate infrastructure that issues user certificates exists, then EAP is the best and most secure option. Note that EAP is supported only by VPN clients running Windows XP, Windows 2000 client, Windows Vista, Windows 7, Windows 2000 Server, Windows Server 2003, Windows Server 2008, and Windows Server 2008 R2.

▶ Use PEAP with EAP-MS-CHAP v2 as a method of easing the deployment burden. In this configuration, certificates are required only for the VPN server infrastructure and not for the clients. However, the key generation is done using Transport Level Security (TLS) with mutual authentication for greatly enhanced security.

▶ Use MS-CHAP v2 and enforce strong passwords using Group Policy if you must use a password-based authentication protocol. Although not as strong of a security protocol as PEAP or EAP, MS-CHAP v2 is supported by computers running Windows Server 2008, Windows Server 2008 R2, Windows Server 2003, Windows 2000 Server, Windows Vista, Windows 7, Windows XP, Windows 2000 client, Windows NT 4.0 with Service Pack 4 and higher, Windows Me, Windows 98, and Windows 95 with the Windows Dial-Up Networking 1.3 or higher Performance and Security Update.

# VPN Protocols

PPTP, L2TP, and SSTP are the communication standards used to manage tunnels and encapsulate private data. It is important to note that data traveling through a tunnel must also be encrypted to be a VPN connection. Windows Server 2008 R2 includes PPTP, L2TP, and SSTP tunneling protocols.

To establish a tunnel, both the tunnel client and tunnel server must be using the same tunneling protocol. Tunneling technology can be based on either a Layer 2 or Layer 3 tunneling protocol that corresponds to the Open System Interconnection (OSI) reference model. Layer 2 protocols correspond to the Data-link layer and use frames as their unit of exchange. PPTP and L2TP are Layer 2 tunneling protocols that encapsulate the payload in a PPP frame before it is sent across the Internet. Layer 3 protocols correspond to the

Network layer and use packets. IPSec tunnel mode is a Layer 3 tunneling protocol that encapsulates IP packets in an additional IP header before sending them across the Internet.

Windows 7, Windows Vista, Windows XP, and Windows 2000 workstation VPN client and server computers support both L2TP/IPSec and PPTP by default. Both PPTP and L2TP/IPSec use PPP to provide an initial envelope for the data and then append additional headers for transport through the Internet. PPTP and L2TP also provide a logical transport mechanism to send PPP payloads and provide tunneling or encapsulation so that PPP payloads based on any protocol can be sent across the Internet. PPTP and L2TP rely on the PPP connection process to perform user authentication and protocol configuration.

There are a few differences between the three protocols. First, when using PPTP, the data encryption begins after the PPP connection process is completed, which means PPP authentication is used. With L2TP/IPSec, data encryption begins before the PPP connection process by negotiating an IPSec security association. In SSTP, the session is encrypted by SSL before authentication begins. In DirectAccess, communications are encrypted transparently before user data begins to flow.

Second, PPTP connections use MPPE, a stream cipher that is based on the Rivest-Shamir-Adleman (RSA) RC-4 encryption algorithm and uses 40-, 56-, or 128-bit encryption keys. Stream ciphers encrypt data as a bit stream. L2TP/IPSec connections use the Data Encryption Standard (DES), which is a block cipher that uses either a 56-bit key for DES or three 56-bit keys for 3DES. Block ciphers encrypt data in discrete blocks (64-bit blocks, in the case of DES). SSTP uses SSL with RC4 or AES. DirectAccess uses 3DES or AES.

Finally, PPTP connections require only user-level authentication through a PPP-based authentication protocol. L2TP/IPSec connections require the same user-level authentication as well as computer-level authentication using computer certificates. In contrast, SSTP and DirectAccess only require computer-level certificates for the VPN servers.

Table 24.2 compares some of the characteristics of the three tunneling protocols.

TABLE 24.2   Comparing VPN Protocols

| Characteristics | PPTP | L2TP/IPSec | SSTP |
|---|---|---|---|
| Encapsulation | GRE | L2TP over UDP | SSTP over TCP |
| Encryption | Microsoft Point-to-Point Encryption (MPPE) with RC4 | IPSec ESP with Triple Data Encryption Standard (3DES) or Advanced Encryption Standard (AES) | SSL with RC4 or AES |
| Tunnel maintenance protocol | PPTP | L2TP | SSTP |
| When user authentication occurs | Before encryption begins | After the IPSec session is established | After the SSL session is established |

TABLE 24.2    Comparing VPN Protocols

| Characteristics | PPTP | L2TP/IPSec | SSTP |
| --- | --- | --- | --- |
| Certificates needed | None | Computer certificates on both the VPN client and VPN server | Computer certificate on the VPN server and root CA certificate on the VPN client |
| Client | Windows 9x and above | Windows 2000 and above | Windows Server 2008, Windows XP SP3, and Windows Vista SP1 |

## Tunneling Within a Windows Server 2008 R2 Networking Environment

For Layer 2 tunneling technologies, such as PPTP, L2TP, and SSTP, a tunnel is similar to a session; both of the tunnel endpoints must agree to the tunnel and must negotiate configuration variables, such as address assignment or encryption or compression parameters. In most cases, data transferred across the tunnel is sent using a datagram-based protocol. A tunnel maintenance protocol is used as the mechanism to manage the tunnel.

Layer 3 tunneling technologies generally assume that all the configuration settings are preconfigured, often by manual processes. For these protocols, there might be no tunnel maintenance phase. For Layer 2 protocols (PPTP, L2TP, and SSTP), however, a tunnel must be created, maintained, and then terminated.

After the tunnel is established, tunneled data can be sent. The tunnel client or server uses a tunnel data transfer protocol to prepare the data for transfer. For example, as illustrated in Figure 24.4, when the tunnel client sends a payload to the tunnel server, the tunnel client first appends a tunnel data transfer protocol header to the payload. The client then sends the resulting encapsulated payload across the internetwork, which routes it to the tunnel server. The tunnel server accepts the packets, removes the tunnel data transfer protocol header, and forwards the payload to the target network. Information sent between the tunnel server and tunnel client behaves similarly.

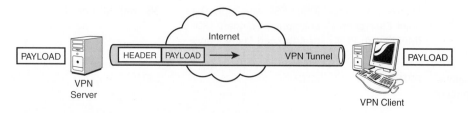

FIGURE 24.4    Tunneling payload through a VPN connection.

## Point-to-Point Tunneling Protocol

The Point-to-Point Tunneling Protocol (PPTP) is a Layer 2 protocol that encapsulates PPP frames in IP datagrams for transmission over the Internet. PPTP can be used for remote access and router-to-router VPN connections. It uses a TCP connection for tunnel maintenance and a modified version of Generic Routing Encapsulation (GRE) to encapsulate PPP frames for tunneled data. The payloads of the encapsulated PPP frames can be encrypted and/or compressed. Figure 24.5 shows the structure of a PPTP packet containing user data.

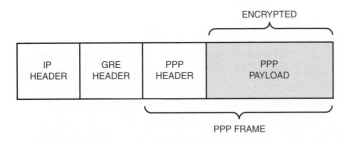

FIGURE 24.5    Structure of the PPTP packet.

## Layer 2 Tunneling Protocol

Layer 2 Tunneling Protocol (L2TP) is a combination of the Point-to-Point Tunneling Protocol (PPTP) and Layer 2 Forwarding (L2F), a technology proposed by Cisco Systems, Inc. L2TP encapsulates PPP frames that are sent over IP, X.25, frame relay, and ATM networks. The payloads of encapsulated PPP frames can be encrypted and/or compressed. When sent over the Internet, L2TP frames are encapsulated as User Datagram Protocol (UDP) messages, as shown in Figure 24.6.

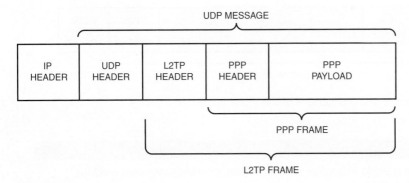

FIGURE 24.6    Structure of the L2TP packet.

L2TP frames include L2TP connection maintenance messages and tunneled data. L2TP connection maintenance messages include only the L2TP header. L2TP tunneled data includes a PPP header and PPP payload. The PPP payload can be encrypted or compressed (or both) using standard PPP encryption and compression methods.

In Windows Server 2008 R2, L2TP connections do not negotiate the use of PPP encryption through Microsoft Point-to-Point Encryption (MPPE). Instead, encryption is provided through the use of the IP Security (IPSec) Encapsulating Security Payload (ESP) header and trailer.

## IP Security

IP Security (IPSec) was designed as an end-to-end mechanism for ensuring data security in IP-based communications. Illustrated in Figure 24.7, the IPSec architecture includes an authentication header to verify data integrity and an encapsulation security payload for both data integrity and data encryption. IPSec provides two important functions that ensure confidentiality: data encryption and data integrity. IPSec uses an authentication header (AH) to provide source authentication and integrity without encryption and the Encapsulating Security Payload (ESP) to provide authentication and integrity along with encryption. With IPSec, only the sender and recipient know the security key. If the authentication data is valid, the recipient knows that the communication came from the sender and that it was not changed in transit.

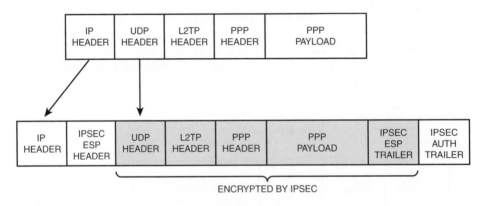

FIGURE 24.7    Structure and architecture of the IPSec packet.

## Secure Socket Tunneling Protocol

Introduced in Windows Server 2008, SSTP was specifically developed to get around the difficulties of setting up VPN tunnels through corporate firewalls, which block many of the ports and protocols used by PPTP and L2TP. The SSTP tunnel uses the HTTP over SSL (HTTPS) protocol, which is widely supported for secure web traffic. SSTP uses port 443 for the connection.

The tunneling protocol functions by encapsulating the original IP packet with a PPP header and then an SSTP header. The SSTP header, the PPP header, and the original IP packet are all encrypted by the SSL session. Finally, an IP header is added to the packet and it is routed to the destination. The structure of the packet is shown in Figure 24.8.

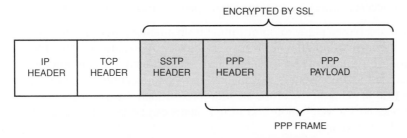

FIGURE 24.8   Structure and architecture of the SSTP packet.

> **NOTE**
>
> Interestingly, even though SSTP is based on the HTTPS web protocol, the VPN server does not have to be configured with IIS. The RRAS VPN server listens for SSTP connections on the uniform resource identifier (URI) /sra_{BA195980-CD49-458b-9E23-C84EE0ADCD75}/. This does not conflict with or require IIS, so IIS can be installed if needed for other purposes.

Unfortunately, SSTP does not support tunneling through web proxies that require authentication. Another limitation of SSTP is that it does not support site-to-site connections in Windows Server 2008 R2, which both PPTP and L2TP do.

# DirectAccess in Windows Server 2008 R2

DirectAccess is a new remote access protocol in Windows Server 2008 R2 that provides network node connectivity to remote systems without any user login requirements. DirectAccess addresses several challenges with traditional VPN, including the following:

▶ The need for the user to manually connect to the VPN.

▶ The delay the user experiences when connecting to the VPN while health checks are completed during the connection process.

▶ The need for the user to reconnect manually if an established VPN connection is lost.

▶ The slow performance when all traffic (intranet and Internet) is routed through the VPN connection.

These challenges can cause users to limit the use of traditional VPN solutions. DirectAccess has been designed from the ground up to address those challenges. DirectAccess hides all the connection processes from the users and intelligently routes intranet versus Internet traffic, thereby alleviating the challenges of traditional VPNs. It connects as soon as the computer starts up and conducts the health checks, rather than when the user is logging in. The connection process is transparent to the user and the user never needs to explicitly connect to DirectAccess. Finally, DirectAccess has built-in options to control how DNS requests are handled, effectively bifurcating the Internet and intranet traffic to avoid burdening the remote access connection and improving performance.

DirectAccess creates an encrypted point-to-point tunnel from a remote user—in this case, specifically a remote user on Windows 7—to the internal "enterprise" network. The difference is that the connection is transparent to the user. Once configured, the computer will automatically connect to the office from any available Internet connection. The user experience is almost identical to being in the office. In addition, through the use of the Windows Server 2008 R2 NPS server, remote-connected clients can be securely managed similarly to internal client systems.

> **NOTE**
>
> Although positioned as an alternative to a VPN, the DirectAccess technology has all the elements of a VPN. It establishes a secure private tunnel through public networks using IPSec and certificates, with an end result functionally not much different from L2TP. The differences are mainly administrative rather than technical.

DirectAccess uses IPv6, IPSec, and certificates to establish secure connections from the DirectAccess clients to intranet resources via the DirectAccess server. To traverse public IPv4 networks, DirectAccess uses IPv6 transition technologies such as ISATAP, Teredo, and 6to4.

DirectAccess has some specific requirements, as follows:

▶ The server running Windows Server 2008 R2 needs to have two network cards: one attached to the intranet and one attached to the Internet.

▶ The Internet network card must have two consecutive public IPv4 addresses.

▶ The Intranet resources and applications must support IPv6.

▶ The DirectAccess clients need to be running Windows 7; older clients are not supported.

▶ A domain controller and DNS server that the systems are connected to need to be running Windows Server 2008 SP2 or Windows Server 2008 R2.

▶ A PKI needs to be available to issue certificates with a published Internet available certificate revocation list (CRL).

These requirements are somewhat stringent and might prevent many organizations from deploying DirectAccess. However, for an organization with an up-to-date infrastructure, servers, and clients, DirectAccess can be an excellent solution.

## DirectAccess and IPv6

DirectAccess is designed on top of IPv6 and requires that all endpoint devices support IPv6. It is one of the first services to require this modern protocol.

DirectAccess is most likely to be deployed in an IPv4 world, given the prevalence of IPv4 on the Internet today. This creates an IPv4 gap (shown in Figure 24.9) across which IPv6 devices like DirectAccess clients need to communicate.

FIGURE 24.9   The IPv4 gap between IPv6 devices.

Most organizations will need to use IPv6 transition technologies to bridge the IPv4 gap from their IPv6 enlightened devices to communicate. This, in effect, routes the IPv6 communications through the IPv4 protocol stack, as shown in Figure 24.10. The packets traveling down the IPv6 protocol stack take a sharp turn and move across the protocol stack to the IPv4 protocol stack, allowing them to transit the IPv4 network. On the other side, the same packets come in via the IPv4 protocol stack, but are routed to the IPv6 stack.

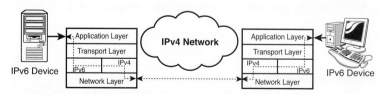

FIGURE 24.10   Bridging the IPv4 gap with transition technologies.

Communications between IPv6 devices like DirectAccess clients over IPv4 networks is accomplished with IPv6 over IPv4 tunneling. In tunneling, the IPv6 packets are encapsulated in an IPv4 packet by the source device and routed through the IPv4 network. When the encapsulated packet arrives at the boundary between the IPv4 and IPv6 networks, the IPv4 encapsulation is stripped off and the IPv6 packet continues on its way. The most common tunneling protocols are ISATAP, 6to4, and Teredo.

For organizations, the IPv6 tunneling protocols are used for the following purposes:

▶ **ISATAP**—This protocol is used to automatically assign IPv6 addresses within the organization's IPv4 intranet.

▶ **6to4**—This protocol is used to automatically assign IPv6 addresses and route across the public IPv4 Internet.

▶ **Teredo**—This protocol is used to automatically assign IPv6 addresses and route across the public IPv4 Internet to devices behind Network Address Translation (NAT) firewalls.

For organizations that have not deployed IPv6 natively, Microsoft Windows Server 2008 R2 and Windows 7 support ISATAP, 6to4, and Teredo transition protocols. However, even while DirectAccess clients are using IPv6 transitional technologies like Teredo or 6to4, it is ultimately communicating from IPv6 clients to IPv6 hosts.

Internally, DirectAccess can use Network Address Translation-Protocol Translation (NAT-PT) devices, which can be used to provide access to IPv4 resources. Resources that don't support IPv6 natively can be accessed through the use of a Network Address Translation-Protocol Translation (NAT-PT) device. Microsoft Windows Server 2008 R2 does not currently include that capability, so a third-party device would be needed for this functionality.

> **NOTE**
>
> NAT-PT is covered in IETF RFC-2766 (http://tools.ietf.org/html/rfc2766), but was reclassified from a Proposed Standard to Historic due to issues with the standard. RFC4966 (http://tools.ietf.org/html/rfc4966) contains the details of these issues. These include difficulty with integrity mechanisms, inability to redirect protocols that lack demultiplexing capabilities, premature state timeouts, loss of information due to IPv4 and IPv6 header incompatibilities, packet fragmentation issues, and an inability to handle multicast traffic. NAT-PT devices are only recommended as a stop-gap measure due to these issues.

For organizations that have not deployed IPv6, the deployment of DirectAccess is an excellent project to test the IPv6 waters with. The infrastructure can be deployed in parallel with existing remote access solutions and without impacting the existing IPv4 addressing scheme, providing IT personnel with a chance to learn IPv6 and its integration with IPv4 in a low-impact production setting.

See Chapter 10, "Domain Name System and IPv6," for a detailed discussion of the IPv6 protocol and the transition technologies needed to bridge the IPv4 gap.

## A Tale of Two Tunnels

The DirectAccess client establishes two tunnels, which are key to the versatility of this method of remote access. These tunnels are IPSec Encapsulating Security Payload (ESP) tunnels that are authenticated with certificates and encrypted to ensure the confidentiality. These tunnels are as follows:

▶ **Computer tunnel**—The computer tunnel is established first when the DirectAccess client starts up. This tunnel is authenticated with the computer certificate only and provides access to the intranet DNS and domain controllers. This tunnel is also used to download the computer group policy and request user authentication.

▶ **User tunnel**—This tunnel is authenticated with the computer certificate and the user credentials and provides access to the intranet resources. This tunnel is used to download user group policy as well.

Both these tunnels are established transparently to the user. The user does not have to present credentials above and beyond the normal Windows logon to establish remote access. The two tunnels are shown in Figure 24.11.

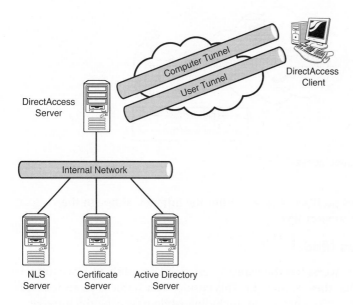

FIGURE 24.11   The two DirectAccess tunnels.

These tunnels allow for the transparent establishment of remote access, essentially allowing the computer to connect to the intranet even when no user is logged on. This allows the DirectAccess client to receive Group Policy remotely and be managed by the management servers in the intranet. When a user logs on, they are authenticating to the intranet and, thus, ensuring that users are subject to the latest requirements, password changes, and policies. In contrast, other VPN solutions typically have users authenticating using cached credentials against the local machine and then establishing the remote access connection.

## End-to-Edge DirectAccess Model

The end-to-edge model of DirectAccess has the DirectAccess client establish an IPSec tunnel to the DirectAccess server. The DirectAccess server then forwards unprotected traffic to the intranet resources. This is the most common form of DirectAccess and closely follows a standard remote access methodology.

Figure 24.12 shows the end-to-edge connection model. Note that there is a single protected (solid line) connection through the tunnel to the DirectAccess server, which then is forwarded to each of the application servers in three separate unprotected (dashed line) connections.

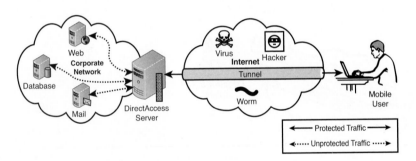

FIGURE 24.12    End-to-edge DirectAccess.

The end-to-edge model requires no IPSec support within the intranet, although the intranet resources still need to support IPv6.

## End-to-End DirectAccess Model

The end-to-end model of DirectAccess has the DirectAccess client establish an IPSec tunnel with each application server that they connect to. This ensures that traffic is protected end to end (hence the name) by the IPSec encryption, including while traversing the intranet.

Figure 24.13 shows the end-to-end connection model. Note that there is a protected (solid line) connection through the tunnel and the DirectAccess server to each of the application servers. This indicates that there are separate IPSec connections to each server, which are protected by encryption not only through the Internet but also through the intranet.

The end-to-end model requires that each application server run on Windows Server 2008 or Windows Server 2008 R2, as well as use IPv6 and IPSec. There is also some additional overhead for the IPSec connections.

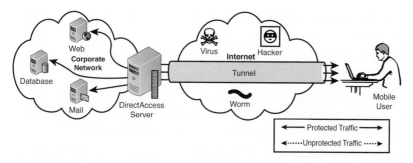

FIGURE 24.13   End-to-end DirectAccess.

The requirement that all application servers be Windows Server 2008 or higher is a difficult hurdle to overcome in today's heterogeneous IT environments. This makes the end-to-end model of DirectAccess less common than the end-to-edge model.

## Internet Versus Intranet Traffic with DirectAccess

One of the benefits of DirectAccess is the ability to separate the intranet traffic (destined for internal servers) from the Internet traffic (destined for external servers). This conserves the corporate bandwidth for access to corporate resources. By specifying the domains and subdomains for which the DirectAccess server provides access, traffic for those domains is directed through the DirectAccess connection. Other traffic is routed through the default routes and bypasses the DirectAccess connection. This is the highest performance configuration and is the default mode of operation.

However, in some cases, administrators might want to have all traffic route through the DirectAccess connection. Examples of this include organizations that want to control or monitor their client communications or prevent access to certain Internet sites. In these cases, the DirectAccess client can be configured to route all traffic through the DirectAccess connection.

## DirectAccess Components

DirectAccess leverages IPv6 technology along with PKI to provide a seamless secure connection to the enterprise network. DirectAccess runs at boot and connects as soon as Internet connectivity is established. There's no need for a user to configure a VPN client or logon. From an administrative perspective, this technology allows system administrators to manage and monitor remote systems through tools like Microsoft System Center Configuration Manager (SCCM) and Group Policy. DirectAccess finally puts remote workers on equal ground with traditional office employees.

The following list depicts the components found in a DirectAccess deployment:

▶ **DirectAccess server**—This is the server that connects to the internal network and the Internet. It has to be running Windows Server 2008 R2 with two physical interfaces: one on the public Internet and one for the internal network. The public interface must have two consecutive public IP addresses assigned.

▶ **DirectAccess client**—This is a computer running Windows 7. It must be a domain member with a certificate.

▶ **Corporate IPv6 network**—The IPv6 network to which DirectAccess clients will be connecting remotely.

▶ **Certificate server**—This server issues the certificates that support the tunnel creation, authentication, and security. This certificate server must have a published certificate revocation list (CRL) that is available internally and externally.

▶ **Network Location Server (NLS)**—This is an HTTPS site that serves as the indicator to the DirectAccess client if it is connected to the Internet or the intranet.

▶ **Active Directory and DNS server**—This server must be running Windows Server 2008 SP2 or Windows Server 2008 R2. The AD and DNS role can be separate servers, although most organizations will have these services on the same server.

Figure 24.14 shows the components and their connections.

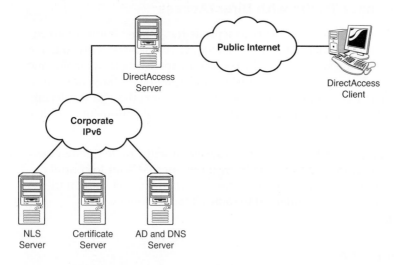

FIGURE 24.14    DirectAccess components.

Smart cards or NAP protection can also be implemented for additional security if desired. In its most simple configuration, DirectAccess requires each client to have a valid computer certificate for authentication to the internal network. This takes the place of a traditional username and password.

DirectAccess requires IPv6 on the internal enterprise network. It leverages conversion technology like Teredo, 6to4, and also the new IP-HTTPS for remote clients using IPv4 to connect to the IPv6 enterprise network. These new technologies are described in the following list:

▶ Teredo is the most common method for DirectAccess. It allows IPv6 traffic to pass through NAT devices that transition out to an IPv4 public network. A good example is many "hot spot" connections at coffee shops and many home networks.

▶ 6to4 directly translates IPv6 addresses into IPv4 addresses. If remote clients are directly connected to the Internet and have only IPv4 public IP addresses, 6to4 is the preferred method for connectivity.

▶ IP-HTTPS is a new protocol in Windows 7 and Windows Server 2008 R2. It tunnels IPv6 traffic over an IPv4 HTTPS tunnel between a DirectAccess client and a DirectAccess server. Although this might seem like the simplest option, it comes at a large performance cost due to network overhead and should be used only as a last resort.

The DirectAccess protocol is very robust and will transparently attempt multiple methods of access to establish a connection.

## Network Location Service

The Network Location Service (NLS) is a critical component for the DirectAccess architecture. This is a website that clients attempt to connect to determine if they are currently connected to the Internet or to the intranet. It is the URL of a highly available website in the corporate intranet.

There are two behaviors that would be experienced for the DirectAccess client system. They are as follows:

▶ If the DirectAccess client can reach the NLS URL, it assumes that it is connected to the corporate network and no further action is necessary.

▶ If the DirectAccess client cannot reach the NLS URL, it assumes that it is not connected to the corporate network and then begins the DirectAccess connection process.

The NLS service is normally a highly available website, such as servers in a Network Load Balanced (NLB) cluster or a Windows cluster.

> **NOTE**
>
> As you can see, if the NLS website is down, this can result in the disastrous situation of all the DirectAccess clients suddenly thinking they are on the Internet, even though they are really in the intranet. They would all then begin the DirectAccess connection process. That's why the NLS website must be highly available.

## DirectAccess Connection Process

The DirectAccess client is very robust and will try a variety of methods to connect to the corporate network. The connection process is started when the DirectAccess client detects that it is connected to a network—that is, a network transition such as the connection to a LAN, wireless access point, or other connection becomes active.

The DirectAccess client goes through the following connection process when it detects that it is connected to a network:

1. The DirectAccess client attempts to connect to the NLS website. If it can reach the site, it determines that it is connected to the intranet and stops the DirectAccess process. If it cannot reach the NLS website, it determines that it is connected to the Internet and continues with the DirectAccess process.

2. The DirectAccess client establishes an IPSec tunnel to the DirectAccess server using IPv6. If there is an intervening IPv4 network, the client uses the Teredo or 6to4 protocols to tunnel IPv6 over IPv4.

3. If the DirectAccess client is unable to connect using the Teredo or 6to4 protocols, the client will attempt to connect using the IP-HTTPS protocol.

4. The DirectAccess client establishes an IPSec tunnel to the DirectAccess server using IPv6. The DirectAccess client and the DirectAccess server mutually authenticate using certificates in the process of setting up the IPSec computer tunnel.

5. The DirectAccess client contacts the domain controller and obtains the computer group policy.

### NOTE

The user does not have to be logged on to the computer for this process to complete to this point in the process.

6. The DirectAccess user logs on or the logged-on credentials are used in conjunction with the certificates to establish the IPSec user tunnel. The user group policy is applied to the DirectAccess client.

7. The DirectAccess server begins forwarding traffic from the DirectAccess client to authorized intranet resources.

This entire process is transparent to the user and requires no user interaction. In the event of an interruption in network connectivity, the DirectAccess client will reestablish the connection through this process when it detects network connectivity again.

# Choosing Between Traditional VPN Technologies and DirectAccess

One of the choices to make when you're deploying Windows Server 2008 R2-based remote access is the choice between a traditional VPN technology and the new DirectAccess.

Within the VPNs technologies are a number of choices, primarily whether to use L2TP/IPSec or PPTP.

## Advantages of L2TP/IPSec

Although PPTP users significantly outnumber L2TP/IPSec users, because of a higher level of security in L2TP/IPSec as well as several other benefits of L2TP/IPSec, organizations that are seeking to improve secured remote connectivity are beginning to implement L2TP/IPSec VPN as their remote and mobile access standard. The following are the advantages of using L2TP/IPSec over PPTP:

▶ IPSec provides per-packet data authentication (proof that the data was sent by the authorized user), data integrity (proof that the data was not modified in transit), replay protection (prevention from resending a stream of captured packets), and data confidentiality (prevention from interpreting captured packets without the encryption key). PPTP provides only per-packet data confidentiality.

▶ L2TP/IPSec connections provide stronger authentication by requiring both computer-level authentication through certificates and user-level authentication through a PPP authentication protocol.

▶ PPP packets exchanged during user-level authentication are never sent unencrypted because the PPP connection process for L2TP/IPSec occurs after the IPSec security associations are established. If intercepted, the PPP authentication exchange for some types of PPP authentication protocols can be used to perform offline dictionary attacks and determine user passwords. If the PPP authentication exchange is encrypted, offline dictionary attacks are possible only after the encrypted packets have been successfully decrypted.

## Advantages of PPTP

Although L2TP/IPSec is more secure than a PPTP VPN session, there are significant reasons organizations choose PPTP over L2TP/IPSec. The following are advantages of PPTP over L2TP/IPSec:

▶ PPTP does not require a certificate infrastructure. L2TP/IPSec, SSTP, and DirectAccess require a certificate infrastructure for issuing computer certificates to the VPN server computer (or other authenticating server) and all VPN client computers.

▶ PPTP can be used by all Windows desktop platforms (Windows Server 2008, Windows Server 2008 R2, Windows Server 2003, Windows 2000 Server, Windows 7,

Windows Vista, Windows XP, Windows 2000 client, Windows NT 4.0, Windows Millennium Edition [Me], Windows 98, and Windows 95 with the Windows Dial-Up Networking 1.3 Performance and Security Update). Windows Server 2008 R2, Windows Server 2008, Windows Server 2003, Windows 2000 Server, Windows 7, Windows Vista, Windows XP, and Windows 2000 Workstation VPN clients are the only clients that support L2TP/IPSec and the use of certificates. Windows 7 is the only client that supports DirectAccess.

IPSec functions at a layer below the TCP/IP stack. This layer is controlled by a security policy on each computer and a negotiated security association between the sender and receiver. The policy consists of a set of filters and associated security behaviors. If a packet's IP address, protocol, and port number match a filter, the packet is subject to the associated security behavior.

## Advantages of SSTP

The SSTP protocol in Windows Server 2008 R2 gives administrators the capability to establish tunnels across the majority of corporate networks, bypassing many of the technical hurdles that stop PPTP and L2TP.

The advantages of SSTP are as follows:

▶ SSTP helps lower administrative costs by reducing the technical steps needed to tunnel between organizations. Because HTTPS is allowed through most firewalls and proxy servers, there is no additional infrastructure changes needed to support SSTP.

▶ SSTP is certificate-based security implemented via SSL. However, certificates only need to be issued to the servers rather than the clients. This provides the security benefits of L2TP, but with almost the ease of configuration of PPTP.

The benefits are offset by the requirement that the client Certificate Authority requirements and the operating system requirement. The client requirement is that it trusts the CA issuing the certificates and that it can access the certificate revocation list.

Support for SSTP in clients is available in Windows Server 2008, Windows Server 2008 R2, Windows 7, Windows XP SP3 or later, and Windows Vista SP1 or later.

## Advantages of DirectAccess

DirectAccess is a new technology introduced with Windows Server 2008 R2 and is a completely new idea for remote access. Essentially, DirectAccess is a transparent always-on remote access. It allows users to always appear to be on the corporate network and appear as if they are in the office. In addition, it allows administrators to manage systems as local systems through tools like Group Policy and Microsoft System Center Configuration Manager (SCCM). From a user perspective, this is the easiest remote access solution. Once configured, they don't need to perform any action; it just works. From an administrator point of view, however, this solution is the most complex due to the IPv6 and certificate requirements.

The advantages of DirectAccess are as follows:

▶ DirectAccess provides seamless connectivity wherever a remote system has an Internet connection. No user interaction is required.

▶ System administrators can manage remotely connected systems as if they were internal systems.

▶ DirectAccess allows folder redirection so that all critical data is maintained inside the corporate network and backed up using enterprise tools.

▶ DirectAccess uses a new technology, Name Resolution Policy Table (NRPT), to determine the appropriate DNS server for connection requests. Combined with split-tunneling, this makes for a truly transparent solution.

Despite these benefits, DirectAccess can be somewhat complex to implement. If most of the pieces, such as IPv6, PKI, and Windows 7 on the desktop are already in place, DirectAccess might be the best overall remote access solution for Windows Server 2008 R2.

**NOTE**

One advantage of DirectAccess is the fact that it uses IPv6. For organizations that have been looking to deploy IPv6 and gain experience with this new addressing scheme, the DirectAccess technology provides a good IPv6 learning platform that is self-contained and integrates well with existing IPv4 technologies.

## Ports Affecting the VPN Connectivity

Frequently, RRAS servers operating as VPN servers have two network cards, one of which is plugged into the external network or DMZ. This is simpler, as there are typically few restrictions on communicating with that externally facing interface. The RRAS server is firewalled and the externally facing interface is hardened as a matter of best practice to mitigate the potential risks. In fact, this is a requirement for DirectAccess servers.

However, even with mitigation steps, this externally facing interface can present an unacceptable level of risk to some organizations. In those cases, the VPN infrastructure must remain entirely within the internal network. In that configuration, the firewall must be configured to allow the appropriate traffic to the RRAS server.

Table 24.3 and Table 24.4 list the relevant firewall rules needed for the PPTP and L2TP protocols. The IP address for each of the rules is the RRAS server address, which is the destination if the direction is inbound and the source if the direction is outbound.

TABLE 24.3   Firewall Rules for the RRAS Server for PPTP

| Direction | Protocol | Port or ID | Why? |
|-----------|----------|------------|------|
| Inbound | TCP | 1723 | Allows PPTP tunnel maintenance traffic from the PPTP client to the PPTP server |

TABLE 24.3　Firewall Rules for the RRAS Server for PPTP

| Direction | Protocol | Port or ID | Why? |
|-----------|----------|------------|------|
| Inbound | IP | 47 | Allows tunneled PPTP data from the PPTP client to the PPTP server |
| Outbound | TCP | 1723 | Allows PPTP tunnel maintenance traffic from the PPTP server to the PPTP client |
| Outbound | IP | 47 | Allows tunneled PPTP data from the PPTP server to the PPTP client |

TABLE 24.4　Firewall Rules for the RRAS Server for L2TP

| Direction | Protocol | Port or ID | Why? |
|-----------|----------|------------|------|
| Inbound | UDP | 500 | Allows IKE traffic to the VPN server |
| Inbound | UDP | 4500 | Allows IPSec NAT-T traffic to the VPN server |
| Inbound | IP | 50 | Allows IPSec ESP traffic to the VPN server |
| Outbound | UDP | 500 | Allows IKE traffic from the VPN server |
| Outbound | UDP | 4500 | Allows IPSec NAT-T traffic from the VPN server |
| Outbound | IP | 50 | Allows IPSec ESP traffic from the VPN server |

> **NOTE**
>
> Interestingly, because the DirectAccess server must be a dual-homed server with a network interface on the public network, there are no ports needed on the firewall for DirectAccess. In effect, it bypasses the firewall completely.

The SSTP protocol is simple and only requires that TCP port 443 be permitted inbound to the RRAS server.

# Traditional VPN Scenario

The best way to illustrate the concepts in this chapter is to walk through a sample VPN scenario. The example will walk through the setup and testing of a VPN infrastructure that will include health checks and remediation of a client. The sample VPN scenario architecture is shown in Figure 24.15.

The scenario will use the systems with the basic configuration shown in Table 24.5. These examples assume that an Active Directory domain companyabc.com has been created and that DC1 is the domain controller.

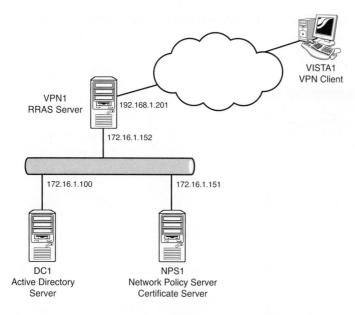

FIGURE 24.15   VPN scenario diagram.

TABLE 24.5   VPN Scenario Servers

| Server | Roles | Operating System | IP Address |
| --- | --- | --- | --- |
| DC1 | Directory server | Windows Server 2008 R2 | 172.16.1.100 |
| NPS1 | Network Policy Server Certificate server | Windows Server 2008 R2 | 172.16.1.151 |
| VPN1 | RRAS server | Windows Server 2008 R2 | 172.16.1.152 (internal) 192.168.1.201 (external) |
| VISTA1 | VPN client | Windows Vista SP1 | |

The steps to configure the VPN architecture will consist of the following:

▶ Set up the certificate server.

▶ Set up the Network Policy Server.

▶ Configure the Network Policy Server.

▶ Set up the RRAS.

▶ Set up the VPN client.

▶ Test the VPN connection.

▶ Control unhealthy VPN clients.

In Windows Server 2008 R2 Active Directory, the users would need to be enabled in the Dial-in tab of the account properties. As you can see in Figure 24.16, the default option is Control Access Through NPS Network Policy.

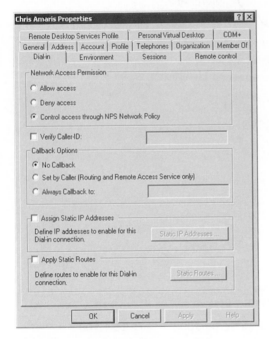

FIGURE 24.16    Dial-in tab in Windows Server 2008 R2 Active Directory.

We'll now step through the setup, configuration, and testing of a Windows Server 2008 R2 traditional VPN infrastructure.

## Setting Up the Certificate Server

The first step is to configure the certificate server. This server will be used to issue certificates for the VPN infrastructure. The example uses Microsoft Certificate Services, but a third-party CA and certificates could be used as well.

The NPS1 server was chosen for this example, as it will be the centralized policy server and so is well situated to provide certificate services. A completely separate server could have been configured as well. The procedure assumes that the Windows Server 2008 R2 operating system has been installed and that the NPS1 server has joined the companyabc.com domain.

Install the Active Directory Certificate Services role on the NPS1 server using the following steps:

1. Launch Server Manager.

2. In the Roles Summary pane, select Add Roles to start the wizard.

3. Click Next.

4. Select Active Directory Certificate Services, and click Next.

5. Click Next.

6. Check the Certification Authority Web Enrollment to add the check mark.

7. A window opens with an additional set of role services and features required to support web enrollment. Click Add Required Role Services to add these prerequisites.

8. Click Next.

9. Leave the Enterprise option to create an enterprise CA, and click Next.

10. Leave the Root CA option selected, and click Next.

11. Leave the Create a New Private Key option selected, and click Next.

12. Click Next to accept the cryptography options for the CA.

13. Click Next to accept the CA name.

14. Click Next to accept the default validity period of five years.

15. Click Next to accept the default directories.

16. Click Next.

17. Click Next to accept the default web server role services.

18. Click Install to install the roles.

19. When the installation finishes, click Close to close the wizard.

This certificate server will be used on each of the components in the VPN infrastructure.

## Certificate Autoenrollment

Next, configure the root CA so that computer certificates are issued automatically through a group policy using a GPO named Cert Auto Enrollment Group Policy Object.

To configure the computer certificate autoenrollment using the enterprise CA, use the following steps:

1. On the domain controller DC1, launch Server Manager.

2. Expand Features, Group Policy Management, Forest: companyabc.com, Domains, and select companyabc.com.

3. In the console tree, right-click the domain companyabc.com and select Create a GPO in the Domain and Link It Here.

4. Enter the name `Cert Auto Enrollment Group Policy Object` and then click OK.

5. Right-click the Cert Auto Enrollment Group Policy Object and select Edit.

6. In the console tree of the Group Policy Management Editor, open Computer Configuration, Policies, Windows Settings, Security Settings, and select Public Key Policies.

7. In the details pane, right-click Automatic Certificate Request Settings, point to New, and then click Automatic Certificate Request.

8. In the Automatic Certificate Request Wizard, click Next.

9. On the Certificate Template page, click Computer (shown in Figure 24.17), click Next, and then click Finish.

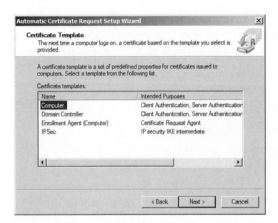

FIGURE 24.17   Certificate autoenrollment.

10. Close the Group Policy Management Editor and Group Policy Management Console.

Now each computer that is a member of the domain will be enrolled automatically with a computer certificate.

## Setting Up the Network Policy Server

The next major step is to install the Network Policy Server (NPS) on the NPS1 server, which will provide services to create and enforce NAP policies. To install the NPS, complete the following steps:

1. Launch Server Manager.
2. In the Roles Summary pane, select Add Roles to start the wizard.
3. Click Next.
4. Select the Network Policy and Access Services role, and click Next.
5. Click Next.
6. Select the Network Policy Server role service, and click Next.
7. Click Install to install the role service.
8. When the installation finishes, click Close to exit the wizard.

The NPS role could be installed on the VPN server, which will be installed next. However, the NPS system would likely be used by multiple entities, so a best practice is to host it on a separate server.

## Configuring the Network Policy Server

The next step is to configure the NPS with the appropriate policies to validate and enforce security. This consists of the following elements:

- ▶ Health validators
- ▶ Health policy
- ▶ Network policy
- ▶ Connection request policies
- ▶ RADIUS client

Because of the interdependencies, they should be configured in the order presented. To set up the health validators in the NPS, execute the following steps:

1. On the NPS system, select Start, Administrative Tools, Network Policy Server to launch the MMC.
2. Expand the Network Access Protection folder, and expand the System Health Validators folder.
3. Expand the Windows Security Health Validation folder and click Settings.
4. Right-click the default configuration and select Properties.
5. Uncheck all options except for the Firewall option. The configuration should look like the example shown in Figure 24.18.
6. Click OK.

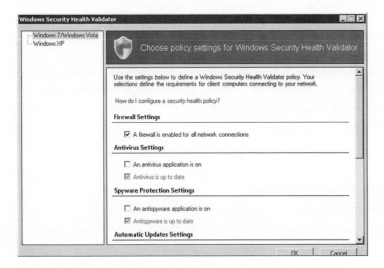

FIGURE 24.18   Validator configuration.

The validator properties are now configured and a health policy needs to be created to use the validator. To configure the health policy, execute the following steps:

1. In the Network Policy Server MMC, expand the Policies folder and select the Health Policies folder.

2. Select Action, New to create a new health policy.

3. Enter Pass for the policy name.

4. Under Client SHV Checks, ensure that the Client Passes All SHV Checks is selected.

5. Select the Windows Security Health Validator in the SHVs Used in This Health Policy window.

6. Click OK to save the health policy.

7. Select Action, New to create a new health policy.

8. Enter Fail for the policy name.

9. Under Client SHV Checks, ensure that the Client Fails One or More SHV Checks option is selected.

10. Select Windows Security Health Validator in the SHVs Used in This Health Policy window.

11. Click OK to save the health policy.

Now the conditions (that is, that the firewall is enabled) for the health of a connecting system are established. Now the network policies for systems that pass or fail the health validation need to be created. These policies are separate, so there will be one policy for passing and one policy for failing.

The first part is to configure a network policy that will allow clients that pass the health validation to connect to the network:

1. In the Network Policy Server MMC, expand the Policies folder, and select the Network Policies folder.

2. Disable the two default policies in the middle pane by selecting each one and then selecting Action, Disable. They should both show as grayed out when this is done.

3. Select Action, New to create a new network policy.

4. Enter Pass Allow Access for the policy name.

5. Select Remote Access Server (VPN Dial-Up) for the type of network access server.

6. Click Next.

7. Click the Add button to specify conditions.

8. Select Health Policies and click the Add button.

9. Select the previously created Pass health policy from the drop-down list, and click OK.

10. Click Next.

11. Leave the default Access Granted option, and click Next.

12. Leave the default authentication methods, and click Next.

13. Leave the default constraints, and click Next.

14. In the Configure Settings options, select NAP Enforcement.

15. Leave the default Allow Full Network Access, which will allow the clients that pass the health validation to connect, and click Next.

16. Click Finish to complete the network policy.

The next step is to configure a network policy for those clients that fail the health validation:

1. With the Network Policies folder highlighted, select Action, New to create a new network policy.

2. Enter `Fail Limit Access` for the policy name.

3. Select Remote Access Server (VPN Dial-Up) for the type of network access server.

4. Click Next.

5. Click the Add button to specify conditions.

6. Select Health Policies and click the Add button.

7. Select the previously created Fail Health Policy from the drop-down list, and click OK.

8. Click Next.

9. Leave the default Access Granted option, and click Next. It might be counterintuitive to grant access, but we will be configuring the policy to remediate the condition rather than deny access outright.

10. Leave the default authentication methods, and click Next.

11. Leave the default constraints, and click Next.

12. In the Configure Settings options, select NAP Enforcement.

13. Select Allow Limited Access, which will limit the clients that fail the health validation.

14. Ensure that the default Auto-remediation option is set to Enable Auto-remediation of Client Computers.

15. Click the IP Filters option in the Settings window.

16. Click the Input Filters button in the IPv4 window.

17. Click New to add a filter for the domain controller DC1, which is 172.16.1.100 in this example.

18. Check the Destination Network check box, and enter the IP address for the domain controller (172.16.1.100) and a subnet mask of 255.255.255.255.

> **NOTE**
>
> The subnet mask of 255.255.255.255 restricts the access to a single IP address. If a range of IP addresses were needed—for example, a class C subnet (192.168.99.x) that the quarantined client could access—then an address such as 192.168.99.0 and a subnet mask of 255.255.255.0 could be used to permit the clients to access the entire IP address range.

19. Click OK to close the window.

20. Select Permit Only the Packets Listed Below, and click OK.

21. Click the Outbound Filters button in the IPv4 window.

22. Click New to add a filter for the domain controller DC1.

23. Check the Source Network check box, and enter the IP address for the domain controller (172.16.1.100) and a subnet mask of 255.255.255.255.

24. Click OK to close the window.

25. Select Permit Only the Packets Listed Below, and click OK.

26. Click Next.

27. Click Finish to complete the network policy.

Now that the health and network policies have been configured, the next step is to configure the connection request policy. To configure the connection policy, execute the following steps:

1. In the Network Policy Server MMC, expand the Policies folder, and select the Connection Request Policies folder.

2. Highlight the Use Windows Authentication for All Users policy, and select Action, Disable.

3. Select Action, New to create a new connection request policy.

4. Enter RAS connections for the policy name.

5. Select Remote Access Server (VPN Dial-Up) for the type of network access server, and click Next.

6. In the Specify Conditions window, click the Add button to create a new condition.

7. Select Client IPv4 Address and click the Add button.

8. Enter the IP address of the RADIUS client, which is the VPN server VPN1 in this example (172.16.1.152), and click OK.

9. Click Next.

10. Leave the default Authenticate Requests on This Server, and click Next.

11. In the Specify Authentication Methods window, check the Override Network Policy Authentication Settings check box.

12. Click the Add button in the EAP Types window.

13. Select Microsoft: Protected EAP (PEAP), and click OK.

14. Click the Add button again in the EAP Types window.

15. Select Microsoft: Secured Password (EAP-MS-CHAP v2), and click OK.

16. Select Microsoft: Protected EAP (PEAP) in the EAP Types window, and click Edit.

17. Verify that the certificate requested earlier in the section is selected based on the FQDN in the friendly name.

18. Click OK to close the window.

19. Click Next at the Configure Settings window.

20. Verify settings to ensure that they look similar to Figure 24.19.

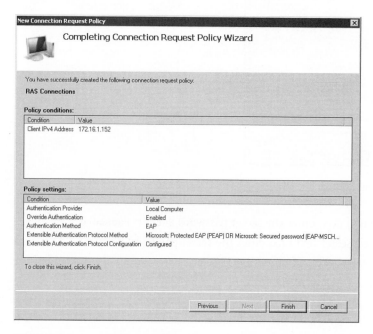

FIGURE 24.19    PEAP properties.

21. Click Finish to create the connection request policy.

The next step is to configure the RRAS server as a RADIUS client on the NPS system. This requires using a shared secret password, which in this example is "Secret Password." To configure the RADIUS client, execute the following steps:

1. In the Network Policy Server MMC on NPS1, expand the RADIUS Clients and Servers folder.

2. Select the RADIUS Clients folder and select Action, New RADIUS Client.

3. Enter the friendly name for the client—in this example, VPN1.

4. Enter the FQDN or IP address for the client—in this example, 172.16.1.152, as shown in Figure 24.20.

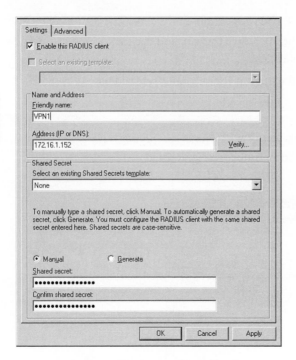

FIGURE 24.20    RADIUS client configuration.

5. In the Shared Secret text box, enter the secret password `Secret Password`.

6. In the Confirm Shared Secret text box, enter the secret password again.

7. Select the Advanced tab and check the RADIUS Client Is NAP-Capable check box.

8. Click OK to create the RADIUS client.

The Network Policy Server configuration is now complete on NPS1. The next step is to create the RRAS server.

## Setting Up the RRAS Server

The RRAS server is the entity that will actually connect to the Internet or DMZ, providing the direct communications with the VPN clients, although the NPS system will be authenticating and authorizing those connections.

The following steps assume that Windows Server 2008 R2 is already installed, that the VPN1 server is configured with an internal network interface card (NIC; 172.16.1.152) and an external NIC (192.168.1.201), and that the VPN1 server is a member of the companyabc.com Active Directory domain. In addition, the network interfaces have been renamed to Internal and External to reflect their connection.

The next step is to add and configure the Routing and Remote Access role to the VPN server:

1. Launch Server Manager on the VPN server, and select Add Roles in the Roles Summary window.

2. Click Next.

3. Select the Network Policy and Access Services role, and click Next.

4. Click Next.

5. Select the Remote Access Service check box, and click Next.

6. Click Install to install the role.

7. Click Close to exit the wizard.

8. Click Start, Administrative Tools, and Routing and Remote Access to launch the RRAS MMC.

9. Right-click on the VPN server name, and select Configure and Enable Routing and Remote Access.

10. Click Next.

11. Select Remote Access (Dial-Up or VPN), and click Next.

12. Check the VPN check box, and click Next.

13. Select the Internet-facing network interface—in this example, the interface named External.

14. Uncheck the Enable Security on the Selected Interface by Setting Up Static Packet Filters, and click Next.

15. Leave the IP Address Assignment as Automatically, and click Next.

16. Select Yes, Set Up This Server to Work with a RADIUS Server, and click Next.

17. Enter the NPS system FQDN into the Primary RADIUS Server Name field, which in this example is nps1.companyabc.com.

18. Enter the secret password in the Shared Secret field, which is the same password used earlier in the RADIUS Client setup.

19. Click Next and then click Finish.

20. A message box appears, indicating that the properties of the DHCP Relay Agent will need to be configured. This is because of the selection to automatically assign IP addresses. Click OK to close the message box.

21. Select the VPN server in the Routing and Remote Access MMC.

22. Select Action and Properties.

23. Select the Security tab.

24. Click on the Authentication Methods button and confirm that Extensible Authentication Protocol (EAP) and Microsoft Encrypted Authentication Version 2 (MS-CHAP v2) are selected.

25. Click OK to close the Authentication Methods window.

26. Select the IPv4 tab.

27. Verify that the correct adapter is selected for the VPN server to obtain DHCP services—in this case, the Internal adapter.

28. Click OK to close the Properties window.

The RRAS server is now configured and ready to accept VPN client connections.

## Setting Up the VPN Client

The next step is to set up the VPN client. The four major tasks in this process are as follows:

▶ Enable Security Center

▶ Enable the System Health Agent (SHA)

▶ Configure certificate trusts

▶ Configure the VPN client

These tasks prepare the client to connect and also validate, enforce, and remediate health policies.

If the client is a domain member, the Security Center will be disabled. This can be enabled in the local security policy through the following procedure:

1. On the VPN Client computer, select Start, Run.

2. Enter `gpedit.msc` and click OK.

3. Expand Local Computer, Computer Configuration, Administrative Templates, Windows Components, and select Security Center.

4. Double-click on Turn on Security Center (Domain PCs Only).

5. Select Enabled and click OK.

6. Close the Group Policy Edit tool.

The Remote Access Quarantine Enforcement Client is normally disabled, so it will need to be enabled on the client. This is done with the NAP Client Configuration MMC (`napclcfg.msc`).

1. On the client, select Start, Run.

2. Enter `napclcfg.msc` and click OK.

3. Select the Enforcement Clients folder.

4. Select the Remote Access Quarantine Enforcement Client. (In Windows 7, use EAP Quarantine Enforcement Client.)

5. Select Action, Enable to enable the client.

6. Exit the NAP Client Configuration MMC.

The Network Access Protection Agent service is normally set to manual, so it will need to be started and set to start automatically.

1. On the client, select Start, Run and then enter `Services.msc`.

2. Highlight the Network Access Protection Agent service, and select Action, Properties.

3. Change the Startup Type to Automatic, and click Start.

4. Click OK to exit the service properties.

For PEAP to function correctly, the client will need to trust the Certificate Authority. This can be done using automatic enrollment for Active Directory domain members, via the certificate enrollment site, or manually by exporting and importing the certificate. For this example, we assume that the client is not a domain member and that the certificate needs to be distributed manually, such as via email.

To export the certificate from the Certificate Authority, execute the following steps:

1. On the Certificate Authority server, select Start, Administrative Tools, and then Certification Authority.
2. Highlight the Certificate Authority (in this case, companyabc-NPS1-CA) and select Action, Properties.
3. Click on the View Certificate button.
4. Select the Details tab, and click the Copy to File button.
5. Click Next.
6. Click Next to accept the default Export File Format.
7. Enter a name for the certificate (in this case, `c:\nps1 ca certificate`) and click Next.
8. Click Finish to export the certificate.
9. Click OK to acknowledge the export, and then exit the Certification Authority MMC.

This certificate will be used to certify the NPS1 Certificate Authority to the client, which will allow the client to trust certificates issued by the Certificate Authority. This will require that the client import the certificate into the local computer trusted Certificate Authority store. To import a certificate into the local computer trusted Certificate Authority store, do the following:

1. Copy the CA certificate file to the VPN client.
2. Select Start, Run.
3. Type `mmc` and click OK.
4. Select File, Add or Remove Snap-ins.
5. Select the Certificates snap-in and click the Add button.
6. Select Computer Account and click Next.
7. Click Next to select the Local computer.
8. Click OK.
9. Expand the Certificates (Local Computer) folder.
10. Expand the Trusted Root Certification Authorities folder, and highlight the Certificates subfolder.
11. Right-click the Certificates subfolder, and select All Tasks, Import.
12. Click Next.
13. Click the Browse button and navigate to the CA certificate file—in this example, `nps1 ca certificate.cer`.
14. Click OK.
15. Click Next.
16. Click Next to place the certificate in the Trusted Root Certification Authorities folder.
17. Click Finish and then click OK to acknowledge the certificate installation.
18. Exit the console without saving.

This allows the client to trust the certificates issued by the NPS1 Certificate Authority. The next step is to set up and configure the VPN connection on the VPN client:

1. On the client, select Start, Control Panel.

2. Click on Network and Internet.

3. Click on Network and Sharing Center.

4. Click on Set Up a Connection or Network.

5. Select Connect to a Workplace, and click Next.

6. Click on Use My Internet Connection (VPN).

7. Enter the Internet address—in this case, `192.168.1.201`. You can also enter the FQDN `vpn1.companyabc.com`.

8. Enter a destination name, such as `Company ABC VPN Connection`.

9. Check the Don't Connect Now check box, as we will need to configure additional settings.

10. Click Next.

11. Enter the username, the password, and the domain, and check the Remember This Password check box.

12. Click Create to create the connection.

13. Click Close.

14. Click Manage Network Connections.

15. Right-click on the Company ABC VPN Connection, and select Properties.

16. Select the Security tab.

17. In the Security Options window, select the Advanced (Custom Settings) option button.

18. Click the Settings button.

19. In the Logon Security window, select the Use Extensible Authentication Protocol (EAP) option button.

20. Select Protected EAP (PEAP) (Encryption Enabled) from the drop-down list, and click the Properties button.

21. Uncheck the Connect to These Servers check box.

22. Check the box next to the previously imported CA certificate in the Trusted Root Certification window—in this example, companyabc-NPS1-CA.

23. Verify that Secured Password (EAP-MS-CHAP v2) is selected in the Select Authentication Method drop-down list.

24. Uncheck the Enable Fast Reconnect check box.

25. Check the Enable Quarantine Checks check box. The result should look like Figure 24.21.

26. Click OK to close the Protected EAP Properties dialog box.

27. Click OK to close the Advanced Security Settings dialog box.

28. Click OK to close the connection properties.

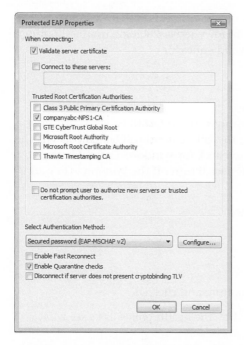

FIGURE 24.21    VPN connection security options.

The connection is now ready for use. The next step is to test the connection.

## Testing the VPN Connection

The next step in the working with a VPN connection is to test the configuration to make sure the system can properly VPN into the network. To test the VPN connection, do the following:

1. On the client, right-click on the Company ABC VPN Connection, and select Connect.

2. Click the Connect button.

3. Click OK to accept the credentials. The connection will be established.

The connection can be tested by pinging the domain controller dc1.companyabc.com. Because the system passed the health validation checks, the connection is granted full access to all intranet resources. To test the connection, complete the following steps:

1. With the Company ABC VPN Connection connected, select Start, All Programs, Accessories, and click on Command Prompt.

2. Enter ping dc1.companyabc.com and press Enter.

3. You should get a reply from the IP address of DC1.

4. Select Start, Connect To and choose to open the Connections window.

5. Select the Company ABS VPN Connection, and click Disconnect.

6. Click Close.

The NPS system presents a wealth of information on the connection that was sorely lacking in previous versions of Windows. With Windows Server 2008 R2, troubleshooting traditional VPN connection issues is a straightforward endeavor.

## Controlling Unhealthy VPN Clients

The previous example had everything going smoothly with no health issues. However, if the client had failed the health validation checks, the failing items will be remediated. The health validation check that was configured was to check for Windows Firewall being enabled. To test the health remediation capabilities, we'll turn off the Windows Firewall and then connect again:

1. On the VPN client, select Start, Control Panel.
2. Click on Security.
3. Click on Windows Firewall.
4. Click on Change Settings.
5. Select the Off (Not Recommended) option button, and click OK.

The client is now in an unhealthy state, as defined by the health policy. Let's see what happens when the client connects to the VPN:

1. On the client, select Start, Connect To, and then choose to open the Connections window.
2. Right-click on the Company ABC VPN Connection, and select Connect.
3. Click the Connect button.
4. Click OK to accept the credentials.
5. The client firewall will be enabled by the NAP client and then connected to the VPN.

The NAP client continues enforcing the health policy even after the initial connection. You can test this by leaving the connection active and then turning off the Windows Firewall:

1. On the VPN client, select Start, Control Panel.
2. Click on Security.
3. Click on Windows Firewall.
4. Click on Change Settings.
5. Select the Off (Not Recommended) option button, and click OK.

The Windows Firewall will be off briefly and then be turned back on. Just like magic, the EAP agent will fix the problem to ensure that the client stays compliant with the health policy even after the initial connection.

If the client should fall out of compliance with the health policy in such a way as to be irremediable, the connection will drop to a reduced connectivity state as defined by the health policies. For example, if an intrepid user disables the Windows Firewall, the EAP agent will detect that condition and take the appropriate action. The following example illustrates this:

1. On the client, connect to the Company ABC VPN Connection.
2. Select Start, Run.
3. Enter services.msc and click OK.
4. Select the Windows Firewall service in the list of services.
5. Select Action, Properties.
6. Change the startup type to Disabled, and click OK.
7. Select Action, Stop to stop the Windows Firewall.

The connection icon will change to show a yellow warning triangle with an exclamation point to indicate limited connectivity. As shown in Figure 24.22, a NAP agent icon will appear in the system tray with the message: "This computer does not meet the requirements of this network. Network access is limited."

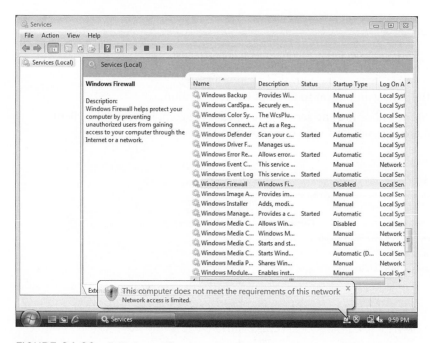

FIGURE 24.22    Failed compliance.

Thus, even if the remediation steps fail, the internal network is protected from noncompliant systems. Even better, when the client returns to compliance, the EAP agent detects that and reestablishes full connectivity. To illustrate that, complete the following steps:

1. Select the Windows Firewall service in the list of services.
2. Select Action, Properties.

3. Change the startup type to Automatic, and click OK.

4. Close the Services MMC.

5. Click on the NAP agent icon in the system tray. A message will appear, indicating that remediation had previously failed, as shown in Figure 24.23.

FIGURE 24.23    Network Access Protection remediation message.

6. Click on the Try Again button to attempt the remediation.

7. The NAP agent will restart the service and update the compliance of the client, showing a message similar to the one shown in Figure 24.24.

FIGURE 24.24    Successful compliance message.

8. Click Close to close the NAP agent window.

The NPS and NAP combination is a very powerful tool for ensuring the health of the systems that are connecting to the VPN infrastructure.

## SSTP Troubleshooting

The VPN scenario up to now was using the PPTP protocol for establishing the tunnel. The Secure Socket Tunneling Protocol (SSTP) is configured by default and should function; however, there are frequently problems with the configuration and utilization of the certificates. The two main problems are as follows:

▶ Incorrect RRAS Computer Certificate Bound to the Listener

▶ Certificate Revocation Site Not Available to VPN Clients

This section covers troubleshooting these common problems with SSTP.

The RRAS computer certificate must be added before the RRAS role is added to the VPN server for SSTP to function properly. Otherwise, the wrong certificate will be bound to the protocol.

You can check the listener using the following procedure:

1. On the RRAS server, open a command prompt.

2. Execute the command `netstat -aon ¦ findstr 443`.

3. Verify that the command returns TCP [::]:443 [::]:0 LISTENING 4. This indicates that the server is listening on port 443.

The next item to check is that the listener is bound to the correct certificate. The listener can be bound to a certificate that no longer exists in the certificate store of the local computer, which can be a troubleshooting headache.

You can check the SSL binding using the following procedure:

1. On the RRAS server, open a command prompt.

2. Execute the command `netsh http show sslcert`.

The result will show the SSL certificate bindings, similar to the following text:

```
SSL Certificate bindings:
    IP:port                 : 0.0.0.0:443
    Certificate Hash        : f3919870176049e87b1ea2cf4bf148d1c3c6e922
    Application ID          : {ba195980-cd49-458b-9e23-c84ee0adcd75}
    Certificate Store Name  : MY
    Verify Client Certificate Revocation    : Enabled
    Verify Revocation Using Cached Client Certificate Only    : Disabled
    Usage Check    : Enabled
    Revocation Freshness Time : 0
    URL Retrieval Timeout    : 0
    Ctl Identifier          : (null)
    Ctl Store Name          : (null)
    DS Mapper Usage    : Disabled
    Negotiate Client Certificate    : Disabled

    IP:port                 : [::]:443
```

```
Certificate Hash          : 9be2b8db741e08838ede5ee83c62c7b3e5f7ac0b
Application ID            : {ba195980-cd49-458b-9e23-c84ee0adcd75}
Certificate Store Name    : MY
Verify Client Certificate Revocation     : Enabled
Verify Revocation Using Cached Client Certificate Only    : Disabled
Usage Check     : Enabled
Revocation Freshness Time : 0
URL Retrieval Timeout     : 0
Ctl Identifier            : (null)
Ctl Store Name            : (null)
DS Mapper Usage     : Disabled
Negotiate Client Certificate     : Disabled
```

The relevant areas to check are the certificate hash and the application ID fields, which are listed in two places. The application ID {ba195980-cd49-458b-9e23-c84ee0adcd75} in each of the bindings indicates that it was added by the RRAS SSTP. The 40-character hexadecimal certificate hash for both bindings needs to match the appropriate certificate in the RRAS server certificate store. As you can see in the listing, one binding shows a hash value of f3919870176049e87b1ea2cf4bf148d1c3c6e922 and the other binding shows a hash value of 9be2b8db741e08838ede5ee83c62c7b3e5f7ac0b. Because they are different, it is clear that one or both must be bound to the wrong certificate.

To get the certificate hash from the certificate store, execute the following steps:

1. Select Start, Run.

2. Type mmc and click OK.

3. Select File, Add or Remove Snap-ins.

4. Select the Certificates snap-in, and click the Add button.

5. Select Computer Account and click Next.

6. Click Next to select the Local computer.

7. Click OK.

8. Expand the Certificates (Local Computer) folder.

9. Expand the Personal folder.

10. Select the Certificates folder.

11. Right-click on the appropriate certificate, and select Open.

12. Select the Details tab.

13. Select the Thumbprint field and write down the 40-character hexadecimal value. In the case of VPN1 in this example, the thumbprint is f3919870176049e87b1ea2cf4bf148d1c3c6e922.

This is the certificate hash and should match the certificate hash from the previous Netsh command. If it does, the correct certificate is bound to the listener. If the thumbprint does not match the certificate hash, the binding can be corrected using the following steps.

In this case, the hash does not match, so the binding needs to be remediated. This will be done by deleting the bindings and re-creating them. The four commands are as follows:

```
netsh http delete sslcert ipport=0.0.0.0:443
netsh http delete sslcert ipport=[::]:443
netsh http add sslcert ipport=0.0.0.0:443
        certhash=f3919870176049e87b1ea2cf4bf148d1c3c6e922
        appid={ba195980-cd49-458b-9e23-c84ee0adcd75} certstorename=MY
netsh http add sslcert ipport=[::]:443
        certhash=f3919870176049e87b1ea2cf4bf148d1c3c6e922
        appid={ba195980-cd49-458b-9e23-c84ee0adcd75} certstorename=MY
```

The first two commands delete the bindings and the second two commands re-create the bindings with the correct certificate hash. We could have only done (deleted and added) the "[::]:443" ipport binding because that was the incorrect one.

Finally, the Certificate Authority revocation list must be available for SSTP to function correctly. If it is not available, SSTP clients will generate the error shown in Figure 24.25. The solution to this is to make the Certificate Authority revocation site available to clients over the Internet.

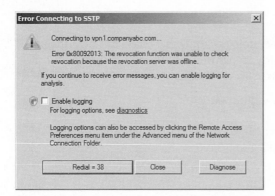

FIGURE 24.25   SSTP client revocation check error.

This is quite a stringent requirement and is due to the combination of the firewall piercing quality of SSTP and the potential to have disparate networks connected at Layer 3. This revocation list requirement can present problems for organizations using internal CAs, as the CA website must be published. This could potentially present a security risk and would be an argument for using a third-party Certificate Authority for the SSTP connections.

### Preventing SSTP Connections

The SSTP tunneling protocol can help VPN clients traverse through NATs and firewalls. This is a huge benefit of the protocol, but this is also a potential security risk. This is because it in effect creates an OSI Layer 3 connection between two networks, which might be against the security policy of the originating network or destination network. For example, a consultant might initiate a connection from a client site to their corporate network, in effect connecting the two networks.

Because SSTP uses HTTPS (TCP port 443), a port-based firewall cannot block the protocol without also blocking all other HTTPS traffic. This is widely used by secure websites, so this is not normally an option. This is one of the benefits of the SSTP technology.

However, SSTP connections can be prevented if the client traffic passes through an application-level web proxy, which is a common configuration for enterprises today. When a VPN client using SSTP connects, the client will send an HTTP "CONNECT" request with a custom HTTP header named "SSTPVERSION" with a value of "1.0."

To prevent SSTP connection through a web proxy, simply block those requests with the customer HTTP header to disable SSTP.

# DirectAccess Scenario

Although the prerequisites and associated technologies for DirectAccess can be difficult to implement, DirectAccess configuration is fairly straightforward through a simple wizard. The example walks through the DirectAccess Wizard in Windows Server 2008 R2.

The scenario accomplishes two major goals, as follows:

1. Allow a workstation to seamlessly move between internal, public, and home networks while retaining access to application servers.
2. Enable IPv6 in an IPv4 network using IPv6 transition technologies.

It is important to note that the scenario does not require that you have deployed IPv6 throughout the internal network to begin using DirectAccess. The scenario leverages the Windows Server 2008 R2 and Windows 7 technologies that will automatically enable and configure IPv6 using transitional technologies like ISATAP, 6to4, and Teredo.

This scenario assumes that Windows Server 2008 R2 Active Directory and DNS are already deployed. The DirectAccess server must have two physical network interfaces. The first is connected directly to the Internet, no NAT, and must have two consecutive public IP addresses. The second interface is connected to the internal network. This scenario also assumes you have an internal enterprise PKI deployment with CRLs published on the Internet.

There are five servers and a client in the scenario shown in Figure 24.26. These are the systems that will be configured and tested against during the scenario. The systems are as follows:

▶ **DC1**—Domain controller, DNS, and enterprise Certificate Authority server running Windows Server 2008 R2. The Active Directory domain is companyabc.com. The CA must have an Internet available certificate revocation list (CRL). The DC1 IP address is 192.168.3.200.

▶ **DA1**—DirectAccess server domain member running Windows Server 2008 R2, with two network interface cards, and two public IP addresses (12.155.166.2 and 12.155.166.3) assigned. The internal IP address is 192.168.3.211. This server should also have the Web Server role installed to support IP-HTTPS.

> **NOTE**
>
> The reason for two consecutive public IPv4 addresses on the DirectAccess server's public Internet interface is so that Teredo-based DirectAccess clients can detect the type of NAT that they are located behind.

▶ **SERVER1**—The application server that the DirectAccess client is accessing. The server also hosts the NLS role, using the URL https://nls.companyabc.com. The application server has been assigned the internal IP address 192.168.3.201.

▶ **NS1**—External DNS server hosting the external companyabc.com zone. The NS1 IP address is 12.155.166.1.

▶ **WS3**—DirectAccess client domain member running Windows 7. This system will travel between the internal, public, and home networks.

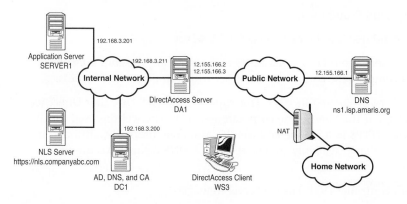

FIGURE 24.26   DirectAccess scenario.

The scenario assumes that split-brain DNS is being used—that is, that there is an internal companyabc.com zone and an external companyabc.com zone. There should be a DNS A record for da1.companyabc.com (12.155.166.2) in the external companyabc.com zone, as well as the DNS record for the CRL for the certificate authority (typically crl.companyabc.com).

There are three networks in the scenario. The DirectAccess client is WS3 and will be roaming between these networks, but must be able to access the application server no matter which network they are in. The three networks are as follows:

▶ **Internal network**—This is the corporate network and is using an IPv4 address in the 192.168.3.x range.

▶ **Public network**—This is the Internet, and the servers being configured are using the IPv4 12.155.166.x range.

▶ **Home network**—This is a network behind a NAT firewall, and the IP address range is not known.

The client WS3 will be tested while connected to the internal network, the public network, and, finally, to the home network. In all cases, the client WS3 will seamlessly transition between the networks with no interruption in access to internal resources.

## Configuring the Infrastructure

Next, configure the DNS service to remove the ISATAP name from its default global block list. This allows the DNS to service ISATAP requests.

To remove ISATAP from the DNS global query block list, complete the following steps:

1. On the domain controller server, open a command prompt.
2. In the Command Prompt window, enter the command `dnscmd /config /global-queryblocklist wpad` and then press Enter.
3. Close the Command Prompt window.

The preceding command needs to be run on each DNS server.

This scenario assumes split-brain DNS—that is, there is a companyabc.com domain internally, and there is a companyabc.com on the Internet with a limited set of records.

The NLS record needs to be created in DNS. This supports the NLS URL that DirectAccess clients use to determine if they are in the corporate network. The website used for the NLS needs to support HTTPS and can be any website available internally, although it is a best practice that it be highly available. To create an NLS DNS record, execute the following steps:

1. On the domain controller DC1, launch Server Manager.
2. Expand Roles, DNS Server, DNS, DC1, Forward Lookup Zones, and select the companyabc.com zone.
3. Right-click company abc.com and then click New Host (A or AAAA).

4. In the Name field, type nls. In the IP address field, type the IP address of the NLS website, click Add Host, click OK, and then click Done.

The next step is to create a security group for DirectAccess client computers. This allows the DirectAccess clients to be specified. The group will be named DirectAccessClients. To create the group, execute the following steps:

1. On the domain controller, launch Server Manager.
2. Expand Roles, Active Directory Domain Services, Active Directory Users and Computers, expand the companyabc.com domain, and select the Users container.
3. Right-click on Users, select New, and then click Group.
4. In the Group Name field, type DirectAccessClients and click OK.

This group will be used later to assign Group Policy to the DirectAccess clients.

## Using a GPO to Configure Firewall Rules

The next step is to create and enable firewall rules for ICMPv4 and ICMPv6 traffic. ICMP messages need to be sent and received to provide connectivity for Teredo-based DirectAccess clients, which is needed if the DirectAccess clients will be behind a NAT.

The ICMP firewall rules will be deployed with a GPO named "DirectAccess Group Policy Object." To create and enable firewall rules for ICMPv4 and ICMPv6 traffic, execute the following steps:

1. On the domain controller DC1, launch Server Manager.
2. Expand Features, Group Policy Management, Forest: companyabc.com, Domains, and select companyabc.com.
3. In the console tree, right-click the domain companyabc.com and select Create a GPO in the Domain and Link It Here.
4. Enter the name DirectAccess Group Policy Object and then click OK.
5. Right-click the DirectAccess Group Policy Object and select Edit.
6. In the console tree of the Group Policy Management Editor, expand Computer Configuration, Policies, Windows Settings, Security Settings, Windows Firewall with Advanced Security, and select Windows Firewall with Advanced Security.
7. In the console tree, select and then right-click Inbound Rules, and then click New Rule.
8. On the Rule Type page, click Custom, and then click Next and Next.
9. On the Protocols and Ports page, for Protocol Type, select ICMPv4, and then click Customize.
10. In the Customize ICMP Settings dialog box, click Specific ICMP Types, select Echo Request, and then click OK.

11. Click Next, Next, Next, and Next.

12. On the Name page, in the Name field, type `Inbound ICMPv4 Echo Requests`, and then click Finish.

13. In the console tree, right-click Inbound Rules, and then click New Rule.

14. On the Rule Type page, click Custom, and then click Next and Next.

15. On the Protocols and Ports page, for Protocol Type, select ICMPv6 (shown in Figure 24.27), and then click Customize.

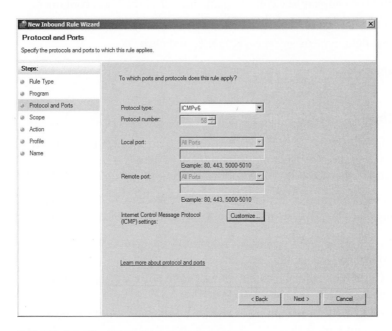

FIGURE 24.27    ICMPv6 inbound firewall rule.

16. In the Customize ICMP Settings dialog box, click Specific ICMP Types, select Echo Request, and then click OK.

17. Click Next, Next, Next, and Next.

18. On the Name page, in the Name field, type `Inbound ICMPv6 Echo Requests`, and then click Finish.

19. In the console tree, right-click Outbound Rules, and then click New Rule.

20. On the Rule Type page, click Custom, and then click Next and Next.

21. On the Protocols and Ports page, for Protocol Type, click ICMPv4, and then click Customize.

22. In the Customize ICMP Settings dialog box, click Specific ICMP Types, select Echo Request, and then click OK. Click Next and Next.

23. On the Action page, click Allow the Connection, and then click Next and Next.

24. On the Name page, in the Name field, type `Outbound ICMPv4 Echo Requests`, and then click Finish.

25. In the console tree, right-click Outbound Rules, and then click New Rule.

26. On the Rule Type page, click Custom, and then click Next and Next.

27. On the Protocols and Ports page, for Protocol Type, click ICMPv6, and then click Customize.

28. In the Customize ICMP Settings dialog box, click Specific ICMP Types, select Echo Request, and then click OK. Click Next and Next.

29. On the Action page, click Allow the Connection, and then click Next and Next.

30. On the Name page, in the Name field, type `Outbound ICMPv6 Echo Requests`, and then click Finish.

31. Close the Group Policy Management Editor and Group Policy Management Console.

This new group policy will take effect on all domain computers, allowing ICMPv4 and ICMPv6 through the operating system firewall.

## Custom Certificate Template for IP-HTTPS

Next, create a certificate template so that requesting computers can specify the subject name and subject alternative name of a certificate. This certificate will be used by the DirectAccess server to set up IP-HTTPS sessions.

To create and enable a custom Web Server 2008 certificate template, execute the following steps:

1. On the domain controller DC1, launch Server Manager.

2. Expand Roles, Active Directory Certificate Services, and select Certificate Templates.

3. In the contents pane, right-click the Web Server template, and then click Duplicate Template.

4. Click Windows Server 2008 Enterprise, and then click OK.

5. In the Template Display Name field, type `Web Server 2008`.

6. Click the Security tab.

7. Click Authenticated Users, and then select Enroll in the Allow column.

8. Click the Add button, type `Domain Computers`, and then click OK.

9. Click Domain Computers, and then select Enroll in the Allow column.

10. Click the Request Handling tab.

11. Select Allow Private Key to Be Exported and click OK.

12. Select the companyabc-DC1-CA in the Active Directory Certificate Services, right-click Certificate Templates, point to New, and then click Certificate Template To Issue.

13. In the list of certificate templates, click Web Server 2008, and then click OK.

14. Confirm that the new certificate template, Web Server 2008, is listed (shown in Figure 24.28).

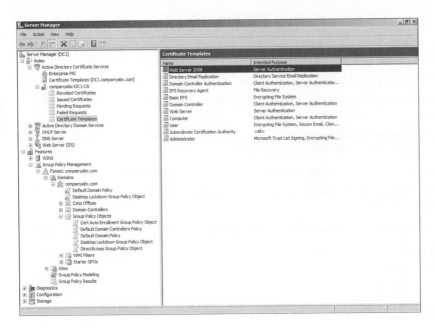

FIGURE 24.28    Web Server 2008 certificate.

Now the certificate server will be able to issue a Web Server 2008 certificate for the DirectAccess server to use for IP-HTTPS. The certificate will be requested later in the process.

## Certificate Autoenrollment

Next, configure the root CA so that computer certificates are issued automatically through a group policy using a GPO named Cert Auto Enrollment Group Policy Object. These certificates will be used to secure the IPSec tunnels established.

To configure computer certificate autoenrollment, complete the following steps:

1. On the domain controller DC1, launch Server Manager.

2. Expand Features, Group Policy Management, Forest: companyabc.com, Domains, and select companyabc.com.

3. In the console tree, right-click the domain companyabc.com and select Create a GPO in the Domain and Link It Here.

4. Enter the name Cert Auto Enrollment Group Policy Object and then click OK.

5. Right-click the Cert Auto Enrollment Group Policy Object and select Edit.

6. In the console tree of the Group Policy Management Editor, open Computer Configuration, Policies, Windows Settings, Security Settings, and select Public Key Policies.

7. In the details pane, right-click Automatic Certificate Request Settings, point to New, and then click Automatic Certificate Request.

8. In the Automatic Certificate Request Wizard, click Next.

9. On the Certificate Template page, click Computer (shown in Figure 24.29), click Next, and then click Finish.

FIGURE 24.29    Certificate autoenrollment.

10. Close the Group Policy Management Editor and Group Policy Management Console.

Now, each computer that is a member of the domain will be enrolled automatically with a computer certificate.

## IP-HTTP Certificate

Next, obtain an additional certificate for DA1 with a customized subject and alternative name for IP-HTTPS connectivity. This certificate is in addition to the computer certificate that was obtained through the autoenrollment configured earlier.

To obtain the additional certificate for the DirectAccess server DA1, execute the following steps:

1. On the DirectAccess server DA1, click Start, type mmc, and then press Enter.

2. Click File and select Add/Remove Snap-Ins.

3. Select Certificates, click the Add button, select Computer Account, click Next, select Local Computer, click Finish, and then click OK.

4. In the console tree of the Certificates snap-in, expand Local Computer, Personal, and select Certificates.

5. Right-click Certificates, point to All Tasks, and then click Request New Certificate.

6. Click Next twice.

7. On the Request Certificates page, click Web Server 2008, and then click the button More Information Is Required to Enroll for This Certificate.

8. On the Subject tab of the Certificate Properties dialog box, in the Subject Name section, for Type, select Common Name.

9. In the Value field, type da1.companyabc.com, and then click the Add button.

10. In the Alternative Name section, for Type, select DNS.

11. In the Value field, type da1.companyabc.com, and then click the Add button.

12. Click OK, click Enroll, and then click Finish.

13. In the details pane of the Certificates snap-in, verify that a new certificate with the name da1.contoso.com was enrolled with Intended Purposes of Server Authentication.

14. Right-click the certificate and select Properties.

15. In the Friendly Name field, type IP-HTTPS and click OK.

## Installing the DirectAccess Feature on DA1

Before you can run the DirectAccess Setup Wizard, you must install the DirectAccess feature on DA1. To install the DirectAccess feature, execute the following steps:

1. On the DirectAccess server DA1, launch Server Manager.

2. Right-click on Features and select Add Features.

3. On the Select Features page, select DirectAccess Management Console.

4. At the pop-up, click Add Required Features. This adds the Group Policy Management feature.

5. Click Next.

6. Click Install.

7. Click Close to finish.

The DirectAccess feature has been installed, but still needs to be configured.

## Configuring DirectAccess Feature

Next, run the DirectAccess Setup Wizard to configure DA1 and the Group Policy settings for DirectAccess clients.

To run the DirectAccess Setup Wizard, complete the following steps:

1. On the DirectAccess server DA1, launch Server Manager.

2. Expand Features, DirectAccess, and select the Setup node. The screen will show the four-step DirectAccess setup, as shown in Figure 24.30.

3. On the Select Features page, select DirectAccess Management Console.

4. In Step 1 Remote Clients, click Configure.

5. On the DirectAccess Client Setup page, click the Add button.

6. In the Select Group dialog box, type DirectAccessClients and click OK. The screen will show the group, as shown in Figure 24.31.

7. Click Finish.

8. In Step 2 DirectAccess Server, click Configure.

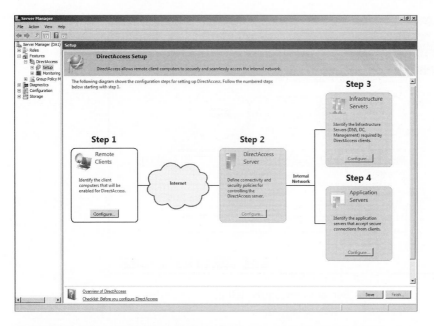

FIGURE 24.30    DirectAccess Setup screen.

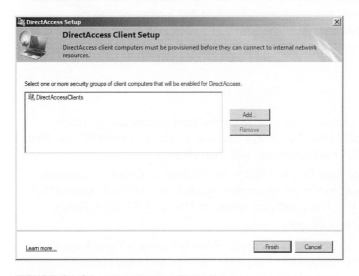

FIGURE 24.31    DirectAccess Client Setup.

9. On the Connectivity page, for Interface Connected to the Internet, ensure that the correct interface is selected. For Interface Connected to the Internal Network, ensure that the correct interface is selected. The wizard will attempt to select the best interfaces based on the IP address ranges. In Figure 24.32, the public address 12.155.166.3 has been assigned to the Internet interface and the private address 192.168.3.211 has been assigned to the internal interface.

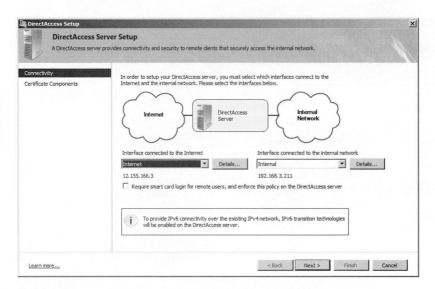

FIGURE 24.32 DirectAccess Server Connectivity Setup.

The DirectAccess Setup Wizard has an informational note that it detected that the internal network is IPv4-based and will enable IPv6 transition technologies as part of the setup. The DirectAccess server will be configured as the ISATAP server.

10. Click Next.

11. On the Certificate Components page, for Select the Root Certificate to Which Remote Client Certificates Must Chain, click Browse. In the list of certificates, click the companyabc-DC1-CA root certificate, and then click OK.

12. For Select the Certificate That Will Be Used to Secure Remote Client Connectivity over HTTPS, click Browse. In the list of certificates, click the certificate named IP-HTTPS, and then click OK. The results are shown in Figure 24.33. Click Finish.

13. In Step 3 Infrastructure Servers, click Configure.

14. On the Location page, click Network Location Server Is Run on a Highly Available Server, type `https://nls.companyabc.com`, click Validate, and then click Next. You should get a green check mark with a Validation Successful message.

15. On the DNS and Domain Controller page (shown in Figure 24.34), note the entry for the name companyabc.com with the IPv6 address 2002:c9b:a602:1:0:5efe:192.168.3.200. This is the 6to4 IPv6 address for the DC1 domain controller. All DirectAccess client requests to the domain companyabc.com will be forwarded to this domain controller. The nls.companyabc.com is also listed with a blank DNS server, which ensures that DirectAccess clients will not forward the requests to this host.

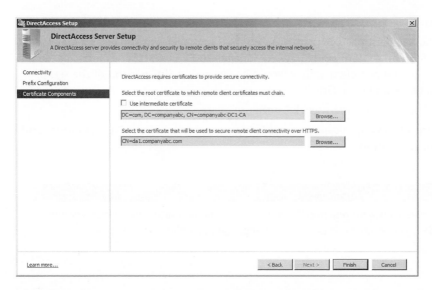

FIGURE 24.33    DirectAccess Server certificate components.

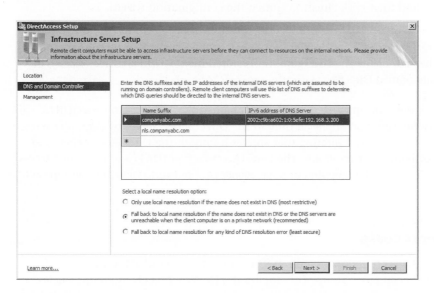

FIGURE 24.34    DirectAccess Infrastructure Server Setup for DNS.

**NOTE**

The blank DNS for the Network Location Service (NLS) is needed so that DirectAccess clients can use the URL to determine if they are inside the corporate network or on the Internet. When inside the network, the DirectAccess clients will be able to access the site. When remote and connected via DirectAccess, the clients will be unable to reach the site due to the blank DNS entry, although they can reach all other internal resources.

**16.** Click Next.

**17.** On the Management page, if there were internal management servers, such as Microsoft System Center Configuration Manager 2007 (SCCM) servers that needed to reach the DirectAccess clients, they would be entered in this portion of the setup. Leave this blank and click Finish.

**18.** In Step 4 Application Servers, click Configure.

**19.** On the DirectAccess Application Server Setup page, leave Require No Additional End-to-End Authentication.

---

**NOTE**

If end-to-end protection were required, Step 4 is where the permitted application servers would be added. This scenario is doing end-to-edge, so no configuration is needed.

---

**20.** Click Finish.

**21.** Click Save, and then click Finish to launch the configuration wizard.

**22.** In the DirectAccess Review dialog box, click Apply. The configuration will be applied.

**23.** In the DirectAccess Policy Configuration message box, click OK. The configuration has now been applied. The configuration is stored in %WinDir%\DirectAccess\ in an XML file named DirectAccessConfig.xml.

There will be two new Group Policy Objects, each named DirectAccess Policy-<GUID>. One has security filtering that applies it only to the DirectAccess server by computer name (DA1$). The other has security filtering that applies it only to the DirectAccess clients in the DirectAccessClients security group. The DirectAccess server (DA1) and the DirectAccess clients (WS3) will need to be rebooted or have gpupdate.exe run to have their group policies applied.

## Testing DirectAccess

To test the DirectAccess functionality, the WS3 computer will be added to the DirectAccessClients computer group. This applies the DirectAccess client group policies.

To add CLIENT1 to the DirectAccess client computers security group, complete the following steps:

**1.** On the DC1 domain controller, launch Server Manager.

**2.** Expand Roles, Active Directory Domain Services, Active Directory Users and Computers, the domain companyabc.com, and select the container Users.

**3.** Right-click the group DirectAccessClients and select Properties.

4. Select the Members tab, and then click the Add button.

5. In the Select Users, Contacts, Computers, or Groups dialog box, click Object Types, check Computers, and click OK.

6. Under Enter the Object Names to Select (Examples), type WS3, and click OK.

7. Click OK to save.

8. Restart the WS3 computer to have the changes take effect.

The DirectAccess group policies will now be in effect on the WS3 computer.

You might need to run gpupdate.exe on the DirectAccess server DA1 to get the group policies to take effect on it.

On all the internal servers, the commands net stop iphlpsvc and net start iphlpsvc will need to be run to restart the IP Helper service and have the new ISATAP configuration be recognized. This includes DC1, SERVER1, and DA1. When the IP Helper service starts, the systems will resolve the isatap.companyabc.com DNS entry installed by the DirectAccess setup and will enable their ISATAP interfaces.

### NOTE

Of course, many administrators will simply reboot all the systems, which will have the same effect as restarting the IP Helper service and applying group policies.

Following the configuration and the restart of the IP Helper service on all the components, the IPv6 network should be fully functional. All systems should be able to reach each other using the IPv6 addresses as well as the IPv4 addresses. If there is a problem with the IPv6 access, DirectAccess will not function.

### NOTE

The ping.exe tool can be used to verify that IPv6 is working. The -6 option forces ping to use IPv6. The -4 option forces ping to use IPv4. The command to ping a computer DC1 using IPv6 is ping dc1.companyabc.com -6. The command to ping a computer DC1 using IPv4 is ping dc1.companyabc.com -4. Each computer should be successfully pinged with both commands. This can be a very useful technique when troubleshooting DirectAccess and IPv6.

As shown in the arrows in Figure 24.35, we will test (A) the connection to the internal network, (B) the connection to the public network, and, finally, (C) the connection to the home network.

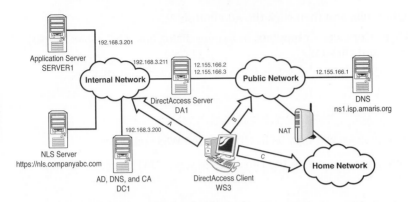

FIGURE 24.35   Testing client connection to networks.

For Test A, the connection to the internal network, execute the following steps:

1. Connect the DirectAccess client WS3 to the internal network.

2. Select Start, enter cmd, and press Enter.

3. At the command prompt, enter ipconfig and press Enter. Figure 24.36 shows that WS3 has been assigned an IPv4 address (192.168.3.102) on the internal network and that an ISATAP address has been automatically generated in the ISATAP tunnel adapter.

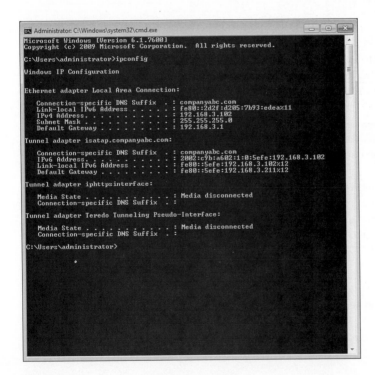

FIGURE 24.36   Test A—internal network.

**4.** Launch Explorer and access a share on the application server to demonstrate access.

This demonstrates that WS3 is connected to the internal network and is able to access resources and that the IPv6 transitional technologies are working internally, specifically ISATAP.

For Test B, the connection to the public network, execute the following steps:

**1.** Connect the DirectAccess client WS3 to the public network.

**2.** Select Start, enter cmd, and press Enter.

**3.** At the command prompt, enter ipconfig and press Enter. Figure 24.37 shows that WS3 has been assigned an IPv4 address (12.155.166.101) on the public network and that a 6to4 address has been automatically generated with the 6to4 2002: prefix in the 6to4 tunnel adapter.

FIGURE 24.37    Test B—public network.

**4.** Launch Explorer and access a share on the application server to demonstrate access.

This demonstrates that WS3 is connected to the public network and is able to access resources and that the IPv6 transitional technologies are working publicly, specifically 6to4.

For Test C, the connection to the home network, execute the following steps:

1. Connect the DirectAccess client WS3 to the home network.

2. Select Start, enter cmd, and press Enter.

3. At the command prompt, enter ipconfig and press Enter. Figure 24.38 shows that WS3 has been assigned an IPv4 address (192.168.137.147) on the home network and that a Teredo address has been automatically generated with the Teredo 2001: prefix in the Teredo tunnel adapter.

FIGURE 24.38    Test C—home network.

4. Launch Explorer and access a share on the application server to demonstrate access.

This demonstrates that WS3 is connected to the home network and is able to access resources and that the IPv6 transitional technologies are working publicly, specifically Teredo.

In the course of the testing, no additional configuration was needed, no logon credentials needed to be supplied, and resources were transparently available. This is the seamless nature of DirectAccess, which completely hides the connection complexity from the end user.

## Monitoring the DirectAccess Server

The DirectAccess server includes an excellent tool to monitor the activity of the DirectAccess clients. Shown in Figure 24.39, it provides an overall status of the DirectAccess server, status and activity of the individual DirectAccess components, and detailed statistics on the components. The figure shows that the Teredo components are active, indicating that there are DirectAccess clients using Teredo but none using IP-HTTPS.

FIGURE 24.39    DirectAccess component status.

The DirectAccess monitoring provides information on the traffic activity, data, and control traffic counters for the following components:

- ▶ Teredo Relay
- ▶ Teredo Server
- ▶ 6to4
- ▶ IPHTTPS
- ▶ ISATAP
- ▶ Network Security
- ▶ DNS Server

The status is updated every 10 seconds. The status indicators for the components will change depending on the health and activity of the component. The various states are as follows:

- ▶ Green indicates current activity in the component.
- ▶ Orange indicates the component is idle.
- ▶ Yellow indicates the component is experiencing issues.
- ▶ Red indicates that the component has failed.

To use the DirectAccess server monitoring, run the following steps:

1. Launch Server Manager on the DirectAccess server DA1.

2. Expand Features, DirectAccess, and select Monitoring.

3. The details window will show the component status screen. As connections are made, the status will update every 10 seconds to show the activity.

4. To see the performance metrics for any given component, click on the Details button to launch Performance Monitor with the appropriate counters. For example, click ISATAP Details.

5. Select the Change Graph Type pull-down menu to change between the different graph types. The Line Graph is shown in Figure 24.40. From the selected Packets/sec, it looks like there was a maximum of six thousand packets per second during the measuring window.

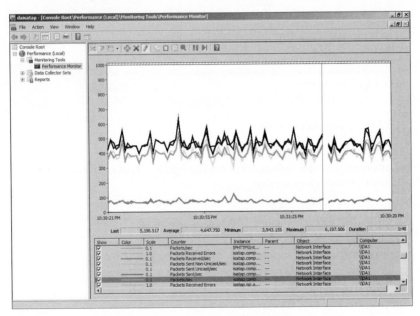

FIGURE 24.40    DirectAccess performance monitoring.

The DirectAccess Monitoring tool gives access to dozens of key performance metrics in graphical or tabular format. These metrics are invaluable for monitoring and troubleshooting the DirectAccess infrastructure.

# Connection Manager

The connection manager allows VPN administrators to deploy an easy-to-use, preconfigured interface for their end users.

▶ Connection Manager Client Dialer

▶ Connection Manager Administration Kit (CMAK)

The Connection Manager (CM) client dialer is installed on the VPN clients, whereas the CMAK can be installed anywhere and be used to generate the CM profiles.

## Connection Manager Client Dialer

The Connection Manager client dialer is software that is installed on each remote access client. It includes advanced features that make it a superset of basic dial-up and VPN networking. CM simplifies the client configuration for the users by enabling them to do the following:

▶ Select from a list of phone numbers or IP addresses to use, based on physical location.

▶ Use customized graphics, icons, messages, and help.

▶ Automatically create a dial-up connection before the VPN connection is made.

▶ Run custom actions during various parts of the connection process, such as preconnect and postconnect actions.

A customized CM client dialer package (CM profile) is a self-extracting executable file created by the CMAK. The CM profile can be distributed to VPN users via CD-ROM, email, website, or file share. The CM profile automatically configures the appropriate dial-up and VPN connections. The Connection Manager profile does not require a specific version of Windows and will run on the following platforms: Windows 7, Windows Vista, Windows XP, Windows 2000, Windows NT 4.0, and Windows Millennium Edition.

## Connection Manager Administration Kit

The Connection Manager Administration Kit (CMAK) enables administrators to preconfigure the appearance and behavior of the CM. With CMAK, client dialer and connection software allow users to connect to the network using only the connection features that are defined for them. CMAK also enables administrators to build profiles customizing the Connection Manager Installation package sent to remote access users.

The CMAK feature is installed independent of any Windows Server 2008 R2 roles. To install CMAK, add the CMAK feature by following these steps:

1. On the server that will generate the CM profiles, launch Server Manager.
2. Click on Add Features to launch the wizard.
3. Select Connection Manager Administration Kit, and click Next.
4. Click Install.
5. Click Close.

To use the CMAK to create CM profiles, you run the CMAK wizard. To create a profile, execute the following steps:

1. Select Start, Administrative Tools, and click Connection Manager Administration Kit.
2. Click Next.
3. Select the operating system for the target client (in this case, Windows 7 or Windows Vista) and click Next.

4. Select New Profile and click Next.

5. Enter a service name—in this example, Company ABC VPN.

6. Enter a filename (in this example, abcvpn) and click Next. The filename must be eight characters or less.

7. Select Add a Realm Name to the User Name to enter a domain name.

8. Enter the FQDN of the Active Directory domain (in this example, companyabc.com) and click Next.

9. Click Next to skip merging information from other profiles.

10. Select the Phone Book from this Profile check box to add support for VPN connection.

11. Select the Always Use the Same VPN Server option button in the VPN server name or IP address section.

12. Enter the VPN server's external FQDN or IP address, which is vpn1.companyabc.com in this example.

> **NOTE**
>
> The CMAK supports multiple addresses for VPN servers. A text file of the various addresses must be created in the proper format. The Allow the User to Choose a VPN Server Before Connecting check box is selected and the text file is imported using the Browse button.

13. Click Next.

14. Click Next.

15. Uncheck the Automatically Download Phone Book Updates check box, and click Next.

16. Click Next.

17. Click Next to skip the routing table updates configuration.

18. Click Next to skip the proxy configuration.

19. Click Next to skip the custom actions.

20. Click Next to accept the default logon graphic.

21. Click Next to accept the default phone book graphic.

22. Click Next to accept the default icons.

23. Click Next to leave the default Help file.

24. Enter the custom support number for users to dial when experiencing problems connecting, and click Next.

25. Click Next to skip the import of a custom licensing agreement.

26. Click Next to skip the import of additional files.

27. Click Next to build the profile.

28. Note the directory where the profile was saved—in this example, c:\Program Files\CMAK\Profiles\Windows 7 and Windows Vista\abcvpn\abcvpn.exe.

29. Click Finish to close the wizard.

The profile executable is now ready to be distributed to clients and executed to create the Company ABC VPN Connection. This example was relatively simple, but for many organizations, the ability to add various customizations such as the Help file, licensing agreement, or predefined VPN addresses will help drive down support costs.

# Summary

Remote and mobile connectivity has increased over the years because the extended office now includes hotels, airports, client sites, other campus buildings, and even wireless coffee shop users. With the expansion of the network from which users need to connect to a Windows Server 2008 R2 environment, the improvement of security, reliability, compatibility, and performance becomes extremely important for an organization. The Windows Server 2008 R2 VPN technologies meet the needs of these increasingly mobile and remote users.

Windows Server 2008 R2 contains all the VPN technologies from the previous version of Windows and adds DirectAccess as a compelling solution for enterprises with extensive infrastructure already in place.

These new technologies allow the Windows Server 2008 R2 VPN to extend further with increased security and reliability, while making the end user experience painless.

# Best Practices

The following are best practices from this chapter:

▶ Use the Network Policy Server to validate and remediate the health of clients.

▶ Use certificates for authentication where possible.

▶ For increased security, choose DirectAccess, SSTP, or L2TP with IPSec as the VPN protocol.

▶ Use PEAP as the preferred authentication protocol.

▶ Use the more secure MS-CHAP v2 if password authentication must be used.

▶ Use DirectAccess to provide remote users a simpler no-touch method of securely connecting back to the office.

▶ Use the DirectAccess Monitoring to troubleshoot and monitor DirectAccess clients.

▶ Always install the computer certificate on the RRAS server before adding the RRAS role.

# Remote Desktop Services

Remote Desktop Services (previously named Terminal Services) is a component of Microsoft Windows (server and client operating systems) that enables users to remotely run applications or manage a server from any machine that has the Remote Desktop Connection (RDC) client and network access. In a Remote Desktop Services session, whether a client requires a complete Remote Desktop environment or just needs to run a single application, the Remote Desktop Session Host uses its hardware resources to perform all the application processing. In a basic Remote Desktop Services session, the client sends out only keyboard and mouse signals and receives screen images, which requires only a small amount of bandwidth on the network. For a more robust session that might need access to local resources, Remote Desktop Services can provide audio, local printer, COM port, local disk, and Plug and Play Device Redirection (for media players and digital cameras) to provide ease of data transfer between the client and server through a single network port. Remote Desktop Services also provides local time zone redirection, which allows users to view time stamps of email and files relative to their location. Lastly, Remote Desktop Services can also support higher-resolution desktop computers (up to 4096x2048) and spanning multiple monitors horizontally to form a single, large desktop, and using the Client Experience feature, users can be given a Remote Desktop Services desktop experience that feels and looks like Windows 7.

Remote Desktop Services was first introduced in Windows NT 4.0 Terminal Server Edition. Through subsequent versions of Windows, both Remote Desktop Services and its subject protocol Remote Desktop Protocol (RDP) have been significantly improved. These improvements have culminated with the Windows Server 2008 R2 and Windows 7 release rebranding of Terminal Services to Remote Desktop Services and the introduction of a number of new features, such as the following:

▶ Remote Desktop Services management support via Windows PowerShell

▶ Per-user RemoteApp program filtering for Remote Desktop Web Access

▶ Remote Desktop Virtualization Host, which is a component of Microsoft's Virtual Desktop Infrastructure (VDI) offerings

▶ The introduction of RemoteApp and Desktop Connection, which is designed to provide a seamless user experience on Windows 7

▶ Support for Single Sign-On between RD Session Host and RD Web Access

▶ Improved audio and video playback support

This chapter reviews features and how to plan, implement, and support a Windows Server 2008 R2 Remote Desktop Services deployment. This chapter addresses not only the new features added in Windows Server 2008 and Windows Server 2008 R2, but also how these new technologies can be leveraged to improve remote access services by users and by network administrators.

# Why Implement Remote Desktop Services

Remote Desktop Services is a versatile product that can be implemented to meet many different business needs. In some cases, it is implemented to give administrators the ability to remotely administer a server, group of servers, or applications. Remote Desktop Services can also be used to allow users access to applications and network resources through a terminal session. Or, Remote Desktop Services can be implemented by an application service provider (ASP) to create managed application services, eliminating the need for its customers to buy server hardware, software, and support.

Regardless of the reason why Remote Desktop Services is implemented, there are several benefits to implementing it:

▶ **Centralized deployment of applications**—By deploying applications using Remote Desktop Services, those applications reside only on Remote Desktop Services and can be centrally managed. In addition, deploying applications in this manner allows them to be rapidly deployed and updated.

▶ **Remote access to applications**—Remote Desktop Services allows users to access applications within a local network and remotely. Connections can even be made to applications in bandwidth-constrained connections, such as dial-up or shared wide area network (WAN) links, and over Hypertext Transfer Protocol Secure (HTTPS).

▶ **Windows Anywhere**—Remote Desktop Services allows users to access feature-rich Windows applications from many different devices. These devices can include underpowered hardware, non-Windows desktops, thin clients (terminals), and even mobile devices.

▶ **Virtual desktops**—Using Remote Desktop Services in conjunction with Remote Desktop Virtualization, users can be allocated their own personal virtual desktop or given access to a virtual desktop instance within a virtual desktop pool.

> **NOTE**
>
> Windows XP Professional, Windows XP Media Center and Tablet PC Editions, Windows Vista Ultimate, Enterprise, and Business Editions, and Windows 7 Ultimate, Business, and Professional include a scaled-down version of Remote Desktop Services that can be enabled and used for remote administration or remote workstation access.

## Remote Desktop for Administration

As a remote administration tool, Remote Desktop Services gives an administrator the option of performing server administration from a server console or from any other server or workstation using the Remote Desktop Connection client (previously known as the Terminal Services Client). Remote Desktop is installed by default, but is not automatically enabled. Using Remote Desktop can simplify server administration for an IT department by allowing personnel to do their jobs from almost any console on the network. This can improve IT response times to complete trouble tickets concerning access to network resources or user account management. Server maintenance tasks such as reviewing logs or gathering server performance data can be accomplished through the client.

Applications and updates can be installed through a Remote Desktop session, but should be done only when the installation does not involve a Windows component installation or when users are running Remote Desktop server sessions. Installing applications from the local server console is recommended, but if an application must be installed remotely, some changes with Session 0 introduced in Windows Vista and Windows Server 2008 make doing so easier. (These changes are explained later in this chapter in the section "Session 0 Isolation.")

> **NOTE**
>
> With the release of the Terminal Services Client 6.0, the client was renamed Remote Desktop Connection.

## Remote Desktop for Users

There are many benefits of making Remote Desktop available to users. For example, company hardware costs can be reduced, application availability and licensing management can be simplified, and network performance can increase.

Because a Remote Desktop session is really a remote session running on the Remote Desktop Session Host, all Remote Desktop users run applications on a Windows server, utilizing the processing power of the server while reducing the load on the local workstation. This can extend the life of an underpowered machine whose deficient resources might impede workflow through high processor, memory, or disk utilization.

From a desktop support perspective, a Remote Desktop Session Host can be put in place and used as a secondary means of providing users access to their applications if problems are encountered with the applications on their local workstations. Although this approach might seem to be overkill, providing a secondary means of application access can be vital to user productivity and company revenue when support personnel might not be readily available to fix end-user application issues.

Providing centralized applications for users though Remote Desktop Services can also simplify application management by reducing the number of machines on which application upgrades, security updates, and fixes need to be installed. Because all the applications run on the Remote Desktop Session Host, only the server itself needs to be updated, and the entire user base benefits from the change immediately. This way, the updates can be performed for all Remote Desktop Session Host users at one time.

## Remote Desktop for Remote User Support

Remote Desktop can be used to provide application support for end users within a Remote Desktop session. When users are running in a Remote Desktop session, an administrator can configure remote control or shadowing functionality to view or completely interact with a user's session. This feature can be used to train users, provide application support, or create configuration changes, such as installing a printer or connecting to a network file share. This capability can greatly reduce the number of administrators needed during the regular workday because multiple users can be assisted from one location.

> **NOTE**
>
> To comply with many organizations' security and privacy policies, Remote Desktop Services provides an option for the remote control function to be completely disabled. Alternatively, rather than completely disabling the function for all users, Remote Desktop Services can be configured to give users the ability to choose whether to allow an administrator to interact with their Remote Desktop session.

## Remote Desktop for Application Service Providers

Installing the Remote Desktop Services role service allows applications and services to be made available to users in any location. Companies that provide services to businesses through proprietary applications can standardize and provide their applications exclusively through Remote Desktop Services and gain all the benefits outlined in the preceding sections. An added bonus for these companies is that Remote Desktop Services reduces the need to send application media out to each client, and end-user support can be provided in a way never before possible.

Application service providers that make several applications available to clients can use Remote Desktop Services to service hundreds or thousands of users from different organizations while charging a fee for application usage or terminal session time usage.

> **NOTE**
>
> Windows Server 2008 R2 does not provide a standard reporting mechanism to present Remote Desktop session data. However, some valuable information can be gathered by filtering the security event log for user logon and logoff events, using the Remote Desktop Licensing Manager tool, as well as teaming this information with data gathered by creating performance logs configured to monitor Terminal Services (an item not renamed) session counters using the Performance Monitor Microsoft Management Console (MMC) snap-in or through information provided by Windows System Resource Manager (WSRM), included with Windows Server 2008 R2. It is also important to note that System Center Operations Manager 2007 and some third-party solutions for Remote Desktop Services provide exceptional reporting functionality.

# How Remote Desktop Works

Remote Desktop allows users to connect to a remote machine and access applications or an entire desktop. To establish their client/server session, users utilize the Remote Desktop Connection client. The RDC client, in turn, uses a multichannel protocol called the Remote Desktop Protocol (RDP), which is an extension of the ITU T.120 family of protocols. By default, RDP-based connections are made over TCP 3389, or if Remote Desktop Gateway is used, then the connections are made over TCP 443 (HTTPS).

When a user uses RDP, client mouse and keyboard events are redirected from the client to the remote machine. On the remote machine, RDP uses its own onscreen keyboard and mouse driver to receive these keyboard and mouse events from RDC clients. Then to render a user's actions, RDP uses its own video driver. Using this video driver, RDP constructs the display output into network packets, which are then redirected back to the RDC client. On the client, the rendering data is received and translated into corresponding Microsoft Win32 graphics device interface (GDI) application programming interface (API) calls.

Because RDP is multiple-channel capable, separate virtual channels are used for carrying device communication, presentation data, and encrypted client mouse and keyboard data between the RDC client and a remote machine. RDP's virtual channel base is extensible and supports up to 64,000 separate channels for data transmissions or multipoint transmissions.

> **NOTE**
>
> Using a multipoint transmission data from an application can be sent to multiple clients in real time without sending the same data to each session individually (for example, virtual whiteboards).

## Modes of Operation

Remote Desktop can be run in two different modes of operation. The first mode is called the Remote Desktop for Administration and the other is called Remote Desktop Services.

### Remote Desktop for Administration

Remote Desktop for Administration is included and installed with the Windows Server 2008 R2 operating system and only needs to be enabled. This eases automated and unattended server deployment by allowing an administrator to deploy servers that can be managed remotely after the operating system has completed installation. This mode can also be used to manage a headless server, which reduces the amount of space needed in any server rack. More space can be dedicated to servers instead of switch boxes, monitors, keyboards, and mouse devices.

The Remote Desktop for Administration limits the number of terminal sessions to only two parallel connections (three, if the administrator uses session 0, the local console), and only local administrators can connect to these sessions by default. No additional licenses are needed to run a server in this Remote Desktop mode, which allows an administrator to perform almost all the server management duties remotely.

Even though Remote Desktop for Administration is installed by default, it has to be enabled. Some organizations might see using this feature as an unneeded security risk and choose to keep it disabled or limit access to remote sessions. However, Remote Desktop for Administration can also easily be enabled by using a group policy, a PowerShell-based command/script, or good old manual means. Lastly, this mode of Remote Desktop is available in every Windows Server 2008 R2, Windows Server 2008, and Windows Server 2003 version and, as mentioned before, Windows XP Professional, Windows XP Media Center and Tablet PC Editions, Windows Vista Ultimate, Enterprise, and Business Editions, and Windows 7 Ultimate, Business, and Professional.

> **NOTE**
>
> Starting with Windows Vista/Windows Server 2008 and on to Windows 7/Windows Server 2008 R2, there have also been a number of changes to how Remote Desktop works. A listing of these changes can be found in the "Why Implement Remote Desktop Services" section found earlier in this chapter.

### Remote Desktop Services

Remote Desktop Services allows any authorized user to connect to the server and run a single application or a complete desktop session from their client workstation. Running Remote Desktop Services requires the purchase of a Remote Desktop Services client access license (CAL) for each simultaneous connection. To manage these CALs, a Remote Desktop licensing server is needed to allocate and track the licenses for Remote Desktop Services. The Remote Desktop Licensing role service can be installed on any Windows Server 2008 R2 Standard, Enterprise, or Datacenter Edition member server.

It should also be noted that before installing applications that will be used in Remote Desktop Services, it is recommended that administrators follow a strict validation process to ensure that each application runs as it should in multiple user sessions. Some applications might not be properly suited to run on a Remote Desktop server; in such cases, extensive Remote Desktop Services application compatibility testing should take place before deployment. The results of such testing can both determine if an application is compatible and if any custom installation steps or scripts need to be created for these applications to run correctly.

> **NOTE**
>
> Remote Desktop Services is not available in Windows Server 2008 R2 Web and Windows Server 2008 R2 Itanium Editions.

## Client-Side Remote Desktop Services

Windows XP Professional, Windows XP Media Center and Tablet PC Editions, Windows Vista Ultimate, Enterprise, and Business Editions, and Windows 7 Ultimate, Business, and Professional all have a scaled-down version of Remote Desktop. This version of Remote Desktop allows a user to connect to a workstation and remotely take over the workstation to run applications that he or she would normally run from their desk locally. As an administration tool, this client-side Remote Desktop can be used to install software on an end user's workstation from a remote machine. Also, it can be used to log on to a user's desktop environment to remotely configure a user's profile settings.

### Remote Assistance

Remote Assistance is a feature that has been present in Windows since Windows Server 2003 and Windows XP Professional. This feature allows a user to request assistance from a trusted friend or administrator to help deal with desktop issues and configurations. This feature gives the end user the power to control what level of participation the remote assistant can have. The remote assistant can be granted the ability to chat with the end user, view the desktop, or remotely control the desktop. During remote assistance sessions, both the end user and remote assistant can hand off control of the keyboard and mouse. Remote assistance uses the underlying Remote Desktop Protocol (RDP) used by Remote Desktop.

### Remote Desktop Connection

The Remote Desktop Connection client is the newly improved and renamed Terminal Server client. This full-featured client allows the end user to control Remote Desktop session settings such as local disk, audio, and port redirection, plus additional settings such as running only a single program or logging on automatically and so on. Remote Desktop Connection information can be saved and reused to connect to Remote Desktop Services with previously defined session specifications.

# Understanding the Name Change

As mentioned earlier in this chapter, Windows Terminal Services was renamed to Remote Desktop Services in Windows Server 2008 R2. Table 25.1 lists the Terminal Services role, role services, and related components that have been renamed and their new Windows Server 2008 R2 name.

TABLE 25.1    Parameters and Values for Creating an Unattended Answer File

| Previous Name | Windows Server 2008 R2 Name |
| --- | --- |
| Terminal Services | Remote Desktop Services |
| Terminal Server | Remote Desktop Session Host (RD Session Host) |
| Terminal Services Licensing (TS Licensing) | Remote Desktop Licensing (RD Licensing) |
| Terminal Services Gateway (TS Gateway) | Remote Desktop Gateway (RD Gateway) |
| Terminal Services Session Broker (TS Session Broker) | Remote Desktop Connection Broker (RD Connection Broker) |
| Terminal Services Web Access (TS Web Access) | Remote Desktop Web Access (RD Web Access) |
| Terminal Services Manager | Remote Desktop Services Manager |
| Terminal Services Configuration | Remote Desktop Session Host Configuration |
| TS Gateway Manager | Remote Desktop Gateway Manager |
| TS Licensing Manager | Remote Desktop Licensing Manager |
| TS RemoteApp Manager | RemoteApp Manager |

# Understanding Remote Desktop Services

Although some of the features in Remote Desktop Services have already been touched on, this section covers features that are important, new, or improved in Windows Server 2008 R2–based Remote Desktop Services.

## RD Session Host

The Remote Desktop Session Host (RD Session Host) role service was previously known as the Terminal Server role service in Windows Server 2008. This role service is used to host Windows-based applications or a full Windows desktop for users who connect to an RD Session Host using either Remote Desktop Connection or RemoteApp.

The new features that have been introduced in Windows Server 2008 R2 for the RD Session Host role service are discussed in the following sections.

### Per-User RemoteApp Filtering

Using per-user RemoteApp filtering, an administrator can now filter the list of RemoteApp programs that are available to users when they log on to RD Web Access. Prior to this feature being introduced, each user was presented with a list of all RemoteApp programs regardless of whether they had rights.

### Fair Share CPU Scheduling

In previous versions of Terminal Services, the Windows scheduler had a fair scheduling policy that distributed processor time evenly across all threads of the same priority level. Although this scheduling methodology was a good mechanism to prevent any one user from completely monopolizing the CPU, it was not able to evenly distribute the processor time based on dynamic loads. To better handle dynamic loads, the Fair Share CPU Scheduling feature in Remote Desktop Services uses a Windows Server 2008 R2 kernel-level scheduling mechanism to dynamically distribute processor time across sessions based on the number of active sessions and load on those sessions.

> **NOTE**
>
> By default, the Fair Share CPU Scheduling feature is enabled. To disable this feature, set the following Registry entry as 0:
> `HKEY_LOCAL_MACHINE\SOFTWARE\Policies\Microsoft\Windows\SessionManager\DFSS\EnableDFSS`.

### Windows Installer RDS Compatibility

In previous versions of Terminal Services, only one Windows Installer installation was supported at a time. This meant that user-related MSI actions (like personalization) were limited to one concurrent run per Terminal Server. To streamline application deployments to RS Session Host servers, the Windows Installer RDS Compatibility feature is designed so that per-user application installations are queued by the RD Session Host server and then handled by the Windows Installer.

> **NOTE**
>
> Windows Installer RDS Compatibility is enabled by default. You can disable this feature by configuring the following Registry entry to 0:
> `HKEY_LOCAL_MACHINE\Software\Policies\Microsoft\Windows NT\Terminal Services\TSAppSrv\TSMSI\Enable`.

### Client Experience Configuration Page

During the installation of the RD Session Host role service using Server Manager, one of the steps in the wizard is the Client Experience Configuration page. Using this page, an administrator can configure the following client experience features:

- Audio and video playback redirection
- Audio recording redirection

▶ Desktop composition (user-interface elements of the Windows Aero desktop experience within an RD Session Host session)

> **NOTE**
>
> When any of these features are configured using the installation wizard, the Desktop Experience role service is also installed and Windows Audio service is started on the RD Session Host server.

### Roaming User Profile Cache Management

Caching of roaming profiles is often enabled in a Remote Desktop Services deployment to improve end-user experience. Unfortunately, the profile cache tends to grow very large and in certain cases can consume all the available disk space on a server. Roaming user profile cache management is a new Remote Desktop Services feature that is designed to limit the overall size of the roaming profile cache. When enabled and the roaming profile cache has exceeded the specified size, Remote Desktop Services will continue deleting the least recently used profiles until the cache size is below the defined quota.

> **NOTE**
>
> The profile cache size can be limited using the Group Policy setting `Computer Configuration\Policies\Administrative Templates\Windows Components\Remote Desktop Services\Remote Desktop Session Host\Profiles\Limit the Size of the Entire Roaming User Profile Cache`. When enabling this setting, both monitoring interval (in minutes) and a maximum size (in gigabytes) must be defined.

### Remote Desktop IP Virtualization

In certain cases, an application might require that each initialized instance of that application must be assigned a unique IP address; for example, a CRM application that binds to a temporary database instance, which is listening on a network port. In previous versions of Terminal Services, these types of applications presented a deployment challenge for administrators. However, by using the new Remote Desktop IP Virtualization, an IP address can now be assigned to a remote desktop connection on a per-session or per-program basis.

## RD Virtualization Host

The Remote Desktop Virtualization Host (RD Virtualization Host) role service works in conjunction with Hyper-V to host virtual machines for Remote Desktop Services. Users can connect to a virtual machine using either RemoteApp and Desktop Connection or Remote Desktop Web Access (RD Web Access). These virtual machines can either be deployed as a personal virtual desktop (each user is assigned a unique virtual machine) or part of a shared virtual desktop pool (a virtual machine is dynamically assigned).

Personal virtual desktops are assigned to individual users by using the Remote Desktop Connection Manager. Users can only be assigned one virtual desktop; additionally, a virtual desktop can only be assigned to one user. By keeping the relationship one-to-one, all customizations that are made to a personal virtual desktop by a user are preserved and available for future use.

In contrast, the goal with a virtual desktop pool is to have the same user experience across all virtual desktops regardless of the virtual desktop that a user is connected to. To achieve this type of experience, all virtual machines in a virtual desktop pool must be configured identically (in addition to not already being assigned as a personal virtual desktop). Additionally, virtual desktop pools can be configured to roll back changes to a previous state when a user logs off of the virtual machine.

To redirect users to the correct virtual machine, the RD Virtualization Host uses the Remote Desktop Connection Broker (RD Connection Broker). When a user is assigned to a personal virtual desktop, the RD Connection Broker redirects a user's session request to the appropriate virtual machine. For cases when the virtual machine is not powered on, the RD Virtualization Host will power on the virtual machine before completing the session request. When a user attempts to open up a connection to a shared virtual desktop pool, the RD Connection Broker does either of the following:

1. If the user already has a disconnected session to a virtual machine, the RD Connection Broker simply redirects the connection request to that virtual desktop.

2. If the user doesn't already have a disconnected session, the RD Connection Broker dynamically assigns a virtual machine from the pool.

> **NOTE**
>
> Using the RD Virtualization Host role service requires that Hyper-V also be installed.

## RD Gateway

The Remote Desktop Gateway (RD Gateway) role service allows users to access network resources (like RD Session Host servers, RD Session Host servers running RemoteApp programs, RD Virtualization Host–based virtual machines, or computers with Remote Desktop enabled) that are located behind firewalls in a private network from any Internet-based client (or internally based clients if TCP 3389 is an internally restricted port). To do this, the RD Gateway employs something that is called an SSL relay (also known as an SSL VPN). In short, an SSL relay allows clients to connect to internal resources over a secure, encrypted HTTPS connection. In this case, the traffic that is being passed through the SSL relay is just RDP (TCP 3389).

> **NOTE**
>
> RD Gateway must be installed on Windows Server 2008 R2 servers, but it can perform SSL relay for both Windows Server 2008 R2 RD Session Host servers and Windows Server 2008/2003 Terminal Servers.

RD Gateway was first introduced in Windows Server 2008 as the TS Gateway. The reason Microsoft has included this feature in Windows Server 2008 was because security measures were typically put into place to block traffic such as RDP (TCP 3389). In other words, IT security departments typically blocked RDP or were reluctant to open ports on their firewalls for it. Microsoft took a card from networking companies and built an SSL VPN solution into their Remote Desktop Services offerings. The result of this effort is the RD Gateway, which allows users to gain access to the services that are provided by Remote Desktop Services, regardless of their location.

As hinted previously, the RD Gateway uses an HTTP Secure Sockets Layer/Transport Layer Security (SSL/TLS) tunnel to transmit RDP traffic. Because the RD Gateway server is using HTTPS, a server authentication certificate needs to be installed. Furthermore, the certificate that is installed needs to be issued by a certificate authority (CA) that is trusted on clients accessing the RD Gateway. In other words, the certificate of the CA that signed the RD Gateway server certificate must be located in the client's Trusted Root Certification Authority store. A trusted certificate can either be obtained from a publicly trusted CA or an internal CA to your organization that is already trusted by clients.

The following are some additional requirements that should be taken into account when using the RD Gateway:

▶ The Remote Procedure Call (RPC) over HTTP Proxy service must be installed (this is installed when you install the RD Gateway role service).

▶ Internet Information Services 7.5 must be installed and running for the RPC over HTTP Proxy service to function.

▶ The Network Policy Server (NPS) service must be installed or an existing NPS server must be present that can be used by the RD Gateway.

▶ RD Gateway servers and Remote Desktop Services clients can be configured to use Network Access Protection (NAP).

▶ Active Directory Domain Services is required if the RD Gateway authorization policy is defined such that clients must be a member of a domain-based group.

> **NOTE**
>
> The RD Gateway feature is only supported on clients running Windows Server 2008 (R2), Windows 7, Windows Vista, Windows XP with Service Pack 2 or higher, or Windows Server 2003 with Service Pack 1 or higher that have the Remote Desktop Connection (RDC) client installed.

The new features that have been introduced in Windows Server 2008 R2 for the RD Gateway role service are discussed in the following sections.

### Configurable Idle and Session Timeouts

In Windows Server 2008 R2, an administrator can now configure idle and session timeouts for an RD Gateway server. An idle timeout is used to reclaim unused resources. If a user's session is idle longer than the specified time, that user's RD Gateway session is disconnected. When this occurs, a user will still be able to reestablish the session, if they choose to. A session timeout allows for the ability to periodically enforce new policies on active user connections. Policy refreshes mean that Remote Desktop connection authorization policy (RD CAP) changes or Remote Desktop resource authorization policy (RD RAP) changes can be enforced on existing sessions.

### Background Session Authentication and Authorization

If a timeout is reached, a session can either be disconnected or silently reauthenticated and reauthorized. When enabled for background authentication and authorization, the authentication and authorization requests for the session are automatically done in the background with no interaction.

### System and Logon Messages

Now when a user starts a new RD Gateway session, an administrator can define system and logon messages. System messages can be used to inform users about system status changes, upcoming server maintenance, and so on, whereas a logon message can be used to display a legal-logon notice to users before they gain access to any protected resources.

### Device Redirection Enforcement

RD Gateway now has the option to only allow Remote Desktop clients to connect to RD Session Host and RD Virtualization Host servers that enforce secure device redirection. This change was put in place to prevent non-Microsoft Remote Desktop clients from overriding the gateway device redirection controls. However, this new feature is only supported on RDC 7.0 or later clients.

### Network Access Protection (NAP) Remediation

When using a Windows Server 2008 R2 RD Gateway server, clients that are found out-of-compliance with a health policy can now be brought into compliance via software updates. By using this feature, an administrator can use a CAP policy to ensure that remote clients that connect to internal resources through an RD Gateway are always kept current with the latest software updates.

### Pluggable Authentication and Authorization

The pluggable authentication and authorization feature exposes a set of APIs that allow organizations custom or third-party authentication and authorization plug-ins that integrate with RD Gateway. By using this feature, RD Gateway authentication and authorization can be tailored to fit a wide range of security requirements.

### Windows Server 2008 R2 Feature Requirements

For an administrator to utilize the new RD Gateway features introduced in Windows Server 2008 R2, the following requirements must be met:

- RD Session Host servers must be Windows Server 2008 R2.

- RD Gateway servers must be Windows Server 2008 R2.

- Users must use the Remote Desktop Connection (RDC) 7.0.

# RD Web Access

The Remote Desktop Web Access role service is designed to allow users (internally and remotely) to access RemoteApp programs, session-based remote desktops, or virtual desktops from within a website. Using RD Web Access, a user accessing a website (hosting the RD Web Access web part) would be presented with a single consolidated list of published RemoteApps. This list consists of the application icons for each RemoteApp that has been published either from a single RD Session Host server or RD Session Host server farms. By clicking on one of these icons, a session would then be launched on the remote RD Session Host or RD Virtualization Host that is hosting the published resource. RD Web Access is especially useful to administrators who want to deploy Remote Desktop Services–based programs from a central location, from a customized web page, or from a Windows SharePoint Services site.

To use RD Web Access, clients must meet the following requirements:

▶ Internet Explorer 6.0

▶ Remote Desktop Connection (RDC) that supports at least Remote Desktop Protocol (RDP) 6.1

The version of the RDC client on Windows 7 and Windows Server 2008 R2 supports RDP 7.0. The RDC client that is being used determines which RD Web Access features will be available to users. Additionally, the Remote Desktop Services ActiveX Client control must be enabled.

The new features that have been introduced in Windows Server 2008 R2 for the RD Session Host role service are discussed in the following sections.

### Forms-Based Authentication

Forms-based authentication (FBA) is an ASP.NET authentication service that enables applications to provide their own logon page and do their own credential verification. Additionally, this service authenticates users, redirects unauthenticated users to the logon page, and performs all the necessary cookie management. Like Outlook Web Access (OWA), by supporting FBA, RD Web Access users will now have an improved logon experience. For example, administrators can customize the RD Web Access logon page to include such things as branding stylization and other important look-and-feel items.

### Single Sign-On Between RD Session Host and RD Web Access

An important feature that was missing from the Windows Server 2008 Terminal Services version of Web Access was support for Single Sign-On. In that version, when a user connected to a RemoteApp program using Web Access, they were prompted for their credentials twice. Needless to say, the double credential prompting led to a poor user experience. However, with the Windows Server 2008 R2 version of Web Access (RD Web Access), support for Single Sign-On has been added. When used correctly, users will only have to provide their credential information once when connecting to a RemoteApp program using RD Web Access.

**NOTE**

To use RD Web Access Single Sign-On, several dependencies must be met. First, the certificate used to sign the RemoteApp programs must be trusted. Second, Single Sign-On is only supported from clients running Remote Desktop Connection (RDC) 7.0.

### Public and Private Computer Option

Like OWA, the RD Web Access Web page can now be accessed via either a public or private mode. If the public computer option is used, cookies storing the username are available for about 20 minutes. If the cookie is left to expire, the user's information is technically purged from the system being used. When the private computer option is used, cookies storing the username are available for about 4 hours.

**NOTE**

A user's password is never cached on a system when either the public or private RD Web Access options are used.

## RD Connection Broker

In Windows Server 2003, the feature named Session Directory was introduced to maintain user connection states across load-balanced Terminal Servers. This feature kept a list of sessions indexed by username. Then, when a user became disconnected from that session and attempted to reconnect, the Session Directory redirected the user back to the same Terminal Server that held their disconnected session.

In Windows Server 2008, the Session Directory was renamed to the Terminal Services Session Broker (TS Session Broker). The renamed TS Session Broker also contains a new feature called TS Session Broker load balancing. Microsoft introduced the load-balancing feature to allow administrators to distribute session loads between Terminal Servers without having to use Windows Network Load Balancing (NLB). A typical deployment for the TS Session Broker load-balancing feature is for Terminal Server farms that consist of 2 to 10 servers.

For Windows Server 2008 R2, TS Session Broker was again renamed, this time to RD Connection Broker. Like before, the RD Connection Broker role service still performs load balancing and ensures that users get connected to the correct Remote Desktop session. However, the RD Connection Broker also supports load balancing and session state management for session-based desktops, virtual desktops, and RemoteApp programs accessed by using RemoteApp and Desktop Connection.

**NOTE**

When the RD Connection Broker role service is installed, the RD Web Access role service is also installed.

To track user sessions in a load-balanced RD Session Host server farm, an RD Connection Broker server stores information in its local database for each and every session. This session information includes where the session resides, its state, the session ID, and the username associated with the session. Using this information, the RD Connection Broker redirects users with an already existing session to the correct RD Session Host server or virtual desktop.

With RD Connection Broker Load Balancing, users with existing sessions are still redirected to those sessions if they attempt to reconnect to them. However, for new session connections, the RD Connection Broker will attempt to distribute the session load between more-powerful and less-powerful servers in the farm based on an assigned server weight value and which server has the least load.

To configure RD Connection Broker Load Balancing, an administrator must create an A or AAAA record for each RD Session Host in a farm. The hostname for the record is then set to the farm's name and the IP address to the RD Session Host server that is being added. The RD Connection Broker then uses round-robin DNS to distribute a user's initial connection to an RD Session Host server farm. After the user has connected and authenticated to the initial RD Session Host server, that server then queries the RD Connection Broker for where to redirect the user to. The final RD Session Host server that is returned from the RD Connection Broker is based on the following two decisions:

▶ Does the user have an existing session? If so, redirect that user to the RD Session Host server where that session exists.

▶ If the user doesn't have an existing session, which RD Session Host server has the least load? Redirect that user to the RD Session Host server with the least load.

---

**CAUTION**

RD Connection Broker Load Balancing does not work with Windows Server 2003 Terminal Servers, but does with work Windows Server 2008–based Terminal Servers.

---

In addition, there are also a couple of features that allow an administrator some control over the two previously listed decision paths. First, as mentioned, server weight can be assigned to each RD Session Host server that has been added to the RD Connection Broker. Configuring a server weight allows differences in load to be spread across RD Session Host servers that might not have the same hardware configuration. Less-powerful RD Session Host servers would then have a lower weight and fewer sessions, whereas more-powerful RD Session Host servers would have a higher weight and more sessions. Second, an administrator can also configure an RD Session Host server to act as a dedicated redirector. A dedicated redirector is an RD Session Host server that is configured to process initial session requests, but does not accept any user sessions. By using a dedicated redirector(s), the time associated with the initial connection into a farm and the resulting redirection is decreased, which results in faster logon times.

> **NOTE**
>
> By default, RD Connection Broker Load Balancing has a limit of 16 maximum pending logon requests per RD Session Host server. The limit is in place to prevent RD Session Host servers from becoming overwhelmed with logon requests either when they are coming back online or being added into a farm.

### Windows System Resource Manager

Windows System Resource Manager (WSRM) is a feature in Windows Server 2008 R2 that allows administrators to control how resources are allocated to applications, services, and processes. When being used in conjunction with Remote Desktop Services, WSRM allows administrators to precisely control the amount of resources each user or session is allowed to consume on an RD Session Host server. By limiting resources a session or user can use, an administrator can reduce the chances of a user maxing out an RD Session Host server's resources, which might impact other users on that server.

### Using Network Load Balancing (NLB)

Since Windows 2000 Server Terminal Services, Terminal Services nodes could be "clustered" using Network Load Balancing (NLB) to split the client load across several servers. With the introduction of RD Connection Broker Load Balancing, this clustering technique is no longer the only method by which to facilitate RD Session Host load balancing. As a general recommendation, RD Connection Broker Load Balancing should be used for RD Session Host server farms that need to facilitate load balancing.

> **NOTE**
>
> Do not confuse NLB-based clustering for Windows Server 2008 RD Session Host servers with the use of Microsoft Cluster Service (MSCS). It is recommended that you don't cluster your RD Session Host servers using MSCS. Clustering does not support memory failover for a node. In the event of a failover, information in memory is lost.

## RD Licensing

In addition to purchasing a Windows Server 2008 R2 server license, administrators must also have the correct number of Windows Server client access licenses (CALs). When utilizing Remote Desktop Services functionality, an additional set of Terminal Services client access licenses (TS CALs) or Remote Desktop Services client access licenses (RDS CALs) is needed for each user or device. For certain types of deployments, RDS External Connector or Service Providers License Agreement (SPLA) licenses can be purchased as well.

> **NOTE**
>
> New CALs are not required to deploy Windows Server 2008 R2 Remote Desktop Services. Both Windows Server 2008 TS CALs and Windows Server 2008 R2 RDS CALs provide access to Remote Desktop Services. However, Windows Server 2008 SP2 is required to install RDS CALs on a TS licensing server. Therefore, Microsoft recommends installing and using a Windows Server 2008 R2–based RD licensing server.

### Understanding Remote Desktop Services License Types

The following Remote Desktop Licensing types are available for use:

▶ **RDS Device CAL**—This CAL type permits one device (used by any user) to utilize Remote Desktop Services functionality on any server.

▶ **RDS User CAL**—This CAL type permits one user (using any device) to utilize Remote Desktop Services functionality on any server.

▶ **RDS External Connector**—Using this type of license allows for multiple external users to access a single Remote Desktop server; when multiple servers are being used, additional RDS External Connectors and Windows Server External Connectors must be purchased.

▶ **Service Providers License Agreement (SPLA)**—Using this type of license provides a service provider with a more flexible and robust licensing solution when hosting Remote Desktop Services to a number of different organizations and end users.

> **NOTE**
>
> Any combination of RDS Device CALs and RDS User CALs can be simultaneously used.

### Understanding Remote Desktop Services Client Access Licensing Mode

When using RDS CALs (Per-User or Per-Device modes), a separate RDS CAL is required for each user or device that is accessing Remote Desktop Services. CALs may be reassigned from one user or device to another. This assignment can be either permanent or temporary, depending on the need at the time.

### Understanding Virtual Desktop Infrastructure (VDI) Licensing

To correctly license a VDI environment also requires the purchase of licenses for both the Windows operating system being used for the virtual machine(s) and the infrastructure/management components needed for an end-to-end VDI deployment.

To license Windows as a guest operating system for any VDI environment, regardless of the choice of infrastructure or hypervisor vendor, a Virtual Enterprise Centralized Desktop (VECD) licensing agreement must be purchased. This agreement is available both for client devices that are covered by Software Assurance (VECD for SA) or just VECD for devices such as thin clients.

To license the rest of a VDI environment requires using one of two paths. The VDI infrastructure components can be licensed using RDS CALs, whereas the VDI management components are separately licensed. Or, the environment can be licensed using either Microsoft Virtual Desktop Infrastructure Standard Suite or the Microsoft Virtual Desktop Infrastructure Premium Suite. Both suites are volume license offerings that combine the products for an optimum VDI experience in a value package.

### Understanding New RD Licensing Features

The new features that have been introduced in Windows Server 2008 R2 for the RD Licensing role service are discussed in the following sections.

**Automatic License Server Discovery No Longer Supported for Remote Desktop Servers**    In previous versions of Windows Server, the licensing server was automatically discovered on the network. In Windows Server 2008 R2, automatic discovery is no longer supported. Instead, administrators must now specify the name of a licensing server to use for each RD Session Host server.

**Changes to the Licensing Tab in Remote Desktop Server Configuration**    When configuring an RD Session Host server, an administrator can use the Licensing tab in the Remote Desktop Server Configuration tool to specify the licensing server. When using this tab, a licensing server can be chosen from a list of servers that have been registered as a service connection point in Active Directory or can be manually defined by entering its name. For cases where more than one license is added, an RD Session Host server will attempt to contact licensing servers in the order in which they appear in the Specified License Servers box.

**The Manage RDS CALs Wizard**    A new wizard has been introduced in the RD Licensing Manager, which allows the following tasks to be performed:

▶ Migrate RDS CALs from one licensing server to another.

▶ Rebuild the RD Licensing database.

It is important to understand that the Manage RDS CALs Wizard can only be used against licensing servers running Windows Server 2008 R2. Therefore, if a licensing server is not running Windows Server 2008 R2, the original CALs on that server should be manually removed as part of the migration process to a Windows Server 2008 R2 licensing server.

**CAUTION**

When rebuilding the RD Licensing database, all RDS CALs are deleted and, therefore, will need to be reinstalled.

**Service Connection Point Registration**    While installing the RD Licensing role service, the licensing server will attempt to register itself as a Service Connection Point (SCP) in Active Directory. Once registered, the licensing server will then show up as a known licensing server in the Remote Desktop Server Configuration tool's Licensing tab. If Active Directory is not available during the role service installation, or the SCP registration fails, an administrator must manually register the licensing server by using Review Configuration in the RD Licensing Manager.

## RemoteApp and Desktop Connection

Windows Server 2008–based Terminal Services introduced a new feature called RemoteApp (TS RemoteApp) or "Seamless Windows." This feature allows applications that are accessed through Terminal Services to appear as if they are running locally on an end user's machine. By using this feature, a user would run their remote application side by side other applications allowing them to minimize, maximize, and resize the application window as if it were a location application. In addition, if a user were to launch more than one RemoteApp, each RemoteApp would reuse the existing Terminal Services session.

In Windows Server 2008 R2 Remote Desktop Services, the RemoteApp feature has been expanded to include the ability to group and personalize RemoteApp programs, session-based desktops, and virtual desktops while making them available to users on the Windows 7 or Windows Server 2008 R2 Start menu. As a result, the expanded RemoteApp feature has been renamed to RemoteApp and Desktop Connection.

To deploy RemoteApp and Desktop Connection, an administrator must first deploy and configure both the RD Connection Broker and the RD Web Access role services. Then, once RemoteApp programs have been defined on a source, administrators can use the Remote Desktop Connection Manager tool to configure virtual desktops or define which RemoteApp sources will be used for RemoteApp and Desktop Connection.

Once configured by and deployed by administrators, users on Windows 7 or Windows Server 2008 R2 machines are able to use RemoteApp programs, session-based desktops, and virtual desktops that were defined as part of the RemoteApp and Desktop Connection. The items from the connection can be found by users on the Start menu. As changes are made to RemoteApp and Desktop Connection, such as adding or removing RemoteApp programs, these changes are then automatically reflected on the Start menu. Additionally, users can use the RemoteApp and Desktop Connection notification area icon in the taskbar to do the following:

▶ See the connection status for RemoteApp and Desktop Connection.

▶ Manage the connection status (disconnect) for RemoteApp and Desktop Connection if needed.

## Granular Session Configuration Control

With the addition of many great features in Remote Desktop Services also comes the ability for an administrator to granularly control the configuration of Remote Desktop sessions. All the features available to the end user's Remote Desktop session can be managed, limited, and overridden by the administrator. Configuring administrative settings through Group Policy or Remote Desktop Management tools can override/control most user-configurable settings. This can greatly benefit an RD Session Host server by freeing up valuable server resources for features that might not be required in an enterprise deployment, such as audio redirection or high-color resolution. With this granular administrative capability, the administrator can also improve RD Session Host server or virtual desktop security by requiring high encryption for sessions, force certain types of strong authentication, or even lock the session down to prevent users from making operating system changes.

## Session 0 Isolation

In Windows Server 2003, Windows XP, and earlier versions of Windows, a console session was called Session 0. In addition to being an interactive logon session, Session 0 was also the session where all services were running. Unfortunately, having services run within the same session that hosted interactive logons presented a possible attack vector. Services run with elevated rights. Because of this, Session 0 services were a target for a malicious agent attempting to elevate their rights.

Microsoft addressed this threat in Windows Vista and Windows Server 2008 (and carried over to Windows 7 and Windows Server 2008 R2) by making Session 0 a non-interactive session. Now, when a user logs on to an interactive session, they are given Session 1, the next parallel user is given Session 2, and so on. As a result of this change, there are a number of consequences with how Remote Desktop for Administration works in Windows 7 and Windows Server 2008 R2. These consequences are as follows:

- ▶ **No /`console` switch**—The /`console` switch does not work when connecting to a Windows 7 or Windows Server 2008 R2 Remote Desktop session.

- ▶ **Only two Remote Desktop sessions can connect at the same time**—In Windows Server 2003, two Remote Desktop sessions and one remote console session were allowed at any given time. With the Session 0 change, there is now only a maximum of two parallel Remote Desktop sessions allowed in Windows 7 or Windows Server 2008 R2.

- ▶ **Session 0 user interface (UI) interaction**—What if a service presents a user with a UI to interact with? Because Session 0 is no longer interactive, Windows 7 and Windows Server 2008 R2 allow the user to interact with the Session 0 UI in a special desktop.

- ▶ **Disconnected session dialog box**—In the new Remote Desktop Connection client, there have been some changes in how a connection made to a Terminal Server with too many sessions is handled. In Windows Server 2003, the client just displayed a message: "The Terminal Server has exceeded the maximum number of connections." Now, when there are too many parallel sessions, the client displays a selection dialog box that allows an administrator to disconnect an existing session.

▶ **Users are restricted to one session by default**—By default in Windows Server 2008 R2 Remote Desktop Services, all users are restricted to one interactive session. This setting can be changed through the management console or Group Policy.

---

**NOTE**

When connecting to a Windows Server 2003 Terminal Server, the /console switch can still be used.

---

## Local Resource Redirection

Remote Desktop Services enables an RDC client to redirect many of the local resources so they can be easily used within a Remote Desktop session. Serial and printer ports can be made available in Remote Desktop sessions to allow a user to send RD Session Host server print jobs to locally configured printers, as well as access serial devices such as modems from within the Remote Desktop session. Audio can also be redirected from a session to local sound cards to enable sound from the Remote Desktop session to be heard from local speakers. Also, the Windows Clipboard can be redirected to allow cutting and pasting between the Remote Desktop session and the local workstation console.

Each of these resource redirections works only if the operating system and the RDC client on the end user's workstation support these configurations. Some of these local resource redirections require user modification or reconfiguration for proper use.

The various redirection support features built in to Remote Desktop Services are described in the following sections.

### Disk Drive Redirection

Local disk drives can be redirected to Remote Desktop sessions and appear in Windows Explorer as networked drives using the naming convention local drive letter on computer name—for example, C on workstation5. To access from a graphical window, simply browse the drive as you would a local or networked drive. Accessing this drive from the command prompt requires a little bit of education. Within a command prompt, the redirected local drives are referenced as \\tsclient\Drive letter. Directory listings can be created using this Universal Naming Convention (UNC), but for file transfer or quick browsing, a client should map a network drive letter to this local drive resource. To do so, follow these steps:

1. Open a command prompt.
2. Type net use * \\tsclient\c, where the local C: drive is the disk you want to access within the Command Prompt window. The local drive is automatically mapped to the next available drive letter, starting from drive letter Z: and working backward through the alphabet.
3. At the command prompt, type Z: and press Enter to connect directly to the mapped local drive and begin using this drive.
4. After you finish working with this resource, disconnect the drive by typing net use Z: /delete, where the Z: drive is the local mapped drive.
5. Close the Command Prompt window.

> **CAUTION**
>
> The preceding steps refer to a machine called `tsclient`. You should not replace this name with the actual machine account name. The Remote Desktop session recognizes the machine's local disk resources only from within a command window as `tsclient`, so do not consider this a substitute for the actual machine name.

### Printer Redirection

Locally defined print devices can also be redirected. This includes printers directly attached to the client workstation as well as network printers. When a client opens a Remote Desktop session that is configured to redirect Windows printers as well as LPT ports, the RD Session Host server attempts to install each printer for use in the Remote Desktop session.

In Windows Server 2003, managing printer drivers for printer redirection was the bane of administrators. Either a client's printer had to be using a printer driver native to Windows Server 2003 or the printer driver had to be manually installed beforehand by an administrator. If neither of these were true, printer redirection would fail. In Windows Server 2008, a new feature called TS Easy Print was introduced to reduce the difficulties involved with managing Terminal Services printer redirection.

TS Easy Print (renamed RD Easy Print in Windows Server 2008 R2) enables users to reliably print from a Remote Desktop session to their printer on their client computer. RD Easy Print does this by accomplishing the following things:

▶ It uses a universal printer driver. Because it is universal, this driver supports legacy and new printer drivers without the need for administrators to install these drivers on the RD Session Host server.

▶ The RD Easy Print driver allows users to view their local printer driver's printing preferences. This is accomplished because the driver acts as a proxy and redirects all calls for the GUI to the actual driver on the client side. The result is the RDC client actually just launches the GUI for the client-side printer on top of the remote session.

In Windows Server 2008 Terminal Services (and carried over to Windows Server 2008 R2 Remote Desktop Services), other changes were also introduced aimed at improving a user's experience with printer redirection. These changes are as follows:

▶ **Scope limitations for redirected printers**—In Windows Server 2003, if a user had multiple sessions open, all the redirection printers from all the sessions were visible to each individual session. Furthermore, administrators could see all the redirected printers for every user connected to a Terminal Server. In Windows Server 2008, the visibility of redirected printers is limited to the session where they are installed. With this change, the spooler service doesn't need to enumerate as many redirected printers. This reduction both improves the time when a user tries to enumerate their printers during a session and during initial logon.

▶ **Per-session default printers**—In Windows Server 2008 or later, a user's default printer is on a per-session basis. This is a change from Windows Server 2003 where the default printer for a user was the same for all sessions.

▶ **Redirected printer names are shorter**—In Windows Server 2003, redirected printer names were "%PRINTER_NAME% (from %CLIENT_MACHINE_NAME%) in session %Session_ID%." In Windows Server 2008 or later, these names have been shortened to "%PRINTER_NAME% (%SESSION_ID%)."

Clients must meet the following requirements to use the RD Easy Print driver:

▶ Using Remote Desktop Connection (RDC) 6.1 or later

▶ Have at least Microsoft .NET Framework 3.0 Service Pack 1 installed

### Local Time Zone Redirection

Remote Desktop Services also supports local time zone redirection. This feature allows RDC clients connecting from a separate time zone to have the session time reflect the user's local time, enabling users to more easily comprehend the times, especially when reviewing emails.

### Plug and Play Device Redirection

Using Plug and Play Device Redirection, a user can redirect Windows Portable Devices that support the Media Transfer Protocol (MTP) and digital cameras that support the Picture Transfer Protocol (PTP). Plug and Play Device Redirection works so that when a terminal session is launched, a user's plug-and-play devices are automatically installed on the RD Session Host server, virtual machine, or remote computer if just Remote Desktop for Administration is being used. After being connected, any plug-and-play notifications will then appear above the taskbar in the Remote Desktop session.

Users can also configure Plug and Play Device Redirection so that devices connected after a session has already been established are then redirected. To do this, a user would select the Devices That I Plug in Later check box in the Remote Desktop Connection client before connecting to a remote machine. Then after a device has been redirected, it will become available for use within the current session. For example, if a digital camera is redirected, that device would be directly accessible from an application such as the Scanner and Camera Wizard on the remote machine.

> **NOTE**
>
> Plug and Play Device Redirection is not supported over cascaded Remote Desktop sessions. A cascading session is when a user connects to one remote machine and then from within that session connects to a second remote machine.

### .NET Device Redirection

.NET Device Redirection allows a device that uses Microsoft Point of Service (POS) for .NET 1.11 to be redirected in a Remote Desktop session. This redirection feature is important to organizations that are deploying Remote Desktop Services to clients that use POS peripheral devices, such as bar-code scanners, biometrics, magnetic card readers, receipt printers, and so on.

> **NOTE**
>
> .NET Device Redirection is only supported on Terminal Servers or RD Session Host servers running an x86-based version of Windows Server 2008 or Windows Server 2008 R2.

### New Redirection Features

The following are new redirection features that are introduced in Windows Server 2008 R2 Remote Desktop Services:

▶ **Multimedia redirection**—This feature redirects multimedia files and streams such that audio and video content is received in its original form from the server to a client. By doing this, multimedia content is then rendered using a client's local media playback capabilities.

▶ **Audio input and recording**—This feature enables audio recording support for remote clients using Voice over IP (VoIP) or speech-recognition applications.

▶ **Language bar redirection**—Users can now control the language setting (for example, right to left) for RemoteApp programs using the local language bar.

## Single Sign-On

This feature allows a user with a domain account to log on once (via a password or smart card) and access RD Session Host servers and virtual desktops without being prompted for credentials again.

The following are some important considerations when using Single Sign-On:

▶ Single Sign-On is supported from Windows 7, Windows Vista, or Windows XP with Service Pack 3 clients to a Windows Server 2008 Terminal Server or Windows Server 2008 R2 RD Session Host server. This feature is also supported between Windows Server 2008 R2 to Windows Server 2008 servers or vice versa.

▶ The remote machine that a client is connecting to must be authenticated via Kerberos or a server authentication certificate such as SSL. Or, an administrator must enable the Allow Default Credentials with NTLM-Only Server Authentication policy.

▶ When saved credentials for a remote machine are already present, those credentials take precedence over the current credentials.

## Remote Desktop Connection Display

In the Remote Desktop Connection 6.0 client (and carried over to RDC 7.0), support was added for several new features that are geared toward improving the end-user experience: custom display resolutions, horizontal monitor spanning across multiple monitors, Desktop Experience, Font Smoothing, and Display Data Prioritization.

25

### Custom Display Resolutions

In the previous Terminal Services Client, only 4:3 display resolution ratios and a maximum resolution of 1600x1200 were supported. In the new client, additional display resolution ratios, such as 16:9 or 16:10, and maximum resolution of 4096x2048 are now supported.

There are two ways to set a custom display resolution. The first method is to edit an `.rdp` file with a text editor. In the file, add or change the following settings:

- `desktopheight:i:<value>`

- `desktopwidth:i:<value>`

The variable `<value>` should be defined as the desired resolution. The second method is to define the custom resolution from the command prompt:

- `mstsc.exe /w:<width> /h:<height>`

### Monitor Spanning

With the monitor spanning feature, a Remote Desktop session can now be spanned across multiple monitors. To use this feature, the monitors used must meet the following requirements:

- The monitors must use the same resolution.

- The monitors must be aligned horizontally.

- The total resolution across all monitors cannot exceed 4096x2048.

Monitor spanning can be enabled using two methods. The first method is to edit an `.rdp` file with a text editor. In the file, add or change the following setting: `Span:i:<value>`.

- `<value>` = 0, monitor spanning is disabled

- `<value>` = 1, monitor spanning is enabled

The second method is to enable spanning from the command prompt:

- `mstsc.exe /span`

### Desktop Experience

The Desktop Experience feature is used to make a desktop session on an RD Session Host server look and feel like a Windows 7 desktop. When enabled, this feature does the following things:

- Installs a Windows 7–like desktop, which then enables features such as Windows Media Player, desktop themes, photo management, and so on

- Allows another feature called Desktop Composition to function; Desktop Composition is used for Windows Aero over a Remote Desktop Connection

> **NOTE**
>
> Desktop Composition is not supported on a multiple monitor–based Remote Desktop session.

### Font Smoothing

An RD Session Host server can provide ClearType functionality to clients via a feature called Font Smoothing. ClearType is a feature that is used to display fonts such that they are clearer and smoother on displays such as an LCD monitor.

By default, ClearType is enabled in Windows Server 2008 and Windows Server 2008 R2. To enable Font Smoothing, use the following procedure on a Remote Desktop Connection client:

1. Open the Remote Desktop Connection client.
2. In the Remote Desktop Connection dialog box, click Options.
3. Now select the Experience tab, and select the Font Smoothing check box.

### Display Data Prioritization

In past versions of Terminal Services, a user's remote session would often become frozen when printing or transferring files. In Windows Server 2008, a feature called Display Data Prioritization was introduced. By design, this feature gives display, keyboard, and mouse data a higher priority over other virtual channel traffic. The result of this design is that virtual channel traffic, such as disk or file transfers, does not adversely affect a user's ability to interact with a remote session.

By default, the bandwidth ratio with the Display Data Prioritization feature is 70:30. This means that 70% of the bandwidth is reserved for display and input data and 30% is reserved for all other traffic. An administrator can adjust the bandwidth ratios by changing the following Registry values on a Terminal Server or RD Session Host server under the `HKEY_LOCAL_MACHINE\SYSTEM\CurrentControlSet\Services\TermDD` subkey:

▶ **FlowControlDisable**—Enables and disables flow control

▶ **FlowControlDisplayBandwidth**—Determines relative bandwidth priority for display (and input data)

▶ **FlowControlChannelBandwidth**—Determines relative bandwidth priority for other virtual channels

▶ **FlowControlChargePostCompression**—Determines bandwidth allocation based on precompression or postcompression bytes

### New RDC Display Features

The following are new RDC display features that are introduced in Windows Server 2008 R2 Remote Desktop Services:

▶ **True multiple-monitor support**—Now up to 16 monitors of almost any size, resolution, or layout are supported with RemoteApp and Remote Desktop.

## Planning for Remote Desktop Services

To successfully deploy a Remote Desktop Services environment requires thorough planning and testing prior to production rollout. Criteria such as application resource usage, security requirements, physical location, network access, licensing, fault tolerance, and

25

information indicating how users will be utilizing their sessions all contribute to the way Remote Desktop Services implementation should be designed.

## Planning for Remote Desktop for Administration

Unless Remote Desktop Services is viewed as a security risk, it is recommended to enable Remote Desktop for Administration on all internal servers to allow for remote administration. For servers that are on the Internet and for demilitarized zone (DMZ) networks, Remote Desktop Services can be used, but access should be limited to predefined separate IP addresses using firewall access lists to eliminate unauthorized attempts to log on to a server. In addition, those servers should be closely monitored for unauthorized attempts to access the system.

## Planning for RD Session Host Requirements

Deploying RD Session Host servers can require a lot of planning. Because the goal is to make applications and entire desktops available to end users, server hardware specification and application compatibility are key components to test before a production rollout.

### User Requirements

It is important to determine user requirements based on typical usage patterns, the number of users accessing the system, and the number of applications that are required to run. For instance, the more applications that a user will run in a session, the more processing power and memory will be required to optimize session performance. On average, a Remote Desktop user who runs one application might take 10MB of RAM and use little more than 3% of a server's total processing time per session. A power user who runs three or more applications simultaneously might require 40MB of RAM or much more, depending on the applications and features being used. Use the Performance Monitor MMC snap-in to test and validate usage statistics. The key is to not overload the server to the point where performance is too slow to be cost effective. Additionally, the bandwidth required by each user session will also affect how well the system performs under various workloads.

### Antivirus on Remote Desktop Services

Just as standard servers require operating system (OS)–level antivirus software, so do Remote Desktop Services servers. When choosing an antivirus product, be sure to choose one that is certified to run on Windows Server 2008 R2 Remote Desktop Services. Additionally, for RD Session Host servers, install the antivirus software after adding the role service so that scanning will work for all Remote Desktop sessions. Be sure to also follow installation guidelines for installing applications as outlined in the "Installing Applications" section later in this chapter.

### Application Compatibility

In Remote Desktop Services, application compatibility is a term used to describe a number of issues that might be encountered when trying to deploy an application on an RD Session Host server. For example:

1.  Some applications are written such that only a single user can use the application at a time. With such applications, conflicts with system resources—such as files,

Registry entries, pipes, IP addresses, and ports, which are used concurrently by multiple instances of applications—might prevent an application from being concurrently executed on an RD Session Host server.

2. In some cases, an application's preferences might persist or manifest from one user to the next. When this scenario occurs, there is concern with user data privacy because settings (data) are transiting from one user to the next.

3. Additionally, an application might be written such that execution of the application requires administrative privileges. However, in most Remote Desktop Services deployments, regular users are not granted administrative access on an RD Session Host server.

4. Applications might also be written such that network bandwidth or hardware constraints cause application performance to suffer in a multiuser usage scenario. For example, a large amount of video or animation content might overwhelm the RD Session Host's network connection, video card, and so on, thus reducing response time. Or, the application was simply written such that it requires a large amount of CPU or memory, thus monopolizing resources.

5. In some cases, an application might require devices that are not redirected by default, for example, devices such as CD drives, hard disk drives, and other special devices that are not available as native devices.

6. Or, an application is written for a particular version of Windows and, thus, its API usage and behavior might differ on Windows Server 2008 R2.

To help administrators determine if an application is compatible before it is deployed on an RD Session Host server, Microsoft provides a tool called the Remote Desktop Services Application Analyzer. When this tool is executed against an application, it uses Microsoft Application Verifier to analyze an application via intercepted function calls from that application into the operating system and notes the calls and the parameters passed. Then based on the information returned from the Microsoft Application Verifier, the Remote Desktop Services Application Analyzer generates a summary report of any RDS incompatible behavior and recommendations about deploying the application on an RD Session Host server. For example:

1. Any shared resources such as files and Registry entries that the application might require

2. Any type of access privileges issues that might be encountered

3. Any API usage requirements that might conflict with RDS

## Planning for RD Session Host Sizing and Optimizing

An RD Session Host server can be sized to deliver high-performance Remote Desktop sessions by estimating the amount of resources each user will require and the number of users who will utilize Remote Desktop Services. Performing frequent performance testing on the RD Session Host server helps generate accurate information on Remote Desktop session usage. You should perform performance testing during both peak and nonpeak times to ensure proper data collection. Increase memory and processors or introduce additional RD Session Host servers as necessary. Understanding the users' resource needs and the number of users will help you decide how to specify the server hardware requirements and determine how many RD Session Host servers you need to support the load.

### Scaling RD Session Host Servers

Scaling RD Session Host servers can be achieved by increasing server resources, such as the number of processors and the amount of memory, as well as by increasing the number of servers that are servicing requests. When determining how to scale, also consider manageability, cost, and how end users might be affected if a server goes offline. For instance, using a greater number of servers might decrease manageability (such as updating applications, keeping up with operating system updates, and other maintenance), but if a server goes down, fewer users will be affected. The solution will vary depending upon your organization's needs and circumstances.

Another consideration is the amount of flexibility your organization requires. Using more instead of bigger servers gives more flexibility because of the redundancy as well as the capability to take servers offline for maintenance. In this scenario, it is important to use servers with enough power to sustain slightly greater workloads during those times when other servers in the farm go offline.

> **NOTE**
>
> For more information on scaling Terminal Services, refer to Microsoft's "Windows Server 2003 Terminal Server Capacity and Scaling" whitepaper. Although the information found in this whitepaper refers to Windows Server 2003 Terminal Servers, the information provided in this document is still a good base until Microsoft releases updated information.

### Optimizing RD Session Host Performance

Optimizing performance on an RD Session Host is a challenging task because of the complexities in any environment. Hardware resources, applications, usage, the number of users to support, and much more can affect how well a Remote Desktop session responds to user interaction. There are rarely cases where there is one "silver bullet" that can improve overall performance; it takes a combined approach. For instance, from a user perspective, video, color depth, audio redirection, printer redirection, and encryption level all affect how well a system performs.

The following are best practices for ensuring that an RD Session Host server runs as efficiently and effectively as possible:

- Limit users to a single session.

- Log off disconnected or idle sessions after a specified period of time.

- If using vendor printer drivers, only use drivers that have been certified for Windows Server 2008 R2.

- Use applications that are certified to run on Windows Server 2008 R2 RD Session Host servers.

- Use System Center Operations Manager 2007 or other operations management software to monitor an RD Session Host server farm.

- For medium and enterprise deployments, use a separate server or group of servers with a fast disk subsystem to store redirected folders.

- Block Internet websites that use a lot of animation.

- Prevent the usage of applications that use a lot animation.

- Prevent users from installing applications such as games or desktop enhancements/themes.

- Utilize folder redirection to roam user data between RD Session Host servers.

**Monitoring RD Session Host Servers**    The Performance Monitor MMC snap-in can be used to monitor a Remote Desktop Session Host server and to gather session statistics. The two specific performance monitoring objects for an RD Session Host server are Terminal Services and Terminal Services Session.

> **NOTE**
>
> These performance monitoring objects have not been renamed in Windows Server 2008 R2 and as such reflect the old "Terminal Services" naming convention.

The first object, Terminal Services, has only three counters: active sessions, inactive sessions, and total sessions. Gathering this session data and teaming it with information such as Server Memory\Available Bytes and Processor\% Idle can give an administrator a clear understanding of RD Session Host usage and load. This information can be used to determine whether additional resources or servers need to be added to accommodate load or enhance performance. For example, one adjustment that can be made after taking readings from these counters is the implementation of disconnected session time limits to free server hardware resources for active sessions. The second performance object, Terminal Services Session, has a number of different performance counters available in relation to Remote Desktop sessions. When using this performance object, an administrator can then gather statistical information, such as how much memory and processor time the average Remote Desktop session uses. Lastly, be sure to also monitor network interfaces for available bandwidth to ensure that the RD Session Host server is not creating a bottleneck between clients and other back-end servers.

**Using Windows System Resource Manager to Control Resources**    As mentioned previously in this chapter, the Windows System Resource Manager (WSRM) can be used to limit the amount of CPU and memory an application can use. On a Remote Desktop Session Host server, you can assign distinct settings based not only on an application, but also on a specific user or group as well. This helps to enforce consistency among user sessions and prevent rogue applications or sessions from negatively affecting other user sessions. For more information on using the Windows Resource Manager, refer to Chapter 34, "Capacity Analysis and Performance Optimization."

## Planning for RD Session Host Upgrades

Upgrading an RD Session Host server can be tricky and should be handled with caution. Before any operating system or application updates or patches are applied on a production RD Session Host server, they should be thoroughly tested in an isolated lab server. This process includes knowing how to properly test the application before and after the update to be sure the update does not cause any problems and, in some cases, adds the functionality that you intended to add.

When an RD Session Host server's operating system is to be upgraded to the next version, many issues can arise during the upgrade process. Applications might not run properly in the next version because key system files might be completely different. Even printer drivers can be changed drastically, causing severe performance loss or even loss of functionality. Lastly, you need to consider that the existing RD Session Host server could have been modified or changed in ways that can cause the upgrade to fail, requiring a full restore from backup.

> **NOTE**
>
> Complete disaster recovery and rollback plans should be available during upgrades. This way, if problems arise, the administrator does not have to create the plan on the spot, ensuring that no important steps are overlooked.

As a best practice and to ensure successful upgrades of RD Session Host servers, replace existing servers with cleanly built RD Session Host servers with the latest updates. This includes re-creating each of the file shares and print devices and using the latest compatible drivers to support each of your clients. If necessary, an existing server can also be rebuilt from scratch and redeployed to the production environment if the hardware can still meet performance requirements.

## Planning the Physical Placement of Remote Desktop Services

Place your Remote Desktop Services servers where they can be readily accessed by the clients that will primarily be using them. Also, to keep network performance optimized, try to place RD Session Host and RD Virtualization Host servers on the same network segment as other servers that clients might use in their session, such as domain controllers, database servers, and mail servers. This way, you can reduce traffic on the network and improve Remote Desktop session performance. However, if security, as opposed to performance, is of concern, you should also take any appropriate steps needed to secure a Remote Desktop Services deployment such as deploying Application-layer firewalls like Forefront Threat Management Gateway or any other needed network controls.

## Planning for Networking Requirements

To keep Remote Desktop sessions running efficiently, adequate available network bandwidth is a must. Additionally, it's important to remember that a Remote Desktop session not only requires network access to the RD Session Host, but might need access to other servers depending on the application being used. For optimum performance for multi-tiered applications, install two or more network cards on an RD Session Host server and either configure the server to use one exclusively for Remote Desktop session connectivity and the other(s) for back-end server communication or consider leveraging teaming technology to aggregate the bandwidth provided by all the network cards.

## Planning for RD Session Host Tolerance

A fault-tolerant RD Session Host farm can be created using NLB, using other hardware vendor load-balancing technologies, or using the RD Connection Broker. If the RD Connection Broker is being used, an administrator needs to create the correct DNS records for the RD Session Host farm and all of its servers. Additionally, an administrator will need to add each RD Session Host server to the RD Connection Broker's Session Broker Computers Local Group. If a third-party load-balancing technology is being used, a preference should be for a technology that can either manage Remote Desktop sessions or use information from the RD Connection Broker. Lastly, if NLB is being used, load balancing of the Windows Server 2008 R2 servers should be configured per best practices that are outlined in Chapter 29, "System-Level Fault Tolerance (Clustering/Network Load Balancing)."

# Deploying Remote Desktop Services

After the Remote Desktop Services deployment has been planned, it is a best practice to then install and configure RDS in a lab environment. Then after the deployment has been verified, the next step is to install it into production and have it tested by IT personnel or a designated pilot group. Lastly, after being tested by these groups, the deployment can finally be released into full production to end users. By following this best-practice method, administrators can reduce many of the inherent risks associated with deploying Remote Desktop Services while also verifying the infrastructure is ready to support end users.

The following subsections contain detailed instructions on how to install and configure Windows Server 2008 R2–based Remote Desktop Services for a typical enterprise deployment that only includes several RDS servers.

## Enabling Remote Desktop for Administration

Remote Desktop for Administration is installed on all Windows Server 2008 R2 servers by default and only needs to be enabled. To enable this feature, follow these steps:

1. Log on to the desired server with local administrator privileges.
2. Click Start, and then click Run.
3. In the Run dialog box, type in ServerManager.msc and click OK.
4. After the Server Manager console is displayed, select the Configure Remote Desktop task.
5. In the Systems Properties dialog box, on the Remote tab, and in the Remote Desktop section, select the Allow Connections Only from Computers Running Remote

Desktop with Network Level Authentication (More Secure) option button, as shown in Figure 25.1.

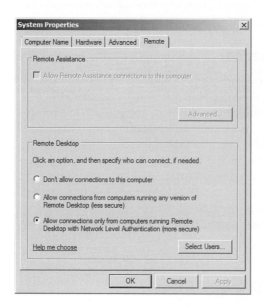

FIGURE 25.1    Allowing users to connect to the system remotely.

6. Click OK in the Systems Properties dialog box to complete this process.

**NOTE**

In the Remote Desktop section on the Remote tab of the System Properties dialog box, there are two different settings for enabling Remote Desktop. The first option, Allow Connections from Computers Running Any Version of Remote Desktop (Less Secure), allows a client using any version of the Remote Desktop Connection client to connect to Remote Desktop Services. The second option, Allow Connections Only from Computers Running Remote Desktop with Network Level Authentication (More Secure), only allows a client that is using a version of the Remote Desktop Connection client that supports Network Level Authentication (NLA) to connect to Remote Desktop Services.

Alternatively, Remote Desktop for Administration can also be enabled via GPO using the following policy options:

▶ Computer Configuration\Policies\Administrative Templates\Windows Components\Remote Desktop Services\Remote Desktop Session Host\Connections\Allow allows users to connect remotely using Remote Desktop Services.

▶ Computer Configuration\Policies\Administrative Templates\Windows Components\Remote Desktop Services\Remote Desktop Session Host\Security\Require requires user authentication for remote connections by using Network Level Authentication.

Or, administrators can also use PowerShell and the following commands to enable Remote Desktop for Administration:

▶ (Get-WmiObject -Class "Win32_TerminalServiceSetting" -Namespace root\cimv2\terminalservices).SetAllowTsConnections(1)

▶ (Get-WmiObject -class "Win32_TSGeneralSetting" -Namespace root\cimv2\terminalservices -Filter "TerminalName='RDP-tcp'").SetUserAuthenticationRequired(1)

> **NOTE**
>
> Although the Server Manager method described previously will also configure the required host firewall rules for Remote Desktop, the other two methods leave it to the administrator to configure the necessary firewall rules.

## Enabling Remote Assistance

To configure remote assistance, follow these steps:

1. Log on to the desired machine with local administrator privileges.
2. Click Start, right-click the Computer shortcut, and then click Properties.
3. Next, select the Remote Settings task and in the Remote Assistance Settings section, select the Allow Remote Assistance Connections to This Computer option.
4. Click the Advanced button to configure whether remote control will be allowed, the maximum amount of time an invitation can remain open, and if invitations can only be used from computers running Windows Vista or later, as shown in Figure 25.2.

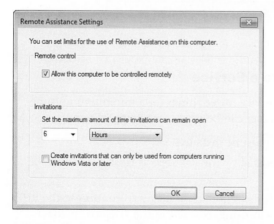

FIGURE 25.2    Enabling a computer for remote assistance.

25

**NOTE**

The previous steps assume that a Windows 7/Vista client is being used. For Windows XP clients, the steps will be slightly different.

5. Click OK in the Advanced window, and click OK on the System Properties page to complete this process.

Remote assistance for clients that are members of a domain can be configured using Group Policy. All of the remote assistance settings are located in Computer Configuration\Policies\Administrative Templates\System\Remote Assistance, as shown in Figure 25.3.

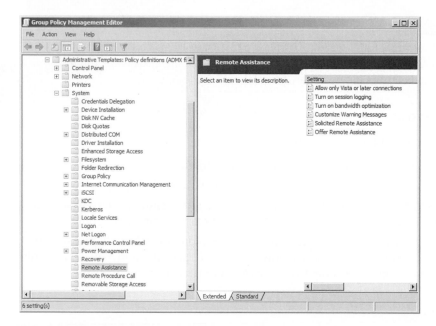

FIGURE 25.3    Group Policy administrative templates for remote assistance.

## Deploying the RD Session Host Role Service

When deploying the RD Session Host role service, three things (at a minimum) must be done, in order, before an RD Session Host server can be used to host applications:

1. First, the RD Session Host role service must be installed.

2. Next, the applications that are to be hosted by the RD Session Host server must be installed.

3. Finally, you must grant users or groups the required privileges to connect to the RD Session Host server and configure RD Licensing, covered in the "Deploying RD Licensing" section later in this chapter.

### Installing the RD Session Host Role Service

To install the RD Session Host role service, follow these steps:

1. Log on to the desired server with local administrator privileges.

2. Click Start, and then click Run.

3. In the Run dialog box, type in `ServerManager.msc` and click OK.

4. In the Roles Summary section, click the Add Roles task.

5. After the Add Roles Wizard loads, click Next.

6. On the Select Server Roles page, select the Remote Desktop Services role, and click Next, as shown in Figure 25.4.

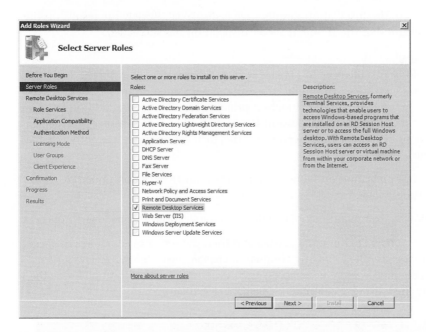

FIGURE 25.4    Selecting the Remote Desktop Services role.

7. On the Remote Desktop Services page, click Next.

8. Now, on the Select Role Services page, only select the Remote Desktop Session Host role service. This is the only role service that is being installed at this time. Click Next.

9. On the Uninstall and Reinstall Applications for Compatibility page, click Next.

10. Now, on the Specify Authentication Method for Remote Desktop Session Host page, select an authentication option for this RD Session Host server (the decision about which method should be made based on what type of clients will be connecting), and then click Next.

11. On the Specify Licensing Mode page, select the Configure Later licensing option (Remote Desktop licensing is reviewed later in this chapter in the section "Deploying RD Licensing"), and then click Next.

12. On the Select User Groups Allowed Access to This RD Session Host Server page, leave the default Administrators group, and then click Next.

13. On the Configure Client Experience page, choose the desired level of "Client Experience" functionality that will be available to remote clients when they connect to this RD Session Host server, and then click Next.

14. On the Confirm Installation Selections page, review the selections made, and then click Install.

15. On the Installation Results page, review the results, and click Close.

16. When prompted to restart the server, click Yes.

17. After the server restarts, log on to the server with local administrator privileges.

18. After logging on, the Installation Results page is displayed. Review the results on the page and confirm that the Terminal Server installation has succeeded.

### Installing Applications

Applications should be installed on an RD Session Host server only after the RD Session Host role service has been installed. Applications that are installed prior to installing the RD Session Host role service might not function properly for all users. In addition, applications must only be installed on an RD Session Host server when it is in a special installation mode. To put an RD Session Host server into this installation mode, use either of the following methods:

▶ Use the Install Application on Remote Desktop Session Host option under Programs in Control Panel.

▶ Use the following command before installing an application: change user /Install.

If the change user /Install command is used and then the server needs to be changed back to Execute mode, use the following command: change user /Execute. The server should be in Execute mode before users access the newly installed application. To see the current mode, use the following command: change user /Query.

---

**NOTE**

When installing applications that use an .msi package from Microsoft, an RD Session Host server typically doesn't need to be switched to Install mode. Instead, just install the application using the .msi package or the related installation executable.

---

### Granting Users or Groups Access

To grant users or groups access to an RD Session Host server, as shown in Figure 25.5, use the following steps:

1. Log on to the desired server with local administrator privileges.

2. Click Start, and then click Run.

3. In the Run dialog box, type in ServerManager.msc and click OK.

4. After the Server Manager console is displayed, select the Configure Remote Desktop task.

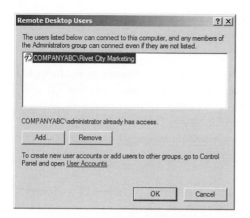

FIGURE 25.5   Granting a domain local group access to this RD Session Host server.

5.  In the Systems Properties dialog box, on the Remote tab, and in the Remote Desktop section, click the Select Users button.

6.  Next, click the Add button, and in the Select Users or Groups dialog box, choose to find the users or groups you want to grant access to, and click OK.

7.  Click OK, and in the System Properties dialog box, click OK.

**NOTE**

Completion of the previous steps actually just results in the modification of the local Remote Desktop Users group. When managing a number of RD Session Host servers in a farm, it is recommended that access to these servers be controlled using a Restricted Groups policy in a Group Policy Object.

## Additional RD Session Host Server Configuration Tasks

In addition to just installing the RD Session Host role service, there are several additional configuration tasks that administrators might want to complete on an RD Session Host server. These tasks are described in the following sections.

### Denying New User Logons

Called "Terminal Services Server Drain mode" in Windows Server 2008, an RD Session Host server can be configured to prevent new user sessions from being created. Reasons why an administrator might want to prevent new user sessions from being created include planned server outages for maintenance or to install new applications. Called User Logon mode in Windows Server 2008 R2, the following modes can be used:

▶  **Allow All Connections**—This is the default setting that is selected and allows users to connect remotely to the RD Session Host server.

▶  **Allow Reconnections, but Prevent New Logons**—When selected, users are prevented from creating new sessions on an RD Session Host server. However, users that already have a Remote Desktop session running can still use and even reconnect to their session. Once the RD Session Host server is rebooted, no users will be able to connect to that server.

▶ **Allow Reconnections but Prevent New Logons Until the Server Is Restarted—** When selected, users who already have a remote session can connect to the RD Session Host server. However, new users without a session will not be able to create new sessions. Then once the RD Session Host server is restarted, the User Logon mode is reset to Allow All Connections.

Use the following steps to configure the User Logon mode on an RD Session Host server:

1. Open the Remote Desktop Session Host Configuration tool by clicking Start, Administrative Tools, Remote Desktop Services and then select Remote Desktop Session Host Configuration.

2. In the Edit Settings area, double-click the User Logon Mode setting.

3. On the General tab of the Properties dialog box, select the desired User Logon mode.

Additionally, the User Logon mode can be configured using the command line:

▶ `change logon /drain`—No additional users will be able to log on to this system.

▶ `change logon /drainuntilrestart`—After the server is restarted, user logons will automatically be reenabled.

▶ `change logon /enable`—User logons are enabled.

### Setting Up Printer Support

By default, when printer redirection is enabled, an RD Session Host server will first attempt to use the Remote Desktop Easy Print driver. If the client cannot use this driver, the server will then attempt to match the printer driver on the client. To support the usage of other printer drivers, administrators mush either preinstall the matching printer driver on an RD Session Host server or create a custom printer mapping file.

To change the default printer driver behavior, an administrator can use GPOs to modify the Use Remote Desktop Services Easy Print Printer Driver First policy setting. This setting is located under the following node: `Computer Configuration\Policies\Administrative Templates\Windows Components\Remote Desktop Services\Remote Desktop Session Host\Printer Redirection`. When enabled or set to Do Not Configure, this policy setting forces the RD Session Host server to use the Remote Desktop Easy Print driver first. If that fails, the server then looks for a matching printer driver. Conversely, when disabled, the policy setting forces the RD Session Host server to look for a matching printer driver first. If that fails, the server attempts to use the Remote Desktop Easy Print driver.

Other printer redirection policy settings available under the noted node include the following:

- ▶ Do Not Allow Client Printer Redirection

- ▶ Do Not Set Default Client Printer to Be Default Printer in a Session

- ▶ Redirect Only the Default Client Printer

### Defining Remote Desktop IP Virtualization

To configure Remote Desktop IP Virtualization, use the Remote Desktop Session Host Configuration tool. On the RD IP Virtualization tab, administrators can define the following settings:

- ▶ Enable or disable RD IP Virtualization.

- ▶ Select the network adapter to be used for RD IP Virtualization.

- ▶ Define if RD IP Virtualization is per session or per program.

- ▶ For per-program virtualization, a list of programs can be defined that can use RD IP Virtualization.

## Deploying RD Web Access

Before installing RD Web Access, you need to take a few considerations into account:

- ▶ The RD Web Access is a role service of the Remote Desktop Services role.

- ▶ The RD Web Access needs to be a Windows Server 2008 R2 machine, but does not need to have the RD Sessions Host role service installed.

- ▶ To run the RD Web Access role service, Microsoft Internet Information Services (IIS) 7.5 must/will be installed.

- ▶ Clients must meet the previously noted requirements that were discussed earlier in this chapter.

### Installing the RD Web Access Role Service

Use the following steps to install the RD Web Access role service:

1. Log on to the desired server with local administrator privileges.
2. Click Start, and then click Run.
3. In the Run dialog box, type in ServerManager.msc and click OK.
4. In the Roles Summary section, click the Add Roles task.
5. After the Add Roles Wizard loads, click Next.
6. On the Select Server Roles page, select the Remote Desktop Services role, and click Next.
7. On the Remote Desktop Services page, click Next.
8. Now, on the Select Role Services page, only select the Remote Desktop Web Access role service. This is the only role service that is being installed at this time, as shown in Figure 25.6.

25

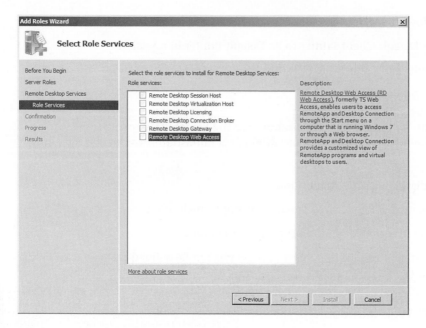

FIGURE 25.6    Selecting the RD Web Access role service.

9. When prompted with the Add Roles Wizard dialog box, click the Add Required Role Services button (any missing required role services or features for RD Web Access role service will now be added), as shown in Figure 25.7.

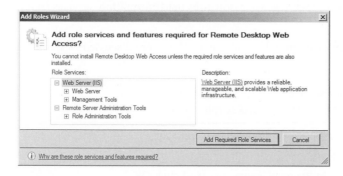

FIGURE 25.7    Adding prerequisite role services and features.

10. On the Select Role Services page, click Next.

11. On the Web Server (IIS) page, click Next.

12. On the Select Role Services page, click Next (do not change the defaults).

13. On the Confirm Installation Selections page, review the selections made, and then click Install.

14. On the Installation Results page, review the results, and click Close.

### Defining the RemoteApps Programs Source

Before users can use RemoteApp and Desktop Connection, the source for RemoteApps programs must be defined for an RD Web Access server. A RemoteApp source can be either of the following:

▶ RD Connection Broker server

▶ RD Session Host server or farm (with identically configured RD Session Host servers)

Use the following steps to define the RemoteApp source:

1. Connect to the RD Web Access Web site using either of the following methods:

    ▶ On the RD Web Access server, click Start, Administrative Tools, Remote Desktop Services, Remote Desktop Web Access Configuration.

    ▶ Using Internet Explorer, connect to the RD Web Access website using the following URL: https://<server_fqdn>/rdweb.

2. When prompted with the RD Web Access forms-based authentication logon page, log on to the site using a domain account that is a member of the local RD Web Access server's TS Web Access Administrators group.

3. Ensure that the Configuration page is selected, and choose either the "An RD Connection Broker Server" option or the "One or More RemoteApp Sources" option, as shown in Figure 25.8.

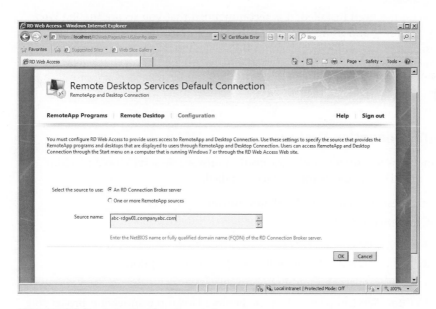

FIGURE 25.8    Selecting the RemoteApp source.

    ▶ If the "An RD Connection Broker Server" option is selected, the NetBIOS name or FQDN of the RD Connection Broker must be defined in the Source Name box.

> ► If the "One or More RemoteApp Sources" option is selected, the NetBIOS name or FQDN of an RD Session Host server or DNS name of the RD Session Host server farm must be entered. If multiple RemoteApp sources are being used, each name must be separated using a semicolon.

4. Click OK to save the changes.

When defining a RemoteApp source, certain requirements must be met depending on the option used. For example, if an RD Session Host is used as the source, the RD Web Access server must be added to the TS Web Access Computers security group on the RD Session Host server. Or, when using an RD Connection Broker server as the source, the RD Connection Broker server must be installed, configured, and online.

Additionally, if the "One or More RemoteApp Sources" option is used, a connection name and connection ID must be defined on the RD Web Access server, and the RDWebAccess.config file needs to be modified. This file is found under the: %windir%\Web\RDWeb\App_Data\ directory. The contents of this file include instructions as to how to define the connection name and connection ID. Once a connection name has been defined, it is used to identify the RemoteApp and Desktop Connection that comes from that RD Web Access server. Conversely, if the "An RD Connection Broker Server" option is used, the connection name and connection ID are defined using the Remote Desktop Connection Manager tool on the RD Connection Broker server.

### Securing RD Web Access

After RD Web Access has been installed, it is recommended that you secure the RD Web Access traffic by installing and using a Server Authentication (SSL) certificate. To complete this task, refer to the IIS 7.5 online help section titled "Request an Internet Server Certificate." After a certificate has been requested, installed, and bound to the website hosting the RD Web Access role service, that website should then be configured to only accept SSL connections.

## Deploying RD Connection Broker

Use the following steps to install the RD Connection Broker role service on a machine that already has the RD Web Access role service installed:

1. Log on to the desired server with local administrator privileges.
2. Click Start, and then click Run.
3. In the Run dialog box, type in ServerManager.msc and click OK.
4. Under Roles Summary, select the Remote Desktop Services option.
5. Under Role Services, select the Add Role Services task.
6. On the Select Role Services page, select the Remote Desktop Connection Broker role service, and then click Next.
7. On the Confirm Installation Selections page, review the selections made, and then click Install.
8. On the Installation Results page, review the results, and click Close.

25

> **NOTE**
>
> If the RD Connection Broker role service is installed, and the RD Web Access role service is not already installed, this role service will also be installed.

### Joining an RD Session Host Server(s) to an RD Session Host Server Farm

1. Log on to the RD Connection Broker server that will be managing sessions for the RD Session Host server farm with local administrator privileges.

2. Click Start, and then click Run.

3. In the Run dialog box, type in ServerManager.msc and click OK.

4. Under the Configuration/Local Users and Groups node, click Groups.

5. Next, double-click the Session Broker Computers group.

6. Click the Add button.

7. In the Select Users, Service Accounts, or Groups dialog box, click Object Types.

8. Select the Computers check box, and then click OK.

9. Locate and then add the computer account for each RD Session Host server that is being added to the farm, and then click OK.

10. Log on to the RD Session Host server that will be added to the RD Session Host server farm with local administrator privileges.

> **NOTE**
>
> RD Connection Broker settings, shown in Figure 25.9, can either be configured using Group Policy or the RD Session Host Configuration tool. For purposes of this example, the Remote Desktop Session Host Configuration tool is used.

11. Click Start, Administrative Tools, Remote Desktop Services, Remote Desktop Session Host Configuration.

12. In the details pane, in the RD Connection Broker section, double-click the Member of Farm in RD Connection Broker option.

13. Next on the RD Connection Broker tab, click the Change Settings button.

14. Now in the Remote Desktop Services section, select the Farm Member option and define the following values:

    ▶ **RD Connection Broker server name**—The server name of the RD Connection Broker server

    ▶ **Farm Name**—The name that will be used to identify the farm; this needs to be the same across all RD Session Host servers that will be joining the farm

15. Click OK.

16. Next select the Participate in Connection Broker Load-Balancing check box.

17. If a relative weight needs to be defined for this RD Session Host server, do so by modifying the relative weight of this server in the farm settings.

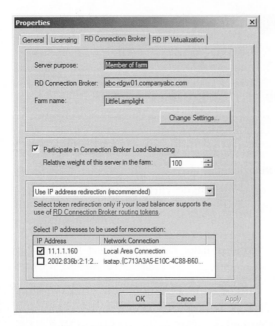

FIGURE 25.9    Configuring the RD Connection Broker settings.

18. Ensure that IP address redirection is enabled, and then in the Select IP Addresses to Be Used for Reconnection text box, select the IP address that is to be used for reconnection.

19. Click OK to finish.

---

**NOTE**

Relative weight settings and the IP addresses to be used for reconnection cannot be defined using Group Policy. To configure these settings, the Remote Desktop Session Host Configuration tool must be used.

---

### Configuring DNS for RD Connection Broker Load Balancing

1. Connect to the appropriate DNS server using the DNS Management snap-in.

2. Expand the server name, the Forward Lookup Zones node, and the appropriate domain name.

3. Right-click the domain and then click New Host (A or AAAA).

4. Within the Name field, type in the name for the RD Session Host server farm.

---

**CAUTION**

Do not enter in the name for an existing RD Session Host server.

---

5. Next, in the IP Address text box, enter in the IP address for an RD Session Host server in the farm, and click Add Host.

6. Click OK, and repeat the process for each RD Session Host server in the farm.

## Deploying RemoteApp and Desktop Connection

To deploy RemoteApp and Desktop Connection, use the following steps.

### Adding RD Session Broker to the TS Web Access Computers Group

On every RD Session Host server that is being used as a source for the RD Session Broker server, complete the following steps:

1. Log on to the RD Session Host server that is a RemoteApp source for the RD Session Host server farm with local administrator privileges.

2. Click Start, and then click Run.

3. In the Run dialog box, type in ServerManager.msc and click OK.

4. Under the Configuration/Local Users and Groups node, click Groups.

5. Next, double-click the TS Web Access Computers group.

6. Click the Add button.

7. In the Select Users, Service Accounts, or Groups dialog box, click Object Types.

8. Select the Computers check box, and then click OK.

9. Locate and then add the computer account for RD Connection Broker server, and then click OK.

### Adding a RemoteApp Source for RemoteApp and Desktop Connection

1. Log on to the RD Connection Broker server with local administrator privileges.

2. Click Start, Administrative Tools, Remote Desktop Services, Remote Desktop Connection Manager.

3. Click RemoteApp Sources, and then in the Actions pane, click Add RemoteApp Source, as shown in Figure 25.10.

4. In the RemoteApp Source Name box, enter the FQDN of the RD Session Host server that is a RemoteApp source for the RD Session Host server farm.

### Configuring RemoteApp and Desktop Connection Properties

1. Log on to the RD Connection Broker server with local administrator privileges.

2. Click Start, Administrative Tools, Remote Desktop Services, Remote Desktop Connection Manager.

3. Click the root node, and then in the Actions pane, click Properties.

4. In the RemoteApp and Desktop Connection Properties dialog box, on the Connection Settings tab, define the following:

   ▶ **Display name**—The name that users will use to identify the customized view of RemoteApp programs and virtual desktops provided by this server

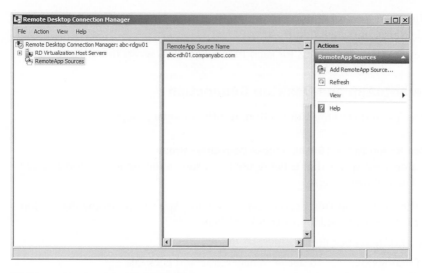

FIGURE 25.10    Adding a RemoteApp source for RemoteApp and Desktop Connection.

> ▶ **Connection ID**—The ID that is used to identify the customized view of RemoteApp programs and virtual desktops provided by this server

5. Next select the RD Web Access tab, and then in the Server Name text box, enter in the FQDN for the RD Web Access server.

6. Click the Add button.

7. Click Apply and then click OK.

### Adding Programs to the RemoteApp Programs

1. Log on to the RD Session Host server that is a RemoteApp source for the RD Session Host server farm with local administrator privileges.

2. Click Start, Administrative Tools, Remote Desktop Services, RemoteApp Manager.

3. In the Actions pane, click Add RemoteApp Programs.

4. On the Welcome page for the RemoteApp Wizard, click Next.

5. On the Choose Programs to Add to the RemoteApp Programs List page, select the program(s) that are to be added to the RemoteApps list from the list as shown in Figure 25.11.

**NOTE**

The applications that are shown on this page are shortcuts that are found in the All Users Start Menu folder. If there is an application that is not listed on this page, an administrator can click on the Browse button, and then specify the location to that application's executable.

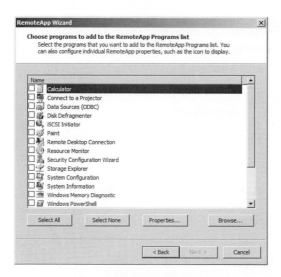

FIGURE 25.11    Adding applications to the RemoteApps list.

6. After selecting an application or applications to add to the RemoteApps list, an administrator can then choose to configure the different RemoteApp properties for that application or applications, as shown in Figure 25.12. To do this, select the application name, click Properties, make any needed modifications, and then click OK.

FIGURE 25.12    Modifying a RemoteApp program's properties.

> **NOTE**
>
> It is important to note that, by default, the RemoteApp Program Is Available Through RD Web Access option is enabled. Also, only system environment variables can be used in the pathname for an application (such as %windir%). Per-user environment variables cannot be used. Lastly, if needed, using the User Assignment tab, an administrator can define which users/groups have access to the RemoteApp program.

7. Click Next.

8. Finally, review the settings on the Review Settings page, and then click Finish.

9. The RemoteApps list will then appear, as shown in Figure 25.13.

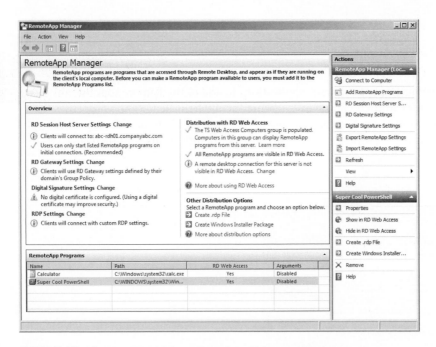

FIGURE 25.13    The RemoteApps list after adding applications.

### Configuring Global Deployment Settings

In the RD RemoteApp Manager interface, an administrator can also configure a number of deployment settings that globally apply to all RemoteApp programs in the RemoteApps list. The settings are grouped into the following categories:

▶ **RD Session Host Server Settings**—These settings are used to define how users will connect to an RD Session Host server or RD Session Host server farm to access RemoteApp programs, as shown in Figure 25.14.

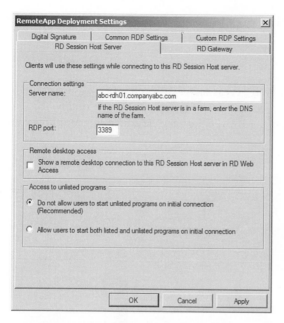

FIGURE 25.14    Modifying global deployment settings.

▶ **RD Gateway Settings**—These settings are used to define RD Gateway deployment settings.

▶ **Digital Signature Settings**—This setting is used to define the digital certificate that is used to digitally sign .rdp files.

▶ **RDP Settings**—These settings are used to define common RDP settings for RemoteApp connections, such as device and resource redirection.

#### Accessing RemoteApp and Desktop Connection

When using Windows 7 or Windows Server 2008 R2, users can also access RemoteApp and Desktop Connection using two methods. The first method is to use a RemoteApp and Desktop Connection URL, which is provided by administrators. For example, such a URL might be formatted as: https://remotedesk.companyabc.com/RDWeb/Feed/webfeed.aspx. Using this URL, a user can then create a new connection to RemoteApp and Desktop Connection using the Control Panel, RemoteApp and Desktop Connection.

The second method to access RemoteApp and Desktop Connection is to use a configuration file that is generated by an administrator. These configuration files are generated using the Remote Desktop Configuration Manager tool. Once the configuration file is given to a user, the user just has to double-click the configuration file and the connection to RemoteApp and Desktop Connection is created.

RemoteApp and Desktop Connection connections are also created when a user logs on to RD Web Access and accesses RemoteApp programs, session-based remote desktops, or virtual desktops. To access RemoteApp and Desktop Connection, users would log on to RD Web Access using the following URL:

```
https://<name>/rdweb
```

The <name> might be the FQDN of the RD Web Access server or some other known name that refers to that server or group of servers, as shown in Figure 25.15. Additionally, for centralized portal deployments, an RD Web Access web part can be added to a Windows SharePoint Services site.

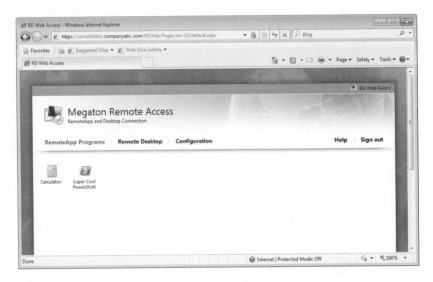

FIGURE 25.15    Using the default RD Web Access web page.

## Deploying RD Gateway

As described previously in this chapter, a number of requirements must be met before the RD Gateway role service can be installed. Additionally, it is highly recommended that the following task be completed:

▶ A trusted SSL certificate must be obtained for and installed on the RD Gateway server(s). For more information about this process, review Chapter 13, "Server-Level Security."

Next, use the following steps to install and configure the RD Gateway role service on a machine that already has the RD Web Access and RD Connection Broker role services installed:

1. Log on to the desired server with local administrator privileges.

2. Click Start, and then click Run.

3. In the Run dialog box, type in ServerManager.msc and click OK.

4. Under Roles Summary, select the Remote Desktop Services option.

5. Under Role Services, select the Add Role Services task.

6. On the Select Role Services page, select the Remote Desktop Gateway role service.

7. When prompted with the Add Roles Wizard dialog box, click the Add Required Role Services button (any missing required role services or features for the RD Gateway role service will now be added).

8. On the Select Role Services page, click Next.

9. On the Choose a Server Authentication Certificate for SSL Encryption page shown in Figure 25.16, choose one of the following certificate options:

   ▶ Choose an Existing Certificate for SSL Encryption (Recommended)

   ▶ Create a Self-Signed Certificate for SSL Encryption

   ▶ Choose a Certificate for SSL Encryption Later

10. On the Create Authorization Policies for RD Gateway page, select the Now option, and click Next.

11. On the Select User Groups That Can Connect Through RD Gateway page, click the Add button and define the local or domain groups that are allowed to connect through RD Gateway, click OK, and then click Next.

12. On the Create an RD CAP for RD Gateway page shown in Figure 25.17, either accept the default RD CAP name or define a new one. Then select the supported Windows authentication methods, and then click Next.

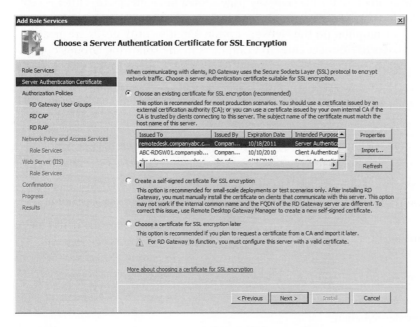

FIGURE 25.16   Choosing a server authentication certificate for SSL encryption.

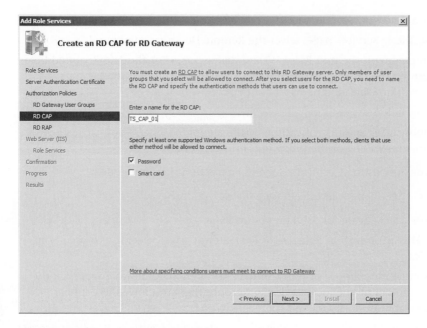

FIGURE 25.17    Creating an RD CAP.

13. On the Create an RD RAP for RD Gateway page shown in Figure 25.18, either accept the default RD RAP name or define a new one. Then select the Allow Users to Connect to Any Computer on the Network option. Or, if security needs are greater, use the Allow Users to Connect Only to Computers in the Following Groups option.

14. Click Next.

15. On the Network Policy and Access Services page, click Next. This page will be displayed if the NPS role is not installed beforehand.

16. On the Select Role Services page, click Next.

17. On the Web Server (IIS) page, click Next. This page will be displayed if the Web Server role is not installed beforehand.

18. On the Select Role Services page, click Next.

19. On the Confirm Installation Options page, verify the information presented and click Install.

20. When the installation is finished, review the Installation Results page, and then click Close.

To test RD Gateway, use the following steps to configure a Remote Desktop Connection client:

1. Log on to the desired client.

2. Click Start, click Run, type in `mstsc`, and click OK.

3. After the Remote Desktop Connection client has loaded, click Options.

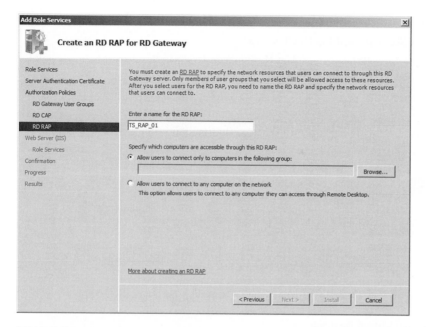

FIGURE 25.18    Creating an RD RAP

4. Select the Advanced tab, and then click the Settings button.

5. In the Connection Settings dialog box, select the Use These RD Gateway Server Settings option.

6. Set the server name equal to the FQDN of the RD Gateway server.

7. Unselect the Bypass RD Gateway Server for Local Addresses option.

8. Now, select the General tab, enter in the name of the RD Session Host server, and click Connect.

9. When prompted, provide the Remote Desktop credentials, and click Submit.

10. When prompted for the RD Gateway credentials, provide the correct credentials, and click Submit.

11. When connected to the specified RD Session Host server, the connection through the RD Gateway is complete.

## Deploying Virtual Desktops

The steps in this section describe how to deploy virtual desktops.

### Installing the RD Virtualization Host Role Service

1. Log on to the desired Hyper-V server that will be hosting the RD Virtualization Host role service with local administrator privileges.

2. Click Start, and then click Run.

3. In the Run dialog box, type in `ServerManager.msc` and click OK.

4. In the Roles Summary section, click the Add Roles task.

5. After the Add Roles Wizard loads, click Next.

6. On the Select Server Roles page, select the Remote Desktop Services role, and click Next, as shown in Figure 25.4.

7. On the Remote Desktop Services page, click Next.

8. Now, on the Select Role Services page, only select the Remote Desktop Virtualization Host role service. This is the only role service that is being installed at this time. Click Next.

> **NOTE**
>
> If Hyper-V is not installed, it will be installed automatically by the installation wizard.

9. On the Confirm Installation Selections page, review the selections made, and then click Install.

10. On the Installation Results page, review the results, and click Close.

### Configuring a Personal Virtual Desktop

Personal virtual desktops are specific virtual machines hosted on an RD Virtualization Host server that have been assigned to a user account in Active Directory. The following steps describe how to assign an existing virtual machine to a user. These steps should be carried out on the server that has the RD Connection Broker role service installed:

1. Log on to the desired server with local administrator privileges.

2. Click Start, Administrative Tools, Remote Desktop Services, Remote Desktop Connection Manager.

3. Next, in the Actions pane click the Configure Virtual Desktops Wizard option.

4. Once the wizard has loaded, click Next.

5. Now, on the Specify an RD Virtualization Host Server page, define the name of the RD Virtualization Host server in the Server Name field, click the Add button, and then click Next.

6. On the Configure Redirection Settings page, define the name of an RD Session Host server running in Redirection mode in the Server Name field, click the Add button, and then click Next.

7. On the Specify an RD Web Access Server page, click Next.

8. On the next page, click Apply, ensure that the Assign Personal Virtual Desktop check box is selected, and then click Finish.

9. Next, on the Assign Personal Virtual Desktop page, click Select User.

10. In the Enter the Object Name to Select box, enter the user's account name and click OK.

11. Next, in the Virtual Machine box, select the name of the virtual machine being defined to the user, and click Next.

12. Now, confirm the information is correct, and click Assign.

13. Finally, clear the Assign Another Virtual Machine to Another User check box, and then click Finish.

### Configuring a Virtual Desktop Pool

A virtual desktop pool is a grouping of identically configured virtual machines that reside on an RD Virtualization Host server. The following steps describe how to create a virtual desktop pool using existing virtual machines that reside on an RD Virtualization Host server. These steps should be carried out on the server that has the RD Connection Broker role service installed and the Configure Virtual Desktops Wizard has not been executed:

1. Log on to the desired server with local administrator privileges.

2. Click Start, Administrative Tools, Remote Desktop Services, Remote Desktop Connection Manager.

3. Next, in the Actions pane click the Configure Virtual Desktops Wizard option.

4. Once the wizard has loaded, click Next.

5. Now, on the Specify an RD Virtualization Host Server page, define the name of the RD Virtualization Host server in the Server Name field, click the Add button, and then click Next.

6. On the Configure Redirection Settings page, define the name of an RD Session Host server running in Redirection mode in the Server Name field, click the Add button, and then click Next.

7. On the Specify an RD Web Access Server page, click Next.

8. On the next page, click Apply, clear the Assign Personal Virtual Desktop check box, and then click Finish.

9. Next, in the Actions pane of the Remote Desktop Connection Manager, click the Create Virtual Desktop Pool option.

10. On the Welcome page, click Next.

11. Now, select all of the virtual machines that will be part of the virtual desktop pool, and then click Next.

12. On the Set Pool Properties page, define the following and then click Next:

   ▶ **Display Name box**—Define the name for the virtual desktop pool.

   ▶ **Pool ID box**—Define the ID used for the virtual desktop pool.

13. Lastly, click Finish.

## Deploying RD Licensing

RD Licensing is a required component of any Remote Desktop Services deployment. To deploy RD Licensing, the following tasks must be completed:

1. Determine the type of RDS CALs that will be used.

2. Install the RD Licensing role service.

3. Activate the RD licensing server.

25

4. Install RDS client access licenses (RDS CALs) on the RD licensing server.

5. Configure the RD Session Host servers to use the licensing server.

### Installing the RD Licensing Role Service

To use the RD Licensing service, the RD Licensing role service needs to be installed on the system. To install the RD Licensing role service, do the following:

1. Log on to the desired server with local administrator privileges.

2. Click Start, and then click Run.

3. In the Run dialog box, type in `ServerManager.msc` and click OK.

4. Under Roles Summary, select the Remote Desktop Services option.

5. Under Role Services, select the Add Role Services task.

6. On the Select Role Services page, select the Remote Desktop Licensing role service.

7. On the Configure Discovery Scope for RD Licensing page, do not choose a scope option and click Next.

8. On the Confirm Installation Selections page, verify the settings, and then click Install.

9. On the Installation Results page, confirm that the installation was successful, and then click Close.

### Activating the RD Licensing Server

An RD licensing server can be activated automatically if the server has Internet access, through a web page from any computer with Internet access, or by the administrator calling a Microsoft Clearing House using an 800 number. The licensing server is activated by contacting the Microsoft Clearing House server that will send the RD licensing server a digital certificate. To activate an RD licensing server, follow these steps:

1. Click Start, Administrative Tools, Remote Desktop Services, Remote Desktop Licensing Manager.

2. Right-click the RD licensing server and select Activate Server.

3. Click Next on the Welcome page.

4. Choose the proper connection method, and click Next.

   ▶ If you choose the Web Browser or Phone Connection method, follow the instructions in the window to complete the activation. Click Finish when you are done.

   ▶ If you choose Automatic Activation, enter the appropriate company information to send to the Microsoft Clearing House, and click Next at each window.

5. After the server is activated, uncheck the Install Licenses Wizard Now check box, and click Finish to return to the Remote Desktop Licensing Manager.

### Installing Client Access Licenses

After the RD licensing server is activated, CALs must be installed using the following steps:

1. Click Start, Administrative Tools, Remote Desktop Services, Remote Desktop Licensing Manager.

2. Right-click the RD licensing server, and click Install Licenses.

3. Click Next on the Welcome page, and depending on the default connection method, the CAL Installation Wizard will try to connect to the Microsoft activation server.

4. When the wizard connects to the activation server, choose the license program that the organization participates in, and click Next. For example, select License Pack (Retail Purchase), Open License, or Select License, as shown in Figure 25.19.

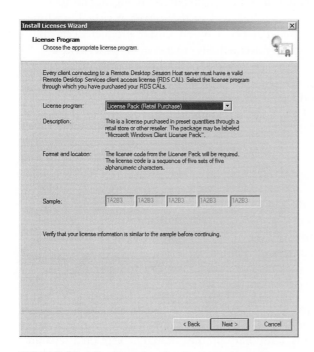

FIGURE 25.19   Choosing the license program.

5. On the Licensing Code page, enter the license number or agreement number for your licensing pack, click the Add button, and then click Next.

6. After the licensing information is verified and the CALs are installed, click Finish to close the CAL Installation Wizard.

Now that the licenses are installed, each RD Session Host server must be configured to use the RD licensing server.

## Securing Remote Desktop Services

Remote Desktop Services should be secured using standard security guidelines and policies defined by an organization. In addition to an organization's security standards and guidelines, it is advisable that administrators use recommended best practices compiled by Microsoft, as well as the National Institute of Standards and Technologies (NIST) and the

National Security Agency (NSA). Both NIST and NSA provide security lockdown configuration standards and guidelines that can be downloaded from their websites (http://www.nist.gov and http://www.nsa.gov, respectively).

## Securely Building Remote Session Services

When building security into Remote Desktop Services, keep in mind that you are giving users certain levels of access to a shared resource. Essentially, users are logging on to a system and using the applications and services installed on that server or virtual machine. With this in mind, it is important to strike a balance between a user's productive capability and what the user can do (intentionally or accidentally) to a system. Otherwise, a single session can significantly affect other user sessions, as well as the entire RD Session Host server or an individual shared virtual machine. Additionally, administrators should also consider that depending on their deployment strategy, users might be accessing Remote Desktop Services from external systems. Therefore, a comprehensive approach around end-to-end security (from the client to RD Session Host/virtual machine) needs to be implemented.

## Segmenting Resources

RD Session Host server resources should be segmented in such a way that users can only modify specific settings. This sounds simple, but requires careful planning. For instance, partitioning the server's disk subsystem can keep the operating system, logs, applications, and profiles separated. Each of these partitions should also be formatted with NTFS so that the proper permissions can be applied. This also makes it easier for administrators to manage and lock down specific resources.

The profile partition should be given particular attention because of the nature of the content it stores. For smaller installations, profiles can be stored on the local server on a separate partition. For larger installations, temporary profiles should be kept on a separate partition and folder redirection should be used for data that needs to roam with a user. This not only improves security, but it can also significantly improve performance.

Typically, these temporary RDS profiles are stored under %SystemDrive%\Users\%Username%, even if roaming profiles are used in the network environment. To change the location to another partition, do the following:

1. Create a Users folder on the partition.
2. Modify `HKEY_LOCAL_MACHINE\SOFTWARE\Microsoft\Windows NT\CurrentVersion\ProfileList\ProfilesDirectory Reg_Sz` to the new location.
3. Restart the server.

## Securing Remote Desktop Services with GPOs

As mentioned later in the "Group Policy for RD Session Host Servers" section, GPOs can and should be used to secure the Remote Desktop Services environment. For instance, if an application or department working with sensitive information uses Remote Desktop Services, the Remote Control setting can be disabled to ensure that only authorized users can view these sessions. Group Policy can also be used to set disconnect timeout values and allow reconnections from only the original client. For more complex security requirements, Group Policy can also be used to secure and customize a user's session. For example:

▶ GPO can be used to create a secure desktop that gives users limited Windows functionality based on their needs.

▶ Or, if supported, a GPO can be used to customize and restrict individual application features.

## Network Level Authentication

In RDP 6.0, a feature called Network Level Authentication was introduced. This feature enhanced RDP security by providing an interface for user authentication earlier in the connection process of a session (before a Remote Desktop connection and the logon screen appears). The following are the benefits of configuring Remote Desktop Services to require Network Level Authentication:

▶ Fewer resources are used validating users before presenting them with a full session.

▶ Remote computer authentication can be used to preauthenticate servers as well.

▶ It can reduce the risk of a denial-of-service attack.

## Changing the RDP Port

As mentioned earlier, Remote Desktop Services securely communicates over TCP port 3389 using RDP. Organizations requiring even greater security can change the default port by modifying the following Registry key:

```
HKEY_LOCAL_MACHINE\System\CurrentControlSet\Control\Terminal
Server\WinStations\RDP-Tcp\PortNumber
```

Or, if RemoteApp programs are being used, the RDP settings can be modified to specify a different port for RDP traffic.

> **NOTE**
>
> Only clients using RDP version 5.1 or later can connect to the nonstandard port. Also, after the port is changed, the RD Session Host server or RD Virtualization Host server must be restarted.

# Supporting Remote Desktop Services

Supporting Remote Desktop Services involves more than just proper configuration; it also involves supporting end users, installing and maintaining applications, and securing and optimizing Remote Desktop settings, among other server duties.

## Using the Role Administration Tools

For the Remote Desktop Services role, a number of different role administration tools can be used to manage the role and its role services. When the role or role service is installed, its corresponding Role Administration Tool is also installed. However, in some cases, an administrator might want to manage a role service using a remote Windows Server 2008 R2 or Windows 7 machine. In these cases, using Server Manager, an administrator can install the Remote Server Administration Tools for the Remote Desktop Services role and all of its corresponding role services.

## Using the Remote Desktop Services Manager

The Remote Desktop Services Manager (tsadmin.msc) can be used to manage sessions on a Remote Desktop Session Host server. Process and resource usage on the RD Session Host server can be monitored here on a server or per-user basis. Also when an administrator wants to remote control an existing Remote Desktop session, he or she can complete this task from within the Remote Desktop Services Manager. Lastly, this tool can also be used to send messages to active session users, disconnect, reset, or log off sessions.

## Managing RDS Using the Command Line

In Windows Server 2008 R2, a number of command-line tools make Remote Desktop Services administrative tasks much more flexible and scriptable. For a complete listing of these commands, refer to the Windows Server 2008 R2 and the Windows Server 2008 online help. A few of the more useful commands are as follows:

- ▶ tskill.exe—This tool can be used to kill hung or stuck processes or applications in any active session without having to connect to the session using remote control.

- ▶ Shadow.exe—This tool initiates a shadow or remote control session from a command prompt or script.

- ▶ Query.exe {Process, Session, Termserver, User}—This tool allows the administrator to query a particular server to get a list of current active and inactive sessions and processes.

## Remotely Managing a Remote Desktop Session

Remote Desktop users might require support for tasks such as mapping to a file share, installing a third-party printer driver, or just troubleshooting issues within the terminal session. While using the remote control features of Remote Desktop Services, an administrator can interact with users in active sessions with view-only access or complete remote control functionality. The amount of access given to an administrator during a remote control session can be set by the user, but it can be configured at the server level by the administrator.

An administrator can remotely control a user's session only from within a separate Remote Desktop session. The remote control command can be initiated using Remote Desktop Services Manager or the command-line tool Shadow.exe.

## Managing Remote Desktop Services with PowerShell

When the Remote Desktop Services role is installed, a PowerShell provider is also installed that allows administrators to manage Remote Desktop settings using PowerShell. Once installed, and a PowerShell console is opened, administrators can access the resulting RDS: drive to manage a number of different settings that are organized into the following directories:

- ▶ **RDSConfiguration**—Contains settings that apply to the RD Session Host role service

- ▶ **Gateway**—Contains settings that apply to the RD Gateway role service

- ▶ **LicenseServer**—Contains settings that apply to the RD Licensing role service

- ▶ **ConnectionBroker**—Contains settings that apply to the RD Connection Broker role service

- ▶ **RemoteApps**—Contains a list of published applications and their settings

- ▶ **RDFarms**—Contains settings that apply to RD Session Host server farms

## Group Policy for RD Session Host Servers

Group Policy contains several Remote Desktop Services user and computer settings to configure Remote Desktop sessions. An administrator can modify existing group policies or create new group policies to manage Remote Desktop Services machine and user settings. These Group Policy Objects (GPOs) can then be applied to RD Session Host servers, virtual machines, or users located in an Active Directory site, domain, or organizational unit (OU) or based on a GPO filter.

Group Policy is the preferred method of standardizing Remote Desktop Services configurations throughout Active Directory because user and machine configurations can be centrally administered. Because so many Remote Desktop Services settings are available in Group Policy, the following list outlines where Remote Desktop Services settings can be found:

- ▶ `Computer Configuration\Windows Settings\Security Settings\Local Policies\User Rights Assignment`—User rights assignment can allow logon through Remote Desktop Services as well as deny logon through Remote Desktop Services, depending on the configuration setting.

- ▶ `Computer Configuration\Administrative Templates\Windows Components\Remote Desktop Services`—Almost all Remote Desktop Services settings can be configured here. Settings here override user or client configurations and also override settings made in the User Configuration section of Group Policy.

- ▶ `User Configuration\Administrative Templates\Windows Components\Remote Desktop Services`—User session settings can be configured in this section. Settings here override user or client configurations.

A simple and effective way to manage the GPOs for your RD Session Host servers is to create an OU for your RD Session Host servers and apply GPOs to the OU. Enabling the

25

Computer Configuration\Administrative Templates\System\Group Policy\User Group Policy Loopback Processing mode is very important if you want the user-context GPO settings to take effect. The loopback processing can be set to either merge or replace. Merging allows existing domain-based GPOs to merge with the ones for Remote Desktop Services, whereas the replace option overrides all other settings and the Remote Desktop Service–specific settings are only applied.

### Applying Service Packs and Updates

Applying service packs and updates on an RD Session Host server or virtual machine should follow the same strategy as outlined in the previous section "Installing Applications." Test all service packs and updates in an isolated lab environment prior to production release and always create a backup of the system first to allow for rollback, if necessary.

### Performing Disaster Recovery

The steps for backing up and restoring an RD Session Host server or virtual machine should follow the same procedures as backing up and restoring a standalone server. Administrators must be sure to back up any local user data, including profiles, and back up the current server System State. The data and System State backup, accompanied with a server build document, are all that an administrator needs to recover the RD Session Host server or virtual machine. For detailed steps concerning the creation of server build documents and Windows Server 2008 R2 backup and recovery techniques, refer to Chapter 22, "Documenting a Windows Server 2008 R2 Environment," Chapter 30, "Backing Up the Windows Server 2008 R2 Environment," and Chapter 31, "Recovering from a Disaster."

## Summary

Windows Server 2008 R2 Remote Desktop Services is a flexible tool that can be used to provide administrative, server-based computing, and virtual desktop functionality. Depending on the needs of your organization, Remote Desktop Services can be deployed to meet needs that range from centralized administration to remote access for business-critical applications. With features like RD Web Access, RD RemoteApp, RD Gateway, RD Virtualization Host, and so on, the ease and simplicity of using Remote Desktop Services has never been more compelling.

Remote Desktop Services enables users and system administrators alike to perform job functions productively from the office or remotely with simplicity.

# Best Practices

The following are best practices from this chapter:

▶ Drain Remote Desktop connections when performing scheduled maintenance on an RD Session Host server.

▶ When an RD Session Host server or virtual machine is due for an operating system upgrade, if possible replace the server with a clean build and test all applications, instead of performing in-place upgrades to avoid server or application failures.

▶ Place your RD Session Host and RD Virtualization Host servers where they can be readily accessed by the clients that will primarily be using them.

▶ Whenever possible, choose applications that have been tested and certified by the vendor to run on Windows Server 2008 R2 Remote Desktop Services.

▶ For optimum performance for multitiered applications, install two or more network cards on an RD Session Host server and configure the server to use one exclusively for RDC client connectivity and the others for back-end server communication.

▶ Use Group Policy to limit client functionality as needed to enhance server security, and if increased network security is a requirement, consider requiring clients to run sessions in 128-bit high encryption mode.

▶ When possible, try to never install the Remote Desktop Services role and then host applications on a domain controller.

▶ It is recommended that applications always be grouped together based on usage. If an application behaves badly or isn't certified to run Remote Desktop Services, it should be separated to dedicated servers in a farm.

▶ Try to treat RD Session Host servers as nodes that are dispensable. As such, try to always build your RD Session Host servers using the same hardware and install the same applications on them.

25

# CHAPTER 26

# Windows Server 2008 R2 Administration Tools for Desktops

Windows Server 2008 R2 contains several services and features that can be leveraged to simplify desktop and user management for an organization's computer and network infrastructure. Effectively managing an organization's computer and network infrastructure requires the ability to support users locally and from remote locations; to perform remote configuration and administration of servers, workstations, and networking services and applications; and to deploy or replace servers and workstations when systems fail or are replaced with new hardware.

When a computer and network infrastructure utilizes Windows Server 2008 R2 systems and Active Directory Domain Services (AD DS), many of the included services and features can simplify administrative tasks. For example, domain group policies can be created and applied to different sets of users and computers to automatically deploy printers, configure wireless networking, redirect user folders to server shares, set default security policies, and much more. Having an Active Directory infrastructure allows organizations to deploy a role called Windows Deployment Services. Windows Deployment Services (WDS) provides administrators with the ability to deploy Windows Server 2008, Windows Server 2008 R2, Windows 7, Windows Vista, and other legacy operating systems such as Windows Server 2003 and Windows XP Professional to servers and workstations (both physical and virtual machines) across the network from a central console using unicast or multicast communications. There are several requirements to make the WDS deployment process work, but, essentially, a system is booted up using PXE boot, connects to the WDS system, selects an installation image, and the operating system is deployed across the network automatically.

Setting up and creating custom operating system deployments that suit a particular organization's server and workstation deployment requirements requires some time and a lot of testing, but when tens or hundreds of machines are deployed each year, taking the time to deploy and configure WDS and WDS images will definitely simplify the deployment of systems and improve system standardization and recoverability.

This chapter focuses on using Windows Deployment Services (WDS) to automate the deployment of operating systems to workstations. Also included in this chapter are some general overviews of the different services and applications provided with Windows Server 2008 R2 that can assist with the management, configuration, and support of servers and workstations after they are already deployed on the production network.

# Managing Desktops and Servers

When planning how the information technology department will manage desktops and servers for a particular organization, many different support scenarios should be considered. Deploying operating systems is only one of the many tasks that fall under the managing desktops and servers umbrella. Additional tasks include deploying and updating software to existing systems, generating reports that detail the status of the overall computer and network infrastructure, supporting end users, and managing backup and recovery processes. There are, of course, many more tasks, but this chapter is limited to these types of IT-related tasks and primarily focuses on the automation of operating system deployment using Windows Server 2008 R2 Windows Deployment Services.

## Operating System Deployment to Bare-Metal Systems

When choosing to deploy an operating system to a bare-metal system, all you need is the operating system media, the correct product key, and the supporting driver disks for your hardware. This is the traditional way to deploy a system—in today's computer and network infrastructure, many workstations come with operating systems preinstalled and servers usually contain vendor-specific installation disks that not only deploy the operating system, but also install vendor-specific drivers, services, and applications specific to the particular server hardware. Deploying operating systems to bare-metal systems, or systems with no existing operating system, is still a common scenario when organizations want to ensure that a very clean, unmodified operating system is deployed without any unnecessary applications or services. Also, this method might be required to meet specific security requirements or to be able to easily leverage WDS to quickly roll out new servers and desktops.

## Managing Updates and Applications

Up until a few years ago, deploying security and application updates to Microsoft Windows workstation and server operating systems was very challenging. Any attempt to centralize the management and deployment of these updates required third-party suites or custom development and scripts. This challenge did not apply only to systems already deployed on the network, but it also applied to systems recently deployed from a WDS server.

Now many organizations utilize domain group policies to configure the Windows Update settings on the organization's servers and desktops to ensure that all systems adhere to a policy that automatically keeps the systems updated and secure. The Windows Server 2008 R2 Windows Server Updates Services role can be used in conjunction with the Windows Updates settings in domain policies to allow an organization to centrally manage and report on which updates will be deployed and which client and server systems are in and out of security update compliance. Regarding WDS images, if any custom images will need to be deployed to systems, they must be updated and recaptured to ensure that the WDS images maintain a high level of security whenever they are deployed.

### Supporting End Users and Remote Administration

Supporting end users and performing administration of the computer and network infrastructure from remote workstations is a necessity for most organizations. Each organization should determine what the particular end-user support requirements will be and how support will be provided. If remote support of end users is the preferred approach, the organization needs to decide on whether Microsoft-specific tools will be used or if third-party products will be necessary to meet the support requirements. Also, the organization needs to determine how or if remote administration of the computer and network infrastructure will be supported.

## Operating System Deployment Options

When new servers or workstations need to be deployed, one of the big decisions to make is whether these systems will be built and deployed manually or if the system deployment process will be automated. Automating system deployment is not a task that can be completed in a few hours or days, at least not the first time. On the contrary, building a functional operating system deployment infrastructure takes careful planning, sometimes expensive licenses, and many hours and days or weeks worth of testing and tuning the images and the automation. There are a few different ways Windows server and business desktop operating system deployments can be performed, including manual installation, unattended installations, manufacturer-assisted or customized unattended installations, and through the deployment of prebuilt and possibly customized operating system images.

### Manual Installation Using Installation Media

Manual installation is rather straightforward. Insert the installation media and run through the step-by-step installation, documenting all of your settings as you move forward. This method is sometimes required when administrators do not have an image suitable for the particular hardware platform or when only a small number of systems are regularly deployed and taking the time to create unattended or image type installations is unnecessary and provides no real value to the organization.

## Unattended Installation

Unattended installations can be helpful when deploying a large number of desktops and servers that have the same hardware specifications. An unattended file is simply a file created that answers all the questions asked during a manual installation. Unattended configuration files were historically referred to as answer files. Options in some unattended answer files can include accepting the end-user licensing agreement, entering a volume license product key, choosing to format the drive, specifying a particular partition or volume size for the operating system, and much more. This is now referred to as an unattended installation file.

## Manufacturer-Assisted Installation

Some manufacturers provide automated installation media that, upon bootup, prompts the administrator to answer a few questions and the remainder of the installation is automated. This is a very common scenario encountered in the retail sector for home user and business desktops and servers that are shipped with preinstalled operating systems. These types of installations usually include original equipment manufacturer (OEM) licensed software. One important point to note is that when an organization wants to move toward the automated deployment of servers or desktops using an imaging or deployment system, an OEM operating system license and media cannot be used as it usually violates the licensing agreement.

## Cloning or Imaging Systems

Cloning or imaging systems can be helpful when deploying a series of identical desktops and servers. You build up a desktop or a server, prepare the system for cloning/imaging, and copy/capture the system image using third-party tools or Microsoft deployment tools such as Windows Deployment Services. Microsoft only supports the cloning and imaging of servers and desktops when Sysprep is used to generate new machine security identifiers (SIDs). Windows Deployment Services can be used to deploy both base installation images and customized or captured installation images to Windows servers and desktops.

### System Center Configuration Manager 2007 R2

For medium- and enterprise-sized organizations, additional deployment options can be leveraged when the organization has deployed System Center Configuration Manager 2007 R2 or System Center Configuration Manager 2007. Utilizing the Operating System Deployment feature, organizations can leverage a zero-touch or lite-touch deployment of operating systems. As evident by the name zero-touch, if configured properly, the workstation or server does not ever need a visit. As an example of how this can be used, an existing Windows XP or Windows Vista SP1 system can be tested for Windows 7 compatibility and if the tests pass, the user state can be exported and saved, a customized Windows 7 image can be pushed down to the system followed by postimage processing to install applications, and, finally, restoring the exported user state if compatible. The end result delivers Windows 7 to the end-user desktop with the user's profile already configured. More information on this and many of the other valuable features included with System Center Configuration Manager 2007 R2 can be found at http://www.microsoft.com/systemcenter/configurationmanager/en/us/default.aspx.

### Remote Installation Services

Remote Installation Services (RIS) was released with Windows 2000 Server and was Microsoft's first successful "over the network" operating system deployment services. Windows 2000 Server RIS did not support server operating systems and had many limitations, but it was a very functional and valuable tool.

### Automated Deployment Services

Automated Deployment Services was an add-on to Windows Server 2003 Enterprise Edition, and was designed to assist with the rapid deployment of Windows 2000/2003 server operating systems only. For organizations that utilized Windows Server 2003 and required desktop deployment options, Windows Server 2003 Remote Installation Services was still required.

### Windows Server 2003 SP2 Windows Deployment Services

With the release of Windows Server 2003 Service Pack 2, administrators could upgrade their Windows Server 2003 RIS systems to Windows Server 2003 Windows Deployment Services (WDS). If RIS had previously been deployed with existing images, the upgrade took the existing RIS (RIPREP and RISETUP) images and placed them in the Legacy Image folder within the WDS MMC snap-in and upon your initial launch of the WDS console, the administrators were prompted to choose whether the WDS system would run in Legacy or Mixed mode. After a few more simple configurations, existing RIS images would work successfully in the environment.

### Windows Server 2008 R2 Windows Deployment Services (WDS)

Windows Deployment Services (WDS) running on Windows Server 2008 or Windows Server 2008 R2 systems provides many of the same features and functions of RIS, Automated Deployment Services, and Windows Server 2003 SP2 WDS combined. Windows Server 2008 R2 WDS also provides additional functionality not included in any of its predecessors. Two of the distinct features of Windows Server 2008 and Windows Server 2008 R2 Windows Deployment Services are that both server and desktop operating systems can be deployed and images can be deployed using multicast communication. New specifically on Windows Server 2008 R2 WDS systems is the ability to support directly adding drivers or driver provisioning to Windows 7 and Windows Server 2008 R2 boot images using the WDS console and the support for network booting on x64-based computers with Extensible Firmware Interface (EFI) support. The proceeding sections, and the bulk of the remainder of this chapter, detail Windows Server 2008 R2 WDS installation and configuration.

## Windows Server 2008 R2 Windows Deployment Services

Windows Server 2008 R2 WDS is a server role that is designed to assist organizations that utilize Active Directory Domain Services with the deployment of Windows systems. The WDS system typically is set up to provide the storage and image retrieval services necessary for image deployment, the client components such as the PXE boot images, and the management components used to configure WDS settings, including adding images to the WDS server and creating multicast transmissions.

As previously stated, Windows Server 2008 R2 WDS includes the best features of all of its predecessors released with Windows 2000 Server, Windows Server 2003, and Windows Server 2008. Some of the features include, but are not limited to, the following:

▶ Support for Windows Server 2008, Windows 7, Windows Vista SP1, and Windows Server 2008 R2 operating systems images.

▶ Support for Windows Server 2003 and Windows XP Professional images.

▶ The ability to deploy images using multicast communication.

▶ The ability to use boot and installation images included with the Windows Server 2008, Windows Vista SP1, Windows 7, and Windows Server 2008 R2 media using the .wim extension. These can be copied directly from the respective installation media right into the WDS server to provide base images for these operating systems within minutes, without any customization.

▶ Support for both 32- and 64-bit operating system deployment.

Before an organization can consider deploying Windows 2008 R2 WDS, Active Directory Domain Services (AD DS) must be deployed. Also, due to the nature of the Preboot Execution Environment (PXE), Dynamic Host Configuration Protocol (DHCP) and domain name system (DNS) services are also required. Of course, for WDS to function properly, the desktop or server hardware must also be compatible and must support PXE boot and have at least 512MB of RAM, as this is the minimum RAM requirement to install Windows Server 2008 R2, Windows 7, and Windows Vista or Windows Server 2008 using the Windows PE environment. Although the WDS server can be configured to use IPv6, all client and WDS server communication will use IPv4.

## WDS Image Types

Windows Server 2008 R2 WDS includes several different image types. WDS administrators need to understand each of these image types to understand the documentation and how WDS works and also to be able to communicate the inner workings of WDS to management and other administrators or clients as required. WDS image types include boot images, installation images, discover images, and capture images.

## Boot Images

A boot image contains the Windows Deployment Services client and the Windows Preinstallation Environment (Windows PE), which is basically a mini operating system used to connect the system to the WDS server and provide the means to select and install a WDS installation image. The boot image included in the Windows Server 2008 R2 installation media, as an example, is appropriately named boot.wim and can be used to boot systems that will install Windows Server 2008 R2, Windows Vista SP1 x64, Windows 7 x64, or Windows Server 2008 x64 images. The Windows Server 2008 R2 boot image can also be used to install images using multicast transmissions. If x86 images will be deployed, it is a best practice to boot those systems using the compatible x86 Windows 7 or Windows Vista SP1 boot image. This will help simplify issues with driver provisioning and manual driver injection as necessary. Also, even if a Windows XP or Windows Server 2003 custom install image will be deployed, the boot image from Windows Automated Installation Kit, or Windows Vista SP1 or greater will be required as well as the appropriate storage, system bus, and networking drivers for that boot image. To be very specific, if a hardware plat-form that will be used for a Windows XP or Windows Server 2003 system does not contain storage, network, and system bus hardware that has a compatible driver that matches the boot image, that hardware might not be a candidate for WDS deployment.

## Installation Images

The installation images are the actual Windows installation media, packaged into a single WIM file. Depending on the actual media used to provide the WIM files, many different installation images might be included. For example, organizations that receive volume license media from Microsoft might have received a Microsoft Windows Server 2008 R2 DVD that contains the full installation and the Server Core images for Standard Edition, Enterprise Edition, and Datacenter Edition. On a WDS server, normally only a single boot image is required per platform, x86 or x64, but it can contain many different installation images.

## Discover Images

A discover image is created from a boot image and is used to boot a system and load the Windows Preinstallation Environment (Windows PE) and locate and connect to a WDS server. A discover image is commonly used when the network does not support PXE boot or the system does not support it. Discover images can be exported to ISO files and then burned or stored on removable media, such as CDs, DVDs, or USB memory sticks, for portability. In some cases when hardware is not booting and connecting properly to a WDS server using a boot image, a Discover image can be tested as an alternative for both deploying installation images and capturing a system to an image.

## Capture Images

A capture image is also created from a boot image, but instead of running setup like an installation image, the capture image runs the WDS capture utility. The WDS capture utility is used to connect to a system that has been prepared for imaging or cloning, using the appropriate system preparation tools, to the WDS system to create a new installation image that can be deployed later to WDS clients. Before a capture image is used, a system with an operating system is customized by adding applications, custom configurations, and other system changes that are required by the particular organization. When the

26

system is ready for imaging, it is prepared using Sysprep, a Microsoft deployment tool used to clear the machine's SID and operating system configurations that are specific to the system that will be imaged.

# Installing Windows Deployment Services (WDS)

You can install WDS on Windows Server 2008 R2 using the Initial Configuration Wizard, the Server Manager console, or the command-line utility Servermanagercmd.exe. Windows Deployment Services can be installed on the Standard, Enterprise, or Datacenter Edition of Windows Server 2008 R2, but it is not included on any Server Core editions. Before installing the WDS role, ensure that all volumes on the WDS server are formatted as NTFS volumes. Also, it is not recommended to install the WDS images into the same volume as the operating system to allow for customized security and to remove any risk of filling up the system drive when adding images to the WDS server. To add the WDS role using Server Manager, perform the following steps:

1. Log on to the Windows Server 2008 R2 system that will have the WDS role installed with an account with local administrator and domain administrator rights.
2. Click Start, click All Programs, click Administrative Tools, and select Server Manager.
3. When Server Manager opens, in the tree pane, select the Roles node.
4. In the tasks pane, click the Add Roles link.
5. Click Next on the Before You Begin page.
6. On the Select Server Roles page, check the box next to the Windows Deployment Services role, and click Next to continue.
7. On the Overview of Windows Deployment Services page, read the introduction and notes, and click Next to continue.
8. On the Select Role Services page, verify that both the Deployment Server and the Transport Server are checked, and click Next to continue.
9. On the Confirm Installation Selections page, review the selections and click Install to continue.
10. Review the results on the Installation Results page, and click Close to complete the installation. Close Server Manager and log off of the server.

## Configuring the WDS Server

After the WDS role is installed, the initial boot and installation image can be added. Locate the Windows 7 Enterprise x64 installation media as the boot image from this media can and will be used to deploy Windows Vista SP1, Windows 7 Ultimate, and Windows 7 Enterprise 64-bit edition images. Add x86-based boot images if both x86 and x64 install images will be deployed using WDS. To install the initial boot image, perform the following steps:

1. Log on to the Windows Server 2008 R2 system that has the WDS role installed with an account with local administrator and domain administrator rights.

2. Click Start, click All Programs, click Administrative Tools, and select Windows Deployment Services.

3. When the Windows Deployment Services console opens, in the tree pane, expand Servers.

4. The WDS server will be listed in the tree pane with a warning symbol on it indicating that the WDS server needs to be configured. Right-click the server and select Configure Server, as shown in Figure 26.1.

FIGURE 26.1    Initiating the WDS server configuration.

5. Review the requirements that are detailed on the Before You Begin page, and click Next to continue.

6. On the Remote Installation Folder Location page, specify the default installation path for the WDS images. For our example, we will use a separate drive and specify the path of E:\RemoteInstall and then click Next.

> **NOTE**
>
> If the WDS server only has a single disk and is selected for the installation folder, a pop-up notification opens stating that it is recommended that you create the remote installation disk on a different volume and, if possible, a different disk.

7. On the PXE Server Initial Settings page, review the options for PXE boot settings:

   ▶ **Do Not Respond to Any Client Computer**—This option essentially disables the WDS server from responding to any PXE boot attempts.

   ▶ **Respond Only to Known Client Computers**—This option requires that each system that will have an image deployed or captured will need to have an existing Active Directory computer account with a predefined globally unique identifier (GUID). This is the desired configuration after the WDS infrastructure is tested and working properly and after the WDS administrator understands how to locate the GUID of a system and pre-create a computer account in Active Directory.

   ▶ **Respond to All Client Computers (Known and Unknown)**—This option allows any machine that is PXE boot capable to connect to the WDS server and load a boot image. Of course, to install an image, the user needs to specify domain credentials.

   When Respond to All Client Computers (Known and Unknown) is selected, the WDS administrator can also select an additional check box that would require WDS administrators to approve connected WDS clients in the console before an image can be deployed to that system. This added security removes the requirement for the collection of system GUIDs before a system can connect to WDS but also adds the necessary security to allow the WDS administrator to control the deployment of WDS images.

8. For the initial WDS installation, select the Respond to All Client Computers (Known and Unknown) option button, and click Next, as shown in Figure 26.2.

9. The Operation Complete page appears and an Add Images to the Server Now check box is displayed. Uncheck the check box and click Finish to close the wizard.

After the wizard closes, the Windows Deployment Services console is displayed. Review each of the nodes that are now displayed beneath the WDS server, such as the Install Images, Boot Images, Pending Devices, Multicast Transmissions, and the new Drivers node. As we move forward in our WDS server configuration, each of these nodes will be reviewed, but at this time, additional configuration of the WDS server might be required. To review the WDS server settings, perform the following steps:

1. Log on to the Windows Server 2008 R2 system that has the WDS role installed with an account with local administrator and domain administrator rights.

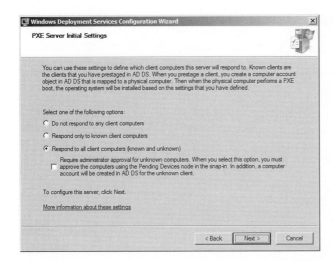

FIGURE 26.2   Configuring WDS to respond to all PXE clients.

2. Click Start, click All Programs, click Administrative Tools, and select Windows Deployment Services.

3. When the Windows Deployment Services console opens, if the local server is not listed under the Servers node, it must be added by right-clicking on Servers in the tree pane and selecting Add Server. Specify the local server and click OK to add it to the console.

4. When the WDS server is listed in the tree pane, right-click the server and select Properties.

5. Review each of the property pages to become familiar with the WDS server configuration options and update as necessary or click Cancel to close the property pages.

## DHCP Configuration

You must have a working DHCP server with an active scope on the network and, of course, DNS and Active Directory Domain Services are also required. The DHCP services are used to supply the PXE client computer with an IPv4 address during the installation of the image. When the WDS server is installed, it automatically registers in Active Directory with a DHCP server to allow for PXE clients to locate the WDS server without having to reconfigure any DHCP options. Of course, the WDS server also registers with the DNS server so it can be located during the network boot process. If this registration process by the WDS server is successful, it should have a DNS record and it should be listed as an authorized DHCP server when viewing the authorized DHCP server using the DHCP console. If the WDS server is not listed as an authorized server, the properties of the WDS server should be reviewed again for the settings in the Advanced tab, to authorize the DHCP server, as detailed in a previous section of this chapter. If, for some reason, the WDS server is also the DHCP server, the WDS server property pages will need to be opened and the DHCP page will need to be enabled so that the DHCP server does not listen on Port 67 and so DHCP option 60 is added to the DHCP server, as shown in Figure 26.3.

26

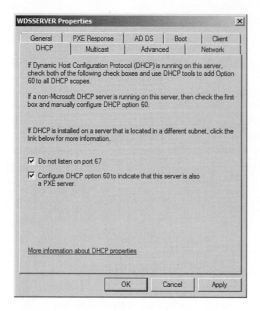

FIGURE 26.3    Configuring WDS server DHCP settings when Microsoft DHCP is installed on the WDS server.

If a DHCP server is running on the network but it is not a Microsoft DHCP server, option 60 will need to be added and configured on the DHCP server to enable PXE clients to locate the WDS server.

## Adding a Boot Image to the WDS Server

After the WDS server is configured as desired, it is time to add the initial boot image to the server. When a system is booted using PXE boot and connects to a WDS server, a boot image is used to prepare the client system to install a Windows image. The boot image contains the WDS client and Windows PE. Legacy imaging systems utilized a flavor of DOS and DOS-based network drivers to boot a system and connect it to the imaging server. With the Windows 7 default boot image, boot.wim, the Windows PE contains an extensive list of network drivers and most systems can be booted to WDS and successfully install an image. Using the Windows 7 or Windows Server 2008 R2 boot.wim images allows for the largest inclusion of network and storage drivers for image deployment. Boot images are also used to create capture images and discover images. One important point to note is that the boot.wim from Windows 7 x86 architecture will list both x86 and x64 install images if the WDS client architecture can support both. x64 boot images will only list x64 install images once connected to the WDS server even if the hardware supports both x86 and x64. To add a boot image to the WDS server, perform the following steps:

1. Log on to the Windows Server 2008 R2 system that has the WDS role installed with an account with local administrator and domain administrator rights.

2. Click Start, click All Programs, click Administrative Tools, and select Windows Deployment Services.

3. When the Windows Deployment Services console opens, if the local server is not listed under the Servers node, it must be added by right-clicking on Servers in the tree pane and selecting Add Server. Specify the local server and click OK to add it to the console.

4. In the tree pane, select and expand the WDS server.

5. Right-click the Boot Images node and select Add Boot Image.

6. When the Add Image Wizard opens, the first page prompts for the location of the boot image file. If the Windows 7 installation media is not in the WDS server's local CD/DVD drive, locate it on the network.

7. Click the Browse button to locate the Windows installation media on the server or on the network. After the media is located, open the Sources folder on the root of the Windows 7 installation media, select the `boot.wim` file, and click Open to add it.

8. Back in the Add Image Wizard window, if the boot image path and file are listed, click Next to continue.

9. On the Image Metadata page, either accept the default boot image name and description or type in a new one, and click Next to continue.

10. Next review the summary page and click Next to continue. This starts the process of adding the boot image to the WDS server.

11. After the process completes, click Finish on the Task Progress page to close the wizard.

12. Back in the Windows Deployment Services console, select the Boot Images node in the tree pane and in the tasks pane verify that the new boot image has been added.

13. Close the Windows Deployment Services console and log off of the server.

## Adding Install Images to the WDS Server

After the initial boot image is added to the WDS server, installation images can be added. Windows Server 2008, Windows 7, Windows Vista SP1, and Windows Server 2008 R2 installation media contain the compatible Windows Imaging (WIM) format file. These WIM files can be directly added to the WDS server as install images. To install the initial install image, perform the following steps:

1. Log on to the Windows Server 2008 R2 system that has the WDS role installed with an account with local administrator and domain administrator rights.

2. Click Start, click All Programs, click Administrative Tools, and select Windows Deployment Services.

3. When the Windows Deployment Services console opens, if the local server is not listed under the Servers node, it must be added by right-clicking on Servers in the tree pane and selecting Add Server. Specify the local server and click OK to add it to the console.

4. In the tree pane, select and expand the WDS server.

26

5. Right-click the Install Images node and select Add Install Image.

6. On the Image Group page, either select an existing image group to store the file in, or create a new image group by typing in a valid name. For this example, we will create a new image group named Windows 7. When you are finished, click Next.

7. On the Image File page, browse to the location of the `install.wim` Install Image file. For our example, in the Windows 7 installation media, browse to the Sources folder, select the `install.wim` file, and click Open.

8. Back on the Image File page, verify the path, and click Next to continue.

9. On the Available Images page, depending on the particular `install.wim` file, several images might be listed. Select only the images that the company or organization is licensed for. Select each of the desired images to install in the Windows 7 image group by checking the boxes next to the desired install images, as shown in Figure 26.4. Click Next to continue.

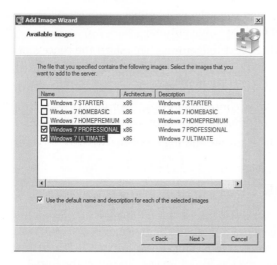

FIGURE 26.4   Selecting the appropriate install images available in the `install.wim` image file.

10. On the Summary page, review the list of install images that will be loaded into the WDS server, and click Next to begin the process.

11. After the images are uploaded into the WDS server, click Finish on the Task Progress page to return to the WDS console.

If necessary or desired, the WDS administrator can now also add additional boot and install images for both x86 and x64 architectures.

## Deploying the First Install Image

After a WDS server has at least one boot image and one install image, the imaging process should be tested before any additional configurations are performed. Prior to testing the imaging process, we need to check the properties of the WDS server and the DHCP server scope options. To verify these settings, perform the following tasks:

- ▶ Using the WDS console, open the properties of the WDS server and click on the Advanced tab to verify or to select the appropriate option buttons to ensure that both the Authorize This Windows Deployment Services Server in DHCP and the Allow Windows Deployment Services to Dynamically Discover Valid Domain Servers (Recommended) check boxes are checked. Click OK to update the server settings if any changes were made; otherwise, click Cancel to close the WDS server property pages.

- ▶ Using the WDS console, open the properties of the WDS server again and click on the PXE Response tab and verify that the Respond to All Client Computers (Known and Unknown) option button is selected and verify that the check box that would require administrator approval is not checked. Click OK to update the server settings if any changes were made; otherwise, click Cancel to close the WDS server property pages.

- ▶ Using the DHCP console on the appropriate DHCP server, open the properties of the appropriate IPv4 DHCP scope, assuming a Microsoft Windows Server 2008 R2 DHCP server is deployed, and verify that the DNS domain name and DNS server DHCP options contain the proper values for your company's environment. DHCP option 60 is not required if the DHCP server is on the same subnet as the WDS server and both of the servers are running Windows Server 2008 or Windows Server 2008 R2.

After these precheck steps are completed, the imaging process can begin. To deploy an image to a system using PXE boot, perform the following steps:

1. Select the desired system that will be imaged using WDS and connect the system's primary network adapter to a live switch port that is on the same network as the DHCP and WDS server.

2. Boot up the system and enter the system BIOS. Verify that PXE network boot is enabled for the primary adapter and verify that PXE network boot is listed in the boot menu before the system hard disk or disk arrays. Depending on an organization's server or workstation configuration and build specifications, configuring PXE boot to be listed before the hard disk in the BIOS boot order might not be the desired configuration, but for this testing it will help put all the administrators and different systems into a similar configuration so this process can proceed.

3. Save the BIOS settings and exit the BIOS to start a system bootup sequence. When the PXE network boot starts, keep a close eye on it to verify that the PXE client is obtaining a DHCP IPv4 lease. When prompted with the Press F12 for Network Boot message, press the F12 key to start the WDS imaging process. If PXE boot is getting an IPv4 address from the DHCP server but the system never prompts to press F12 for

26

network boot, there is most likely some issue with the DHCP server configuration and defined options. This needs to be resolved before moving forward or an alternative is to create and use a discover image to start the imaging process. Creating and using discover images are detailed in the next section "Creating Discover Images."

4. If the system is able to connect to the WDS server after the Press F12 for Network Boot prompt and after the F12 key is pressed, the boot image is downloaded from the WDS server to the client, and the imaging process starts. If multiple boot images have been added to the WDS server, pressing F12 will use the network boot to connect to the WDS server to get the list of boot images, then the boot image selected will be loaded, including the appropriate network drivers to allow the WDS client to connect to the WDS server to locate and begin installation of the install image selected.

5. After the system completes loading the boot image system files, the Windows Preinstallation Environment is loaded and the WDS client install application is started. The page name that appears is named Windows Deployment Services. Select the desired locale and keyboard or input method, and click Next to continue.

6. An authentication window opens. Enter the domain and username of the account used to install WDS and the password, and click OK. For a domain with a NetBIOS name of COMPANYABC, the username should be entered as COMPANYABC\username along with the correct password for that user account. If the authentication window never opens or does not connect to the WDS server after the correct username and password combination are entered, this most likely means that the boot image does not contain suitable network drivers for the client hardware and network drivers will need to be added to the boot image and this process should be started over.

7. On the Install Windows page, each of the install images loaded in the WDS server that match the boot image architecture, x86 or x64, will be listed as available selections. Select the desired operating system install image, and click Next to continue.

8. The next page lists the available or detected disks that can be used for the image installation. If no disks are listed, this is a red flag for WDS imaging and requires adding disk controller driver files to a boot image for WDS imaging to work on this particular hardware platform. Select the disk to install the operating system on, click Next to allow the imaging process to create the volume, format it, and install Windows 7 on the WDS client system.

**NOTE**

When selecting hardware for server and desktops that will be deployed using WDS images, ensure that the hardware is certified to work with Windows Server 2008, Windows 7, Windows Vista SP1, and/or Windows Server 2008 R2 and verify that all of the drivers are certified and signed by the Windows Hardware Quality lab to simplify operating system deployment to these systems.

9. After the disk selection is made and the Next button is clicked, the disk volume is created and formatted and the operating system installation begins by expanding

and copying the necessary files and installing the default operating system selections. When this phase of the installation completes, Windows Setup begins.

10. On the Set Up Windows page, select the correct country, time & currency and keyboard layout, and click Next to continue.

11. Depending on the install image selected and if any unattended files have been created the next few pages will ask for input to set the PC name, product key, accepting the end-user licensing agreement, Windows Update settings, date and time, and network zone settings. These pages will appear in a different order depending on the install image, and some pages might not appear at all if Windows XP or Windows Server 2003 images are being deployed. Follow the necessary steps to complete the installation of this image to the WDS client.

12. Most install images will be able to join the domain automatically, but some might not and, most likely, the default name of the PC will need to be updated using the WDS server property pages or custom unattended file.

This completes the installation process of a default WDS image.

## WDS Boot and Install Image Troubleshooting

Getting a WDS system to work the first time will either work without issue or it can be a real hassle. This section provides a short list of issues and troubleshooting steps that might help make the implementation of WDS more successful.

**Issue 1**: WDS clients never prompt to boot from network by pressing F12.

When this occurs, the issue might be related to the boot order on the client. Go into the BIOS on the client and first verify that the network interface card has network boot functionality enabled. Next set the boot order to make the network interface card first in the boot list or boot priority and try again.

If the PXE boot option starts, the administrator should see the IP address that is leased from the DHCP server. If no IP address is leased, check to see that the WDS server is listed as an authorized DHCP server using the Microsoft Windows Server 2008 R2 DHCP console. If it is not listed, add it by changing the DHCP server advanced property page settings. If DHCP is on the same server as WDS, check the WDS server DHCP property page settings to ensure that both check boxes are checked. Also verify normal DHCP server operation by checking that a client on the same network can acquire a DHCP IP address.

**Issue 2**: WDS clients can press F12 and get the list of boot images. After the boot image is loaded and the locale and keyboard layout are chosen, they are never prompted for credentials or cannot proceed any further even after entering the correct credentials.

When this occurs, the most likely issue is that the boot image selected does not contain a suitable network card driver for that workstation or server network interface card. To determine if this is the case, after the boot image is loaded at the Windows Deployment Services page, press Shift and F10 to drop to a command prompt. Type in Ipconfig and press Enter. If an IP address is listed, run Ipconfig /all to check the DNS server settings as the DHCP server might not be giving the correct scope options. If no IP address is listed, the network interface card drivers for this hardware will need to be manually injected or the drivers can be added using the Windows Server 2008 R2 WDS console, which is detailed later in this chapter.

Another issue that can cause this is if the NTFS and share permissions of the deployment share on the WDS server are not configured correctly. The share and NTFS permissions should allow all desired user groups to read and execute. These groups might be limited based on the delegation of administration desired to control who can deploy WDS images.

**Issue 3**: After entering credentials, the list of install images only shows x64 images.

This issue is by design if the boot image selected is an x64-based boot image. Selecting an x86 boot image, for example from Windows 7 Ultimate, allows the WDS client to show both x86- and x64-based images.

**Issue 4**: Regardless of whether the x86 boot image or the x64 boot image is selected from an x64-compatible WDS client, some install images still are not listed.

This issue can be caused by architecture discovery being disabled on the WDS server. Before changing this setting, however, it is a good idea to restart the WDS server after any new boot or install images are loaded as the first step in troubleshooting. If after restarting the WDS server, if some install images are still not showing, toggle the architecture discovery settings, restart the server, and check the client. Toggle the setting back, restart the server, and check again to see if all the install images are listed. To check and, if necessary, modify the architecture discovery and other WDS server settings, perform the following steps from the WDS server:

1. Log on to the desired WDS server with an account that has local administrator membership.

2. Open a command prompt and type the command `WDSUTIL /get-server /show:config ¦more` and press Enter. This shows the WDS configuration in the Command Prompt window one page at a time.

3. On the second or third page look for architecture discovery and note whether it is enabled or disabled. Change the value and restart the server and check the client. If there is no effect, change the value back.

4. If the WDS server architecture discovery is shown as disabled, type in the command in the Command Prompt window `WDSUTIL /Set-Server /architecturediscovery:Yes` and press Enter.

5. If the WDS server architecture discovery is shown as enabled, type in the command in the Command Prompt window `WDSUTIL /Set-Server /architecturediscovery:No` and press Enter.

6. After changing the architecture discovery setting, restart the WDS server in the Command Prompt window by typing in `Net Stop Wdsserver` and press Enter to stop the service. Then type the command `Net Start Wdsserver` and press Enter to start the service.

**Issue 5**: The WDS client can boot into the boot image and select the install image, but no disks are listed as options to install the WDS image on to.

This issue is most likely caused by a missing storage controller driver in the boot image. The resolution to this issue is to add storage controller drivers to the boot image the same way network card drivers are added.

**Issue 6**: After selecting the install image and the destination disk, the installation starts but after the install completes, many devices are listed as unknown in Device Manager.

This issue indicates that the drivers for these unknown devices are not included in the install image and they should be added to the desired install image the same way drivers are added to the boot image.

# Creating Discover Images

In cases when PXE boot is not supported on the system or on the network, it might be necessary to use bootable media to start a WDS imaging process. This can be accomplished with a WDS discover image. A discover image is created from an existing WDS boot image that contains Windows PE and the WDS client, but can be stored on removable media making it easier to deploy images to older systems or on heterogeneous networks that have PXE issues. To create a discover image, perform the following steps:

1. Log on to the Windows Server 2008 R2 system that has the WDS role installed with an account with local administrator and domain administrator rights.
2. Click Start, click All Programs, click Administrative Tools, and select Windows Deployment Services.
3. When the Windows Deployment Services console opens, in the tree pane, select and expand the WDS server and select the Boot Images node.
4. In the tasks pane, locate and right-click the desired boot image, and select Create Discover Image, as shown in Figure 26.5.
5. On the Discover Image Metadata and Location page, enter a name and description for the new discover boot image. In the Location and File Name section, browse to a folder on the local system where the new discover boot image can be created, type in a name for the discover image, and click Open to return to the Discover Image Metadata and Location page.
6. Enter the fully qualified domain name of the WDS server that the discover image will connect to after booting into the Windows PE and loading the WDS client. Figure 26.6 shows the discover metadata that will be used for this example; the path to the file is important as it will be required later. Click Next to create the discover image.
7. When the discover image is created, click Finish to close the window and return to the WDS console.

At this point, a new discover image has been created, but a few additional steps are required before it can be used to boot a system and connect to a WDS server.

The discover image can now be added to the WDS server as a boot image, by following the steps in the previous section on adding boot images to the WDS server. You might ask why a WDS administrator would want to do this—there have been documented issues where a WDS client PC cannot connect to the WDS server using a standard boot image

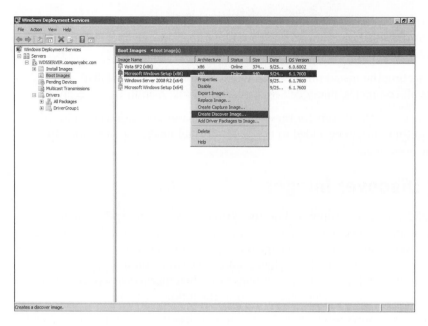

FIGURE 26.5    Creating a discover boot image.

FIGURE 26.6    Sample discover boot image metadata.

but can connect using a discover image. Perhaps it has to do with the fact that the WDS server is already selected, but this is an out-of-the-ordinary case that is only listed here because it might add value to a WDS administrator troubleshooting an implementation.

An alternate and more common use of discover images is to create bootable media that can be used on client or server hardware that does not support PXE boot. To create a bootable CD or DVD that will use the new discover boot image, the tools included in the Windows Automated Installation Kit (WAIK) are required. The WAIK for Windows 7 and Windows Server 2008 R2 is new and includes many updated features and settings. The remainder of this chapter, when referencing the WAIK, references this newest edition of the kit.

## Creating Bootable Media with Discover Boot Images and the Windows Automated Installation Kit (WAIK)

After a new discover image has been created, it is pretty useless until we can actually boot a system and connect to a WDS server using it as a WDS boot image or by creating a bootable removal media. To create bootable media that loads a discover image, the Windows Automated Installation Kit (WAIK) needs to be downloaded from Microsoft and installed on a Windows Server 2008 R2 system. The WAIK can be installed on other operating systems, but several prerequisites must be met before it can be installed.

The Windows Automated Installation Kit is used primarily to help OEM computer builders deploy Windows operating systems onto new hardware. It contains deployment tools that are compatible with the latest version of Windows. Download and install the WAIK on a Windows Server 2008 R2 system. After the WAIK is installed, to create a bootable ISO file that boots the discover boot image, perform the following steps:

1. Log on to the Windows Server 2008 R2 system with an account with administrative rights.

2. Download and install the latest version of the Windows Automated Installation Kit that is compatible with Windows Server 2008 R2 and Windows 7.

3. After the WAIK is installed, copy the discover image created previously to a local drive and folder path. For this example, the file path of our discover image is `E:\RemoteInstall\Win7x86-boot-discover.WIM`.

4. Click Start, click All Programs, click Accessories, and select Command Prompt.

5. Type `cd \` and press Enter to focus the command prompt to the root of the C: drive.

6. Type `cd "Program Files\Windows AIK\Tools\PETools\"` and press Enter to change the command prompt focus to the PETools folder.

7. Type `CopyPe x86 E:\RemoteInstall\Winpe` and press Enter. This creates the WinPE folder and a copy of the Windows Preinstallation Environment, also known as Windows PE or WinPE for short, for x86-based systems on the specified destination on the E: drive. The process copies several files to the destination folder and when completed returns the cursor back to the command prompt, which is now focused in the destination folder.

26

8. Now we have the WinPE files necessary to boot a system and we need to copy the discover image into the correct folder. Type the following command based on the folder and files paths presented in the previous steps: `Copy /y E:\RemoteInstall\Win7x86-boot-discover.WIM E:\RemoteInstall\WinPE\ISO\Sources\Boot.wim` and press Enter. This command copies the created discover boot file and creates or overwrites the default `boot.wim` file that is contained in the WinPE installation folder.

9. After the file copy completes successfully, type in `C:` and press Enter. The focus should be returned back to `c:\program files\Windows AIK\Tools\PETools`, but if not, change to the PETools directory.

10. At this point, we have a WinPE installation ready to create a bootable ISO image that includes our custom discover image. Type the following command and then press Enter:

   `oscdimg -n -bE:\RemoteInstall\Winpe\ISO\Boot\etfsboot.com`
   ↪ `E:\RemoteInstall\Winpe\ISO`
   ↪ `E:\RemoteInstall\Win7-x86-bootable-Discover-image.ISO`

11. The previous command should be entered as a single line and there is no space between the –b and the path to the `etfsboot.com` file. The –b option defines the media used to make the ISO bootable and the –n command allows for the use of long filenames. Each of the options is used for ISO image creation but this utility can be used to create other types of media. After the ISO is created, copy it to a system that has the necessary CD/RW or DVD/RW drive and the necessary software to burn a CD using an ISO image.

12. After the bootable CD is created, boot a system using it to verify that it functions and boots as intended.

This might seem like a tedious process, but it really only needs to be performed once for every WDS server deployed on the network.

## Adding Drivers to Boot and Discover Images

Windows Server 2008 R2 WDS supports adding drivers to Windows Server 2008 R2 and Window 7 boot images from within the WDS console. This also includes any Windows Server 2008 R2 or Windows 7 discover and capture images that are loaded as boot images on a WDS system. For all other boot, discover images, and capture images, drivers will need to be injected manually to the WIM file using the tools in the Windows Automated Installation Kit. To add drivers into a Windows Server 2008 R2 WDS infrastructure into a Windows Server 2008 R2 or Windows 7 boot image, perform the steps detailed in the following sections.

### Adding Drivers to the WDS Server Console

When drivers need to be added to Windows 7 or Windows Server 2008 R2 boot images, they can be installed using the WDS console by performing the following steps:

1. Log on to the Windows Server 2008 R2 system that has the WDS role installed with an account with local administrator and domain administrator rights.

2. Download the appropriate drivers and save the drivers to a folder on WDS server or a network location. Expand the drivers download to reveal the folder that contains the necessary INF, SYS, and other files that are required for the particular driver and note the exact location.

3. On the WDS server, click Start, click All Programs, click Administrative Tools, and select Windows Deployment Services.

4. When the Windows Deployment Services console opens, in the tree pane, select and expand the WDS server.

5. Right-click the Drivers node and select Add Driver Package.

6. On the Driver Package Location page, select the Select Driver from an .inf File option button.

7. In the Location Form field, click the Browse button and browse to the folder that contains the drivers INF, SYS, and other files. Once back on the Driver Package Location page, click Next to continue.

8. On the Available Driver Packages page, check or uncheck the desired drivers that will be added to the WDS server and click Next to continue. Many drivers are packaged together and the driver file may include many different drivers. As a best practice, limit the drivers added to the WDS server and the boot images to only the necessary drivers and no more to avoid unnecessary driver conflicts or file size bloat.

9. Review the selections on the Summary page and click Next to continue.

10. On the Task Progress page, once the driver(s) are added, click Next to continue.

11. On the Drivers Group page, if a driver group exists, the driver can be added to the group; otherwise, a new driver group can be created or the driver can be added to the root without creating a group. Select the desired option button, enter or select the driver group, and/or click Next to continue.

12. On the Task Completed page, click Finish to complete the driver addition.

**Adding Drivers to Windows 7 and Windows Server 2008 R2 Boot Images Using the WDS Console**
If drivers need to be added to existing Windows 7 or Windows Server 2008 R2 boot images on a Windows Server 2008 R2 WDS server, they can be added using the WDS console. The drivers will need to be added to the WDS server as detailed in the previous section before performing the following steps. To add drivers from the WDS server to existing Windows 7 and/or Windows Server 2008 R2 boot images, perform the following steps:

1. Log on to the Windows Server 2008 R2 system that has the WDS role installed with an account with local administrator and domain administrator rights.

2. On the WDS server, click Start, click All Programs, click Administrative Tools, and select Windows Deployment Services.

3. When the Windows Deployment Services console opens, in the tree pane, select and expand the WDS server.

4. Select and expand the Boot Images node and in the tasks pane select the desired boot image.

5. If you do not have a copy of the existing boot image, it is a good idea to back it up by right-clicking on the boot image, selecting Export Image, and following the steps to make a copy/export of the boot image before any drivers are added to the image.

6. Once a backup of the boot image is copied, right-click the desired boot image and select Add Driver Packages to Image.

7. Click Next on the Before You Begin page if you have a good backup of the boot image; otherwise, click Cancel.

8. On the Select Driver Packages page, click the Search for Packages button to list all compatible packages for this boot image. Check any desired drivers listed in the Search Results section, uncheck any drivers that should not be added to the boot image, and click Next to continue.

9. On the Selected Driver Packages page, review the list of drivers that will be added to the boot image, and click Next to continue.

10. On the Operation Complete page, review the results and click Finish to complete the driver addition to the boot image.

11. Repeat this process for any other Windows Server 2008 R2 or Windows 7 boot images that need drivers added, close the WDS console, and log off the server when completed.

12. Now boot up a WDS client using this boot image and verify that the driver is working correctly.

**Manual Driver Injection for Windows 7 and Windows Server 2008 R2 Boot Images**
In situations where a WDS server is not available or not implemented, administrators might still want to add drivers to boot images to create custom installation media with the necessary drivers. When this is the case, the Windows Automated Installation Kit should be used. To inject drivers into a Windows 7 or Windows Server 2008 R2 boot image, perform the following steps:

1. Download the necessary drivers and the WAIK from the Internet to a local server.

2. Log on to a Windows 7 or Windows Server 2008 R2 system with an account with administrator group membership and create a folder called C:\MountImage. Substitute C for a drive letter with ample space to mount the boot image but a few gigabytes of free space should suffice.

3. Install the WAIK on the system in the default folder location.

4. Copy the desired drivers to the system. Make sure the driver files have been expanded and the folder containing the INF, SYS, and other necessary driver files can be located through Windows Explorer on the local machine.

5. Copy the Windows 7 or Windows Server 2008 R2 boot.wim from the installation media to the system on a local drive that can be located through Windows Explorer. Browse to the file location, right-click on the file, and select Properties. Uncheck the read-only attribute and click OK to save the setting.

   For our example, the Windows 7 x86 boot.wim will be located in the C:\Win7Boot\ folder and the network card driver we will add is located in the

C:\Drivers\NIC\Win7\32\ folder. When viewed, this folder contains an INF, SYS, and CAT file that make up the driver set.

6. On the system, open a command prompt. Change directories to the C:\Program Files\Windows AIK\Tools\x86 folder. If the boot image that will be modified is an x64-based image, the amd64 folder would be substituted for the x86 folder in our example.

7. Based on the location of our drivers and boot image, type in the command `DISM /Get-Wiminfo /Wimfile:C:\Win7Boot\Boot.wim` and press Enter.

8. The previous command lists the information about the `boot.wim` file and specifically shows that this Windows 7 x86 `boot.wim` file contains two images, Microsoft Windows PE (Image Index 1) and Microsoft Windows Setup (Image Index 2). We will be mounting and adding drivers to the Image Index 2. This info step should be run on each boot image file that will have drivers added to ensure that the correct image index number is referenced when the file is mounted.

9. In the Command Prompt window, type the command `DISM /Mount-Wim /WimFile:C:\Win7Boot\boot.wim /Index:2 /MountDir:C:\MountImage` and press Enter to mount the boot image file.

10. If the process is successful, the command prompt will state that the operation completed successfully.

11. In the Command Prompt window, type the command `DISM /Image:C:\MountImage /Add-Driver:C:\Drivers\NIC\Win7\32` and press Enter.

12. If the driver addition completes successfully, enter the command `DISM /Unmount-Wim /MountDir:C:\MountImage /Commit` and press Enter to save the changes back to the `boot.wim` file. The results will show in the Command Prompt window, as shown in Figure 26.7.

13. Copy the updated `boot.wim` file to the WDS server, add it as a boot image, and test the image to verify the driver addition was successful.

**Manual Driver Injection for Windows Vista, WinPE, and Windows Server 2008 Boot Images**
There might be situations when WDS administrators need to use a boot image other than a Windows 7 or Windows Server 2008 R2 boot image, and drivers need to be added to these images. In these cases, it is necessary to add or inject those drivers manually to the WIM files. This can be accomplished using the tools included in the Windows Automated Installation Kit (WAIK) for Windows Vista and Windows Server 2008. The WAIK for Windows 7 and Windows Server 2008 R2 does not support injecting drivers to boot images from Windows Vista. To manually inject drivers into a Vista boot image, as an example, perform the following steps:

1. Download the necessary drivers and the Windows Vista WAIK from the Internet to a local server.

2. Log on to a system with an account with administrator group membership and follow the steps noted in the previous section to copy the drivers and `boot.wim` file, and create a folder to mount the image into.

3. Install the Windows Vista WAIK on the system.

26

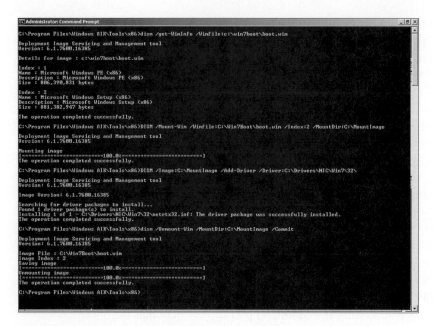

FIGURE 26.7    Manually injecting drivers to Windows 7 boot images.

For our example, the Windows Vista SP2 x86 boot.wim will be located in the C:\VistaBoot\boot.wim and the network card driver we will add is located in the E:\Drivers\NIC\WinVista\32\ folder. When viewed, this folder contains an INF, SYS, and CAT file that make up the driver set. The image will be mounted in a newly created folder named C:\MountImage.

4. On the system, open a command prompt. Change directories to the C:\Program Files\Windows AIK\Tools\x86 folder. If the boot image that will be modified is an x64-based image, the amd64 Tools subfolder would be substituted for the x86 folder in our example.

5. Based on the location of our drivers and boot image, type in the command IMAGEX /info C:\VistaBoot\boot.wim and press Enter. Make sure this boot.wim file is not set to read only.

6. The previous command lists the information about the boot.wim file and specifically shows that this Vista x86 SP2 boot.wim file contains two images, Windows Longhorn WinPE (Image Index 1) and Windows Longhorn Setup (Image Index 2). We will be mounting and adding drivers to the Image Index 2. This info step should be run on each boot image file that will have drivers added to ensure that the correct image index number is referenced when the file is mounted.

7. In the Command Prompt window, type the command IMAGEX /Mountrw C:\Vistaboot\boot.wim 2 C:\MountImage and press Enter to mount the boot image file.

8. If the process is successful, the command prompt will state that the operation completed successfully.

9. In the Command Prompt window, type the command `PEIMG` `/Inf=C:\Drivers\NIC\WinVista\32\netrtx32.inf C:\MountImage\Windows` and press Enter. Also, make sure to substitute the correct INF file that is located in the driver folder.

10. If the process completes successfully, type the command `IMAGEX /Unmount /Commit C:\MountImage` and press Enter.

11. Save the updated `boot.wim` to the necessary WDS server and install as a boot image if desired.

## Pre-creating Active Directory Computer Accounts for WDS

Without doing any extensive customization to the imaging process, you can include customizations to boot images, install images, or the WDS server configuration settings. WDS automatically generates the name of the computer and uses the credentials specified during the image deployment to add the imaged system to the Active Directory domain of which the WDS server is a member. WDS uses the configuration settings in the WDS Properties, AD DS tab, as shown in Figure 26.8, to define the Client Naming Policy format for computers and to define which domain and container the new computer accounts will be created in.

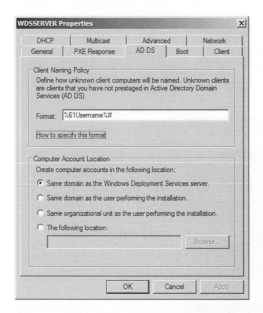

FIGURE 26.8   WDS Properties page for new computer account, AD DS tab.

The configuration options in the WDS Property page, AD DS tab work well for new computer account placement, but are not very flexible for naming computer accounts. When many computers will be deployed and will require predefined computer names in Active Directory, the computer accounts can be pre-created. For the pre-created computer accounts to be linked to the actual systems, the GUID associated with the system's network adapter is required. On most systems, the GUID will be displayed during the PXE boot sequence, as shown in Figure 26.9. After the GUID has been identified and recorded, the Active Directory computer account can be created. The account will need to be created before the system is imaged using WDS. To create an Active Directory computer account for use with WDS, perform the following steps:

1. Log on to the Windows Server 2008 R2 system running WDS with an account with administrative rights.

2. If the Remote Server Administration tools for the Active Directory Domain Services AD DS role are not installed on the WDS server, they must be installed now.

3. After the domain services tools are installed, click Start, click All Programs, click Administrative Tools, and select Active Directory Users and Computers.

4. Expand the domain and select the container that the WDS server will place new computer accounts in, as specified in the WDS Properties page, AD DS tab. By default, all new computer accounts will be placed in the domain's Computers container.

5. Right-click on the domain's Computers container, click New, and select Computer.

6. When the New Object – Computer window opens, type in the desired name of the new computer account in the Computer Name field, and click Next.

7. On the Managed page, check the This Is a Managed Computer check box.

8. After the check box is checked, enter the previously recorded GUID associated with the network card on the system that will be imaged, as shown in Figure 26.10, and click Next to continue. The dashes will need to be removed and should not be typed into the GUID field.

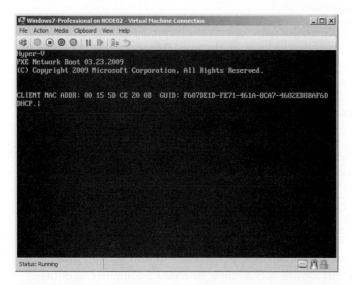

FIGURE 26.9    Gathering a system's network adapter GUID to pre-create Active Directory computer accounts.

**FIGURE 26.10**   Populating the GUID into the Active Directory computer account properties.

9. The next page is the Host Server page where a specific WDS server can be specified to provide images to this host. Either specify a WDS server or leave the default of allowing any WDS server to provide images to this client, and click Next.

10. Review the settings and click Finish to complete the process.

11. After the computer account is created, the system can be imaged and will join the domain using the preconfigured computer account name.

### Migration Path from Win2k3 RIS to W2k3-Sp2 WDS to Win2k8-WDS

Windows Server 2003 Remote Installation Services (RIS) is included with the release of the product and with Service Pack 1. With the release of Windows Server 2003 Service Pack 2, RIS services were upgraded to Windows 2003 Windows Deployment Services. The first time the new WDS console is opened on a Windows Server 2003 SP2 system, a prompt appears asking if the WDS server should be configured to run in Legacy or Mixed mode. If you plan to use previously created RIS images only, Legacy mode can be used. If you want to use your RIS images as well as the Windows Vista, Windows Server 2008, Windows 7, and Windows Server 2008 R2 Windows Imaging Format files (WIM), Mixed mode should be selected.

There are three different modes of WDS within Windows Server 2003: Legacy, Mixed, and Native. Legacy mode is primarily used for RIS image compatibility, Mixed mode is used for utilizing both RIS and WIM files or images, and Native mode is used primarily for WIM files. To upgrade to Windows Server 2008 R2 WDS, your Windows Server 2003 WDS server must be in WDS Native mode.

To upgrade your server from Legacy to Mixed mode, open up the WDS console on the WDS server, locate and right-click the server, and select Initialize Server. After the process completes, the server will be in Mixed mode.

26

To upgrade your server from Mixed mode to Native mode, first decide whether you want to keep your existing RISETUP and RIPREP images. RISETUP images are the base installation images created from Windows 2000, 2003, and XP installation media; RIPREP images are those images created from custom installations that have been pushed up to the RIS server. If you want to remove these images, simply delete the images. If you want to convert them, you have two options: offline conversion, which is used for RIPREP images only, and deploy and recapture, which is used for RIPREP and RISETUP images. Run the `WDSUTIL /SET-Server /ForceNative` command to convert the WDS to Native mode. After the Windows Server 2003 WDS server is running in Native mode, the operating system might be upgradeable to Windows Server 2008 R2 if no other issues prevent the upgrade and if the Windows Server 2003 system is running the 64-bit edition.

### Upgrading a RIS Image to a Windows Server 2008 R2 WDS Image

If you have a working RIS environment and have images that will need to be maintained, these images can be manually imported into a Windows Server 2008 R2 WDS server using a capture image and a detailed process. The following list includes the high-level steps to support this process for migrating Windows XP and Windows Server 2003 RIS images to a Windows Server 2008 R2 WDS server:

1. Deploy the image to a system using the legacy RIS server.
2. Prepare the newly deployed system using the Sysprep utility and, as required, the Setup Manager utility to prepare the system for imaging.
3. Create a capture boot image on the Windows Server 2008 R2 WDS server. Add the capture boot image to the WDS boot images.
4. Boot the system that will be imaged, using PXE boot.
5. Select the capture image when the list of available images is presented.
6. Follow the capture imaging prompts to create the new custom install image.

# Creating Custom Installations Using Capture Images

When the default install images included with Windows Server 2008, Windows Vista, Windows 7, or Windows Server 2008 R2 do not meet the deployment requirements for an organization, custom install images can be created by preparing the system using `Sysprep.exe` and then using capture boot images to upload the new image to the WDS server. To create a new capture image, perform the following steps:

1. Log on to the Windows Server 2008 R2 system that has the WDS role installed with an account with local administrator and domain administrator rights.
2. Click Start, click All Programs, click Administrative Tools, and select Windows Deployment Services.
3. When the Windows Deployment Services console opens in the tree pane, select and expand the WDS server.
4. Select the Boot Images node and in the tasks pane, right-click the desired boot image, and select Create Capture Image.

5. On the Capture Image Metadata and Location page, enter a name and description for the new capture boot image. In the Location and File Name section, browse to a folder on the local system where the new capture boot image can be created, type in a name for the capture image, and click Open to return to the Capture Image Metadata page. Click Next to continue.

6. When the capture boot image is created, we will add the new capture image to the WDS boot images. On the Task Progress page, check the Add Image to the Windows Deployment Server Now check box, and click Finish to close the Create Capture Image Wizard.

7. In the Add Image Wizard window that opens, on the Image File page, verify that the file path represents the capture file path and filename and click Next to continue.

8. On the Image Metadata page, be certain to change the name so that it reflects a capture image, as shown in Figure 26.11. Click Next to continue.

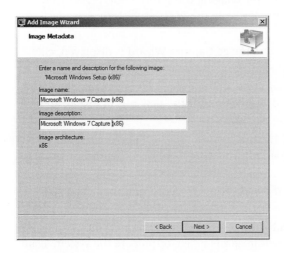

FIGURE 26.11    Naming the new capture boot image.

9. Review the settings on the Summary page, and click Next to import the capture boot image to the WDS server.

10. After this process completes, click Finish, and close the WDS console and log off of the server.

Typically, when organizations decide to use a product to image servers and/or desktops, the main driving force is to reduce the effort required to deploy the systems. If only base operating systems were deployed using WDS, the time-savings would not be much, but when several hours of post operating system software installations and custom configurations are part of this process, creating and deploying customized images can be very valuable. To create an image of a preconfigured Windows Server 2008 R2 or a Windows 7 system, the steps are similar to the steps required to upgrade an RIS image to a WDS image, as follows:

1. Deploy the image to a system using a default boot and install image from the WDS server.

2. Prepare the newly deployed system for imaging by installing any necessary applications or drivers and customizing the system based on the organization's requirements.

3. Run the Sysprep.exe utility from the c:\windows\system32\sysprep folder. In the System Preparation Tool 3.14 window, select the Enter System Out-of-Box Experience (OOBE) option in the System Cleanup Action menu. Check the Generalize check box, select the Shutdown option in the Shutdown Options menu, and click OK. After this completes, it shuts down the system.

4. On the WDS server, create a capture boot image and add the capture boot image to the WDS boot images.

5. Boot the system that has been prepared for imaging using PXE boot, press F12 when required, and when the available boot images are presented, select the previously created capture image.

6. When the Windows Deployment Services Image Capture Wizard is displayed, click Next on the Welcome page to continue.

7. On the Image Capture Source page, select the volume that will be captured from the drop-down menu, type in a name and description for the new install image, and click Next to continue.

8. Next, select the check box to upload the image to the server. Enter credentials when prompted and the image should upload to the server. Complete the capture process and shut down the system.

9. Log on to the WDS server and from the WDS console, verify that the new install image that was just created is listed in the designated install image group.

10. Boot a system using PXE into a WDS boot image, and select the new install image to test the deployment of this image. Customize the image or prepare the system again and recapture.

Additional customization to captured install images might be required using the System Image Manager included in the Windows Automated Installation Kit.

## Customizing Install Images Using Unattended Answer Files

Using the default install images, or install images created from the WDS capture process, there are still several options available that allow administrators to interact and manipulate how the install image will be deployed. If the imaging process needs to be customized to remove options from the end-user experience, such as entering the product key, wiping out any existing partitions on a hard drive, and creating a custom partition size for the operating system, these can be accomplished by creating a customized unattended answer file using the Windows Automated Installation Kit (WAIK).

To create an answer file, you need to copy the install image that will be customized. This can be accomplished by exporting an install image from the WDS console if the install image is custom, or by simply copying the `install.wim` file from the Windows 7 or Windows Server 2008 R2 installation media. After the install image is copied to the server, if the WAIK is not installed, it needs to be downloaded from Microsoft and installed on the server.

The WAIK programs group contains documentation that can be used to provide all of the necessary information on how to create and customize an unattended answer file. This is by no means a quick-and-easy process; it requires several iterations of the file and several tests until the desired result is achieved. For detailed information on how to create and configure unattended answer files using the WAIK, install the WAIK and reference the Unattended Windows Setup reference Help file and the Getting Started for IT Professionals HTML document included with the WAIK installation.

## Creating Multicast Images

A feature of Windows Deployment Services is that images can be deployed to servers and desktops using multicast transmissions. For multicast imaging to work properly, the network devices that connect the WDS multicast clients to the WDS server providing the multicast transmission must support and allow multicast traffic. Creating a multicast transmission is a very straightforward process and can be created within a few minutes, if the WDS server already contains tested boot and install images. To create a multicast transmission, perform the following steps:

1. Log on to the Windows Server 2008 R2 system that has the WDS role installed with an account with local administrator and domain administrator rights.

2. Click Start, click All Programs, click Administrative Tools, and select Windows Deployment Services.

3. When the Windows Deployment Services console opens, if the local server is not listed under the Servers node, it must be added by right-clicking on Servers in the tree pane and selecting Add Server. Specify the local server and click OK to add it to the console.

4. In the tree pane, select and expand the WDS server, and select the Multicast Transmissions node.

5. Right-click Multicast Transmissions and select Create Multicast Transmission.

6. On the Transmission Name page, enter a name for the multicast transmission, and click Next. For example, enter `MC-Win7-Pro`. Click Next to continue.

7. On the Image Selection page, select one of the WDS install images that will be transmitted to clients through this multicast transmission, and click Next. If the desired image is not listed, pull down the image group pull-down menu and select the correct image group that contains the desired install image.

8. On the Multicast Type page, select Auto-Cast, which will start the transmission automatically when a client connects to the WDS server and selects the install image that is defined within this multicast transmission, and click Next. Alternatively, select Scheduled-Cast to define a number of clients or a start time that will kick off the multicast transmission, as shown in Figure 26.12. Click Next after the multicast type is selected.

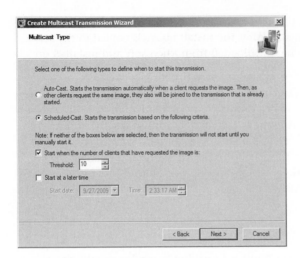

FIGURE 26.12   Selecting the desired multicast transmission type.

9. On the Operation Complete page, click Finish to return to the WDS console.

10. In the tree pane, select and expand the Multicast Transmissions node to reveal the new multicast transmission.

11. Select the new multicast transmission and in the tasks pane, after clients connect to the transmission, each client will be listed and their progress can be tracked.

12. When the multicast transmission is no longer required, right-click the multicast transmission, and select Delete. Confirm the deletion by clicking Yes, and then close the WDS console and log off of the server.

When WDS clients need to connect to the multicast transmission, they only need to select the install image used to create the multicast transmission and they will connect appropriately. This also means that this install image cannot be used by unicast clients until the multicast transmission is removed.

# General Desktop Administration Tasks

Aside from deploying operating systems to servers and desktops, managing or remotely updating the systems and the end users after deployment can be an even more challenging task. Windows Server 2008 R2 provides several tools to assist with the management of the computer and network infrastructure, but for managing users and desktops, one of the most functional tools is domain-based group policies. With group policies, Windows Update settings can be configured, network configurations can be managed from a central console, end-user data can be migrated to the server and synchronized with the local desktop folder for mobile users, and much more. For more information on how group policies can be used to manage Windows systems and users, refer to Chapter 27, "Group Policy Management for Network Clients."

Additionally, when end users need one-on-one support, Windows systems deployed in an Active Directory Domain Services domain can easily leverage the Remote Assistance application. This application allows administrators and end users to share their desktop in either a view-only or fully interactive sessions. Remote Assistance works outside of domain deployments, but within a domain, the IT staff can offer Remote Assistance to the user. To start the process, the user only needs to accept the offer by clicking on the link. Going even one step further, when organizations leverage Remote Desktop Services Host systems, administrators can also interact with end users within their session using a remote control function that allows both the end user and administrator to view and share control of the shared desktop.

## Summary

Windows Server 2008 R2 provides administrators and organizations with many features, applications, and services that can be used to help deploy and manage Windows servers and desktops. Tools such as Windows Deployment Services and domain group policies allow organizations to define configurations and security settings as standards once, and automate the process to reduce the risk of user error or inconsistent configurations across the infrastructure. Of course, as with any powerful technology or service, before any new applications or services are introduced in an existing computer and network infrastructure, the applications and services should be carefully tested and reviewed in an isolated lab environment to ensure that it is really necessary and will increase productivity or enhance the infrastructure's functionality or security.

## Best Practices

The following are best practices from this chapter:

- ▶ Deploy Windows Deployment Services on the computer and network infrastructure only if the organization frequently deploys many servers or desktops or wants to ensure consistent and quickly recoverable systems.

- ▶ Place the WDS image repository on a NTFS volume that is not the system volume, to improve server performance and to also reduce the risk of filling up the system drive.

- ▶ When customized desktop images will be captured to the WDS server as new install images, ensure that the Sysprep utility is run before booting into a capture image; otherwise, the image will be a duplicate of the workstation and there will be name and computer SID conflicts.

- ▶ Instead of re-creating RIS images from scratch, deploy the images to compatible systems, prepare the systems using Sysprep, and boot into a WDS capture boot image to save the system image to the WDS server in the WIM format.

▶ Update images when hardware platforms change enough that heavy customization to the install and boot images are required to support the deployment of WDS images to the systems or when major operating system upgrades have been released.

▶ When selecting new server and desktop hardware, ensure that the systems and all related hardware components are certified to work with Windows 7, Windows Server 2008, Windows Vista, or Windows Server 2008 R2 and that all the necessary drivers are digitally signed by the Windows Hardware Quality labs.

▶ After images are deployed, the systems should be placed on isolated networks until postimaging deployment tasks can be completed, including installing any security updates and software packages to provide adequate security to the production network and the newly deployed system.

# CHAPTER 27

# Group Policy Management for Network Clients

The management and configuration of Windows Server 2008 R2, Windows 7, and some legacy Windows systems can be simplified and standardized with the use of group policies. Group policies are designed to simplify and centralize the configuration and management of Windows systems and the users who log on to the systems. Group Policy management is segmented into two policy nodes including the Computer Configuration and the User Configuration nodes. The policy settings contained in the Computer Configuration node can be used to configure Registry and file system permissions, define user password policies, change network configuration and firewall settings, manage system services, define and control power profiles, and much more. The User Configuration node contains policy settings that can manage desktop environment settings, including automatically enforcing a standard screensaver and lockout duration, installing printers, running logon scripts, redirecting user folders to a network share and configuring folder synchronization, locking down the desktop environment, and much more.

Windows systems can be managed individually with local group policies, and when the systems are members of Active Directory domains, they can also be managed using domain group policies. Local group policies and domain group policies are similar in function but domain group policies provide additional functionality, as many of the settings included within the policy templates apply only to Active Directory domains. One of the reasons many organizations deploy Active Directory domains is to leverage the capabilities of domain Group Policy Objects. Chapter 19, "Windows Server 2008 R2 Group Policies and Policy

Management," details Group Policy infrastructure concepts and how to create, link, back up, and manage Group Policy Objects.

This chapter provides an overview and examples of how local and domain Group Policy Objects can be used to manage and configure Windows systems and users.

# The Need for Group Policies

Many businesses today are challenged and short-staffed when it comes to managing and properly configuring their information technology (IT) systems. For IT staff, managing the infrastructure involves standardizing and configuring application and security settings, keeping network resources readily available, and having the ability to effectively support end users. Providing a reliable computer and network infrastructure is also a key task for these administrators and part of that requirement includes deploying reliable servers and end-user workstations.

Providing reliable servers and workstations often includes tuning the system settings, installing the latest security updates and bug fixes, and managing the end-user desktop. For small environments, performing these tasks manually can be effective and the right approach, but, in most cases, this can result in inconsistent configurations and an inefficient use of the technical staff member's time.

Using group policies to control the configuration of computer and user settings and centrally managing these settings can help stabilize the overall computer network and greatly reduce the total number of hours required to manage the infrastructure. For example, if a network printer is replaced, the new printer can be deployed using Group Policy; the next time a user logs on, the printer can be automatically installed and the original can be automatically removed. Without Group Policy, each user desktop would need a visit to manually install and replace the printers.

Only 10 years ago, the bulk of computer and user configuration and management tasks were performed on a per-user and per-computer basis. Organizations that required higher efficiency had to hire specialized staff to develop and support standard desktop building and cloning procedures and had to create their own applications and scripts to perform many of the management functions that are now included with Windows Server 2008 R2 and Windows 7 group policies. With more specialized technical staff members, the ratio of technical staff to end users commonly ranged from 5 to 8 technical resources for every 200 employees. Even at this ratio, however, when corporatewide changes were necessary, outside consultants and contractors were commonly brought on board to provide expertise and extra manpower to develop custom applications or processes and to implement the necessary changes.

In many of today's organizations, with the advancements in systems and end-user management, it is not uncommon to find organizations now able to support an average of 100 to 250 users with 1 to 2 technical resources. This is only possible when desktop and end-user management policy and procedural standards are developed and group policies are leveraged to support these standards.

# Windows Group Policies

Windows Server 2008 R2 and Windows 7 provide several different types of policies that can be used to manage computer systems and user accounts. Depending on the security groups a user account is a member of, and whether or not the computer system is a member of an Active Directory domain or a Windows workgroup, the number of policy settings applicable will vary.

## Local Computer Policy

Every Windows system will contain a default local computer policy. The local computer policy is a Local Group Policy Object (LGPO). The local computer policy contains separate Computer and User Configuration nodes. The local computer policy, as its name states, only applies configured settings to the individual local computer system and the users who log on. The local computer policy on a new system is blank, except for the default settings defined within the Computer Configuration\Windows Settings\Security Settings policy node. The Security Settings policy node is also the local security policy.

## Local Security Policy

The local security policy of a system contains the only configured policy settings on newly deployed Windows systems. Settings such as user rights assignments, password policies, Windows Firewall with advanced security settings, and system security settings are managed and configurable within the local security policy. Furthermore, the local security policy can be exported from one system as a single text file and imported to other systems to simplify security configuration in workgroup environments and to customize security for new system deployments.

## Local Administrators and Non-Administrators User Policies

Windows Server 2008 R2 and Windows 7 support multiple local group policies for user accounts. If any settings are configured in the User Configuration node of the local computer policy, the settings are applied to all users who log on to the system, including the local Administrators group. In previous versions of Windows, if the local computer policy restricted an administrator from performing a specific function, the policy would need to be changed and reapplied before the administrator could perform the function. Starting with Windows Vista and Windows Server 2008 including continued support in Windows 7 and Windows Server 2008 R2, additional user-only policies can be created to provide override settings to either further restrict or reduce security to allow the particular user to perform their tasks. As an example, if the local computer policy setting was enabled to remove the Display applet from Control Panel, no users would be able to access and modify the display settings of the system. If an Administrators local group policy was created, this same setting could be set to disabled and any users who are members of the local Administrators group would then have access to the Display Control Panel settings.

For local administrators, the Administrators local group policy can be configured as stated previously. Additionally, separate local user policies can be created for the Non-Administrators users. If the system has local user accounts, specific local user policies can be created for each user. This allows for very granular assignment of rights and functionality for systems that use local accounts but require specific configurations and security settings on a per-user basis.

By default, users logging on to Windows Server 2008, Windows Server 2008 R2, Windows Vista, or Windows 7 will apply the local computer policy, followed by either the Administrators or Non-Administrators policy and any local user-specific policy. An example of how to use multiple policies can be a local computer policy that denies all users from writing to removable storage and the Administrators local user policy that allows read and write access to removable storage. Because the Administrators local user policy is applied after the local computer policy, only administrators will be able to write to removable storage media.

## Domain Group Policies

Domain group policies are very similar to local group policies, but many additional settings are included and these policies are managed and applied within an Active Directory environment. For clarification, documentation might refer to local policies as Local Group Policy Objects and group policies as domain-based policies. For the remainder of this chapter, they will be referred to as local policies and domain policies.

Local policies are very close to domain policies, but there are several key differences. Domain policies are managed using the Group Policy Management Editor, which allows administrators to view all available settings or to filter out only configured settings when managing a policy. Also, domain policies can be used to install software applications for computers and users. Many settings that only apply to a domain environment are still available in a local policy but when configured will not function if the computer is not a member of an Active Directory domain. One of the biggest differences between domain and local group policies is the separation of settings into the Policies and Preferences nodes, which is detailed later in this chapter in the "Policies and Preferences" section.

## Security Configuration Wizard

Windows Server 2008 R2 contains a tool called the Security Configuration Wizard (SCW). The SCW contains different templates that can be applied to systems that meet specific criteria.

For example, on a system running only the Windows Server 2008 R2 File Services role, when examined and secured by the SCW, a File Server role template will be applied that will configure the firewall, disable unnecessary services, and tune the system to provide access to the necessary functions of the File Services role but not much else. The SCW should be used only when properly tested because the security changes can impact functionality if incorrect settings are applied to a system. Also, it is highly recommended to configure the server 100% ready for production then run the Security Configuration Wizard to perform the final lockdown. Alternatively, the SCW can be used to create the necessary security template, which can then be exported and later imported into a domain policy and applied to the necessary servers that match the appropriate configuration. Additional information on how to use the Security Configuration Wizard is detailed in Chapter 13, "Server-Level Security."

## Policy Processing Overview

When a Windows system contains multiple local policies or is a member of an Active Directory domain, more than one policy will be processed when the computer boots or when a user logs on. Each policy that applies to the particular computer or user is processed sequentially and it is important to understand the policy processing order. In cases where multiple policies have the same settings configured, but with different values, the resulting setting value will match the last policy processed.

### Policy Processing for Computers

Policy settings are applied to computers during computer startup, shutdown, and background refresh intervals. Policy processing for computer objects is performed in the following order:

1. Local computer policy
2. Domain policies linked to the Active Directory site
3. Domain policies linked to the Active Directory domain
4. Domain policies linked to the organizational unit hierarchy in which the computer account is located

### Policy Processing for Users

Policy settings are applied to users during user logon, logoff, and background refresh intervals. Policy processing for domain and local users is performed in the following order:

1. Local computer policy
2. Local Non-Administrators policy or local Administrators policy if these policies exist
3. Local user-specific policy; only applies if the user is a local user account and a policy exists for the user
4. Domain policies linked to the Active Directory site
5. Domain policies linked to the Active Directory domain
6. Domain policies linked to the organizational unit hierarchy in which the user account is located

### Group Policy Order of Processing

When multiple policies are linked to a single Active Directory site, domain, or organizational unit, each policy will be applied sequentially. The order of policy application or processing is based on the policy link order. The policy link with the number 1 associated to the policy name is the last policy applied at the container and, therefore, takes precedence for policy link order of processing; see Chapter 19.

**Loopback Processing**

When a user is processing domain policies, the policies that apply to that user are based on the location of the user object in the Active Directory hierarchy. The same goes for domain policy application for computers. There are situations, however, when administrators or organizations want to ensure that all users get the same policy when logging on to a particular computer or server. For example, on a computer that is used for training or on a Remote Desktop Session Host, also known as a Terminal Server, when the user desktop environment must be the same for each user, this can be controlled by enabling loopback processing in Replace mode on a policy that is applied to the computer objects. To explain a bit further, if a domain policy has the loopback settings enabled and set to Replace mode, any settings defined within that policy in the User Configuration node are applied to all users who log on to the computer this particular policy is applied to. When loopback processing is enabled and configured in Merge mode on a policy applied to a computer object and a user logs on, all of the user policies are applied and then all of the user settings within the policy applied to the computer object are also applied to the user. This ensures that in either Replace or Merge mode, loopback processing applies the settings contained in the computer-linked policies last.

# Group Policy Feature Set

The Group Policy Feature set is the collection of all the available settings within a group policy. The available policy settings are created from the basic policy template, which includes the general hierarchy, the local security policy, and the default administrative templates stored in the local file system. The administrative templates that present their settings within a policy are referenced from the files stored in the c:\windows\policydefinitions folder or in the Active Directory domain central store.

The policy settings available within a particular policy or all policies can be extended by importing additional administrative templates. This can be accomplished by simply adding the correct ADMX and ADML files to the PolicyDefinitions folder on the local system or in the central store or by importing a legacy administrative template file with the ADM extension into a particular policy. For more information on the central store and how to import ADM files to existing policies, refer to Chapter 19.

By default, the Windows Server 2008 R2 group policies administrative templates contain approximately 1,650 settings in the Computer Configuration node and another 1,450 in the User Configuration node. There are many more settings in the Windows Settings nodes and the Preferences node that extend this number dramatically. This, of course, makes detailing each of the settings a very inconvenient and lengthy process. Instead of covering every setting, this section and many of the following sections in this chapter highlight the types of settings available that might be the most common and useful settings for managing Windows environments.

Many of the policy settings contained in both the Computer and User Configuration policy nodes apply only to specific Windows Server 2008 R2 role services such as the Encrypting File System, Remote Desktop Services, Network Access Protection, or the Distributed File System role services. For these particular services, as with any Group

Policy settings, it is very important that the administrator understands the potential impact of configuring these settings. Before any production group policies are created, modified, or linked, the policy should be tested in an isolated environment and a rollback plan should be created and also tested. For more information on how to plan for Group Policy deployment, see Chapter 19.

## Computer Configuration Policy Node

The Computer Configuration node of a group policy contains settings that are designed to configure and manage a Windows system. Many of the settings found in this node also exist in the User Configuration node, and when both settings are configured, different outcomes will result. In some cases, computer policy settings will always be used even if the user configuration policy setting is configured as well. In other cases, the last policy setting applied will be used. For example, in a local group policy, within each node under Administrative Templates\System\Scripts, there is a setting named Run Logon Scripts Synchronously and if this setting is configured in the Computer Configuration section, it will be enforced regardless of how the setting is configured in the User Configuration policy node.

At the root of the Computer Configuration node, there are three policy nodes named the Software Settings node, the Windows Settings node, and the Administrative Templates node. In domain group policies, these three nodes are located beneath the Computer Configuration\Policies node.

### Computer Configuration Software Settings Node
The Software Settings node is used to add software application packages to the computers that process the particular policy. Prepackaged or custom Windows Installer MSI software packages can be added to this Software Settings node and used to automatically install software on the computer during the next reboot cycle. This is known as an assigned software package. More information regarding deploying software using Group Policy is detailed later in this chapter in the "Deploying Software Packages Using Domain Group Policy Objects" section.

### Computer Configuration Windows Settings Node
The Windows Settings node provides administrators with the ability to manage the overall security and configuration of the Windows system. The settings contained beneath the Windows Settings node can be used to define how local and domain users can interact with and manage the system and how the system will communicate across the network. The five nodes contained within the Windows Settings node are as follows:

- **Name Resolution Policy**—This node allows Group Policy administrators to create rules to build the content of the Name Resolution Policy Table to support DNSSEC implementations and to configure Windows Server 2008 R2 DirectAccess DNS settings centrally.

▶ **Scripts (Startup/Shutdown)**—The Scripts node allows administrators to add startup or shutdown scripts to computer objects.

▶ **Deployed Printers**—This node allows administrators to automatically install and remove printers on the Windows systems. Using the Group Policy Object Editor on Windows Server 2008 or Windows Server 2008 R2 systems, this node might not appear unless the Print Management console is also installed.

▶ **Security Settings**—This node is a replica of the local security policy, although it does not sync or pull information from the local security policy. The settings in this node can be used to define password policies, audit policies, software restrictions, Services configuration, Registry and file permissions, and much more.

▶ **Policy-base QoS**—The Policy-base QoS node can be configured to manage, restrict, and prioritize outbound network traffic between a source Windows system and a destination host based on an application, source, or destination IP address and/or source and destination protocols and ports.

### Security Settings

The Security Settings node allows a security administrator to configure security levels assigned to a domain or Local Group Policy Object. This can be performed manually or by importing an existing security template.

The Security Settings node of the Group Policy Object can be used to configure several security-related settings, including file system NTFS permissions and many more settings contained in the nodes beneath Security Settings as follows:

▶ **Account Policies**—These computer security settings control password policy, lockout policy, and Kerberos policy in Windows Server 2008 R2, Windows Server 2008, Windows Server 2003, and Windows 2000 Server domains and local systems.

▶ **Local Policies**—These security settings control audit policy, user rights assignment, and security options, including setting the default User Account Control settings for systems the policy applies to.

▶ **Event Log**—This setting controls security settings and the size of the event logs for the application, security, and system event logs.

▶ **Restricted Groups**—These settings allow the administrator to manage local or domain group membership from within this policy node. Restricted group settings can be used to add members to an existing group without removing any existing members or it can enforce and overwrite membership based on the policy configuration.

▶ **System Services**—These settings can be used to control the startup mode of a service and to define the permissions to manage the service configuration or state. Configuring these settings does not start or stop any services.

▶ **Registry**—This setting is used to configure the security permissions of defined Registry keys and, if desired, all subkeys and values. This setting is useful in supporting legacy applications that require specific Registry key access that is not normally allowed for standard user accounts.

▶ **File System**—This setting is used to configure NTFS permissions on specified folders on NTFS formatted drives. Also, enabling auditing and configuring folder ownership and propagating these settings to subfolders and files is an option.

▶ **Wired Network (IEEE 802.3) Policies**—This policy node can be used to configure additional security on wired network adapters to allow for or require smart card or computer-based certificate authentication and encryption.

▶ **Windows Firewall with Advanced Security**—This policy node allows administrators to configure the Windows Firewall on Windows client and Windows server systems. The configured settings can configure specific inbound or outbound rules and can define how the firewall is configured based on the firewall profile or network the system is connected to. The configuration can overwrite the local firewall rules or the group policy and local rules can be merged.

▶ **Network List Manager Policies**—Windows Firewall on Windows 7, Windows Vista, Windows Server 2008, and Windows Server 2008 R2 uses firewall profiles based on the network. This setting node can be used to define the permissions end users have regarding the identification and classification of a new network as public or private to allow for the proper firewall profile to be applied.

▶ **Wireless Network (IEEE 802.11) Policies**—These policies help in the configuration settings for a wide range of devices that access the network over wireless technologies, including predefining the preferred wireless network, including the service set identifier (SSID) and the security type for the network. This node includes Windows Vista and later releases and Windows XP compatible policies.

▶ **Public Key Policies**—These settings are used to specify that computers automatically submit a certificate request to an enterprise certification authority and install the issued certificate. Public Key Policies are also created and are used in the distribution of the certificate trust list. Public Key Policies can establish common trusted root certification authorities. Encrypting File System settings use this policy node as well.

▶ **Software Restriction Policies**—These policies enable an administrator to control the applications that are allowed to run on the Windows system based on the file properties, including the filename. Additionally, software restrictions can be created based on certificates or the particular network zone from which the application is being accessed or executed. For example, a rule can be created to block application installations from the Internet zone as defined by Microsoft Internet Explorer.

▶ **Network Access Protection**—This setting can be used to deploy the configuration of the Network Access Protection client. These policy settings allow an administrator to require a client health check before granting access to the network.

27

▶ **Application control policies**—This node enables Group Policy administrators to create rules that define which security groups or specific users can run executables, scripts, or Windows Installer files and can also be used to granularly define which file paths, filenames, and digitally signed publishers of files will be allowed or denied on the computers these policy settings apply to.

▶ **IP Security Policies on Active Directory**—IP Security (IPSec) policies can be applied to the GPO of an Active Directory object to define when and where IPSec communication is allowed or required.

▶ **Advanced Audit Policy Configuration**—This node can be used to define more detailed and granular audit settings for use on Windows Server 2008 R2 and Windows 7 systems.

### Computer Configuration Administrative Templates Node

The Computer Configuration Administrative Templates node contains all of the Registry-based policy settings that apply to the Windows system. These settings are primarily used to control, configure, and secure how the Windows system is set up and how it can be used. This is not the same as the security settings configuration where specific users or groups are granted rights because the configuration settings available within the administrative templates apply to the system and all users who access the system. Many settings, however, are not applied to users who are members of the local administrators group of a system.

## User Configuration Policy Node

The User Configuration node contains settings used to configure and manage the user desktop environment on a Windows system. Unlike the computer configuration settings that define system settings and restrict what users can do on a particular system, the user configuration settings can customize the desktop experience for a user, including setting Start menu options, hiding or disabling Control Panel applets, redirecting folders to network shares, restricting write access to removable media, and much more. At the root of the User Configuration node are three policy nodes named the Software Settings node, the Windows Settings node, and the Administrative Templates node, but the settings contained within these nodes are different from the settings included in the Computer Configuration node, and in a domain group policy, these nodes are located beneath the User Configuration\Policies\ node.

### User Configuration Software Settings Node

The Software Settings node in the User Configuration section of a policy allows administrators to publish or assign software applications to individual users to which the policy applies. When a packaged software application is assigned to a user, it can be configured to be installed automatically at user logon or it can just be available in the Control Panel Programs applet for installation by the user the same as when it is published. When a packaged application is published to a user, it can be installed by that user by accessing the application in the following section of Control Panel:

▶ **Windows Server 2008 and Windows Server 2008 R2**—Control Panel, Get Programs

▶ **Windows Vista**—Control Panel, Programs, Get Programs and Features

▶ **Windows 7**—Control Panel, Programs, Get Programs

▶ **Windows XP**—Control Panel, Add or Remove Programs, Add New Programs

### User Configuration Windows Settings Node

The Windows Settings node in the User Configuration section of a policy allows administrators to configure logon scripts for users, configure folder redirection of user profile folders, define software restriction policies, automatically install and, if necessary, remove printers, and configure many Internet Explorer settings and defaults.

### User Configuration Administrative Templates Node

User Configuration Administrative Templates are the most commonly configured policy settings in domain group policy deployments. Settings contained within the User Configuration Administrative Templates node can be used to assist administrators with the automated configuration of a user's desktop environment. Of course now with domain group policy preferences, many of these newly available settings will also be highly used once Group Policy administrators begin to explore and find the best ways to use preference settings.

# Planning Workgroup and Standalone Local Group Policy Configuration

Many organizations deploy Windows servers and workstations in workgroup configurations and for these organizations, local group policies can play a vital role in simplifying Windows system administration. Some of the benefits of leveraging local group policies in workgroup deployments include, but are not limited to, the following:

▶ **Standardizing workgroup and image deployments**—Define the base local computer, Administrators, and Non-Administrators local policies on a machine that will be used as a template for a desktop or server image to reduce security exposure, improve standardization, and reduce user error when many systems are deployed.

▶ **Standardizing User Configuration settings**—The User Configuration section of the local computer policy can be configured to install specific printers for users, customize the Start menu and display settings, predefine settings for Windows programs such as Remote Desktop Connection, and much more. For the most part, however, the settings are standardized to give every user the same experience.

▶ **Preconfiguring policies for shared or public Windows systems**—Systems that are made available for public use or are utilized by several different users require more restrictive configurations to increase the security and reliability of the system. In these types of deployments, Windows administrators can configure tight security settings in the local computer policy, very restrictive settings in the non-administrators policy, and less restrictive settings in the administrators policy to allow for updates and management. Also, audit settings can be enabled to track logon/logoff, file and folder access, and much more.

▶ **Preconfiguring security updates and remote administration settings**—Windows systems that are deployed in workgroups can be difficult to remotely support and administer if the proper configurations are not created prior to deployment. Using the local computer policy, firewall rules can be created to allow for remote management, Remote Desktop can be enabled and enforced, and Windows Update settings can also be configured to enable automated security update installation and remote management options.

## Creating Local Administrators and Non-Administrators Policies

When a Windows system is first deployed, only the local computer group policy is created. Local group policies for administrators, nonadministrators, and individual local users need to be manually created if they are to be utilized. The process of creating the Administrators or Non-Administrators policy must be performed from the local machine using the Group Policy Object Editor. In the following example, create a local group policy for the Administrators group. To create a local user group policy for administrators, perform the following steps:

1. Log on to the Windows Server 2008 R2 system with an account with administrator privileges.

2. Click Start, click in the Search pane, type MMC, and press Enter.

3. When the Microsoft Management Console opens, click File from the menu bar, and select Add/Remove Snap-In.

4. In the Add or Remove Snap-Ins window, in the Available Snap-Ins pane on the left, scroll down and select the Group Policy Object Editor, and click the Add button.

5. The Select Group Policy Object window opens and defaults to the local computer policy. Click the Browse button to choose a different policy.

6. In the Browse for a Group Policy Object window, select the Users tab.

7. On the Users tab, each local user account will be listed as well as Administrators and Non-Administrators. Select Administrators and click OK, as shown in Figure 27.1.

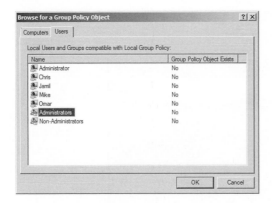

FIGURE 27.1    Selecting the local group policy for administrators.

8. Back in the Select Group Policy Object window, the Group Policy Object name should reflect Local Computer\Administrators. If the name matches, click Finish to return to the Add or Remove Snap-Ins window.

9. In the Add or Remove Snap-Ins window, click OK to complete adding snap-ins to this console window.

10. In the MMC window, the Local Computer\Administrators policy will be available for editing. Because this policy only applies to users in the Administrators group, only the User Configuration node is present.

11. Configure at least one setting in this policy to create it and close the MMC window when the configuration of the local user group policy for administrators is complete.

12. When prompted to save the console, click No and log off of the server.

13. Log back on to the server with an account with local Administrator rights.

14. Click Start, click in the Search pane, type cmd, and press Enter.

15. Type gpresult /h LGPO-Administrators.html and press Enter. The gpresult command with the /h option generates an HTML file that will be used to determine if the local user group policy for administrators has been applied. This option is only available on Windows Vista, Windows 7, Windows Server 2008, and Windows Server 2008 R2 systems, but the tool can be run against remote systems with the proper permissions and firewall settings configured.

16. After gpresult completes, in the command prompt type the name of the file created, in this example LGPO-Administrators.html, and press Enter.

17. The previous command will launch Internet Explorer; notice that the browser might require permission to allow the Active X content to load.

18. After allowing the Active X content and functionality, scroll down to the User Configuration Summary section and click on the Group Policy Objects link.

19. Click on Applied GPOs and Denied GPOs to reveal which policies were applied to the user, as shown in Figure 27.2.

27

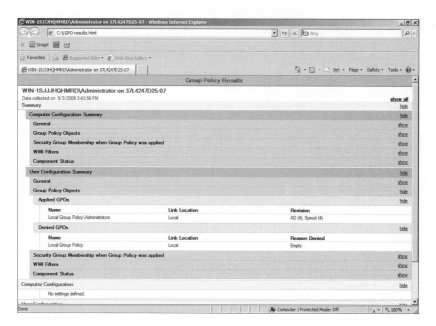

FIGURE 27.2    Verifying GPO application using the `gpresult` HTML report.

**20.** Review the HTML report and when finished, close Internet Explorer and log off.

The same procedure can be used to create local group policies for nonadministrators or individual local user accounts.

# Planning Domain Group Policy Objects

Group Policy Objects (GPOs) can be used to perform many functions across a diverse or standard computer and network infrastructure built on Microsoft Windows and Active Directory Domain Services. Considering how to best utilize group policies to manage any one particular environment and deciding on which GPO settings to leverage can be a lengthy process. To simplify this process and to keep from rethinking GPO usage each time, a base set of GPOs should be created and stored as starter GPOs.

A starter GPO is a feature of the Group Policy infrastructure that first became available with the release of the Windows Server 2008 Group Policy Management Console. A starter GPO can contain a set of Group Policy administrative template settings that have been preconfigured or defined to meet an organization's security and/or configuration requirements. When a new GPO is created, a starter GPO can be leveraged to prepopulate the defined settings into the new GPO. The benefit is that each time a GPO is needed, it does not have to be created from scratch and the administrator does not need to search for each of the settings that are necessary to meet the specific object of the new GPO. Windows Server 2008 R2 provides several starter GPOs for Windows XP and Windows Vista systems that have been created to provide preconfigured security settings to meet the best-practice recommendations outlined in the Windows Vista and Windows XP security guides. For more information on starter GPOs, refer to Chapter 19. The remainder of this section outlines common scenarios for GPO usage to assist administrators with the planning, deployment, and configuration of GPOs across an organization's Active Directory infrastructure.

## Policies and Preferences

Windows 2008 Group Policy introduced a brand-new set of configurable settings known as Preferences. Group Policy Objects are now organized into Policy settings and Preference settings, as shown in Figure 27.3. Preferences provide many of the features that the Group Policy infrastructure was lacking in previous versions, and preferences also provide many functions that were commonly handled with complex logon and startup scripts, with Registry file import tasks, and by administrators configuring the default user profile on workstations and servers. Many preference settings, such as Registry keys and Drive Maps, would have previously been applied with scripts that required the workstation to be logged on to or started up on the internal network. With preference settings in domain group policies, these settings can now be applied during the Group Policy refresh interval, which can greatly increase the successful application of these types of settings.

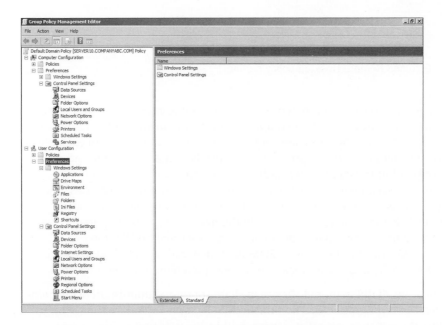

FIGURE 27.3   Group Policy User Configuration Preferences.

Policy settings and Preference settings have different characteristics. Policy settings are enforced and all users are commonly restricted from changing any configured policy setting. If a policy setting contains a graphic interface, when configured, the setting is normally grayed out to the end user, as shown in Figure 27.4 for the policy-configured

Remote Desktop settings. Policy settings such as software installations and computer or user scripts are only processed during computer startup or shutdown and user logon and logoff cycles.

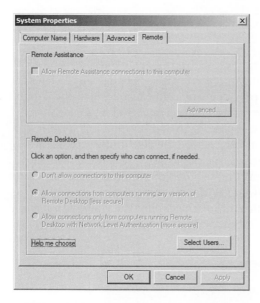

FIGURE 27.4   Enforced Remote Desktop policy setting.

Preference settings are applied to computers and users the same as policy settings: during startup, shutdown, and refresh cycles for computers and logon, logoff, and refresh cycles for users. Preferences settings, however, are configured but not enforced. As an example of this, using a user printer preference, a printer can be installed in a user profile and set to be the default printer but the end user will still retain the ability to define a different default printer if necessary. Preference settings are applied during refresh intervals, but certain settings, such as creating Registry keys and values, might require a computer reboot or user logoff/logon cycle to actually apply the new setting. One important point to note is that the domain group policy preferences are supported on Windows 7, Windows Server 2008, and Windows Server 2008 R2, but Windows XP, Windows Server 2003, and Windows Vista all need an update to support preference settings.

Preference settings are all different, but they each share common administrative functionality. Each preference setting will either be presented in a graphic interface similar to, if not exactly, what the end user can see and access within the user profile. This is one distinction between preference and policy settings, as most policy settings are enabled, disabled, or not configured whereas a preference setting can contain several configuration features. Furthermore, each preference settings can have multiple items defined within it, each with a separate configuration value. As an example, a Drive Map preference can have a setting item of a mapped drive P and a mapped drive U defined within the single domain group policy preference setting.

In addition to the specific setting options that are unique to each preference, such as the drive letter designation for a Drive Map or a folder path to a Network Share preference, each setting also contains a set of common options and many also include a preference action.

### Preference Actions

Preference actions determine how a preference setting will be applied to a user or computer. Many preference settings also contain an option called the preference action. The most common preference actions include the Create, Replace, Update, and Delete actions:

▶ **Create**—The Create action creates or configures the preference setting if the setting does not already exist. If the setting already exists, no action is taken.

▶ **Replace**—The Replace action deletes and recreates the setting on the computer or within the user profile.

▶ **Update**—The Update action creates the setting if it does not exist, but if the setting already exists, part or all of the setting configurations are updated to match the preference setting. Update is the default action and is less intrusive than the Replace action. It can be used to ensure that the setting is configured as desired, but processing speed will be optimized because if the setting already matches it will be skipped.

▶ **Delete**—The Delete action simply deletes the preference setting from the computer or user profile. For example, a Delete action can remove a mapped drive, delete a Registry key, or delete a printer from a computer or a user profile.

### Preference Common Options

Each preference setting contains a common tab that contains several options that can be enabled for the particular setting. A list of the common options is shown in Figure 27.5. Common options include the ability to process the setting only once, which is great for setting default configurations for new user profiles or a new preference setting on existing domain group policies.

### Item-Level Targeting

One of the most functional preference common options is the item-level targeting option. Item-level targeting allows administrators to define the scope of application for a particular preference setting item such as a Drive Map. So with item-level targeting an administrator can create a single domain group policy and have a single Drive Map preference defined that will apply different preference setting items to subsets of computers or users based on the specifications of the item-level target. For example, a Drive Map preference that defined the G drive for groups can be configured to map \\server10\Sales to members of the domain security group named sales, based on the item-level targeting option configuration settings. The same preference can also define the G drive to \\server10\HR for members of the domain Human Resources group based on a different configuration for item-level targeting.

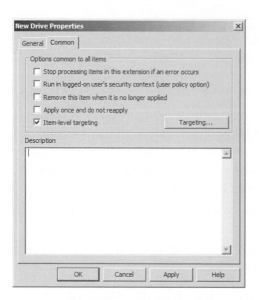

FIGURE 27.5   Group policy preference common options.

## Domain GPOs

When an Active Directory domain is deployed, a default domain policy and a default domain controller policy are created. The default domain policy defines the password and account policies for all domain user accounts and local user accounts for domain member servers and workstations. A few additional settings are also defined within the default domain policy regarding the Encrypting File System, Kerberos authentication, and a few other network-related security settings.

As a best practice, the only changes that should be made to the default domain policy should be modifying the password and account policy settings and nothing else. Additional settings that are required at the domain level should be defined in separate policies linked to the domain. The settings configured on domain-linked GPOs will be applied to all computer and user accounts in the domain, including all domain controllers. Settings configured at the domain level should be deployed as default settings and not as organizational standards. For example, as a domain default, the organization might want to configure all computers to enable Windows Update and get updates from the Windows Software Update Services (WSUS) at headquarters and to configure a few default firewall exceptions to allow for remote administration from the IT department. Common default settings applied at the domain level, but not in the default domain policy, can include the following:

▶ Default screensaver settings

▶ Default Windows Update settings

▶ Default firewall profile and rule configurations

▶ Default Encrypting File System settings and recovery agent

- Trusted root certification authorities

- Certificate enrollment configurations

All Windows systems that are members of an Active Directory domain will inherit the user password and account policies from the domain and apply this policy to local accounts on these systems. In some cases, it might be necessary to leverage local user accounts on systems with a less-restrictive password policy to support a particular service or application. This task can be accomplished by adding a GPO at the organizational unit that defines a less-restrictive password and account lockout policy. This particular password and account lockout policy will only apply to local user accounts on the computers contained within the linked organizational unit. The only thing that will break this configuration is if the default domain policy is enforced. For more information on domain policy enforcement, refer to Chapter 19.

In situations when special or specific domain user accounts cannot adhere to the domain password policy, if the domain is operating in Windows Server 2008 or Windows Server 2008 R2 domain functional level, a fine-grained password policy can be created and applied to the necessary user accounts. Fine-grained password policies are new to Active Directory and are detailed later in this chapter in the section "Fine-Grained Password Policies."

## Domain Controller GPOs

When an Active Directory domain is deployed, a default domain controller policy is created. This is different from the default domain policy in many ways, but the most prevalent distinction is that this policy is applied to the domain controllers organizational unit and not the entire domain. The default domain controller policy only applies to objects in this organizational unit, which should contain all of domain controllers of the specific domain, and no other objects.

The domain controllers organizational unit inherits all policies linked to the domain and each domain controller also inherits any site-linked GPOs if any exist. These policies will be applied by the domain controllers and might not be desirable. As a best practice, to avoid impacting domain controller security and reliability, try to limit the configuration settings defined within domain-linked policies or specifically deny the application of these group policies to the enterprise domain controllers security group within each domain of the forest.

> **NOTE**
>
> Moving a domain controller out of the domain controllers organizational unit is not recommended as adverse effects could result, including compromising the security of the entire domain as well as breaking authentication and replication functionality.

The default domain controller policy defines user rights assignment settings for domain controller management as well as defines settings to control the security of network communication. Most organizations do not require any changes made to the default domain controller policy or any additional policies linked to the domain controllers organizational unit. Common settings applied at the domain controller organizational unit level can include the following:

- ▶ User rights assignment updates for domain controllers (commonly used for backup agent accounts)

- ▶ Restricted group policies for domain security groups

- ▶ Event Viewer settings

- ▶ Audit settings for domain controllers

- ▶ Domain controller–specific Windows Update settings

- ▶ Remote administration settings for domain controllers

## Active Directory Site GPOs

By default, no group policies are created for Active Directory sites. Policies linked to Active Directory sites will be applied to all computers that connect to the domain from the particular subnets associated with the site and, of course, the users who log on to these particular computers. If computers are moved to new sites, these computers will pick up and process any policies linked to the new site and none from the original site. For example, if an Active Directory site is created for the virtual private network (VPN), when a computer is connected to the corporate network using the VPN, any policies linked to the VPN site will be applied to the computer.

Site policies can be a very effective way to simplify administration of mobile users, but if used incorrectly, site policies can cause a lot of issues. For example, using site policies to deploy printers can simplify end-user management for visiting employees. On the other hand, installing software for all computers in a site or enforcing networking settings might impact mobile computers if these settings are not overwritten or restored when the user and the system return back to the main office or disconnect from the corporate network. Site GPOs are not commonly used, but when they are, some of the common settings can include the following:

- ▶ Wireless and Wired Network Policies

- ▶ Deployed Printers (User Configuration)

- ▶ Internet Explorer Proxy Configuration

## Small Business

Many small businesses run Windows Server systems and Active Directory domains. Unless these businesses run an edition of Small Business Server, most small business Active Directory infrastructures do not effectively leverage local or domain group policies using the default configuration. Many of these Active Directory deployments are flat and all computers and users remain in the default containers and only apply the default domain policy. For small businesses with limited IT resources and budget, aside from updating the password and account lockout settings in the default domain policy, there are a few GPO settings that can enhance management and reliability. Please keep in mind that the following small business group policies are not recommended for Small Business Server (SBS) or Essential Business Server (EBS) deployments, as SBS and EBS deploy a number of preconfigured policies that provide some of the features included in the following policies and much more.

Group Policy management for small businesses should be kept simple. The following list of recommendations should be considered for small business Group Policy configurations:

1. Review and, if necessary, adjust the password and account lockout policy in the default domain policy to match the requirements of the organization.

2. Create a new policy named Corporate Computer Policy and disable the User Configuration section of this policy. Within this policy, configure Windows Update settings, deploy network printers, enable remote administration, and configure firewall exceptions or rules to allow for proper communication between the servers and workstations on the network. If necessary, also configure Internet Explorer Security Zone settings. Link this policy to the domain.

3. Create a new policy named Corporate User Policy and disable the Computer Configuration section of this policy. Within this policy, configure user mapped drives, default screensaver settings, and, if necessary, lock down the desktop, Start menu, and Control Panel. In some cases, folder redirection configuration would also be recommended, but this is an advanced configuration and might not be feasible for small businesses. Link this policy to the domain.

4. Edit the default domain controller policy and configure the Windows Update settings to download and notify the administrator when updates are ready. Many organizations configure Windows Update on workstations to autoinstall and autoreboot, but on a domain controller (or any server for that matter), this might be risky. For a small business, allowing for autoinstall and autoreboot might present more of a risk than having a tech regularly perform a manual update task.

## Delegated Administration

Delegating administration to perform Active Directory functions is becoming a very common task in medium- and large-size organizations. Delegation tasks, such as allowing the telecom group to update telephone numbers for all Active Directory user accounts or allowing help desk staff to unlock user accounts and reset user passwords, are simple to implement using the Active Directory Users and Computers snap-in. To configure delegation of Active Directory objects such as user accounts, security and distribution groups, and computer objects, this task is not best handled with domain policies. Instead, these delegation tasks are handled by configuring security permissions at the domain level, organizational unit level, or on the particular object itself. One way to simplify or clarify this concept is to remember that if the task will be performed using the Active Directory Users and Computers snap-in, this is delegated by configuring security permissions on a container or object. If the task would normally be performed by logging on to a computer and configuring settings or configuring the profile of a user or group of users, most functions related to this type of task can be performed using domain policies.

Group Policy Objects are, in fact, Active Directory objects and delegating Group Policy administration rights is also performed by configuring security access on Active Directory containers, such as domains and organizational units. Group Policy management includes several tasks, which can be delegated in the following configurations:

▶ **New domain group policy creation**—This is performed by adding the user account or security group to the domain Group Policy Creator Owners security group or delegating this right using the Group Policy Management Console (GPMC) at the Group Policy Objects container. Although delegating this right allows the user to create new policies, this user or group is not granted the right to edit settings or modify security on existing GPOs.

▶ **Edit settings on an existing GPO**—After a GPO is created, the right to edit that particular GPO can be delegated using the GPMC.

▶ **Edit settings, modify security, and delete a GPO**—These tasks are delegated using the GPMC on a single GPO at a time. The Modify security right allows the designated user to change the security filtering, basically defining which users and computer objects will apply the policy if these objects are in containers linked to that particular GPO.

▶ **Link existing GPOs**—The ability to link GPOs to Active Directory containers is performed by editing the security settings on the particular Active Directory site, domain, or OU. This is known as the Manage Group Policy Links security right.

▶ **Create and edit WMI filters**—The right to create new WMI filters or have full control over all WMI filters in a domain can be delegated at the WMI Filters container using the GPMC. Also, the right to edit or grant full control over an existing WMI filter can be delegated to a user or group. Delegating the right to edit or to grant full control does not enable linking WMI filters to GPOs as that requires edit rights permissions on a particular GPO.

▶ **Perform GPO modeling using GPMC**—GPO modeling delegation is performed by editing the security settings on the particular Active Directory site, domain, or OU. This task allows a designated user the ability to perform dry runs or simulated tests to determine the results of linking a policy to a particular container or moving a user or computer object to a different container in Active Directory. This is also known as the Generate Resultant Set of Policy (Planning) security right. If the user running GPMC is not running GPMC on the domain controller, the user needs to be added to the domain's Distributed COM Users security group to run Group Policy Modeling from another system.

▶ **Perform GPO results using GPMC**—This task can be performed on local machines if the user is a local administrator and the GPMC is installed. It can also be run by using the GPresult.exe from the command line or by loading the rsop.msc Microsoft Management Console snap-in. By default, local administrators can run this tool against all users on a machine. To delegate this right in Active Directory, edit the security settings on the particular Active Directory domain or OU that contains the computer and user accounts. This task allows the user to remotely connect to the computer to query the Group Policy logs to generate a historical report of previously logged Group Policy processing events. This is also known as the Generate Resultant Set of Policy (Logging) security right. To run this task against a remote computer, aside from having this right in Active Directory, the user also needs to be a member of the computer's local Distributed COM Users security group, or the domain group if running modeling or results against a domain controller. Additional configuration might also include possible firewall policy changes on the required computers to enable the remote administration firewall exception.

# Managing Computers with Domain Policies

Managing the configuration and settings of domain servers and workstations can be standardized using domain group policies. Domain group policies offer the advantage of taking user error and mistakes out of the loop by pushing out the configuration and security of computers from a single or a set of group policies. Of course, with this much control it is essential that group policies are tested and tested again to verify that the correct configuration and desired results are achieved with the policies. In the early days of Active Directory domain based group policies, a few organizations, which will go unnamed in this book, found themselves locked out of their own computers and Active Directory domain controllers because of overrestrictive Group Policy security settings and application of these settings to all computers and users, including the domain administrators. When this situation occurs, a domain controller can be rebooted into Directory Services Restore mode and an authoritative restore of Active Directory might be required.

Before domain group policies can be created and managed, the Group Policy Management Console needs to be installed. Also, if printers will be installed using the Deploy Printer function of Group Policy, the Print Services Tools should also be installed. To install the GPMC and Print Services Tools, perform the following steps:

1. Log on to a designated administrative system running Windows Server 2008 R2.
2. Open Server Manager from the Administrative Tools menu.
3. After Server Manager loads, click on the Features node in the tree pane.
4. Select Add Features in the right pane.
5. Scroll down and check the box next to Group Policy Management.
6. Expand Remote Server Administration Tools and expand Role Administration Tools.
7. Check the box next to Print and Document Services Tools and click Next.
8. Confirm the selection and click Install to begin the process.
9. After the process completes, click Close to complete the installation.

## Creating a New Domain Group Policy Object

To create a new domain Group Policy Object, perform the following steps:

1. Log on to a designated Windows Server 2008 R2 administrative server.
2. Click Start, click All Programs, click Administrative Tools, and click on Group Policy Management.

3. If necessary, expand the forest node, the domains node, and the correct domain.

4. Right-click the Group Policy Objects container, and select New.

5. Type in a name for the new GPO.

6. If the starter GPO functionality in the domain is enabled and if a suitable starter GPO exists, click the Source Starter GPO drop-down list arrow, and select either (None) or the desired starter GPO.

7. Click OK to create the GPO. In the tree pane of the Group Policy Management Console window, expand the Group Policy Objects container to reveal the newly created GPO.

8. After the GPO is created, it can be edited by right-clicking on the GPO and selecting Edit.

9. Close the Group Policy Management Console and log off of the server.

## Creating and Configuring GPO Links

After a GPO is created and configured, the next step is to link the GPOs to the desired Active Directory containers. To link an existing GPO to an Active Directory container, perform the following steps:

1. Log on to a designated Windows Server 2008 R2 administrative server.

2. Click Start, click All Programs, click Administrative Tools, and click on Group Policy Management.

3. Add the necessary domains or sites to the GPMC as required.

4. Expand the Domains or Sites node to expose the container to which the GPO will be linked.

5. Right-click the desired site, domain, or organizational unit, and select Link an Existing GPO.

6. In the Select GPO window, select the desired domain and GPO, and click OK to link it.

## Managing User Account Control Settings

Windows 7, Windows Vista, Windows Server 2008, and Windows Server 2008 R2 contain a security feature called User Account Control (UAC). UAC was created primarily to reduce or prevent unauthorized changes to the operating system configuration or file system. UAC interacts with both nonadministrators and administrators in their desktop environment and runs almost all applications in Standard User mode. When an administrator, regular user, or application attempts to perform an action that can result in a system configuration change or require access to sensitive areas of the operating system or file system, UAC interrupts the change and prompts for authorization or credentials to validate the change or requested access or elevation desired by the end user.

UAC settings are pretty flexible in allowing applications to run as desired but can require some tuning on the part of the desktop administrator. Many independent software vendors have been able to produce applications that can interact with UAC but in some cases where functionality or usability of a PC is impacted by UAC, some administrators or organizations may decide to disable UAC completely or just certain UAC settings to optimize the user experience. For situations when UAC is causing undesired issues with applications, if adjusting file security, user rights assignments, or running applications in legacy XP mode do not work, it might be necessary to adjust or disable User Account Control settings. The likely candidates are applications that formerly required the end user to be a member of the local Power Users or Administrators group. UAC settings should not adversely affect the functionality and operation of standard users. On the contrary, UAC actually allows standard users to be prompted for credentials to allow elevation of rights to install software or components that would have failed with previous operating systems with an Access Denied message. If, for some reason, the end user requires local administrator rights to run a legacy application and all other options have failed, then changing UAC security settings in a local computer policy or domain group policy object is required. When UAC security setting changes are required, perform the following steps:

1. Log on to a designated Windows Server 2008 R2 administrative server.

2. Open the Group Policy Management Console from the Administrative Tools menu.

3. Add the necessary domains to the GPMC as required.

4. Expand the Domains node to reveal the Group Policy Objects container.

5. Either create a new GPO or edit an existing GPO.

6. After the GPO is opened for editing in the Group Policy Management Editor, expand the Computer Configuration node, expand the Policies node, select the Windows Settings node, and expand it.

7. Expand the Security Settings node, expand Local Policies, and select Security Options.

8. In the Settings pane, scroll to the bottom of the pane to locate the UAC settings. The following list displays the default UAC settings in the Local Computer Policy for Windows Server 2008 R2:

   ▶ **Admin Approval Mode for the Built-In Administrator Account**—Disabled

   ▶ **Allow UIAccess Applications to Prompt for Elevation Without Using the Secure Desktop**—Disabled

   ▶ **Behavior of the Elevation Prompt for Administrators in Admin Approval Mode**—Prompt for consent for non-Windows binaries

   ▶ **Behavior of the Elevation Prompt for Standard Users**—Prompt for credentials

   ▶ **Detect Application Installations and Prompt for Elevation**—Enabled

   ▶ **Only Elevate Executables That Are Signed and Validated**—Disabled

   ▶ **Only Elevate UIAccess Applications That Are Installed in Secure Locations**—Enabled

   ▶ **Run All Administrators in Admin Approval Mode**—Enabled

   ▶ **Switch to the Secure Desktop When Prompting for Elevation**—Enabled

27

> ▶ **Virtualize File and Registry Write Failures to Per-User Locations—** Enabled

9. To disable all UAC functionality using domain policies, create and link a new GPO for UAC and edit the setting named Run All Administrators in Admin Approval Mode, and configure the setting value to Disabled. If this setting is configured as Disabled, all other UAC settings are ignored. Also, this setting change will be applied during startup, shutdown, and background refresh, but a reboot will be required to complete the setting change.

10. To disable UAC prompts when logged on with an account with Local Administrator rights and leave all other settings functional, using domain policies, create and link a new GPO for UAC and edit the setting named Behavior of the Elevation Prompt for Administrators in Admin Approval Mode, and configure the setting value to Elevate Without Prompting, as shown in Figure 27.6. Click OK to save the setting and close the Group Policy Management Editor window.

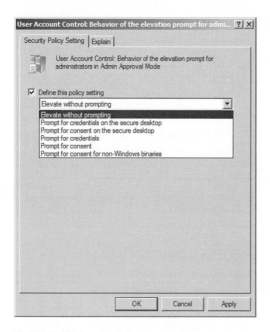

FIGURE 27.6    Configuring User Account Control to allow administrators to elevate privileges without prompting.

11. After the GPO is configured as desired, save the GPO and link it to an organizational unit that has a test Windows Vista, Windows 7,Windows Server 2008, or Windows Server 2008 R2 system to verify that the desired functionality has been achieved.

12. After the testing is completed, configure security filtering and possibly also WMI filtering to limit the application scope of this policy and link it to the desired organizational unit(s).

## Creating a Software Restriction Policy

Many business owners and organizations want to ensure that their employees are as productive as possible. This might require restricting users from playing computer games and surfing the Internet, or just providing a highly reliable computer system. Due to the restrictive nature of previous Windows operating systems and poor development practices by software vendors and independent programmers, many applications also required end users to have local administrator rights. When local users have the ability, through administrative group membership or reduced file system security, to perform administrative tasks, it can be helpful to implement software restriction policies to prevent users from running undesired programs that might impact system configuration and reliability. One important point to note about software restriction policies is that even after the policy is applied, the system will need to be rebooted before the new policy settings are applied. For example, restricting access to a certain Registry path, Registry editor, or any particular executable application can reduce undesired system configuration changes. Group Policy contains very specific Microsoft Management Console policy settings, but for undefined or standard built-in utilities and applications, it might be necessary to define and enforce a specific software restriction policy.

> **NOTE**
>
> For Windows 7 and Windows Server 2008 R2 only, new settings within domain policies named "application control policies" replace software restriction policies and this is discussed in the next section. Although software restriction policies will be processed and applied to Windows 7 and Windows Server 2008 R2 systems, it is recommended to use AppLocker on these systems and software restriction policies for all older operating systems.

To create a software restriction policy for a computer using a domain group policy, perform the following steps:

1. Log on to a designated Windows Server 2008 R2 administrative server.
2. Open the Group Policy Management Console from the Administrative Tools menu.
3. Add the necessary domains to the GPMC as required.
4. Expand the Domains node to reveal the Group Policy Objects container.
5. Either create a new GPO or edit an existing GPO.
6. After the GPO is opened for editing in the Group Policy Management Editor, expand the Computer Configuration node, expand the Policies node, expand the Windows Settings node, and select the Security Settings node.
7. Expand the Security Settings node, and select Software Restriction Policies.
8. Right-click on the Software Restriction Policies node in the tree pane, and select New Software Restriction Policies.

27

9. After the previous task is completed, two subordinate policy setting nodes are created as well as three settings. In the Settings pane, double-click the Enforcement setting to open the properties of that setting.

10. In the Enforcement Properties dialog box, define whether this software restriction policy should apply to all users or if local administrators should be excluded from the policy, as shown in Figure 27.7. Click OK when finished.

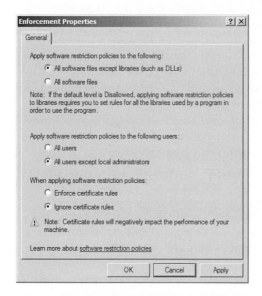

FIGURE 27.7    Excluding local administrators from the software restriction policies.

11. Open the Security Levels settings node to reveal the three default levels of Disallowed, Basic User, or Unrestricted. The default configuration is the Unrestricted security level, which defines that all software will run based on the access rights of the user. If this is acceptable, do not make any changes; otherwise, select the desired security level, right-click the level, and select Set as Default.

12. Regardless of which security level was selected as the default, additional rules will most likely need to be defined to block or allow access. For this example, the ability to block access to the Remote Desktop Connection client is outlined. Right-click on the Additional Rules node in the tree pane beneath Software Restriction Policies, and select New Hash Rule.

13. When the New Hash Rule window opens, click the Browse button to locate the desired file. For this example, the filename is mstsc.exe and is located in the c:\windows\system32 folder. After the file is located, select it and click Open to add it to the hash rule.

**14.** Select the desired security level of Disallowed for this particular file, and then click OK to complete the creation of the new hash rule, as shown in Figure 27.8.

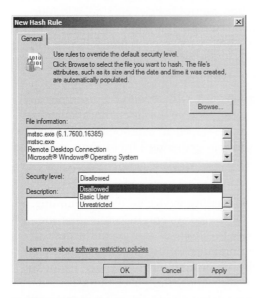

FIGURE 27.8    Configuring the security level for a software restriction hash rule.

**15.** The file properties will be used to generate the hash rule and will be added to the Additional Rules, and this completes the software restriction policy for this exercise. Close the Group Policy Management Editor window.

> **NOTE**
>
> A hash rule uses the filename and the file's specific properties when the rule is created. If a specific application or file needs to be restricted with a hash rule, each version of that file stored on the computer's operating system should be added to the policy because different versions of the same file will exist in client and server operating systems and in different service pack levels.

**16.** Back in the Group Policy Management Console, link the new software restriction GPO to an OU with a computer that can be used to test the policy.

**17.** Log on to a test system that the new policy has been applied to, reboot the system, and verify that the software restriction policy is working by attempting to launch the Remote Desktop client on the test system.

**18.** If the policy is working as desired, the user will receive a message stating that the program is blocked by Group Policy.

27

## Creating Application Control Policies (AppLocker)

Application control policies are new for Windows 7 Enterprise and Ultimate Editions and all editions of Windows Server 2008 R2. Application control policies are similar in function to software restriction policies but they should not be deployed in the same policy that has software restriction policies defined. As a best practice, configure policies with application control policies to be processed by machines only running Windows 7 Enterprise and Ultimate operating systems and/or Window Server 2008 R2 systems.

Application control policies or AppLocker, when enabled, will not allow users to run any executables except those defined as allowed. This can, of course, cause serious functionality issues if deployed improperly, so Microsoft has developed an audit-only mode that can be used to test a policy with AppLocker settings to start gathering a list of applications end users need to run to perform their job.

Before AppLocker policies can function and be applied to the desired Windows 7 and Windows Server 2008 R2 systems, the Application Identity service needs to be running. This service can be set to automatic startup on the desired systems by configuring and applying domain policies. To configure this service to automatic startup on the desired systems, create a new domain policy and in the Computer Configuration node beneath Windows Settings and System Services, locate the Application Identity service, define the policy setting, and set the startup mode to Automatic. Apply this policy to the desired systems but understand that the service, even when set to automatic, will not start until the next reboot or until the service is started by a local user, through a remote management console or script, or through the use of a scheduled or immediate task, which is discussed later in this chapter.

To configure AppLocker settings, perform the following steps:

1. Log on to a designated Windows Server 2008 R2 administrative server.

2. Open the Group Policy Management Console from the Administrative Tools menu.

3. Add the necessary domains to the GPMC as required.

4. Expand the Domains node to reveal the Group Policy Objects container.

5. Either create a new GPO or edit an existing GPO.

6. After the GPO is opened for editing in the Group Policy Management Editor, expand the Computer Configuration node, expand the Policies node, expand the Windows Settings node, and select the Security Settings node.

7. Expand the Security Settings node and select application control policies.

8. Expand the application control policies node and select AppLocker.

9. In the Settings pane, click on the Configure Rule Enforcement link in the center of the page.

10. In the AppLocker Properties window, check the three check boxes for Executable Rules, Windows Installer Rules, and Script Rules, select the Audit Only option from the pull-down menus, as shown in Figure 27.9, and click OK to define the rule enforcement properties.

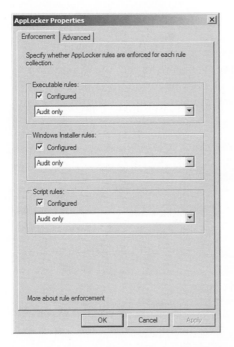

FIGURE 27.9    Configuring the AppLocker enforcement rules to audit only.

11. Now before any auditing can be logged, new rules will need to be created. For this example, right-click on the Executable Rules node beneath AppLocker and select Create New Rule.

12. On the Permissions page, set the Action to Deny and leave the default group of Everyone, and then click Next to continue.

13. On the Conditions page, select the Path option button to define a folder path that will contain executables to which we want to prevent access, and click Next to continue.

14. On the Path page, type in %ProgramFiles%\* and click Create to define the rule. This defines the c:\Program Files folder as an example.

15. Once this is completed, save the domain policy and link it to an organizational unit that contains Windows 7 Enterprise or Ultimate or Windows Server 2008 R2 systems.

16. Log on to the desired test system, verify that the new AppLocker policy has been applied and that the Application Identity service is set to automatic and is running on the desired machine. Reboot the machine.

17. Log back on to the test machine and run Internet Explorer or any other executable that is located beneath the c:\Program Files folder.

18. Now open the Event Viewer console using an elevated account so the audit events can be reviewed.

19. In the Event Viewer window, expand Applications and Services Logs, expand Microsoft, and expand AppLocker.

20. Select the EXE and DLL log and in the Settings pane, verify that warning events are logged, as shown in Figure 27.10. If no warning events are logged, the Application Identity service might not be running and/or a reboot might not have been performed after the initial AppLocker policy was applied.

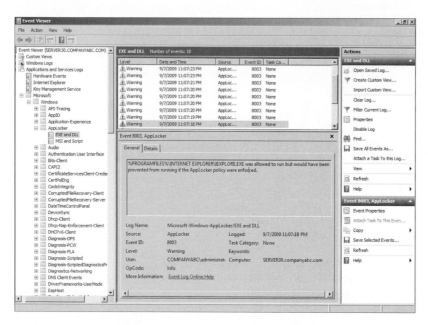

FIGURE 27.10    Viewing AppLocker EXE and DLL event log audit events.

21. Close the event log on the test machine to complete this exercise.

AppLocker rules are applied to the computer object only but unlike software restriction policies, AppLocker rules applied to a computer can be defined or configured to apply on a per-user or per-security group basis. Using software restriction policies, this functionality would apply to all users who log on to the system based on the enforcement settings. AppLocker will block all executables, Windows Installer files, and scripts once each of those rules are enforced. Under each of the rules nodes beneath AppLocker in the tree pane, policy administrators can use the built-in function of creating rules based on a wizard and by creating the default rules. The default executable rules, as an example, once created will define that everyone can run executables in the Program Files and Windows folders, including all subfolders, but only administrators can run executables without path restrictions. To create or populate the default rules for executables, in the tree pane under

AppLocker, expand AppLocker and right-click on the Executable Rules node and click Create Default Rules. This generates the three rules described previously.

## Deploying Printers

Starting with Windows Server 2003 R2 edition, and the release of the Print Management console, Windows administrators are now able to easily deploy printers to multiple computers and users using domain policies. Printers can be deployed to computers and/or users and when a printer is removed from a deployed printer domain policy, it is also removed from the computer or user profile during the next startup or logon cycle. Of course, this means that this setting also requires the Windows XP and Windows Vista systems to wait for the network to start before running this policy because the printer is deployed using Group Policy settings as well as a startup or logon script. Also it must be noted that simply removing the policy does not remove the printer.

Deploying a printer using domain policies can be performed by using the GPMC on a Windows Server 2008 R2 system that also has the Print Services Tools installed. Deploying printers with group policies can also be performed using the Print Management console, which is one of the Print Services Tools, and using this tool actually provides more functionality during printer deployment. Because of the added functionality, the recommended deployment method for Group Policy deployed printers is to use the Print Management console. To deploy a printer to a computer using Group Policy, perform the following steps:

1. Log on to a designated Windows Server 2008 R2 administrative server.

2. If necessary, install the Group Policy Management Console and Print Services Tools features on the system, as detailed previously in this chapter and in Chapter 19.

3. After the tools are installed, click Start, click All Programs, click Administrative Tools, and select Print Management.

4. In the tree pane, expand the Print Servers node to reveal domain print servers. If no servers are listed, right-click the Print Servers node and select Add/Remove Servers. Browse to find a print server or type the server name, click Add to List, and then click OK to return to the Print Management console.

5. After a print server is added, expand the server and select the Printers node in the tree pane. If no printers are listed in the Printers pane, a printer must be installed. Please refer to the Print Management console Help file if assistance with printer installation is required.

6. In the Printers pane, right-click a desired printer, and select Deploy with Group Policy.

7. When the Deploy with Group Policy window opens, click the Browse button to locate the group policy that will contain the deployed printer settings.

8. When the Browse for a Group Policy Object window opens, select the All tab and select the desired group policy. To create a new GPO for this task, select the Create a New Group Policy Object icon near the upper right of the window.

27

9. The new group policy will be created with the default name of New Group Policy Object; right-click the policy and rename it to DeployPrinterGPO. Select the renamed policy, and click OK to return to the Deploy with Group Policy window.

10. Back in the Deploy with Group Policy window, check the "The Computers That This GPO Applies to (per Machine)" check box, and click the Add button to load the printer into the policy, as shown in Figure 27.11.

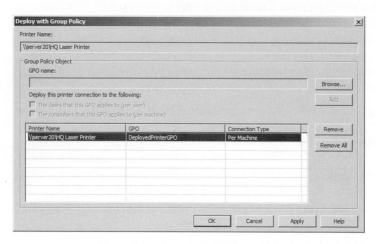

FIGURE 27.11    Configuring the printers for GPO computer deployment.

11. Click OK to apply the changes. A window opens to display the results of the printer deployment. Click OK if the operation succeeded; otherwise, click the Details button to review the log for possible errors.

12. Click OK again to close the Deploy with Group Policy window and return to the Print Management console.

13. In the tree pane, select the Deployed Printers node and verify in the Printers pane that the printer is now listed.

14. Close the Print Management console.

15. Open the Group Policy Management Console and locate the new GPO and link it to the domain, site, or organizational unit that contains the desired computers this policy will apply to.

---

**NOTE**

Only Windows Vista, Windows 7, Windows Server 2008, and Windows Server 2008 R2 are capable of adding printers through policies using built-in functionality. Older operating systems must use startup scripts for computers or logon scripts for users and must run the pushprinterconnections.exe utility from a Windows Server 2008 system.

To support deployed printer domain policies for systems other than Windows Vista, Windows 7, Windows Server 2008, and Windows Server 2008 R2, perform these additional steps:

1. On a Windows Server 2008 NOT R2 system, open Windows Explorer and browse to the c:\Windows\System32 folder.

2. Locate the pushprinterconnections.exe file and copy it to the Clipboard.

3. Browse to the domain Netlogon share in the Windows Explorer window. For this example, it will be \\companyabc.com\Netlogon. Paste the pushprinterconnections.exe file into this share and close the Windows Explorer window.

4. Open the Group Policy Management Console.

5. Expand the domain and expand the Group Policy Objects container.

6. Select the DeployPrintersGPO policy and open it for editing.

7. Expand the Computer Configuration node, expand the Policies node, and expand the Windows Settings node.

8. Select the Scripts (Startup/Shutdown) node, and in the Settings pane double-click the Startup setting.

9. In the Startup Properties window, click the Add button. In the Add a Script window that opens, click the Browse button to search for the file.

10. In the Browse window, browse to the \\companyabc.com\netlogon share, select the pushprinterconnections.exe file, and click Open.

11. Back in the Browse window, leave the script parameters blank, verify the path and executable name are correct, and click OK.

12. Click OK again to close the Startup Script Properties window, and close the Group Policy Management Editor also.

13. Back in the Group Policy Management Console, link the DeployPrinterGPO to a test OU that contains a computer on which the printer can be installed.

14. Reboot the computer to which the DeployPrinterGPO applies.

15. After reboot, log on and verify that the printer was successfully installed. If the printer was not installed, the system might require an additional reboot or Synchronous Foreground Group Policy Processing might need to be enabled.

16. After the GPO testing is complete, log back on to the Windows Server 2008 R2 system, open the GPMC, and link the DeployPrinterGPO to the necessary OUs.

Deploying printers using GPOs to users follows mostly the same process; except when deploying the printer, the check box to deploy in the user section should be checked and instead of a computer startup script a user logon script should be defined. Deploying printers using GPOs for computers or users simplifies the installation and removal of printers but does not set the default printer if multiple printers are installed on the computer or in the user profile. Setting the default printer should be performed by the

27

end user, or the new Printer settings available in the User Configuration Preferences node can be used to install and set the default printer.

## Mapping Drives Using Preferences User Drive Maps Extension

Using the new Preferences User Drive Maps extension in domain policies, administrators can now map network drives for end users without scripts. To define a mapped drive for a user using the Preferences User Drive Maps extension in a domain policy, perform the following steps:

1. Log on to a designated Windows Server 2008 R2 administrative server.

2. If necessary, install the Group Policy Management Console on the system, as detailed previously in this chapter.

3. After the tools are installed, click Start, click All Programs, click Administrative Tools, and select Group Policy Management.

4. Add the necessary domains to the GPMC, as required.

5. Expand the Domains node to reveal the Group Policy Objects container.

6. Create a new GPO called UserDriveMapGPO.

7. Open the GPO for editing and, in the Group Policy Management Editor window, select and expand the User Configuration node in the tree pane.

8. In the tree pane, expand the Preferences node and the Windows Settings node.

9. Select the Drive Maps preference setting, right-click the setting and select New – Mapped Drive.

10. When the New Drive Properties window opens, select the Replace action from Actions pull-down menu.

11. Type in the location of the network share that will be mapped to a drive letter with this setting. For this example, we will use \\companyabc.com\UserFolders\Sales.

12. In the Drive Letter section, select the Use option button and select the desired drive letter by choosing it from the pull-down menu. For this example, select the S drive.

13. Check the Reconnect check box to reconnect the Drive Map, enter the Label as Sales, and click OK to complete the creation of the Drive Map setting item, as shown in Figure 27.12.

14. Close the Group Policy Management Editor.

15. In the Group Policy Management Console, link the GPO to the desired domain, site, or organizational unit that contains a user account for testing.

16. Test the new policy and when the policy delivers the desired results, create the necessary GPO links from the administrative server, close the Group Policy Management Console window, and log off of the server.

## Configuring Preference Item-Level Targeting

There are many instances in group policy deployments when an administrator desires to apply a particular preference setting to only a subset of computers or users. When this is the case, Preference Item-Level Targeting can be used. For example, a Group Policy admin-

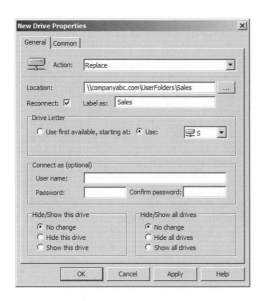

FIGURE 27.12    Configuring a new Drive Map GPO Preference item.

istrator can create a single domain policy named UserDriveMapGPO and leave the policy filtering set to authenticated users, and it can be linked to the domain. In this case, if a Drive Map preference is defined, all users in the domain will map the same drive. Now within this single policy, several Drive Maps can be created but each Drive Map can be applied to only specified users or security groups using item-level targeting with the Drive Map preference options. The following steps detail segmenting the application of a Drive Map setting to a security group using item-level targeting:

1. Log on to a designated Windows Server 2008 R2 administrative server used to create the UserDriveMapGPO, as detailed in the previous section.

2. Click Start, All Programs, Administrative Tools, and select Group Policy Management.

3. Add the necessary domains to the GPMC, as required.

4. Expand the Domains node to reveal the Group Policy Objects container.

5. Select the UserDriveMapGPO and open it for editing.

6. In the Group Policy Management Editor window, select and expand the User Configuration node in the tree pane, and expand the Preferences node and Windows Settings node.

7. Select the Drive Maps preference setting in the tree pane and locate the S drive map in the Settings pane that was previously created.

8. Right-click the S drive map and select Properties.

9. Select the Common tab and check the Item-Level Targeting check box, as shown in Figure 27.13.

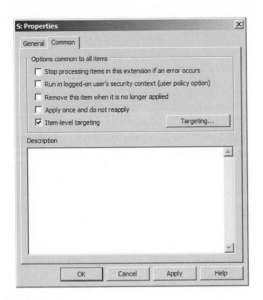

FIGURE 27.13    Enabling item-level targeting for a GPO Preference setting.

10. Click the Targeting button to open the Targeting Editor.

11. In the Targeting Editor window, click the arrow in the New Item pull-down menu to reveal each of the different options that can be used for item-level targeting and select Security Group.

12. When the security group item is added to the window, click the "..." button to locate and add a security group from the domain, as shown in Figure 27.14; for this example, it is the companyabc\sales security group.

13. Click OK when completed and close the Group Policy Management Editor.

14. Test the application of the policy on a test system with a test user account in the sales group to verify that the desired functionality is being delivered.

## Configuring Remote Desktop and Remote Administration Support

A common Group Policy request from IT administrators who need to support Windows XP, Windows Server 2003, Windows Vista, Windows 7, Windows Server 2008, and Windows Server 2008 R2 systems with the Windows Firewall enabled is to allow for remote administration. Group Policy can manage this task with minimal configuration. To enable Remote Desktop on Windows XP, Windows 2003, Windows Vista, or Windows Server 2008 systems, enable the Allow Users to Connect Remotely Using Remote Desktop Services setting. This setting is located in Computer Configuration\Policies\ Administrative Templates\Windows Components\Remote Desktop Session Host\ Connections node, as shown in Figure 27.15. When this GPO is saved and linked to a GPO with computers in it, all the computers will have Remote Desktop enabled. By default, only members of the Administrators group will be able to connect using

Remote Desktop. If this needs to be changed, additional users can be added to the local
Remote Desktop Users group.

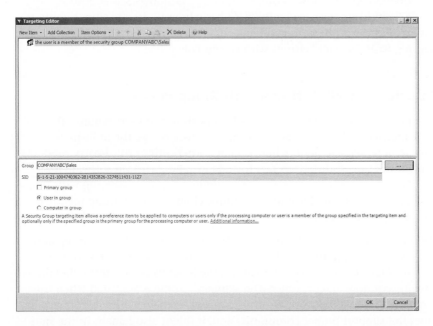

FIGURE 27.14    Specifying the companyabc\sales security group as an item-level target for a
GPO Preference setting.

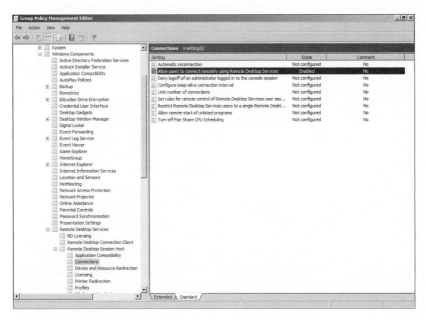

FIGURE 27.15    Enabling Remote Desktop using a GPO.

After Remote Desktop is enabled on a system, the firewall exceptions still need to be configured—otherwise, Remote Desktop is not possible. Remote Desktop is a built-in exception in the Windows XP, Windows Vista, Windows 7, Windows Server 2003, Windows Server 2008, and Windows Server 2008 R2 basic firewall. In addition, remote administration is a built-in exception; to configure these exceptions, see the following section, "Configuring Basic Firewall Settings with Group Policy."

## Configuring Basic Firewall Settings with Group Policy

In many organizations, part of the responsibility of supporting end users requires the ability to remotely manage the desktop. Many organizations leverage the built-in Windows tools for remote management, whereas many others utilize third-party products. Remote management tasks of workstations can include installing custom software for a particular user or group of users, manually running Windows Update, assisting with the installation of local printers, adding local user accounts, changing local group membership, or troubleshooting reported issues.

The Microsoft Windows Firewall includes multiple firewall profiles that contain separate firewall rules and firewall exceptions. Windows XP and Windows Server 2003 contain a domain and standard firewall profile. The domain profile is activated when the desktop is on the same network as a domain controller. The standard profile is activated when the desktop is on a remote or public network, or in many cases, if the machine is connected to a VPN that does not support proper communication, it might also remain in the standard firewall profile. Windows Vista, Windows 7, Windows Server 2008, and Windows Server 2008 R2 contain three firewall profiles, including the domain profile, the private profile, and the public profile. The domain profile remains the same, but the previous standard profile has now been segmented into the private and public profiles. Any network that is different from the domain network is initially categorized as an untrusted network and the public firewall profile is activated. End users, with the appropriate rights, can define a public network as a private network, which can then activate the private firewall profile and the appropriate firewall rule set, which is likely to be less restrictive and might allow the necessary traffic for the remote client to work correctly on the network they are connected to. Windows Firewall design and configuration planning is a very important task for Windows administrators to execute and should not be taken lightly. Also, disabling firewalls in any profile is not recommended and is a poor approach to enabling systems and applications to function on an organization's network.

To allow Windows administrators to continue to manage and administer Windows server and desktop systems remotely, certain firewall exceptions should be defined. Aside from enabling Remote Desktop, as outlined in the previous section, remote administrators might need to copy files to and from systems and utilize Microsoft Management Console snap-ins such as Windows Server Backup, Event Viewer, Computer Management, and many others from remote administrative workstations. To enable the Remote Desktop and Remote Administration exceptions in the Windows Firewall using domain group policies, perform the following steps:

1. Log on to a designated Windows Server 2008 R2 administrative server.

2. If necessary, install the Group Policy Management Console on the system, as detailed previously in this chapter.

3. After the tools are installed, click Start, click All Programs, click Administrative Tools, and select Group Policy Management.

4. Add the necessary domains to the GPMC as required.

5. Expand the Domains node to reveal the Group Policy Objects container.

6. Either create a new GPO or edit an existing GPO.

7. After the GPO is opened for editing in the Group Policy Management Editor, expand the Computer Configuration node, expand the Policies node, and select the Administrative Templates.

8. Expand the Administrative Templates node, expand the Network node, expand the Network Connections node, and select the Windows Firewall node. Configurations made in this section apply to Windows XP, Windows Vista, Windows 7, Windows Server 2003, Windows Server 2008, and Windows Server 2008 R2. However, for more granular firewall configuration for Windows Vista and later operating systems, the Windows Firewall with Advanced Security setting can be used.

9. In the tree pane, expand the Windows Firewall node to reveal the Domain Profile node, and select it.

10. In the Settings pane, locate the setting named Windows Firewall: Allow Inbound Remote Administration Exception, and double-click on it to open the setting for editing.

11. In the Setting window, click the Enabled option button, and type in the network from which inbound remote administration will be allowed. For this example, consider an organization that utilizes the 10.0.0.0 network with a subnet mask of 255.0.0.0. This would be defined as 10.0.0.0/8 in the properties of this exception, as shown in Figure 27.16. When finished, click OK to update the setting.

12. After the previous setting has been configured, back in the Settings pane, select the Windows Firewall: Allow Inbound Remote Desktop Exceptions, and double-click on it to open the setting for editing.

13. In the setting window, click the Enabled option button, and type in the network from which inbound Remote Desktop connections will be allowed. When finished, click OK to update the setting.

14. If necessary, repeat the process of configuring the inbound remote administration and Remote Desktop exception in the standard profile to ensure that remote management from the defined network will function regardless of which firewall profile is currently activated on the client.

27

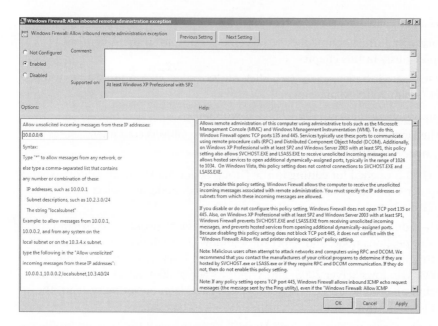

FIGURE 27.16    Enabling the Windows Firewall remote administration exception from the 10.0.0.0/8 network.

> **NOTE**
>
> If the network defined within a Windows Firewall exception is a common network, such as 192.168.0.0/24, the configuration of these exceptions in the standard profile is considered risky and should not be performed. Instead, work with the networking group and VPN configurations to ensure that when users connect remotely to the network from remote sites and through VPN connections, the system will always recognize and apply the domain profile.

15. Back in the GPMC, link the new remote administration firewall exception GPO to an OU with a computer that can be used to test the policy.

16. After the testing is completed, configure security filtering and possibly also WMI filtering to limit the application scope of this policy and link it to the desired organizational unit(s).

### Configuring Advanced Firewall Settings

Windows Vista, Windows 7, Windows Server 2008, and Windows Server 2008 R2 have a new and improved firewall that enables administrators to define granular inbound and outbound firewall rules and exceptions in the default firewall profiles. Even though the Windows Firewall is enabled and active by default on Windows Server 2008 R2, when the Add Roles Wizard is run and a role, role service, and/or feature is added to the Windows Server 2008 R2 system, the necessary firewall exceptions are also configured as part of the process. This is a major advantage compared with what was included in Windows Server 2003. However, be aware that when adding additional applications or services (that are not included with the product) to a Windows Server 2008 system, unless the installation of that product also has a built-in feature to enable and configure the necessary exceptions in the firewall, the exceptions will need to be defined and configured manually. When custom firewall rules, exceptions, and changes to the default behavior and configuration of the firewall profiles are required, the settings need to be defined using the Windows Firewall with Advanced Security console. If these settings need to be defined using a domain policy, access to these policy settings are included in the Computer Configuration\Policies\Windows Security\Security Settings\Windows Firewall with Advanced Security settings node. One advantage of using Windows Firewall with Advanced Security is that when a system is configured manually and all of the necessary exceptions and rules are defined within the firewall, these rules can be exported from the firewall and imported into a domain policy and applied from the central location to all of the desired servers. More information on the Windows Firewall is available in Chapter 13.

## Configuring Windows Update Settings

Many organizations utilize the Internet services provided by Microsoft known as Windows Update and Microsoft Update. The main difference between the two is that Microsoft Update also includes updates for other products such as Microsoft Office, Microsoft Exchange Server, Microsoft SQL Server, Microsoft Internet Security and Acceleration Server, and many more. Starting with Windows XP and Windows Server 2003, all Windows systems are now capable of downloading and automatically installing Windows updates out of the box. To upgrade the Windows Update client to support updates for other Microsoft applications through Microsoft Update, these machines might need to be upgraded manually, upgraded using a GPO software installation, or upgraded using Microsoft Windows Server Update Services (WSUS). A WSUS server can be configured to update the client software automatically, which is the preferred approach. Depending on whether the organization utilizes an internal WSUS server or wants to utilize the Windows/Microsoft Internet-based services to configure these settings using group policies, the settings are located in the following sections:

- ▶ Computer Configuration\Policies\Administrative Templates\Windows Components\Windows Update

- ▶ User Configuration\Policies\Administrative Templates\Windows Components\Windows Update

For more information and recommendations on best practices for configuring Windows Updates, please refer to the WSUS website located at www.microsoft.com/wsus and also located at http://technet.microsoft.com/wsus.

## Creating a Wireless Policy

Wireless networks are becoming more and more common in both public and private networks. Many organizations are choosing to deploy secure wireless networks to allow for flexible connections and communications for mobile users, vendors, and presentation rooms. As a best practice, organizations commonly deploy wireless networks as isolated network subnets with only Internet access or the ability to connect to the company network via VPN. As wireless networks become more sophisticated and secure, the configuration of a wireless network on an end user's machine becomes complicated. In an effort to simplify this task, wireless network configurations can be saved on USB drives and handed off to users to install and they can also be preconfigured and deployed to Windows systems using domain policies. Group Policy wireless policies can be created for Windows Vista or Windows XP compatible systems as each treats and configures wireless networks differently. Windows 7 and Windows Server 2008 systems will use the Windows Vista wireless policies. If defined in domain policies, these wireless network settings will only be used if no third-party wireless network management software is installed and activated on the desired systems.

Wireless networks are commonly unique to each physical location, and the GPO-configured wireless policies should be applied to systems in an Active Directory site or to a specific location-based organizational unit that contains the desired computer accounts. Furthermore, if the wireless policy GPO contains only Windows Vista workstations for the wireless policy, WMI filtering should be applied to the GPO so that only Windows Vista, Windows 7, and Windows Server 2008 systems process and apply the policy. To create a wireless network for a Windows Vista, Windows 7, and Windows Server 2008 system using a domain policy, perform the following steps:

1. Log on to a designated Windows Server 2008 R2 administrative server.

2. Click Start, click All Programs, click Administrative Tools, and select Group Policy Management.

3. Add the necessary domains to the GPMC as required.

4. Expand the Domains node to reveal the Group Policy Objects container.

5. Create a new GPO called WirelessPolicyGPO and open it for editing.

6. After the WirelessPolicyGPO is opened for editing in the Group Policy Management Editor, expand the Computer Configuration node, expand the Policies node and select Windows Settings.

7. Expand Windows Settings, expand Security Settings and select Wireless Network (IEEE 802.11) Policies.

8. Right-click Wireless Network (IEEE 802.11) Policies and select Create a New Wireless Network Policy for Windows Vista and Later Releases. Because this is a new group policy, this option appears, but if the group policy already has a wireless network policy for Windows Vista and later releases, the Windows Vista policy will be available beneath the Wireless Network policy node.

9. When the New Wireless Network Policy window opens, type in an acceptable name and description for the policy.

10. If Windows will manage the wireless network configuration and connection of the Windows Vista systems, check the Use Windows WLAN AutoConfig Service for Clients check box, if it is not already checked.

11. In the Wireless Network Profile section near the bottom of the window, click the Add button to define a new wireless network, and click the Infrastructure link, as shown in Figure 27.17.

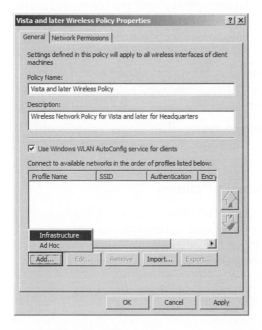

FIGURE 27.17    Selecting to create a new infrastructure wireless network.

12. When the new profile opens, type in a descriptive name and in the Network Name(s) SSID section, type in the SSID name of the network, and click the Add button.

13. If there is an existing "NEWSSID" network name, select it and click Remove.

14. If the client machine should automatically connect to this wireless network when the network is within range, and if the SSID of the wireless network is not broadcasted, check the Connect Even If the Network Is Not Broadcasting check box and check the Connect Automatically When This Network Is in Range check box.

15. Select the Security tab and configure the security properties of the wireless network, including the default authentication and encryption specifications. When finished, click OK to close the profile window.

16. Back in the Wireless Network Policy window, select the Network Permissions tab. From this tab, administrators can restrict the configuration. Click OK to close out of the Vista and Later Wireless Policy Properties window.

17. Back in the Group Policy Management Editor window, close the GPO.

18. In the Group Policy Management Console, link the new WirelessPolicyGPO GPO to an OU with a Windows Vista or later system that can be used to test the policy.

19. On the client workstation, after the group policy applies, in the Available Wireless Network, the network matching the wireless profile name should be listed. Click on this profile and if a security key is required, enter this key now. If a key is required, it must be provided by an administrator as certain authentication and encryption schemes in GPO wireless policies that require keys do not allow the keys to be entered into the GPO.

20. After the testing is completed, configure security filtering and possibly also WMI filtering to limit the application scope of the WirelessPolicyGPO policy and link it to the desired organizational unit(s), domain, or site.

One important point to note is that for Windows to manage the wireless networks and populate wireless profiles via Group Policy, the WLAN AutoConfig service needs to be installed and started on Windows Vista and later operating systems.

## Configuring Power Options Using Domain Policies

Using group policies to manage the power profiles on Windows systems is a feature that has been missing and desired for many years. Starting with Windows Server 2008 R2, Windows Vista and Windows 7 power plans can be defined and applied using domain policies using computer preference settings. To configure a centrally managed power plan for Windows Vista and later operating systems, perform the following steps:

1. Log on to a designated Windows Server 2008 R2 administrative server.

2. Click Start, click All Programs, click Administrative Tools, and select Group Policy Management.

3. Add the necessary domains to the GPMC as required.

4. Expand the Domains node to reveal the Group Policy Objects container.

5. Create a new GPO called PowerProfileGPO and open it for editing.

6. After the PowerProfileGPO is opened for editing in the Group Policy Management Editor, expand the Computer Configuration node and expand the Preferences node.

7. Expand the Control Panel Settings, right-click the Power Options node, and select New – Power Plan (Windows Vista and Later).

8. On the Advanced Settings page, change the default action to Update, change the default power plan from Balanced to High Performance, check the Set as the Active Power Plan check box, and click OK to complete the settings. If desired, change any of the default settings to other values.

9. Close the Group Policy Management Editor and link the policy in the Group Policy Management Console to a test organizational unit.

10. Once the new policy passes validation testing, link it to a production organizational unit as desired.

## Managing Scheduled Tasks and Immediate Tasks with Domain Policies

There are many times when Group Policy administrators would have liked to run an application or a command on a remote machine without having to reboot or log on to that particular system. For example, there might be a critical security or application update that needs to be rolled out and executed immediately. Historically, this would require a new group policy with a script or software package assigned and the machine would need to be rebooted to run the script or install the application. Now with Windows Server 2008 R2, this can be accomplished with the new Scheduled Task and Immediate Task preference settings for both Windows XP and Windows Vista and later operating systems. As an example of this that ties to the previous section on AppLocker, the policy administrators can create a policy that sets the Application Identity service to Automatic Startup mode, and they can create another policy that uses the computer Scheduled Task Immediate Task preference to start the service by running the command Net Start AppIDSvc. To create a Scheduled Task or Immediate Task preference setting for a computer, create a new domain policy, open the policy for editing and navigate to the Computer Configuration\Preferences\Control Panel\Scheduled Tasks node. Right-click on the node and select New – Immediate Task (Windows Vista and Later). Configure and save the task settings, as shown in Figure 27.18. Save the policy and test it out to verify it works as desired, and then deploy it in production or recreate it as a starter GPO so that it can be updated and reused as a template.

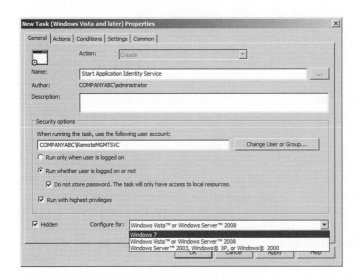

FIGURE 27.18    Defining a new Immediate Task preference setting for Windows 7 systems.

# Managing Users with Policies

Group Policy enables administrators to define how the end-user experience and desktop will be configured. Also, with user-based group policies, end users can be granted or denied access to certain Windows applications and features and even can be limited from reading or writing to removable media. Common user group policy configurations include, but are not limited to, the following:

- ▶ Start menu configuration

- ▶ Restricting Control Panel and display settings

- ▶ Internet Explorer settings

- ▶ Software restrictions

- ▶ Microsoft Management Console restrictions

- ▶ Screensaver settings

- ▶ Mapping network drives

- ▶ Installing printers

- ▶ Creating desktop shortcuts

- ▶ Application-specific configurations, including customizing Microsoft Office if the administrative templates are loaded and used in the policy

- ▶ Network configuration settings

- ▶ Folder redirection and offline file settings

Managing the user environment and desktop with group policies, for the most part, can be used to configure the graphical user interface for the user and to impose security restrictions to increase the reliability of the computer systems in use. In some cases, application shortcuts can be added to the desktop and applets can be hidden from view in the Control Panel or Start menu, but in more restrictive cases, they can be hidden and restricted from execution. Many organizations would like the end-user desktop to be very simple and present the end users with only the necessary applications relevant to their job. Although this is an extreme case, it can be performed by configuring the settings located in the User Configuration\Policies\Administrative Templates\Start Menu and Taskbar Settings node. A more functional Start menu GPO extension can also be used to manage the configuration of the Start menu for Windows XP, Windows Vista, and Windows 7 by configuring settings located in the User Configuration\Preferences\Control Panel Settings\Start Menu node.

Desktop security is also a very big concern for companies, now more than ever. One easy configuration organizations can use to better secure end-user desktops is to implement a password-locking screensaver. Automatic desktop locking with screensavers can be a very handy configuration, but sales and remote users should be granted extended computer idle time before a screensaver kicks in and locks the system in the middle of a sales presentation or a web-based meeting. Screensaver settings can be configured in the User Configuration\Policies\Administrative Templates\Control Panel\Personalization Settings node. To enable a password-protected screensaver with a blank screen screensaver that works on every version of Windows, the following four settings must be configured:

▶ **Enable Screen Saver**—Enabled

▶ **Password Protect the Screen Saver**—Enabled

▶ **Force Specific Screen Saver**—Enabled "scrnsave.scr"

▶ **Screen Saver Time Out**—Enabled "900", to go to screensaver after 15 minutes of inactivity

Another of the biggest pain points for companies is being able to back up end-user data, which, by default, is stored on the local drive of the computer system the user logs on to. When users log on to multiple computers or Remote Desktop Services systems, administrators can configure users with roaming profiles and/or specific Remote Desktop Services profiles, which follow them between systems and are stored on server shares. This configuration is set on the actual user object and is not necessarily a Group Policy setting.

Remote Desktop Services profiles are great for Remote Desktop Services systems, but implementing roaming profiles for an entire company on every computer can introduce challenges because each time the user logs on to a system, the entire profile is copied to the local computer and when the user logs off, the profile is copied back to the server. The larger the profile gets, the longer it takes to copy the profile between the server shares and the computer system. On Remote Desktop Services systems, it is very easy for administrators to remotely log off and complete the copy of the profile back to the server share. However, for end-user workstations, when roaming profiles get large, many users do not wait for the profile copy to complete and manually shut down the system or unplug it from the network. This, of course, can cause profile corruption and, even worse, data loss. Group Policy settings can be used to mitigate these issues somewhat and restrict the data that is included in the roaming profile. To improve Remote Desktop Services profile and standard roaming profile performance, administrators can use Group Policy to redirect user folders to server shares using folder redirection.

## Configuring Folder Redirection

Folder redirection can be used to redirect certain special folders in the end user's profile to server shares. Special folders such as the Documents folder, which is the default folder for users to store and access their data, can be redirected to server shares. The following are some basic rule-of-thumb guidelines when using this Group Policy extension:

▶ **Allow the system to create the folders**—If the folders are created by the administrator, they will not have the correct permissions. But properly configuring the share and NTFS permissions on the server share is essential in providing a functional folder redirection experience.

▶ **Enable client-side caching or offline file synchronization**—This is important for users with portable computers but is not the desired configuration for folder redirection on Remote Desktop Services systems. Furthermore, when storing data on end-user workstations, it may violate regulatory and/or security requirements to allow for cached local copies.

▶ **Use fully qualified (UNC) paths or DFS paths for server share locations**—For example, use \\Server1.companyabc.com\UserProfiles or \\companyabc.com\UserProfiles\ if DFS shares are deployed.

Before folder redirection can be expected to work, share and NTFS permissions must be configured appropriately. For folder redirection to work properly, configure the NTFS as follows:

▶ Configure the share folder to not inherit permissions and remove all existing permissions.

▶ Add the file server's local Administrators group with Full Control of This Folder, Subfolders, and Files.

▶ Add the Domain Admins domain security group with Full Control of This Folder, Subfolders, and Files.

▶ Add the System account with Full Control of This Folder, Subfolders, and Files.

▶ Add the Creator/Owner with Full Control of Subfolders and Files.

▶ Add the Authenticated Users group with both List Folder/Read Data and Create Folders/Append Data – This Folder Only rights. The Authenticated Users group can be replaced with the desired group, but do not choose the Everyone group as a best practice.

The share permissions of the folder can be configured to grant administrators Full Control and Authenticated Users Change permissions.

To redirect the Documents folder to a network share for Windows Vista, Windows 7, Windows Server 2008, and Windows Server 2008 R2 systems, perform the following steps:

1. Log on to a designated Windows Server 2008 R2 administrative server.
2. Click Start, click All Programs, click Administrative Tools, and select Group Policy Management.
3. Add the necessary domains to the GPMC as required.
4. Expand the Domains node to reveal the Group Policy Objects container.
5. Create a new GPO called UserFolderRedirectGPO and open it for editing.
6. After the UserFolderRedirectGPO is opened for editing in the Group Policy Management Editor, expand the User Configuration node, expand Policies, expand Windows Settings, and select the Folder Redirection node to display the user profile folders that are available for redirection, as shown in Figure 27.19. Keep in mind

that the folders in this section and detailed in Figure 27.19 represent the folders available in Windows Vista, Windows 7, Windows Server 2008, and Windows Server 2008 R2 user profiles. If Windows 2000, Windows XP, or Windows Server 2003 profiles require folder redirection, configuring the Documents folder for redirection is supported work but will require additional testing against each edition and service pack level of the legacy operating system that the policy applies to.

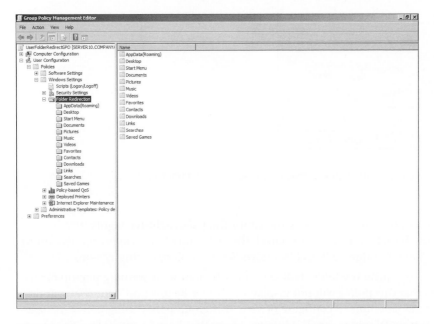

FIGURE 27.19   Windows Server 2008 R2 and Windows Vista folder redirection.

7. In the Settings pane, right-click the Document folder and select Properties.

8. On the Target tab, click the Setting drop-down list arrow, and select Basic – Redirect Everyone's Folder to the Same Location, which reveals additional options. There is another option to configure folder redirection to different locations based on group membership, but for this example, select the basic redirection option.

9. In the Target Folder Location section, there are several options to choose from and each should be reviewed for functionality; for this example, select Create a Folder for Each User Under the Root Path. This is very important if multiple folders will be redirected; more details are explained in the following steps.

10. In Root Path field, type in the server and share name, for example \\companyabc.com\UserFolders, as shown in Figure 27.20. Notice how the end-user name and Document folder will be created beneath the root share folder. This requires that the end users have at least Change rights on the share permissions and they must also have the Create Folder and Create File NTFS permissions on the root folder that is shared.

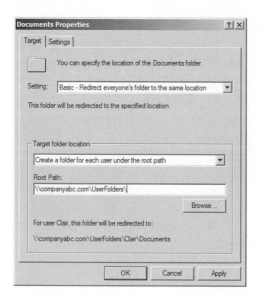

FIGURE 27.20   Folder redirection with basic redirection to a target root folder.

11. Select the Settings tab and uncheck the Grant the User Exclusive Rights to Documents check box. If necessary, check the check box to also apply redirection to Windows 2000, Windows XP, and Windows Server 2003 operating systems.

12. Click OK to complete the folder redirection configuration. A warning pop-up opens that states that this policy will not display the Folder Redirection node if an administrator or user attempts to configure or view this group policy using policy management tools from Windows 2000, Windows XP, or Windows Server 2003. Click Yes to accept this warning and configure the folder redirection.

13. Back in the Group Policy Management Editor window, close the GPO.

14. In the GPMC, link the new UserFolderRedirectGPO policy to an OU with a user account that can be used to test this policy.

15. Log on to a Windows Vista, Windows 7, or a Windows Server 2008 system with the test user account. After the profile completes loading, click the Start button, and locate and right-click the Documents folder. Select the Location tab and verify the path. For example, for a user named Khalil, the path should be `\\companyabc.com\UserFolders\Khalil\Documents`.

If the folder is not redirected properly, the Windows Vista or later system might need to have a domain policy applied that forces Synchronous Foreground Refresh of group policies. Also a very common configuration error is the NTFS and share permissions on the root folder. In most cases, however, a few logons by the particular user will get the settings applied properly.

Each of the default folder redirection folders will automatically be configured to synchronized with the server and be available offline. When additional server folders need to be configured to be available offline, perform the following steps:

1. Locate the shared network folder that should be made available offline.

2. Right-click the folder and select Always Available Offline.

As long as the server share allows offline synchronization and the client workstation also supports this, as they both do by default, that is all that is necessary.

## Removable Storage Access

Windows Server 2008 R2, Windows Vista, and Windows 7 group policies provide several settings that can be used to control how removable devices and removable storage can be used. Some of these settings apply to CD and DVD drives and media, but many are designed to control the read and write permission to removable disks such as external USB drives and memory sticks. These settings can be configured in a computer group policy but can also be configured in the User Configuration node to deny write access to removable media, as shown in Figure 27.21. The settings are located in User Configuration\Policies\Administrative Templates\System\Removable Storage Access.

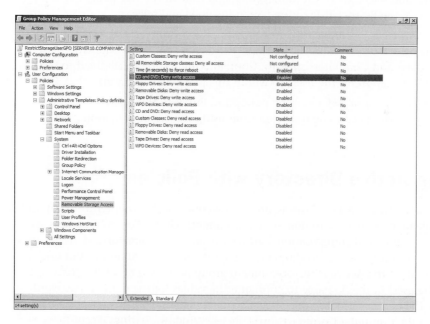

FIGURE 27.21    Restricting write access to removable storage for users.

## Managing Microsoft Management Console Access

Microsoft has standardized the deployment of management and configuration tools to use Microsoft Management Console (MMC) snap-ins. By default, all users can open a blank MMC and add snap-ins to the console. The snap-ins loaded on a particular machine are the only ones that can be added. Having access to each snap-in can unnecessarily expose configuration information to undesired individuals. Also, depending on the function of the snap-in, functions might be available to standard users that can impact the performance of production systems. For example, a user can add the Active Directory Users and Computers snap-in to an MMC console and can then create queries that run against the domain controller, causing unnecessary load on the system. To restrict access to the MMC or specific MMC snap-ins using domain group policies, perform the following steps:

1. Log on to a designated Windows Server 2008 R2 administrative server.

2. Open the Group Policy Management Console from the Administrative Tools menu.

3. Add the necessary domains to the GPMC as required.

4. Expand the Domains node to reveal the Group Policy Objects container.

5. Either create a new GPO or edit an existing GPO.

6. After the GPO is opened for editing in the Group Policy Management Editor, expand the User Configuration node, expand the Policies node, and select Administrative Templates.

7. Expand the Administrative Templates node and select Windows Components.

8. Scroll down and select Microsoft Management Console in the tree pane. Expand this node to reveal the Restricted/Permitted Snap-Ins node and select it.

9. With the Restricted/Permitted Snap-Ins node selected in the tree pane, a list of well-known snap-ins is displayed in the Settings pane. Select and open the Active Directory Users and Computers snap-in. Configure the setting to Disabled to block the use of this snap-in for the users to whom this policy will apply and click OK.

10. After the snap-in is disabled, close the policy and link it to the desired OU that contains the users who need to be restricted from using the disabled snap-in.

## Managing Active Directory with Policies

Many Group Policy settings detailed in the previous sections of this chapter for computer and user management apply only to domain environments. Group Policy can and is also used to manage security and configuration settings within Active Directory. Many settings apply to server role configurations to standardize security and configurations, but one main configuration of the Active Directory domain group policies is to set the password policy for all the users in the domain. To configure the values for the domain password policy settings, the default domain policy needs to be edited. The password policy settings are contained in the Computer Configuration\Policies\Windows Settings\Security Settings\Account Policies\Password Policy settings node. Figure 27.22 displays the default password policy settings for Windows Server 2008 R2 domains.

When administrators review or need to update the domain password policy, an account lockout policy should also be defined. The account lockout policy determines how many failed password attempts will be tolerated before a user account is locked, and whether the

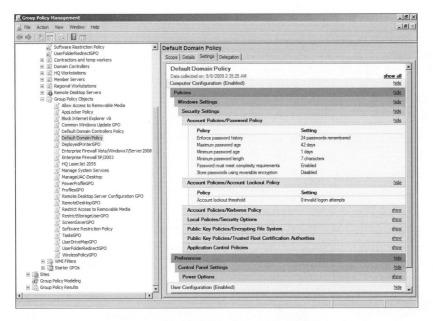

FIGURE 27.22   Default domain password policy settings.

account will be automatically unlocked. The following list contains the three account lockout settings:

▶ **Account Lockout Duration**—This setting defines how many minutes an account will remain locked out before it is automatically unlocked by the system.

▶ **Account Lockout Threshold**—This setting defines the number of failed logon attempts that will be allowed before the user account is locked out.

▶ **Reset Account Lockout Counter After**—This setting defines the number of minutes before the bad logon count is returned to zero.

## Fine-Grained Password Policies

New for Windows Server 2008 and also included with Windows Server 2008 R2 domains is a feature called fine-grained password policies. This feature is only available in domains operating in Windows Server 2008 or later domain functional level. A fine-grained password policy is a password policy that can be defined and applied to a single user or a set of users. This can be a very valuable feature for organizations that require interoperability with legacy systems or applications that require service accounts that cannot adhere to the standard domain password policy. Fine-grained password policies are stored in the domain Password Settings Container and are defined as Password Settings Objects. To create a new Password Settings Object, perform the following steps:

1. Log on to a designated Windows Server 2008 R2 administrative server.

2. Click Start, click in the Search pane, type in MMC, and press Enter.

3. When the Microsoft Management Console opens, click the File menu and select Add/Remove Snap-In.

4. In the Add/Remove Snap-In window, in the Available Snap-Ins list, locate and double-click on ADSI Edit to add it to the Selected Snap-Ins list. Click OK to close the Add/Remove Snap-In window. If the ADSI Edit snap-in is not listed, install the Remote Server Administration Tools from the Add Features option in Server Manager, and then repeat this step again.

5. Back in the MMC, in the tree pane, right-click the ADSI Edit node and select Connect To.

6. When the window opens to select a naming context, the default naming context will be the default selection; do not make any changes and click OK.

7. In the tree pane, expand the default naming context to reveal the domain naming context; in this example, it is named dc=companyabc,dc=com.

8. Expand the domain naming context to reveal the CN=System node. Expand the System node to reveal the Password Settings Container, as shown in Figure 27.23.

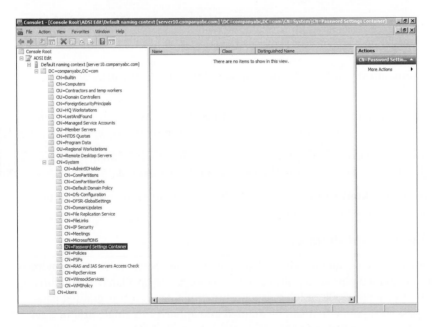

FIGURE 27.23    Locating the Password Settings Container.

9. Right-click the Password Settings Container and select New Object.

10. When the Create Object window opens, select the msDS-PasswordSettings object class, and click Next.

11. On the Common-Name page, type in Fine-GrainedPSO and click Next.

12. On the Password Setting Precedence page, type in 5 and click Next.

13. On the msDS-PasswordReversibleEncryptionEnabled page, set the value to `False` and click Next.

14. On the msDS-PasswordHistoryLength page, set the value to 5 and click Next.

15. On the msDS-PasswordComplexityEnabled page, set the value to `False` and click Next.

16. On the msDS-MinimumPasswordLength page, set the value to 6 and click Next.

17. On the msDS-MinimumPasswordAge page, set the value to -864000000000 and click Next. This is the equivalent of 1 day and the negative symbol must be added.

18. On the msDS-MaximumPasswordAge page, set the value to -77760000000000 and click Next. This is the equivalent of 90 days.

19. On the msDS-LockoutThreshold page, set the value to 0 and click Next. Setting this value to zero keeps the account unlocked.

20. On the msDS-LockoutObservationWindow page, set the value to -9000000000 and click Next. This is the equivalent of 15 minutes.

21. On the msDS-LockoutDuration page, set the value to -9000000000 and click Next. This is the equivalent of 15 minutes.

22. On the final page, click Finish to create the Password Settings Object (PSO).

23. After the PSO is created, select the Password Settings Container in the tree pane. In the Settings pane, right-click the new Fine-GrainedPSO object, and select Properties.

24. When the Fine-GrainedPSO opens, click the Filter button and check the Show Only Attributes That Have Values check box.

25. Review the configured settings, as shown in Figure 27.24, and click OK when finished.

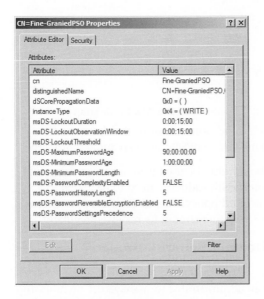

FIGURE 27.24    Reviewing the PSO settings.

Now that a new fine-grained password policy is created, the Fine-GrainedPSO, the policy can be applied to specific user accounts. To apply this PSO to a user account, perform the following steps:

1. Open the properties of the Fine-GrainedPSO. If necessary, click the Filter button and uncheck the Show Only Attributes That Have Values check box.

2. Scroll down and locate the msDS-PSOAppliesTo attribute and double-click it to open the property pages.

3. Click on the Add Windows Account button to locate users using the Select Users, Computers or Groups window.

4. In the Select Users, Computers or Groups window, type in the name of a user and click OK.

5. If the user is located, the logon and distinguished name of the user is added to the msDS-PSOAppliesTo window, as shown in Figure 27.25. Click OK. Repeat the process to add additional users if required.

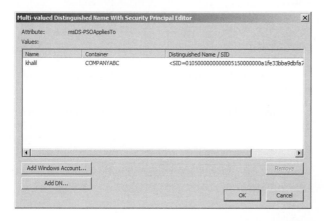

FIGURE 27.25    Configuring users who will apply the fine-grained Password Settings Object.

6. Click OK again to close the Fine-GrainedPSO and close the ADSI Edit snap-in.

7. Log on to a workstation or server with a user account added to the policy and change the password to verify that the Fine-GrainedPSO has been applied properly.

Even though fine-grained password policies should only be used if necessary and sparingly, after administrators know about it, many accounts will suddenly need to be added to a PSO that is less restrictive than the domain password policy. To audit the users to whom PSOs apply, the PSOs in the Password Settings Container should be reviewed regularly.

## Configuring Restricted Groups for Domain Security Groups

A great feature of group policies that commonly goes unused is restricted groups. Restricted groups Group Policy settings allow an administrator to manage the membership of local groups on domain member servers and workstations. Restricted groups can also be leveraged to manage the membership of domain security groups when applied to the appropriate domain or the domain controllers organizational unit.

---

**NOTE**

Unless the impact is completely understood and desired, never link a group policy with restricted group settings to a domain or a site object because the settings will be inherited by all computers in the domain or site, including domain controllers and Active Directory security groups. If linking this policy to a domain or site is required, make sure to use security or WMI filtering to exclude domain controllers and any additional systems as required if Active Directory security groups should not be managed by the policy.

---

Restricted groups can be used to populate and control the members of a designated group, or they can be used to add members to a specific group. Using restricted groups requires a deep understanding of how the settings work and GPO modeling should always be used before linking a restricted group GPO to an Active Directory site, domain, or organizational unit. There are a few scenarios that Group Policy administrators and organizations commonly utilize restricted groups domain policies for and these scenarios include, but are not limited to, the following:

▶ Define and restrict the membership of a local or domain security group by adding users or other groups using the members setting of restricted groups.

▶ Add universal and global domain groups to local computer or local domain groups using the member of setting of restricted groups.

Of course, defining the membership of groups is still limited by the domain functional level when it comes to group nesting.

### Controlling Group Membership Using Restricted Groups

Restricted groups can be used to control the membership of a group using the member setting, which is detailed next. When this setting is defined for a group, only the members added to this list will be a member of the group and any existing members will be removed when the policy is applied or refreshed. The only exception to this rule is when the local Administrator user account is a member of a member server Administrators local group or the Administrators domain security group. The same exception applies to managing the membership of domain groups, if the Administrator account in the domain is a member of the Administrators domain group, this account will remain even when a restricted group member setting is defined that does not include the Administrator account. This does not apply to any other security group that the Administrator account is a member of.

The restricted groups Administrator account exception was added as a fix with specific service pack revisions so if the computers in the organization are not up to date on supported operating systems and current service pack revisions, the administrator account can be removed by a restricted groups member policy. As a best practice, when the local or domain administrator account needs to be a member of a restricted group, do not count on the GPO to leave it in; instead, define it within the member policy setting. As an example of how to control membership of a local group on a member server or workstation using restricted groups, perform the following steps:

1. Log on to a designated Windows Server 2008 R2 administrative server.

2. Open the Group Policy Management Console from the Administrative Tools menu.

3. Add the necessary domains to the GPMC as required.

4. Expand the Domains node to reveal the Group Policy Objects container.

5. Create a new GPO named NetCfgOpsRestrictedGroupGPO.

6. Open the NetCfgOpsRestrictedGroupGPO policy for editing and in the Group Policy Management Editor, expand the Computer Configuration node, expand Policies, expand Windows Settings, expand the Security Settings node, and select Restricted Groups.

7. In the tree pane, right-click the Restricted Groups node and select Add Group.

8. When the Add Group window opens, do not browse; just type in Network Configuration Operators and click OK.

9. When the Network Configuration Operators window opens, click the Add button in the Members of This Group section.

10. When the Add Member window opens, type in the name of a user or group and click OK, or click the Browse button to locate and select users and/or groups, click OK, and click OK again. Domain accounts should be entered as domain\username and multiple entries should be separated by semicolons.

11. After all the entries are added, click OK to finalize the settings, as shown in Figure 27.26.

12. Back in the Group Policy Management Editor window, close the GPO.

13. In the GPMC, link the new NetCfgOpsRestrictedGroupGPO policy to an OU with a computer account that can be used to test this policy. Network Configuration Operators groups exist in Windows XP, Windows Server 2003, Windows Server 2008, Windows Vista, and Windows 7 systems.

14. Log on to a system to which the policy applies with an account with administrative privileges and verify the membership of the group. If the policy has not yet been applied, run the gpdate.exe /force command in a Command Prompt window.

15. Add additional users to the group and reapply the GPO by running the gpupdate.exe /force command in a Command Prompt window. Verify that the new users have been removed by the domain group policy.

16. Log off of the workstation and log back on to the Windows Server 2008 R2 system. Link the GPO to the appropriate organizational unit to complete this task.

Using this function of restricted groups is not recommended for the Administrators local group on domain workstations or in Active Directory unless the organization is certain that no users have been added to allow for legacy application or other additional rights. For this example, the Network Configuration Operators group membership has been

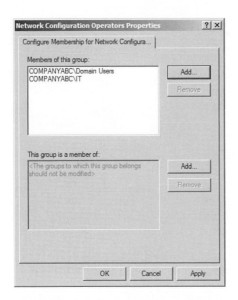

FIGURE 27.26    Configuring members using restricted groups.

defined by the policy. This group has the rights to completely manage and configure network settings of the computer.

### Modifying Group Membership Using Restricted Groups

When defining the membership of a group is not the desired change, the Restricted Groups Member of function can be used. This is a less-invasive method of updating or modifying group membership using domain policies. As an example, if an organization wants to add the COMPANYABC\IT domain security group to the local Administrators group of all computers in the HQ Workstations organizational unit, the following process can be followed:

1. Create an OU called HQ Workstations and place all the necessary computer accounts into the OU.

2. Create a new domain group policy called HQWorkstationsRestrictedGroupGPO and open it for editing.

3. Click the Computer Configuration node, expand Policies, expand Windows Settings, expand Security Settings, and then select Restricted Groups. Add a group but do not specify the Administrators group; instead, specify the COMPANYABC\IT group.

4. In the properties of the COMPANYABC\IT restricted group, click the Add button in the This Group Is a Member Of section. In the Add window, do not browse; simply type in Administrators and click OK. The properties of the group should appear, as shown in Figure 27.27.

27

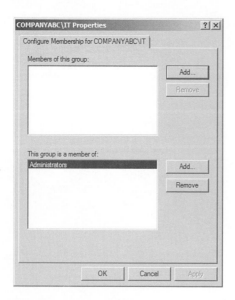

FIGURE 27.27    Adding members to the local Administrators group using the Restricted Group Member of function.

5. Click OK again to close the COMPANYABC\IT Restricted Group Properties window.

6. Back in the Group Policy Management Editor window, close the GPO.

7. In the Group Policy Management Console, link the new HQWorkstationsRestrictedGroupGPO policy to an OU with a computer account that can be used to test this policy.

8. Log on to a system that the policy applies to using an account with Administrators group membership, and verify the membership of the local Administrators group, as shown in Figure 27.28.

9. Log off of the workstation and log back on to the Windows Server 2008 R2 system. Link the GPO to the appropriate organizational unit.

Configuring restricted groups to manage domain groups can be performed using the same steps as previously outlined. The only difference is that the GPO will need to be linked to the Domain Controllers organizational unit, or the domain itself. Even if membership or member of configuration of a group is managed with restricted groups, it does not prevent users with the correct access from modifying the membership of these groups between Group Policy refresh cycles. To mitigate this, try to keep the membership of Administrators, Domain Admins, Account Operators, and Enterprise Admins in the domain to a minimum. On the local systems, try to keep the local Administrators group membership limited as well.

FIGURE 27.28    Verify that the restricted groups policy has updated the local Administrators group membership.

## Extending Group Policy Functionality

When the settings included in Group Policy do not provide the necessary settings or configuration options, Group Policy can be extended by adding additional administrative templates. Many third-party software vendors, and Microsoft, provide administrative templates that can be imported into group policies to add functionality. As detailed in Chapter 19, Windows Vista, Windows 7, Windows Server 2008, and Windows Server 2008 R2 support a new administrative template format consisting of an ADMX file that contains the administrative template settings, and a corresponding ADML file that contains the language-specific information that allows for the editing of the administrative template settings in the local language of the system administrator. To extend Group Policy functionality to manage Office 2007 settings as an example, perform the following steps:

1. Follow the procedure outlined in Chapter 19 to create a domain central store.

2. Download the Office 2007 administrative templates from Microsoft.

3. Execute the download and select a target folder.

4. Open this folder to locate the ADMX folder and open it to reveal the ADMX files and the language-specific subfolders that contains the respective ADML language files.

5. For this example, our Group Policy management will only be performed using the English language templates. Select all of the ADMX files at the root of the folder and also select the en-us folder, as shown in Figure 27.29.

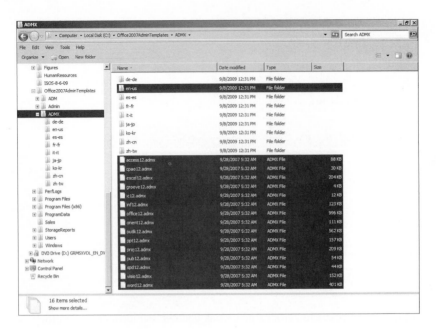

FIGURE 27.29    Selecting all of the Office 2007 ADMX files and the English United States language-specific folder.

6. Copy the selected ADMX files and the en-us folder to the Clipboard by right-clicking and choosing Copy.

7. Navigate to the domain central store network location and open the folder. For the domain companyabc.com, the location of the central store is
`\\companyabc.com\sysvol\companyabc.com\Policies\PolicyDefinitions`.

8. Right-click on a blank spot in this folder and choose Paste to copy the ADMX files and the en-us ADML folder to the central store. Because an en-us folder already exists, a prompt opens stating that if any files exist in the folder with the same name as the files being placed in that folder they will be merged. Check the Do This for All Current Items check box, and click the Yes button.

9. Close the window and open the Group Policy Management Console.

10. Create a new policy named Office2007TestGPO and open it for editing.

11. Navigate to the Computer Configuration\Policies\Administrative Templates settings node and select it.

12. In the Settings pane, if the process worked correctly, there should be several new Office 2007–related settings nodes, as shown in Figure 27.30.

13. Navigate to the User Configuration\Policies\Administrative Templates settings node and select it.

14. Note all of the new Office 2007 user settings.

15. Close the Group Policy Management Editor and close the Group Policy Management Console.

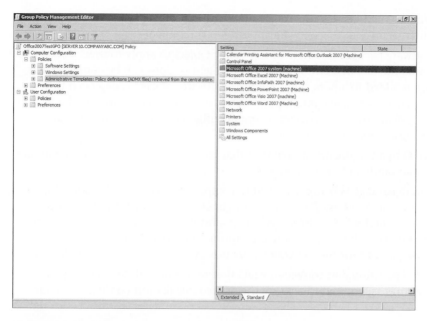

FIGURE 27.30    Reviewing the new Office 2007 Computer
Configuration\Policies\Administrative Templates.

The main reason to use the central store when extending group policies with new administrative templates is so that any administrator who attempts to create, view, or edit a
domain policy will be able to view all of the available settings.

## Deploying Software Packages Using Domain Group Policy Objects

Domain Group Policy Objects can be used to deploy Windows Installer compatible MSI
software application packages. Many software vendors provide their desktop and sometimes even their server applications as MSI packages, which can make deploying these
applications using domain policies very easy. Some applications, however, are not so
nicely packaged and require the use of a third-party MSI packaging product or must be
deployed using a different method. Software deployment with domain policies is functional but does not provide very flexible configuration and deployment options, such as
those included in Windows Server Update Services for Windows and System Center
Configuration Manager 2007 R2, formerly Systems Management Server, for all types of
applications and several other third-party software vendors that provide software deployment software suites. Deploying a software package using Group Policy requires the
following steps:

1.  Define the parameters of the installation and locate, create, and customize the
    Windows Installer MSI package.

2.  Place the MSI package on a network share that allows the necessary Active Directory
    computer and/or user accounts to read the package and any other necessary files
    during installation. This includes configuring the share and NTFS permissions as

required and, in many cases, selecting the Authenticated Users group works well unless tighter security of the software application is required.

3. Add the software package to a new Group Policy Object to apply to users or computers and define the deployment options. Deployment options can be defined when the package is added to a policy, but after the software package is deployed to a system, any changes to the configuration of the software package will not be picked up by that system unless the package is then configured to reapply the package, which can cause some undesirable results.

4. Link the GPO to a test organizational unit that contains only one or a few computer and/or user accounts to test the policy.

5. If the software package is being deployed to computers, including Windows XP, Windows Vista, or Windows 7 systems, configure Group Policy settings to force these systems to perform Synchronous Foreground Refresh, which forces the system to wait for the network to start before attempting to process Group Policy Objects. Windows servers wait for the network before processing group policies by default.

6. Verify GPO application and software installation results and, if necessary, update the GPO settings as required to achieve the desired installation configuration and behavior.

7. After the software package has been verified or updated to run correctly, remove the link from the test OU, and link the GPO to the desired domain, site, or organizational unit(s).

### Creating a New Software Installation GPO

Deploying software applications using a Group Policy Object is a simple task after the package is created and any necessary customizations to the installation behavior are defined. In many cases, the desired deployment option is to deploy the application to computer objects. When applications are deployed to computers, the applications are installed during the startup cycle of the system. This, of course, requires that the system starts while connected to the organization's network over a fast link and waits for the network to start before attempting to process group policies with the software package.

To deploy a packaged MSI software application using a domain group policy to a computer, perform the following steps:

1. Log on to a designated Windows Server 2008 R2 administrative server.

2. Locate the MSI package that will be deployed using the new Group Policy Object and copy it to a network share. Ensure that the Authenticated Users group has at least Read Share permissions and Read and Execute NTFS permissions in the shared folder.

3. Open the Group Policy Management Console from the Administrative Tools menu.

4. Expand the domain to expose the Group Policy Objects container and select it.

5. Right-click the Group Policy Objects container and select New.

6. Type in a name for the new GPO such as CorporateSoftwareGPO and click OK to create the new GPO. Do not select a starter GPO as this GPO will only contain the software package and does not need to have any prepopulated information.

7. After the GPO is created, right-click on the new GPO and select Edit.

8. When the Group Policy Management Editor opens, expand Computer Configuration, expand Policies, and double-click on Software Settings.

9. Right-click on the Software Installation node and select New, Package.

10. A Browse window opens. Locate the MSI package and click OK to add the package to the GPO. The package must be available on a network share and should be referenced using a UNC path.

11. When the Deploy Software window opens, select the Assigned option button, and click OK to complete the process.

12. After the process completes, which can take a few minutes, the package will be listed in the right pane. Right-click the new package and select Properties to open the advanced property pages.

13. In the property pages for the package, review the settings on the Deployment tab to determine if the package should be automatically uninstalled if the computer is removed from the application of this policy, as shown in Figure 27.31.

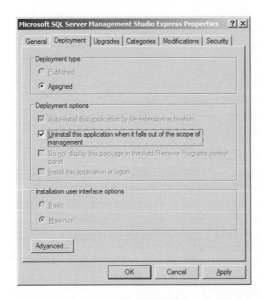

FIGURE 27.31   Configuring autouninstall of software packages with GPO removal.

14. With the property pages still open, review the settings on the remaining tabs and make any required changes to the way the application package will function.

15. After the package is configured, click OK to close the property pages, and close the Group Policy Management Editor.

16. Return to the Group Policy Management Console, and link the GPO to an organizational unit that has a few test or pilot systems on which the package can be installed.

17. Locate and log on to a system in the linked OU and reboot it to attempt to apply the new GPO and install the software package.

18. Troubleshoot and repair the GPO and package as necessary to achieve the desired functionality.

19. After the GPO is working as desired, link it to the intended site, domain, or OU.

20. Back up the GPO and log off of the test system and the administrative workstation.

## Synchronous Foreground Refresh

Group Policy processing occurs at computer startup, shutdown, and periodically during the background refresh interval for computers. Processing for users occurs at user logon and logoff and periodically during the background refresh interval. Certain functions of Group Policy, including software installation, user folder redirection, computer startup and shutdown scripts, and user logon and logoff scripts, require the network to be available during processing. Windows XP, Windows Vista, and Windows 7 systems do not wait for the network during computer startup and user logon by default and by design. This feature provides faster computer reboots and faster user logon processes but can also cause some Group Policy processing issues. When software installations, folder redirection, computer startup, and/or user logon scripts are defined within domain group policies, it might be required to also enable the Always Wait for the Network at Computer Startup and Logon setting within group policies. The setting is stored in the Computer Configuration node and must be applied as follows:

▶ GPOs that define computer startup scripts or computer-assigned software installations should have this setting enabled within the policy. Software installations that are assigned should be set to this configuration but published software installation GPOs can be left with the default processing configuration.

▶ If GPOs exist that define user logon scripts, assigned software installations, or folder redirection settings that require processing before Windows Explorer is opened, the computers that the users will log on to must have a GPO that applies this setting. Configuring this setting within the policy that contains the user settings will not have the desired effect unless the user's computer is also in the container that is linked to the GPO or unless a different policy that applies to the user enables this setting.

To configure Synchronous Foreground Processing of group policies, perform the following steps:

1. Log on to a designated Windows Server 2008 R2 administrative server.

2. Open the Group Policy Management Console from the Administrative Tools menu.

3. Expand the domain to expose the Group Policy Objects container and select it.

4. Right-click the Group Policy Objects container and select New or select an existing policy to update.

5. If a new GPO is being created, type in a name for the new GPO, and click OK to create the new GPO.

6. After the GPO is created or if an existing GPO will be updated, right-click on the desired GPO and select Edit.

7. When the Group Policy Management Editor opens, expand Computer Configuration, expand Policies, and select the Administrative Templates node.

8. Beneath the Administrative Templates node, expand System, and select Logon in the tree pane.

9. In the Settings pane, double-click on the Always Wait for the Network at Computer Startup and Logon setting.

10. On the setting tab, select the Enabled option button, and click OK, as shown in Figure 27.32.

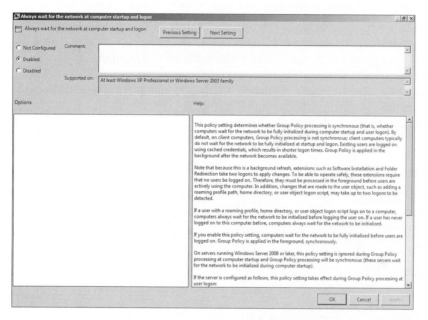

FIGURE 27.32    Enabling Synchronous Foreground Group Policy processing.

11. Close the Group Policy Management Editor, and return to the GPMC.

12. In the GPMC, if necessary, adjust the links to the updated GPO and close the GPMC when finished.

## GPO Modeling and GPO Results in the GPMC

When an organization decides to perform administrative and management tasks using group policies, it is essential that the system administrators understand how to check to see if Group Policy processing is working correctly. In the case when Active Directory hier-archies are being restructured, or if new policies are being deployed, performing a simu-lated application of group policies to review the results can help avoid unexpected issues. To perform Group Policy simulations, an administrator can use Group Policy Modeling, available in the GPMC. Group Policy Modeling is the equivalent of Resultant Set of Policies (Planning), which is the name of the administrative right that must be delegated in Active Directory to run this tool. To perform Group Policy Modeling, perform the following tasks:

1. Log on to a designated Windows Server 2008 R2 administrative server.

2. Open the Group Policy Management Console from the Administrative Tools menu.

3. In the tree pane, select the Group Policy Modeling node, right-click the node, and select Group Policy Modeling Wizard.

4. On the Welcome page, click Next to continue.

5. On the Domain Controller Selection page, specify a domain controller or accept the default of using any domain controller, and click Next.

6. On the User and Computer Selection page, the Group Policy Modeling Wizard can be used to run a simulation based on a specific user and computer in their current locations, or containers can be specified for either the user or computer to simulate GPO processing of a specific user, logging on to a Computer in a specific container. For this example, select the Users container and the Computers container of the domain to determine which policies and settings will be applied by default, as shown in Figure 27.33. Click Next to continue.

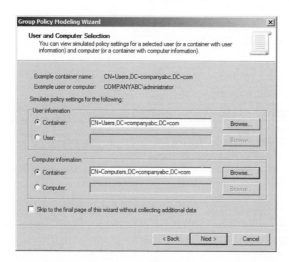

FIGURE 27.33    Selecting the default user and computer containers for Group Policy Modeling.

7. On the Advanced Simulations page, loopback processing, slow network connections, and site-specific testing can be specified. Accept the defaults and click Next to continue.

8. On the User Security Groups page, specific security groups can be specified to run policy modeling against. Accept the defaults and click Next to continue.

9. On the Computer Security Groups page, specific security groups can be specified to run policy modeling against. Accept the defaults and click Next to continue.

10. On the WMI Filters for Users page, select the All Linked Filters option button, and click Next to continue.

11. On the WMI Filters for Computers page, select the All Linked Filters option button, and click Next to continue.

12. On the Summary of Selections page, review the choices and if everything looks correct, click Next to run the GPO modeling tool.

13. When the process completes, click Finish to return to the GPMC and review the modeling results.

14. In the Settings pane, the summary of the computer and user policy processing will be available for view. Review the information on this page and then click on the Settings tab to review the final GPO settings that would be applied, as shown in Figure 27.34.

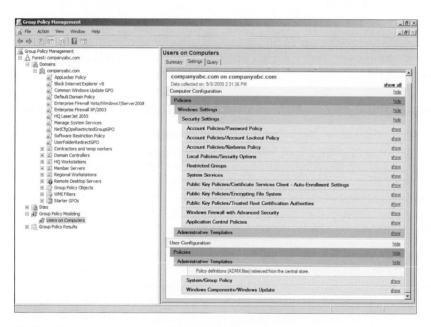

FIGURE 27.34   Reviewing the GPO modeling resultant settings.

15. Close the GPMC and log off.

In situations when Group Policy is not delivering the desired results, GPO Results can be run to read and display the Group Policy processing history. GPO Results are run against a specific computer, but can also be used to collect user policy processing. To run GPO Results to review the GPO processing history, perform the following steps:

1. Log on to a designated Windows Server 2008 R2 administrative server.

2. Open the Group Policy Management Console from the Administrative Tools menu.

3. In the tree pane, select the Group Policy Results node, right-click the node, and select Group Policy Results Wizard.

4. On the Welcome page, click Next to continue.

5. On the Computer Selection page, choose to run the policy against another computer and locate a Windows 7 system that a user has already logged on to. Also be sure to uncheck the Do Not Display Policy Settings for the Selected Computer in the Results check box, and click Next.

6. On the User Selection page, select the Display Policy Settings For option button, and then select the Select a Specific User option button. Select a user from the list, and click Next to continue. Only users who have previously logged on to the selected computer will be listed and they will only be listed if the user running the tool is a domain admin or has been granted the right to run Resultant Set of Policies (Logging) for the particular users.

7. On the Summary of Selections page, review the choices and click Next to start the GPO Results collection process.

8. When the process completes, click Finish to return to the GPMC.

9. When the process completes, the results will be displayed in the Settings pane on the Summary, Settings, and Policy Events tabs. Review the results and close the GPMC when finished.

## Managing Group Policy from Administrative or Remote Workstations

It is very common for Windows system administrators to manage group policies from their own administrative workstations. To manage a Windows Server 2008 R2 environment properly, domain group policy administration should be performed using a Windows Server 2008 R2 or Windows 7 system with the Group Policy Management tools and the Print Services tools installed. The main reason for this is that by using the latest version of the tools possible, the administrator ensures that all possible features are available and that the most stable version of the tools are being used.

Group Policy management, aside from creating and managing policies, provides administrators with the ability to simulate policy processing for users and computers in specific containers in Active Directory using the Group Policy Modeling node in the GPMC. Furthermore, the previous application of Group Policy for users and computers can be collected and reviewed in the Group Policy Management Console using the Group Policy Results node in the GPMC. For an administrator, even a member of the Domain Admins group, to perform remote Group Policy Modeling using the GPMC from a machine other than a domain controller, the following requirements must be met:

▶ The administrator must be a member of the domain Distributed COM Users security group.

▶ The administrator must be delegated the Generate Resultant Set of Policy (Planning) right in Active Directory, as shown in Figure 27.35. This right must be applied to the domain, OU, container, or site that contains all of the computers and users the administrator will run simulated GPO processing against.

▶ The administrator must have the right to read all the necessary group policies, and this should be allowed by default.

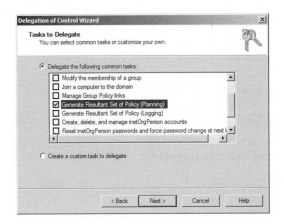

FIGURE 27.35    Delegating the Generate Resultant Set of Policy (Planning) right.

To perform remote Group Policy Results tasks using the GPMC from a machine other than a domain controller, the following requirements must be met:

▶ The administrator must be a member of the remote computer's local Distributed COM Users security group.

▶ The administrator must be a member of the remote computer's local Administrators security group for legacy desktop platforms and the remote system must be accessible on the network.

▶ The Windows Firewall must be configured to allow the inbound Remote Administration exception and the remote workstation must be on a network that is defined within this exception.

▶ The administrator must be delegated the Generate Resultant Set of Policy (Logging) right in Active Directory. This right must be applied to the domain, OU, container, or site that contains all of the computers and users the administrator will run simulated GPO processing against.

▶ The administrator must have the right to read all the necessary group policies, and this should be allowed by default.

## Summary

Windows Server 2008 R2 Group Policy provides administrators with many options to standardize configuration and management of users and computer settings. Management policies can be fine tuned based on the function, location, and security needs of the users or the security requirements of the organization. This chapter offers many suggestions and examples of how Group Policy can be leveraged in any organization. Although group policies are very functional and can be a very attractive option for user and computer management, the planning and testing of group policies is essential in delivering the desired

27

configuration and security settings to users and computers in an Active Directory or Windows workgroup environment.

# Best Practices

The following are best practices from this chapter:

▶ The only changes that should be made to the default domain policy should be modifying the password and account policy settings and nothing else.

▶ When the local or domain Administrator user account is a member of a group that will be managed with domain group policy restricted groups, do not count on the GPO to leave it in; instead, define it within the member policy setting of a restricted group.

▶ When naming group policies, try to use naming conventions that will more easily help identify the function of the policies for the organization.

▶ Assign or publish software to high-level Active Directory objects. Because Group Policy settings apply by default to child containers, it is simpler to assign or publish applications by linking a Group Policy Object to a parent organizational unit or domain as long as each of the objects in the child containers requires the application.

▶ Assign or publish just once per Group Policy Object. When multiple packages are included in a single policy, often only one package gets applied and they do not necessarily get processed in order.

▶ When using folder redirection for user profile folders, allow the system to create the folders and ensure that the share and root folder permissions are set up appropriately to allow this.

▶ Configure policies with application control policies to be processed by machines running Windows 7 Enterprise and Ultimate operating systems and/or Window Server 2008 R2 systems.

▶ Use fully qualified (UNC) paths, such as `\\server.companyabc.com\share` or DFS links such as `\\companyabc.com\share`.

▶ Have systems administrators use standard user accounts to do their day-to-day tasks and use User Account Control to allow for prompting of elevation when administrator privileges are required.

# CHAPTER 28

# File System Management and Fault Tolerance

Computer networks were created to share data. The most primitive form of sharing data on computer networks, of course, is accessing files and folders stored on networked systems or central file servers, such as Windows Server 2008 R2 file servers.

As data storage needs and computer services have evolved in the past 20 or so years, many different methods have become available to present, access, secure, and manage data. As an example, data can be accessed through a web browser; by accessing data stored on external storage media, such as USB drives, floppy disks, CDs, and DVDs; and by accessing data stored on any of the different types of media for the many different operating systems, network storage devices, and file systems available.

This chapter covers the file system features and services included with Windows Server 2008 R2. The goal of this chapter is to introduce administrators to the Windows Server 2008 R2 file services and give them the tools they require to deploy fault-tolerant and reliable enterprise file services for their organizations using Windows Server 2008 R2.

## Windows Server 2008 R2 File System Overview/Technologies

Windows Server 2008 R2 provides many services that can be leveraged to deploy a highly reliable, manageable, and fault-tolerant file system infrastructure. This section of the chapter provides an overview of these services.

## Windows Volume and Partition Formats

When a new disk is added to a Windows Server 2008 R2 system, it must be configured by choosing what type of disk, type of volume, and volume format type will be used. To introduce some of the file system services available in Windows Server 2008 R2, you must understand a disk's volume partition format types.

Windows Server 2008 R2 enables administrators to format Windows disk volumes by choosing either the file allocation table (FAT) format, FAT32 format, or NT File System (NTFS) format. FAT-formatted partitions are legacy-type partitions used by older operating systems and floppy disk drives and are limited to 2GB in size. FAT32 is an enhanced version of FAT that can accommodate partitions up to 2TB and is more resilient to disk corruption. Data stored on FAT or FAT32 partitions is not secure and does not provide many features. NTFS-formatted partitions have been available since Windows NT 3.51 and provide administrators with the ability to secure files and folders, as well as the ability to leverage many of the services provided with Windows Server 2008 R2.

## NTFS-Formatted Partition Features

NTFS enables many features that can be leveraged to provide a highly reliable, scalable, secure, and manageable file system. Base features of NTFS-formatted partitions include support for large volumes, configuring permissions or restricting access to sets of data, compressing or encrypting data, configuring per-user storage quotas on entire partitions and/or specific folders, and file classification tagging, which is discussed later in this chapter.

Several Windows services require NTFS volumes; as a best practice, we recommend that all partitions created on Windows Server 2008 R2 systems are formatted using NT File System (NTFS).

## File System Quotas

File system quotas enable administrators to configure storage thresholds on particular sets of data stored on server NTFS volumes. This can be handy in preventing users from inadvertently filling up a server drive or taking up more space than is designated for them. Also, quotas can be used in hosting scenarios where a single storage system is shared between departments or organizations and storage space is allocated based on subscription or company standards.

The Windows Server 2008 R2 file system quota service provides more functionality than was included in versions older that Windows Server 2008. Introduced in Windows 2000 Server as an included service, quotas could be enabled and managed at the volume level only. This did not provide granular control; furthermore, because it was at the volume level, to deploy a functional quota-managed file system, administrators were required to create several volumes with different quota settings. Windows Server 2003 also included the volume-managed quota system, and some limitations or issues with this system included the fact that data size was not calculated in real time. This resulted in users exceeding their quota threshold after a large copy was completed.

Windows Server 2008 and Windows Server 2008 R2 include the volume-level quota management feature but also can be configured to enable and/or enforce quotas at the folder level on any particular NTFS volume using the File Server Resource Manager service. Included with this service is the ability to screen out certain file types, as well as real-time calculation of file copies to stop operations that would exceed quotas thresholds. Reporting and notifications regarding quotas can also be configured to inform end users and administrators during scheduled intervals, when nearing a quota threshold, or when the threshold is actually reached.

## Data Compression

NTFS volumes support data compression, and administrators can enable this functionality at the volume level, allowing users to compress data at the folder and file level. Data compression reduces the required storage space for data. Data compression, however, does have some limitations, as follows:

▶ Additional load is placed on the system during read, write, and compression and decompression operations.

▶ Compressed data cannot be encrypted.

## Data Encryption

NTFS volumes support the ability for users and administrators to encrypt the entire volume, a folder, or a single file. This provides a higher level of security for data. If the disk, workstation, or server the encrypted data is stored on is stolen or lost, the encrypted data cannot be accessed. Enabling, supporting, and using data encryption on Windows volumes and Active Directory domains needs to be considered carefully as there are administrative functions and basic user issues that can cause the inability to access previously encrypted data.

## File Screening

File screening enables administrators to define the types of files that can be saved within a Windows volume and folder. With a file screen template enabled, all file write or save operations are intercepted and screened and only files that pass the file screen policy are allowed to be saved to that particular volume or folder. The one implication with the file screening functionality is that if a new file screening template is applied to an existing volume, files that would normally not be allowed on the volume would not be removed if they are already stored on it. File screening is a function of the File Server Resource Manager service, covered in the "File Server Resource Manager (FSRM)" section later in this chapter.

## File Classification Infrastructure

Windows Server 2008 R2 includes a new feature called the File Classification Infrastructure (FCI). The FCI enables administrators to create classification policies that can be used to identify files and tag or classify files according to properties and policies defined by the file server administrators. FCI can be managed by using the File Server Resource Manager

28

console and allows for file server administrators to identify files and classify these files by setting specific FCI property values to these files based on the folder they are stored in and/or based on the content stored within the file itself. When a file is classified by FCI, if the file is a Microsoft Office file, the FCI information is stored within the file itself and follows the file wherever it is copied or moved to. If the file is a different type of file, the FCI information is stored within the NTFS volume itself, but the FCI information follows the file to any location it is copied or moved to, provided that the destination is an NTFS volume hosted on a Windows Server 2008 R2 system. More information on FCI is detailed later in this chapter.

## Volume Shadow Copy Service (VSS)

Windows Server 2003 introduced a file system service called the Volume Shadow Copy Service (VSS). The VSS enables administrators and third-party independent software vendors to take snapshots of the file system to allow for faster backups and, in some cases, point-in-time recovery without the need to access backup media. VSS copies of a volume can also be mounted and accessed just like another Windows volume if that should become necessary.

### Shadow Copies of Shared Folders

Volume shadow copies of shared folders can be enabled on Windows volumes to allow administrators and end users to recover data deleted from a network share without having to restore from backup. The shadow copy runs on a scheduled basis and takes a snapshot copy of the data currently stored in the volume. In previous versions of Windows prior to Windows Server 2003, if a user mistakenly deleted data in a network shared folder, it was immediately deleted from the server and the data had to be restored from backup. A Windows Server 2003, Windows Server 2008, or Windows Server 2008 R2 NTFS volume that has shadow copies enabled allows a user with the correct permissions to restore deleted or overwritten data from a previously stored shadow copy backup. It is important to note that shadow copies are stored on local volumes and if the volume hosting the shadow copy becomes inaccessible or corrupted, so does the shadow copy. Shadow copies are not a replacement for backups and should not be considered a disaster recovery tool.

### Volume Shadow Copy Service Backup

The Volume Shadow Copy Service in Windows Server 2008 R2 also provides the ability for Windows Backup and third-party software vendors to utilize this technology to improve backup performance and integrity. A VSS-compatible backup program can call on the Volume Shadow Copy Service to create a shadow copy of a particular volume or database, and then the backup can be created using that shadow copy. A benefit of utilizing VSS-aware backups is that the reliability and performance of the backup is increased as the backup window will be shorter and the load on the system disk will be reduced during the backup. More information on volume shadow copy backups is detailed in Chapter 30, "Backing Up the Windows Server 2008 R2 Environment."

## Remote Storage Service (RSS)

The Remote Storage Service was included with Windows 2000 Server and Windows Server 2003. The Remote Storage Service enables administrators to migrate or archive data to lower-cost, slower disks or tape media to reduce the required storage space on file servers.

This service, however, has been discontinued in Windows Server 2008 and is not included in Windows Server 2008 R2 either. Many organizations that required this sort of functionality have turned to third-party vendors to provide this type of hierarchical storage management. However, the New File Management Tasks node within the File Server Resource Manager console provides a function that allows administrators to schedule processes that will report on files that might be candidates for moving to alternate storage through a function called file expiration. This can be configured to notify both administrators and end-user file owners of upcoming files that will be expired and moved to alternate volumes. One main difference, however, is that file expiration does not leave a link in the original file location as the Remote Storage Service previously did. File expiration is covered later in this chapter in the "File Management Tasks" section.

> **CAUTION**
>
> If a Windows Server 2003 32- or 64-bit system is running Remote Storage Service, upgrading this system to Windows Server 2008 32- or 64-bit or Windows Server 2008 R2 causes any data stored on Remote Storage media to become inaccessible.

## Distributed File System (DFS)

As the file services needs of an organization change, it can be a challenging task for administrators to design a migration plan to support the new requirements. In many cases when file servers need additional space or need to be replaced, extensive migration time frames, scheduled outages, and, sometimes, heavy user impact results.

In an effort to create highly available file services that reduce end-user impact and simplify file server management, Windows Server 2008 R2 includes the Distributed File System (DFS) service. DFS provides access to file data from a single namespace that can be used to represent a single server or a number of servers that store different sets or replicated sets of the same data. For example, when using DFS in an Active Directory domain, a DFS namespace named \\companyabc.com\UserShares could redirect users to \\Server10\UserShares or to a replicated copy of the data stored at \\Server20\UserShares.

Users and administrators both can benefit from DFS because they only need to remember a single server or domain name to locate all the necessary file shares. DFS is described in detail later in this chapter.

28

## Distributed File System Replication (DFSR)

With the release of Windows 2003 R2 and continuing with Windows Server 2008 and Windows Server 2008 R2, DFS has now been upgraded. In previous versions, DFS Replication was performed by the File Replication Service (FRS). Starting with Windows Server 2003 R2, DFS Replication is now performed by the Distributed File System Replication service, or DFSR. DFSR uses the Remote Differential Compression (RDC) protocol to replicate data. The RDC protocol improves upon FRS with better replication stability, more granular administrative control, and additional replication and access options. Also, starting with Windows Server 2008 R2, RDC improves replication by only replicating the portions of files that have changed, as opposed to replicating the entire file, and replication can now be secured in transmission. DFSR and RDC are discussed in detail in the section, "The Distributed File System," later in this chapter.

## File System Management Tools

Windows Server 2008 R2 provides several tools administrators can leverage to manage Windows Server 2008 R2 file servers. Administrators can install these tools on Windows Server 2008 R2 systems by adding the File Services tools feature to the system. The File Services tools can be added by invoking the Add Features applet located in Server Manager. The tools are located in the Add Features, Remote Server Administration Tools, Role Administration Tools hierarchy. The File Services tools installed in this group include the following:

- ▶ Distributed File System tools
- ▶ File Server Resource Manager tools
- ▶ Services for Network File System tools

These tools are detailed in the section, "File Server Resource Manager (FSRM)," later in this chapter.

## File System Monitoring and Reporting

Windows Server 2008 R2 includes the ability for administrators to enable automated monitoring and reporting of the file system. This includes reporting on storage and quota usage, file screening, file group by types as well as owners, and file properties. Also, new to Windows Server 2008 R2 is the ability to produce reports on file classification and file expiration file management tasks. The aforementioned reports can be configured using the File Server Resource Manager tool detailed in the section, "File Server Resource Manager (FSRM)," later in this chapter.

# File System Access Services and Technologies

Windows Server 2008 R2 provides administrators with many different options to present file data to end users. These, of course, include the traditional file sharing methods, but also include presenting file data using web services. By default, Windows Server 2008 R2 systems running the File Services role support Windows 2000 clients and later. To support legacy Windows clients, UNIX clients, or legacy Apple Mac clients might require additional services and security modifications to the data. Several of the options available for presenting file data to end users are included in the proceeding sections.

## Windows Folder Sharing

This is the traditional and most commonly used method to access server data using the server message block (SMB) protocol over TCP/IP. Windows systems, many UNIX systems, and current Apple Mac systems can access Microsoft servers using this protocol. The path to access the data uses the Universal Naming Convention (UNC) path of `\\server\sharename`.

## Distributed File System (DFS) Namespaces and Replication

This method utilizes Windows folder sharing under a unified namespace. The main difference between standard Windows Server folder sharing and DFS shares is that the actual server name is masked by a unified name, commonly the Active Directory domain name, but in some cases, a single server name and share can be used to access data stored on several servers. Also with DFS, the underlying data can be replicated or synchronized between servers. One limitation of DFS is that the client accessing the DFS namespace must be a DFS-aware client so it can utilize the benefits of DFS and, in some cases, just locate and access the data.

## WWW Directory Publishing

Using this method, administrators can make folders and files available through a web browser for read and/or write operations. This can be a useful tool to make files available to remote users with only Internet access. Some common types of files typically published in websites can include employee handbooks, time sheets, vacation requests, company quarterly reports, and newsletters. Additionally, file publishing through the web can be performed using Windows SharePoint Services and Microsoft Office SharePoint Server. Microsoft Exchange 2007 and 2010 also enable administrators to provide access to designated file shares through the Outlook Web Access interface.

## File Transfer Protocol Service

The File Transfer Protocol (FTP) service is one of the oldest services available to transfer files between systems. FTP is still commonly used to make large files available and to present remote users and customers alike with a simple way to send data to the organization. FTP is very efficient, and that is why it still has a place in today's computer and network infrastructure. Standard FTP, however, is not secure by default and should only be used with secure and monitored connections. FTP is compatible with most web browsers, making it very easy to include and utilize links to FTP data within websites to improve file transfer performance. Some common types of files typically made available using FTP sites include company virtual private network (VPN) clients, software packages, product manuals, and to present a repository for customers and vendors to transfer reports, large databases, and other types of data.

28

## Secure File Transfer Protocol (FTPS)

As security becomes more and more of an expectation rather than a necessity for a simple service, Microsoft supports Secure File Transfer Protocol, or Secure FTP, for data transfer services. Using an encryption algorithm for data security and integrity purposes, FTPS provides a method to upload and download data with a significantly more secure FTPS than was typically done in the past using unsecured FTP.

## Windows SharePoint Services (WSS)

Windows SharePoint Services (WSS) can be used to present files in document libraries, but the data is stored in Microsoft SQL databases and not in the file system. Because WSS stores file data in SQL databases, separate backups are required and the data stored in WSS is not directly accessible in the file system, except in the form of web links. WSS does have some benefits to managing file data, including document management features such as version history, check-in and checkout functionality, and the ability to notify users or groups when a document has been added, updated, or removed from a WSS document library. For more information on WSS, see Chapter 35, "Windows SharePoint Services."

## Services for NFS

"Services for NFS" is a suite of services that provides the ability for Windows administrators to simplify the integration of Windows systems into legacy UNIX networks. In previous versions of Windows, Services for NFS or Services for UNIX (SFU) included User Name Mapping services, gateway for NFS, client for NFS, and server for PCNFS (IBM's implementation of NFS). With Windows Server 2008 R2, the only components included are the client and server for NFS. Mapping UNIX users to Active Directory users is now available as a feature of the Identity Management for UNIX role services, which are part of the Active Directory Domain Services role. Services for NFS allows UNIX systems running the NFS protocol to access data stored on Windows Server 2008 R2 systems. Client for NFS allows the Windows system to access data stored on UNIX systems running the NFS protocol.

> **NOTE**
>
> Most of the current UNIX systems can access Windows systems using the Server Message Block protocol.

## Services for Mac

This service was removed in Windows Server 2008 as current Apple Mac devices can connect to Microsoft servers by default using the SMB protocol. To support legacy Apple Mac clients, Windows administrators would need to deploy Windows Server 2003 systems with file and/or print services for Mac installed or provide alternate ways for Mac users to access data, such as FTP or web access.

# Windows Server 2008 R2 Disks

Windows Server 2008 R2 enables administrators to define how disks are presented and used within the system. Depending on the type and size of a disk, administrators can determine which particular type of disk and volumes they should consider deploying on their systems.

Windows disks can be defined as basic or dynamic disks. Furthermore, these same disks can be defined as Master Boot Record (MBR) or GUID Partition Table (GPT) disks. A simple way to clearly differentiate how to choose between these disk types is to consider that basic disks only support simple volumes, whereas dynamic disks allow logical volumes to be created across multiple physical disks. Choosing between MBR and GPT disks depends on the size of the disk, as well as understanding how many partitions you will need to create on the disk.

Windows Server 2008 R2 also supports VHD or virtual hard disks, for Hyper-V virtual machines. VHD disks can now also be created and mounted directly within a Windows host operating system, regardless of whether the Windows Server 2008 R2 system is hosting the Hyper-V role.

## Master Boot Record Disks

Master Boot Record (MBR) disks utilize the traditional disk configuration. The configuration of the disk, including partition configuration and disk layout, is stored on the first sector of the disk in the MBR. Traditionally, if the MBR became corrupted or moved to a different part of the disk, the data became inaccessible. MBR disks have a limitation of three primary partitions and a single extended partition that can contain several logical drives. Choosing to create an MBR disk should provide administrators with a more compatible disk that can easily be mounted and/or managed between different operating system platforms and third-party disk management tools.

## GUID Partition Table (GPT) Disks

GPT disks were first introduced in Windows with Windows Server 2003 Service Pack 1. GPT disks are recommended for disks that exceed 2TB in size. GPT disks can support an unlimited number of primary partitions and this can be very useful when administrators are leveraging large external disk arrays and need to segment data for security, hosting, or distributed management and access. GPT disks are only recognized by Windows Server 2003 SP1 and later Windows operating systems. Attempting to manage a GPT disk using a previous operating system or third-party MBR disk management tool will be blocked and virtually inaccessible.

## Basic Disk

A Windows disk is defined as a basic or a dynamic disk regardless of whether the disk is an MBR or a GPT disk. A basic disk supports only simple volumes or volumes that exist on a single disk and partition within Windows. Basic disks contain no fault tolerance managed by the Windows operating system, but can be fault tolerant if the disk presented to

28

Windows is managed by an external disk controller and is configured in a fault-tolerant array of disks.

Basic disks are easier to move across different operating systems and usually are more compatible with Windows and third-party disk and file system services and management tools. Basic disks also support booting to different operating systems stored in separate partitions. Furthermore, and most important, if the disk presented to Windows is from a SAN that includes multiple paths to the disk, using a basic disk will provide the most reliable operation as a different path to the disk might not be recognized if the disk is defined within Windows as a dynamic disk.

## Dynamic Disk

Dynamic disks extend Windows disk functionality when managing multiple disks using Windows Server 2008 R2 is required. Windows administrators can configure dynamic disks to host volumes that span multiple partitions and disks within a single system. This allows administrators to build fault-tolerant and better performing volumes when RAID controllers are not available or when a number of smaller disks need to be grouped together to form a larger disk.

In some server deployments, dynamic disks are required as the disk controllers do not support the necessary performance, fault-tolerance, or volume size requirements to meet the recommended system specifications. In these cases, dynamic disks can be used to create larger volumes, fault-tolerant volumes, or volumes that can read and write data across multiple physical disks to achieve higher performance and higher reliability. Dynamic disks are managed by the operating system using the Virtual Disk Service (VDS).

## Virtual Hard Disks

Virtual hard disks or VHDs are used by virtual machines to emulate Windows disks. Virtual hard disks can be created on an existing Windows Server 2008 R2 system using the Hyper-V Management console or they can be created directly using the Disk Management console. VHDs are primarily created on the Windows host system as a file on an existing Windows volume that has a .vhd extension. VHD disks can be created to be fixed size or dynamically expanding. A fixed-sized VHD that is 10GB in size will equate to a 10GB file on the Windows host server volume. A dynamically expanding VHD file will expand as files are stored on it, only as necessary. VHD files can easily be moved across servers and between virtual machines, and also can be expanded quite easily, granted that the VHD is not in use and there is ample free space on the host volume. VHD files can be attached directly to a Windows Server 2008 R2 host using the Disk Management console, unlike in previous releases, which required scripts to mount the file. This added functionality is a needed improvement to the integrated VSS Hyper-V backup functionality, included with Windows Server Backup and available to third-party backup software vendors. Creating and attaching a VHD file to a Windows Server 2008 R2 host is detailed later in this chapter, but for more information on VHD files and their management, refer to Chapter 37, "Deploying and Using Windows Virtualization."

## Partition or Volume

When referring to Windows disks, administrators might consider partitions and volumes interchangeable. In fact, even though the graphical user interface makes no clear distinction and might refer to everything as a volume, volumes only exist on dynamic disks and partitions only exist on basic disks. This is especially important when managing disks using the diskpart.exe command-line utility, which defines a clear delineation between partitions and volumes.

## Mount Point

When a new volume is created in Windows, it can be assigned a drive letter or mounted into an existing empty folder on an existing volume. When a volume is mounted into a folder, this is known as a mount point or junction point. Mount points can be very useful in situations where administrators want to simplify disk access for end users, but must also make use of a number of small disks versus a single large disk. For example, on a database server with three disks, an administrator might assign disk1 the D drive, disk2 would be mounted in d:\data, and disk3 would be mounted in d:\logfiles. Any administrator would only need to connect to the D drive to access the databases or log files. One thing that administrators must test before using mount points is to see that all clients, applications, and backup agents support the use of mount or junction points and can successfully access and back up data stored within them. With many backup applications, enabling a backup job to back up data stored on a mounted volume is not the default and can cause major problems if the correct backup configuration is not selected before a failure occurs.

## Simple Volumes

A simple volume is a single partition created on a single basic or dynamic disk. On a basic disk, simple volumes can be extended to include free, unallocated space that exists in a sequential section of the disk. To extend a simple volume to a noncontiguous, unallocated space on the same disk or a different disk, the disk will need to be upgraded to a dynamic disk.

## Spanned Volumes

A spanned volume is treated as a single drive, but the volume spans two or more disks or different noncontiguous areas of the same disk. Spanned volumes provide no disk fault tolerance but can be used to meet disk storage needs that exceed the capacity of a single disk or volume. Spanned volumes are slowest when it comes to reading and writing data and are recommended only when the space of more than a single disk is necessary or an existing simple volume needs to be extended to add disk space and there is no available, unallocated space located next to the volume. For instance, if an application, file share, or service is dependent on the drive letter, does not support the moving of data or system files to another drive, and the current drive is nearly full, a simple volume can be upgraded to a spanned volume and extended with unallocated space on the same or another disk to add additional disk space. A simple volume that has been extended with unallocated space on the same disk is still considered a simple volume. If the simple volume is extended to a different disk, it is automatically converted to a spanned volume.

The allocated space on each of the disks can be different sizes, and there is no space lost when creating a spanned volume. One thing to keep in mind, though, is that a spanned volume can never be reverted to a simple volume.

## Striped Volumes

A striped volume or RAID-0 compatible volume requires two or more Windows dynamic disks and provides the fastest of all disk configurations. Striped volumes read and write data from each of the disks simultaneously, which improves disk access time. Striped volumes utilize all the space allocated for data storage but provide no disk fault tolerance. If one of the disks should fail, the entire data set would become inaccessible. Stripe sets require the exact amount of disk space on each of the allocated disks. For example, to create a 15GB stripe set array with three disks, 5GB of unallocated space would be required on each disk.

## Fault-Tolerant Volumes

When fault-tolerant disk arrays managed by hardware controllers are not available, fault-tolerant volumes can be created using multiple Windows dynamic disks. Fault-tolerant volumes in Windows are able to maintain data availability in the event of a single disk failure. Windows Server 2008 R2 supports two types of fault-tolerant volumes, including mirrored volumes and RAID-5 volumes.

## Mirrored Volumes

Mirrored or RAID-1 compatible volumes require two separate disks to create. Furthermore, the size of the volume must be equal and available in one contiguous, unallocated section of each of the disks. Mirrored volumes duplicate data across each disk and can withstand the failure of a single disk. Because the mirrored volume is an exact replica of the first disk, the total space capacity is the capacity of one disk.

## RAID-5 Volumes

Software-based RAID-5 volumes require three or more Windows dynamic disks and can provide faster disk read access than a single disk because all disks in the set can be read at the same time. Write performance can be slower than a single disk because of the parity stripe that must be generated and written. The space allocated to the RAID-5 volume on each disk in the volume must be equal and contiguous unallocated space. For example, to create a RAID-5 volume that requires 100GB on each disk, a disk with two separate areas of 50GB of unallocated space cannot be used to participate in the volume.

RAID-5 sets can withstand the failure of a single disk in the volume. During a disk failure, the remaining disks in the volume will continue to provide access to data but at a slower or degraded rate. This capability is achieved by reserving a small portion of each disk's allocated space to store data parity information that can be used to rebuild a failed disk and to continue to provide data access. This is called a parity stripe. RAID-5 parity information requires the total space of a single disk in the array. For example, if five 10GB dynamic disks are used to create a single RAID-5 volume, 40GB would be available for data storage. The reserved 10GB would be spread evenly across all five disks. The formula for usable capacity of a RAID-5 array is $(N - 1) * S$, where N is the total number of drives in the array and S is the capacity of the smallest drive in the array.

# Utilizing External Disk Subsystems

Windows Server 2008 R2 is capable of utilizing and, in some cases, managing disks stored in external storage area networks (SANs) or disk subsystems. Many enterprise organizations, and actually many midsize organizations, deploy Windows systems connected to external disk storage. As organizations move toward consolidating and virtualizing servers, the need to provide fault-tolerant disk storage at the organization level instead of at the server level has become more common.

## Hardware-Based Disk Arrays

As a best practice, whenever possible, use RAID-compatible disk controllers or SANs to provide fault-tolerant disk volumes to Windows Server 2008 R2 systems. Using externally managed RAID arrays will reduce server processing requirements and can also improve the recoverability of the system if operating system corruption is encountered.

## Boot from Storage Area Networks

Many SAN vendors and Microsoft tout the ability to deploy diskless servers that boot from SAN disks. This configuration allows SAN vendors to completely manage the Windows system disks and can simplify the recovery or replacement of a server based on hardware failure or scheduled replacement.

## Managing External Storage

Windows Server 2008 R2 provides a tool called "Storage Manager for SANs" to assist administrators in managing SAN-based disks. In most cases, however, SAN vendors provide and recommend the use of their own vendor-based management tools.

## External Storage Support Requirements

Microsoft has very tight specifications when it comes to supporting external storage for Windows servers. Administrators who plan to utilize external storage should review the Windows Server 2008 R2 Hardware Compatibility List for external storage devices, storage controllers, driver types, driver versions, and controller firmware versions to verify supported compatibility before purchasing any external storage devices—that is, if the administrators want to be supported by Microsoft in the event of disk or data corruption.

# Managing Windows Server 2008 R2 Disks

Disks in Windows Server 2008 R2 can be managed using a few different tools included with the operating system. Most disk-related tasks can be performed using the Disk Management console, the Share and Storage Management console, or the diskpart.exe command-line utility, but to manage a new disk just added to Windows, the Disk Management console must be used.

## The Disk Management MMC Snap-In

The Disk Management console, or snap-in, can be used to initialize and configure new disks; import previously configured disks; convert basic disks to dynamic disks; create, extend, and shrink disk volumes; format disk volumes; enable shadow copies; and many more disk-related tasks. Disk Management can also be used to create and attach or mount VHD files to the host operating system for quick volume access and data management. This snap-in is included as part of the Computer Management console and the Server Manager console, but it can also be added to a separate Microsoft Management Console window. The Disk Management console can be used to manage disks on remote machines as well as local disks.

## Diskpart.exe Command-Line Utility

Diskpart.exe is a command-line utility that administrators can use to manage Windows disks. Most disk tasks that can be performed using the Disk Management console can also be performed using this command-line utility except for initializing new disks. When issues are encountered with a Windows Server 2008 R2 that won't boot, diskpart.exe might be the only option available when booting into the recovery environment, so administrators should be well versed and comfortable with this tool.

## Adding a New Disk to Windows

When a disk is added to a Windows Server 2008 R2 system, the only tool that can be used to get the disk configured is the Disk Management snap-in. Windows Server 2008 R2 is able to detect most disks without a reboot. This, of course, depends on the disk type and the disk controller type. For example, if a new disk is added to a system with a RAID-compatible disk controller, it will not be detected or available to Windows until the new disk is configured using the RAID controller configuration utility. When a new disk is ready to be added into the Windows Server 2008 R2 operating system, perform the following steps:

1. Log on to the Windows Server 2008 R2 system with an account with administrator privileges.
2. Click Start, click All Programs, click Administrative Tools, and select Server Manager.
3. In the tree pane, double-click the Storage node, and select Disk Management.

> **NOTE**
>
> In many cases, when a new disk is added to Windows, it is automatically detected and an Initialize Disk pop-up Window opens; please close this window.

4. Right-click Disk Management and select Rescan Disks, as shown in Figure 28.1.

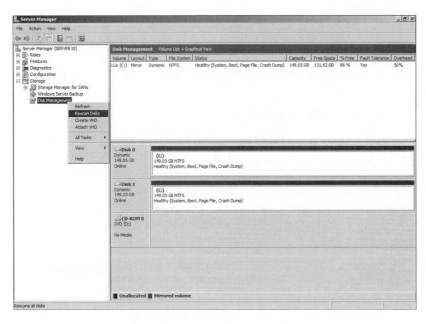

FIGURE 28.1    Rescanning disks using Disk Manager.

5. After the disk scan completes, scroll down in the tasks pane to locate the new disk that was just added. Right-click the disk and select Online.

6. The new disk will be listed as Unknown and Not Initialized. Right-click the disk and select Initialize Disk.

7. When the Initialize Disk window opens, check the disk or disks to initialize, and select the option button to create either an MBR or GPT type disk, as shown in Figure 28.2.

FIGURE 28.2    Initializing a new Windows disk.

8. After the disk initialization completes, the disk will be listed as a basic disk. Repeat the online and initialize task for any additional disks that were added to the Windows Server 2008 R2 system.

At this point, the disk is ready to have a volume defined, formatted, and added to Windows.

## Converting Basic Disks to Dynamic Disks

In many cases, if disk fault tolerance is desired in a server configuration, the disks need to be converted from the default basic disk configuration to a dynamic disk configuration. After the disks are set to Dynamic, the fault-tolerance configuration can be applied. To convert basic disks to dynamic disks, perform the following steps:

1. To convert a disk to a dynamic disk, right-click the basic disk to be converted, and select Convert to Dynamic Disk.

---

**CAUTION**

After a disk is converted to a dynamic disk, it cannot be changed back to a basic disk without removing all the volumes and losing the data.

---

2. When the Convert to Dynamic Disk window opens, select the disk to convert by checking the box next to the desired disk and clicking OK to convert the disk.

## Creating Fault-Tolerant Volumes Using Disk Management

Windows Server 2008 R2 supports fault-tolerant disk arrays configured and managed on a RAID disk controller or configured within the operating system using dynamic disks. To create arrays using a RAID controller, refer to the manufacturer's documentation and use the appropriate disk utilities. To create a fault-tolerant volume within the Windows Server 2008 R2 operating system using the Disk Management snap-in, perform the following steps:

1. Log on to the Windows Server 2008 R2 system with an account with administrator privileges.

2. Click Start, click All Programs, click Administrative Tools, and select Server Manager.

3. In the tree pane, double-click the Storage node, and select Disk Management.

4. In the tasks pane, verify that each of the disks that will be part of the fault-tolerant volume is listed as online. If the disks are not online or initialized, perform the steps in the previous section, "Adding a New Disk to Windows," before proceeding.

---

**NOTE**

If the disks that will be members of the fault-tolerant array are not dynamic, when the fault-tolerant volume is created, the wizard can convert the disks as part of the process.

---

5. After all of the necessary disks are online and initialized, they should be converted to dynamic disk using the steps in the preceding section, "Converting Basic Disks to Dynamic Disks." Once all of the disks are ready, right-click any of the disks and select either New Mirrored Volume or New RAID-5 Volume to create a fault-tolerant volume. For this example, we will be creating a RAID-5 volume, but the steps would be the same for a spanned or striped volume.

> **NOTE**
>
> To create a striped or RAID-5 volume, a minimum of three disks are required.

6. After selecting New RAID-5 Volume, a New RAID-5 Volume window opens; click Next on the Welcome page.

7. The disk that was right-clicked will already be selected. For each remaining disk that will be part of the RAID-5 volume, select the disk in the Available section, and click the Add button to move it to the Selected section. For this example, we will create a RAID-5 volume using disks two through seven, as shown in Figure 28.3.

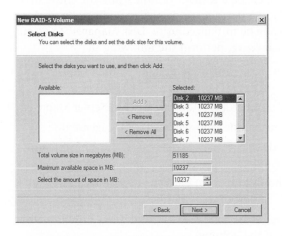

FIGURE 28.3    Selecting disks for the RAID-5 volume.

8. After all the necessary disks are listed in the Selected section, unless only a section of the disk will be used in the volume, the entire disk space will be used. Click Next to continue.

9. On the Assign Drive Letter or Path page, select the drive letter to assign or browse to a folder location to mount the volume into an empty folder, and then click Next.

10. On the Format Volume page, accept the defaults to format the volume as NTFS, accept the default allocation size, and type in the volume label as required to easily identify the drive in Disk Manager, diskpart.exe, and Explorer. Uncheck the Perform a Quick Format check box, and click Next.

> **TIP**
>
> When you're formatting RAID-5 volumes, perform a complete format to avoid loss of disk performance later when data is first copied to the volume.

11. On the Completing the New RAID-5 Volume Wizard page, review the settings and click Finish to create and format the volume.

12. If any of the disks were not previously converted to dynamic disks before the start of the volume creation, a window opens to confirm that all disks will be converted; click the Yes button to accept the conversion of the necessary disks.

Because a quick format was not selected, the time it takes to format the volume might be extensive, so please plan accordingly.

## Creating a Fault-Tolerant Volume Using Diskpart.exe

This section provides step-by-step instructions for creating the same RAID-5 volume as in the preceding section using diskpart.exe. For reference, these steps will be used to converts disks 2 through 7 to dynamic disks, create a RAID-5 volume using the entire disk, add a volume label, format the drive as NTFS, and assign a drive letter to the volume. As a prerequisite, each of the disks needs to already be initialized using Disk Manager. To create a fault-tolerant RAID-5 volume using diskpart.exe, perform the following steps:

1. Log on to the Windows Server 2008 R2 system with an account with administrator privileges.

2. Click Start, click All Programs, click Administrative Tools, and select Server Manager.

3. In the tree pane, double-click the Storage node, and select Disk Management.

4. In the tasks pane, verify that each of the disks that will be part of the fault-tolerant volume is initialized and listed as dynamic.

5. Any disk that is listed as unknown and offline, right-click the disk, and select Online. Repeat for each disk that will be part of the volume.

6. Any disk that is listed as not initialized, right-click the disk, and select Initialize Disk. Repeat for each disk that will be part of the volume.

7. Close Disk Manager.

8. Click Start, All Programs, Accessories, and double-click the Command Prompt shortcut. Each of the remaining steps will be typed in the command prompt window.

9. Type diskpart.exe and press Enter.

10. Type List Disk and press Enter. Note which disks are listed as online and dynamic. As an example, Figure 28.4 shows that disks 0, 1, 2, 3, 4, and 5 are online and dynamic

and disks 6 and 7 are online and basic. The online or offline status is listed in the Status column and a dynamic disk is shown in the Dyn column with a * symbol.

FIGURE 28.4   Listing disk status using `diskpart.exe`.

11. Based on the disk configuration detailed in Figure 28.4, disk 6 and disk 7 need to be converted to dynamic disks.

12. In the Command Prompt window, type `select disk 6` and press Enter.

13. In the Command Prompt window, type `convert dynamic` and press Enter.

14. In the Command Prompt window, type `select disk 7` and press Enter.

15. In the Command Prompt window, type `convert dynamic` and press Enter. Leave `diskpart.exe` running in the Command Prompt window.

16. Now that all of the disks are initialized, online, and dynamic, we can create the RAID-5 volume.

17. In the Command Prompt window, type `Select disk 2` and press Enter.

18. In the Command Prompt window, type `Create volume RAID disk 2,3,4,5,6,7` and press Enter.

19. Now that the RAID-5 volume is created, we will format it, but the volume will need to be identified. In the Command Prompt window, type `List volume` and press Enter.

20. The new volume should be listed as a RAID-5 volume. In Figure 28.5, the new volume is listed as volume 2.

28

FIGURE 28.5    Identifying the new RAID-5 volume using `diskpart.exe`.

21. In the Command Prompt window, type `Select volume 2` and press Enter.

22. In the Command Prompt window, type `Format FS=NTFS label=New_RAID5_Volume`, and press Enter to format the volume. This will perform a full format of the volume.

23. When the format completes, the window details if the format completed successfully. If the format completed successfully, once the volume is formatted, type `Assign Letter=F` and press Enter to assign the new volume the letter F.

24. When the drive letter is assigned, in the Command Prompt window, type `Exit`, and press Enter to close `diskpart.exe`.

25. In the Command Prompt window, type `Exit`, and press Enter to close the Command Prompt window.

The new RAID-5 volume should now be accessible from the operating system.

## Working with Virtual Hard Disks

Virtual hard disks have been around since virtual machines appeared on the scene in the late 1990s. Windows Server 2008 R2 can create and directly attach Microsoft virtual hard disks or VHD files. VHD files are used in Windows Server 2008 and Windows Server 2008 R2 Hyper-V guest machines, as well as Microsoft Virtual Server 2005 and Microsoft Virtual PC, although not all VHD versions are 100% interchangeable. Starting with Windows Server 2008 R2, VHD files can be easily created and attached to the host operating system using Disk Manager. To create and attach a new VHD file, perform the following steps:

1. Log on to the Windows Server 2008 R2 system with an account with administrator privileges.

2. Click Start, click All Programs, click Administrative Tools, and select Server Manager.

3. In the tree pane, double-click the Storage node, and select Disk Management.

4. Right-click Disk Management and select Create VHD.

5. In the Create and Attach Virtual Hard Disk window, click Browse to select the volume and folder to place the new VHD file.

6. In the Browse Virtual Disk Files window, locate the correct volume and folder, type in the name of the new VHD file, and click Save.

7. Back in the Create and Attach Virtual Hard Disk window, enter the size of the new virtual hard disk and pull down the menu to select MB, GB, or TB. For our example, we will create a 10GB file on the E: drive called NEW-Virtual-Disk.vhd.

8. In the Create and Attach Virtual Hard Disk window, after the location, name, and size of the new virtual disk are defined, select the Fixed Size option button to create the file and allocate all the space to file, as shown in Figure 28.6, and click OK to create the new virtual hard disk.

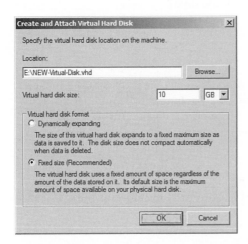

FIGURE 28.6    Creating and attaching a new virtual hard disk.

9. Once the process completes, scroll down in the Disk Management tasks pane to locate the new virtual hard disk, which should be listed as the last disk and should be listed as Unknown and Not Initialized. Right-click the disk in the left section of the tasks pane and select Initialize Disk.

10. In the Initialize Disk window, choose to create an MBR partition style for the disk, ensure that the correct disk is checked in the window, and click OK to initialize the disk.

11. Once initialized, the disk will be listed as basic and online. Right-click the unallocated space in the tasks pane and select New Simple Volume.

12. Follow the steps to format the disk as NTFS and assign a drive letter.

28

13. Once the process has completed, the virtual hard disk will be available in My Computer and Windows Explorer just as any other local drive.

14. Once the usage of the disk is complete, from within Disk Manager, right-click the attached virtual hard disk and select Detach VHD.

15. In the Detach Virtual Hard Disk window, the disk that was selected will be listed; if the virtual hard disk file will be used again, do not check the box to delete the virtual disk as part of detaching it. Click OK to detach the disk.

Once the virtual hard disk is detached, if the disk was not deleted, it can be copied to any other Windows Server 2008 R2 system and mounted or attached to the host operating system or a Hyper-V guest virtual machine. One use of this new feature is to easily preload software and files on virtual disks that will be used for Hyper-V guest machines or to mount up virtual disk for disk repair, data copies, backup, or a number of different functions.

To attach an existing virtual disk to a Windows Server 2008 R2 system, the server administrator can open Server Manager, right-click the Disk Management node, and select Attach VHD, and then the administrator can choose to attach the VHD in read-only mode to avoid changing or modifying any data stored within the disk.

# System File Reliability

In each release of Microsoft Windows for the workstation or server, Microsoft has made great attempts to increase the reliability of the system by extending the number of included hardware drivers. This holds true today for Windows Server 2008 R2 and Windows 7, which to date have the most complete set of hardware and device drivers. Of course, Windows Server 2008 R2 is only available in 64 bit, which does limit hardware compatibility to a certain degree. Microsoft works hand in hand with software and hardware manufacturers to provide the means for these manufacturers to create the best drivers for Windows that will provide the highest level of reliability for the client and server operating systems.

## System File Stability

Windows Server 2008 R2 and Windows 7 allow an administrator to control the level of security associated with hardware drivers. Because Microsoft works closely with independent hardware vendors (IHVs), Windows Server 2008 R2 and Windows 7 support extensive brands of hardware and client/server peripherals. When an IHV tests its hardware and passes certain Microsoft requirements, its hardware driver is certified, digitally signed by Microsoft, and, in most cases, added to the Hardware Compatibility List (HCL) for the particular platform or operating system. If the driver is certified early enough in the operating system development process, the driver is included with the operating system.

Most new hardware will be detected by Windows and will prompt to search the local file system or Windows Update to find the driver. If the hardware was tested and verified by Microsoft before the production release of Windows, it should be found and added automatically. If the hardware was certified after the release of Windows, it might be included in Windows Update or the administrator might be required to locate, download, and install the driver right from the manufacturer's website.

In most cases, administrators should only install drivers provided by Microsoft and digitally signed by Microsoft Windows Hardware Compatibility Publisher. In other cases, however, especially when it comes to connecting to external disk storage, it might be preferential and required to use the driver provided by the manufacturer. Unsigned drivers are not accepted by default on Windows Vista, Windows 7, Windows Server 2008, and Windows Server 2008 R2. These drivers are not fully tested and can cause issues. Make sure to check with the hardware manufacturer for compatibility before purchasing any new or used hardware that will be attached to a new Windows Server 2008 R2 system. In particular, disk controllers and disk access are critical to server stability and administrators should always try to configure their disk controller firmware version and driver version to match the recommended manufacturer and Microsoft specification; otherwise, data corruption or loss might result.

### File Signature Verification (`Sigverif.exe`)

File Signature Verification is a graphic-based utility that can be used when it is suspected that original, protected, and digitally signed system files or drivers have been replaced or overwritten after an application or device installation. This tool checks the system files and drivers to verify that all the files have a Microsoft digital signature. When unsigned or incorrect version files are found, the information, including filename, location, file date, and version number, is saved in a log file and displayed on the screen.

To run this tool, click Start, Run, and in the search pane, type `Sigverif.exe`, and press Enter. When the window is open, click Start to run a check for signed drivers and system files in the operating system. This starts a scan of the devices drivers and if they all pass, a window will open stating that the files have been scanned and verified and digitally signed. Click OK to close the pop-up and click Close to close the File Signature Verification window.

### System File Checker (`Sfc.exe`)

The System File Checker is a command-line tool that is similar in function to the File Signature Verification tool, but any detected incorrect files are automatically replaced with the Microsoft version of the detected file. This tool can be dangerous and cause serious problems if the administrator is not sure if certain Windows files or unsigned drivers are required for the operating system to function properly. This tool should be used if operating systems become unstable and drivers or system files are suspected or logged as possible causes of problems.

> **NOTE**
>
> `Sfc.exe` scans and replaces any system files that it detects are incorrect. If any unsigned drivers are necessary for operation, do not run this utility; otherwise, the files might be replaced and cause your hardware to operate incorrectly, producing data corruption, loss of functionality, or actually producing different problems.

`Sfc.exe` can be configured to run using Group Policy. `Sfc.exe` options are configurable using Group Policy with settings found in `Computer Configuration\Policies\Administrative Templates\System\Windows File Protection`. This might be a good option for supporting workstations to maintain system stability. It might also prove to be useful for servers, but as a general guideline, use is on workstations and servers only when system file corruption or driver issues have been reported as problematic.

# Adding the File Services Role

Windows Server 2008 R2 systems, out of the box, can be used to share folder data right after installation. To get the most out of the system, the File Services role should be added. Adding the File Services role not only configures settings to optimize the system for file sharing, but also enables the administrator to choose which file server options as well as which tools for managing the file system will be installed. To install the File Services role, perform the following steps:

1. Log on to the Windows Server 2008 R2 system with an account with administrator privileges.

2. Click Start, click All Programs, click Administrative Tools, and select Server Manager.

3. In the tree pane, click on the Roles node.

4. In the tasks pane, click on the Add Roles link.

5. When the Add Roles window opens, read the information on the Before You Begin page and if the system meets the recommendations to have a strong administrator password, static IP address, and be updated with the latest Windows security updates, click Next to continue.

6. On the Select Server Roles page, check the File Services check box, and click Next to continue.

7. The next page provides a short introduction to the File Services role and notes the fact that the Windows Search Service and the indexing service cannot be installed on the same system. Click Next to continue with the installation of the File Services role.

8. The Role Services page enables administrators to select which File Services role services will be installed on the system. The File Server service is selected by default. In addition to this service, also check Windows Search Service to set up indexing of the file system for faster searches and also check the File Server Resource Manager to enable quota, file screening, file classification, and reporting functionality, as shown in Figure 28.7. After checking the desired services, click Next to continue.

> **NOTE**
>
> When additional File Services role services are chosen, the corresponding tools to manage the services are also installed.

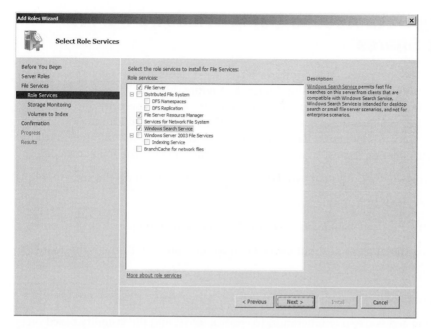

FIGURE 28.7    Selecting the File Services role services.

9. Because the File Server Resource Manager was selected, the next page is the Configure Storage Usage Monitoring page. Check the box next to each drive letter that will have storage reporting enabled and when completed, accept the default settings for monitoring, and click Next to continue.

10. On the Set Report Options page, accept the defaults of storing reports on the root folder, Storage Reports, and click Next to continue.

### NOTE

Detailed configuration of the File Server Resource Manager reports and monitor settings are outlined in the "File Server Resource Manager (FSRM)" section later in this chapter.

11. Because the Windows Search Service was selected, the next page will be the Select Volumes to Index for Windows Search Service. Check the volumes that will contain user data that should be indexed, and click Next to continue.

12. The Confirm Installation Selections page enables the administrator to review the chosen settings. After confirming that the settings are correct, click Install to install and configure the services and tools chosen.

13. Review the details on the results page and click Close to complete the installation.

28

# Managing Data Access Using Windows Server 2008 R2 Shares

Providing access to data stored on a Windows Server 2008 R2 server can be very simple to configure using Windows shares. Existing folders and entire drives can be shared with a few clicks, but understanding who can access that data is critical to security and, in some cases, licensing. Server shares are accessed using the UNC or Universal Naming Convention of \\server\sharename. Administrators can configure a few different settings when creating or updating shares. Share options or features include the following:

▶ Determining whether the share will be visible or hidden, based on the share name

▶ Setting the description of the share

▶ Configuring the type of share; if Server for NFS is installed, there will be two options

▶ Configuring the number of simultaneous connections allowed through the share

▶ Configuring the cache or offline sync settings of the share

▶ Enabling or disabling BranchCache

▶ Configuring access-based enumeration to control folder and file visibility based on NTFS permissions

▶ Configuring NTFS permissions on the folder or volume hosting the file share

▶ Configuring share permissions to manage whether users can read, change, or have full control over a share

Because sharing can be performed for CD drives, DVD drives, and FAT and NTFS volumes, the configurable share permissions are limited to Full Control, Change, and Read. Full Control permissions allow users to manage all data and to reset permissions. Change allows users to manage all data and Read only allows users to read the data. Because share permissions are not very granular, folder shares should be created only on NTFS volumes, when possible, to increase the security of data.

When shares are created on NTFS volumes, both the Share and NTFS folder and file permissions are applied to the user. Windows Server 2008 R2 will combine the permissions, and the most restrictive permissions will apply. For example, if a folder located at c:\users is shared and testuser1 is granted Read permission at the share and Change or Modify permissions on the NTFS folder, testuser1 will only have Read permission when accessing the data across the network through the share. If testuser1 logs on to the system console and accesses the c:\users folder directly, testuser1 will have Change or Modify permissions.

## Access-Based Enumeration

A new sharing feature included with Windows Server 2008 and Windows Server 2008 R2 is called access-based enumeration. Access-based enumeration, when enabled on a share, hides the folders or files within the share from view for users who do not have access to the data. Access-based enumeration, however, does not hide the share itself. This feature can simplify data access for end users as they will only see what they can access, but, on the flip side, users who are collaborating and trying to instruct their co-workers on where to locate the data might be confused when the folders cannot be located.

## Client-Side Caching and Offline Files

To provide flexibility for mobile users and to provide centralized storage for end-user data, Windows Server 2008 R2 shares can be configured to allow, enforce, or disable client-side caching of shared server data. Client-side caching (CSC) is a feature that enables data shared on a server to be synchronized between the server and end-user workstations. This enables end users to access data when the server is unavailable or when the workstation is not connected to the company network. This feature also can be used to ensure that any data stored in a synchronized end-user workstation folder is copied to the server for centralized storage and backup and recoverability.

For CSC to function properly, both the workstation and the server must be configured to support it. CSC from the workstation and server side is more commonly referred to as Offline Files. Depending on the workstation operating system version, different synchronization options are available. A common usage of offline files is to couple offline files with a Group Policy setting called Folder Redirection.

Folder Redirection can be used to redirect the end user's My Documents or Documents folder to a server share. When an end user's My Documents or Documents folder is redirected to a server share with offline files enabled, enforced or not, the folder is automatically configured to synchronize with the server. This functionality ensures that any file an end user saves to their default documents folder will be copied up to the server during synchronization. Folder Redirection is covered in Chapter 27, "Group Policy Management for Network Clients." The default offline file synchronization settings for Windows 7 and Windows Server 2008 R2 will synchronize with the server at logon, logoff, and when a file is opened or saved. Additionally, synchronization can be configured to run when a computer has been idle or when a user locks or unlocks a workstation.

Offline files can be configured on a per-share basis using the shared folder's share property page. By default, all shares allow end users to configure offline file synchronization as they desire. Certain folders—for example, the My Documents or Documents folders—when redirected to a Windows Server 2003, Windows Server 2008, or Windows Server 2008 R2 system, will automatically enable and configure the folder to be synchronized. To synchronize additional shares, perform the following steps on the server and the workstation:

1. Log on to the Windows Server 2008 R2 system with an account with administrator privileges.

2. Click Start, click All Programs, click Administrative Tools, and select Server Manager.

3. Double-click on Roles, and then double-click on File Services.

4. Select Share and Storage Management.

5. In the tasks pane, right-click the share that needs to be available offline, and select Properties.

6. On the Sharing tab, click the Advanced button.

7. Select the Caching tab, and verify that one of the following option buttons is selected:

   ▶ Only the Files and Programs That Users Specify Are Available Offline

   ▶ All Files and Programs That Users Open from the Share Are Automatically Available Offline

8. Close the Share Properties dialog box and the Share and Storage Management console.

9. Log on to the Windows 7 workstation with an account with administrator privileges.

10. Click the Windows flag, or Start button, and select Control Panel.

11. Near the upper-right corner of the Control Panel window, pull down the View By menu and choose to view the window by Small Icons instead of Categories.

12. Scroll down in the window as necessary to locate Sync Center and click on the link.

13. When the Sync Center window opens, click on the Manage Offline Files link in the left pane of the window.

14. When the Offline Files window opens, verify that the top button on the General tab is labeled Disable Offline Files, which means that offline file functionality is enabled. If the button is labeled Enable Offline Files, click the button and click OK to save the settings and reboot the workstation.

## BranchCache

BranchCache is a new feature for Windows Server 2008 R2 and Windows 7. BranchCache allows a branch office that has no server to allow local workstations to locate and locally store copies of files and folders hosted on remote Windows Server 2008 R2 BranchCache file servers. When BranchCache is installed on a Windows Server 2008 R2 file server, and BranchCache is enabled on a particular file share, when a remote branch office user on a Windows 7 workstation requests the file from the file server, it broadcasts the request on the local network. If no copy exists, it will pull a copy to the local machine. The updates to that file will be sent across the network as changes are made. When the next Windows 7 workstation attempts to access this same file from across the network, the broadcast for that file will be sent on the local network, and in this particular example, the file will be referenced from the original workstation that copied the file over during the initial request, thus improving access performance to the file and reducing network traffic. More detailed information on BranchCache is included in Chapter 32, "Optimizing Windows Server 2008 R2 for Branch Office Communications." To enable BranchCache on a Windows Server 2008 R2 system, perform the steps in the following sections.

### Install the BranchCache Service

Before BranchCache can be utilized, the service must be installed on a Windows Server 2008 R2 system. To install the BranchCache service, perform the following steps:

1. Log on to the Windows Server 2008 R2 system with the File Services Role installed with an account with administrator privileges.

2. Click Start, click All Programs, click Administrative Tools, and select Server Manager.

3. Double-click on Roles in the tree pane to expand the role services. In the tasks pane on the right, scroll down to Role Services until you reach the File Services Role section. Under the File Service Role section, check to see whether the BranchCache for network files is installed.

4. If the service is not installed, click on Add Role Services and follow the steps to check and install the BranchCache for network files service.

### Enable BranchCache on a File Share

Once the BranchCache for network files service is installed on the Windows Server 2008 R2 system, the service can be enabled on a share-by-share basis. To enable BranchCache functionality on a particular server share, perform the following steps:

1. Log on to the Windows Server 2008 R2 system with an account with administrator privileges.

2. Click Start, click All Programs, click Administrative Tools, and select Server Manager.

3. Double-click on Roles, and then double-click on File Services.

4. Select Share and Storage Management.

5. In the tasks pane, right-click the share that needs to have BranchCache functionality enabled and select Properties.

6. On the Sharing tab, click the Advanced button.

7. Select the Caching tab, and verify that the Only the Files and Programs That Users Specify Are Available Offline option button is selected. Check the Enable BranchCache check box, and click OK to close the Advanced window.

8. Click OK again to save the settings to the share and close the Server Manager window.

Before BranchCache functionality is enabled, network administrators need to understand the service in greater detail, especially because it is currently only supported on Windows 7 workstations and Windows Server 2008 R2, and any lower-level client will not be able to make use of this feature. In cases where Windows Vista or older clients still exist on remote or branch office networks, administrators should continue to deploy remote file servers with replicated DFS file shares when access to large or numerous files is required.

## Managing Folder Shares

Folders can be shared on FAT, FAT32, and NTFS volumes. When a folder is shared, as stated earlier, share options can be configured, including the share name, description, share permissions, access-based enumeration, limiting the number of simultaneous connections, the default offline file settings, and BranchCache if the service is already installed on the Windows Server 2008 R2 system. There are many ways to create a share, but to provide the most functionality during the share creation task, administrators should use the Share and Storage Management console located in Server Manager.

28

The Share and Storage Management console can be used to create shares and provision storage, including tasks such as creating volumes on existing Windows disks. To create a new share using the Share and Storage Management console, perform the following steps:

1. Log on to the Windows Server 2008 R2 system with an account with administrator privileges.

2. Click Start, click All Programs, click Administrative Tools, and select Server Manager.

3. Double-click on Roles, and then double-click on File Services.

4. Select Share and Storage Management.

5. In the Actions pane, click Provision Share to invoke the Provision a Shared Folder Wizard.

6. For this example, a new folder called HumanResources will be created and shared on the C: drive. Type `c:\HumanResources` in the location area, and click Next.

7. A pop-up window opens, stating that the folder does not exist; click Yes to create the folder.

8. On the NTFS Permissions page, select the No, Do Not Change NTFS Permissions option button, and click Next to continue. If desired, click to change the permissions and add the Human Resources department members or security groups to limit access to the share.

9. On the Share Protocols page, select the SMB protocol to share the folder to Windows and other compatible SMB clients, type in the name of the share if the default is not desired, and click Next to continue. If the Services for NFS is installed, the administrator can also enable the NFS protocol for this share by checking the NFS check box and entering a share name.

10. On the SMB Settings page, click the Advanced button to configure the advanced share settings.

11. In the Advanced Settings window, select the User Limits tab to configure the maximum number of connections to the share and check the Enable Access-based Enumeration check box.

12. On the Caching tab, select the No Files or Programs from the Share Are Available Offline option button, as shown in Figure 28.8, and click OK. Because we are sharing a folder that will contain Human Resources data, users should only be able to access the folders and files when connected to the company network and that is why we are disabling caching. Also, due to the secure nature of some Human Resources data, we have also enabled access-based enumeration to ensure that the users who do not have access to the data do not even see the folders or files hosted within the share.

13. Back on the SMB Settings page, click Next to continue.

14. On the SMB Permissions page, select the Administrators Have Full Control; All Other Users and Groups Have Only Read Access option button, and click Next. This permission setting is preferred on some networks to allow administrators to upload new data to the share from the network to simplify administration. If tighter security is required, as would be typical with a Human Resources folder, the administrator can select the users and groups that have custom share permissions and

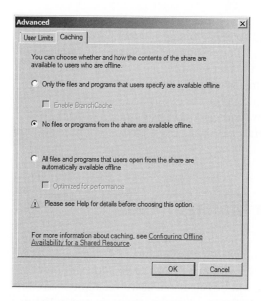

FIGURE 28.8    Disabling caching on a file share.

configure the permissions to allow only the network administrators and Human Resources department members access to the share.

15. If the File Server Resource Manager is installed, the Quota Policy page is displayed. On the Quota Policy page, configure the Apply Quota check box as necessary, and click Next to continue.

16. If the File Server Resource Manager is installed, the File Screen Policy page is displayed on the next page. On the File Screen Policy page, configure the Apply File Screen check box as necessary, and click Next to continue.

17. On the DFS Namespace Publishing page, clear the check box, and click Next to continue.

18. On the Review Settings and Create Share page, review the chosen settings and if everything appears correct, click Create to continue.

19. The Confirmation page is displayed to show the results of the share creation. Click Close to complete the share creation.

Using the Share and Storage Management console on Windows Server 2008 R2 systems with the File Server Resource Manager (FSRM) installed enables administrators to fully configure a share's properties and security settings. That is why no file server should be deployed without the FSRM and why shares should only be created using the Share and Storage Management console.

As a best practice, always define share permissions for every share regardless of the volume format type. When a share is first created using the Share and Storage Management console, the administrator is provided three standard permissions configuration options as well as the ability to customize the permissions. The three preconfigured permissions options use the local Administrators group and the Everyone group for share permissions. Using any of the three preconfigured settings and not customizing permissions might not be acceptable for companies that must adhere to strict security requirements as the Everyone group can enable guest and anonymous share access and viewing. Even though the guest account is disabled by default, and anonymous access is disabled by default, using a best-practice recommendation is to always replace the Everyone group with at least the Authenticated Users, local server Users, or Domain Users group to require authentication before accessing a share.

# Volume-Based NTFS Quota Management

Quotas can be enabled and configured at the volume level and applied to user and group objects. This is the same quota management included with Windows 2000 Server, Windows Server 2003, Windows Server 2003 R2, Windows Server 2008, and Window Server 2008 R2. Quotas enabled at the volume will be calculated based on all files saved to the volume by a particular user who is not part of the server administrators group. Volume quotas can only be enabled on NTFS volumes and cannot be applied to any lower level, such as a subfolder. The key to a successful implementation of quotas on a volume is setting the correct file permissions for the entire volume and folders and to limit the data transferred to a volume for an end user by a third party, such as a desktop or server administrator.

The steps required to enable and implement quotas based on folders and not an entire volume are detailed later in the chapter in the "Configuring Quotas with File Server Resource Manager" section. The quota management features available in the File Server Resource Manager are different from the features included with NTFS volume quotas; Table 28.1 details the differences.

TABLE 28.1   Quota Differences Between FSRM and NTFS

| Quota Capabilities | FSRM Quotas | NTFS Quotas |
| --- | --- | --- |
| Quota tracking | By folder or by volume | Per user on a specific volume only |
| Calculation of storage usage | By actual disk space used | By the logical file size on the volume |
| Notification method | By email, custom reports, and event log entries | By event log only |

**NOTE**

Prior to the release of FSRM, organizations used to depend on NTFS volume quotas or third-party products to provide their quota storage management capabilities; however, FSRM has effectively replaced the use of NTFS volume quotas. The coverage of NTFS volume quotas in this section is merely to describe the process and use of NTFS volume quotas; however, most organizations should consider using FSRM quotas and should avoid using NTFS volume quotas or both types because they are not complementary to each other.

To enable quotas for an NTFS volume, perform the following steps:

1. Log on to the Windows Server 2008 R2 system with an account with administrator privileges.
2. Click Start, click All Programs, click Administrative Tools, and select Server Manager.
3. In the tree pane, double-click the Storage node, and select Disk Management.
4. In the tasks pane, scroll down to locate the desired volume, right-click the volume, and select Properties.
5. Select the Quota tab and check the Enable Quota Management check box.
6. Enter the appropriate quota limit and warning thresholds and decide whether users will be denied write access when the limit is reached, as shown in Figure 28.9.

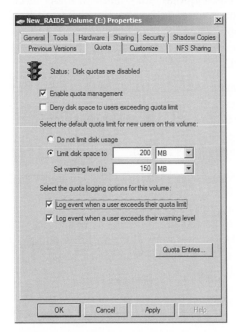

FIGURE 28.9   Enabling NTFS volume quotas.

28

7. Click OK to complete the quota configuration for the NTFS volume.

8. A window opens, prompting you to confirm the enabling of quotas; click OK to enable the quota and scan the volume to update quota statistics.

9. After you configure quotas, open the properties of the volume, select the Quota tab, and click the Quota Entries button to review the existing quotas based on data already stored on the volume.

# File Server Resource Manager (FSRM)

Windows Server 2008 R2 includes a file system management and reporting configuration tool named the File Server Resource Manager (FSRM). This service and tool was first introduced in Windows Server 2003 R2 and provides administrators with the ability to configure quota management at the volume and folder level, create and apply file screening policies, generate alert notifications and reports on a schedule and in real time, and classify files and folders based on administratively defined criteria.

With the volume-level quota management, previously included with Windows Server versions, administrators were very limited on how quotas could be applied and several issues were encountered. Many organizations that required tighter control of their storage were forced to utilize third-party quota management software to get the functionality they required. With the quota management functionality included with the FSRM service in Windows Server 2008 R2, administrators can now create quotas at a volume or folder level and create exceptions or tighter restrictions as required in subfolders. With this sort of functionality, a standard quota size can be established and specific managers, executives, or administrators or specific departments or collaborative groups could have different quota policies applied on the folders that require different storage settings.

With the file screening functionality of FSRM, organizations can restrict all users from storing certain types of files on server storage; for example, music, video, or executables are common files that are screened for end users. Of course, this can be overridden using file screen exceptions to allow these file types in a specific folder or set of folders beneath the parent folder or volume to which the file screen policy is applied.

The new feature included with Windows Server 2008 R2 FSRM is the File Classification Infrastructure. This new functionality can be used to run scheduled tasks that identify and tag or classify files based on their storage location and/or the content stored within the file. Of course, FCI can only search through the content of certain file types, which does not include encrypted files. As this is the first implementation or release of the FCI on the Windows platform, expect that future releases will detail the types of files that can be classified by content and the built-in actions that can be performed after classification is performed on a set of files.

## Uses of File Server Resource Manager

FRSM allows administrators to set quotas on volumes and folders as well as implementing file screening functionality or file classification by location or content. Even though in today's market disk storage is much more affordable than in previous years, the amount of time required to back up and restore the data still needs to be managed. Furthermore, many more organizations need to ensure that their file systems meet certain security and regulatory compliance policies and FSRM can assist with these tasks. Some of the most common uses of FSRM are as follows:

▶ **Setting limits on storage**—An administrator can set the limit on how much disk space a user or group of users can store within a system volume or folder. This is the traditional quota limit item that can limit users to store, for example, 100MB of files on the network.

▶ **Providing storage limit flexibility of group data**—When a user or group of users need to have different storage limits, rather than allowing these users unlimited access, FSRM can be configured to allow the extension of storage usage beyond the default within specific, designated folders. This can be achieved by applying a strict quota policy on a parent folder and either disabling the quota on a subfolder or applying a less-restrictive quota policy on the necessary folder or folders.

▶ **Enforcing storage policies**—FSRM does more than just define storage policies, but can also help administrators enforce the policies by creating reports and generating notifications of policy violations and predefined storage threshold limits, on a real-time or scheduled basis, that can be sent via email, stored in event logs, or stored in designated report folders.

▶ **File screen policies**—Administrators can block the storing of a particular type of file or sets of files. In previous years, many organizations were surprised to discover that a significant source of increased data storage requirements had to do with end users downloading and storing music files on the server. File screen exceptions can be created and applied to subfolders as necessary.

▶ **File classification**—Administrators can define file classification properties and rules that can be manually run or scheduled to check files and define file classification property values based on the administratively defined rules. This can be useful in identifying data based on usage characteristics or identifying data based on content to ensure higher security and management of sensitive data.

## Installing the File Server Resource Manager Tools

The File Server Resource Manager tools can be installed separately or it can be installed during the installation of the File Services role. If the FSRM tools needs to be installed on a system that is not a file server or just installed separately, perform the following steps:

1. Log on to the Windows Server 2008 R2 system with an account with administrator privileges.

2. Click Start, click All Programs, click Administrative Tools, and select Server Manager.

3. Click on the Features node in the tree pane, and then click on Add Features in the tasks pane.

4. The Add Features Wizard opens. On the Select Feature page, click the plus symbol next to Remote Server Administration Tools.

5. Click the plus symbol next to Role Administration Tools.

28

**6.** Click the plus symbol next to File Services tools, check the File Server Resource Manager Tools check box, as shown in Figure 28.10, and click Next to continue.

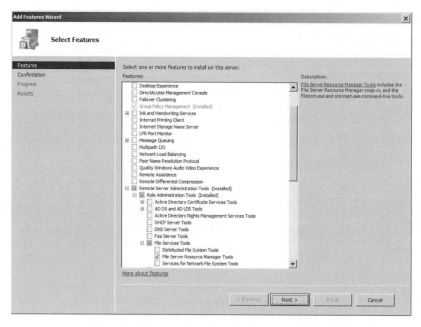

FIGURE 28.10    Selecting the File Server Resource Manager tools.

**7.** On the Confirm Installation Selections page, review the selections made and click Install to continue.

**8.** On the Installation Results page, review the result summary, and click Close to complete the installation.

On a system with the FSRM tools installed but not the File Server role and File Server Resource Manager services, FSRM will only be available from the Administrative Tools menu to manage remote servers. On systems with the File Server role and File Server Resource Manager services installed, FSRM will be available in the Server Manager console in the File Services group under Roles.

> **NOTE**
>
> If the File Services role is installed but the File Server Resource Manager tool cannot connect to the system, chances are that during the File Services role installation, File Server Resource Manager was not selected. To add this functionality, the File Service Resource Manager service will need to be added using the Add Role Services from the tasks pane in the Server Manager Role node.

## FSRM Global Options

To enable the full functionality of the FSRM service, FSRM notifications, and FSRM auditing and reporting, FSRM global options need to be configured. FSRM settings such as the SMTP server to use for email notifications, notification limits, the location of reports, and enabling file screen auditing can be configured by right-clicking the File Server Resource Manager node in Server Manager, and selecting Configure Options. FSRM settings apply to only the single server they are configured on. These settings can be configured on remote servers using the FSRM console, but settings cannot be created and applied to multiple servers using the FSRM interface.

## Configuring Quotas with File Server Resource Manager

After the File Server Resource Manager service and tool has been installed, an administrator can launch the tool and begin creating FSRM quota and file screening policies. To open the FSRM console, perform the following steps:

1. Log on to the Windows Server 2008 R2 system with an account with administrator privileges.
2. Click Start, click All Programs, click Administrative Tools, and select Server Manager.
3. Double-click on Roles.
4. Double-click on File Services.
5. Double-click on Share and Storage Management.
6. Double-click on the File Server Resource Manager console.

To create a new quota using the File Server Resource Manager console, continuing from the preceding set of steps, perform the following steps:

1. Double-click the Quota Management node under the FSRM console.
2. Select the Quotas node in the tree pane.
3. In the Actions pane, click the Create Quota link to begin the process.
4. When the Create Quota window opens, specify the path for the quota, such as E:\UserShares.
5. Select the Auto Apply Template and Create Quotas on Existing and New Subfolders option button.
6. In the Quota Properties section of the window, select the Derive Properties from This Quota Template option button and from the drop-down menu, select the 200 MB Limit Reports to User template, and click Create, as shown in Figure 28.11.
7. After the quota is created, click the Refresh link in the Actions pane.
8. In the tasks pane, the new quota will be listed, along with the quotas applied to all existing subfolders and the current status of each quota.
9. Review the quotas as desired and close the Server Manager console.

28

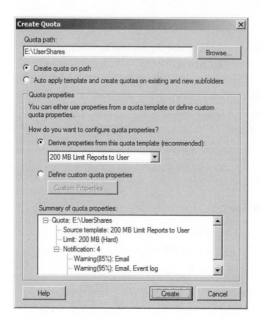

FIGURE 28.11    Creating a new FSRM quota.

## Adjusting Quotas

When an auto apply quota is created on a folder, all new subfolders of that parent folder will inherit the quota. In some cases, it might be necessary to exclude a particular subfolder from the parent folder quota or to modify the quota of that particular subfolder. When this is necessary, an administrator simply needs to right-click the quota of the particular folder and select Edit Quota Properties. In the Quota Properties window, the quota can be disabled by checking the Disable Quota check box or the quota space limit can be adjusted, as shown in Figure 28.12.

## Creating a Quota Template

When working with quotas, rather than defining the storage limits on each and every folder being issued a quota, an administrator can create a quota template and apply the template to the folder, simplifying the quota policy creation process. Within the quota template, the administrator can define the following:

▶ **Amount of disk space of the quota**—The administrator can define in KB, MB, GB, or TB the amount of space to be set as the quota for the template.

▶ **Hard limit or soft limit**—A hard limit does not allow a user to extend beyond the hard limit for storage, whereas a soft limit gives the user a warning they have

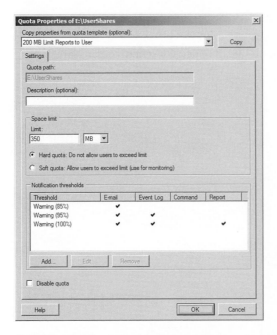

FIGURE 28.12   Adjusting the quota space limit of a quota managed folder.

exceeded the policy limit; however, it allows the user to continue to save files beyond the limit.

▶ **Notification thresholds**—When the storage limit nears or reaches the quota limit, a series of events can occur, such as the automatic generation of an email warning, event log entry, or a script can be executed.

To create a new quota template, click on the Quota Templates node beneath the FSRM console within the Server Manager File Services Role node, and perform the following steps:

1. Click on Create Quota Template in the Actions pane to open the Create Quota Template window.

2. Type in a name of the template—for example, `500mb Hard Limit for Sales`—and enter a label of Quota `Template for Sale Staff Users`.

3. Specify the storage limit for the quota; for this example, enter `500` and choose MB from the list.

4. Pick whether you want a hard limit or soft limit for the quota; for this example, select Hard Quota: Do Not Allow Users to Exceed Limit.

5. Create notification thresholds by clicking the Add button and defining limits. A common threshold is an 85% limit that notifies users via email that they have

28

achieved 85% of their limit and to consider deleting files so they do not exceed their limit.

6. The quota limit will look similar to Figure 28.13. Click OK when you are satisfied with your settings.

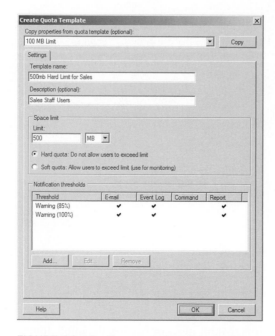

FIGURE 28.13    New quota template settings.

The administrator can now create quotas and apply this template or other templates to the quota settings.

## Creating File Screens

Another function of the File Server Resource Manager is the ability to create file screens. A file screen applied to a folder inspects the file to be stored and either allows or disallows a user from saving the file based on the file screen. A file screen blocks files from being stored within folder and all subfolders. As an example, an organization can allow the storage of all undefined documents and deny the storage of *.mp3 audio files and *.mpg video files by applying a file screen that contains these two file types to a particular folder or set of folders.

To create a file screen, perform the following steps:

1. Open the File Server Resource Manager and expand it.

2. Double-click File Screening Management.

3. Select the File Screens node. In the Actions pane, click Create File Screen.

4. In the Create File Screen window, specify the path for the file screen, such as E:\UserShares.

5. In the File Screen Properties section of the window, select the Derive Properties from This File Screen Template option button, or choose Define Custom File Screen Properties depending on whether you want to apply a template or create a custom screen. For this example, choose the Derive Properties from This File Screen Template option button, and select Block Audio and Video Files from the drop-down menu, as shown in Figure 28.14. Click Create to create the new file screen.

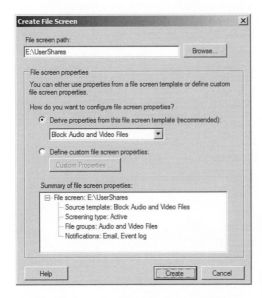

FIGURE 28.14    Creating a new file screen.

## Creating a File Screen Template

Windows Server 2008 R2 provides several functional file screen templates, but when customized file screens are required, administrators can create new file screen templates. A file screen template includes file groups, screening policies, and notification settings:

▶ **File groups**—The administrator can define the file types into groups, such as Office 2007 file groups containing *.docx Microsoft Word files and *.xlsx Microsoft Excel files.

▶ **Active screening and passive screening**—An active screen does not enable a user to save file types by design, whereas a passive screen allows the file type, but it is logged for monitoring and reporting functionality.

▶ **Notifications**—When a user attempts to save a file that matches the file screen designation, a notification can be generated. The notification can be the automatic generation of an email warning or event log, a script can be executed, and a report can be generated and sent out immediately.

To create a new file screen template, perform the following steps:

1. Open the File Server Resource Manager and expand it.

2. Double-click File Screening Management.

3. Select File Screen Templates. In the Actions pane, click Create File Screen Template.

4. In the Create File Screen Template window, enter a name for the template—for example, `Company Standard File Screen Template`.

5. Select the Active Screening option button.

6. In the File Group section, check the boxes next to the following file groups:

   ▶ Audio and Video Files

   ▶ Backup Files

   ▶ Executable Files

   ▶ System Files

7. Configure the notification settings on the E-mail, Event Log, Command, and Report tabs, as required.

8. On the Settings tab, review the configuration, and click OK to create the new file screen, as shown in Figure 28.15.

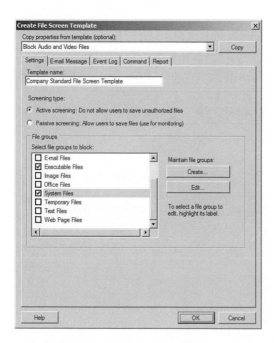

FIGURE 28.15   New file screen template settings.

The new file screen template can now be used to create a new file screen.

> **NOTE**
>
> It is important to note that file screens are based on the filename or filename extensions defined within the file groups applied to the file screen. A savvy end user can simply rename a screened file to bypass the file screen, but Windows Server 2008 R2 has the ability to detect some files by their characteristics and not necessarily by the file extension name, so extended testing should be performed when very strict file screening enforcement is required to ensure the highest level of reliability.

## File Screen Exceptions

In many cases, as with quotas, file screen standards can be created and applied to server storage, but certain file types might be required or certain users might require storage of blocked file types. In these cases, file screen exceptions can be created and applied to subfolders of a file-screened parent folder. For example, in the previous example, a template was created to block executables but a file screen exception could be created to allow executable files in a subfolder. Of course, the subfolder should be secured by NTFS permissions to limit who can save these types of files to the folder.

## Generating Storage Reports with FSRM

The File Server Resource Manager provides the ability to create or automatically generate reports for quota and file screen activity. The various reports that can be generated include the following:

- ▶ Duplicate Files
- ▶ File Screening Audit
- ▶ Files by File Group
- ▶ Files by Owner
- ▶ Files by Property
- ▶ Large Files
- ▶ Least Recently Accessed Files
- ▶ Most Recently Accessed Files
- ▶ Quota Usage

### Generating Reports in Real Time

Reports can be generated on a real-time basis to view the file storage information on demand. To generate a report, right-click the Storage Reports Management node of the FSRM utility, and choose Generate Reports Now. Then do the following:

1. Click on the Add button to define the scope of the volumes or folders that the report will be based on (for example E:\UserShares) and click OK to return to the Storage Report Task Properties window.

28

2. Choose which report or reports will be generated by checking the check box for the particular report type.

3. Choose the report format for the new report (for example, the default option of DHTML) by checking the appropriate check box in the Report Formats section of the window.

4. Click OK when the report options are configured.

5. A new window opens, prompting you to decide to wait for the report to generate and automatically display the report or to generate the report in the background and store it in the default report location. Select the Wait for Reports to be Generated and Then Display Them option and click OK.

6. Each report will be displayed in a separate browser window or tab; close or save the reports as desired.

### Scheduling Reports to Be Generated on a Regular Basis

Reports can be generated on a regular basis (such as weekly or monthly), typically for the purpose of reporting file storage information to management. To schedule a report, right-click the Storage Reports Management node of the FSRM utility, and choose Schedule a New Report Task. Then do the following:

1. Click on the Add button to choose the volume or file share that you want to generate a report, such as R:\UserShares.

2. Choose which report or reports will be generated; by default, all reports will be selected except the Files by Property report.

3. Choose the report format you want to use—for example, the default option of DHTML.

4. Select the Delivery tab if the report should be emailed as well as stored in the global StorageReports folder.

5. Select the Schedule tab, and click the Create Schedule button to create a schedule for the automated report generation. Click OK when the desired schedule or schedules are defined.

6. Click OK when you are finished.

The report or reports specified will be generated at the scheduled intervals and any email addresses specified on the Delivery tab will have the reports emailed to them when the reports are generated. The scheduled report will be listed in the tasks pane when the Storage Reports Management node is selected. The scheduled report can be generated at will by right-clicking on the scheduled report and selecting Run Report Task Now.

## File Classification Management

As stated earlier in this chapter, Windows Server 2008 R2 FSRM includes a new feature called file classification, based on the new File Classification Infrastructure or FCI. File classification allows an organization to define properties and rules that will add specific file properties to better define the characteristics of the classified files. File classification properties are supported on a Windows Server 2008 R2 NTFS partition and the file classification properties will follow Microsoft Office 2007 files and SharePoint files when moved around. All other files that are classified will have their properties stored within the NTFS volume they are hosted on, but if the files are moved to other Windows Server 2008 R2 NTFS volumes, these properties will follow the files.

File classification in Windows Server 2008 R2 is the first release of this feature and is sure to be more and more valuable as third-party Microsoft partners and independent software vendors extend the functionality included with the default framework provided. Currently, out of the box, Microsoft Windows Server 2008 R2 allows administrators to create file properties and automatically classify files with these properties based on the file location and, in some cases, based on the content stored within the file. The steps to file classification include, first, enabling and defining file properties that can be used for classification and, second, creating classification rules that will actually classify files according to the criteria defined within the rule, and properties and values that are applied to this rule. Once files are classified, file management tasks can be created to perform tasks upon classified files, such as moving files to designated folders or performing custom tasks such as running automated scripts to perform any number of tasks related to the particular file classifications.

The best way to understand file classification is to start defining file classification properties, file classification rules, and file management tasks on data that has been copied from a server share to an isolated lab server running Windows Server 2008 R2. Once a file is classified and has properties defined, these properties cannot be removed—they can only be overwritten or merged with other properties, so performing any sort of learning or testing on production data can result in undesired changes that would require heavy manual work to reverse. To begin using the file classification features of Windows Server 2008 R2, install the File Server Resource Manager service and tool as previously described in this chapter, then perform the steps outlined in the proceeding sections.

## Classification Properties

Classification properties are used to categorize files to be used later for file management tasks or reporting. A classification property, as included with Windows Server 2008 R2, includes the following classification property types:

- ▶ Yes/No
- ▶ Date-time
- ▶ Number
- ▶ Ordered List
- ▶ String
- ▶ Multichoice
- ▶ Multistring

To get a good understanding of how classification can be used, this section and the following sections provide an example of how classification can be used to classify files based on content that includes the word *password*. To do this, we will create a file property type of Yes/No and create a classification rule to search the E:\ITDept folder for any files containing the word and to classify these files as necessary. To perform this task, we must first create the classification property. Perform the following steps to create the classification property:

1. Log on to a Windows Server 2008 R2 system with the FSRM service and tool installed, with an account with administrative rights.

2. Click Start, click All Programs, click Administrative Tools, and select Server Manager.

3. Expand Roles, expand File Services, expand Share and Storage Management, and double-click on the File Server Resource Manager node beneath it.

4. Double-click Classification Management and select the Classification Properties node.

5. In the Actions pane, click on the Create Property link to start the creation of the classification property.

6. In the Create Classification Property Definition window, type `Files with Passwords` in the Property name section, enter a description, and choose the Property type of Yes/No.

7. In the Value section, enter a description as desired and click OK to create the classification property, as shown in Figure 28.16.

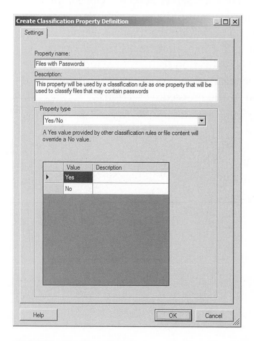

FIGURE 28.16    Creating a new classification property.

Once the new classification property is created, we can create a classification rule that will use this property to classify files that the rule determines to meet the criteria.

## Classification Rules

Once the file administrator has created the necessary file classification properties, they can proceed in creating classification rules that will actually process and classify the files that meet the rule criteria, by applying the necessary classification property values to the file collections. To create a new classification rule, perform the following steps:

1. Log on to the same Windows Server 2008 R2 system that the Files with Passwords classification property was previously defined on, with an account with administrative rights.

2. Click Start, click All Programs, click Administrative Tools, and select Server Manager.

3. Expand Roles, expand File Services, expand Share and Storage Management, and double-click on the File Server Resource Manager node beneath it.

4. Double-click Classification Management and select the Classification Rules node.

5. In the Actions pane, click on the Create a New Rule link to start the creation of a new classification rule.

6. In the Classifications Rule Definitions window, type in the name of the rule as Classify files with passwords and enter a description.

7. In the Scope section of the page, click the Add button to define the volumes and or folders that this classification rule will be applied to. For our example, we will apply this rule to E:\ITDept. When the location is specified, all subfolders will be included.

8. Once the name, description, and file locations are defined, click on the Classification tab and select Content Classifier from the Classification mechanism drop-down menu.

9. In the Property Name section, select the Files with Passwords property and set the property value to be assigned as Yes, as shown in Figure 28.17.

10. Click the Advanced button to set the additional parameters that will actually be used to determine if the files match the criteria and should be classified with the property defined in this rule.

11. In the Additional Rule Parameters window, select the Additional Classification Parameters tab. On this tab, administrators can define three different types of criteria used to search with a files content. These three types are as follows:

   ▶ **RegularExpression**—The RegularExpression is the same as is used with .NET programming and can be used to find complex or multiple types of data formats, for more complex searches.

   ▶ **String**—The String type is used to find a very specific string, such as *password* that will not be dependent on the case of the string, although the string must be an exact match. For example, the string *password* will not match *passwords*, as that is a different string.

   ▶ **StringCaseSensitive**—The StringCaseSensitive is the same as the string, in that the entire string must be an exact match, but the case must match. For example, the StringCaseSensitive string of *Password* will not match the string *password*.

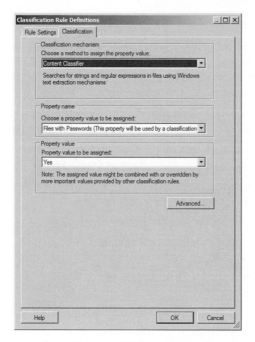

FIGURE 28.17    Defining the classification criteria on a file classification rule.

**12.** For our example, we will specifically look for the word *password* and will not care about the case. In the Name section, type in String and in the value type in password, as shown in Figure 28.18. Click OK when completed.

**13.** Back on the Classification Rule Definitions page, click OK to complete the rule creation.

Once the rule is created, it can be scheduled or run manually. To run all of the rules manually, in the tasks pane, right-click on the Classification Rules node and select Run Classification with All Rules Now. Follow the steps to select the type of report that will be generated and whether the administrator will wait for the classification to complete and display the window or to have the process run in the background. If a schedule or a manual run is performed, any files that meet the properties of any enabled classification rules will be classified, unless these files have been previously classified.

## File Management Tasks

File Management tasks is a new feature within the FSRM console. File Management tasks can be run out of the box on a Windows Server 2008 R2 system, to either expire classified files that meet a certain criteria, by moving these files to a designated folder location, or to perform a custom task. This can be a handy tool to automatically move files that have not been accessed in an extended period of time. Or, in the case of sensitive data, such as files that might contain passwords, this tool can be used to create a custom script to move the

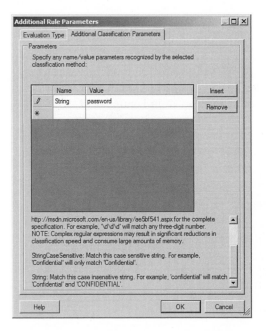

FIGURE 28.18    Defining the additional content parameter for content classification by string.

classified files to a designated, secured folder, and leave a link or note in the original location to instruct any users on how to regain access to that file. Of course, this logic would
need to be created by an administrator because this functionality is not included out of
the box. As an example, to create a new File Management Task to move files that have not
been accessed in over a year, perform the following steps on a Windows Server 2008 R2
system with the FSRM service and tool installed:

1. Log on to a Windows Server 2008 R2 system with the FSRM service and tool
   installed, with an account with administrative rights.

2. Click Start, click All Programs, click Administrative Tools, and select Server Manager.

3. Expand Roles, expand File Services, expand Share and Storage Management, and
   double-click on the File Server Resource Manager node beneath it.

4. Double-click File Management Tasks node beneath the File Server Resource
   Manager node.

5. In the Actions pane, click the Create File Management Task link to start the process.

6. In the Create File Management Task window, on the General tab, type in a task
   name of Move Data not accessed in 1 year and enter a description as desired.

7. In the Scope section, click the Add button to locate and add the folder, folders, or
   volumes to this task.

28

8. Click on the Action tab and for action type, choose File Expiration, and in the expiration directory, type or browse to a volume and folder location to where the files that meet this criteria should be moved.

9. Click on the Notification tab and click the Add button to add notifications to users and administrators so they can be notified of when particular files will be considered expired and moved to the expiration directory, as shown in Figure 28.19.

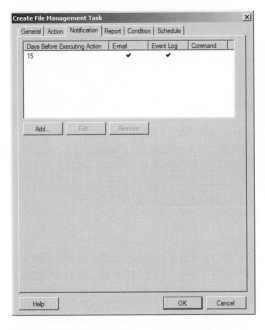

FIGURE 28.19 Defining the notification settings for a File Management Task.

10. Back in the Create File Management Task window, click on the Condition tab and check the Day Since File Was Last Accessed check box and enter a value of 365.

11. In the Effective Starting section, enter the date that files will actually begin expiration; this date should be more than the amount of days included in any notification.

12. Click on the Schedule tab, click the Create button and create a new schedule. Click OK until the windows are closed to complete the creation of the file management task. Depending on the date chosen for the effective date, a pop-up might open stating that the effective date must be pushed forward to ensure that users are notified in advance before their data is moved.

Once the task is completed, it will run on the designated schedule and will begin notifying administrators and users when files will be moved. One important point to consider is that once a file is expired and moved, there will be no indication of where or when that file was moved when users go to the original location of the expired file. Much more can be done with file management tasks, including performing custom actions on files that have been previously classified, and it is recommend that any organization wanting to leverage this new File Classification Infrastructure test it thoroughly on copied data in an isolated lab network.

# The Distributed File System

To improve the reliability and availability of file shares in an enterprise network, Microsoft has developed the Distributed File System (DFS). DFS improves file share availability by providing a single, unified namespace to access shared folders hosted across one or more servers. A user needs to only remember a single server or domain name and share name to connect to a DFS shared folder.

DFS has many benefits and features that can simplify data access and management from both the administrator and end-user perspective. DFS provides three main functions, as follows:

▶ **Data redundancy**—DFS can provide access to a single share that is hosted on multiple servers. This allows clients to get referred to or fail over to a different server if the primary server cannot be contacted.

▶ **Automated data replication**—DFS can be configured to utilize the Distributed File System Replication (DFSR) service, and can be configured to automatically synchronize folders between DFS servers to provide data redundancy or centralized storage of branch office data.

▶ **Distributed data consolidation**—DFS can be used to provide a single namespace that can contain several distinct or unique data sets, which can be hosted on separate servers. This enables administrators to provide access to existing file shares hosted on many different file servers, from the single namespace, without adding replication or redundant data sets.

## DFS Namespaces

DFS can be used in a few different ways, but it will usually require the creation of a DFS namespace. A DFS namespace can be the name of a single server and share folder or the DNS and NetBIOS name of an Active Directory domain and share folder. The DFS namespace is also referred to as the namespace root. The namespace allows connections to automatically be redirected to different servers without user knowledge. Using Figure 28.20 as an example, when a client connects to the domain DFS namespace named \\Companyabc.com\Apps, the client will be redirected to \\Server10\Apps, and the client will be unaware of this redirection.

28

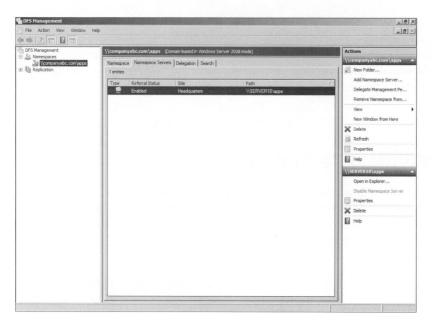

FIGURE 28.20    Domain DFS namespace.

For DFS to function properly with regard to client redirection and just basic connectivity, a compatible DFS client is required. In a network that supports different versions of Windows, Apple Mac, and UNIX clients, DFS should be tested on all clients before it is released to production. DFS-compatible clients are currently available for the following Microsoft Windows operating systems:

- Windows 2000 Professional and Server.

- Windows XP Professional.

- Windows Server 2003 and Windows Server 2003 R2.

- Windows Vista Business, Ultimate, and Enterprise.

- Windows 7 Professional, Ultimate, and Enterprise.

- Windows Server 2008 and Windows Server 2008 R2.

- Windows NT Server and Workstation 4.0 with Service Pack 6a and the Active Directory Client Extension found on the Windows 2000 Server CD.

- Windows 98 can support DFS domain namespaces with the installation of the Active Directory Client Extension found on the Windows 2000 Server CD.

Because DFS clients do not connect to the actual server by name, administrators can move shared folders to new servers and user logon scripts and mapped drive designations never need to be changed. In fact, DFS data presented in a single namespace can be hosted on multiple servers to provide redundancy and distribution of large amounts of data.

### Standalone DFS Namespace

A standalone DFS namespace utilizes the name of the server hosting the DFS namespace. Standalone DFS namespaces should be used when file system access needs to be simplified and the amount of data exceeds the capacity of a single server. Also, if no Active Directory domain exists, a standalone DFS namespace is still supported. When a standalone DFS namespace is created on a Windows Server 2008 R2 server that is a member of an Active Directory domain, DFS replication can be configured.

### Domain-Based DFS Namespace

A domain-based DFS namespace utilizes the name of the Active Directory domain the DFS namespace server is a member of. A domain-based DFS namespace is created upon deployment of an Active Directory domain at the location of \\domain\SYSVOL to replicate the domain group policies and logon script folders. Domain-based DFS namespaces support replication using either the File Replication Service or the new Distributed File System Replication service.

### Domain-Based DFS Namespace Windows 2008 Mode

When a new domain-based DFS namespace is created on a Windows Server 2008 R2 system, an option to enable Windows Server 2008 mode is presented. This option is available on Windows Server 2008 and Windows Server 2008 R2 systems when the namespace is hosted on either operating system, and the domain the system is a member of must be running in Windows Server 2008 domain functional level and at least Window Server 2003 forest functional level. This means that the domain must have only Windows Server 2008 domain controllers and the entire forest must have only Windows 2003 and/or Windows 2008 domain controllers.

Windows Server 2008 mode enables the namespace to contain more than 5,000 DFS folders and it also enables access-based enumeration within the DFS namespace. Historically, many organizations ran into issues when deploying DFS because over time, the number of folders beneath a namespace grew too large and they had to create multiple namespaces and segregate the data, which in some cases defeated the purpose for deploying DFS. Windows Server 2008 namespace mode surpasses this previous limitation and with the added bonus of access-based enumeration, it allows for users to locate the data that is relevant to them much easier.

It is important to note that the same functionality enabled for a Windows 2008 mode domain-based namespace exists on standalone DFS namespaces when the namespace server is hosted on a Windows Server 2008 R2 server, so this functionality can be leveraged immediately, even in organizations that are far from meeting the requirements for Windows 2008 mode domain-based namespaces.

## DFS Replication

When an Active Directory domain exists, standalone and domain-based DFS namespaces support the replication of DFS data stored on multiple servers. This can be a valuable tool used to distribute company applications to each site or to provide centralized storage of remote office data for redundancy, centralized backup, and to support users who travel and work in different offices.

With the release of Windows Server 2003 R2 and further improved in Window Server 2008 R2, a service to extend the functionality and optimize DFS Replication has been created. This service is called the Distributed File System Replication (DFSR) service, which utilizes the new Remote Differential Compression (RDC) protocol. DFSR replaces the legacy File Replication Service (FRS) that was previously used to replicate DFS data. As long as all of the DFS servers defined in a DFS replication group are running Windows Server 2003 R2 or later, the DFSR service will be used to replicate the data. If any of the systems are running a previous version operating system, DFS data will be replicated using the File Replication Service. There is one exception to this rule: The Domain System Volume (SYSVOL) will be replicated between domain controllers using the File Replication Service, even if all the domain controllers are running Windows Server 2008 R2, until the domain functional level is raised to the Windows Server 2008 level and the SYSVOL is migrated from FRS to DFSR.

DFS Replication and DFS namespaces are independent of one another, but they can be used together, as they are commonly deployed in this fashion. Replication of folders can be set up between servers that do not host any DFS namespaces or namespace folders but the DFS Replication service must be installed on all systems participating in the replication. Windows Server 2008 R2 increases DFS Replication security and performance because all DFS Replication is compressed and encrypted. Note that the data stream cannot be set to run unencrypted.

## DFS Terminology

To properly understand DFS, a number of technical terms are used when deploying, configuring, and referencing DFS. Although the DFS namespace and DFS Replication have already been described, the remaining terms should also be understood before reading the remainder of this chapter or deploying a new DFS infrastructure:

▶ **DFS namespace**—A unified namespace that presents a centralized view of shared folder data in an organization.

▶ **DFS namespace server**—A Windows server that hosts a DFS namespace.

▶ **DFS namespace root**—The top level of the DFS tree that defines the namespace for DFS and the functionality available. The namespace root is also the name of the DFS namespace. A domain-based root adds fault-tolerant capabilities to DFS by allowing several servers to host the same DFS namespace root.

> **NOTE**
>
> Depending on which Server version, service pack, and edition of Window Server 2003 or 2008 is used will determine how many namespaces are supported on a single server. Please refer to online Microsoft documentation to determine which edition is right for your organization's implementation of DFS.

▶ **DFS folder**—A folder that will be presented under the root when a DFS client connects. When a root is created, folders can be created within the file system, but

DFS folders allow the system to redirect clients to different systems other than the namespace server hosting the root.

▶ **Folder target**—A shared folder hosted on a Windows server. The DFS folder name and the share name do not need to be the same but for troubleshooting purposes it is highly recommended. Multiple folder targets can be assigned to a single DFS folder to provide fault tolerance. If a single folder target is unavailable, clients will be connected to another available target. When DFS folders are created with multiple folder targets, replication can also be configured using DFS replication groups to keep the data across the targets in sync. Folder targets can be a share name or a folder beneath a share. For example, \\server1\userdata or \\server1\userdata\ Finance are both valid folder targets.

▶ **DFS tree**—The hierarchy of the namespace. For example, the DFS tree begins with the DFS root namespace and contains all the defined folders below the root.

▶ **Referrals**—A configuration setting of a DFS namespace and/or folder that defines how DFS clients will connect to the namespace server, a folder in the namespace, or a particular folder target server. Referral properties include limiting client connections to servers in the local Active Directory site and how often to check the availability of a DFS server. Disabling a target's referral keeps it from being used by clients. Target referral can be disabled when maintenance will be performed on a server.

## DFS Replication Terminology

DFS uses either the File Replication Service or the Distributed File System Replication service to automatically replicate data contained in DFS folder targets. To understand the replication concepts, you must understand some key DFS replication terminology. Here are some important terms:

▶ **Replication**—The process of copying data from a source server folder to a destination server folder.

▶ **Replication connection**—The directory object that defines and manages the replication between a sending and receiving replication member server. The replication connection defines the replication schedule, which service will replicate the data, the sending and receiving members, and any bandwidth restrictions for the connection. Each replication connection has only a single sending and receiving replication member.

▶ **Replication member**—A server that shares a common replication connection. The receiving replication server receives data from a sending member server specified in the replication connection. The sending replication partner sends data to the receiving member specified in the replication connections.

▶ **Read-only replication folders**—Windows Server 2008 R2 introduces support for read-only replicas. This can be useful for auditing, centralized backup, or managing data sets. Only the replication members that are not defined as the primary source can host read-only replication folders. Read-Only Domain Controllers host the SYSVOL as a read-only replication folder. When read-only replication folders exist, it

28

is a best practice to ensure that replication is only one-way to the read-only replication folder.

▶ **Replication group**—All the servers, folders, and connections that define a replication set of data.

▶ **Multimaster replication**—This defines two-way replication between multiple servers in a replication group. With multimaster replication, data changed on any server in the group will be replicated to every other server in the group.

# Planning a DFS Deployment

Planning for a DFS implementation requires an administrator to understand the different types of Distributed File System namespaces and the features and limitations of each type, including which operating system versions and domain functional levels are required to enable certain functionality. Also, the administrator must understand which tasks can be automated using DFS and which must be configured manually. For instance, DFS can create the file share for namespace roots, folders, or folder targets, including setting share permissions, but the NTFS permissions and additional share features cannot be configured during this process. As a best practice, DFS administrators should create and define shares, share permissions, and NTFS permissions on the shared folder prior to defining these shares as DFS folder targets.

When an organization wants automated file replication, domain-based DFS and standalone DFS namespaces deployed in an Active Directory domain can utilize Windows Server 2008 DFS Replication using the Remote Differential Compression to replicate shared folders if all of the participating DFS servers are running Windows Server 2008 or later.

## Configuring File Share and NTFS Permissions for DFS Root and Folder Targets

The DFS Management console is not currently capable of configuring advanced share features or setting or synchronizing NTFS permissions for namespace root shares or folder targets. This means that for administrators to ensure proper folder access, administrators should first configure the advanced share features and NTFS permissions on folders that will host namespace roots and folder targets before configuring DFS. If multiple namespace root servers or folder target servers will be utilized, permissions between the servers will need to be manually synchronized to match; otherwise, undesired access or lack or access might result.

## Choosing a DFS Type

As mentioned previously, DFS namespaces can be based on the server name (standalone) or the domain name hosting the namespace. Both provide a single namespace, but only domain namespaces can provide redundancy at the namespace root level.

### Standalone DFS Namespace

A standalone DFS namespace provides the characteristic DFS single namespace. The namespace is defined by the name of the server that hosts the root target and the share. Standalone roots can support only a single root target, but an administrator can configure multiple folder targets. Data stored within multiple folder targets must be kept in sync manually unless the standalone namespace server and all of the folder target servers are members of a single Active Directory domain and will utilize DFS Replication. Standalone roots are normally deployed in environments that do not contain Active Directory domains and can be used to enable access-based enumeration of DFS folders as well as enabling the ability to host more than 5,000 folders within the namespace.

### Domain-Based DFS Namespace

For an administrator to create a domain DFS root, the initial namespace root server must be a member of an Active Directory domain. A domain-based DFS namespace provides a single namespace that is based on the DNS and NetBIOS domain name plus a root name, when the namespace is created. Domain-based DFS namespaces can utilize DFS Replication to replicate data between multiple folder targets.

### Windows 2008 Mode for Domain-based DFS Namespace

Windows 2008 mode for domain-based namespaces enables the namespace to contain more than 5,000 folders and access-based enumeration can also be enabled. To enable this functionality, the forest must be set to Windows Server 2003 or greater forest functional level and the domain that contains the namespace servers must be in Windows Server 2008 domain functional level.

## Planning for DFS Replication

When an organization wants to replicate data stored on Windows Server 2008 R2 systems published in DFS namespaces, administrators must create the namespaces on servers that are members of an Active Directory domain. Replication can be configured between multiple targets on a DFS folder or on Windows Server 2008 or Windows Server 2008 R2 systems that do not participate in a DFS namespace. When multiple targets are defined for a folder, DFS can utilize the FRS or the DFSR service to create replication connection objects and automatically synchronize data between each target.

### Initial Master

When replication is first configured using the DFS console and the New Replication Group Wizard, the administrator can choose which target server will be the initial master. The data contained on the initial master is replicated to the remaining targets. For targets on servers other than the initial master, existing data is moved to a hidden directory, and the current folder is filled with the data contained only in the initial master folder. After initial replication is complete, the administrator can restore data moved to the hidden folder back to the working directory, where it can trigger replication outbound to all the other replicas in the replica set, if replication is two-way and neither target is set to read-only. As a best practice, when adding additional targets to a replica set, try to start with empty folders.

### The Staging Folder

The staging folder is the location where a DFS Replication member stores the data that will be replicated to other replication members within a replication group. In a fully synchronized replication group, the staging folder on all servers will be empty. Because replication data will travel through this folder, the drive hosting the staging folder must have sufficient free space to accommodate the maximum size of the staging folder and should be able to handle the additional disk load. By default, the staging folder is limited to 4GB. The default location for the staging folder will be located in the target share folder in a hidden directory named c:\Apps\DfsrPrivate\Staging, if the target is located in c:\Apps as an example. The staging folder and its 4GB limit is unique to each target on each server.

## Determining the Replication Topology

Windows Server 2008 R2 DFS provides a number of built-in replication topologies to choose from when an administrator is configuring replication between DFS folder targets or replication group members; they're described next. As a general guideline, it might be prudent to configure DFS Replication connections and a schedule to follow current Active Directory site replication topology connections or the existing network topology when the organization wants true multimaster replication.

### Hub and Spoke

A hub-and-spoke topology is somewhat self-descriptive. A single target is designated as the replication hub server, and every other target (spoke target) replicates exclusively with it. The hub target has two replication connections with each spoke target: sending and receiving. A hub-and-spoke topology requires three or more servers, and when the hub target is unavailable, replication updates stop between all replication members. Windows Server 2008 R2 introduces the ability to specify more than one hub when creating a hub-and-spoke replication topology. In previous releases, this required creating a custom topology.

### Full Mesh

Using a full mesh topology, each target has a connection to every other target in the replication group. This enables replication to continue among available replication members when any member becomes unavailable. Because each member has a connection to every other member, replication can continue with as few as two replication members. Using this topology with read/write replication sets can lead to data conflicts if data is being changed in multiple sites so this topology should be used with caution.

### No Topology and Custom Topology

During the creation of a replication group, one of the topology options is the No Topology option. Selecting this option enables an administrator to create a custom replication topology after the replication group is created. A custom topology allows an administrator to define specific replication connections for each target. This option can be useful if an organization wants to define one-way replication for centralized backup or to optimize read-only replicated folders. Also, this can be most useful when creating a topology for a network that is connected using different speed WAN links or each connection needs to have a specific schedule and bandwidth setting.

### Replication Schedule and Bandwidth Throttling

Windows Server 2003 R2, Windows Server 2008, and Windows Server 2008 R2 DFS Replication support scheduling replication, as well as restricting the amount of bandwidth a replication connection can utilize. In the original version of DFS that came with Windows 2000 and the initial release of Windows 2003, administrators were limited in their replication scheduling options and forced to limit replication to after hours for large data sets as opposed to trickling data replication all day long using only a portion of the wide area network (WAN) link between sites. For large data sets that will initially replicate across the WAN, the initial replication connections can be configured to run limited bandwidth during business hours and full bandwidth after hours until replication has completed and restrictions can be removed if desired.

# Installing DFS

To install DFS, an administrator of a file server on the network needs to install the File System role and select the necessary DFS-related role services. Also, when the DFS role services are selected, the necessary DFS tools will be installed as part of the installation. To install the DFS services, please refer to the steps detailed in the "Adding the File Services Role" section earlier in this chapter, but on the Select Role Services page, select Distributed File System, DFS Namespaces, and DFS Replication. When installing the DFS services, a new namespace can be created. Skip namespace creation during installation to ensure a successful installation and create the namespace later to ensure proper configuration.

## Creating the DFS Namespace and Root

When creating a DFS namespace, the administrator requires local Administrator group access on each of the servers hosting the namespace, and if a domain namespace is selected, the administrator also requires domain-level permissions because the domain-namespace information is stored in Active Directory.

A DFS namespace root requires a file share. When the DFS root is created, the name can be matched to an existing file share name or a custom name can be selected. The wizard searches the specified server for an existing file share matching the DFS root name; if it does not locate one, the wizard can create the share as part of the process.

As a best practice, the file share should be created and have share and NTFS permissions configured prior to the DFS namespace creation. One thing to keep in mind, though, is that the share name must match the DFS namespace name. Preconfiguring the NTFS permission will help simplify troubleshooting and administration of the namespace.

To create a file share for a DFS root, follow the steps outlined in the "Managing Folder Shares" section earlier in this chapter.

Before attempting to create a new DFS namespace, if the DFS services have just been installed, ensure that the DFS services are running. In addition, for the DFS Management console to appear in Server Manager, all instances of Server Manager might have to be closed and reopened before following the proceeding steps.

To create a DFS namespace and root, follow these steps:

1. Log on to the Windows Server 2008 R2 system with an account with local server administrator privileges. If a domain DFS namespace and root will be created, ensure that the account has the necessary permissions to the DFS-Configuration container in Active Directory.

2. Pre-create the share and set share and NTFS permissions on the servers and shares that will host the DFS namespace root.

3. Click Start, click All Programs, click Administrative Tools, and select DFS Management.

4. Select the Namespaces node, and in the Actions pane, click on the New Namespace link.

5. When the New Namespace Wizard opens, type in the name of the server that will host the namespace, and click Next.

6. On the Namespace Name and Settings page, type in the name of the share previously created, and click Next.

7. A pop-up window opens, asking whether the existing share should be used, as shown in Figure 28.21. Click Yes to use the previously configured share.

FIGURE 28.21    Using an existing share for the DFS namespace.

> **NOTE**
>
> The initial DFS root name must match the name of the file share created previously. If the share does not exist, the wizard will prompt you to create a file share from an existing folder or a new folder. Although the wizard can simplify the process by automating this task, it does not provide a method of configuring NTFS permissions.

8. On the Namespace Type page, to create a domain-based namespace, select the appropriate option button and check the Enable Windows Server 2008 Mode check box to enable scalability and allow for access-based enumeration within the namespace, as shown in Figure 28.22.

9. On the Review Settings and Create Namespace page, review the namespace settings and if everything looks correct, click Create to start the namespace creation.

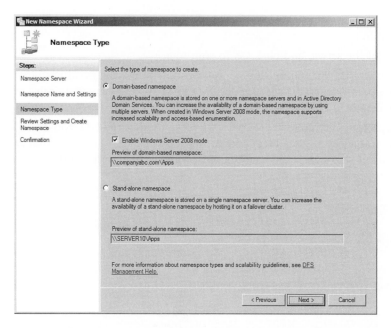

FIGURE 28.22    Creating a Windows 2008 mode domain-based namespace.

10. On the Confirmation page, if the result status is reported as a success, click Close to complete the process. If the creation failed, select the Errors tab to review the issues, repair the problems, and attempt the namespace creation again.

## Adding an Additional Namespace Server to a Domain-Based Namespace

After a domain namespace has been successfully created, it is a best practice to add an additional server to host the namespace. To add an additional server to an existing domain-based namespace, perform the following steps:

1. Log on to the Windows Server 2008 R2 system with an account with local server administrator privileges. If a domain DFS namespace and root will be configured, ensure that the account has the necessary permissions to the DFS-Configuration container and child objects in Active Directory.

2. Pre-create and set NTFS permissions on the servers and shares that will host the DFS namespace root.

3. Click Start, click All Programs, click Administrative Tools, and select DFS Management.

4. Select the Namespaces node, and then double-click the Namespaces node to expose the existing namespaces.

5. If the desired namespace does not appear, in the Actions pane, click on the Add Namespaces to Display link and follow the steps to search for and add an existing namespace to the console view.

28

6. Select the desired existing namespace, and in the Actions pane, click on the Add Namespace Server link.

7. Type in the name of the server, and click OK to continue.

8. If the share already exists, click OK on the pop-up window to use the existing share and existing share permissions. If the share does not exist, it will be created under `c:\DFSRoots\` by default.

9. In the tasks pane, select the Namespace Servers tab to verify that the additional namespace server was successfully added, as shown in Figure 28.23. Also note that at the top of the pane, it shows that the namespace is a domain-based in Windows Server 2008 mode.

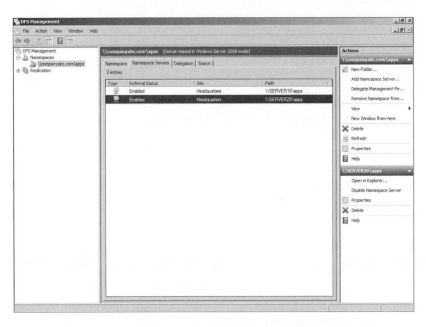

FIGURE 28.23    Verify the successful addition of a namespace server.

## Creating a DFS Folder and Replication Group

Creating a DFS folder is similar to creating the DFS root. A folder can be created to target existing shares or folders beneath shares, or a new share can be created on the desired server or servers. As recommended previously, pre-create the file share on an NTFS folder and properly configure the share and NTFS permissions for each folder target that will be added to the folder.

When a new folder is created with multiple folder targets, a replication group can be created at the same time. To create a folder within an existing namespace, perform the following steps:

1. Log on to the Windows Server 2008 R2 system with an account with local server administrator privileges.

2. Pre-create and set NTFS permissions on the servers and shares that will host the DFS namespace folder.

3. Click Start, click All Programs, click Administrative Tools, and select DFS Management.

4. Select the Namespaces node, and then double-click the Namespaces node to expose the existing namespaces.

5. If the desired namespace does not appear, in the Actions pane, click on the Add Namespaces to Display link and follow the steps to search for and add an existing namespace to the console view.

6. Select the desired existing namespace, and in the Actions pane, click on the New Folder link.

7. When the New Folder window opens, type in the name of the folder and click the Add button to locate the folder targets.

8. After all the folder target servers have been added to the New Folder window, click OK to continue, as shown in Figure 28.24.

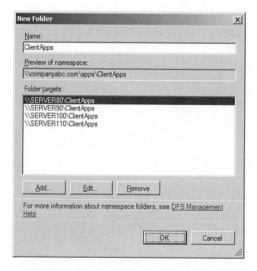

FIGURE 28.24    Defining a new folder and folder targets.

9. When a new folder is created and multiple targets are specified, a Replication pop-up window opens, asking if a replication group should be created. Click Yes to create a new replication group for the folder targets.

10. When the Replication Group and Replicate Folder Name window opens, review the name of the proposed replication group name and the replicated folder name, and click Next to continue. The prepopulated names will match the namespace and folder names.

11. The Replication Eligibility page will display whether or not each of the folder targets are capable of DFS Replication. If all targets are eligible, click Next to continue.

28

12. On the Primary Member page, click the Primary Member drop-down list arrow and select the folder target server that will be used to populate the remaining member folder targets. The data that exists in the folder of the primary target member will be replicated to each of the other targets. After selecting the desired primary server, click Next to continue.

13. On the Topology Selection page, select the desired replication topology. For this example, select the Hub and Spoke option button, as shown in Figure 28.25, and click Next to continue.

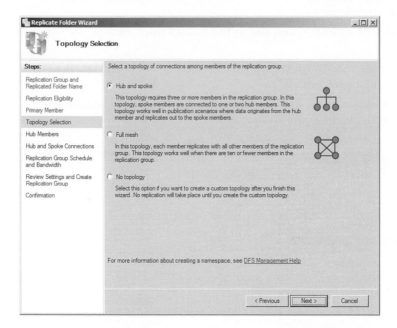

FIGURE 28.25    Selecting the hub and spoke replication topology.

14. On the Hub Members page, all servers will initially be listed in the Spoke Member section. Double-click the desired servers to move them to the Hub Member section, if they will be used as a hub server. Hub servers will replicate with all other servers and spoke servers will only replicate with the hub servers defined on this page. Once all the necessary hub servers are in the Hub Member section, click Next to continue.

15. On the Hub and Spoke Connections page, each of the spoke servers will be listed with their required hub member and an optional hub member. Optional hub members will only be populated if multiple servers are selected as hub members in the previous step. Even though the hub servers are listed as required and optional, the spoke servers will replicate with both and a connection between each hub

server and spoke system will be created. Also, hub servers will replicate with one another as well.

16. On the Replication Group Schedule and Bandwidth page, select the desired bandwidth limitation if desired or set the hours replication to allowed, and click Next to continue.

17. On the Review Settings and Create Replication Group page, review the selections and if everything looks correct, click Create.

18. On the Confirmation page, if the replication group creation tasks were all completed successfully, click Close. Otherwise, select the Errors tab and review and repair the errors, and rerun the Replication Group Creation Wizard.

19. Once the window is closed, back in the DFS Management console, double-click on the Replication node to reveal the new replication group and select it.

20. In the tasks pane, with the new replication group selected in the tree pane, select the Connections tab to review the connections created from the previous steps.

## Best Practices for DFS Replication

Following best practices for DFS Replication can help ensure that replication occurs as expected. Because file replication is triggered by a file version change or last-saved or modified time stamp, a standard file share might generate many replication changes, which can saturate the network bandwidth if no bandwidth constraints are placed within DFS Replication connections. To avoid such scenarios, follow as many of these suggestions as possible:

▶ Start with empty DFS namespace folders and targets to keep from having to replicate any data at the root level. Also, this can simplify the restore process of a DFS root folder because it contains only folders that are managed by DFS.

▶ Do not replicate data between DFS namespace shares because the namespace shares will try to replicate the data in the namespace folders as well as the data contained within the folder targets. Replication is not necessary if the folder targets are already replicating. Because the roots will not replicate for redundancy, deploy domain DFS namespaces and add additional namespace servers.

▶ Back up at least one DFS folder target and configure the backup to not update the archive bit. Changing the archive bit might trigger unnecessary replication.

▶ Thoroughly test server operating system antivirus programs to ensure that no adverse effects are caused by the scanning of files on a replicated DFS target. Also, configure server antivirus to scan at write operations only and configure clients to scan on read operations to ensure complete antivirus protection for DFS servers and clients.

▶ Verify that the drive that will contain the staging folder for a replication connection contains ample space to accept the amount of replicated data sent and received by the server.

28

Having a high number of read-write operations is not desirable because it causes heavy replication, and in a scenario like this, DFS Replication should be performed during off-peak hours unless Windows Server 2008 R2 DFS Replication can be used in conjunction with bandwidth constraints.

### Configuring DFS Read-Only Replication

Windows Server 2008 R2 now allows for a replicated folder to be defined as read-only. This can be configured once a replication group is defined. As a best practice, when read-only replicated folders are desired, select the No Topology option button on the Topology Selection page when running the Replicate Folder Wizard. Once a replication group is created, select the replication group in the tree pane, and in the tasks pane select the Memberships tab. Right-click the desired Replicated Folder member and select Make Read-only, as shown in Figure 28.26.

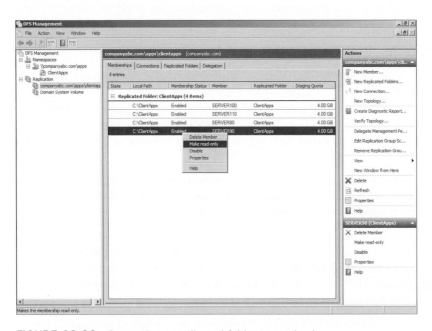

FIGURE 28.26   Converting a replicated folder to read-only.

As a best practice, when using read-only replicated folders, configure replication connections to be one-way to the read-only folder.

### Enabling Access-Based Enumeration on a Domain-Based Namespace in Windows Server 2008 Mode

When a domain-based namespace is created and Windows 2008 mode is enabled, access-based enumeration can be enabled, but it is not by default. To enable access-based enumeration on a domain-based namespace in Windows Server 2008 mode, locate the namespace in DFS Management. Right-click the namespace and select Properties. Select the Advanced tab and check the Enable Access-Based Enumeration for This Namespace check box at the bottom of the window. Click OK to complete the change. One thing to keep in mind is that this will apply to the entire namespace and any and all folders and folder targets defined in the namespace.

# Managing and Troubleshooting DFS

DFS can be managed through the DFS Management console included in the Windows Server 2008 R2 Administrative Tools program group and in the Server Manager console. DFS can also be managed in a command-line environment using the DFS command-line utilities. These utilities include the following:

▶ **DfsUtil**—Can be used to manage DFS namespaces, servers, and clients. DfsUtil can also be used to export DFS namespaces to XML files so they can be migrated to new systems.

▶ **DfsCmd**—Can be used to manage the folders and targets within an existing DFS namespace.

▶ **DfsrAdmin**—Can be used to perform actions on existing DFS Replication groups, including adding new replication group folders and generating reports on existing replicated folder members.

▶ **DfsrDiag**—Can be used to force replication, stop replication, or report on replication health.

Using the DFS management console, DFS standalone and domain-based roots can be shown and managed in a single DFS console window. The administrator can check DFS root and folder targets for availability by checking the Connection status of all targets for a particular replication group. Using the DFS Management console, a DFS administrator can also create a DFS Replication Diagnostic report. To create a diagnostic report for replication, perform the following steps:

1. Open the DFS Management console and expand it.

2. Double-click on Replication to reveal the desired replication group. If the desired replication group is not shown, right-click the Replication node, select Add Replication Groups to Display, and follow the steps to add the desired group.

3. Right-click the desired replication group, and select Create Diagnostic Report.

4. When the Diagnostic Report Wizard window opens, select either the health report, propagation test, or propagation report, and click Next.

5. If a report was selected, the report will be saved to the c:\DFSReports folder with a default name; if necessary, change the report name and location and click Next.

6. On the Members to Include page, add or remove the desired folder target servers for the report, and click Next.

28

7. On the Options page, select the desired options for the report details, to count or not count backlogged files and whether or not to count the replicated files and folders, including data set size on each member, and click Next.

8. Review the selections and if everything looks correct, click Create to generate and display the report.

9. The report will be displayed in the default browser; close the browser and DFS Management console when you are finished.

## Taking a Target Offline for Maintenance

When a target needs to be rebooted or just taken offline for a short maintenance window, the connected users must be gracefully referred to another replica, or they must be disconnected from the DFS server.

To take a folder target offline for maintenance, follow these steps:

1. Open the DFS Management console and locate the namespace and expand it to reveal the desired folder and select the folder.

2. Once the folder is selected in the tree pane, in the tasks pane, select the Folder Targets tab and select the target that will be taken offline.

3. Right-click the appropriate target, and select Enable or Disable Folder Target, as shown in Figure 28.27. This option changes the current referral status of a target.

FIGURE 28.27    Disabling DFS referral to free a server for maintenance.

4. Repeat the preceding steps for any additional DFS root or folder targets on the server on which you are disabling referrals.

5. Wait long enough for all the existing connections to close. Usually, after you make the referral change, all users should be disconnected after the cache interval has been exceeded. Start counting after the referral is disabled. One way to know for sure that all users have been disconnected from a target is to open Share and Storage Management on the target server and use the Manage Sessions and Manage Open Files links in the Actions pane to determine if any users and systems are connected.

6. When all connections are closed on the target server, perform the necessary tasks and enable the target from the DFS Management console when maintenance is completed and server functionality has been restored.

## Disabling Replication for Extended Downtime

When a server containing a replicated folder target will be offline for an extended period of time, for upgrades or due to unexpected network downtime, removing that server's targets from all replication groups is recommended. Doing this relieves the available replica servers from having to build and store change orders and staging files for this offline server. Because the staging folder has a capacity limit, an offline server might cause the active server's staging folders to reach their limit, essentially shutting down all replication.

When the server is once again available, the administrator can add this server back to the list of targets and configure replication. The data will be moved to the preexisting folder where it can be compared with file IDs sent over on the change orders from the initial master. If the file ID is the same, it will be pulled from the preexisting folder instead of across the WAN to reduce network traffic.

## Limiting Connections to Site DFS Targets

In previous versions of DFS, prior to Windows Server 2003 R2 and Windows Server 2008, one issue administrators faced was that users could connect to a folder target across a WAN link for an extended period of time, after only a short network disruption. To enhance performance and keep this situation down to a minimum, DFS administrators can set referral priority and restrict folder target access to local Active Directory site DFS folder target servers. To set referral priority or restrict access to local site target servers, perform the following steps:

1. Open the DFS Management console, and add the necessary namespace to the console.

2. Expand the namespace to reveal the desired folder, right-click the DFS folder, and select Properties.

28

3. Select the Referrals tab, and check the Exclude Targets Outside of the client's site and click OK, as shown in Figure 28.28.

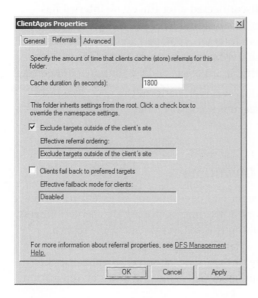

FIGURE 28.28    Restricting client connections to local Active Directory site for DFS folder targets.

# Backing Up DFS

Administrators do not need to perform any special steps to back up DFS data other than backing up the actual data in the folders as well as the System State of the servers that host and participate in the DFS namespace. The following elements should be backed up:

▶ **Folder Target data**—This is the actual data that is being accessed by end users. With a true multimaster replication topology, only one target needs to be backed up for each DFS folder target.

▶ **DFS hierarchy**—For standalone DFS namespaces, the System State of the root server and System State of all servers containing DFS targets should be backed up. For domain-based DFS namespaces, the System States of domain controllers and all other servers containing DFS targets should be backed up. Active Directory stores all the DFS hierarchy and DFSR replication connection information. Active Directory is backed up with the domain controller System State.

To back up the DFS Hierarchy only, the DFSutil can be used to export the settings. To perform this task, follow these steps:

1. Log on to the Windows Server 2008 R2 system that has the DFS services installed, with an account with local server administrator privileges.

2. Click Start, Run; then type cmd in the search pane and press Enter to open a Command Prompt window.

3. In the Command Prompt window, type dfsutil domain companyabc.com and press Enter to list all of the namespaces in the companyabc.com domain as an example. For our example, we returned the Apps name space located at \\companyabc.com\apps.

4. Once the namespace name is determined, type dfsutil root export \\companyabc.com\apps c:\dfs-export-namespace-Apps.xml and press Enter to export this namespace.

5. In the Command Prompt window, type c:\dfs-export-namespace-Apps.xml to review the exported information.

This process should be performed on all DFS server and domain-based namespaces for reference. Also, this file can be used to migrate a DFS namespace from a set of namespace servers to a different set of servers by deleting the original namespace, editing this file, and using the dfsutil root import command.

# Using the Volume Shadow Copy Service

The Windows Server 2008 R2 Volume Shadow Copy Service (VSS) is a feature available for NTFS volumes. VSS is used to perform a point-in-time backup of an entire volume to the local disk. This backup can be used to quickly restore data that was deleted from the volume locally or through a network-mapped drive or network file share. VSS is also used by Windows Server Backup and by compatible third-party backup applications to back up local and shared NTFS volumes.

VSS can make a point-in-time backup of a volume, including backing up open files. This entire process is completed in a very short period of time but is powerful enough to be used to restore an entire volume, if necessary. VSS can be scheduled to automatically back up a volume once, twice, or several times a day. This service can be enabled on a volume that contains DFS targets and standard Windows Server 2008 R2 file shares.

## Using VSS and Windows Server Backup

When the Windows Server Backup program runs a backup of a local NTFS volume, VSS is used by default to create a snapshot or shadow copy of the volume's current data. This data is saved to the same or another local volume or disk. The Backup program then uses the shadow copy to back up data, leaving the disk free to support users and the operating system. When the backup is complete, the shadow copy is automatically deleted from the local disk. For more information on VSS and Windows Server Backup, please refer to Chapters 30 and 31, "Backing Up the Windows Server 2008 R2 Environment" and "Recovering from a Disaster," respectively. One important point is that in order for VSS backups to work properly, shadow copies should be enabled on every volume and enough free space should exist to store the shadow copies. Even if the schedule is set to once a year, enabling shadow copies on the volume defines the shadow copies with the Volume Shadow Copy provider and reduces VSS errors on backups.

## Configuring Shadow Copies

Enabling shadow copies for a volume can be very simple. Administrators have more options when it comes to recovering lost or deleted data and, in many cases, can entirely avoid restoring data to disk from a backup tape device or tape library. In addition, select users can be given the necessary rights to restore files that they've accidentally deleted.

The Volume Shadow Copy Service is already installed and is automatically available using NTFS-formatted volumes.

To enable and configure shadow copies, follow these steps:

1. Log on to the Windows Server 2008 R2 system with an account with administrator privileges.

2. Click Start, click All Programs, click Administrative Tools, and select Server Manager.

3. In the tree pane, double-click the Storage node, and select Disk Management.

4. In the tasks pane, scroll down to locate the desired volume, right-click the volume, and select Properties.

5. Select the Shadow Copies tab, and in the Select a Volume section, click on the desired volume, and click the Settings button.

6. The Settings page allows you to choose an alternate volume to store the shadow copies. Select another volume to store the shadow copies in line with best practices and set the storage space limit for the shadow copies. The default is usually set to 10% of the volume size; accepting the defaults is recommended.

7. After the location and maximum size are configured, click the Schedule button and define the schedule. The defaults create a shadow copy at 7:00 a.m. and 12:00 p.m., but for this example, set up an additional shadow copy to run at 5:00 p.m., as shown in Figure 28.29.

8. Click OK to close the Schedule window and click OK again to close the Volume Shadow Copy Settings window. The shadow copy for the originally selected volume is now enabled.

9. If necessary, select the next volume and enable shadow copying; otherwise, click the Create Now button to create the initial shadow copy.

10. If necessary, select the next volume and immediately create a shadow copy by clicking the Create Now button.

11. After the shadow copies are created, click OK to close the Disk Volume window, close Server Manager, and log off the server.

For more detailed information concerning the Volume Shadow Copy Service and how to recover data using previously created volume shadow copies, refer to Chapters 30 and 31.

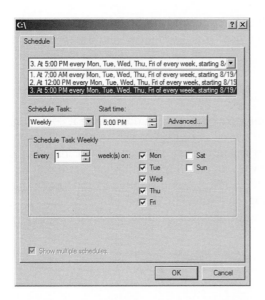

FIGURE 28.29   Creating an additional schedule for Volume Shadow Copies.

## Recovering Data Using Shadow Copies

The server administrator or a standard user who has been granted permissions can recover data using previously created shadow copies. The files stored in the shadow copy cannot be accessed directly, but they can be accessed by connecting the volume that has had a shadow copy created.

To recover data from a file share, follow these steps:

1. Log on to a Windows Server 2008 R2 system, Windows XP SP1, or later workstation with either administrator rights or with a user account that has permissions to restore the files from the shadow copy.

2. Click Start and select Run or type in the server and share name in the Search pane.

3. At the Run prompt or Search pane, type \\servername\sharename, where server-name represents the NetBIOS or fully qualified domain name of the server hosting the file share. The share must exist on a volume in which a shadow copy has already been created.

4. When the folder opens, right-click on the folder that contains the data that will be restored and select Properties.

5. When the window opens, if necessary, select the Previous Versions tab, select the desired folder version, and click the Open button.

6. An Explorer window then opens, displaying the contents of the folder when the shadow copy was made. If you want to restore only a single file, locate the file, right-click it, and select Copy.

28

7. Open the server share location in which the restored file will be placed, right-click, and choose Paste. Overwrite the file as required and close all the windows as desired.

## Summary

Windows Server 2008 R2 file services give administrators several options when it comes to building fault-tolerant servers and data storage as well as fault-tolerant file shares. Through services such as the Volume Shadow Copy Service, deleted or overwritten files can be restored automatically or by an administrator without restoring from backup. Using services such as the Distributed File System and DFS Replication, administrators have more flexibility when it comes to deploying, securing, and providing high-availability file services. Using just one or a combination of these file system services, organizations can truly make their file systems fault tolerant.

## Best Practices

The following are best practices from this chapter:

▶ Use the Volume Shadow Copy Service to provide file recoverability and data fault tolerance to minimize the number of times you have to restore from backup.

▶ Try to provide disk fault tolerance for your operating system and data drives, preferably using hardware-based RAID sets.

▶ Do not use a quick format when creating RAID-5 volumes to avoid loss of disk performance later when data is being first copied to the volumes.

▶ Use NTFS on all volumes to enable additional file system functionality and security.

▶ Always define share permissions for every share, regardless of the volume format type.

▶ Replace the Everyone group with the Domain Users group when shares are created on domain servers and anonymous or guest access is not required, and set the share permissions accordingly.

▶ Use File Server Resource Manager (FSRM) quotas at the folder level instead of NTFS quotas at the volume for better quota management capabilities.

▶ Use domain-based DFS roots whenever possible.

▶ Use DFS to provide a unified namespace to file data.

▶ Use Window Server 2008 mode on domain-based namespaces to enable access-based enumeration and improved scalability.

▶ Start with an empty DFS root folder to keep from having to replicate any data at the root level and do not create any replication groups based on the namespace root folder.

▶ When deploying domain-based DFS namespaces, add additional namespace servers for redundancy.

▶ DFS administrators should create and define shares, share permissions, and NTFS permissions on the shared folder prior to defining these shares as DFS folder targets.

▶ Replicate DFS data only during off-peak hours to reduce network congestion or restrict replication with bandwidth constraints if WAN links are heavily used during business hours.

▶ When utilizing read-only replicated folders, ensure that replication is only one-way to the read-only replication folder.

▶ Back up at least one DFS folder target and configure the backup to not update the archive bit to avoid possible unnecessary replication.

▶ Test antivirus programs thoroughly to ensure that no adverse effects are caused by the scanning of files on a replicated DFS folder target.

▶ Verify that the drive containing the staging folder for a replication connection contains ample space to accept the amount of replicated data inbound and outbound to this server.

28

# CHAPTER 29

# System-Level Fault Tolerance (Clustering/Network Load Balancing)

Many businesses today rely heavily on their computer and network infrastructure. Internet access, email, instant messaging, file and print services, and networking services such as domain name system (DNS), Dynamic Host Configuration Protocol (DHCP), and virtual private networking are just a few of the core computer and networking services that are critical to many businesses. If one of these critical systems is down or unexpectedly offline, the impact to the business can be huge. When businesses cannot withstand extended periods of unexpected or unplanned downtime, deploying a fault-tolerant computer and network infrastructure might be necessary.

Windows Server 2008 R2 provides several methods of improving system- and service-level fault-tolerance by leveraging some of the roles, role services, and features included in the different editions of the operating system. As an example, as detailed in Chapter 28, "File System Management and Fault Tolerance," the Distributed File System (DFS) can be used to create and deploy redundant and automatically synchronized file data through DFS shares and DFS Replication. Another example of providing redundant services is to design an infrastructure that includes multiple domain controllers and print services in each major site and for remote sites, configuring the Active Directory site properties to utilize remote site domain controllers when local services become unavailable.

Windows Server 2008 R2 provides many functions and services that can extend and enhance the reliability and resilience of computer and networking services. Many services, however, are only available when deployed on specific hardware platforms and when deployed on the

Enterprise or Datacenter Editions of Windows Server 2008 R2. This chapter covers system-level fault tolerance using Windows Server 2008 R2 Network Load Balancing (NLB) and failover clusters. NLB is available in Standard, Enterprise, and Datacenter Editions of Windows Server 2008 R2. Failover clusters are available only in the Enterprise and Datacenter Editions of Windows Server 2008 R2. These built-in clustering technologies provide load-balancing and failover capabilities that can be used to increase fault tolerance for many different types of applications and network services. Each of these clustering technologies is different in many ways. Choosing the right Windows Server 2008 R2 clustering technology depends on the services and applications that will be hosted by the cluster.

Windows Server 2008 R2 technologies such as NLB and failover clusters improve fault tolerance for services, but before these clustering technologies can be leveraged effectively, basic server or system stability best practices must be used.

This chapter focuses on the setup and deployment of the Windows Server 2008 R2 clustering technologies, NLB, and failover clusters, including predeployment checklists to ensure that the server hardware is more reliable.

# Building Fault-Tolerant Windows Server 2008 R2 Systems

Building fault-tolerant Windows Server 2008 R2 systems by utilizing the built-in clustering technologies consists of carefully planning and configuring server hardware and software, planning and configuring the network devices that connect the server to the network, and providing reliable power for the server. Purchasing high-quality server and network hardware is a good start to building a fault-tolerant system, but the proper configuration and selection of this hardware is equally important. Also, providing this equipment with reliable power and redundant backup power from battery sources and possibly generators can increase reliability of the servers as well as the networking infrastructure. Last, but not least, properly tuning the server operating systems to streamline performance for the desired roles, role services, features, and applications helps enhance server availability and stability.

## Powering the Computer and Network Infrastructure

Powering Windows Server 2008 R2 servers and network hardware with battery or generator-backed power sources not only provides these devices with conditioned line power by removing voltage spikes and providing steady line voltage levels, but it also provides alternative power when unexpected blackouts or brownouts occur. Many organizations cannot afford to implement redundant power sources or generators to power the offices, data centers, and server rooms. For these organizations, the best approach to providing reliable power to the computer and network infrastructure is to deploy uninterruptible power supplies (UPSs) with battery-backed power. With a UPS, power is normally supplied from the batteries, which are continually charged by the utility line power. When the line power fails, a properly sized UPS provides ample time for end users to save their data to the server and to gracefully shut down the server or network device without risk of damaging hardware or corrupting data.

UPS manufacturers commonly provide software that can send network notifications, run scripts, or even gracefully shut down servers automatically when power thresholds are reached. Of course, if end-user data is important, each end-user workstation and the network switches that connect these workstations to the computer and network infrastructure should also be protected with UPSs that can provide at least 5 to 10 minutes of battery-backup power.

One final word on power is that most computer and network hardware manufacturers offer device configurations that incorporate redundant power supplies designed to keep the system powered up in the event of a single power supply failure.

## Designing Fault-Tolerant IP Networks

Network design can also incorporate fault tolerance by creating redundant network routes and by utilizing technologies that can group devices together for the purposes of load balancing and device failover. Load balancing is the process of spreading requests across multiple devices to keep individual device load at an acceptable level. Failover is the process of moving services offered on one device to another upon device failure, to maintain availability. Common scenarios for creating fault-tolerant IP networks can include, but are not limited to, the following:

▶ **Acquiring multiple network connections between the data center and the Internet**—This includes using different Internet service providers and, hopefully, each of the connections is not connected to the same external telco box on the street as this becomes the single point of failure if hit by a car, truck, or cut off from communications.

▶ **Deploying multiple and redundant firewalls, virtual private networks (VPNs), and network routers that will failover to one another**—This usually involves software or hardware configurations that allow each of the devices to communicate with one another to detect failures. These devices, when deployed in redundant configurations, can be leveraged in an active/passive configuration where only a single primary device is used and the secondary device only comes online when the primary fails. Alternatively, in many cases these devices can be used in an active/active configuration that disperses or distributes the load and requests across each device and when a single device fails, the remaining device handles the entire load.

▶ **Deploying critical servers with multiple network adapters connected to separate network switches**—This allows a server to be connected and available on different switches in case a single network card in the server fails or if the port or the entire network switch or blade fails.

▶ **Deploying hardware-based NLB devices**—Many network switches, routers, and certain devices created just for this purpose can provide some, if not all, of the functionality included in Windows Server 2008 R2 NLB. This, of course, might be the best choice for load balancing at the network level when organizations deploy and support systems other than Windows Server 2008 R2 and when they also need to load-balance network devices, such as firewalls and VPN devices.

▶ **Deploying servers with multiple network adapters using third-party network teaming software**—This configuration uses third-party software installed and configured on a server to create a new virtual network adapter that is used to provide access to the server system through a single or all of the physical network adapters on the server that are part of this configuration. Windows Server 2008 R2 supports teamed network adapters as long as the drivers and software are certified to work with Windows Server 2008 R2.

> **NOTE**
>
> If the Windows Server 2008 R2 system utilizes iSCSI storage, the network adapters designated for iSCSI communications are not supported on teamed network adapters.

## Designing Fault-Tolerant Server Disks

Many Windows Server 2008 R2 systems that will be used for NLB or failover clusters are deployed with local disk storage. The local disks commonly store the operating system files as well as the necessary service or application files. Each system that will participate in a cluster should have the local disks and volumes configured exactly the same, including drive letters and any mount point assignments. When local disks are used to provide the operating system and application or service core files, the local disks should be deployed using redundant, fault-tolerant configurations. There are mainly two different ways to add fault tolerance to the local disks in a Windows Server 2008 R2 system. The first is creating redundant arrays of inexpensive disks (RAID) using disk controller configuration utilities (also known as hardware-level RAID), and the second is creating RAID volumes using dynamic disks using the Disk Management console from within the operating system (known as software-level RAID).

Using two or more disks, different RAID-level arrays can be configured to provide fault tolerance that can withstand disk failures and still provide uninterrupted disk access. Implementing hardware-level RAID configured, stored, and managed by the system's disk controllers is preferred over the software-level RAID configurable within Windows Server 2008 R2. Windows Server 2008 R2 dynamic disk mirrored and RAID-5 volumes are managed by the system and add some load to the system. Additionally, another good reason to provide hardware-level RAID is that the configuration of the disks does not depend on the operating system, which gives administrators greater flexibility when it comes to recovering server systems and performing upgrades. For more information on disk configuration options, refer to Chapter 28 of this book. For detailed information on how to best configure RAID arrays using local disk controllers, refer to the manufacturer's documentation.

As a best practice, Windows Server 2008 R2 can be deployed with the operating system disks stored on RAID-1, or mirrored, disks and presented to the operating system as the "C" volume. A second volume in the system can be used to store application data and files and, when possible, this data should be placed on different redundant disks or at least on separate volumes to prevent impact to the space available in the operating system volume.

## Increasing Service and Application Availability

A service and/or application's reliability is greatly dependent on the underlying software code, the hardware the system is running on, and how it interacts with the host operating system. Windows Server 2008 R2 is a very stable platform partly because third-party applications and services must use only the system files provided by Microsoft when interacting with the operating system and the system hardware. Furthermore, when third-party services and applications require additional drivers, these drivers must be certified for Windows Server 2008 R2 and the drivers must be digitally signed by the Windows Quality Hardware labs to ensure the highest reliability. Administrators can disable the strict device driver signing requirements, but on failover clusters, this would place the system in an unsupported configuration and is not advisable. Remember that the only reason to deploy failover clusters or NLB clusters is to provide high availability or very scalable services; deploying systems using unsigned or untested drivers can reduce the overall reliability of each system and the entire cluster.

# Windows Server 2008 R2 Clustering Technologies

Windows Server 2008 R2 provides two clustering technologies, which are both included on the Enterprise and Datacenter Editions. Clustering is the grouping of independent server nodes that are accessed and viewed on the network as a single system. When a service and/or application is run from a cluster, the end user can connect to a single cluster node to perform his work, or each request can be handled by multiple nodes in the cluster. In cases where data is read-only, the client might request data from one server in the cluster and the next request might be made to a different server and the client would never know the difference. Also, if a single node on a multiple node cluster fails, the remaining nodes will continue to service client requests and only the clients that were originally connected to the failed node may notice either a slight interruption in service, or their entire session might need to be restarted depending on the service or application in use and the particular clustering technology that is in use for that cluster.

The first clustering technology provided with Windows Server 2008 R2, Enterprise and Datacenter Editions is failover clustering. Failover clusters provide system fault tolerance through a process called failover. When a system or node in the cluster fails or is unable to respond to client requests, the clustered services or applications that were running on that particular node are taken offline and moved to another available node where functionality and access are restored. Failover clusters, in most deployments, require access to shared data storage and are best suited, but not necessarily limited to, the deployment of the following services and applications:

▶ **File services**—File services deployed on failover clusters provide much of the same functionality a standalone Windows Server 2008 R2 system can provide, but when deployed as clustered file services, a single data storage repository can be presented and accessed by clients through the currently assigned and available cluster node without replicating the file data.

▶ **Print services**—Print services deployed on failover clusters have one main advantage over a standalone print server: If the active print server fails, each of the shared printers is made available to clients using another designated print server in the cluster. Although deploying and replacing printers to computers and users is easily managed using Group Policy deployed printers, when standalone print servers fail, the impact can be huge, especially when servers, devices, services, and applications that cannot be managed with group policies access these printers.

▸ **Database services**—When large organizations deploy line-of-business applications, e-commerce, or any other critical services or applications that require a back-end database system that must be highly available, deploying database services on failover clusters is the preferred method. Also, in many cases configuring enterprise database services can take hours and the size of the databases, indexes, and logs can be huge, so deploying database services on a standalone system encountering a system failure may results in several hours of undesired downtime during repair or restore, instead of quick recovery as with a failover cluster.

▸ **Back-end enterprise messaging systems**—For many of the same reasons as cited previously for deploying database services, enterprise messaging services have become critical to many organizations and are best deployed in failover clusters.

▸ **Hyper-V virtual machines**—As many organizations move toward server consolidation and conversion of physical servers to virtual servers, providing a means to also maintain high availability and reliability has become even more essential when a single physical Hyper-V host has several critical virtual machines running on it.

The second Windows Server 2008 R2 clustering technology is Network Load Balancing (NLB), which is best suited to provide fault tolerance for front-end web applications and websites, Remote Desktop Services Session Host server systems, VPN servers, streaming media servers, and proxy servers. NLB provides fault tolerance by having each server in the cluster individually run the network services or applications, removing any single points of failure. Depending on the particular needs of the service or application deployed on an NLB cluster, there are different configuration or affinity options to determine how clients will be connected to the back-end NLB cluster nodes. For example, on a read-only website, client requests can be directed to any of the NLB cluster nodes; during a single visit to a website, a client might be connected to different NLB cluster nodes. As another example, when a client attempts to utilize an e-commerce application to purchase goods or services provided through a web-based application on an NLB cluster, the client session should be initiated and serviced by a single node in the cluster, as this session will most likely be using Secure Sockets Layer (SSL) encryption and will also contain specific session data, including the contents of the shopping cart and the end-user specific information.

**NOTE**

Microsoft does not support running failover clusters and Network Load Balancing on the same Windows Server 2008 R2 system.

## Windows Server 2008 R2 Cluster Terminology

Before failover or NLB clusters can be designed and implemented, the administrator deploying the solution should be familiar with the general terms used to define the clustering technologies. The following list contains the many terms associated with Windows Server 2008 R2 clustering technologies:

▶ **Cluster**—A cluster is a group of independent servers (nodes) that are accessed and presented to the network as a single system.

▶ **Node**—A node is an individual server that is a member of a cluster.

▶ **Cluster resource**—A cluster resource is a service, application, IP address, disk, or network name defined and managed by the cluster. Within a cluster, cluster resources are grouped and managed together using cluster resource groups, now known as Services and Applications groups.

▶ **Services and Applications group**—Cluster resources are contained within a cluster in a logical set called a Services and Applications group or historically referred to as a cluster group. Services and Applications groups are the units of failover within the cluster. When a cluster resource fails and cannot be restarted automatically, the Services and Applications group this resource is a part of will be taken offline, moved to another node in the cluster, and the group will be brought back online.

▶ **Client Access Point**—A Client Access Point is a term used in Windows Server 2008 R2 failover clusters that represents the combination of a network name and associated IP address resource. By default, when a new Services and Applications group is defined, a Client Access Point is created with a name and an IPv4 address. IPv6 is supported in failover clusters but an IPv6 resource either needs to be added to an existing group or a generic Services and Applications group needs to be created with the necessary resources and resource dependencies.

▶ **Virtual cluster server**—A virtual cluster server is a Services or Applications group that contains a Client Access Point, a disk resource, and at least one additional service or application-specific resource. Virtual cluster server resources are accessed either by the domain name system (DNS) name or a NetBIOS name that references an IPv4 or IPv6 address. A virtual cluster server can in some cases also be directly accessed using the IPv4 or IPv6 address. The name and IP address remain the same regardless of which cluster node the virtual server is running on.

▶ **Active node**—An active node is a node in the cluster that is currently running at least one Services and Applications group. A Services and Applications group can only be active on one node at a time and all other nodes that can host the group are considered passive for that particular group.

▶ **Passive node**—A passive node is a node in the cluster that is currently not running any Services and Applications groups.

▶ **Active/passive cluster**—An active/passive cluster is a cluster that has at least one node running a Services and Applications group and additional nodes the group can

29

be hosted on, but are currently in a waiting state. This is a typical configuration when only a single Services and Applications group is deployed on a failover cluster.

▶ **Active/active cluster**—An active/active cluster is a cluster in which each node is actively hosting or running at least one Services and Applications group. This is a typical configuration when multiple groups are deployed on a single failover cluster to maximize server or system usage. The downside is that when an active system fails, the remaining system or systems need to host all of the groups and provide the services and/or applications on the cluster to all necessary clients.

▶ **Cluster heartbeat**—The cluster heartbeat is a term used to represent the communication that is kept between individual cluster nodes that is used to determine node status. Heartbeat communication can occur on a designated network but is also performed on the same network as client communication. Due to this internode communication, network monitoring software and network administrators should be forewarned of the amount of network chatter between the cluster nodes. The amount of traffic that is generated by heartbeat communication is not large based on the size of the data but the frequency of the communication might ring some network alarm bells.

▶ **Cluster quorum**—The cluster quorum maintains the definitive cluster configuration data and the current state of each node, each Services and Applications group, and each resource and network in the cluster. Furthermore, when each node reads the quorum data, depending on the information retrieved, the node determines if it should remain available, shut down the cluster, or activate any particular Services and Applications groups on the local node. To extend this even further, failover clusters can be configured to use one of four different cluster quorum models and essentially the quorum type chosen for a cluster defines the cluster. For example, a cluster that utilizes the Node and Disk Majority Quorum can be called a Node and Disk Majority cluster.

▶ **Cluster witness disk or file share**—The cluster witness or the witness file share are used to store the cluster configuration information and to help determine the state of the cluster when some, if not all, of the cluster nodes cannot be contacted.

▶ **Generic cluster resources**—Generic cluster resources were created to define and add new or undefined services, applications, or scripts that are not already included as available cluster resources. Adding a custom resource provides the ability for that resource to be failed over between cluster nodes when another resource in the same Services and Applications group fails. Also, when the group the custom resource is a member of moves to a different node, the custom resource will follow. One disadvantage or lack of functionality with custom resources is that the Failover Clustering feature cannot actively monitor the resource and, therefore, cannot provide the same level of resilience and recoverability as with predefined cluster resources. Generic cluster resources include the generic application, generic script, and generic service resource.

▶ **Shared storage**—Shared storage is a term used to represent the disks and volumes presented to the Windows Server 2008 R2 cluster nodes as LUNs. In particular, shared storage can be accessed by each node on the cluster, but not simultaneously.

▶ **Cluster Shared Volumes**—A Cluster Shared Volume is a disk or LUN defined within the cluster that can be accessed by multiple nodes in the cluster simultaneously. This is unlike any other cluster volume, which normally can only be accessed by one node at a time, and currently the Cluster Shared Volume feature is only used on Hyper-V clusters but its usage will be extended in the near future to any failover cluster that will support live migration.

▶ **LUN**—LUN stands for Logical Unit Number. A LUN is used to identify a disk or a disk volume that is presented to a host server or multiple hosts by a shared storage array or a SAN. LUNs provided by shared storage arrays and SANs must meet many requirements before they can be used with failover clusters but when they do, all active nodes in the cluster must have exclusive access to these LUNs.

▶ **Failover**—Failover is the process of a Services and Applications group moving from the current active node to another available node in the cluster when a cluster resource fails. Failover occurs when a server becomes unavailable or when a resource in the cluster group fails and cannot recover within the failure threshold.

▶ **Failback**—Failback is the process of a cluster group automatically moving back to a preferred node after the preferred node resumes operation. Failback is a nondefault configuration that can be enabled within the properties of a Services and Applications group. The cluster group must have a preferred node defined and a failback threshold defined as well, for failback to function. A preferred node is the node you would like your cluster group to be running or hosted on during regular cluster operation when all cluster nodes are available. When a group is failing back, the cluster is performing the same failover operation but is triggered by the preferred node rejoining or resuming cluster operation instead of by a resource failure on the currently active node.

▶ **Live Migration**—Live Migration is a new feature of Hyper-V that is enabled when Virtual Machines are deployed on a Windows Server 2008 R2 failover cluster. Live Migration enables Hyper-V virtual machines on the failover cluster to be moved between cluster nodes without disrupting communication or access to the virtual machine. Live Migration utilizes a Cluster Shared Volume that is accessed by all nodes in the group simultaneously and it transfers the memory between the nodes during active client communication to maintain availability. Live Migration is currently only used with Hyper-V failover clusters but will most likely extend to many other Microsoft services and applications in the near future.

▶ **Quick Migration**—With Hyper-V virtual machines on failover clusters, Quick Migration provides the option for failover cluster administrators to move the virtual machine to another node without shutting the virtual machine off. This utilizes the virtual machine's shutdown settings options and if set to Save, the default setting, performing a Quick Migration will save the current memory state, move the virtual machine to the desired node, and resume operation shortly. End users should only encounter a short disruption in service and should reconnect without issue depending on the service or application hosted within that virtual machine. Quick Migration does not require Cluster Shared Volumes to function.

▶ **Geographically dispersed clusters**—These are clusters that span physical locations and sometimes networks to provide failover functionality in remote buildings and data centers, usually across a WAN link. These clusters can now span different networks and can provide failover functionality, but network response and throughput must be good and data replication is not handled by the cluster.

▶ **Multisite cluster**—Geographically dispersed clusters are commonly referred to as multisite clusters as cluster nodes are deployed in different Active Directory sites. Multisite clusters can provide access to resources across a WAN and can support automatic failover of Services and Applications groups defined within the cluster.

▶ **Stretch clusters**—A stretch cluster is a common term that, in some cases, refers to geographically dispersed clusters in which different subnets are used but each of the subnets is part of the same Active Directory site—hence, the term stretch, as in stretching the AD site across the WAN. In other cases, this term is used to describe a geographically dispersed cluster, as in the cluster stretches between geographic locations.

# Determining the Correct Clustering Technology

For either of the Windows Server 2008 R2 fault-tolerant clustering technologies to be most effective, administrators must carefully choose which technology and configuration best fits their application or service requirements. NLB is best suited to provide connectivity to TCP/IP-based services such as Remote Desktop Services, web-based services and applications, VPN services, streaming media, and proxy services. NLB is easily scalable and the number of clients that can be supported is based on the number of clients a single NLB cluster node can support multiplied by the number of nodes in the cluster. Windows Server 2008 R2 failover clusters provide system failover functionality for mission-critical applications, such as enterprise messaging, databases, file servers, print services, DHCP services, Hyper-V virtualization services, and many other built-in Windows Server 2008 R2 roles, role services, and features.

Although Microsoft does not support using both NLB and failover clusters on the same server, multitiered applications can take advantage of both technologies by using NLB to load-balance front-end application servers and using failover clusters to provide failover capabilities to back-end databases that contain data too large to replicate during the day or if the back end cannot withstand more than a few minutes of downtime if a node or service encounters a failure.

## Failover Clusters

Windows Server 2008 R2 failover clusters are a clustering technology that provides system-level fault tolerance by using a process called failover. Failover clusters are best used to provide access to resources such as file shares, print queues, email or database services, and back-end applications. Applications and network services defined and managed by the failover cluster, along with cluster hardware including shared disk storage and network cards, are called cluster resources. When services and applications are cluster-aware or certified to work with Windows Server 2008 R2 failover clusters, they are monitored and managed by the cluster service to ensure proper operation.

When a problem is encountered with a cluster resource, the failover cluster service attempts to fix the problem by restarting the resource and any dependent resources. If that doesn't work, the Services and Applications group the resource is a member of is failed over to another available node in the cluster, where it can then be restarted. Several conditions can cause a Services and Applications group to failover to a different cluster node. Failover can occur when an active node in the cluster loses power or network connectivity or suffers a hardware or software failure. In most cases, the failover process is either noticed by the clients as a short disruption of service or is not noticed at all. Of course, if failback is configured on a particular Services and Applications group and the group is simply not stable but all possible nodes are available, the group will be continually moved back and forth between the nodes until the failover threshold is reached. When this happens, the group will be shut down and remain offline by the cluster service.

To avoid unwanted failover, power management should be disabled on each of the cluster nodes in the motherboard BIOS, on the network interface cards (NICs), and in the Power applet in the operating system's Control Panel. Power settings that allow a display to shut off are okay, but the administrator must make sure that the disks, as well as each of the network cards, are configured to never go into Standby mode.

Cluster nodes can monitor the status of resources running on their local system, and they can also keep track of other nodes in the cluster through private network communication messages called heartbeats. Heartbeat communication is used to determine the status of a node and send updates of cluster configuration changes and the state of each node to the cluster quorum.

The cluster quorum contains the cluster configuration data necessary to restore a cluster to a working state. Each node in the cluster needs to have access to the quorum resource, regardless of which quorum model is chosen or the node will not be able to participate in the cluster. This prevents something called "split-brain" syndrome, where two nodes in the same cluster both believe they are the active node and try to control the shared resource at the same time or worse, each node can present its own set of data, when separate data sets are available, which causes changes in both data sets and a whirlwind of proceeding issues. Windows Server 2008 R2 provides four different quorum models, which are detailed in the section "Failover Cluster Quorum Models" later in this chapter.

## Network Load Balancing

The second clustering technology provided with Windows Server 2008 R2 is Network Load Balancing (NLB). NLB clusters provide high network performance, availability, and redundancy by balancing client requests across several servers with replicated configurations. When client load increases, NLB clusters can easily be scaled out by adding more nodes to the cluster to maintain or provide better response time to client requests. One important point to note now is that NLB does not itself replicate server configuration or application data sets.

Two great features of NLB are that no proprietary hardware is needed and an NLB cluster can be configured and up and running literally in minutes. One important point to remember is that within NLB clusters, each server's configuration must be updated independently. The NLB administrator is responsible for making sure that application or service configuration, version and operating system security, and updates and data are kept consistent across each NLB cluster node. For details on installing NLB, refer to the "Deploying Network Load Balancing Clusters" section later in this chapter.

# Overview of Failover Clusters

After an organization decides to cluster an application or service using failover clusters, it must then decide which cluster configuration model best suits the needs of the particular deployment. Failover clusters can be deployed using four different configuration models that will accommodate most deployment scenarios and requirements. The four configuration models in this case are defined by the quorum model selected, which include the Node Majority Quorum, Node and Disk Majority Quorum, Node and File Share Majority Quorum, and the No Majority: Disk Only Quorum. The typical and most common cluster deployment that includes two or more nodes in a single data center is the Node and Disk Majority Quorum model. Another configuration model of failover clusters that utilizes one of the previously mentioned quorum models is the geographically dispersed cluster, which is deployed across multiple networks and geographic locations. Geographically dispersed clusters or stretch clusters will be detailed later in this chapter in the "Deploying Multisite or Stretch Geographically Dispersed Failover Clusters" section.

## Failover Cluster Quorum Models

As previously stated, Windows Server 2008 R2 failover clusters support four different cluster quorum models. Each of these four models is best suited for specific configurations but if all the nodes and shared storage are configured, specified, and available during the installation of the failover cluster, the best-suited quorum model is automatically selected.

### Node Majority Quorum
The Node Majority Quorum model has been designed for failover cluster deployments that contain an odd number of cluster nodes. When determining the quorum state of the cluster, only the number of available nodes is counted. A cluster using the Node Majority Quorum is called a Node Majority cluster. A Node Majority cluster remains up and

running if the number of available nodes exceeds the number of failed nodes. As an example, in a five-node cluster, three nodes must be available for the cluster to remain online. If three nodes fail in a five-node Node Majority cluster, the entire cluster is shut down. Node Majority clusters have been designed and are well suited for geographically or network dispersed cluster nodes, but for this configuration to be supported by Microsoft, it takes serious effort, quality hardware, a third-party mechanism to replicate any back-end data, and a very reliable network. Once again, this model works well for clusters with an odd number of nodes.

### Node and Disk Majority Quorum

The Node and Disk Majority Quorum model determines whether a cluster can continue to function by counting the number of available nodes and the availability of the cluster witness disk. Using this model, the cluster quorum is stored on a cluster disk that is accessible and made available to all nodes in the cluster through a shared storage device using Serial Attached SCSI (SAS), Fibre Channel, or iSCSI connections. This model is the closest to the traditional single-quorum device cluster configuration model and is composed of two or more server nodes that are all connected to a shared storage device. In this model, only one copy of the quorum data is maintained on the witness disk. This model is well suited for failover clusters using shared storage, all connected on the same network with an even number of nodes. For example, on a 2-, 4-, 6-, 8-, or 16-node cluster using this model, the cluster continues to function as long as half of the total nodes are available and can contact the witness disk. In the case of a witness disk failure, a majority of the nodes need to remain up and running for the cluster to continue to function. To calculate this, take half of the total nodes and add one and this gives you the lowest number of available nodes that are required to keep a cluster running when the witness disk fails or goes offline. For example, on a 6-node cluster using this model, if the witness disk fails, the cluster will remain up and running as long as 4 nodes are available, but on a 2-node cluster, if the witness disk fails, both nodes will need to remain up and running for the cluster to function.

### Node and File Share Majority Quorum

The Node and File Share Majority Quorum model is very similar to the Node and Disk Majority Quorum model but instead of a witness disk, the quorum is stored on file share. The advantage of this model is that it can be deployed similarly to the Node Majority Quorum model but as long as the witness file share is available, this model can tolerate the failure of half of the total nodes. This model is well suited for clusters with an even number of nodes that do not utilize shared storage or clusters that span sites. This is the preferred and recommended quorum configuration for geographically dispersed failover clusters.

### No Majority: Disk Only Quorum

The No Majority: Disk Only Quorum model is best suited for testing the process and behavior of deploying built-in or custom services and/or applications on a Windows Server 2008 R2 failover cluster. In this model, the cluster can sustain the failover of all nodes except one, as long as the disk containing the quorum remains available. The limitation of this model is that the disk containing the quorum becomes a single point of failure and that is why this model is not well suited for production deployments of failover clusters.

As a best practice, before deploying a failover cluster, determine if shared storage will be used, verify that each node can communicate with each LUN presented by the shared storage device, and when the cluster is created, add all nodes to the list. This ensures that the correct recommended cluster quorum model is selected for the new failover cluster. When the recommended model utilizes shared storage and a witness disk, the smallest available LUN will be selected. This can be changed, if necessary, after the cluster is created.

## Choosing Applications for Failover Clusters

Many applications can run on failover clusters, but it is important to choose and test those applications wisely. Although many can run on failover clusters, the application might not be optimized for clustering or supported by the software vendor or Microsoft when deployed on Windows Server 2008 R2 failover clusters. Work with the vendor to determine requirements, functionality, and limitations (if any). Other major criteria that should be met to ensure that an application can benefit and adapt to running on a cluster are the following:

▶ Because clustering is IP-based, the cluster application or applications must use an IP-based protocol.

▶ Applications that require access to local databases must have the option of configuring where the data can be stored so a drive other than the system drive can be specified for data storage that is separate from the storage of the application core files.

▶ Some applications need to have access to data regardless of which cluster node they are running on. With these types of applications, it is recommended that the data is stored on a shared disk resource that will failover with the Services and Applications group. If an application will run and store data only on the local system or boot drive, the Node Majority Quorum or the Node and File Share Majority Quorum model should be used, along with a separate file replication mechanism for the application data.

▶ Client sessions must be able to reestablish connectivity if the application encounters a network disruption or fails over to an alternate cluster node. During the failover process, there is no client connectivity until an application is brought back online. If the client software does not try to reconnect and simply times out when a network connection is broken, this application might not be well suited for failover or NLB clusters.

Cluster-aware applications that meet all of the preceding criteria are usually the best applications to deploy in a Windows Server 2008 R2 failover cluster. Many services built in to Windows Server 2008 R2 can be clustered and will failover efficiently and properly. If a particular application is not cluster-aware, be sure to investigate all the implications of the application deployment on Windows Server 2008 R2 failover clusters before deploying or spending any time prototyping the solution.

**NOTE**

If you're purchasing a third-party software package to use for Windows Server 2008 R2 failover clustering, be sure that both Microsoft and the software manufacturer certify that it will work on Windows Server 2008 R2 failover clusters; otherwise, support will be limited or nonexistent when troubleshooting is necessary.

## Shared Storage for Failover Clusters

Shared disk storage is a requirement for Windows Server 2008 R2 failover clusters using the Node and Disk Majority Quorum and the Disk Only Quorum models. Shared storage devices can be a part of any cluster configuration and when they are used, the disks, disk volumes, or LUNs presented to the Windows systems must be presented as basic Windows disks.

All storage drivers must be digitally signed and certified for use with Windows Server 2008 R2. Many storage devices certified for Windows Server 2003 or even Windows Server 2008 might not work with Windows Server 2008 R2 and either simply cannot be used for failover cluster shared storage, or might require a firmware and driver upgrade to be supported. One main reason for this is that all failover shared storage must comply with SCSI-3 Architecture Model SAM-2. This includes any and all legacy and serial attached SCSI controllers, Fibre Channel host bus adapters, and iSCSI hardware- and software-based initiators and targets. If the cluster attempts to perform an action on a LUN or shared disk and the attempt causes an interruption in communication to the other nodes in the cluster or any other system connected to the shared storage device, data corruption can occur and the entire cluster and each storage area network (SAN)–connected system might lose connectivity to the storage.

When LUNS are presented to failover cluster nodes, each LUN must be presented to each node in the cluster. Also, when the shared storage is accessed by the cluster and other systems, the LUNs must be masked or presented only to the cluster nodes and the shared storage device controllers to ensure that no other systems can access or disrupt the cluster communication. There are strict requirements for shared storage support, especially with failover clusters. Using SANs or other types of shared storage must meet the following list of requirements and recommendations:

▶ All Fibre, SAS, and iSCSI host bus adapters (HBAs) and Ethernet cards used with iSCSI software initiators must obtain the "Designed for Microsoft Windows" logo for Windows Server 2008 R2 and have suitable signed device drivers.

▶ SAS, Fibre, and iSCSI HBAs must use StorPort device drivers to provide targeted LUN resets and other functions inherent to the StorPort driver specification. SCSIport was at one point supported for two-node clusters, but if a StorPort driver is available, it should be used to ensure support from the hardware vendors and Microsoft.

▶ All shared storage HBAs and back-end storage devices, including iSCSI targets, Fibre, and SAS storage arrays, must support SCSI-3 standards and must also support persistent bindings or reservations of LUNs.

29

▶ All shared storage HBAs must be deployed with matching firmware and driver versions. Failover clusters using shared storage require a very stable infrastructure and applying the latest storage controller driver to an outdated HBA firmware can cause very undesirable situations and might disrupt access to data.

▶ All nodes in the cluster should contain the same HBAs and use the same version of drivers and firmware. Each cluster node should be an exact duplicate of each other node when it comes to hardware selection, configuration, and driver and firmware revisions. This allows for a more reliable configuration and simplifies management and standardization.

▶ When iSCSI software initiators are used to connect to iSCSI software- or hardware-based targets, the network adapter used for iSCSI communication should be connected to a dedicated switch, should not be used for any cluster communication, and cannot be a teamed network adapter as teamed adapters are not supported with iSCSI.

For Microsoft to officially support failover clusters and shared storage, in addition to the hardware meeting the requirements listed previously, the entire configuration of the server brand and model, local disk configuration, HBA or network card controller firmware and driver version, iSCSI software initiator software, storage array, and storage array controller firmware or SAN operating system version must be tested as a whole system before it will be considered a "Windows Server 2008 R2 Failover Cluster Supported Configuration." The point to keep in mind is that if a company really wants to consider using failover clusters, they should research and find a suitable solution that will meet their budget. If a tested and supported solution cannot be found within their price range, the company should consider alternative solutions that can restore systems in about an hour or a few hours if not within a few minutes. The truth is that failover clusters are not for everyone, they are not for the faint of heart, and they are not within every organization's information technology budget from an implementation, training, and support standpoint. Administrators who want to test failover cluster configurations to gain knowledge and experience can leverage several low-cost shared storage alternatives, including using the Windows iSCSI initiator and a software-based iSCSI target, but they must remember that the configuration may not be supported by Microsoft in case a problem is encountered or data loss results.

### Serial Attached SCSI (SAS) Storage Arrays

Serial Attached SCSI or SAS storage arrays provide organizations with affordable, entry-level, hardware-based direct attached storage arrays suitable for Windows Server 2008 R2 clusters. SAS storage arrays commonly are limited to four hosts, but some models support extenders to add additional hosts as required. One of the major issues with direct attached storage is that replication of the data within the storage is usually not achievable without involving one of the host systems or software provided by the hardware vendor.

### Fibre Channel Storage Arrays

Using Fibre Channel (FC) HBAs, Windows Server 2008 R2 can access both shared and nonshared disks residing on a SAN connected to a common FC switch. This allows both the shared storage and operating system volumes to be located on the SAN, if desired, to provide diskless servers. In many cases, however, diskless servers might not be desired if the operating system performs many paging actions because the cache on the storage controllers can be used up very fast and can cause delays in disk read and write operations for dedicated cluster storage. If this is desired, however, the SAN must support this option and be configured to present the operating system dedicated LUNs to only a single host exclusively. The LUNs defined for shared cluster storage must be zoned and presented to every node in the cluster, and no other systems. The LUN zoning or masking in many cases is configured on the Fibre Channel switch that connects the cluster nodes and the shared storage device. This is a distinct difference between direct attached storage and FC or iSCSI shared storage. Both FC and iSCSI require a common fiber or Ethernet switch and network to establish and maintain connections between the hosts and the storage.

A properly configured FC zone for a cluster will include the World Wide Port Number (WWPN) of each cluster host's FC HBAs and the WWPN of the HBA controller(s) from the shared storage device. If either the server or the storage device utilizes multiple HBAs to connect to a single or multiple FC switches to provide failover or load-balancing functionality, this is known as Multipath I/O (MPIO) and a qualified driver for MPIO management and communication must be used. Also, the function of either MPIO failover and/or MPIO load balancing must be verified as approved for Windows Server 2008 R2. Consult the shared storage vendor, including the Fibre Channel switch vendor, for documentation and supported configurations, and check the cluster Hardware Compatibility List (HCL) on the Microsoft website to find approved configurations.

### iSCSI Storage

When organizations want to utilize iSCSI storage for Windows Server 2008 R2 failover clusters, security and network isolation is highly recommended. iSCSI utilizes an initiator on the host that requires access to the LUNs or iSCSI targets. Targets are located or hosted on iSCSI target portals. Using the target portal interface, the target must be configured to be accessed by multiple initiators in a cluster configuration. Both the iSCSI initiators and target portals come in software- and hardware-based models, but both models utilize IP networks for communication between the initiators and the targets. The targets need to be presented to Windows as a basic disk. When standard network cards will be used for iSCSI communication on Windows Server 2008 R2 systems, the built-in Windows Server 2008 R2 iSCSI initiator can be used, provided that the iSCSI target can support the authentication and security options provided, if used.

Regardless of the choice of the Microsoft iSCSI initiator, software- or hardware-based initiators, or targets, iSCSI communication should be deployed on isolated network segments and preferably dedicated network switches and network interface cards. Furthermore, the LUNs presented to the failover cluster should be masked and secured from any systems that are not nodes participating in the cluster, by using authentication and IPSec communication, when possible. Within the Windows Server 2008 R2 operating system, the iSCSI HBA or designated network card should not be used for any failover cluster configuration and cannot be deployed using network teaming software—or it will not be supported by Microsoft.

Hopefully by now, it is very clear that Microsoft only wants to support organizations that deploy failover clusters on tested and approved entire systems, but in many cases, failover clusters can still be deployed and can function, as the Create a Cluster Wizard will allow a cluster to be deployed that is not in a supported configuration.

### Multipath I/O

Windows Server 2008 R2 supports Multipath I/O to external storage devices such as SANs and iSCSI targets when multiple HBAs are used in the local system or by the shared storage. Multipath I/O can be used to provide failover access to disk storage in case of a controller or HBA failure, but some drivers also support load balancing across HBAs in both standalone and failover cluster deployments. Windows Server 2008 R2 provides a built-in Multipath I/O driver for iSCSI that can be leveraged when the manufacturer conforms to the necessary specifications to allow for the use of this built-in driver. The iSCSI initiator built in to Windows Server 2008 R2 is very user friendly and makes adding iSCSI targets simple and easy by making new targets reconnect by default. Multipath I/O (MPIO) support is also installed by default, and this is different from previous releases of the iSCSI initiator software.

### Volume Shadow Copy for Shared Storage Volume

The Volume Shadow Copy Service (VSS) is supported on shared storage volumes. Volume Shadow Copy can take a point-in-time snapshot of an entire volume, enabling administrators and users to recover data from a previous version. Furthermore, failover clusters and the entire Windows Server Backup architecture utilize VSS to store backup data. Many of today's services and applications that are certified to work on Windows Server 2008 R2 failover clusters are VSS compliant; careful choice and consideration should be made when choosing an alternative backup system, unless the system is provided by the shared storage manufacturer and certified to work in conjunction with VSS, Windows Server 2008 R2, and the service or application running on the failover cluster.

## Failover Cluster Node Operating System Selection

Windows Server 2008 R2 supports only the 64-bit operating systems but the nodes must be running either the Enterprise or Datacenter Edition. If any services or applications require deployment on 32-bit operating systems, and if this application is deployed on a Windows Server 2008 R2 failover cluster, performance of that application might suffer and should be performance tested thoroughly before deploying these applications on production failover clusters. Also, verify that these 32-bit applications are indeed supported on Windows Server 2008 R2 failover clusters and not just on Windows Server 2008 failover clusters or Windows Server 2003 server clusters.

# Deploying Failover Clusters

The Windows Server 2008 R2 Failover Clustering feature is not installed on a system by default and must be installed before failover clusters can be deployed. Remote management on administrative workstations can be accomplished by using the Remote Server Administration Tools feature, which includes the Failover Cluster Manager snap-in, but the feature needs to be installed on all nodes that will participate in the failover cluster. Even before installing the Failover Clustering features, several steps should be taken on each node of the cluster to help deploy a reliable failover cluster. Before deploying a failover cluster, perform the following steps on each node that will be a member of the failover cluster:

▶ Configure fault-tolerant volumes or LUNs using local disks or SAN-attached storage for the operating system volume.

▶ Configure at least two network cards, one for client and cluster communication and one for dedicated cluster communication.

▶ For iSCSI shared storage, configure an additional, dedicated network adapter or hardware-based iSCSI HBA.

▶ For Hyper-V clusters, configure an additional, dedicated network adapter on each node for virtual guest communication.

▶ Rename each network card property for easy identification within the Failover Cluster Manager console after the failover cluster is created. For example, rename Local Area Connection to PRODUCTION, Local Area Connection 2 to iSCSI NIC, and Local Area Connection 3 to HEARTBEAT, as required and possible. Also, if network teaming will be used with third-party software, configure the team first and rename each physical network adapter in the team to TEAMMEMBER1 and 2. The virtual team adapter should then get the name of PRODUCTION. Remember, teaming is not supported or recommended for iSCSI and heartbeat connections.

▶ Configure all necessary IPv4 and IPv6 addresses as static configurations.

▶ Verify that any and all HBAs and other storage controllers are running the proper firmware and matched driver version suitable for Windows Server 2008 R2 failover clusters.

▶ If shared storage will be used, plan to utilize at least two separate LUNs, one to serve as the witness disk and one to serve as the cluster disk for a high-availability Services and Applications group.

▶ If applications or services not included with Windows Server 2008 R2 will be deployed in the failover cluster, as a best practice, add an additional fault-tolerant array or LUN to the system to store the application installation and service files.

▶ Ensure that proper LUN masking and zoning has been configured at the FC or Ethernet switch level for FC or iSCSI shared storage communication, suitable for failover clustering. Each node in the failover cluster, along with the HBAs of the shared storage device, should have exclusive access to the LUNs presented to the failover cluster.

▶ If multiple HBAs will be used in each failover node or in the shared storage device, ensure that a suitable Multipath I/O driver has been installed. The Windows Server 2008 R2 Multipath I/O feature can be used to provide this function if approved by the HBA, switch, and storage device vendors and Microsoft.

▶ Shut down all nodes except one and on that node, configure the shared storage LUNs as Windows basic disks, format as a single partition/volume for the entire span of the disk, and define an appropriate drive letter and volume label. Shut down the node used to set up the disks and bring each other node up one at a time and verify that each LUN is available, and, if necessary, configure the appropriate drive letter if it does not match what was configured on the first node.

▶ As required, test Multipath I/O for load balancing and/or failover using the appropriate diagnostic or monitoring tool to ensure proper operation on each node one at a time.

▶ Designate a domain user account to be used for Failover Cluster Manager, and add this account to the local Administrators group on each cluster node. In the domain, grant this account the Create Computer Accounts right at the domain level to ensure that when the administrative and high-availability Services and Applications groups are created, the account can create the necessary domain computer accounts.

▶ Create a spreadsheet with the network names, IP addresses, and cluster disks that will be used for the administrative cluster and the high-availability Services and Applications group or groups that will be deployed in the failover cluster. Each Services and Applications group requires a separate network name and IPv4 address, but if IPv6 is used, the address can be added separately in addition to the IPv4 address or a custom or generic Services and Applications group needs to be created.

After the tasks in the preceding list are completed, the Failover Clustering feature can be installed. Failover clusters are deployed using a series of steps, including the following tasks:

1. Preconfigure the nodes, as listed previously and create a domain user account to be used as the cluster service account.

2. Install any necessary Windows Server 2008 R2 roles, role services, or features that will be deployed on the failover cluster. If any wizards are included with the role installation, like creating a DFS namespace or a DHCP scope, skip those wizards. Repeat this installation on all nodes that will be in the cluster.

3. Install the Failover Clustering feature on each node logged on with the cluster service account.

4. Run the Validate a Configuration Wizard and review the results to ensure that all tests pass successfully. If any tests fail, the configuration will not be supported by Microsoft and can be prone to several different types of issues and instability.

5. Run the Create a Cluster Wizard to actually deploy the administrative cluster.

6. Customize the failover cluster properties.

7. Install any Microsoft or third-party applications that will be added as application-specific cluster resources, so the application can be deployed using the High Availability Wizard.

8. Run the High Availability Wizard to create a high-availability Services and Applications group within the failover cluster, such as a file server, print server, DHCP server, virtual machine, or another of the included or separate services or applications that will run on a Windows Server 2008 R2 failover cluster.

9. Test the failover cluster configuration, and back it up.

## Installing the Failover Clustering Feature

Before a failover cluster can be deployed, the necessary feature must be installed. To install the Failover Clustering feature, perform the following steps:

1. Log on to the Windows Server 2008 R2 cluster node with an account with administrator privileges.

2. Click Start, click All Programs, click Administrative Tools, and select Server Manager.

3. When Server Manager opens, in the tree pane select the Features node.

4. In the tasks pane, select the Add Features link.

5. In the Select Features window, select Failover Clustering, click Next, and click Install on the Confirm Installation Selections page to install the feature.

6. When the installation completes, click Close to complete the installation and return to Server Manager.

7. Close Server Manager and install the Failover Clustering feature on each of the remaining cluster nodes.

## Running the Validate a Configuration Wizard

Failover Cluster Manager is the MMC snap-in used to administer the Failover Clustering feature. After the feature is installed, the next step is to run the Validate a Configuration Wizard from the tasks pane of the Failover Cluster Manager console. All nodes should be up and running when the wizard is run. To run the Validate a Configuration Wizard, perform the following steps:

1. Log on to one of the Windows Server 2008 R2 cluster nodes with an account with administrator privileges over all nodes in the cluster.

2. Click Start, click All Programs, click Administrative Tools, and select Failover Cluster Manager.

3. When the Failover Cluster Manager console opens, click the Validate a Configuration link in the Actions pane under the Management heading.

4. When the Validate a Configuration Wizard opens, click Next on the Before You Begin page.

5. On the Select Servers or a Cluster page, enter the name of a cluster node, and click the Add button. Repeat this process until all nodes are added to the list, as shown in Figure 29.1, and click Next to continue.

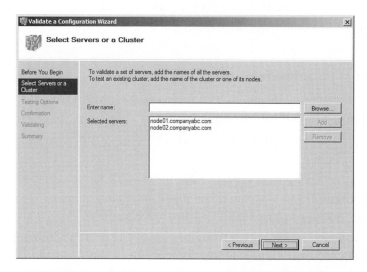

FIGURE 29.1   Adding the servers to be validated by the Validate a Configuration Wizard.

6. On the Testing Options page, read the details that explain the requirements for all tests to pass in order to be supported by Microsoft. Select the Run All Tests (Recommended) option button, and click Next to continue.

7. On the Confirmation page, review the list of servers that will be tested and the list of tests that will be performed, and click Next to begin testing the servers.

8. When the tests complete, the Summary page displays the results and if the tests pass, as shown in Figure 29.2, click Finish to complete the Validate a Configuration Wizard. If the test failed, click the View Report button to review the details and determine which test failed and why the test failed.

Even if the Validate a Configuration Wizard does not pass every test, depending on the test, creating a cluster might still be possible. After the Validation a Configuration Wizard is completed successfully, the cluster can be created. One common mistake is that the disks that will be used for the cluster are not defined on any of the cluster nodes, and these should be defined and active on at least one node, and listed as offline on the

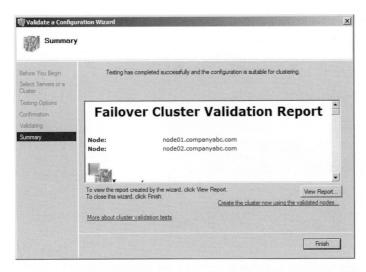

FIGURE 29.2    A successful result of the Validate a Configuration Wizard is required for Microsoft failover cluster support.

remaining nodes. Alternatively, the cluster can be deployed with only a single node, the cluster can be created, and additional nodes can be added later.

## Creating a Failover Cluster

When the failover cluster is first created, all nodes in the cluster should be up and running. The exception to that rule is when failover clusters utilize direct attached storage such as Serial Attached SCSI devices that require a process of creating the cluster on a single node and adding other nodes one at a time. For clusters that will not use shared storage or clusters that will connect to shared storage using iSCSI or Fibre Channel connections, all nodes should be powered on during cluster creation. To create the failover cluster, perform the following steps:

1. Log on to one of the Windows Server 2008 R2 cluster nodes with an account with administrator privileges over all nodes in the cluster.

2. Click Start, click All Programs, click Administrative Tools, and select Failover Cluster Manager.

3. When the Failover Cluster Manager console opens, click the Create a Cluster link in the Actions pane under the Management heading.

4. When the Create Cluster Wizard opens, click Next on the Before You Begin page.

5. On the Select Servers page, enter the name of each cluster node, and click the Add button. When all the nodes are listed, click Next to continue.

6. On the Access Point for Administering the Cluster page, type in the name of the cluster, complete the IPv4 address, and click Next, as shown in Figure 29.3.

29

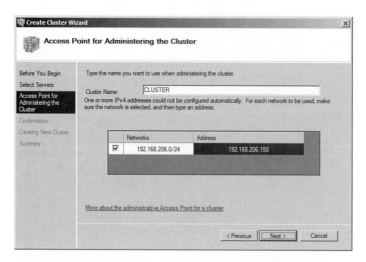

FIGURE 29.3    Defining the network name and IPv4 address for the failover cluster.

7. On the Confirmation page, review the settings, and click Next to create the cluster.

8. On the Summary page, review the results of the cluster creation process, and click Finish to return to the Failover Cluster Manager console. If there are any errors, you can click the View Report button to reveal the detailed cluster creation report.

9. Back in the Failover Cluster Manager console, select the cluster name in the tree pane, if not already selected by default, and in the tasks pane, review the configuration of the cluster.

10. In the tree pane, select and expand the cluster to reveal the Nodes group to list all of the cluster nodes.

11. Select Storage and review the cluster storage in the tasks pane listed under Storage, as shown in Figure 29.4.

12. Expand Networks in the tree pane to review the list of networks. Select each network and review the names of the adapters in each network.

13. When reviewing is completed, the initial cluster deployment is complete. Close the Failover Cluster Manager console and log off of the cluster node.

After the cluster is created, additional tasks should be performed before any Services and Applications groups are created using the High Availability Wizard. These tasks can include, but might not require, customizing the cluster networks, adding storage to the cluster, adding nodes to the cluster, and changing the cluster quorum model.

## Configuring Cluster Networks

After the cluster is created, several steps should be taken to improve cluster management. One of these tasks includes customizing the cluster networks. Each node in the cluster should have the same number of network adapters and each adapter should have already

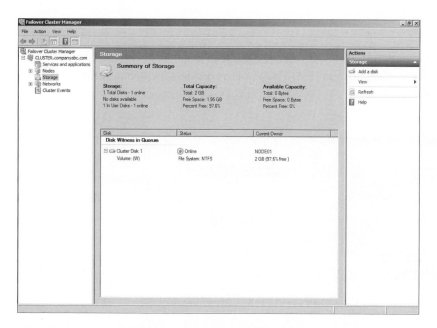

FIGURE 29.4    Displaying the dedicated cluster storage.

been renamed to describe a network or to easily identify which network a particular network adapter belongs to. After the nodes are added to the failover cluster, for each network card in a cluster node, there will be a corresponding cluster network. Each cluster network will be named "Cluster Network 1," "Cluster Network 2," and so forth for each network. Each network can be renamed and can also be configured for use by the cluster and clients, for internal cluster use only, or the network can be excluded from any cluster use. Networks and network adapters used for iSCSI communication must be excluded from cluster usage. Now excluding iSCSI networks from cluster usage might seem strange, especially if iSCSI disks are used for the cluster, but this is intended to ensure that only iSCSI communication is passed to that network and no unnecessary cluster communication is competing for NIC resources when disk access might be critical. To customize the cluster networks, perform the following steps:

1. Log on to one of the Windows Server 2008 R2 cluster nodes with an account with administrator privileges over all nodes in the cluster.

2. Click Start, click All Programs, click Administrative Tools, and select Failover Cluster Manager.

3. When the Failover Cluster Manager console opens, if necessary type in the name of the local cluster node to connect to the cluster.

4. When the Failover Cluster Manager console connects to the cluster, select and expand the cluster name.

29

5. Select and expand Networks in the tree pane, and select Cluster Network 1 as an example.

6. In the tasks pane, review the name of the network adapters in the network, as shown in Figure 29.5, for the HEARTBEAT network adapters that are members of Cluster Network 1.

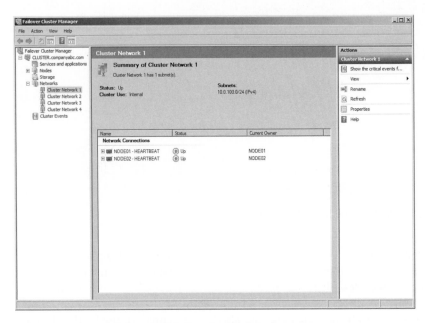

FIGURE 29.5    Displaying the network adapters in a cluster network.

7. Right-click Cluster Network 1, and select Rename. Rename the cluster to match the network adapter name.

8. For this example, right-click the renamed HEARTBEAT network, and select Properties.

9. Select the Allow Cluster Communication on This Network option button, and do not check the check box to allow clients to connect through this network. Click OK when completed.

10. Back in the Failover Cluster Manager console, rename the remaining cluster networks and verify that each network is configured for the proper cluster only or cluster and client communication. iSCSI network interface cards should be configured to not allow cluster network communication and production networks should be configured to allow cluster network communication and to allow clients to connect through the network.

11. When all of the networking changes are complete, click on the Networks node in the tree pane and the networks should be listed similarly to Figure 29.6. Close the Failover Cluster Manager console and log off of the server.

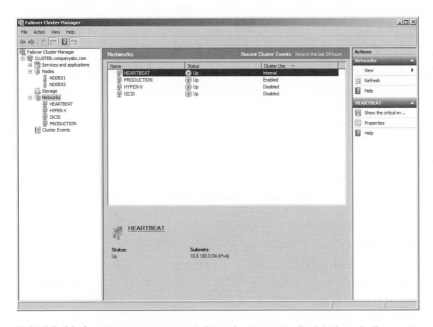

FIGURE 29.6    Cluster networks defined for internal, disabled, and client communication.

## Adding Nodes to the Cluster

If additional nodes need to be added to the cluster after the initial cluster creation process, first join that server to the domain, add the failover clustering feature, configure the network interface cards and storage configuration per cluster specifications, and then perform the following steps:

1. Log on to one of the Windows Server 2008 R2 cluster nodes with an account with administrator privileges over all nodes in the cluster.

2. Click Start, click All Programs, click Administrative Tools, and select Failover Cluster Manager.

3. When the Failover Cluster Manager console opens, if necessary type in the name of the local cluster node to connect to the cluster.

4. When the Failover Cluster Manager console connects to the cluster, select and expand the cluster name.

5. Select and expand Nodes in the tree pane.

6. Right-click Nodes and select Add Node.

29

7. When the Add Node Wizard opens, click Next on the Before You Begin page.

8. On the Select Server page, type in the name of the cluster node, and click the Add button. After the node is added to the list, click Next to continue.

9. If this node was not previously included with the original run of the Cluster Validation Wizard, a Validation Warning page appears. Select the Yes option button to check this node for cluster validation before adding it to the cluster or select No if support from Microsoft is not desired or required, and click Next to continue. If you selected Yes, the validation wizard will open and all nodes will be tested again. Once completed and validation results are successful, continue with the remaining steps in this process.

10. On the Confirmation page, review the names of the node or nodes that will be added, and click Next to continue.

11. When the process completes, review the results on the Summary page, and click Finish to close the wizard.

12. Close the Failover Cluster Manager console and log off of the server.

## Adding Storage to the Cluster

When shared storage is used with failover clusters, all of the LUNs or targets presented to the cluster hosts might not have been added to the cluster during the initial configuration. When this is the case, and additional storage needs to be added to the cluster, perform the following steps:

1. Log on to one of the Windows Server 2008 R2 cluster nodes with an account with administrator privileges over all nodes in the cluster.

2. Click Start, click All Programs, click Administrative Tools, and select Failover Cluster Manager.

3. When the Failover Cluster Manager console opens, if necessary type in the name of the local cluster node to connect to the cluster.

4. In the tree pane, expand the desired cluster Services and Applications group, select Storage, right-click Storage, and select Add a Disk.

5. If suitable storage is ready to be added to the cluster, it will be listed in the Add Disks to a Cluster window. If a disk is listed, check the box next to the desired disk or disks, and click OK to add the disk(s) to the cluster. The disks will need to be basic disks and set to online in Disk Manager on one of the cluster nodes and should already have a single partition and drive letter. It is essential that drive letters used for cluster disks are not in conflict with any drive letters on any node in the cluster, including optical or external drives.

6. After the process completes, if necessary change the drive letter of the new disk. Once this process completes, if Disk Manager is opened on the cluster nodes, disks will show as Basic and Reserved on all cluster nodes, but only the active cluster node will show the disk partition and drive letter information.

7. Close the Failover Cluster Manager console.

8. Click the Start button and select Computer.

9. Review the list of disks on the cluster node and note that disks managed by the cluster are listed as Clustered Disks instead of Local Disks, as shown in Figure 29.7.

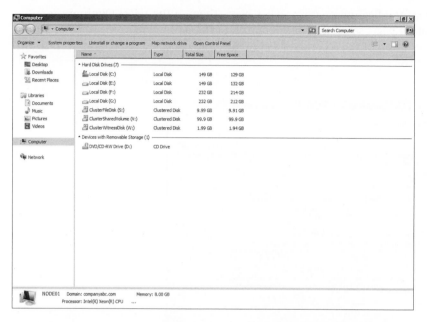

FIGURE 29.7   Displaying the local and clustered disks on a cluster node.

10. Close the Explorer windows and log off of the server.

## Cluster Quorum Configuration

If all cluster nodes and shared storage were available during the creation of the cluster, the best-suited quorum model would have been automatically selected during the cluster creation process. In some cases, the selected quorum model might need to be changed if the cluster configuration changes by adding or removing nodes or by deploying geographically dispersed clusters. When the existing cluster quorum needs to be validated or changed, perform the following steps:

1. Log on to one of the Windows Server 2008 R2 cluster nodes with an account with administrator privileges over all nodes in the cluster.

2. Click Start, click All Programs, click Administrative Tools, and select Failover Cluster Manager.

3. When the Failover Cluster Manager console opens, if necessary type in the name of the local cluster node to connect to the cluster.

4. In the tree pane, select the cluster name; in the tasks pane, the current quorum model is listed.

29

5. Review the current quorum model, and if it is correct, close the Failover Cluster Manager console.

6. If the current quorum model is not the desired model, right-click the cluster name in the tree pane, click More Actions, and select Configure Cluster Quorum Settings.

7. If the Before You Begin page opens, click Next, then on the Select Quorum Configuration page, select the option button of the desired quorum model or select the option button of the recommended model, and click Next to continue, as shown in Figure 29.8.

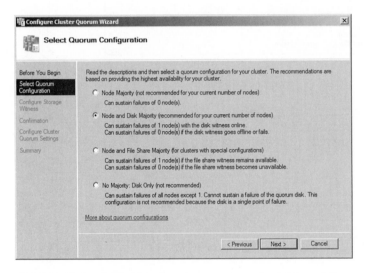

FIGURE 29.8    Configuring the cluster quorum model for a failover cluster.

8. If a quorum model contains a witness disk or file share, select the designated disk or specify the path to the file share, and click Next.

9. On the Confirmation page, review the settings, and click Next to update the cluster quorum model for the failover cluster.

10. Review the results on the Summary page, and click Finish to return to the Failover Cluster Manager console.

11. Close the Failover Cluster Manager console and log off of the server.

## Enabling Cluster Shared Volumes

When Hyper-V virtual machines will be deployed on Windows Server 2008 R2 failover cluster nodes and shared storage is used, the new Cluster Shared Volumes can be enabled for use with Hyper-V Live Migration configurations for designated virtual machines. Cluster Shared Volumes are currently only supported on failover clusters for Hyper-V and unlike other cluster shared storage, these designated volumes can be read and written to by all nodes in the cluster simultaneously. Obvious to some is the fact that when two separate systems can write to a single disk, corruption can occur and that is why this feature is only currently supported for Hyper-V and Live Migration. One important point to note is that for a virtual machine to use a Cluster Shared Volume, this feature must be enabled on the cluster and the virtual machine must use storage that has been added to the Cluster Shared Volume storage group prior to virtual machine creation. To learn how to enable Cluster Shared Volumes and deploy virtual machines using CSV storage, refer to Chapter 37, "Deploying and Using Windows Virtualization."

## Deploying Services or Applications on Failover Clusters

After the desired cluster configuration is achieved, the cluster is ready for the deploying of Services and Applications groups. Windows Server 2008 R2 provides several out-of-the-box cluster resources that can be used to deploy Windows services and applications using failover clusters, as shown in Figure 29.9.

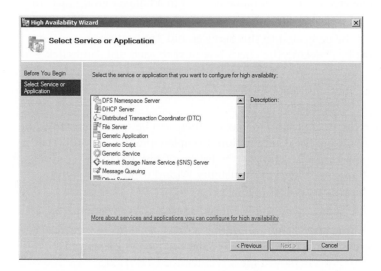

FIGURE 29.9    Windows Server 2008 R2 built-in cluster services and applications resources.

Before a particular built-in service or application can be deployed in the cluster, the role, role service, or feature associated with it needs to be installed on each node prior to running the High Availability Wizard. For example, before a File Services server can be deployed on a failover cluster for high availability, the File Services role will need to be installed on each node in the cluster. After the prerequisites are installed on each cluster node, perform the following steps to deploy the service or application on the failover cluster:

1. Log on to one of the Windows Server 2008 R2 cluster nodes with an account with administrator privileges over all nodes in the cluster.

2. Click Start, click All Programs, click Administrative Tools, and select Failover Cluster Manager.

3. When the Failover Cluster Manager console opens, if necessary type in the name of the local cluster node to connect to the cluster.

4.  In the tree pane, select the cluster name, expand it, and select Services and Applications.

5.  Right-click Services and Applications, and select Configure a Service or Application.

6.  In the High Availability Wizard that opens, click Next on the Before You Begin page.

7.  Select the desired service or application on the Select a Service or Application page, and click Next to continue. If the necessary roles, role services, or features are not installed on each node prior to selecting the desired entry, an error is displayed and the process cannot continue. For this example, we have selected File Server as the service or application that will be managed by the failover cluster.

8.  On the Client Access Point page, type in the name and IP address for the new file server, and click Next. This is the name and IP address used to publish or host the service or application. Also, a computer account in the Active Directory domain and DNS entries will be created for each name defined in a failover group's Client Access Point.

9.  Select the disk that will be dedicated to this Services and Applications group on the Select Storage page by checking the check box next to each disk, and click Next to continue

10. Review the settings on the Confirmation page, and click Next to deploy the service or application in the failover cluster.

11. Depending on the service or application deployed, there can be specific postcreation wizards that open to complete the configuration. Complete the steps in the wizards as required or close the wizard and return to the Failover Cluster Manager console. Otherwise, click Finish to close the High Availability Wizard window and return to the Failover Cluster Manager console.

12. In the tree pane, expand Services and Applications to reveal the new group.

13. Select the new group in the tasks pane, and in the Actions pane, review the available management commands, such as Add a Shared Folder or Manage Shares and Storage, as shown in Figure 29.10, for a deployed file server named CLUSTERFS.

14. Complete the configuration of the newly deployed service or application, close the Failover Cluster Management console, and log off of the cluster node.

## Configuring Failover and Failback

Clusters that contain two or more nodes automatically have failover configured for each Services and Applications group as long as each node has the necessary services or applications installed to support running the group locally. Failback is never configured by default and needs to be manually configured for each Services and Applications group if desired. Failback allows a designated preferred server or "preferred owner" to always run a particular cluster group on the preferred node, when it is available. When the preferred owner fails and the affected groups failover to alternate nodes, once the preferred node is back online and functioning as desired, the failback configuration options are used to determine if the group will automatically failback immediately or after a specified time period. Also, with regard to failover and failback configuration, the Failover and Failback properties define how many failures in a specified number of hours will be tolerated

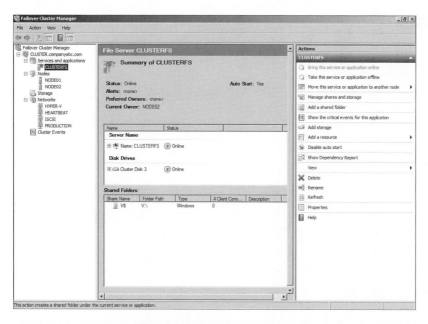

FIGURE 29.10    Reviewing the available actions for a file server failover cluster group.

before the group is taken offline and remains offline. To review and if necessary change the failover and failback configuration options on a particular Services and Applications group, perform the following steps:

1. Log on to one of the Windows Server 2008 R2 cluster nodes with an account with administrator privileges over all nodes in the cluster.

2. Click Start, click All Programs, click Administrative Tools, and select Failover Cluster Manager.

3. When the Failover Cluster Manager console opens, if necessary type in the name of the local cluster node to connect to the cluster.

4. In the tree pane, select the cluster name, expand it, and select Services and Applications.

5. Expand Services and Applications, right-click the desired group, and select Properties. For this example, the CLUSTERFS file server group will be used.

6. In the CLUSTERFS group properties on the General tab, in the Preferred Owner section, check the box next to the desired node if failback will be configured. Do not close the group property window.

7. Select the Failover tab and review the number of allowed failures in a specified number of hours. The default is one group failure allowed in six hours.

8. In the lower section of the tab, if desired, enable failback and configure whether failback will be allowed and whether it will occur immediately when the preferred node is online or if the failback can only occur during after hours, such as between the hours of 9:00 p.m. and 6:00 a.m. or 17 and 6, as shown in Figure 29.11.

29

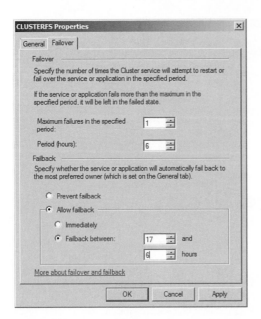

FIGURE 29.11    Configuring a Services and Applications group's failover threshold and failback configuration.

---

**NOTE**

To reduce the chance of having a group failing back to a node during regular business hours after a failure, configure the failback schedule to allow failback only during non-peak times or after hours using settings similar to those made in Figure 29.11 based on the organization's work hours and backup schedule.

---

## Testing Failover Clusters

After all the desired cluster nodes to the failover cluster are added and failover and failback configuration options are set for each Services and Applications group, each group should be verified for proper operation on each cluster node. For these tests to be complete, failover and, when applicable, failback of cluster groups need to be tested. They can be tested by simulating a cluster resource failure or by manually moving the Services and Applications groups between nodes.

### Testing Services and Applications Groups Using Manual Failover

To manually failover or move a Services and Applications group between failover cluster nodes, perform the following steps:

1. Log on to one of the Windows Server 2008 R2 cluster nodes with an account with administrator privileges over all nodes in the cluster.

2. Click Start, click All Programs, click Administrative Tools, and select Failover Cluster Manager.

3. When the Failover Cluster Manager console opens, if necessary type in the name of the local cluster node to connect to the cluster.

4. In the tree pane, select the cluster name, expand it, and select Services and Applications.

5. Expand Services and Applications and select the desired group. For this example, the CLUSTERFS file server group will be used.

6. In the tasks pane, note the current owner of the group.

7. In the tree pane, right-click the desired group, select Move This Service or Application to Another Node, and select any of the desired available nodes, as shown in Figure 29.12, to move the group to NODE02. A confirmation dialog box will open to confirm moving the group to the alternate node; confirm the move to continue by pressing the Move CLUSTERFS to NODE02 button.

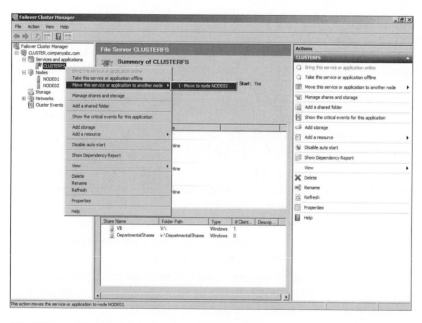

FIGURE 29.12    Moving a Services and Applications group to another available node.

8. The group will be moved to the chosen node and when the group is back online it will be reflected as Status: Online in the tasks pane. Close the Failover Cluster Manager console and log off of the server.

### Simulating the Failure of a Cluster Resource

Simulating a cluster resource failure can be easily accomplished using the Failover Cluster Manager console. Each resource has its own properties and simulating a failure usually initiates the startup or restoration of the resource back to an online state. After the failure threshold is reached, the Services and Applications group is taken offline, moved to another available node, and brought back online. To simulate the failure of a cluster resource and test the failover of a group, perform the following steps:

1. Log on to one of the Windows Server 2008 R2 cluster nodes with an account with administrator privileges over all nodes in the cluster.

2. Click Start, click All Programs, click Administrative Tools, and select Failover Cluster Manager.

3. When the Failover Cluster Manager console opens, if necessary type in the name of the local cluster node to connect to the cluster.

4. In the tree pane, select the cluster name, expand it, and select Services and Applications.

5. Expand Services and Applications and select the desired group. For this example, the CLUSTERFS file server group will be used.

6. In the tasks pane, scroll down to locate the File Server cluster resource.

7. Right-click the File Server resource, and select Properties.

8. On the File Server Property page, select the Policies tab and review the resource failure configuration. The default configuration allows for one service restart after failure within a period of 15 minutes. If a second failure occurs within the threshold of 15 minutes, the entire group is taken offline, moved to an alternate node, and brought back online. This is controlled by checking the If Restart Is Unsuccessful, Fail Over All Resources in This Service or Application check box.

9. Close the File Server Property pages.

10. Back in the tasks pane of the Failover Cluster Manager console, right-click the File Server resource, select More Actions, and click Simulate Failure of This Resource, as shown in Figure 29.13. The resource will be failed and the cluster will attempt to automatically restart the File Server resource.

11. When the simulation is started, a confirmation is required; click the appropriate button to allow for the resource failure simulation to be processed.

12. After the File Server resource is automatically restarted, perform the resource failure simulation again within 15 minutes. This time, the entire group is taken offline and moved to the other node where it will be brought back online.

13. When the simulation is started, a confirmation is required; click the appropriate button to allow for the resource failure simulation to be processed.

14. If necessary, scroll up in the tasks pane to verify that the group has been moved to the alternate cluster node.

15. Close the Failover Cluster Manager console and log off of the server.

## Failover Cluster Maintenance

Services and applications are deployed on failover clusters based on the fact that they are critical to business operations. The reliability of each cluster node is very important and making any changes to the software or hardware configuration of each node can compro-

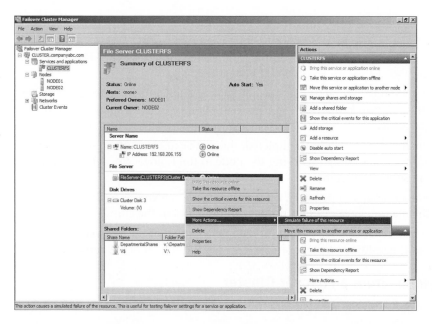

FIGURE 29.13    Simulating a failure of the File Server cluster resource.

mise this reliability. Before any changes are implemented on a production failover cluster, a few premaintenance tasks should be performed.

### Premaintenance Tasks

Before maintenance is run on a cluster node or the entire failover cluster, several tasks should be completed. To prepare a cluster node for maintenance, do the following:

1. Whether you're planning a software or hardware upgrade, research to see whether the changes will be supported on Windows Server 2008 R2 failover clusters.

2. Log on to one of the Windows Server 2008 R2 cluster nodes with an account with administrator privileges over all nodes in the cluster.

3. Click Start, click All Programs, click Administrative Tools, and select Failover Cluster Manager.

4. When the Failover Cluster Manager console opens, if necessary type in the name of the local cluster node to connect to the cluster.

5. In the tree pane, select the cluster name, and in the tree pane, note the Current Host Server. If the Current Host Server is the node that will be taken offline for maintenance, the cluster will be automatically moved to an alternate node if the maintenance node is rebooted.

6. In the tree pane, select and expand Services and Applications to reveal each of the groups.

7. Select each group and in the tasks pane, note which node is the Current Owner of the move. Manually move each group to the node that will remain online if any of the groups are currently running on the node that will be taken offline for maintenance.

29

8. After all the groups are moved to a node that will remain online, in the tree pane, expand Nodes to reveal all of the nodes in the failover cluster.

9. Locate the node that will be taken offline for maintenance, right-click the node, and select Pause.

10. When the node is paused, resources cannot failover and come online and the system can have the software and/or hardware configuration or updates applied and, if necessary, rebooted.

11. After the maintenance tasks are completed, the node can be configured to be active in the failover cluster by right-clicking the node in the Failover Cluster Manager console and selecting Resume.

12. When the node resumes operation, if necessary, move the groups to this node and perform the maintenance tasks on the remaining nodes in the cluster.

13. When the maintenance tasks have been completed on all of the failover cluster nodes, close the Failover Cluster Manager console and log off of the server.

## Removing Nodes from a Failover Cluster

Cluster nodes can be removed from a cluster for a number of reasons, and this process can be accomplished quite easily.

> **NOTE**
>
> If you're removing nodes from a cluster that utilizes the Node Majority Quorum model, be sure that a majority of the nodes remain available; otherwise, the cluster might be shut down. If this is not possible, the Quorum model might need to be changed before a node is removed from the failover cluster.

To remove a node from a failover cluster, perform the following steps:

1. Log on to one of the Windows Server 2008 R2 cluster nodes with an account with administrator privileges over all nodes in the cluster.

2. Click Start, click All Programs, click Administrative Tools, and select Failover Cluster Manager.

3. When the Failover Cluster Manager console opens, if necessary type in the name of the local cluster node to connect to the cluster.

4. In the tree pane, select the cluster name, expand it, and select Nodes.

5. Expand Nodes to reveal all of the cluster nodes.

6. Right-click on the node that will be removed from the cluster, select More Actions, and click Evict.

7. A confirmation window opens. Select the option to evict the desired node from the cluster. After the process starts, if the cluster and/or any Services and Applications groups are running on this node, they will be moved to a remaining node before this node is removed from the cluster.

8. After the node is removed, close the Failover Cluster Manager console and log off of the server.

## Cluster Migration and Upgrades

If an organization currently supports Windows Server 2003 clusters, the nodes in the cluster cannot be upgraded to Windows Server 2008 R2 failover cluster nodes. This is mainly because the requirements of Windows Server 2003 server clusters and Windows Server 2008 R2 failover clusters are very different. Even hardware requirements between Windows Server 2008 and Windows Server 2008 R2 are different in terms of what actual configurations have been tested and are certified for failover clusters on each operating system version. Windows Server 2008 R2 does provide a tool that can be used to collect data and migrate built-in Windows services between Windows Server 2003 server clusters or other Windows Server 2008 or Windows Server 2008 R2 failover clusters to a destination Windows Server 2008 R2 failover cluster. For more information on migrating services between Windows Server 2003 and Windows Server 2008 failover clusters to Windows Server 2008 R2, review the Help topic "Migrating Settings to a Failover Cluster Running Windows Server 2008 R2" in the failover clusters Help file. Note that any application or service that was able to run on a Windows Server 2008 failover cluster will also work on a Windows Server 2008 R2 failover cluster; only the hardware that is supported may be different.

# Backing Up and Restoring Failover Clusters

Windows Server 2008 R2 contains a rebuilt backup program appropriately named Windows Server Backup. Windows Server Backup can be used to back up each cluster node and any cluster disks that are currently online on the local node. Also, the System State of the cluster node can be backed up individually or as part of a complete system backup.

To successfully back up and restore the entire cluster or a single cluster node, the cluster administrator must first understand how to troubleshoot, back up, and restore a standalone Windows Server 2008 R2 system using Windows Server Backup. Some basic and some advanced Windows Backup and Restore topics and procedures are detailed in Chapters 30 and 31, "Backing Up the Windows Server 2008 R2 Environment" and "Recovering from a Disaster," respectively. The process of backing up cluster nodes is the same as for a standalone server, but restoring a cluster might require additional steps or configurations that do not apply to a standalone server. To be prepared to recover different types of cluster failures, you must take the following steps on each cluster node:

▶ Back up each cluster node's local disks.

▶ Back up each cluster node's System State.

▶ Back up the cluster quorum from any node running in the cluster.

▶ For failover clusters using shared storage, back up shared cluster disks from the node on which the disks are currently hosted.

29

## Failover Cluster Node—Backup Best Practices

As a backup best practice for cluster nodes, administrators should strive to back up everything as frequently as possible. Because cluster availability is so important, here are some recommendations for cluster node backup:

▶ Back up each cluster node's System State daily and immediately before and after a cluster configuration change is made.

▶ Back up cluster local drives and System State daily if the schedule permits or weekly if daily backups cannot be performed.

▶ Back up cluster shared drives daily if the schedule permits or weekly if daily backups cannot be performed.

▶ Using Windows Server Backup, perform a full system backup before any major changes occur and monthly if possible. If a full system backup is scheduled using Windows Server Backup, this task is already being performed.

For detailed information on how to perform any of the backup tasks previously listed, refer to Chapter 30.

## Restoring an Entire Cluster to a Previous State

Changes to a cluster should be made with caution and, if at all possible, should be tested in a nonproduction isolated lab environment first. When cluster changes have been implemented and deliver undesirable effects, the way to roll back the cluster configuration to a previous state is to restore the cluster configuration to all nodes. This process is simpler than it sounds and is performed from only one node. There are only two caveats to this process:

▶ All the cluster nodes that were members of the cluster previously need to be currently available and operational in the cluster. For example, if Cluster1 was made up of Server1 and Server2, both of these nodes need to be active in the cluster before the previous cluster configuration can be rolled back.

▶ To restore a previous cluster configuration to all cluster nodes, the entire cluster needs to be taken offline long enough to restore the backup, reboot the node from which the backup was run, and manually start the cluster service on all remaining nodes.

To restore an entire cluster to a previous state, perform the following steps:

1. Log on to one of the Windows Server 2008 R2 cluster nodes with an account with administrator privileges over all nodes in the cluster. (The node should have a full system backup available for recovery.)

2. Click Start, click All Programs, click Accessories, and select Command Prompt.

3. At the command prompt, type `wbadmin get versions` to reveal the list of available backups. For this example, our backup version is named 09/16/2009-08:30 as defined by the version identifier.

4. After the correct backup version is known, type the following command wbadmin Start Recovery -version: 09/16/2009-08:30 -ItemType:App -Items:Cluster (where version is the name of the backup version name), and press Enter.

5. Wbadmin returns a prompt stating that this command will perform an authoritative restore of the cluster and restart the cluster services, as shown in Figure 29.14. Type in Y and press Enter to start the authoritative cluster restore.

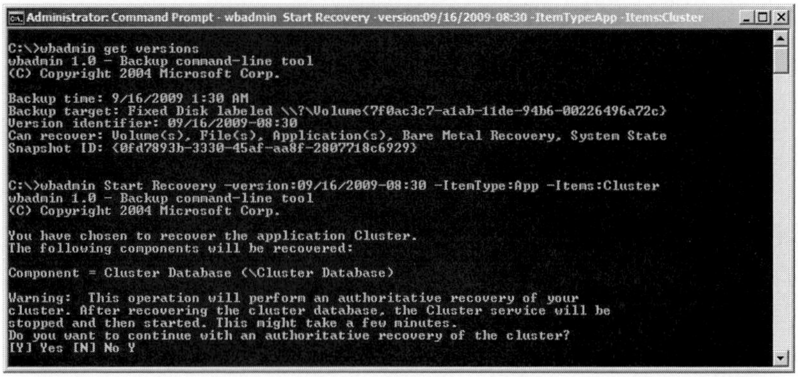

FIGURE 29.14    Performing an authoritative restore of the cluster configuration.

6. When the restore completes, each node in the cluster needs to have the cluster service started to complete the process. This might have been performed by the restore operation, but each node should be checked to verify that the cluster service is indeed started.

7. Open the Failover Cluster Manager console to verify that the restore has completed successfully. Close the console and log off of the server when you are finished.

## Deploying Multisite or Stretch Geographically Dispersed Failover Clusters

Geographically dispersed failover clusters are failover clusters that include cluster nodes deployed in multiple physical locations. The multisite or stretch term defines whether the two locations share a common network that is extended across the WAN, stretch, or multisite, in which cluster nodes are members of different Active Directory sites. By definition of an Active Directory site, these sites are defined by the different networks they reside on. Geographically dispersed failover clusters are not easy to deploy as each organization's network configuration might require different tuning parameters within the failover cluster services and Applications group resource properties. Some special considerations for geoclusters are as follows:

▶ Data replication is not performed by the cluster and must be performed using a third-party hardware or software solution.

▶ If an even number of nodes will be deployed with an equal amount of nodes in each location and the Node and File Share Majority Quorum configuration is used, if the

29

file share is hosted in either of the sites, and that site becomes inaccessible, the remote site will not be able to return to operation. In this case, it might be necessary to host the file share in another site to add some resilience to the multisite cluster.

▶ If the failover cluster will span multiple subnets, how will the IP address resources be configured? You can create multiple IP address resources in the Services and Applications group, one for each network, but you will need to carefully define that each IP address can only run on nodes in the group that are in the respective subnet.

▶ For multisite failover clusters with different IP address resources for each network, the Network Name resource dependency will need to be adjusted to allow for starting up when either of the IP address resources are online, but not both. In other words, all IP address resources should be added as dependencies of the Network Name resource but should be listed as OR dependencies, as shown in Figure 29.15.

FIGURE 29.15    Adjusting the Network Name resource dependencies for Services and Applications groups with multiple IP address resources.

▶ DNS record registration settings might need to be adjusted, particularly for Services and Applications groups that contain Network Name resources with multiple IP addresses in different subnets. Changing the DNS record TTL settings that the Network Name resource will use when it performs dynamic registration can directly affect client communication after a failover. If the client cannot resolve the network name to the correct IP address, it does not matter if the failover cluster is online or not. These settings can be changed using the cluster.exe utility.

▶ Cluster heartbeat communication settings might need to be adjusted based on the network usage and response. This would need to be determined by performing exhaustive testing during different network conditions to determine if the default heartbeat settings will be sufficient and will not unexpectedly determine that the nodes in a site are offline due to network latency. These settings can be changed using the cluster.exe utility.

# Deploying Network Load Balancing Clusters

The other clustering technology included in Windows Server 2008 R2 is Network Load Balancing (NLB). NLB clusters can easily be deployed on Windows Server 2008 R2 systems. Before an NLB cluster can be deployed, the Network Load Balancing feature needs to be installed on all servers that will be members or nodes in the NLB cluster. To properly configure an NLB cluster, the administrator needs to research the type of network traffic the application or service utilizes. For example, a standard website uses TCP Port 80 and standard Remote Desktop Services utilize port 3389.

## NLB Applications and Services

NLB is well equipped to distribute user connections and create fault tolerance for a number of different applications and network services. Because NLB does not replicate data across cluster nodes—and neither does failover clustering for that matter—using applications that require access to local data that is dynamic or frequently changes is not recommended for NLB clusters.

Applications well suited for NLB clusters are web-based applications and services, proxy services, virtual private network, SMTP gateways, streaming media, and Remote Desktop Services Session Host server systems. Many other applications and services can also run well on NLB clusters, but the preceding list is what most organizations utilize NLB clusters for.

NLB clusters are based on client connections made to a specific DNS name, IP address, and TCP and/or UDP port using either IPv4 or IPv6. It's important to read the vendor's application documentation regarding how the client communicates with the application and how this communication can be configured on load-balancing devices or services such as Microsoft Windows Server 2008 R2 NLB clusters. For instance, certain applications use cookies or other stateful session information that can be used to identify a client throughout the entire session and it is important that the client maintains a connection to the same cluster node during the entire session. Other applications, such as a website that serves up static pages, can respond to a single client's requests from multiple nodes in the NLB cluster. For a web-based application, such as an e-commerce application, an encrypted SSL session, or an application that is authenticated by the actual web server, the NLB cluster would need to direct all communication between the client and a specific cluster node. Considering these types of scenarios in advance helps determine how the NLB cluster will be defined.

29

## Installing the Network Load Balancing Feature

Before an NLB cluster can be created, the feature needs to be installed on all servers that will participate in the cluster. To install the Network Load Balancing feature, perform the following steps:

1. Log on to each Windows Server 2008 R2 system with an account that has local administrator rights.

2. Click Start, click All Programs, click Administrative Tools, and select Server Manager.

3. In the tree pane, select Features, and in the Actions pane, click the Add Features link.

4. On the Before You Begin page, click Next to continue.

5. On the Add Features page, check the box for Network Load Balancing, and click Next to continue.

6. On the Confirm Installation Selections page, review the list of features that will be added, and click Install to begin the installation.

7. On the Installations Results page, review the results, and click Close to return to Server Manager.

8. Close the Server Manager console and log off of the server.

9. Log on and repeat this process on the remaining servers that will participate in the cluster as required.

## Creating Port Rules

When an NLB cluster is created, one general port rule is also created for the cluster. The NLB cluster port rule or rules define what type of network traffic the cluster will load-balance across the cluster nodes and how the connections will be managed. The Port Rules Filtering option defines how the traffic will be balanced across each individual node. As a best practice, limiting the allowed ports for the clustered IP addresses to only those needed by the cluster load-balanced applications can improve overall cluster performance and security. In an NLB cluster, because each node can answer for the clustered IP address, all inbound traffic is received and processed by each node. When a node receives the request, it either handles the request or drops the packet if another node has already established a session or responded to the initial request.

When an administrator discards the default NLB cluster port rule and creates a rule that only allows specific ports to the clustered IP address or addresses, plus an additional rule to block all other traffic destined for the cluster IP address, each cluster node can quickly eliminate and drop packets that do not meet the allow port rule and in effect improve network performance of the cluster. The security benefit of this configuration also removes any risk of attacks on any other port using the cluster IP address.

## Port Rules Filtering Mode and Affinity

Within an NLB cluster port rule, the NLB administrator must configure the appropriate filtering mode. This allows the administrator to specify whether only one node or multiple nodes in the cluster can respond to requests from a single client throughout a session. There are three filtering modes: Single Host, Disable This Port Range, and Multiple Host.

### Single Host Filtering Mode

The Single Host filtering mode ensures that all traffic sent to the cluster IP address that matches a port rule with this filtering mode enabled is handled exclusively in the cluster by one particular cluster node.

### Disable This Port Range Filtering Mode

The Disable This Port Range filtering mode tells the cluster which ports are not active on the cluster IP address. Any traffic requests received on the cluster IP address that match a port rule with this filtering mode result in the network packets getting automatically discarded or dropped. Administrators should configure specific port rules and use this filter mode for ports and port ranges that do not need to be load-balanced across the cluster nodes.

### Multiple Hosts Filtering Mode

The Multiple Host filtering mode is probably the most commonly used filtering mode and is also the default. This mode allows traffic to be handled by all the nodes in the cluster. When traffic is balanced across multiple nodes, the application requirements define how the Affinity mode should be set. There are three types of multiple host affinities:

- ▶ **None**—This affinity type can send unique clients' requests to all the servers in the cluster during the entire span of the session. This can speed up server response times but is well suited only for serving static data to clients. This affinity type works well for general web browsing, read-only file data, and FTP servers.

- ▶ **Network**—This affinity type routes traffic from a particular class C address space to a single NLB cluster node. This mode is not used too often but can accommodate client sessions that use stateful applications and when different client requests are serviced by down-level proxy servers. This is a useful affinity type for companies that direct traffic from several remote offices, through proxies before connecting to the services, and/or applications managed by the port rules in the NLB cluster.

- ▶ **Single**—This affinity type is the most widely used. After the initial request is received by the cluster nodes from a particular client, that node will handle every request from that client until the session is completed. This affinity type can accommodate sessions that require stateful data such as an encrypted SSL web application or a Remote Desktop session. This is the default filtering mode on a port rule and is well suited to handle almost any NLB clustered service or application.

## Using Cluster Operation Mode

There are three different cluster operation modes: Unicast, Multicast, and IGMP Multicast. Most traditional network traffic is unicast traffic where clients and servers maintain a one-to-one network connection. Multicast networking allows a server to send out information to one multicast address that is then processed by a number of clients. To receive multicast data, a client joins a multicast group associated with the multicast address and one data feed or transmission is presented to the group by the server, thereby streamlining and improving network performance of the application. Multicast traffic is usually one direction and when the multicast client joins the group, it begins to receive the transmission.

29

Common applications that use multicast are streaming music and video websites, Internet radio, and Internet training or online noninteractive courses. IGMP Multicast can be used in place of multicast and enhances overall network performance when multicast is required. Selecting this management protocol allows for the multicast clients to register with the IGMP Multicast server and afterward, the multicast traffic will only be sent to the switch ports or trunks that connect to the multicast clients, reducing traffic on the remaining ports of the network switches. One more important point to mention about multicast traffic is that the network switches and routers that the traffic will pass through must support multicast traffic and allow it. Many enterprise class switches and routers have multicast support disabled by default.

## Configuring Network Cards for NLB

Configuring the network cards on the NLB cluster nodes is the first step in building the cluster. Although these steps can be performed during cluster creation using the NLB Manager, the same result can be achieved by editing the TCP/IP properties of each of the cluster node's network cards. Best practice for NLB cluster nodes running in Unicast mode is to have two network cards to allow host communication to occur on one NIC while cluster communication is isolated on the cluster NIC. Multiple NICS can also add greater flexibility when it comes to controlling traffic and managing network security.

## Creating an NLB Cluster

Before an NLB cluster can be created, a few bits of information are required. The NLB cluster is actually clustering based on a defined IP address, the DNS name, and the TCP/IP ports that will be used. Each NLB cluster node can also be configured with multiple network cards. Each card can be associated with a different NLB cluster and a single card can support multiple clusters, but each cluster must have a different DNS name and IP address(es). One configuration that cannot be performed is creating a single NLB cluster that uses multiple network adapters in a single node. To designate multiple adapters for a single NLB cluster, third-party network teaming software must be loaded prior to configuring the NLB cluster; the cluster will use the Virtual Team Network adapter and the teamed physical adapters should not be configured with NLB. For this example, a new NLB cluster will be created for the name www.companyabc.com using the IP address of 192.168.206.50. To create an NLB cluster, perform the following steps:

1. Log on to a Windows Server 2008 R2 system with an account that has local administrator rights and that has the NLB feature already installed.

2. Click Start, click All Programs, click Administrative Tools, and select Network Load Balancing Manager.

3. When the Network Load Balancing Manager console opens, click the Cluster menu, and select New to create a new cluster.

4. When the New Cluster window opens, type in the name of the first server that will be added to the new NLB cluster, and click Connect. If the server is a remote system and cannot be contacted, ensure that the Inbound Remote Administration exception has been enabled in the remote system's firewall.

5. When the server is contacted, each of the network adapters will be listed, select the adapter that will be used for the NLB cluster, as shown in Figure 29.16, and click Next.

FIGURE 29.16    Selecting the network adapter that will be used for the NLB cluster.

6. On the Host Parameters page, accept the defaults of giving this first server the Host ID of 1 and select the dedicated IP address that will be used when communication is received for the NLB cluster IP address, which will be specified next. Click Next to continue.

7. On the Cluster IP Addresses page, click the Add button to specify an IPv4 address and subnet mask or an IPv6 address to use for the NLB cluster, and click OK. For our example, we will use the IPv4 configuration of 192.168.206.50/255.255.255.0.

8. Back on the Cluster IP Addresses page, add additional cluster IP addresses as required, and click Next to continue.

9. On the Clusters Parameters page, enter the fully qualified DNS name that is associated with the IP address specified on the previous page, and select whether it will be used for Unicast traffic, Multicast traffic, or IGMP Multicast. This choice depends on the network communication of the service or application that will be used in this NLB cluster. For this example, we are creating an NLB cluster for standard web traffic, so we will use www.companyabc.com as the Internet name and select Unicast as the cluster operation mode, as shown in Figure 29.17.

29

FIGURE 29.17   Specifying the DNS/Internet name associated with an NLB cluster IP address.

**10.** If multiple IP addresses were defined on the previous page, the IP address can be chosen from the IP address drop-down list, and the Internet name and cluster operation mode can be defined for each additional address. When all the IP addresses have had their properties defined, click Next to continue.

**11.** On the Port Rules page, a default rule is precreated that allows all traffic on all ports to be load-balanced across the NLB cluster between the cluster IP address and the dedicated IP address of the local server's dedicated IP address. Select this rule and click the Remove button to delete it.

**12.** Click the Add button to create a new port rule.

**13.** When the Add/Edit Port Rule window opens, type in the starting and ending port range, for example 80 and 80 for a single HTTP port rule, but do not close the window.

**14.** Under protocols, select the TCP option button, but do not close the window.

**15.** In the Filtering Mode section, select Multiple Host, and select Single Affinity, but do not close the window.

**16.** Finally, review the settings, and click OK to create the port rule, as shown in Figure 29.18.

**17.** Back on the Port Rules page, click the Add button to create an additional port rule.

**18.** Specify the starting port as 0 and the ending port as 79, select Both for the protocol's configuration, select the Disable This Port Range Filtering mode, and click OK to create the rule.

**19.** Back in the Port Rules page, click the Add button to create one more port rule.

**20.** Specify the starting port as 81 and the ending port as 65535, select Both for the protocol's configuration, select the Disable This Port Range Filtering mode, and click OK to create the rule.

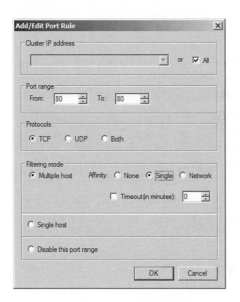

FIGURE 29.18   Defining a port rule for TCP port 80 with multiple host, single affinity.

21. Back on the Port Rules page, review the list of port rules and if the rules look correct, click Finish.

22. Back in the Network Load Balancing Manager window, the cluster will be created and brought online. The cluster IP addresses are automatically added to the TCP properties of the designated network adapter. Close the NLB Manager and log off of the server.

## Adding Additional Nodes to an Existing NLB Cluster

After an NLB cluster is created, additional nodes can be added to it. To add nodes to an existing cluster, perform the following steps:

1. Log on to the Windows Server 2008 R2 system with an account that has local administrator rights.

2. Click Start, click All Programs, click Administrative Tools, and select Network Load Balancing Manager.

3. When the Network Load Balancing Manager console opens, click the Cluster menu, and select Connect to Existing.

4. When the Connect page opens, type in the hostname of a cluster node in the cluster that will have nodes added to it. For this example, the hostname is NODE02. Type in NODE02 and click Connect to retrieve a list of all NLB clusters running on the specified host.

5. In the Clusters section of the Connect page, select the cluster that will be loaded into the management console, and click Next.

29

6. Back in the Network Load Balancing Manager window, in the tree pane, select and right-click the cluster, and select Add Host to Cluster.

7. When the Connect page opens, type in the hostname of the Windows Server 2008 R2 system that will be added to the cluster, and click Connect.

8. After the system is connected, a list of all of the available network adapters is shown. Select the desired adapter to use for the NLB cluster, and click Next.

9. On the Host Parameters page, review the details of the page, and click Next to continue. The default settings should be sufficient unless the Host ID needs to be changed or if multiple IP addresses are already bound to the adapter; select the desired IP address to use for dedicated NLB cluster communication, and click Next to continue.

10. On the Port Rules page, the existing port rules for the cluster are listed. Unless this node will handle different traffic on this cluster, accept the defaults and click Finish.

11. The node will be added to the cluster and if the node addition is successful, both nodes will be listed under the cluster with a green background, as shown in Figure 29.19.

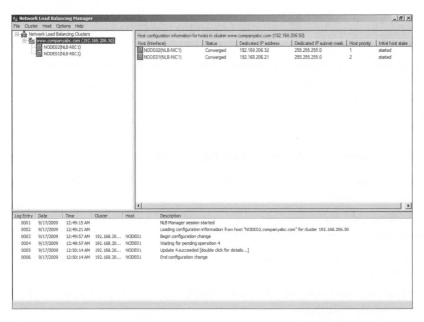

FIGURE 29.19    Verifying that all NLB cluster nodes are operating properly.

12. Close the Network Load Balancing Manager and log off of the server.

# Managing NLB Clusters

An NLB cluster can be managed using the Network Load Balancing Manager from a local cluster node or from a remote machine with the Remote Administration tools installed. Network Load Balancing can also be managed using the command-line tool NLB.exe and by using some of the new PowerShell commands included with Windows Server 2008 R2. Using the NLB Manager, a node can be added, removed, or suspended from cluster operation to perform maintenance, including hardware or software updates. Because data is not replicated between cluster nodes, any data that is required by all nodes in the cluster either needs to be replicated to each node or the application needs to be configured to access data on a system that is not in the NLB cluster.

## Backing Up and Restoring NLB Nodes

The procedure for backing up and restoring NLB nodes is no different than for standalone servers. A full system backup using Windows Server Backup or the organization's Windows Server 2008 R2 approved backup software should be created before and after any major server or NLB cluster configuration changes are implemented. An NLB configuration can be restored when the System State of a particular node is restored. If a full node recovery is necessary, the System State and local disks should be restored using a full system restore.

For detailed backup and restore procedures, refer to Chapters 30 and 31.

## Performing Maintenance on an NLB Cluster Node

To perform maintenance on an NLB cluster node, the administrator can temporarily stop the NLB service on the node in the cluster, perform the upgrade, and start it back up later. Stopping the cluster node without impacting user connections requires the use of the Drainstop option from the Network Load Balancing Manager. The Drainstop option informs the NLB cluster that the particular node will be stopped and no new connections should be directed toward this node. All existing connections will remain up and running and when all of the sessions are closed, the NLB service will be shut down on the designated node. After the maintenance has completed, the NLB service can be restarted on the NLB node and client connections can be initiated. To perform maintenance on a cluster node, perform the following steps:

1.  Log on to each Windows Server 2008 R2 system with an account that has local administrator rights.

2.  Click Start, click All Programs, click Administrative Tools, and select Network Load Balancing Manager.

3.  When the Network Load Balancing Manager console opens, click the Cluster menu, and select Connect to Existing.

4.  When the Connect page opens, type in the hostname of a cluster node in the cluster that has the node that requires maintenance, and click the Connect button. Do not

type in the name of the node that will be taken down for maintenance as the NLB manager will lose connections to the cluster.

5. After the system is connected, select the desired NLB cluster and click Finish to connect to the NLB cluster.

6. In the tree pane, expand the cluster to reveal all of the nodes in the cluster.

7. Locate the node that will be taken offline for maintenance. Right-click the node, select Control Host, and select Drainstop, as shown in Figure 29.20.

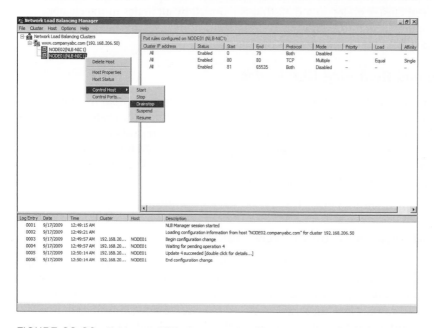

FIGURE 29.20    Taking an NLB cluster node offline using the Drainstop option.

8. After all connections are closed, the node will be highlighted in red and the status will be changed to "Host is Stopped." Perform the necessary maintenance on the NLB cluster node.

9. After the maintenance has been performed, open NLB Manager, connect to the cluster, and expand the cluster to reveal the nodes.

10. Select the node that has been stopped, right-click the node, select Control Host, and select Start.

11. After the host starts up, it will have a green background and will immediately be ready to accept client connections.

12. Close the Network Load Balancing Manager and log off of the server.

To perform the Drainstop using PowerShell, perform the following steps:

1. Open PowerShell from the Accessories/System Tools folder in the All Programs Start menu group on a Windows Server 2008 R2 system.

2. Type the command `import-module networkloadbalancingclusters` and press Enter.

3. To stop the NLB service on NODE01, using Drainstop as an example, type the command `Stop-NlbClusterNode NODE01 -Drain` and press Enter.

4. The PowerShell cmdlet will return the status of the command once the server has stopped.

5. To resume operation on this node, type the command `Start-NlbClusterNode NODE01` and press Enter.

6. When completed, close the PowerShell window and log off of the server.

To get a list of all PowerShell NLB cmdlets, from within a PowerShell window after running the import-module command for NLB, type the command `Get-Command -Module NetworkLoadBalancingClusters` and press Enter.

# Summary

Windows Server 2008 R2 provides two very different clustering technologies that enable organizations to create system-level fault tolerance and provide high availability for mission-critical applications and services. Although failover clusters and Network Load Balancing are each characteristically different and are best deployed on very different types of applications, between them they can increase fault tolerance for almost any service or application.

# Best Practices

The following are best practices from this chapter:

▶ Purchase quality server, network hardware, and shared storage devices and HBAs that are certified for Windows Server 2008 R2 when deployed on failover clusters.

▶ Deploy cluster node operating systems on fault-tolerant disk arrays.

▶ Deploy only services and applications that are certified to work on Windows Server 2008 R2 failover clusters or NLB clusters whenever possible.

▶ Thoroughly understand the application that will be used before determining which clustering technology to use.

▶ Use Windows Server 2008 R2 failover clusters to provide system-level fault-tolerance for mission-critical applications, such as enterprise messaging, databases, file and print services, and other networking services.

▶ If iSCSI is used for shared storage, ensure that any network adapters used for iSCSI communication are excluded from any cluster usage.

29

▶ Use NLB to provide connectivity to TCP/IP-based services, such as Remote Desktop Services, websites, VPN services, SMTP gateways, and streaming media services.

▶ Rename and clearly label all network adapters on each cluster node and configure static IPv4 and if necessary IPv6 addresses.

▶ Configure the appropriate power management settings for the system and network adapters on all cluster nodes.

▶ Configure the appropriate cluster quorum model that is right for the deployment and, hopefully, the recommended model.

▶ Use multiple network cards in each node so that one card can be dedicated to internal cluster communication (heartbeat network) while the other can be used only for client connectivity and cluster communication.

▶ If failback is required, configure the failback schedule to allow failback only during nonpeak times or after hours to reduce the chance of having a group failing back to a node during regular business hours.

▶ Thoroughly test failover and failback mechanisms.

▶ Be sure that a majority of the nodes remain running to keep the cluster in a working state if you're removing a node from a cluster that leverages the Node Majority Quorum model.

▶ Carefully consider backing up and restoring a cluster and do not deploy any clusters until a tested and documented backup and recovery plan exists.

▶ For NLB clusters, create a port rule that allows only specific ports to the clustered IP address and an additional rule blocking all other ports and ranges.

# CHAPTER 30

# Backing Up the Windows Server 2008 R2 Environment

W indows Server 2008 R2 is a very powerful and feature-rich operating system that can provide many organizations with the tools they require from their computer and network infrastructure. Some of the functions a Windows Server 2008 R2 system can provide include centralized directory services, email services, file and print services, web services, networking and VPN services, streaming media services, and many more. Of course, before any new system, service, or application is deployed in an organization's computer and network infrastructure, the responsible parties should understand how to set up, optimize, administer, and properly back up and recover data and functionality in the event of a failure.

As is the case with many organizations' computer and network infrastructures, new services, servers, or applications are deployed before a valid backup and recovery plan to support them have been created or tested. As a result of this, some organizations are just not prepared when a critical business system unexpectedly fails or when disasters strike. Lack of backup and recovery planning can result in the unrecoverable loss of data, employees unable to perform their job, and even the loss of revenue or customers.

To avoid this, information technology (IT) managers and administrators who are responsible for the different aspects of the computer and network infrastructure should create a backup and disaster recovery plan.

This chapter provides IT decision makers and their technical staff with the information they require to start planning and implementing viable backup strategies for a Windows Server 2008 R2 infrastructure.

# Understanding Your Backup and Recovery Needs and Options

A key to creating a valuable backup and recovery plan is to have a clear understanding of how the computer and network infrastructure is configured, as well as having an understanding of how the business operates and utilizes the infrastructure. This discovery process involves mapping out both the computer and network systems in place and also documenting and understanding the business processes that depend on the infrastructure. For example, an organization might process incoming orders from field sales representatives via fax transmissions of contracts that are accepted by a Windows Server 2008 R2 fax service. If the fax service is not available, no orders are processed. This is just a simple example of when downtime of a Windows server can directly affect business operations. Understanding which systems and services are most important to the business can help IT staff set the order or prioritize which systems will be recovered first, in the event of a large-scale disaster.

## Identifying the Different Services and Technologies

Each deployed role, role service, feature, or application provided by a Windows Server 2008 R2 system provides a key system function, which in many cases is critical to the organization. Each application, role service, role, and feature installed on a Windows Server 2008 R2 system should be identified and documented so the IT group can have a clear view of the complexity of the environment as backup and recovery plans are being developed. It is very common for server and web-based applications to require special backup and restore procedures, and these are especially important to identify for disaster recovery purposes.

## Identifying Single Points of Failure

A single point of failure is a device, application, or service on a computer and networking infrastructure that provides an exclusive function with no redundancy. A common single point of failure in smaller organizations is a network switch that provides the connectivity between all of the servers, client workstations, firewalls, wireless access points, and routers on a network. Within a Windows Server 2008 R2 Active Directory infrastructure as an example, Active Directory Domain Services (AD DS) inherently comes with its own set of single points of failure, with its Flexible Single Master Operations (FSMO) roles. These roles provide an exclusive function to the entire Active Directory forest or just a single domain, and if the designated domain controller hosting that role fails, these hosted FSMO roles become unavailable. Even though the FSMO roles are single points of failure, recovering a domain controller can be very simple and painless if proper backup and recovery planning is performed. For more information on FSMO roles, refer to Chapter 7, "Active Directory Infrastructure."

# Evaluating Different Disaster Scenarios

Before a backup and disaster recovery plan can be formulated, IT managers and administrators should meet with the business owners to discuss and decide on which types of failures or disasters should be planned for. This section of the chapter provides a high-level description of common disaster scenarios to consider. Of course, planning for every disaster scenario is nearly impossible or, more commonly, will exceed an organization's backup and recovery budget, but discussing the likelihood of each scenario and evaluating how the scenario can impact the business is necessary.

### Physical Disaster

A physical disaster is anything that can keep employees or customers from reaching their desired office or store location. Examples include natural disasters such as floods, fires, earthquakes, hurricanes, or tornadoes that can destroy an office. A physical disaster can also be a physical limitation, such as a damaged bridge or highway blockage caused by a car accident. When only physical access is limited or restricted, a remote access solution could reestablish connectivity between users and the corporate network. Refer to Chapter 24, "Server-to-Client Remote Access and DirectAccess," for more information in this area.

### Power Outage or Rolling Blackouts

Power outages can occur at any time unexpectedly. Some power outages are caused by bad weather and other natural disasters, but other times they can be caused by high power consumption that causes system overloads. When power systems are overloaded, rolling blackouts may occur. A rolling blackout is when a power company shuts off power to certain power subscribers or areas of service, so that it maintains power to critical services, such as fire departments, police departments, hospitals, and traffic lights. The rolling part of rolling blackouts is that the blackout is managed; after a predetermined amount of the time, the power company will shut down a different power grid and restore power to a previously shutdown grid. Of course, during power outages, many businesses are unable to function because the core of their work is conducted on computers or even telephone systems that require power to function.

### Network Outage

Organizations that share data and applications between multiple offices and require access to the Internet as part of their daily business operations are susceptible to network outages that can cause severe loss of employee productivity and possibly revenue. Network outages can affect just a single computer, the entire office, or multiple offices depending on the cause of the outage. IT staff must take network outages into consideration when creating the backup and recovery plans.

### Hardware Failures

Hardware failures seem to be the most common disaster encountered and coincidentally are the most common type of problem organizations plan for. Server hardware failures include failed motherboards, processors, memory, network interface cards, network cables, fiber cables, disk and HBA controllers, power supplies, and, of course, the hard disks in the local server or in a storage area network (SAN). Each of these failures can be dealt with differently, but to provide system- or server-level redundancy, key services should be

30

deployed in a redundant cluster configuration, such as is provided with Windows Server 2008 R2, Enterprise Edition Failover Clustering, or Network Load Balancing (NLB).

### Hard Drive Failure

Hard drives are indeed the most common type of computer- and network-related hardware failure organizations have to deal with. Windows Server 2008 R2 supports hot-swappable hard drives and two types of disks: basic disks, which provide backward compatibility, and dynamic disks, which allow software-level disk arrays to be configured without a separate hardware-based disk array controller. Also, both basic and dynamic disks, when used as data disks, can be moved to other servers easily to provide data or disk capacity elsewhere if a system hardware failure occurs and the data on these disks needs to be made available as soon as possible. Windows Server 2008 R2 also contains tools to provision, connect, and configure storage located on a SAN and can easily mount VHD files as operating system disks using Disk Manager or diskpart.

> **NOTE**
>
> If hardware-level RAID is configured, the controller card stores the disk array configuration and the manufacturer should be contacted to provide the necessary tools or documentation necessary to back up, restore, rebuild, or re-create the configuration should a controller failure occur or if the disk needs to be moved to a different machine with the same type of controller.

### Software Corruption

Software corruption can occur at many different levels. Operating system files could be corrupted, antivirus software can interfere with the writing of a file or database causing corruption, or a new application or driver installation could overwrite a critical file leaving a system unstable or in a failed state. Also, more commonly found in today's networks, a security, application, or system update conflicts with an existing application or service causing undesirable issues.

## Prioritizing the Recovery

After all of the computer services and applications used on a network are identified, as well as deciding which typical disaster scenarios will be considered in the backup and recovery plan, the next step is to organize or prioritize how the recovery of critical systems and services will be executed. The prioritization usually involves getting the most critical services up and running first; this usually requires networking services such as DNS and DHCP, as well as Active Directory domain controllers, especially on corporate networks that utilize Microsoft Windows servers and client operating systems.

Maintaining up-to-date backup and recovery plans requires following strict processes when changing an organization's computer and network infrastructure. With an up-to-date technology priority list, administrators can tackle the planning for the most important services first to ensure that if a disaster strikes sooner rather than later, the most important systems are always protected and recoverable.

## Identifying Bare Minimum Services

The bare minimum services are the fewest possible services and applications that must be up and running for business operations to continue. Only the top few services and applications in the technology prioritized list will become part of the bare minimum services list. For example, a bare minimum computer service for a retail outlet could be a server that runs the retail software package and manages the register and receipt printer. For a web-based company, it could be the web and e-commerce servers that process online orders.

## Determining the Service-Level Agreement and Return-to-Operation Requirements

A service-level agreement (SLA) is an estimated planned uptime or availability time frame for a system, service, or application. SLAs are usually defined by hours per day, week, month, or year and are expressed in percentages. For example, if the corner grocery store claims to be open 24 hours a day, every day of the year, the grocery store SLA is 100%. Another example could be an organization's electronic fax services that should be available 7 days a week between the hours of 5:00 a.m. and 11:00 p.m.

Many organizations hope to achieve and maintain operation of the most critical services 24 hours a day, 7 days a week or 100% planned uptime as logistically possible. A few common SLA targets are included in the following list:

▶ 99.999% planned uptime results in 5.25 minutes of planned downtime or maintenance per year.

▶ 99.99% planned uptime results in 52.5 minutes of planned downtime or maintenance per year.

▶ 99.9% planned uptime results in 8 hours, 45.6 minutes of planned downtime or maintenance per year.

▶ 99.7% planned uptime results in 26 hours and 17 minutes of planned downtime or maintenance per year.

▶ 99% planned uptime results in 87 hours and 36 minutes of planned downtime or maintenance per year.

Executives and managers alike all know that maintaining 100% of planned uptime is not usually possible because of a number of factors. Also, many professionals might also consider that the SLA must account for the time to recover after a failure or disaster is encountered. Ensure that the definition of the SLA is understood by all as "planned" uptime or "planned and unplanned." The difference is huge. A recommendation is that an SLA is defined as planned uptime. The unplanned recovery time frame is defined as the Return to Operation (RTO) number for the remainder of this section.

The RTO defines how long it will take to recover a system, service, application, or business operation after a failure or disaster has occurred. Of course, the shorter the RTO time frame is, the more likely the backup and recovery solution costs will increase. For example, deploying a Windows Server 2008 R2 failover cluster can provide system recovery within seconds or minutes, but the hardware and software licensing costs would easily exceed the costs of a recovery plan that included diagnosing a hardware issue and waiting for a replacement part to arrive within a 4-hour window. The business owners or executives of an organization need to clearly understand how long it will take to recover from certain failures and that will help derive the final accepted backup and recovery solution.

Separating the SLA and RTO in disaster recovery documentation can be a very valuable tool to use when presenting the current or proposed computer and network infrastructure disaster recovery solution to executives, managers, auditors, and customers. For example, a service might be presented to customers with a 99.99% SLA. The same system can be presented in the finer details to have a maximum of an 8-hour RTO, which will still meet a 99.9% uptime in the event of a major disaster. This can also be worded as "This service will provide 99.9% to 99.99% availability."

# Creating the Disaster Recovery Solution

When administrators understand what sorts of failures can occur and know which services and applications are most critical to their organization, they have gathered almost all the information necessary to create a preliminary high-level disaster recovery solution. Many different pieces of information and several documents will be required, even for the preliminary solutions. Some of the items required within the solution are listed in the following sections.

## Disaster Recovery Solution Overview Document

The Disaster Recovery Solution Overview document is a short narrative of the solution in action, including presentations with quality graphics and/or Microsoft Visio diagrams. This document first provides an executive summary, including only high-level details to provide executives and management with enough information to understand what steps are being taken to provide business continuity in the event of a disaster. The remainder of the document should contain detailed information related to the plan, including many of the following items:

▶ Current computer and network infrastructure review.

▶ Detailed history of the planning meetings and the information that was presented and discussed in those meetings.

▶ The list of which disaster and outage scenarios will be greatly mitigated by this plan, and which scenarios will not be addressed by this plan.

> **NOTE**
>
> Scenarios that will not be addressed in your organization's disaster recovery solutions should still be referenced in the document to show that it was presented, discussed, and considered very unlikely to occur, too expensive to mitigate up front, or not important enough to dedicate budget or staff resources.

▶ The list of the most critical applications, systems, and services for the organization and the potential impact to the business if these systems encounter a failure or are not available.

▶ Description of the high-level solution, including how the proposed disaster recovery solution will enhance the organization by improving the reliability and recoverability.

▶ Defined SLA and RTO time estimates this solution provides to each failure and disaster scenario.

▶ Associated computer and network hardware specifications, including initial purchasing and ongoing support and licensing costs.

▶ Associated software specifications and licensing costs for initial purchase and ongoing support and maintenance costs.

▶ Additional WAN links costs.

▶ Additional outside services costs, including hosting services, data center lease costs, offsite disk and tape storage fees, consulting costs for the project, technical writing, document management, and ongoing support or lease costs.

▶ Estimated internal staffing resource assignment and utilization for the solution deployment, as well as the ongoing utilization requirements to support the ongoing backup and recovery tasks.

▶ The initial estimated project schedule and project milestones.

## Getting Disaster Recovery Solutions Approved

Prioritizing and identifying the bare minimum services are not only the responsibility of the IT staff; these decisions belong to management as well. The IT staff is responsible for identifying single points of failure, gathering the statistical information of application and service usage, and possibly also understanding how an outage can affect business operations.

Before the executives can make a decision regarding budget for an organization's disaster recovery plan, they should be presented with as much information as possible to make the most informed decision. As a general guideline, when presenting the preliminary disaster recovery solution, make sure it includes the "In a perfect world with unlimited budget" plan, along with one or two lower-cost plans with clearly highlighted extended downtime or reduced functionality. Presenting alternate plans highlighting different costs and results might help ensure that the solution gets approval in one form or another.

Getting the budget approved for a secondary disaster recovery solution is better than getting no budget for the preferred solution. The staff should always try to be very clear on the SLA for a chosen solution and to document or have a paper trail concerning all disaster recovery solutions that have been accepted or denied. If a failure that could have been planned for occurs but budget was denied, IT staff members or IT managers should make sure to have all their facts straight and documentation to prove it.

30

# Documenting the Enterprise

So far, in the backup and recovery preparation, computer and network discovery has been performed, different failure scenarios have been considered, and the most critical services have been identified and prioritized. Now, it is time to start actually building the backup and disaster recovery plan that a qualified individual will use in the event of a failure. To begin creating the plan, the current computer and network infrastructure must be documented. Information on documenting a Windows Server 2008 R2 system can be found in Chapter 22, "Documenting a Windows Server 2008 R2 Environment." Documentation should include, but not be limited to, the following:

> **Server configuration document**—This document details which services and applications the system provides, as well as the network settings, software installed, and hardware specifications.

> **Server build document**—This document contains step-by-step instructions on how to build a Windows Server 2008 R2 system for a specific role, such as domain controller or file server, including which software is required and hardware specifications. This document will also include specific security configurations, hardware and software configurations, and other organizational server configuration standards.

> **Network diagrams**—Network diagrams should contain network configurations, as well as the hardware included in the infrastructure and the WAN links.

> **Network device configuration**—These documents contain the configurations of the network devices, including the switches, firewall, and routers on the network.

> **SAN configuration**—Most medium- and large-size organizations utilize one form of centralized storage or another. When storage devices are utilized, these device configurations should be documented so they can be recovered in the event of a device issue.

> **Software documentation**—This document contains a list of all the software used in the organization, possibly including the licensing information and the storage location.

> **Service accounts and password document**—A master list of user accounts and network device usernames and passwords should be created and kept in a sealed envelope in a secured onsite and offsite location.

> **Contact and support documentation**—This document should contain all IT staff and vendor contact information required to support the infrastructure.

# Developing a Backup Strategy

Determining not only what needs to be backed up, but also how the backups will be performed and stored, is an important task. Many organizations back up data to tape media and have that media shipped to offsite storage locations on a weekly basis. Windows Server 2008 R2 Server Backup is built to support backup to local internal and externally connected disks and network shares for scheduled backups. Windows Server Backup does not natively support tape devices for backup. If an organization wants to use tape storage and simplify onsite and offsite media management, Microsoft System Center Data Protection Manager or a third-party backup suite is recommended.

## Assigning Tasks and Designating Team Members

To make sure that Windows Server 2008 R2 systems are getting backed up properly, IT staff should train and assign at least two IT staff members to monitor and manage backups. Windows Server 2008 R2 systems, by default, allow users in the local Administrators or "Backup Operators" security groups to back up and restore data. On domain controllers, the domain-based security groups have these same rights on the Active Directory domain controllers in the respective domain(s).

## Creating Regular Backup Procedures

Creating a regular backup procedure helps ensure that the entire enterprise is backed up consistently and properly. When a regular procedure or checklist is created, the assigned staff members will soon become accustomed to the procedure, and it will become second nature. If there is no documented procedure, certain items or systems might be overlooked or might not be backed up, which can turn out to be a major problem if a failure occurs. An example of a backup checklist or procedure could be as simple as configuring backups on Windows systems to run a full backup of a server every night, reviewing the backup status of each system every morning, and regularly swapping backup managed disks and shipping the disks to offsite disk and tape storage facilities. Additional steps in the backup checklists should include performing test restores of data and applications hosted on Windows Server 2008 R2 systems.

# Windows Server Backup Overview

Windows Server 2008 R2 contains a built-in powerful backup program appropriately named Windows Server Backup. Windows Server Backup is installed as a system feature and it allows administrators to back up and restore system, file, folder, and application data for Windows Server 2008 R2 systems.

Windows Server Backup includes a graphical user interface (GUI) MMC snap-in, as well as a very functional command-line utility. Windows Server Backup includes a few new functions but also has new restrictions. Windows Server Backup replaces the previous version of backup included with Windows Server 2003 and earlier Windows operating systems, known as Ntbackup, but the features and functions are much different.

## Backup Storage Support and Media Management

Windows Server Backup allows administrators to back up to locally attached disks, network shares, and DVD writable media. Tape devices are not supported by Windows Server Backup, and to back up to DVD media, the system requires a local writable DVD drive.

Using Ntbackup.exe in previous versions of Windows Server editions, media management was one of the biggest challenges administrators faced. Tape media needed to be prelabeled if any logical media management was required for backups. Also, if disk-based file backups were used, the file could end up filling up the server disk if the media was configured to append instead of overwrite when new backups were performed. The other option for backup media was to overwrite the media when a backup was run, but that also relabeled the media and any stickers on the tape would no longer match. Media management was possible, but just very tedious.

Windows Server Backup greatly improves media management by taking full control of the media, including labeling, efficiently storing data, cataloging the backup media, and managing the free disk space. Performing backups using remote server shares or local volumes as backup destinations has the risk of filling up the destination volume. When local disks are dedicated for Windows Server Backup and the utilized disk space is nearing capacity, the backup system will overwrite the oldest backup data on the disk to keep the disk from filling and to keep the backup job from failing.

### External Disks

Windows Server Backup supports backup data to be stored on locally attached disks and writable DVD media located in local writable DVD drives. Locally attached disks include internal disk drives, hot-swappable disk drives, and drives externally connected via USB 2.0 or IEEE 1394 interfaces. Also, SAN-attached disks can be used as backup destinations. Storing backups on SAN storage enables faster rotation or replication of backup disks volumes to other SAN storage without impacting Windows system performance.

### CD/DVD Writer Drives

Windows Server 2008 R2 contains many features that can take advantage of DVD writer drives. These include the Windows Server Backup feature to capture backups to DVD and Windows Deployment Services, which can be used to create boot, capture, and discover images on DVD media. With regard to Windows Server Backup, a manual backup can be created to contain a volume or entire system backup, and might span multiple DVDs. This can be a valuable option as data from remote servers can be synchronized across the network using Distributed File System Replication, but creating a full system backup across a WAN link usually is not an option. Branch office administrators can be tasked with creating full system DVD backups monthly, quarterly, or more frequently to provide full system recovery options, and the media can easily be copied, archived, and shipped to offsite storage locations or to a central office.

### Remote Shared Folder and Folder on Local Volume

Shares on remote servers or folders on local volumes can be designated as backup targets for manual and scheduled backup jobs. Designating a remote shared folder allows an administrator to create a backup not stored on media physically mounted in the system, and also allows for the backup of multiple servers to be stored on a central server. Choosing to back up using a folder on a local volume removes the restriction of having to dedicate an entire volume for backup usage. There are two very important catches to be aware of when using remote shared folders and folders on local volumes:

▶ When using a remote shared folder, only one copy of the backup can be stored within the folder, and each backup will perform a full overwrite backup.

▶ When a folder on a local volume is selected as a backup destination, the performance of that volume will be severely impacted during backup, which could cause poor system performance if any user data is stored and accessed on the same volume.

### Tape Devices

Tape devices are not supported in Windows Server Backup. Administrators who want to back up data to tape will require Microsoft System Center Data Protection Manager or third-party backup applications, or they will be forced to create manual backups to disk and then copy the data to tape drives.

## Backup Media Files

In the previous backup application, Ntbackup.exe, backup data stored on disks was stored in a single file with a .bkf extension. This file contained the data as well as the catalog and could easily be moved and mounted in an Ntbackup.exe console on any server on the network. Windows Server Backup stores system backup data in a folder named WindowsImageBackup. Beneath this folder is subfolder named after the server that was backed up. Included in the server folder is a set of Extensible Markup Language (XML) files that detail the backup history, catalog, and system configuration details of the media. Also included in the server folder are one or more virtual hard disk (VHD) files. The VHD files are close to exact duplicates of the backed-up server volumes.

The VHD file can quickly be added and viewed in a virtual machine, so protecting the backup folders is critical to server security.

> **NOTE**
>
> Windows Server Backup does not encrypt the backup data stored on DVDs or disks. Administrators should take all precautions to ensure that any disks, DVD media, or remote server shares that store backup data are secured with NTFS permissions on remote shares and physically secure on disks and DVDs.

## Backup Options

Windows Server 2008 R2 has made creating and managing backups simple within the Windows Server Backup interfaces. Using the GUI-based console, the Wbadmin command-line utility, or through PowerShell cmdlets, backups can be run to protect disk volumes, full systems, the System State only, or set to back up just individual files and folders. In addition, specific files and folders can be excluded from a backup.

30

**Manual Backup Options**

Windows Server Backup allows for backups to be created on a recurring schedule or manually using the Backup Once option available in the Windows Server Backup console. Manual backups can be stored on local disks, burned to DVD media, or stored on remote shares. Manual backups on remote shares can be used for complete PC restore operations if the system to be recovered can access the network location during the restore operation.

**Scheduled Backup Options**

Scheduled backup operations allow administrators to create a backup schedule that adds backup automation to a Windows Server 2008 R2 system. Scheduled backups can be configured to run once a day or multiple times per day to provide the required level of recoverability.

## Windows Server Backup MMC Snap-In

The Windows Server Backup feature includes a Microsoft Management Console snap-in. The file is named wbadmin.msc and is available from the Administrative Tools menu. Most backup-related tasks can be performed using this console, including creating backups, reviewing backup history, and restoring data.

The Windows Server Backup snap-in can be used to connect and manage backups on remote Windows Server 2008 R2 systems with the Windows Server Backup feature installed.

## Windows Backup Command-Line Utility

All editions of Windows Server 2008 R2 include the option of installing the Windows Server Backup feature's command-line tools. The primarily utility included is wbadmin.exe, which provides more granular control of backup- and recovery-related tasks. As more and more administration of Windows systems moves back into the shell or command prompt environment, this utility will provide administrators with the functions they require to manage backups within this environment. Wbadmin provides the ability for administrators to start backups and recoveries of systems, get information, and configure new backup storage and schedule backup policies.

## Windows Server Backup PowerShell Cmdlets

Windows Server 2008 R2 includes several PowerShell cmdlets for managing Windows Server Backup. The PowerShell cmdlets are installed with the Windows Server Backup feature command-line tools option. Unlike wbadmin.exe, PowerShell cmdlets for Windows Server Backup provide much more flexibility when managing remote systems. Most command-line executable files are being removed and replaced with PowerShell cmdlets, and administrators should consider this when creating and documenting backup and recovery tasks. One function that is not included in the current set of cmdlets is the ability to perform data recovery. This still needs to be performed using the MMC snap-in or the wbadmin.exe command-line utility. Examples of using a few of the PowerShell cmdlets for Windows Server Backup are included in proceeding sections of this chapter.

# Using Windows Server Backup

When an organization decides to use Windows Server Backup, the type of backup and the storage media for the backups must be determined. For example, if scheduled backups will be used, an organization will need to determine the correct storage destination for their Windows Server 2008 R2 backups as each destination has its own set of requirements and implications that should be understood and considered.

## Installing Windows Server Backup

Although the Windows Server Backup console is listed in Administrative Tools, the Windows Server Backup feature still needs to be installed. The easiest way to install the Windows Backup tools is to use the Add Features function within Server Manager. Of course, for Server Core deployments, installing using PowerShell is preferred.

### Installing Windows Server Backup Using Server Manager

On every edition of Windows Server 2008 R2, except for Server Core installations, the Windows Server Backup feature can be installed using Server Manager. To install the Windows Server Backup feature, perform the following steps:

1. Log on to the Windows Server 2008 R2 system with an account with administrator privileges.

2. Click Start, click All Programs, click Administrative Tools, and select Server Manager.

3. In the tree pane, select the Features node, and select the Add Features link in the tasks pane.

4. When the Add Features Wizard opens, scroll down and click on the plus sign next to Windows Server Backup Features. Check both boxes to ensure that the command-line tools are also selected, as shown in Figure 30.1. Click Next to continue.

5. On the Confirm Installation Selections page, review the summary, and click Install to continue.

6. On the Installation Results page, review the results, and click Close to complete the installation.

### Installing Windows Server Backup Using Windows PowerShell ServerManager Module

In many cases, administrators might choose to use the Windows PowerShell environment to manage a server and as a preference when installing roles, role services, or features. When a particular feature or role is installed using the Windows PowerShell ServerManager module, all features, role services, and role dependencies are also added. To install the Windows Server Backup features, including the Windows Server Backup PowerShell cmdlets using Windows PowerShell, perform the following steps:

1. Log on to the Windows Server 2008 R2 system with an account with administrator privileges.

2. Click Start, click All Programs, click Accessories, and click the Windows PowerShell folder to reveal the application shortcuts.

30

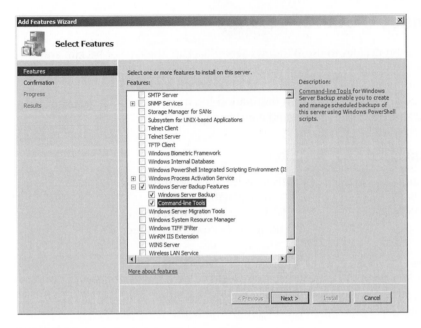

FIGURE 30.1    Selecting the Windows Server Backup features.

3. Right-click Windows PowerShell and select Run As Administrator. If a User Account Control window opens, click Continue to open the PowerShell window.

4. Type cd \ and press Enter.

5. Type Import-Module ServerManager and press Enter.

6. Type Add-WindowsFeature Backup-Tools and press Enter. After the installation completes, the results will be listed in the window, as shown in Figure 30.2.

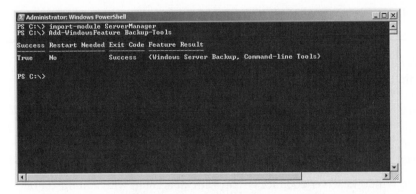

FIGURE 30.2    Installing Windows Server Backup using Windows PowerShell.

7. Type `Get-WindowsFeature ¦More` and press Enter to get a list of the installed roles, role services, and features. Review the list to verify that Windows Server Backup and Windows Server Backup command-line tools are now installed.

8. Type `exit` in the PowerShell window and press Enter.

### Installing Windows Server Backup on Server Core Installations

On a Windows Server 2008 R2 Server Core deployment, if the Windows Server Backup feature is not installed, it can be installed by performing the following steps:

1. Log on to the Windows Server 2008 R2 Server Core system with an account with administrator privileges.

2. In the Command Prompt window, type `cd \` and press Enter.

3. Type in `Start /w ocsetup.exe WindowsServerBackup` and press Enter.

4. Log on to a different Windows Server 2008 R2, Enterprise Edition system with an account with administrator privileges on the local system as well as the Server Core system. It is assumed that both systems are part of the same domain and the Server Core system can access other resources on the network from the Server Core system.

5. Click Start, click All Programs, click Administrative Tools, and select Windows Server Backup.

6. In the Actions pane, click the Connect to Another Computer link.

7. In the Computer Chooser window, select the Another Computer option button, type in the name of the Server Core system, and click OK.

8. If you can connect to the Server Core system, the installation is successful. If the connection fails, either the Server Core firewall is preventing connectivity or Windows Server Backup has not been installed. Troubleshoot as necessary.

## Scheduling a Backup Using Windows Server Backup and Allocating Disks

After Windows Server Backup has been installed, no backups will be automatically scheduled. The fastest way to get a backup configured and define any dedicated disks for backups is to run the Backup Schedule Wizard. This wizard enables administrators to not only select and exclude which backup items will be contained within a backup, but it also allows the administrator to configure a recurring backup schedule and allocate a dedicated disk for scheduled backups if used. One thing to keep in mind is that if the configuration will support backing up to multiple dedicated disks, to provide some level of backup media rotation, it is recommended that all of the disks be available during the running of the wizard.

When dedicated disks will be used for Windows Server Backup jobs, these disks will be erased, reformatted, and from there on, assigned and managed by Windows Server

30

Backup. The disk allocation process will create a single NTFS formatted volume that spans the entire disk and will set the disk volume label to include the server name, the date and time the disk is allocated, and the disk number for each disk. For example, if disk 1 is assigned to the backup of SERVER10 on October 8, 2009 at 6:10 p.m., the label will be SERVER10 2009_10_08 18:10 DISK_01. To allocate disks for Windows Server Backup, perform the following steps:

1. Log on to the Windows Server 2008 R2 system with an account with administrator privileges.

2. Click Start, click All Programs, click Administrative Tools, and select Windows Server Backup.

3. In the Actions pane, click on the Backup Schedule link to start the Backup Schedule Wizard. Selecting the Backup Schedule link is the only way multiple disks can be allocated to Windows Server Backup in one process.

4. Click Next on the Getting Started page.

5. Select the Full Server (Recommended) option button, and click Next to continue.

6. On the Specify Backup Time page, select the time to run the scheduled backup from the Once a Day or the More Than Once a Day selections, and click Next to continue. Figure 30.3 details a backup that will run every day at 9:00 p.m.

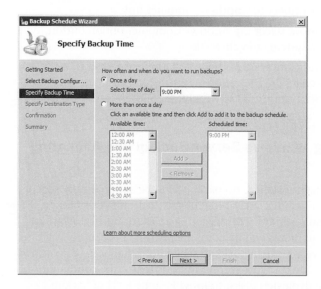

FIGURE 30.3    Setting the scheduled backup to run every day at 9:00 p.m.

7. On the Specify Destination Type page, select the Back Up to a Hard Disk That Is Dedicated for Backups (Recommended) option button and click Next. On this page, a backup to a nonsystem volume or a shared network folder could have been selected. When utilizing volumes for backup, performance might be degraded severely during an active backup process if the disk hosting the backup volume is

also used to store production data. Storing scheduled backups on a shared network folder results in backups being overwritten during each backup cycle.

8. Because we selected to use dedicated backup disks, the next page is the Select Destination Disk page. Click the Show All Available Disks button to select the desired disks.

9. In the Show All Available Disks window, check each of the disks that will be dedicated to the scheduled backup, and click OK to save the settings, as shown in Figure 30.4.

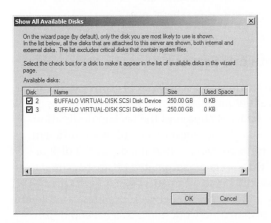

FIGURE 30.4   Selecting local disks to be used for scheduled backups.

---

**NOTE**

When multiple disks are assigned to a single scheduled backup, any of the disks will be used and that is not in the control of the administrator. If a disk is removed for off-site storage, the remaining disks will be used for the next scheduled backup.

---

10. Back on the Select Destination Disk page, check all of the disks that have been added, and click Next to continue.

11. A Windows Server Backup warning window opens requiring confirmation that the selected disks will be reformatted and used by Windows Server Backup exclusively; click Yes to assign the disks for backup.

12. On the Confirmation page, verify the settings, and click Finish to save the new scheduled backup and backup settings and to reformat and label each of the assigned disks.

13. On the Summary page, review the results, and click Close to complete the process.

Creating a scheduled backup using Windows Server Backup enables an administrator to automate the backup process, and with the backup and VSS managing the dedicated disks, the administrator only needs to verify that backups have been run successfully.

30

### Manually Running a Scheduled Backup

After the scheduled backup is created for a server, an administrator can let the backup run as scheduled or the backup can be run manually using the Backup Once link. To manually run a scheduled backup, simply use the Backup Once link and select the Scheduled Backup Options option button on the Backup Options page. Click Next and click Backup on the Confirmation page to start the backup. One important point to note is that if multiple disks are allocated to a scheduled backup, running a manual backup does not allow the administrator to select which disk to use. The only way to control which disk is used for scheduled backup is to either remove all the other allocated disks from the system or mark the disks as offline using Disk Management or Diskpart.exe.

## Running a Backup to a Shared Network Folder

Starting with Windows Server 2008 R2, both manual and scheduled backups can use dedicated backup disks, a specific folder on a local volume, or a shared network folder as a backup destination. When a shared network folder is chosen as the backup destination, a system administrator can store full backups on alternate locations to allow for different recovery scenarios. Also, something important to consider is that if a dedicated disk or specific folder on a local volume is selected, this offers no automated offsite backup. Using a shared network folder can enable offsite backup if the destination system is located in a remote data center, and the backup window and bandwidth between the sites can tolerate the over the wire network backup. To select a shared network folder as a backup destination for a manual backup as an example, perform the following steps:

1. Log on to the Windows Server 2008 R2 system with an account with administrator privileges.

2. Click Start, click All Programs, click Administrative Tools, and select Windows Server Backup.

3. In the Actions pane, click on the Backup Once link to start the Backup Once Wizard.

4. On the Select Backup Configuration page, select either the Full Server (Recommended) option button to back up all of the drives on the Windows Server 2008 R2 system, including the System State, or select the Custom option button to select specific volumes and include or exclude certain files, folders, or backup items. For this example, select Full Server (Recommended), and click Next.

5. On the Specify Destination Type page, select Remote Shared Folder, and click Next, as shown in Figure 30.5.

6. On the Specify Remote Folder page, type in the UNC path of the remote server share, and select the Do Not Inherit option button to set the permissions on the destination folder that will be created and will store the backup.

7. Click Next on the Specify Remote Folder page. A window might open, asking for credentials to use when connecting to the share. Enter the appropriate username and password that can create subfolders and write to the share, and click OK.

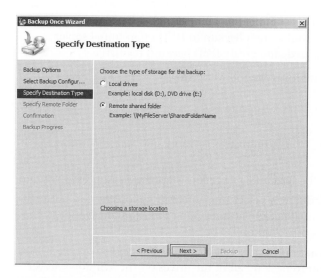

FIGURE 30.5    Selecting to store the backup on a remote shared folder.

**NOTE**

If a remote folder is specified as the backup destination, ensure that the folder does not already contain a WindowsImageBackup folder as the permissions might be overwritten by the new backup. If the permissions are not a worry and will remain as is, selecting the Inherit option button on the Specify Remote Folder page is preferred.

8. On the Confirmation page, review the settings and click Backup to start the manual backup.

9. On the Backup Progress page, the progress can be viewed in real time, or the Close button can be clicked and the progress can be tracked in the tasks pane back in the Windows Server Backup console. Click Close when the backup completes.

## Storing a Backup on DVD

On a Windows Server 2008 R2 system with a local DVD writer drive, backups can be directed to a DVD for storage. Backups stored on DVD media can be used to restore the entire system or entire volumes; files and folders or any other granular restores cannot be performed using a DVD backup media.

When an administrator has a DVD backup of a system, it can be used to restore the entire system, but the Windows Server 2008 R2 bootable installation media must also be available. With a DVD backup, additional steps and documentation will be required to restore

30

a system from a failed state back into operation. As a best practice, whenever a system contains a DVD writer drive, create a full system backup to DVD upon initial server deployment and when disks are changed, and create DVD backups regularly.

To create a backup on DVD media, perform the following steps:

1. Log on to the Windows Server 2008 R2 system with an account with administrator privileges.

2. Click Start, click All Programs, click Administrative Tools, and select Windows Server Backup.

3. In the Actions pane, click on the Backup Once link to start the Backup Once Wizard.

4. When the Backup Once Wizard opens, select the Different Options option button, and click Next. Running a manual backup and selecting the Different Options option is the only way to store a backup on DVD.

5. On the Select Backup Configuration page, select either the Full Server (Recommended) option button to back up all of the drives on the Windows Server 2008 R2 system or select the Custom option button to select specific volumes, files, folders, or other backup items. For this example, select Full Server (Recommended), and click Next.

6. On the Specify Destination Type page, select the Local Drives option button, and click Next.

7. On the Backup Destination page, select the DVD drive from the pull-down menu, check the Verify After Writing (Recommended) check box, and click Next.

8. On the Confirmation page, review the settings and click Backup to start the manual backup to DVD.

9. On the Backup Progress page, a shadow copy of the volumes is created first. After the shadow copy is created, a window opens prompting the administrator to insert a labeled DVD in the drive. Label the DVD with the name presented in the window; then insert the blank DVD and click OK to continue.

10. If additional DVDs are required, label them and place them in the drive as prompted.

11. Overall backup progress should be viewed in real time, and the window can be closed after the backup completes.

# Managing Backups Using the Command-Line Utility wbadmin.exe and PowerShell Cmdlets

Windows Server 2008 R2 systems can use either the Windows Server Backup command-line tool, wbadmin.exe, or the PowerShell Windows Server Backup cmdlets. The command-line backup tool used for this example is named wbadmin.exe and can be accessed using a Command Prompt window. Wbadmin.exe is very functional and can be used to perform most of the functions available in the GUI.

Understanding and becoming familiar and fluent with the command-line options of wbadmin.exe is very useful for administrators who need to manage Windows Server 2008 R2 Server Core systems or who need advanced automation capabilities. The following sections detail a few common tasks that can be performed using wbadmin.exe.

## Viewing Backup History

To view the backup history of a system, perform the following steps:

1. Log on to the Windows Server 2008 R2 system with an account with administrator privileges.
2. Open a command prompt.
3. Type in wbadmin.exe Get Versions and press Enter to list the backup history.

To perform the same task using Windows PowerShell, perform the following steps:

1. Log on to the Windows Server 2008 R2 system with an account with administrator privileges.
2. Click Start, click All Programs, click Accessories, click the Windows PowerShell folder, right-click on Windows PowerShell, and select Run As Administrator.
3. Type cd \ and press Enter.
4. Type Add-PsSnapin Windows.ServerBackup and press Enter.
5. To get the list of all of the available Windows Server Backup PowerShell cmdlets, type the command Get-Command *wb* -Commandtype cmdlet and press Enter.
6. To get the history list, type Get-WbBackupSet and press Enter.

## Running a Manual Backup to Remote Storage Using wbadmin.exe

Using wbadmin.exe to run backups can be tedious. To understand each of the options available for a manual backup in a Command Prompt window, type wbadmin.exe Start Backup /? and press Enter. To run a manual backup and store it on a remote server share, a few options are required. The data will be stored on the remote server share \\Server30\NetworkBackup, the Bare Metal Recovery item, referred to as the AllCritical option used in our example, will be selected for backup. This item includes all volumes in

30

use by the system, including volumes that contain applications and shared data folders, as well as the System State. For this example, the companyabc\administrator account will be used to connect to the remote share. To run the manual backup using the preceding criteria, perform the following steps:

1. Log on to the Windows Server 2008 R2 system with an account with administrator privileges.

2. Open a command prompt.

3. Type `wbadmin.exe Start Backup –backuptarget:\\Server2\NetworkBackup –AllCritical -user:companyabc\administrator –password:My$3cretPW!` and press Enter to start the backup.

4. The backup window will state that the network share cannot be securely protected, press Y, and then press Enter to allow the backup to run to this network share.

5. The backup progress will be detailed in the Command Prompt window. After the backup completes, type `exit` to close the Command Prompt window.

To perform the previous backup task using Windows PowerShell is a much more detailed task and requires several steps to make this work. To perform a manual backup to a network share capable of Bare Metal Recovery, perform the following steps:

1. Log on to the Windows Server 2008 R2 system with an account with administrator privileges.

2. Click Start, click All Programs, click Accessories, click the Windows PowerShell folder, right-click on Windows PowerShell, and select Run As Administrator.

3. Type `cd \` and press Enter.

4. Type `Add-PsSnapin Windows.ServerBackup` and press Enter.

5. Type `$BMRPolicy=New-WbPolicy` and press Enter.

6. Type `$BMRCred=Get-Credential` and press Enter.

7. A Windows dialog box opens; enter the username and password combination that will be used to connect to the network share, and click OK to save the credentials and return to the PowerShell window.

8. Back in the PowerShell window, type `$NetShareBackup=New-WbBackupTarget –NetworkPath \\Server30\NetworkBackup -Credential $BMRCred` and press Enter.

9. Type `Add-WbBackupTarget –policy $BMRPolicy –Target $NetShareBackup` and press Enter.

10. Type `Add-WbBareMetalRecovery –policy $BMRPolicy` and press Enter.

11. Type `Start-WbBackup –policy $BMRPolicy` and press Enter. The backup should start, as shown in Figure 30.6.

# Backing Up Windows Server 2008 R2 Role Services

Many Windows Server 2008 R2 role services store configuration and status data in separate files or databases located in various locations on the boot volume. If a scheduled backup is configured to run a full backup or a Bare Metal Recovery backup, this includes all boot,

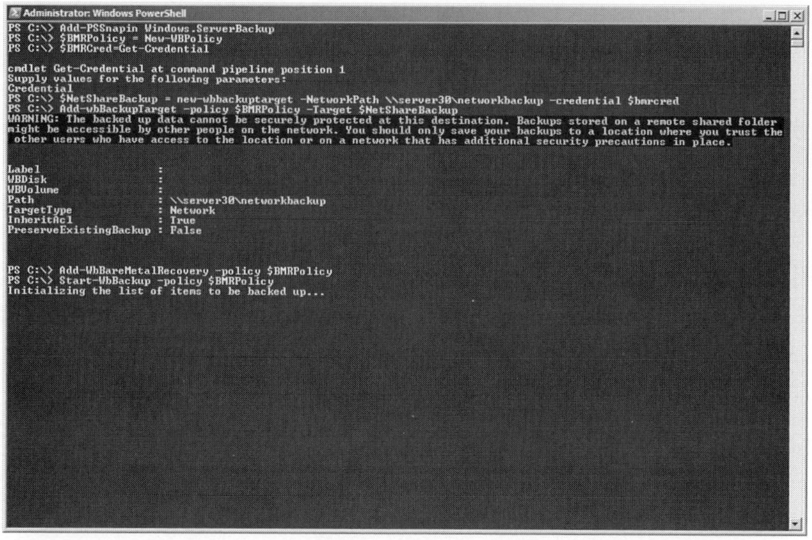

```
Administrator: Windows PowerShell
PS C:\> Add-PSSnapin Windows.ServerBackup
PS C:\> $BMRPolicy = New-WBPolicy
PS C:\> $BMRCred=Get-Credential

cmdlet Get-Credential at command pipeline position 1
Supply values for the following parameters:
Credential
PS C:\> $NetShareBackup = new-wbbackuptarget -NetworkPath \\server30\networkbackup -credential $bmrcred
PS C:\> Add-wbBackupTarget -policy $BMRPolicy -Target $NetShareBackup
WARNING: The backed up data cannot be securely protected at this destination. Backups stored on a remote shared folder
might be accessible by other people on the network. You should only save your backups to a location where you trust the
other users who have access to the location or on a network that has additional security precautions in place.

Label            :
WBDisk           :
WBVolume         :
Path             : \\server30\networkbackup
TargetType       : Network
InheritAcl       : True
PreserveExistingBackup : False

PS C:\> Add-WbBareMetalRecovery -policy $BMRPolicy
PS C:\> Start-WbBackup -policy $BMRPolicy
Initializing the list of items to be backed up...
```

FIGURE 30.6   Running a manual backup to a network share using PowerShell.

system, and data volumes used by the system as well as any application data and the
System State necessary for a complete PC restore. A few services also provide alternative
backup and restore options, and should be leveraged to provide additional recovery
options in the event of a service failure, as opposed to a full system failure.

## Backing Up the System State

The System State of a Windows Server 2008 R2 system contains, at a minimum, the
system Registry, boot configuration files, system files that are protected by Windows File
Protection (WFP), and the COM+ class registration database. Backing up the System State
creates a point-in-time backup that can be used to restore a server to a previous working
state. Having a copy of the System State is essential if a server restore is necessary. A
System State backup is included in a full server backup and is also included in the Bare
Metal Recovery selection, but it can also be backed up separately. To create a separate
System State backup using the GUI, perform the following steps:

1. Log on to the Windows Server 2008 R2 system with an account with administrator
   privileges.

2. Click Start, click All Programs, click Administrative Tools, and select Windows
   Server Backup.

3. Click on Backup Once in the Actions pane.

4. On the Backup Options page, select the Different Options option button and click
   Next to continue.

5. On the Select Backup Configuration page, select the Custom option button and click
   Next to continue.

30

6. On the Select Items for Backup page, click the Add Items button. In the Select Items window, check the box next to System State, as shown in Figure 30.7.

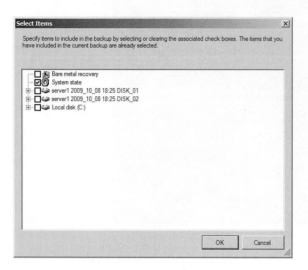

FIGURE 30.7    Selecting a System State only backup.

7. On the Select Items for Backup page, click Next to continue.

8. Complete the backup by selecting the desired destination for the backup and complete the required steps.

## Excluding Items from Backup

When full backups are not an option or if a particular folder on a volume needs to be excluded from a backup, this can be accomplished by creating a custom backup set. As an example, to back up the C volume and exclude the C:\Downloads folder, perform the following steps:

1. Log on to the Windows Server 2008 R2 system with an account with administrator privileges.

2. Click Start, click All Programs, click Administrative Tools, and select Windows Server Backup.

3. Click on Backup Once in the Actions pane.

4. On the Backup Options page, select the Different Options option button and click Next to continue.

5. On the Select Backup Configuration page, select the Custom option button and click Next to continue.

6. On the Select Items for Backup page, click the Add Items button. In the Select Items window, check the box next to Local Disk (C:) and click OK. This assumes that the C volume does not have a custom volume label.

7. Back on the Select Items for Backup page, click the Advanced Settings button.

8. On the Exclusions tab, click the Add Exclusions button. Select and expand the Local Disk (C:), select the Downloads folder, and click OK.

9. Back in the Advanced Settings window, the excluded folder should be listed, as shown in Figure 30.8.

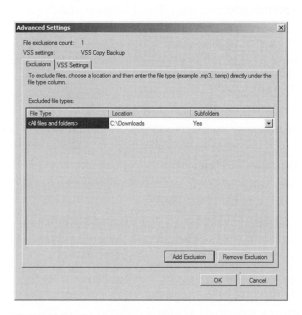

FIGURE 30.8   Excluding folders from backup.

10. Complete the backup by selecting the desired destination for the backup and complete the required steps.

## Backing Up Active Directory

Active Directory domain controllers contain a copy of the database that stores all Active Directory-related information. This is stored by default on the C: drive but it is included in the System State and Bare Metal Recovery backup. Also critical on Active Directory servers are the files and folders stored in the sysvol folder on the boot drive. The sysvol folder is also included in a System State backup. To properly back up a domain controller, a full backup should be scheduled to run nightly or multiple times per day. In addition to scheduled backups, text file exports and securing the most important objects can assist with reliability as well as recovery efforts. If full backups cannot be performed daily due to time or backup storage constraints, taking daily System State backups would be sufficient for Active Directory recovery, but might not provide enough protection to recover the entire domain controller after a hardware issue or serious software problem.

30

## LDIFDE and CSVDE Command-Line Tools

Ldifde.exe and csvde.exe are two command-line utilities that can be used to export and import Active Directory object information. For example, these tools can be used to export a list of all user accounts, groups, organizational units (OUs), and computer objects in an Active Directory domain.

When a restore of a deleted object is required, or when an object's attribute or property values are changed, having a text file export to reference the original location and distinguished name of the object, or the values of the object's attributes, is very valuable. To restore a single object, or an OU with all the objects contained within the OU, the distinguished name (DN) of the object is required. Using LDIFDE or CSVDE to export objects to a text file will contain the DN for all objects in the query. Either tool can be run from the command line. To export a list of all objects in Active Directory to a file called AllObjects.ldf, perform the following steps:

1. Log on to the Windows Server 2008 R2 system with an account with administrator privileges.
2. Click Start, click All Programs, click Accessories, and select Command Prompt.
3. Type cd \ and press Enter. The command prompt should reflect the local boot drive. For this example, we assume that this drive is the C: drive.
4. Type ldifde.exe –f AllObjects.ldf and press Enter.
5. The root of the C: drive now contains a file named AllObjects.ldf. Open this file using Notepad and review the export.
6. Back in the Command Prompt window, type ldifde.exe –f AllUsers.ldf –r "(objectclass=user)" and press Enter.
7. The root of the C: drive now contains a file named AllUsers.ldf. Open this file using Notepad and review the export to see that only the user objects have been exported to this file.
8. Type logoff and press Enter to log off of the server.

Ldifde.exe and csvde.exe have similar switches, but the export file format will be different. Also, each of these tools has a number of options that can be used to perform advanced queries and only export a select list of objects. For more information on these utilities, please reference the Help feature by typing ldifde /? or csvde /? and pressing Enter in a Command Prompt window.

> **NOTE**
>
> This process does not include security information, nor does it change the backup date on the database; therefore, it does not provide the same level of data protection as a "real" backup.

### Exporting Active Directory Object Data Using PowerShell

Windows Server 2008 R2 includes many PowerShell cmdlets for managing Active Directory. A few examples of these include the following cmdlets:

- **Get-AdObject**—This cmdlet is used to read AD object data and return it to the screen for reading, exporting, or piping into another cmdlet as a variable value. Some other useful cmdlets that are close in functionality include Get-AdUser, Get-ADComputer, Get-AdGroup, and several more.

- **Set-AdObject**—This cmdlet enables administrators to update attribute values on specified Active Directory objects. Some other useful cmdlets that are close in functionality include Set-AdUser, Set-ADComputer, Set-AdOrganizationalUnit, and several more.

- **Remove-ADObject**—This cmdlet can be used to delete an object or several objects from Active Directory, provided of course that deletion protection is not configured for the desired objects. Some other useful cmdlets that are close in functionality include Remove-AdUser, Remove-ADGroupmember, Remove-AdOrganizationalUnit, and several more.

- **New-AdObject**—This cmdlet can be used to create new Active Directory objects. Some other useful cmdlets that are close in functionality include New-AdUser, New-ADGroup, New-AdOrganizationalUnit, and several more.

- **Restore-AdObject**—This cmdlet can be used to restore an Active Directory object that has been previously deleted granted that the Active Directory Recycle Bin has been enabled before the object was deleted. More details on this particular cmdlet are included in Chapter 31, "Recovering from a Disaster."

More AD cmdlets that can be used for common tasks include Unlock-AdAccount, Search-AdAccount, and several more. All in all, more than 50 Active Directory-related cmdlets are included with Windows Server 2008 R2 PowerShell. To perform a few basic Active Directory export tasks using PowerShell, perform the following steps:

1. Log on to the Windows Server 2008 R2 system with an account with administrator privileges.

2. Click Start, click All Programs, click Accessories, click the Windows PowerShell folder, right-click on Windows PowerShell, and select Run As Administrator.

3. Type cd \ and press Enter.

4. Type Import-Module ActiveDirectory and press Enter.

5. Type Get-Command *AD* -CommandType cmdlet and press Enter. This returns all the Active Directory-related cmdlets and also returns a few more cmdlets not related to Active Directory.

6. Type Get-ADObject –Filter * and press Enter. This returns all the Active Directory objects to the PowerShell window with a default list of attributes.

30

7. Type Get-ADObject -Filter * ¦ Export-csv All-ADObjects.csv and press Enter. This returns all the Active Directory objects, writes the output to a .csv file instead of the window, and includes a default list of attributes.

8. Type Get-ADObject -Filter * -Properties *¦ Export-csv All-ADObjects.csv and press Enter. This returns all the Active Directory objects, writes the output to a .csv file, and includes all populated attributes for each object.

The previous command is similar to the ldifde -f allobjects.ldf command run in the previous section. For more granular exports, the following list provides a few more examples of Active Directory cmdlets commands that can be run in a PowerShell window with the Active Directory module installed:

▶ get-adobject -LdapFilter "(&(objectcategory=person)(objectclass=user))" -properties * ¦export-csv all-users.csv

▶ get-adobject -LdapFilter "(&(objectcategory=person)(objectclass=contact))" ¦export-csv all-contacts.csv

▶ get-adobject -LdapFilter "(&(objectcategory=computer)(objectclass=computer))" ¦export-csv all-computers.csv

▶ get-adobject -LdapFilter "(&(objectcategory=group)(objectclass=group))" ¦export-csv all-groups.csv

### Accidental Deletion Protection

A feature first released with the Windows Server 2008 Active Directory Users and Computers snap-in and included in the Windows Server 2008 R2 edition is an option to protect an object from accidental deletion. Setting this option defines a Deny permission to object deletion, so the result is not new, just the simplicity in configuring it is new. To protect an object from accidental deletion, perform the following steps of configuring this option on the Administrator user account:

1. Log on to the Windows Server 2008 R2 domain controller system with an account with administrator privileges.

2. Click Start, click All Programs, click Administrative Tools, and select Active Directory Users and Computers.

3. Select the View menu, and select Advanced Features.

4. In the tree pane, select the Users container.

5. In the right pane, locate the Administrator account, and double-click the user account to open the property pages.

6. Select the Object tab, check the Protect Object from Accidental Deletion check box, and click OK to apply the changes, as shown in Figure 30.9.

### Using the Directory Services Restore Mode Password

When a Windows Server 2008 R2 system is promoted to a domain controller, the Directory Services Restore mode (DSRM) password is created. This password is used only when booting into Directory Services Restore mode. Restore mode is used when the Active

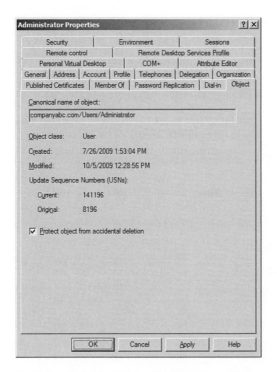

FIGURE 30.9   Enabling accidental deletion protection on an Active Directory user account.

Directory database is in need of maintenance or needs to be restored from backup. Many administrators have found themselves without the ability to log on to Restore mode when necessary and have been forced to rebuild systems from scratch to restore the System State data. Many hours can be saved if this password is stored in a safe place, where it can be accessed by the correct administrators. Now with Windows Server 2008 R2, if a full authoritative restore of the entire Active Directory database and sysvol folder is required, this can be performed using the Windows Server Backup GUI. To perform the restore, the domain controller will need to be booted into Directory Services Restore mode. If a single object or a container with objects within is accidentally deleted, it can be granularly restored by booting a domain controller in DSRM, restoring the System State, and performing an authoritative restore of the desired object(s). The issue with this is that the domain controller is offline to client requests during the entire time it is running in Directory Services Restore mode. To avoid this, Windows Server 2008 R2 has a new feature called the AD Recycle Bin, which allows for object recovery while the domain controller is online. This is detailed in the next section.

There can still be cases where restores will require booting domain controllers into DSRM and the DSRM password will be required. To make sure this password is known, the password can be updated regularly on all domain controllers. The Restore mode password is server specific and created on each domain controller. If the password is forgotten, and the domain controller is still functional, it can be changed using the command-line tool ntdsutil.exe from the command prompt. To update the DSRM password on a domain controller named dc1.companyabc.com, perform the following steps:

1. Log on to the Windows Server 2008 R2 system with an account with administrator privileges.

2. Click Start, click All Programs, click Accessories, and select Command Prompt.

3. Type cd \ and press Enter.

4. Type NTDSutil.exe and press Enter.

5. Type Set DSRM Password and press Enter.

6. Type Reset Password on Server dc1.companyabc.com and press Enter.

7. Type the new DSRM password, and press Enter.

8. Type the new DSRM password again for confirmation, and press Enter.

9. Repeat the previous three steps for any additional domain controllers that will have the DSRM password updated. To close out from NTDSutil.exe, type quit, press Enter, type quit again, and press Enter.

10. Back at the command prompt, type logoff to log off of the domain controller.

## Active Directory Recycle Bin

Windows Server 2008 R2 includes a feature that can be enabled called the Active Directory Recycle Bin. When enabled, this feature can allow for a deleted Active Directory object to be restored without having to restore the System State of a domain controller and boot to Directory Services Restore mode to perform a selective authoritative restore of that object. Enabling the Active Directory Recycle Bin requires that all domain controllers are running Windows Server 2008 R2, the forest functional level must be set to Windows Server 2008 R2, and then functionality can be enabled manually. To enable the Active Directory Recycle Bin, perform the following steps:

1. Log on to a Windows Server 2008 R2 domain controller in the forest root domain with an account with domain administrator privileges.

2. Click Start, click All Programs, click Accessories, click the Windows PowerShell folder, right-click on Windows PowerShell, and select Run As Administrator.

3. Type cd \ and press Enter.

4. Type Import-Module ActiveDirectory and press Enter.

5. Type Get-ADForest and press Enter. Review the ForestMode value, which should be set to Windows2008R2Forest.

6. If the ForestMode is not set to Windows2008R2Forest, for a forest named companyabc.com as an example, type Set-ADForestMode –Identity companyabc.com -ForestMode Windows2008R2Forest and press Enter. Type a Y and press Enter to confirm the change.

7. Once the forest functional level is confirmed to be at the Windows Server 2008 R2 level, type in Get-ADOptionalFeature –Filter * and press Enter. This returns the list of optional features, including the Active Directory Recycle Bin. If this feature is enabled, the EnabledScopes setting will have a value.

8. Assuming that this functionality has not been enabled, as it is not enabled by default, type `Enable-ADOptionalFeature 'Recycle Bin Feature' -Scope ForestorConfigurationSet -Target companyabc.com` and press Enter.

9. When prompted that this is an irreversible action, type `Y` and press Enter to enable the Active Directory Recycle Bin feature.

10. After the command completes, type `Get-ADOptionalFeature -Filter *` and press Enter. Note that the EnabledScopes setting is now populated with a value, as shown in Figure 30.10.

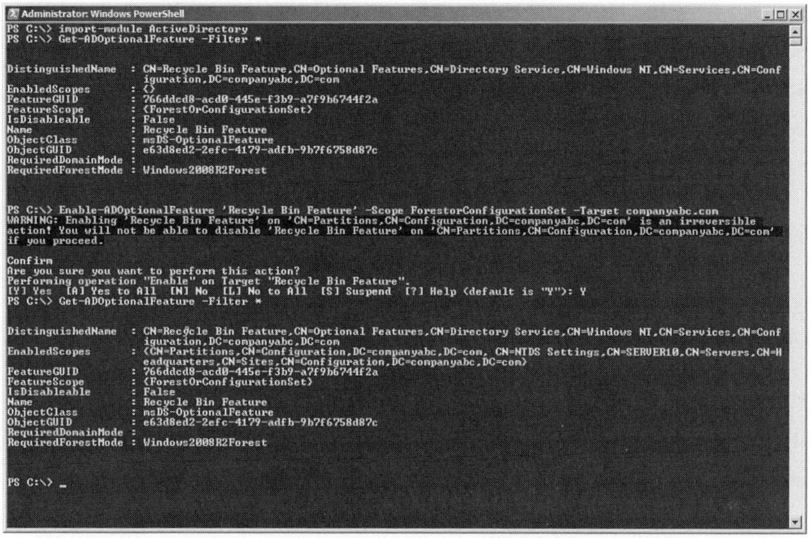

FIGURE 30.10   Enabling the Active Directory Recycle Bin feature.

11. Type `exit` and press Enter to close the PowerShell window.

After the Active Directory Recycle Bin is enabled, it should be tested with test organizational units, groups, users, or any desired objects. To perform a restore, the Restore-ADObject cmdlets will be used along with a few other cmdlets to get the preliminary information needed to restore. This restore process is detailed in Chapter 31.

## Certificate Services

When the Active Directory Certificate Services role and role servers are installed on a Windows Server 2008 R2 system, a Certification Authority is created. The Certification Authority or CA is used to manage and allocate certificates to users, servers, and workstations when files, folders, email, or network communication needs to be secured or encrypted.

When the CA allocates a certificate to a machine or user, that information is recorded in the certificate database on the local drive of the CA. If this database is corrupted or deleted, all certificates allocated from this server become invalid or unusable. To avoid this problem, the certificates and Certificate Services database should be backed up frequently. Even if certificates are rarely allocated to new users or machines, backups should still be performed regularly. The certificate authority database is backed up with a full system backup but can be backed up using the Certification Authority console. To perform a manual backup of the certificate authority, perform the following steps:

1. Log on to the Windows Server 2008 R2 Certification Authority server system with an account with administrator privileges.

2. Click Start, click All Programs, click Administrative Tools, and select Certification Authority.

3. Double-click on the Certification Authority server to initiate the connection in the console.

4. Right-click on the server, click All Tasks, and select Back Up CA.

5. When the Certification Authority Backup Wizard opens, click Next on the welcome page.

6. On the Items to Back Up page, check both check boxes, and in the Back Up to This Location text box, type `c:\Windows\System32\CABackup\` and click Next, as shown in Figure 30.11.

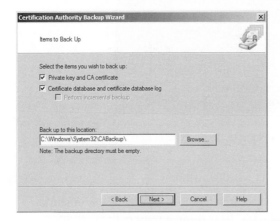

FIGURE 30.11    Specifying the options for the Certification Authority Backup Wizard.

7. A window opens stating that the destination folder does not exist; click OK to create the folder and continue.

8. On the Select a Password page, enter a password, confirm the password, and click Next to continue. This password is very important because it will be required to restore the database should that be necessary—so store this password in a safe place.

9. On the Completing the Certification Authority Backup Wizard page, review the settings, and click Finish to create the backup.

10. After the backup completes, the focus is returned to the Certification Authority console. Close the console.

11. Log off of the server.

## Domain Name System

Domain name system (DNS) configuration data is stored in the Registry and is backed up with the System State backup. For each DNS zone that is hosted on the Windows Server 2008 R2 server that is not an Active Directory-integrated zone, a backup zone file is created and stored in the %systemroot%\DNS\Backup folder. These files can be backed up and used to restore a DNS zone to the same server after a restore or they can be used to create new zones on a different server using these files to import the latest saved records. For Active Directory-integrated DNS zones, these zones are backed up with the domain controller System State and can be troublesome to restore. To back up the DNS zones manually and selectively, perform the following steps:

1. Log on to the Windows Server 2008 R2 domain controller running DNS services with an account with administrator privileges. These steps also work on primary zones that are not Active Directory-integrated and also on non-domain controller DNS servers.

2. Click Start, click All Programs, click Accessories, and select Command Prompt.

3. Type `Dnscmd /ZoneExport companyabc.com companyabc.com.txt` and press Enter. The previous example exports the companyabc.com DNS zone and the export file named companyabc.com.txt will be saved to `c:\Windows\System32\DNS\companyabc.com.txt`.

4. Repeat this command for any other DNS zones that will be backed up.

5. When completed, type `exit` and press Enter when completed.

> **NOTE**
>
> This method does not capture several elements of the zone, including security and delegate information. It also does not capture DNS server configuration information, including primary/secondary relationships, forwarding, and the like.

## Windows Internet Naming Service

Windows Internet Naming Service (WINS) is a database composed of NetBIOS names and their corresponding IP addresses. The NetBIOS names include domain, server, and workstation names, along with other records used to identify services such as the master browser. The WINS database is backed up by performing a System State backup of the WINS server or by initiating a backup using the WINS console.

30

Because the WINS database is populated by servers and workstations dynamically, in some cases backing up might not be necessary. When WINS contains static mappings, a WINS backup is essential because records will not be re-created automatically if the WINS database is corrupted or rebuilt from scratch. To create a backup using the WINS console, perform the following steps:

1. Log on to the Windows Server 2008 R2 WINS server system with an account with administrator privileges.

2. Click Start, click All Programs, click Administrative Tools, and select WINS.

3. Double-click on the WINS server to initiate the connection in the console.

4. Right-click on the WINS server in the tree pane, and select Back Up Database.

5. Browse to the folder location to store the backup, and click OK. The default location that should be specified is c:\windows\system32\WINS.

6. The backup will run and create a subfolder called wins_bak.

7. Click OK on the Confirmation page indicating that the backup was successful, and close the WINS console.

8. Log off of the Windows Server 2008 R2 WINS server system.

## Dynamic Host Configuration Protocol

The Dynamic Host Configuration Protocol (DHCP) server is responsible for assigning IP addresses and options to devices on the network in need of network configuration. DHCP allocates IP configurations, including IP addresses, subnet masks, default gateways, DNS servers, WINS servers, WDS servers, TFTP servers, and boot filenames. Other IP options can be configured, depending on the organization's needs.

These IP address scope properties and options are stored in the DHCP database. This database also stores the information concerning IP address leases and reservations. The DHCP database is backed up with a server System State backup, but it can also be backed up using the DHCP console.

To back up the DHCP database from the console, perform the following steps:

1. Log on to the Windows Server 2008 R2 DHCP server system with an account with administrator privileges.

2. Click Start, click All Programs, click Administrative Tools, and select DHCP.

3. Double-click on the DHCP server to initiate the connection in the console.

4. Right-click on the DHCP server in the tree pane, and select Backup.

5. When the Browse for Folder window opens, it will default to the systemroot\System32\DHCP\Backup folder; click OK to accept this location and start the backup.

6. There will be no confirmation of a successful backup. To verify if a backup was completed, open the folder and check the date and time stamps of the subfolders and files. The default subfolder name will be New.

7. Log off of the DHCP server system.

## Distributed File System

The Distributed File System (DFS) is a Windows Server 2008 R2 service that improves file share availability by providing a single unified namespace to access shared folders hosted across different servers. When DFS domain namespaces are used, DFS folders can be configured to replicate with one another using the DFS Replication service. Domain namespaces servers store the DFS folders, targets, and replication group configurations in Active Directory. When a stand-alone namespace is used, the configuration is stored in the namespace server's Registry. Backing up the System State of a stand-alone DFS server backs up the DFS configuration. For domain DFS namespaces, backing up the System State of a domain controller accomplishes this task. More information on DFS can be found in Chapter 28, "File System Management and Fault Tolerance."

## Internet Information Services

Internet Information Services (IIS) 7.5 is Windows Server 2008 R2's web application and FTP server. It is included on every version of the Windows Server 2008 R2 platform, but it is not installed by default. IIS stores configuration information for web and FTP site configurations and security in a set of XML files stored in the system root folder. The IIS configuration is automatically backed up with full system backups and with separate System State backups.

## Windows SharePoint Services

Windows SharePoint Services (WSS) runs on top of IIS 6.x and 7.x. Version 3.0 with SP2 can be downloaded and installed separately for use with Windows Server 2008 and Windows Server 2008 R2. WSS stores configuration- and site-related data (application data) within Microsoft SQL databases or within the internal Windows Server 2008 R2 database, also known as the SQL 2005 Express Edition. When WSS is installed, it can be configured to use the internal database or it can be connected to a fully functional SQL database server running on the local or a remote system.

Windows Server Backup currently supports the backup and restore of WSS configuration and application data natively, if the data is stored within the internal database. For WSS deployments or Microsoft Office SharePoint Server deployments that utilize SQL servers, the databases need to be backed up using a compatible SQL backup agent, or the backup functionality included within the SQL Management tools. To perform a manual backup of Windows SharePoint Services, perform the following steps:

1. Log on to the Windows Server 2008 R2 Windows SharePoint Services server system with an account with administrator privileges.

2. Click Start, click All Programs, click Administrative Tools, and select SharePoint 3.0 Central Administration.

3. When the browser opens, if prompted, enter a username and password for an account with administrative privileges on the WSS server.

4. When the SharePoint 3.0 Central Administration website opens, select the Operations tab.

30

5. Scroll down in the window, and on the right side, under the Backup and Restore section, click on the Perform a Backup link.

6. Near the top of the window, check the Farm check box to back up the entire contents and configuration data for the Windows SharePoint Services on this server, and click on the Continue to Backup Option link located right above the Farm check box, as shown in Figure 30.12.

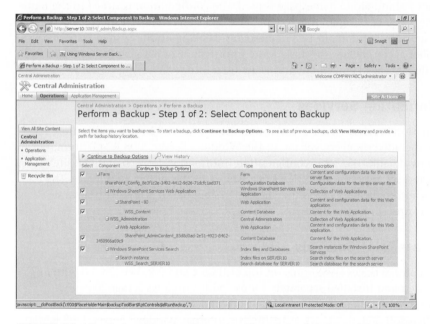

FIGURE 30.12    Performing a backup using SharePoint 3.0 Central Administration.

7. On the next page, scroll down and enter the UNC path to store the backup, and click OK to start the backup.

8. On the next page, click on the Timer Job Status link to view the status of the backup job. When the new page opens, review the status of the backup job, as shown in Figure 30.13, as an initialized job.

9. After the job has completed, it will be removed from the Timer page upon refresh. Click the browser's Back button to return to the Backup and Restore Status page, and click the Refresh button. Scroll down on the page to review the result of the backup.

10. Close the browser and log off of the system.

## Volume Shadow Copy Service (VSS)

Window Server 2008 R2 Volume Shadow Copy Service (VSS) provides some great features that can be used to enhance backup and recovery for Windows disks. One great feature of VSS, called Shadow Copies for Shared Volumes, captures and stores copies of the files and folders at a specific point in time.

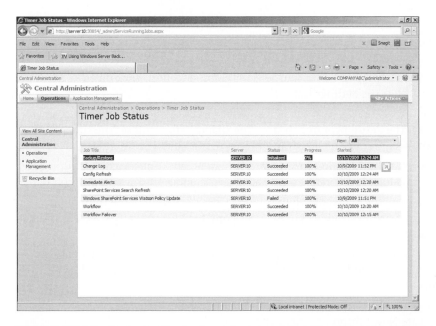

FIGURE 30.13    Reviewing the backup job status using SharePoint 3.0 Central Administration.

Administrators and end users with the correct permissions can browse the shadow copies based on the time and date of creation and essentially restore a specific folder, file, or entire volume without restoring from tape. The shadow copies are very space efficient, as the first copy is a complete compressed version of the data on the volume, and subsequent copies store only the changes made since the last shadow copy was created.

Another great feature of the VSS is the tight integration it provides for third-party software vendors and to the Windows Server Backup tools. VSS enables manual backups created using Windows Server Backup to store shadow copies on remote server shares. Windows Server Backup also utilizes VSS to manage the storage space of the backup by using the space-efficient and intelligent storage functions of VSS.

## Enabling Shadow Copies for Shared Volumes

Enabling shadow copies on a volume can be very simple. Administrators have more options when it comes to recovering lost or deleted data and, in many cases, can entirely avoid restoring data to disk from a backup tape device or tape library. In addition, select users can be given the necessary rights to restore files that they've accidentally deleted.

The Volume Shadow Copy Service is already installed and is automatically available using NTFS-formatted volumes.

To enable and configure shadow copies, follow these steps:

1. Log on to the Windows Server 2008 R2 system with an account with administrator privileges.

2. Click Start, click All Programs, click Administrative Tools, and select Server Manager.

30

3. In the tree pane, double-click the Storage node, and select Disk Management.

4. In the tasks pane, scroll down to locate the desired volume, right-click the volume, and select Properties.

5. Select the Shadow Copies tab; in the Select a Volume section, click on the desired volume, and click the Settings button.

6. The Settings page enables you to choose an alternate volume to store the shadow copies. Select the desired volume to store the shadow copy and set the storage space limit for the volume. The default is usually set to 10% of the volume size.

7. After the location and maximum size are configured, click the Schedule button and define the schedule. The defaults create a shadow copy at 7:00 a.m. and 12:00 p.m.

8. Click OK to close the Schedule window, and click OK again to close the Volume Shadow Copy Settings window. The shadow copy for the originally selected volume is now enabled.

9. If necessary, select the next volume and enable shadow copying; otherwise, select the enabled volume and immediately create a shadow copy by clicking the Create Now button.

10. If necessary, select the next volume and immediately create a shadow copy by clicking the Create Now button.

11. After the shadow copies are created, click OK to close the Shadow Copies page, close the Server Manager, and log off of the server.

To learn how to recover lost or overwritten data using Shadow Copies for Shared Folders, refer to Chapter 31.

# Windows Server 2008 R2 Startup Options

When a Windows Server 2008 R2 system has startup issues, a few different startup options can be used to troubleshoot the problem. On every server, when the boot loader is shown, the administrator can press the F8 key to list several boot configurations, including Safe mode to load only the core drivers and applications. The different options can be used to disable or change a suspected driver or application that is causing normal system startup to fail. The different startup options are detailed in Chapter 31.

## Emergency Management Services Console Redirection

Windows Server 2008 R2 enables administrators to remotely manage or troubleshoot a system when normal operating system functionality is not available. Using out-of-band connections, such as a serial COM port, information can be redirected to other servers to resolve startup or operating system problems. Emergency Management Services (EMS) can be used when physical access to a server is not available and remote administrative options through network connections are not working properly.

Some hardware requirements must be met before Emergency Management Services console redirection can be used. For example, the system motherboard BIOS must support Serial Port Console Redirection (SPCR). Emergency Management Services is enabled and installed on servers during operating system installation if the motherboard supports SPCR. To enable and configure EMS on existing Windows Server 2008 R2 systems, use the `bcdedit.exe` utility.

Refer to the Windows Server 2008 R2 Help and Support documentation for the specific switches and settings for Bcdedit.

## Summary

When it comes to disaster recovery planning and backing up Windows Server 2008 R2 systems, there are many options to consider. Specialized utilities can be leveraged for specific backup tasks, but for complete server backup, the graphic and command-line utilities of Windows Server Backup take care of all of the Windows Server 2008 R2 role services requirements. Third-party applications might require additional backup programs or tasks to be backed up properly.

## Best Practices

The following are best practices from this chapter:

▶ Make sure that disaster recovery planning includes considerations for the physical site, power, entire system failure, server component failure, and software corruption.

▶ Identify the different services and technologies, points of failure, and critical areas; then prioritize in order of importance.

▶ Make sure that the disaster recovery solution contains costs associated with additional hardware, complex configurations, and a service-level agreement estimating how long it will take to recover the service should a failure occur. Different options should also be presented.

▶ Document the server configuration for any environment, regardless of size, number of servers, or disaster recovery budget.

▶ Verify that any backup disks or remote server shares used to store backups are both physically secure and secured by NTFS and share permissions to reduce the risk of compromising or losing company data.

30

# Recovering from a Disaster

When organizations need to recover data or restore business services and operations after a disruption in business operations, having a well-formulated and validated recovery plan is vital to success. This requires a disciplined process of creating and maintaining backup and recovery procedures and documentation, as well as periodically validating the recovery tasks by simulating different failure scenarios and recovering data and applications.

In addition to having a disaster recovery plan, many organizations—not just the organizations that are required by law—should also implement and follow a strict change management system to evaluate the benefits and risks associated with proposed changes to current business systems, services, applications, and operational processes.

This chapter, as a complement to Chapter 30, "Backing Up the Windows Server 2008 R2 Environment," details how to recover a Windows Server 2008 R2 environment using Windows Server Backup after a failure or disaster has occurred. In addition to system recovery, this chapter also provides some best practices and ideas organizations should consider when planning how to support and restore operation to the computer and network infrastructure when system failures and disasters occur.

## Ongoing Backup and Recovery Preparedness

Creating and documenting processes that detail how to properly back up and recover from a disaster is an essential step in a disaster recovery project. Equally important as creating these processes is periodically reviewing, validating, and updating the processes. Disaster recovery planning should not be considered a project for the current calendar year; instead, it should be considered an essential part of regular business operations and should have dedicated annual budget and assigned staff.

Each year, many businesses, business divisions, or departments update their computer and network infrastructure and change the way they provide services to their staff, vendors, and clients. In many of these cases, the responsible information technology staff, cross-departmental managers, executives, and employees are not involved or properly informed in advance of the execution or implementation of these changes. Computer and network infrastructure changes can have ripple effects throughout an entire organization during transition and during disaster and failure situations, so proper planning and approval of changes should always be performed and documented.

To reduce the risk of a change negatively impacting business operations, many organizations implement processes that require new projects and system changes to be submitted, evaluated, and either approved or rejected based on the information provided. Although this chapter does not focus or even really discuss project management, all organizations that utilize computer and network infrastructures should consider implementing a Project Management Office and a change-control committee to review and oversee organizational projects and infrastructure changes.

## Project Management Office (PMO)

In recent years, many organizations have introduced Project Management Offices (PMOs) into their business operations. A PMO is used to provide somewhat of a project oversight committee to organizations that frequently operate several projects simultaneously. Organizations that utilize a proven project methodology can further extend this methodology to include workflow processes that include checkpoints with the PMO staff.

The role of the PMO can be different in almost every organization, but most include a few key functions. The role of the PMO usually involves reviewing proposed projects to determine how or if the project deliverables coincide with the organization's current or future business plans or strategies. PMO membership can also be very different among organizations. PMO membership can include departmental managers, directors or team leads, executive staff, employee advocates, and, in some cases, board members. Having the PMO staff represent views and insight from the different levels and departments of an organization enables the PMO to add value to any proposed project.

Having diverse staff included in the PMO staff enables the organization to evaluate and understand current and proposed projects and how these projects will positively or negatively affect the organization as a whole. Some of the general functions or roles a PMO can provide include the following:

> ▶ **High-level project visibility**—All proposed projects are presented to the PMO and if approved, the project is tracked by the PMO. This provides a single entity that is knowledgeable and informed about all ongoing and future projects in an organization and how they align to business and technical objectives.

▶ **Project sounding board**—When a new project is proposed or presented to the PMO, the project will be scrutinized and many questions will be asked. Some of these questions might not have been considered during the initial project design and planning phases. The PMO improves project quality by constantly reviewing and monitoring projects from when the project is proposed and during regular scheduled project status and PMO meetings.

▶ **Committee-based project approval or denial**—The PMO is informed of all the current and future projects, as well as business direction and strategy, and is the best-equipped group to decide on whether a project should be approved, denied, or postponed.

▶ **Enterprise project management**—The PMO tracks the status of all ongoing projects and upcoming projects, which enables the PMO to provide additional insight and direction with regard to internal resource utilization, vendor management for outsourced projects, and, of course, project budget and scheduling.

## Change Control

Whereas a PMO improves project management and can provide the necessary checkpoints to verify that backup and recovery requirements are addressed within the new projects, an organization with a change-control system can ensure that any proposed changes have been carefully evaluated and scheduled before approval or change execution. Change control involves a submittal, review, and approval process for each change that typically includes the following information:

▶ **Change description**—Includes which systems will be changed, what the change is, and why it is proposed or required.

▶ **Impact of the change**—Details if any systems or services will be unavailable during the execution of the change and who will be affected or impacted by the change.

▶ **Change duration**—Details how long it will take to execute and complete the change and, if necessary, revert or roll back the change.

▶ **Change schedule**—Includes the proposed date and time to execute the change.

▶ **Change procedure**—Details how the change will be executed, including a detailed description; this usually also includes detailed steps or an accompanying document.

▶ **Change rollback plan**—Details the steps necessary to recover or roll back the change in the event that the change causes undesirable results.

▶ **Change owners**—Includes who will execute the change and is responsible for communicating the status and results of the change back to the change-control committee.

A change-control committee, similar to a PMO, is made up of managers, executives, and employee advocates who will review and determine if the change is approved, denied, or needs to be postponed. Proposed changes are submitted in advance. A day or two later, a change-control review meeting is held where each change is discussed by the change-control committee and the change owner, and the change will be approved, denied, postponed, or closed, or more information will be requested.

During failure or disaster situations, going through the normal change-control process might not be an option due to the impact of the failure. During these situations, emergency change-request processes should be followed. An emergency change request usually involves getting the particular departmental manager and the responsible information technology manager, director, or CIO to sign off on the change before it is executed. In short, all changes need to be considered and approved, even in failure scenarios when time is of the essence. When an administrator is troubleshooting and trying to resolve a failure or trying to recover from a disaster, especially in a stressful situation, making changes without getting approval can lead to costly mistakes. Following the proper change-control and emergency change-control processes to inform and involve others, getting approval from management, and following documented processes will provide accountability and might even save the administrator's job.

## Disaster Recovery Delegation of Responsibilities

At this point, the organization might have a documented and functional backup and recovery plan, a PMO, and a change-control committee, but the ownership and maintenance of disaster recovery operations is not yet defined or assigned. Disaster recovery roles, functions, or responsibilities might be wrapped up into an existing executive's or manager's duties or a dedicated staff member might be required. Commonly, disaster recovery responsibilities are owned by the chief information officer, operations manager, chief information security officer, or a combination of these positions. Of course, responsibilities for different aspects of the overall disaster recovery plan are delegated to managers, departmental leads, and staff volunteers as necessary. An example of delegating disaster recovery responsibilities is contained in the following list:

▶ The chief information officer is responsible for disaster recovery planning and maintaining and executing disaster recovery-related tasks for the entire telecom, desktop and server computer infrastructure, network infrastructure, and all other electronic and fax-related communication.

▶ The manager of facilities or operations is responsible for planning alternate office locations and offsite storage of original or duplicates of all important paper documents, such as leases, contracts, insurance policies, stock certificates, and so on, to support disaster recovery operations to alternate sites or offices.

▶ The manager of human resources is responsible for creating and maintaining emergency contact numbers for the entire company, storing this information offsite, and communicating with employees to provide direction and information prior to disasters striking and during a disaster recovery operation.

The list of responsibilities can be very granular and extensive and disaster recovery planning should not be taken lightly or put on the back burner. Although there are many aspects of disaster recovery planning, the remainder of this chapter focuses only on the disaster recovery responsibilities and tasks that should be assigned to qualified Windows administrators who need to support a Windows Server 2008 R2 environment.

**31**

## Achieving 99.999% Uptime Using Windows Server 2008 R2

When the topic of disaster recovery comes up, many people think of the phrase "five nines" or "99.999% uptime." Although understanding this concept is reasonably simple, actually providing five nines for a server or a network can be quite a large and expensive task. Achieving 99.999% uptime means that the server, application, network, or whatever is supposed to have this amount of uptime can only be down for just over five minutes per year. Having such success is quite a claim to make, so administrators should make it with caution and document it, citing explicitly what this service depends on. For example, if a power failure occurs and the battery backups will last only two hours, a dependency for a server could be that if a power outage occurs, it can withstand up to two hours without power.

To provide 99.999% uptime for services available on Windows Server 2008 R2, administrators can build in redundancy and replication on a data, service, server, or site level. Many Windows Server 2008 R2 services outlined in other chapters of this book, including Failover Clusters, Network Load Balancing, and the Distributed File System, can provide redundancy for the specific services available.

# When Disasters Strike

When a failure or disaster strikes is when not only having, but also following, a disaster recovery plan is most important. Having a procedure or checklist to follow allows all involved parties to be on the same page and understand what steps are being taken to rectify the situation. The following sections detail steps that can be followed to ensure that no time is wasted and resources are not being led in the wrong direction.

## Qualifying the Disaster or Failure

When a system failure occurs or is reported as failed, the information can come from a number of different sources and should be verified. The reported issue can be caused by user or operator error, network connectivity, or a problem with a specific user account configuration or status. A reported system failure should be verified as failed by performing the same steps reported by the reporting party.

If the system is, in fact, in a failed state, the impact of the failure should be noted, and this information should be escalated within the organization so that a formal recovery plan can be created. This can be known as qualifying the disaster or failure. An example of qualifying a failure includes a short description of the failure, the steps used to validate the failure, who is affected, how many end users are affected, which dependent applications or systems are affected, which branch offices are affected, and who is responsible for the maintenance and recovery of this system.

## Validating Priorities

When a disaster strikes that affects an entire server room or office location, the priority of restoring systems and operations should already be determined. First and foremost are the core infrastructure systems, such as networking and power, followed by authentication systems, and the remaining core bare minimum services. In the event of a failure that involves multiple systems—for example, a web server failure that supports 10 separate applications—the priority of recovery should be presented and approved by management. If each of these 10 applications takes 30 minutes to recover, it could be 5 hours before the system is fully functional, but if one particular application is critical to business operations, this application should be recovered first. Always perform checkpoints and verification to ensure that the priorities of the organization are in line with the recovery work that is being performed.

## Assume and Be Doomed

Disaster, system failures, and data corruption issues tend to create a lot of stress and havoc among technical business personnel. Recovery administrators and managers should always be on the same page regarding the priority of recovery and the process. Also, get this communication in paper or electronic format because it might be required later to justify why a choice was made. Those administrators who decide to move forward on resolving an issue based on assumptions and not by first communicating with their managers might find themselves in a very sticky situation, especially if the results of their actions prove to be unsuccessful or end up causing more problems.

## Synchronizing with Business Owners

Prioritizing the recovery of critical and bare minimum business systems is part of disaster recovery planning. When a situation strikes that requires an entire data center or group of systems to be restored or recovered, the steps that will be followed need to be put back in front of the business owners again. Please remember that between the time a disaster recovery plan is created and the time the failure occurs, business priorities might have shifted and the business owners might be the only ones aware of this change. During a recovery situation, always take the time to stay calm and focused and communicate with the managers, executives, and business owners so that they can be informed of the progress. An informed business owner is less likely to stay in the server room or data center if they feel that recovery efforts are in good hands.

## Communicating with Vendors and Staff

When failures or disasters strike, communication is key. Regardless of whether customers, vendors, employees, or executives are affected, some level of communication is required or suggested. This is where the soft skills of an experienced manager, sales executive, technical consultant, and possibly even lawyers can be most valuable. Providing too much information, information that is too technical, or, worst of all, incorrect or no information, is a mistake technical staff frequently make. My recommendation to technical staff is to only communicate with your direct manager or his or her boss if they are not available. If the

CEO or an end user asks for an update, try to defer to the manager as best you can, so that focus can be kept on restoring services.

## Assigning Tasks and Scheduling Resources

The situation is that we have a failure, we have an approved plan, we have communicated the situation, and we are ready to begin fixing the issue. The next step is to delegate the specific tasks to the qualified staff members for execution. As stated previously, hand off communication to a manager or spokesperson and only communicate through them if possible. Determining who will restore a particular system is as important if not more important than assigning communication responsibilities. Only certain technical staff members might be qualified to restore a system, so selecting the correct resource is essential.

When a serious failure has occurred, recovery efforts might require multiple technical resources onsite for an extended period of time. Furthermore, there might be dependencies that affect which systems can be restored, and, of course, the order or priority of restore will advance or delay the recovery of a system. Mapping out the extended recovery timeline and technical resource scheduling ensures that a technical resource is not onsite until their skills and time are required. Also, rotating technical resources after six to eight hours of time helps to keep progress moving forward.

## Keeping the Troops Happy

This section goes out to all technical leads, project managers, IT managers, business owners, and executives. If you have technical resources working for you in an effort to recover from a failure, you should do all you can to ensure that these technical resources are kept happy and focused. For starters, try to keep the end users and any other business owners or executives from bothering this staff. Regular communication will help with this task tremendously. Next, and possibly more important, provide all the bottled water, soda, coffee, snacks, food, breaks, and anything else that will keep these professionals happy, healthy, and focused on the task at hand. Technical staff will work very hard during disaster situations, so don't forget to pat them on the back and let them know how much the organization and you personally appreciate their time and commitment.

## Recovering the Infrastructure

After the failure has been validated, the initial communications meetings have been held, restore tasks have been confirmed and possibly reprioritized, and recovery task assignment of resources has been completed, the recovery efforts can finally begin. Verify that each technical resource has all the documentation, phone numbers, software, and hardware they require to perform their task. Hold periodic checkpoint meetings, starting every 15 minutes and tapering off to every 30 or 60 minutes as recovery efforts continue.

## Postmortem Meeting

After a system failure or disaster strikes, and the recovery has been completed, an organization should hold a meeting to review the entire process. The meeting might just be an event where individuals are recognized for their great work; however, the meeting will most likely involve reviewing what went wrong and identifying how the process could be improved in the future. A lot of interesting things will happen during disaster recovery situations—both unplanned and simulated—and this meeting can provide the catalyst for ongoing improvement of the processes and documentation.

# Disaster Scenario Troubleshooting

This section of the chapter details the high-level steps that can be taken to recover from particular types of disaster scenarios. As this book and chapter focuses on Windows Server 2008 R2 environments, so shall the following sections.

## Network Outage

When an organization is faced with a network outage, the impact can affect a small set of users, an entire office, or the entire company. When a network outage occurs, the network administrators should perform the following tasks:

▸ Test the reported outage to verify if the issue is related to a wide area network (WAN) connection between the organization and the Internet service provider (ISP), the router, a network switch, a firewall, a physical fiber or copper network connection or network port, or line power to any of the aforementioned devices.

▸ After the issue is isolated or, at least, the scope of the issue is understood, the network administrator should communicate the outage to the necessary managers and/or business owners and, as necessary, open communication to outside support vendors and ISP contacts to report the issue and create a trouble ticket. And no—this should not go out in an email if the network is down.

▸ Create a logical action plan to resolve the issue and execute the plan.

▸ Create and distribute a summary of the cause and result of the issue and how it can be avoided in the future. Close the trouble ticket as required.

## Physical Site Failure

In the event a physical site or office cannot be accessed, a number of business operations might be suspended. Planning how to mitigate issues related to physical site limitations can be extensive, but should include the considerations discussed in the following sections.

### Physical Site Access Is Limited but Site Is Functional

This section lists a few considerations for a situation where the site or office cannot be accessed physically, but all systems are functional:

▸ Can the main and most critical phone lines be accessed or forwarded remotely?

▸ Is there a remote access solution to allow employees with or without notebooks/laptop computers to connect to the organization's network and perform their work?

## 31

▶ Are there any other business operations that require onsite access that are tied to a service-level agreement, such as responding to paper faxes or submitted customer support emails, phone calls, or custom applications?

### Physical Site Is Offline and Inaccessible

This section lists a few considerations for a situation where the resources in a site are nonfunctional. This scenario assumes that the site resources cannot be accessed across the network or Internet and the data center is offline with no chance of a quick recovery. When planning for a scenario such as this, the following items should be considered:

▶ Can all services be restored in an alternate capacity—or at least the most critical systems, such as the main phone lines, fax lines, devices, applications, system, and remote access services?

▶ If systems are cut over to an alternate location, what is the impact in performance, or what percentage of end-user load can the system support?

▶ If systems are cut over to an alternate location, will there be any data loss or will only some data be accessible?

▶ If the decision to cut over to the alternate location is made, how long will it take to cut over and restore the critical services?

▶ If the site outage is caused by power loss or network issues, how long of an outage should be sustained before deciding to cut over services to an alternate location?

▶ When the original system is restored, if possible, what will it take to failback or cut the systems back to the main location, and is there any data loss or synchronization of data involved?

These short lists merely break the surface when it comes to the planning of or dealing with a physical site outage, but, hopefully, they will spark some dialogue in the disaster recovery planning process to lead the organization to the solution that meets their needs and budget.

## Server or System Failure

When a server or system failure occurs, administrators must decide on which recovery plan of action will be the most effective. Depending on the particular system, in some cases, it might be more efficient to build a new system and restore the functionality or data. In other cases, where rebuilding a system can take several hours, it might be more prudent to troubleshoot and repair the problem.

### Application or Service Failure

If a Windows Server 2008 R2 system is still operational but a particular application or service on the system is nonfunctional, in most cases troubleshooting and attempting repair or restoring the system to a previous backup state is the correct plan of action. The Windows Server 2008 R2 event log is much more useful of a tool than in previous versions, and it should be one of the first places an administrator looks to determine the cause of a validated issue. Following troubleshooting or recovery procedures for the particular application is the next logical step. For example, if an end user deleted a folder from a network share, the preferred recovery method might be to use Shadow Copy backups to restore the data instead of the Windows Server Backup.

For Windows services, using Server Manager to review the status of the role and role services assists administrators in identifying and isolating problems because the Server Manager tool displays a filtered representation of Event Viewer items and service state for each role installed on the system. Figure 31.1 details that the File Services role SERVER10 logged several errors and warnings in the last 24 hours.

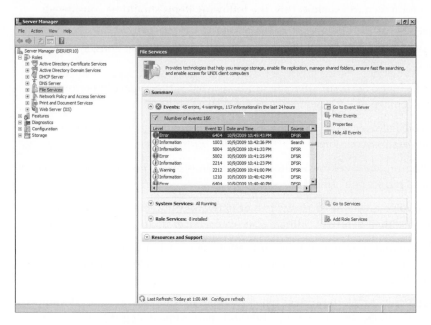

FIGURE 31.1   File Services role and role status.

### Data Corruption or Loss

When a report has been logged that the data on a server is missing, is corrupted, or has been overwritten, Windows Server 2008 R2 administrators have a few options to deal with this situation. Shadow Copies for Shared Folders can be used to restore previous versions of selected files or folders and Windows Server Backup can be used to restore selected files, folders, or the entire volume on a Windows disk. Using Shadow Copies for Shared Folders, administrators and end users with the correct permissions can restore data right from their workstation. Using the restore features of Windows Server Backup, administrators can place the restored data back into the same folder by overwriting the existing data or placing a copy of the data with a different name based on the backup schedule date and time. For example, to restore a file called ClientProprosal.docx that was backed up on 10-9-09 at 12:30 p.m., Windows Server Backup will restore the file as 2009-10-09 12-30

Copy of `ClientProposal.docx`, and the time representation will be the current time zone of the server.

### Hardware Failure

When hardware failure occurs, a number of issues and symptoms might result. The most common issues related to hardware failures include system crashes, services or drivers stopping unexpectedly, frozen (hung) systems, and systems that are in a constant reboot cycle. When hardware is suspected as failed or failing on a Windows Server 2008 R2 system, administrators should first review the event logs for any related system or application event warnings and errors. If nothing apparent is logged, hardware manufacturers usually provide several different diagnostic utilities that can be used to test and verify hardware configuration and functional state. Don't wait to call Microsoft and involve their professional support services department because they can be working in conjunction with your team to capture and review debugging data.

When a system is suspected of having hardware issues and it is a business-critical system, steps should be taken to migrate services or applications hosted on that system to an alternate production system, or the system should be recovered to new hardware. Windows Server 2008 R2 can tolerate a full system restore or a complete PC restore to alternate hardware if the system is an exact or close hardware match with regard to the motherboard, processors, hard disk controller, and network card. Even if the hardware is exact and the disk arrays, disk IDs, and volume or partition numbers do not match, a complete PC restore to alternate hardware might fail if no additional steps are taken during the restore or recovery process. This is detailed in a later section of this chapter named "Complete PC Restore to Alternate Hardware."

# Recovering from a Server or System Failure

When a failure or issue is reported regarding a Windows Server 2008 R2 system, the responsible administrator should first perform the standard validation tests to verify that there is a real issue. The following sections include basic troubleshooting steps when failure reports are based around data or application access issues, network issues, data corruption, or recovery issues.

## Access Issues

When end users report issues accessing a Windows Server 2008 R2 system but the system is still online, this is categorized as an access issue. Administrators should start troubleshooting access issues by first verifying that the system can be accessed from the system console and then verifying that it can be accessed across the network. After that is validated, the access issue should be tested to reveal whether the access issue is affecting everyone or just a set of users. Access issues can be system or network related, but they can also be related to security configurations on the network or local system firewall or application, share, and/or NTFS permissions. The following sections can be used to help troubleshoot access issues.

### Network Access Troubleshooting

Troubleshooting access to a system that is suspected to be network related can involve the networking group as well as the Windows Server 2008 R2 system administrators. When networking is a suspect, the protocol and system IP information should be noted before any tests are performed. Tests should be performed from the Windows system console to determine if the system can access other devices on the local network and systems on neighboring networks located across a gateway or router. Tests should be performed using both the system DNS names as well as IP addresses and, if necessary, IP Next Generation IPv6 addresses.

> **NOTE**
>
> Testing connectivity for web-based applications should be performed using system host-names, fully qualified domain names, and IP addresses to ensure that tests yield the proper results. Many web servers and/or firewalls can receive a properly formed header in the web GET request and will not respond to a request made from an IP-based uniform resource locator (URL).

If the system can communicate out but users still cannot access the system, possible causes could be an incorrect IP subnet mask default gateway or routing table or a restriction configured in the Windows or network firewall. Windows Firewall is enabled by default on Windows Server 2008 R2 systems and the new firewall supports multiple firewall profiles simultaneously. If a network is identified incorrectly as a public network instead of a domain network, depending on the firewall profile settings, this might restrict access undesirably. When administrators follow the proper procedures for installing roles and role services, during the installation of the roles, exceptions will be added to the firewall. Administrators can review the settings using the Windows Firewall applet from Control Panel but to get very detailed firewall information, the Windows Firewall with Advanced Security console should be used. This console is located in the Administrative Tools program group.

### Share and NTFS Permissions Troubleshooting

If network connectivity and firewall configurations check out, the next step in troubleshooting access issues is to validate the configured permissions to the affected application, service, or shared folder. For application access troubleshooting, refer to the section,

"Application Access Troubleshooting," and the application vendors' administration and troubleshooting guides. For Windows services and share folder permission troubleshooting, Event Viewer can assist tremendously, especially if auditing is enabled. Auditing can be enabled within an Active Directory group policy on the Windows Server 2008 R2 local computer policy, but auditing must also be enabled on the particular NTFS folder. For information on local and domain Group Policies, refer to Chapter 27, "Group Policy Management for Network Clients." To troubleshoot share and NTFS permissions, please review the following sections.

**Validating Share Permissions**   When share permissions need to be validated, there are several ways to accomplish this task. One way to accomplish this task is to use the Share and Storage Management snap-in, as detailed in the following steps:

1.  Log on to the Windows Server 2008 R2 system with an account with administrator privileges.
2.  Click Start, click All Programs, click Administrative Tools, and select Share and Storage Management.
3.  When the window opens, locate the desired share in the tasks pane, right-click the share, and choose Properties.
4.  Select the Permissions tab and click the Share Permissions button.
5.  Review and, if necessary, reconfigure the share permissions as required.
6.  Click OK to close the Share Permissions window and click OK again to close the share properties pages.
7.  Close the Share and Storage Management console.

**Enabling Auditing for NTFS Folders**   Enabling auditing on an NTFS folder can be a helpful aid in troubleshooting access to server folders. Enabling auditing for NTFS folders is a two-part configuration involving either Group Policy or local computer policy audit settings, as well as configuring auditing on the folder itself. To enable auditing for a folder on a Windows Server 2008 R2 system, perform the following steps:

1.  Log on to the Windows Server 2008 R2 system with an account with administrator privileges.
2.  Click Start, click All Programs, click Administrative Tools, and select Local Security Policy.
3.  In the tree pane, double-click on Local Policies, and double-click on Audit Policy.
4.  In the tasks pane, double-click on Audit Object Access.
5.  When the Audit Object Access Properties window opens, check the Failure check box, and click OK, as shown in Figure 31.2.

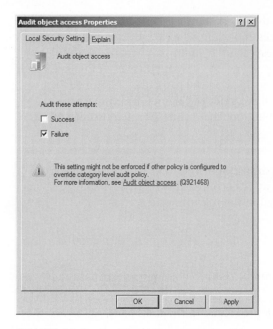

FIGURE 31.2    Enabling failure audit for object access.

6. Close the Local Security Policy window.

7. Click Start and click on Computer.

8. Browse to the drive and folder on which you will enable auditing; for this example, use the c:\HumanResources folder.

9. Right-click the folder and select Properties.

10. Select the Security tab and click the Advanced button near the bottom of the window.

11. Select the Auditing tab and click the Edit button to enable audit changes.

12. In this particular example, we want to log failed attempts to access the folder, so we will use the Everyone group and enable all failure audits. Click the Add button in the Advanced Security Settings window for the HumanResources folder.

13. When the Select User, Computer, Service Account, or Group window opens, type in Everyone and click OK.

14. In the Auditing Entry window for everyone, check the Failed check box next to Full Control, check the box at the bottom of the window to apply the Audit policy to all objects contained within the HumanResources folder, and click OK, as shown in Figure 31.3.

15. In the Advanced Security Settings window, check the Replace All Existing Inheritable Auditing Entries check box, and click OK.

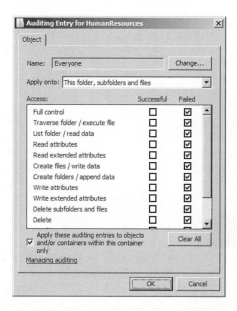

FIGURE 31.3    Configuring an audit entry for the HumanResources NTFS folder.

**16.** Click OK again to close the Advanced Security Settings window, and then click OK one more time to close the property pages of the HumanResources folder.

When a user attempts to access the HumanResources folder and fails based on permissions, a failed audit entry will be logged on the server in the Security event log.

**Validating Permissions on NTFS Folders**    When permissions seem to be configured correctly but an end user still cannot properly access a folder or file within a folder because of group membership or some other factor, perform the following steps:

**1.** Log on to the Windows Server 2008 R2 system with an account with administrator privileges.

**2.** Click Start and click on Computer.

**3.** Browse to the drive and folder on which you will validate the end user's permission. For this example, use the c:\HumanResources folder and check permissions for a user named Khalil Droubi.

**4.** Right-click the folder and select Properties.

**5.** Select the Security tab and click the Advanced button near the bottom of the window.

**6.** Select the Effective Permissions tab, and click the Select button to add the end user.

**7.** In the Select User, Computer, or Group window, type in the end user's name, and click OK. For this example, use Khalil Droubi.

8. On the Effective Permissions tab, the resulting permissions will be displayed, as shown in Figure 31.4. This example displays that Khalil Droubi only has Read permissions and cannot create files or folders.

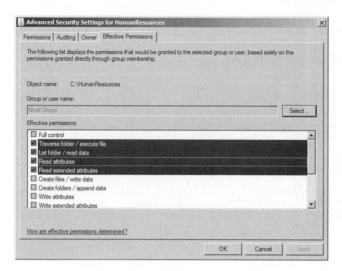

FIGURE 31.4    Display the effective permissions on a folder for a specific end user.

### Application Access Troubleshooting

If the issue revolves around an application running on a Windows Server 2008 R2 system, troubleshooting the application according to the application administration guide is the recommended approach. Many applications can be configured to use authentication using Active Directory via LDAP, Kerberos, or NTLM authentication. Also, applications might use custom application or database user accounts and might still require NTFS permissions via application pool identities and service accounts. Each application is different and should be treated as such. Specific troubleshooting guides and backup and recovery documentation should be created for applications before they are deployed on a network.

## Data Corruption and File and Folder Recovery

When data is reported as corrupted or deleted, administrators have the option of restoring the data from backup using Windows Server Backup or Shadow Copies for Shared Folders. An alternative to simply restoring a corrupted file from a shadow copy or backup, the CHKDSK tool can be run on a disk if multiple users are reporting issues or if disk errors have been reported in the System event log. CHKDSK is a utility that will scan a disk for file corruption and bad sectors. If any errors are found, repair attempts will be made and the details will be available in the Completed Status window. When data has been overwritten or deleted, the only options are to recover from shadow copies or from backup media.

### Recovering File and Folder Data Using Shadow Copies

To recover individual files and folders using previously created shadow copies of shared folders, perform the following steps:

1. Log on to a Windows Server 2008 R2 system, Windows XP SP1, or later workstation with either administrator rights or with a user account that has permissions to restore the files from the shadow copy.

2. Click Start and select Run or type in the server and share name in the search pane.

3. At the Run prompt or search pane, type \\servername\sharename, where *servername* represents the NetBIOS or fully qualified domain name of the server hosting the file share. The share must exist on a volume in which a shadow copy has already been created.

4. Right-click the folder that will be restored or the folder that contains the file or folder that will be restored, and select Restore Previous Versions.

5. When the window opens, if necessary, select the Previous Versions tab, and select the particular folder version to be restored.

6. After the folder or file is selected, click Open.

7. An Explorer window then opens, displaying the contents of the folder when the shadow copy was made. If you want to restore only a single file, locate the file, right-click it, and select Copy.

8. Open the server share location in which the restored file will be placed, right-click in an empty location, and choose Paste. Overwrite the file as required and close all the windows as desired.

### Recovering File and Folder Data Using Windows Server Backup

To recover individual files and folders using backup media created with Windows Server Backup, perform the following steps:

1. Log on to the Windows Server 2008 R2 system with an account with administrator privileges.

2. Click Start, click All Programs, click Administrative Tools, and select Windows Server Backup.

3. In the Actions pane, select Recover to start the Recovery Wizard.

4. On the Getting Started page, select either to restore data previously backed up from the local computer or a different computer. For this example, select This Server (Servername), and click Next to continue. If no previous backup was performed using a local disk, choose a different disk and locate the backup folder, which will be scanned and will present all available backups for any system that stored a backup in that folder.

5. On the next page, select the date of the backup by selecting the correct month and click on the particular day.

6. After the month and day are selected, if multiple backups were run in a single day, click the Time drop-down list arrow, and select the correct backup, as shown in Figure 31.5. Click Next to continue after the month, day, and time are selected.

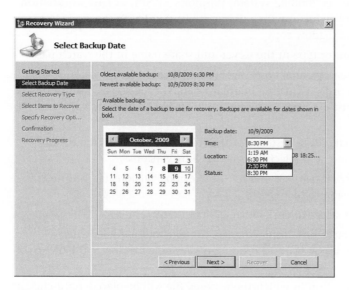

FIGURE 31.5    Selecting the correct backup.

7. On the Select Recovery Type page, select the Files and Folders option button, and click Next to continue.

8. On the Select Items to Recover page, expand the server node; select the disks, folders, and files to be restored; and click Next to continue.

> **NOTE**
>
> Unlike other backup utilities, Windows Server Backup does not contain check boxes to select items for recovery. To select an item or multiple items, simply click on the item to highlight it and use the Shift or Ctrl keys to make multiple sections.

9. On the Specify Recovery Options page, specify whether the files will be restored to the original location or an alternate location. Do not click Next.

10. On the Specify Recovery Options page, if the restore will be placed in the original location, specify how to deal with existing files by choosing to either create copies in the same folder, overwrite the existing data with restore data, or do not recover items that already exist, as shown in Figure 31.6.

11. On the Confirmation page, verify the restore selections and options. If everything is correct, click the Recover button to start the recovery process.

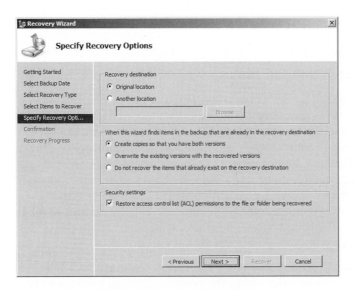

FIGURE 31.6   Selecting the restore options.

**12.** On the Recovery Progress page, verify the success of the recovery or troubleshoot the errors if the recovery fails.

**13.** Click Close to complete the recovery and close Windows Server Backup.

**14.** Browse to the location of the restore to verify the recovery, and if the create copies option was selected, notice that there are two copies: the original and the restored, which is named after the date and time the backup was taken. When you are finished, log off of the server.

# Managing and Accessing Windows Server Backup Media

Microsoft has completely changed the way backups and backup media are managed with the release of Windows Server 2008. In previous editions of Windows Server versions, the NT Backup utility could back up the entire system or just a set of folders and files. The backup could be stored on tapes or they could be stored in a single .bkf file that is saved on a local disk or on a network shared folder. Starting with Windows Server Backup for Windows Server 2008 and Windows Vista, backups can be taken of only the entire system or volumes but not of granular folders or files. With Windows Server 2008 R2, Windows Server Backup supports backing up individual files and folders, and exclusions can be added to backup jobs as well. Windows Server Backup can store backups on dedicated locally attached disks on a DVD disk or a set of disks, or the backup can be stored on a network shared folder.

Windows Server Backup can be configured to run a scheduled backup or a manual backup. Either can be run from the graphical user interface or the command-line utility, but the backup options, including where the backup can be stored and the recovery options available, are different.

## Windows Server Backup Managed Disks

Windows Server Backup can be used to run a manual backup or it can be used to run a scheduled backup. Scheduled backups can be stored on locally attached disks that are dedicated to Windows Server Backup, a folder on a local volume, or a network shared folder. When a scheduled Windows Server Backup job is created, the administrator can define which locally attached disks, folder, or network share will be used to store the backups. During the creation of the scheduled job, if dedicated disks are selected, which is recommended, the allocated disks will each be repartitioned and reformatted. Windows Server Backup will stamp the disk volume to match the time and date the scheduled job is created. By default, this disk will only be available on the local system through the Windows Server Backup program.

A Windows Server Backup disk can have a drive letter added after the initial backup is created if the disk needs to be accessed from within the operating system, from across the network, or if the backup data needs to be copied to additional disks or network folders for offsite storage. Although adding a drive letter to a dedicated Windows Server Backup disk is not recommended, it might be the only way or the most efficient way to make the backup media available to an alternate system if the disk cannot be locally attached to the alternate system. Getting access to this backup data, however, might prove to be challenging from Windows Explorer and might need to be accessed through Windows Server Backup. Backups contained on a Windows Server Backup dedicated disk can be used to restore an entire system, an entire volume, or a set of specified files and folders.

## DVD Media

When Windows Server 2008 R2 systems have a local DVD writer drive, which is highly recommended, backups of Windows volumes and the complete system can be stored on DVD media. Backups stored on DVD media will span several DVDs and can be used when data needs to be restored to offsite servers or systems in an isolated network. Backups stored on DVD media can only be used to restore the entire Windows system or entire volumes. Selective restore of files and folders cannot be performed using DVD backup media.

## Network Shared Folders

When Windows Server Backup is configured to back up to a network shared folder, backup administrators need to consider a few things. First, the share and NTFS permissions should be configured so that only backup administrators and specific service accounts can access and read this data. Also, if this share contains data that will be replicated by a third-party provider, special permissions might need to be added to support this. Another very important point to note about network shared folders for Windows Server Backup is that only the most recent copy of the backup will be stored there because each backup overwrites the previous. This is unlike backup to dedicated disks, which can store multiple versions and copies of a Windows Server 2008 R2 system backup.

# Windows Server Backup Volume Recovery

When an entire disk or disk volume has been corrupted or has failed and needs to be replaced and recovered, Windows Server Backup can be used to restore the disk or volume. Local disks, local folder backups, network backups, and DVD backups can be used to restore an entire volume using Windows Server Backup. When an entire volume needs to be recovered, unless the volume contains system data, the volume can be restored using the Windows Server Backup program from within a running operating system. If the volume contains system folders, the restore needs to be restored using the Repair Your Computer option when booting the system using the Windows installation media.

## Windows Server 2008 R2 Data Volume Recovery

When a data volume on a Windows Server 2008 R2 system has failed and needs to be restored using Windows Server Backup, perform the following steps:

1. Log on to the Windows Server 2008 R2 system with an account with administrator privileges.

2. Click Start, click All Programs, click Administrative Tools, and select Windows Server Backup.

3. In the Actions pane, select Recover to start the Recovery Wizard.

4. On the Getting Started page, select either to restore data previously backed up from the local computer or a different computer. For this example, select This Server (Servername), where *Servername* is the name of the server Windows Server Backup is connected to, and click Next to continue.

5. On the Select Backup Date page, select the correct date and time of the backup you will use to restore the data, and click Next to continue. Days with a successful backup are formatted in boldface.

6. On the Select Recovery Type page, select the Volumes option button, and click Next to continue.

7. On the Select Volumes page, the window displays each of the volumes contained in the backup that was previously chosen. Check the box next to the desired volume that will be restored, and select the destination volume to which you will restore the backed up volume. Figure 31.7 displays that the backed-up G: volume will be restored to the existing G volume; click Next to continue after the correct selections are made.

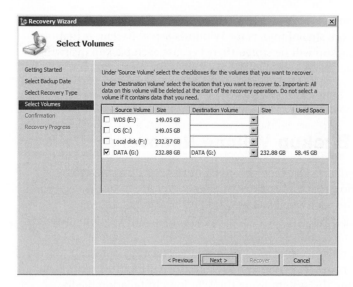

FIGURE 31.7    Selecting the source and destination volumes for volume recovery.

8.  After clicking Next on the Select Volumes page, a window opens, requesting confirmation that the data on the volume(s) will be lost by the recovery process; click Yes to continue with the volume recovery process.

9.  On the Confirmation page, review the selections. If everything looks correct, click the Recover button to start the volume recovery.

10. On the Recovery Progress page, the recovery status of the volume will be displayed. After the recovery completes, review the results and click Close if the recovery was successful; otherwise, select the Errors tab to review the errors.

11. If the volume recovery was successful, the only additional step that might be required is to reboot the system if the data on the volume is shared or used by any applications or services. Reboot as required.

## Windows Server 2008 R2 System Volume Recovery

Restoring a system volume cannot be performed using Windows Server Backup. System volumes can only be restored using the Windows recovery environment from the Windows installation media. System volumes should only be restored separately when the system volume is corrupted or failed but the system hardware has not changed and data disks remain intact. Any Windows disk that contains system volumes will be erased and restored as part of this process. If a single disk contains two volumes including the system volume and a separate data volume, the data volume will also be erased and restored by this process. To restore the system volume, perform the following steps:

1.  Boot up your system using the Windows Server 2008 R2 installation media. If necessary, configure the BIOS to allow booting from the CD/DVD drive and, if prompted, press a key to boot from the DVD.

2. When the Install Windows interface opens, select the correct language, time, and keyboard settings, and click Next to continue.

3. On the next page, click the Repair Your Computer link located in the lower-left corner of the window.

4. On the System Recovery Options page, the operating system drive that will be recovered should be listed. If not, click the Load Drivers button, and install the necessary hard drive controller files. If the system is listed, select the Restore Your Computer Using a System Image That You Created Earlier option button located at the bottom of the window, and click Next to continue.

5. On the Select a System Image Backup page, if a local disk was used for the backup, the most recent backup will be listed and the Use the Latest Available System Image check box will be automatically selected by default. Select the Select a System Image option button and click Next to continue.

6. The next page presents the list of backups stored on the local dedicated backup disk. Select the desired backup and click Next to continue.

> **NOTE**
>
> If no local backup disks exist, the administrator can select to use a different backup and can then click the Advanced button to enable the network and connect to a network shared folder that contains a valid backup, as detailed in the next section of this chapter.

7. The following page lists which volumes are contained within the known backups. Select the desired backup again and click Next to continue.

8. On the Choose Additional Restore Options page, check the Only Restore System Drives check box, and click Next to continue. This leaves any other disks intact, but any volumes that are hosted on the same disks that contain system volumes will be formatted, re-created, and restored as well.

9. The next page details the date and time of the backup that will be restored, the server that will be restored, and the volumes that are contained in this restore set. Review the information and click Finish to continue with the recovery of the system volumes.

10. A dialog box appears, stating that all drives selected will be restored with the data in the system image; click Yes to approve this and continue.

11. The recovery time frame will vary depending on the size of the system volume, the performance of the volume, and the restore disk or network share. After the recovery completes, the system will automatically reboot.

12. After the system reboots, log on and verify functionality. If everything is back up and running, run a full backup and log off.

## System Volume Recovery Using Network Shared Folder Backups

If the backup data is stored on a network shared folder, alternate recovery steps are required to restore the system volume. If recovering a system volume from a network shared folder, perform the following steps:

1. Boot up your system using the Windows Server 2008 R2 installation media. If necessary, configure the BIOS to allow booting from the CD/DVD drive and, if prompted, press a key to boot from the DVD.

2. When the Install Windows interface opens, select the correct language, time, and keyboard settings, and click Next to continue.

3. On the next page, click the Repair Your Computer link located in the lower-left corner of the window.

4. On the System Recovery Options page, the operating system drive that will be recovered should be listed. If not, click the Load Drivers button, and install the necessary hard drive controller files. If the system is listed, select the Restore Your Computer Using a System Image That You Created Earlier option button located at the bottom of the window, and click Next to continue.

5. If there is no local backup disk or volume, an error window will appear; click Cancel. On the Select a System Image Backup page, click the Select a System Image option button and click Next.

6. On the Select the Location page, click the Advanced button.

7. In the pop-up window, click on the Search for a System Image on the Network button and confirm that you want to connect to the network and understand the security implications.

8. Enter the UNC path to the network shared folder and click OK. When prompted, enter the appropriate network credentials to access the backup folder.

9. Once connected, the window will list the backup stored on the specified network folder. Select this backup and click Next to continue.

10. The following page lists which volumes are contained within the known backups. Select the desired backup again and click Next to continue.

11. On the Choose Additional Restore Options page, check the Only Restore System Drives check box, and click Next to continue. This leaves any other disks intact, but any volumes that are hosted on the same disks that contain system volumes will be formatted, re-created, and restored as well.

12. The next page details the date and time of the backup that will be restored, the server that will be restored, and the volumes that are contained in this restore set. Review the information and click Finish to continue with the recovery of the system volumes.

13. A dialog box appears stating that all drives selected will be restored with the data in the system image; click Yes to approve this and continue.

14. The recovery time frame will vary depending on the size of the system volume, the performance of the volume, and the restore disk or network share. After the recovery completes, the system will automatically reboot.

15. After the system reboots, log on and verify functionality. If everything is back up and running, run a full backup and log off.

### Windows Complete PC Restore

In the event of a complete system failure, it might be necessary to restore a Windows Server 2008 R2 system in its entirety. If this is the case, perform the same steps as a system volume recovery, except on the Choose Additional Restore Options page, check the Format and Repartition Disks check box and uncheck the Only Restore System Drives check box. This restores all of the disks and also performs the disk partitioning, drive letter assignment, and mounted volume configuration. If different size disks are provided, the restore only partitions the disks based on the original size of the disk volumes. Smaller disks cause the restore to fail, but larger disks can easily be extended after the recovery completes successfully.

### Complete PC Restore to Alternate Hardware

Microsoft does not officially support recovering Windows Server 2008 R2 systems to alternate hardware. However, recovering a Windows Server 2008 R2 system to different hardware can be accomplished—but it can be a very challenging and painful task. As a best practice recommendation, if an organization has not or cannot standardize on server hardware platforms or if systems will be used in production even when the hardware is at its end of life or maintenance on a system has expired—consider moving critical physical systems to virtual servers.

When a system is migrated to a virtual server, migrating or restoring that system to an alternate host running on different hardware is fairly straightforward and simple, as long as the different host systems run the same version of the virtualization host software. Configuration files and disks created in Virtual PC 2007 or Virtual Server 2005 R2 will move right over into Windows 2008 or Windows Server 2008 R2 Hyper-V virtualization, but importing or restoring systems from alternate third-party virtualization software might not work. If moving virtual systems between platforms is required, System Center Virtual Machine Manager provides some functionality in this area. If virtualizing servers is on the company road map, it is highly recommended to review the Hyper-V virtualization functionality of Windows Server 2008 R2 as well as Microsoft Systems Center Virtual Machine Manager. For more information about Microsoft virtualization solutions, see Chapter 37, "Deploying and Using Windows Virtualization."

## Recovering Role Services and Features

Each particular role on a Windows Server 2008 R2 system can have very specific backup and recovery procedures. As a general rule, though, performing full backups using Windows Server 2008 R2 Windows Server Backup will enable the restore of a system to a previous point in time, including restoring all Windows Server roles, role services, features, and configuration to that previously backed-up state. Most role services can be restored using a System State recovery; however, a System State recovery cannot be restored in part—only the complete System State can be restored.

## Windows Server 2008 R2 System State Recovery

When operating systems become corrupt or unstable or a role service needs to be rolled back to a previously backed-up state, the quickest and easiest way to perform this task is to restore the System State. The System State can be backed up independently but is also contained within a full server backup. To restore the System State on a Member Server from a previous backup, perform the following steps:

1. Log on to the Windows Server 2008 R2 system with an account with administrator privileges.

2. Click Start, click All Programs, click Administrative Tools, and select Windows Server Backup.

3. In the Actions pane, select Recover to start the Recovery Wizard.

4. On the Getting Started page, select either to restore data previously backed up from the local computer or a different computer. For this example, select This Server (*Servername*), where *Servername* is the name of the server Windows Server Backup is connected to, and click Next to continue.

5. On the Select Backup Date page, select the correct date and time of the backup you will use to restore the data, and click Next to continue. Days with a successful backup are formatted in boldface.

6. On the Select Recovery Type page, select the System State option button, and click Next to continue.

7. On the Select Location for System State Recovery page, click the Original Location option button and click Next to continue. If this system was a domain controller, more options would be available, but that is covered later in this chapter.

8. On the Confirmation page, review the section and ensure that the check box to automatically reboot the server to complete the recovery process is checked, and then click Recover to start the process.

9. After the system reboots, log on to the server to verify functionality. If the system is working properly, perform a full system backup.

## Active Directory Recycle Bin Recovery

Let's begin this section with a very clear statement: If you need to recover a deleted Active Directory object and the Active Directory Recycle Bin was not enabled before the object was deleted, skip this section and proceed to the "Active Directory Authoritative Restore" section. Now if the Active Directory Recycle Bin feature was enabled before an Active Directory object was deleted, follow the proceeding steps to recover objects using the

Active Directory Recycle Bin. Before completing the following steps, you should know a few important things:

▶ Restoring a deleted object using the Recycle Bin requires that the object's distinguished name or object GUID is known.

▶ When restoring an object, the object will be restored into the original location, unless the -TargetPath option is used. If the original location does not exist, the restore will fail.

▶ Restoring a container or organizational unit using the Restore-ADObject cmdlet does not restore any objects that were contained within the container or OU when it was deleted. For this functionality, either all objects need to be restored after the container or OU is restored or a domain controller can be booted into DSRM and an authoritative restore can be performed using the Restore Subtree option.

Now, if you know that an object was mistakenly deleted and it should be recovered, the following steps can be followed. For this example, we will restore a user account named Khalil Droubi. To discover the properties of this deleted object, we will use the Get-ADObject cmdlet and will filter based on the name of Khalil. Also, when running the Get-AdObject cmdlet, using the -properties switch will expand the attributes listed for the query or search results. To restore a single deleted user object, perform the following steps:

1. Log on to the Windows Server 2008 R2 domain controller system with an account with domain administrator privileges.

2. Click Start, click All Programs, click Accessories, click the Windows PowerShell folder, right-click on Windows PowerShell, and select Run As Administrator.

3. Type `cd \` and press Enter.

4. Type `Import-Module ActiveDirectory` and press Enter.

5. Type `Get-Command *AD* -CommandType cmdlet` and press Enter. This returns all of the Active Directory-related cmdlets and also returns a few more cmdlets not related to Active Directory.

6. Type `Get-ADObject -Searchbase "CN=Deleted Objects,DC=Companyabc,DC=com" -Filter * -IncludeDeletedObjects` and press Enter. This returns all of the deleted Active Directory objects on the local domain controller in the companyabc.com domain to the PowerShell window with a default list of attributes.

7. Because we are trying to restore a deleted user account named Khalil Droubi, we can filter the previous command by typing `Get-AdObject -Searchbase"CN=Deleted Objects,DC=Company,DC=com" -LdapFilter "Name=*Khalil*" -IncludeDeletedObjects` and pressing Enter. This command returns all of the deleted objects that contain Khalil in the name.

8. As stated previously, if the deleted object will be restored to the original location, as is the case with a default `Restore-ADObject` command, the parent OU or container must be present. To determine the parent container of the deleted user object, type `Get-AdObject -Searchbase"CN=Deleted Objects,DC=Company,DC=com" -LdapFilter "Name=*Khalil*" -IncludeDeletedObjects -Properties LastknownParent` and then press Enter.

9. When the `LastKnownParent` property value is returned, if the value returns a proper distinguished name, it exists. If the name includes CN=Deleted Objects in the value, the parent OU or container has also been deleted. If the LastKnownParent has been deleted, it either needs to be restored before the deleted user object or the user object needs to be restored to an alternate location using the `-TargetPath` option in the Restore-ADObject cmdlet.

10. Assuming that the LastKnownParent value returns an existing container to restore the object, copy the ObjectGUID of the deleted user account to the Clipboard, type `Restore-ADObject -Identity` and paste the ObjectGUID, and press Enter to restore the object, as shown in Figure 31.8.

FIGURE 31.8 Restoring a deleted Active Directory user object from the AD Recycle Bin using the Restore-ADObject cmdlet.

## System State Recovery for Domain Controllers

Performing a System State recovery for a domain controller is similar to the recovery of a member server, but a few more options are presented during the selection process and the domain controller needs to be booted into Directory Services Restore mode. Recovering the System State of a domain controller should only be performed if objects were deleted from Active Directory and need to be restored and the Active Directory Recycle Bin is not enabled, or if the Active Directory database on the particular domain controller is corrupt and the Active Directory Domain Services service will not start properly, or if data in the SYSVOL is missing or corrupted and needs recovery.

Before a domain controller can be booted into DSRM, the DSRM password will be required. This password is configured when a system is promoted to a domain controller and is stored locally on each domain controller. The DSRM username is administrator with no domain designation and the password can manually be changed on a working domain controller by using the NTDSUTIL utility. To restore the System State of a domain controller, perform the following steps:

1. Log on to the Windows Server 2008 R2 domain controller system with an account with administrator privileges.

2. Click Start, click All Programs, click Administrative Tools, and select System Configuration.

3. Select the Boot tab. In the Boot Options section, check the Safe Boot check box, select the Active Directory Repair option button, as shown in Figure 31.9, and then click OK.

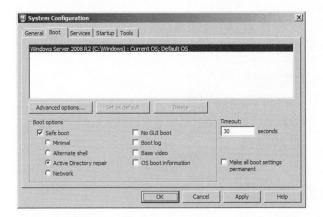

FIGURE 31.9    Using the System Configuration utility to boot a domain controller into Directory Services Restore mode.

4. The System Configuration utility will ask for a reboot, and if there are no additional tasks to perform, click the Restart button to boot the system into DSRM.

5. When the system completes a reboot, log on as administrator with the DSRM password. Make sure to specify the local server as the logon domain—for example, server10\administrator instead of companyabc\administrator.

6. Click Start, click All Programs, click Administrative Tools, and select Windows Server Backup.

7. In the Actions pane, select Recover to start the Recovery Wizard.

8. On the Getting Started page, select This Server (Servername), where *Servername* is the name of the server to which Windows Server Backup is connected, and click Next to continue.

9. On the Select Backup Date page, select the correct date and time of the backup you will use to restore the data, and click Next to continue. Days with a successful backup are formatted in boldface.

10. On the Select Recovery Type page, select the System State option button, and click Next to continue.

11. On the Select Location for System State Recovery page, select the Original Location option button. Do not check the Perform an Authoritative Restore of Active Directory Files check box unless the sysvol folder and content will be marked as the definitive/authoritative copy and replicated to all other domain controllers. For our example, we will recover the System State but not mark the SYSVOL as an authoritative restore, as shown in Figure 31.10. Click Next to continue.

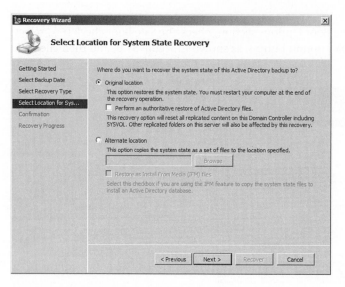

FIGURE 31.10    Restoring a domain controller System State without marking the sysvol data as authoritative.

12. A dialog box opens that states that this recovery option will cause the server to resynchronize after recovery; click OK to continue.

13. On the Confirmation page, verify that the System State is listed and that the check box to automatically reboot the server is not checked. Click Recover to start the System State recovery of the domain controller.

14. A dialog box opens, detailing that once the recovery is started, it cannot be paused, and a restart will be required to complete the recovery. Click Yes to start the recovery. System State recovery can take a long time to complete; please be patient.

15. Once the System State restore completes, even if the check box to automatically reboot is not checked, Windows Server Backup will present a dialog box with a Restart button and no other option. Restart the server now.

16. Once the server reboots, it will reboot into DSRM again. Log on with the DSRM local username and password.

17. Once logged in, a wbadmin command prompt opens, stating that the restore completed successfully. Close the command prompt.

18. Click Start, click All Programs, click Administrative Tools, and select System Configuration.

**19.** Select the Boot tab. In the Boot Options section, uncheck the Safe Boot check box and click OK.

**20.** If an authoritative restore of Active Directory objects is not required, click the Restart button in the dialog box and allow the server to reboot normally.

**21.** If an authoritative restore is required, click the Exit Without Restart button in the dialog box and perform the steps outlined in the "Active Directory Authoritative Restore" section.

### Active Directory Authoritative Restore

When Active Directory has been modified and needs to be restored to a previous state, and this rollback needs to be replicated to all domain controllers in the domain and possibly the forest, an authoritative restore of Active Directory is required. An authoritative restore of Active Directory can include the entire Active Directory database, a single object, or a container, such as an organizational unit including all objects previously stored within the container. To perform an authoritative restore of Active Directory, perform the System State restore of a domain controller, but when you are finished, reboot as directed and when the reboot completes follow these additional steps:

**1.** Open a command prompt on the domain controller that is running in DSRM and has just completed a System State recovery and a reboot.

**2.** In the Command Prompt window, type `NTDSUTIL` and press Enter.

**3.** Type `Activate Instance NTDS` and press Enter.

**4.** Type `Authoritative Restore` and press Enter.

**5.** To restore a single object, type `Restore Object` followed by the distinguished name of the previously deleted object. For example, to restore an object named Khalil Droubi in the Users container of the companyabc.com domain, type `Restore Object "cn=Khalil Droubi,cn=users,dc=companyabc,dc=com"`.

**6.** To restore a container or organizational unit and all objects beneath it, replace the "restore object" with "restore subtree" followed by the appropriate distinguished name.

**7.** After the appropriate command is typed in, press Enter. A window opens, asking for confirmation of the authoritative restore; click the Yes button to complete the authoritative restore of the object or subtree.

**8.** The NTDSUTIL tool displays the name of the text file that may contain any back-links for objects just restored. Note the name of the file(s) and whether any back-links were contained in the restored objects.

**9.** Type `quit` and press Enter; type `quit` again to close out of the NTDSUTIL tool.

**10.** Click the Restart button in the Windows Server Backup dialog box and reboot. Make sure to set the boot option back to normal boot if not changed previously.

**11.** After the domain controller reboots into normal boot mode, log on to verify that the authoritatively restored objects are replicating to the other domain controllers. If things are working properly, run a full backup of the domain controller and log off.

### Authoritative Restore Backlinks

When an object is authoritatively restored to Active Directory and if the object was previously a member of groups in other domains in an Active Directory forest, a file will be created that defines the restored object backlinks. A backlink is a reference to a cross-domain group membership. When an object that was previously deleted is authoritatively restored, the file can be used to update that object's group membership in the other domains that contain the groups in question. The NTDSUTIL, upon completion of the authoritative restore, will list the name of the file that contains the backlink information. This file can be copied over the domain controller in the different domains and can be processed by running the command ldifde -i -k -f FileName, where *FileName* represents the text file created by the NTDSUTIL authoritative restore.

### Restoring the Sysvol Folder

When a domain controller System State is restored, the SYSVOL is also restored to the point in time the backup was taken. If the SYSVOL that has replicated across the domain needs to be rolled back, an authoritative restore of the SYSVOL, known previously as a primary restore of SYSVOL, must be performed. To perform an authoritative restore of the SYSVOL, restore the System State of a domain controller using Windows Server Backup, as outlined in the previous section, "System State Recovery for Domain Controllers," but on the Select Location for System State Recovery page, check the Perform an Authoritative Restore of Active Directory Files check box. Follow the steps to recover the System State of the domain controller, and then boot the domain controller normally. Once the domain controller is returned to operation, the Active Directory database will sync with other domain controllers, but the SYSVOL of this particular domain controller will be pushed out to all other domain controllers in the domain as the authoritative copy and will overwrite the other copies. No other steps are required.

### Restoring Group Policies

When group policies need to be restored, performing a restore of the SYSVOL as well as the Active Directory database is required. Group Policy Object information is stored in a container in the domain-naming context partition called the Group Policy Objects container, and the files are stored in the sysvol folder on each domain controller. The most effective way to back up and restore group policies is to use the backup and restore features built in to the Group Policy Management Console included with Windows Server 2008 R2 Group Policy Management tools. For detailed information on how to back up and recover group policies using the Group Policy Management Console, refer to Chapter 19, "Windows Server 2008 R2 Group Policies and Policy Management."

## DHCP

In situations when DHCP services fail and need to be restored, the fastest recovery option is to restore the System State of the DHCP system. In many cases, however, DHCP services are not hosted on systems dedicated only to the DHCP service and the DHCP service will need to be recovered independently. The DHCP service itself when in a failed state will need to be investigated and repaired just like any other application or service. If only the configuration details of the DHCP server need to be restored and a previous backup was made, perform the following steps:

1. Log on to the Windows Server 2008 R2 DHCP server system with an account with administrator privileges.

2. Click Start, click All Programs, click Administrative Tools, and select DHCP.

3. Double-click on the DHCP server to initiate the connection in the console.

4. Right-click on the DHCP server in the tree pane, and select Restore.

5. When the Browse for Folder window opens, it defaults to the systemroot\System32\DHCP\Backup folder; click OK to accept this location and start the restore. If more recent backups have been created, they might be located in subfolders of the Backup folder.

6. A window opens, requiring confirmation to restart the DHCP service; click Yes to stop the DHCP service, restore the data, and restart the DHCP service.

7. After the restore completes, click OK on the window and then verify that the DHCP scopes and other data have been restored to the state when the backup was performed.

8. Log off of the DHCP server system.

## Windows SharePoint Services

When Windows SharePoint Services (WSS) is installed on Windows Server 2008 R2 using the default options, WSS stores configuration and content data in SQL databases on SQL servers or in databases included in the Windows Internal Database feature, which are essentially SQL databases with some limited functionality. When WSS databases need to be restored, this can be performed using the SharePoint 3.0 Central Administration Backup and Recovery Operations functions if a backup using this tool was previously performed. Restore of databases can also be performed using full system backups created using Windows Server Backup.

### Recovering WSS Data Using SharePoint 3.0 Central Administration

If a previous WSS backup was performed using the SharePoint 3.0 Central Administration tool, recovery can be performed using this tool as well. To recover WSS using a SharePoint 3.0 Central Administration backup, perform the following steps:

1. Log on to the Windows Server 2008 R2 Windows SharePoint Services server system with an account with administrator privileges.

2. Click Start, click All Programs, click Administrative Tools, and select SharePoint 3.0 Central Administration.

3. When the browser opens, if prompted, enter a username and password for an account with administrative privileges on the WSS server.

4. When the SharePoint 3.0 Central Administration website opens, select the Operations tab.

5. In the window, scroll down; on the right side, in the Backup and Restore section, click on the Restore from backup option.

6. Near the top of the window, enter the UNC network path of the backup, and click OK. For example, enter \\server30\wssbackup\ and click OK.

7. On the next page, select the desired backup by selecting the appropriate option button, and click the Continue Restore Process link.

8. On the next page, select the appropriate databases or components of the WSS farm that will be restored by checking the appropriate check boxes, and then click the Continue Restore Process link. For this example, the entire farm will be restored by clicking the check box next to Farm.

9. On the next page, in the Type of Restore section, select the Same Configuration option button because you are trying to restore an existing system back to a functional state. When this option button is selected, a window opens stating that the selected objects will be overwritten with the data from the restore; click OK to continue.

10. Scroll to the bottom of the page, and click OK to submit the restore job to the SharePoint Services Timer Service.

11. You will be directed to the Backup and Restore Status page. Click the Refresh link to view and get updates on the status of the job.

12. After the job completes, open the restored SharePoint sites and check functionality. IIS might need to be restarted, and if the system can tolerate a system reboot, it might be helpful in case other dependent services are not running because of SharePoint issues.

13. If WSS is restored back to normal operation, run a full backup and log off.

### Recovering WSS Databases Using Windows Server Backup

If full system backups have been run on systems running Windows SharePoint Services, because SharePoint and Windows Server Backup are both support and use the Volume Shadow Copy Service (VSS), the databases files can be used for restore purposes. To restore a Windows Internal Database for Windows SharePoint Services from a Windows Server full system backup, perform the following steps:

1. Log on to the Windows Server 2008 R2 system with an account with administrator privileges.

2. Click Start, click All Programs, click Administrative Tools, and select Internet Information Services (IIS manager).

3. Double-click on the server in the tree pane, and double-click on Sites.

4. Locate the WSS site that will be restored, right-click the site, choose Manage Web Site, and click Stop. This stops the website. Leave IIS Manager open.

5. Click Start, click All Programs, click Administrative Tools, and select Services.

6. Locate the Windows SharePoint Services Timer Service, right-click the service, and select Stop.

7. Scroll up and locate the Windows Internal Database (MICROSOFT##SSEE) service, right-click the service, and select Stop. Leave the services console open.

8. Click Start, click All Programs, click Administrative Tools, and select Windows Server Backup.

9. In the Actions pane, select Recover to start the Recovery Wizard.

10. On the Getting Started page, select either to restore data previously backed up from the local computer or a different computer. For this example, select This Server (Servername), and click Next to continue.

11. On the next page, select the date of the backup by selecting the correct month and click on the particular day.

12. After the month and day are selected, if multiple backups were run in a single day, click the Time drop-down list arrow, and select the correct backup.

13. On the Select Recovery Type page, select the Files and Folders option button and click Next to continue.

14. On the Select Items to Recover page, expand the server node; select the disks, folders, and files to be restored; and click Next to continue. For example, select the c:\windows\SYSMSI\SSEE\MSSQL.2005\MSSQL\Data\WSS_Content.MDF and WSS_Content_log.LDF, as shown in Figure 31.11.

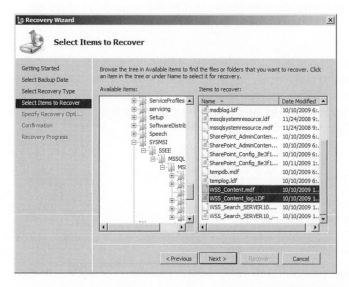

FIGURE 31.11    Selecting the WSS_content database and log files for restore.

15. On the Specify Recovery Options page, specify whether the files will be restored to the original location or an alternate location. Do not click Next.

16. On the Specify Recovery Options page, choose to recover the files to the original location and choose to overwrite the existing versions with the recovered versions. Ensure that the check box to restore access control list permissions is checked and click Next to continue.

17. On the Confirmation page, verify the restore selections and options. If everything is correct, click the Recover button to start the recovery process.

18. On the Recovery Progress page, verify the success of the recovery or troubleshoot the errors if the recovery fails.

19. Click Close to complete the recovery and close Windows Server Backup.

20. Open the Services window and start the Windows Internal Database Service and start the Windows SharePoint Services Timer Service. Close the Services console.

21. Open the IIS Manager console, locate the SharePoint site, right-click the site, choose Manage Web Site, and click Start to start the website.

22. Open a web browser and connect to the SharePoint site. If everything looks okay, perform a full backup of the system.

## Summary

This chapter covered many aspects of recovery with regard to Windows Server 2008 R2. Administrators and IT managers responsible for disaster recovery tasks, including planning and execution, should test all plans regularly to ensure that in the event of a failure, the critical systems and most important data are backed up, and can be recovered properly and efficiently.

Many technologies and solutions built in to Windows Server 2008 R2 were covered in this chapter to provide readers with useful recovery processes for Windows Server Backup or Shadow Copies to recover data and systems. Also covered were the tasks involved in creating the recovery plan, testing it, and making sure that what you think will happen in a recovery process actually can happen through tested procedures.

## Best Practices

The following are best practices from this chapter:

▶ Document all backup and recovery procedures.

▶ Periodically test the restore procedures to verify accuracy and test the backup media to ensure that data can actually be recovered.

▶ Validate reported system failures before attempting to restore data or fix an issue.

▶ Allocate the appropriate hardware devices, including servers with enough processing power and disk space to accommodate the restored machines' resources.

▶ Store a copy of all disaster recovery documentation and copies of dedicated Windows Server Backup disks at secure offsite locations.

▶ Understand the dependencies of the applications and services to the operating system to choose whether to rebuild or restore from backup.

▶ Identify and document special restore requirements for each server.

▶ If an organization has not or cannot standardize on server hardware platforms or if systems will be used in production even when the hardware is at its end of life or the maintenance on a system has expired—consider moving critical physical systems to virtual servers.

▶ When planning for recovery scenarios, ensure that a proper chain of communication is established to allow the technical staff to focus on their tasks and not be inundated with requests for status updates.

# CHAPTER 32

# Optimizing Windows Server 2008 R2 for Branch Office Communications

Today's organizations are likely to consist of many branch offices. On average, a branch office is a small office hosting fewer than 50 employees in a remote location. Typically, a branch office infrastructure is connected to the headquarters site, centralized data center, or hub site by means of a wide area network (WAN) link in a distributed fashion. Due to the high costs associated with purchasing bandwidth, these WAN links are usually slow, unreliable, and inefficient. Finally, most branch offices lack physical security and IT support personnel.

For many organizations, maintaining branch offices generates significant operational costs and administrative challenges. Two scenarios exist when dealing with branch offices because of the high costs of securing high-speed links between the branch office and hub site. Either the organization implements server infrastructure at the branch office or IT services are provided to the branch office from a centralized site such as the company headquarters.

By providing branch offices with their own infrastructure productivity increases; however, operational and management costs typically rise. When providing services to a branch office from a centralized site, its productivity is reduced as all branch office users must obtain services over a slow and unreliable WAN link. In addition, if the WAN link becomes unavailable, productivity at the branch office can come to a halt until the WAN link is repaired. As you can see, each scenario has cost and efficiency trade-offs.

Challenges like the one just described might, however, become a thing of the past for branch offices. Windows Server 2008 R2 provides new technology solutions that allow organizations to integrate branch offices seamlessly

into the organization's infrastructure. This chapter covers the use of built-in Windows
Server 2008 R2 technologies that help improve the operations, management, administration, and support for branch offices in any organization. In particular, this chapter
includes the implementation and use of Read-Only Domain Controllers, the use of two-
state domain controller (DC) promotion, an introduction to DFS read-only replicated
folders, and the ability to configure administrative role separation. Also covered in this
chapter is information enabling BitLocker Drive Encryption, BranchCache, and the latest
technologies, which improve WAN utilization between branch offices and hub sites.

# Understanding Read-Only Domain Controllers (RODCs)

One of the new features that received close attention in Windows Server 2008 was a new
breed of domain controllers referred to as Read-Only Domain Controllers, also known as
RODCs. The RODC hosts a copy of the Active Directory (AD) database like any other
writable domain controller, but as its name implies, the contents replica of the domain
database residing on the domain controller is read-only and write operations are not
supported. It is equally important to mention that the RODCs do not participate in Active
Directory replication in the same fashion as writable domain controllers. The fundamental
difference between RODC replication and the typical multimaster replication model
between writable domain controllers is that RODC replication is unidirectional. This
means all changes from a writable domain controller are propagated to the RODCs. As a
result, the RODC receives changes, but does not partake in or perform outbound replication with other domain controllers. This characteristic of RODCs provides an extra layer
of security as any unauthorized data changes, especially changes made with the intent to
hurt the organization, will not replicate out to other domain controllers. Unidirectional
replication also reduces the workload of bridgehead servers in the hub site and the effort
required to monitor replication.

Another new RODC functionality that improves security is commonly witnessed when
replication transpires between a writable domain controller and an RODC. Here, user
account information is replicated, but account passwords are not replicated. This is a new
phenomenon because of the existence of Windows domain controllers. Security is
bolstered in this situation as the only password that resides on the RODC is the local
administrator's password and Krbtgt accounts (the account used for Kerberos authentication). In essence, the read-only philosophy of an RODC is similar to the NT 4.0 Backup
Domain Controller (BDC); however, with the NT 4.0 BDC, all user information is replicated from the Primary Domain Controller (PDC), including passwords.

---

**NOTE**

If needed, it is also possible to configure credential caching of passwords for a specific
user account to an RODC. Moreover, by default, security groups with high privileges
such as Domain Administrators and Enterprise Administrators are configured to never
allow their passwords to replicate to RODCs.

---

Although Microsoft fields numerous questions on this new Active Directory technology, the question that is asked the most is where does the RODC fit in? RODCs are most often used to provide Active Directory Domain Services (AD DS) to remote locations and branch offices where heightened security is essential, where Windows Active Directory administrators are lacking, and where the promise of physical security is practically nonexistent. In many cases, RODCs offer a practical headache-free solution for branch office environments that in the past had to endure solutions that always put them in compromising situations.

## Organizations' Branch Office Concerns and Dilemmas

The next section illustrates typical branch office concerns about having domain controllers onsite. This section makes it evident why the RODC is becoming popular if not extremely necessary for branch offices.

### Lack of Physical Security at the Branch Office

Typically, branch office locations do not have the facilities to host a data center. For that reason, it is common to find domain controllers hiding in closets, tucked away in the kitchen next to the fridge, or even in a restroom. As such, branch offices lack physical security when it comes to storing domain controllers, which results in these servers being prime targets for thieves.

### Domain Controllers Stolen from the Branch Office

With inadequate physical security in the branch offices, it was very common for domain controllers to be stolen. This posed a major security threat to organizations because domain controllers contain a copy of all the user accounts associated with the domain. Confidential items such as highly privileged administrator accounts, DNS records, and the Active Directory schema could fall into the hands of the wrong people in this situation.

### Removing Domain Controllers from the Branch Office

Because of a lack of physical security and concerns over domain controller theft, branch offices often had their domain controllers removed from their site. After being removed, users were forced to authenticate over the WAN to a domain controller residing at their corporate headquarters or to the closest hub site. Although this action solved the security issue, it also cultivated a new problem. If the WAN link between the branch office and hub site was unreliable or unavailable, users could not log on to the workstations at the branch office or the amount of time required to log on was greatly increased. This resulted in a loss of productivity for users in the branch office or outages that resulted in downtime if the WAN link was severed. These types of outages commonly lasted for days.

### Lack of Administration Role Separation at the Branch Office

In small branch offices, it is also very common for multiple server functions to be hosted on a single server to reduce costs. For example, a single server might provide domain controller, file, print, messaging, and other line-of-business (LOB) functionality. In such cases, it is necessary for the administrators of these applications to log on to the system to manage their applications. By granting administrators privileges to the domain controller, these individuals also received full access to the Active Directory domain, which is considered to be a major security risk.

### Lack of IT Support Personnel at the Branch Office

It is very common for secretaries, receptionists, or even high-level personnel such as managers and directors without any prior knowledge of IT management or maintenance to manage servers in a branch office. Typically, these individuals get nominated or promoted to a branch office IT support role because a local IT administrator does not exist. Unfortunately, even when conducting basic administration tasks like restarting an unresponsive server, these individuals can inadvertently wreak havoc on the Active Directory domain when granted administrator privileges on a domain controller. In a Windows Server 2003 environment, there was little that could be done about this situation. You just had to be careful about who you promoted to the exclusive club of domain administrators.

## Understanding When to Leverage RODCs

As you can see, branch offices were faced with numerous challenges. Because of the many features of RODCs, however, branch offices can now have domain controllers on site without compromising security.

The main benefits of running RODC in branch offices are associated with the following:

▶ Read-only Active Directory Domain Services

▶ Reduced replication workload over the network

▶ Credential caching

▶ Administrator role separation

▶ Read-Only DNS

▶ Read-Only SYSVOL

These features of RODCs, which are discussed in detail in the following sections, assist in alleviating concerns and dilemmas for organizations.

### Read-Only Active Directory Domain Services

Poor physical security is typically the most common rationale for deploying an RODC at a branch office. A read-only copy of the domain controller provides fast and reliable authentication, while simultaneously protecting against data loss in the event the server is compromised or stolen. Because no changes can originate from an RODC, a malicious hacker or IT support personnel with little knowledge of Active Directory administration cannot make changes at the branch level. On a writable domain controller, not only can changes be made, but these changes would propagate to all other domain controllers, eventually damaging or polluting the Active Directory domain and forest.

### Reduced Replication Workload over the Network

As mentioned earlier, RODCs do not participate in Active Directory replication in the same fashion as writable domain controllers. Replication with RODC is one-way, meaning all changes from a writable domain controller are propagated to the RODC. An RODC receives changes, but does not partake in or perform any outbound replication to other domain controllers. This results in the replication workload being minimized over the network because changes do not have to be pulled from an RODC and because Active Directory replication is unidirectional. Also reduced is the amount of time required to monitor replication, which is another plus for having an RODC.

### Credential Caching

Credential caching with an RODC provides numerous security enhancements for a domain controller residing at a branch office. Take, for example, a new functionality in RODCs that increases security in the event an RODC is stolen. When replication transpires between a writable domain controller and an RODC, only a user's account information is replicated—not the user's password. Equally important, passwords are not stored on an RODC. In the event the RODC is stolen, the only accounts that can be hacked and compromised are the local administrator accounts and the RODC account, which is specific to the RODC server. These accounts are not considered to be highly privileged, nor do they have access authorization on the forest and domain. On the other hand, traditional writable domain controllers store both the user's account information and password on a domain controller, ultimately leaving users very vulnerable.

Because an RODC by default does not store user accounts or passwords locally, branch office users must authenticate against a writable domain controller in a hub site. This is often not practical for branch office users, especially if the WAN link between the sites is slow or unavailable. In this case, it is possible to configure password replication caching for specific branch office users on the branch office RODC. After the credentials are cached on the RODC, the domain controller will service users the next time they try to log on and every other time after that until the credentials change. Typically, a branch office only has a few users, so only a subset of an organization's users' accounts are cached on the RODC at the branch office, limiting the exposure of credentials in the event of a system breach.

To provide an additional level of security and at the same time reduce the amount of information exposed in the event an RODC is stolen, a domain administrator can use tools within Active Directory Users and Computers to delete the RODC from the Active Directory domain/forest and reset the passwords for user accounts cached on the RODC.

### NOTE

By default, security groups with high privileges such as Domain Administrators and Enterprise Administrators are configured to never allow their passwords to replicate to RODCs.

### Administrator Role Separation

Organizations are encouraged to use RODCs when there is a need to satisfy unique administrative requirements and to maintain administrator role separation and isolation. The use of an RODC is especially encouraged if the domain controller situated in a branch office hosts more than one server function or server role, such as a print server, messaging server, file server, and much more. The use of an RODC is also recommended when there are other applications installed on the domain controller. Traditionally, in this situation the administrator of these applications has privileges not only to the applications, but also to the entire Active Directory, which can pose a threat. With RODC, however, you can delegate permissions to local administrators, granting them rights to a particular server, roles, or LOB applications without ever granting them access to Active Directory or domain resources beyond the scope of the branch. As a result, the local administrator at the branch can perform his or her administrator work activities effectively without compromising the entire Active Directory environment.

### Read-Only DNS

When using RODCs, it is possible to add the DNS role/service to the RODC. After the DNS service is added to an RODC, the RODC will replicate Active Directory–integrated DNS information such as DNS-related AD partitions, including both the ForestDNS and DomainDNS zones.

Running DNS on an RODC is very similar to running DNS on a writable domain controller. Users can query the local DNS server residing on the branch office RODC for A records and other DNS-related items such as Internet requests. However, unlike traditional writable domain controllers, DNS on RODC does not support dynamic updates. The DNS zone information is entirely read-only.

If a client wants to update their DNS A or PTR record in the local branch office, the RODC will send a DNS replicate-single-object change request to a writable domain controller running the traditional DNS service. The DNS change for the client will occur on the writable DNS server and, eventually, the change will be propagated back to the RODC via unidirectional Active Directory replication.

> **NOTE**
>
> It is a best practice to have clients in the branch office point to their local RODC DNS server for DNS lookups. This can be achieved via an Active Directory group policy or DNS lookup list based on DHCP.

### Read-Only SYSVOL

In Windows Server 2008, it was still possible for changes to be made to the sysvol folder of an RODC. When changes were made to the contents of the sysvol folder, those changes persisted until being overwritten by the next DFS Replication cycle. In Windows Server 2008 R2, Microsoft made changes to the RODC functionality such that the sysvol folder is now read-only on an RODC.

## Installing a Read-Only Domain Controller

RODCs can be implemented on a full or core installation of Windows Server 2008 or Windows Server 2008 R2. The installation can be performed in a standard or in a staged manner. Because RODCs are tailored toward branch office implementations where physical security and theft are a concern, it is a best practice to heighten security even further by installing an RODC on a Server Core installation. A Server Core installation minimizes surface attacks and provides the maximum amount of protection in the event of a system breach.

The upcoming sections include step-by-step procedures for installing an RODC on a full installation of Windows Server 2008 R2, installing an RODC on a Windows Server 2008 R2 Server Core installation, and performing a staged installation. Before launching into the procedures, however, let us examine the prerequisites associated with installing RODCs and understanding the limitations associated with using an RODC.

> **NOTE**
>
> The following steps assume an RODC install is being performed using Windows Server 2008 R2. However, RODC functionality was first introduced in Windows Server 2008 and as such the installation can also be completed using that version of Windows Server.

## Examining Prerequisite Tasks When Deploying an RODC

The following bullets list the items you should review and complete before installing RODCs:

▶ Active Directory running on Windows Server 2003 or Windows Server 2008 R2 must already exist in the environment.

▶ The Active Directory schema must support the Windows Server 2008 R2 server extensions.

▶ The forest and domain functional level must be running Windows Server 2003 or higher.

▶ At least one domain controller within the domain must be running Windows Server 2008 R2.

▶ The PDC Emulator FSMO role must be running Windows Server 2008 R2.

▶ A regular non-read-only (writable) domain controller must already exist within the Active Directory infrastructure.

▶ The RODC cannot be the first domain controller within the Active Directory infrastructure.

▶ If the DNS service will be configured on a Server Core installation, a non-read-only DNS server must be present within the domain.

## Limitations Associated with Windows Server 2008 R2 RODCs

There are situations when RODCs cannot be used. This is the case with bridgehead servers and operations master role holders. For example, a Windows Server 2008 R2 bridgehead server is responsible for managing Active Directory replication from a physical site. Because an RODC can only perform inbound unidirectional replication, it cannot be designated as a bridgehead server because these servers must support both inbound and outbound replication.

An RODC also cannot function as a Flexible Single Master Operations (FSMO) role holder. Each FSMO role needs to write information to an Active Directory domain controller. As an example, consider extending the Active Directory schema for Microsoft Exchange Server 2007. The new schema extensions would be written on a domain controller to support Exchange 2007. The schema extensions would fail on an RODC because the domain controller is not writable, which, of course, explains why an RODC cannot perform the FSMO role.

To add to its limitations, out-of-the-box RODCs cannot authenticate a smart card logon. This is because the Enterprise Read-Only Domain Controller (ERODC) group is not defined in the domain controller certificate template by default. Because the ERODC is not associated with the default group defined in the template, the RODC is not automatically enrolled in the certificate process, which is a requirement for authenticating smart card logons. Unlike the limitations of RODCs stated in the previous two paragraphs, there is a way to work around this particular drawback so an RODC can authenticate a smart card logon. The following changes must be orchestrated in the certificate templates for an RODC to support smart card logons:

▶ ERODC group permissions for Enroll must be set to Allow on the Domain Controller certificate template.

▶ ERODC group permissions for Enroll and Autoenroll must be set to Allow on the Domain Controller Authentication and Directory E-Mail Replication certificate template.

▶ The Authenticated Users group permissions must be set to Allow Read on the Domain Controller Authentication and Directory E-Mail Replication certificate template.

## Conducting an RODC Installation

As mentioned earlier, an RODC can be implemented on either a full installation of Windows Server 2008 R2 or on a Windows Server 2008 R2 Server Core installation. The upcoming sections include step-by-step instructions on installing an RODC for both types of scenarios.

### Installing an RODC on a Full Installation of Windows Server 2008 R2

Before installing an RODC within your Active Directory infrastructure, ensure the prerequisites are met and you fully understand the circumstances under which the RODC should not be used or else you will jeopardize the success of your installation.

Now, let's look at how to install an RODC; this example assumes the base Windows Server 2008 R2 system has already been installed. The installation is very similar to a traditional domain controller installation; however, the final steps include Read-Only Domain Controller settings. To conduct the installation with the Active Directory Domain Services Wizard, follow these steps:

1. Log on to the new branch office Windows Server 2008 R2 system with an account that has domain administrative privileges.

2. Click Start, Run, and type dcpromo.exe. Click OK to commence the full installation of an RODC. Alternatively, you can add the Active Directory Domain Services role via Server Manager.

> **NOTE**
>
> The Active Directory Domain Services Wizard checks to see if the Active Directory Domain Services binaries are installed. If they are not, the wizard will begin installing them.

3. On the Welcome to the Active Directory Domain Services Wizard page, click Next to commence the installation of Active Directory Domain Services (AD DS) on the server.

4. Review the warning on the Operating System Compatibility page, and then click Next.

5. On the Choose a Deployment Configuration page, ensure the Existing Forest option is selected, and then specify Add a Domain Controller to an Existing Domain. Click Next to continue, as illustrated in Figure 32.1.

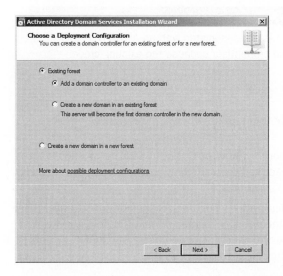

FIGURE 32.1    Adding a new RODC to an existing domain.

6. On the Network Credentials page, type the name of any domain in the forest where you plan to install the domain controller. After the domain name is entered, specify the account credentials that have permissions to conduct the dcpromo process and that will be used to perform the installation. You can either use the current logged-on credentials or specify alternate credentials. Click Next to continue, as displayed in Figure 32.2.

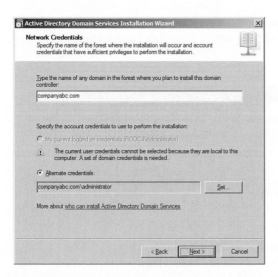

FIGURE 32.2    Specifying network credentials for the RODC installation.

**NOTE**

If the computer is part of a workgroup and is not associated with an Active Directory domain, you must specify alternate domain credentials because the existing credentials are associated with the local server.

7. On the Select a Domain page, specify the domain where the new RODC will be added, and then click Next.

8. On the Select a Site page, specify whether the wizard should add the new RODC to a site based on the subnet defined in Active Directory Sites and Services. Alternatively, select a site manually. Click Next to continue.

9. On the Additional Domain Controller Options page, select the additional options for the domain controller. The options include DNS Server, Global Catalog, and Read-Only Domain Controller (RODC). Ensure that, at the very least, the RODC option is selected, as shown in Figure 32.3. Click Next to continue.

**NOTE**

The RODC option will not be available if a writable domain controller does not already exist in the domain.

10. At the next step of the installation, the Active Directory Domain Services Wizard prompts you to enter a user or group on the Delegation of RODC Installation and Administration page. Ultimately, the user or group you specify will be responsible for

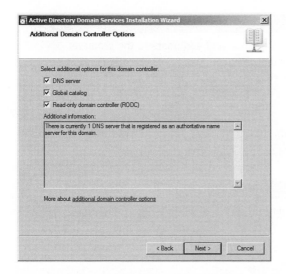

FIGURE 32.3    Ensuring the RODC option is selected.

attaching a server to the RODC account and subsequently managing the RODC after
the installation is complete. If a user or group is not specified, the installation wizard
will automatically allow the Domain Admin or Enterprise Admin group to attach to
the RODC. Enter a group on the Delegation of RODC Installation and
Administration page, and then click Next, as displayed in Figure 32.4.

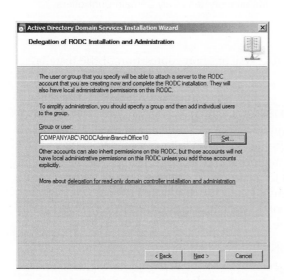

FIGURE 32.4    Specifying a group on the Delegation of RODC Installation and Administration
page.

> **NOTE**
>
> For simplicity, it is a best practice to specify a group and add users to the group as needed. Each user associated with the group will have the opportunity to log on to the RODC and will have full control over the server.

11. Enter the folder location of the database, log files, and sysvol files on the Location for Database, Log Files, and sysvol page, and then click Next to continue.

> **NOTE**
>
> For maximum performance and recoverability, it is a best practice to store the database and log files on separate volumes.

12. On the next page, enter a Directory Services Restore Mode administration password, and then click Next.

13. Review the selections on the Summary page, and then click Next to finalize the installation.

> **NOTE**
>
> It is possible to export the RODC selections to an answer file if needed. This comes in handy when creating additional Server Core installation Read-Only Domain Controllers.

14. Click Finish and reboot the new RODC system upon completion of the installation wizard.

### Installing an RODC on a Windows Server 2008 R2 Server Core Installation

As mentioned in Chapter 3, "Installing Windows Server 2008 R2 and Server Core," one of the most innovative and anticipated security features of Windows Server 2008 R2 is Windows Server Core, a scaled-down installation option that uses command-line prompts instead of graphical user interfaces (GUIs) to manage the server. Because a Server Core installation is able to provide a minimal environment by only installing a subset of the Windows Server 2008 R2 binaries, to support server roles, it is especially ideal for remote locations such as branch offices where only the bare essentials need to be installed.

Operating with a lean server has its benefits. Through Windows Server Core, a minimal environment is created that decreases the amount of maintenance and management an administrator is required to perform when running specific server roles such as Active Directory Domain Services. This comes in handy at branch offices as organizations don't typically want inexperienced administrators managing the branch office domain controller. Therefore, the reduced amount of administration is an advantage. In addition, by having a minimal environment, the attack surface for the server roles residing on the Server Core installation is also reduced. It is also worth mentioning that Server Core is in line with Microsoft's Trustworthy Computing initiative.

Unlike installing other Windows Server 2008 R2 roles on a Server Core installation, installing AD DS—which is part of the RODC installation—on a Server Core installation of Windows Server 2008 R2 requires an unattended answer file to first be created. The unattended answer file provides answers to questions that might be asked during the installation of an Active Directory Domain Services installation. After the unattended answer file is created, the next step is to run dcpromo from the RODC and reference the unattended answer file by using the following syntax at the command prompt: dcpromo /unattend:<unattendfile>.

> **NOTE**
>
> It is possible to create an unattended answer file by exporting settings on the Summary page when using the Active Directory Domain Services Installation Wizard. This answer file can be used for creating subsequent installations of Active Directory domain controllers on Server Core installations.

The following example depicts installing an RODC on a Server Core installation. The first step creates the unattended answer file based on settings included in Table 32.1. The second step conducts the dcpromo process on the Server Core installation by referencing the answer file created in the first step. This example assumes a Windows Server 2008 R2 Server Core installation already exists at the branch office.

TABLE 32.1    Parameters and Values for Creating an Unattended Answer File

| Parameter | Value |
| --- | --- |
| Site | Toronto |
| Additional options | Read-only DC: Yes<br>Global catalog: Yes<br>DNS server: Yes |
| Update DNS delegation | No |
| Source DC | Any writable domain controller |
| Password Replication Policy | Allow: COMPANYABC1\Allowed RODC Password Replication Group<br>Deny: BUILTIN\Administrators<br>Deny: BUILTIN\Server Operators<br>Deny: BUILTIN\Backup Operators<br>Deny: BUILTIN\Account Operators<br>Deny: COMPANYABC1\Denied RODC Password Replication Group |

| | |
|---|---|
| Delegation for RODC installation and administration | COMPANYABC1\RODC-Admins-BranchOffice-10 |
| Active Directory file placement | Database folder: c:\Windows\NTDS<br>Log file folder: c:\Windows\NTDS<br>sysvol folder: c:\Windows\SYSVOL |
| DNS server settings | The DNS service will be installed on this computer.<br>The DNS service will be configured on this computer.<br>This computer will be configured to use this DNS server as its preferred DNS server. |

**NOTE**

For more information on understanding and conducting a Server Core installation, review Chapter 3.

### Creating the Unattended Answer File Based on the Values in Table 32.1

1. First create an unattended answer file similar to the following example. The parameters and values found in this example have been summarized in Table 32.1.

```
; DCPROMO unattend file (automatically generated by dcpromo)
; Usage:
;    dcpromo.exe /unattend:C:\Temp\RODCAnswerFile.txt
;
;
[DCInstall]
; Read-Only Replica DC promotion
ReplicaOrNewDomain=ReadOnlyReplica
ReplicaDomainDNSName=companyabc1.com
ServerAdmin="COMPANYABC1\RODC-Admins-BranchOffice-10"
SiteName=Toronto
InstallDNS=Yes
ConfirmGc=Yes
DNSDelegation=No
UserDomain=companyabc1.com
UserName=*
Password=*
DatabasePath=C:\Windows\NTDS
LogPath=C:\Windows\NTDS
SYSVOLPath=C:\Windows\SYSVOL
; Set SafeModeAdminPassword to the correct value prior to using the unattend
file
SafeModeAdminPassword=
; Run-time flags (optional)
; CriticalReplicationOnly=Yes
```

```
; RebootOnCompletion=Yes
TransferIMRoleIfNecessary=No
```

**NOTE**

This example represents the unattended answer file for the RODC installation, which also includes parameters and values for installing DNS, a global catalog, Password Replication Policy, administrator delegation, Active Directory file placement, and DNS settings. Modify the values as needed.

32

**NOTE**

You might need to fill in password fields prior to using the unattended file. If you leave the values for "Password" and/or "DNSDelegationPassword" as "*", you will be asked for credentials at runtime.

2. Save the unattended file and copy it to the Windows Server 2008 R2 Server Core installation system that will be the new branch office RODC server.

### Implementing the RODC on a Server Core Installation by Using an Unattended Answer File

3. Now that the unattended answer file is created, you must run the following syntax `dcpromo /unattend:<unattendfile>` from a Server Core installation command prompt.

For a full list of Active Directory Domain Services installation options, review this web link: http://technet.microsoft.com/en-us/library/cc772074(WS.10).aspx.

### Performing a Staged RODC Installation

A staged approach can also be leveraged to install an RODC in a branch office. There are two steps to the new approach. Each step is described in the following list from a high-level perspective:

▶ The first step involves creating a computer account for the RODC in Active Directory. After the computer account is created, you must delegate its installation and management to a user at the branch office. The person being delegated does not require elevated privileged rights within the Active Directory forest like Domain Administrators or Enterprise Administrators.

▶ The next step requires branch office personnel to complete the RODC installation by attaching a server to the RODC account created in the previous step.

By delegating the installation of the RODC to a regular user account at the branch office, you eliminate the need to stage the RODC in a hub site and physically ship the server to the branch office. This was a common approach to configuring domain controllers for branch offices when using previous versions of Windows because administrators did not want to grant regular users at the branch office elevated administrative privileges to conduct the installation. In addition, if the domain controller was traditionally built at the branch office, using this new staged approach eliminates the need to ship sensitive Windows Server 2008 R2 media and product keys.

**NOTE**

Another alternative to performing a staged RODC installation is to have the branch office prepare a base installation of the Windows Server 2008 R2 operating system. After this installation is complete and the server is on the network, a domain administrator from the hub site can use the Remote Desktop Protocol (RDP) and remotely perform the dcpromo process. This strategy also eliminates the need to use branch personnel in any facet of the domain controller installation process.

Complete the following steps to create an account for a Read-Only Domain Controller (RODC). You will be using the Active Directory Users and Computers interface in the first step of this staged approach.

1. On a writable Windows Server 2008 R2 domain controller, invoke Active Directory Users and Computers by selecting it from the Administrative Tools.

2. In Active Directory Users and Computers, expand the domain tree, and then select the Domain Controllers Organizational Unit folder.

3. Right-click the Domain Controllers OU container, and then select Pre-Create Read-Only Domain Controller Account.

4. The Active Directory Domain Services Installation Wizard is invoked. Review the Welcome page, and then click Next to continue.

5. On the Network Credentials page, specify the account credentials that will be used to perform the installation. The options include either My Current Logged On Credentials or Alternate Credentials. Click Next to continue.

6. Enter a computer name for the RODC in the Computer Name text box located on the Specify the Computer Name page. This is illustrated in Figure 32.5. Click Next.

**NOTE**

This procedure creates a computer account in Active Directory Domain Services. The RODC computer name specified in this step should be the name of the server you plan on promoting to an RODC. As part of the prerequisite tasks and also to minimize server name conflicts, do not join the server you plan on using as an RODC to the domain. The server should reside in a workgroup.

7. On the Select a Site page, select a site for the new domain controller installation, and then click Next.

8. On the Additional Domain Controller Options page, select the additional options for the domain controller. Additional items could include a DNS server and a global

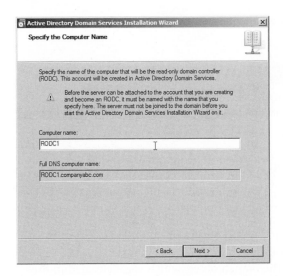

FIGURE 32.5    Specifying the computer name of the RODC system.

catalog server. Also, notice that the Read-Only Domain Controller is selected automatically and cannot be unselected.

> **NOTE**
>
> In general, to minimize unnecessary WAN utilization, it is a best practice to also make the RODC a DNS server and a global catalog server.

9. On the Delegation of RODC Installation and Administration page, specify a user or group who will ultimately manage and attach the server to the RODC account being created. Do this by selecting Set and enter the desired user account or group. Click Next to continue.

10. Review the summary of the Active Directory installation, and click Next on the Summary page to finalize the inauguration of the RODC.

11. Click Finish to finalize the creation of the RODC account.

At this point, the RODC account has been created. The next step is to run the Active Directory Domain Services Installation Wizard on a server that will eventually become the RODC by leveraging the user or group the RODC installation was delegated to in the previous steps. To attach a server to an RODC account, follow these simple steps:

1. Using someone with local administrative privileges, log on to the server that will be the RODC in the branch office.

> **NOTE**
>
> To reaffirm, make sure this server is in a workgroup and not associated with the Active Directory domain.

**2.** Click Start, Run, type the command dcpromo/UseExistingAccount:Attach, and
then click OK.

> **NOTE**
>
> The Active Directory Domain Services binaries will be installed. After this is complete,
> the Active Directory Domain Services Installation Wizard will be invoked.

**3.** On the Welcome to the Active Directory Domain Services Installation Wizard page,
click Next to attach the server to a corresponding domain controller account created
in the previous steps.

**4.** On the Network Credentials page, first specify the name of the forest where the
RODC installation will occur. Then click Set to specify the alternate account credentials that will be used to perform the installation. Provide the username and password of the IT support personnel at the branch office, which was delegated in the
previous steps, as shown in Figure 32.6. Click Next.

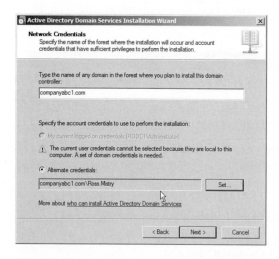

FIGURE 32.6    Entering the domain and alternate credentials information for the RODC
installation.

> **NOTE**
>
> If the source server computer account name deviates from the RODC name that was
> created in the previous step, the installation is sure to fail. The two account names
> must be identical.

**5.** On the Select Domain Controller page, the wizard will automatically link and match
the server name to the account name of the RODC created in the previous step.

Ensure the Computer Name, DC Type, and Domain and Site information located in the Account Details section is correct. If it is, click Next to continue.

6. Validate the folder location for the Database, Logs Files, and sysvol folder, and then click Next.

7. Enter and confirm the password for the Directory Services Restore mode administrator account, and click Next.

8. Review the summary of the Active Directory installation, and click Next on the Summary page to finalize the inauguration of the RODC.

9. Click Finish and restart the RODC system.

# Understanding BitLocker Drive Encryption

Microsoft added Windows BitLocker Drive Encryption to Windows Server 2008 mostly as a result of organizations demanding protection not only for their operating systems in remote locations, but also for the vital data stored on the system volume, data volumes, and USB flash drives that were used in these locations. BitLocker Drive Encryption, commonly referred to as just BitLocker, is a software-based Full Disk Encryption (FDE) data-protection security feature included in all versions of Windows Server 2008 and Windows Server 2008 R2, as well as in the Ultimate and Enterprise Editions of Windows Vista and Windows 7. It is an optional component that must be installed if you choose to use it.

BitLocker increases data at rest protection for an operating system by merging two concepts together: encrypting a volume and guaranteeing the integrity of the operating system's boot components. The first component, drive encryption, safeguards data residing on the system volume and configured data volumes by preventing unauthorized users from compromising Windows system files encrypted with BitLocker. The second component provides integrity verifications of the early boot components, which essentially refers to components used during the startup process, by validating that the hard disk has not been tampered with or removed from its original server. Equally important, when you use BitLocker, confidential data on a protected server cannot be viewed even if the hard disks are transferred to another operating system. If these two conditions are met, only then will data on a BitLocker volume be accessible and the system allowed to boot.

If you have worked with previous versions of Windows Server, you will recognize immediately that BitLocker is a great addition to Windows Server 2008 R2 as it protects all of the data residing on a server's hard disks because everything written to the disk including the operating system is encrypted. In previous versions of Windows Server, encryption based on integration with integrity controls was not supported, which meant personal information could be compromised. In addition, with BitLocker now on the map, branch offices concerned over the physical security and theft of their domain controllers stand to benefit the greatest from leveraging BitLocker because this feature further bolsters security and ensures confidential data is not disclosed without authorization.

---

**NOTE**

Many professionals are posing questions as they wonder about the differences
between BitLocker and Encrypting File System (EFS). Both technologies offer tools for
encryption; however, BitLocker is intended to protect all personal and system files on a
system and after it is enabled, it is transparent as well as automatic. EFS, on the other
hand, encrypts individual files based on an administrator's judgment call.

---

## Examining BitLocker's Drive Encryption

BitLocker was first introduced with the release of Windows Vista. Since entering the
Windows Server 2008 family of operating systems, Microsoft has continued to improve
BitLocker by adding new features, for example: support for data volumes, smart card certifi-
cates, data recovery agents, USB flash drives, a new RSAT BitLocker interface, and so on.

### Understanding Its Benefits

By using BitLocker in conjunction with Windows Server 2008 R2, an organization can
enjoy a number of benefits:

▶ Prevention of unauthorized access to data at rest, which is located on Windows
managed system volumes, data volumes, and USB flash drives.

▶ Support for integrity checking of early boot components using Trusted Platform
Module (TPM) to ensure that a machine has not been tampered with and that
encrypted materials are located on the original machine.

▶ Protection against cold boot attacks by requiring an interactive form of authentication (including a PIN or a USB key) in addition to the presence of the TPM hardware
before a machine will boot or resume from hibernation.

▶ Support for escrow of BitLocker recovery materials in Active Directory.

▶ A streamlined recovery process, which can be delegated to non-Domain
Administrators.

▶ Windows Server 2008 R2 and Windows 7 automatically creates the necessary
BitLocker disk partitions during installation.

▶ Support for BitLocker protection on USB flash drives. This feature is called
BitLocker To Go.

▶ Lastly, support for Data Recovery Agent (DRA) support so that authorized IT administrators will always have access to BitLocker protected volumes.

### Understanding TPM

The term Trusted Platform Module (TPM) is used to refer to both the name of a published
specification by the Trusted Computing Group for a secure cryptoprocessor and the implementation of that specification in the form of a TPM chip. A TPM chip's main purpose in
life is the secure generation of cryptographic keys, the protection of those keys, and the
ability to act as a hardware pseudo-random number generator. In addition, a TPM chip

can also provide remote attestation and sealed storage. Remote attestation is a feature in which a hash key summary is created based on a machine's current hardware and software configuration. Typically, remote attestation is used by third-party applications such as BitLocker to ensure a machine's state has not been tampered with. Sealed storage is used to encrypt data such that it may only be decrypted once the TPM chip releases the appropriate decryption key. This release is only done by TPM chip once the required authenticator for that data has been provided. Lastly, a TPM chip can also be used to authenticate hardware devices.

In BitLocker, a TPM chip is used to protect the encryption keys and provide integrity authentication for a trusted boot pathway (that is, BIOS, boot sector, and so on). This type of TPM-supported protection is only performed when BitLocker is in either Transparent Operation mode or User Authentication mode. When in either of these modes, BitLocker uses the TPM chip to detect if there are unauthorized changes to the preboot environment (trusted boot pathway protection) such as the BIOS and MBR. If unauthorized changes were made, BitLocker will then request that a recovery key be provided before the Volume Master Key can be decrypted and bootup of the machine can continue.

> **NOTE**
>
> Because of how a TPM chip is used, it is often referred to as a "root of trust."

## Comprehending BitLocker's Drive Encryption Hardware Requirements

Configuring BitLocker Drive Encryption is not as simple as clicking through a few screens on a Windows Server 2008 R2 wizard. A number of prerequisite steps must be fulfilled before BitLocker can be configured and implemented.

Before you implement BitLocker Drive Encryption, make certain the following hardware requirements and prerequisites are met and understood:

- The system should have a Trusted Platform Module (TPM) version 1.2 or higher.

- A Trusted Computing Group (TCG)-compliant BIOS, which can also support USB devices during startup.

- If the system does not have TPM, a removable USB memory device can be used to store the encryption key.

- There must be a minimum of at least two partitions on the system. One partition is an active partition, referred to as the "system partition," which is used by bootmgr to boot Windows. This partition should be at least 100MB and not be encrypted. The second "primary partition" is where the Windows binaries are installed.

- All drives and partitions must be formatted with the NTFS file system.

> **NOTE**
>
> The TPM and BIOS requirements only come into play when you want to use the TPM as a root of trust for a machine's BitLocker configuration.

### Understanding BitLocker Deployment Scenarios

Similar to an RODC, branch office domain controllers are great candidates for implementing BitLocker. BitLocker can be exploited at the branch office to protect against physical breaches or theft of a domain controller or hard drive, and it can secure data during shipment of a branch office domain controller from a hub site to a branch office location. BitLocker can also be used to protect against data theft using disk cloning by maintenance or outsourcing techniques.

## Configuring BitLocker Drive Encryption on a Windows Server 2008 R2 Branch Office Domain Controller

The following sections cover step-by-step procedures on how to implement BitLocker by first configuring the system partitions, installing the BitLocker feature, and then enabling BitLocker Drive Encryption. The enabling section includes steps for enabling BitLocker when using TPM hardware, when not using TPM hardware, and enabling BitLocker on additional volumes beyond the scope of the volume hosting the operating system. The final step-by-step procedures include how to utilize the BitLocker recovery password in the event of an issue and how to remove BitLocker after it has been installed and configured.

### Installing the BitLocker Drive Encryption Feature

Now that the system partition has been configured, there are different ways to install BitLocker. Install it during the initial configuration through Server Manager or through a command prompt. The next sections illustrate how to execute both of these installations.

#### Installing BitLocker with Server Manager

To install the BitLocker server role using Server Manager, follow these steps:

1. Click Start, Administrative Tools, and Server Manager. The Server Manager tools appear.
2. Right-click Features in the left pane of Server Manager, and then select Add Features.
3. On the Select Features page, install BitLocker by selecting BitLocker Drive Encryption in the Features section, as shown in Figure 32.7, and then click Next.
4. On the Confirm Installation Selections page, review the roles, services, and features selected for installation, and then click Install to initiate the installation process.
5. Ensure the installation succeeded by reviewing the messages on the Installation Results page, and then click Close.
6. After the BitLocker feature has finished installing, restart the system.

> **NOTE**
>
> Alternatively, the BitLocker Drive Encryption feature can also be installed by selecting Add Features in the Initial Configuration Tasks Wizard.

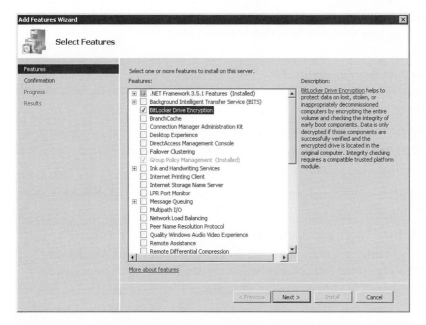

FIGURE 32.7    Selecting the BitLocker feature for installation.

### Installing BitLocker via the Command Line

Another alternative to installing BitLocker is via the command line (PowerShell). This methodology should be reserved for branch office implementations using Windows Server 2008 R2 Server Core installation because a graphical interface to manage the server does not exist. To install the BitLocker feature using PowerShell, follow these steps:

1. From within a PowerShell console session, execute the `ImportSystemModules` function.

2. After the PowerShell has finished loading all of the system modules, execute the following command: `Add-WindowsFeature BitLocker`.

3. After the BitLocker feature has finished installing, restart the system.

## Configuring the System Partitions for BitLocker

As mentioned earlier, one of the prerequisite tasks when configuring an operating system for BitLocker is configuring a nonencrypted active partition also referred to as a system partition. In Windows 7 and Windows Server 2008 R2, the necessary disk partitions are automatically created when Windows is installed.

## Enabling BitLocker Drive Encryption

By default, BitLocker is configured to use a Trusted Platform Module. To recap, however, BitLocker's full functionality will not be witnessed unless the system being used is compatible with the TPM chip and BIOS. This next section looks at how to enable BitLocker Drive Encryption with TPM. Microsoft recognizes that many laptops and computers do not have TPM chips (or are not "TPM enabled"). If you are in this situation, don't despair because you can use BitLocker without a compatible TPM chip and BIOS. As such, this section also covers information on how to enable BitLocker without TPM.

### Enabling BitLocker Drive Encryption with TPM

The first step to enabling BitLocker with TPM is to turn ON the TPM. Use the following steps to complete this task:

1. Go into the system's BIOS setup and set TPM Security to ON.

2. Next, save the changes in the BIOS setup, and reboot the system.

3. Lastly, reenter the system's BIOS setup and activate the TPM.

Once the TPM has been enabled, the next step is to enable BitLocker. Use the following steps to complete this task:

1. Click Start, Control Panel, and double-click BitLocker Drive Encryption.

2. Enable BitLocker Drive Encryption for the operating system volume by clicking Turn On BitLocker on the BitLocker Drive Encryption page. This is displayed in Figure 32.8.

FIGURE 32.8    Turning on BitLocker via Control Panel.

> **NOTE**
>
> The Initialize TPM Security Hardware screen will be displayed if the TPM is not initialized. Launch the wizard to initialize the hardware and then restart your computer.

3. Review the message on the BitLocker Drive Encryption Platform Check page, and then click Continue with BitLocker Drive Encryption to start the BitLocker process.

4. Because TPM hardware is present on this system, select the option to Use BitLocker Without Additional Keys, and then click Next. This option can be found on the Set BitLocker Startup Preferences page, as displayed in Figure 32.9. Additional keys such as a PIN or USB are not required as BitLocker stores both encryption and decryption keys within the TPM chip.

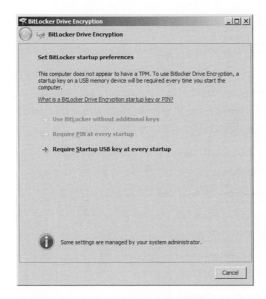

FIGURE 32.9   Specifying BitLocker startup preferences.

5. The Save the Recovery Password page is invoked. The administrator has the ability to save the BitLocker recovery password on a USB drive or to a folder on the system. In addition, the third option allows for printing of the password. Choose the desired storage alternative for saving the recovery password, and then click Next to continue.

6. On the Encrypt the Volume page, ensure the Run BitLocker System Check option is enabled, and then click Continue. The system check guarantees that BitLocker can access and read the recovery and encryption keys before encrypting the volume.

7. The Encryption in Progress status bar is displayed. Restart the system when the encryption process is finalized.

### Enabling BitLocker Drive Encryption when TPM Is Not Available

If TPM hardware is not available on the system, BitLocker must be configured to leverage a USB key at startup. The following example configures a local group policy for the Group Policy Object titled "Enabling Advanced Startup Options: Control Panel Setup."

1. Click Start, Run, and then type gpedit.msc. Click OK and the Local Group Policy Object Editor is invoked.

2. In the Local Group Policy Object Editor, expand Local Computer Policy, Computer Configuration, Administrative Templates, Windows Components, BitLocker Drive Encryption, and then select Operating System Drives.

3. In the right pane, double-click Require Additional Authentication at Startup.

4. Enable the BitLocker Group Policy settings by selecting the Enabled option, and then click OK, as displayed in Figure 32.10.

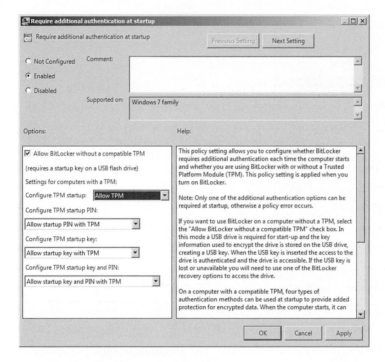

FIGURE 32.10    Enabling additional authentication options for BitLocker support.

5. Apply the new Group Policy settings by typing gpupdate.exe /force at the command prompt.

BitLocker Drive Encryption utilizing a USB device can now be configured by completing the following steps:

1. Click Start, Control Panel, and double-click BitLocker Drive Encryption.

2. Enable BitLocker Drive Encryption by clicking Turn On BitLocker on the BitLocker Drive Encryption page.

3. Review the message on the BitLocker Drive Encryption Platform Check page, and then click Continue with BitLocker Drive Encryption to start the BitLocker process.

4. If necessary, the installation will prepare the system for BitLocker, then click Next.

5. Because a TPM does not exist in this example, select the option Require a Startup USB Key at Every Startup, and then click Next. This option can be found on the Set BitLocker Startup Preferences page.

6. Ensure a USB memory device has been inserted into the system. Then on the Save Your Startup Key page, specify the removable drive to which the startup key will be saved, and then click Save.

7. The Save the Recovery Password page is then invoked. The administrator has the ability to save the BitLocker recovery password on a USB drive or to a folder on the system. In addition, the third option allows for printing of the password. Choose the desired storage alternative for saving the recovery password, and then click Next to continue.

**NOTE**

It is a best practice to make additional copies of the recovery password and store them in a secure location like a vault. For maximum security, the recovery password should not be stored on the local system nor should the password be printed on paper. In addition, do not store the recovery password and the startup key on the same media.

8. On the Encrypt the Volume page, ensure the Run BitLocker System Check option is enabled, and then click Continue. The system check guarantees BitLocker can access and read the recovery and encryption keys before encrypting the volume.

**NOTE**

Do not bypass the option to run a system check before encrypting the volume. Data loss can occur if there is an error reading the encryption or recovery key.

9. Insert the USB memory device containing the startup key into the system, and then click Restart Now. The Encryption in Progress status bar is displayed showing the completion status of the disk volume encryption.

**NOTE**

The USB device must be plugged in to the system every time the system starts to boot and gain access to the encrypted volume. If the USB device containing the startup key is lost or damaged, you must use the Recovery mode and provide the recovery key to start the system.

### Enabling BitLocker Drive Encryption on Additional Data Volumes

There might be situations when BitLocker Drive Encryption is warranted not only on the volume containing the operating system files, but also on the data volumes. This is especially common with domain controllers in branch offices where a lack of physical security and theft are concerns.

When encrypting data volumes with BitLocker, the keys generated for the operating system volume are independent of the drive volume. However, encryption of a data volume is similar to the encryption process of the operating system volume.

Follow these steps to enable BitLocker Drive Encryption for server data volumes:

1. Click Start, Run, and then type cmd. Click OK to launch a command prompt.

2. From within the command prompt, type `manage-bde -on <volume>: -rp –rk <removable drive>:\`.

---

**NOTE**

Replace the <volume> argument with the desired volume drive letter that you want to encrypt. In addition, replace the <removable drive> argument with the drive letter of a USB device. The USB device is utilized to store the recovery key.

---

The data volume must be unlocked each time the server is rebooted. This can be accomplished through a manual or automatic process. The syntax to manually unlock a data volume after every restart consists of the following two options:

▶ `manage-bde -unlock <volume>: -rp <recovery password>`

▶ `manage-bde -unlock <volume>: -rk U:\<recovery-key-file name>`

The first option uses the recovery password, whereas the second option takes advantage of passing the recovery key to decrypt the data volume. As mentioned in the previous paragraph, it is possible to enable automatic unlocking of a data volume by utilizing the following syntax at the command prompt:

`manage-bde –autounlock –enable <volume>:`

This command creates a recovery key and stores it on the operating system volume. The data volume is automatically unlocked after each system reboot.

## Utilizing the BitLocker Recovery Password

There might be situations when you need to leverage the recovery password to gain access to a volume that is encrypted with BitLocker. This situation might occur when there is an error related to the TPM hardware, one of the boot files becomes corrupt or modified, or if TPM is unintentionally cleared or disabled. The following instructions outline the recovery steps:

1. Restart the system and the BitLocker Drive Encryption console will come into view.

2. Insert the USB device containing the recovery password, and then press Esc. If the USB device is not available, bypass step 2 and proceed to step 3.

3. Press Enter. You will be prompted to enter the recovery password manually.

4. Type in the recovery password, press Enter, and then restart the system.

### Scenarios for when the Recovery Password Is Required

There are a number of different scenarios where a BitLocker recovery would need to be performed; these include (but are not limited to):

▶ Changing or replacing the motherboard with a new TPM

▶ Changing the status of the TPM

▶ Updating the BIOS and or any other ROM on the motherboard

▶ Attempting to access a BitLocker-enabled drive on a different system.

▶ Entering the wrong PIN information too many times

▶ Losing or damaging the USB startup key

## Removing BitLocker Drive Encryption

The course of action for turning off BitLocker Drive Encryption is the same for both TPM-based hardware configurations and USB devices. When turning off BitLocker, two options exist. You can either remove BitLocker entirely and decrypt a volume or you can temporarily disable BitLocker so changes can still be made. The following steps depict the process for removing and disabling BitLocker:

1. Click Start, Control Panel, and double-click BitLocker Drive Encryption.

2. Turn off BitLocker Drive Encryption by clicking Turn Off BitLocker on the BitLocker Drive Encryption page.

3. The What Level of Decryption Do You Want dialog box will be invoked. Choose either Disable BitLocker Drive Encryption or Decrypt the Volume.

# Understanding and Deploying BranchCache

BranchCache is a new feature in Windows Server 2008 R2 and Windows 7 that is designed to optimize wide area network (WAN) bandwidth usage by branch offices. To accomplish this, BranchCache copies content from central office content servers and caches the content at the branch office. Once cached, clients no longer have to traverse a WAN connection to access content. Instead, the content is accessed directly from within the branch office from caches on other peer Windows 7 machines or servers running the BranchCache feature of Windows Server 2008 R2. Therefore, BranchCache helps improve content access times by branch office servers and clients while also reducing the amount of traffic on a WAN link.

> **NOTE**
>
> BranchCache is only supported on Windows Server 2008 R2 and Windows 7.

## Important BranchCache Concepts

When working with BranchCache, the following important concepts should be taken into consideration:

▶ There are two modes of operation in BranchCache: Distributed Cache mode and Hosted Cache mode. If cached content is only being distributed using client computers, this is called Distributed Cache mode. Hosted Cache mode, however, is when the content cache is being hosted by a server that is located within the branch office.

▶ BranchCache supports the optimization of file access as well as downloads over HTTPS and IPSec.

▶ BranchCache protects content that is cached by encrypting it. Content can then only be accessed by using identities, which are provided by the originating server to authenticated clients that are members of the same domain as the content server.

## Distributed Cache Mode

Distributed Cache mode is a peer-to-peer caching scheme that is used to cache intranet website (communicating over HTTP or HTTPS) or file server (communicating over the standard SMB protocol) content within a branch office without the need of a local hosted cache server.

### Server-Side Configuration

By default, BranchCache is not enabled. To enable it on a Web server or a file server, the following steps need to be performed:

1. **Web (IIS) Server**—You would need to enable the BranchCache feature using Server Manager.

2. **File Server (SMB)**—You would need to enable the BranchCache for Remote Files role service, which is part of the File Services role using Server Manager.

Additionally, for file servers, the following things need to be completed:

1. Configure the Hash Publication for BranchCache GPO setting (Computer Configuration\Policies\Administrative Templates\Network\Lanman Server). Set this to: Allow Hash Publication Only for Shared Folders on Which BranchCache Is Enabled.

2. Specify the HashStorageLimitPercent Registry value (HKLM\CurrentControlSet\Service\LanmanServer\Parameters). This is the maximum percentage of physical disk space used to store the publication hashes.

3. Lastly, tag your file shares by enabling BranchCache support for them. On the Caching tab, select Only the Files and Programs That Users Specify Are Available Offline. Then select Enable BranchCache, as shown in Figure 32.11.

### Client-Side Configuration

Like the server-side configuration, the BranchCache feature must be enabled on Windows 7 clients. To enable this feature in Distributed Cache mode, there are two methods. The

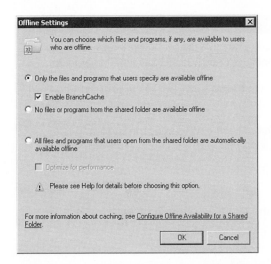

FIGURE 32.11   Enabling file share BranchCache support.

first method is via Netsh. For example, run a command prompt (Run As Administrator) and execute:

```
netsh branchcache set service mode=DISTRIBUTED
```

**NOTE**

Executing the previous command not only turns on and configures BranchCache, but also configures Windows Firewall with the appropriate rules to allow BranchCache to operate in this mode.

Needless to say, running a Netsh command is not the most efficient way of turning on BranchCache. That is why most people will use the second method for configuring BranchCache on clients in Distributed Cache mode, which is a GPO. Use the following steps to complete this task:

1. Enable the Turn On BranchCache GPO setting (Computer Configuration\Policies\Administrative Templates\Network\BranchCache).

2. Enable the Set BranchCache Distributed Cache Mode GPO setting (Computer Configuration\Policies\Administrative Templates\Network\BranchCache).

3. Enable and configure the BranchCache for Network Files GPO setting (Computer Configuration\Policies\Administrative Templates\Network\BranchCache). Here, the latency value that determines when the network files aspect of BranchCache will kick in must be specified. The default is 80.

> **NOTE**
>
> The latency value can be set to 0, which forces BranchCache for network files (SMB) to be turned on all the time. Also, when you configure BranchCache via GPO, it overrides any configuration that is done via `Netsh`.

Lastly, once the BranchCache GPO settings have been configured, the next step is to configure Windows Firewall to allow incoming HTTP and WS-Discovery traffic:

▶ Allow TCP HTTP - 80 Inbound (from all other BranchCache clients—at the branch office).

▶ Allow UDP WS-Discovery - 3702 Inbound (from all other BranchCache clients—at the branch office).

### Understanding WS-Discovery

WS-Discovery (Web Services Dynamic Discovery, or WSD) is a technical specification for a multicast discovery protocol that is used to locate services on a local network. WSD, which is not proprietary to Microsoft, is used by BranchCache to discover locally cached content. For example, BranchCache clients will initiate multicast WSD Probe messages with the hashes of the content probes to other BranchCache clients (also known as peers). If these peers have the content, they will then reply with a unicast Probe-Match message.

To understand how this all works, here is the basic flow:

1. Client2 will first contact the content server FileServer1 for a document named `File.doc`.
2. FileServer1 will respond with list of hashes that make up the indices of the requested content.
3. Client2 will then send out a WSD Probe message to other clients in their local network.
4. If there is a match on another peer, it responds to the Probe message with a Probe-Match.
5. Client2 then will decide on where to get the content from (content server or other peers).

> **NOTE**
>
> If content is retrieved from other peers, this is done via HTTP.

### Testing Distributed Cache Mode

To test BranchCache in Distributed Cache mode, the following must be in place:

1. A Windows Server 2008 R2–based content server and content to put on that server.
2. Two different network segments with some sort of latency.
3. Two or more Windows 7 clients across continents from the content server.

Next, after the previously mentioned requirements are in place and BranchCache has been correctly configured for Distributed Cache mode, BranchCache can be tested using the following steps:

1. On Client1, copy a file from the share on the content server to your desktop.

2. Next, on Client2, copy the same file from the share on the content server to your desktop.

**NOTE**

These steps assume that BranchCache for network files is being tested.

## Hosted Cache Mode

Hosted Cache mode is still kind of peer-to-peer. However, in this deployment mode, all the content that is cached on each peer is also cached on a central server in the branch office. This hosted cache then becomes the central point of reference for peers to validate locally cached content and then to retrieve that content from the cache. In other words, a Hosted Cache server is kind of a glorified caching proxy server.

### Server-Side Configuration

The server-side configuration for a Hosted Cache deployment is exactly the same as a Distributed Cache deployment. However, there is one difference; a Hosted Cache server must be deployed. Use the following steps to complete this task:

1. Install the BranchCache feature.

2. Next, execute the following `Netsh` command:

   ```
   netsh BranchCache set service mode=HOSTEDSERVER
   ```

3. Install an SSL server authentication certificate where the subject name is set to the FQDN of the Hosted Cache server.

4. Lastly, configure the Hosted Cache server to use the server authentication certificate. To do that, get the certificate hash from the certificate you just installed, and execute the following command:

   ```
   netsh HTTP ADD SSLCERT IPPORT=0.0.0.0:443 CERTHASH="cert-hash" APPID=
   ➥{d673f5ee-a714-454d-8de2-492e4c1bd8f8}
   ```

### Understanding the SSL Certificate

As mentioned before, BranchCache peers do not upload content to the Hosted Cache server. Instead, they advertise the content in their cache, and the Hosted Cache server then downloads the content it needs from the client. The SSL certificate is required because clients "advertise" their content to the Hosted Cache server by doing an HTTP post over TLS.

32

### Client-Side Configuration

Like Distributed Cache mode, there are two methods for configuring Hosted Cache mode. The first method is via `Netsh`. For example, run a command prompt (Run As Administrator) and execute the following command:

```
netsh branchcache set service mode=HOSTEDCLIENT LOCATION="FQDN of Hosted
➥Cache Server"
```

The second method for configuring BranchCache on clients in Hosted Cache mode is GPO. Use the following steps to complete this task:

1. Enable the Turn On BranchCache GPO setting (`Computer Configuration\Policies\Administrative Templates\Network\BranchCache`).

2. Enable the Set BranchCache Hosted Cache Mode GPO setting (`Computer Configuration\Policies\Administrative Templates\Network\BranchCache`).

3. Enable and configure the BranchCache for Network Files GPO setting (`Computer Configuration\Policies\Administrative Templates\Network\BranchCache`). Here, the latency value that determines when the network files aspect of BranchCache will kick in must be specified. The default is 80.

Lastly, once the BranchCache GPO settings have been configured, the next step is to configure Windows Firewall to allow incoming HTTP:

▶ Allow TCP HTTP - 80 Inbound (from all other BranchCache clients—at the branch office).

## Troubleshooting (Is BranchCache Doing Something?)

Unfortunately, BranchCache is kind of a black box. When it's working, users shouldn't notice anything. On the flip side, when BranchCache is not working, users will still probably not really notice anything (besides a performance hit). Therefore, to determine if BranchCache is functioning, the following might be performed:

▶ Load up NetMon and watch the traffic flows. Or, if a tool is being used that can monitor bandwidth across the WAN, improvements in bandwidth usage should be seen.

▶ Watch the BranchCache event logs. However, this is only partly useful as a majority of the BranchCache event messages are not very meaningful.

▶ Run the `netsh branchcache show status` command. The results from this command are actually a really good starting point to see how BranchCache is configured on a BranchCache client or Hosted Cache server.

▶ Look at the BranchCache performance counters (the BranchCache Kernel mode and BranchCache counters). Just keep in mind that Kernel mode counters are only seen server side.

# Enhancing Replication and WAN Utilization at the Branch Office

Windows Server 2008 R2 introduces new technologies and refines existing ones to maximize performance, replication, and file sharing and to reduce WAN bandwidth utilization consumed between branch offices and hub sites. The following technologies that address and improve bandwidth utilization, latency, and reliability of the WAN links at a branch office include the following:

- ▶ Read-Only Domain Controllers
- ▶ Next Generation TCP/IP
- ▶ Distributed File System
- ▶ DirectAccess
- ▶ Virtualization
- ▶ Group Policy
- ▶ SMB v2

## Read-Only Domain Controllers

As revealed earlier in this chapter, the amount of information replicated over the WAN between a Read-Only Domain Controller residing at a branch office and a writable domain controller at a hub site is significantly minimized. This is because changes do not originate at an RODC, eliminating the need to replicate data from an RODC to a writable domain controller replication partner at a hub site, resulting in a reduction of bandwidth and WAN utilization being used.

## Next Generation TCP/IP Stack

A tremendous amount of improvement is seen in the Next Generation TCP/IP stack introduced in Windows Server 2008 R2. Some of the features for the new TCP/IP stack that directly impact and improve branch office WAN utilization and replication include the following:

- ▶ **Receive Window Auto-Tuning**—Support for Receive Window Auto-Tuning is new in the Next Generation TCP/IP stack. Receiver-side throughput is improved through Receive Window Auto-Tuning because this feature is able to calculate the best possible receive window size for each connection by taking into account bandwidth, latency connection, and application retrieval rate. Bandwidth performance naturally improves with better throughput. Bandwidth performance can improve even more if all applications receive TCP data.

- ▶ **Compound TCP/IP (CTCP)**—Compound TCP/IP, which is most often used for TCP connections that have a large receive window size in addition to a large bandwidth delay product, ultimately improves receiver-side throughput. With CTCP, the amount of data sent across connections is significantly greater; however, TCP connections are not impacted negatively. If CTCP and Receive Window Auto-Tuning are used together, even more benefits, including increased link utilization and performance gains for large bandwidth delay connections, can be witnessed.

▶ **ECN support**—When a TCP segment is lost, TCP assumes that it was because of congestion at a router, so it performs congestion control. This lowers the TCP sender's transmission rate. With Explicit Congestion Notification (ECN) in the routing infrastructure, routers experiencing congestion mark the packets as they forward them. TCP peers receiving marked packets lower their transmission rate to ease congestion and prevent segment losses. This increases the overall throughput between TCP peers.

▶ **Improved routing**—Path maximum transmission unit (PMTU) black-hole router detection automatically adjusts the PMTU for a connection when large TCP segments are detected.

▶ **RFC optimizations**—The TCP/IP stack has better support for RFCs related to TCP communications.

▶ **Neighbor detection**—The Next Generation TCP/IP stack supports neighbor unreachability detection for IPv4 traffic. A computer such as a branch office maintains status about whether neighboring computers such as a hub site are reachable. This provides better error detection and recovery when computers are not available.

▶ **Dead Gateway support**—Unlike the previous Windows versions of Dead Gateway Detection, the Next Generation TCP/IP Dead Gateway support now provides a failover and failback mechanism when encountering dead gateways.

For more information on the new TCP/IP stack, review Chapter 10, "Domain Name System and IPv6."

## Distributed File System (DFS)

DFS in Windows Server 2008 R2 builds upon the completely revised replication engine in Windows Server 2003 R2. DFS, which was first introduced with Windows 2000 Server, provides a robust multimaster file replication service that is significantly more scalable and efficient in synchronizing file servers than its predecessor, File Replication Service (FRS).

With Windows Server 2008 R2, DFS includes an impressive list of benefits for both Active Directory and branch office server management, including simplified branch server management, reduction of backups, and more efficient storage management. In addition, DFS Replication (DFSR) enhances branch office implementations because it is possible to schedule and throttle replication schemes, support multiple replication topologies, and utilize Remote Differential Compression (RDC) to increase WAN efficiency. If WAN connections fail, data can be stored and forwarded until WAN connections become available. As a result, WAN replication is reduced and optimized, branch office mission-critical files can be replicated among branch offices, hub sites can reduce the amount of IT management that takes place in the branch office, and the need for backups can also be reduced.

Additionally, a new feature that was introduced in Windows Server 2008 R2 is support for read-only copies of information stored in Distributed File System (DFS) replicas. Because information that is stored on a read-only DFS replica is read-only, users are not able to modify/delete/create the replicated content. Therefore, information that is stored in a read-only DFS replica is protected at branch office locations from accidental modification.

For more information on understanding and deploying DFSR, review Chapter 28, "File System Management and Fault Tolerance."

## Group Policies

Windows Server 2008 R2 now uses DFSR to replicate Group Policy Objects between domain controllers within a domain. By leveraging DFSR differential replication, changes only occur between two domain controllers and not all of the domain controllers as in the past. As a result, the amount of bandwidth required during Group Policy replication is greatly reduced.

Group policies, which are the traditional Administrative Template files, are now replaced with new XML-based files called ADMX in Windows Server 2008 R2. Moreover, the new ADMX files are stored in a centralized store within SYSVOL. Thus, the new templates, storage of group policies, and utilization of DFSR for replication improve branch office solutions because less data needs to be replicated between the branch office and hub site.

For more information on understanding and implementing Group Policy Objects, see Chapter 27, "Group Policy Management for Network Clients."

## SMB Version 2.0

Another enhancement for Windows Server 2008 R2 branch office deployments is the server message block (SMB) protocol version 2.0. SMB, originally invented at IBM, is an application-level network file-sharing protocol mainly applied when accessing files, printers, serial ports, and miscellaneous communications between computers on a network.

The protocol hasn't evolved much since it was originally created 15 years ago. As a result, the protocol is considered to be overly chatty and generates unnecessary network traffic between computers on a network. This especially hinders users at branch office implementations when accessing files over the WAN to a hub site, especially if the WAN link is slow or already congested.

Microsoft understands the concerns and limitations with the existing version of SMB and has completely rewritten SMB to meet the demand of today's branch office needs. The benefits and improvements of the new SMB version 2.0 protocol on WAN network performance and end-user experience when transferring data between the branch office and hub sites include the following:

▶ Efficiency, performance, and data streaming are improved and are four to five times faster than the older version of SMB.

▶ The client can increase parallel requests.

▶ Offline capabilities are included, which is beneficial on slow networks and improves the end-user experience.

▶ Synchronization performance for offline files is improved.

▶ Multiple client requests can be compounded into a single round-trip.

▶ Users can now work in offline mode and synchronize changes on demand.

▶ Server scalability has been increased by reduced per-connection resource usage.

▶ The amount of bandwidth required for network communications has been dramatically reduced.

# Summary

Windows Server 2008 R2 provides fundamental technologies that assist organizations in implementing solutions for their branch offices. When dealing with branch offices that lack physical security and IT personnel, it is a best practice for organizations to combine the new Windows Server 2008 R2 technologies such as RODCs and BitLocker when deploying domain controllers at their remote locations. These combined technologies provide the strongest solution when security, ease of management, and prevention of data loss are concerns or business requirements.

Finally, with Windows Server 2008 R2, organizations can maintain the performance, availability, and productivity benefits of a local branch office server while avoiding the negative issues typically associated with branch office environments, including, but not limited to, connectivity setbacks and management overhead.

# Best Practices

The following are best practices from this chapter:

▶ Utilize the latest Windows Server 2008 R2 technologies to improve support and return on investment at the branch office.

▶ Leverage Read-Only Domain Controllers when there is a lack of experienced IT support personnel supporting the domain controller at the branch office and to reduce replication workload between the branch office and hub site.

▶ Use RODCs at the branch office to maintain administrator role separation and isolation because the domain controller is hosting more than one application.

▶ Conduct a staged implementation of an RODC if there is a need to have a non–highly privileged administrator conduct the RODC installation at the branch office.

▶ Exploit BitLocker to encrypt domain controller volumes at the branch office when theft and a lack of physical security are concerns.

▶ When implementing BitLocker at the branch office, leverage more than one factor for maximizing security and protection during bootup of the Windows Server 2008 R2 domain controller.

▶ For maximum protection, combine all of the new Windows Server 2008 R2 branch office technologies, such as RODCs, BitLocker, and Server Core installation, when deploying domain controllers at branch offices.

▶ Employ DFSR to the branch office and replicate branch office data back to a hub site to eliminate the need for branch office backups.

▶ Take advantage of the Next Generation TCP/IP stack, including SMB version 2, to reap the benefits of increased WAN performance between a branch office and hub sites.

32

# CHAPTER 33

# Logging and Debugging

$\bigcup$p until this chapter, the book has focused on planning, designing, implementing, and migrating to Windows Server 2008 R2. This chapter pays attention to the built-in management tools for monitoring, logging, debugging, and validating reliability, which help organizations identify and isolate problems in their networking environments.

Many of the tools identified in this chapter are similar to those used in previous versions of Windows; however, as with most features of the Windows Server family of products, the features and functionality of the tools have been improved and expanded upon in Windows Server 2008 R2.

This chapter covers the Task Manager for logging and debugging issues, the Event Viewer for monitoring and troubleshooting system issues, Performance Monitor, the new Best Practices Analyzer tool, the Task Scheduler for automation, and additional debugging tools available with Windows Server 2008 R2.

## Using the Task Manager for Logging and Debugging

The Task Manager is a familiar monitoring tool found in Windows Server 2008 R2. Ultimately, the tool is very similar to the Task Manager included with previous versions of Windows such as Windows Server 2003. It still provides an instant view of system resources, such as processor activity, process activity, memory usage, networking activity, user information, and resource consumption. However, there are some noticeable changes, including the addition of a Services tab and the ability to launch the Resource Monitor directly from the Performance tab.

The Windows Server 2008 R2 Task Manager is very useful for an immediate view of key system operations. It comes in handy when a user notes slow response time, system problems, or other nondescript problems with the network. With just a quick glance at the Task Manager, you can see whether a server is using all available disk, processor, memory, or networking resources.

There are three methods to launch the Task Manager:

▶ **Method 1**—Right-click the taskbar and select Task Manager.

▶ **Method 2**—Press Ctrl+Shift+Esc.

▶ **Method 3**—Press Ctrl+Alt+Del and select Start Task Manager.

When the Task Manager loads, you will notice six tabs, as shown in Figure 33.1.

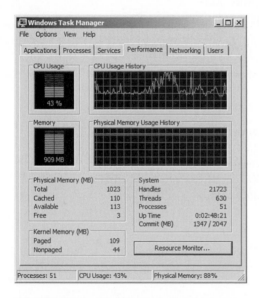

FIGURE 33.1   The Windows Task Manager.

---

**TIP**

If you are working on other applications and want to hide the Task Manager, deselect Always on Top in the Task Manager's Options menu. In addition, select Hide When Minimized to Keep the Task Manager off the taskbar when minimized.

---

The following sections provide a closer look at how helpful the Task Manager components can be.

## Monitoring Applications

The first tab on the Task Manager is the Applications tab. The Applications tab provides a list of tasks in the left column and the status of these applications in the right column. The status information enables you to determine whether an application is running and allows you to terminate an application that is not responding. To stop such an application, highlight the particular application and click End Task at the bottom of the Task Manager. You can also switch to another application if you have several applications running. To do so, highlight the program and click Switch To at the bottom of the Task Manager. Finally, you can create a dump file that can be used when a point-in-time snapshot of every process running is needed for advanced troubleshooting. To create a dump file, right-click on an application and select Create Dump File.

## Monitoring Processes

The second Task Manager tab is the Processes tab. It provides a list of running processes, or Image Names, on the server. It also measures the performance in simple data format. This information includes CPU percent used, memory allocated to each process, and username used in initiating a process, which includes system, local, and network services.

You can sort the processes by clicking the CPU or Memory (Private Working Set) column header. The processes are then sorted in order of usage. This way, you can tell which one is using the most of these resources and is slowing down performance of your server. You can terminate a process by selecting the process and clicking the End Process button.

Many other performance or process measures can be removed or added to the Processes tab. They include, but are not limited to, process identifier (PID), CPU time, session ID, and page faults. To add these measures, select View, Select Columns to open the Select Column property page. Here, you can add process counters to the process list or remove them from the list.

## Monitoring Services

With the release of Windows Server 2008, the newest edition to the family of Task Manager tabs was the Services tab. When selected, you can quickly assess and troubleshoot a specific service by viewing whether it has stopped or is still running. The Services tab also offers additional key details, including the service name, service description, and service group. In addition, it is also possible to launch the Services snap-in if there is a need to make changes to a specific service. For example, if you know a given service should be running and you don't see it running on the Processes tab (a common one is spoolsv.exe, which is the Windows Print Spooler service executable), you can just go to the Services tab and attempt to start the service from there. It's very rudimentary, but in keeping with what Task Manager is typically used for—it does offer a quick overview of system status and preliminary problem resolution.

## Monitoring Performance

The Performance tab enables you to view the CPU and physical memory usage in graphical form. This information is especially useful when you need a quick view of a CPU or memory performance bottleneck.

The Performance tab makes it possible to graph a percentage of processor time in Kernel mode. To show this, select View, Show Kernel Times. The kernel time is represented by the red line in the graph. The kernel time is the measure of time that applications are using operating system services. The other processor time is known as User mode. User mode processor time is spent in threads that are spawned by applications on the system.

If your server has multiple CPU processors installed, you can view multiple CPU graphs at a time by selecting View, CPU History and choosing either One Graph Per CPU or One Graph, All CPUs.

Also on the Performance tab, you will find a button labeled Resource Monitor. You can invoke Resource Monitor for additional analysis of the system.

## Monitoring Network Performance

The Networking tab provides a measurement of the network traffic for each adapter on the local server in graphical form, as shown in Figure 33.2.

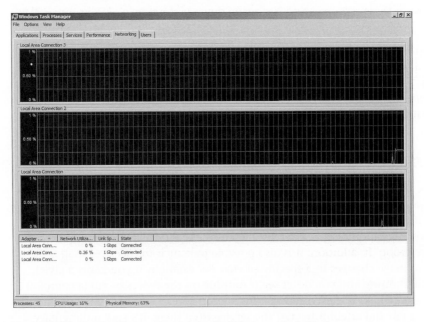

FIGURE 33.2    The Networking tab in the Windows Task Manager.

For multiple network adapters—whether they are dial-up, a local area network (LAN) connection, a wide area network (WAN) connection, a virtual private network (VPN) connection, or the like—the Networking tab displays a graphical comparison of the traffic for each connection. It provides a quick overview of the adapter, network utilization, link speed, and state of your connection.

To show a visible line on the graph for network traffic on any interface, the view automatically scales to magnify the view of traffic versus available bandwidth. The graph scales from 0% to 100% if the Auto Scale option is not enabled. The greater the percentage shown on the graph, the less is the magnified view of the current traffic. To auto scale and capture network traffic, select Options, Auto Scale.

It is possible to break down traffic on the graph into Bytes Sent, Received, and Total Bytes by selecting View, Network Adapter History and checking the selections you want graphed. This can be useful if you determine the overall throughput is high and you need to quickly determine if inbound or outbound traffic is an issue. In this situation, the default setting is displayed in Total Bytes.

You can also add more column headings by selecting View, Select Columns. Various network measures can be added or removed; they include Bytes Throughput, Bytes Sent/Interval, Unicast Sent and Received, and so on.

33

> **TIP**
>
> If you suspect a possible network server problem, launch the Task Manager and quickly glance at the CPU utilization, memory available, process utilization, and network utilization information. When the utilization of any or all of these items exceeds 60% to 70%, there might be a bottleneck or overutilization of a resource, causing pressure. However, if all the utilization information shows demand being less than 5%, the problem is probably not related to server operations.

## Monitoring User Activity

The final tab on the Task Manager is the Users tab, which displays a list of the users who are connected to or logged on to the server, session status, and names. The following five columns are available on the Users tab:

▶ **User**—Shows the users logged on the server. As long as the user is not connected via a console session, it is possible to remote control the session or send a message. Remote control can be initiated by right-clicking the user and selecting Remote Control. The level of control is dictated by the security settings configured in Remote Desktop.

▶ **ID**—Displays the numeric ID that identifies the session on the server.

▶ **Status**—Displays the current status of a session. Sessions can be either Active or Disconnected.

▶ **Client Name**—Specifies the name of the client computer using the session, if applicable.

▶ **Session**—Displays which session the user is logged on with.

# Using Event Viewer for Logging and Debugging

Event Viewer is the next tool to use when debugging, problem solving, or troubleshooting to resolve a problem with a Windows Server 2008 R2 system. Event Viewer, as shown in Figure 33.3, is a built-in Windows Server 2008 R2 tool completely rewritten based on an Extensible Markup Language (XML) infrastructure, which is used for gathering troubleshooting information and conducting diagnostics. Event Viewer was completely rewritten in Windows Server 2008 and many new features and functionality were introduced, including a new user interface and a home page, which includes an overview and summary of the system.

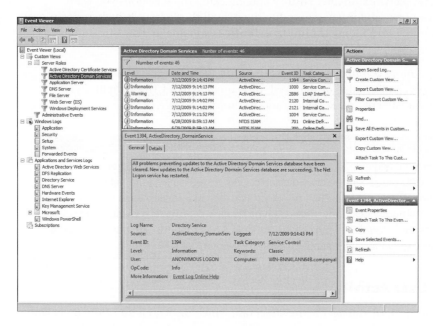

FIGURE 33.3    Event Viewer, including the Overview and Summary pane.

The upcoming sections focus on the basic elements of an event, including detailed sections covering the new features and functionality.

Microsoft defines an event as any significant occurrence in the operating system or an application that requires tracking of the information. An event is not always negative. A successful logon to the network, a successful transfer of messages, or replication of data can also generate an event in Windows. It is important to sift through the events to determine which are informational events and which are critical events that require attention.

When server or application failures occur, Event Viewer is one of the first places to check for information. Event Viewer can be used to monitor, track, view, and audit security of your server and network. It is used to track information of both hardware and software contained in your server. The information provided in Event Viewer can be a good starting point to identify and track down the root cause of any system errors or problems.

Event Viewer can be accessed through the Administrative Tools menu or by expanding the Diagnostics section of the new Server Manager MMC snap-in. You can also launch Event Viewer by running the Microsoft Management Console (Start, Run, mmc.exe) and adding the snap-in or through a command line by running eventvwr.msc.

Each log has common properties associated with its events. The following bullets define these properties:

- ▶ **Level**—This property defines the severity of the event. An icon appears next to each type of event. It helps to quickly identify whether the event is informational, a warning, or an error.

- ▶ **Date and Time**—This property indicates the date and time that the event occurred. You can sort events by date and time by clicking this column. This information is particularly helpful in tracing back an incident that occurred during a specific time period, such as a hardware upgrade before your server started experiencing problems.

- ▶ **Source**—This property identifies the source of the event, which can be an application, remote access, a service, and so on. The source is very useful in determining what caused the event.

- ▶ **Event ID**—Each event has an associated event ID, which is a numeral generated by the source and is unique to each type of event. You can use the event ID on the Microsoft Support website (www.microsoft.com/technet/) to find topics and solutions related to an event on your server.

- ▶ **Task Category**—This property determines the category of an event. Task Category examples from the Security log include Logon/Logoff, System, Object Access, and others.

## Examining the New Event Viewer User Interface

The interface for Event Viewer in Windows Server 2008 R2 has changed significantly from earlier versions. Although the information produced by logged events remains much the same, it's important to be familiar with the new interface to take advantage of the new features and functionality.

Administrators accustomed to using the latest Microsoft Management Console (MMC) 3.0 will notice similarities in the new look and feel of the Event Viewer user interface. The navigation tree on the left pane of the Event Viewer window lists the event logs available to view and also introduces new folders for creating custom event views and subscriptions from remote systems. The central details pane, located in the center of the console, displays relevant event information based on the folder selected in the navigation tree. The home page central details pane also includes a new layout to bolster the administrator's experience by summarizing administrative events by date and criticality, providing log summaries and displaying recently viewed nodes. Finally, the tasks pane, located on the extreme right side of the window, contains context-sensitive actions depending on the focus in the Event Viewer snap-in.

The folders residing in the left pane of the Event Viewer are organized by the following elements:

▶ Custom Views

▶ Windows Logs

▶ Applications and Services Logs

▶ Subscriptions

### The Custom Views Folder

Custom views are filters either created automatically by Windows Server 2008 R2 when new server roles or applications such as Active Directory Certificate Services and DHCP Server are added to the system or manually by administrators. It is important for administrators to have the ability to create filters that target only the events they are interested in viewing to quickly diagnose and remediate issues on the Windows Server 2008 R2 system and infrastructure. By expanding the Custom Views folder in the Event Viewer navigation tree and right-clicking Administrative Events, selecting Properties, and clicking the Edit Filter button, you can see how information from the event log is parsed into a set of filtered events. The Custom View Properties Filter tab is displayed in Figure 33.4. In the built-in Administrative Events custom views, all critical, error, and warning events are captured for all event logs. Rather than looking at the large number of informational logs captured by Windows Server 2008 R2 and cycling through each Windows log, this filter gives the administrator a single place to go and quickly check for any potential problems contained on the system.

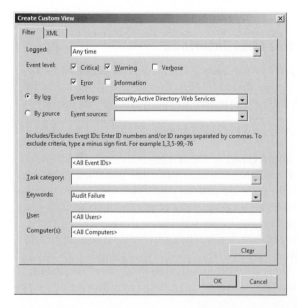

FIGURE 33.4   The Filter tab located in the Custom View Properties page.

Also listed in the Custom View section of Event Viewer are predefined filters created by Windows Server 2008 R2 when new roles are added to the system. These queries cannot be edited; however, they provide events related to all Windows Server 2008 R2 roles and the logical grouping can be used to quickly drill down into issues affecting the performance of the system as it relates to specific server roles. Again, this is a way of helping an administrator find the information needed to identify and ultimately resolve server problems quickly and efficiently.

The filter was first introduced with Windows Server 2008. The new Administrative Events filter groups all events associated with the system from an administrative perspective. By drilling down to the Administrative Events filter, an administrator can quickly decipher issues associated with all administrative events.

### Creating a New Custom View

To create a new custom view, in Event Viewer, right-click on the Custom View folder and select Create Custom View. Alternatively, select Custom View from the Action menu. This results in the Custom View Properties box, as illustrated in Figure 33.4.

First, decide whether you want to filter events based on date; if so, specify the date range by using the Logged drop-down list. Options include Any Time, Custom Range, and specific time intervals. The next step is to specify the Event Level criteria to include in the custom view. Options include Critical, Error, Warning, Information, and Verbose. After the Event Level settings are specified, the next area to focus on is the By Log and By Source sections. By leveraging the drop-down lists, specify the event log and event log sources to be included in this custom filter. To further refine the custom filter, enter specific event IDs, task categories, keywords, users, computers, and then click OK and save the filter by providing it a name, description, and the location of where to save the view.

---

**TIP**

Performance and memory consumption might be negatively affected if you have included too many events in the custom view.

---

After the custom view is defined, it can be exported as an XML file, which can then be imported into other systems. Filters can also be written or modified directly in XML but keep in mind, after a filter has been modified using the XML tab, it can no longer be edited using the GUI described previously.

### The Windows Logs Folder

The Windows Logs folder contains the traditional application, security, and system logs. Windows Server 2008 R2 also includes two out-of-the-box logs, which can also be found under the Windows Logs folder—the Setup and Forwarded Events logs. The following is a brief description of the different types of Windows logs that are available:

▶ **Application log**—This log contains events based on applications or programs residing on the system.

33

- ▶ **Security log**—Depending on the auditing settings configured, the security log captures events specific to authentication and object access.

- ▶ **Setup log**—This log captures information tailored toward installation of applications, server roles, and features.

- ▶ **System log**—Events associated with Windows system components are logged to the system log. This might include driver errors or other components failing to load.

- ▶ **Forwarded Events log**—Because computers can experience the same issues, this feature consolidates and stores events captured from remote computers into a single log to facilitate problem isolation, identification, and remediation.

### The Applications and Services Logs Folder

The Applications and Services Logs folder introduces a new way to logically organize, present, and store events based on a specific Windows application, component, or service instead of capturing events that affect the whole system. An administrator can easily drill into a specific item such as DFS Replication or DNS Server and easily review those events without being bombarded or overwhelmed by all the other systemwide events.

These logs include four subtypes: Admin, Operational, Analytic, and Debug logs. The events found in Admin logs are geared toward end users, administrators, and support personnel. This log is very useful because it not only describes a problem, but also identifies ways to deal with the issues. Operational logs are also a benefit to systems administrators but they typically require more interpretation.

Analytic and Debug logs are more complex. Analytic logs trace an issue and often a high number of events are captured. Debug logs are primarily used by developers to debug applications. Both Analytic and Debug logs are hidden and disabled by default. To view them, right-click Applications and Services Logs, and then select View, Show Analytic and Debug Logs .

### The Subscriptions Folder

The final folder in the Event Viewer console tree is called Subscriptions. Subscriptions is another new feature included with the Windows Server 2008 R2 Event Viewer. It allows remote computers to forward events; therefore, they can be viewed locally from a central system. For example, if you are experiencing issues between two Windows Server 2008 R2 systems, diagnosing the problem becomes challenging as both systems typically log data to their respective event logs. In this case, it is possible to create a subscription on one of the servers to forward the event log data from the other server. Therefore, both system event logs can be reviewed from a central system.

**Configuring Event Subscriptions**    Use the following steps to configure event subscriptions between two systems.

First, each source computer must be prepared to send events to remote computers:

1. Log on to the source computer. Best practice is to log on with a domain account that has administrative permissions on the source computer.

2. From an elevated command prompt, run `winrm quickconfig`. Exit the command prompt.

3. Add the collector computer to the local administrators group of the source computer.

4. Log on to the collector computer following the steps outlined previously for the source system.

5. From an elevated command prompt, run `wecutil qc`.

6. If you intend to manage event delivery optimization options such as Minimize Bandwidth or Minimize Latency, then also run `winrm quickconfig` on the collector computer.

After the collector and source computers are prepared, a subscription must be made identifying the events that will be pulled from the source computers. To create a new subscription, do the following:

1. On the collector computer, run Event Viewer with an account with administrative permissions.

2. Click on the Subscriptions folder in the console tree and select Create Subscription or right-click and select the same command from the context menu.

3. In the Subscription Name box, type a name for the subscription.

4. In the Description box, enter an optional description.

5. In the Destination Log box, select the log file where collected events will be stored. By default, these events are stored in the forwarded events log in the Windows Logs folder of the console tree.

6. Click Select Computers to select the source computers that will be forwarding events. Add the appropriate domain computers, and click OK.

7. Click Select Events and configure the event logs and types to collect. Click OK.

8. Click OK to create the subscription.

## Conducting Additional Event Viewer Management Tasks

Now that we understand the functionality of each of the new folders associated with the newly improved Event Viewer included with Windows Server 2008 R2, it is beneficial to review the upcoming sections for additional management tasks associated with Event Viewer. These tasks include the following:

▶ Saving event logs

▶ Organizing data

▶ Viewing logs on remote servers

▶ Archiving events

▶ Customizing the event log

▶ Understanding the security log

### Saving Event Logs

Event logs can be saved and viewed at a later time. You can save an event log by either right-clicking a specific log and choosing Save Events As or by picking individual events from within a log, right-clicking on the selected events, and choosing Save Selected Items. Entire logs and selected events can also be saved by selecting the same command from the Actions pane. After being saved, these logs can be opened by right-clicking the appropriate log and selecting Open Saved Log or by clicking on the same command in the Actions pane. After a log has been opened, it will be displayed in a new top-level folder called Saved Logs from within Event Viewer.

### Organizing Data

Vast numbers of logs can be collected by Windows and displayed in the central pane of Event Viewer. New tools or enhancement to old ones make finding useful information much easier than in any other iteration of Event Viewer:

- ▶ **Sorting**—Events can be sorted in many ways, for example, by right-clicking the folder or Custom View icon and then selecting View, Sort By, or by selecting the column name on which to sort in the left pane or clicking the column to be sorted or the heading. Sorting is a quick way to find items at a very high level (for example, by time, source, or event ID). The new features for finding and sorting data are more robust and well worth learning.

- ▶ **Selection and sorting of column headings**—Various columns can be added to or removed from any of the event logs. The order in which columns are displayed from left to right can be altered as well by selecting the column in the Select Column dialog box and clicking the up or down arrow button.

- ▶ **Grouping**—A new way to view event log information is through the grouping function. By right-clicking on column headings, an administrator can opt to group the event log being viewed by any of the columns in view. By isolating events, desired and specific criteria trends can be spotted that can help in isolating issues and ultimately resolving problems.

- ▶ **Filtering**—As mentioned earlier, filtering, like grouping, provides a means to isolate and only display the data you want to see in Event Viewer. Filtering, however, gives the administrator many more options for determining which data should be displayed than grouping or sorting. Filters can be defined based on any or all of the event levels, log or source, event ID(s), task category, keywords, or user or computer(s). After being created, filters can be exported for use on other systems.

- ▶ **Tasks**—By attaching tasks to events, logs, or custom views, administrators can bring some automation and notification into play when certain events occur. To create a task, simply right-click on the custom view, built-in log, or specific event of your choice, then right-click on Attach a Task to This Custom View, Log, or Event. The Create a Basic Task Wizard then launches; on the first tab, simply select a name and description for the task. Click Next to view the criteria that will trigger the task action (this section cannot be edited and is populated based on the custom view, log, or task selected when the wizard is initiated). Click Next and select Start a Program, Send an E-mail or Display a Message as desired.

### Viewing Logs on Remote Servers

You can use Event Viewer to view event logs on other computers on your network. To connect to another computer from the console tree, right-click Event Viewer (Local) and click Connect to Another Computer. Select Another Computer and then enter the name of the computer or browse to it and click OK. You must be logged on as an administrator or be a member of the Administrators group to view event logs on a remote computer. If you are not logged on with adequate permissions, you can select the Connect as Another User check box and set the credentials of an account that has proper permissions to view the logs on the remote computer.

### Archiving Events

Occasionally, you might need to archive an event log. Archiving a log copies the contents of the log to a file. Archiving is useful in creating benchmark records for the baseline of a server or for storing a copy of the log so it can be viewed or accessed elsewhere. When an event log is archived, it is saved in one of four forms:

▶ **Comma-delimited text file (.csv)**—This format allows the information to be used in a program such as Microsoft Excel.

▶ **Text-file format (.txt)**—Information in this format can be used in a program such as a word processing program.

▶ **Log file (.evtx)**—This format allows the archived log to be viewed again in the Windows Server 2008 R2 or Windows 7 Event Viewer. Note that the new event log format is XML, which earlier versions of Windows cannot read.

▶ **XML (.xml)**—This format saves the event log in raw XML. XML is used throughout Event Viewer for filters, tasks, and logging.

The event description is saved in all archived logs. To archive, right-click the log to be archived and click Save Log File As. In the File Name field of the resulting property page, type in a name for the archived log file, choose a file type from the file format options of .csv, .txt, .evtx, or .xml, and then click Save.

> **NOTE**
>
> You must be a member of the Backup Operators group at the minimum to archive an event log.

Logs archived in the new log-file format (.evtx) can be reopened using the Windows Server 2008 R2 Event Viewer utility. Logs saved in log-file format retain the XML data for each event recorded. Event logs, by default, are stored on the server where the Event Viewer utility is being run. Data can, however, be archived to a remote server by simply providing a UNC path (such as \\servername\share\) when entering a filename.

Logs archived in comma-delimited (.csv) or text (.txt) format can be reopened in other programs such as Microsoft Word or Excel. These two formats do not retain the XML data or formatting.

### Customizing the Event Log

The properties of an event log can be configured. In Event Viewer, the properties of a log are defined by general characteristics: log path, current size, date created, when last modified or accessed, maximum size, and what should be done when the maximum log size is reached.

To customize the event log, access the properties of the particular log by highlighting the log and selecting Action and then Properties. Alternatively, you can right-click the log and select Properties to display the General tab of the log's property page, as shown in Figure 33.5.

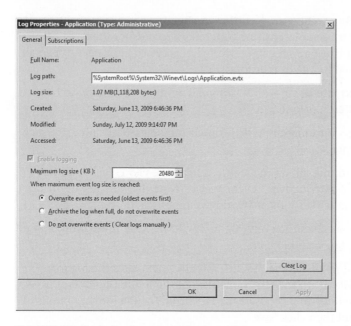

FIGURE 33.5    Selecting properties for the event log.

The Log Size section specifies the maximum size of the log and the subsequent actions to take when the maximum log size limit is reached. The three options are as follows:

- ▶ Overwrite Events as Needed (Oldest Events First)

- ▶ Archive the Log When Full, Do Not Overwrite Events

- ▶ Do Not Overwrite Events (Clear Logs Manually)

If you select the Do Not Overwrite Events option, Windows Server 2008 R2 stops logging events when the log is full. Although Windows Server 2008 R2 notifies you when the log is full, you need to monitor the log and manually clear the log periodically so new events can be tracked and stored in the log file.

In addition, log file sizes must be specified in multiples of 64KB. If a value is not in multiples of 64KB, Event Viewer automatically sets the log file size to a multiple of 64KB.

When you need to clear the event log, click the Clear Log button in the lower right of the property page.

### Understanding the Security Log

Effectively logging an accurate and wide range of security events in Event Viewer requires an understanding of auditing in Windows Server 2008 R2. It is important to know events are not audited by default. You can enable auditing in the local security policy for a local server, the domain controller security policy for a domain controller machine, and the Active Directory (AD) Group Policy Object (GPO) for a domain. Through auditing, you can track Windows Server 2008 R2 security events. It is possible to request that an audit entry be written to the security event log whenever certain actions are carried out or an object such as a file or printer in AD is accessed. The audit entry shows the action carried out, the user responsible for the action, and the date and time of the action.

# Performance and Reliability Monitoring

Performance is a basis for measuring how fast application and system tasks are completed on a computer and reliability is a basis for measuring system operation. How reliable a system is will be based on whether it regularly operates at the level at which it was designed to perform. Based on their descriptions, it should be easy to recognize that performance and reliability monitoring are crucial aspects in the overall availability and health of a Windows Server 2008 R2 infrastructure. To ensure maximum uptime, a well-thought-through process needs to be put in place to monitor, identify, diagnose, and analyze system performance. This process should invariably provide a means for quickly comparing system performances at varying instances in time, detecting, and potentially preventing a catastrophic incident before it causes system downtime.

Performance Monitor, which is a Microsoft Management Console (MMC) snap-in, provides a myriad of tools for administrators so they can conduct real-time system monitoring, examine system resources, collect performance data, and create performance reports from a single console. This tool is literally a combination of three legacy Windows Server monitoring tools: System Monitor, Performance Monitor, and Server Performance Advisor. However, new features and functionalities have been introduced to shake things up, including Data Collector Sets, resource view, scheduling, diagnostic reporting, and wizards and templates for creating logs. To launch the Performance Monitor MMC snap-in tool, select Start, All Programs, Administrative Tools, Performance Monitor, or type `perfmon.msc` at a command prompt.

The Performance Monitor MMC snap-in is composed of the following elements:

- Overview Screen
- Performance Monitor
- Data Collector Sets
- Report Generation

The upcoming sections further explore these major elements found in the Performance Monitoring tool.

## Performance Monitor Overview

The first area of interest in the Performance Monitor snap-in is the Overview of Performance Monitor screen, also known as the Performance icon. It is displayed as the home page in the central details pane when the Performance Monitor tool is invoked.

The Overview of Performance Monitor screen presents holistic, real-time graphical illustrations of a Windows Server 2008 R2 system's CPU usage, disk usage, network usage, and memory usage, as displayed in Figure 33.6.

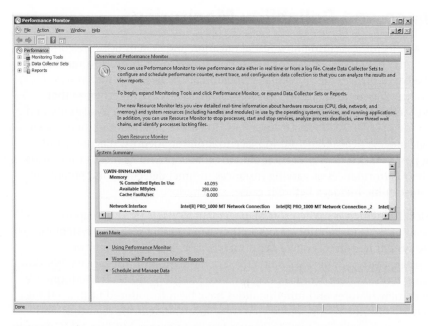

FIGURE 33.6   Viewing the Overview of Performance Monitor screen.

Additional process-level details can be viewed to better understand your system's current resource usage by reviewing subsections beneath each metric being displayed. For example, the Memory section includes % Committed Bytes in Use, Available Mbytes, and Cache Faults/sec.

The Overview of Performance Monitor screen is the first level of defense when there is a need to get a quick overview of a system's resources. If quick diagnosis of an issue cannot be achieved, an administrator should leverage the additional tools within Performance Monitor. These are covered in the upcoming sections.

## Performance Monitor

Windows Server 2008 R2 comes with two tools for performance monitoring. The first tool is called Performance Monitor and the second tool is known as Reliability Monitor. In the previous release of Windows, the Reliability Monitor tool was included in the Reliability and Performance snap-in. With Windows Server 2008 R2, the Reliability Monitor tool has been removed from the Performance Monitor console. The improved Performance Monitor tool provides performance analysis and information that can be used for bottleneck, performance, and troubleshooting analysis.

First, defining some terms used in performance monitoring will help clarify the function of Performance Monitor and how it ties in to software and system functionality. The three components noted in Performance Monitor, Data Collector Sets, and Reports are as follows:

▶ **Object**—Components contained in a system are grouped into objects. Objects are grouped according to system functionality or by association within the system. Objects can represent logical entities such as memory or a physical mechanism such as a hard disk drive. The number of objects available in a system depends on the configuration. For example, if Microsoft Exchange Server is installed on a server, some objects pertaining to Exchange would be available.

▶ **Counter**—Counters are subsets of objects. Counters typically provide more detailed information for an object such as queue length or throughput for an object. The System Monitor can collect data through the counters and display it in either a graphical format or a text log format.

▶ **Instances**—If a server has more than one similar object, each one is considered an instance. For example, a server with multiple processors has individual counters for each instance of the processor. Counters with multiple instances also have an instance for the combined data collected for the instances.

Performance Monitor provides an interface that allows for the analysis of system data, research performance, and bottlenecks. Performance Monitor displays performance counter output in line graphs, histogram (bar chart), and report format.

The histogram and line graphs can be used to view multiple counters at the same time, as shown in Figure 33.7. However, each data point displays only a single value that is independent of its object. The report view is better for displaying multiple values.

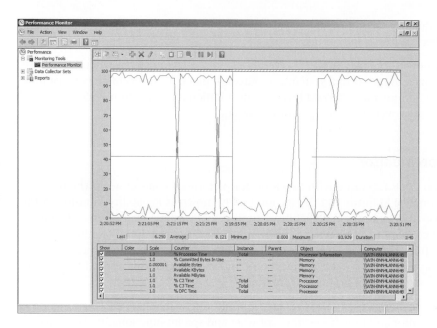

FIGURE 33.7    The graph view of Performance Monitor.

Launching Performance Monitor is accomplished by selecting Performance Monitor from the Monitoring Tools folder in the Performance Monitor MMC snap-in. You can also open it from a command line by typing Perfmon.msc. When a new Performance Monitor session is started, it loads a blank system monitor graph into the console with % Processor Time as the only counter defined.

### Adding Counters with Performance Monitor

Before counters can be displayed, they have to be added. The counters can be added simply by using the menu bar. The Counter button on the toolbar includes Add, Delete, and Highlight. You can use the Add Counter button to display new counters. On the other hand, use the Delete Counter button to remove unwanted counters from the display. The Highlight Counter button is helpful for highlighting a particular counter of interest; a counter can be highlighted with either a white or black color around the counter.

The following step-by-step procedures depict how to add counters to Performance Monitor:

1. In the navigation tree of Performance Monitor, first expand Performance, Monitoring Tools, and then Performance Monitoring.

2. Either click the Add icon in the menu bar or right-click anywhere on the graph and select Add Counters.

**NOTE**

Typical baseline counters consist of Memory - Pages/Sec, PhysicalDisk - Avg. Disk Queue Length, and Processor - % Processor Time.

3. The Add Counters dialog box is invoked, as shown in Figure 33.8. In the Available Counters section, select the desired counters, and click the Add button.

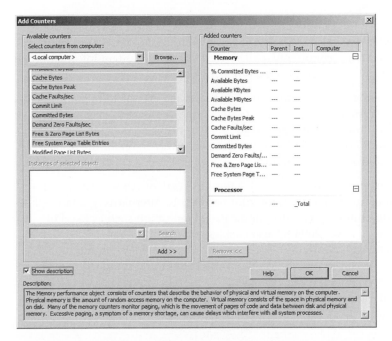

FIGURE 33.8    Adding counters to Performance Monitor.

> **NOTE**
>
> Windows Server 2008 R2 includes a tremendous amount of counters to choose from when conducting performance monitoring. It is challenging to fully explain what each counter offers in this section. If you are interested in finding out more about a counter, enable the Show Description option in the Add Counters dialog box and highlight a specific counter to obtain a detailed explanation of it.

4. Review the selected counters in the Added Counters section, and then click OK.

> **NOTE**
>
> When adding counters, it is possible to conduct remote monitoring by selecting counters from another system. To simplify things, it is also possible to search for instances of a counter and add a group of counters.

### Managing Performance Monitor Settings

While back on the Performance Monitor display, update displays by clicking the Clear Display button. Clicking the Freeze Display button or pressing Ctrl+F freezes displays, which suspends data collection. Data collection can be resumed by pressing Ctrl+F or clicking the Freeze Display button again. Click the Update Data button to display an updated data analysis.

It is also possible to export and import a display by using the Cut and Paste buttons. For example, a display can be saved to the Clipboard and then imported into another instance of Performance Monitor. This is commonly used to view or analyze system information on a different system, such as information from a production server.

The Properties page of Performance Monitor has five additional tabs of configuration: General, Source, Data, Graph, and Appearance. Generally, the Properties page provides access to settings that control the graph grid, color, style of display data, and so on. Data can be saved from the monitor in different ways. The easiest way to retain the display features is to save the control as an HTML file.

Performance Monitor enables you to also save log files in HTML or tab-separated (.tsv) format, which you can then analyze by using third-party tools. Alternatively, a tab-separated file can be imported into a spreadsheet or database application such as Excel or Microsoft Access. Windows Server 2008 R2 also enables you to collect data in SQL database format. This is useful for performance analysis at an enterprise level rather than a per-server basis. Reports displayed in Excel can help you better understand the data as well as provide reports to management. As well as saving log files, you can save the results from Performance Monitor as an image. This is great when you need to obtain a point-in-time depiction of a performance graph.

## Data Collector Sets

The Data Collector Sets is a vital new feature available as a subfolder within the Performance Monitor snap-in. The purpose of a Data Collector Set is to review or log system performance data. This is achievable through a single component that encompasses organized multiple data collection points. This information can then be analyzed to diagnose problems, correct system performance issues, or create baselines.

Performance counters, event trace data, and system configuration information are all data collector elements that can be captured and contained in a Data Collector Set. Data Collector Sets can be based on a predefined template, from a Data Collector Set that already exists, by creating it manually, with a wizard, or it can be user defined. Data Collector Sets can be exported and used for multiple systems, easing the administrative load involving the configuration of new systems producing more effective monitoring. Wizards facilitate the creation of Data Collector Sets and enable an administrator to quickly create collections based on server roles or the type of information that is required.

**NOTE**

To create Data Collector Sets, you must be a member of the Administrators group or logged on with an account that is a member of the Performance Log Users group.

## Creating Data Collector Sets

Data Collector Sets can be created manually from a template or from Performance Monitor. The following examples will help you to gain an understanding of the different methods for creating Data Collector Sets.

To create a Data Collector Set from Performance Monitor, do the following:

1. In the Performance Monitor snap-in, navigate to Performance Monitor.

2. Add counters based on items you want to capture. For this example, the following counters were used: Memory - Pages/Sec, Physical Disk - Avg.Disk Queue Length, and Processor - % Processor Time.

3. After the counters are added, right-click on Performance Monitor in the navigation tree, select New, and then select Data Collector Set. The Create New Data Collector Set Wizard is launched.

4. Enter a name for this new Data Collector Set on the Create New Data Collector Set page, and then click Next.

5. On the next page, specify where you want the data to be saved. The default path is the %systemdrive%\PerfLogs\. Click Finish to save the current settings and exit or click Next to enter a user account to run as.

6. Click the Change button to enter a user for this data set.

7. Select the option to Save and Close or Start This Data Collector Set Now, and then click Finish to complete the Data Collector Set creation process.

The resulting Data Collector Set can be configured to run immediately by right-clicking the new Data Collector Set and selecting Start. The properties of the Data Collector Set can be viewed by right-clicking and selecting Properties.

Data Collector Sets can be created, saved, or restored from templates. Many templates are built in and can be created using the Create New Data Collector Set Wizard in Windows Performance Monitor. This wizard is invoked by right-clicking on the User Defined folder, the Event Trace Sessions folder, or the Startup Event Trace Sessions folder under Data Collector Sets and selecting New, Data Collector Set.

To create a Data Collector Set from a template, do the following:

1. Expand the Data Collector Sets folder and then the User Defined subfolder in the Performance Monitor snap-in.

2. Right-click the User Defined subfolder and select New Data Collector Set to launch the Create New Data Collector Set Wizard.

3. Enter a name for this new Data Collector Set, select the Create from a Template option, and then click Next.

4. On the next page, select the desired template to use, and then click Next.

---

**NOTE**

The Create New Data Collector Set Wizard offers three templates for creating Data Collector Sets. The templates include Basic, System Diagnostics, and System Performance. Use the Basic template when there is a need to create a basic Data Collector Set. The System Diagnostics template generates a report detailing the status of local hardware resources, system response times, system information, and configuration data. The Systems Performance template is leveraged when you want to not only generate a report detailing the status of local hardware resources and system response times, but also processes on the local computers. In summary, typically the Basic template provides basic diagnostics, whereas the Systems Diagnostics template is good for maximizing performance and streamlining system operations, and the System Performance template is a good choice when you want to identify performance issues. Each of the templates can be edited after they have been created. In addition, it is possible to select the Browse button and import templates from other servers.

---

5. On the next page, specify where you want the data to be saved. The default path is the %systemdrive%\PerfLogs\. Click Finish to save the current settings and exit or click Next to enter a user account to run as.

6. Click the Change button to enter a user for this data set.

7. Select the option to Save and Close, Start This Data Collector Set Now, or Open Properties for This Data Collector Set, and then click Finish to complete the Data Collector Set creation process.

## Reports

The final folder in the Performance Monitor snap-in is Reports. The Reports folder provides diagnostic reports to support administrators in troubleshooting and diagnosing system performance problems including reliability. Reports are viewed in the central details pane of the Performance Monitor snap-in.

The reports are based on Data Collector Sets that were previously defined by users or preconfigured and included with Windows Server 2008 R2 Performance Monitor. The report console's features and functionality are very similar to those seen by means of the reports introduced with Server Performance Advisor in Windows Server 2003.

The Reports folder is broken into two main subfolders: User Defined reports and System reports. The default System reports typically include reports relating to LAN Diagnostics, System Diagnostics, and System Performance. Additional System reports are automatically generated depending on the server role installed on the Windows Server 2008 R2 system. For example, an Active Directory Diagnostics system report is automatically included in the console when the Active Directory Domain Services server role is installed on the Windows Server 2008 R2 system.

### Creating a User Defined Report

The first step in creating a User Defined report is creating a User Defined Collector Set and defining the parameters for a collection. After the User Defined Collector Set is created, data collection must be manually started or scheduled to run at a specific date. At this time, a report folder is automatically generated under the User Defined folder. After the report is created, you can review the contents by selecting it. When viewing reports, it is possible to expand specific items such as the report summary, diagnostic results, or CPU for additional information. This is depicted in the sample System Performance Report in Figure 33.9.

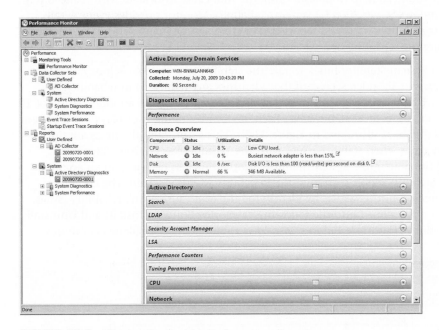

FIGURE 33.9    Viewing the System Performance Report.

### Viewing Predefined System Reports

Another option for assessing system health and troubleshooting system anomalies is to leverage the predefined system reports. The following steps illustrate how to view these system reports:

1. In the Performance Monitor navigation tree, expand the Data Collector Sets folder and then System.

2. Right-click one of the predefined Data Collector Sets such as System Diagnostics, and then click Start. This starts the data collection process.

3. Now expand the Reports folder, System, and then System Diagnostics.

4. Highlight the newly created report and review the contents of the report in the central details pane.

### NOTE

The report generates and appears when the data collection process is complete. The report is automatically tagged with the current date.

## Reliability Monitor

The Reliability Monitor was a brand-new tool first introduced with the release of Windows Vista and then reintroduced with Windows 2008. This enhanced system management tool is the second monitoring tool available within a Windows Server 2008 R2 system. The tool can be invoked by selecting View Reliability History from within the Action Center. Use this tool when you need help troubleshooting the root cause associated with reduced reliability of a Windows Server 2008 R2 system. Reliability Monitor provides event details through system stability charts and reports that help diagnose items that might be negatively impacting the reliability of a system.

The tool uses a System Stability Index to rate the stability of a system each day over its lifetime by means of an index scorecard that identifies any reduction in reliability. An index rating of 1 represents a system in its least stable stage, whereas an index rating of 10 indicates a system in its most stable stage. Each day's index rating is displayed in a System Stability Chart graph, as illustrated in Figure 33.10. This graph typically helps administrators to identify dates when stability issues with the Windows Server 2008 R2 system occurred. Additional itemized system stability information can be found in an accompanying System Stability Report section of the Reliability Monitor screen. The additional stability information further assists by identifying the root cause of the reliability issues. This information is grouped into the following categories: Software Installs and Uninstalls, Application Failures, Hardware Failures, Windows Failures, and Miscellaneous Failures.

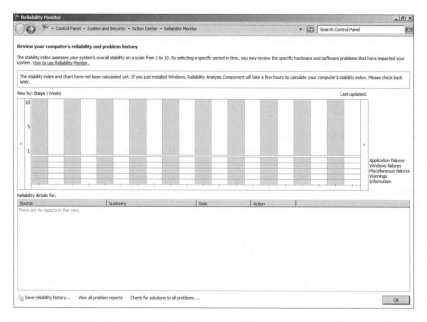

FIGURE 33.10    The Reliability Monitor screen.

Reliability Monitor is an essential tool for identifying and correlating problems with Windows Server 2008 R2. With Reliability Monitor, an administrator can quickly identify changes in a system that caused a negative trend with system reliability. As such, this tool can also help administrators anticipate other problems, which ultimately leads to solving issues efficiently and effectively.

# Setting Baseline Values

A baseline is a performance level that can be used as a starting point to compare against future network performance operations. When a server is first monitored, there is very little to compare the statistics against. After a baseline is created, information can be gathered at any time in the future and compared against the baseline. The difference between the current statistics and the baseline statistics is the variance caused by system load, application processing, or system performance contention.

To be able to set a baseline value, you need to gather a normal set of statistics on each system that will eventually be monitored or managed in the future. Baselines should be created for normal and stressed times. The workload on a machine at night when there are fewer users connected to it provides a poor baseline to compare real-time data in the middle of the day. Information sampled in the middle of the day should be compared with a baseline of information collected at around the same time of day during normal load prior to the sample comparison.

Creating baselines should be an ongoing process. If an application or a new service is added to a server, a new baseline should be created so that any future comparisons can be made with a baseline with the most current status of system performance.

## Reducing Performance Monitoring Overhead

Performance monitoring uses system resources that can affect the performance of a system as well as affect the data being collected. To ensure that performance monitoring and analyzing do not affect the machines being monitored themselves, you need to decrease the impact of performance monitoring. Some steps can be taken to ensure that performance monitoring overhead is kept to a minimum on the server being monitored to create as accurate of an analysis on a system as possible:

▶ Use a remote server to monitor the target server. Servers can actually be dedicated to monitoring several remote servers. Although this might also lead to an increase in network bandwidth, at least the monitoring and tracking of information do not drastically degrade CPU or disk I/O as if the monitoring tool were actually running on the server being monitored.

▶ Consider reducing the frequency of the data collection interval because more frequent collection can increase overhead on the server.

▶ Avoid using too many counters. Some counters are costly in terms of taxing a server for system resources and can increase system overhead. Monitoring several activities at one time also becomes difficult.

▶ Use logs instead of displaying graphs. The logs can then be imported into a database or report. Logs can be saved on hard disks not being monitored or analyzed.

## Important Objects to Monitor

The numbers of system and application components, services, and threads to measure in Windows Server 2008 R2 are so extensive that it is impossible to monitor thousands of processor, print queue, network, or storage usage statistics. Defining the roles a server plays in a network environment helps to narrow down what needs to be measured. Servers could be defined and categorized based on the function of the server, such as application server, file and print server, or services server such as DNS, domain controller, and so on.

Because servers perform different roles, and hence have different functions, it makes sense to monitor the essential performance objects. This helps prevent the server from being overwhelmed from the monitoring of unnecessary objects for measurement or analysis.

Overall, four major areas demand the most concern: memory, processor, disk subsystem, and network infrastructure. They all tie into any role the server plays.

The following list describes objects to monitor based on the roles played by the server:

▶ **Active Directory Domain Services**—Because the DC provides authentication, stores the Active Directory database, holds schema objects, and so on, it receives many requests. To be able to process all these requests, it uses up a lot of CPU resources, disks, memory, and network bandwidth. Consider monitoring memory, CPU, system, network segment, network interface, and protocol objects such as TCP, UDP, NBT, NetBIOS, and NetBEUI. Also worth monitoring are the Active Directory NTDS service and site server LDAP service objects. DNS and WINS also have applicable objects to be measured.

▶ **File and print server**—The print servers that process intensive graphics jobs can utilize extensive resources of system CPU cycles very quickly. The file server takes up a lot of storage space. Monitor the PrintQueue object to track print spooling data. Also monitor CPU, memory, network segment, and logical and physical disks for both file and print data collection.

▶ **Messaging collaboration server**—A messaging server such as an Exchange Server 2010 uses a lot of CPU, disk, and memory resources. Monitor memory collection, cache, processor, system, and logical and physical disks. Exchange objects are added to the list of objects after Exchange is installed, such as message queue length or name resolution response time.

▶ **Web server**—A web server is usually far less disk intensive and more dependent on processing performance or memory space to cache web pages and page requests. Consider monitoring the cache, network interface, processor, and memory usage.

▶ **Database server**—Database servers such as Microsoft SQL Server 2008 can use a lot of CPU and disk resources. Database servers can also use an extensive amount of memory to cache tables and data, so RAM usage and query response times should be monitored. Monitoring objects such as system, processor, logical disk, and physical disk is helpful for overall system performance operations.

# Using the Debugging Tools Available in Windows Server 2008 R2

Several useful tools are available in Windows Server 2008 R2 for troubleshooting and diagnosing various problems ranging from TCP/IP connection issues to verification and maintenance issues. These tools also make it much easier for IT professionals and administrators, allowing IT personnel to focus on business improvement tasks and functions, not on simply running specific tools in the networking environment.

## Best Practices Analyzer Tools

Many years ago, Microsoft introduced Best Practices Analyzer (BPA) tools for server products such as SQL Server and Exchange. The tools would enable an IT professional to conduct a scan against a product to ensure it was configured based upon industry best practices. For many years, IT professionals wanted a similar tool to scan their Windows infrastructure; however, one did not exist. Windows Server 2008 R2 now introduces a Best Practice Analyzer tool, which is included with all editions of the server except for Server Core. When scanning Server Roles to find best-practice violations, the BPA tool will measure a server role's compliance based upon eight different rule categories. The rule categories include Security, Performance, Configuration, Policy, Operation, Predeployment, Postdeployment, and BPA Prerequisites. Compliance is measured based upon three severity levels: Noncompliant, Compliant, and Warnings. It is worth noting that only a select few server roles are supported with BPA.

Note: The Windows BPA tool should be run on a regular basis to alleviate incorrect configurations, poor performance, poor reliability, and security violations.

Follow these steps to launch the Best Practice Analyzer tool:

1. Click Start, All Programs, and then select Server Manager.
2. In the tree pane, expand the Roles section.
3. Select a server role that you want to scan—for example, Active Directory Domain Services (AD DS).
4. In the details pane, open the Best Practice Analyzer section and then select Scan This Role.
5. Once the scan is complete, review the results in the same Best Practices Analyzer section, as displayed in Figure 33.11. Each result is categorized by Noncompliant, Excluded, Compliant, and All tabs.

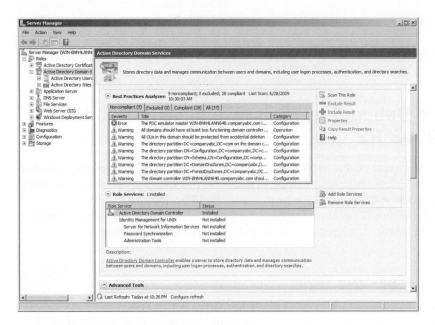

FIGURE 33.11    The Best Practices Analyzer Results screen.

When using the GUI to run a Best Practices Analyzer scan, it is possible to exclude scan results for a specific role. This can be achieved by selecting a result from the Noncompliant, Compliant, or All tabs and then clicking the Exclude link. Alternatively, you can exclude more than one result by holding down the CTRL key, selecting more than one result and then clicking Exclude.

## TCP/IP Tools

TCP/IP forms the backbone of communication and transportation in Windows Server 2008 R2. Before you can communicate between machines, TCP/IP must be configured.

In Windows Server 2008 R2, TCP/IP is installed by default during the OS installation and also makes it impossible to add or remove TCP/IP through the GUI.

If a TCP/IP connection fails, you need to determine the cause or point of failure. Windows Server 2008 R2 includes some dependable and useful tools that can be used to troubleshoot connections and verify connectivity. The tools described in the following ten sections are very useful for debugging TCP/IP connectivity problems. Most of these tools have been updated to include switches for IPv4 and IPv6.

### Ping

Ping means Packet Internet Groper. It is used to send an Internet Control Message Protocol (ICMP) echo request and echo reply to verify the availability of a local or remote machine. You can think of Ping as a utility that sends a message to another machine asking: "Are you still there?" By default, in Windows Server 2008 R2, Ping sends out four ICMP packages and waits for responses back in one second. However, the number of packages sent or time to wait for responses can be changed through the options available for Ping.

Besides verifying the availability of a remote machine, Ping can help determine a name resolution problem.

To use Ping, go to a command prompt and type `Ping Targetname`. Different parameters can be used with Ping. To display them, type `Ping /?` or `Ping` (without parameters).

The parameters for the Ping command are as follows:

- ▶ `-4`—Specifies that IPv4 is used to ping. This parameter is not required to identify the target host with an IPv4 address. It is required only to identify the target host by name.

- ▶ `-6`—Specifies that IPv6 is used to ping. Just like –4, this parameter is not required to identify the target host with an IPv6 address. It is required only to identify the target host by name.

- ▶ `-a`—Resolves the IP address to the hostname. The hostname of the target machine is displayed if this command is successful.

- ▶ `-f`—Requests that echo back messages are sent with the Don't Fragment flag in packets. This parameter is available only in IPv4.

- ▶ `-i ttl`—Increases the timeout on slow connections. The parameter also sets the value of the Time to Live (TTL). The maximum value is 255.

- ▶ `-j HostList`—Routes packets using the host list, which is a series of IP addresses separated by spaces. The host can be separated by intermediate gateways (loose source route).

- ▶ `-k HostList`—Similar to `-j` but hosts cannot be separated by intermediate gateways (strict source route).

- ▶ `-l size`—Specifies the length of packets in bytes. The default is 32. The maximum size is 65,527.

- ▶ `-n count`—Specifies the number of packets sent. The default is 4.

- ▶ `-r count`—Specifies the route of outgoing and incoming packets. It is possible to specify a count that is equal to or greater than the number of hops between the source and destination. The count can be between 1 and 9 only.

- ▶ `-R`—Specifies that the round-trip path is traced (available on IPv6 only).

- ▶ `-s count`—Sets the time stamp for the number of hops specified by count. The count must be between 1 and 4.

- ▶ `-S SrcAddr`—Specifies the source address to use (available on IPv6 only).

- ▶ `-t`—Specifies that Ping should continue sending packets to the destination until interrupted. To stop and display statistics, press Ctrl+Break. To stop and quit PING, press Ctrl+C.

33

▶ -v TOS—Specifies the value of the type of service in the packet sent. The default is zero. TOS is specified as a decimal value between 0 and 255.

▶ -w timeout—Specifies the time in milliseconds for packet timeout. If a reply is not received within the timeout, the Request Timed Out error message is displayed. The default timeout is four seconds.

▶ TargetName—Specifies the hostname or IP address of the destination to ping.

> **NOTE**
>
> Some remote hosts can be configured to ignore Ping traffic as a method of preventing acknowledgment as a security measure. Therefore, your inability to ping a server might not necessarily mean that the server is not operational, just that the server is not responding for some reason.

### Tracert

Tracert is generally used to determine the route or path taken to a destination by sending ICMP packets with varying Time to Live (TTL) values. Each router the packet meets on the way decreases the value of the TTL by at least one; invariably, the TTL is a hop count. The path is determined by checking the ICMP Time Exceeded messages returned by intermediate routers. Some routers do not return Time Exceeded messages for expired TTL values and are not captured by Tracert. In such cases, asterisks are displayed for that hop.

To display the different parameters that can be used with Tracert, open a command prompt and type tracert (without parameters) to display help or type tracert /?. The parameters associated with Tracert are as follows:

▶ -4—Specifies that tracert.exe can use only IPv4 for the trace.

▶ -6—Specifies that tracert.exe can use only IPv6 for the trace.

▶ -d—Prevents resolution of IP addresses of routers to their hostname. This is particularly useful for speeding up results of Tracert.

▶ -h maximumHops—Specifies the maximum number of hops to take before reaching the destination. The default is 30 hops.

▶ -j HostList—Specifies that packets use the loose source route option. Loose source routing allows successive intermediate destinations to be separated by one or multiple routers. The maximum number of addresses in the host list is nine. This parameter is useful only when tracing IPv4 addresses.

▶ -R—Sends packets to a destination in IPv6, using the destination as an intermediate destination and testing reverse route.

▶ -S—Specifies the source address to use. This parameter is useful only when tracing IPv6 addresses.

▶ -w timeout—Specifies the time in milliseconds to wait for each reply.

Tracert is a good utility to determine the number of hops and the latency of communications between two points. Even if an organization has an extremely high-speed connection to the Internet, if the Internet is congested or if the route a packet must follow requires forwarding the information between several routers along the way, the performance and, ultimately, the latency (or delay in response between servers) will cause noticeable communications delays.

## Pathping

Pathping is a route tracing tool that combines both features of Ping and Tracert commands with some more information that neither of those two commands provides. Pathping is most ideal for a network with routers or multiple routes between the source and destination hosts. The Pathping command sends packets to each router on its way to a destination, and then gets results from each packet returned from the router. Because Pathping computes the loss of packets from each hop, you can easily determine which router is causing a problem in the network.

To display the parameters in Pathping, open a command prompt and type `Pathping /?`. The parameters for the Pathping command are as follows:

- `-4`—Specifies that tracert.exe can use only IPv4 for the trace.

- `-6`—Specifies that tracert.exe can use only IPv6 for the trace.

- `-g Host-list`—Allows hosts to be separated by intermediate gateways.

- `-h maximumHops`—Specifies the maximum number of hops before reaching the target. The default is 30 hops.

- `-i address`—Uses the specified source address.

- `-n`—Specifies that it is not necessary to resolve the address to the hostname.

- `-p period`—Specifies the number of seconds to wait between pings. The default is a quarter of a second.

- `-q num_queries`—Specifies the number of queries to each host along the route. The default is three.

- `-w timeout`—Specifies the timeout for each reply in milliseconds.

## Ipconfig

Ipconfig displays all TCP/IP configuration values. It is of particular use on machines running DHCP. It is used to refresh DHCP settings and to determine which TCP/IP configuration values have been assigned by DHCP. If Ipconfig is used without parameters, it displays IP addresses, subnet masks, and gateways for each of the adapters on a machine. The adapters can be physical network adapters or logical adapters such as dial-up connections.

Some of the parameters for Ipconfig are as follows:

▶ /all—Displays all TCP/IP configuration values.

▶ /displaydns—Displays the contents of the DNS client resolver cache.

▶ /flushdns—Resets and flushes the contents of the DNS client resolver cache. This includes entries made dynamically.

▶ /registerdns—Sets manual dynamic registration for DNS names and IP addresses configured on a computer. This is particularly useful in troubleshooting DNS name registration or dynamic update problems between a DNS server and client.

▶ /release[Adapter]—Sends a DHCP release message to the DHCP server to discard DHCP-configured settings for adapters. This parameter is available only for DHCP-enabled clients. If no adapter is specified, IP address configuration is released for all adapters.

▶ /renew[Adapter]—Renews DHCP configuration for all adapters (if an adapter is not specified) and for a specific adapter if the Adapter parameter is included. This parameter is available only for DHCP-enabled clients.

▶ /setclassid Adapter [classID]—Configures the DHCP class ID for a specific adapter. You can configure the DHCP class ID for all adapters by using the wildcard (*) character in place of Adapter.

▶ /showclassid Adapter—Displays the DHCP class ID for a specific adapter.

▶ /allcompartments—Displays information about all compartments.

▶ /allocmpartments /all—Displays detailed information about all compartments.

> **NOTE**
>
> Ipconfig displays the assigned configuration for a system such as the default gateway, DNS servers, local IP address, subnet mask, and so on. When you're debugging network problems, you can use Ipconfig to validate that the proper TCP/IP settings have been set up for a system so that a server properly communicates on the network.

### Arp

Arp stands for Address Resolution Protocol. Arp enables the display and modification of the Arp table on a local machine, which matches physical MAC addresses of machines to their corresponding IP addresses. Arp increases the speed of connection by eliminating the need to match MAC addresses with IP addresses for subsequent connections.

Some of the parameters for Arp are as follows:

▶ -a[InetAddr] [-N IfaceAddr]—Displays the Arp table for all adapters on a machine. Use Arp –a with the InetAddr (IP address) parameter to display the ARP cache entry for a specific IP address.

▶ -dInetAddr [IfaceAddr]—Deletes an entry with a specific IP address (InetAddr). Use the IfaceAddr parameter (IP address assigned to the interface) to delete an entry in a table for a specific interface. Use the wildcard character in place of `InetAddr` to delete all entries.

▶ `-g[InetAddr] [-N IfaceAddr]`—Similar to the –a parameter.

▶ `-sInetAddr EtherAddr [IfaceAddr]`—Adds a static entry to the ARP cache that resolves the IP address (InetAddr) to a physical address (EtherAddr). To add a static ARP cache entry to the table for a specific interface, use the IP address assigned to the interface (IfaceAddr).

### Netstat

As its name implies, Netstat (or Network Statistics) is used to display protocol statistics for any active connections, monitor connections to a remote host, and monitor IP addresses or domain names of hosts with established connections.

The parameters for Netstat are as follows:

▶ `-a`—Displays all connections and listening ports by hostname.

▶ `-b`—Displays the executable involved in creating each connection.

▶ `-e`—Displays Ethernet packets and bytes to and from the host.

▶ `-n`—Displays address and port numbers without resolving the address to the hostname.

▶ `-o`—Displays TCP connections and includes the corresponding process ID (PID). Used in combination with –a, -n, and –p. Not available in previous Windows versions.

▶ `-p protocol`—Displays statistics based on the protocol specified. Protocols that can be specified are TCP, UDP, TCPv6, or UDPv6. It can be used with –s to display TCP, UDP, ICMP, IP, TCPv6, UDPv6, ICMPv6, or IPv6.

▶ `-s`—Displays statistics on a protocol-by-protocol basis. Can be used with the –p parameter to specify a set of protocols.

▶ `-t`—Displays the current connection offload state.

▶ `-r`—Displays the route table. Information displayed includes network destination, netmask, gateway, interface, and metric (number of hops).

▶ `[Parameter] Interval`—Displays the information at every interval specified. Interval is a numeral in seconds. Press Ctrl+C to stop the intervals.

### Route

Route is particularly useful for troubleshooting incorrect static routes or for adding a route to a route table to temporarily bypass a problem gateway. Static routes can be used in place of implicit routes specified by a default gateway. Use Route to add static routes to forward packets going to a gateway specified by default to avoid loops, improve traffic time, and so on.

The parameters for Route are as follows:

- ▶  -add—Adds a route to a table. Use -p to make the route persistent for subsequent sessions.

- ▶  -Delete—Deletes a route from the table.

- ▶  -Print—Prints a route.

- ▶  -change—Modifies an existing route.

- ▶  -destination—Specifies the host address.

- ▶  -gateway—Specifies the address of gateway for Route.

- ▶  IF interface—Specifies the interface for the routing table to modify.

- ▶  -mask Netmask—Uses the subnet mask specified by Netmask. If mask is not used, it defaults to 255.255.255.255.

- ▶  -METRIC Metric—Specifies the metric, or cost, for the route using the value Metric.

- ▶  -f—Clears the routing table of all gateway entries.

- ▶  -p—Used with -add to create a persistent route.

### Nslookup

Nslookup is used to query DNS. You can think of Nslookup as a simple diagnostic client for DNS servers. It can operate in two modes: Interactive and Noninteractive. Use Noninteractive mode to look up a single piece of data. To look up more than one piece of data, use Interactive mode. To stop Interactive mode at any time, press Ctrl+B. To exit from the command, type exit. If Nslookup is used without any parameters, it uses the default DNS name server for lookup.

The parameters for Nslookup are as follows:

- ▶  -ComputerToFind—Looks up information for the specified ComputerToFind. By default, it uses the current default DNS name server.

- ▶  -Server—Specifies the server as the DNS name server.

- ▶  -SubCommand—Specifies one or more Nslookup subcommands as a command-line option. Type a question mark (?) to display a list of subcommands available.

### DCDiag

The Domain Controller Diagnostic (DCDiag) tool analyzes the state of domain controllers and services in an Active Directory forest. It is installed when the Active Directory Domain Services (AD DS) role is added to a Windows Server 2008 R2 installation. This is a great general-purpose test tool for checking the health of an Active Directory infrastructure.

Tests include domain controller connectivity, replication errors, permissions, proper roles, and connectivity, and other general Active Directory health checks. It can even run non-domain controller-specific tests, such as whether a server can be promoted to a domain controller (the dcpromo test), or register its records properly in DNS (RegisterInDNS test).

DCDiag is run on domain controllers exclusively, with the exception of the dcpromo and RegisterInDNS tests.

When run without any parameters, the tests will be run against the current domain controller. This runs all the key tests and is usually sufficient for most purposes.

The parameters for DCDiag are as follows:

- `/s:DomainController`—Uses the domain controller as the home server.

- `/n:NamingContext`—Uses the specified naming context (NetBIOS, FQDN, or distinguished name) to test.

- `/u:Domain\UserName /p:{*¦Password¦""}`—Uses the supplied credentials to run the tool.

- `/a`—Tests all domain controllers in the site.

- `/e`—Tests all domain controllers in the enterprise.

- `/q`—Displays quiet output (errors only).

- `/v`—Displays verbose output.

- `/I`—Ignores minor error messages.

- `/fix`—Fixes minor problems.

- `/f:LogFile`—Logs to the specified log file.

- `/ferr:ErrorLogFile`—Logs errors to the specified log file.

- `/c`—Comprehensively runs all tests.

- `/test:TestName`—Runs the specified tests only.

- `/skip:TestName`—Skips the specified tests.

When specifying tests to run or to skip, nonskippable tests will still be run.

---

**NOTE**

DCDiag is automatically included on a Windows Server 2008 R2 system when the Active Directory Domain Services role is added. Otherwise, on non-domain controllers, the utility can be added by adding the Remote Server Administration Tools feature in Server Manager.

---

## System Startup and Recovery

The System Startup and Recovery utility stores system startup, system failure, and debugging information. It also controls the behavior (what to do) when a system failure occurs.

To open System Startup and Recovery, launch Control Panel, select System and Security, select System, Advanced System Settings, click the Advanced tab in the Systems Settings dialog box, and then click Settings under Startup and Recovery to display a property page similar to the one shown in Figure 33.12.

FIGURE 33.12   The Startup and Recovery page.

The Default Operating System field contains information that is displayed at startup. This information is typically the name of the operating system such as Windows Server 2008 R2. You can edit this information using bcdedit from a command prompt. If the machine is dual-booted, there will be an entry for each operating system. The Time to Display List of Operating Systems option specifies the time the system takes to display the name of the operating system at startup. The default time is 30 seconds. This can be increased or reduced. The Time to Display Recovery Options When Needed is unchecked by default but can be selected and an interval in seconds entered.

You can set the action to be taken when system failure occurs in the System Failure section. There are two options. The first option is Write an Event to the System Log. This action is not editable in Windows Server 2008 R2 because this action occurs by default every time a stop error occurs. The next option, Automatically Restart, reboots the system in the event of a system failure.

The Write Debugging Information section tells the system where to write debugging information when a system failure occurs. The options available include where the debugging information can be written to and the level of debugging information: Small Memory Dump (128KB), Kernel Memory Dump, Complete Memory Dump, or (None). The Write Debugging Information To option requires a paging file on the boot volume, which should be large enough to contain the select debugging option.

## Windows Memory Diagnostics Tool

Many troubleshooting scenarios revolve around memory-related issues associated with a system. Typical memory issues can involve an errant application, a specific process consuming too much memory, or failing hardware such as bad RAM or the memory system on the motherboard. Thankfully, Windows Server 2008 R2 includes a tool for diagnosing problems associated with system memory.

By using Windows Memory Diagnostics Tool, an administrator has another means for isolating root issues when a server is performing poorly, subject to crashes, or other abnormal behavior not caused by issues with the OS or installed applications.

The Windows Memory Diagnostics Tool can be launched by following the instructions below:

1. First, save all work and close down open applications and utilities.

2. To invoke the tool, select Start, All Programs, Administrative Tools, Windows Memory Diagnostic, or type MdSched at a command prompt.

3. Select whether you want to Restart Now and Check for Problems or Check for Problems the Next Time I Start My Computer, as displayed in Figure 33.13.

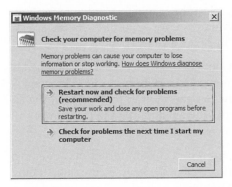

FIGURE 33.13    The options associated with running the Windows Memory Diagnostics tool.

4. When the system is rebooted, the Diagnostics tool automatically launches and conducts a Basic test by using default settings. Additional Test Mix options, Cache

options, and Pass Count can be selected by pressing F1. The Test Mix options consist of Basic, Standard, and Extended, whereas the Cache option includes Default, On, or Off. In addition, set the Pass Count value. The value represents the number of times the entire test mix will be repeated. Note a value of 0 represents infinitely. Press F10 to apply the settings and start the memory tests. Status is reported throughout the test indicating results.

---

**TIP**

The Windows Memory Diagnostics Tool might not detect all the problems with the system RAM. Just because no errors are reported doesn't mean the RAM or even the motherboard is working properly. Typically, the manufacturer of the hardware device will have additional diagnostics utilities that enable an administrator to conduct a deeper analysis of the root problems at the hardware level.

---

### Resources and Support Tools

Software errors can be reported in Windows Server 2008 R2. The Windows Error Reporting mechanism makes this happen. Additionally, the Customer Experience Improvement Program (CEIP) enables the system to report information to Microsoft about computer hardware and usage.

The errors reported in the error-reporting mechanism and information derived from the Customer Experience Improvement Program can be sent automatically or when the user is prompted to notify Microsoft to help improve its future products.

You can manage the Software Error-Reporting Mechanism by selecting the Enable Automatic Updating link in the Update This Server section on the Initial Configuration Tasks screen. To change Windows Error Reporting, select the Manually Configure Settings link and click the Change Settings button in the Windows Error Reporting section. Select the appropriate participation option, as displayed in Figure 33.14.

The Customer Experience Improvement Program Configuration screen can be launched by clicking the Change Settings button in the Customer Experience Improvement Program section. When the dialog box is invoked, select whether you want to participate in the Windows Server Customer Experience Improvement Program and indicate the number of servers, desktops, and industry that best represents your organization.

Finally, the combination of the resources and support tools help administrators better log, troubleshoot, and solve issues with a Windows Server 2008 R2 system. At the same time, Microsoft collects this information to improve the product.

## Task Scheduler

The Task Scheduler in Windows Server 2008 R2 replaces the Scheduled Tasks tool that was literally unchanged since the release of Windows 98. The main focal point of the tool is to assist administrators by automating tasks. In addition, by consolidating standard and reoc-

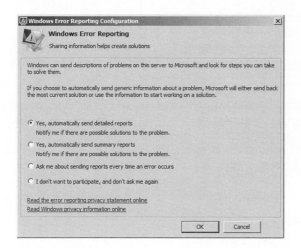

FIGURE 33.14    The error reporting screen.

curring tasks into a central location, administrators gain insight into system functionality and control over their Windows Server 2008 R2 infrastructure through automation. These things together assist administrators in the areas of logging and debugging.

Windows Server 2008 R2 improves upon the previous version of the Scheduled Task tools included in Windows Server 2003 by allowing scheduled jobs to run more securely and with greater predictability. One of the most compelling new features of the Task Scheduler is that it fully integrates with Event Viewer. As such, a task can be triggered based on an event captured in the event log. This is a great feature because administrators can be automatically notified when a specific event transpires.

## Understanding Task Scheduler

Scheduling tasks involves triggers and actions. A task runs once it is triggered. Tasks are initiated by triggers that are based on an event or time. Multiple triggers can be associated with a task as defined by an administrator. An action represents the work being performed as the task is being executed. Examples of actions include starting a program or sending an email. When a task is running multiple actions, up to 32 can be performed.

An additional functionality is task conditions. When a task is triggered, it will only run if specific defined conditions are met. Task conditions eliminate ambiguous situations by providing criteria-based functions. By improving on the Task Scheduler's functionality, it has become a very powerful and extensive development and activation tool for automating and assisting with troubleshooting tasks.

With Windows Server 2008 R2, Task Scheduler has been moved from Control Panel to Administrative Tools. The new user interface is displayed in Figure 33.15.

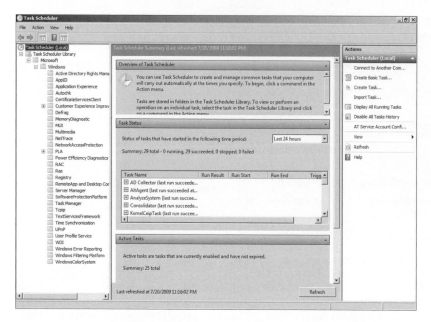

FIGURE 33.15    The Task Scheduler user interface.

Tasks are created by selecting Create Basic Task, Create Task, or Import Task from the Actions pane in the Task Scheduler snap-in. When creating a task, there are five tabs of options that must be configured. They include general settings, triggers, actions, conditions, and additional settings. The upcoming sections explain the options when creating tasks.

## Understanding Trigger Options and Settings

The first thing to consider when configuring a task is what triggers will cause the task to execute. Triggers can be based on time, events, or various system states. As noted earlier, each task can contain multiple triggers. With more than one trigger, the task will launch when any of the conditions in any of the triggers is met.

The following describes the various trigger types and the settings that can be configured for each type:

▶ **On a Schedule**—Triggers for a schedule allow tasks to run on a specific date (one time), Daily, Weekly, or Monthly. For reoccurring tasks, the start time can be configured along with reoccurring options to completely customize when the task will run.

▶ **At Log On**—Tasks scheduled to run when At Log On is set for any user or for a specific user or group of users.

▶ **At Startup**—There are no specific settings for tasks configured to run at startup. This type of trigger runs whenever the system starts and the only settings are the advanced ones, which are described later in the chapter.

▶ **On Idle**—The settings for tasks set to run when the computer is idle are set on the Conditions tab.

▶ **On an Event**—This trigger causes a task to run when specific events are created in an event log. You can choose either a basic event trigger or custom event settings. Basic settings fire based on a single event from a specific event log. You choose which log contains the event, the publisher name, and the event ID. If you specify the custom event trigger settings, you can specify an XML event query or custom event filter to query for events that will fire the task.

---

**NOTE**

It's easier to create event-based triggers from within the event log unless you know exactly what event(s) you want to trigger. See the section "Customizing the Event Log" earlier in this chapter for a detailed explanation of how to create events from within the event log.

---

▶ **At Task Creation/Modification**—Tasks created with this trigger are fired as soon as they are created or whenever they are modified. The only settings for this trigger are the advanced settings as described in the next section, "Understanding the Advanced Settings Associated with Triggers."

▶ **On Connection to User Session**—The trigger fires when a user connects to the system using the Remote Desktop Connection program from another system and can be set to run when any user connects, or when a specific user or group connects to the server.

▶ **On Disconnect from User Session**—This trigger works the same as the On Connection to User Session; however, it fires when users disconnect from the server from a Remote Desktop Connection session. The trigger can be set to run for all users or a specific user or group.

▶ **On Workstation Lock**—The trigger fires when the workstation is locked. The settings for this trigger enable you to set it for all users or a specific user or group.

▶ **On Workstation Unlock**—This trigger fires when the workstation is unlocked. The settings for this trigger enable you to set it for all users or a specific user or group.

## Understanding the Advanced Settings Associated with Triggers

Advanced settings exist when creating triggers. Familiarize yourself with these advanced settings to ensure trigger creation and the workflow process is fully optimized. The following bullets explain each of the advanced settings associated with triggers:

▶ **Delay Task for or Delay Task for Up To (Random Delay)**—Tasks can be delayed randomly so that they do not start immediately when the schedule triggers a task. For systems that might run the same tasks, this ensures there is some load balancing and that all systems do not run tasks at exactly the same time. Random delays can be set for 30 seconds, 1 minute, 30 minutes, 1 hour, 8 hours, or up to 1 day.

▶ **Repeat Task Every**—Tasks can also be set to repeat at regular intervals and for a set duration (for example, a task could be set to ping a particular system every minute for 1 day, write an event to the event log in the case of a failure, and email a distribution group to notify the IT team about the issue).

▶ **Stop Any Task If It Runs Longer Than**—Tasks can be stopped if they run past a defined amount of time and can be set to expire at a certain date and time.

▶ **Start and Expire**—Start and Expiration times can be set to synchronize across time zones to ensure tasks set to run on systems in multiple time zones start and stop at the same time.

▶ **Enabled**—Tasks can be enabled or disabled by checking or unchecking the enabled box.

## Understanding the Actions Associated with a Task

As mentioned earlier, an action is the work conducted when a task runs. Tasks can have a single action or up to a maximum of 32 actions. The Actions tab of a task contains a list of actions associated with a particular task. An administrator can edit each action as follows:

▶ **Start a Program**—This action starts a program or script. In the Program/Script text box, type either the name of the program or script that should be run. Alternatively, the administrator can browse the application or script. If further command-line arguments are required, these can be specified in the Add Arguments (Optional) text box. In the Start In (Optional) text box, the working directory can be specified for the command line that executes the program or script. This path is either the path to the program or script or to the files that are used by the executable.

▶ **Send an E-mail**—This action sends an email when the task is triggered. In the Edit Action dialog box, you enter who the email is from, who it should be sent to, a subject, and any desired text. You must also enter a valid SMTP server.

▶ **Display a Message**—This action simply displays a message on the console of the system where the task is created. You can enter a title for the message as well as any text that should be displayed. This type of action only launches if the Run Only If User Is Logged On security option has been selected on the General tab of the Task Properties in the Create Task dialog box.

## Understanding Conditions Associated with a Task

Conditions in conjunction with triggers determine whether the task will run. Tasks will not run if any condition associated with a given task is not fulfilled. The following sections illustrate the types of conditions associated with a task:

▶ **Idle Conditions**—A trigger can be based on idle time of a computer. Idle time is checked by the Task Scheduler service every 15 minutes. Computers are idle if a screensaver is running. When a screensaver is not running, the computer is considered to be idle if for 15 minutes the CPU usage and disk input or output were at 0% for 90% of the overall time. In this situation, mouse or keyboard input should also be nil during this period of time. The Task Scheduler service only waits for user input to mark the end of an idle state.

▶ **Power Conditions**—Administrators can specify that tasks run only on computers operating on AC power. If administrators do not want a task to run when a computer is on battery power, a condition must be set to stop the task. Also, if the computer is off, a condition can be set to awaken the computer from a Sleep or Hibernate mode so the task can run. Although this is unlikely in a server environment, it's still an option.

▶ **Network Conditions**—Administrators can choose to start a task only if a specified network connection is available. This setting is appropriate if the action requires access to a remote system or network.

> **NOTE**
>
> The Network Conditions do not support interoperability with Windows 2000 or XP.

## Understanding Task Settings

The Settings tab of the Tasks Properties or Create Task dialog box offers settings that help you control how the task is run, restarted, stopped, or deleted, as follows:

▶ **Allow Task to Be Run on Demand**—If selected, this setting enables the administrator to manually start the task regardless of triggers or conditions by selecting the tasks and clicking Run in the Actions pane or right-clicking the task and selecting Run from the context menu.

▶ **Run Task as Soon as Possible After a Scheduled Start Is Missed**—If this option is selected, a task that has been scheduled to start at a specific time but did not run (for example, the computer was off or the scheduler service was busy) will be started, but only after 10 minutes has elapsed from the original start time.

▶ **If the Task Fails, Restart Every**—This setting controls what to do when a task does not run (for example, if a task fails to start a service due to an undetermined system problem). If this option is selected, an administrator can also configure the number of attempts that should be made to initiate the task.

▶ **If the Running Task Does Not End When Requested, Force It to Stop**—If a task does not respond to a request to stop, an administrator can set a condition to force it to stop.

▶ **Stop the Task If It Runs Longer Than**—If this item is checked, a limit on how long the task can run is enforced. As a result of this setting, a task might not be completed when it is stopped.

▶ **If the Task Is Not Scheduled to Run Again, Delete It After**—This selection helps the administrator keep the Task Scheduler MMC free from old tasks that might have been put in place to accomplish a specific action but are no longer needed or will never be repeated. Note that a trigger must contain an expiration task.

▶ **If the Task Is Already Running: Do Not Start a New Instance**—The task will not start a new instance if an instance of the task is already running.

▶ **If the Task Is Already Running: Run a New Instance in Parallel**—A new task will run in parallel if one instance is running and the triggers and conditions cause the task to be triggered again.

▶ **If the Task Is Already Running: Queue a New Instance**—A new task will queue, but it will not start until the first instance is complete and will not stop the instance that is already running.

▶ **If the Task Is Already Running: Stop the Existing Instance**—A new task is triggered and conditions specified in the task will first stop the current instance and then start a new instance of the task.

### Understanding Task History

The History tab on the properties page for a task contains events filtered from the Operational events for the Task Scheduler in the Event Viewer and enables an administrator to see success and failures for any given task without having to review all task-related event information for a system or collection of systems.

---

**NOTE**

Although the Task Scheduler enables an administrator to create folders for organizing tasks and new tasks can be given meaningful names, after a folder or task is created, it cannot be renamed. Further, tasks cannot be moved from one folder to another. However, tasks can be exported and then imported into a new folder or another system.

---

# Summary

Logging and debugging tools help administrators monitor, manage, and problem solve errors on a Windows Server 2008 R2 system and infrastructure. Many of the tools used to identify system problems in a Windows Server 2008 R2 environment have been improved from previous versions of the applications in earlier releases of the Windows operating system. In addition, new tools have been introduced to enhance the administration logging and debugging experience. Key to problem solving is enabling logging and monitoring the logs to identify errors, research the errors, and perform system recovery based on problem resolution.

In addition to the tools and utilities that come with the Windows Server 2008 R2 environment are resources such as the Microsoft TechNet database (www.microsoft.com/technet/).

Between utility and tool improvements as well as online technical research databases, problem solving can be simplified in a Windows Server 2008 R2 infrastructure.

# Best Practices

The following are best practices from this chapter:

- ▶ Use the Task Manager to provide an instant view of system resources, such as processor activity, process activity, memory usage, and resource consumption.

- ▶ Use Event Viewer to check whether Windows Server 2008 R2 is experiencing problems.

- ▶ To mitigate configuration issues, server roles should be scanned with the Best Practices Analyzer tool on a regular basis.

- ▶ Use filters, grouping, and sorting to help isolate and identify key events.

- ▶ Create custom filters to expedite problem identification and improve monitoring processes.

- ▶ Create alerts using triggers and actions to identify issues quickly.

- ▶ Archive security logs to a central location on your network and then review them periodically against local security logs.

- ▶ Use subscriptions to consolidate logs from multiple systems to ensure that problems are identified quickly.

- ▶ Set an auditing policy to shut down the server immediately when the security log is full. This prevents generated logs from being overwritten or old logs from being erased.

- ▶ Establish a process for monitoring and analyzing system performance to promote maximum uptime and to meet service-level agreements.

- ▶ Run System Monitor from a remote computer to monitor servers.

- ▶ Use logging when monitoring a larger number of servers.

- ▶ Establish performance baselines.

- ▶ Create logging jobs based on established baselines to ensure performance data is captured during times when the system is having resource issues and to facilitate altering for proactive system management.

- ▶ Create new baselines as applications or new services are added to a server.

- ▶ Consider reducing the frequency of data collection to reduce the amount of data that must be collected and analyzed.

- ▶ Use logs to capture performance data.

- ▶ Use the Reliability Monitor to identify a timeline of system degradation to facilitate expeditious investigation of root issue causes.

- ▶ Use the Memory Diagnostics Tool to facilitate hardware troubleshooting.

33

# CHAPTER 34

# Capacity Analysis and Performance Optimization

Capacity analysis and performance optimization is a critical part of deploying or migrating to Windows Server 2008 R2. Capacity analysis and performance optimization ensures that resources and applications are available, uptime is maximized, and systems scale well to meet the growing demands of business. The release of Windows Server 2008 R2 includes some new and some refreshed tools to assist IT administrators and staff with properly assessing server capacity and performance—before and after Windows Server 2008 R2 is deployed on the network. If you invest time in these processes, you will spend less time troubleshooting or putting out fires, thus making your life less stressful and also reducing business costs.

## Defining Capacity Analysis

The majority of capacity analysis is working to minimize unknown or immeasurable variables, such as the number of gigabytes or terabytes of storage the system will need in the next few months or years, to adequately size a system. The high number of unknown variables is largely because network environments, business policy, and people are constantly changing. As a result, capacity analysis is an art as much as it involves experience and insight.

If you've ever found yourself having to specify configuration requirements for a new server or having to estimate whether your configuration will have enough power to sustain various workloads now and in the foreseeable future, proper capacity analysis can help in the design and configuration. These capacity-analysis processes help weed out the unknowns and assist you while making decisions as accurately as possible. They do so by giving you a greater understanding of your Windows Server 2008 R2 environment. This knowledge and understanding can then be used to reduce time and costs associated with supporting and designing an infrastructure. The result is that you gain more control over the environment, reduce maintenance and support costs, minimize firefighting, and make more efficient use of your time.

Business depends on network systems for a variety of different operations, such as performing transactions or providing security, so that the business functions as efficiently as possible. Systems that are underutilized are probably wasting money and are of little value. On the other hand, systems that are overworked or can't handle workloads prevent the business from completing tasks or transactions in a timely manner, might cause a loss of opportunity, or keep the users from being productive. Either way, these systems are typically not much benefit to operating a business. To keep network systems well tuned for the given workloads, capacity analysis seeks a balance between the resources available and the workload required of the resources. The balance provides just the right amount of computing power for given and anticipated workloads.

This concept of balancing resources extends beyond the technical details of server configuration to include issues such as gauging the number of administrators that might be needed to maintain various systems in your environment. Many of these questions relate to capacity analysis, and the answers aren't readily known because they can't be predicted with complete accuracy.

To lessen the burden and dispel some of the mysteries of estimating resource requirements, capacity analysis provides the processes to guide you. These processes include vendor guidelines, industry benchmarks, analysis of present system resource utilization, and more. Through these processes, you'll gain as much understanding as possible of the network environment and step away from the compartmentalized or limited understanding of the systems. In turn, you'll also gain more control over the systems and increase your chances of successfully maintaining the reliability, serviceability, and availability of your system.

There is no set or formal way to start your capacity-analysis processes. However, a proven and effective means to begin to proactively manage your system is to first establish systemwide policies and procedures. Policies and procedures, discussed shortly, help shape service levels and users' expectations. After these policies and procedures are classified and defined, you can more easily start characterizing system workloads, which will help gauge acceptable baseline performance values.

## The Benefits of Capacity Analysis and Performance Optimization

The benefits of capacity analysis and performance optimization are almost inconceivable. Capacity analysis helps define and gauge overall system health by establishing baseline performance values, and then the analysis provides valuable insight into where the system is heading. Continuous performance monitoring and optimization will ensure systems are stable and perform well, reducing support calls from end users, which, in turn, reduces costs to the organization and helps employees be more productive. It can be used to uncover both current and potential bottlenecks and can also reveal how changing management activities can affect performance today and tomorrow.

Another benefit of capacity analysis is that it can be applied to small environments and scale well into enterprise-level systems. The level of effort needed to initially drive the capacity-analysis processes will vary depending on the size of your environment, geography, and political divisions. With a little up-front effort, you'll save time, expense, and gain a wealth of knowledge and control over the network environment.

## Establishing Policy and Metric Baselines

As mentioned earlier, it is recommended that you first begin defining policies and procedures regarding service levels and objectives. Because each environment varies in design, you can't create cookie-cutter policies—you need to tailor them to your particular business practices and to the environment. In addition, you should strive to set policies that set user expectations and, more important, help winnow out empirical data.

Essentially, policies and procedures define how the system is supposed to be used—establishing guidelines to help users understand that the system can't be used in any way they see fit. Many benefits are derived from these policies and procedures. For example, in an environment where policies and procedures are working successfully and where network performance becomes sluggish, it would be safe to assume that groups of people weren't playing a multiuser network game, that several individuals weren't sending enormous email attachments to everyone in the Global Address List, or that a rogue web or FTP server wasn't placed on the network.

The network environment is shaped by the business more so than the IT department. Therefore, it's equally important to gain an understanding of users' expectations and requirements through interviews, questionnaires, surveys, and more. Some examples of policies and procedures that you can implement in your environment pertaining to end users could be the following:

- ▶ Email message size, including attachments can't exceed 10MB.

- ▶ SQL Server databases settings will be enforced with Policy Based Management.

- ▶ Beta software, freeware, and shareware can be installed only on test equipment (that is, not on client machines or servers in the production environment).

- ▶ Specify what software is allowed to run on a user's PC through centrally managed but flexible group policies.

- ▶ All computing resources are for business use only (in other words, no gaming or personal use of computers is allowed).

- ▶ Only business-related and approved applications will be supported and allowed on the network.

- ▶ All home directories will be limited in size (for example, 500MB) per user.

- ▶ Users must either fill out the technical support Outlook form or request assistance through the advertised help desk phone number.

Policies and procedures, however, aren't just for end users. They can also be established and applied to IT personnel. In this scenario, policies and procedures can serve as guidelines for technical issues, rules of engagement, or an internal set of rules to abide by. The following list provides some examples of policies and procedures that might be applied to the IT department:

▶ System backups must include System State data and should be completed by 5:00 a.m. each workday, and restores should be tested frequently for accuracy and disaster preparedness.

▶ Routine system maintenance should be performed only outside of normal business hours, for example, weekdays between 8:00 p.m. and 12:00 a.m. or on weekends.

▶ Basic technical support requests should be attended to within two business days.

▶ Priority technical support requests should be attended to within four hours of the request.

▶ Any planned downtime for servers should follow a change-control process and must be approved by the IT director at least one week in advance with a five-day lead time provided to those impacted by the change.

## Benchmark Baselines

If you've begun defining policies and procedures, you're already cutting down the number of immeasurable variables and amount of empirical data that challenge your decision-making process. The next step to prepare for capacity analysis is to begin gathering baseline performance values. The Microsoft Baseline Security Analyzer (MBSA) is an example of a tool that performs a security compliance scan against a predefined baseline.

Baselines give you a starting point with which you can compare results. For the most part, determining baseline performance levels involves working with hard numbers that represent the health of a system. On the other hand, a few variables coincide with the statistical representations, such as workload characterization, vendor requirements or recommendations, industry-recognized benchmarks, and the data that you collect.

### Workload Characterization

Workloads are defined by how processes or tasks are grouped, the resources they require, and the type of work being performed. Examples of how workloads can be characterized include departmental functions, time of day, the type of processing required (such as batch or real-time), companywide functions (such as payroll), volume of work, and much more.

It is unlikely that each system in your environment is a separate entity that has its own workload characterization. Most, if not all, network environments have systems that depend on other systems or are even intertwined among different workloads. This makes workload characterization difficult at best.

So, why is workload characterization so important? Identifying systems' workloads allows you to determine the appropriate resource requirements for each of them. This way, you can properly plan the resources according to the performance levels the workloads expect and demand.

**Benchmarks**

Benchmarks are a means to measure the performance of a variety of products, including operating systems, virtually all computer components, and even entire systems. Many companies rely on benchmarks to gain competitive advantage because so many professionals rely on them to help determine what's appropriate for their network environment.

As you would suspect, Sales and Marketing departments all too often exploit the benchmark results to sway IT professionals over their way. For this reason, it's important to investigate the benchmark results and the companies or organizations that produced the results. Vendors, for the most part, are honest with the results, but it's always a good idea to check with other sources, especially if the results are suspicious. For example, if a vendor has supplied benchmarks for a particular product, check to make sure that the benchmarks are consistent with other benchmarks produced by third-party organizations (such as magazines, benchmark organizations, and in-house testing labs). If none are available, you should try to gain insight from other IT professionals or run benchmarks on the product yourself before implementing it in production.

Although some suspicion might arise from benchmarks because of the sales and marketing techniques, the real purpose of benchmarks is to point out the performance levels that you can expect when using the product. Benchmarks can be extremely beneficial for decision making, but they shouldn't be your sole source for evaluating and measuring performance. Use the benchmark results only as a guideline or starting point when consulting benchmark results during capacity analysis. It's also recommended that you pay close attention to their interpretation.

Table 34.1 lists companies or organizations that provide benchmark statistics and benchmark-related information, and some also offer tools for evaluating product performance.

TABLE 34.1    Organizations That Provide Benchmarks

| Company/Organization Name | Web Address |
| --- | --- |
| The Tolly Group | www.tollygroup.com |
| Transaction Processing | www.tpc.org/ |
| Lionbridge (Veritest) | www.etestinglabs.com/ |
| Computer Measurement Group | www.cmg.org/ |

# Using Capacity-Analysis Tools

Analyzing system capacity and performance requires a handful of tools and the knowledge to use them properly to obtain valuable data. Windows Server 2008 R2 includes several tools to assist with this initiative, and even more are available for download or purchase from Microsoft. In addition, several other companies also have performance and capacity-analysis solutions available. Some of these tools are even capable of forecasting system capacity, depending on the amount of information they are given.

A number of sizing tools exist from various companies. A sizing tool takes data relative to the networking environment and returns recommended hardware configurations, usually in a Microsoft Excel spreadsheet or similar reporting application. An example of one such tool is the Microsoft Assessment and Planning (MAP) Toolkit for Windows Server 2008 R2. This tool, available for download from Microsoft at http://technet.microsoft.com/en-us/solutionaccelerators/dd537573.aspx, assists you when planning your migration to Windows Server 2008 R2 by creating an inventory of your current server infrastructure; therefore, you can determine hardware and device compatibility and Windows Server 2008 R2 readiness.

Another free tool offered from Microsoft is the Virtualization Solution Accelerators. For example, the Microsoft Assessment and Planning (MAP) Toolkit for Hyper-V can be leveraged to accelerate your migration to Hyper-V on Windows Server 2008 R2 by identifying underutilized servers within your infrastructure, which can be potential virtualization candidates.

Microsoft also offers several useful utilities that are either inherent to Windows Server 2008 R2 or are sold as separate products. Some of these utilities are included with the operating system, such as Task Manager, Network Monitor, Performance Monitor, and the enhanced Event Viewer. Data that is collected from these applications can be exported to other applications, such as Excel or Microsoft Access, for inventory and analysis. Other Microsoft utilities like System Center Configuration Manager (SCCM) and System Center Operations Manager (OpsMgr) can also be used; however, they are sold separately.

## Task Manager

The Windows Server 2008 R2 Task Manager is similar to its Windows Server 2008 and Windows Server 2003 predecessors in that it offers multifaceted functionality. You can view and monitor processor, memory, application, network, services, user, and process-related information in real time for a given system. This utility is a well-known favorite among IT personnel and is great for getting a quick view of key system health indicators with the lowest performance overhead.

To begin using Task Manager, use any of the following methods:

▶ Press Ctrl+Shift+Esc.

▶ Right-click on the taskbar and select Start Task Manager.

▶ Press Ctrl+Alt+Delete and then click Start Task Manager.

When you start Task Manager, you'll see a screen similar to that shown in Figure 34.1.

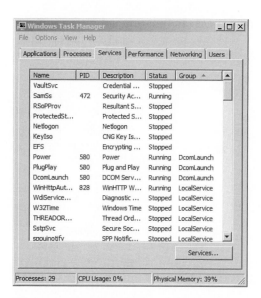

FIGURE 34.1    Services tab in the Windows Server 2008 R2 Task Manager.

The Task Manager window contains the following six tabs:

▶ **Applications**—This tab lists the applications that are currently running. You can start and end applications from this tab.

▶ **Processes**—On this tab, you can find performance metric information of the processes currently running on the system. Sorting the processes by CPU or memory usage will reveal which processes are consuming the most system resources.

▶ **Services**—A recent addition to Windows is the Services tab in Task Manager. As shown in Figure 34.1, administrators can now see what services are running without having to load Computer Management or the Services Management Console (services.msc) separately.

▶ **Performance**—This tab can be a graphical or tabular representation of key system parameters such as kernel usage, paging, CPU cycles, and more—in real time.

▶ **Networking**—This tab displays the network traffic coming to and from the machine. The displayed network usage metric is a percentage of total available network capacity for a particular adapter.

▶ **Users**—This tab displays users who are currently logged on to the system.

In addition to the Task Manager tabs, the Task Manager is, by default, configured with a status bar at the bottom of the window. This status bar, shown in Figure 34.2, displays the number of running processes, CPU utilization percentage, and the amount of memory currently being used.

FIGURE 34.2    Windows Server 2008 R2 Task Manager status bar.

As you can see, Task Manager presents a variety of valuable real-time performance information. This tool is particularly useful for determining what processes or applications are problematic and gives you an overall picture of system health with quick access to terminate applications and processes, or identify potential bottlenecks.

There are limitations, however, which prevent it from becoming a useful tool for long-term or historical analysis. For example, Task Manager can't store collected performance information for future analysis and viewing; it is capable of monitoring only certain aspects of the system's health, and the information that is displayed pertains only to the local machine. For these reasons alone, Task Manager doesn't make a prime candidate for capacity planning.

## Network Monitor

Network Monitor is a crucial tool that system administrators should have in their arsenal. Network Monitor, now in its third version, has been overhauled to support the new networking changes introduced with both Windows Server 2008 R2 and Windows 7. Network Monitor 3.3 includes several enhancements for capturing network traffic and parsing the captured data for use in troubleshooting, capacity analysis, and performance tuning. The next few sections cover using Network Monitor to capture network traffic between two computers, on a wireless connection, over remote access connections; how to analyze captured data; and how to parse captured data for analysis. Network Monitor 3.3, shown in Figure 34.3, can be downloaded from the System Tools section in the Microsoft Download Center at www.microsoft.com/downloads/.

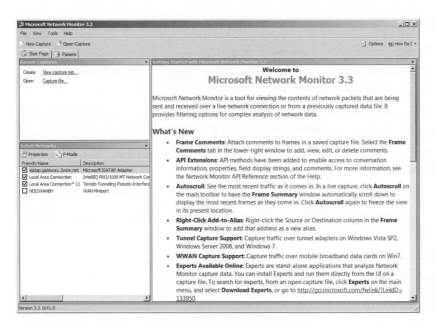

FIGURE 34.3    The Network Monitor 3.3 interface.

**NOTE**

The Network Monitor TechNet blog located at http://blogs.technet.com/netmon contains a wealth of information regarding Network Monitor, capturing, and analyzing data.

**NOTE**

Network Monitor 3.3 is available in ia64, x64, and x86 versions and can run on Windows Server 2008 R2, Windows Server 2008, Windows Server 2003, Windows 7, Windows Vista, and Windows XP systems.

### What's New in Network Monitor 3.3

Network Monitor 3.3 expands on the capabilities of the previous versions of Network Monitor by including several more features and fixes for issues that were discovered in the 3.x versions. Network Monitor 3.3 is very flexible and can even stop a capture based on an event log entry in Event Viewer.

The previous versions of Network Monitor included the following:

▶ An optimized interface that included network conversations and an expandable tree view of frames for the conversation(s)

▶ A real-time display and updating of captures

▶ The ability to capture traffic on multiple network cards simultaneously

▶ The ability to run multiple capture sessions simultaneously

▶ A script-based protocol parser language

▶ Support for Windows Server 2008, Windows Vista, Windows XP, and Windows Server 2003 on 32- or 64-bit platforms

▶ The ability to capture wireless traffic, scan one or all wireless channels supported by the network card, and view signal strength and transfer speed of the connection

▶ The ability to trace traffic inside of a Windows Vista virtual private network (VPN) tunnel by capturing remote access server (RAS) traffic

▶ The ability to right-click in the Frame Summary pane and click Add to Filter

▶ Support for the Windows Update service by periodically checking for updates to the Network Monitor program

▶ A redesigned filter toolbar

▶ A redesigned engine for supporting more protocol schemes

▶ New public parsers like ip1394, ipcp, PPPoE, and more

Some of the new features in Network Monitor 3.3 include the following:

▶ Support for Windows Server 2008 R2, Hyper-V, and Windows 7

▶ The ability to capture WWAN and tunnel traffic on Window 7 computers

▶ Support for both IPv4 and IPV6

### Using Network Monitor 3.3

Before you can start using the advanced features of Network Monitor, analyzing captured data, and identifying potential issues and bottlenecks, a basic understanding of Network Monitor and how it works is necessary.

To capture network traffic, install Network Monitor 3.3 and do the following:

1. Run Network Monitor (Start, All Programs, Microsoft Network Monitor 3.3, Microsoft Network Monitor 3.3).
2. Click the Create a New Capture Tab link in the left pane.
3. Click the Start button or press F5 to start capturing traffic.

To apply filters to a captured stream of information, do the following:

1. With a capture running and the tab selected, as shown in Figure 34.4, click the Filter menu in the menu bar at the top of the Network Monitor program.

   ▶ **To create a capture filter**—Click on Capture Filter, Load Filter, Standard Filters to select a preconfigured filter that will capture traffic relative to a specific item such as DNS.

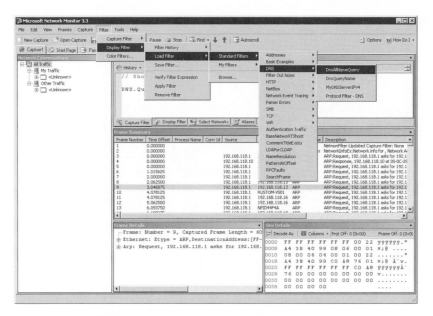

FIGURE 34.4    Capturing and Configuring Filters in Network Monitor 3.3.

▶ **To create a display filter**—Click on Display Filter, Load Filter, Standard Filters to select a preconfigured filter that will only display information relative to a specific item such as DNS from captured data.

▶ **To create a color filter**—Click on Color Filter, Load Filter, Standard Filters to apply a color effect to specific items such as DNS.

2. After a filter has been added, it must be applied. Filters can be applied by clicking the Apply button in the Capture Filter pane, pressing the Ctrl+Enter keys simultaneously, or clicking Apply in the Filter menu for the added filter.

3. Apply the filter(s) by clicking the Filter menu at the top of the Network Monitor program.

▶ To apply a capture filter, highlight Capture Filter, and click Apply Filter.

▶ To apply a display filter, highlight Display Filter, and click Apply Filter.

▶ To add a color filter, click Color Filter, click Add, add an expression (for example, RDP or 192.168.1.5), and format the font for your preference. Click OK, and click OK again to apply the filter and close the Color Filter window.

Alternatively, a capture or display filter can be applied by right-clicking on an item in the Frame Summary pane and selecting Add Cell to Display Filter, as shown in Figure 34.5. Figure 34.6 shows a sample capture with a DNS capture filter applied and all RDP packets color-coded in red using a color filter.

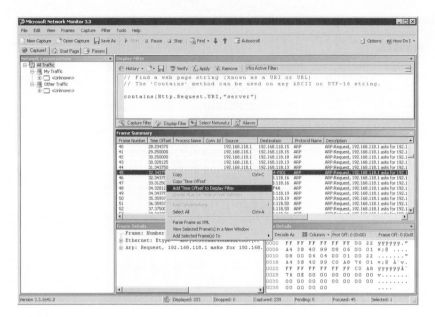

FIGURE 34.5    Choosing to add a cell to display filter.

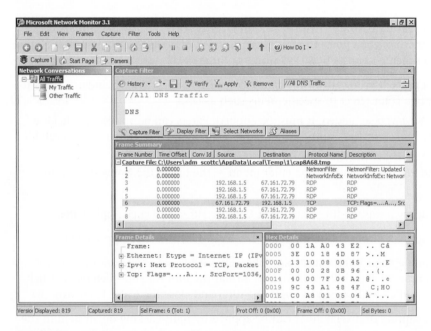

FIGURE 34.6    Sample capture with red highlighted filtered data.

To remove a filter, simply highlight the correct filter type from the Filter menu and select Remove Filter, click the Remove button in the Capture Filter pane, or press the Ctrl+Shift+Enter keys simultaneously.

**NOTE**

Removing a filter does not remove it from the filter list. It just removes it from being applied.

### Capturing Network Traffic Between Computers

As outlined previously, Network Monitor 3.3 includes the ability to capture wireless, remote, local area network (LAN), and wide area network (WAN) traffic using a remote agent. In some cases, network administrators want to diagnose or monitor a conversation between two computers. The steps necessary to monitor traffic between two different computers are outlined in the following list.

To capture network traffic between two different computers using IPv4 source and destination addresses, as shown in Figure 34.7, do the following:

1. In Network Monitor, click the Create a New Capture Tab button on the left.

2. Click the Filter menu, select Capture Filter, Load Filter, Standard Filters.

3. Select Addresses, and then IPv4 Addresses.

4. Edit the filter to specify the IP addresses that should be filtered in the Capture Filter window (for example, 192.168.0.100 and Any).

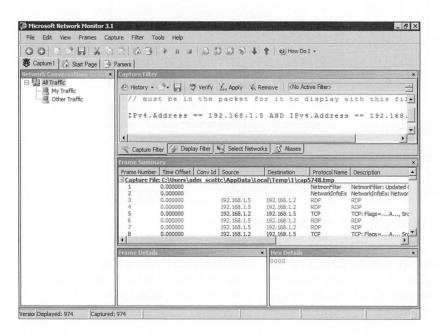

FIGURE 34.7    Network Monitor capture of network traffic between two IP addresses.

5.  Click the Apply button in the Capture Filter pane.

6.  Click the Start button on the main Network Monitor menu bar or press the F5 key to start the capture.

### Parsing Captured Network Traffic Data

Parsing captured data allows the information to be converted into a format that is more legible to the naked eye. Parsing captured data makes analysis of the captured data easier—in fact, it's almost essential. The Network Monitor parsing engine was completely rewritten to support the new functionality of Network Monitor 3.3.

To modify parsing of captured data in Network Monitor 3.3, do the following:

1.  With a capture running or loaded from a saved file, select the Parsers tab in Network Monitor, as shown in Figure 34.8.

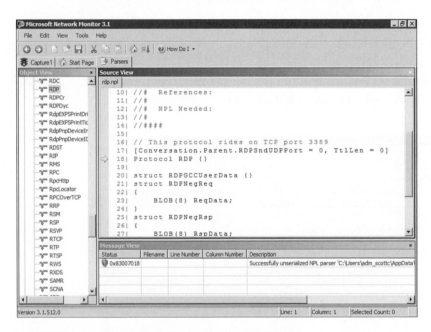

FIGURE 34.8    Parsers tab of Network Monitor 3.3.

2.  Expand the appropriate parsing category and double-click on the desired parser to load the parser code into the editor. Parsers use Network Monitor Parser Language (NPL), a simple-to-use language. Help for NPL is included in the Network Monitor 3.3 Help file.

## Windows Performance Monitor

The Performance Monitor in Windows Server 2008 R2, shown in Figure 34.9, has been modified since Windows Server 2008 as it no longer includes the Reliability Monitor snap-in. The Performance Monitor is composed of three main components: monitoring tools such as Performance Monitor, Data Collector Sets, and a reporting component. The Performance Monitor can be launched from within the Windows Server 2008 R2 Server Manager or from the Start, All Programs, Administrative Tools menu.

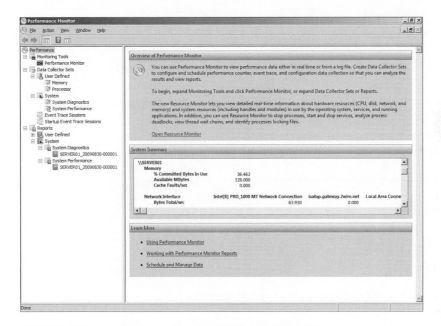

FIGURE 34.9   Performance Monitor in Windows 2008 R2.

Using Performance Monitor, administrators can identify bottlenecks and pinpoint resource issues with applications, processes, or hardware. Monitoring these items can help identify and resolve issues, plan for capacity changes, and help establish baselines that can be used for analysis in the future. Upon launching the Performance Monitor, a summary of system performance is displayed, showing current memory, disk, processor, and network loads.

### Performance Monitor

Many IT professionals rely on the Performance Monitor because it is bundled with the operating system, and it allows you to capture and monitor every measurable system object within Windows Server 2008 R2. Using the tool involves little effort to become familiar with it. You can find and start the Performance Monitor from within the

Performance Monitor program under Monitoring Tools in the console view. The Performance Monitor, shown in Figure 34.10, is by far the best utility provided in the operating system for capacity-analysis purposes. With this utility, you can analyze data from virtually all aspects of the system both in real time and historically. This data analysis can be viewed through charts, reports, and logs. The log format can be stored for use later so that you can scrutinize data from succinct periods of time.

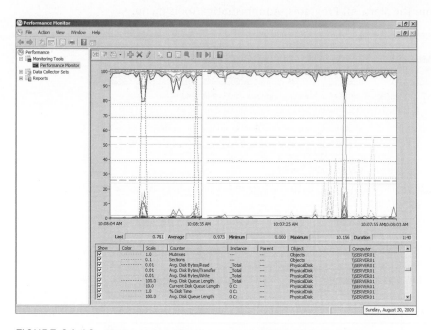

FIGURE 34.10   Performance Monitor expanded Data Collector Sets.

### Data Collector Sets

As mentioned previously, Data Collector Sets are a collective grouping of items to be monitored. You can use one of the predefined sets or create your own to group together items that you want to monitor. Data Collector Sets are useful for several reasons. First, data collectors can be a common theme or a mix of items. For example, you could have one Data Collector Set that monitors only memory or a Data Collector Set that contains a myriad of items such as memory, disk usage, processor time, and more. Data Collector Sets can also be scheduled to run when needed. The Data Collector Sets section of the Performance Monitor is shown in Figure 34.11.

### Reports

As previously discussed, the Performance Monitor includes an updated reporting mechanism and several template performance and diagnostic reports for use. In addition, reports can also be created manually or generated from Data Collector Sets. Three system reports are included for diagnosing and assessing system performance: LAN Diagnostics, System Diagnostics, and System Performance. The following steps outline the process to view a System Diagnostics report. Figure 34.12 shows a sample System Diagnostics report.

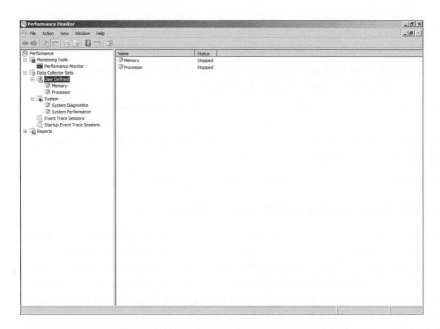

FIGURE 34.11    Data Collector Sets in Performance Monitor.

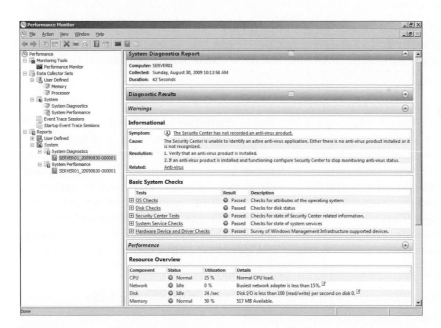

FIGURE 34.12    System Diagnostics report in Performance Monitor.

34

To create and view reports in Performance Monitor, do the following:

1. Expand Data Collector Sets and System in the console tree of Performance Monitor.

2. Right-click on either the System Diagnostics or System Performance sets and select Start. Windows will begin collecting data for the report.

3. When you have collected enough data, right-click the collection set again, and select Stop.

4. Expand Reports, System and click the collection set you chose earlier. Double-click the report listed under that performance set.

5. The report will be compiled and displayed, as in Figure 34.12.

## Other Microsoft Assessment and Planning Tools

Several other products and tools are available from Microsoft to assist with proper capacity analysis and performance monitoring. Some of these tools are available for purchase separately or can be downloaded for free. Selecting the right tool or product depends on the goal you are trying to accomplish. For example, the Windows System Resource Manager (WSRM) would be used if you want to implement thresholds for the amount of resources an application or process is allowed to consume, and System Center Operations Manager might be deployed if you want to be notified when critical processes behave abnormally on production servers.

Discussing each of these tools in depth is beyond the scope of this book; however, a basic understanding and overview of their purposes will help you make an informed decision when selecting the right technologies for analyzing system resources, availability, and performance.

### Windows System Resource Manager

Windows System Resource Manager is included in the feature set of Windows Server 2008 R2 and provides an interface that allows you to configure how processor and memory resources are allocated among applications, services, and processes. Having the ability to control these items at such a granular level can help ensure system stability, thus improving system availability, improving the user experience. Assigning thresholds to services, applications, and processes can prevent issues like high CPU consumption. System Resource Manager is installed as a feature in Server Manager. System Resource Manager can manage multiple items on the local system and remote computers (if Remote Desktop Services is installed). The System Resource Manager interface is shown in Figure 34.13.

To install System Resource Manager, do the following:

1. Launch Server Manager by choosing it in the Administrative Tools folder.

2. Click Features in the Scope pane on the left.

3. Click Add Features in the central Details pane; the Select Features window opens.

4. Scroll down and select Windows System Resource Manager.

5. If it isn't already installed, a notification window opens stating that the Windows Internal Database feature must also be installed. Click the Add Required Features button to accept the addition of the feature.

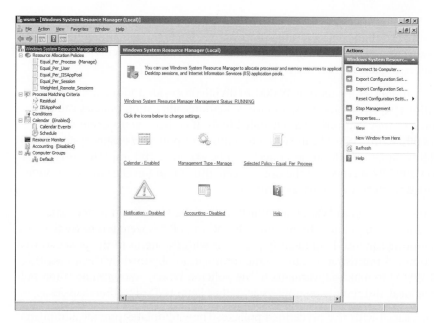

FIGURE 34.13    Windows System Resource Manager.

6. Click Next.

7. Click Install to install the Windows System Resource Manager and required components.

8. Click Close when the installation completes.

**NOTE**

A warning appears in Server Manager if the Windows System Resource Manager service is not started. This service must be running to use Windows System Resource Manager.

After WSRM is installed, you can start fine-tuning the Windows Server 2008 R2 server's processes, services, applications, and other items to ensure CPU cycles and memory usage are allocated appropriately. WSRM provides administrators with a means of adjusting the system to meet the demands of those accessing it. WSRM can allocate CPU time and memory usage through the use of the included resource allocation policies or a customized one. Observed system usage and data obtained from tools like Performance Monitor can be applied directly to WSRM policies. For example, if system monitoring reveals that a particular application is in high demand but the same server is busy providing other services, making the application sluggish, the WSRM can allocate enough resources to both items to ensure that neither the system nor the items being used are negatively impacted. It is very common for WSRM to be implemented in conjunction with SQL Server to improve sustainability in a consolidated environment. For example, if 10 WSRM-managed SQL Server instances exist, each instance can be granted 10% of the total processor. Each instance can use its entire share of the processor, but if nine instances are using less than their allocated processor resource, the remaining instance can use more processor resources. If demand for processor resources then increases on one of the other instances, WSRM returns the resources as needed.

Resource allocation policies are used in WSRM to divide processor and memory usage among applications, services, processes, and users. Resource allocation policies can be in effect at all times, or they can run on a scheduled basis. If certain events occur or the system behaves differently, WSRM can switch to a different policy to ensure system stability and availability. Resource allocation policies can be exported and imported between Windows Server 2008 R2 servers and the policies can also contain exclusions when something doesn't require specific resource assignments.

When accounting is enabled in WSRM, administrators of the servers can review data collected to determine when and why resource allocation policies were too restrictive or too loose. Accounting can also help identify problems with the items in the policy as well as peak access times. Administrators can use the information obtained by the accounting component of WSRM to make adjustments to the policies. WSRM resource allocation policies can manage local and remote computers as well as Remote Desktop Services sessions.

WSRM comes packaged with five predefined policies. These templates provide administrators with a way to quickly allocate resources, leaving room for fine-tuning at a later time. The predefined resource allocation policy templates are as follows:

- ▶ **Equal per Process**—Allocates resources equally among all running processes, preventing one process from consuming all available CPU and memory resources

- ▶ **Equal per User**—Allocates resources equally among all users, preventing one user from consuming all available CPU and memory resources

- ▶ **Equal per Session**—Allocates resources equally among all Remote Desktop Services sessions, preventing one session from consuming all available CPU and memory resources

- ▶ **Equal per IIS Application Pool**—Allocates resources equally among all IIS application pools, preventing one session from consuming all available CPU and memory resources

- ▶ **Weighted Remote Sessions**—Controls priority for users who are remotely connected to the system

> **NOTE**
>
> WSRM policies are only enforced when CPU usage climbs above 70%. The WSRM policies are never active on processes owned by the core operating system or any items in the exclusion list.

> **TIP**
>
> Memory limits should be applied in policies only when the application, service, or process is having issues or not allocating memory usage properly on its own.

A common task performed in WSRM is to create matching criteria rules. Matching criteria rules allow an administrator to define (or exclude) processes, services, or applications that should be monitored by WSRM. This definition is used later in the WSRM management process. To create a matching criteria rule, do the following:

1. Launch Windows System Resource Manager by clicking Start, All Programs, Administrative Tools, Windows System Resource Manager.

2. Right-click the Process Matching Criteria item in the WSRM console and select New Process Matching Criteria.

3. Enter a unique name for the matching criteria in the Criteria Name box at the top and click Add under the Rules section.

   ▶ Enter the processes, services, or applications in the Included Files or Command Lines section of the Files or Command Lines tab.

   *Or*

   ▶ Select the object type (process, service application, or IIS application pool) from the drop-down list, and click the Select button and select the policy to apply.

4. To exclude items from the policy, check the Excluded Files or Command Lines check box.

   ▶ Enter the processes, services, or applications in the Included Files or Command Lines section of the Files or Command Lines tab.

   *Or*

   ▶ Select the object type (process, service application, or IIS application pool) from the drop-down list, and click the Select button and select the policy to apply.

5. Repeat the preceding steps to add all of the exclusions and items that should be managed by or excluded from a WSRM policy.

Another task that is commonly performed is creating custom resource allocation policies. Similar to "matching criteria rules" that look for specific process, service, and application criteria, the custom resource allocation policy provides the administrator the ability to define how much of a resource should be allocated to a specific process, service, or application. As an example, if only 20% of the system processing should be allocated to a print process, the resource allocation would be defined to limit the allocation of resources to that process. To create a custom resource allocation policy, do the following:

1. Launch Windows System Resource Manager by clicking Start, All Programs, Administrative Tools, Windows System Resource Manager.

2. Right-click the Resource Allocation Policies option in the WSRM console, and select New Resource Allocation Policy.

3. Provide a name for the policy, and click the Add button in the Allocate These Resources section.

4. On the General tab, select the Process Matching Criteria and specify the percentage of processor time that will apply.

5. On the Memory tab, specify the maximum committed memory and working set limits.

34

6. The Advanced tab allows you to select which processors the policy should be assigned to as well as suballocating processor resources. If you want to edit these parameters, make the changes and click OK.

7. Click OK when you are finished.

The calendar component of WSRM can be used to schedule policy enforcement on a regular basis and by one-time or recurring events. For example, policy enforcement might only be necessary during normal business hours. Calendar control is enabled by default and can be controlled by right-clicking the Calendar item in the WSRM console and selecting the Enable or Disable option. To create calendar items based on scheduled times, do the following:

1. Launch Windows System Resource Manager by clicking Start, All Programs, Administrative Tools, Windows System Resource Manager.

2. Expand the Calendar item in the WSRM console by clicking the plus sign.

3. Right-click the Schedule option and select New Schedule.

4. Enter a name and description for the schedule.

5. Double-click on a time slot in the New Schedule window, specify the policy, start, and stop times, and click OK.

Rather than creating a calendar item based on scheduled times, you can create the calendar item based on a specific triggered event. To create calendar items based on specific events, do the following:

1. Launch Windows System Resource Manager by clicking Start, All Programs, Administrative Tools, Windows System Resource Manager.

2. Expand the Calendar item in the WSRM console by clicking the plus sign.

3. Right-click the Calendar Event option, and select New One Time Event.

4. Enter a name for the event.

5. Select Policy Name or Schedule Name, and select the appropriate policy.

6. Specify a start and end date and time (not available if associated with a schedule), and click OK.

For calendar events that you want to trigger based on recurring events, a rule can be created for this to happen. To create recurring events, do the following:

1. Launch Windows System Resource Manager by clicking Start, All Programs, Administrative Tools, Windows System Resource Manager.

2. Expand the Calendar item in the WSRM console by clicking the plus sign.

3. Right-click the Calendar Event option, and select New Recurring Event.

4. Enter a name for the event.

5. Select Policy Name or Schedule Name, and select the appropriate policy.

6. Specify a start and end time and specify a recurrence schedule, such as every Monday (not available if associated with a schedule), and click OK.

One example of where WSRM is useful is when an administrator wants to allocate system resources to sessions or users who are active on a Windows Server 2008 R2 Remote Desktop Services system. Configuring a WSRM policy for Remote Desktop Services can ensure the sessions will not behave erratically and system availability will be stabilized for all who use the Remote Desktop Services server. This is accomplished using the Equal per User or Equal per Session policy templates provided with WSRM. To allocate resources to a Windows Server 2008 R2 Remote Desktop Services system, do the following:

1. Launch Windows System Resource Manager by clicking Start, All Programs, Administrative Tools, Windows System Resource Manager.

2. Expand the Resource Allocation Policies option in the WSRM console.

3. Right-click Equal_Per_Session or Equal_Per_User, and select Set as Managing Policy.

4. A dialog box opens indicating that the calendar function will be disabled; click OK.

5. Click OK.

### Assessment and Planning Solution Tool

As mentioned earlier in the chapter, the Microsoft Assessment and Planning Toolkit (MAP) provides a solution to IT personnel when faced with questions like "Which product should we buy or deploy?" or "Are we ready for Windows Server 2008 R2?" Granted, there are multiple approaches to tackling questions like these; however, Microsoft has again developed a tool that will do most of the work for you. The Assessment and Planning Solution Tool inventories and assesses systems, hardware, and software and makes product and technology recommendations based on those results. The discovery and readiness tools included in the latest version of MAP include Windows Server 2008 R2 Readiness, Windows 7 Readiness Assessment, Windows Vista Hardware Assessment, Office 2007 Assessment, SQL Server Discovery, Windows Server Role Discovery, Virtual Machine Inventory, Power Savings Assessment, Security Assessment, and Application Virtualization Assessment. The Assessment and Planning Solution Tool can be downloaded from the Microsoft Download site at www.microsoft.com/downloads/.

### System Center Capacity Planner (SCCP) 2007

System Center Capacity Planner 2007 Infrastructure Planning and Tools are tools for IT staff to plan their migration or deployment of System Center Operations Manager (OpsMgr) 2007, SharePoint Server 2007, and Exchange 2007/2010. SCCP can determine and recommend the necessary changes for deploying SharePoint, Exchange 2007/2010, and OpsMgr 2007. This includes in-depth analysis of hardware, network architecture, placement of servers, and much more. SCCP 2007 can even advise on changes after deployment, whether they are planned or unplanned such as the addition of new users, new features like Outlook WebApp (OWA), or changes to the network. More information about SCCP 2007 can be found at the following website: http://www.microsoft.com/systemcenter/en/us/capacity-planner.aspx.

### System Center Operations Manager 2007

System Center Operations Manager (OpsMgr) 2007 has replaced its popular predecessor, Microsoft Operations Manager (MOM). OpsMgr 2007 is a comprehensive monitoring and reporting solution that reports on conditions related to services, system, and network performance, and alerts administrators when problems arise, for example, when critical services have failed to start, when CPU usage consistently stays above a designated threshold, or when excessive paging is observed by the OpsMgr agent. OpsMgr integrates directly with Active Directory, Windows Server 2008 R2, and most other Microsoft technologies to provide an overall solution to help automate monitoring of critical systems and processes. OpsMgr uses management packs specific to the technology, such as the Windows Server 2008 R2 baseline operating system, Exchange 2007/2010 or Internet Information Services 7.5 (IIS), so little configuration is needed out of the box. More information regarding OpsMgr 2007 can be found in Chapter 23, "Integrating System Center Operations Manager 2007 R2 with Windows Server 2008 R2."

## Third-Party Toolset

Without a doubt, many third-party utilities are excellent for capacity-analysis and performance monitoring purposes. Most of them provide additional functionality not found in Windows Server 2008 R2's Performance Monitor and other tools, but they have a cost and might have special requirements for deployment and integration into the organization's network. You might want to evaluate some third-party utilities to get a more thorough understanding of how they might offer more features than Microsoft solutions. Generally speaking, these utilities enhance the functionality that's inherent to Microsoft monitoring solutions, such as scheduling, an enhanced level of reporting functionality, superior storage capabilities, the ability to monitor non-Windows systems, or algorithms for future trend analysis. Some of these third-party tools are listed in Table 34.2.

TABLE 34.2   Third-Party Capacity-Planning and Monitoring Tools

| Utility Name | Company | Website |
| --- | --- | --- |
| AppManager Suite | NetIQ Corporation | http://www.netiq.com/products/am/default.asp |
| BMC Performance Manager | BMC Software | www.bmc.com/ |
| HP BTO Software | HP | https://h10078.www1.hp.com/cda/hpms/display/main/hpms_home.jsp?zn=bto&cp=1_4011_100__ |
| Robomon/ Longitude | Heroix | www.robomon.com/ |
| NSM | CA | www.ca.com/ |

Although it might be true that most third-party capacity-analysis and performance monitoring products might add more or different functionality to your capacity-analysis and performance monitoring procedures or goals, there are still pros and cons to using them over the free tools included with Windows Server 2008 R2 or other solutions available from Microsoft. The key is to decide what you need to adequately and efficiently perform capacity-analysis and performance monitoring procedures in your environment. Taking the time to research and experiment with the different solutions available today, from Microsoft and others, will only benefit you in making an informed decision for managing your Windows Server 2008 R2 environment.

# Monitoring System Performance

Capacity analysis is not about how much information you can collect; it is about collecting the appropriate system health indicators and the right amount of information. Without a doubt, you can capture and monitor an overwhelming amount of information from performance counters. There are more than 1,000 counters, so you'll want to carefully choose what to monitor. Otherwise, you might collect so much information that the data will be hard to manage and difficult to decipher. Keep in mind that more is not necessarily better with regard to capacity analysis. This process is more about efficiency. Therefore, you need to tailor your capacity-analysis monitoring as accurately as possible to how the server is configured.

Every Windows Server 2008 R2 server has a common set of resources that can affect performance, reliability, stability, and availability. For this reason, it's important that you monitor this common set of resources, namely CPU, memory, disk, and network utilization.

In addition to the common set of resources, the functions that the Windows Server 2008 R2 server performs can influence what you should consider monitoring. So, for example, you would monitor certain aspects of system performance on file servers differently than you would for a domain controller running on Windows Server 2008 R2 AD DS. There are many functional roles (such as file and print sharing, application sharing, database functions, web server duties, domain controller roles, and more) that Windows Server 2008 R2 can perform, and it is important to understand all those roles that pertain to each server system. By identifying these functions and monitoring them along with the common set of resources, you gain much greater control and understanding of the system.

The following sections go more in depth on what specific items you should monitor for the different components that constitute the common set of resources. It's important to realize, though, that there are several other items that should be considered regarding monitoring in addition to the ones described in this chapter. You should consider the following material a baseline of the minimum number of things to begin your capacity-analysis and performance-optimization procedures.

## Key Elements to Monitor for Bottlenecks

As mentioned, four resources compose the common set of resources: memory and pagefile usage, processor, disk subsystem, and network subsystem. They are also the most common contributors to performance bottlenecks. A bottleneck can be defined in two ways. The most common perception of a bottleneck is that it is the slowest part of your system. It can either be hardware or software, but generally speaking, hardware is usually faster than software. When a resource is overburdened or just not equipped to handle higher workload capacities, the system might experience a slowdown in performance. For any system, the slowest component of the system is, by definition, considered the bottleneck. For example, a web server might be equipped with ample RAM, disk space, and a high-speed network interface card (NIC), but if the disk subsystem has older drives that are relatively slow, the web server might not be able to effectively handle requests. The bottleneck (that is, the antiquated disk subsystem) can drag the other resources down.

A less common, but equally important, form of bottleneck is one where a system has significantly more RAM, processors, or other system resources than the application requires. In these cases, the system creates extremely large pagefiles, has to manage very large sets of disk or memory sets, yet never uses the resources. When an application needs to access memory, processors, or disks, the system might be busy managing the idle resource, thus creating an unnecessary bottleneck caused by having too many resources allocated to a system. Thus, performance optimization means not having too few resources, but also means not having too many resources allocated to a system.

## Monitoring System Memory and Pagefile Usage

Available system memory is usually the most common source for performance problems on a system. The reason is simply that incorrect amounts of memory are usually installed on a Windows Server 2008 R2 system. Windows Server 2008 R2 tends to consume a lot of memory. Fortunately, the easiest and most economical way to resolve the performance issue is to configure the system with additional memory. This can significantly boost performance and upgrade reliability.

There are many significant counters in the memory object that could help determine system memory requirements. Most network environments shouldn't need to consistently monitor every single counter to get accurate representations of performance. For long-term monitoring, two very important counters can give you a fairly accurate picture of memory pressure: Page Faults/sec and Pages/sec memory. These two memory counters alone can indicate whether the system is properly configured and experiencing memory pressure. Table 34.3 outlines the counters necessary to monitor memory and pagefile usage, along with a description of each.

TABLE 34.3    Important Counters and Descriptions Related to Memory Behavior

| Object | Counter | Description |
| --- | --- | --- |
| Memory | Committed Bytes | Monitors how much memory (in bytes) has been allocated by the processes. As this number increases above available RAM so does the size of the pagefile as paging has increased. |
| Memory | Pages/sec | Displays the amount of pages that are read from or written to the disk. |
| Memory | Pages Output/sec | Displays virtual memory pages written to the pagefile per second. Monitor this counter to identify paging as a bottleneck. |
| Memory | Page Faults/sec | Reports both soft and hard faults. |

TABLE 34.3   Important Counters and Descriptions Related to Memory Behavior

| Object | Counter | Description |
|--------|---------|-------------|
| Process | Working Set, _Total | Displays the amount of virtual memory that is actually in use. |
| Paging file | %pagefile in use | Reports the percentage of the paging file that is actually in use. This counter is used to determine if the Windows pagefile is a potential bottleneck. If this counter remains above 50% or 75% consistently, consider increasing the pagefile size or moving the pagefile to a different disk. |

By default, the Memory tab in Resource Monitor, shown in Figure 34.14, provides a good high-level view of current memory activity. For more advanced monitoring of memory and pagefile activity, use the Performance Monitor snap-in.

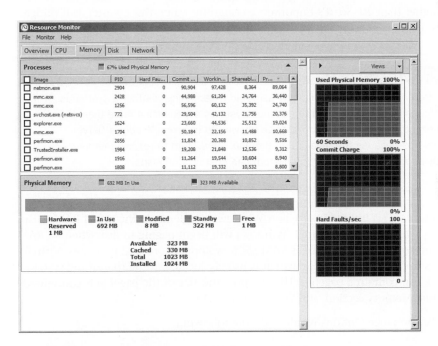

FIGURE 34.14   Memory section of the Resource Monitor.

Systems experience page faults when a process requires code or data that it can't find in its working set. A working set is the amount of memory that is committed to a particular process. When this happens, the process has to retrieve the code or data in another part of physical memory (referred to as a soft fault) or, in the worst case, has to retrieve it from the disk subsystem (a hard fault). Systems today can handle a large number of soft faults without significant performance hits. However, because hard faults require disk subsystem access, they can cause the process to wait significantly, which can drag performance to a crawl. The difference between memory and disk subsystem access speeds is exponential even with the fastest hard drives available. The Memory section of the Resource Monitor in Performance Monitor includes columns that display working sets and hard faults by default.

The Page Faults/sec counter reports both soft and hard faults. It's not uncommon to see this counter displaying rather large numbers. Depending on the workload placed on the system, this counter can display several hundred faults per second. When it gets beyond several hundred page faults per second for long durations, you should begin checking other memory counters to identify whether a bottleneck exists.

Probably the most important memory counter is Pages/sec. It reveals the number of pages read from or written to disk and is, therefore, a direct representation of the number of hard page faults the system is experiencing. Microsoft recommends upgrading the amount of memory in systems that are seeing Pages/sec values consistently averaging above 5 pages per second. In actuality, you'll begin noticing slower performance when this value is consistently higher than 20. So, it's important to carefully watch this counter as it nudges higher than 10 pages per second.

> **NOTE**
>
> The Pages/sec counter is also particularly useful in determining whether a system is thrashing. Thrashing is a term used to describe systems experiencing more than 100 pages per second. Thrashing should never be allowed to occur on Windows Server 2008 R2 systems because the reliance on the disk subsystem to resolve memory faults greatly affects how efficiently the system can sustain workloads.

System memory (RAM) is limited in size and Windows supplements the use of RAM with virtual memory, which is not as limited. Windows will begin paging to disk when all RAM is being consumed, which, in turn, frees RAM for new applications and processes. Virtual memory resides in the pagefile.sys file, which is usually located in the root of the system drive. Each disk can contain a pagefile. The location and size of the pagefile is configured under the Virtual Memory section, shown in Figure 34.15.

To access the Performance Options window, do the following:

1. Click Start.
2. Right-click on Computer and select Properties.
3. Click on the Advanced System Settings link on the left.
4. When the System Properties window opens, click the Settings button under the Performance section.
5. Select the Advanced tab.
6. Click Change under Virtual Memory.

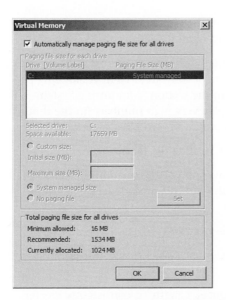

FIGURE 34.15    Virtual Memory configuration options.

---

**TIP**

Windows will normally automatically handle and increase the size of pagefile.sys as needed; however, in some cases you might want to increase performance and manage virtual memory settings yourself. Keeping the default pagefile on the system drive and adding a second pagefile to another hard disk can significantly improve performance.

Spanning virtual memory across multiple disks or simply placing the pagefile.sys on another, less-used disk, will also allow Windows to run faster. Just ensure that the other disk isn't slower than the disk pagefile.sys is currently on. The more physical memory a system has, the more virtual memory will be allocated.

---

## Analyzing Processor Usage

Most often, the processor resource is the first one analyzed when there is a noticeable decrease in system performance. For capacity-analysis purposes, you should monitor two counters: % Processor Time and Interrupts/sec.

The % Processor Time counter indicates the percentage of overall processor utilization. If more than one processor exists on the system, an instance for each one is included along with a total (combined) value counter. If this counter averages a usage rate of 50% or greater for long durations, you should first consult other system counters to identify any processes that might be improperly using the processors or consider upgrading the processor or processors. Generally speaking, consistent utilization in the 50% range doesn't necessarily adversely affect how the system handles given workloads. When the average processor utilization spills over the 65% or higher range, performance might become intolerable. If you have multiple processors installed in the system, use the % Total Processor Time counter to determine the average usage of all processors.

The Interrupts/sec counter is also a good guide of processor health. It indicates the number of device interrupts that the processor (either hardware or software driven) is handling per second. Like the Page Faults/sec counter mentioned in the section "Monitoring System Memory and Pagefile Usage," this counter might display very high numbers (in the thousands) without significantly impacting how the system handles workloads.

Conditions that could indicate a processor bottleneck include the following:

▶ "Average of % Processor Time" is consistently over 60%–70%. In addition, spikes that occur frequently at 90% or greater could also indicate a bottleneck even if the average drops below the 60%–70% mark.

▶ "Maximum of % Processor Time" is consistently over 90%.

▶ "Average of the System Performance Counter; Context Switches/second" is consistently over 20,000.

▶ The "System Performance Counter; Processor Queue Length" is consistently greater than two.

By default, the CPU tab in Resource Monitor, shown in Figure 34.16, provides a good high-level view of current processor activity. For more advanced monitoring of processors, use the Performance Monitor snap-in with the counters discussed previously.

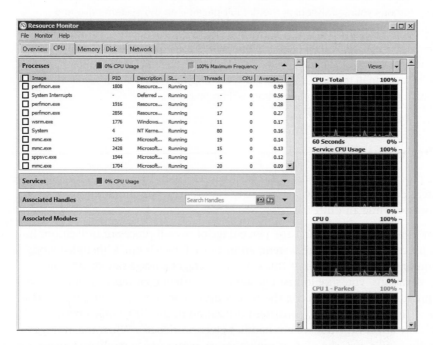

FIGURE 34.16   CPU section of the Resource Monitor.

## Evaluating the Disk Subsystem

Hard disk drives and hard disk controllers are the two main components of the disk subsystem. The two objects that gauge hard disk performance are Physical and Logical Disk. Although the disk subsystem components are becoming more and more powerful, they are often a common bottleneck because their speeds are exponentially slower than other resources. The effects, though, can be minimal and maybe even unnoticeable, depending on the system configuration.

To support the Resource Monitor's Disk section, the physical and logical disk counters are enabled by default in Windows Server 2008 R2. The Disk section in Resource Monitor, shown in Figure 34.17, provides a good high-level view of current physical and logical disk activity (combined). For more advanced monitoring of disk activity, use the Performance Monitor component with the desired counters found in the Physical Disk and Logical Disk sections.

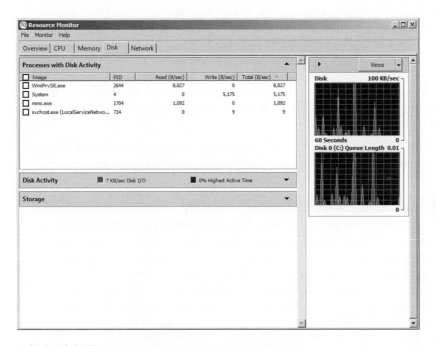

FIGURE 34.17    Disk section of the Resource Monitor.

Monitoring with the Physical and Logical Disk objects does come with a small price. Each object requires a little resource overhead when you use them for monitoring. As a result, you might want to keep them disabled unless you are going to use them for monitoring purposes.

So, what specific disk subsystem counters should be monitored? The most informative counters for the disk subsystem are % Disk Time and Avg. Disk Queue Length. The % Disk Time counter monitors the time that the selected physical or logical drive spends servicing read and write requests. The Avg. Disk Queue Length monitors the number of requests not yet serviced on the physical or logical drive. The Avg. Disk Queue length value is an interval average; it is a mathematical representation of the number of delays the drive is experiencing. If the delay is frequently greater than 2, the disks are not equipped to service the workload and delays in performance might occur.

## Monitoring the Network Subsystem

The network subsystem is by far one of the most difficult subsystems to monitor because of the many different variables. The number of protocols used in the network, network interface cards, network-based applications, topologies, subnetting, and more play vital roles in the network, but they also add to its complexity when you're trying to determine bottlenecks. Each network environment has different variables; therefore, the counters that you'll want to monitor will vary.

The information that you'll want to gain from monitoring the network pertains to network activity and throughput. You can find this information with the Performance Monitor alone, but it will be difficult at best. Instead, it's important to use other tools, such as Network Monitor, discussed earlier in this chapter in the section "Network Monitor," in conjunction with Performance Monitor to get the best representation of network performance as possible. You might also consider using third-party network analysis tools such as network sniffers to ease monitoring and analysis efforts. Using these tools simultaneously can broaden the scope of monitoring and more accurately depict what is happening on the wire.

Because the TCP/IP suite is the underlying set of protocols for a Windows Server 2008 R2 network subsystem, this discussion of capacity analysis focuses on this protocol.

> **NOTE**
>
> Windows Server 2008 R2 and Windows 7 deliver enhancement to the existing Quality of Service (QoS) network traffic–shaping solution that is available for XP and Windows Server 2003. QoS uses Group Policy to shape and give priority to network traffic without recoding applications or making major changes to the network. Network traffic can be "shaped" based on the application sending the data, TCP and/or UDP addresses (source and/or destination), TCP or UDP protocols, and the ports used by TCP or UDP or any combination thereof. More information on QoS can be found at Microsoft TechNet: http://technet.microsoft.com/en-us/network/bb530836.aspx.

Several different network performance objects relate to the TCP/IP protocol, including ICMP, IPv4, IPv6, Network Interface, TCPv4, UDPv6, and more. Other counters such as FTP Server and WINS Server are added after these services are installed. Because entire books are dedicated to optimizing TCP/IP, this section focuses on a few important counters that you should monitor for capacity-analysis purposes.

First, examining error counters, such as Network Interface: Packets Received Errors or Packets Outbound Errors, is extremely useful in determining whether traffic is easily traversing the network. The greater the number of errors indicates that packets must be present, causing more network traffic. If a high number of errors are persistent on the network, throughput will suffer. This can be caused by a bad NIC, unreliable links, and so on.

If network throughput appears to be slowing because of excessive traffic, keep a close watch on the traffic being generated from network-based services such as the ones described in Table 34.4. Figure 34.18 shows these items being recorded in Performance Monitor.

TABLE 34.4    Network-Based Service Counters Used to Monitor Network Traffic

| Object | Counter | Description |
| --- | --- | --- |
| Network Interface | Current Bandwidth | Displays used bandwidth for the selected network adapter |
| Server | Bytes Total/sec | Monitors the network traffic generated by the Server service |
| Redirector | Bytes Total/sec | Processes data bytes received for statistical calculations |
| NBT Connection | Bytes Total/sec | Monitors the network traffic generated by NetBIOS over TCP connections |

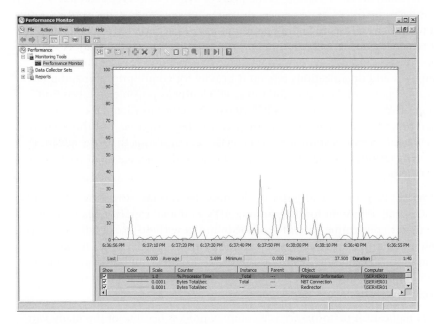

FIGURE 34.18    Network-based counters in Performance Monitor.

# Optimizing Performance by Server Roles

In addition to monitoring the common set of bottlenecks (memory, processor, disk subsystem, and network subsystem), the functional roles of the server influence what other counters you should monitor. The following sections outline some of the most common roles for Windows Server 2008 R2 that require the use of additional performance counters for analyzing system behavior, establishing baselines, and ensuring system availability and scalability.

Microsoft also makes several other tools available that will analyze systems and recommend changes. Ensuring a system is properly configured to deliver services for the role it supports is essential before performance monitoring and capacity planning can be taken seriously.

## Domain Controllers

A Windows Server 2008 R2 domain controller (DC) houses Active Directory Domain Services (AD DS) and may have additional roles such as being responsible for one or more Flexible Single Master Operations (FSMO) roles (schema master, domain naming master, relative ID master, PDC emulator, and/or infrastructure master) or a global catalog (GC) server. Also, depending on the size and design of the system, a DC might serve many other functional roles such as DNS and WINS. In this section, AD, replication, and DNS monitoring will be explored.

### Monitoring Active Directory and Active Directory Replication

Active Directory Domain Services (AD DS) is the heart of Windows Server 2008 R2 domains and has been the directory of choice for years. Active Directory has continuously been improved with each release, including performance enhancements. AD DS is used for many different facets, including, but not limited to, authentication, authorization, encryption, and Group Policies. Because AD plays a vital role in a Windows Server 2008 R2 network environment and organizations rely on it heavily for communication and user management, it must perform its responsibilities as efficiently as possible. You can find more information on Windows Server 2008 R2's Active Directory in Chapter 4, "Active Directory Doman Services Primer." Each facet by itself can be optimized, but this section focuses on the Directory Services and Database objects. Organizations that take advantage of System Center Operations Manager can take advantage of the management pack available for Active Directory.

The Directory Services Performance Monitor object provides various AD performance indicators and statistics that are useful for determining AD's workload capacity. Many of these counters can be used to determine current workloads and how these workloads can affect other system resources. There are relatively few counters in this object, so it's recommended that you monitor each one in addition to the common set of bottleneck objects. With this combination of counters, you can determine whether the system is overloaded and Active Directory performance is impacted.

Measuring AD DS replication performance is a complex process because of the many variables associated with replication. They include, but aren't limited to, the following:

▶ Intrasite versus intersite replication

▶ The compression being used (if any)

▶ Available bandwidth

▶ Inbound versus outbound replication traffic

Fortunately, there are performance counters for every possible AD replication scenario. These counters are located within the Directory Services object and are prefixed by the primary process that is responsible for AD DS replication—the Directory Replication Agent (DRA). Therefore, to monitor AD replication, you need to choose those counters beginning with DRA.

Like most other server products, AD DS uses a database and its performance should also be monitored to provide an accurate reflection of AD DS performance. Understanding a domain controller's overall system resource usage and the performance of AD DS will help you align future upgrades and changes with capacity and performance needs. As companies continue to grow, it is essential that the systems be able to grow with them, especially in regard to something critical like AD DS. Although many counters exist, some of the relevant counters necessary to monitor AD DS and the database are in Table 34.5. This is only a sample list and additional counters might need to be added, depending on the desired outcome of the monitoring and specific AD DS functionality.

**TABLE 34.5**   Performance Counters Relative to AD DS Performance and Replication

| Object | Counter | Description |
| --- | --- | --- |
| Directory Services | DRA Inbound Full Sync Objects Remaining | Objects remaining before synchronization is marked complete. |
| Directory Services | DRA Inbound Object Updates Remaining in Packet | Objects remaining that need to be processed by the domain controller. Indicates delay in applying changes to the database. |
| Directory Services | DRA Remaining Replication Updates | Objects that have been received during replication but have not yet been applied. Indicates slow replication. |
| Directory Services | DRA Pending Replication Synchronizations | Number of queued directory synchronizations remaining. Indicates replication backlog. |
| Directory Services | LDAP Client Sessions | Sessions generated from LDAP clients. |
| Directory Services | LDAP Searches/sec | Search queries performed by LDAP clients per second. |
| Directory Services | LDAP Writes/sec | Amount of writes per second from LDAP clients. |
| Security Systemwide Statistics | Kerberos Authentications/sec | Client authentication tickets passed to the domain controller per second. |
| Security Systemwide Statistics | NTLM Authentications/sec | NTLM authentication requests served per second. |

34

TABLE 34.5    Performance Counters Relative to AD DS Performance and Replication

| Object | Counter | Description |
|---|---|---|
| Database | Database Cache % Hit | Percentage of page requests for the database file that were fulfilled by the database cache without causing a file operation. If this percentage is low (85% or lower), you might consider adding more memory. |
| Database | Database Cache Page Fault Stalls/sec | Number of page faults per second that cannot be serviced because there are no pages available for allocation from the database cache. This number should be low if the system is configured with the proper amount of memory. |
| Database | Database Cache Page Faults/sec | Number of page requests per second for the database file that require the database cache manager to allocate a new page from the database cache. |
| Database | Database Cache Size | Amount of system memory used by the database cache manager to hold commonly used information from the database to prevent file operations. |

### Monitoring DNS

The domain name system (DNS) has been the primary name resolution mechanism in almost all networks and this continues with Windows Server 2008 R2. For more information on DNS, refer to Chapter 10, "Domain Name System and IPv6." Numerous counters are available for monitoring various aspects of DNS in Windows Server 2008 R2. The most important categories in terms of capacity analysis are name resolution response times and workloads, as well as replication performance.

The counters listed in Table 34.6 are used to compute name query traffic and the workload that the DNS server is servicing. These counters should be monitored along with the common set of bottlenecks to determine the system's health under various workload conditions. If users are noticing slower responses, you can compare the query workload usage growth with your performance information from memory, processor, disk subsystem, and network subsystem counters.

TABLE 34.6    Performance Counters to Monitor DNS

| Counter | Description |
|---|---|
| Dynamic Update Received/sec | Dynamic Update Received/sec is the average number of dynamic update requests received by the DNS server in each second. |
| Recursive Queries/sec | Recursive Queries/sec is the average number of recursive queries received by the DNS server in each second. |
| Recursive Query Failure/sec | Recursive Query Failure/sec is the average number of recursive query failures in each second. |

TABLE 34.6   Performance Counters to Monitor DNS

| Counter | Description |
|---------|-------------|
| Secure Update Received/sec | Secure Update Received/sec is the average number of secure update requests received by the DNS server in each second. |
| TCP Query Received/sec | TCP Query Received/sec is the average number of TCP queries received by the DNS server in each second. |
| TCP Response Sent/sec | TCP Response Sent/sec is the average number of TCP responses sent by the DNS server in each second. |
| Total Query Received/sec | Total Query Received/sec is the average number of queries received by the DNS server in each second. |
| Total Response Sent/sec | Total Response Sent/sec is the average number of responses sent by the DNS server in each second. |
| UDP Query Received/sec | UDP Query Received/sec is the average number of UDP queries received by the DNS server in each second. |
| UDP Response Sent/sec | UDP Response Sent/sec is the average number of UDP responses sent by the DNS server in each second. |

Comparing results with other DNS servers in the environment can also help you to determine whether you should relinquish some of the name query responsibility to other DNS servers that are less busy.

Replication performance is another important aspect of DNS. Windows Server 2008 R2 supports legacy DNS replication, also known as zone transfers, which populate information from the primary DNS to any secondary servers. There are two types of legacy DNS replication: incremental (propagating only changes to save bandwidth) and full (the entire zone file is replicated to secondary servers).

Asynchronous full zone transfers (AXFR) occur on the initial transfer and then the incremental zone transfers (IXFR) are performed thereafter. The performance counters for both AXFR and IXFR (see Table 34.7) measure both the requests and successful transfers. It is important to note that if your network environment integrates DNS with non-Windows systems, it is recommended that those systems support IXFR.

**NOTE**

If your network environment is fully Active Directory–integrated, the counters listed in Table 34.7 will all be zero because AD–integrated DNS replicates with AD DS.

## Remote Desktop Services Server

Remote Desktop Services Server has its own performance objects for the Performance Monitor called the Remote Desktop Services Session and Remote Desktop Services objects.

TABLE 34.7   DNS Zone Transfer Counters

| Counter | Description |
| --- | --- |
| AXFR Request Received | Total number of full zone transfer requests received by the DNS service when operating as a master server for a zone |
| AXFR Request Sent | Total number of full zone transfer requests sent by the DNS service when operating as a secondary server for a zone |
| AXFR Response Received | Total number of full zone transfer requests received by the DNS service when operating as a secondary server for a zone |
| AXFR Success Received | Total number of full zone transfers received by the DNS service when operating as a secondary server for a zone |
| AXFR Success Sent | Total number of full zone transfers successfully sent by the DNS service when operating as a master server for a zone |
| IXFR Request Received | Total number of incremental zone transfer requests received by the master DNS server |
| IXFR Request Sent | Total number of incremental zone transfer requests sent by the secondary DNS server |
| IXFR Response Received | Total number of incremental zone transfer responses received by the secondary DNS server |
| IXFR Success Received | Total number of successful incremental zone transfers received by the secondary DNS server |
| IXFR Success Sent | Total number of successful incremental zone transfers sent by the master DNS server |

It provides resource statistics such as errors, cache activity, network traffic from Remote Desktop Server, and other session-specific activity. Many of these counters are similar to those found in the Process object. Some examples include % Privileged Time, % Processor Time, % User Time, Working Set, Working Set Peak, and so on.

**NOTE**

A comprehensive list of all performance counters and descriptions relative to Remote Desktop Services can be found at http://support.microsoft.com/kb/186536. More information on Remote Desktop Services can also be found in Chapter 25.

Three important areas to always monitor for Terminal Server capacity analysis are the memory, processor, and application processes for each session. Application processes are by far the hardest to monitor and control because of the extreme variances in programmatic behavior. For example, all applications might be 32-bit, but some might not be certified to run on Windows Server 2008 R2. You might also have in-house applications running on Remote Desktop Services that might be poorly designed or too resource intensive for the workloads they are performing.

## Virtual Servers

Deployment of virtual servers and consolidation of hardware is becoming more and more prevalent in the business world. When multiple servers are running in a virtual environment on a single physical hardware platform, performance monitoring and tuning becomes essential to maximize the density of the virtual systems. If three or four virtual servers are running on a system and the memory and processors aren't allocated to the virtual guest session that could use the resources, virtual host resources aren't being utilized efficiently. In addition to monitoring the common items of memory, disk, network, and CPU, two performance counters related to virtual sessions are added when virtualization is running on the Windows Server 2008 R2 host. These counters are shown in Figure 34.19.

The performance counters related to virtualization include the following:

▶ **Allocated MB**—Displays the amount of physical memory (RAM) allocated to each virtual server

▶ **Allocated Pages**—Displays the amount of memory pages per virtual machine

The Virtual session object and its counters are available only when a virtual machine is running. Counters can be applied to all running virtual sessions or to a specific virtual session.

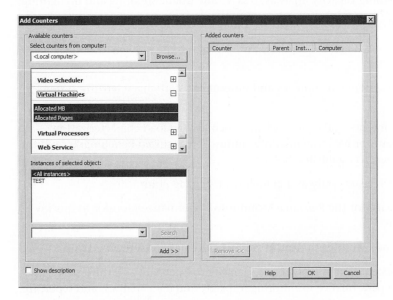

FIGURE 34.19   Performance Monitor counters for virtualization.

# Summary

Capacity planning and performance analysis are critical tasks in ensuring that systems are running efficiently and effectively in the network environment. Too much capacity being allocated to systems indicates resources are being wasted and not used efficiently, which in the long run can cause an organization to overspend in their IT budgets and not get the value out of IT spending. Too little capacity in system operations, and performance suffers in serving users as well as creates a hardship on servers that can ultimately cause system failure.

By properly analyzing the operational functions of a network, a network administrator can consolidate servers or virtualize servers to gain more density in system resources, which can result in additional physical servers that can ultimately be used for other purposes, such as disaster recovery failover servers or cluster servers providing high availability of IT resources.

Although it's easy to get caught up in daily administration and firefighting, it's important to step back and begin capacity-analysis and performance-optimization processes and procedures. These processes and procedures can minimize the environment's complexity, help IT personnel gain control over the environment, assist in anticipating future resource requirements, and, ultimately, reduce costs and keep users of the network happy.

# Best Practices

The following are best practices from this chapter:

- Spend time performing capacity analysis to save time troubleshooting and firefighting.

- Use capacity-analysis processes to help weed out the unknowns.

- Establish systemwide policies and procedures to begin to proactively manage your system.

- After establishing systemwide policies and procedures, start characterizing system workloads.

- Use performance metrics and other variables such as workload characterization, vendor requirements or recommendations, industry-recognized benchmarks, and the data that you collect to establish a baseline.

- Use the benchmark results only as a guideline or starting point.

- Use the Task Manager or the Resource Monitor in Performance Monitor to quickly view performance.

- Use the Performance Monitor to capture performance data on a regular basis.

- Consider using System Center Operations Manager or Microsoft and third-party products to assist with performance monitoring, capacity and data analysis, and reporting.

▶ Carefully choose what to monitor so that the information doesn't become unwieldy.

▶ At a minimum, monitor the most common contributors to performance bottlenecks: memory and pagefile usage, processor, disk subsystem, and network subsystem.

▶ Identify and monitor server functions and roles along with the common set of resources.

▶ When monitoring specific roles like virtual servers or Active Directory Domain Services, include the common performance counters such as memory, CPU, disk, and network as well as counters specific to the role of the server.

▶ Examine network-related error counters.

# Windows SharePoint Services

Windows SharePoint Services 3.0 (WSS) is the foundation for SharePoint Server 2007, provides much of the functionality of the more complete version of the product, and is well suited for organizations interested in exploring the collaboration and document management capabilities of the product. Windows SharePoint Services 3.0 builds upon the previous version of the product (Windows SharePoint Services 2.0) by greatly expanding the power of the tools available, and adding a wealth of new features.

This chapter focuses on how Windows SharePoint Services can be used to extend the functionality of Windows Server 2008 R2 so that it can function as a powerful document management and collaboration platform. This chapter introduces Windows SharePoint Services 3.0 features using a bottom-up methodology that starts with a history of the evolution of the product, then the installation process, and an introduction to the building blocks of organization— document libraries and lists—and then works up to sites and workspaces. This approach will help you understand how different groups of users benefit from the new and improved features of Windows SharePoint Services 3.0.

To learn more about the full range of features that can be found in the SharePoint product line, you might consider purchasing the book titled *SharePoint 2007 Unleashed* (Sams Publishing, ISBN: 978-0672329470).

# Understanding the History of SharePoint Technologies

Most readers will have run into SharePoint in one incarnation or another, but a brief review of the history of the product is helpful to understand the maturation process of the product line and differences between the Windows SharePoint Services and SharePoint Server products.

## SharePoint Origins

In 2001, Microsoft released SharePoint Portal Server 2001. The intent was to provide a customizable portal environment focused on collaboration, document management, and knowledge sharing. The product carried the "digital dashboard" web part technology a step further to provide an out-of-the-box solution. SharePoint Portal was the product that could link together the team-based websites that were springing up. SharePoint Team Services was a separate product that offered a subset of features of the "Portal" product.

Having two separate products with similar names confused many people. "SharePoint" was often discussed in a generic manner, and people weren't sure whether the topic was SharePoint Portal or SharePoint Team Services, or the two technologies together.

Then, in the 2003 version of the SharePoint products, Microsoft developed Windows SharePoint Services as the engine for the team collaboration environment. Windows SharePoint Services 2.0 replaced SharePoint Team Services, and it included many new and enhanced features, some of which were previously part of SharePoint Portal Server 2001. Windows SharePoint Services 2.0 was also included as an optional component to the Windows Server 2003 operating system at the same time.

SharePoint Portal Server 2003 remained a separate server-based product. It built upon the Windows SharePoint Services technology platform and was intended as an enterprise solution for connecting internal and external sources of information. SharePoint Portal Server 2003 allowed the creation of portal "areas," searching across multiple sites, and enabled the integration of business applications into the portal.

These versions of SharePoint integrated more closely with Microsoft Office 2003 products, making it easier for users to leverage SharePoint 2003 features without leaving the comfort of the Office 2003 applications. For example, users could create meeting and document workspaces directly from Office 2003 products. Most Office 2003 applications also included the Shared Workspace Task Pane, which allowed users to see information stored on the site if the document they were editing was opened.

When the SharePoint 2007 products were released, many organizations already had experience with the first and second iterations of the products, and were eagerly awaiting the "v3" products, knowing that the product was even more mature and that many new features had been added. The SharePoint 2007 family includes SharePoint Server 2007, and Windows SharePoint Services 3.0, and abandoned the often confusing term *Portal* from the product title. The "v3" SharePoint products also continued the trend of close integration with Office products, and although they work well with Office 2003 products, are optimized for use with Office 2007 products. Microsoft also broke out a key component from the server product, and made it available separately: SharePoint Server 2007 for Search. Microsoft also introduced a set of features that were only available when the Enterprise features were activated during or after the SharePoint Server 2007 installation process: primarily Excel Services, Business Data Catalog, and Web Based InfoPath forms.

## Understanding the Need for SharePoint 2007 Products

Organizations have increasingly recognized the need for collaboration and document management products over the last decade, and most organizations have implemented one or more products to meet these needs. An overarching goal was to enhance productivity of the information workers in the organization, manage documents for legal and efficiency reasons, provide better search capabilities, and to expose information to Internet and external users.

Most organizations have solutions in place that provide intranet solutions, or portals that often overlap with intranet functionality and features, but typically provide access to software services and applications. As the SharePoint product line matured and provided enhanced feature sets, security, and performance, many clients decided to replace one or more other technologies with SharePoint-based technologies.

Cost effectiveness was, and still is, a driving factor for SharePoint implementation. Windows SharePoint Services became known as the "free" version of SharePoint and was often implemented to test-drive the features. WSS isn't technically free because the organization must still purchase the Windows Server operating system that houses the WSS sites and must purchase the SQL Server software and licenses if the full version of SQL Server is being used. WSS does not require the purchase of the SharePoint Portal Server 2003 or SharePoint Server 2007 software, nor does it require that the organization pay for the client access licenses (CALs). However, the implementation cost is lower than the full version of SharePoint Server and this was a key factor in the adoption of SharePoint software. With this less-expensive option, organizations were able to test-drive the features of the SharePoint family at very low software costs, test migrations from other collaboration/intranet/portal/document management solutions, and determine whether their needs would be met. In many cases, this resulted in savings of tens of thousands of dollars over competing products.

Another driving factor was the close integration of SharePoint products with the Office product line, which a large percentage of organizations use. Their knowledge workers could easily publish documents to their SharePoint sites from their familiar applications like Word and Excel, and could "connect" to calendar or task data in SharePoint lists and libraries from their Outlook clients. Many competitors' products sought to offer the same level of integration, but were typically several steps behind in features and ease of use.

For organizations requiring the full set of features, they could upgrade to SharePoint Portal Server 2003 or SharePoint Server 2007, and then would need to purchase CALs for each user (internal or external) that would be accessing the SharePoint sites. Typically, "enterprise class" SharePoint implementations would use the full version of SQL Server and benefit from enhanced features, management tools, performance, and scalability.

35

Organizations that had been experimenting with SharePoint technologies gradually came to depend upon them for managing large amounts of data and enhancing existing business processes, and as SharePoint dabblers evolved into power users, requests came up for features that SharePoint 2003 didn't provide out of the box. Fortunately, third-party companies quickly evolved to offer new, cutting-edge features, such as an undelete capability, workflow tools, enhanced navigation tools, roll-up web parts, and many more. FrontPage 2003 allowed customization of SharePoint pages and sites, and developers could also turn to the Visual Studio products for more advanced development.

Enter the SharePoint 2007 product line, which builds on the many strengths of the previous version, introduces features that end users have requested, and provides new features that many users might never have dreamed of.

# What Are the Differences Between Windows SharePoint Services 3.0 and SharePoint Server 2007?

A fundamental question that has caused many inquisitive IT personnel many hours of research is "What exactly is the difference between Windows SharePoint Services 3.0 and SharePoint Server 2007?" To answer this question, it is helpful to look at what the basic features of Windows SharePoint Services 3.0 are, and because SharePoint Server 2007 includes Windows SharePoint Services 3.0 as part of the installation, those features are all included in SharePoint Server 2007. However, the "Server" version of the product adds a large number of features to these base capabilities, a sampling of which are listed in this section. Although these features are not explored in depth in this chapter, they give examples of the features that make the Server version of the product appealing to organizations with more complex needs.

## Basic Features of Windows SharePoint Services 3.0

The following list provides an overview of the standard features included in Windows SharePoint Services 3.0, many of which are examined in more detail throughout this chapter. This is a very basic list, and ignores a number of features, such as the administrative toolset, management features, search features, and others, but gives a basic summary:

▶ **Document libraries**—This basic component of a SharePoint site is designed to store and manage documents, and allows the administrator to add additional columns of data to the library (called metadata) as well as create custom views, track versions of the documents, and control access on a document level. Many other features are available in a document library, such as requiring checkout before a document can be edited or creating alerts that send email when certain conditions are met, such as a document changing. Other standard libraries include the form library, wiki page library, and picture library.

> **NOTE**
>
> Metadata is data about data. So, for example, a Microsoft Word document has metadata associated with it, such as author, creation date, and modification date. Windows SharePoint Services 3.0 document libraries allow administrators to define other columns that can contain a wide variety of other information that is associated with a document.

- ▶ **Lists**—Another basic component of a SharePoint site, a list can take many forms, but is essentially data arranged in spreadsheet format that can be used to meet a virtually limitless array of needs. For example, standard lists include announcements, contacts, discussion boards, events, tasks, and surveys.

- ▶ **Web pages**—Web pages include basic pages and web part pages, each of which organize navigational and design components and include web parts. These are the pages that users see and use when interacting with Windows SharePoint Services 3.0 sites. Web parts are modular components that can be placed on pages and perform functions such as displaying data that resides in a document library or list.

- ▶ **Sites and workspaces**—Sites and workspaces are essentially groupings of lists, libraries, and basic web part pages that provide a variety of features and functions to the users. For example, there might be a site for human resources or information technology, or a workspace that enables users to collaborate on a document or a workspace could be created for a specific event, such as a company quarterly meeting.

- ▶ **Site management tools**—These come in a variety of forms, including the browser-based page editing tools, subsite management tools, and site collection management tools.

- ▶ **Central Administration console tools**—These tools allow a SharePoint farm administrator to configure the server or servers to perform properly and to perform backups and restores of data.

## What Is Not Included in Windows SharePoint Services 3.0 but Is Included in SharePoint Server 2007

The Server product includes Windows SharePoint Services 3.0 as part of the installation and so includes all of Windows SharePoint Services 3.0 features and adds a host of additional features on top of these. Many IT administrators, departmental managers, and power users are curious about what is not included in Windows SharePoint Services 3.0 as they need to justify the cost of SharePoint Server 2007 and want to better understand what the more complete product includes. Bear in mind that there are two possible installations of SharePoint Server 2007: the Standard installation and the Enterprise installation.

An overview of the main features that require the purchase of SharePoint Server 2007 is provided in the following list:

▶ My Sites is only available in SharePoint Server 2007. If enabled, My Sites allows users to create their own site and customize personal information that can be shared with the organization.

▶ The Site Directory feature is only available in the SharePoint Server 2007 product and can be very helpful if a large number of sites will be created. Each time a site is created, it can be included in the Site Directory and categories can be applied to each site for grouping and sorting purposes.

▶ User profiles are included in the SharePoint Server 2007 product. SharePoint Server 2007 connects to Active Directory (AD) and pulls in user information on a regular basis, which is then stored in the profiles database. Additional SharePoint-specific fields are added to this database creating a new database of user information that can be leveraged and customized in SharePoint Server 2007.

▶ Content sources outside of the SharePoint content databases can be searched and indexed with SharePoint Server 2007. SharePoint Server 2007 can index file shares, websites, Exchange public folders, and other sources out of the box.

▶ Windows SharePoint Services 3.0 is very limited in out-of-the-box workflows, offering only the Three-state workflow, whereas SharePoint Server 2007 offers more flexibility with Approval, Collect Feedback, Collect Signatures, and Disposition Approval workflows.

▶ If integration with Microsoft Information Rights Management (IRM) is needed, the SharePoint Server 2007 product is required.

▶ SharePoint Server 2007 is required for retention and auditing policies, and for logging all actions on sites, content, and workflows.

▶ If policies, auditing, and compliance features are needed, SharePoint Server 2007 allows for the creation of document retention and expiration policies, workflow processes to define expiration, tracking and auditing, and other tools.

▶ If browser-based forms are required, the Enterprise Edition of SharePoint Server 2007 provides the tools needed to publish browser-based forms. More important, InfoPath is not required on the end users' desktops to fill out forms.

▶ Excel Services are only available in SharePoint Server 2007, Enterprise Edition. Through Excel Services, a Microsoft Excel 2007 user can publish a spreadsheet, or portions of it, to a SharePoint Server 2007 document library so that it can be accessed via the Excel Web Access web part.

▶ Microsoft offers the Business Data Catalog (BDC) only in SharePoint Server 2007, Enterprise Edition. The BDC enables SharePoint Server 2007 to mine data from external databases via application definition files. A number of dedicated web parts then enable SharePoint Server 2007 to display this data to form advanced dashboards.

▶ Microsoft single sign-on integration is only available with SharePoint Server 2007.

A common question revolves around size limitations of the databases that can be supported by WSS 3.0. If the Basic installation option is followed as shown in this chapter, there is no hard limit for the size of the databases. The only installation option that brings with it a size limit is if SharePoint Server 2007 is installed using the SQL Server Express Edition, where there is a 4GB limit. This is confusing to many new SharePoint users and worth clarifying. If either WSS 3.0 or SharePoint Server 2007 are connected to any full version of SQL Server 2005 or 2008 (such as SQL Server 2005 Standard or Enterprise, or SQL Server 2008 Standard or Enterprise), there are no hard limits for database sizes.

Microsoft does recommend as a best practice that the content databases that store the documents uploaded to document libraries and content stored in SharePoint lists not exceed 50GB–100GB in size, but this is for performance and maintenance reasons, and is not a hard limit.

An excellent document is available on the Microsoft website with additional information comparing the products: http://office.microsoft.com/en-us/sharepointserver/ HA101978031033.aspx.

# Identifying the Need for Windows SharePoint Services

A number of organizational needs have spurred the adoption of SharePoint technologies. Many organizations see SharePoint technologies as the next evolution in document management and sharing, where the silo is more intelligent, controls access to, and use of, documents better, tracks usage information, and alerts users of certain conditions. The files stored in SharePoint can have data attached to them (metadata) to enhance management and categorization of the files. Workflows in lists and libraries can be kicked off automatically or started manually for a variety of business processes. The somewhat amorphous term *collaboration* can be enhanced with these tools, as can the ability to quickly create sites for smaller groups of users to share ideas, work on a document, or store data pertaining to a specific event. Some of the most common requirements include the following:

▶ **A need for better document management than the file system can offer—** This includes document versioning, checkout and check-in features, adding metadata to documents, and better control of document access (by using groups and granular security). The high-level need is simply to make it easier for users to find the latest version of the document or documents they need to do their jobs, and, ultimately, to make them more efficient in those jobs.

▶ **Improved collaboration among users with a minimal learning curve—** Although virtually everyone has a different definition of what collaboration is, a functional definition is a technology solution that allows users to interact efficiently with each other using software products to share documents and information in a user-friendly environment. In regard to SharePoint, this typically refers to document and meeting workspaces, site collections, discussion lists, integration of instant messaging and presence information, and integration with the Office suite of applications. Integration with Office applications is a key component: Most organizations do not want to force users to learn a new set of tools to collaborate more effectively because users generally resist such requirements.

▶ **A better intranet**—Although most companies have an intranet in place, common complaints are that it is too static, that it is not user friendly, and that every change has to go through IT or the "web guy." These complaints generally comes from a departmental manager, team lead, or project manager frustrated with their inability to publish information to a select group of users and regularly update resources their team needs to do their jobs.

▶ **A centralized way to search for information**—Rather than using the "word-of-mouth" search engine, there should be an engine in place that allows the user to quickly and efficiently find particular documents. The user can search for documents that contain certain words; documents created or modified during a certain time frame; documents authored by a specific person; or documents that meet other criteria, such as file type.

▶ **Creation of a portal**—Many definitions exist for the term *portal*, but a general definition is that a portal is a web-enabled environment that allows internal and, potentially, external users to access company intellectual resources and software applications. A portal typically extends standard intranet functionality by providing features such as single sign-on, powerful search tools, and access to other core company applications, such as help desk, human resources software, educational resources, and other corporate information and applications.

### Customizing WSS to Suit Organizational Needs

If the default functionality in Windows SharePoint Services 3.0 is not enough, or does not satisfy the specific business requirements of an organization, the product can easily be customized. Easily customizable or downloadable web parts can be "snapped-in" to a WSS site, without the need to understand HTML code. The more basic web parts allow the site designer or administrator to choose what information from document libraries and lists is displayed on the home page, or on web part pages. More complex web parts roll up or filter data, or provide data to other web parts (for example, the user's name or choices from a drop-down menu) to customize the data they present.

More advanced developers can use ASP.NET or other programming tools to produce custom code to work with Windows SharePoint Services 3.0. Further enhancement of Windows SharePoint Services 3.0 sites can be accomplished using SharePoint Designer 2007, which is a free download from Microsoft, and allows for a great deal of customization with relative ease. Later sections in this chapter give examples of some of the customization possibilities in Windows SharePoint Services 3.0.

# Installing Windows SharePoint Services

Installation of Windows SharePoint Services 3.0 is fairly straightforward once Windows Server 2008 R2 has been installed, assuming it is a single Windows SharePoint Services 3.0 installation, rather than a more complex SharePoint farm. If the Windows SharePoint Services 3.0 server will be part of a SharePoint farm, the installation is more complex and you should consider purchasing the *SharePoint 2007 Unleashed* book mentioned earlier for specifics on complex SharePoint farm designs and implementations.

The following steps assume that Windows Server 2008 R2 has been successfully installed and has been added to an existing production domain or test network environment, and has the latest patches and updates applied. It is not generally recommended that Windows SharePoint Services 3.0 be used for production purposes when installed on a domain controller or server running processor-intensive applications such as Exchange.

## Outlining WSS Requirements

Windows SharePoint Services 3.0 designs can range from single-server installations to multiple servers that make up a SharePoint farm. To make matters more complicated, Windows SharePoint Services 3.0 can be installed on Windows Server 2003 as well as on Windows Server 2008 and Windows Server 2008 R2 servers. For this section, the assumption is that Windows SharePoint Services 3.0 is being installed on a Windows Server 2008 R2 server, so the server must meet the minimum hardware requirements, as outlined in Chapter 1, "Windows Server 2008 R2 Technology Primer."

The following is a list of the Microsoft minimum recommendations for Windows SharePoint Services 3.0. It is important to note that this list indicates only the bare minimum necessary for support. In most cases, servers deployed for WSS should be more robust than the minimum requirements dictate.

### Hardware and Software
The following are the minimum hardware and software recommendations for the implementation of Windows SharePoint Services 3.0:

▶ Server with a processor speed of at least 2.5GHz, dual processors that are 3GHz or faster recommended

▶ RAM capacity of 1GB minimum, 2GB recommended

▶ NTFS file system–formatted partition with a minimum of 3GB of free space, plus adequate free space for your websites

▶ DVD drive or the source copied to a local or network-accessible drive

▶ 1024 × 768 or higher resolution monitor

▶ 56Kbps or faster connection between client computers and server

▶ Windows Server 2003 SP1 (assumption is that Windows Server 2008 R2 will be used for this chapter)

▶ The Web Server role, the Microsoft .NET Framework version 3.0, and Windows Internal Database

After these requirements have been satisfied, WSS can be installed on a Windows Server 2008 R2 system.

Clients access WSS through a web browser. Microsoft supports several different web browsers for use with Windows SharePoint Services 3.0 and classifies them as either "Level 1" or "Level 2" browsers. Level 1 browsers offer full functionality on all SharePoint sites, including the Central Administration website and include the following:

▶ Level 1 web browsers for WSS 3.0 with SP2 are as follows:

  ▶ Internet Explorer 6.x (32-bit) (Windows)

  ▶ Internet Explorer 7.x (32-bit) (Windows)

  ▶ Internet Explorer 8.x (32-bit) (includes running in compatibility mode) (Windows)

▶ Level 1 web browsers for WSS 3.0 original release and Service Pack 1 (SP1) are as follows:

  ▶ Internet Explorer 6.x (32-bit) (Windows)

  ▶ Internet Explorer 7.x (32-bit) (Windows)

Level 2 browsers provide basic functionality so that users can both read and write in SharePoint sites and perform site administration. However, ActiveX controls are supported only in Level 1 browsers and there are functionality differences between different browsers. Thus, the user experience will be different from that in Level 1 browsers.

▶ Level 2 web browsers for WSS 3.0 with SP2 are as follows:

  ▶ Internet Explorer 7.x (64-bit) (Windows)

  ▶ Internet Explorer 8.x (64-bit) (Windows)

  ▶ Firefox 3.x (Linux/UNIX/Macintosh OS X Leopard)

  ▶ Safari 3.x (Macintosh OS X Leopard)

▶ Level 2 web browsers for WSS 3.0 original release and Service Pack 1 (SP1) are as follows:

  ▶ Firefox 1.5 (Windows/Linux/UNIX/Macintosh O SX)

  ▶ Mozilla 1.7 (Windows)

  ▶ Netscape Navigator 7.2 (Linux/UNIX)

  ▶ Netscape Navigator 8.1 (Windows)

  ▶ Safari 2.0 (Macintosh OS X)

## Performing a Windows SharePoint Services Installation

The installation of WSS is a straightforward process that consists of the following steps:

1. Install and configure the Web Server (IIS) role and .NET Framework 3.5.1 features.
2. Download and install Windows SharePoint Services 3.0 with SP2.
3. Install optional components such as SMTP services.

Configuration must be performed by the server administrator and includes adding the Web Server (IIS) role and role services.

You must make one major decision before the setup begins: whether to use Microsoft SQL Server 2005 Express Edition or to connect to an already deployed instance of SQL Server 200x Standard/Enterprise. The initial process detailed here installs WSS with the free Microsoft SQL Server 2005 Express Edition, which is suitable for small or test Windows SharePoint Services 3.0 implementations.

The WSS installation process begins by installing the Web Server (IIS) role using the following steps:

1. Open Server Manager (click Start, Administrative Tools, Server Manager).

2. Select Roles from the left pane, and then click Add Roles under Roles Summary.

3. Review the prerequisites on the Before You Begin page and then click Next.

4. Select Web Server (IIS) from the list of available roles and click Next.

5. Click Next on the Web Server (IIS) page.

6. On the Select Role Services page, the following role services should be checked:

    ▶ Common HTTP Features:

        ▶ Static Content

        ▶ Default Document

        ▶ Directory Browsing

        ▶ HTTP Errors

    ▶ Health and Diagnostics:

        ▶ HTTP Logging

        ▶ Request Monitor

    ▶ Security:

        ▶ Request Filtering

    ▶ Performance:

        ▶ Static Content Compression

    ▶ Management Tools:

        ▶ IIS Management Console

7. After verifying the above IIS role services have been selected, click Next.

8. Review the Installation Selections and click Install, as shown in Figure 35.1.

9. When the installation completes, review the installation results and click Close.

Next, you must install the Windows Server 2008 R2 .NET Framework 3.5.1 feature to support WSS. Features describe an auxiliary or supporting function of a server and augment the functionality of an existing role.

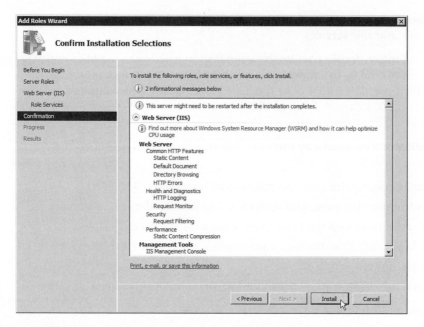

FIGURE 35.1    Add Roles Wizard Confirm Installation Selections screen.

1. In Server Manager, select Features and click Add Features.

2. Expand .NET Framework 3.5.1 Features and select .NET Framework 3.5.1.

3. Click Next.

4. Review the installation selections and click Install, as shown in Figure 35.2.

5. When the installation completes, click Close.

Now that the Web Server role and required features have been installed, you are ready to install Windows SharePoint Services 3.0.

1. Download Windows SharePoint Services 3.0 with SP2 from the Microsoft download site at http://sharepoint.microsoft.com/product/related-technologies/Pages/windows-sharepoint-services.aspx.

2. From the Download section, choose 32- or 64-bit as appropriate to your server, and select the appropriate language (assumption is that English will be downloaded) and the country you are downloading to. Click Download Now.

3. Click Save, choose a local destination to save to (for example, C:\Temp), and click Save. The file will now download, which will take several minutes or more depending upon your Internet connection speed. For this installation, the version downloaded was 12.0.6425.1000.

4. Click Open Folder, right-click on the application (SharePoint.exe), and choose Run as Administrator.

5. Check the I Accept the Terms of This Agreement check box, and click Continue.

6. Then next screen allows you to choose Basic or Advanced. For the purposes of this installation, choose the Basic button. The installation will start and includes the

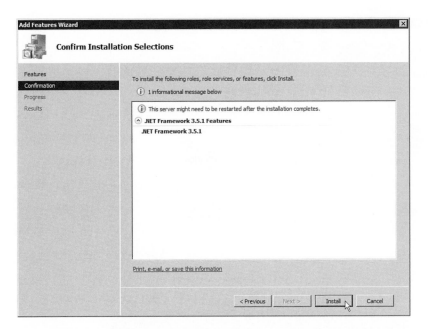

FIGURE 35.2   Add Features Wizard Confirm Installation Selections screen.

installation of SQL Server 2005 Express Edition. This will take several minutes depending upon the speed of your server.

7. Once the installation process completes, the Microsoft Windows SharePoint Services 3.0 window will appear, and the check box next to Run the SharePoint Products and Technologies Configuration Wizard will now be checked. Click Close.

8. The Welcome to SharePoint Products and Technologies Configuration Wizard will open. Click Next.

9. Click Yes in the warning window that lists the services that might need to be started or reset. The Configuration Wizard will proceed with the basic install of WSS 3.0. This includes creating the configuration database, securing resources in the Registry, registering SharePoint services, provisioning the Central Administration Web Application, creating sample data, installing application content files, and finalizing the install.

10. The Configuration Successful message should appear. Click Finish to close the wizard.

11. The default Team Site should now open, as shown in Figure 35.3, and you might need to authenticate using the account you performed the installation with.

12. To ensure the installation is fully completed, click the Start button, and click the SharePoint 3.0 Central Administration link. If this link isn't available here, click All Programs, Administrative Tools, SharePoint 3.0 Central Administration. The Central Administration console should open, as shown in Figure 35.4.

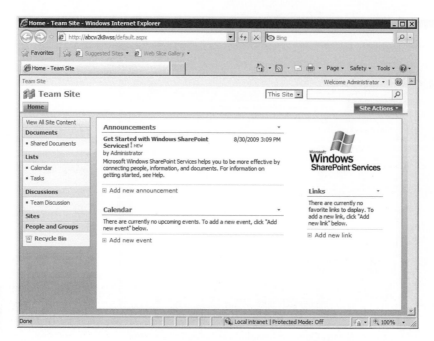

FIGURE 35.3    Default Team Site after new installation of WSS 3.0.

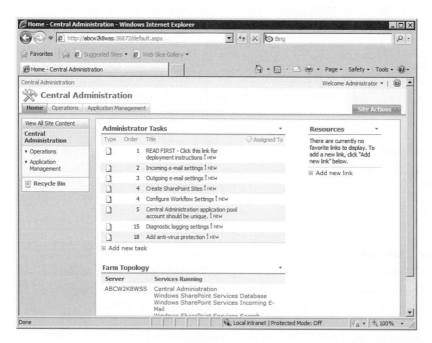

FIGURE 35.4    Default Central Administration console after new installation of WSS 3.0.

## Reviewing the Internet Information Services (IIS) Configuration

During the installation process, websites are created in IIS. A brief walk-through of these changes is helpful to provide an overview of what websites are created following the WSS 3.0 installation. In general, it is recommended to not change the settings at this point, assuming WSS 3.0 has just been installed for testing purposes. If WSS 3.0 was installed for production uses, changes might be required, such as adding host headers, changing bindings, or adding SSL certificates to one or more websites, but such steps are not included in this chapter.

Follow these steps to review the IIS configuration:

1. Click the Start button, click Administrative Tools, and click on Internet Information Services (IIS) Manager. The IIS Manager tool will open.

2. Expand the node for your server in the left pane, and expand the Sites node. You should see the Default Web Site with a square icon next to it indicating that it is stopped, a SharePoint – 80 site below it, and a SharePoint Central Administration v3 below it.

3. Highlight the SharePoint – 80 site node, and clink on the Bindings link in the Actions pane on the right. This should show the type of site as http and the port as 80. Click Close.

4. With this node still selected, click on the Browse :80 (http) link in the right pane under Manage Web Site. The default Team Site should open.

5. Next, highlight the SharePoint Central Administration v3 site node and click on the Bindings link. This will show you the http type and the random port assigned to the Central Administration site. It is a good idea to make a note of this port in case you are having trouble accessing the Central Administration site.

The right pane in the IIS Administration tool proves to be very useful for daily administrative tasks. For example, the bindings of the website can be edited (for example, the website can be bound to a different port, or a host header can be applied); the site can be stopped, started, or restarted; and advanced settings can be accessed. The center pane provides access to ASP.NET tools, IIS tools, and management tools. So, settings such as authentication, compression, logging, and Secure Sockets Layer (SSL) can be accessed. Additional exploration of IIS 7 is covered in more depth in Chapter 12, "Internet Information Services."

## Reviewing Installed Software and Databases After the Installation

Now that the software is installed, many administrators want to get a better sense of what software was actually installed, and where the WSS 3.0 databases "live." Reviewing the Programs and Features tool is helpful as a starting point. Installing SQL Server Management Studio Express is a helpful step for more curious administrators as it allows the administrator to see the databases that were installed and delve more into the configuration settings of the version of SQL Server that was installed.

Follow these steps to review Programs and Features:

1. Click the Start button, click Control Panel, click the Programs category, and then click Programs and Features.

2. Microsoft Windows SharePoint Services 3.0 will show, but no reference to SQL Server software will be provided.

3. Next click on View Installed Updates in the left pane, and Windows SharePoint Services 3.0 SP2 (SP2) will be in the list, assuming the SP2 version was actually installed.

The version of SQL Server that is installed with the Basic installation of WSS 3.0 is the SQL Server 2005 Express Edition (also known as SSEE) and no management tools are provided with it. A helpful step to take at this point is to download and install the Microsoft SQL Server Management Studio Express tools by completing the following steps:

1. Visit the following page:
   http://www.microsoft.com/downloadS/details.aspx?familyid=C243A5AE-4BD1-4E3D-94B8-5A0F62BF7796&displaylang=en

2. Scroll down the page and select either the 32- or 64-bit version of the application as appropriate. Click the Download button, and click Run.

3. The wizard will open. Click Next.

4. Accept the license agreement and click Next.

5. Enter your name and company information and click Next.

6. Click Next to accept the default feature selection and installation path.

7. Click Install to complete the installation.

8. Once the installation has completed, click Finish to close the wizard.

9. Click the Start button, click All Programs, and now there will be a Microsoft SQL Server 2005 entry. Click that entry and then select SQL Server Management Studio Express.

10. From the Connect to Server window, enter the following:
    `\\.\pipe\mssql$microsoft##ssee\sql\query` and click Connect.

11. The Management Studio Express will then connect to the WSS 3.0 databases, as shown in Figure 35.5.

12. Right-click the top-level node in the left pane and click Properties to see more information about the installation, including the location of the root directory, which actually contains the database files. The default root directory is C:\Windows\SYSMSI\SSEE\MSSQL.2005\MSSQL. Navigate to this directory and the `.mdf` and `.ldf` files will be visible.

An experienced SQL administrator can delve more into the features of the Management Studio Express, but less-experienced administrators should tread lightly as changes made in the Management Studio Express tool can affect WSS 3.0 performance and can cause failures in the installation.

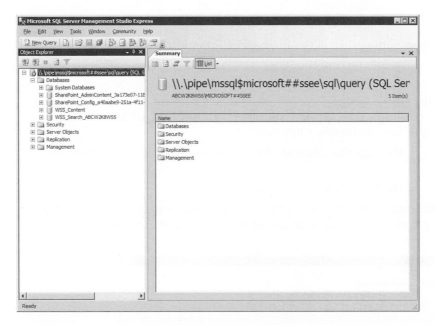

FIGURE 35.5    SQL Server Management Studio Express.

## Using the Central Administration Console to Complete the Installation

The Central Administration console is designed to make it easy for a SharePoint administrator to finish the configuration of the Windows SharePoint Services 3.0 environment and to perform administrative tasks outside of the user interface provided in Windows SharePoint Services 3.0 site collections. The tool offers a Home page, as well as two tabs—Operations and Application Management—which provide access to tools that help configure features such as services, security, logging and reporting, backup and restore, site management, workflow management, and external connections. This section walks through some of the basic tasks needed to finish the WSS 3.0 installation.

### Configure Incoming E-Mail Settings

To enable incoming email, the SMTP service needs to be installed. Installing the SMTP service is only required if the Windows SharePoint Services 3.0 sites need to be enabled to receive incoming email. This is generally considered to be a more advanced feature, as a certain amount of configuration is required, and both site end users will need to understand that new email addresses are needed and then understand what the results are. Fully configuring incoming email in WSS 3.0 typically involves coordination with the Exchange or email administrator, so the following covers the basic steps only.

> **CAUTION**
>
> Some organizations have policies in place that prohibit the installation of SMTP services on production servers that are not dedicated mail servers.

To install the SMTP service, follow these steps:

1. Click the Start button, then click All Programs, Administrative Tools, Server Manager.

2. Click on the Features node in the Server Manager pane. Click on Add Features in the Features Summary pane.

3. Click on the box next to SMTP Server, and the Add Features Wizard window opens clarifying which role services and features need to be installed. Click the Add Required Role Services button. Click Next.

4. Click Next on the page that discusses the Web Server (IIS) role, which is already installed.

5. Click Next on the Select Role Services page.

6. Review the installation selection on the next page, and note that ODBC Logging and SMTP Server will be installed, as shown in Figure 35.6, and click Install.

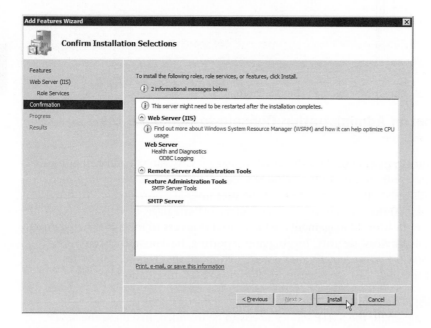

FIGURE 35.6   Adding the SMTP feature to the server.

7. Make sure that the installation is fully successfully, and then click Close.

### Completing the Configuration for Incoming E-Mail Settings

Now that SMTP Server features have been installed, the Incoming E-Mail Settings can be configured. To finish the configuration, follow these steps:

1. Open the Central Administration console by clicking the Start button, then clicking All Programs, Administrative Tools, and SharePoint 3.0 Central Administration. Provide your username and password if needed. After you have successfully logged on to the Central Administration console, the Home tab displays.

2. Click the Incoming E-Mail Settings task.

3. Click the Configure Incoming E-Mail Settings link.

4. Click Yes under Enable Sites on This Server to Receive E-Mail.

5. Under Settings Mode, leave Automatic selected. (Note: If Automatic can't be selected, a reboot of the server might be needed because the SMTP service configuration might not be registered by the Central Administration console.)

6. In the Directory Management Service section, leave No selected. If Yes is selected, users can create distribution groups and contacts, but an AD container needs to be identified where new distribution groups and contacts will be created and additional settings configured. This is a more complex configuration to administer and is not recommended for most test implementations unless this feature is of specific interest.

7. In the Incoming E-Mail Server Display Address section, either leave the default email suffix or enter a desired display address. A general best practice is to leave the WSS 3.0 server name unless the mail administrator is going to be involved in the configuration.

8. In the Safe E-Mail Servers section, either select Accept Mail from All E-Mail Servers or Accept Mail from These Safe E-Mail Servers. If the second option is selected, the FQDN of the "safe" email server needs to be entered.

9. Click OK when you are finished.

Note that there are typically configuration steps needed on the mail server as well for this feature to work, and then individual document libraries need to be enabled for incoming emails. These steps will vary based on whether Exchange Server 2003 or Exchange Server 2007 is being used, or whether another SMTP mail server is being used.

**Configure Outgoing E-Mail Settings**

From the Home tab for the Central Administration console, a link for Outgoing E-Mail Settings will be visible. Outgoing email enables WSS 3.0 lists and libraries to send alerts to users, and to send workflow forms and perform other mail-based communications when needed. This is a simpler configuration than incoming emails and is generally considered a "must-have" for WSS 3.0 testing and production configurations.

Follow these steps to configure outgoing emails:

1. From the Home tab for the Central Administration console, click on the Outgoing E-Mail Settings link in the Administrator Links section.

2. Once the form opens, click on the Configure Outgoing E-Mail Settings link in the Actions section.

3. From the Outgoing E-Mail Settings page, provide information in the Outbound SMTP Server, From Address, and Reply-to Address fields. Leave the character set as 65001 (Unicode UTF-8) unless a different character set is required.

4. Click OK to complete.

Once this is complete, the administrator should test to make sure that alerts are functional by visiting a document library, creating an alert for the library, and then performing an action that will trigger the alert. If the alert emails are not sending properly, additional troubleshooting will be required.

## Exploring the Default Site Collection

When Windows SharePoint Services 3.0 is installed, an empty top-level site is created, as seen in Figure 35.3. Access this site by opening a browser on the server or from a workstation with access to the server and entering the URL you saw after completing the basic installation (typically the FQDN of the server). Enter the username and password of the account that was used to configure Windows SharePoint Services 3.0 and you should see a page identical to the one shown in Figure 35.7.

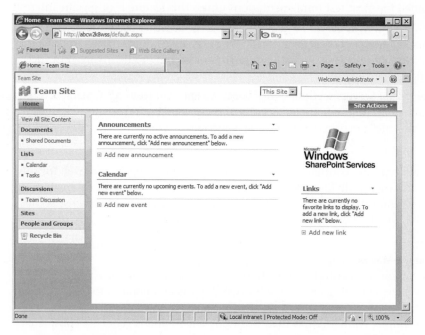

FIGURE 35.7    Default top-level site in Windows SharePoint Services 3.0.

The main components of this site are as follows:

▶ **Current user**—In the upper-right corner, the identity of the currently logged-on user is listed. Clicking this link opens a menu that gives options such as My Settings, Sign In as Different User, Request Access, and Personalize This Page.

▶ **Help icon**—You can click the question mark icon to gain access to Windows SharePoint Services 3.0 Help and how-to information. This information is actually quite useful and is a good place to start when getting familiar with WSS 3.0.

▶ **Drop-down search options**—The drop-down menu next to the search field offers only the option to search This Site, but depending on the context will offer other choices, such as searching only a specific document library.

▶ **Quick Launch area**—On the left side of the page is the Quick Launch area, which by default lists the option to View All Site Content, or access Documents, Lists, Discussions, Sites, People and Groups, and the Recycle Bin.

▶ **Web parts**—To the right of the Quick Launch area are several web parts, including Announcements, Calendar, the Windows SharePoint Services logo, and Links. If the titles of Announcements, Calendar, or Links are clicked, the list it is connected to opens, allowing more interaction with the data. For example, new items can be created, existing ones edited, alerts set, workflows started, and other actions.

▶ **Site actions**—This menu is only available to users who have a certain level of privileges on the site, and allows access to Create, Edit Page, and Site Settings options.

It is important for a future Windows SharePoint Services 3.0 administrator to understand these basic elements and features of the standard team site, so these will be reviewed in more detail in the following sections.

By clicking on the View All Site Content link at the top of the Quick Launch area on the left side of the screen, the full contents of the current site that the logged-in user has access to will be revealed. An example of this is shown in Figure 35.8. The libraries, lists, and subsites, if any, are shown in this view. This is a great place to check when visiting a new site to see which lists, libraries and subsites are available for the current user to access. As shown in Figure 35.8, the name of the list or library is shown, along with a description of the purpose and/or content of the list or library, how many items are stored in it, and the last modified date. With this information, it is very easy to tell how active the site is, the number of documents or list items available, and the most recently modified list and libraries. Clicking on the title of the list or library will open it so the contents can be viewed, and if your account has the appropriate privileges, new items can be added or existing items can be modified.

The Create link is provided for users with appropriate privileges on the site, and it gives access to the create.aspx page, as shown in Figure 35.9. The items that can be created are divided into the following groups: Libraries, Communications, Tracking, Custom Lists, and Web Pages. Note that the very last item under the Web Pages header is Sites and Workspaces, which allows you to pick a site or workspace template from the available templates.

# Lists and Libraries in Windows SharePoint Services 3.0

Lists and libraries are two key components of the Windows SharePoint Services 3.0 environment. They allow users to manage documents by uploading them to libraries or to manage rows and columns of information in a list, which is similar to a spreadsheet in many ways. This section reviews the basic features of Windows SharePoint Services 3.0 document libraries and lists. As the name suggests, a document library is designed to store documents, and each document can have metadata attached to it. This metadata allows a visitor to the library to get a sense for when the document was added or modified, by whom, and to better understand the purpose or content of the document in question. A Windows SharePoint Services 3.0 list is essentially a "spreadsheet on steroids" and is

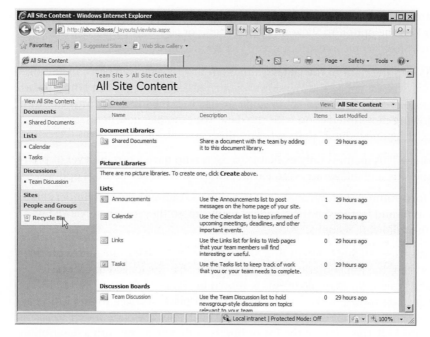

FIGURE 35.8    All Site Content page.

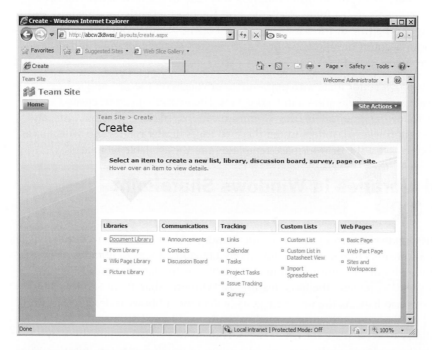

FIGURE 35.9    The Create page.

designed to store data in much the same way as an Excel spreadsheet does. The following sections provide an overview of the capabilities of these two key components of Windows SharePoint Services 3.0.

## Libraries in Windows SharePoint Services 3.0

Many users wonder what the difference is between simply continuing to store their files in a file share on a network server, keeping them on their local hard drives to make sure they are close at hand, or emailing them to people when needed. Windows SharePoint Services 3.0 document libraries offer a variety of features that have proven to be useful to a wide range of users and projects and that empower the site administrators to customize the storage and collaborative features of the library and enhance user productivity. Some of the advantages provided by a SharePoint document library include the following:

▶ The administrator of a document library can customize who can add, modify, and delete documents in a document library, or just read them.

▶ Versioning can be turned on for a document library that keeps a complete copy of previous versions of the documents for reference or recovery purposes.

▶ Alerts can be set on a document within the library or for the entire library so the user receives an email notification if a document is modified, added, or deleted.

▶ Documents can be checked out, and the name of the person who has the document checked out can be listed in the library, so that other users can't modify the document and know who has it reserved.

▶ A template can be stored in the document library that can be used to create a new document in the library.

▶ Metadata can be added to a document library that enables users to better describe what the document contains, by, for example, clarifying which client it belongs to, key words in the document, or pretty much any other kind of textual or numerical information.

▶ Views can be created that group documents by certain criteria, sort them by any of the columns in the library, or only display documents that meet certain criteria.

▶ The library can be searched for text contained within the document, a feature often not available on a corporate network. In addition, the metadata associated with a document can be searched.

▶ If the organization decides on certain standards for the customization of a document library, it can create a template that can be used in other sites.

In Windows SharePoint Services 3.0, the standard document libraries provided are as follows:

▶ Document library

▶ Form library

▶ Wiki page library

▶ Picture library

The following section walks through the main features of a document library. Form libraries are designed to store InfoPath-based forms, whereas wiki page libraries contain pages that provide wiki-like functionality (multiple people can modify the content and changes are tracked) and the picture library is designed to store and manage graphic file types.

### A Tour of a Document Library

To access a document library, a user first needs to have a level of privileges that allows access to the site that houses the library, and also have privileges to open the library. Figure 35.10 shows the AllItems.aspx view of a document library (note the uniform resource locator [URL] in the address bar of Internet Explorer in the figure). Note that many of the features on this web page are similar to the home page of the site itself, including the look and feel of the home page and the Quick Launch area on the left side, but it now displays library-specific data in the main body of the page, where three documents are visible that were uploaded to this sample library. Note that the document titled "Test PDF Document" does not have the PDF icon assigned to it, which is expected. This PDF icon file needs to be placed in the proper directory, and the appropriate XML file edited, for the icon to appear.

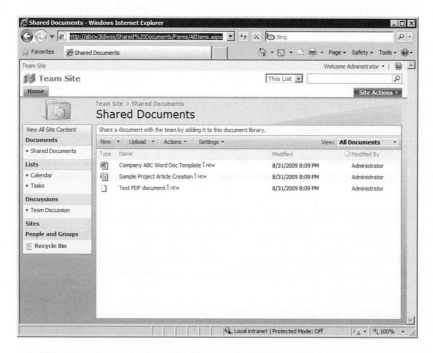

FIGURE 35.10   The AllItems.aspx view of the document library.

Following is a summary of the features offered in the different toolbar menus in a document library. These tools allow the user to perform a great number of tasks quickly and easily within the library, from adding new documents from a template, to uploading one or multiple documents, to connecting to Outlook, to adding columns, to exporting to Microsoft Access.

**The New Menu**    The New menu allows a user with the Add Items permission for lists and libraries to launch a template document that can be modified and saved by default back to the library, or to create a New Folder in the document library. Other users won't see this option on the toolbar.

**The Upload Menu**    The Upload menu offers the Upload Document option, and if the appropriate version of Office is installed, the Upload Multiple Documents option is provided. Only users with the Add Items permission for the library will see this menu on the toolbar. If a user chooses to Upload Multiple Documents, an interface allows multiple documents from within the same folder to be uploaded. Note that whole folders cannot be checked, nor can files from multiple folders be uploaded at once.

**The Actions Menu**    The Actions menu offers a number of different and powerful options and is context sensitive based on the privileges of the logged-on user. This menu is visible to all users who can access the document library, but users with lesser privileges will have fewer options available to them. The following list gives a brief overview of the features provided:

▶ **Edit in Datasheet**—When a user selects this option, the contents of the document library are displayed in a spreadsheet fashion, assuming the appropriate Office components are installed on the computer. Generally, the Datasheet view is used to rapidly enter recurring text for columns of metadata that are editable. There are also additional tools available in Datasheet view. To access these additional tools, click the arrow on the right side of the document library to expand the tasks pane. This tasks pane includes the following tools as indicated by icons in the upper portion of the tasks pane: Cut, Copy, Paste, Undo, Sort, Remove Filter/Sort, and Help. Below these tools in the Office Links section of the tasks pane, the user can access additional tools: Track This List in Access, Export to Access, Report with Access, Query List with Excel, Print with Excel, Chart with Excel, and Create Excel Pivot Table Report. Using the Print with Excel option is also handy because printing directly from Internet Explorer doesn't provide much flexibility.

**35**

**NOTE**

Make sure that the standard desktop is compatible with Datasheet view, or users will be filing help desk tickets when they try to access this feature. The following are requirements for Datasheet view:

▶ Per Microsoft, Office 2007 must be installed on your computer. However, testing with Office 2003 showed normal functionality, but with the "old" tasks pane from SharePoint 2003.

▶ Install the Microsoft Office Access Web Datasheet Component that is included with the 2007 Office release on your computer. This is also a requirement for Office 2003, and is found on the Office 2003 Professional CD.

▶ **Open with Windows Explorer**—When this option is selected, a separate Explorer window opens, which provides standard Explorer functionality, such as Open, Edit, New, Print, Copy, and Paste. The user's rights in the document library are still respected, so right-clicking an item and deleting it doesn't delete it from the library if the user doesn't have appropriate rights.

▶ **Connect to Outlook**—This option allows the user to connect a SharePoint library to Outlook 2007. This is very handy if a user wants to take the contents of the library offline in Outlook so she can access it when not connected to the network or the Internet.

▶ **Export to Spreadsheet**—Similar to the commands available from the tasks pane that is available in Datasheet view, the Export to Spreadsheet option opens Excel 2007 (or Excel 2003).

▶ **View RSS Feed**—When selected, this option opens the `listfeed.aspx` page, as shown in Figure 35.11, which gives the user a chance to see what the content of the document library will look like when accessed through the RSS feeder functionality in Windows SharePoint Services 3.0. If the user clicks on the Subscribe to This Feed link in Internet Explorer 7 or 8, he will be prompted for the following information in an Internet Explorer window: name for the feed, folder to create the feed in, and the option to create a new folder.

---

**CAUTION**

Note that the View RSS Feed functionality is not supported in Internet Explorer 6—only in Internet Explorer 7 or 8.

---

▶ **Alert Me**—Windows SharePoint Services 3.0 can send an email alert if certain conditions are met in a document library. As shown in Figure 35.12, the alerting feature allows the user to add multiple names to the alert or even distribution lists. The user can specify the conditions that will send them an alert, such as all changes, new items are added, and other conditions such as only if someone else changes a document created by me. The email alert can be sent immediately, in a daily summary, or even in a weekly summary at a given day and time.

**The Settings Menu** The Settings menu is only available to site visitors with Manage Lists permissions. This menu offers the Create Column, Create View, and Document Library Settings options. Figure 35.13 shows the `listedit.aspx` page that will open if the Document Library Settings choice is selected. By glancing at the options on this page, it is

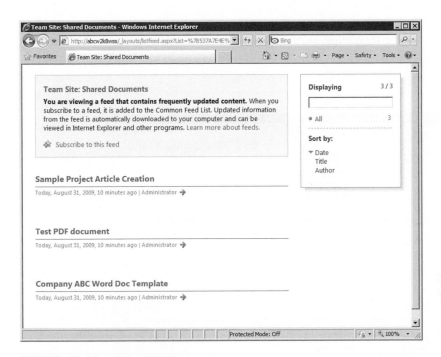

FIGURE 35.11    View RSS Feed page.

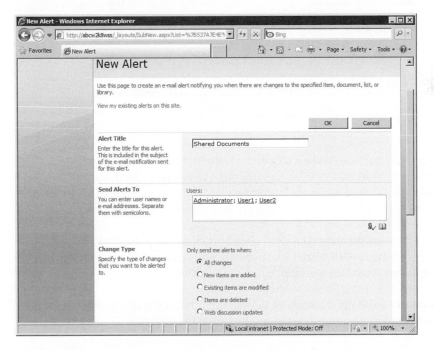

FIGURE 35.12    Alert options in a document library.

clear that many different types of changes can be made from the Document Library Settings page, including versioning, permissions, workflows, RSS, creating new columns, editing existing columns, and, barely visible at the bottom of Figure 35.13, creating or modifying views.

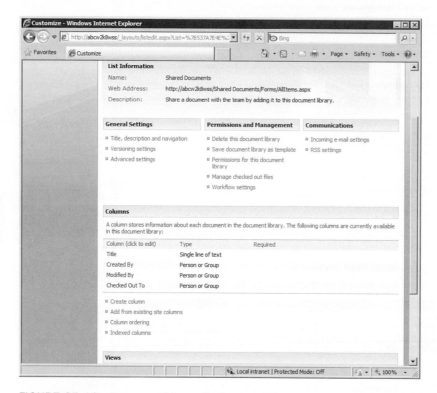

FIGURE 35.13    Document Library Settings page.

Figure 35.14 shows the previously viewed document library after a new column titled Type of Document has been added. Compare this view to Figure 35.10 to see the difference. By adding a column, the administrator provides additional metadata about the different documents, to help visitors more quickly find the document they require.

**The View Menu**    The View menu on the right edge of the toolbar is available to members of all groups, but only users with Manage Lists permissions can add or remove public views of a list or library. Standard views include the following:

▶ **All Documents**—The All Documents view is a standard view that provides the user with basic information about the documents stored in the library: Type, Name,

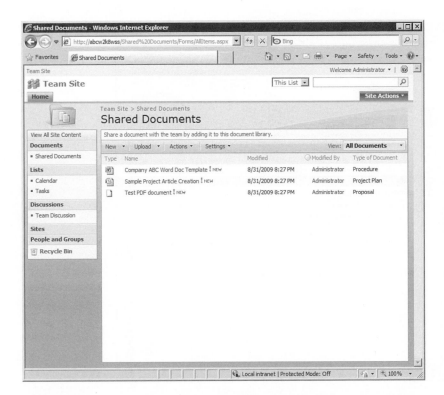

FIGURE 35.14    Document library with a new column added.

Modified, and Modified By. The All Documents view can be modified by an administrator with sufficient privileges.

▶ **Explorer**—The Explorer view (which is different from the Open with Windows Explorer action) displays the contents of the document library in an Explorer-type environment, where certain standard commands are available, and right-clicking on an item brings up standard Explorer commands.

▶ **Modify This View**—This option is only available to users with Manage Lists permissions.

▶ **Create View**—As with the preceding option, this is only available to users with Manage Lists permissions.

### Understanding the Edit Menu Options in a Document Library

In addition to the other library features reviewed in the previous sections, additional interactions with documents stored in a document library are possible through the Edit menu, which is accessed by hovering over the document name, as shown in Figure 35.15.

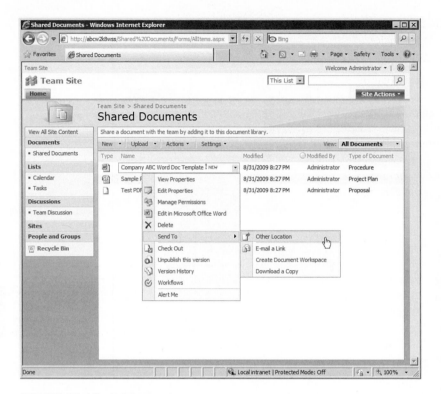

FIGURE 35.15 Edit menu.

These options reflect an additional level of power and functionality offered by a document library. A brief summary of each of the standard Edit menu items is as follows:

▶ **View Properties**—A variety of tools are made available when View Properties is selected from the drop-down menu, including Edit Item, Delete Item, Manage Permissions, Manage Copies, Check In, Workflows, and Alert Me. The user must have sufficient permissions to see these options.

▶ **Edit Properties**—This option displays the metadata associated with the item, and allows the user, if he has the appropriate permissions, to modify this data.

▶ **Manage Permissions**—A user with the Manage Lists permissions is able to use this tool to change which permissions different Windows SharePoint Services 3.0 users or groups have to the document. For example, a human resources document library manager might change permissions on certain documents to Read for the Members group, even though, by default, they can modify or delete other documents in the library.

▶ **Edit in Microsoft Application**—Windows SharePoint Services 3.0 will search for the association of the file type to an application, and if it is a Microsoft application, the application will be opened, allowing editing of the document.

▶ **Delete**—This moves the document to the Recycle Bin for the document library if the user has sufficient permissions.

▶ **Send To**—As shown in Figure 35.15, the default options are Other Location, E-Mail a Link, Create Document Workspace, and Download a Copy. The Other Location option actually makes a copy of the document in another SharePoint document library that is defined in the Advanced Settings for the library accessible from the Document Library Settings page. Emailing a link shares the document with another user without a full copy of the document being sent to that user. A document workspace is a SharePoint site that contains a copy of the document and encourages collaboration on a specific document. Downloading a copy allows the user to specify a location on their computer where a copy will be saved.

▶ **Check Out**—This is widely considered one of the more important features of a document management system. Administrators can now force a checkout before editing can take place from the Versioning Settings accessible from the Document Library Settings page. A user can check out a document and save it to a SharePoint Drafts folder in the My Documents folder. If the user chooses this option, she can edit the document even if she is offline and can't connect to the SharePoint 2007 server. A user can check out a document simply to make sure no one else modifies it, and if they forget, an administrator can force a check-in later from the Manage Checked Out Files link on the Document Library Settings page.

▶ **Unpublish This Version**—Versioning needs to be configured in this library to allow major and minor drafts for this option to be available. With these versioning options available, "unofficial" minor draft versions of documents can be posted to the library that may still be in need of editing, or published as major drafts that should be considered complete. The unpublish option allows a user to revert the status of the document to minor from major. Note that a document library administrator can choose to hide minor versions of documents from users with only Read access to the library.

▶ **Version History**—If versioning is turned on for a document library, every time a document is changed and saved, SharePoint keeps the entire previous version of the document. Published versions are considered to be major versions, whereas unpublished versions are considered minor versions. The number of each type of version retained can be set by the administrator. As an example, a site administrator might decide to allow both major and minor versions. The administrator may choose to keep 10 major versions as well as keep the minor versions for only the last 2 major versions. This granularity in version history allows for some rollback and history of the most recent major versions, but discards minor versions for all other major versions. When a user chooses Publish a Major Version, he can then add comments that can describe the changes made.

▶ **Workflows**—One or more workflows can be created in a document library in Windows SharePoint Services 3.0. This option is only available if a workflow has

35

been created by an administrator for the document library. Only one template is available, however: the Three-state workflow. This assigns states to a document based on the values in a column that the administrator chooses (such as draft, final, approved, or in review). When the first assignee completes their review, it is set to the middle state, and when the next person reviews it, it is set to the final state. Although limited, this workflow gives Windows SharePoint Services 3.0 users an understanding of the workflow process.

▶ **Alert Me**—This process was covered previously with reference to a whole document library. If selected for a document or file, the alert will only execute if the document or file is changed.

### Summarizing the Challenges and Benefits of Document Libraries

As the previous sections summarized, there are many, many features and options available in a document library. Although it only takes a few minutes to understand the basic processes of uploading and checking out documents, it can take many months of using and managing document libraries to master the more complex features (some of which, such as content types, aren't even presented in this section because of space constraints). Because document libraries are such a critical component of the Windows SharePoint Services 3.0 ecosystem, ample time should be given to testing them, exploring the different features, and coming up with some standards that meet the needs of the user community.

For example, an organization that has never used Windows SharePoint Services 3.0 before shouldn't immediately try to leverage all of the advanced features of a document library, such as minor and major drafts, item-level security, RSS feeds, and complex columns (such as lookup or calculated columns). Instead, the organization should add one or two new columns to a document library that meet the needs of the user group (such as a column titled Client Name or Part Number), create a custom view, and then provide some training to the pilot users. The best way to promote the adoption of SharePoint is to limit the complexity, add value to the users, and provide training.

## Windows SharePoint Services 3.0 Lists Demystified

Arguably just as important as document libraries, lists provide a huge range of tools to end users and administrators, project managers, customers, and partners. A list presents information in columns and rows, much as a spreadsheet does, and then provides special features suited to the purpose of the list. A number of people can work on a Windows SharePoint Services 3.0 list at the same time, facilitating collaboration much more easily than trying to share an Excel spreadsheet.

The standard lists available in SharePoint 2007 and Windows SharePoint Services v3 are as follows:

▶ Announcements list

▶ Contacts list

▶ Discussion board list

▶ Links list

▶ Calendar list

▶ Tasks list

▶ Project tasks list

▶ Issue tracking list

▶ Survey list

▶ Custom list

▶ Custom list in Datasheet view

▶ Import spreadsheet

The Calendar list is covered in the following section to provide an overview of the basic features of a commonly used list. Following that, a tasks list will be reviewed to provide additional insight into the features and capabilities of a list.

### Reviewing the Calendar List

A Windows SharePoint Services 3.0 Calendar list looks quite a bit like an Outlook calendar, but is based on an Excel-like array of information. Figure 35.16 shows the calendar.aspx page with a few sample entries. The presentation of the calendar provides a mini calendar in the Quick Launch area, which allows the user to jump quickly from one year to another or from one month to another by clicking the arrows. As reviewed in the previous section on document libraries, the menu bar offers New, Actions, and Settings drop-down menus, as well as a View drop-down menu. Note in the example shown in Figure 35.16 that there is a recurring team meeting that happens each Wednesday, and vacations are shown for two team members, which can clearly be seen to overlap.

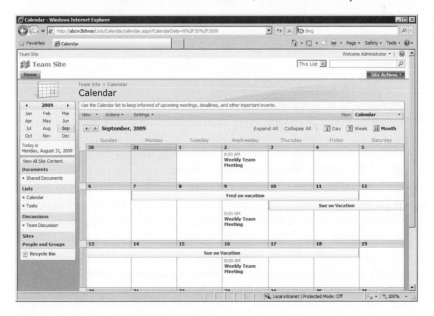

FIGURE 35.16   Calendar list.

35

The department manager wants to create a meeting workspace for the recurring weekly team meeting, and can do so by following these steps:

1. Assuming a recurring event has already been created in a Calendar list, click on the link to the event and then click the Edit Series tool on the toolbar.

2. As shown in Figure 35.17, the EditForm.aspx page will open. This page allows the editing of the title for the event, location, start time, end time, description, recurrence, and allows for the creation of a Meeting Workspace, visible at the bottom of the page.

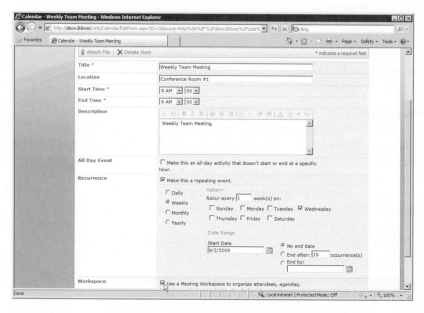

FIGURE 35.17     Editing a calendar item.

3. If the box is checked next to Use a Meeting Workspace to Organize Attendees, Agendas, Documents, Minutes and Other Details for This Event and OK is clicked, the New Meeting Workspace form will open, allowing the user to change the title, give a description, modify the URL (but not the location of the new workspace, which is a subsite of the current site), and either Use Same Permissions as the Parent Site or Use Unique Permissions. Click OK to continue.

4. The next screen allows the user to select a template to use: Basic Meeting Workspace, Blank Meeting Workspace, Decision Meeting Workspace, Social Meeting Workspace, or Multipage Meeting Workspace. Select Multipage Meeting Workspace and click OK.

5. Figure 35.18 shows the resulting Multipage Meeting Workspace. A visitor to this workspace can easily choose from the different meetings in the left pane, or toggle between different pages by clicking on the tabs. Of course, the manager needs to populate the site with content to encourage visits to the workspace. For example, he could post notes from each meeting to make them easily accessible for attendees.

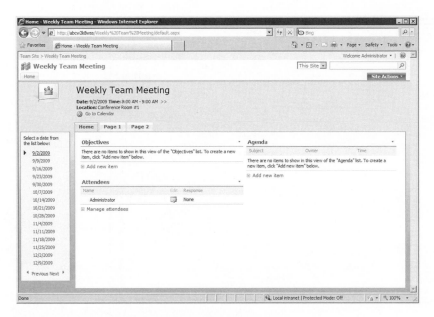

FIGURE 35.18    Multipage Meeting Workspace.

Finally, Figure 35.19 shows the All Events view in the Calendar list, which contains the new event titled "Really Important Meeting with the Boss." The icon to the left of the title links to the meeting workspace and the icon to the left of that indicates that it is a recurring meeting. Individual meetings can be modified, start and end times can be changed, and the workspace will reflect these changes, which is helpful for typical business requirements.

Hopefully, it is evident from the All Events view in Figure 35.19 that the Calendar list contains cells of data (Title, Location, Start Time, End Time, Link to a Site That Is a Meeting Workspace) and each item (or row of information) can be managed in a similar fashion to the metadata tagged to a document in a document library. So, many of the skills learned from working with a document library translate directly to a list.

If a user clicks on View Item from the Edit menu when in the All Events view, he has the option to Export Event, which saves the item to an .ics iCalendar file in the location of their choosing. This can then be dragged into an Outlook 2007 calendar. Or, the user can connect the whole calendar to Outlook by clicking Connect to Outlook from the Actions menu in All Events view. A new calendar will be created containing the events in the SharePoint 2007 Calendar list. Clients have been very excited to hear that users can now add appointments in Outlook to this calendar, and these events will be synchronized to the SharePoint 2007 Calendar list, assuming they have appropriate rights. Some Outlook features, such as reminders, are not supported in the SharePoint 2007 Calendar list, but the basic events are synchronized. An Outlook 2007 user can also drag and drop an appointment from their personal calendar to the SharePoint 2007 exported calendar, and will be warned that "any incompatible content will be removed during the next synchronization."

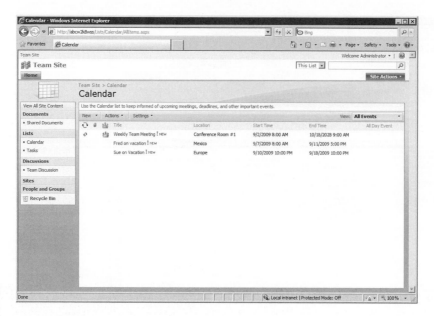

FIGURE 35.19    All Events view in a Calendar list.

### A Brief Look at the Tasks List

Tasks lists are an essential management tool that facilitate day-to-day operations of a department, activities that need to be performed by a group, or specific, well-defined steps that need to take place in a project, such as a marketing, engineering, or IT project. Project managers are typically great people to involve in pilot testing of WSS 3.0 configurations because tools such as the Tasks lists and Calendars are extremely helpful for managing projects of any size.

Figure 35.20 shows a New Item page for a Tasks list. The fields are fairly self-explanatory, and, of course, new fields can be added if the existing fields don't provide enough granularity. The choices in drop-down menus—Priority and Status—can also be modified. A list administrator has the option to Send E-Mail when Ownership Is Assigned, which will send an email to the user in the Assigned To field. The Actions menu provides the Connect to Outlook tool. If selected, this will ask the user if they want to Connect This SharePoint Task List to Outlook, and provide access to the Advanced options. The tasks will then be displayed in an Outlook 2007 Tasks list. These tasks can be dragged and dropped to the user's own Tasks list in Outlook 2007.

### Custom Lists Provide a Blank Slate

If one of the template lists doesn't offer the right combination of elements, you can create one from scratch by selecting the Custom List or Custom List in Datasheet View option. This allows you to choose how many columns make up the list, determine what kind of data each column will contain, such as text, choices (a menu to choose from), numbers, currency, date/time, lookup (information already on the site), yes/no, hyperlink or picture, or calculations based on other columns. With this combination of contents available and the capability to link to other data contained in the site from other lists, a database of

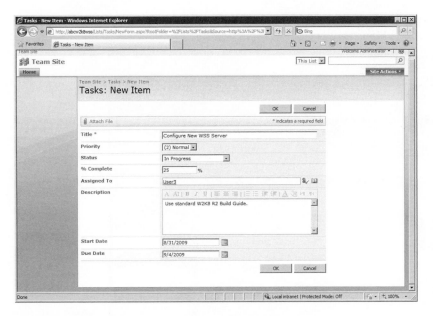

FIGURE 35.20    New Item page for a Tasks list.

information that pertains to the site can be created that can get quite complex. For example, a custom list could include events from the Events list, tracking the cost of each event and which task corresponds to the event.

# Integrating Office 2007 Applications with Windows SharePoint Services 3.0

A key design goal for Windows SharePoint Services 3.0 was to have it more tightly integrated with Microsoft Office applications. Although Windows SharePoint Services 3.0 supports earlier versions of Office, the most complete integration will—no surprise—come with Office 2007 products. However, many organizations tend to have a mixture of different versions of Office. Some clients still have Office 2000 products, 2003 products, and are just starting (at the time of this writing) to implement Office 2007 products, so it is important to test the performance of the installed versions with Windows SharePoint Services 3.0.

## Using Word 2007 with Windows SharePoint Services 3.0

When Word 2007 is used to open a document from a SharePoint 2007 document library, the user can access metadata and other information stored in Windows SharePoint Services 3.0. To view the Document Properties Ribbon, as shown in Figure 35.21, click the Office Button, then select Prepare, and Properties. To show the Document Management pane, which is visible on the right side of Figure 35.21, click the Office Button, then select Server, and Document Management Information.

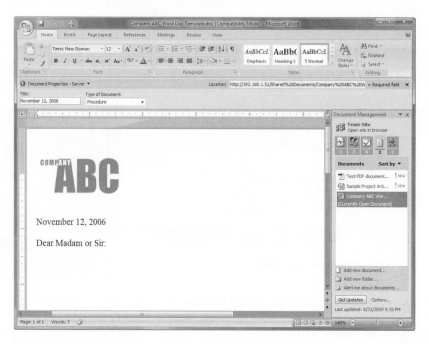

FIGURE 35.21    Document Properties Ribbon and Document Management pane in Word 2007.

As shown in Figure 35.21, the Type of Document metadata column created previously for this document library is visible under the Document Properties – Server title. In the Document Management pane on the right, five options are available, each of which provides data from SharePoint:

▶ **Status option**—Lists important status information about the current document.

▶ **Members option**—Lists which individuals and groups have access to the document library, and which users are online or not online. An email can be sent to all members from this tab.

▶ **Tasks option**—Shows tasks from the primary Tasks list on the Windows SharePoint Services 3.0 site that houses the document library. New tasks can be added, alerts can be set, and workflow tasks can be viewed.

▶ **Documents option**—Shows the other documents in the home library for the open document. New documents and new folders can be added, and alerts can be created.

▶ **Links option**—Displays any links that are present in a Links list on the home site. A new link can be added, or an alert can be created.

The Publish link from under the Office button can also be used. Two standard options offered are to publish to a blog or to a document management server. If the Blog option is selected, the user is shown a preview and is asked to select the SharePoint blog site to publish to. If the Document Management Server option is chosen, the Save As window opens with a list of possible locations.

Another entry option in the Office button in Word 2007 is the Server entry. It provides some additional tools, which are available when a document has been opened from SharePoint 2007. One of these is Check Out, if the document is not already checked out. Another is View Version History, which allows the user to see the version number, modified date, user who made the changes, size of the document, and any comments. And if any workflows are available in the document library that houses the document, a View Workflow Tasks option will be available.

This ease of use for accessing information encourages users to share, collaborate, and communicate together on projects, initiatives, or ideas without having to leave the comfort of the Word 2007 application.

## Using Excel 2007 with Windows SharePoint Services 3.0

Excel 2007 offers the same level of connectivity as Word 2007 in terms of the Document Properties Ribbon and Document Management pane. Excel 2007 also has some additional ways of linking to Windows SharePoint Services 3.0 lists, quite possibly because Excel data is so similar to data stored in SharePoint lists, or because Microsoft understands the importance of encouraging users to adopt SharePoint technologies as an alternative to Excel spreadsheets, and to enhance collaboration.

One way of sharing data in an Excel workbook with SharePoint 2007 users is to export the contents to a SharePoint list. For this to work, you first need to create a table in Excel 2007, populate it, and then initiate the export process. An extremely powerful feature of SharePoint lists is that multiple people can edit them at the same time, which can be an advantage over users fighting to check out, edit, and check in documents one at a time. So the following exercise is helpful as a way of demonstrating the collaboration capabilities of a list that houses Excel data.

To export an Excel 2007 table to a Windows SharePoint Services 3.0 list, follow these steps:

1. On a worksheet with data, select the range of cells that you want to make into a table. From the Insert tab, in the Tables group, click Table.
2. The Create Table window opens. Define the range, and check the My Table Has Headers check box, if needed.
3. Click OK. A table is created that includes the data in the defined range, as shown in Figure 35.22.

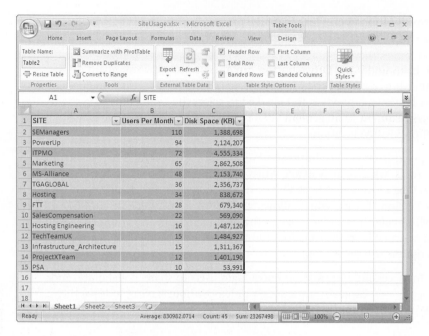

FIGURE 35.22 Converting a range of cells to a table.

4. If necessary, select a cell in the table, so that the Design tab becomes active, access the Export drop-down menu, and select Export Table to SharePoint List. The Step 1 of 2 window opens, as shown in Figure 35.23. Enter the address of the site to be published to and the name of the table. Click Next.

FIGURE 35.23 Export Table to SharePoint List from Excel 2007.

5. The Step 2 of 2 window opens, and it summarizes the data types that will be used (for example, Text(single line) or Number or Date). Formulas are stripped at this point, and only the values are kept. Click Finish.

6. A summary window opens stating "The table was successfully published" and provides a URL to the new list. Click this URL to open the new list.

7. Figure 35.24 shows the new list, in this case titled Site Usage Data. Note that because the data was exported, there is no longer a link between Excel and this data.

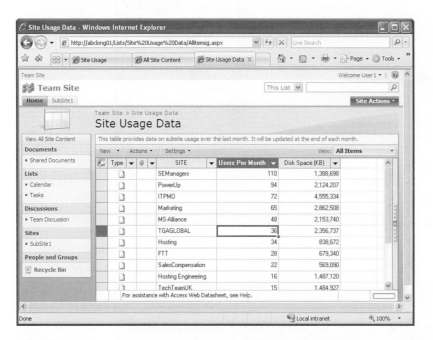

FIGURE 35.24   List created from an exported Excel 2007 table.

---

**CAUTION**

Using the Export Table to SharePoint List option is a great way to quickly publish data to a Windows SharePoint Services 3.0 table. However, this is a one-time export, so if the spreadsheet is updated later, you cannot re-export it to the same SharePoint list!

---

### Exporting to Access 2007 from a SharePoint 2007 List

A Windows SharePoint Services 3.0 list also provides the ability to export list data to an Access 2007 list so that the administrator can leverage some of the powerful analysis tools of Access 2007. The administrator can create forms, pivot charts, reports, or queries.

Simply click on Export to Access from the Office Links, which can be accessed on the right side of the screen in Datasheet view of a list, as shown in Figure 35.25. After the data is opened in Access 2007, you can easily create a report with a few mouse clicks, as shown in Print Preview mode in Figure 35.26.

35

FIGURE 35.25    Exporting list data to Access 2007.

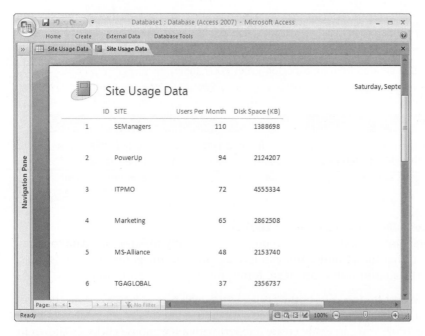

FIGURE 35.26    Report created in Access 2007 in Print Preview mode.

Many other tools are available in Access 2007, which makes it well suited for repurposing data from Windows SharePoint Services 3.0. For example, data can be exported to

- Excel 2007

- SharePoint 2007 or Windows SharePoint Services 3.0 list

- Rich Text Format File (ideal for then using in Word 2007)

- Text file

- Other formats, including XML file, ODBC database, HTML document, or merged with Word

Many users saw little if any use for Access with SharePoint data in the past, but Microsoft has worked hard to improve the effectiveness of the tools provided in Access 2007, which now makes it an ideal companion to Windows SharePoint Services 3.0.

# Managing the Site Collection

The previous sections gave some insight into the different components of a site, including lists and libraries, and an overview of many of the features of these components. This section provides an overview of the tools a Windows SharePoint Services 3.0 farm administrator, site collection administrator, and subsite administrator have available. These tools allow her to control many of the elements of the Windows SharePoint Services 3.0 farm (which can consist of one server or a collection of servers), the collection of sites from the top-level site (which is linked to an IIS website and a specific port number on the server—typically port 80), and subsites beneath the top-level site.

These different toolsets provide insight into what tools are available at each strata of the Windows SharePoint Services 3.0 environment and help to clarify what can easily be changed from within the different interfaces and what might require other products, such as SharePoint Designer or command-line tools (such as the `stsadm.exe` tool).

## Using the Site Settings Pages to Manage Top-Level Sites and Subsites

Figure 35.27 shows the tools available on the Site Settings page (`settings.aspx`) for the top-level site (http://abcw2k8wss/default.aspx) that we have been working with in this chapter. The tools are divided into Users and Permissions, Look and Feel, Galleries, Site Administration, and Site Collection Administration. Figure 35.28 shows the Site Settings page for a subsite, which has fewer options, and only includes the same headers but with fewer tools. For example, the top-level site Site Settings page offers the Site Collection Administration tool, where individuals or groups can be made administrators for the top-level site and all sites beneath it, whereas the subsite Site Settings page does not offer this option. The top-level Site Settings page offers a number of additional galleries—Site Templates, List Templates, Web Parts, Workflows—as well as additional Site Collection Administration tools, such as the Recycle Bin, Site Collection Features, Site Hierarchy, and

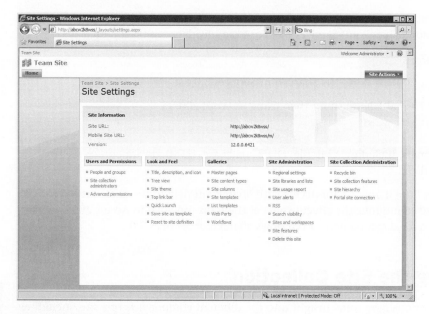

FIGURE 35.27    Site Settings page for a top-level site.

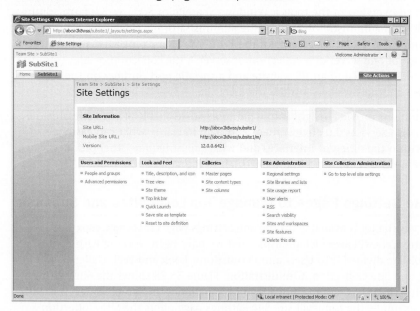

FIGURE 35.28    Site Settings page for a subsite.

Portal Site Connection. These differences illustrate some of the key features of a site collection:

▶ A site collection administrator can manage the top-level site and all subsites, whereas a subsite administrator can manage that site and sites below it.

▶ The top-level site has additional galleries that store components that can be accessed by subsites, including Site Templates, List Templates, Web Parts, and Workflows.

▶ The Recycle Bin is managed at the top-level site.

▶ Site Collection Features are managed at the top-level site. For example, the Three-state workflow is a feature that can be deactivated on the Site Collection Features page.

▶ The Site Hierarchy shows all of the websites that have been created under the top-level site.

▶ A Portal Site Connection can be created if needed, which connects the site collection to another SharePoint farm to provide additional resources to the users of the current site collection, assuming they have rights on the other farm.

## Using the Edit Page Interface to Customize Pages

Although the tools discussed in the previous section allow the subsite administrator or site collection administrator to perform much of the functional configuration for the site or site collection, there are still many tasks that need to be done on a day-to-day basis to meet the needs of the user community, and to make the site look appealing and professional. The previous sections on document libraries and lists gave some examples of changes that could be made within these building blocks of the SharePoint environment, but users also expect to be able to access single pages (such as home pages for a top-level site or subsite) that provide navigational tools and customized views of data stored in lists or libraries so they have a summary or introduction to the content of the site. The analogy of the front page of a magazine can be used here. The front page of a magazine has a title and other basic information identifying the type of content, as well as graphics, snippets of stories to intrigue the reader, and often page numbers of the full articles. In a similar way, the home page of a site (such as http://abcw2k8wss/default.aspx) should provide a similar level of information.

The following example shows how the browser interface can be used to customize the home page of the Team Site (such as http://abcw2k8wss/default.aspx) that has been used as an example throughout the chapter. Follow these steps on your own site for similar results:

1. Click on the Site Actions drop-down menu on the default.aspx page of the site (requires sufficient privileges on the site). Click on Edit Page. The resulting page will resemble Figure 35.29. A notice is provided above the editable region that states "You are editing the Shared Version of the page," and the editable zones are highlighted and contain the Add a Web Part link.

2. Click on an Add a Web Part link to see a list of web parts that are available. For this example, add the Shared Documents list view web part to the page by checking the box next to Shared Documents. Click the Add button. Figure 35.30 shows the results, while still in editing mode.

3. To see what other options are available for the Shared Documents list view web part, click on Edit on the right side of the title bar, and click on Modify Shared Web Part. This task pane allows the administrator to select a different view that will change

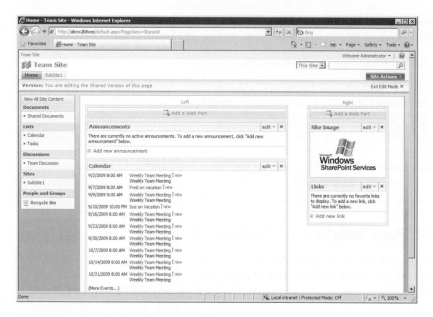

FIGURE 35.29    Edit mode for a site home page.

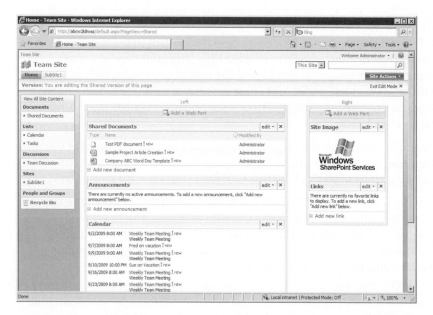

FIGURE 35.30    Results of adding a document library list view web part to a home page.

how the data is displayed; modify the toolbar type; and change the appearance, layout, and Advanced settings.

### Reviewing the Tools Provided in the Central Administration Console

Windows SharePoint Services 3.0 provides the Central Administration console, which allows the Windows SharePoint Services 3.0 farm administrator to perform high-level configuration tasks and manage the overall health of the environment. These tools are broken into Operations and Application Management tools and include numerous tools in the following categories:

- ▶ Topology and Services
- ▶ Security Configuration
- ▶ Logging and Reporting
- ▶ Global Configuration
- ▶ Backup and Restore
- ▶ Data Configuration
- ▶ SharePoint Web Application Management
- ▶ Application Security
- ▶ Workflow Management
- ▶ SharePoint Site Management
- ▶ External Service Connections

Figures 35.31 and 35.32 show the interfaces and tools that are available in each one of the categories just listed.

Each of these topics is fairly advanced and a thorough discussion of them is beyond the scope of this chapter, but the range of tools available gives some insight into the power of Windows SharePoint Services 3.0 from Microsoft.

# Summary

Windows SharePoint Services 3.0 is a powerful and free add-on to Windows Server 2008 R2 that many companies and organizations are considering a must-have in their network environments. This chapter summarized the differences between Windows SharePoint Services 3.0 and SharePoint Server 2007, giving insight into reasons that organizations will invest in extending the capabilities of Windows SharePoint Services 3.0. The chapter then moved into providing an overview of the basic capabilities of document libraries and lists in Windows SharePoint Services 3.0 to give a peek at the amazing array of tools and features that are offered. Examples of how Word 2007, Excel 2007, and Access 2007 can be

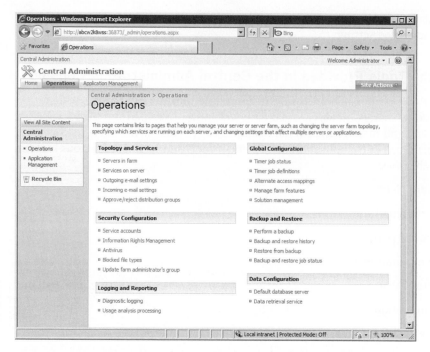

FIGURE 35.31   Operations tab in the Central Administration console.

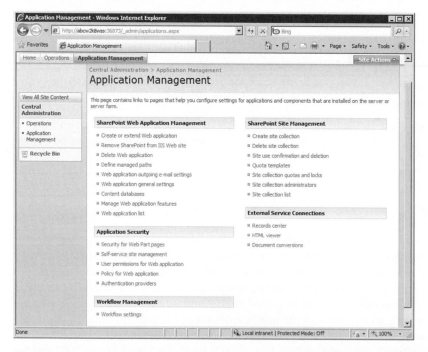

FIGURE 35.32   Application Management tab in the Central Administration console.

used with Windows SharePoint Services 3.0 were provided, as well as tools that site collection and site administrators can use on a daily basis. Finally, the highest-level tools that a SharePoint farm administrator would use to maintain the overall health and performance of the environment were summarized.

# Best Practices

The following are best practices from this chapter:

▶ Although Windows SharePoint Services 3.0 can work with the SQL Server 2005 Express Edition software that is free and installed by default, consider using the full version of SQL Server 2005 if Windows SharePoint Services 3.0 will be used extensively by the organization and contain mission-critical data.

▶ Keep the Windows SharePoint Services 3.0 Server up to date with all patches and updates of Windows Server 2008 R2 to reduce the risk of attacks or malfunctions.

▶ Use the full SharePoint Server 2007 application when you need to add enterprise-level tools to Windows SharePoint Services 3.0 sites, or to add other features as summarized in this chapter.

▶ Document libraries are building blocks of Windows SharePoint Services 3.0 sites and provide tools such as document versioning, checkout and check-in features, alerts, and RSS feed capabilities.

▶ Lists are similar to Excel spreadsheets in many ways, and are customized in Windows SharePoint Services 3.0 to offer calendaring, task management, discussion group, and other types of functionality.

▶ The Office 2007 products offer extensive integration with Windows SharePoint Services 3.0 sites. However, Office 2003 products can also be used with Windows SharePoint Services 3.0 sites, but the integration is more limited.

▶ Windows SharePoint Services 3.0 offers different tiers of management tools for the farm administrator, top-level site administrator, and site administrator. Design tools can be used from the browser for many page layout and formatting tasks.

# Windows Media Services

Digital content has taken society to fascinating new levels. It's not surprising as today's digital media solutions allow individuals and organizations alike to use various devices to capture, download, present, and stream digital content in a matter of minutes.

The move away from conventional forms of communication has placed a heavy demand on companies like Microsoft to introduce products that not only give people and organizations more efficient ways to communicate, but also provide a mechanism to publish digital content while also reducing costs.

As a result, Microsoft introduced Windows Media Services— a free, optional component for Windows Server 2008 R2 that takes full advantage of the Internet and intranet to stream live or on-demand digital content. Microsoft also provides two major tools, both of which are freely downloadable, that perform media conversion (Windows Media Encoder) as well as content customization for presentations.

Organizations, small and large, are seeing the impact the streaming media solution has on communication and their pockets. It has improved communication by ensuring information broadcast and rebroadcast is consistent. For example, employees in an organization's most remote location can watch a presentation live. Equally important, the presentation remains available on demand for those who missed the live presentation or wanted to review it. As this example demonstrates, everyone receives the same information. Employee downtime has also significantly decreased. Employees are traveling less for company meetings, career development workshops, and other events. The benefits do not stop there as organizations are saving money by taking advantage of their existing networks. By building upon what they already have instead of investing in other products, including satellite or television, organizations are seeing financial benefits. Not to mention some organizations' business models, such as YouTube, bring in millions every year by offering digital media publishing services to their consumers.

This chapter covers both the server component of Windows Media Services as well as the downloadable tools that provide editing and publishing support for users and administrators.

# Understanding Windows Media Services

Windows Media Services is no longer a built-in component on the Windows Server 2008 R2 operating system. As such, it will be necessary for those working with the Windows Server 2008 R2 family of operating systems to obtain Windows Media Services directly from the Microsoft website. It will also be necessary to install and configure the Windows Media Services role on a Windows Server 2008 R2 system. Windows Media Services enables the administrators of an organization to organize video and audio files to be published to other users. The publishing function sets the bandwidth that will be used during the file distribution, controls the number of users accessing audio and video files at the same time, and manages the overall bandwidth demands of the Windows Media Services functions.

By properly configuring and optimizing media services functions, an organization can minimize the excessive demands of media services distribution over the network. The decisions that need to be made include whether distribution will be:

▶ Real-time live broadcasts

▶ Single broadcasts at a time

▶ Multiple files combined to a single broadcast

▶ Multiple files in a single directory for selective broadcasting

The various publishing options are highlighted throughout this chapter as best practices, tips, and tricks on configuring and implementing the publishing services to meet various organizational needs.

## Features Included with Windows Media Services Running on Windows Server 2008 R2

Windows Media Services running on Windows Server 2008 R2 offers a plethora of features and functionality:

▶ **Cache/Proxy Management**—To bolster presentation experience, a plug-in can be used to provide cache or reverse proxy functionality of digital media content. This new feature reduces network infrastructure costs by decreasing the amount of bandwidth required and used.

▶ **Server Core installation**—IT professionals have the option of installing the Windows Media Services components on a Server Core installation of Windows

Server 2008 R2. A Server Core installation of Windows Server 2008 R2 is a scaled-down version of the installation offering specific administrative roles without the management interfaces and tools, which reduces management and surface area attacks.

---

**NOTE**

Review Chapter 3, "Installing Windows Server 2008 R2 and Server Core," for more information on Windows Server 2008 R2 Server Core installation.

---

▶ **Multicast for Silverlight**—Windows Media Services can now deliver multicast streams to Silverlight with the new Silverlight Multicast plug-in.

▶ **Single Installation Package**—Unlike Windows Server 2008, a single package is offered to make the deployment of Windows Media Server on Windows Server 2008 R2 much easier.

▶ **Tighter Integration with Hyper-V**—Streaming, performance, and manageability has improved when running Windows Media Services on Hyper-V on Windows Server 2008 R2.

▶ **Advanced Fast Start**—This new feature associated with Windows Server 2008 R2 leverages the maximum available bandwidth allowed during the initial connection to a stream, resulting in end users being able to see content as soon as they connect. As soon as the playback begins, bandwidth is throttled back to a regular amount.

▶ **Play While Archiving**—This new feature, which is only supported when running the Enterprise Edition or Datacenter Edition, allows transmitted content to be archived to a file. It is interesting to note here that the file can be accessed on demand or rebroadcast even before the archiving is finished.

▶ **Advanced FF/RW**—When using this feature, independent files are used for fast-forward and rewind functionality. Separate files increase performance playback and reduce bandwidth contention.

▶ **Broadcast AutoStart**—This feature aims to minimize end-user disruption and downtime. The key is to configure the broadcast publishing points to run automatically so the stream automatically restarts in the event of a disruption.

▶ **Absolute Playlist Time**—Leverage this feature if there is a need to start a stream or playlist at a certain time by indicating a specific value for time, such as 12:00 a.m. The time entry is based on Coordinated Universal Time (UTC).

▶ **Encoder Failover URL Modifiers**—It is possible to leverage more than one encoder to increase reliability and redundancy of the source content. The result is that Windows Media Services can be configured to pull source content from an alternate location in the event of a failure.

## System Requirements for Windows Media Services

Besides requiring a Windows Server 2008 R2 system (Web Edition, Standard Edition, Enterprise Edition, or Datacenter Edition), the basic requirements for Windows Media Services are as follows:

▶ **Processor**—One or more processors running at 550MHz or higher

▶ **Memory**—512MB of RAM or higher

▶ **Hard disk space**—A minimum of 2GB

▶ **File system**—NTFS

▶ **Ethernet network adapter running TCP/IP**

> **NOTE**
>
> It is important for readers to know that some features such as the Advanced Fast Start and the Cache/Proxy Management functionality only operate if Windows Media Services is installed on a Windows Server 2008 R2, Enterprise Edition or Datacenter Edition.

Although these are the minimum hardware specifications provided by Microsoft, most server class systems today typically consist of Dual Quad-Core, a minimum of 8GB of RAM, and at least a gigabit network adapter.

What's key to the Windows Media Services system is having enough processing speed to handle the media streaming requests, enough RAM to cache the media streams, and enough disk space to store the video files being shared and published. In addition, it is a best practice to use a dedicated server for streaming, limit the total number of users to 50% of the maximum user capacity achieved by the load tests, and ensure the overall network utilization is less than 50% of the maximum network interface capacity.

> **TIP**
>
> To improve the performance of a Windows Media Services system, place the operating system and program files on one volume and place the video files on another volume to distribute the normal server processes from the read/write access of the video files. In addition, placing striped drive sets with ample hard drive controller cache can improve both the sequential and parallel read/write requests of the video files as Windows Media Services is more I/O intensive than processor intensive.

## Determining Which Windows Server 2008 R2 Version to Utilize

Unlike the majority of the Microsoft products, the bells and whistles are included with the Enterprise Edition or Datacenter Edition. This tradition deviates with Windows Media Services on Windows Server 2008 R2. Many of the Windows Media Services features that were only included with Windows Server 2008, Enterprise and Datacenter Editions are now included with the Windows Server 2008 R2, Standard, Foundation, and Web Editions. Therefore, the feature sets with the Windows Server 2008 R2, Standard, Foundation, and Web Editions are no longer limited in comparison with the Enterprise Edition or Datacenter Edition.

Windows Media Services supports the following editions of Windows Server 2008 R2: R2 Datacenter, R2 Enterprise, R2 Standard, R2 Foundation, and Web Server 2008 R2.

> **NOTE**
>
> Unfortunately, Windows Media Services is not supported on the Itanium-based versions of Windows Server 2008 R2. However, there have been significant improvements for performance and manageability when streaming media with Hyper-V for Windows Server 2008 R2.

To further assist readers and organizations in choosing the right version of Windows Server 2008 R2, Table 36.1 compares the features available with Windows Media Services based on each edition of the Windows Server 2008 R2 family.

TABLE 36.1   Comparing the Editions of Windows Media Services

| Feature Item | Standard, Foundation, and Web Editions | Enterprise and Data Center Editions |
| --- | --- | --- |
| Absolute Playlist Time | X | X |
| Advanced Fast Start | X | X |
| Advanced FF/RW | X | X |
| Advertising server support | X | X |
| Broadcast AutoStart | X | X |
| Cache/proxy support | X | X |
| Custom plug-in support | X | X |
| Event-based scripting support | X | X |
| Fast Cache | X | X |
| Fast Reconnect | X | X |
| Fast Recovery | X | X |
| Fast Start | X | X |
| Fast Streaming | X | X |
| Internet authentication method (Digest) | X | X |
| Internet Group Management Protocol version 3 (IGMPv3) support | X | X |

36

TABLE 36.1    Comparing the Editions of Windows Media Services

| Feature Item | Standard, Foundation, and Web Editions | Enterprise and Data Center Editions |
|---|---|---|
| Internet Protocol version 6 (IPv6) support | X | X |
| Intranet authentication methods (Negotiate authentication, Anonymous access) | X | X |
| Multicast content delivery | | X |
| Multiple authorization methods (NTFS ACL, IP Address) | X | X |
| Multiple control protocol support (MMS, HTTP, RTSP) | X | X |
| Multiple media parser support (Windows Media, MP3) | X | X |
| Multiple playlist parser support (WSX, Directory) | X | X |
| Play While Archiving | X | X |
| RTSP streaming | X | X |
| Robust event notification (WMI, SNMP) | X | X |
| Server-based content repacketization | X | X |
| Unicast content delivery | X | X |

To end this section on a high note, there isn't a need to purchase a separate license for Windows Media Services because the software is included as a free download from Microsoft's website. For this reason, a separate client access license (CAL) is not required to run the services. However, there is still a need to license the server product for Windows Server 2008 R2.

## Updating the Windows Media Services Platform to Windows Server 2008 R2

It will likely be necessary for most organizations to upgrade their systems running the Windows Media Services platform to Windows Server 2008 R2. For those currently running Windows Server 2003, it is a matter of upgrading to Windows Server 2008 R2. However, a direct upgrade from Windows NT 4.0 or Windows 2000 Server is not supported. Organizations in this predicament that are running a legacy version of Windows Media Services on Windows NT 4.0 or Windows 2000 Server will need to first upgrade the Windows Media Services platform to Windows Server 2003 and then upgrade again to Windows Server 2008 R2.

> **TIP**
>
> It is a best practice to first back up the legacy Windows Media Services platform before upgrading to Windows Server 2008 R2. This includes capturing and backing up the configuration settings, log files, and digital media content.

## Determining Which Windows Media Services Administration Tools to Leverage

When planning to run Windows Media Services on Windows Server 2008 R2, organizations should consider the numerous ways it can be administered and managed to find their best fit. The following bullets identify the tools available for administering Windows Media Services:

▶ **Windows Media Service snap-in**—This is the most common interface for managing Windows Media Services. This interface is based on the traditional Microsoft Management Console (MMC). It can be added as a snap-in to any server running Windows Server 2008 R2, Windows Vista, or Windows 7.

▶ **Windows Media Services Administrator for the web**—Organizations can choose to administer Windows Media Services over the web. The web interface for administration is particularly useful and appreciated by users who manage Windows Media Services from a non-Windows machine over the Internet or on a network with low latency.

▶ **Command-line scripts**—Like many of the Windows Server products, Windows Media Services administration tasks can be automated through the command line by using a series of scripts.

When the full installation option for Windows Media Services is utilized, both the Windows Media Service snap-in and the Windows Media Services Administrator for the web are included. It should be noted that the Windows Media Service Administrator for the web requires the Web Server (IIS) server role to be installed on the Windows Server 2008 R2 system. Alternatively, the Windows Media Services 2008 R2 Remote Server Administration tool can be downloaded from the Microsoft website.

# Installing Windows Media Services

IT professionals will quickly recognize that the installation process for Windows Media Services on Windows Server 2008 R2 is not as simplistic as it was with previous Windows Server operating systems. In the past, an IT professional would simply add the Windows Media Services component through Add and Remove Programs as it was included with the

36

base Windows Server operating system. With Windows Server 2008 R2, more steps are involved in the installation process. Windows Media Services is no longer included with the Windows Server 2008 R2 family of operating systems, as it is offered as a separate out-of-band download. Therefore, IT professionals will need to download the Microsoft Update Standalone (MUS) package from the Microsoft website and install it on Windows Server 2008 R2. Unlike Windows Server 2008, there is only one MUS package that needs to be downloaded for all editions of Windows Server 2008 R2. After the installation is complete, the next step is to add the Streaming Media Services role in Server Manager.

## Downloading the Windows Media Services Source Files

As mentioned earlier, the first step when installing the Windows Media Services role on Windows Server 2008 R2 is to obtain the Windows Media Services for Windows Server 2008 R2 installer files from the Microsoft website.

The out-of-band Windows Media Services installation files for Windows Server 2008 R2 can be obtained from the Windows Media Services 2008 website at http://www.microsoft.com/windows/windowsmedia/forpros/serve/prodinfo2008.aspx.

## Conducting the Windows Media Services Installation

To install the Windows Media Services role on a Windows Server 2008 R2 system, perform the following steps:

1. Obtain the appropriate Streaming Media Services installer file from the Microsoft website.

2. Click Download and run the installation immediately by clicking Open in the File Download dialog box or click Save to download the file to your computer. The latter choice allows you to conduct the installation at a later time.

> **NOTE**
>
> If the incorrect installation file is selected, the Windows Update Standalone Installer will provide a warning message to indicate the update does not apply to your system.

3. After the installation for Windows Media Services is complete, click Start, Administrative Tools, Server Manager. If Server Manager was running during the install, close and reopen it to display the newly available role.

4. Select Add Roles by right-clicking Roles in Server Manager, which is located in the left pane.

5. On the Select Server Roles screen, install the role by selecting Streaming Media Services in the Roles section, and then click Next.

6. Review the messages in the Streaming Media Services screen, and click Next.

7. Select the desired Streaming Media Services role services to install. The role services options include Windows Media Server, Web-based Administration, and Multicast

and Logging Agent. For this example, Windows Media Server was selected, as illustrated in Figure 36.1. Click Next to continue.

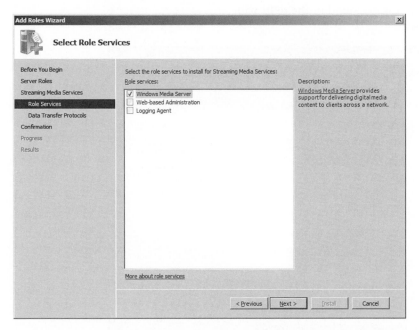

FIGURE 36.1    Selecting the role services to install for Streaming Media Services.

8.  Select the data transfer protocol for streaming media content, and then click Next. The two options available are as follows:

    ▶ **Real Time Streaming Protocol (RTSP)**—Delivers unicast streams to computers running Windows Media Player 9 Series or later, or Windows Media Services 9 Series.

    ▶ **Hypertext Transfer Protocol (HTTP)**—Delivers unicast streams to all versions of Windows Media Player and Windows Media Services, regardless of version. This option is only available to install if Internet Information Services (IIS) is installed.

9.  Confirm the installation selections, and click Install to install the selected roles, role services, and features.

10. To complete the installation, review the installation results, and then click Close.

## Configuring Windows Media Services

After being installed, the services for Windows Media Services are set to start automatically. The next step is to configure Windows Media Services to meet the video and audio publishing requirements of your organization. To do so, launch the Windows Media Services MMC administration tool by selecting Start, All Programs, Administrative Tools,

Windows Media Services. You will see a screen similar to the one shown in Figure 36.2. The Getting Started tab includes informational items on Streaming Media Basics and Resources on the Web. In addition, if you select the server in the left pane, additional Getting Started tabs can be found in the right pane.

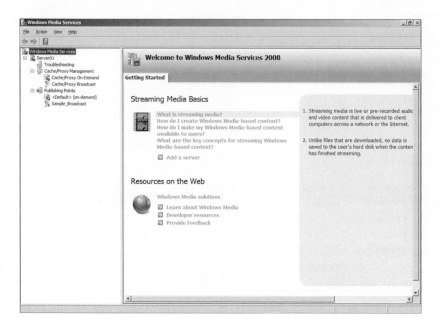

FIGURE 36.2    The Windows Media Services MMC administration tool.

# Using Windows Media Services for Real-Time Live Broadcasts

A Windows Media Services server can be used as the host to broadcast real-time videos. With a camera attached to the broadcasting server, video can be captured and published to multiple users. Real-time live broadcast videos are commonly used for organizational press releases or announcements, distributed broadcasting of conference sessions or training classes, or video-published company meetings.

## Configuring a Server for Real-Time Live Broadcasts

To configure a Windows Media Services system for real-time live broadcasts, a publishing point needs to be configured for live communications. The configuration process is as follows:

1. In the Windows Media Services MMC, right-click on Publishing Points in the navigation tree, and select Add Publishing Point (Wizard).

2. Click Next to move past the Welcome screen.

3. Enter a publishing point name that describes the function. In the case of this live broadcast, you might choose something like `Live Company Mtg 09-05-09`. Click Next to continue.

---

**NOTE**

The name of a publishing point should not have special characters, such as <, >, \, ?, %, &, ', #, ", {, }, [, ], or *. These characters can interfere with the successful publishing of the broadcast over the Internet.

---

4. Select Encoder (A Live Stream) and click Next.
5. Select Broadcast Publishing Point and click Next.
6. Select Unicast or Multicast as the delivery option for the broadcasting publishing point, and then click Next.

**Unicast Versus Multicast**

The Unicast delivery option sets up a one-to-one video stream between the Windows Media server and each client system, whereas the Multicast delivery option sends a single video stream that can be accessed by multiple users simultaneously.

The unicast delivery method is simpler to configure and more likely to work without much network infrastructure (router, firewall, system configuration) changes. However, unicast is a significantly more bandwidth-intensive environment. Because each client-to-server session is a separate video stream, a broadcast with 10 users would have 10 video streams from the server to the clients, and a broadcast with 100 users would feature 100 video streams from the server to the clients. For a relatively small or low-demand Windows Media server environment, unicast delivery is easier to implement, but be careful when using unicast delivery in large or broadly distributed environments.

The multicast delivery method sends a single video stream out on the network, which can be accessed by multiple client systems simultaneously. With a multicast delivery stream, whether 10 users or 100 users need to access the system, there is only a single broadcast either way. However, for a multicast delivery to work, the routers must be configured to support multicast routing. The client systems receiving the multicast broadcasts need to be running Windows 2000 Professional, Windows XP Professional, Windows Vista, Windows 7, Windows 2000 Server, Windows Server 2003, Windows Server 2008, or Windows Server 2008 R2.

An additional consideration for choosing between the unicast and multicast delivery methods is the number of clients that expect to connect to the broadcast stream and the variation of client configurations. If the compatibility to accept broadcasts from various systems is important and the number of connections to a broadcast stream is limited, the unicast method will provide better compatibility. If the organization controls the desktop configurations and knows the client systems can accept multicast broadcasts and the organization is broadcasting a video to be received by many users, the multicast delivery method will lessen the demand on network bandwidth.

36

7. Enter the uniform resource locator (URL) for the encoder. This is typically the name of the Windows Media server, such as `http://server1` or `http://media.companyabc.com`, depending on whether the server has been added to DNS for naming. Click Next to continue.

8. Select the Enable Logging option if you want to log media events, and then click Next.

9. The next screen shows a summary of the created publishing point, similar to the one shown in Figure 36.3. You can choose to start the publishing point when the wizard is finished, and if you want to capture and archive the live event, select the Start Archiving When Publishing Point Starts option. Click Next.

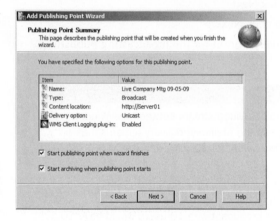

FIGURE 36.3    Creating a publishing point.

10. Before finishing with the Add Publishing Point Wizard, you are prompted to choose between three file creation options:

   ▶ **Create an Announcement File (.asx) or Web Page (.htm)**—An announcement file is similar to an invitation file that can be used to notify users of a pending live broadcast or the availability of an on-demand video playback session.

   ▶ **Create a Wrapper Playlist (.wsx)**—A wrapper playlist is content that can be added to either the start or end of a broadcast. An example of wrapper content might be a welcome or closing message, advertisements, or broadcast identification.

   ▶ **Create a Wrapper Playlist (.wsx) and Announcement File (.asx) or Web Page (.htm)**—Choosing this option launches both the Announcement File and Wrapper Playlist Wizards to create the invitation announcement, as well as the capability to add content at the start or end of a broadcast.

   Choose one of these three options or deselect the After the Wizard Finishes check box if you don't want to choose any of the options. Click Finish when complete.

### Starting a Real-Time Live Broadcast

A live broadcast can be started immediately or at a later time. Many organizations create the live broadcast publishing point and test the session to ensure that the session process is working properly. Some key aspects to test include making sure the camera and lighting are acceptable for view, ensuring that the microphone is working, and ensuring the audio quality and volume are acceptable.

After the live broadcast is tested, the session can be stopped and started at the time of the live broadcast. To start a broadcast, right-click on the publishing point, and select Start, as shown in Figure 36.4.

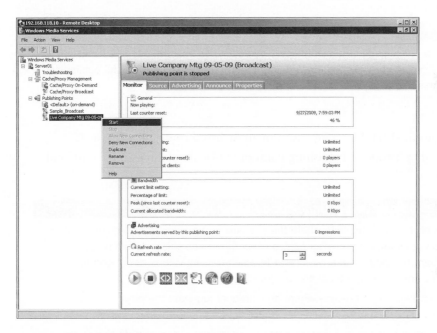

FIGURE 36.4    Starting a publishing point.

When the broadcast is complete, clicking the Stop button stops the broadcast session.

## Broadcasting Stored Single Files

A Windows Media Services system can be set up to host the broadcasting of a single video file. A single video file broadcast is typically set up on demand, meaning that a user requests the playback of the video file on request. On-demand video playbacks are commonly used for replays of video files, such as on-demand training classes, or viewing captured meetings or presentations.

## Configuring a Server for Single On-Demand Video Playback

To configure a Windows Media server for on-demand video playback broadcasts, a publishing point needs to be configured for on-demand communications. The configuration process is as follows:

1. In the Windows Media Services MMC, right-click on Publishing Points in the navigation tree, and select Add Publishing Point (Wizard).

2. Click Next to move past the Welcome screen.

3. Enter a publishing point name that describes the function. In the case of this on-demand single file broadcast, you might choose something like Company Mtg 11-16-2009. Click Next to continue.

---

**NOTE**

The name of a publishing point should not have special characters, such as <, >, \, ?, %, &, ', #, ", {, }, [, ], or *. These characters can interfere with the successful publishing of the broadcast over the Internet.

---

4. Select One File (Useful for a Broadcast of an Archived File), and click Next.

5. Choose either Broadcast Publishing Point or On-Demand Publishing Point, and click Next.

---

**Broadcast Publishing Versus On-Demand Publishing**

Broadcast publishing is a process where the publishing of a video is scheduled, similar to a television program. A time is scheduled when the stored video file will be played back. This might be used in an environment in which training videos are played back during specific times during the day for employees to view.

On-demand publishing is a process where an individual requests the playback of a video file. This allows users the flexibility of deciding when they watch a video.

As each session is independent with on-demand video, there is no benefit to doing a multicast session because the video will only be viewed by an individual. Therefore, the default delivery option for on-demand published videos is unicast, and the multicast option is not provided.

When choosing a broadcast published video, because multiple users are likely to access the broadcast at the same time, the organization can choose to multicast the video as long as the remote client systems and network infrastructure support multicast video routing. With multicast delivery, the Enable Unicast Rollover option provides a unicast delivery stream if the remote client does not support multicast broadcasts.

---

At this point, whether you selected Broadcast Publishing Point or On-Demand Publishing Point in step 5 will determine what options are available in the remaining steps of the wizard.

If you selected On-Demand Publishing Point in step 5, you will be prompted to either add a new publishing point (which will start the wizard over at step 2), or you can select Use an Existing Publishing Point and then click Next to finish the on-demand file publishing point.

If you selected Broadcast Publishing Point in step 5, you will be prompted with several other options:

1. Select Unicast or Multicast as the delivery option for the broadcasting publishing point, and then click Next.

2. You will then be prompted for the name of the file that you want to publish. Select the file and then click Next.

3. Select the Enable Logging option if you want to log media events, and then click Next.

4. The next screen shows a summary of the created publishing point. You can choose to start the publishing point when the wizard is finished, and if you want to capture and archive the live event, select the Start Archiving When Publishing Point Starts option. Click Next to continue.

5. Before finishing the Add Publishing Point Wizard, you are prompted to choose between three file creation options:

   ▶ **Create an Announcement File (.asx) or Web Page (.htm)**—An announcement file is similar to an invitation file that can be used to notify users of a pending live broadcast or the availability of an on-demand video playback session.

   ▶ **Create a Wrapper Playlist (.wsx)**—A wrapper playlist is content that can be added to either the start or end of a broadcast. An example of wrapper content might be a welcome or closing message, advertisements, or broadcast identification.

   ▶ **Create a Wrapper Playlist (.wsx) and Announcement File (.asx) or Web Page (.htm)**—Choosing this option launches both the Announcement File and Wrapper Playlist Wizards to create the invitation announcement, as well as the capability to add content at the start or end of a broadcast.

Choose one of these three options or deselect the After the Wizard Finishes check box if you don't want to choose any of the options. Click Finish when complete.

## Starting a Single File Publishing Point

A single file publishing point can be started immediately or at a later time. Unless the broadcast is to be scheduled at a different time, usually single file publishing points are started immediately so that they can be accessed at any time. Testing a file publishing point ensures that the session process is working properly. Some key aspects to test include making sure the multicast delivery broadcasting is working properly, and that the video and audio quality and volume are acceptable.

# Hosting a Directory of Videos for On-Demand Playback

If the organization wants to publish an entire directory of files, the Windows Media server can be configured to publish a number of video files. The hosting of a directory of videos is typically set up on an on-demand basis to provide users with access to a number of videos. Whereas the single file broadcast has a single file associated to a publishing point, the hosting of a directory eliminates the need to selectively publish each file. Instead, the directory is published and files can simply be copied to the directory, where users can then request them.

## Configuring a Server to Host a Directory of Videos for Playback

To configure a Windows Media server for on-demand video playback of any file in a directory on the server, a publishing point needs to be configured for publishing a directory of files. The configuration process is as follows:

1. In the Windows Media Services MMC, right-click on Publishing Points in the navigation tree, and select Add Publishing Point (Wizard).
2. Click Next to move past the Welcome screen.
3. Enter a publishing point name that describes the function. When broadcasting a directory of files, you might choose something like `Company Training Files`. Click Next to continue.

> **NOTE**
>
> The name of a publishing point should not have special characters such as <, >, \, ?, %, &, ', #, ", {, }, [, ], or *. These characters can interfere with the successful publishing of the broadcast over the Internet.

4. Select the Files (Digital Media or Playlists) in a Directory (Useful for Providing Access for On-Demand Playback Through a Single Publishing Point) option and click Next.
5. Choose either Broadcast Publishing Point or On-Demand Publishing Point. Refer to the "Broadcast Publishing Versus On-Demand Publishing" sidebar for decisions on publishing points. Click Next to continue.

At this point, whether you selected Broadcast Publishing Point or On-Demand Publishing Point in step 5 will determine what options are available in the remaining steps of the wizard.

If you selected On-Demand Publishing Point in step 5, you will be prompted with a series of questions:

1. You will be prompted to add the name of the directory where the published files will be stored. You can also choose to allow access to the subdirectory using wildcards. Click Next to continue.

2.  A choice to select content playback gives you the option to loop videos, shuffle videos, both, or none. Make your choices and click Next to continue.

3.  Select the Enable Logging option if you want to log media events, and then click Next.

4.  The next screen shows a summary of the created publishing point. You can choose to start the publishing point when the wizard is finished, and if you want to capture and archive the live event, select the Start Archiving When Publishing Point Starts option. Click Next to continue.

### Loop, Shuffle, Both, or None

*Looping* videos means that when the video is complete, it will start from the beginning and play again. This is a good option for kiosks or other public systems where a video will be played over and over.

*Shuffle* means that the video being played will be randomly selected from any one of the videos in the directory. This option provides an organization with the choice of selecting the streaming files it wants to display. This might be a good option for advertisements or for public kiosk systems. However, the shuffle process only randomly plays the videos in the directory once. The videos will stop after all the files have been played back.

If both looping and shuffle are selected, the videos in the directory will be played randomly, and the publishing of videos will be continuous. This is the best option for organizations that want different videos displayed continuously.

You can also choose neither of these options. This is the best option for the publishing and on-demand playback of any of the videos in the directory. The videos are selected individually and they play once. Upon completion, the video stops and allows the user to choose another video to play back.

If you selected Broadcast Publishing Point in step 5, you will be prompted with several other options:

1.  Select Unicast or Multicast as the delivery option for the broadcasting publishing point, and then click Next.

2.  You will then be prompted for the name of the directory that you want to publish. Select the directory and then click Next.

3.  A choice to select content playback gives you the option to loop videos, shuffle videos, both, or none. Make your choices and click Next to continue.

4.  Select the Enable Logging option if you want to log media events, and then click Next.

5.  The next screen shows a summary of the created publishing point, as shown in Figure 36.5. You can choose to start the publishing point when the wizard is finished, and if you want to capture and archive the live event, select the Start Archiving When Publishing Point Starts option. Click Next to continue.

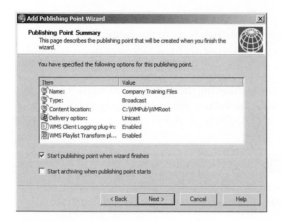

FIGURE 36.5    Viewing the summary of a directory publishing point.

For either the broadcast or on-demand publishing options, before finishing the Add Publishing Point Wizard, you are prompted to choose between three file creation options:

▶ **Create an Announcement File (.asx) or Web Page (.htm)**—An announcement file is similar to an invitation file that can be used to notify users of a pending live broadcast or the availability of an on-demand video playback session.

▶ **Create a Wrapper Playlist (.wsx)**—A wrapper playlist is content that can be added to either the start or end of a broadcast. An example of wrapper content might be a welcome or closing message, advertisements, or broadcast identification.

▶ **Create a Wrapper Playlist (.wsx) and Announcement File (.asx) or Web Page (.htm)**—Choosing this option launches both the Announcement File and Wrapper Playlist Wizards to create the invitation announcement, as well as the capability to add content at the start or end of a broadcast.

Choose one of these three options or deselect the After the Wizard Finishes check box if you don't want to choose any of the options. Click Finish when complete.

## Starting a File from Within the Directory Publishing Point

A single file can be viewed from within the directory publishing point. Depending on the option selected, a user simply enters the URL of the directory publishing point (such as mms://media.companyabc.com/pubpoint/) followed by the name of the individual file in the directory (like Training-Jan-21st.wmv). The full URL would be mms://media.companyabc.com/pubpoint/training-jan-21.wmv. The advantage of the directory publishing point is that a media administrator can simply copy more files to the directory and the initial publishing point directory URL remains the same—only the filename changes for each file being accessed. A single publishing point can also be created without the need of individually publishing files one by one.

# Combining Multiple Files for a Combined Single Broadcast

There are times when a broadcast administrator wants to combine several media files but only has the ability to publish just one video stream. The individual media files are added to a playlist, and the playlist is then published so that a single publishing point will play back the entire playlist of files. The playlist concept is frequently used for audio files where a playlist of music files are combined, yet only a single stream is distributed. Or the playlist file can be constantly updated to include new media files that are needed for publishing and distribution. The benefit of creating a playlist and combining the content into a single broadcast is the ability to have just a single broadcast point that brings multiple files to users.

## Configuring a Server for Playlist Broadcasting of Multiple Files

To configure a Windows Media server for broadcasting multiple files into a single stream, a publishing point needs to be configured for playlist broadcasting. The configuration process is as follows:

1. In the Windows Media Services MMC, right-click on Publishing Points in the navigation tree, and select Add Publishing Point (Wizard).

2. Click Next to move past the Welcome screen.

3. Enter a publishing point name that describes the function. When broadcasting a playlist of multiple files, you might choose something like `Playlist of Conf Content`. Click Next to continue.

> **NOTE**
>
> The name of a publishing point should not have special characters such as <, >, \, ?, %, &, ', #, ", {, }, [, ], or *. These characters can interfere with the successful publishing of the broadcast over the Internet.

4. Select the Playlist (A Mix of Files and/or Live Streams That You Combine into a Continuous Stream) option, and click Next.

5. Choose either Broadcast Publishing Point or On-Demand Publishing Point. Refer to the "Broadcast Publishing Versus On-Demand Publishing" sidebar for decisions on publishing points. Click Next.

At this point, whether you selected Broadcast Publishing Point or On-Demand Publishing Point in step 5 will determine what options are available in the remaining steps of the wizard.

36

If you selected On-Demand Publishing Point in step 5, you will be prompted with a series of questions:

1. You will be prompted whether you want to add a new publishing point (or playlist), which you will typically want to do, or create an existing playlist. Select Add a New Publishing Point, and click Next.

2. You will be prompted to add the name of a playlist where the published files will be listed and stored. Enter the name of an existing playlist, or select the Create a New Playlist option. Click Next to continue.

3. If you choose to create a new playlist, you will be prompted to add media and add advertisements into your playlist file, as shown in Figure 36.6. Click Next.

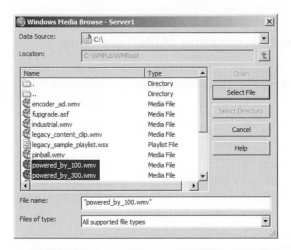

FIGURE 36.6    Choosing media to add to the playlist.

4. Enter a name for your playlist, and then click Next.

5. A choice to select content playback gives you the option to loop videos, shuffle videos, both, or none. For more information on these options, see the "Loop, Shuffle, Both, or None" sidebar earlier in this chapter. Click Next to continue.

6. Select the Enable Logging option if you want to log media events, and then click Next.

7. The next screen shows a summary of the created publishing point. You can choose to start the publishing point when the wizard is finished, and if you want to capture and archive the live event, select the Start Archiving When Publishing Point Starts option. Click Next to continue.

If you selected the Broadcast Publishing Point option in step 5, you will be prompted with several other options:

1. Select Unicast or Multicast as the delivery option for the broadcasting publishing point, and then click Next.

2. If you choose to create a new playlist, you will be prompted to add media and add advertisements into your playlist file. Click Next.

3. Enter a name for your playlist, and then click Next.

4. A choice to select content playback gives you the option to loop videos, shuffle videos, both, or none. For more information on these options, see the "Loop, Shuffle, Both, or None" sidebar earlier in this chapter. Click Next to continue.

5. Select the Enable Logging option if you want to log media events, and then click Next.

6. The next screen shows a summary of the created publishing point. You can choose to start the publishing point when the wizard is finished, and if you want to capture and archive the live event, select the Start Archiving When Publishing Point Starts option. Click Next to continue.

For either the broadcast or on-demand publishing options, before finishing the Add Publishing Point Wizard, you are prompted to choose between three file creation options:

▶ **Create an Announcement File (.asx) or Web Page (.htm)**—An announcement file is similar to an invitation file that can be used to notify users of a pending live broadcast or the availability of an on-demand video playback session.

▶ **Create a Wrapper Playlist (.wsx)**—A wrapper playlist is content that can be added to either the start or end of a broadcast. An example of wrapper content might be a welcome or closing message, advertisements, or broadcast identification.

▶ **Create a Wrapper Playlist (.wsx) and Announcement File (.asx) or Web Page (.htm)**—Choosing this option launches both the Announcement File and Wrapper Playlist Wizards to create the invitation announcement, as well as the capability to add content at the start or end of a broadcast.

Choose one of these three options or deselect the After the Wizard Finishes check box if you don't want to choose any of the options. Click Finish when complete.

## Starting a Playlist from Within the Playlist Publishing Point

A playlist can be launched to initiate the playback of media contained within the playlist file. Depending on the option selected, a user simply enters the URL of the directory publishing point (such as mms://media.companyabc.com/Corp Playlist). The playlist of files will begin to publish the first of the media clips and will continue through the entire playlist until the list is complete. If the loop option was selected in the publishing point configuration settings, the playlist will continuously loop the media content of the playlist. If shuffle was selected, the files within the playlist will be played randomly.

Any of the options selected from within the configuration setting can be modified at any time to change or reconfigure settings initially created in the wizard installation process.

36

# Understanding Windows Media Encoder

For any media content producer that is working with audio and video content, the Microsoft free Windows Media Encoder is a must-have tool for capturing and converting media content. Although the Windows Media server can be used to capture and publish video files, it's unlikely that a content producer will want to travel around with a media server everywhere. Instead, you can download Windows Media Encoder and install it on Windows Server 2008, Windows Vista, Windows XP, Windows Server 2003, or Windows 2000 Server. Either the 32-bit or 64-bit edition can be downloaded and installed.

> **NOTE**
>
> Windows Media Encoder can be downloaded from http://www.microsoft.com/windows/windowsmedia/forpros/encoder/default.mspx.

In addition, Windows Media Encoder provides tools to convert files from one video format to another, such as from AVI format to MPG format. One of the biggest limitations of Windows Media Encoder is its inability to perform simple edits to the media files. For this, you need to download and use third-party tools.

> **Editing Tools**
>
> Because Microsoft does not provide freely downloadable video-editing tools, content producers need to look for other tools to perform basic cropping at the start or end of a video file, or when merging video files. There are dozens of professional video editing and content production programs available, such as Adobe's Premiere Pro or Ulead's VideoStudio. There are also hundreds of third-party shareware and freeware tools that can be downloaded from the Internet for little or no money.
>
> The biggest challenge video producers face is selecting a utility that meets all their needs. Most downloadable tools offer trial versions with trial periods that allow you to try the software before buying it. If you don't find the tool you're looking for at first, jump back on the Internet and keep searching. Tools for every video and audio editing need seem to be readily available.

## Understanding the Requirements for Windows Media Encoder

Windows Media Encoder runs on Windows Vista, Windows 2000, and Windows XP desktops, as well as on Windows 2000 Server and Windows Server 2003 systems. The basic configuration of the system depends on the task being performed by the Windows Media Encoder software. Microsoft recommends the system configurations shown in Table 36.2. Because Windows Media Encoder does not work on Windows Server 2008 R2 servers or Windows 7 client systems, for media encoding using this tool, install it on an earlier release of Windows that is supported and transfer the encoded file to a Windows Server 2008 R2 Media Server system.

## Installing Windows Media Encoder

After downloading Windows Media Encoder from the Microsoft website, the software can be installed on any system meeting the requirements noted in Table 36.2. The installation process is as follows:

1. Run the `wmencoder.exe` file to begin the installation process.

2. Click Next to move past the Welcome screen.

3. To accept the licensing agreement, click the I Accept the Terms of the License Agreement option, and click Next.

4. Select a custom installation folder, or just click Next to choose the default folder. Then click Install to begin the installation.

5. Click Finish when prompted.

After being installed, Windows Media Encoder can be launched by selecting Start, All Programs, Windows Media, Windows Media Encoder. Upon launching Windows Media Encoder, you will see a New Session screen.

TABLE 36.2     Requirements for Windows Media Encoder

| Encoding Task | 32-Bit Recommendation | 64-Bit Recommendation |
|---|---|---|
| Conversion of files | 500MHz processor or higher and at least 128MB of RAM or higher | 1800MHz processor or higher and at least 512MB of RAM or higher |
| Capture and broadcast of audio files | 866MHz processor or higher and at least 128MB of RAM or higher | 2000MHz processor or higher and at least 512MB of RAM or higher |
| Capture and broadcast of audio and video files for dial-up modem and mid-bandwidth audiences using Windows Media Audio 9 and Windows Media Video 7 codecs | 866MHz processor or higher, 128MB of RAM, and a single stream bit rate of 100Kbs through 500Kbs | Dual 2000Mhz processor or higher, 512MB of RAM, and a single stream bit rate of 100Kbs through 500Kbs |
| Capture and broadcast of audio and video files for dial-up modem and mid-bandwidth audiences using Windows Media Audio and Video 9 codecs | Dual 1Ghz processor or higher, 256MB of RAM, and a single stream bit rate of 100Kbs through 500Kbs | Dual 2000Mhz processor or higher, 768MB of RAM, and a single stream bit rate of 100Kbs through 500Kbs |
| Capture and broadcast of audio and video files for high-bandwidth audiences using Windows Media Audio and Video 9 codecs | Dual 2Ghz processor or higher, 256MB of RAM, and a single stream bit rate of 500Kbs through 2Mbps | Dual 2400Mhz processor or higher, 1024MB of RAM, and a single stream bit rate of 500Kbs through 2Mbps |

36

# Broadcasting a Live Event

Windows Media Encoder can be used in conjunction with a Windows Media server to broadcast a live event. This gives an organization the capability to use the Windows Media server as the back-end server to publish the live content to multiple users. Also, a laptop or some other mobile or portable device can then act as the system capturing the video/audio content that will be published by the Windows Media server.

## Preparing for a Live Broadcast

To prepare for a live broadcast, a Windows Server 2008 server or Windows Vista workstation with a compatible camera and microphone, or a system with a video/audio capture card, must be configured and tested for basic functionality. The camera and audio devices should be able to capture and record video and audio content at the desired level of quality.

After the remote system is working properly, the live broadcast can be initiated.

## Initiating a Live Broadcast

To start a live broadcast, Windows Media Encoder should be launched on the broadcasting system. After being launched, follow these steps:

1. Select Broadcast a New Event, and then click OK.

2. Select the video and audio device source that will be capturing the event. Click Next when you are ready.

> **NOTE**
>
> For systems with only a single video and audio source, the options should default to the only devices in the system. However, for systems with an audio and video capture card installed, the onboard audio might also be an option, so be certain that the correct video and audio devices are selected.
>
> When choosing the audio device, you might want to click Configure and confirm that the microphone has been enabled. Many systems automatically have the microphone disabled, so although the correct device has been selected, no sound will be captured.

3. The next setting allows the Windows Media Encoder system to either push the video/audio stream to a Windows Media server on the network, or allows the Windows Media server to initiate a pull from the encoder system. Make the choice and then click Next to continue.

**NOTE**

The choice of whether to push or pull media content depends on what you are closer to. If you are closest to the Windows Media Encoder system (you are in the room where the event is taking place), you probably want to push the video/audio stream to the Windows Media server. A push from the encoder system causes the Windows Media server to automatically start publishing the session.

If the Windows Media Encoder system is set up in a room and you are with the server, but not necessarily where the encoder system is located, you can initiate the capture remotely by choosing to have the Windows Media server initiate the session.

If you choose to push to the Windows Media server, you will be prompted with the following steps:

1. You will be prompted to enter the name of the Windows Media server and the publishing point, and you have the option of copying the publishing point settings from another configuration. Click Next when ready.

2. The next screen will prompt for the encoding options. The various bit rates for encoding will be shown, displaying Total Bit Rate, Frame Rate, and Output Size. Choose the desired bit rate or bit rates, and then click Next to continue.

**Choosing the Bit Rate(s)**

When given the option of choosing the bit rate or bit rates supported, keep in mind the quality desired as well as the bandwidth available to publish the media files.

If users are dialing in to receive the published content, you do not want a total bit rate that exceeds the available bandwidth of the dial-up modem session. Just because a user has a 56KB modem does not mean that user is getting a 56KB bit-rate speed. You should choose a bit rate lower than the available bandwidth.

Multiple bit rates can be selected for the encoding options so that a modem rate (possibly 24Kbps or 37Kbps), a DSL/cable modem rate (possibly 135Kbps or 240Kbps), or high-quality rate (possibly 500Kbps or greater) can be selected. With multiple bit rates, the bit rate that meets the transmission speed of the remote client system will be used. Therefore, a user coming in over DSL might get a 135Kbps transmission, and a user coming in over a dial-up modem might get the same transmission at 24Kbps.

When selecting multiple bit rates, one thing to consider is the size of the captured file. The more bit rates that are selected, the larger the file will be. Each bit-rate encoding option selected will capture a video and audio stream for that mode. So if 12 bit-rate encoding options are selected, 12 streams of the content will be stored in the file.

Another point to consider is the desired available bandwidth. Even if all the users have high-speed network connections and can accept a 768Kbps bit-rate encoded stream, if the file is published using unicast broadcasting, a network might become oversaturated with too much data. A lower captured video stream can allow more users access to the information.

**36**

3. For live broadcasts, an archive copy of the broadcast file can be captured and saved to disk. This allows for future playback of the session. Select the check box to archive the file and enter a filename to capture the session. Click Next to continue.

4. Information can be added to the broadcast file, such as title, author, copyright information, rating, and description. This information is optional. Enter the desired information and click Next to continue.

5. The next screen gives you the option to begin the broadcast when the Finish button is clicked, or to simply finish the configuration and start the session later. Make the appropriate selection and click Finish.

If you choose to pull where the session is initiated by the Windows Media server from the encoder, you will be prompted with the following steps:

1. You will be prompted to enter a free HTTP port that can be used to communicate between the Windows Media server and the Windows Media Encoder system. Port 8080 is the default, but by clicking the Find Free Port button, you can search for an open port. Click Next to continue.

2. The next screen prompts you for the encoding options. The various bit rates for encoding will be shown, displaying Total Bit Rate, Frame Rate, and Output Size. Choose the desired bit rate or bit rates. Refer to the "Choosing the Bit Rate(s)" sidebar for more details. Click Next to continue.

3. For live broadcasts, an archive copy of the broadcast file can be captured and saved to disk. This allows for future playback of the session. Select the check box to archive the file and enter a filename to capture the session. Click Next to continue.

4. Information can be added to the broadcast file, such as title, author, copyright information, rating, and description. This information is optional. Enter the desired information and click Next to continue.

5. The next screen gives you the option to begin the broadcast when the Finish button is clicked, or to simply finish the configuration and start the session later. Make the appropriate selection and click Finish.

For live broadcasts, it's usually preferable to test the broadcast process to make sure that the lighting, sound quality, and video quality are at the desired level. Playing around with the different bit rates can provide better results based on the needs of the organization. Although a producer can choose a higher bit rate to get better quality, the results might not be better than those obtained at a lower bit rate and with presumably lower-quality published media. If the lower bit rate produces results that are still acceptable, lowering the bit rate can minimize bandwidth demands on the network, creating less demand on the network and allowing the organization to have more simultaneous media streams.

## Capturing Audio or Video for Future Playback

If you want to capture a session but there is no need for an immediate live broadcast, choosing the Capture Audio or Video option enables Windows Media Encoder to capture and encode the session for future playback. This option can be used to capture training or conference sessions, press releases that will be broadcast at a later time and date, or organizational activities such as parties. The captured content can be stored and played back either on a scheduled broadcast basis or on demand.

## Preparing for a Captured Session

To prepare for a captured broadcast, a Windows Vista, Windows XP, Windows 2000 workstation, Windows Server 2008, Windows 2003, or Windows 2000 server with compatible camera and microphone, or a system with a video/audio capture card, must be configured and tested for basic functionality. The camera and audio devices should be able to capture and record video and audio content at the desired level of quality.

After the remote system is working properly, a session can be captured.

## Capturing a Session for Future Broadcast

To capture a session, Windows Media Encoder should be launched on a system that has a camera, microphone, and enough disk space to capture the content. After being launched, follow these steps:

1. Select Capture Audio or Video, and then click OK.

2. Select the video and audio device source that will be capturing the event. Refer to the "Choosing the Bit Rate(s)" sidebar for more details on choosing the capture options. Click Next.

> **NOTE**
>
> Don't worry about adding an extension to the filename. A .wmv file extension will be initially created for video files (Windows Media Video), and a .wma file extension will be initially created for audio files (Windows Media Audio).

### Choosing the Distribution Content Method

When given the option of choosing the content distribution method, the various options determine the options given on the next screen of the wizard.

When the Windows Media Server (Streaming) option is selected, the capture of the media will have multiple bit-rate options because Windows Media servers support variable bit rates, and multiple users can receive a different media stream based on their connection bandwidth.

When the Web Server (Progressive Download) option is selected, a recommended option is selected because web servers only support a single bit-rate distribution. Typically, the Web Server option chooses a lower bit-rate option to take the variable bandwidth capabilities of web users into consideration.

The Windows Media Hardware Profiles option provides the option of choosing a single video and audio bit rate at a higher bit rate than the Web Server option. When a Windows Media hardware profile has been defined on the system, a specific bandwidth and quality can be generated.

36

PocketPC devices typically have limited cache, buffer, and storage space, so a lower bit-rate option is recommended. This becomes the lowest common denominator for media capture and playback.

Lastly, the File Archive option creates the smallest captured file. However, the quality of the video is typically poor, although the audio is of good quality. The assumption on this setting is that the audio information is more important than the video information.

Choosing the right method of recording produces better results for the system playing back the content.

3. Enter a name for the file to be saved. Click Next to continue.

4. Choose how you want to distribute your content. Your choices are Windows Media Server (Streaming), Web Server (Progressive Download), Windows Media Hardware Profiles, PocketPC, or File Archive. Click Next to continue.

5. Optional information can be added to the captured file, such as title, author, copyright, rating, and description information. Enter the desired information and click Next to continue.

6. The next screen gives you the option to begin the capture when the Finish button is clicked, or to simply finish the configuration and start the session later. Make the appropriate selection and click Finish.

Because a live session is not being viewed, sometimes it's hard to know what the resulting quality of the captured video and audio will be. Testing the various capture methods and fiddling with the bit rates can confirm whether the resulting video and distribution of the video content will be acceptable.

# Using Other Windows Media Encoder Options

Windows Media Encoder can also convert videos as well as capture screen content from a video session. These functions are useful utility features that give media producers some basic tools for editing and publishing content.

### Capturing Screen Content with the Windows Media Encoder Software

Capturing screen content from video is not as simple as you might think. Simply pressing Ctrl+Print Screen does not capture video content. This usually results in a grayed-out box where the video was being played. Third-party screen capture tools also typically do not capture video screens—they typically capture bit images of a video screen, and the DirectX video or streaming video caches video content that does not show up on the active screen.

A tool like the one built in to Windows Media Encoder allows users to capture video screens. The screen capture function in Windows Media Encoder can capture an entire streaming video session. This is useful if you are watching a webcast, a video stream, or some other session that you might not otherwise be able to download for replay later. By capturing the entire video and audio session using Windows Media Encoder, you can bypass any access limitations to the streaming information.

To capture a screen using Windows Media Encoder, do the following:

1. Click the Capture a Screen option, and then click OK.

2. On the Screen Capture Session window, choose to capture a specific window, a region of the screen, or the entire screen. Choose to capture audio from the default audio device by selecting the appropriate check box and then click Next.

3. Depending on the option selected in step 2, choose the window or region you want to capture, and then click Next.

4. Enter the name of the file to which you want to capture the file, and then click Next.

5. Choose the quality setting: low, medium, or high. Click Next to continue.

6. Optional information can be added to the captured file, such as title, author, copyright information, rating, and description. Enter the desired information and click Next to continue.

7. The next screen gives you the option to begin the capture when the Finish button is clicked, or to simply finish the configuration and start the session later. Make the appropriate selection and click Finish.

After the session has been captured, it can be played back by opening the file with Windows Media Player or another video playback tool.

## Converting Videos to Windows Media Video Format

Converting a file might be necessary for the producer of media content. Many times, a video file is stored in a format or has been encoded with a codec that is not widely or easily distributed. A video file might also be stored in a format that does not support the Windows Media server publishing capabilities. One way to convert the file is to use the screen-capturing capability of Windows Media Encoder, as covered in the section "Capturing Screen Content with the Windows Media Encoder Software." The other way to convert the video is to use the conversion functionality built in to Windows Media Encoder.

Windows Media Encoder can convert files from the ASF, AVI, BMP, JPG, MPG, MP3, WAV, WMA, and WMV formats to a WMV video format supported by the Windows Media server. To initiate a file conversion, do the following:

1. Click the Convert a File option in the Windows Media Encoder software, and then click OK.

2. Select the source file of the file you want to convert. Choose the directory and filename where you want the output written. Click Next to continue.

3. Choose how you want to distribute your content. Your choices are File Download, Hardware Devices (CD, DVD, Portable), Windows Media Server (Streaming), Web Server (Progressive Download), Windows Media Hardware Profiles, PocketPC, or File Archive. Refer to the "Choosing the Distribution Content Method" sidebar for more details. Click Next to continue.

36

4. The next screen will prompt you for the encoding options. The various bit rates for encoding will be shown, displaying Total Bit Rate, Frame Rate, and Output Size. Choose the desired bit rate or bit rates and click Next to continue.

5. Optional information can be added to the captured file, such as title, author, copyright information, rating, and description. Enter the desired information and click Next to continue.

6. The next screen gives you the option to begin the capture when the Finish button is clicked, or to simply finish the configuration and start the session later. Make the appropriate selection and click Finish.

After the file has been converted, it can be played back by opening the file with Windows Media Player or another video playback tool.

## Summary

Windows Media Services is a combination of server components and tools that help organizations go beyond text-based communications to include audio and video communications. Windows Media Services is a component that can be added to the Windows Server 2008 R2 family of operating systems and can easily be enabled on a server system. However, the server component is predominantly a publishing and distribution function—it relies on add-ins such as Windows Media Encoder to provide capture and conversion functionality.

Even with what Microsoft provides in the Windows Media Services server function and the Windows Media Encoder download tools, there's still a need for third-party editing and cropping tools.

Windows Media Services provides a new way for organizations to conduct employee training and broadcast live meetings, and integrate audio and video content into PowerPoint presentations.

## Best Practices

The following are best practices from this chapter:

▶ For faster performance on a Windows Media Services system, place the system and application files on one hard drive set, and place the data files stored on a separate hard drive set.

▶ Use the Windows Media Load Simulator to test the real-time performance capabilities of a Windows Media Services system.

▶ Use standard DNS characters (A–Z, a–z, 0–9, and the minus sign) for publishing point names so that when you need to access the published access, you can access it over the Internet.

▶ If you are publishing a broadcast to dozens of users over a network infrastructure that supports multicast broadcasting, use the Multicast function of Windows Media Services to minimize system bandwidth demands.

▶ Use the loop function in the video playback options if the video you are publishing should run continuously, such as in public kiosks or advertising systems.

▶ Combine files for publishing by using the playlist function in the Windows Media Services MMC Publishing Point Configuration option.

▶ Download Windows Media Encoder to access freely available file capture and conversion tools.

▶ Run Windows Media Encoder on a system with as much RAM, processing speed, and disk space as possible. When a system is underpowered, a video capture or conversion might be forced to drop frames and ultimately lower the quality of the video.

▶ When capturing content using Windows Media Encoder, ensure that the microphone has been turned on to properly capture audio content because the microphone is normally disabled by default.

▶ Select a bit rate for capture and conversion that matches the needs of the users. Although the highest quality might be preferable, the bandwidth demands of multiple users accessing the content at high quality might saturate the available network bandwidth.

36

# Deploying and Using Windows Virtualization

Windows Hyper-V virtualization continues to make inroads in the server virtualization market. Although Microsoft has had a virtual server technology for several years, the features and capabilities of Microsoft's hypervisor virtualization poise Microsoft to leap past rival virtual server technologies like EMC's VMware. Windows Server 2008 R2 was written to provide enhanced virtualization technologies through a rewrite of the Windows kernel itself to support virtual server capabilities equal to, if not better than, other options on the marketplace. This chapter focuses on the Windows virtualization on a Windows Server 2008 R2 system.

## Understanding Microsoft's Virtualization Strategy

Server virtualization is the ability for a single system to host multiple guest operating system sessions, effectively taking advantage of the processing capabilities of a very powerful server. Most servers in data centers run under 5%–10% processor utilization, meaning that there is excess capacity on the servers that is unused. By combining the capabilities of multiple servers, an organization can better utilize the processing power available in the networking environment.

Some might suggest that an organization should just put more users on existing server systems to take advantage of the excess server capacity. From a load-balancing perspective, however, most organizations prefer to not combine more users on a single system, but rather have multiple systems distributing the workload to provide some level of distributed processing. This also minimizes single points of failure for an organization and provides distribution of processing across multiple systems. Server virtualization can provide server consolidation while still providing multiple physical host systems to distribute the processing load.

## History of Windows Virtualization

Microsoft's position in the virtualization marketplace prior to the release of Windows 2008 R2 wasn't one where Microsoft particularly had a bad product; it was because Microsoft jumped into the virtualization space just four to five years before the release of Windows 2008 R2 virtualization. Being relatively new to the virtualization space, Microsoft had some catching up to do.

### Acquisition of Virtual PC

Microsoft jumped into the virtualization marketplace through the acquisition of a company called Connectix in 2003. At the time of the acquisition, Virtual PC provided a virtual session of Windows on either a Windows system or on a Macintosh computer system. Virtual PC was used largely by organizations testing server software or performing demos of Windows systems on desktop and laptop systems—or in the case of Virtual PC for the Mac, the ability for a Macintosh user to run Windows on their Macintosh computer.

Microsoft later dropped the development of Virtual PC for the Mac; however, it continues to develop virtualization for Windows systems with the release of Virtual PC 2007. Virtual PC 2007 enables users running Windows XP or Windows Vista to install, configure, and run virtual guest sessions of Windows server or even non-Windows operating systems.

### Microsoft Virtual Server

Virtual PC, however, is targeted at operating under an operating system that is typically optimized for personal or individual applications, so Virtual PC does not scale for a data center wanting to run four, eight, or more sessions on a single system. At the time of the acquisition of Connectix, Connectix was in development of a virtual server solution that allows for the operation of virtualization technologies on a Windows 2003 host server system.

Because a Windows Server 2003 system provides more RAM availability, supports multiple processors, and generally has more capacity and capabilities than a desktop client system, Microsoft Virtual Server provided organizations with more capabilities for server-based virtualization in a production environment.

### Virtual Server 2005

Although the initial Virtual Server acquired through the Connectix acquisition provided basic server virtualization capabilities, it wasn't until Virtual Server 2005 that Microsoft had its first internally developed product. Virtual Server 2005 provided better support and integration into a Windows 2003 environment, better support for multiprocessor systems and systems with more RAM, and better integration and support with other Microsoft server products.

In just two years, Microsoft went from having no virtual server technologies to a second-generation virtual server product; however, even with Virtual Server 2005, Microsoft was still very far behind its competitors.

**Virtual Server 2005 R2**

Over the subsequent two years, Microsoft released two major updates to Virtual Server 2005 with the release of an R2 edition of the Virtual Server 2005 product and a service pack for the R2 edition. Virtual Server 2005 R2 Service Pack 1 provided the following capabilities:

- ▶ **Virtual Server host clustering**—This technology allows an organization to cluster host systems to one another, thus allowing guest sessions to have higher redundancy and reliability.

- ▶ **x64 host support**—x64 host support means that organizations had the capability to use the 64-bit version of Windows 2003 as the host operating system, thus providing better support for more memory and system capacity found in x64-bit systems. Guest operating systems, however, are still limited to x86 platforms.

- ▶ **Hardware-assisted virtualization**—New to processors released from Intel (Intel VT) and AMD (AMD-V) are processors that provide better distribution of processor resources to virtual guest sessions.

- ▶ **iSCSI support**—This technology allows virtual guest sessions to connect to iSCSI storage systems, thus providing better storage management and storage access for the guest sessions running on a virtual server host.

- ▶ **Support for more than 16GB virtual disk sizes**—Virtual disk sizes can reach 2TB in size, thus allowing organizations the ability to have guest sessions with extremely large storage capacity.

These capabilities—among other capabilities of the latest Virtual Server 2005 product—brought Microsoft closer to its competition in the area of server virtualization.

# Integration of Hypervisor Technology in Windows Server 2008

To leap beyond its competition in the area of server virtualization, Microsoft had to make some significant changes to the operating system that hosted its next-generation virtual server technology. With the original Windows 2008 in development, Microsoft took the opportunity to add in a core technology to Windows 2008 (and extended it in Windows 2008 R2) that provided the basis of Microsoft's future dominance in server virtualization. The core technology is called hypervisor, which effectively is a layer within the host operating system that provides better support for guest operating systems. Microsoft calls their hypervisor-based technology Hyper-V.

Prior to the inclusion of Hyper-V in Windows 2008 and Windows 2008 R2, the Virtual Server application sat on top of the host operating system and effectively required all guest operating systems to share system resources, such as network communications, video-processing capabilities, memory allocation, and system resources. In the event that the host operating system has a system failure of something like the host network adapter driver, all guest sessions fail to communicate on the network. This monolithic approach is similar to how most server virtualization technologies operate.

37

Technologies like VMware ESX as well as Hyper-V leverage a hypervisor-based technology that allows the guest operating systems to effectively bypass the host operating system and communicate directly with system resources. In some instances, the hypervisor will manage shared guest session resources, and in other cases will pass guest session requests directly to the hardware layer of the system. By providing better independence of systems communications, the hypervisor-supported environment provides organizations better scalability, better performance, and, ultimately, better reliability of the core virtual host environment.

Hyper-V is available in Windows Server 2008 R2 Standard, Enterprise, and Datacenter Editions. Each of these SKUs are available with and without Hyper-V.

> **NOTE**
>
> Hyper-V in Windows Server 2008 R2 is only supported on x64-bit systems that have hardware-assisted virtualization support. CPUs must support Intel VT or AMD-V option and Data Execution Protection (DEP). Also, these features must be enabled in the computer BIOS. Fortunately, almost all new servers purchased since late 2006 include these capabilities.

## What's New in Windows Server 2008 R2 Hyper-V

There are many long-awaited features and technologies built in to Hyper-V that provide Microsoft the ability to compete with other server virtualization products on the market. Some of the key additions to Hyper-V include the following:

- ▶ **Live Migration**—Live Migration is the number-one most-requested feature by customers. Live Migration enables administrators to migrate highly available Hyper-V guests between clustered hosts with nearly zero downtime.

- ▶ **Support for up to eight physical processors**—Windows 2008 Server R2 virtualization provides the capability to have up to eight physical processors—twice the number of physical processors supported by Hyper-V V1 in Windows Server 2008. Note that this refers to physical sockets, not cores.

- ▶ **Support for up to 64 logical cores per guest session**—Windows Server 2008 R2 virtualization provides the capability to have up to 64 logical processors (cores) allocated to a single guest session—four times better than in Windows Server 2008.

- ▶ **Support for greater physical host memory**—Windows Server 2008 R2 virtualization supports up to 1TB physical memory allocation per host—a huge increase from the 32GB supported in Windows Server 2008.

- ▶ **Support for greater virtual guest memory**—Virtual guests can now access up to 64GB per VM. This is a huge scalability improvement from Windows Server 2008, where VMs were limited to 32GB total RAM per host.

> **NOTE**
>
> Although Hyper-V provides the capability to host guest operating systems for Windows servers, client systems, and non-Windows systems, many of the tools enterprises use in virtual server environments require the addition of the System Center Virtual Machine Manager (VMM) tool.
>
> VMM provides a more centralized view and administration of multiple virtual guest sessions, the tools to do physical-to-virtual image creation, virtual-to-virtual image copying, and load balancing of virtual images across VMM servers. VMM adds the administrative tools that take the basic virtual server sessions, and provides administrators the ability to better manage the guest sessions.

## Microsoft Hyper-V Server as a Role in Windows Server 2008 R2

Hyper-V is enabled as a server role just as Windows Server 2008 R2 Remote Desktop Services, DNS Server, or Active Directory Domain Services are added to the server.

The installation of the Microsoft Hyper-V Server role is covered later in this chapter in the section, "Installation of the Microsoft Hyper-V Server Role."

# Planning Your Implementation of Hyper-V

For the organization that chooses to leverage the capabilities of Windows Server 2008 R2 virtualization, a few moments should be spent to determine the proper size, capacity, and capabilities of the host server that would be used as the virtual server host system. Many server system applications get installed with little assessment on resource requirements of the application itself, because most servers in a data center are running less than 10% server utilization, so there is plenty of excess server capacity to handle server workload capabilities.

With Hyper-V, however, because each guest session is a discretely running operating system, the installation of as few as three or four high-performance guest sessions could quickly bring a server to 50% or 60% of the server performance limits. So, the planning phase is an important step in a Hyper-V implementation.

## Sizing Your Windows Server 2008 R2 Server to Support Virtualization

Although the minimum requirements for server compatibility for Windows Server 2008 R2 applies, because server virtualization is the focus of this server system, the minimum Windows Server 2008 R2 server requirements will not be sufficient to run Hyper-V virtualization.

Additionally, although Windows Server 2008 R2 supports up to 64 processor cores, 1TB of RAM, and 384 concurrently running virtual machines, the reality on the scaling of

Windows virtualization comes down to the raw capabilities of network I/O that can be driven from a single host server. In many environments where a virtualized guest system has a relatively low system utilization and network traffic demand, a single host system could easily support a dozen, two dozen, or more guest sessions. Other environments where a virtualized guest session has an extremely high system utilization, lots of disk I/O, and significant server network I/O, the organization might find that a single host server would maximize its capacity with as few as seven or eight guest sessions.

### RAM for the Host Server

The rule of thumb for memory of a Windows Server 2008 R2 server running Hyper-V is to have 2GB of RAM for the host server, plus enough memory for each guest session. Therefore, if a guest session needs to have 2GB of RAM, and there are three such guest sessions running on the host system, the host system should be configured with at least 8GB of RAM. If a guest session requires 8GB of memory and three of those systems are running on the system, the server should be configured with 24GB of memory to support the three guest sessions, plus at least 2GB of memory for the host system itself.

### Processors for the Host Server

The host server itself in Windows Server 2008 R2 virtualization has very little processor I/O requirements. In the virtualized environment, the processor demands of each guest session dictate how much processing capacity is needed for the server. If a guest session requires two cores to support the processing requirements of the application, and seven guest sessions are running on the system, the server should have at least 15 cores available in the system. With quad-core processors, the system would need four physical processors. With dual-core processors, the system would need at least eight physical processors.

With Windows Server 2008 R2 virtualization, each guest session can have up to 64 cores dedicated to the session, or processing capacity can be distributed, either equally or as necessary to meet the performance demands of the organization. By sharing cores among several virtual machines that have low processing needs, an organization can more fully utilize their investment in hardware systems.

### Disk Storage for the Host Server

A host server typically has the base Windows Server 2008 R2 operating system running on the host system itself with additional guest sessions either sharing the same disk as the host session or the guest sessions virtual disks being stored on a storage area network (SAN) or some form of external storage.

Each guest session takes up at least 7GB of disk space. For guest sessions running databases or other storage-intensive configurations, the guest image can exceed 10GB, 20GB, or more. When planning disk storage for the virtual server system, plan to have enough disk space to support the host operating system files (typically about 7GB of actual files plus space for the Pagefile) and then disk space available to support the guest sessions.

## Running Other Services on the Hyper-V System

On a system running Hyper-V, typically an organization would not run other services on the host system, such as making the host server also a file and print server, making the host server a SharePoint server, or so on. Typically, a server running virtualization is already going to be a system that will maximize the memory, processor, and disk storage capabilities of the system. So, rather than impacting the performance of all the guest sessions by having a system-intensive application like SharePoint running on the host system, organizations choose to make servers running virtualization dedicated solely to the operation of virtualized guest sessions.

Of course, there are exceptions to this general recommendation. If a system will be used for demonstration purposes, frequently the host system is set up to run Active Directory Domain Services, DNS, DHCP, and other domain utility services. So, effectively, the host server is the Active Directory system. Then, the guest sessions are created to run things like Microsoft Exchange 2010, SharePoint 2007, or other applications in the guest sessions that connect back to the host for directory services.

Other organizations might choose to not make the host system the Active Directory server, but rather put the global catalog functions in yet another guest session and keep the host server dedicated to virtualization.

## Planning for the Use of Snapshots on the Hyper-V System

A technology built in to Hyper-V is the concept of a snapshot. A snapshot uses the Microsoft Volume Shadow Copy Service (VSS) to make a duplicate copy of a file; however, in the case of virtualization, the file is the virtual server guest virtual disk.

The first time a snapshot is taken, the snapshot contains a compressed copy of the contents of RAM on the system along with a bitmap of the virtual disk image of the guest session. If the original guest image is 8GB in size, the snapshot will be significantly smaller in size; however, the server storage system still needs to have additional disk space to support both the original disk image, plus the amount of disk space needed for the contents of the snapshot image.

Subsequent snapshots can be taken of the same guest session; however, the way VSS works, each additional snapshot just identifies the bits that are different from the original snapshot, thus reducing the required disk space for those additional snapshots to be just the same as needed for the incremental difference from the original snapshot to the current snapshot. This difference might be just megabytes in size.

The use of snapshots in a Windows virtualization environment is covered in more detail later in this chapter in the section titled "Using Snapshots of Guest Operating System Sessions."

# Installation of the Microsoft Hyper-V Role

With the basic concepts of Windows virtualization covered so far in this chapter, and the background on sizing and planning for server capacity and storage, this section now focuses on the installation of the Microsoft Hyper-V Server role on a Windows Server 2008 R2 system.

## Installing Windows Server 2008 R2 as the Host Operating System

The first step is to install Windows Server 2008 R2 with Hyper-V as the host operating system. The step-by-step guidance for the installation of the Windows operating system is covered in Chapter 3, "Installing Windows Server 2008 R2 and Server Core." Typically, the installation of a Windows Server 2008 R2 to run the Hyper-V role is a new clean server installation, so the section in Chapter 3, "Installing a Clean Version of Windows Server 2008 R2 Operating System," is the section to follow for getting Windows Server 2008 R2 set up for virtualization.

## Running Server Manager to Add the Hyper-V Role

After the base image of Windows Server 2008 R2 has been installed, some basic initial tasks should be completed as noted in Chapter 3. The basic tasks are as follows:

1. Change the server name to be a name that you want the virtual server to be.
2. Configure the server to have a static IP address.
3. Join the server to an Active Directory domain (assuming the server will be part of a managed Active Directory environment with centralized administration).
4. Run Windows Update to confirm that all patches and updates have been installed and applied to the server.

After these basic tasks have been completed, the next step is to add the Hyper-V role to the server system. Do the following to add the server role to the system:

1. Make sure you are logged on to the server with local Administrator or Domain Admin privileges.
2. Start the Server Manager console if it is not already running on the system.
3. Right-click on Roles in the left pane of the console, and select Add Roles, as shown in Figure 37.1.
4. After the Add Roles Wizard loads, click Next to continue past the Welcome screen.
5. On the Select Server Roles page, select the Hyper-V role, and click Next.

> **NOTE**
>
> Hyper-V requires a supported version of hardware-assisted virtualization. Both Intel VT and AMD-V chipsets are supported by Hyper-V. In addition, virtualization must be enabled in the BIOS. Check your server documentation for details on how to enable this setting.

FIGURE 37.1     Adding a role to the Server Manager console.

6. On the Hyper-V page, read the notes and information about the role; then click Next.

7. On the Create Virtual Networks page, select the LAN adapter(s) you want to have shared with guest sessions. Click Next to continue.

**NOTE**

It is recommended that you reserve one network adapter for remote access to the host server. To reserve a network, do not select it to be used as a virtual network.

8. On the Confirm Installation Selections page, review the selections made, and then click Install.

9. On the Installation Results page, review the results, and click Close.

10. When prompted to restart the server, click Yes.

11. After the server restarts, log on to the server with local Administrator or Domain Admin privileges.

12. After logging on, the installation and configuration will continue for a few more moments. When complete, the Installation Results page will be displayed. Review the results on the page and confirm that the Windows Hyper-V role has been installed successfully. Click Close.

> **NOTE**
>
> The server's network configuration will change when virtual networking is installed. When network adapters are used in virtual networks, the physical network adapter becomes a Microsoft virtual switch and a new virtual network adapter will be created. By default, this virtual network adapter is shared between the host and the guest VMs.
>
> It is important to note that the new virtual adapter will not inherit the old physical adapter's IP settings. It will become a DHCP client, which can be reconfigured to use the old physical adapter's configuration.

# Becoming Familiar with the Hyper-V Administrative Console

After Hyper-V has been installed, the next step is to install guest images that will run on the virtual server. However, before jumping into the installation of guest images, here is a quick guide on navigating the Hyper-V Administrative console and the virtual server settings available to be configured that apply to all guest sessions on the server.

## Launching the Hyper-V Administrative Console

There are two ways to open the Hyper-V Administrative console and access the server's configuration options. One way is to use the Server Manager tool and administer the host server through Server Manager, and the other option is to launch the freestanding Hyper-V Manager Microsoft Management Console (MMC) to perform administrative tasks for the host system.

> **NOTE**
>
> The functions and settings between the Server Manager console and the stand-alone MMC application are the same. Administrators who manage several server roles tend to use the Server Manager console because they have easy access to more than just the virtualization role; they can also manage DNS, Remote Desktop Services, Network Policy and Access Services, or other roles that might be applicable to their job. For those whose sole job is to administer Windows virtualization systems, they might choose the freestanding MMC application for administering and managing the Windows virtual server systems.

### Using the Server Manager Tool to Manage Hyper-V Systems

For administrators who want to manage their Hyper-V systems from a centralized console, the Server Manager tool provides a common administrative interface for all the server roles installed on a particular system. To start the Server Manager tool to view and edit Hyper-V Settings, do the following:

1. Click the Server Manager icon in the Windows Server 2008 R2 taskbar. This will start the Server Manager application if it is not already running on the system.

2. Expand the Roles section of the tree by clicking on the +.

3. Expand the Hyper-V branch of the tree, and expand the Hyper-V Manager branch of the tree.

### Using the Hyper-V MMC Tool to Manage Hyper-V Systems

For administrators who want to manage their Hyper-V systems from a dedicated console just for Hyper-V administration, the Hyper-V tool should be used. To start the Hyper-V administration tool, do the following:

1. Click Start, All Programs, Administrative Tools, and then choose Hyper-V Manager for the tool to launch.

2. Click on Hyper-V Manager to see the virtual servers to which you are connected.

3. Click on the name of one of the virtual hosts and then select one of the virtual machines listed to see snapshots, details, and actions available for the guest system. By default, the Hyper-V MMC will have the local virtual server system listed, as shown in Figure 37.2.

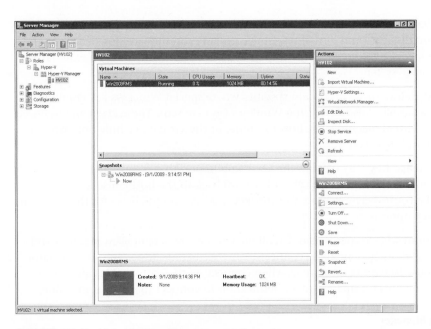

FIGURE 37.2    Virtualization Management Console.

### Connecting to a Remote Hyper-V Host

If you want to administer or manage a remote Hyper-V host system, you can connect to that server using the Hyper-V Manager. To connect to a remote virtual server, do the following:

1. From within the Hyper-V Manager Console, click on the Hyper-V Manager object in the left pane.

2. In the Actions pane, click Connect to Server.

3. Select Another Computer and either enter in the name of the server and click OK, or click on Browse to search Active Directory for the name of the Hyper-V server you want to remotely monitor and administer.

4. When the server appears in the Hyper-V Manager Console, click to select the server to see the actions available for administering and managing that server.

## Navigating and Configuring Host Server Settings

Regardless of whether you have chosen to use Server Manager or the MMC tool, the configuration options and settings are the same. When you click on the virtual server system you want to administer, action settings become available. These action settings allow you to configure the host server settings for the system you have chosen to administer.

### Hyper-V Settings

When you select the Hyper-V Settings action item in the Actions pane, you have access to configure default paths and remote control keyboard settings. Specifics on these settings are as follows:

▶ **Default Paths**—This option enables you to set the drive path for the location where virtual hard disk files and virtual machine configuration files are stored. This might be on the local C: volume of the server system or could be stored on an external SAN or storage system.

▶ **Keyboard Behavior**—This option specifies where special Windows key combinations (for example, Alt+Tab and the Windows key) are sent. These keys can always be sent to the virtual machine, the host machine, or the virtual machine only when it is running in full screen.

▶ **Mouse Release Key**—By default, the key combination that releases the guest session so the administrator can gain keyboard control back to the host console is Ctrl+Alt+Left Arrow. The Remote Control/Release Key option allows for the selection of other key options.

▶ **User Credentials**—Hyper-V uses default credentials, by default. This means it will use the logged-on credentials to connect to any virtual machine. The administrator might choose to require credentials when connecting to a virtual machine. This is necessary when using smart card authentication to connect to a virtual machine.

### Virtual Network Manager

By selecting the Virtual Network Manager action item, you have access to configure the virtual network switches, as shown in Figure 37.3. Here is where you configure the local area network (LAN) and WAN connections available for the guest sessions of the virtual server host.

Specific to these settings are as follows:

▶ **Add New Virtual Network**—This configuration option allows for the addition of a new external, internal, or private network segment available to the guest sessions. An external network binds to the physical network so the virtual machines can

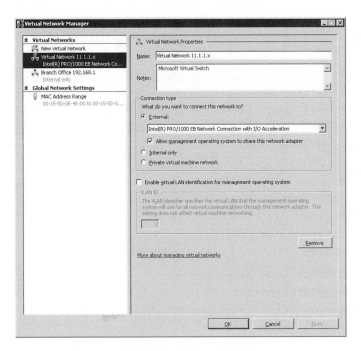

FIGURE 37.3    Virtual network switch management.

access the physical network, just like any other host on the network. An internal network segment would be a connection that is solely within the virtual server system, where you might want to set up a virtual LAN so that the virtual server guests within a system can talk to each other and the host, but not with the physical network. A private network segment can only be used by the virtual machines that run on that host. They are completely isolated and cannot even communicate directly with the host server.

> **NOTE**
>
> A new feature in Windows Server 2008 R2 is the option to "Allow Management Operating System to Share This Network Adapter" in external networks. By deselecting this option, you isolate the management operating system from communications between virtual machines and other computers on a physical network.

Here, the administrator can also choose to configure virtual LAN identification (VLAN ID) for the management operating system. This enables the administrator to tag the virtual network for a specified VLAN.

▶ **Existing virtual networks**—If the system you are managing already has virtual networks configured, they will be listed individually in the left pane of the Virtual Network Manager dialog box. By selecting an existing virtual network switch, you can change the name of the virtual network; change the internal, private, or external connection that the network has access to; or remove the network altogether.

▶ **MAC Address Range**—Every virtual network adapter must have a unique Media Access Control (MAC) address to communicate on an Ethernet network. The administrator can define the range of MAC addresses that can be assigned dynamically to these adapters.

### Edit Disk

The Edit Disk option in the Virtual Network Manager action item menu enables you to modify an existing virtual hard disk (VHD) image. Specifically, the options are as follows:

▶ **Compact**—This option enables you to shrink a virtual hard disk to remove portions of the disk image file that are unused. This is commonly used when a disk image will be archived and stored, and having the smallest disk image file possible is preferred.

▶ **Convert**—This option enables you to convert a dynamic virtual hard disk file to a fixed-size virtual hard disk by copying the contents to a new file.

▶ **Expand**—This option enables you grow the size of a dynamic disk image. For example, you might have initially created the disk image to only be 8GB maximum in size, and now that you've added a lot of applications to the guest image, you are running out of space in the VHD file. By expanding the image file, you effectively have the ability to add more applications and data to the guest session without having to re-create the guest session all over again.

### Inspect Disk

The Inspect Disk option in the Virtual Network Manager action item menu enables you to view the settings of an existing virtual image file. For the example shown in Figure 37.4, the disk image is currently 4MB in size, can dynamically grow up to the maximum limit of 2040GB, and is located on the local hard drive in the directory C:\vpcs.

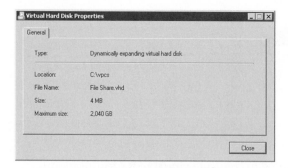

FIGURE 37.4    Virtual Hard Disk Properties shown in the Inspect Disk option.

### Stop Service

The Stop Service option in the Hyper-V Manager Actions pane provides for the ability to stop the Hyper-V Virtual Machine Management on the Hyper-V host machine being managed. You might choose to stop the service if you needed to perform maintenance or begin the shutdown process of an administered system.

### New Configuration Wizard

One of the wizards listed in the Hyper-V Manager Actions pane allows for the creation of new virtual machines, hard disks, and floppy disks. Specifics of this configuration option are as follows:

- ▶ **New – Virtual Machine**—This option enables you to create a new virtual guest session. The whole purpose of running Windows virtualization is to run virtual guest sessions, and this option is the one that enables you to create new guest sessions.

- ▶ **New – Hard Disk**—This option enables you to create a new virtual hard disk (VHD) image. When you create a new virtual machine in the first option, this includes creating a hard disk image for the operating system; however, some servers will need additional virtual hard disks. This wizard walks you through the configuration of a new virtual hard disk image.

- ▶ **New – Floppy Disk**—This option enables you to take an existing floppy disk and create a virtual floppy disk image from the physical disk. This might be used to create an image of a bootable floppy disk that would later be used in configuring or managing a guest image, or used to create a floppy disk image of a disk that has drivers or utilities on it that will be used in a virtual guest session.

# Installing a Guest Operating System Session

One of the key tasks noted in the previous section is to begin the installation of a new guest operating system session. The guest operating system installation is wizard driven and provides the administrator with the ability to configure settings for the guest session, and to begin the installation of the guest operating system software itself. A guest session could be a server-based session running Windows Server 2003 or Windows Server 2008 R2, a client-based session running Windows 7, Windows XP, or Windows Vista, or a guest session running a non-Windows operating system.

## Gathering the Components Needed for a Guest Session

When creating a guest operating system, the administrator needs to make sure they have all of the components needed to begin the installation. The components needed are as follows:

- ▶ **Operating system media**—A copy of the operating system installation media is required for the installation of the guest image. The media could be either a DVD or an ISO image of the media disc itself.

- ▶ **License key**—During the installation of the operating system software, if you are normally prompted to enter in the license key for the operating system, you should have a copy of the license key available.

Other things you should do before starting to install a guest operating system on the virtual server system:

▶ **Guest session configuration settings**—You will be prompted to answer several core guest session configuration setting options, such as how much RAM you want to allocate for the guest session, how much disk space you want to allocate for the guest image, and so on. Either jump ahead to the next section on "Beginning the Installation of the Guest Session" so you can gather up the information you'll need to answer the questions you'll be asked, or be prepared to answer the questions during the installation process.

▶ **Host server readiness**—If you will be preplanning the answers to the questions that you'll be asked, make sure that the host system has enough RAM, disk space, and so on to support the addition of your guest session to the virtual server system. If your requirements exceed the physical capacity of the server, stop and add more resources (memory, disk space, and so on) to the server before beginning the installation of the guest operating system.

## Beginning the Installation of the Guest Session

After you are ready to begin the installation of the guest operating system, launch the guest operating system installation wizard. This is done by doing the following:

1. From the Actions pane, choose New, Virtual Machine. The New Virtual Machine Wizard will launch.

2. Click Next to continue past the initial Welcome screen.

3. Give your virtual machine a name that will be descriptive of the virtual guest session you are creating, such as AD Global Catalog Server, or Exchange 2010 Client Access Server 1, or ISA Proxy Server.

4. If you had set the default virtual machine folder location where guest images are stored, the new image for this virtual machine will be placed in a subfolder of that default folder. However, if you need to select a different location where the image files should be stored, click Store the Virtual Machine in a Different Location, and select Browse to choose an existing disk directory or to create a new directory where the image file for this guest session should be stored. Click Next to continue.

5. Enter in the amount of RAM you want to be allocated to this guest image (in megabytes), and then click Next.

6. Choose the network segment to which you want this guest image to be initially connected. This would be an external, internal, or private network segment created in the section "Virtual Network Manager" earlier in this chapter. Click Next.

**NOTE**

You can also choose Not Connected during this virtual machine creation process and change the network segment option at a later date.

7. The next option enables you to create a new virtual hard disk or use an existing virtual hard disk for the guest image file. Creating a new virtual hard disk creates a VHD disk image in the directory you choose. By default, a dynamic virtual disk image size setting is set to 127GB. The actual file itself will only be the size of the data in the image (potentially 4GB or 8GB to start, depending on the operating system) and will dynamically grow up to the size indicated in this setting. Alternately, you can choose an existing hard disk image you might have already created (including an older image you might have created in Windows Server 2008 Hyper-V or Microsoft Virtual Server 2005), or you can choose to select a hard disk image later. To use a fixed-size disk, select the last option and create the virtual disk later from the Virtual Machine Settings window. The options for this configuration are shown in Figure 37.5. Click Next to continue.

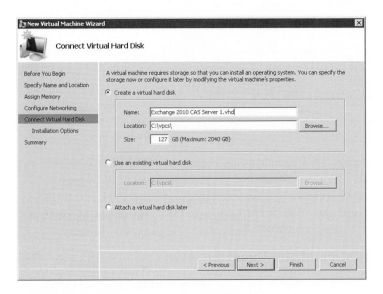

FIGURE 37.5    Creating a new virtual hard disk.

**NOTE**

Dynamic VHD performance in Windows Server 2008 R2 has been greatly enhanced, essentially equaling that of fixed disks. This means you can now seriously consider using dynamic disks instead of fixed disks in production environments.

8. The next option, shown in Figure 37.6, allows for the installation of an operating system on the disk image you created in the previous step. You can choose to install an operating system at a later time, install an operating system from a bootable CD/DVD or ISO image file, install an operating system from a floppy disk image, or install an operating system from a network-based installation server (such as

Windows Deployment Services). Typically, operating system source discs are on either a physical disc or ISO image file, and choosing a CD or DVD or an associated ISO image file will allow for the operating system to be installed on the guest image. Select your option, and then click Next to continue.

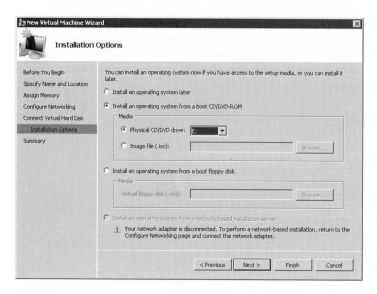

FIGURE 37.6    Selecting the operating system installation options.

9. Review the summary of the options you have selected and either click Finish if the settings you've chosen are fine, or click Previous to go back and make changes. Click Finish to create the new virtual machine.

## Completing the Installation of the Guest Session

When the new virtual machine is started, the guest operating system installation will proceed to install just like the process of installing the operating system on a physical system. Typically, at the end of an operating system installation, the guest session will restart and bring the session to a logon prompt. Log on to the guest operating system and configure the guest operating system as you would any other server system. This typically has you do things such as the following:

1. Change the system name to a name that you want the virtual server to be. For many versions of operating systems, you will be prompted to enter the name of the system during the installation process.

2. Configure the guest session with an appropriate IP address. This might be DHCP issued; however, if you are building a server system, a static IP address is typically recommended.

3. Join the system to an Active Directory domain (assuming the system will be part of a managed Active Directory Domain Services environment with centralized administration).

4. Download and apply the latest patches and updates on the guest session to confirm that all patches and updates have been installed and applied to the system.

The installation of the guest operating system typically requires yet another reboot, and the operating system will be installed and operational.

# Modifying Guest Session Configuration Settings

After a guest session has been installed, whether it is a Microsoft Windows server guest session, a Microsoft Windows client guest session, or a guest session running a non-Windows operating system, the host configuration settings for the guest session can be changed. Common changes to a guest session include things such as the following:

▶ Adding or limiting the RAM of the guest session

▶ Changing network settings of the guest session

▶ Mounting a CD/DVD image or mounting a physical CD/DVD disc

## Adding or Limiting the RAM of the Guest Session

A common configuration change that is made of a guest session is to increase or decrease the amount of memory allocated to the guest session. The default memory allocated to the system frequently is fine for a basic system configuration; however, with the addition of applications to the guest session, there might be a need to increase the memory. As long as the host server system has enough memory to allocate additional memory to the guest session, adding memory to a guest session is a very simple task.

To add memory to the guest session, do the following:

1. From the Server Manager console or from the Hyper-V Manager MMC snap-in, click to select the guest session for which you want to change the allocated memory.

2. Right-click the guest session name, and choose Settings.

3. Click on Memory and enter in the amount of RAM you want allocated for this guest session (in megabytes).

4. Click OK when you are finished.

**37**

### NOTE

You cannot change the allocated RAM on a running virtual guest session. The guest session must be shut down first, memory reallocated to the image, and then the guest image booted for the new memory allocation to take effect.

## Changing Network Settings for the Guest Session

Another common configuration change made to a guest session is to change the network setting for the guest session. An administrator of a virtual server might choose to have each guest session connected directly to the network backbone with an external network, just as if the guest session had a network adapter connected to the backbone, or the network administrator might choose to set up an isolated (internal or private) network just for the guest sessions. The configuration of the internal, private, and external network segments that the administrator can configure the guest sessions to connect to is covered earlier in this chapter in the section "Virtual Network Manager."

The common configuration methods of the virtual network configurations can be broken down into two groups, as follows:

▶ **Direct addressing**—The guest sessions can connect directly to the backbone of the network to which the virtual server host system is attached. In this instance, an administrator would configure an external connection in the Virtual Network Manager and have an IP address on that external segment.

▶ **Isolated network**—If the administrator wants to keep the guest sessions isolated off of the network backbone, the administrator can set up either an internal or private connection in the Virtual Network Manager and the guest sessions would have an IP address of a segment common to the other guest sessions on the host system. In this case, the virtual server acts as a network switch connecting the guest sessions together.

> **NOTE**
>
> To connect the internal network segment with the external network segment, a guest session can be configured as a router or gateway between the internal network and external network. This router system would have two virtual network adapters, one for each network.

To change the connected network used by a guest session adapter, do the following:

1. From the Server Manager console or from the Hyper-V Manager MMC snap-in, click to select the guest session for which you want to change the network configuration.

2. Right-click the guest session name, and choose Settings.

3. Click on the network adapter that requires reconfiguration. From the list in the Network field, select the desired network.

4. Click OK when you are finished.

## Mounting a Physical CD/DVD Image or Mounting a CD/DVD Image File

When installing software on a guest session of a virtual server system, the administrator would either insert a CD or DVD into the drive of the physical server and access the disc from the guest session, or mount an ISO image file of the disc media.

To access a physical CD or DVD disc or to mount an image of a CD or DVD, do the following:

1. From the Server Manager console or from the Hyper-V Manager MMC snap-in, click to select the guest session for which you want to provide access to the CD or DVD.

2. Right-click the guest session name, and choose Settings.

3. Click on DVD Drive and choose Physical CD/DVD Drive if you want to mount a disc in the physical drive of the host system, or click on Image File and browse for the ISO image file you want to mount as a disc image.

4. Click OK when you are finished.

### Other Settings to Modify for a Guest Session Configuration

There are other settings that can be changed for a guest session. These options can be modified by going into the Settings option of the guest session and making changes. These other settings include the following:

▶ **BIOS**—This setting allows for the selection of boot order on the guest machine to boot in an order that can include floppy, CD, IDE (disk), or network boot.

▶ **Processor**—Hyper-V provides the ability to allocate core processors to the guest image, so a guest image can have up to four core processors allocated for each session. Additionally, resource control can be weighted between guest sessions by allocating system resource priority to key guest server sessions versus other guest sessions.

> **NOTE**
>
> Windows Server 2008 R2 provides a processor compatibility check box to limit processor functionality for virtual machines that will be Live Migrated between dissimilar hosts. Live Migration is discussed later in this chapter.

**37**

▶ **IDE Controller**—The guest session initially has a single virtual hard drive associated with it. Additional virtual hard drives can be added to a virtual guest session.

▶ **SCSI Controller**—A virtual SCSI controller can be associated with a virtual guest session as well providing different drive configuration options for the different drive configurations.

▶ **COM Ports**—Virtual communication ports such as COM1 or COM2 can be associated with specific named pipes for input and output of information.

# Launching a Hyper-V Guest Session

After a Hyper-V guest session has been created, and the settings have been properly modified to meet the expected needs of the organization, the virtual guest session can now be launched and run. Decisions need to be made whether you want the guest session to automatically launch as soon as the host server is booted, or whether you want to manually launch a guest session. Additionally, a decision needs to be made on the sequence in which guest sessions should be launched so that systems that are prerequisites to other sessions come up first. As an example, you'd want a global catalog server session and DHCP server session to come up before an application server that logs on and authenticates to Active Directory comes online and needs to authenticate to Active Directory before the server service begins.

## Automatically Launching a Guest Session

One option for launching and loading guest sessions is to have the guest session boot right after the physical host server completes the boot cycle. This is typically the preferred option if a guest session is core to the network infrastructure of a network (such as a domain controller or host server system) so that in the event of a physical server reboot, the virtual guest sessions boot up automatically as well. It would not be convenient to have to manually boot each virtual server session every time the physical server is rebooted.

The option for setting the startup option for a virtual session is in the configuration settings for each guest session.

To change the startup action, do the following:

1. From the Server Manager console or from the Hyper-V Manager MMC snap-in, right-click the virtual machine for which you want to change the setup option, and select Settings.

2. In the Management section of the settings, click Automatic Start Action.

3. You are provided with three options, as shown in Figure 37.7, of what to do with this virtual guest session upon startup of the physical host server. Either click Nothing (which would require a manual boot of the guest session), click Automatically Start If It Was Running When the Service Stopped, or click Always Start This Virtual Machine Automatically. To set the virtual session to automatically start after the physical server comes up, choose the Always Start This Virtual Machine Automatically option.

4. Also on this setting is the ability to have an automatic start delay. This enables you to sequence the startup of virtual machines by having some VMs take longer to automatically start than others. Click OK to save these settings.

## Manually Launching a Guest Session

Another option for guest session startup is to not have a guest session automatically start after a physical server boots up. This is typically the preferred option if a guest session will be part of a demonstration or test server where the administrator of the system wants to control which guest sessions are automatically launched, and which sessions need to be manually launched. It would not be convenient to have a series of demo or test sessions automatically boot up every time the system is booted. The administrator of the system would typically want to choose to start these guest sessions.

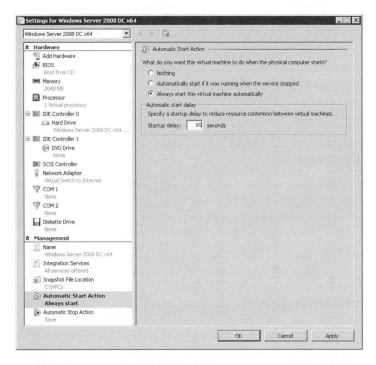

FIGURE 37.7   Automatic start actions.

To set the startup action to manually launch a guest session, do the following:

1. From the Server Manager console or from the Hyper-V Manager MMC snap-in, right-click the virtual machine for which you want to change the setup option, and select Settings.

2. In the Management section of the settings, click Automatic Start Action.

3. When provided the three options of what to do with this virtual guest session upon startup of the physical server, either click Nothing (which would require a manual boot of the guest session), click Automatically Start If It Was Running when the Service Stopped, or click Always Start This Virtual Machine Automatically. Choose the Nothing option, and the session will need to be manually started.

## Save State of a Guest Session

In Windows Server 2008 R2 Hyper-V, there are two concepts for saving guest images: being snapshots and being a saved state. At any time, an administrator can right-click a guest session and choose Save. This Save function is similar to a Hibernate mode on a desktop client system. It saves the image state into a file with the option of bringing the saved state image file back to the state the image was in prior to being saved.

# Using Snapshots of Guest Operating System Sessions

A highly versatile function in Windows Server 2008 R2 Hyper-V is the option to create a snapshot of a guest session. A snapshot in Windows Hyper-V uses Microsoft Volume Shadow Copy Service (VSS) technology that captures an image of a file on a server—in this case, the file is the VHD image of the virtual server itself. At any point in time in the future, the snapshot can be used for recovery.

## Snapshots for Image Rollback

One common use of a guest image snapshot is to roll back an image to a previous state. This is frequently done with guest images used for demonstration purposes, or test labs where a scenario is tested to see the results and compared with identical tests of other scenarios, or for the purpose of preparing for a software upgrade or migration.

In the case of a guest image used for demonstration purposes, a user might run through a demo of a software program where they add information, delete information, make software changes, or otherwise modify information in the software on the guest image. Rather than having to go back and delete the changes, or rebuilding the image from scratch to do the demo again, with a snapshot, the user can simply roll the image back to the snapshot that was available before the changes were made to the image.

Image rollback has been successfully used for training purposes where an employee runs through a process, then rolls back the image so they can run through the same process all over again repeating the process on the same base image but without previous installations or configurations.

In network infrastructures, a snapshot is helpful when an organization applies a patch or update to a server, or a software upgrade is performed and problems occur; the administrator can simply roll back the image to the point prior to the start of the upgrade or migration.

## Snapshots for Guest Session Server Fault Tolerance

Snapshots are commonly used in business environments for the purpose of fault tolerance or disaster recovery. A well-timed snapshot right before a system failure can help an organization roll back their server to the point right before the server failed or problem occurred. Rather than waiting hours to restore a server from tape, the activation of a snapshot image is nothing more than choosing the snapshot and selecting to start the guest image. When the guest image starts up, it is in the state that the image was at the time the snapshot was created.

## Creating a Snapshot of a Guest Image

Snapshots are very easy to create. To create a snapshot, do the following:

1.  From the Server Manager console or from the Hyper-V Manager MMC snap-in, click to select the guest session for which you want to create a snapshot.

2. Right-click the guest session name, and choose Snapshot. A snapshot of the image will immediately be taken of the guest image and the snapshot will show up in the Snapshots pane, as shown in Figure 37.8.

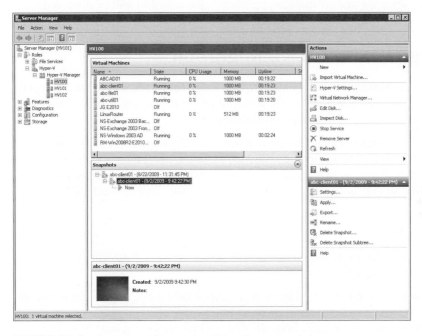

FIGURE 37.8    Snapshot of a running Hyper-V guest session.

## Rolling Back a Guest Image to a Previous Snapshot Image

The term used in Windows Server 2008 R2 Hyper-V to roll back an image is called "applying" a snapshot to an existing image. When an image is rolled back, the image that is currently running has the snapshot information applied to the image, thus bringing the image back to an earlier configuration state. To apply a snapshot, do the following:

1. From the Server Manager console or from the Hyper-V Manager MMC snap-in, click the snapshot to which you want to revert the running guest image.

2. Right-click the snapshot image and choose Apply. The configuration state of the image will immediately be reverted to the state of the image when the snapshot was taken.

### NOTE

By default, the name of the snapshot image takes on the date and time the image was created. As an example, if the virtual machine is called "Windows 2008 R2 IIS," an image taken on September 2, 2009 at 9:42 p.m. would show up as "Windows 2008 R2 IIS - (9/2/2009 - 9:42:22 PM)." Snapshots can be renamed to something more meaningful, if desired, such as "Clean Build with All Patches".

## Reverting a Snapshot Session

When working with snapshots, if you snapshot a session, the revert action can be used on the virtual machine to revert the guest session's state to the last created or applied snapshot. All changes since the last creation or application of a snapshot will be discarded.

# Quick Migration and Live Migration

There are two forms of automated migration provided by Windows Server 2008 R2 Hyper-V: Quick Migration and Live Migration. These migration processes can be used to increase service availability for planned and unplanned downtime.

Although both technologies achieve the same thing—moving virtual servers between Hyper-V hosts—they use different methods and mechanisms to achieve it. Both require at least two Hyper-V host servers in a cluster, attached to the same shared storage system. Usually, the shared storage is an iSCSI or Fibre Channel storage area network (SAN).

## Quick Migration

Quick Migration provides a way to quickly move a virtual machine from one host server to another with a small amount of downtime.

In a Quick Migration, the guest virtual machine is suspended on one host and resumed on another host. This operation happens in the time it takes to transfer the active memory of the virtual machine over the network from the first host to the second host. For a host with 8GB of RAM, this might take about two minutes using a 1GB iSCSI connection.

Quick Migration was the fastest migration available for Windows Server 2008 Hyper-V. Microsoft made considerable investments in Hyper-V migration technologies, trying to reduce the time required to migrate virtual machines between Hyper-V hosts. The result was Live Migration, which has the same hardware requirements as Quick Migration, but with a near instantaneous failover time.

## Live Migration

Since the release of Hyper-V V1 with Windows Server 2008, the number-one most-requested feature by customers is the ability to migrate running virtual machines between hosts, with no downtime. VMware's VMotion has been able to do this for some time. Finally, with Windows Server 2008 R2, it can be done natively with Hyper-V for no extra cost. This makes it a compelling reason to move to Hyper-V.

Live Migration uses failover clustering. The quorum model used for your cluster will depend on the number of Hyper-V nodes in your cluster. In this example, we will use two Hyper-V nodes in a Node and Disk Majority Cluster configuration. There will be one shared storage LUN used as the cluster quorum disk and another used as the Cluster Shared Volume (CSV) disk, described later in this chapter. For more details on clustering, see Chapter 29, "System-Level Fault Tolerance (Clustering/Network Load Balancing)."

> **NOTE**
>
> If there is only one shared storage LUN available to the nodes when the cluster is formed, Windows will allocate that LUN as the cluster quorum disk and it will not be available to be used as a CSV disk.

This section describes how to use Hyper-V Live Migration to move virtual machines between clustered Hyper-V hosts.

## Configuring the Cluster Quorum Witness Disk

Live Migration requires a Windows Server 2008 R2 cluster configured to use shared storage. Typically, these are LUNs provisioned on an iSCSI or Fibre Channel SAN. One LUN will be used as the witness disk for quorum and another will be used as a Cluster Shared Volume (CSV) to store the virtual machine images. The CSV will be configured later in this chapter.

The LUN for the shared witness quorum disk must be configured before the cluster is formed, so that cluster manager can configure the cluster properly. Connect this LUN via iSCSI or Fibre Channel to both nodes you will use for the cluster. The disk must be initialized and formatted with an NTFS file format prior to cluster use. When properly configured, both nodes share the same online Basic disk and can access the disk at the same time.

> **IMPORTANT**
>
> The Windows cluster service will always use the first shared disk as the cluster quorum disk. Provision this disk first on each node.

Now that the shared storage witness disk has been configured, we can move on to installing the Windows cluster.

## Installing the Failover Clustering Feature

Before a failover clustering can be deployed, the necessary feature must be installed. To install the Failover Clustering feature, perform the following steps:

1. Log on to the Windows Server 2008 R2 cluster node with an account with administrator privileges.
2. Click the Server Manager icon in the Windows taskbar.
3. Select the Features node in the tree pane when Server Manager opens.
4. In the tasks pane, select the Add Features link.
5. In the Select Features window, select Failover Clustering, click Next, and click Install on the Confirm Installation Selections page to install the feature.

6. When the installation completes, click Close to complete the installation and return to Server Manager.

7. Close Server Manager and install the Failover Clustering feature on each of the remaining cluster nodes.

## Running the Validate a Configuration Wizard

Failover Cluster Management is used to administer the Failover Clustering feature. It can be run from Server Manager or as a separate MMC console. After the feature is installed, run the Validate a Configuration Wizard from the tasks pane of the Failover Cluster Management console. All nodes should be up and running when the wizard is run. To run the Validate a Configuration Wizard, perform the following steps:

1. Log on to one of the Windows Server 2008 R2 cluster nodes with an account with administrator privileges over all nodes in the cluster.

2. Click Start, click All Programs, click Administrative Tools, and select Failover Cluster Management.

3. When the Failover Cluster Management console opens, click the Validate a Configuration link in the Actions pane.

4. When the Validate a Configuration Wizard opens, click Next on the Before You Begin page.

5. On the Select Servers or a Cluster page, enter the name of a cluster node, and click the Add button. Repeat this process until all nodes are added to the list, as shown in Figure 37.9, and click Next to continue.

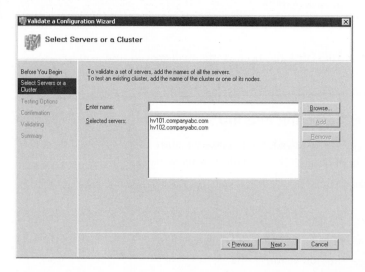

FIGURE 37.9    Adding the servers to be validated by the Validate a Configuration Wizard.

6. On the Testing Options page, read the details that explain the requirements for all tests to pass in order to be supported by Microsoft. Select the Run All Tests (Recommended) option button, and click Next to continue.

7. On the Confirmation page, review the list of servers that will be tested and the list of tests that will be performed, and click Next to begin testing the servers.

> **NOTE**
>
> For years, administrators have complained that the Validate a Configuration Wizard window is too small. In Windows Server 2008 R2, administrators can finally resize the window by dragging the lower-right corner. This is not obvious, but try it—it works!

8. When the tests complete, the Summary page displays the results, and if the tests pass, click Finish to complete the Validate a Configuration Wizard. If the tests failed, click the View Report button to review the details and determine which test failed and why the test failed.

Even if the Validate a Configuration Wizard does not pass every test, depending on the test, creating a cluster might still be possible. After the Validation a Configuration Wizard is completed successfully, the cluster can be created.

## Creating a Node and Disk Majority Cluster

When the failover cluster is first created, all nodes in the cluster should be up and running. To create the failover cluster, perform the following steps:

1. Log on to one of the Windows Server 2008 R2 cluster nodes with an account with administrator privileges over all nodes in the cluster.

2. Click Start, click All Programs, click Administrative Tools, and select Failover Cluster Management.

3. When the Failover Cluster Management console opens, click the Create a Cluster link in the Actions pane.

4. When the Create Cluster Wizard opens, click Next on the Before You Begin page.

5. On the Select Servers page, enter the name of each cluster node, and click the Add button. When all the nodes are listed, click Next to continue.

6. On the Validation Warning page, select No. I Do Not Require.... The validation test can be run after the configuration is complete. Click Next to continue.

7. On the Access Point for Administering the Cluster page, type in the name of the cluster, complete the IPv4 address, and click Next, as shown in Figure 37.10. The name you choose for the cluster will become a cluster computer account in Active Directory.

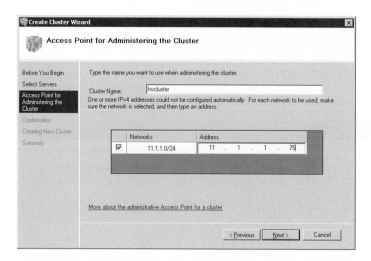

FIGURE 37.10    Defining the network name and IPv4 address for the failover cluster.

8. On the Confirmation page, review the settings, and click Next to create the cluster.

9. On the Summary page, review the results of the cluster creation process, and click Finish to return to the Failover Cluster Management console. If there are any errors, you can click the View Report button to reveal the detailed cluster creation report.

10. Back in the Failover Cluster Management console, select the cluster name in the tree pane. In the tasks pane, review the configuration of the cluster.

11. In the tree pane, select and expand Nodes to list all the cluster nodes.

12. Select Storage and review the cluster storage in the tasks pane. The shared storage disk will be listed as the witness disk in quorum. This disk is used to maintain quorum.

13. Expand Networks in the tree pane to review the list of networks. Select each network and review the names of the adapters in each network.

14. Click Validate Configuration in the Actions pane to start an automated review of the cluster configuration. See the previous section, "Running the Validate a Configuration Wizard," for more details. Keep in mind that Microsoft support for the cluster will require a successful execution of the validation process.

## Adding Additional Shared Storage

At this point, we have a Node and Disk Majority cluster using a shared witness disk to maintain quorum. We can now add the shared storage that will be used as a Cluster Shared Volume.

Another LUN must be provisioned for the Cluster Shared Volume to hold the virtual machine images used in Live Migration. This LUN may be a new unpartitioned volume or one that already contains virtual machine images and data.

Connect this LUN via iSCSI or Fibre Channel to both nodes in the cluster. The disk must be initialized and formatted with an NTFS file format prior to cluster use in the cluster. When properly configured, the disk will show in Disk Management on both nodes.

Next, we add the new shared disk to the cluster.

1. On one of the cluster nodes, open Failover Cluster Management.
2. Expand the Cluster and select Storage.
3. Click Add a Disk in the Actions pane.
4. Select the disk to add and click OK. The disk will be added to available storage.

## Configuring Cluster Shared Volumes

Cluster Shared Volumes (CSVs) are a new concept for Windows Server 2008 R2. They provide the new capabilities required for Hyper-V Live Migration to work, and is why only Windows Server 2008 R2 nodes can participate in the cluster.

With CSV, any node can host the virtual machine and any node can access the VHD on shared storage, so virtual machine and disk ownership can move freely across cluster nodes without impacting any other resources on that shared disk.

To enable and configure Cluster Shared Volumes, perform the following steps from the Failover Cluster Management console:

1. Select the cluster name in the Failover Cluster Management console.
2. Click Enable Cluster Shared Volumes in the Actions pane.
3. The Enable Cluster Shared Volumes information dialog box will be displayed. Read the important information, shown in Figure 37.11, explaining that CSVs are only supported for the Hyper-V role on Windows Server 2008 R2 servers. Click the check box that you have read the notice and click OK.

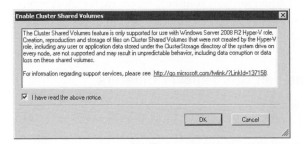

FIGURE 37.11   Enabling Cluster Shared Volumes on a cluster.

4. A new item, Cluster Shared Volumes, will be added to the tree view. Select Cluster Shared Volumes.
5. Click Add Storage in the Actions pane. The Add Storage window is displayed.

37

6. Click the check box to select the shared cluster disk and click OK. The shared disk will be added to Cluster Shared Storage, as shown in Figure 37.12.

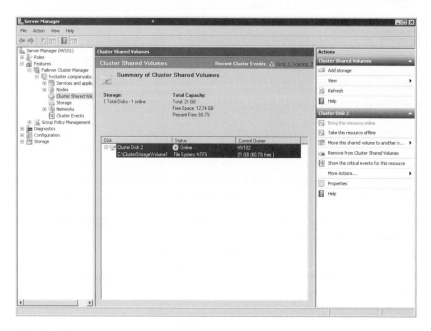

FIGURE 37.12    New Cluster Shared Volume.

Unlike other shared volume disks, Cluster Shared Volumes are presented to the nodes as a folder in the local C: drive of each node.

From either node, open Windows Explorer and navigate to the path indicated in the Cluster Shared Volume disk, usually C:\ClusterStorage\Volume1, where each CSV is given a unique number beginning with 1. If another CSV disk is added to the same cluster, it will be accessible from C:\ClusterStorage\Volume2.

## Deploying New Virtual Machines on CSV Failover Clusters

After the desired cluster configuration is achieved, the cluster is ready for the deploying of virtual machines:

1. On one of the cluster nodes, open Failover Cluster Management.

2. Expand the Cluster and select Services and Applications.

3. Now that Cluster Storage Volumes have been configured, the Virtual Machines application is available in the Actions pane. Click Virtual Machines, New Virtual Machine and select the cluster node on which to deploy the virtual machine.

4. The New Virtual Machine Wizard will launch, as it does from the Hyper-V Manager described earlier in this chapter. Click Next at the introduction screen.

5. Provide a name for the new virtual machine and click the Store the Virtual Machine in a Different Location check box. Enter the path to the C:\ClusterStorage\Volume1, as shown in Figure 37.13, and click Next.

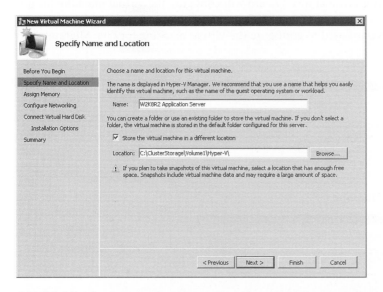

FIGURE 37.13     Specify the name and location of the virtual machine.

**NOTE**

It is recommended on Hyper-V servers using Live Migration to change the default location to store virtual machines to the Cluster Shared Volume path. This is configured in Hyper-V Settings of the Hyper-V Manager console, as described earlier in this chapter.

6. Assign the desired amount of memory for the new virtual machine.

7. Select the virtual network, or choose Not Connected to configure it later. Click Next.

8. Create a new virtual hard disk in the C:\ClusterStorage\Volume1 folder or select an existing VHD and click Next.

**NOTE**

Both the virtual machine configuration file and its associated virtual hard disk (VHD) files must reside in the CSV folder location for Live Migration to work.

9. Select how you will install the operating system for the new virtual machine, either using a boot CD-DVD ROM, ISO image, floppy disk, or from a network-based installation server, and click Next.

10. Review the summary of the options you have selected and either click Finish if the settings you've chosen are fine, or click Previous to go back and make changes.

11. Click Finish to create the new virtual machine. After the virtual machine is saved to the CSV path, the High Availability Wizard will configure the virtual machine for use in Live Migration, as shown in Figure 37.14. Click View Report to review the step the High Availability Wizard used to configure the virtual machine for Live Migration.

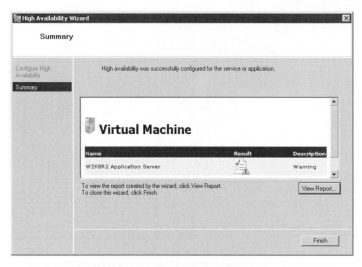

FIGURE 37.14   The High Availability Wizard.

---

**NOTE**

It is normal for the High Availability Wizard to report a warning if the operating system for the virtual machine will be installed from the host's physical CD-DVD ROM, an ISO file, or a floppy drive. This is because the drive or file used for installation is not in a location available to the cluster. Most of the time, this does not matter, but it can be overcome if needed by installing the operating system from an ISO located on the CSV location.

---

12. Click Finish to complete the configuration of the new virtual machine.

13. Change the virtual machine settings, if desired, to increase the number of virtual processors, change the drive configuration, and so on.

14. Right-click the virtual machine in Failover Cluster Manager and select Start Virtual Machines to start the virtual machine and install the operating system.

Once the operating system is installed, Live Migration can be used to move the cluster from one node to another.

## Deploying Existing Virtual Machines on CSV Failover Clusters

If the LUN provisioned as a CSV disk in the cluster contains existing virtual machine images, these can be made highly available. You can also copy any virtual hard disk to the CSV volume and make it highly available:

1. On one of the cluster nodes, open Failover Cluster Management.

2. Expand the cluster and select Services and Applications.

3. Right-click Services and Applications and select Configure a Service or Application. This will open the High Availability Wizard.

4. Click Next on the Before You Begin page.

5. On the Service or Application page, click Virtual Machine and click Next.

6. Select the virtual machine(s) to be made highly available and click Next.

7. Review the Summary page in the wizard and click Finish.

8. Select the virtual machine in the Service and Application pane and click Start Virtual Machines in the Actions pane.

## Performing a Live Migration

The virtual machine runs on one of the cluster nodes, known as the owner. When a Live Migration is performed, multiple steps are performed. These steps can be broken down into three stages: preflight migration, virtual machine transfer, and final transfer/startup of the virtual machine.

The first step in Live Migration occurs on the source node (where the virtual machine is currently running) and the target node (where the virtual machine will be moved) to ensure that migration can, in fact, occur successfully.

The detailed steps of Live Migration are as follows:

1. Identify the source and destination machines.

2. Establish a network connection between the two nodes.

3. The preflight stage begins. Check if the various resources available are compatible between the source and destination nodes:

   ▶ Are the processors using similar architecture? (For example, a virtual machine running on an AMD node cannot be moved to an Intel node, and vice versa.)

   ▶ Are there a sufficient number of CPU cores available on the destination?

   ▶ Is there sufficient RAM available on the destination?

   ▶ Is there sufficient access to required shared resources (VHD, network, and so on)?

   ▶ Is there sufficient access to physical device resources that must remain associated with the virtual machine after migration (CD drives, DVDs, and LUNs or offline disks)?

37

Migration cannot occur if there are any problems in the preflight stage. If there are, the virtual machine will remain on the source node and processing ends here. If preflight is successful, migration can occur and the virtual machine transfer continues.

4. The virtual machine state (inactive memory pages) moves to the target node to reduce the active virtual machine footprint as much as possible. All that remains on the source node is a small memory working set of the virtual machine.

   The virtual machine configuration and device information are transferred to the destination node and the worker process is created. Then, the virtual machine memory is transferred to the destination while the virtual machine is still running. The cluster service intercepts memory writes and tracks actions that occur during the migration. This page will be retransmitted later. Up to this point, the virtual machine technically remains on the source node.

5. What remains of the virtual machine is briefly paused on the source node. The virtual machine working set is then transferred to the destination host, storage access is moved to the destination host, and the virtual machine is reset on the destination host.

The only downtime on the virtual machine occurs in the last step, and this outage is usually much less than most network applications are designed to tolerate. For example, an administrator can be accessing the virtual machine via Remote Desktop while it is being Live Migrated and will not experience an outage. Or a virtual machine could be streaming video to multiple hosts, Live Migrated to another node, and the end users don't know the difference.

Use the following steps to perform a Live Migration between two cluster nodes:

1. On one of the cluster nodes, open Failover Cluster Management.

2. Expand the Cluster and select Services and Applications.

3. Select the virtual machine to Live Migrate.

4. Click Live Migrate Virtual Machine to Another Node in the Actions pane and select the node to move the virtual machine to. The virtual machine will migrate to the selected node using the process described previously.

---

**NOTE**

If there are processor differences between the source and destination node, Live Migration will display a warning that the CPU capabilities do not match. To perform a Live Migration, you must shut down the virtual machine and edit the settings of the processor to "Migrate to a Physical Computer with a Different Processor Version".

---

# Summary

Microsoft Hyper-V has come a long way in just a few short years, and even further since Windows Server 2008 was released. As recently as 2003, Microsoft wasn't even in the virtualization game, and now with Windows Server 2008 R2, virtualization provides organizations with a way to consolidate server applications onto a fewer number of virtual server systems and provide enterprise-level fault tolerance. Key to the release of Windows Server 2008 R2 Hyper-V is the ability to perform Live Migrations, reducing failover times from minutes to nearly instantaneous. This technology competes directly with other competitors, such as VMware, head-to-head, but at a much lower cost.

Hyper-V in Windows Server 2008 R2 provides the ability of hosting Windows server, Windows client, and non-Windows guest sessions with the ability of consolidating dozens of physical servers into a single virtual server system. By adding additional virtual server systems to an enterprise, an organization can drastically reduce the number of physical servers it has, plus provide a method of implementing server redundancy, clustering, and disaster recovery without the need to double the number of physical servers the organization requires to provide better computing services to the organization.

# Best Practices

The following are best practices from this chapter:

- ▶ Plan for the number of virtual guest sessions you plan to have on a server to properly size the host system with respect to memory, processor, and disk requirements.

- ▶ Have the installation media and license keys needed for the installation of the guest operating system handy when you are about to install the guest operating system session.

- ▶ Apply all patches and updates on guest sessions soon after installing the guest operating system, just as you would for the installation of updates on physical systems.

- ▶ For Microsoft Windows guest sessions, install the Windows add-in components to improve the use and operation of the guest session.

- ▶ After installing the guest session and its associated applications, confirm whether the memory of the guest session is enough, and adjust the memory of the guest session accordingly to optimize the performance of the guest session.

- ▶ Allocate enough disk space to perform snapshots of images so that the disk subsystem can handle both the required guest image and the associated snapshots of the guest session.

- ▶ Consider using snapshots before applying major patches, updates, or upgrades to an image session to allow for a rollback to the original image.

- ▶ Consider Live Migration instead of Quick Migration to quickly migrate virtual servers between hosts with little to zero downtime.

- ▶ Ensure that the hardware used in Live Migration is on the Windows Server 2008 R2 compatibility list and is using the same Intel or AMD platform.

- ▶ Use Cluster Shared Volumes only for Hyper-V Live Migration clusters.

37

▶ Configure the Windows failover cluster before adding shared storage, which will be provisioned as Cluster Shared Volumes.

▶ For Live Migration nodes, change the default location to store virtual machines to the Cluster Shared Volume path.

▶ Ensure that both the virtual machine configuration file and its associated virtual hard disk (VHD) files reside in the CSV folder location for Live Migration virtual machines.

# SYMBOLS

# A

*How can we make this index more useful? Email us at indexes@samspublishing.com*

FTP, 396-403

IIS, 408-409

IPSec, 857

Kerberos, 133, 420

support, 247

L2TP, 857

Network Level Authentication, RDS, 981

PEAP, 857

placeholder domain model, 169

PPTP, 857

RODCs, 22

RRAS, 856-858

selecting, 858-859

SSL, 410

Authentication feature page, 394

Authentication Rules feature page, 395

AuthenticationLevel property, 751

authoritative restores

Active Directory, 1297

backlinks, 1298

authorization

background sessions, 933

DHCP, 360

HCAP, 462

Authorize DHCP Server page, 335

autoenrollment, certificates, 879-880, 904-905

Automated Deployment Services, 991

Automatic Private IP Addressing. See APIPA

automatic updates, 682-684

Automatic Updates clients, deployment, 434

automation

DHCP database backup and restore, 337-338

DNS, creating zones, 287

guest sessions, launching, 1536-1537

PowerShell, 697-699. See also PowerShell

replication, 1147

Task Scheduler, 1383

updating, enabling, 96-97

WAIK, 1007, 1018

AutoStart, broadcasts, 1485

autouninstall of software packages, 1089

availability

applications, 1177

High Availability Wizard, 1548

services, 1177

Available section, 1113

avoiding full AD synchronization, 213

awareness, NLA, 587

AXFR (asynchronous full zone transfers), 276, 1427

# B

back-end enterprise messaging systems, 1178

Background Intelligent Transfer Service (BITS), 98, 435

backgrounds

jobs, 720

migration documentation, 70

section, documentation, 65

session authentication, 933

work, reducing, 640

backlinks, authoritative restores, 1298

Backup Domain Controller (BDC), 1306

backups, 1226-1227

accidental deletion protection, 1254-1255

Active Directory, 1251-1256

Big Bang migration, 489

command line, 1252

databases, DHCP automation, 337-338

DFS, 1166-1167, 1261

DFSR, 32

DHCP, 1260

disaster recovery documentation, 787-788

*How can we make this index more useful? Email us at indexes@samspublishing.com*

# E

# F

*How can we make this index more useful? Email us at indexes@samspublishing.com*

# H

# J-K

# L

# N

# O

*How can we make this index more useful? Email us at indexes@samspublishing.com*

*How can we make this index more useful? Email us at indexes@samspublishing.com*

# S

# W

# UNLEASHED

**Unleashed** takes you beyond the basics, providing an exhaustive, technically sophisticated reference for professionals who need to exploit a technology to its fullest potential. It's the best resource for practical advice from the experts, and the most in-depth coverage of the latest technologies.

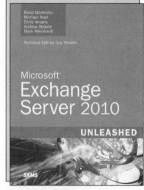

**Microsoft Exchange Server 2010 Unleashed**
ISBN-13: 978-0-672-33046-9

## OTHER UNLEASHED TITLES

**Microsoft SQL Server 2008 Reporting Services Unleashed**
ISBN-13: 978-0-672-33026-1

**ASP.NET MVC Framework Unleashed**
ISBN-13: 978-0-672-32998-2

**SAP Implementation Unleashed**
ISBN-13: 978-0-672-33004-9

**Microsoft XNA Game Studio 3.0 Unleashed**
ISBN-13: 978-0-672-33022-3

**Microsoft SQL Server 2008 Integration Services Unleashed**
ISBN-13: 978-0-672-33032-2

**Microsoft SQL Server 2008 Analysis Services Unleashed**
ISBN-13: 978-0-672-33001-8

**ASP.NET 3.5 AJAX Unleashed**
ISBN-13: 978-0-672-32973-9

**WPF Control Development Unleashed**
ISBN-13: 978-0-672-33033-9

**Windows PowerShell Unleashed**
ISBN-13: 978-0-672-32988-3

**Windows Small Business Server 2008 Unleashed**
ISBN-13: 978-0-672-32957-9

**Silverlight 2 Unleashed**
ISBN-13: 978-0-672-33014-8

**Windows Communication Foundation 3.5 Unleashed**
ISBN-13: 978-0-672-33024-7

**Windows Server 2008 Hyper-V Unleashed**
ISBN-13: 978-0-672-33028-5

**LINQ Unleashed**
ISBN-13: 978-0-672-32983-8

**Microsoft Dynamics CRM 4 Integration Unleashed**
ISBN-13: 978-0-672-33054-4

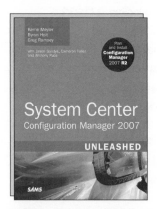

**System Center Configuration Manager (SCCM) 2007 Unleashed**
ISBN-13: 978-0-672-33023-0

## SAMS

informit.com/sams

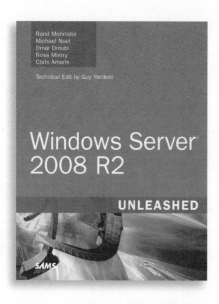

FREE Online Edition

Your purchase of **Windows Server® 2008 R2 Unleashed** includes access to a free online edition for 45 days through the Safari Books Online subscription service. Nearly every Sams book is available online through Safari Books Online, along with more than 5,000 other technical books and videos from publishers such as Addison-Wesley Professional, Cisco Press, Exam Cram, IBM Press, O'Reilly, Prentice Hall, and Que.

**SAFARI BOOKS ONLINE** allows you to search for a specific answer, cut and paste code, download chapters, and stay current with emerging technologies.

## Activate your FREE Online Edition at
## www.informit.com/safarifree

> **STEP 1:** Enter the coupon code: UHDUOXA.

> **STEP 2:** New Safari users, complete the brief registration form.
> Safari subscribers, just log in.

If you have difficulty registering on Safari or accessing the online edition, please e-mail customer-service@safaribooksonline.com